JOYA CHATTERJI

Joya Chatterji is a Fellow of Trinity College, Cambridge, Emeritus Professor of South Asian History at the University of Cambridge and sometime Reader in International History at the London School of Economics. From 2010 to 2021, she was first Editor and then Editor-in-Chief of *Modern Asian Studies*, a leading scholarly journal in the field. Between 2014 and her retirement in 2019, she was Director of the Centre of South Asian Studies at Cambridge. She was elected a

in 2018.

T0332765

Praise for *Shadows at Noon*

'With clarity, wit and charm, [Joya Chatterji] tells the story
of the subcontinent's recent history in a fluent, sweeping
arc that takes us from the great anti-colonial rebellion of
1857 to the rise of the BJP's muscular Hindu
nationalism . . . wide-angled and hugely ambitious,
but also highly personal and pleasingly discursive.
Wonderfully enjoyable to read . . . a brilliant introduction
to modern Indian history . . . [The] tone is non-academic
and conversational, at times even chatty . . . Chatterji's
"compulsion to understand" has resulted in a wonderfully
original, genre-defying work that is sure to become a classic'
William Dalrymple, *Observer*

'Weaves between the personal and the political with the
robust handling of a classic Ambassador Mark III car on
a rural Indian road . . . an innovative history of South
Asia . . . Chatterji brings together the political and cultural
in a way rarely done before . . . Chatterji's scholarship and
enthusiasm shine through – and never bore'
Rana Mitter, *Financial Times*

'This is a book that invents a genre: navigating effortlessly
between the archives, conversations, memoir, newspapers,
swooping out to make magisterial observations and
zooming in to unearth nuggets of gossip. It is like
riding a rollercoaster with a mesmerising guide who
can touch down on any part of South Asia that she
chooses, before taking off again'
Anuradha Roy, author of *All the Lives We Never Lived*

'It's refreshing to read a history of modern India, Pakistan and Bangladesh that rises above the usual national and chronological divisions, and that ends on a surprisingly upbeat note'
Dominic Sandbrook, *Sunday Times*

'A truly magnificent book about the history, politics and culture of twentieth-century South Asia . . . A must-read'
Mihir Bose, author of *The Nine Waves*

'History at its best; blending compelling evidence with deep insight, this is an invitation to enter worlds within worlds in the company of a master storyteller'
Dr Simon Longstaff AO

'This is history as it should be written, but rarely is. Chatterji maps the journey of South Asia from the high noon of empire to today, and in so doing a rich tapestry unfolds that is unlikely to be equalled for some time'
Professor Mahesh Rangarajan

'Original and revealing . . . this is a book which both scholars and the wider public can dip into, enjoy and learn from'
Literary Review

'A wonderful book concentrating for once on what the peoples of different South Asian countries have in common. That's something South Asians and all the rest of us should now concentrate on'
Sir Mark Tully

JOYA CHATTERJI

Shadows at Noon

The South Asian Twentieth Century

VINTAGE

1 3 5 7 9 10 8 6 4 2

Vintage is part of the Penguin Random House group of companies whose
addresses can be found at global.penguinrandomhouse.com

First published in Vintage in 2024
First published in hardback by The Bodley Head in 2023

Copyright © Joya Chatterji 2023

Joya Chatterji has asserted her right to be identified as the author of this Work
in accordance with the Copyright, Designs and Patents Act 1988

Maps by Bill Donohoe

penguin.co.uk/vintage

Printed and bound in Great Britain by Clays Ltd, Elcograf S.p.A.

The authorised representative in the EEA is Penguin Random House Ireland,
Morrison Chambers, 32 Nassau Street, Dublin D02 YH68

A CIP catalogue record for this book is available from the British Library

ISBN 9781529925555

Penguin Random House is committed to a sustainable future
for our business, our readers and our planet. This book is made
from Forest Stewardship Council® certified paper.

Contents

Maps   ix

Note on Names   xiii

Introduction   xv

1 The Age of Nationalisms: Competing Visions   1

2 Citizenship and Nation-building after Independence:
   South Asian Experiences   84

3 The State in South Asia: A Biography   204

4 Migration at Home and Abroad: South Asian Diasporas   293

5 The Household, Marriage and the Family   380

6 Fasting, Feasting, Gluttony and Starvation:
   Consumption, Caste and the Politics of Food in
   South Asia   450

7 Leisure, Twentieth-century Style   539

   Epilogue   635

   A Note on Further Viewing   659

   Acknowledgements   679

   Glossary   687

   Picture Credits   707

   Notes   711

   Index   795

One learns far more from students than one teaches them.

This book is dedicated to my brilliant and beloved graduate students, who are (still) my learned instructors.

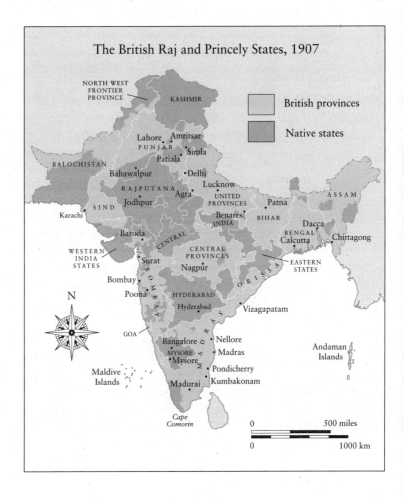

The British Raj and Princely States, 1907

British provinces

Native states

NORTH WEST FRONTIER PROVINCE
KASHMIR
Lahore Amritsar
PUNJAB
Patiala Simla
BALOCHISTAN
Bahawalpur
Delhi
RAJPUTANA
Lucknow
Agra
UNITED PROVINCES
Jodhpur
Benares
INDIA
BIHAR
Patna
ASSAM
SIND
Karachi
Baroda
CENTRAL
Dacca
BENGAL
Calcutta
Chittagong
WESTERN INDIA STATES
Surat
CENTRAL PROVINCES
Nagpur
EASTERN STATES
BOMBAY
ORISSA
Bombay
Poona
HYDERABAD
Hyderabad
Vizagapatam
N
GOA
Bangalore
Nellore
MYSORE
Madras
MADRAS
Mysore
Pondicherry
Maldive Islands
Madurai
Kumbakonam
Andaman Islands
Cape Comorin

0   500 miles

0   1000 km

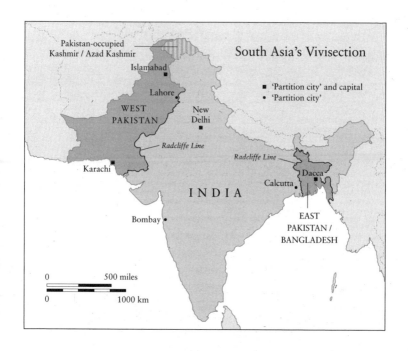

Pakistan-occupied
Kashmir / Azad Kashmir

South Asia's Vivisection

Islamabad

Lahore
New
Delhi
WEST
PAKISTAN

■ 'Partition city' and capital
● 'Partition city'

Radcliffe Line

Radcliffe Line

Dacca

Karachi

Calcutta

I N D I A

EAST
PAKISTAN /
BANGLADESH

Bombay

0   500 miles

0   1000 km

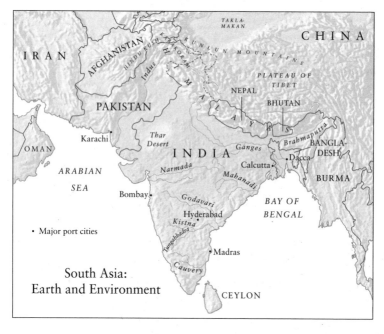

TAKLA-
MAKAN

C H I N A

I R A N

AFGHANISTAN

HINDU KUSH

KARAKORAM

KUNLUN   MOUNTAINS

Indus

PLATEAU OF
TIBET

H
I
M
A
L
A
Y
A
S

PAKISTAN

NEPAL

BHUTAN

Brahmaputra

BANGLA-
DESH

OMAN

Karachi

*Thar
Desert*

I N D I A

Ganges

Calcutta

Dacca

ARABIAN
SEA

Narmada

Mahanadi

BURMA

Bombay

Godavari

BAY OF
BENGAL

Hyderabad

Kistna

● Major port cities

Tungabhadra

Madras

South Asia:
Earth and Environment

Cauvery

CEYLON

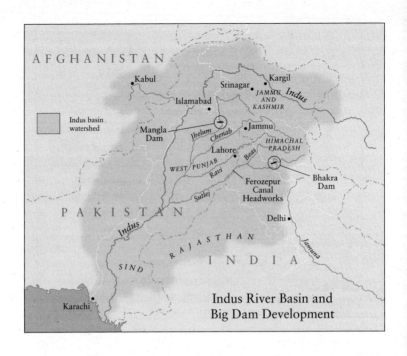

Indus River Basin and Big Dam Development

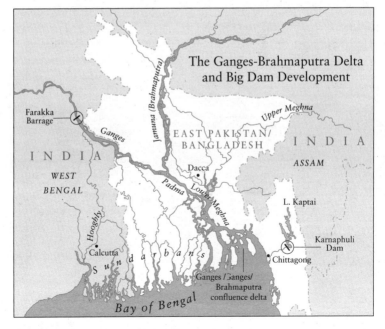

The Ganges-Brahmaputra Delta and Big Dam Development

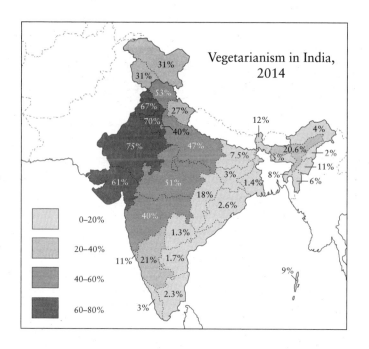

Vegetarianism in India, 2014

31%
31%
53%
67%
70%
27%
40%
75%
47%
12%
4%
20.6%
5%
2%
11%
7.5%
3%
1.4%
8%
6%
61%
51%
18%
2.6%
40%
1.3%
11% 21% 1.7%
9%
2.3%
3%

0–20%
20–40%
40–60%
60–80%

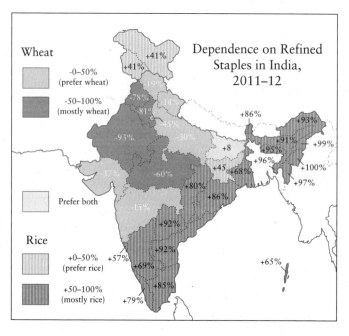

Dependence on Refined Staples in India, 2011–12

Wheat

-0–50%
(prefer wheat)

-50–100%
(mostly wheat)

+41%
+41%
-19%
-78%
-18%
-81%
-45%
-93%
-30%
+8
-37%
-60%
+45
+68%
-15%
+80%
+86%
+92%
+57%
+92%
+69%
+85%
+79%
+86%
+93%
+91%
+95%
+96%
+99%
+100%
+97%
+65%

Prefer both

Rice

+0–50%
(prefer rice)

+50–100%
(mostly rice)

Note on Names

This book covers a century, and in some chapters, decades more than that.

The names of places were either spelled inconsistently over that long timespan, or were changed, and changed again, in tune with changing political events. Given that this book discusses many places, in order not to confuse the reader with that variety of names for one place, I will use the name used at the start of the century for the whole century.

This can lead to some awkward, or ugly, British-era names surviving here, Oudh being a particular pet hate. I do not for a moment suggest these are the *right* names. Thus Calcutta survives the century, as do Madras, Dacca and Bombay. They aid consistency. Above all, they help the reader.

I make exceptions to this rule when places – princes' states, in particular – disappear or are divided by war. Thus when I speak of Hyderabad, I refer to the princely state of that name which existed until the 1950s. That state was later dissolved, and much of it absorbed into Andhra Pradesh, a new entity.

Regarding Kashmir, I use the name to refer to the entire area covering the princely state as it existed, and still exists as a disputed area. The Indian province of Jammu and Kashmir refers to its post-war limits.

I stick to the term 'province' throughout to indicate a unit of government below the centre.

The British invented names of persons from an amalgam of patronyms, village names, caste names and given names, to arrive at something that resembled a 'Christian name, surname' combination. It caused mayhem in the spelling of names. In my own family, we have Chatterjis, Chaterjees, Chatterjeas, Chattopadhays and Chattopadhayas, to give you one confounding example. This is a caste name, and however you spell it, it means the same thing.

The way I have dealt with this is to use the name by which the person in question is best known. So I have used Jinnah instead of Jinnahbhai, Tagore instead of Thakur, Sher-Gil instead of Shergill.

Some of my subjects are not famous. In which case I have used a phonetic transliteration of their names, or their own favoured spelling.

Some interviewees were reluctant to reveal their names. For most, I have used aliases that reflect their social and cultural location. For the most vulnerable of them all, her pseudonym erases all such markers.

Transliteration is a tricky business in a subcontinent of so many languages. I have not used diacritical marks anywhere. My method has been to aim for a phonetic approach without them, approximating sounds as far as possible. So I use *firanghee* instead of *feringhee* for 'foreigner', and *bondhu-baandhob* (Bangla) for 'friends'.

I make exceptions to this rule where their absorption into English has made terms familiar to readers. There is no way of writing the 'sepoy' out of history. Airbrushing out 'box-wallah' would be plain silly in a book that tries to uncover subjects, rather than conceal them.

Introduction

I was born in New Delhi in 1964. We lived on what was then the frontier of the city. As a child, I heard jackals howl at night; each morning I was woken by the peacock's cry. Delhi's clear winter nights were cold: we would wake to frosts of transient beauty. Today the city is shrouded in noxious gases, and the jackals have long since fled. Outside our home today, a solitary peacock puzzles at his reflection in the windowpane. He soon lies down exhausted, on a faux-rattan sofa designed for twenty-first-century smokers.

This book tells the story of South Asia's twentieth century, of which the peacock, like me and two billion other humans, has been part. That history has been turbulent, rich and compelling. It tells us much about how the present came to be.

Unlike many other histories of the subcontinent that concentrate solely on politics, people are at the heart of the book, in all their voluble and often violent relationships with one another.

We meet them in a host of contexts: eating together and apart, living in large and complex households, travelling as migrants to work or to marry, fleeing carnage, competing for space in sprawling cities, enjoying changing forms of leisure. I will look at the common life-worlds, material practices and cultural memories, as well as the shared environments that transcend the borders drawn by a British lawyer on a map in 1947.

This book, then, is not just about South Asia's political history. Where it is, it interprets that history from a bold new perspective: that of relentless nation-making. This remained a priority for the neighbouring states, supposedly different from each other in every respect. That shared history is another recurrent theme.

Carving out new nation states from what had been a common land inhabited by all kinds of folk had two landmark moments: 1947, when independence produced the two separate nations of India and Pakistan; and 1971, when Bangladesh tore itself apart from Pakistan. These were two moments of 'unmixing', in which certain people – whether by virtue of religion or language – were declared the 'national majority'. The rest, woe betide them, became 'national minorities' who could never prove their allegiance to the nation, whatever they did.

These events were apocalyptic in their own right. But they also fired the starting gun for turning people with shared languages – linked by dense webs of social and economic connection, migratory and pilgrimage routes, and common environments and idioms of rule – into citizens of antithetical states.

This was not the work of a day. Making citizens identify with their nation's self-declared character and ambition has dominated South Asian politics for the latter half of the twentieth century. It remains an ongoing project, hotly contested in all three countries, since there is no unanimity about what each nation's character really is. It was ever thus: there never was harmony among nationalists, nor among the new rulers. Nonetheless citizens were produced in their millions.

I was one such product. Taught at school (from a national syllabus) by the age of ten to hate 'the Britishers' and Jinnah of Pakistan, I loved India with such a passion that I still have my Indian passport despite living many years abroad. Yet classmates bullied my brother at Delhi's new blue 'modern' school when forced to admit that our mother was English. Their conclusion, 'Oh, so your father is a traitor and your mother is a Britisher?' – the latter word spat out with hatred – tended to make us more opaque than we should have been as little children. Perhaps it helps explain my intense curiosity about the past. Perhaps it also made me question, in later life, the jingoistic view of history. But I was privileged with many years of further education. Others, the vast majority, were not.

This book brings you a view born in a diasporic location, at a university where young South Asians meet each other – often for the first time – and realise that, in fact, they are more like their neighbours than like students from other countries and continents. I discovered in my first year at university that we cooked the same food, had the same spices on our kitchen shelves, the same packets of rice, lentils, potatoes (bought in bulk: we were all poor) and the same paring knives for cutting onions. That was back in 1985. Today my friends and I watch cricket together, the very same India–Pakistan matches that are allegedly 'like war'. We share our passion for the game and admire the beauty of that *doosra* or the 'wrist' in that cover-drive. We are, after all, South Asians.

As a scholar at that university, I discovered that the British Raj developed into the strongest state that the subcontinent had ever seen. But its agenda had been to promote its own interests and keep the peace, whether by flag-marching villagers, issuing crawling orders or sending noisy Indians into exile. It wasn't interested in trying to make all Indians British, or even to educate or feed them.

India and Pakistan were different from the Raj, albeit in similar ways. Both were far more ambitious than the British had been – they had to be, given the expectations aroused by the many different independence movements before 1947, each with its own imagined utopia. They grew more powerful too, penetrating deeper and further into people's lives than the Raj had ever done. And they invested a good deal of their energy and power in what might be described as the 'citizenship project'.

Thus the people of British India were taught, nudged and cowed into becoming citizens of India, Pakistan and Bangladesh. They were persuaded that certain people, of a particular faith or speaking a particular language, were 'the enemy abroad' (and, indeed, the 'enemy within'). Their neighbouring nations, they learned, were hostile states, posing mortal and ever-present threats.

In fact, the new nations were not irreconcilable foes. They could not afford to be: they had to cooperate on a thousand and one mundane matters. As this book will reveal, India and Pakistan acted more often in step than at odds.

But people of the subcontinent paid a heavy price for their fear and hatred of 'the other'. The three nations were careless of what and who was lost in their determination to turn what was similar into something unique, something modern, something national. 'Sorrow does not have a century,' Deborah Levy writes. But if it did, twentieth-century South Asia could stake a claim.

What, you may wonder, do I mean by the term, 'the South Asian twentieth century'? My point is simple: there are other ways of seeing this era than as 'the American century'. The American story and its turning points are so well known that many of us know them by heart: the two world wars, the Cold War, the fall of the Berlin Wall, the defeat of the Soviet Union and the creation of Russia, and, some thought, 'the end of history'. (We know better than that now.)

The century looks rather different, however, from other vantage points around the world.

It is certainly not the perspective from Jaipur's Jantar Mantar observatory. Or the peak of K2 in Pakistan. Or Shah Jalal's shrine in Bangladesh. Or the Coromandel coast in the southern peninsula, so distinctive that it can be recognised from the moon.

There are overlaps, to be sure. South Asia, too, was caught up in the world wars. It was the keystone in the arch of a global empire and many bloody tides of those wars washed over it. Yet the view from South Asia diverges so much from the standard understanding of the twentieth century that it demands our consideration – not least because divided India grew over that period from being one of the poorest places in the world to one of its wealthiest and most populous. Today one in six people on our planet is a South Asian; and the South Asian diaspora is the size of several countries.

You will find that its turning points are rather different from those of the 'American century'. The partition was a catastrophe of such magnitude that it is still difficult for me to comprehend how the rest of the world – even Britain – knew so little about it. The joys of independence and the agonies of partition make 1947, rather than 1945, a key milestone in South Asian history. The second partition in 1971, and the bloody birth of Bangladesh, is another. Popular protest against British rule, horrific famines, strikes, assassinations and military coups played intermittent but powerful notes. Communal violence – whether against Ahmediya, Shia, Sikh, Christian, Sunni, 'Bihari' or any other minorities – has had potent rhythms beaten on its *dholak* drums. The demolition of the Babri Mosque in 1992 represents a more critical watershed for the region than the events of 9/11.

You might also wonder what I mean by 'South Asia'. My focus is on the territories of the former British Raj and its principalities, which are now divided between three countries: Bangladesh, Pakistan and India. It is only by discussing these places before and after their independence that I can tease out subtle continuities as well as dramatic changes in how they have worked, both before and after the Union Jack came down. To investigate how far one became three. This is my goal in this book. To have included Afghanistan, Ceylon, Burma, Bhutan and Nepal – three of which the British never conquered – would have taken me off this comparative track.

This book makes a fresh and profound argument. Despite partition, India and Pakistan did not fly off to distant corners of the universe. They stayed right where they were, nestled up against each other in the same ecosystems, connected by the Himalayas, the Karakoram ranges and two enormous river systems, by the monsoons, and by a shared legacy of structures of rule. And a lot else – let's call it history.

My aim is to challenge the myth of their incompatible personalities, their ceaseless animosity and mutual belligerence. I suggest that India and Pakistan had more in common than is often understood.

I will pull back South Asia's 'Iron Curtain' to reveal these parallels and continuities despite the partitions of 1947 and 1971. I will shine a spotlight on the region's apparently clashing backcloths to reveal common patterns. Some are like delicate strands of gold *zari* thread woven into the fabric; others are more striking, with vivid colours and emphatic designs.

The structure of the book is unorthodox: it is both thematic and chronological. The first three chapters address various themes in South Asia's political history. They are best read as a foundation on which the later chapters rest. Those later chapters address specific questions that might arise in the mind of a curious reader. But while it focuses on a certain theme, each chapter is chronological within itself, furling out to analyse change over a century in one particular sphere. This format allows the reader to explore particular issues – say, the tensions in South Asia's vast cities or the workings of joint families – over time and in some depth. And each chapter builds on the ones before it.

The book aims to make contemporary South Asia intelligible, without underplaying its complexity. It does not attempt, in facile ways, to simplify the history of a vast, mythically intricate society. Yet it brings complicated processes in its modern history to life through the stories of people. Great men and women figure in it, as they must. But the stories of those on the wrong side of history, and on its margins, also find a place. Uncomfortable subjects that have fallen through the trapdoor of history re-emerge into the light. Princes appear in new guises. An Englishwoman's romantic liaison with an 'untouchable' sweeper questions the much-vaunted 'super-racism' of white women in India, while also shedding light on the lives and experiences of Dalits.

Indeed, although nationalisms and nation-building get detailed attention, those marginalised by these processes are not brushed under the carpet. Readers will meet refugee women like Bibi Ram Pyari, widowed after partition, who set up a tiny kiosk in the front room of her miniscule dwelling in Delhi where she sold home-made candy as she supervised her children's homework; by the end of the century, this shop had grown into one of Delhi's better-known super-stores. Readers will be introduced to the 'Bihari' stateless 'camp boys' in Dacca who fought a landmark case to gain citizenship in 2008. They will meet Salima, who is rooted to the ground in 'the age of migration' and too terrified to move lest she loses her home. Now in her seventies, she has not left for more than fifty years a tiny win-dowless room in which she has squatted with eight dependants. Her story brings home, in raw human terms, the price so many have paid for the nation.

The start and end dates for each chapter vary. Watersheds will not work to rule: they tend not to follow the centennial calendar. In some chapters, 1857, the year of the Mutiny and Rebellion, is the key turning point, having brought an end to the East India Company's rule and see-ing it replaced by the British Raj. The chapter on leisure concentrates largely on the decades after 1913 – the year the first film was made in Bombay (now known as Mumbai). The chapter on nation-building ends in 1992, when the Babri Mosque in Ayodhya came down, marking the start of a new phase of nation creation, which is still unfolding at the time of writing. Some chapters delve deeper into the past for clues to later events. Bear with me: there is a logic to each date.

The book's end date (c.2000) extends far beyond the period for which systematic archival research is possible, and for which a rich body of historical literature exists. Illness and immobility have made it difficult for me to conduct as many oral history interviews as I once might have done.

For this reason, I have used vignettes of autobiography, family lore and my own life history. I have interviewed myself, dredging out memories, recognising that they are as labile as the memories of others. My grandparents were born in the 1880s, my father in 1921, his sister in 1913; and many cousins, nieces and nephews were mid-night's children, born around the time of independence and partition.

My own siblings and I arrived in the 1950s and 60s. We started to produce the next generation in the 1980s and 90s. So this family, like so many, has seen the century and has stories to tell about it.

I was a curious child and teenager. I could not rest until I had 'understood', and I was never satisfied with the explanations I was given. I will introduce you to that inquisitive young person, to the questions she asked and the answers she elicited from a host of interesting people. After all, these could well have been your questions too, when you first picked up this book.

These stories leaven the text; they add intimacy and immediacy. But they also explain why I wrote this book. Many of the questions I ask here have plagued me since I was old enough to ponder. One was about what 'the state' was. Another was why people – who, for the most part, seemed intelligent and warm-hearted – were so full of hatred towards certain groups in society. Another was about the poverty of which I was acutely conscious. Why were people so destitute? What was being done about it?

Other questions popped up when I started teaching at university. I had neither the time nor the stillness needed to dwell on them. Since my retirement from teaching for medical reasons in 2019, I have had both. This is my personal discovery, then, not of India, but of a divided subcontinent that was once called India.

I seek to soar above a subcontinent partitioned by politics and states and observe with a bird's eye its shifting patterns of light and shadows. I recognise that my knowledge of the subcontinent is uneven: I know some parts of it like the back of my hand but others only through secondary work. Yet the work of other scholars who faced similar limitations and painted large canvases with brilliant effect persuaded me that this was not impossible.

If I haven't rushed to archives hither and yon around the subcontinent, and indeed the world, as I might once have done, or read as many official files for the latter years as for the former, it's because official secrets acts and archive weeding pose insurmountable roadblocks. Instead, I have resorted to a parallel archive of amateur films, documentaries, feature films, photographs, stamps, newspaper clippings, private papers, maps, genealogies, handicrafts, calligraphy, amulets, and collections of objects from different places.

A lifetime of reading, thinking, teaching and learning from students at the cutting edge of their subjects helped me envisage this book.

Writing it has been a journey down many winding roads. I have come out of it knowing incomparably more than I did when I began. I have not 'understood' everything, of course, but I have gained insights into much. It has been the most fascinating, thrilling and challenging project on which I have ever embarked.

I hope, through this book, to share with you those insights and that excitement.

I

The Age of Nationalisms:
Competing Visions

In 1907, the annual session of the Indian National Congress at Surat dissolved in pandemonium. The trading town near Bombay with a population of about 120,000 people had witnessed many historical dramas, but nothing quite like this.

The 'extremist' Bal Gangadhar Tilak strode onto the stage, challenging the Congress' 'moderate' leaders. Supporters sprang to their feet in the moderates' defence, 'wildly gesticulating vengeance, shaking their fists and yelling to the air'. 'Suddenly something flew through the air – a shoe! – a Mahratta shoe! – reddish leather, pointed toe, studded with lead. It struck Surendra Nath Banerjea on the cheek; it cannoned off upon Sir Pherozeshah Mehta.' Both men were leading moderates, 'Surrender-not' and 'Ferocious' to their admirers. 'It flew, it fell, and, as at a given signal, white waves of turbaned men surged up ... brandishing long sticks.' Ten thousand men hurled chairs 'as missiles', and 'long sticks clashed and shivered'. 'Blood flowed from broken heads.' Within an hour, 'the vast Pandal [marquee], strewn with broken chairs, sticks and rags of raiment, stood empty as a banquet-hall deserted.'[1]

Anyone watching this scene could scarcely have believed that this was a day in the life of the world's most powerful anti-colonial nationalist movement.

The purpose of nationalism is to unite. Just as often, it divides. My purpose here is not to decry the power of India's imagined national unities; it is to explore why, despite their undoubted energy, India's nationalisms have fragmented again and again. Why was nationalism in South Asia more often like a civil war than a serried rank of troops marching forward in unison? Why did the Republic Day Parade, to which my parents took me on a foggy January morning in New Delhi when I was six years old, ring a false note even to my childish ears?

Troops were marching, to be sure, and bagpipes were playing as MiG fighter jets flew past. Regional dancers in bright hues paraded by on floats, displaying India's 'unity in diversity'. But why did we still have to be persuaded that we were a nation in 1970, two and more decades after independence? As we would say in Hindustani, *daal mein kuchh kala hai* – there is something suspicious going on here (literally, 'there is something black in the lentils'). The nation protested too much.

And why did India break into two upon achieving independence? How did a division so deep open up and grow to the point that it sundered 'the nation' apart?

Two issues have splintered Indian nationalism again and again. The first had to do with methods. What were the right means by which nationalists should pursue their goal – which was to reform, and later to get rid of, the British Empire? Was violence acceptable, given the disproportionate force the British could (and did) wield against unarmed protestors?[2] Was it ethical? The violent scenes at Surat began with a debate in which the 'moderates' refused to condone 'extremist' bloodshed. Such ironies are commonplace in the annals of nationalism.

The second issue related to identity. Many nationalists claimed that 'Indian-ness' was the primary identity, superseding all other affiliations, whether to religion, sect, caste, language or region. Yet the very conditions of modernity under colonialism – the spread of technology, railways, print and ideas – which had fuelled the rise of Indian national identity in the first place, also encouraged the growth of religious, regional, linguistic, sectarian and caste-based identities.

Some of these (Maratha, Bengali-Hindu, Hindu 'upper-caste', Tamil-Brahmin, for instance) nested like Russian dolls within the mother-doll of 'Indian-ness'. Others did not. 'Dravidian' identity and 'Indian' identity were rather like hostile cellmates in a British jail. Other groups – notably 'Indian Muslims', an umbrella identity fashioned in this era – claimed that their 'community' was far too large and important to be considered just another 'little identity' that could be accommodated under the sheltering tree of 'the Indian nation'. They were a nation, some Muslim leaders claimed, in their own right.

Nor should we assume that identity politics ended with independence. It flourished – indeed flowered – until the end of the twentieth century.

How India's nationalists contended with these challenges is a fascinating story. Pragmatic strategies for unity came to the fore at different moments, and these are quite as important to consider as the moments of violence, grand protest and high drama. One was to make the economy the chosen terrain on which to present all Indians as one (however far-fetched that claim might appear to us today). Another was to suggest that India was a 'composite nation', a happy conglomeration of diverse 'nations' and 'peoples'. A third was to work through negotiation and compromise. None of these paths succeeded – nationalism's histories are littered with as many collapses as triumphs. Yet they raised wild hopes and awkward expectations of the nation states that came after the Raj.

Twenty-two years after it first met in Bombay in 1885, the Congress fell apart, in the first of many ruptures in its chequered history. As the century progressed, fresh disagreements came to the fore and gained momentum. In August 1947, by the time the Union Jack finally came down, these had become so intense that not one nation was born, but two. Yet even a radical partition on the grounds of religion could not produce unanimity about what each of the two new 'nations' was about, what they stood for or where they should head. Pakistan, described by its founder as 'moth-eaten' and 'truncated', underwent a second brutal partition in 1971, when its eastern wing seceded from it to form Bangladesh. In the later twentieth century, it is little surprise that the states would seek to replace the story of nationalisms in the subcontinent with the enterprise of nation-building: zealous top-down efforts to weld its diverse peoples into homogeneous citizenries – another grand design not easy to realise.

I

IMPERIAL LIBERALISM AND ITS HYPOCRISIES

'The idea that Indians should take up a common political stance against the iniquities of "Anglo-India" was almost as old as the first stirrings of constitutional politics in India.'[3] But the obstacles in the way of establishing such an organisation are instructive. So too is the fact that the first association to achieve this goal (as so often in the history of anti-colonial nationalisms) was a small student-led body in London. In 1865, a handful of expatriate Indians, mainly students who had come there to sit the bar or civil service examinations, established the London India Association.

The vigorous spirit behind it was Dadabhai Naoroji, the son of a Gujarati-speaking Parsi widow. Among these young pioneers in London were four future presidents of the Indian National Congress, including Surendranath Banerjee and Pherozeshah Mehta, both victims, years later, of that red leather shoe.

At this time, western-educated (and English-speaking) Indians were a miniscule fragment of the country's total population of about 240 million. Although denizens of large towns and cities were often polyglot, there were few such places in the subcontinent in 1900. The overwhelming majority had no common language in which to communicate other than their 'dialects', or new – more formal – 'languages'. Indeed, nineteenth-century Indians spoke in so many tongues that it took George Grierson, linguist and civil servant, over thirty years to record and describe India's 179 languages and 544 dialects in the multi-volume *Linguistic Survey of India*.[4]

To be sure, Persian was still a lingua franca for the scribal elites of the North Indian Mughal heartlands of the empire that the British had displaced, but its penetration into the rest of the subcontinent had been patchy, except in the large state of Hyderabad. Likewise, Brahmins learned in the *shastras* (sacred texts) could read Sanskrit, but they were a select elite, and the language ancient and arcane. Like Latin, it was 'dead'. Many Muslims could recite Arabic, the language of the Quran, but few read, spoke or understood it when the century began.

Urdu, Tamil, Telegu, Gujarati, Bengali, Marathi, Malayam, Pashto and Punjabi (just to name a few) were vibrant, living, growing languages. Many Congressmen and women understood and spoke two or three, but could read only one. You had to be a linguist of talent to achieve command over two (as well as English), since each had a distinctive printed and cursive script, vocabulary and a grammar that was only just being standardised. (Imagine, for a moment, a late-nineteenth-century world in which French, German, Spanish, Italian and American readers did not even share a common Roman *script*.)

In late-colonial India, English emerged as a pontoon bridge spanning this polyphony.

Indians had felt the need for subcontinental unity since the late nineteenth century. Yet the hurdles in forging it seemed insuperable. When gauged by the real-time experience of travel, India was far vaster then than it is now. Before the railway connected Calcutta to Delhi in 1864 (a journey of 1,400 kilometres that now takes about two hours by plane), travel by land for the affluent was by horse-drawn carriage or *gharry*, and for the less wealthy, by bullock cart – an odyssey taking weeks or months.[5] The ancient Grand Trunk Road notwithstanding, all-weather roads were few and far between: a serious road-building programme began only during the Second World War, and that too only in the eastern part of the country.

Until the 1880s, the fastest route between Calcutta, the capital of the British Indian empire, and Bombay, its premier port on the west coast, was by sea. Travellers had to embark at Hooghly, where docks only began to be developed in 1885, and take a steamship all the way round Cape Comorin and up the Arabian Sea coast.[6] Even in the age of steam, sail and oars powered most of the little boats that continued to ply the inland waters or coasts. When the much-vaunted railroads were developed in the later nineteenth and early twentieth century (at a cost nine times higher than the railways in the United States and funded solely by the Indian taxpayer), they were designed to shift imperial troops and British goods rather than Indian passengers.

Thus rail travel for Indians was unimaginably hard. Journeys lasted weeks at a time. Stations along the way were rudimentary structures, their facilities segregated along racial lines. Arrangements for food, water and latrines for 'natives' were dismal, if they existed at all.[7]

In 1866, the British Indian Association of Calcutta complained that railway journeys 'enforced starvation' upon Indian passengers.[8] In his travelogue, Kedarnath Ray, a middle-class Bengali sojourner, describes staying overnight with horses, as accommodation in a stable was all that he could find.[9] Lighting, seats and privies were afforded to middle-class cabin passengers only after years of privation and petitions. There was no provision for eating on the way, except during short halts at stations. So wealthier Indian sojourners (most of them conscious of caste and dietary restrictions) travelled with cooks and servants, which made both travel and accommodation at their destination a logistical nightmare. Gandhi recalls, in his *Autobiography*, his first visit to the Congress session at Calcutta in 1901, looking on with amazement at the untouchability that he saw. 'The Tamilian kitchen was far away from the rest. To the Tamil delegates even the sight of others, whilst they were dining, meant pollution. So a special kitchen had to be made for them in the college compound, walled in by wicker-work.'[10] Given these difficulties – practical, caste-based, sociocultural – it continued to be much easier for Indian students from different parts of the subcontinent to meet face to face in London, as they had in 1865, to discuss how best to create an association that claimed to speak for all India.

Even so, the mental geographies of each nationalist's 'India' were likely to have been forged in a train: a palimpsest of images of landscapes glimpsed from the small windows of carriages; of memories of brief stops at stations where they encountered for the first time unfamiliar languages, headwear, foods and micro-environments; of vast crowds at the great pilgrimage sites of the subcontinent's sacred geography, of the huge red glowing sun setting on parched fields. When Gandhi returned from South Africa hungry to understand India, Gokhale told him to travel its length and breadth. He took a lot of trains.

My own grasp of 'India' also emerged from encounters, by rail, with the subcontinent's diverse vistas, in all their grandeur, beauty and pathos. Whole picture albums of memories, of fragments of journeys travelled, lie in a trunk in my mind, but it is hard to unlock, and harder still to gaze on the images. They come into focus for a second, then blur, fade and disappear into the darkness. Was the 'India' of these early nationalists, then, also a charged series of impressions, a moving magic lantern rather than a painting? Perhaps it was.

Perhaps these pictures (and the emotions attached to them) fuelled the students of the London India Association. Perhaps these blurry snapshots of India – so personal to each traveller – explain why the Association succeeded in generating such a powerful reciprocal push in India itself, in the age of the railways.

But we would be unwise, in the search for new explanations, to overlook the more obvious reason, and that lies in the 'betrayals' and disappointments after the Mutiny (later Rebellion) of 1857. An uprising in the Bengal Army – made up, in the main, of Indian mercenaries – gave a host of Indian kingdoms (some of them uneasy allies of the British), armed landlords with their own private armies as well as peasant insurrectionaries, the chance to wage war to rid the land of the arrogant *firanghee* (foreigner) with his cruel taxes, his meddling in religion and his humiliation of the Nawab of Oudh, the charismatic overlord of the region from which most soldiers enlisted. City-dwellers too, not least in Delhi, became rebels. Their war was violent: they took no prisoners. British legend has attached the worst cruelties on the 'Indian' side – the siege of Lucknow symbolising everything savage about the now detested but also feared 'native'. As for the British, when they rallied with the help of firepower destined for China, their reaction was no less vengeful. They blew rebels out of cannons, just for starters. In the high age of racism's ascendancy, British prejudice in India took on a more anxious and aggressive tenor.

After 1857 it became crystal clear, if any fool had ever thought otherwise, that India could never be held by force alone. So in 1858, when the Mutiny and Rebellion were finally quelled, East India Company rule ended and Parliament took over India's affairs. At this critical juncture, Queen Victoria promised Indians equal status with all her other subjects, and free and impartial access to office. For Indians who could understand it, Victoria's proclamation 'that, so far as may be, Our Subjects, of whatever race or creed, be freely and impartially admitted to Offices in Our Service' was India's 'Bill of Rights', if not her Magna Carta.[11]

'Imperial subjecthood', on this impartial basis, was what many educated Indians of that time would have settled for.[12] But the impartiality promised by London proved a chimera in India. This was a key issue around which the Indian National Congress was formed in 1885.

After the Mutiny and Rebellion, the government put in place a new structure for the governance of India. We will return to it in Chapter 3, so here a sketch must suffice. Ultimate control now lay in the hands of the new Secretary of State for India, based in London in the India Office. In India, the viceroy was in charge and he reported to London. Rule in the provinces lay in the hands of governors, who reported to the viceroy. The structure that undergirded the pyramid was the Indian Civil Service (ICS). District officers were the face of government on the ground.

Among the many impediments preventing Indians joining government service was the fact that recruitment to the ICS was by an examination held in London. Indian contestants were at an unfair disadvantage with British 'competition-wallahs', since the cost of travelling to, and studying in, London was crippling for all but the very wealthiest. British critics mocked the fact that this issue was on the Congress agenda for many years, seeing it as proof, if proof were needed, that Congressmen were 'a microscopic minority' who represented nobody but themselves. But this was, as so often in British caricatures of Indian nationalists, far off the mark.

Why would some Indians *not* want to be part of a benign government that reigned over them and their countrymen? They had more of a stake in the country, after all. Or so they felt and thought, in that era of heightened racial tension.

What infuriated Indians was the discrimination against them, and the failure of the Raj to fulfil the Proclamation's promise of equal opportunities. Indian intellectuals could see the hypocrisy, since all imbibed, and indeed contributed to, liberal thought in this era.[13] What lay behind the British apologia was the paternalistic colonial view that a British civil servant (the district magistrate) was better able to understand and speak for 'the ordinary Indian' than an Indian of high status.

This grated. Pherozeshah Mehta's sharp rejoinder was that 'the microscopic minority can far better and far more intuitively represent the needs and aspirations than the still more microscopic minority of omniscient district officers'.[14]

It also encouraged men like Mehta to fashion an alternative notion of 'the ordinary Indian' and to make their interests the litmus test for just (imperial) rule. For nationalists, 'the ordinary Indian' was a subject with a stake in how the polity was run, who required representation by other Indians, and whose allegiance and loyalty the Raj could not take for granted. This imagined person was 'native to India'; and Indian nationalists could identify with that person because they, too, were 'native to India'.

This confrontation over the fundamental claims of British rule explains why the early Congress was government-regarding. A loose association of elite Indians who met each year at a convention in a different part of India, its members were a particular kind of elite, with a particular relationship with government: most were scions of service families who had worked as scribes and administrators for India's emperors and kings. What united them, to begin with, were their ambitions, and their frustration with the failure of the Raj to become a responsive empire. Their goal was not to replace British rule, but to reform it.

This overriding notion that 'Anglo-India' was failing to deliver Victoria's promises to India underpinned much of early liberal nationalism. In the late nineteenth century, the Raj presented countless instances of what its Indian subjects saw as bad faith.

Two particular instances became notorious.

The first was the Vernacular Press Act of 1878, which discriminated against Indian publishers of newspapers in 'native' languages. In the late nineteenth century, Indians had taken to print culture with brio: by the turn of the century, 'there [was] now scarcely a town of importance which [did] not possess its printing-press or two.'[15] Out of these presses poured a flood of pamphlets, tracts, plays and novels both in English and in Indian languages, which enjoyed wide circulation through the mushrooming of libraries and reading rooms. By the 1910s, one press alone, the Naval Kishore Press in Lucknow, which published in Urdu, Hindi, Arabic and Persian, had printed some 14,000 titles. These writers and their voracious readers began to see themselves as a *vox populi* addressing large issues in public spheres, not all of whose members were educated in the formal way.[16]

More and more, those who ran the 'native press' saw as one of their prime roles to broadcast how 'Anglo-India' mistreated 'the ordinary Indian': poor 'natives' who worked for white men as coolies on their plantations or as *ayahs* (nannies) and 'boys' in their homes. In 1861 the *Hindu Patriot* serialised Dinabandhu Mitra's play *Nil Darpan* ('Mirror of Indigo'), which depicted the brutality of white indigo planters against indentured peasants. After this shocker, the Indian press rammed home the message that there was one rule of law for the whites, and quite another for Indians. When white planters and tea garden managers flogged coolies, this made the headlines. 'Shooting accidents' in which the sahibs 'bagged a native by mistake' rippled through 'native newspapers', as did the scandalously light sentences the courts awarded to the few whites who were ever prosecuted for these crimes.[17]

The indifference of the Raj to the behaviour of the 'unofficial' white community (British persons resident in India but not employed by the Raj) also fuelled nationalist sentiment: Dinshaw Wacha, another Parsi founding father of the Congress, expressed his horror at 'European murders of Natives'.[18] The legal profession, which came into its own in Indian courts after Macaulay's Penal Code was implemented in this period, became a critical focus of this political milieu. As a British civilian remarked in 1878, 'within the [previous] 20 years . . . a feeling of nationality, which formerly had no existence . . . [had] grown up, and the . . . Press [could] now, for the first time in the history of [British] rule, appeal to the whole Native Population of India against their foreign rulers.'[19]

When Edward Lytton, a Tory viceroy, tried to muzzle that press with the Vernacular Press Act of 1878, he succeeded only in uniting Indians against him. Indeed, it had the effect of combining vernacular and English presses behind a common 'liberal' cause: the freedom of expression. Several owners of vernacular presses also owned English-language publications. Tilak, the challenger at Surat, is a case in point: his *Kesari* was a Marathi-language newspaper, whereas the *Mahratta* came out in English. It was no coincidence that of the seventy-two delegates who were at the inaugural meeting of the Congress at the Tejpal Gokuldas Boarding House in Bombay, thirty-nine were lawyers and fourteen were journalists.[20]

Another issue of the day was the Ilbert Bill. By this modest measure in 1883, Lord Ripon, a Liberal viceroy, and his Law member, Sir Courtney Ilbert, proposed that district magistrates who happened to be Indian be given the same powers as their European counterparts. This sparked off a hysterical attack by 'Anglo-India' upon the viceroy and educated 'natives', whom they deemed unfit to sit in judgement over the white man (and 'his' women). The unabashedly racist tenor of the attack on the 'whole d–d nigger party' left educated Indians in no doubt about the contempt and hatred in which 'Anglo-India' held them.

By definition, those Indians who had risen up the ranks of service in the Raj had not only mastered the English language, they had also imbibed the liberal ethos as college students and trainee officers.[21] The Ilbert Bill affair revealed to them the yawning chasm between liberal theory and bigoted practice.[22] It rubbed their faces in the deep racism of imperialism, in India and beyond.

The Mutiny had deepened the racial divide between rulers and ruled. In its aftermath, white men in India segregated themselves from Indians in 'whites only' residential areas, cantonments and clubs, putting as much distance between themselves and the 'Black Towns', which (in contrast to a century before) were now seen as hotbeds of vice and disease. The new generation of British civil servants and the 'box-wallahs' – the white traders, financiers, tea-plantation and jute-mill owners and managers – lived inside their own caste system and treated the 'westernised oriental gentlemen' with the derision the acronym 'wog' implied.

Their racism politicised its victims. It created an imagined 'native' experience that straddled differences of class, caste and creed. After the Ilbert Bill episode, 'friendship between the races' seemed impossible. The Calcutta newspaper *Amrita Bazar Patrika* concluded, in stark terms, that 'we must agitate'.[23] The miasma of failed promises of imperial liberalism, of everyday double standards, generated the fury and frenetic energy that enabled the founders of the Congress to overcome the tremendous hurdles of time and space to organise its first session, and for that experiment to persist, survive and prosper.

In another irony with which the chronicles of nationalism are replete, it was only because the founders were English-educated that they encountered these hurtful views, an exposure some have likened to 'epistemic violence'.[24] English education had introduced them not only to the European enlightenment but also to British prejudice. They would have had to read James Mill's *History of British India*, which condemned the 'savagery and particular brutishness' of Indian culture. They had read Thomas Babington Macaulay who, while Law member of the Supreme Council in India in 1833, pontificated that it was 'no exaggeration to say that all the historical information which has been collected from all the books written in the Sanscrit language is less valuable than what may be found in the most paltry abridgments used at preparatory schools in England'. It was this dismissive assessment of one of the world's oldest and most complex civilisations that lay behind Macaulay's enterprise to persuade the British government in India 'to do our best to form a class who may be interpreters between us and the millions whom we govern – a class of persons Indian in blood and colour, but English in tastes, in opinions, in morals and in intellect'.

Macaulay's vision did not succeed, and could not succeed. Even the most liberal of fin-de-siècle Indians did not transmute, by virtue of their education, into becoming such 'a class of persons'. Instead, their education in English values created generations of Indians never wholly at ease in their own skins, since they belonged to a society whose cultures they had been taught to decry. As Jawaharlal Nehru as a young man would tell a court in 1922, 'I had imbibed most of the prejudices of Harrow and Cambridge and in my likes and dislikes was perhaps more an Englishman than an Indian.'[25] It produced restless reformers, seekers after truth, and violent revolutionaries who sought solace in resurgent, modernised religion. This painful sense of being always at one remove from, and even at odds with, their 'roots' seems to have acted almost like the painful grit within the oyster. It was a productive impulse, leading to remarkable political dynamism and intellectual creativity.

Dadabhai Naoroji is a case in point. A Parsi by religion, born in 1825 into a line of Zoroastrian *mobeds* (priests), Dadabhai was educated at Bombay's most prestigious English-medium school, the Elphinstone Institute. Yet by the age of fourteen he had qualified for Parsi priesthood and married the young girl his mother had chosen for him. At twenty-six, Dadabhai founded the organisation Rahnumai Mazdayasnan Sabha (Guides on the Mazdayasnan Path) to reform the ancient faith the Zoroastrian diaspora had brought with them aeons before when they came to India from Persia, and to rid it of 'accretions'. Throughout his life, he remained invested in this mission of religious and social reform, staying in close touch with his friends and kin in Parsi society. Indeed, without the support of Bombay's small but wealthy Parsi community, it is not clear whether his numerous political projects would have got off the ground.

Yet Dadabhai was also, in many senses, a product of the European enlightenment. He excelled at mathematics (his command over numbers would give point to his indictment of British rule in India, of which more below). A European visitor to Elphinstone described him as 'a little Parsi lad with an overhanging forehead and small sparkling eyes ... [who in class] quickly took a step before the rest, contracted his brows in deep and anxious thought and with parted lips and fingers eagerly uplifted towards the master, rapidly worked his problem and blurted out the solution with startling haste'.[26] That 'little Parsi lad' would go on to hold a Chair in Mathematics and Natural Philosophy at Elphinstone, becoming the first Indian to be elevated to a full professorship.[27] In 1855, he resigned this post to go to Liverpool to open, as a partner in Cama & Co, the office of the first Indian company to be established in Britain. Later in life he was the first Indian elected to the House of Commons, as the Liberal Member for Finsbury. He also held a Chair as Professor of Gujarati at University College London.

A man of many talents, Dadabhai, like so many of his co-adjutors, was brilliantly multilingual, one minute discussing Parsi religious affairs in Gujarati, the next moment speaking in English about cotton duties. Others like him – the 'moderate' Gopal Krishna Gokhale, the social reformer M. G. Ranade, and the bellicose Tilak, and soon Gandhi and Jinnah – were embedded, simultaneously, in quite different social locations. They saw the world, their 'culture' and their 'country' from varying angles of vision. In some sense, they were like fuglemen of a diaspora: occupying and opening up connections between cultures while also exploring, defining and sharpening the differences between them. Proud, able and learned, they were determined to show the British that Indians were just as good as Western Man, while also being very distinct from him. Even if they never left India (though many of the most famous did, for extended stays abroad), they all had some of the exile's perspective on their country: sometimes they were clear-eyed; at other moments, hearts heavy with nostalgia, they bestowed upon 'India' a factitious homogeneity.

Pulled this way and that by their own ambivalence, their clashes with each other were real and sometimes bitter, but their passion, and even their feuding, fired political awareness among the wider public. The arguments among India's nationalists in this period speak volumes about how rich, varied and creative Indian political thinking was in the late nineteenth century, and how it pulled in a host of different directions as the new century began.

The shoe affair was not just some silly fracas, then. It was a mark of this intensity and the contending ideas that animated nationalisms in the early twentieth century. It was also an omen for how difficult it would be to forge a single and united national movement.

II

'INDIANS ARE WORSE OFF THAN AMERICAN SLAVES'

If the failed promises of 'Anglo-India' brought them together, 'economic nationalism' emerged as a glue binding Indian nationalists together. Despite all their differences, and their rows about almost everything else, the increasingly numerous delegates to the Congress' annual sessions had one common article of faith: British rule had impoverished India.

In 1891, the Congress affirmed that 'fully fifty millions of the population, a number yearly increasing, are dragging out a miserable existence on the verge of starvation, and that in every decade, several millions actually perish by starvation'.[28] This allegation came to be the cornerstone of their indictment of British rule, and the ground on which 'Indian' unity could perhaps have been built.

The systematic case that India was being made poorer under the British was the work of many men.[29] Two among them were giants. The first was the indefatigable Dadabhai, whose ground-breaking paper 'Poverty of India' in 1876 stated the powerful claim that 'India is suffering seriously in several ways, and is sinking in poverty'.[30] In 1900, he shocked the world by declaring that Indians were worse off than slaves had been in America: 'the latter were at least taken care of by their masters whose property they were'.[31]

The second was Romesh Chunder Dutt. Born into a distinguished Bengali literary family, Dutt's idyllic childhood was cut short by his father's death in 1861; thereafter he was brought up by an uncle with whom he soon fell out.[32] At the age of nineteen, while still an undergraduate at Presidency College Calcutta (an institution that had already produced a galaxy of stars), Dutt left for England in 1868, without his family's permission, having 'run away from home under cover of night'.[33] His plan was to take the Civil Service examination. In one short year, he qualified in the open examination, having learned Latin, Greek and horse-riding (the bizarre set of qualifications apparently required to govern India). He became only the second Indian to achieve this distinction, and he went on to do as well in the Indian Civil Service as an Indian was then permitted to do.

But this deep and thinking man, whose job involved him in famine relief operations in Nadia in Bengal in 1874, was troubled by the scant rights of the tenantry, and the ruinous level of tax they paid under colonial revenue settlements. A model bureaucrat, he sought a meeting with the viceroy, Lord Curzon, to argue the case for tax reform to prevent famine which so persistently stalked the land. Curzon, whose arrogance was well known, dismissed Dutt's proposals out of hand.

Dutt retired from the ICS at the age of forty-nine. The gag of office now removed, he put his case to the public. In 1898, as a lecturer in Indian History at University College London, he wrote his famous theses on the Indian economy. In the measured tones that were his style, Dutt showed that excessive taxation, and the escalating revenue demands of the Raj, had thrust India's peasants into chronic poverty. In 1900, his stunning *Open Letters to Lord Curzon on Famines and Land Assessments in India* set out, in staccato fashion, the raw facts about each of the twenty-two major famines that had blighted India since the Company had begun to rule in 1770.[34] Between 1860 and 1897 alone, 'at a moderate computation', twenty million people had lost their lives. 'It is a melancholy phenomenon which is not presented in the present day by any other country on earth enjoying a civilised administration.'[35] Damningly, he showed that the famines were becoming more – rather than less – devastating as the nineteenth century progressed, despite the vaunted 'moral and material progress' under *Pax Britannica*. Dutt claimed that 'the famines which have desolated India within the last quarter of the nineteenth century are unexampled in their extent and intensity in the history of ancient or modern times'.[36]

These charges challenged the very core of the Raj's case for its rule over India. Officials tried to counter them by conducting enquiries and writing reports that 'proved' that, in normal times, Indian cultivators were well fed and content, particularly as their 'Hindu' 'spiritual' outlook ensured that, 'judged from their own standpoint, the peasantry are happy and prosperous'.[37] Their condition, the government tried to argue, was getting better year by year. John Strachey, panglossian in his admiration for all things imperial, went further still. Compare, he trumpeted, the average Indian peasant with his counterpart in Europe, and 'it cannot be doubted that the advantage would be greatly in favour of the former'.[38]

But Dadabhai's strategy in rebuttal was crafty. A master of mathematics, he marshalled a wealth of *official* statistics and published *British* reports to arrive at the very first statistical estimate of India's per capita income. This, he concluded, was Rs 20, a shocking £2 a year.[39] In 1901, falling right into his trap, Curzon claimed that the average was, in fact, Rs 30. In the scrap that ensued, nationalists compared India's per capita income with that of other countries, and found that – whether Rs 20 or Rs 30, or somewhere in between – it was a lot lower than that of Russia, Ireland or even Turkey. The 'paradise of the Indies', once fabled for its wealth, was now 'the poor-est country in the civilised world'.[40]

In this escalating war of words, Dadabhai, Dutt, Ganesh Vyankatesh Joshi, G. Subramaniya Iyer (and a host of others) maintained that India's poverty was getting worse: the horrific famines of the turn of the century were a sign of an economy in such distress that a single failed rainfall could lead to mass starvation. The causes of this mal-ady, Dadabhai asserted, were not difficult to grasp. India's wealth was being 'drained' away by 'home charges', as Dadabhai described Brit-ain's imperial levy on India. These were sums that *Indians paid Britain to rule over them*, both in India and in London. Indian subjects paid every *rupee*, *anna* and *pie*, metropolitan as well as Indian, that it cost to run 'the jewel in the crown': the salaries and pensions of colonial officials, the running of the India Office in London,[41] the building and maintenance of its Library and Records, debt services for the con-struction of railways, as well as the British Indian Army, Britain's garrison in the eastern seas, and even the expense of lunatic asylums in Ealing to house 'Tommies' ravaged by syphilis contracted in India.[42]

The ruin of indigenous manufactures, and the abolishment, after 1881, of any tariffs to protect them, were central points in their indict-ment. Writing in 1881 in the *Mahratta*, Tilak made the blunt point that Indian interests were being sacrificed to those of Manchester as a 'penalty' for being 'a conquered nation'. That India was being taxed beyond its capacity was another crucial theme. Dinshaw Wacha told delegates at the seventh session of the Congress in 1891 that 'the *ryot* [peasant] is bled in order that the military tax eater may thrive and gain stars and medals'.[43] Crippled by the weight of land taxation, cultivators found it impossible to save, and this drained the country-side of capital investment. Better soil was exhausted by constant cropping without manure; and the extension of cultivation into infer-ior soil led to chronic underproduction. These factors came together to produce a severe and sustained agricultural depression of which repeated famines were a sign: they were just the tip of a vast iceberg of a pandemic of hunger in the countryside.

The twentieth century opened with a famine that devastated Bom-bay Presidency, the Central Provinces and Berar, with more than one million lives lost in British India alone. It also ravaged the princely states of Hyderabad, Rajputana, Central India, Baroda, Kathiawar and Cutch, where large (never accurately collated) numbers died and many more were forced to migrate. In December 1900, Congress delegates travelling by train to the session in Lahore saw the devastation with their own eyes from carriage windows; at every small station they encountered starving children with bloated bellies, and desperate adults unable to feed them. They witnessed the distress of the dying, they glimpsed the bodies of the dead. These scenes grew more unbearable and more unacceptable with each new crisis. Writing of her travels in 1896, Annie Besant, the Irishwoman who was beginning her 'last four lives' in India as a theosophist and later as a Congresswoman (she would become the party's leader in 1917), wrote of how shocked she was when her train stopped at little railway stations, and she saw 'living skeletons, holding out skinny hands and crying in agony to the passengers for food'.[44]

In each year of the first decade of the new century, there was yet another famine somewhere in India. One part of North India, the Bhojpuri-speaking region, suffered famine in 1903, 1905, 1909, and again in 1910.[45] Every new crisis hammered home Dadabhai's simple message that India was a community of producers who were not producing enough to feed themselves, and Dutt's argument that something was terribly wrong with the colonial system of agrarian taxation.

In this context, British counter-arguments appeared feeble. A paradox, as Annie Besant could see, lay at the heart of imperial rule in India. 'British rule', she wrote, had supposedly 'enlightened her [India's] darkness with Western civilisation', given India 'the best Civil Service in the world', and 'imposed peace and security upon her'. Yet this was 'curiously accompanied with widespread poverty, recurring famines and no possible margin for increased taxation'.[46]

Blaming the weather showed the extent to which the imperialists were losing the argument. Curzon's response that 'to ask any Government to prevent the occurrence of famine in a country, the meteorological conditions of what they are here . . . is to ask us to wrest the keys of the universe from the hands of the Almighty',[47] was blundering at best. Another default position was to pin the blame on Indian peasants for their alleged laziness, or their spendthrift habits. Nor did Curzon's offhand (and sometimes bizarre) remarks persuade these sophisticated critics. In 1904, he compared Gokhale to an amiable eccentric who puts up his umbrella and insists it is raining when the sun is shining. In 1905 his *ex cathedra* declaration that the material progress of India was 'without example in the previous history of

India and rare in the history of any people' required faith in viceregal infallibility in a land of unbelievers.[48] It only infuriated Indians further. The bottom line was that these statements made the British appear to care not a jot about the starving poor, 'the ordinary Indian' – contrary to the public justification for their rule.

Deep wells of 'poverty feeling' irrigated Indian patriotism hereafter.[49] Arguably they have had a critical impact on the structure of South Asian nationalisms ever since. The notion that India had been sucked dry, converted 'into a land of raw produce for the benefit of manufacturers and operatives in England', and overtaxed to the point of mass starvation, became a defining idea that bridged the divides between warring nationalist factions and camps of every hue.

The arguments of these pioneers of economic nationalism – Dadabhai, Dutt, G. V. Joshi and G. Subramaniya Iyer – were nuanced, layered and based on statistics generated by the Raj itself. When translated, via the press, to larger publics, however, the message was starker and more crude. The Tamil 'extremist' Subramaniam Bharati, the first Indian to produce cartoons in his Tamil vernacular paper *India*, depicted a corpulent John Bull literally sucking out India's wealth through a straw, reducing her to a skeleton – making the economic critique of empire available to the non-literate.

Importantly for the politics of this era, one idea lost in translation was the question of intention. For Dadabhai, bad (and hence 'unBritish') rule by 'Anglo-India' had created the crisis of Indian poverty; but he never argued that the government, or the people of Britain, *wanted* Indians to starve. This was why he spent much of his life as an MP in London appealing to the goodwill and sense of justice of the British people. Yet when the emergent media discussed the issue in India, this distinction was often glossed over. More and more, the idea took hold that Britain was *deliberately* exploiting India's economy in her own best interests. It became common currency to believe that the British cared not a fig about the consequences for India's people.

Another vital point needs to be made about 'economic nationalism'. It focused on India's *lack of sufficient production* to feed her people, and pinned the blame for this deficiency on the Raj and its acts of omission and commission. At no stage did they raise the question of unequal *distribution*, or the inequitable treatment of the poor. This particular interpretation of the problem of poverty made it a unifying issue that helped to unite different classes of Indian society, rather than pitting one against the other.[50]

Despite its materialism, therefore, economic nationalism was worlds away from Marxist doctrine. It said little of the many crucial distinctions between Indians, whether as producers or as consumers. The fact that most subsisted on a handful of unpolished millet, while a few decked their families in gold or drove imported motorcars, was not discussed. Paradoxically, economic nationalism was thus a unifying creed. Reinterpreted with different accents across the century, its key propositions endured. Throughout the twentieth century South Asians grew up 'knowing' its 'truths' without ever having studied or analysed them. In this sense they became normative concepts, impossible for the British to dislodge.

When independence came, these concepts formed the bedrock on which Indians, Pakistanis and, later, Bangladeshis based their expectations of their new independent nations. This is when the paradox at the heart of the creed of economic nationalism jumped out of its cage to bite its nationalist legatees.

III

MEANS AND ENDS I: 'WE WILL KILL, THE NATION WILL RISE'

If Indian nationalists shared perceptions of white racism and were agreed that British rule was impoverishing India, what accounts for the violence at Surat? What divided the 'moderates' from the 'extremists'?

Factional conflicts are a part, but only a minor part, of the explanation. Strong personalities are rarely comfortable bedfellows, and the history of nationalisms in the subcontinent is replete with the most vital, vivid, larger-than-life personalities. It is also rife with swordplay between them. There was no love lost between the leading 'moderate', Gopal Krishna Gokhale, and the challenger at Surat, Bal Gangadhar Tilak. Both came from the same stable (in social terms): both were of the Chitpavan Brahmin caste (more on caste in Chapter 6), both were descendants of a scribal elite who had served Shivaji's Maratha empire long before the East India Company took over western India. Both went to Deccan College in Poona, a premier centre of learning in the Bombay Presidency.

But despite their similar background and education, they were very different characters: Gokhale was soft-spoken, sedate and courteous, and knew how to get his own way with honey rather than vinegar. (Gandhi was Gokhale's disciple, and may have learned some of his own political arts from his guru.) Tilak, by contrast, was all vinegar. He was emphatic and belligerent. Often the two men jockeyed for the same positions in the same organisations, and their animus towards each other was no secret. Tilak and his extremist followers begrudged the moderates their domination of the Congress. In these early days, the Congress leadership tended to be something of a closed cabal. Many moderate leaders had been friends since their student days, so those not belonging to this charmed circle felt like outsiders.

But there was much more to Surat than that.

The 'New Party', as Tilak described his group, represented the more culturally assertive mood abroad in India at the turn of the century. Among Hindus this was particularly marked in western India, Bengal and the Punjab, where 'revivalist' voices had begun to challenge the damning British (and Christian missionary) account of Hinduism as a religion rife with superstition and snake oil. In western India, Tilak championed orthodox Hindus, who were dead against raising the age of consent for Hindu girls. Indian social reformers had long demanded that the law raise to twelve the age when a Hindu marriage could be consummated. In 1892, they finally persuaded the government (always chary after the Mutiny and Rebellion of intervening in Indian religious affairs) to draft a bill to this effect. But Tilak, backed by some Poona Brahmins, fought the bill tooth and nail, arguing that 'for 2,500 years the custom had been to consummate a marriage as soon as a girl achieved puberty, whatever her age. Since puberty was often reached before twelve, the proposed [measure] not only attacked religious custom but it undermined the rights of Hindu husbands.'[51]

In a horrific case in Calcutta two years previously, ten-year-old Phulmonee had died as a result of being raped, with unspeakable violence, by her much older husband.[52] Yet Tilak rose to defend the husband against 'diabolical persecution' for a 'harmless act'.[53] The Age of Consent Bill now escalated into a larger issue about the sanctity of Hindu marriage, which Tilak (and others like him) insisted was a sacred space to be protected from the intrusion of colonial law and western values. Hindu marriage began to emerge, in this camp, as the very symbol of India's cultural authenticity. The preservation of the Hindu wife's purity (in both physical and cultural terms) became almost synonymous, in this period, with a certain brand of nationalism. It remains so in contemporary India, having picked up even darker tones during the violence of partition, as this book will show.

Tilak's reputation, forged during the Age of Consent controversy, grew when he campaigned for the Hindu festival of Ganapati. Until then a relatively quiet domestic celebration, he wanted to politicise the festival, turning it into a popular symbol of Hindu resistance: in his Marathi newspaper *Kesari*, he called upon Hindus to convert 'the large religious festivals into mass political rallies'.[54] Today, the Ganapati festival in Bombay is celebrated by hundreds of thousands of boisterous devotees parading through the city's roads carrying massive gaudy idols of the elephant-headed god Ganesh to be immersed in the sea. Visitors from afar might think this is a Hindu custom as old as time but, as with much else apparently ancient in modern India, it is a recent innovation.

Tilak believed that Ganesh, the remover of obstacles, who appealed to 'low' and 'high' castes alike, would unite Hindus in public worship. But in promoting the Ganapati festival, he had another, more menacing, agenda: to compete with Muslims, who had won from the government permission (denied to Hindus) to have public assemblies and processions for religious purposes. By redressing the balance of public visibility for Hindus in this way, Tilak left a profound mark on the public culture of western India, and indeed the subcontinent. He also threw himself behind a cult of Shivaji, the seventeenth-century Hindu Maratha leader who had successfully resisted Mughal (and hence allegedly 'Muslim') forces.

Tilak's attempt to create an annual Shivaji festival failed but his Marathi poem 'Shivaji's Utterances' reveals his preoccupation with national 'degradation':

O, Shiv, Shiv, I see now with my eyes the ruin of the country!
O, to build which I spent money like rain,
And where to acquire which fresh hot blood was spilt.
From which I issued forth attacking through valleys, roaring like a lion.
These forts of mine have toppled down,

What ruin is this?
The foreigners teasingly and forcibly drag Lakshmi by the hand.
With her, plenty has run away and health has followed.[55]

It is hard to go anywhere in Maharashtra today without seeing statues of Shivaji depicted as a Maratha warrior on horseback, complete with turban and beard and brandishing a sword, the emblem of militant Hindu resistance to the foreigner. With an unerring instinct for metaphor and allegory, Tilak created symbols around which Hindu cultural assertion – and indeed aggression – could coalesce. These iconographies had (and were designed to have) an anti-Muslim edge. Tilak's politics were confrontational, designed to destroy unities that liberals had contrived with great care.

There were other revivalist currents abroad throughout India at this time. In the Punjab, the teachings of another social reformer, Dayanand Saraswati, and of his Arya Samaj movement, inspired the extremists with its enthusiasm for cow protection. In Bengal, meanwhile, they drew upon the writings of Bankimchandra Chatterjee (1838–94). A Bengali deputy magistrate, Bankimchandra was a brilliant polymath – an essayist, novelist and playwright – who came to define the Bengal Renaissance of the later nineteenth century. His distinctive thesis was that the sources of national rejuvenation lay not in western culture but were to be found within Hindu tradition. To succeed, he insisted, modern Hindus must recover their lost physical vigour and love of liberty. In significant ways, he began to define 'modern' Hinduism.[56]

Bankimchandra wrote stinging social satire as well as gripping romances in which powerful heroines flouted social norms. In literary terms, he was a genius. Yet the work which had the greatest political impact was one of his least accomplished. The play *Ananda Math* ('The Abbey of Bliss', 1882) tells the story of how a band of young pilgrims fought to rid their motherland of Muslim invaders. Their anthem 'Bande Mataram' ('Hail the Motherland') opens with hauntingly beautiful imagery, evoking, despite its Sanskritised language, the nation as a mother goddess rich with sweet waters, bejewelled with fruit, her serene fields windswept in the dusk.[57] In 1905, 'Bande Mataram' became the hymn of the *swadeshi* movement (of which more to come) and an anthem for Hindu revivalists throughout India. It remains so to this day (see Chapter 2).

Latent in this Hindu revivalist mood was the notion that colonialism was not just the cause of economic impoverishment but was also a consequence of cultural emasculation. Hindus had to recover their vitality through learning the old arts of 'physical culture'. In this call for resistance, there was more than a hint that violence was both necessary and legitimate. Tilak's commentary on the *Gita* – in which Lord Krishna in the *avataar* of a charioteer urges Arjun, hero of the ancient epic, the *Mahabharata*, to go to war against his cousins – was notable in this genre. But long before it was published, the warrior undertones of Hindu revivalism were at work in the many gymnasiums or *akharas* where young boys learned to wrestle and trained to fight with sticks and staves. Tilak's *Gita Rahasya* ('The Meaning of the Mysteries of the Gita'), written in 1915 in a Mandalay prison, validated a mood music already turned up loud.

Thus one issue between the moderates and extremists was the promotion by the latter of these currents of 'muscular Hinduism'.[58] But this is not to suggest that the moderates were irreligious, rationalist or atheist in their view towards religion. Many 'moderates' were deeply religious men. In the Parsi context, Dadabhai was as much a revivalist or fundamentalist as was Tilak among Hindus: he was just not keen to mix these matters of faith with a *constructive* nationalist project. In the late nineteenth century, religious practices had come under intense scrutiny as, with the spread of print, scriptures were translated from the languages of the gods into the demotic tongues of men. Increasingly, as laymen and -women came to challenge the tight grip that theocracies and religious scholars had previously enjoyed over the interpretation of 'the word', every faith underwent a fragmentation of religious authority at much the same time, and for much the same reasons.[59] This process spawned a multitude of revivalist, reformist and fundamentalist strands and sects. Extremists gained inspiration from them, but by no means all revivalists were extremists.

What *was* distinct about the extremists was their accent on violence. Their elision of a particularly 'upper-caste' construction of modern Hinduism with the idea of the nation itself – already much in evidence at the start of the century – would be a toxic legacy for the subcontinent. But at Surat, these issues remained latent. In 1907, the split was mainly about methods and tactics. Moderates insisted that steady and persistent pressure upon the British government in

London for reform in India was the best means of achieving change. Their preferred method was persuasion, armed with reasoned argument based on irrefutable 'facts' and figures gained from British archives and censuses. The extremists dismissed this approach as mendicant and humiliating. As one young Bengali anarchist put it to the Grand Old Man of moderation, Dadabhai, 'While fifty years of preaching and supplication had proved of no avail, half an ounce of lead had worked wonders, and will still work wonders.' Yet Dadabhai found 'the idea [of violence] was wholly repugnant [to his] feelings and convictions'. Despite disappointments, he still wanted to 'believe that India's salvation lies in the hands of the British public'.[60]

Violence as a means, and revulsion against it, had by 1907 become two opposite poles in the nationalist politics of India. From now on, arguments about violence would continue to rage and shape its force fields. These debates were so impassioned that it is easy to miss the common ground shared by protagonists at the two ends of the spectrum.

The *swadeshi* movement of 1905–8, a call to boycott British goods and 'buy Indian', is fascinating because it puts these differences as well as the shared assumptions under the spotlight. The movement was both more popular and more divisive than anything that had preceded it – signalling how uncomfortably popular movements sit within projects of 'national unity'.

The trigger was Curzon's plan to partition Bengal, India's largest and most populous province, on the face of things because the province was simply too unwieldy to be governed. By cutting Bengal into two, officials claimed, the 'backward' province of Assam would, together with eastern Bengal, have a more efficient administration. But behind the scenes, they were conscious that Bengal was home to some of the Raj's most vocal and articulate critics, the Hindu elites or *bhadralok* (gentlefolk). A partition of Bengal, they thought, would neutralise this 'thorn in the side of government'.[61] Prudence and political expediency pointed in the same direction, or so it seemed. It proved to be one of Curzon's biggest political blunders, showing how remote this Most Superior Person was from the India he had been sent to rule.

George Nathaniel Curzon was not a man given to self-doubt. Born in 1859 in the grand surroundings of Kedleston Hall to a line which, he liked to claim, went 'straight back to a Norman who came over with the Conqueror', from his very first days at Eton, Britain's grandest school, Curzon had gained a reputation for arrogance.[62] One can see why. By the age of thirteen, he was complaining to his mother about Windsor's 'silly tradesmen' and 'idiotic' tailors.[63] The youngest viceroy ever to have been sent out to India – he was not yet forty when he arrived in Calcutta – as a typical gentleman-scholar Curzon had travelled widely in Asia before he took up his post, and he regarded himself as an expert on Asia's geopolitics. From that perspective, he was concerned about getting Britain the upper hand in the so-called 'Great Game', repelling the threat to British India from Tsarist Russia's relentless expansion to the east, and after a series of risings on the Afghan frontier in the closing years of the nineteenth century. Irritated as much by the 'carping' Bengalis as by crippling sciatica, he let the bureaucrats persuade him that the best way to 'manage' the problem of Bengal was to divide it. His advisors predicted that once the deed was done, 'the native . . . will quickly become accustomed to the new conditions'.[64]

But the 'natives' – particularly urban 'upper-caste' Bengali Hindus, many of whom had their estates in East Bengal, where Muslims were the majority of the population – did not take the partition lying down. They belonged to a generation brought up on Bankimchandra's ode to the motherland. They had absorbed the arguments marshalled by Dutt and Dadabhai. Even if they had not read the 'Grand Old Man' (as by now Dadabhai was known), most had read Sakharam Ganesh Deuskar's popular summary of his arguments in the Bengali work *Desher Katha* ('The Story of the Country'), which by 1910 had sold more than 10,000 copies. They had consumed the even more succinct and damning pamphlet '*Krishaker sarbanash*' ('The ruin of the peasantry') and had watched street plays dramatising the same powerful message. Economic nationalism had become part of their collective DNA. Thus a key plank of the movement was the boycott of British goods, and in its place, the support of *swadeshi* (domestic) manufactures.

After 1905, when the movement entered its radical phase in the agitation against the partition of Bengal, 'the air [became] full of *swadeshi* schemes – textile mills and improved handlooms, river transport concerns, match and soap factories, education and tanneries.'[65] Handloom weaving revived to such an extent that in the peak years of the *swadeshi* movement, there were sharp falls in the imports to Bengal of

Lancashire's cotton goods and apparel. Imports of tobacco and liquor slumped as well, starting a permanent trend, as Indian manufacturers stepped in fast to take advantage of new markets for their goods.[66]

But it would be a mistake to focus on their opportunistic rise and miss the heady mix of sacrifice and resistance that *swadeshi* conjured into being. My grandfather, a man of considerable commercial initiative, built the Hill Cart Road from the railhead in Jalpaiguri in North Bengal all the way to Darjeeling, to supply coal to British-owned tea gardens. One might describe him as a classic collaborator with the Raj. But it is too easy to judge a man's politics from what he does for a living: my *Dadu* (grandpa) boycotted British goods for years. Abjuring British alcohol was a huge sacrifice for him. He dealt with these privations in an enterprising spirit, setting up a private distillery to show solidarity with the cause. Throughout the *swadeshi* years (and indeed through the Gandhian years of non-cooperation) he and his friends drank his home-made brew instead of imported Scotch. I doubt that Dadu, who loved life's luxuries, enjoyed the stuff – he had a taste for fine teas that were more expensive than champagne. But in the era of *swadeshi*, he bought, ate, wore and drank only *swadeshi* goods. A great many people like him did – including many who looked as though they might be, or ought to be, sympathetic to British rule.

Yet while economic nationalism informed the *swadeshi* project, it also soon developed a religious meaning. For the Bengali revolutionary Aurobindo Ghosh, nationalism was about much more than economics and politics; it was 'a religion by which we are trying to live. It is a religion by which we are trying to realise God in the nation, in our fellow-countrymen.'[67]

Born in 1872 as the son of an atheist surgeon, Aurobindo had an unusual upbringing even in a time of flux and shifting contexts for most Indian elites. His father seems to have been determined to produce boys so thoroughly anglicised that he hired an English nurse and butler, and then sent his sons to Loreto Convent in Darjeeling, a school mainly reserved for the children of European officials in India. When Aurobindo was seven, the boys were packed off to England, where they were placed in the charge of a Reverend Drewett and his wife, who taught them history, Latin, French, geography and mathematics. This curious arrangement might have been influenced by the fact that Swarnalata, Aurobindo's mother, was beginning to show signs of the mental-health troubles that plagued her family, but it left

Aurobindo a grass orphan with a lifelong hatred for Christian preaching.

When the Drewetts migrated to Australia, they left the boys behind with some of their own elderly relatives. Aurobindo somehow contrived to get into St Paul's School in London, and later gained a place at King's College, Cambridge, on an open scholarship, using his grant to help support his brothers – his father having long since stopped sending any money to support his sons.

Aurobindo never spoke of his abandonment by his parents. But his brother Manmohan did, writing to a friend, 'I had no mother. She is insane. You may judge the horror of this, how I strove to snatch a fearful love, but only succeeded in hating and loathing, and at last becoming cold.'[68] The loneliness of the boys, and their dire financial straits in England, make the young Aurobindo's future achievements all the more remarkable. On his return to India, he went to work for the Maharaja of Baroda, Sayaji Rao Gaekwad III, who was among a number of princes who flirted with nationalist and revolutionary endeavours, and more to the point, financed them.[69] (Both Romesh Chunder Dutt and Dadabhai were employed at different times at his court.)

When Aurobindo returned to India, he was neither a revolutionary nor a nationalist. But he was profoundly moved by the country, experiencing 'a tremendous peace' as soon as he 'set foot on Indian soil'.[70] Yet in the Maharaja of Baroda's employ in western India, his outlook began to change. Aurobindo met Tilak but, if anything, his view of the state of the nation was even harsher than that of the older man. India, in Aurobindo's words, was like an old man 'with stores of knowledge, with ability to feel and desire, but paralysed by senile sluggishness, senile timidity, senile feebleness'.[71] His diagnosis was clear, albeit presented in purple prose:

If India is to survive, she must be made young again. Rushing and billowing streams of energy must be poured into her; her soul must become, as it was in the old times, like the surges, vast, puissant, calm or turbulent at will, an ocean of action or of force.[72]

Here again we see the perception of India's fall from past greatness, so characteristic of nationalist thinking of this era, and the urgent need for a project of reconstruction and recovery. Returning to Bengal as a journalist and activist, Aurobindo, together with his more

trigger-happy youngest brother Barin, established Jugantar, a secret
society of young men dedicated to 'the rebirth of the Shakti [force] of
the Mother [Goddess]'. Jugantar was one of many such societies set
up in Bengal between 1905 and 1908, imbued with a spirit of religious dedication to the motherland, which enlisted young men to
make bombs and guns to win freedom.

Between the two poles, with moderately worded requests for reform
at one end and terrorist societies at the other, a host of organisations
promoted self-help (*atma-sakti*) in all manner of forms. Bengal's
iconic poet and India's first Nobel laureate, Rabindranath Tagore,
fashioned his own brand of 'constructive *swadeshi*', which anticipated
a great deal of what Gandhism would be about; but he also created a
new ethics and aesthetics of nationalism that would be profoundly
influential for much of the rest of the twentieth century.[73] In his tract
Swadeshi Samaj ('Our Autonomous Society'), Tagore spelled out with
poetic eloquence a practical programme urging volunteers to spread
enlightenment in India's villages and to revive 'traditional society'.
Only by a huge labour of love and self-sacrifice could the nation ever
achieve its potential, he urged. What 'Young India' needed to do was
renounce luxury, instead accumulating spiritual power by cooperative
enterprises, mass education schemes and grassroots development
projects.

Disparaging modern habits of consumption, by which 'the fatal
embrace' of colonial domination had 'introduced its tentacles through
our social fabric, from our educational institutions to the shops that
provide our daily necessities', Tagore commended, in his inimitable
style, the use of simple, rough, home-made goods.[74] Although he later
rejected much of his early vision of *swadeshi* and in particular the
potential for violence inherent in nationalism, *Swadeshi Samaj* 'created a sensation' when it was published in 1904.[75] Its call for material
sacrifice inspired the innumerable *swadeshi* organisations that sprang
up in this period, including not only industries but national schools,
even a university.

In the first decade of the twentieth century, therefore, nationalism
was no longer just an idea, or a project, it had become a *practice*.
India's elites boycotted British goods, and using indigenous handicrafts assumed a new political and moral significance. Elite tastes
began to change. Nationalist men and women began to promote a
new *swadeshi* material culture. Santiniketan (the 'abode of peace'),

Tagore's experimental school in rural Bolpur, a long way from Calcutta, played a key role in this transformation. Santiniketan's students learned in Bengali, not in English – a volte-face for an intelligentsia that had rushed to embrace western education, western languages, western dress and western habits. At Tagore's school (where the later prime minister of India, Indira Nehru Gandhi, studied for some years), students and teachers wore Indian dress and fabrics, ate Indian food, used Indian handicrafts, and learned to read their own language using his lyrical Bengali primer, *Sahaj Paath* ('Easy Lessons'). Illustrated by woodcuts made by the artist Nandalal Bose, it must be one of the best textbooks in any language anywhere in the world.

Tagore had a passionate love of nature. Santiniketan's curriculum thus included walks through the countryside, with students being encouraged to observe the changing seasons, the flora and the fauna around them. Immersion in the natural environment of Bengal became a way of imbuing pupils with his own love of it, palpable in the song 'Amar Shonar Bangla' ('Our Golden Bengal'). Pupils read Bengali plays and sang Bangla songs, many of them composed by Tagore himself, a genius whose love of the idioms and rhythms of rural Bengal drenched his poetry. Under Tagore's influence, nationalism became a love affair with the country's physical and human geography. Yet it was a love that embraced both India's beauty and its ugliness. Tagore inspired Bipin Chandra Pal, a Bengali extremist, to write in 1907:

Love of India now means a loving regard for the very configuration of this continent – a love for its rivers and mountains, for its paddy fields and its arid sandy plains, its towns and villages however uncouth and unsanitary these might be ... a love for the muddy weed-entangled village lands, the moss-covered stinky village ponds, and for the poor, the starved, the malaria-stricken populations of the country, a love for its languages, its literatures, its philosophies, its religions.[76]

Gandhi's adoption (and adaptation) of Tagore's hand-spun, folk aesthetic would extend its reach and popularity in the next decades, taking it well beyond Bengal. But it was during the *swadeshi* era that a person's politics began to be marked out by what she was eating, drinking or wearing – or not wearing, as the case may be. In October 1905, students at Dacca Government College came barefoot to class to protest against Curzon's partition of Bengal. Students across the country joined them to show sympathy. They were expelled from their schools as a result.

The government's response, as so often in the century that saw the decline and fall of the empire, was blundering. A spate of executive orders tried to prevent the contagion spreading. In East Bengal the Lyon Circulars banned the very words '*Bande mataram*' of Bankimchandra's ode, while the Carlyle Circular threatened to withdraw grants and deny affiliation to schools and colleges that failed to prevent their students from participating in politics. Rangpur and Dacca expelled students and teachers en masse. These ill-conceived measures only upped the ante. Disaffected and often rusticated or expelled from colonial institutions, middle-class students rushed to join Bengal's extremist groups and revolutionary terrorist societies.

Just how influential these societies were has always been controversial. By their very nature official information about them was patchy, garnered from unreliable government spies and self-interested 'approvers'; while the revolutionaries' own memoirs (often published years later, long after independence) are sometimes self-aggrandising. But it is generally agreed that between 1905 and 1908, terrorist societies flourished; that they did not disappear until the mid-1930s; and that a mood of violence was woven into the fabric of Bengal's politics, always palpable in the backcloth. Early in the boycott movement, an obscure Calcutta weekly called *Pratijna* ('Resolve') called on the public to give police informers 'a good thrashing'.[77] The journal *Sandhya* ('Evening'), unique in its use of the demotic language of the streets, abused the *firanghee* (foreigner) and mocked all Indians who aped his ways; by 1901 it had already become Calcutta's most popular vernacular daily.[78] *Yugantar* ('New Age'), advised by Aurobindo himself, began with a tiny circulation but by 1908, when it was banned, its print run had risen to 15,000. It espoused violence, declaring that 'without bloodshed, the worship of the goddess [the motherland] will not be accomplished'.[79]

Most of the terrorists' plots were botched attempts ending in failure; some were almost comical in their incompetence, with home-made devices often failing to go off. A few were well organised and successful. In 1906, Hemchandra Kanungo of the Anushilan Samity sold part of his own land to fund a trip to Paris to learn anarchist methods, and he returned with a 174-page bomb manual and a treatise on revolutionary organisation.[80] Using this knowledge, Kanungo made a bomb, placed it inside a book and posted it to Kingsford, a former magistrate of Calcutta, hated in *swadeshi* circles for ordering that activists be flogged. Kingsford was not a reading man, however, and placed the book, unopened, on his bookshelf. (An imperial irony if there ever was one.)

In October 1908, the Anushilan Samity made a second attempt on the hated official's life. Prafulla Chaki and Khudiram Bose set out to assassinate him. This time, the bomb intended for Kingsford instead killed the hapless wife and daughter of Pringle Kennedy, a leading lawyer of Muzaffarpur. The police hunted down the fifteen-year-old Khudiram and the judge ordered him to be sent to the gallows. His bravery and defiance when arrested electrified the Indian public. Even the pro-government, 'Anglo-Indian' daily, *The Statesman*, acknowledged his popularity and the courage with which he accepted his fate:

The Railway station was crowded to see the boy [Khudiram]. A mere boy of 18 or 19 years old, who looked quite determined. He came out of a first-class compartment and walked all the way to the phaeton, kept for him outside, like a cheerful boy who knows no anxiety . . . on taking his seat the boy lustily cried 'Vandemataram'.[81]

This was the stuff of myth and fable, building up hopes that the nation, inspired by the sacrifice of these young revolutionaries, would rise up. Young girls would be part of that awakening. Many of them are famous today but few were spot on target. Santi Ghosh and Suniti Chowdhury, both sixteen years old, were among the few who were. They succeeded in shooting dead the British district magistrate of Comilla district in 1931. Assassinating district commissioners became a popular sport in areas where secret societies were strong: the British lost several in Midnapore alone. Many Indians well beyond Bengal began to condone – indeed, lionise – assassination as an instrument of politics. The pithy slogan coined by Bagha ('Tiger') Jatin, another revolutionary icon, encapsulated their intent: '*Aamra maarbo, jogoto jaagbe*' ('We will kill, the nation will rise').

The nation did not rise, and rather few were killed. Many applauded from the sidelines, but the revolution they hoped for did not materialise. If names like Bagha Jatin became forces to be reckoned with, their violence disturbed many Indians. And it alienated Muslim enthusiasts, who were barred from joining violent secret Hindu societies; many joined the Communist Party instead. Indeed, the very iconisation of 'nation-as-mother-goddess' challenged the religious belief of Muslims that there is but one god.

Yet without question, the terrorists' call to arms and willingness to die for the motherland gave challenge to more moderate forms of nationalist practice guided by liberal thought and pragmatic accommodation. The clash at Surat hinted at the compelling magnetism of the revolutionary path. The moderates may have won the battle at Surat, but they did not win the war. Even in the age of Gandhi, the debate over means and ends was never resolved. Violence continued to run in underground streams which erupted with sudden bangs, challenging the political and social order.[82] However, the politics of liberalism, negotiation, compromise and working through and around difference was the stuff of Indian nationalism on an everyday basis. This was difficult work, as every alliance was cobbled together over time, and could collapse like a house of cards.

IV

MEANS AND ENDS II: 'A HIMALAYAN MISCALCULATION'

Gandhi's embrace of non-violence is best understood within this context. Born in 1869 in a tiny princely state in present-day Gujarat, the son of a humble *dewan* (chief minister) of the state, Mohandas Gandhi came from a very different India to the metropolitan nationalist intelligentsia of Calcutta, Bombay and Madras described above. Something of a country cousin in their sophisticated and Europeanised world of ideas, he was dumbstruck in the presence of Pherozeshah Mehta, one of the original members of the London India Society and a leading moderate who, Gandhi wrote in his memoirs, 'roared like a lion in court'.[83]

For a start, Gandhi was not a Brahmin, but of a *baniya* (trading) caste, and his father was barely educated in the western sense, although he could read, write and keep accounts. By his own admission, Gandhi was a poor student, albeit a very obedient one. His autobiography gives a picture of a sensitive if eccentric child. While others of his age were busy playing games, young Mohandas puzzled over morality, truth and right conduct. Influenced by his mother's Jain religious austerity, and by her cheerful and apparently endless episodes of fasting, Gandhi came to believe that her spirit of sacrifice defined and ennobled Hindu womanhood – very much in the patriarchal spirit of his times.

But in other ways he was most unusual. When Mohandas looked after his father through his long, and ultimately fatal, illness, he showed a passion for the 'effeminate' business of nursing that characterised much of his life.

The family tried to force this square peg into a round hole, marrying him off at the age of thirteen to the feisty and pragmatic young Kasturbai (with whom he developed a passionate, jealous and complicated relationship) and then sending him to London to become a barrister. But he never lost his innate idiosyncrasy. In London, his obsession was with dietetics; extreme vegetarianism interested him far more than the law, which he studied with diligence but without flair. His interests were eclectic. He joined the London Vegetarian Society. He studied Christianity after reading the New Testament. Aware of his own appetites, he grew interested in sexual – and other forms of – abstinence. He read bits and pieces about Hinduism, mainly in English translation. In fact, it was only after reading Madame Blavatsky's *The Key to Theosophy* – the Russian occultist had taken elite India by storm when Gandhi was still a child – that he yearned to learn about 'his own faith'. Blavatsky's book, he recalled, 'disabused me of the notion fostered by the missionaries that Hinduism was rife with superstition'.[84] Gandhi's Hindu faith was in no sense traditional or orthodox: it was a personal construct, built from watching his mother, from reading a mixed bag of religious texts and commentaries, from conversations with friends with similar interests. It was a highly individual creed which, as the subtitle of his autobiography, *My Experiments with Truth*, suggests, he worked throughout his life to refine.

In 1891, after being called to the bar at London, Gandhi returned to India and set up as a lawyer in Bombay. But his painful shyness left him tongue-tied and trembling when called upon to speak in the courtroom. This diffidence, and his lack of connections in the big city, meant that he got no briefs.

Gandhi's first dealings with a British official in India came at this point in his life: despite his being a barrister, the white *saheb* threw him out of the room when he went to intercede on behalf of his brother.[85] This insult, Gandhi recalls, was 'the first shock', and there were more to come.

In 1893, still with no briefs coming his way, a chance offer of work took him to South Africa. A Porbandar trading firm with a big case in Durban offered to retain him for a year to advise their local lawyers, all expenses paid, for a fee of £105. He stayed on in South Africa until 1914. It was here that he forged close and formative friendships, and that he matured as a lawyer, thinker and activist.[86] In 2003, a sculpture of the young Gandhi in legal robes was erected in Gandhi Square near the courts in Johannesburg, to commemorate his role in South Africa's history.

Yet that contribution, as with so much else about Gandhi, was shot through with ambivalence. In *Hind Swaraj or Indian Home Rule* (1909), which many take to be his defining work, Gandhi held that 'Asiatics' were superior to 'uncivilised' *'kaffirs'* or blacks. Because like the Europeans they came from a great civilisation, they should not be treated on the same footing as Africans.[87] He later applied some of this language of hierarchy and exclusion to Dalits, India's 'untouchables'; while championing their cause, Gandhi urged them to 'purify' themselves by abandoning their 'evil habits'.[88]

In Natal, discrimination against 'Asiatics' – who after the Boer War had to pay a poll tax of £3 to enter the province, could own land only in specially allocated zones, and were denied the franchise – prompted Gandhi to develop his techniques of passive resistance. He had supported the British Empire 'in its hour of need', showing courage and commitment in assembling an Indian ambulance corps during the Boer War, the Zulu rebellion, and later during the First World War. Like his mentor Gokhale, Gandhi still had faith in the British and, in his own way, was a passionate imperial citizen.[89] But in South Africa he was brought face to face with the horrendous conditions of Indian, mainly Tamil- and Telegu-speaking indentured labourers, and took his campaign to improve their lot to India itself. With Gokhale's exhortations in support, the Congress took up the issue. As the campaign against the inequities of indenture gathered momentum in India (we will return to it in Chapter 4), the British deemed it expedient in 1917 to abandon the system.

Meanwhile, Gandhi's championing of the issue won him some recognition in India, particularly in the regions of the south from which most of the workers were recruited, as well as among Muslim merchants and professionals from Gujarat, based in Natal but with connections to their home regions.

Gandhi's first direct engagement with Indian politics came when he wrote *Hind Swaraj*. First composed in Gujarati, while on board a ship on one of his journeys from South Africa to India, this short but crucial work – banned in India in 1910 – takes the form of a dialogue between a questioning Reader and the Editor (Gandhi himself). A central theme was violence and its illegitimacy as a political strategy. In this pithy, deceptively simple work, the Editor insists that British rule in India rested on neither conquest nor force, but on the collusion of Indians seduced by the siren calls of western materialism and modernity: 'The English have not taken India; we have given it to them. They are not in India because of their strength, but because we keep them.'[90]

It followed that to challenge or overthrow British rule, force was not needed. If Indians withdrew their cooperation from the Raj – as they should, he later argued, when the Khilafat and Punjab 'wrongs' convinced him in 1919 that British rule in India was perfidious and immoral – it could not survive. Bluntly stated, 'their arms and ammunition are perfectly useless'.[91]

Gandhi's politics were a mélange: a creative mix of his 'experiments with truth' and what he saw as the best in existing political theory and practice. Added to boycott, non-cooperation and *swadeshi* which had emerged in Bengal, were Gokhale's gentlemanly politics of respect for his opponents, and various forms of passive moral suasion creditors deployed in his home region of Kathiawar; they included a mixed bag of ideas he had picked up in London and South Africa and made his own.[92] In that bag was the muscular Judaism of Max Nordau,[93] John Ruskin's economics in *Unto This Last*, esoteric Christianity, the non-violent resistance advocated by Tolstoy in *The Kingdom of God Is Within You*, Theosophy of course, and the *Bhagavad Gita*, which he read again and again. This bricolage of ideas and practices emerged within a global context in the last decades of the nineteenth century, when many were questioning the efficacy of liberalism and how Indian society would cope with mass democracy and socialism. As one scholar puts it, 'The figure of the *satyagrahi* was forged within this miasma of fears.'[94]

To give his politics a name, Gandhi coined the neologism *satyagraha*, combining *satya* (truth) with *agraha* (force). At a basic level, *satyagraha* was about harnessing the power of truth to win the opponent over without violence, and that meant refusing to retaliate in the face of state brutality. Its deeper, spiritual meaning (which preoccupied Gandhi) remains elusive, despite the efforts of many fine minds to unravel it.[95]

Paradoxically, the Mahatma himself was not a nationalist, if judged by the influential definition of nationalism as a political movement which seeks to capture state power.[96] Gandhi did not look to the state to improve the lot of the people. No admirer of parliamentary democracy, he had little time for liberal ideas of economic development and progress. Indeed, in *Hind Swaraj*, Gandhi comes across as a conservative in the mode of Edmund Burke. He saw himself more as a social and religious reformer than a political leader. Yet Gandhi was a major figure in the growth of all-India nationalism as it became a more broad-based movement. His achievement was to attract the meek and the humble to the cause of the nation. Yet he did so while remaining ambivalent about the 'masses' themselves; their lack of 'hygiene' and above all their lack of 'discipline' troubled him. Gandhi was an ally of capitalists and the caste order, and a friend of patriarchy, *panchaayats* and propriety. As the industrialist Ghanshyam Das Birla told the viceroy, this man of the people was India's greatest force for conservatism.

By the time Gandhi returned to India in 1914, the country had begun to pay a substantial price, in men and money, to support the Allied war effort. In peacetime, the Indian Army recruited about 15,000 men each year; during the First World War, that number rocketed upwards to almost 1.3 million men over four years, almost a million of whom were pressed into service overseas. British India paid for this massive force by doubling down on taxation, already heavy to breaking point before the hostilities began. In 1917 India made a direct contribution of £100 million to its imperial overlord, a sum representing 'nearly two years of her net revenue as it stood at the beginning of the war'.[97] Every form of tax was slapped onto Indians, and merchants particularly resented the heavy new taxes on sales and on 'super profits'.

After the war ended, wealthy peasants hit by price fluctuations and interruptions in essential supplies, demobilised soldiers returning in their hundreds of thousands to their previous avocations, squeezed traders and businessmen, and many others who had previously shown little interest in the politics of the Congress began to look to the party as a vehicle to express their discontents. The Home Rule League movement, established by Tilak and Annie Besant (who had been chosen, some years before, by Blavatsky as her successor to lead the Theosophists), was absorbed into the Congress when Tilak wrested control over it in 1916: its membership swelled to about 60,000.

In this context of extreme economic hardship for many Indians, starving peasants in Champaran in the foothills of the Himalayas (in present-day Bihar) begged Gandhi to intercede on their behalf against white planters of indigo, the dye used in denim cloth. His success in persuading the government to set up a commission of enquiry burnished his reputation for identifying obvious wrongs and putting them to rights.

Then, in 1918, responding to an appeal from peasants in Kaira in Gujarat, Gandhi launched a *satyagraha*. Famine, cholera and the plague all threatened, but the government had refused to postpone collecting the land revenue or to hold an enquiry. The Kaira *satyagraha* is revealing. Gandhi persuaded many wealthier landowners to withhold payment in solidarity with their poorer brethren, which tells us much about his wider vision of moral politics. But the government made only the barest concessions, and those only to maintain some semblance of order during the war.[98] The staunch supporter of the Empire was finally becoming disillusioned by the callousness with which the Raj treated its Indian subjects.

At this stage the British regarded the Mahatma as little more than a nuisance. When Montagu, the Secretary of State for India, met him in 1917, he described Gandhi as 'a pure visionary' who lived on air, 'with a real desire to find grievances and cure them'.[99] Of much more concern to the authorities were signs that the Punjab, since 1856 the chief recruiting ground for their Indian Army and seen as a bastion of support for their rule, was restive, gripped by a new and dangerous political activism. A mysterious transnational revolutionary movement of diasporic Sikhs in Vancouver, the Ghadr, was making trouble in the Land of the Five Rivers.[100] The colonial government in India reacted by extending its draconian wartime control over all Indian political activity. It imposed the Defence of India Regulations, and suspended indefinitely such limited rights to free political expression that their Indian subjects had.

These were the infamous Rowlatt Bills. Gandhi saw this legislation as the ultimate breach of faith, a slap in the face in return for all the help Indians had given their rulers during the war. 'The recommendations of

the Rowlatt Committee', he wrote, were 'altogether unwarranted ...
such that no self-respecting people could submit to them'.[101] Country-
wide agitations to persuade the government to withdraw the Bills
failed because, as Gandhi put it: 'You can wake a man only if he is
really asleep.'[102]

Gandhi was not sure what to do. The answer, he claimed in typical
fashion, came to him in a dream: he would call upon the whole country to observe a general *hartal* (strike) for one day. 'Let all the people
of India suspend their business on that day and observe the day as one
of fasting and prayer.' The date of this 'peaceful hartal' was fixed for
30 March 1919, and later shifted to 6 April, news which did not reach
all parts of India in time. Where it did, 'the whole of India from one
end to the other, towns as well as villages, observed a complete hartal
on that day.'[103]

Gandhi wanted to be in the Punjab for the Rowlatt *satyagraha*, but
the government prevented him from getting there. Contrary to his
plans, violence broke out in some places, notably in the Punjab itself.
Nervous that the 'contagion' of unrest would unsettle the Punjab, the
province that had long been the bulwark of its rule, the government
banned political rallies there. Large public gatherings were held in defiance, or ignorance, of the ban, although their mood seems to have
been cheerful enough: on 9 April, Ram Navami, the birthday of the
'Hindu' god Ram, the brass band leading the procession struck
up 'God Save the King' while marching past the British Deputy
Commissioner.[104]

The government was jittery nonetheless, and called upon the army
to stand by. Troops began to attack protestors. When they beat the
elderly Congress leader, Lala Lapat Rai, to death, in broad daylight,
every Indian was horrified, no matter where they stood on the spectrum of nationalist views. They were enraged. In the Punjab there
were more protests, and 'Whipping Orders' in response to them. The
British were beginning to lose their nerve.

On 13 April 1919, General Dyer ordered his troops to fire on a
peaceful crowd gathered at Jallianwalla Bagh, an enclosed, walled park
in Amritsar in the heart of the Punjab, just a stone's throw from the
Sikh Golden Temple.[105] The park had only one narrow exit, which was
blocked by Dyer's troops. Precise casualty figures are still in dispute,
but in the carnage that day at least 500 people lost their lives.[106]

This massacre marked a profound turning point, an irreversible blow to the Raj's claims to legitimacy in their Indian empire, which went well beyond the Punjab. For a great many Indians outside that province – particularly educated Indians who had put their faith in the liberal possibilities of imperial subjecthood – that dream ended with Jallianwalla Bagh.[107] As Rabindranath Tagore wrote to the viceroy when he gave back his knighthood in protest: 'The time has come when badges of honour make our shame glaring in the incongruous context of humiliation.'[108]

I visited Jallianwalla Bagh in 2016. I had never been there before, although I cannot recall a time when I did not know about it. I was there with my husband, Anil, also a historian of India. Gaurav, a stout young father, drove us there in a large SUV ill-suited to the narrow lanes that lead to the even narrower entrance to the garden. A discreet image of Guru Nanak, the founder of Sikhism, on the dashboard, told me that Gaurav was a Sikh despite his fashionable Bollywood hairstyle. A distracted policeman with kohl-rimmed eyes told us that the entrance to Jallianwalla Bagh was marked by a banner advertising Coca-Cola, and so it was.

Hundreds of people strolled through the park with us, which on first appearance, looked much like any small park in South Asia on an average spring afternoon, slightly scruffy but crowded with families enjoying a day out. But everyone there knew its 'history'. Teenagers took ghoulish selfies by the well into which many victims had jumped in an effort to avoid being gunned down. They pored over and discussed every hole on the park's bullet-marked walls. When we returned to our car, I began to discuss the Rowlatt *satyagraha* with Gaurav, mentioning the confusion over when it had been scheduled to start, and the change of date to 6 April, but he corrected me. 'It was not the 6th, it was the 13th of April, 1919 – the first day of Baisakhi, the start of the Punjabi New Year and the anniversary of the birth of Sikhism,' he said. I was struck not only by his command of 'the facts', but also by how effortlessly his narrative wove together religious and regional histories into a particular story of national sacrifice. The fact that Jallianwalla Bagh is recalled so vividly by so many today, in the shadow of the Golden Temple, speaks volumes. Nationalism may be contested – indeed, civil war broke out in the 1980s over an independent Sikh state of Khalistan – but it is by no means dead.

Jallianwalla Bagh complicated Gandhi's mission of non-violent resistance to British rule. Despite the Mahatma's undeniable popularity, revolutionaries like Bhagat Singh, a Sikh communist from the Punjab who threw a bomb in the central assembly, and Bagha Jatin, who attempted for years to assassinate the despised Lieutenant Governor of Bengal and successfully killed Indian collaborators, became instant martyrs with a popular following rivalling the Mahatma's own.

The heavy-handedness of British repression only strengthened their mass appeal. British 'rule by gallows' made them into folk heroes whom thousands – perhaps tens of thousands – were willing to emulate. Convinced that unconnected instances of violence across India amounted to a massive and concerted Bolshevik conspiracy, the Raj resorted to extrajudicial violence to stamp it out, chasing the will-o'-the-wisps it feared but could not see.[109] A panoply of alternative penal tactics, many of which had no basis even in India's imperfect criminal justice system, were brought into force.[110] Hundreds of Indians went to jail without trial. Many more were flogged in public. Villages suspected of harbouring revolutionaries had to hold 'flag parades' and pay punitive collective fines. As layer upon layer of executive ordinance pushed the 'rule of law' into the background, violent punishments became routine elements of a regime increasingly unsure of its grip.[111] Firing on crowds was now deemed acceptable. Even after the Hunter Commission (which Congress boycotted) rebuked General Dyer for what he did at Jallianwalla Bagh, he became 'Anglo-India's' popular hero – and nationalist India's nemesis.

To regain a semblance of control over this situation, Gandhi had to act and act fast. With characteristic skill and timing, at the Congress session in Nagpur in 1920, he urged Indians not to cooperate with British rule, and to refuse (peacefully, of course) to obey its 'unjust' laws:

> If … the acts of … the Government be wrong … it is clear that we must refuse to submit to this official violence. Appeal to Parliament by all means if necessary, but if the Parliament fails us and we are worthy to call ourselves a nation, we must refuse to uphold the Government by withdrawing cooperation from it.[112]

In this crucial intervention, Gandhi's masterstroke was to urge Congressmen and all Indians with political influence in the provinces to boycott the new provincial Councils promised by the Government of India Act of 1919.

At Nagpur, his 'non-cooperation' resolution was passed by a Congress session packed not only with the usual Congress contingents but also with trainloads of angry Muslim Khilafatists (of whom more below). It was backed by all manner of politicians who calculated that they would not do well in the elections under the new Act, under a franchise calibrated by the British to help *their* friends. By skilful and opportunistic tactics within a brilliant grand strategy, Gandhi captured Congress, outflanking many Congress leaders who were puzzled by his idiosyncracies, alarmed by his alliance with Muslim Khilafatists and unconvinced of the merits of standing back from elected Councils in the provinces.

Non-cooperation, Gandhi stressed at Nagpur, had to be based on *ahimsaa* (non-violence). But *ahimsaa* was never achieved. Violence erupted here, there and everywhere. In 1922 at Chauri Chaura, a small hamlet for ever after notorious in the annals of the nation, the Mahatma's followers, believing Gandhi's victory would usher in a new utopia, burned twenty-two Indian policemen alive for standing in their way as they put an entire station to the torch, fearless because they believed Gandhi's messianic charisma would shield them from bullets, and bring an end to the *kali yuga* (the age of darkness).

This was the most horrific instance of a disorder that prompted some monied men to rethink their support for Gandhi's campaign.[113] Gandhi decided to call off the movement. He would later describe the *satyagraha* as a 'Himalayan miscalculation'.

> I wondered how I could have failed to perceive what was so obvious. I realised that before a people could be fit for offering civil disobedience, they should thoroughly understand its deeper implications. That being so, before restarting civil disobedience on a mass scale, it would be necessary to create a band of well-tried, pure-hearted volunteers who thoroughly understood the strict conditions of Satyagraha. They could explain these to the people, and by sleepless vigilance keep them on the right path.[114]

But despite his efforts after this to 'discipline and mobilise', and to lead only small bands of 'true satyagrahis' at the right place and the right time, the genie of mass protest had been let out.[115] No one, not even the Mahatma, could put it back into the bottle.

During the first decades of the twentieth century, violence became embossed onto the nation's fabric: the Bagha Jatins and Bhagat

Singhs had seen to that. Despite all the clamour, the propaganda, and Gandhi's sincere efforts, the Mahatma's vision of legitimate political means never achieved hegemony. Violence in pursuit of political goals always enjoyed, and continues to enjoy, considerable legitimacy. The bust-up at Surat was a sign of things to come: of a political history punctuated by fire and sword, murder and assassination, riot and revolutionary violence, as well as more everyday forms of brutality.

This violence would be one current of the history of the century, often shaping (as the next chapter will show) the subcontinent's political direction at critical junctures.

V

THE BIRTH AND RISE OF 'MUSLIM NATIONALISM'

A modernised Hinduism dominated the language and imagery of Indian nationhood; and its votaries were almost all 'upper-caste' Hindus. Even the Irishwoman among their ranks, Annie Besant, was convinced that:

> Indian Nationality has, as its original basis, unity of religion, and the daily prayers of her Hindu population keep this unity ever before their eyes. They recite the names of the sacred rivers, the sacred cities from the Himalayan shrines to Rameswaran in the extreme south, and these have, from the dawn of history to the present day, been places of pilgrimage, knitting the whole Hindu population into one nation . . . The differences are superficial; the unity is fundamental.[116]

It is hard to conceive, therefore, why any Muslim should want to join the Congress, daubed as it was in these Hindu Brahminical hues. But many did: at the turn of the century, one in every fifteen delegates to the Congress sessions was Muslim. Muslim support was vital for Gandhi's success at Nagpur and Hindus and Muslims jointly organised the non-cooperation campaign.

But other Muslims developed anti-Congress attitudes and alternative nationalisms. Some were pro-British, tactically or otherwise;[117] others were vehement anti-imperialists who challenged Eurocentric views of the history of civilisations.[118] Ideas of Muslim nationhood proliferated alongside, and sometimes in tension with, the Islamic concept of the global *ummaa* (community). Muslim intellectuals of this period were as deeply at odds with each other about 'the right path', whether political or religious, just as the men (some of them Muslim, of course) hurling chairs at each other at Surat. In today's context of rampant and ignorant Islamophobia, which constructs all Muslims as identical (and dangerous), it is crucial that we understand this heterogeneity.

Before getting to the bottom of these quarrels, we need first to get a feel for the complex life-worlds of the late-nineteenth-century Muslim intelligentsia, and their differences, in temper and outlook, from the Hindu and Parsi literati of their time. Before 1857, even as British power undermined Mughal and other Muslim rulers in India, the Muslim *ashraf* (cultured classes) enjoyed a sense of confidence – even entitlement – that came with knowing that the Mughal emperor still sat on the throne in Delhi. Embedded in networks of religious practice, marriage and service that connected them to the Mughal court and to Muslim elites in Egypt, Yemen and the Hijaz, they saw themselves not only as members of an aristocracy that had for centuries ruled India, but as part of a wider Muslim world whose cultural influence stretched from Cordoba to Java, and whose civilisation rivalled (and indeed surpassed) that of Europe.

The Mutiny was the culmination of a century of shocks (some seismic, some cumulative) that had diminished Islamic power the world over. The Safavid empire had fallen in Iran in 1736, Tipu Sultan's Mysore had been vanquished in 1799, and the end of the Crimean War in 1856 sounded the death knell of the Ottoman empire. Expanding British power in the subcontinent had until 1857 operated behind a fig leaf of Mughal sanction. But in 1858, the last Mughal emperor – the octogenarian figurehead of the revolt – was dethroned, tried at the Red Fort, and packed off to ignominious exile in Rangoon.

Many of the British, civilians and military men alike, regarded the Mutiny as a Muslim conspiracy (which it was not), and in its aftermath reacted against Muslim elites with terrifying ferocity. Much of the Old City of Shahajanabad, the symbolic seat of Mughal 'authority' and still a centre of the old empire's rich cultural and material life, was razed to the ground. Hideous barracks now stand where its most delicate and ornate palace once stood. The Great Mosque was confiscated. The Daryaganj Mosque became, of all things, a bakery. House after house in

Old Delhi was pulled down to make way for British roads, railways and canals.[119] From being a symbol of Mughal grandeur, Delhi became a sad relic, vandalised by a brash and vengeful new power.

For the *ashraf* literati of North India, 1857 turned their world upside down. Their fine culture, their *aadaab* (etiquette), courtly ways, and religious beliefs had prospered under the benign umbrella of Mughal overlordship. Now the British government in India regarded them as a dangerous menace. Overnight, families suspected to have backed the rebels were stripped of their property.[120] Several families associated with the court, or with the rebels, fled Delhi at this time, seeking safety, employment and cultural continuity in a handful of princely states ruled by Muslims, such as Hyderabad and the Rohilla state of Rampur. Some 'troublemakers' and 'fanatics' fled even further afield, to Mecca, Medina, Cairo and Constantinople, using established religious networks.

In the Ottoman empire under Abd-al-Aziz, they found a cautious welcome. Muslim émigrés from India exported the '1857 mood' to centres of Muslim learning in the Ottoman empire, and from those centres they sent their 'brand of cosmopolitanism back to Hindustan via immigrant traders, scholars, pilgrims and publishers who maintained a steady link between British India and Ottoman cities'.[121] Abul Kalam Azad, one of the most significant Indian Muslim voices of the twentieth century, was born in Mecca, where his father, a learned *pir* (spiritual guide), was an émigré. The fact that Azad lies buried in an enclosed garden in Old Delhi, at a spot where the homes of Muslim nobles were razed to the ground in 1858, says a lot about this group and its sense of its place in history.[122]

Their scattering across India and the wider Muslim world would give these learned men a new appreciation of the challenges global Islam faced, something they had hitherto only dimly appreciated. New webs and networks of learning were now forged that linked the *nawabi* courts in Hyderabad, Bhopal and Rampur with hostelries and *madrassas* (theological seminaries) in Mecca, Medina and Cairo. The diasporic consciousness emerging from this dispersal is captured in this poem by Muhammad Iqbal, the iconic poet who is credited with first imagining Pakistan:

> Our Essence is not bound to any place;
> The vigour of our wine is not contained

> In any bowl; Chinese and Indian
> Alike the shard constitutes our jar,
> Turkish and Syrian alike the clay
> Forming our body; neither is our heart
> Of India, or Syria, or Rum,
> Nor any fatherland do we profess
> Except Islam.[123]

It is not hard to imagine why Muslim elites and scholars of the early twentieth century saw themselves as part of this far-flung world, even if they never left the soil of Hindustan. The burgeoning Urdu press of the time showed an intense concern for this wider world, to such an extent that any challenge to it fuelled its expansion. 'When Russia and the Ottoman Empire went to war in the late 1870s, the Press boomed. When the British invaded Egypt in 1882, it boomed again. When the Ottoman Empire entered into terminal stages from 1911 onwards, the Press boomed as never before.'[124] Everywhere, it seemed to Urdu readers, Islamic authority and Muslim ways of life were being threatened and attacked by western powers. The most influential authors were multilingual, and wrote in Urdu, Persian and Arabic, and this made it hard for the linguistically less-than-adept British to police them, particularly since they travelled easily between India, the Hijaz and Cairo. Thus Maulana Rehmatullah Kairanwi, who preached rebellion in 1857 because *mulk khuda ka* ('the country belongs to God'), could for years evade the British Indian authorities.[125]

Given this context, it is easier to appreciate why the Muslim *ashraf* looked askance at the new English education when it began to be fashionable among Hindu 'upper castes' and service elites in the late nineteenth century. Not only did its secular thrust trouble them, but they were also determined in the face of all odds to maintain their own proud traditions of learning. Urdu poets believed themselves to be the product of ancient *silsilas* (lineages) of illustrious predecessors, and fought to sustain their traditions. Iqbal, for example, visited Delhi in 1914 to attend the *urs* (commemoration) of the poet Amir Khusrau, whose golden pen had stunned the literary world of the thirteenth and fourteenth centuries. He wrote verses to celebrate the poets Altaf Hussain Hali (1837–1914) and Mirza Ghalib (1797–1869).[126] Knowledge, whether religious or cultural – these spheres were not sharply distinct – was carefully cultivated, preserved and transmitted through networks and lineages.

The religious tradition was, until the late nineteenth century, almost always transmitted by word of mouth. Its bedrock was the practice of listening to the recitation of the Quran and committing to memory the 'twigs of the burning bush aflame with God'.[127] The *ulema* (trained religious scholars) studied a classical syllabus of the Quran, Hadith (accounts of the deeds and sayings of the Prophet), *fiqh* (jurisprudence), and logic, directly from other *ulema*; once they had graduated and had gained their *ijaazas* (licences to instruct), they transmitted their learning in the same way to their own pupils. Thus powerful personal ties wove through, and strengthened, religious bonds.

Often *ulema* were also Sufi *pirs*, or leaders of Sufi mystical communities, with huge personal followings of *murids*, devotees whose commitment to their leaders knew no bounds. Maulana Abul Kalam Azad, the son of the celebrated *pir* Maulana Khairuddin, tells us his first memories were of 'the aura of dignity and sanctity all around me, and I found my family honoured and reverenced as if they were idols. While I was still a child, thousands of men used to come and kiss my hands and feet as the son of a pir . . . to every word that escaped my lips, no matter how worthless and meaningless, they listened with bowed heads and very great respect.'[128] Authority over knowledge and religion – commanded and controlled by a few men who had immersed themselves in years of scholarship or were heirs to Sufi mystical traditions – thus flowed in strong, controlled ways.

The printed word blew these structures of authority apart. The freely circulated book challenged the old oral traditions of knowledge and undermined their guardians, the *ulema*. By the 1870s, printed editions of the Quran were selling in their thousands, and at least twelve Urdu translations of the holy book were in circulation. Every decade of the twentieth century saw another 4,000–5,000 new books in Urdu, and Urdu newspapers typically attracted readerships of 10,000 and more. All manner of ideas, unsanctioned by *ulema*, were making the rounds. As one scholar puts it, religious books could now be consulted by any 'Ahmad, Mahmud or Muhammad, who could make what they will of them', enabling them to 'claim to speak for Islam'.[129] 'English' knowledge represented, in this milieu, a particular threat.

It was not uncommon for 'traditionalist' fathers at this time to school their sons at home with an almost paranoid zeal, in a vain attempt to prevent them from coming into contact with 'false' ideas.[130] Maulana Abul Kalam Azad's father, Maulana Khairuddin, brought up his sons so that they 'were not permitted the slightest diversion from [the customs of his own childhood]. Going to bed, getting up in the morning, the times of prayer, punctuality at meals – in all these things we were cast in the mould of the procedure he had appointed.'[131] Significantly, these rearguard battles were as much against new and different approaches to Islam as the threat of western thought.[132] (We will return to this theme in Chapter 2.)

This aversion to English schooling among Muslim elites gave the 'high-caste' Hindu literati, who had fewer inhibitions about the new learning, the edge in becoming the intermediaries and service groups on which the Raj relied. Bengali Brahmins and Kayasthas set off to serve the Raj 'upcountry' in government offices around Orissa, Bihar, the United Provinces, Punjab, Rajputana and Bombay;[133] they were also engaged in their thousands as 'surgeons, physicians, postmasters, businessmen [and] contractors'.[134] By the beginning of the twentieth century, there were so many Bengali Hindus in administrative positions in Assam that Bengali had become a medium of instruction in local schools.[135] One leading Muslim who noted these trends, understood their implications and made addressing them the lynchpin of his politics, was Sir Syed Ahmed Khan.

If we use a broad brush, 'Muslim nationalists' of this period (a label that obscures as much as it reveals) can be roughly divided into two groups. Sir Syed Ahmed Khan belonged to the first, whose concern was with 'Muslims' (seen as an ethnic bloc) and their standing and interests 'in this world' in post-Mutiny India, and their relationship with the colonial state. They believed, from various standpoints, that British rule after 1858 was bad for Muslims; that they would soon be outstripped by other communities and slip into irretrievable backwardness. Colonial policies, built on the misconceived idea that India was composed of internally homogenous religious communities with antithetical interests, did much to fuel these fears. Already by the late nineteenth century there was talk that 'Indian Muslims' constituted a separate nation. Sir Syed was the first to make this claim, but he was by no means the last.

The second group, smaller and more diverse, was more concerned with the fate of global Islam than with the declining fortunes of local Muslims. Islam, they believed, faced an existential threat, enfeebled around the world as much by European empires as by the conduct of Muslims themselves, above all by their failure to be 'true Muslims'. Embedded, as many of these thinkers were, in Islamic cosmopolitan networks, they had little investment in *wataniyat* (territorial nationhood). Saiyid Abu-l-Ala Mawdudi, whose family had been close to the Mughal court and suffered in the aftermath of 1857, is perhaps their best-known exponent, although he was only one among hundreds of voices with fresh interpretations of what 'true Islam' was, and what being a 'good Muslim' involved. These divisions within this grouping were so deep that they were unable to unite behind a single political programme.

Among the 'this-worldly' communalists, Sir Syed was a colossus. Like so many Muslim intellectuals of his time, he was from an aristocratic family associated with the Mughal court; but in 1837, much against his family's wishes, he had taken up service with the East India Company. When the Mutiny broke out, he was serving as a *munsif* (judge) in Bijnor, and he ensured the safety of every British person in the district. This made Sir Syed, who was eventually awarded a knighthood, respected among British officers. After 1858 they paid attention to his views.

For Syed Ahmed Khan, the Mutiny delivered a different lesson than that drawn by most of his Muslim peers. This man of extraordinary energy and intellect argued that India's Muslims had no choice but to come to terms with the new realities. In a series of publications that had a searing impact on the many impressionable, and indeed shell-shocked, young men who read them, he founded Islamic modernism in India. This he did by drawing a persuasive distinction between the Quran's eternal 'essence', and all that which was not essential, belonging as it did to the culture of times long past when Islam was revealed to the Prophet. This allowed a 'modern Islam' to step free from that past. It encouraged young Muslims to become 'modern', to keep up to date with new science and fearlessly embrace reform and social change. Maulana Azad recalled being mesmerised by Sir Syed's writings, which he devoured in secret, in a state akin to 'intoxication'.[136]

If Sir Syed's religious modernism was novel, so too were his politics. Muslims, he argued, should accept that British rule was in India to stay, and they should make a tactical alliance with the new rulers in the land. Aware that *ashraf* Muslims would not be persuaded to send their sons to the godless schools being set up, where they would have to rub shoulders with the hoi polloi – his 'Select Committee for the Better Diffusion and Advancement of Learning among Muhammadans of India' recognised the prejudice among the 'noble classes' against their sons sharing schooling with 'boys of low parentage' – he set up his own college.[137] This would offer the best western education and the essentials of the traditional syllabus to Muslim notables unwilling to mix with a 'lesser' sort.

The Muhammadan Anglo-Oriental College at Aligarh, founded in 1875, was modelled on Oxford and Cambridge. A residential college, it had courts and a neo-Gothic arched gateway that mimicked the oldest universities of the West. One of its first principals, Theodore Beck, appointed at the age of twenty-four, was a graduate of Trinity College, Cambridge. Tutors imported from Oxbridge imparted lessons in science (Sir Syed's great love), mathematics, history, geography and English literature. The campus also had a mosque. The Quran, the Hadith and the Islamic sciences were part of the syllabus, but they were not the focus of Aligarh's curriculum. Whereas orthodox *ulema* and many aristocratic families regarded the institution with horror, the pragmatists among the leading families of upper India began to take Sir Syed's point that without an English education and a working relationship with the British, their children had no future in India. Aligarh thrived. For three decades and more, so too did Sir Syed's policy of tactical loyalism towards the British in India.

Stepping back, one can see how remarkable an achievement it was for one man, more or less single-handedly, to persuade the British that far from being implacable opponents of their rule, the Muslims of India were their most dependable allies, and to persuade his co-religionists that this was a wise manoeuvre, not a quisling betrayal of their proud traditions. But this is what happened. More and more, it became government policy to promote Muslim education at Aligarh, and to employ Muslims in the government services, police and army.

Sir Syed regarded the Congress as a threat, and he enjoined Muslims not to be seduced by it. If they joined the Congress, he was convinced the entente between the British and Muslims would founder. But there was more to it than that. Sir Syed held that Muslims were a distinct people – indeed, a nation – and that the 'Hindu' Congress did not, and could not, represent them. He used the word 'nation' much as politicians of a later era would speak of the Muslim 'community', and he thought of India as a 'commonweal' of such 'nations'.[138] For him, the Congress represented a political alliance of the Bengali Hindu, Brahmin (Kashmiri and Tamil) and Maratha 'nations', whose attitudes towards the British, from a Muslim standpoint, were dangerous. While he desired friendship and 'brotherly feeling' between 'the Muslim nation' and the nations represented by the Congress, he urged Muslims to eschew another ruinous political battle against the British. 'What took place in the Mutiny?' he asked in one pointed exchange. 'The Hindus began it; the Mohammedans with their eager disposition rushed into it. The Hindus having bathed in the Ganges became as they were before. But the Mohammedans and all their noble families were ruined.'[139] This would again be the consequence for Muslims, he predicted, if they were seduced into another political agitation against the British.

The Mutiny and its traumatic aftermath shaped Sir Syed's politics. In 1886, he established the Muhammadan Educational Conference to bring together Muslims from all of India to discuss their problems and 'promote national brotherhood'.[140] It was intended to be apolitical, focusing only on Muslim instruction: but it served a political purpose as well. By focusing on Muslims within British India, it turned its face against Muslim cosmopolitanism, claiming to represent, and helping to forge, a pan-Indian Muslim community.

Sir Syed's approach suited British purposes. Victorian liberalism, hard-headed pragmatism and Indian fiscal realities (the imperatives of keeping costs down) all pointed to the need for the British to subcontract governance at the base to Indians. The arguments for bringing more 'able and sensible natives', nominated by local bodies, into the provincial Councils, was that 'if they in their turn had a native party behind them, the government of India would cease to stand up, as it does now, an isolated rock in the middle of a tempestuous sea'.[141] Reforms in the 1880s and the Indian Councils Act of 1892 gave Indians a greater presence in the reconstituted and enlarged councils at the provincial and central level. In a development critical to the growth of all-India nationalism, some of the Indian members of these councils were now indirectly drawn from the district and municipal boards.

From now on, would-be politicians who claimed to speak for their constituents and sought to influence British policy needed a mandate from their countrymen. Those with ambition had to make their mark on the politics of their provinces, to solicit the backing of influential local politicians, mobilise wide networks. They had to be seen to 'represent' their interests and articulate their concerns.

'Local self-government', whether at the base, or in the Indian Councils Act of 1892, was planned by the British to give Indians a limited say in 'safe' areas of governance. But which Indians were to be the representatives? And on what basis? To begin with, Burkean notions about representing 'interest groups' determined how these councils were established; and the Raj showed a clear preference for recruiting onto the Councils' 'solid' conservative elements: rajas, nawabs and landlords as opposed to the chattering classes from the cities – whom, in an ironic twist, they now regarded as 'the deadly legacy of Metcalfe and Macaulay'. This policy flowed from their construct that India was constituted by bounded communities of interest, creed and caste, capable of being sized up in numbers and social importance, each with its own 'natural leaders'. Their participation in the new system of representation was designed to enable the Raj to tax more heavily and intervene more actively in their Indian empire. Inevitably, this led many Indians to claim to speak for such bounded 'communities', and to try to conjure them into existence. And then compete with each other to represent 'them' in the reformed councils.

Soon after, however, the government began to take some account of the size of a 'community'. Its demographic weight, now known with factitious exactitude as a consequence of decennial censuses (the first in 1872, thereafter in 1881 and every tenth anniversary since), became one of the factors determining how it was represented on councils. Time was when power in India had been exercised through carefully calibrated collaborations between rulers and men who commanded authority and extracted wealth at local levels. Now other roads to power were being laid.

The new politics required those who travelled along them to claim that they represented large numbers (constituted as separate and often antagonistic interest groups), and to persuade the imperial state to recognise these claims. Political legitimacy in India had once derived from the capacity to maintain order, help collect revenues, uphold moral norms and husband the resources of the land. Now it came from being the spokesman of 'the people', variously defined. Demography, once a neutral matter, became charged with a novel significance, as the size of 'communities' came to be linked to their share of the cake of representation, as well as to patronage by government, which was as much then as it is now South Asia's largest employer.

The decennial censuses revealed one striking 'fact': that Muslims of all sorts (the census questions were not designed to unpick subtle differences of belief) made up just over twenty per cent of the population, confirming them to be a demographic minority in the country as a whole. Two provinces alone bucked the trend: Bengal, India's largest province in the east, and the Punjab in the west. But even in the Punjab, at just over fifty per cent, the Muslim majority was small rather than overwhelming. These figures stunned many government officials. Even those who worked in Muslim areas in Bengal – men like Sir William Wilson Hunter, who wrote a treatise making the case for a British tactical alliance with the Muslims – realised that he had mistaken Hindu peasants for Muslim ones, and vice versa.

Sir Syed died in 1898, before the new century and before the 'solid men' who backed his pragmatic loyalism began to recognise the implications of the new demographic politics. Hindus – however divided they might be by their political views, by caste, class, language and custom – were a majority in British India, the census showed. Unless a special case was made in terms of their importance, Muslims would be reduced to the position of a permanent minority. As soon as it became clear that the councils were to be reformed, and that elections might be introduced, Muslim elites set about making that case. In 1906 a deputation of seventy influential Muslims, headed by the Aga Khan, called on the viceroy, Lord Minto, in Simla. They demanded separate electorates for Muslims in the new reformed councils. Minto, a gentleman-jockey, was persuaded that Muslims were a 'natural counterweight' to the Congress and gave Muslim leaders everything they asked for. (The *swadeshi* movement was raging in Bengal at the time: that had something to do with his swift acquiescence.)

The Indian Councils Act gave Muslims separate electorates in 1909, as well as weightage in representation. In 1906, the Morley–Minto Reforms had acknowledged that Muslims were a 'community' too significant to be disregarded, and 'national' in scope and presence. The Muslim League, established that same year, declared that it spoke for this 'community'. Of course it did not. No such community existed: it would have to be cajoled into being.

. The 'communities' in twentieth-century India – not only 'Muslims' but others that have since emerged – are best understood as modern political coalitions created in this period. Far from being homogenous, timeless, ancient groups, they are recent constructs with a clear agenda, which was to gain recognition and benefits from the colonial state. Their overriding purpose: to gain concessions from government, and a share of power, in the peculiar context of an evolving colonial policy which was to recognise difference among Indians and the rights of groups (as opposed to individuals).[142]

But these coalitions were challenging to build, and harder still to hold together. In the Muslim case, no sooner had Sir Syed's strategy paid off by the spectacular coup in the Morley–Minto Reforms when the alliance fell apart at its base. National and global events coalesced in ways that made Sir Syed's tactical loyalism seem dated and inadequate. The government repeatedly rejected Aligarh's demand for university status, who knows why. The school's alumni were aggrieved, because without official recognition of its degrees, jobs were hard to find.

In 1900, the governor of the United Provinces, caught in the cross-fire of a debate between supporters of Hindi and Urdu already tinged with communal rivalry, came down in favour of Hindi. Again, who knows why. This novel 'Hindi' language – created by writing Hindustani/Urdu in the Devanagiri/Sanskrit script, and stuffing it full of words with Sanskrit roots – now became the official language of the province. Defending Urdu rapidly became a cause that united North Indian Muslims.

Then, in 1911, the partition of Bengal was revoked, to the consternation of the Muslims of East Bengal who had hoped to benefit from having a province of their own. To this injury, the government added insult: a municipality in the United Provinces demolished part of a mosque complex in order to construct a road, and refused to back down despite furious Muslim protests. Muslim interests and sentiments seemed to be ignored everywhere in India, Sir Syed's legacy notwithstanding.

Events on the world stage nourished this indignation. Given the dense networks connecting India and the Ottoman *madrassas* and towns, this was inevitable. When the Ottoman empire began to fall on its knees, well-informed Indian Muslims felt profound distress, and they neither understood nor sympathised with the Arab nationalisms of desert tribes that challenged its unity. When the European powers declared war against the Sultan in the First World War, they felt placed in an impossible position. In his memoirs, Mohamed Ali wrote:

> We in India who had already lost our own Empire several generations if not a whole century ago, were not probably expected to feel as acutely as we did the loss of our co-religionists in Persia, in Egypt and in Tripoli, and in far-off Morocco. But the temporal losses of Turkey . . . touched a particular chord in our sub-consciousness, the Chord of Religion; for the Ruler of Turkey was the Khalifa or Successor of the Prophet . . . and the Khilafat was as essentially our religious concern as the Qur'an or the *Sunnah* of the Prophet.[143]

Mohamed Ali, a young man from Rampur, had graduated from Aligarh at the top of his class. His remarkable mother Abadi Bano Begum, from a family who had fled the depredations in Delhi, had been quick to see what so many of her contemporaries did not: the value of the 'modern' education on offer at Aligarh. So she sent both her talented sons there, pawning her jewellery to pay their fees. His elder brother, Shaukat, wanted his talented sibling to join the elite ranks of the Indian Civil Service, but Mohamed failed to get in. Instead he became a journalist, launching *The Comrade*, one of the most influential news-sheets of its time; and later, *The Hamdard* ('The Empathetic'). Through these papers, with prolific pen and exciting (if overblown) prose, he demanded that the British protect the Ottoman sultan – the caliph (*khalifa*) – and the holy places of Islam.

Both brothers were remarkable characters. Mohamed Ali's agitation quickly attracted a huge following in India. When London paid no heed to the sentiments of its Indian Muslim subjects in the post-war settlement in the Middle East, he launched the Khilafat campaign. He had the unflagging support of his ebullient brother Shaukat, and that of the young Maulana Abul Kalam Azad, who by now had become a brilliant journalist (his pen name 'Azad' means 'Free'). Azad was far more austere and intellectually rigorous than the Ali brothers; but although he may have lacked the 'common touch', he had the adulation of his *pir* father's hundreds of thousands of disciples. Another ally was Abdul Bari, an influential and excitable *aalim* (religious scholar) from Firangi Mahal, one of India's leading centres of Islamic religious learning. Almost as volatile as Shaukat (who once threatened to burn the Archbishop of Canterbury in oil), Bari brought to the cause many *ulema* who would normally have shied clear of politics. The Ali brothers also enjoyed the Mahatma's support – and he theirs – for a time.

In 1920, despite impassioned appeals from Indian Khilafatists, the Treaty of Sèvres dismembered the Ottoman empire. It placed Syria, Palestine (already promised by the British to both Arabs and Zionists) and Mesopotamia under British and French mandates, ceded Eastern Thrace and Smyrna to Greece, and gave the Dodecanese islands to Italy. Constantinople remained part of the new Turkey, but the strategic Dardanelle Straits were made into international waters.

The Khilafatists responded by joining the Indian National Congress in droves, declaring non-cooperation with perfidious Albion. They also announced that self-government, shoulder to shoulder with Hindus, was their goal. Non-cooperation, therefore, was the means to both political and religious ends: it would enable Indian Muslims to throw off a British Raj, revealed to be an enemy of global Islam, and replace it with an independent nation in which they would be free to follow their faith.

In a famous and eloquent speech, Maulana Azad set out the ethical basis of the Khilafat movement. In a repetitive, ascending cadence which roused his audience, Azad underscored their reasons to oppose British rule:

> They [the British] allow us to pray, a religious duty, but they will not allow us to uphold the temporal power of the *Khilafat*, a more important religious duty. They allow us to perform the pilgrimage, but they pay no attention to our cries when they compel the *Khalifah* to hand over the pilgrimage places to non-Muslims. They are proud of their religious neutrality, but call us seditious when we object to their blatant transgression of that neutrality.[144]

Distinguishing between those non-Muslims who threatened Muslim lands and the true faith, and others, like India's Hindus, who lived in peace with Muslims, Azad urged friendship with the latter, while having no truck with the former.[145] This was an important speech, in which Azad laid out the moral framework for *muttahida qaumiyat* (composite nationalism) that formed the basis for Muslim unity with Hindus in the pursuit of a free nation. He remained committed to it for the rest of his life.

The Khilafatists' strategy, in alliance with the Congress

non-cooperators, was to mobilise India's people to deny cooperation to the government in four stages, each designed to ramp up the pressure on the British. The first, returning titles, was symbolic. Next, Indians would boycott foreign goods, before quitting the army and police. Finally, in the ultimate and most extreme step, they would withhold taxes.

This campaign was the longest, most sustained and dangerous challenge to British rule since the Mutiny. Yet it has curiously fallen through the trapdoor of historiography – perhaps because it had nothing obvious to do with the campaign for Pakistan and little to do with the later history of the Congress. The history of the nation, in India, Bangladesh and Pakistan, as elsewhere, is always teleological.

The Khilafat movement was chaotic. It pulled in this direction and that. It was based on an inherently unstable alliance between urban 'this-worldly' politicians (many with Aligarh connections), journalists, merchants who gave funds but urged caution, *ulema* who were at odds among themselves, the fastidious Gandhi and a Congress party he had captured but did not yet command.

But the Ali brothers, larger-than-life characters both literally and metaphorically, were not put off by these challenges. Their physical bulk contained unbounded and boyish energy. One vignette illustrates the differences in style and personality between the boisterous brothers and the skinny Mahatma, and what an incongruous trio they made. On the innumerable tours with Gandhi across the country by train, they encountered huge crowds at stations. 'Arriving at the Lucknow station, they found the platform a veritable jungle of humanity, all devotees waiting to see them. Gandhi, in his passion for order and nonviolence, refused to descend from the train until the unruly mob had sat down and become quiet. The brothers at once swung into action. Forming a phalanx of two, they sallied forth to clear a path for the Mahatma, grabbing some by the shoulders and seating them on the ground, and generally throwing their weight around. In a few minutes, Gandhi could appear before a rather more orderly crowd.'[146]

Yet despite their differences, the brothers had much in common with Gandhi, and with many of his talents, which they turned into political commodities some years before he did (something that is now little remembered in India). Refusing to accept a sharp distinction between the 'political' and 'religious' spheres of life, they harnessed to their project the piety of many of their co-religionists.

They were natural fund-raisers, cultivating relationships with businessmen and merchants; one key ally was Seth Mian Muhammad Haji Jan Muhammad Chotani, whose wartime profits from trading in lumber and other strategic materials they tapped.[147] They also had a penchant for spending monies with a liberal hand, so that Gandhi had to step in to defend some sloppy accounting of expenditure by the Central Khilafat Committee.[148] Like the Mahatma, they understood sartorial symbolism. In 1913, they hung up their Savile Row suits (the 'fancy pants' for which they had developed a taste in England) and, to show solidarity with the Turkish caliph, they henceforth donned flowing robes embroidered with the crescent badge of the Anjuman-e-Khuddam-e-Kaaba, and astrakhan caps, also emblazoned with the crescent moon of Islam. They wore their regular spells in British jails as (metaphorical) badges of martyrdom, a technique which they in turn borrowed from the revolutionary terrorists.

They also had a rare talent for using the courtroom to stage choreographed shows of resistance. On trial in the 'Karachi Seven' case, Mohamed admitted to proposing and supporting the (non-cooperation) resolutions at Karachi, but argued that he had only followed his faith – a right granted to him, he reminded the court, by Victoria's proclamation. The crowds attending were so large that the trial had to be shifted from the courtroom to a public auditorium, and the brothers milked that situation for all it was worth. Their arrival at the hearing every day was a set piece, with Mohamed and Shaukat waving gaily to the crowds thronging outside the building. Once inside, they refused to stand when the magistrate entered. Why, they asked, should non-cooperators honour a judge serving the British government? 'When their chairs were removed to oblige them to stand, the brothers took off their long handloom cloaks, spread them on the floor, and sat down.'[149]

The Khilafat movement's goal was to unite Indian Muslims behind the symbol of distant holy places to which few (at this stage) had ever been, or had dreamed of going. As such, it was responsive to global events over which its leaders had little control. But the example of resistance sparked off local uprisings of all sorts across the country, and the Khilafat ideal became bound up with local issues and particular injustices that had little to do with Turkey or the Treaty of Sèvres. The Ali brothers soon realised that they could not control local conflagrations which the campaign had helped to set alight but could not put out.

In the summer of 1920, for instance, thousands of Muslims from Sind and the North West Frontier Province sold their property and began to march to Afghanistan in the blazing heat, to perform *hijrat*. A religious procession meant to rescue the faith by migrating to a Muslim country, *hijrat* had been discussed at a number of Khilafat meetings, but had been discouraged as it might weaken the movement in India. However, some local imams and *pirs* – charismatic leaders of local shrine-based communities – seem to have supported the idea.[150] Soon, the Khyber Pass became clogged with caravans. When the number of *muhaajirun* (refugees) crossed 30,000, the Amir of Afghanistan asked that no more should come, but few heard his proclamation. Tribesmen attacked and robbed some of the *muhaajirun*. Others died of thirst and starvation. Those who survived returned home penniless and disillusioned.

In August 1921, thousands of miles to the south in Malabar, rebellion broke out among the Mapilla Muslims. Malabar, a tropical coastal region in the far south-west of the subcontinent, was more closely connected to the wider Muslim world than one might imagine, given its distance from the Mughal heartlands. One of the leaders of the uprising was Sayyid Fadl, scion of a Sufi *pir* family that had migrated from the Hadramaut in southern Yemen to Malabar in the nineteenth century, and who had rich and far-flung connections in the British, Dutch and Ottoman empires.[151] In Malabar, as in many parts of North India, the Khilafat message had become intertwined with local appeals for tenancy reform. Landlords, most of whom were 'upper-caste' Nayyar Hindus, had ignored previous appeals couched in more deferential terms.

Now another failed monsoon, the return home of demobilised soldiers and the arrest of local Khilafatist campaigners produced a combustible admixture. Then, one night, someone burgled a landlord's home. The police, who believed the burglary had something to do with the Khilafat movement, searched the local mosque where they thought the miscreants were hiding. Rumours spread that the mosque had been desecrated. This was like throwing a match on a parched pine forest: a peasant insurgency began to rage.

As with other jacqueries of the time, militant peasants singled out for destruction all markers of colonial authority. They tore up railway lines; they cut telegraph wires; and they robbed and then burned down post offices and police stations. They also targeted and looted

Hindu landlords, their belongings and their estates, and even damaged Hindu temples, destroying all symbols of the structures of power that had long oppressed them.[152]

Then they took to the surrounding hills, where they engaged the army, which had been called out, in guerrilla warfare. The ranks of their supporters swelled – perhaps out of fear of the British, perhaps emboldened by their example. For six months, no less, the rebels held out. Some villages proclaimed Khilafat 'kingdoms'. What sovereign futures they imagined for themselves we will never know: perhaps they hoped to establish realms of righteousness, emancipated from the oppressions of both the rapacious landlords, the *zamindaars*, and the British government. Perhaps these futures were conceived in terms of their own understanding of Islamic justice; perhaps they were more inchoately imagined. But when the (false) rumour began to circulate that the Amir of Afghanistan would send his forces to help them, such little support as they still enjoyed among Hindu Congress leaders evaporated.

Just a few months later, when his supporters attacked the local police station at Chauri Chaura, Gandhi decided to put a stop to non-cooperation. But the writing had been on the wall for some time. The more the Mahatma saw of Indian popular movements inspired by him and other leaders, the less he liked them. What he saw in Malabar and Chauri Chaura persuaded him that the Indian 'masses' lacked the discipline necessary for the rigours of non-cooperation. If attacked by the police, they would retaliate rather than turning the other cheek; and when they hit back, they did so with a bloodthirsty rage that appalled him.

After this, Gandhi backed away for ever from mass mobilisation. He insisted that *satyagraha* was not for the many but for the select few: the handful of disciples he had tutored at his *aashrams* in self-discipline and the rigorous religious practice of seeking truth. The grand dream, that the non-cooperation Khilafat campaign would bring about *swaraj* in a single year, lay in ashes.

Another legacy of the Mapilla rebellion was the end of 'Hindu–Muslim unity', as conceived of by the Mahatma, the Ali brothers and Maulana Azad. These men had accepted that 'Hindus' and 'Muslims' were indeed different communities, each with its different cultures and histories, each with its own internal problems to resolve. But they had believed that 'Hindus' and 'Muslims' could work together, support each other and live peaceably as 'good neighbours'.[153] Heightened religiosity in politics, they hoped, would help achieve this, as better Hindus and better Muslims would be better fellow countrymen, and more ethical Indians. But after the Mapilla rebellion, many leaders concluded that this emphasis on religiosity was in fact heightening communal competition and violence. The failure of the non-cooperation Khilafat model had revealed that practical intercommunal cooperation required forms of leadership and social control that did not exist, and rested on alliances at the top that were simply too weak to withstand buffeting from below.

VI

THE RETURN OF THE LIBERALS

These events created space for the return of liberal constitutionalists to the centre ground of Indian politics. They were ready, waiting in the wings. Another factor that helped them stand forth was the fact that the Raj, weakened by war and demoralised by these events, recognised the need for reform.

The Government of India Act of 1919 introduced the new system of 'diarchy', which distinguished between different 'heads' of power and devolved those it deemed less important to local and municipal councils. It encouraged Indians to run for elections to these councils, where they could raise taxes and spend local monies on local welfare. Many Indians were happy to oblige. While Gandhi and his closest coterie of followers, and also the Ali brothers, called for the boycott of the new councils, they no longer had solid majorities behind them. A large 'Pro-changer' group now emerged in the Congress, which preferred to work in the reformed councils, scrutinising and debating legislation, and resisting the British state from within. The Swarajya party, representing 'Pro-changers' (both Hindus and Muslims), was born. It decided, contra Gandhi, to contest the elections. In the Bengal council, Chittaranjan Das, the province's most admired Congress leader, formed an alliance with Huseyn Shaheed Suhrawardy, a charismatic Muslim politician, against British members of the council.

A new chasm opened up in the Congress as 'No-changers' battled 'Pro-changers' for the soul of the party. The warfare between them was more decorous than the shoe-hurling, head-breaking affair at Surat, but the split was 'deeper and wider'.[154]

These were early signs of a major realignment in the subcontinent's politics. Although mass movements against the *Sarkar* (government) and its local despots would continue to erupt, not least in 1942, leaders like Gandhi and the Ali brothers began to recede into the background. Contrary to legend, Gandhi remained in the wings, for the most part, in the years before Britain's departure in 1947. In these early decades of 'the long decolonisation', different alliances began to be forged, as Indian politicians attempted to build coalitions that could consolidate their influence under a wounded and ever-weaker government.[155] In a trend enhanced by the Government of India Act of 1935, which introduced provincial autonomy and larger electorates, such coalition-building became 'the new normal'. Many of its features would endure until the 1980s.

Most political histories of twentieth-century South Asia focus on the moments of high drama – *swadeshi*, non-cooperation, civil disobedience, partition and the Bangladesh Liberation War of 1971. Yet these moments were exceptional ruptures in the dusty-brown fabric of the routine. If we turn our gaze instead towards the humdrum, to the mundane mechanics of order, what might we learn about the compromises that shaped the 'everyday' in the last decades of the Raj?

With hindsight, it is clear that the lineaments of these new structures – already well established in the era of Gokhale – re-emerged in the 1920s, after the Khilafat movement had collapsed, Gandhi had withdrawn non-cooperation, and this model of Hindu–Muslim unity had revealed its fragility.

At their heart was a set of coalitions between 'liberals' and 'pragmatists', both of whom were keen to ensure the establishment of a political order that they could influence, and which was capable of bringing pressure to bear upon the state without unleashing havoc on the streets, in the mills and fields. These alliances required constant management and negotiation. The dull political routine was thus more fragile than it appeared to be. Each time they were reconstructed, coalitions came again together in slightly new ways. The emergent new order was at once brittle and tenacious.

Indian 'liberal' politics of this period had a different accent from liberalism in the West. Indian liberals examined how its different aspects (positivism, constitutionalism, justice, economic development, social progress) were 'suited to Indian conditions' or could be made so to do.[156] Their liberalism was grounded above all in the particularities of their colonial status, and Queen Victoria's proclamation. Their consciousness of racism – the fact that they were *not* equal in the eyes of the law – made them angrily committed to the liberal principle of legal equality. Inevitably western-educated, often lawyers, they worked for change within the law, putting pressure on the British by using the new councils the diarchy system had created. They were constitutionalists to a man (or indeed woman: Sarojini Naidu, the Bengali poetess, emerging as a major political figure in this period). This was an age in which constitutionalism matured as a robust form of politics in India.[157]

The liberals were aware that, to succeed, they needed the support of the pragmatists: men who wanted stability, who wanted to make money, who knew how 'to get their work done' and call in favours, and who were keen to influence policy on matters that affected them. In this period, businessmen stepped forward in significant numbers to join politics. In the countryside too landlords left the *kutcheries* (accounts offices) to their *naibs* and *aamils* (deputies and chief accountants) and joined the new local and provincial boards. In 1935, after legislative assemblies were established in the provinces, they fought and won elections. This was a new kind of politics for them, but they learned its mechanics soon enough.

These new entrants into the political arena were not always English-educated. Instead of gaining a higher education after rudimentary schooling, many had joined the family firm, on which so much business in South Asia rests. Yet they too wanted change. Above all, they wanted customs barriers to protect Indian industries, lower sales taxes and lower revenue demands in the countryside to open up Indian markets. To bring pressure to bear upon government, they needed political allies who claimed to represent large communities, and liberal friends who could articulate their case with eloquence on the councils. But they were all clear about one thing: they wanted change to come about in an orderly fashion. They had no desire to shake up the status quo. They had too much to lose.

The key liberals of this era were Muhammad Ali Jinnah of Bombay, and Motilal Nehru (father of Jawaharlal) and Tej Bahadur Sapru from the United Provinces. All were lawyers and they were most comfortable with legalistic modes of reasoning. Gokhale and Dadabhai were their role models. Their lifestyles were urbane.

Sapru and Nehru Senior were both Brahmins whose ancestors had migrated from Kashmir to North India in an earlier age, where they were part of a tight-knit expatriate community which came to wield a quite extraordinary influence over Indian politics for much of the rest of century. In many ways, the two men were chalk and cheese. Where Motilal was showy, Sapru did not draw attention to himself. When Motilal thundered, Sapru spoke with calm fluency. He seems to have been far less interested in money and the high life than his Kashmiri fellow liberal.

Sapru, born in Aligarh in 1875, rose to serve a member for law in the Viceroy's Council from 1920 to 1923, when he was knighted; he was appointed a member of the Privy Council in 1934. Fair-minded, able and of an even temperament, Sir Tej Bahadur, as he now was, headed the committee that wrote the Sapru Report in 1944. It proposed a constitution that would prevent a partition of India by including vital protections for minority groups. It fell by the wayside. Thus Sapru's report represents yet another of those roads not taken on the journey to partition.

His granddaughter Amrita and I were at college together: we read history, with unfashionable zeal, at Lady Sri Ram College in Delhi while our more carefree peers had their hands painted with *mehndi* (henna) designs or bought glass bangles in rainbow colours. I visited the Sapru home often, where ease with western lifestyle – mango 'fool' was served regularly for tea, prizes won at Oxbridge were displayed in glass cabinets – sat comfortably with pride in Kashmiri scribal culture and courtly Mughlai ways. Courtesy, even courtliness, of a very particular kind seemed ingrained in family life. The *istri-waali*, the woman who did the locality's ironing under a tree near their house, was always addressed with respect as '*aap*' and thanked for her work, even when she burned a valuable tissue-silk sari just before yet another Kashmiri wedding. Such civility towards poor workers was rare in India in the 1980s, and it gave me an insight, I'd like to think, into the popular appeal of the Nehrus, Saprus and their ilk.

Motilal Nehru was very different, but memorable in his own way. As part of the service elite working for the Mughal court, Motilal's father, Gangadhar Nehru, had been one of the stream of refugees who fled the carnage in Delhi after the Mutiny, and, having lost almost everything he possessed, soon died in his new home in Agra. Motilal, born in 1861 three months after his father's death, had to make his own way in the world. Educated in Arabic and Persian, he only joined an English-medium school at the age of twelve. Supported by an older brother who also died young, his education was entirely in India; unlike Gandhi or Jinnah, he was never called to the bar in London.

Despite these handicaps, Motilal Nehru established a flourishing legal practice at Allahabad. His command of case law, his readiness to play hardball in court and softball outside it, helps explain his rapid rise to the top. His generosity was lavish, his wit pointed, he was courteous, warm and good company. These qualities won him as many admirers as his summations in court. Shrewdly, Motilal specialised in laws of inheritance (whose complexities we will encounter in Chapter 5). He fought civil suits over property for landlords of fabulous wealth – the *nawabzaadas*, *ranis* and *taluqdaars* of upper India – and earned handsome fees by winning cases for them.

He was also a big spender. In 1900 he purchased a property in the 'civil lines', the European part of town. 'Anand Bhavan', as the large Nehru mansion was named, housed the entire extended family and household, including his late older brother's wife and children, as well as sundry tutors and governesses. Motilal loved making improvements to his estates, adding tennis courts, gardens, swimming pools and fountains. Anand Bhavan was the first house in Allahabad to have electricity, running water and a hot-water system. In 1904, he imported a car, the first in the city, and probably the first in the United Provinces. On every trip he made to Europe, he added to his fleet of cars. He was a man who wanted only the best for himself and his family. For his only son and his pride and joy, Jawaharlal, he provided the best English education at Harrow and Trinity College, Cambridge.

Motilal's fascination with things western was such that he once ordered the entire extended family to speak only in English. In the event there was silence, since none of the women of the household, nor the children, could speak it. He scorned Brahminical ritual. He began to eat a packed lunch at the court premises, much to the horror of fellow Brahmin lawyers, who ate, as their caste status required, in complete seclusion and privacy. (We will return to food and caste in Chapter 6.) Worse still, after a trip across the black water to Europe he refused to perform the purification ceremony, the *praayaschitt*. 'My mind is fully made up. I will not (come what may) indulge in the

tomfoolery of Proschit. No, not even if I die for it. I have been provoked and have been dragged from my seclusion into public notice.
But my enemies will find me a hard nut to crack.'[158] He was 'outcast-
ed', or excommunicated, by orthodox Brahmins but refused to
capitulate.

The opaque and reserved Jinnah could hardly have been more different, although he shared Motilal's liberal attitudes. 'Jinnahbhai' was
born in 1876 to a family of Khoja Ismailis, the small sect led by the
Aga Khan. Although he is alleged to have converted later to Shiism,
and then to the Sunni faith, he never disclosed his religious beliefs; we
can't be sure if indeed he had any. Late in life, he married for love
outside the community, having fallen hard for the charms of the Parsi
heiress Ruttie Petit, who was less than half his age. The attraction was
mutual: she left her family for him.

Jinnah was from a middle-income background: his father, a small-
time cloth merchant, came from the minor princely state of Kathiawar
(where Gandhi had also grown up). In 1875, the family moved to
Karachi, then a small port town in Sind, where Jinnah was educated
at the *madrassa*. Like Gandhi, therefore, he was an outsider to mainstream nationalist politics: he did not come from the typical
background or have the typical 'English-educated' training. Perhaps
this explains his legendary prickliness. Tall, with striking looks – his
handsome face lent intensity by luminous, deep-socketed eyes – he
was an elegant dresser who cut a dash in Bombay society when he
set up his law firm there. His acute legal mind – he had a forensic
intelligence – was soon the talk of the town. A frugal man, he dressed
in style, but his 'Savile Row' suits (and later his perfect *sherwaanis*)
were the work of a local master tailor.[159] Women fell for him in droves.
But there was something unreachable, unknowable and intensely private about Jinnah.

His father found his bright son a job with a British managing
agency company, and it was as the firm's representative in London
that Jinnah first travelled to the city in 1892. There politics began
to consume him. He went regularly to Parliament to watch debates,
and became an admirer and friend of Dadabhai, then MP for
Finsbury. He was in the public gallery when Dadabhai made his
maiden speech. Lord Morley, whose liberalism was then in the ascend-
ant, deeply influenced him: 'I grasped that liberalism, which became
part of my life and thrilled me very much.'[160] Jinnah would later

recommend Morley's *On Compromise* as required reading, telling students in 1938: 'I think you ought to read that book not only once but over and over again.'[161] Without consulting his father, he decided to abandon commerce and study law, and in 1893 joined Lincoln's Inn. At the time, and even a century later, it was highly unusual for a young Indian to flout his father's wishes. The firmness of character, such a hallmark of the man, had begun to show through.

In London he learned a very British style of debating, although it did not always play well back in Bombay. As his biographer has noted: 'His barbed, and often witty, comments were seen by the British as unacceptable from an Indian, and by Indians as personal attacks.'[162]

On his return to India Jinnah joined the Congress, serving Dadabhai as secretary at the Congress session in 1906. He soon imbibed the older man's abhorrence for the 'hysteria' of agitational politics. Yet remarkably, although he was a 'moderate', he doted on both Gokhale and Tilak. In turn these two men, who saw eye to eye on almost nothing else, were both his fond admirers. (Just a case in point that it is never a good idea to read history backwards.)

Jinnah was quick to make an impression in nationalist circles in Bombay. His extreme intelligence and courage of conviction marked him out, even in these early years, as someone to watch. Shortly after his election to the Legislative Council, he made a passionate speech on indentured Indian labour in Natal, a system he denounced as 'harsh and cruel'. The viceroy, Lord Minto, interjected, objecting to the use of the word 'cruel' for 'a friendly part of the Empire'. Jinnah shot back: 'Well, my Lord, I should feel inclined to use much harsher language.'[163] Minto was a daunting man, and viceroys were not used to having their views challenged, let alone by 'mere' Indians. Yet Jinnah never retracted his words. His pride, confidence and absolute sense of being an equal in his dealings with British administrators made most of 'Anglo-India' detest him, but won him the admiration and respect of many fellow Indians. These qualities help to explain how this remote man – a man so different from both Gandhi and Mohamed Ali – gained such authority and fame.

Jinnah's career is often seen as having gone through two unconnected, even contradictory, phases. The popular view is that he started out as a liberal Congressman and 'ambassador of Hindu–Muslim unity', playing this role until the 1920s, when he retreated from politics in the face of the growing 'religious hysteria' he found intolerable. Then, after a damascene conversion in the late 1930s, he became the unbending enemy of the Congress and creator of Pakistan.

In fact from 1906, when he returned to India from London, until 1948 when he died broken by tuberculosis, as governor-general of Pakistan, Jinnah remained a liberal constitutionalist with a rare talent for negotiation. What changed, particularly in the 1930s and 40s, was not Jinnah but the Congress, whose leadership became ever more insistent that it represented the entire nation, and after its electoral successes in 1937, grew less interested in the politics of compromise. From the 1930s onwards, the Congress claimed to be the sole spokesman for 'India', and progressively its leadership saw less reason to conciliate those who rejected that claim. This more hegemonic stance drove out those, Jinnah among them, who believed that constitutional safeguards were necessary for minorities in Indian circumstances, and that there were identities other than 'Indian' that demanded recognition, space and respect. It proved impossible, in the end, for the arch-negotiator to bring about a compromise with a party which would not bend.

But more of this in a moment. Two achievements of Jinnah's early career in politics give a flavour of his flair for mediation. The first followed an attack in the privy council on the validity of Muslim *waqfs* – a form of religious trust, as old as Islam itself, by which a Muslim could make a religious endowment in perpetuity for the upkeep of his descendants, or for other charitable or religious purposes. The privy council ruled that *waqfs* for the upkeep of descendants were no different from secular gifts, challenging the notion that 'to help one's family' was a charitable purpose. This angered Muslims, but different camps could not agree about what ought to be done about it. Muslims of different sects had innumerable, often mutually hostile, *waqf* boards to oversee these charities. Jinnah succeeded in persuading them all that the time had come to reform *waqf*, putting forward the Mussalman Wakf Validating Bill in the Central Legislature in 1911. After many amendments, which took into account the views of different Muslim sects, 'a well-balanced compromise' was steered ably by Jinnah onto the statute book in 1913.[164] This is a reminder, if one is needed, of how divided Muslims were on a whole range of matters. That Jinnah could unite them even around a single issue is a high point in his career.

The second, much greater, feat, was the Lucknow Pact of 1916, which brought the Congress and the Muslim League into alliance. Jinnah was conscious that the biggest stumbling block in achieving Indian nationalist unity were Hindu–Muslim differences, and saw that both sides would have to make major concessions for these differences to be overcome. He worked tirelessly to achieve this, in a series of almost balletic moves, building on alliances he had cultivated inside each party. Using his influence with Gokhale, Jinnah first pushed for a conciliatory gesture from the Congress to the Muslim League. Communal electorates – recently promised to the Simla Deputation by Minto, and of which Jinnah did not approve – had become a key stumbling block in the way of collaboration between the two parties. In 1909, Gokhale accepted the principle of separate electorates, recognising that 'unless the feeling of soreness in the minds of the minorities is removed by special supplementary treatment such as proposed by the Government of India, the advance towards a real union will be retarded rather than promoted'.[165]

Next Jinnah tried to extract countervailing concessions from the League, working with young nationalist friends inside that party, the Raja of Mahmudabad and Syed Wazir Hasan. On 31 December 1912, Jinnah argued successfully for the proposal that the League change its objective to 'the attainment of self-government suitable to India ... cooperating with other communities for the said purpose'.[166]

This stance moved the League several steps in the direction of the Congress, and the gesture was duly acknowledged by the Congress, expressing at its Karachi session in 1913 its 'warm appreciation of the adoption by the All-India Muslim League of the ideal of Self Government'. Again Jinnah worked behind the scenes with Gokhale to achieve this.[167]

Next, he manoeuvred to get the Congress and the All-India Muslim League both to meet on his own turf, in Bombay, in 1916. The two national parties were minded to agree, but the Bombay Provincial League – in which Jinnah had bitter enemies, and which was split along sectarian lines between Ismailis, Shias and Sunnis – took umbrage at not having been consulted. Jinnah persuaded the Aga Khan, leader of the Ismailis, to weigh in on his behalf, and the meeting went forward, despite carping from Jinnah's Muslim critics.

What emerged from the meeting was the Lucknow Pact: a groundbreaking agreement that 'Mahomedans and Hindus, wherever they are in a minority ... [should be] given proper and adequate representation having regard to their numerical strength and position'.[168] In the provinces where Muslims were in a minority, they would be given weighted representation – more seats than the demographic facts on the ground warranted. Where Hindus were in a minority, the same principle would be followed in their favour.

The Pact thus proposed a form of positive discrimination in a composite nation, to generate goodwill and trust between the two largest 'communities'. It was not – dare I say it – a bad basis for nationhood for South Asia. Motilal Nehru and Sapru helped cement the compromise, persuading Hindus to relinquish to the Muslims thirty per cent representation in the United Provinces, even though they represented barely thirteen per cent of the population. Annie Besant (whose influence had grown enormously with the establishment of the Home Rule League movement), Motilal Nehru and even Tilak worked together to line up the Congress party behind the Pact.

Jinnah's role then was to persuade Punjabi and Bengali Muslims to surrender the communal majorities that demography on its own would have given them, to bolster the position of Muslims in provinces where they were fewer in number. This took time, but in the end they caved in to the Bombay lawyer's persuasion.

The Pact, achieved through a series of concessions by the central leadership of the two parties, countered majoritarianism in the provinces. While it might have had all the weaknesses of the multicultural politics of a later era, had it survived, the Lucknow Pact may well have had their strengths too: it recognised group rights, and responded to the fears and aspirations of minorities. That it failed makes it one of the great missed opportunities in South Asian history, reminding us once more that partition was not inevitable.

VII

'NATION' VERSUS 'COMMUNITY'

The politics of compromise that made the Lucknow Pact possible continued through the 1920s and early 30s. But a number of developments in this period undermined them.

First, Jinnah's key allies in the Congress died: Gokhale in 1915, aged only forty-nine, and then in 1920, Tilak, whom Montagu described as having 'the greatest influence of any person in India'.[169] Big personalities played a huge role in South Asia's politics, and their death (and the manner of their death) often led to swerves in political direction.

Non-cooperation and Khilafat, meanwhile, had let loose aspirations that they could not satisfy, and created tensions between Hindus and Muslims on a new scale. Communal riots, relatively rare in India in the past, grew more frequent. (These are discussed in detail later, but here they must be borne in mind as part of the backdrop to political shifts.) We have already seen the scale of the uprising, and its religious idioms, in Malabar. During 1923 alone, Amritsar, Moradabad, Meerut, Allahabad, Jabalpur, Agra, Rae Bareilly and Saharanpur suffered violent communal disturbances. Jinnah, who had nothing but contempt for Shaukat Ali, blamed Gandhi and the Khilafatists for the violence. When Gandhi urged Jinnah to 'share in the new life which has opened up before the country', Jinnah replied:

> If by 'new life' you mean your methods and your programmes, I am afraid I cannot accept them; for I am convinced that it must lead to disaster. But . . . your methods have already caused split and division in almost every institution that you have approached hitherto, and in the public life of the country, not only among Hindus and Muslims but between Hindus and Hindus and Muslims and Muslims and even between fathers and sons.[170]

This last phrase ('even between fathers and sons') alluded to the rift that had opened up at the start of the non-cooperation campaign between Motilal Nehru and the apple of his eye, Jawaharlal. The senior Nehru, Jinnah's stalwart ally, opposed Gandhi's methods, while the younger Nehru, who by this time had returned to India from Cambridge, threw himself behind the campaign. The bond between father and son remained deep: their letters show that they often discussed politics and, unusually for an Indian patriarch, Motilal allowed his son to argue against him.[171] Yet their disagreement did not bode well for Jinnah's project.

In the 1920s and 30s, Jinnah's political approach did not change; but much was changing around him, not least inside the Congress party. While he recognised these shifts, his own strategy remained consistent: to seek a grand compromise with solid sensible elements in the Congress. In what could be seen to resemble a tea dance in one of

Simla's colonial ballrooms, he set about waltzing with Liberals, doing the foxtrot with Swarajists, and turns with Motilal.

In the Central Legislative Assembly Jinnah now combined with the Swarajists to form a new alliance, the 'Nationalist Party'. (Jinnah's name for this new grouping is revealing of his grand design.) The viceroy, Lord Reading, had his own uncharitable assessment of the power dynamics in the party:

> The Independents under the Leadership of Jinnah made upon their arrival in Delhi ... a bargain with the Swarajists ... Jinnah evidently thought that by the terms of the alliance he would be sitting in the driving seat of the motor car holding the steering wheel, with Motilal Nehru beside him powerless to control except by means of advice. The exact opposite resulted.[172]

Even though this coalition was as fraught with problems as the one it had replaced, the new party's creation gave the British a shock. In hindsight, one can see that the possibility of such a wide-ranging, moderate, liberal alliance informed the British constitutional manoeuvre leading to the Government of India Act of 1935.

Outside the assembly, meanwhile, Jinnah's goal was to devise an Indian plan for a reformed constitution, based on agreement between the two communities, and dominion status for India. Jinnah, Motilal Nehru and Sapru put their minds to this fiendishly complex task. The problems were manifold. First, there was the challenge of getting agreement between 'Hindus' and 'Muslims', the main areas of disagreement being separate electorates, weightage for minorities in the provinces, and a substantial voice for Muslims at the centre. Second, even if such an agreement were achieved at an all-India level between central leaders, there was the issue of achieving unanimity, or even broad support, among those 'communities' on the ground, who, in the violent context of the times, could easily be encouraged by extremists to think that their interests had been 'sold out'. Jinnah was particularly vulnerable in this respect: his Congress background and nationalist credentials made him suspect in the eyes of many Muslims as communal bitterness grew more intense.

And then there was the small matter of persuading the British viceroy, Secretary of State for India and 'Anglo-India' as a whole that the architects of the agreement truly represented 'Hindus' and 'Muslims' respectively. This was also assuming that the British would play a straight bat in all of this, which they had no intention of doing and no reason to do.

Meanwhile, Jinnah had his private worries as his wife Ruttie, estranged but still dear to him, grew more ill. Motilal was coming under increasing pressure from his son to up the ante against the British, and to abandon what the firebrand saw as wishy-washy *swarajism*. Nonetheless the two men ploughed on, with Sapru's help, to try to square the circle.

In a major move in 1927, Jinnah outlined the 'Delhi Proposals'. These included four points: that Sind be made into a separate (Muslim-majority) province; that the North West Frontier Province and Balochistan be treated on a par with other provinces; that in Punjab and Bengal, representation be based on population; and that there be a third share of Muslim representation in the Central Legislature. He also indicated that if these claims were accepted, the Muslim community would in turn be 'prepared to accept a joint electorate in all provinces so constituted and are further willing to make Hindu minorities in Sind, Balochistan and the North West Frontier Province the same concessions that Hindu majorities in other provinces are prepared to make to Mohammedan minorities'.[173]

Here was the broad outline of Jinnah's strategy: giving up separate electorates as a concession to Hindu opinion, but creating new Muslim-majority provinces, and bringing in Muslims in the provinces as a counterweight to the Hindus' overall national majority, with some weightage for Muslims at the centre.

The Congress Working Committee was minded to accept these proposals. It set up a sub-committee (whose members were all liberals and moderates, friends and admirers of Jinnah, with Motilal at the helm) to examine them. This group accepted Jinnah's proposals with minor alterations. But other powerful players saw to it that they came to nought. On the Hindu side, Madan Mohan Malaviya put up a strong fight against making concessions to Muslims, and the Hindu Mahasabha – a small but vocal organisation, noisy in its opposition to Jinnah – backed him. This party had risen to influence in the 1920s, the decade during which the Hindu nationalist organisation, the Rashtriya Swayamsevak Sangh (RSS, National Self-help Association), was also founded.

All was not lost, or so Jinnah hoped, as he urged Muslims to boycott the all-white Simon Commission which had come out in 1928 to investigate the extension of franchise in India, arguing that 'cooperation with the Commission was a betrayal of India for which they [the Muslim community] will not even get the 30 pieces of silver which Judas got for betraying Christ'.[174] He hoped this stance would move him closer, once again, to the possibility of a new compromise. But this was not to be.

The crucial reason for this was the profound change in the structure of the Congress party. The old 'moderate–extremist' schisms had given way, but this did not mean that the party became more homogeneous. If anything, it had become more divided, but this time along a left–right axis, with each grouping committed to its own version of nationalist fundamentalism.

On the left were socialists or social democrats such as Jawaharlal Nehru, who held that there was no place for 'communal parties' like the Muslim League in the Indian nation. They believed in individuals with an un-hyphenated 'Indian' identity, and in their 'upliftment' through economic 'development'. Several leading Congress socialists were former terrorists who had converted to Marxism while in British jails and they had the zeal of new converts; others were participants in the mass movements of the 1920s and 30s, who felt that these did not go far enough in addressing issues of economic inequality. They all defined themselves as 'secular'.

For many of them, every native of the subcontinent had only one legitimate identity, and that was 'Indian'. All other identities had to be cast aside in the cause of the nation. These other 'little' identities, in their view, were forms of false consciousness: economic malaise disguising itself in religious, regional or casteist garbs, which had to be exposed in the cause of national unity. They had little time for the emerging 'Dravidian' movement, led by Erode Venkatappa Ramasamy (1879–1973), an audacious and outspoken critic of Brahmin power. Known as 'Periyar' ('Great Leader') to his multitudes of followers in South India, he drew women and 'lower-caste' groups into a powerful coalition demanding 'self-respect'; which resisted the 'domination' of 'North India'.[175]

Yet the Congress left wing barely engaged with this radical, failing to note the strength of the disaffections to which he gave voice. As for the Muslim League, they denounced it as being not representative of Muslim minorities but of feudal elites and aristocracies. They would have no truck with it. When the Muslim League proposed a joint session of the two parties in 1924, they received a contemptuously dismissive reply from the Secretary of the Congress.[176] That secretary was Jawaharlal Nehru.

On the right wing of the Congress were two lobbies whose membership often overlapped. One group consisted of economic conservatives, who had their own reasons to join the Congress in the early 1930s and seek to push it in directions that were friendly to Indian capital. After the 1929 crash and the global depression, Indian industrialists had gained both market share and muscle. Hitherto timorous and reluctant to challenge the Raj, they were now so angered by new systems of imperial preference, and by the lack of tariff protection for Indian industries, that they began to speak up against the British government. Emboldened by the crushing of the great strikes of the 1920s, they funded the Civil Disobedience campaign that the Congress launched under Gandhi's leadership in 1931, but were keen to see that the campaign was short-lived and well controlled – serious unrest was not in their interests. Civil disobedience, they believed, was 'a very dangerous weapon in the hands of a population, the majority of whom are illiterate'.[177] They urged Gandhi to meet the viceroy, Lord Irwin, and talk to him. When Irwin conceded some of Gandhi's demands in the Gandhi–Irwin Pact in March 1931, they encouraged him to suspend the movement. He did. They also urged the Mahatma to go to London to participate in the Round Table Conferences to settle India's constitutional future – effectively seeking to push him back onto the path of dialogue and constitutional politics.[178] He took their advice.

The other lobbying group were the social conservatives who pursued a more hardline Hindu 'communal' approach. As 'modern' Hindus, they took the view that India was a self-evidently Hindu nation. Influenced by the ideas of an ever more assertive Hindu revolutionary right wing, and in particular its dynamic ideologue, Vinayak Savarkar (of whom more in Chapter 2), they spoke of Indians as those who worshipped India both as their motherland and as their holy land.[179] This mantra deliberately excluded from national belonging those whose holy lands were in Bethlehem, Persia, Mecca or Medina.

Most right-wingers took a less extreme approach than Savarkar, who announced that Gandhi was his enemy. But they saw little need for the Congress to make concessions to Muslim interests. Any concessions, they felt, should flow in the other directions: Muslims, speakers of languages other than Hindi, and other minorities should relinquish (or at least subordinate) their religious and cultural ways, give up calls for safeguards and integrate into the Indian nation.

None of this should surprise us. Around the world in these decades, from Malaya to Germany, hardline nationalisms flourished in the wake of the Great Depression. India's hardliners were men of their time. Vallabhbhai Patel of Gujarat represented this tendency, as did Rajendra Prasad from Bihar and Charan Singh in the United Provinces.[180] The fact that the three men sat on the Congress party's new executive Working Committee through much of the period says a great deal about the directions in which the party was now moving.

The 1936 elections to the provincial assemblies were won by the Congress in all Hindu-majority provinces. In Bombay and Bihar, a Parsi and a Muslim were passed over for the job of chief minister, despite having the best credentials. Little-known Hindus were promoted instead, with the backing of Patel in Bombay and Prasad in Bihar. Investigations into the affair brushed things under the carpet, with Jawaharlal's knowledge and connivance; indeed, Jawaharlal shouted down the Parsi candidate at a meeting of the Working Committee at which the affair was discussed. As Maulana Azad recalled with some bitterness in the part of his biography supressed for decades: 'We all knew that the truth had been sacrificed in order to satisfy Sardar Patel's communal demands.'[181]

By the time the 1920s had drawn to a close, the Congress party had changed to such an extent that there were few leaders left with whom Jinnah could negotiate. The Nehru Report of 1928 reflected just how much his influence had dwindled. Described by the viceroy, Lord Irwin, as the 'Nehru–Sapru' constitution, the report was drawn up while Jinnah was in London. Motilal Nehru and a few senior Congressmen were worried by Jinnah's not having a hand in the proceedings, with Motilal going so far as to say: 'I can think of no responsible Muslim to take his place.'[182] But Jawaharlal pressed for the conference to continue without Jinnah, and the son prevailed over the father. In the end, what emerged was a 'constitution' that Jinnah had to reject if he was to retain any support among his fractious Muslim following.

While the Nehru Report conceded the demand for the separation of Sind and full provincial status for the North West Frontier Province and Balochistan, it also endorsed the introduction of full adult franchise. In the biggest blow to Jinnah, it recommended that only twenty-five per cent of seats in the Central Legislature be reserved for Muslims, based on their population in the country. Demos was the way the Congress was going, with no safeguards for minorities, it seemed. Jawaharlal's fingerprints were all over the Nehru Report – indeed, Nehru Senior acknowledged his son's contribution to the proceedings.

The Hindu Mahasabha was overjoyed. Jinnah's efforts to amend the recommendations came to nought. While the Liberals were prepared to concede many of Jinnah's amendments, neither the right nor the left of the Congress was willing to budge. Nor, it must be said, was the atmosphere in the Muslim League conducive to compromise. When Jinnah presented his own 'counter-constitution', in the form of 'Fourteen Points' (harking back to Woodrow Wilson's famous speech), all hell broke loose. 'A melee erupted' among angry members of the party, as nationalist Muslims prevented Jinnah from even putting his case forward.[183] Composite nationalism, if not yet dead and buried, lay gravely wounded.

In December 1930, the poet Muhammad Iqbal, as president of the Muslim League, gave composite nationalism a further blow. 'There are communalisms and communalisms,' he said in his opening speech to the conference, a speech that deserves to be quoted at length.

A community which is inspired by feelings of ill-will towards other communities is low and ignoble. I entertain the highest respect for the customs, laws, religious and social institutions of other communities. Nay, it is my duty, according to the teaching of the Quran, even to defend their places of worship, if need be. *Yet I love the communal group which is the source of my life and behaviour; and which has formed me what I am by giving me its religion, its literature, its thought, its culture, and thereby recreating its whole past as a living operative factor, in my present consciousness.*

... Communalism in its higher aspect, then, is indispensable to the formation of a harmonious whole in a country like India. The units of Indian society are not territorial as in European countries ... The principle of European democracy cannot be applied to India without recognising the fact of communal groups. The Muslim demand for the creation of a Muslim India within India is, therefore, perfectly justified. The resolution of the All-Parties Muslim Conference at Delhi is, to my mind, wholly inspired by this noble ideal of a harmonious whole which, instead of stifling the respective individualities of its component wholes, affords them chances of fully working out the possibilities that may be latent in them.

... Personally, I would go farther than the demands embodied in it. *I would like to see the Punjab, North-West Frontier Province, Sind and Baluchistan amalgamated into a single State. Self-government within the British Empire, or without the British Empire, the formation of a consolidated North-West Indian Muslim State appears to me to be the final destiny of the Muslims, at least of North-West India.* The proposal was put forward before the Nehru Committee. They rejected it on the ground that, if carried into effect, it would give a very unwieldy State. ... The idea need not alarm the Hindus or the British. India is the greatest Muslim country in the world.[184]

VIII

SCHISMS IN 'THE PAKISTAN MOVEMENT'

While the grand plans for unity between the Congress and the Muslim League faded from view, the two parties grew ever more fractured in themselves. British policy played a significant part in bringing this about. In a bold move, with the Communal Award of 1932 and the Government of India Act of 1935, British power retreated to the centre, where the Raj strove to hold on only to the most vital aspects of sovereignty. All other powers were devolved to new elected provincial governments in which Indians dominated. Five times as many Indians voted in 1937 as had previously enjoyed the privilege, albeit still only fifteen per cent of the population.[185]

This new electorate was mainly in the countryside and rural voters now emerged as a force in the constitutional arena. Whereas previously only urban and landed elites, educated classes and people who paid significant levels of tax had enjoyed the franchise, the new voters were, in the main, wealthy or middle peasants who had come out of the depression better off, with some land from which they could derive a surplus, who were paying some tax and had aspirations of upward mobility. The British believed that this social group would be conservative and vote for solid loyalist candidates, thereby weakening all-India anti-colonial parties, whether the Congress or the League.[186]

The real sting in the tail, though, were the communal majorities the Communal Award introduced in the new provincial assemblies. In the past, the structure of provincial councils – with their substantial numbers of official and nominated elements – had required Indians to work together in cross-communal alliances if they wanted to bring about any change or reform. But now, in any province, one 'community' was given the power to rule outright. The spectre of perpetual minority status in provinces which Indians would govern, gave an edge to communal animosity. It heightened tension in the provinces. Minorities began to articulate, with rising panic, their fear of the tyranny of the majority.[187]

But it also created a major dilemma for a politician like Jinnah, who already had quite enough difficulties. The Award had satisfied Muslim politicians in the provinces where Muslims were in a majority, above all the Punjab and Bengal, which accounted for the great majority of all India's Muslims. Instead of uniting Muslims throughout India, the 1935 Act strengthened parties with a strongly provincial outlook, particularly in the Punjab, where the Unionists, a conservative, Muslim-dominated party of landed interests willing to cut deals with other communities, rose to the fore. In Bengal, where most of the subcontinent's Muslims were clustered, the Krishak Praja Party, supported by peasants and agrarian tenants, emerged as the dominant voice of Muslims, reflecting the social matrix from which most Bengali Muslims were drawn.

These parties saw no real role in the politics of their provinces for Jinnah. This made the Muslim League all but irrelevant – a fact that was held up for all to see in the party's spectacular debacle in the elections held under the enlarged franchise in 1937. The League was trounced, winning less than five per cent of all Muslim votes polled in India. The emperor was revealed to have no clothes. To make matters worse, the Congress – revitalised by a second wave of civil disobedience from 1932 to 1934 – surpassed expectations, winning comfortably all provinces where Hindus were in a majority. In a move that many have seen as a turning point but was perhaps just the end of a long slippery slope, Jawaharlal Nehru rejected the League's overtures to have some Leaguers join the Congress Ministry in the United Provinces.

Some have claimed that Jinnah's famously ambiguous 'Lahore resolution' of 1940 was a response to these challenges: a bargaining counter by which he hoped to make the best of a bad hand of cards. Others view it as the start of the 'Pakistan movement'.[188] There is little to prove either version: Jinnah played his cards close to his chest. But very late in the day, in December 1946, he signed up to a British plan for a single united India with a centre at which minorities would have a say. This seems to have been what, by this stage, he was ready to settle for.

The problem was that the Congress leaders were so fed up, and so determined to have it all their own way (they had the upper hand, by this stage) that they did not sign up to the plan. They instead pushed for a limited partition of India, in which Muslim-majority states would go to Pakistan, with Punjab and Bengal being divided along religious lines.

Another huge difficulty for Jinnah was that the Lahore resolution sparked off wild hopes and desperate fears that he could do little to manage. Just as with the vision for India, the idea of 'Pakistan' from the moment of its birth engendered as much conflict, anxiety and misgiving among Muslims as it did unity.

A major schism became apparent before long between those Muslims who continued to adhere to the vision of *muttahida qaumiyat* (composite nationalism), which had come powerfully to the fore during the Khilafat movement, and those who did not. If its clearest expositor was Maulana Azad, its most ardent propagandist was Husain Ahmad Madani, a leading *aalim* at Deoband, and a powerful voice in the Congress-leaning Jamiatul-Ulema-i-Hind, the chief organisation of Indian *ulema*. Madani evocatively linked the idea of composite nationalism to the compact forged by Muslims and Jews in the lifetime of the Prophet under the Covenant of Medina.

But he was savaged by other leading *ulema*, including Maulana Thanawi, founder of the proselytising Tablighi Jamaat. Authoritative voices outside the world of the *ulema* also attacked Madani, not least Mawdudi and Iqbal. The clash was so ferocious that it tore the Jamiatul-Ulema-i-Hind apart. A rival group of *ulema* established the Jamiatul-Ulema-i-Islam, which campaigned incessantly for Pakistan, seeking to put theological flesh on the bones of the still-vague idea of a Muslim country.[189]

Perhaps the most persuasive of all was a Sunni *aalim*. Born in 1887

in Bijnor, Shabbir Ahmed Usmani was one of the eleven children of a
deputy inspector of schools. So serious and pious was the young Shabbir that his mother petitioned his teachers to intercede with her son so
that his health would not be broken by his extreme and self-imposed
regimen of study all day and prayer all night.[190] By 1932 he was
appointed vice-chancellor of Deoband – a sign of the esteem in which
he was held by his peers; Deoband had, by this time, emerged as one
of the leading seminaries in Asia.

When Deoband, under the influence of Madani, attacked the
Lahore resolution, Shabbir Usmani orchestrated the split in the
Jamiatul-Ulema-i-Hind. Turning Madani's claims on their head, Usmani argued that Pakistan would be the first Islamic state in history that
would *revive* the utopia created by the Prophet in Medina. Repeatedly
using the words 'Pakistan' and 'Medina' interchangeably, so that they
would be linked together in the minds of followers, he claimed that a
new and glorious chapter of Islamic history would begin with the
birth of Pakistan. Just as the Prophet had spread Islam from Medina
to all of Arabia, so too Pakistan would spread Islam to the whole of
India. The sacred places of Islam all over the subcontinent would be
safe, in consequence, protected from an overweening Hindu Raj.

But the learned *maulanas* were far from being the only Muslim
voices in the debate about Pakistan. Muslims in minority provinces
were profoundly anxious about its implications for their fate. In the
end, for all the high-flown rhetoric of Shabbir Usmani and his ilk,
most Muslims envisaged that Pakistan would be a territorial state, a
watan. That people were alert to this inevitability is shown in the
many maps circulating in India at this time, speculating on the possible boundaries of Pakistan. Yet however the territorial cookie
crumbled, some twenty million Muslims would be left behind in
India. These Muslims could not all migrate to Pakistan, which would
lack the resources to accommodate them.

In a scathing article in *Madina*, for instance, Syed Abu Syed Bazmi
of the United Provinces tore into the idea of a Muslim state, mounting
a powerful economic critique of Pakistan's viability. But interestingly,
he also pointed out that Hindus were not 'inert' like 'rocks and wood',
to be 'sorted, slotted and distributed at will': any apportionment of
territory would have to consider Hindu claims too. He was scathing
about the talk of transfers of population in the popular media, recalling that the largest such transfer ever to have occurred previously was

between Turkey and Greece following a conference at Lausanne after the First World War. 'Who', Bazmi asked, 'has the courage to perform the miracle of migration [*naql-i-watan*] of 50–60 million people?'[191] He demanded to know what these hapless refugees would do for a living. Reminding his readers of a still-recent disaster, he recalled the catastrophe when Indian Muslims had, during the Khilafat movement, migrated to Afghanistan.

Bazmi also attacked Jinnah for sacrificing the twenty million Muslims of the minority provinces (the size of the population of all of Arabia) whom he was willing to see 'crushed'. How could any Muslim countenance such a prospect?[192] All through the Second World War, the debate about Pakistan raged, as nationalist Muslims like Madani and Bazmi 'proved' that it could never be a 'Muslim Zion'.[193]

Nor was that ever part of Jinnah's plan. Once a 'truncated' and moth-eaten Pakistan had been forced into existence, he urged Muslims in non-Pakistan areas to hold their ground. Large migrations were neither expected nor welcomed even after Pakistan was formed, as developments after 1947 would show (see Chapter 2).

But Muslims close to Jinnah also raised questions. Perhaps the most shocking, from Jinnah's point of view, came from his close follower and faux-nephew. The Maharajkumar of Mahmudabad, the younger brother of one of Jinnah's oldest friends and allies, wrote to Jinnah soon after the Lahore resolution demanding religious safeguards for Shias in Pakistan. He listed five demands: i) that Shias would be given a voice in elected bodies and state institutions, and that on matters affecting Shias, justice and equity would prevail rather than the rule of the majority; ii) that the liberty of religious observances and beliefs of Shias would be guaranteed; iii) that the Shia *waqfs* would be controlled exclusively by Shias; iv) that where laws were passed in accordance with the Hanafi tradition, the principles of the Shia Shariat would be taken into consideration; and v) that the governors of provinces would have special powers to favour Shias in instances of injustice done to them.[194]

Jinnah was furious. This was incendiary stuff and it went right to the heart of his claim that Muslims (now) were a nation. The Quaid-i-Azam ('Great Leader', as Jinnah was now known) slapped the young Maharajkumar down with a terse response: 'The proper policy for the Shias is to join the League wholeheartedly. The League is now able to enforce justice and fair play between Musalman and Musalman whatever be his sect or section. The one thing alone that matters is that we are all Musalmans.'[195]

This was a reflection of Jinnah's strategy, of course, which was to unite all Muslims behind him; but in fact, it could well have been Jawaharlal's response to Jinnah. It pointed to the flaws of any majoritarian nation state – India or Pakistan – built around a singular identity, which refused to accommodate (or even acknowledge) difference, let alone accept that difference was legitimate. By definition, any nation state that claimed the unity and integrity of its citizenry as one indivisible people threatened to ride roughshod over particularisms, and other minority forms of self-definition. The younger Mahmudabad spotted this fundamental flaw in the model of Pakistan, just as it was a flaw in the model of India.

Paradoxically, therefore, the 'two nations', came to resemble each other ever more closely as partition approached, rushed through by the reckless and vainglorious Lord Mountbatten, the last Viceroy of India. Jinnah and Jawaharlal, two men who despised each other, came to resemble each other all the more as they strove querulously to subdue those within 'their own ranks' who challenged their claim to speak for the 'nation' as a whole.

And then there came the vivisection, which transformed the subcontinent more profoundly than anyone had anticipated. Violence on a scale few believed possible tore through the fabric of the Punjab, forcing refugees to flee in their millions, and leaving perhaps close to a million dead. Beyond the Punjab, terror drove migrations small and large, as minorities fearful about the future sought the protection of more benevolent states across the border that they thought would accept them (whether they did, is discussed in Chapter 4). Meanwhile, arson, looting, plunder and rape became the currency of power as new structures were established in a time of extraordinary flux.[196]

I discuss the implications and legacies of partition in more depth in Chapter 4. Here I wish only to note that partition did not solve the problem of what 'the nation' was about, or who it was for. It did not resolve tensions between the overriding 'official' identities of India and Pakistan, and the 'little' (or not so little) identities that survived, flourished and struggled with greater intensity after independence. Region and language would become, in both countries, flashpoints around which new alliances would coalesce. New parties would be established in both countries, all demanding recognition, rights and autonomy for this or that linguistic community. But interestingly, between 1947 and 1971, in India, and to a lesser degree in Pakistan, liberals and pragmatists forged (or renewed) alliances among themselves. This enabled their leaders to recreate old power structures and ensure a degree of stability, even a measure of continuity, despite the upheavals of decolonisation and partition.

In the late 1960s these structures began to give way, helping to explain India's slide into authoritarianism in 1975 during the Emergency under Indira Gandhi, and in Pakistan after 1976 under the military ruler/dictator General Zia-ul-Huq. In Pakistan, the inability to resolve tensions between national and 'lesser' identities led to civil war, and the birth of Bangladesh in 1971 – an astonishing occasion in modern history in which the majority seceded from a nation. Yet only five short years after the founding of Bangladesh as a nation, the unities that underpinned its own national movement dissolved, and its founding father, Sheikh Mujibur Rahman, died at the hands of assassins. How the three countries have met these challenges is the subject of the next chapter. Here it is enough to say that because, throughout the subcontinent, state-backed nationalism strives to contain, control and deny 'little' identities and impose from above grand constructs of unity, these conflicts will, in the coming years, surely intensify.

Citizenship and Nation-building after Independence: South Asian Experiences

I was seven years old during the 1971 war between India and Pakistan. My first political memory is of this short war, which lasted barely two weeks from 3 to 16 December. The blacked-out windows of our home in Delhi, the wailing air-raid sirens, the darkened tops of cars' headlamps that made them look like Noddy-cars gazing coyly downwards – these are among my most vivid early recollections.

After lights-out, my nine-year-old brother Ini and I played Monopoly by torchlight under the bed. Delhi is not far from the border of West Pakistan: this fact of geography now entered my consciousness. Our English mother who had survived the Blitz was terrified that the city would be bombed. Over our early supper before lights-out, Ini and I discussed the 'heroic' deeds of India's Indira Gandhi and the 'evil' Yahya Khan of Pakistan. Our *khaansama* (cook), Diwan Singh, a condescending Hindu Rajput with a hennaed handlebar moustache, convinced us that just as Muslims and Hindus were polar opposites, so Pakistan was the obverse of India. Yahya Khan, he told us, ate with his elbows instead of his hands. In Pakistan, according to Diwan Singh, the rain flowed heavenwards instead of falling to the ground. We fell for his fairytales, since our parents were too busy following the 'real' news to tell us what was happening. My father, a Bengali, was desperate to learn about rumoured massacres in East Bengal and was glued to All India Radio. The name 'Sheikh Mujibur Rahman' came up again and again as my parents drank gin, soda and Angostura bitters in the dark.

Anti-Pakistani socialisation, to which we were exposed – even as the children of left-leaning atheists – was intense. My father and his sister had sheltered Maoists on the run, having gone to school with Charu Mazumdar (one of the leaders of the Naxalite movement; Hill Cart Road, their family home, is a few miles from its epicentre in Naxalbari). Our father was also a character witness, at this time, for the left-wing Bombay journalist Arshad Faruqi, during his trial as a 'Pakistani spy'.

Despite this, we fell for Diwan Singh's stories. Post-colonial nationalist regimes on both sides of the border projected messages of difference and enmity so routinely that by 1970 even oddballs like us had come to identify either with India or Pakistan. It was not a smooth process, however. I have a memory of trying to stalk (with my feisty friend Emma) the Pakistani all-rounder Imran Khan, then on a visit to Delhi. How we adored him! By the 2000s, these notions had been naturalised to such an extent that the rare Indian citizen who supported the Bangladeshi cricket team was dismissed as an eccentric, while the many who admired Pakistan's fast-bowlers did so in fear (if they were Muslims), because being branded 'anti-national' by this time was a very serious crime. Go straight to jail – *ek dam* (straight away). 'Anti-nationals' represented, it seems, a vital threat to the Indian state.

How did we become 'Indians', 'Pakistanis' and 'Bangladeshis' after the two divisions of the subcontinent? Given that national identity was so fragile and contested before 1947, how did it become a matter so 'natural' after it? Or did it? Did nation-making projects succeed?

Partition is often thought of as a physical process, a massive earth-quake that sent different segments of the subcontinent hurtling apart in different directions. Because India and Pakistan (and later Bangla-desh) evolved differently in certain important respects, and because the chatter about these differences has been so loud, the facts of their shared predicaments in the early years of nation-building have been all but drowned out. India and Pakistan evolved similar strategies in the face of comparable challenges, albeit on different scales. Common patterns were formed and persist across South Asia, partition not-withstanding. On both sides of the Radcliffe Line, nation-building shared similar premises. It tried, but failed, to produce ersatz citizen-ries. It is as well that we remember this.

I

REFUGEES, VIOLENCE AND PARALLEL CITIZENSHIP

In August 1947, the very survival of both India and Pakistan seemed at stake. The waves of migration sweeping across and within their borders were unlike anything the world had seen before. (Only post-war Europe comes close to it in scale.)[1] The two newborn countries threatened to be engulfed by violence and the fear of violence, which precipitated vast human flows. India and Pakistan began their lives as nation states with a sense of existential peril. They faced many dangers, but the most proximate (in the official view) was the millions of people fleeing their homes, seeking safety. These migrants bore no arms, often they had only a few personal belongings. Some came with nothing. As the scholar Aristide Zolberg tells us, in the face of mass migrations, governments often see their nations as small crafts in danger of being swamped and dragged down below the waterline. The reactions of both Jinnah and Nehru in the face of the refugee crisis bear this out. It was the nation, not the refugee, that had to be saved.

The refugee crisis did not affect every part of the subcontinent in the same way, or to the same extent. The Punjab, as is well known, was its epicentre, with over ten million people crossing its borders in both directions over a period of six months. The land of five rivers and umpteen canals, of peasant-soldiers and *biraadiris* (clans), of rural magnates and urban merchants, of temples, mosques, shrines and Sikh *gurdwaaras*, was aflame. Roving bands of men on horseback set villages alight and butchered their inhabitants. No one was willing or able to stop them. And so people fled for their lives.

But refugees also left Sind, East and West Bengal, Assam and Kashmir in unmanageable millions. Violence welled up in small hitherto peaceful towns, like Garhmukteswar, not far from Delhi.

Migrants fled in streams, large and small, not just to the other dominion, whether India or Pakistan, but also to princely territories within them, in a desperate bid for protection. Just as with the refugee movements, the scale varied from place to place, but its epicentre was Hyderabad in the south. The violence committed upon migrants and 'minorities' (sometimes, indeed increasingly often, by the state itself) was horrifying. Hyderabad – whose Nizam (ruler) was one of the world's richest men – had resisted incorporation into India: it now became the largest destination for internal Muslim refugees. There 25,000–40,000 Muslims are thought to have perished after the Indian government invaded Hyderabad and toppled the Nizam. But even tiny states such as Pataudi, whose Nawab 'Tiger' would later play cricket for India, became a refuge for the displaced.[2] The flight of terrified people left property unguarded, crops untended, livestock and jobs abandoned. Economic devastation loomed.

In both India and Pakistan, the capital cities and major metropolises acted as magnets to the incomers, and became unruly sites of rioting and land-grabbing.[3] Desperate refugees fled to Karachi, Pakistan's new capital, in such numbers that by 1951, in just four years, the city's modest population had almost trebled in size, despite the flight from its *mohallas* (neighbourhoods) of almost all its Hindus. Sindhi Hindus, who had made up more than half the city's numbers in 1941, were reduced to just two per cent by 1951, an embattled and terrified minority.[4] Within the next ten years, Karachi's numbers grew by eighty per cent, its population crossing the two million mark. For its part, in 1947 alone Calcutta attracted over a million refugees from East Bengal. The 1951 census recorded that Delhi's population at 1.43 million had more than doubled in a decade, despite the emigration of more than 300,000 Muslims from the Old City.

In these beleaguered metropolises, refugee hawkers, street-vendors and destitutes occupied pavements during the day, and slept on footpaths or in parks at night. This was enough to prompt panicky officials to begin to seal off these urban spaces and plan the wholesale removal of refugees from them, above all from the prized former 'White Town' zones, now the preserve of the brown ruling elites. In September 1947, the government of India prohibited further immigration into Delhi. Karachi followed suit a month later (although the ban on migrants had to be lifted in a few months). The state government of West Bengal strove officiously to shut down all its refugee camps and prevent new refugees from registering themselves. The governments of both India and Pakistan were determined to rid their capital cities – symbols of national cohesion and state control – of disruptive, and often belligerent, refugees. Neither succeeded.

This was the context in which a remarkable story unfolded, whereby citizenship in both countries assumed similar forms because of the frantic actions of the refugees themselves. Their actions – small but decisive acts of agency by countless ordinary people firmly convinced of the justice of their claims – posed new challenges to the states whose protection they sought, and elicited novel answers to questions for which their leaders were quite unprepared.

When the Constituent Assembly of India first met in December 1946, its first task was to decide who India's citizens were to be. Who were 'the people of India', in Nehru's uplifting words, who were 'giving themselves' a constitution? Until this defining moment, the leaders of the All India Congress often invoked 'the people of India' and even 'the citizens of India', but had taken a very broad-brush approach as to who was to be included in that category. The Constitution of India Bill of 1895 merely stated that all 'those born in India' or naturalised therein would be Indian citizens.[5] Now the question had to be revisited in transformed circumstances.

The Constituent Assembly acted fast. On 24 January 1947, it set up an advisory committee on minorities and fundamental rights to examine the question. Its chairman was Sardar Vallabhbhai Patel, strong man of the Congress party, then home minister in the interim government. The very name of the committee reveals that to begin with, the lawmakers saw 'minority rights' and 'fundamental rights' as allied matters. Its minutes reveal that at this early stage, its members were unanimous in regarding minority rights as *additional* 'safeguards' to be enjoyed by certain communities, *over and above* the fundamental rights that all citizens would enjoy in equal measure.[6]

In April 1947, the committee reported to the Assembly with a simple and elegant formula for Indian citizenship. Its draft proposal suggested that 'every person born in the Union or naturalised according to its laws and subject to the jurisdiction thereof shall be a citizen of the Union'.[7] The committee had taken the principle in English law of *jus soli*, or birth within the realm, as the basis for citizenship of independent India.

The nitty-gritty of debate which led to this outcome took place in a forum outside the Constituent Assembly. Distinguished liberals – not all of them Congressmen – took a hand in the drafting. The clause emerged, in the heart of chaos, out of old-fashioned liberal compromise. Even Patel, no liberal himself, could see the good sense of it.

But powerful figures were troubled by this formula. At their helm was Dr Rajendra Prasad, a long-standing member of the Working

Committee from Bihar, a leading figure in the Congress high command, president of the Constituent Assembly, and soon to be president of the new republic. He led the resistance. 'Suppose', he enquired in his own brand of racism, 'a Jap by birth is travelling through the country [and] while travelling a child is born to him. What happens?'[8] Others raised concerns about the position of children of Indian parents who had been born abroad. Would they be denied citizenship?[9] In their different ways, these questions derived from the notion that the claims of ethnicity or blood should determine citizenship.

Yet Patel stood firm against them. Arguing that it would be inconsistent for the Congress leadership to push for 'narrow nationality', given that it had demanded full rights for Indians born in South Africa, he rebuked Prasad for seeking to introduce 'racial phraseology' into the constitution on account of 'a few foreigners coming here'.[10]

Patel's remark is of huge significance. It shows beyond a shadow of doubt that the Congress high command at this point had not faced the possibility of admitting large and permanent migrant populations into India in the event of a partition that – by this stage – looked very likely. In March 1947, the Congress leadership had already settled for a limited partition of India. By early May, it had persuaded Mountbatten, Britain's last viceroy, that partition on its terms was the only way to break the constitutional impasse between the Congress and the Muslim League. It remained unclear which precise territories would be included in the Indian Union and which would go to Pakistan, but already some of the Assembly's members had begun to recognise the implications of partition for the citizenship question. Despite Patel's brisk attempts to axe debate on the matter, they refused to be silenced. Significantly, it was Rustom K. Sidhwa, a Parsi member from Sind (a Muslim majority province that would soon become part of Pakistan), who asked the critical question. 'I am born in Sind. Supposing Sind is not going to be part of the Union, what will be my position? Am I to lose my citizenship of the Union [of India]?'[11]

Sidhwa's question brought into the open, for the first time, the thorny issue of what would happen to non-Muslims who would be 'stranded', by virtue of their place of birth and domicile, in Pakistan. Were they entitled to Indian citizenship? If so, on what basis? Immediately it became apparent that several members of the Assembly believed that these people were 'obviously' Indians, and hence 'patently' entitled to Indian citizenship.[12] In its turn, this notion ran a coach and horses through the tidy territorial definition of citizenship and nationality that Patel had striven to impose. As soon as it became clear that the issue could not be resolved so easily, discussion of the citizenship clause was postponed. In consequence, when India achieved independence on 15 August 1947, the vital decision on who its citizens were to be had not been settled.

On the other side of the fence, discussions about citizenship in Pakistan only began after the announcement on 3 June 1947 by the British prime minister, Clement Attlee, that British India would be divided into two successor states. So a separate Constituent Assembly for Pakistan had to be set up, and it first met on 10 August 1947, just five days before partition and the transfer of power. Nevertheless, it immediately tackled the question of citizenship, and its deliberations were no less important. On 11 August 1947, Jinnah made a historic speech promising the citizens of Pakistan 'equal rights, privileges and obligations', regardless of their religion.[13]

This speech presented the protagonists of a Pakistan where religion was the sole determinant of nationality with a conundrum that remains to be resolved. Not only did it reveal Jinnah's adherence to a liberal conception of Pakistan, but it also underscored his pragmatism. In fact, Jinnah could at once see the logic of a territorial definition of citizenship as soon as Attlee conceded partition on 3 June. On 9 June 1947, addressing the general assembly of the All-India Muslim League, he had urged Muslims who would be left in India after partition to 'stick to their respective homeland(s)', live as Indian citizens and avoid the 'temptation' to migrate.[14] He clung to this position in the face of vigorous opposition from many members of the Pakistan Assembly who wanted the new nation's constitution to be based on Islamic foundations.[15] Jinnah underlined his seriousness of intent by setting up, and chairing, a committee on the fundamental rights of citizens and minorities. Just as in India, Pakistan's lawmakers saw these two subjects as intertwined; just as in India, they regarded minority rights as additional protections that were to be enjoyed by certain minorities, over and above the fundamental rights enjoyed by all citizens.

So, contrary to the legend of their inherently different personalities, based on their distinctive nationalisms, both India and Pakistan started out with a liberal conception of citizenship. Both did so in response to the same pragmatic imperatives: to restore confidence among their large and terrified minority populations and prevent mass migrations from one country to the other. But by the time their respective advisory committees came back with their recommendations months after partition, Jinnah was dead, Gandhi was dead, and mass migrations had changed the facts on the ground.

On 17 August 1947, violence on an unprecedented scale broke out in the divided province of Punjab and spread to many parts of North India and western Pakistan. Gripped by panic, countless people began to flee from their homes. Thousands tried to cross the new border to seek the protection of the 'right' nation state, but found themselves vulnerable to attack in their refugee convoys and camps. They abandoned their homes to cluster in localities on the side of the border where their co-religionists tended to be concentrated, seeking safety in numbers. Many hoped to go back home when 'normality' returned.

But normality never did return to the subcontinent. In the weeks and months after partition, officials on the ground devised a series of ad hoc measures to deal with the exigencies that mass migration brought in its train. These measures, as much as the acts of the migrants themselves, were informed by commonsense notions about citizenship, belonging and nationality.[16] In a remarkable series of developments, these conceptions swiftly came to push, stretch and reshape policy, and eventually to inform law, constituting a new regime about citizenship that, once put into place, could not be undone.

The plight of 'stranded refugees' prompted the first of these emergency measures. Desperate to flee across the border but unable to do so for want of transport, many hundreds of thousands of migrants huddled together in makeshift camps, terrified at the prospect of being attacked by marauding gangs, or by refugees crossing in the opposite direction thirsty for revenge. Immediately after partition, social workers and local officials began to bombard ministers in India and Pakistan with telegrams warning that the very soldiers and policemen who were supposed to protect these refugees had a hand in the violence that had prompted their flight.

On 24 August 1947, Sushila Nayyar, one of Gandhi's closest aides and disciples, sent an urgent message from Wah near Rawalpindi in Pakistan, alerting India's leaders to the fact that 'Muslim troops and police [were] cooperating in [the] disturbances'.[17] On 25 August 1947, soldiers of the 3rd Baloch Regiment perpetrated what was perhaps the single most gruesome act of violence during partition, mowing down in cold blood 3,000 Hindu and Sikh refugees in Sheikhupura in West Punjab.[18]

After this incident, Sampuran Singh, newly appointed deputy high commissioner for India in Pakistan, wrote to Patel predicting genocide. 'Fifty thousand Hindus and Sikhs are daily butchered by the military and the police here. No high commissioner can save them. All Hindus and Sikhs in West Punjab will be finished.'[19] Singh was responding to floods of appeals from 'stranded' Hindus and Sikhs in West Pakistan who *expected* the Indian high commission to help them: the fortnightly reports from the commission in Karachi are full of references to members of these communities turning up at the commission's headquarters at Damodar Mahal, demanding help and protection.[20]

The Indian side of the border presented a similar picture. On 28 August, Lt Col P. N. Kirpal told Mountbatten that 'Indian officers and men had become ... affected with the communal virus'.[21] During these terrible weeks, Jinnah heard that Indian policemen and soldiers had joined in the bloodletting against Muslims. On 22 August 1947, Salma Tasadduque Hussain,[22] social worker and Secretary of the Central Punjab Muslim League, wrote of 'the most gruesome, inhuman and brutal assaults by Sikhs and non-Muslim soldiers' on 'innocent Muslims'.[23] The Punjab Boundary Force, hastily put together under Brigadier 'Pete' Rees in July 1947 specifically to keep the peace in the border districts, had not only failed spectacularly in its task but some of its members had joined members of their own community in committing atrocities against the other.[24]

In September 1947, the prime minister of India, Jawaharlal Nehru, and the prime minister of Pakistan, Liaquat Ali Khan, decided jointly to set up the Military Evacuation Organisation to protect refugees and escort them across the border. But because the British Indian Army from which it was drawn (itself in the process of being partitioned) was largely recruited from the Punjab, and its soldiers had apparently succumbed to the 'contagion' of communalism which had gripped that province, Nehru and Liaquat agreed that Muslim refugees should be protected and evacuated by Muslim troops, and that Hindu and Sikh refugees would be protected by soldiers of the same faith as themselves. In consequence, that month, Muslim troops from

Balochistan (in Pakistan) were brought in to Delhi (in India) to protect Muslim refugees who had fled from the unfolding carnage in
Rajasthan (in India),[25] and were charged with the task of escorting
across the border those who wished to leave for Pakistan.[26] Within a
month of achieving sovereignty, driven by similar concerns to protect
minorities, both India and Pakistan had thus conceded that the troops
of the other dominion could enter its territory to rescue and protect
its 'own' refugees.[27]

In October 1947, after the Sikh leader Baldev Singh urged Patel to
mount an operation to rescue 'non-Muslim girls' abducted by Muslim
youths in Pakistan, the two dominions stepped forward to act as
patriarchs recovering 'their' abducted women, in a bid to restore a
sense of national pride and communal honour.[28] Women's sexual
chastity and their violation had come to be closely bound up with
these issues during the nationalist movements; and now that two
nation states had been created, India and Pakistan made it their business to hunt these women down, to 'bring them home' to countries
many had never seen – in some cases ripping them out of relationships
they had forged with their 'abductors' (or lovers), whom in many
cases they did not want to leave.[29] They embarked on this mission in
concert.

These measures had far-reaching implications for citizenship in
South Asia. Until this point, India and Pakistan had insisted on taking
responsibility for ensuring the protection and welfare of minorities
within their own territories. The new policy was a (joint) admission
that Hindus and Sikhs 'stranded' by virtue of their birth in Pakistan
had to be protected by the Indian nation state, and vice versa for Muslims in India.

By December 1947, the Military Evacuation Organisation had
evacuated most of the five million refugees in the two Punjabs, Sind
and Delhi, and it seemed that the crisis was over.[30] Yet no sooner had
things begun to settle down in the north-west than violence threatened
to erupt in divided Bengal, sparking fresh exoduses across the eastern
border between India and Pakistan. This was the context in which
India and Pakistan held their first inter-dominion conference in Calcutta in April 1948. At this historic conference,[31] both India and
Pakistan accepted that the high commissioner of the *other* dominion
was the 'proper channel' for the oversight of the protection of minorities in both states.[32]

What this meant in practice was bizarre. If, say, a Hindu girl was abducted in a village in East Pakistan, her family had to report the matter to the deputy high commissioner *for India* in Dacca. This member of India's foreign service would then take the matter up with Pakistan's ministry of external affairs, which would pass the case on to Pakistan's interior ministry to investigate the charges. The interior ministry's findings on the claim, and any action taken by way of redress would then be relayed, by the same circuitous route, back to India's high commission via its external affairs ministry in Delhi.[33]

By agreeing on these measures, India and Pakistan further compromised their stated commitment to the principles of *jus soli* and territorial citizenship. They did this, moreover, in tandem: responding to common pressures, with common aims and common purposes.

These were only the first steps down a slippery slope. Once refugees moved across borders in large numbers (and indeed were assisted by 'national' troops in so doing), this raised big questions about their property in the country they were leaving behind. Who was to protect it and by what means?

Once again, both nations started out with the firm liberal intention to protect properties left behind by emigrants (designated 'evacuees') within their own territories. Both declared that they were determined to keep out looters and squatters, to preserve the 'property and effects of evacuees', and to guarantee their continued rights of ownership over these properties, whether moveable or immoveable. This was all very well in theory, but it posed the urgent problem of how to deal with the innumerable refugees who had *already* occupied evacuee property in the first few weeks after partition. By definition, in India, much of this 'squatter' property had previously been owned by Muslims who had abandoned their homes during the violence. Hindu and Sikh refugee squatters now refused, point blank, to vacate these properties. Instead, they threatened landlords, intimidated policemen sent to enforce the ordinance, and cowed the remaining Muslim families who tried to remonstrate with them.[34] Writing to the district commissioner of Delhi, one landlord in Chandni Chowk in the Old City wrote of refugees squatting in his property: 'They are not paying any attention towards my request of vacating . . . and are now threatening me and are causing . . . much anxiety in the entire *mohalla* [neighbourhood].'[35] In another case, a Muslim landowner wrote repeatedly to the custodian of evacuee property in Delhi, begging for help to recover property forcibly occupied by Sikh refugees:

> All my buildings have been unauthorisingly [*sic*] trespassed by these trespassers and [I have] been deprived of my birthright, income and peaceful living . . . It will not be out of place to mention here that I am a peaceful, loyal and faithful citizen of Delhi and well-wisher of our Benign Government of India.[36]

But policemen all over India and Pakistan encountered fierce resistance when they tried to enforce the ordinance. All too frequently these confrontations ended in violence, with refugees fighting pitched battles against the police and landlords. A celebrated example was the standoff between the refugee resident-squatters of 'Azadgarh' ('the fortress of freedom') and the police and local landlords. For years, the men of Azadgarh armed themselves with staves and brickbats at all times, and they clung to their foothold in Calcutta with the raw desperation of drowning men.[37]

In this pattern of action and response, the refugees' sense of entitlement comes across with force. Hindu and Sikh refugees showed that they believed that they now belonged in India, that its government was obliged to protect them, and that they had a moral claim to the property of Muslim evacuees. In Karachi in Pakistan, Muslim refugees felt similarly entitled.[38] They had sacrificed their all for the nation and they believed they deserved compensation. Refugee squatters were remarkably effective at persuading 'the *pablik*' that they were so entitled.

The way refugees stood their ground against police action shows these encounters to be true 'acts of citizenship', which changed and shaped the political landscape from below.[39] In the thousands of local battles that refugees fought across India and Pakistan at this time, we see these rapid but profound shifts taking place, as illegal acts of forcible appropriation gained legitimacy in the eyes of 'a *pablik*' that sided with the refugees. Instead, it was usually the local *havildaar* (policeman) who had to flee, taking his eviction orders with him. One frightened constable in Calcutta, for instance, reported how his efforts to 'eject' Hindu refugees from Muslim-owned houses evoked a 'threatening response', with the refugees having gained 'public sympathy on their behalf. Their eviction', he concluded, 'would not be an easy task.'[40]

The temper and norms of 'the public' then – the refugees, their numerous sympathisers in local communities, as well as lower-level state functionaries drawn from those communities – were pitted against the official policies and laws of the *Sarkar* in both India and Pakistan. With surprising speed, this climate of opinion began to influence the Indian government. Nehru, who six weeks before had been determined to protect *all* Muslim evacuee properties against *all* squatters, by October 1947 had begun to prevaricate on the issue, increasingly drawing a distinction between refugees and ordinary looters. On 6 October 1947, he told Patel that only squatters who were simply looters 'profiteering at the expense both of the original owner of the house and the Punjabi refugee' had to be evicted and punished.[41]

However, these equivocations raised yet another conundrum. What would happen if Muslim evacuees came back to their homes in India once order was restored? Many were known to want to return: Nehru himself estimated that perhaps half of Old Delhi's Muslim evacuees wished to return to their own *kuchas* (alleys), hutments, *havelis* (townhouses) and neighbourhoods, and had no desire to migrate to Pakistan. But where were they to go if their homes had been captured by refugees? And what would happen to Hindu and Sikh refugees who wanted to return to homes in Pakistan?

In response to this quandary, Nehru's government came to a conclusion with historic consequences: it had to prevent Muslim evacuees from returning to reclaim their homes. The Influx from Pakistan (Control) Ordinance, promulgated in January 1948, laid down that 'No person shall enter India from any place in (West) Pakistan, whether directly or indirectly unless he is in possession of a permit.'[42] The Indian high commission in Karachi would issue a permit only if it was satisfied on one of two conditions: either that the applicant had never intended permanently to migrate to Pakistan, or that he was a Pakistani national wishing to make a short trip to India on legitimate business.[43] The government's intention was plain. Muslim refugees who had fled to Pakistan were not to be readmitted into India. In October 1948, Pakistan followed suit with its own ordinance laying down the same conditions.[44]

India and Pakistan thus, simultaneously, *retreated* from their liberal commitment to uphold the law and to protect the property of evacuees. They did so because, as both governments recognised, they had already lost the argument on the ground.

The permit system, however, proved impossible to administer: it was liable to gross abuse and impossible to enforce. The governments of both India and Pakistan lacked the wherewithal to police the 3,000-kilometre length of the western border, so the business of checking whether people had the right permit devolved to the low-paid functionaries who manned the transport networks in the border regions. Railway guards, ticket collectors and ships' captains now began to demand that passengers who, from their commonsense per-spective, did not look like 'bona fide nationals' produce their permits for inspection, with all the inequities for which such stop-and-search procedures are notorious.

For their part, the targets of their haphazard surveillance found plenty of ways of evading it. Holders of temporary permits simply tore them up, claiming never to have left India in the first place, leav-ing the police 'with no means whatever to identify [them]'.[45] Soon a flourishing trade sprang up in counterfeit permits. By October 1948, the intelligence agencies were reporting that 'we suspect fake permits are being issued', while pointing out how difficult it was to distinguish between fake and genuine papers.[46] In December 1948, the govern-ment of India was forced to instruct all state governments to stop issuing any permits for permanent resettlement. Stern reminders were sent in April 1949, and again in May 1949, but to no avail.[47]

Even where officials succeeded in catching permit-dodgers and tried to deport them, their efforts often foundered because of the access these people had to the protection of the courts. In India, the system provoked thousands of appeals from Muslims facing deporta-tion who insisted that they had never intended to migrate permanently to Pakistan. Judges struggled to establish the required state of mind to prove that the appellants had or had not intended to renounce their Indian citizenship by travelling to Pakistan; for their part, appellants struggled to produce sufficient evidence to disprove such a state of mind.

Take the case of Fazal Dad (alias Sardar Khan Fateh Ali), who was arrested in 1953. Fazal Dad claimed to have lived in a village in the Central Provinces for forty years, where he owned 'considerable immovable property'. According to his deposition, he went to Pakistan on a temporary visit in 1948 to attend a marriage and to bring his children back to India. For reasons beyond his control he had to stay on in Pakistan until 1953, when he re-entered India, using a Pakistani passport. In court he argued that he had 'always been a citizen of India and that he could not, on account of his allegedly temporary visit to Pakistan . . . be deemed to have lost his rights of a citizen of this country'. The case dragged on for almost a decade. Finally, in November 1962, Justices Krishnan and Sharma ruled that he was a Pakistani citizen and dismissed his petition to be allowed to stay in India.[48] Of course these rulings tended to be biased against the plaintiffs, and of course less fortunate Muslims who had no papers or property were seldom given the benefit of the doubt.[49] But the point is that thousands of people charged with violating the permit rules challenged the system in the courts. Their appeals continued to clog the sclerotic arteries of the Indian judiciary long after the permit laws were repealed in 1952, when both India and Pakistan introduced passports, once again in tandem, for travel between the two countries.

This was the context for the promulgation by India of the Evacuee Property Ordinance in June 1949.[50] This draconian ordinance effectively nationalised, at a stroke, all property vacated by Muslims in India, outside Bengal, Assam and the north-eastern states.[51] Such property, the ordinance stated, was to be deployed by the government for the rehabilitation of refugees, and for other 'public purposes'. Any property, or part of a property, that had been abandoned, or appeared to have been abandoned, by its Muslim owners was liable to be 'attached', on the presumption that its owners had migrated to Pakistan. Whether or not this was actually the case, the ordinance gave the Custodian absolute authority to vest ownership of such property in the state.

As with the permit system, the identification of Muslims as evacuees depended on a subjective assessment by an official about their 'state of mind'. A ruling by the Custodian that a Muslim was 'an intending evacuee' would be virtually impossible to challenge. But now, with the bitter experience of being mired in the courts with thousands of permit cases, the Indian government decided to deny jurisdiction over evacuee property to civil or revenue courts. It also refused the courts the power 'to question the legality of any action taken by the Custodian General or the Custodian under this Act'.[52]

Evacuee property was thus made an area of governance outside the rule of law: a state of exception where executive authority was wholly unchecked, with a significance for the status and rights of India's Muslim citizens that can hardly be exaggerated. Even as Thomas

Marshall was writing his classic treatise on citizenship in 1950, which argued that access to courts was a vital attribute of 'civil citizenship', in India this access was being denied to one category of citizen: its Muslims.[53] When the constitution-makers first met early in 1947, they had agreed that minorities needed *additional* safeguards, over and above the fundamental rights enjoyed by all citizens. Now, less than three years later, the act stripped them of a key fundamental right – the right to property – and of the right of appeal against their dispossession. It also undermined their right of free movement, since if they moved anywhere, their property was liable to seizure. This meant that they enjoyed substantially *fewer* rights and protections than 'ordinary' citizens of the new nation.

Officials in Pakistan protested, with justification, that these harsh measures 'disinherited' India's Muslim 'displacees'. (The fact that Jinnah's home in Bombay's Malabar Hill was one of the first to be seized by the Custodian inspired particular outrage.) But soon, in October 1949, Pakistan followed with its own measures appropriating all evacuee Hindu and Sikh property abandoned in Pakistan.[54] In October 1954, India formalised its arrangements with the Displaced Persons (Compensation and Rehabilitation) Act, which subsumed all Muslim evacuee property in a 'compensation pool' to pay for the rehabilitation of Hindu and Sikh refugees.[55] Pakistan followed suit.[56] Evacuee property was thus established as the cornerstone of refugee rehabilitation and, by extension, of the new post-partition order.

These regulatory regimes had a profound impact on South Asia. In a region where mobility and circulation have for centuries been a way of life, they stopped the legitimate movement of populations, forcing them into an unnatural stability.[57] They sealed the western border between India and Pakistan much more effectively than any wall or fence. A series of measures followed, which gradually extended their remit. In 1955, India enacted citizenship laws that created a hierarchy of rights, ruling out citizenship for persons who had at any point migrated to Pakistan or been domiciled there, Pakistan having already legislated along the same lines in 1951. In 1965, India and Pakistan fought a brief war, and in 1968 both promulgated enemy property ordinances that gave the state draconian powers to seize property owned by 'an enemy'. India defined 'an enemy' as any Muslim who had migrated from India to Pakistan in the wake of partition, and Pakistan, for its part, as any Hindu or Sikh who had migrated to India. Both governments extended the scope of the 'enemy acts' to cremation and burial sites, temples and shrines: sacred spaces which had hitherto been spared from the sweeping power of the custodians. The enemy acts applied, moreover, to all the territories of India, bringing East Pakistan, West Bengal, Assam and Tipperah within their remit. Long after the wars of 1965 and 1971 ended, the acts in both countries continued to be strengthened by amendment. They remain in force to this day.

Meanwhile, as we were being fashioned into 'Indians' and 'Pakistanis', we had no idea that the contexts and laws that made us so, were in fact, one and the same.

In 1972, after its secession from Pakistan in a war that spawned ten million refugees, Bangladesh enacted its own Vested Property Ordinance, mirroring the provisions of the evacuee and enemy property acts of its neighbours, with calamitous implications for its large Hindu populations, and also for its Urdu-speaking (Bihari) minorities.[58]

Until the break-up of Pakistan in 1971, then, there was a remarkable symmetry in the way India and Pakistan defined citizens and dealt with 'minority citizens', controlling them by weakening their hold over their property, and curtailing their right to free movement. This situation persisted until 1971, when both countries still contained significant populations of minority citizens. For Pakistan, however, this balance would change dramatically; once bereft of Bangladesh, Pakistan's non-Muslim minority reduced at a stroke to under two per cent. Significant changes in the law followed from this but the stark fact remained that India was the 'seventh largest Muslim country in the world'. Pakistan could not make a single mistake that would trigger these Muslims to flow in its direction.

India and Bangladesh continued to have large minority populations. These big changes in demography have produced new forms of majoritarianism, and new nationalist bellicosities across South Asia, discussed later in this chapter. But, after 1971, hard borders would become the main means by which the three states of South Asia, and India in particular, tried to protect themselves from the influx of 'dangerous' non-nationals from across the frontier.

All three states grew less liberal in their approach to the rights of minorities who, by the end of the century, existed as 'bare citizens'.[59] The notion that India was a unique and glorious success story in a neighbourhood of savages is an Indian nationalist fiction.

II

FOUR DEATHS AND A FUNERAL

The horrors of partition were a wake-up call for Nehru. Some of his self-righteous certitudes were shaken by the violence of partition. He was appalled by the riots in Delhi, which he witnessed with his own eyes. Mass killings in September 1947 drove more than 300,000 Muslims out of the Old City of Shahjahanabad onto trains to Pakistan, or into makeshift refugee camps and shelters in the city itself. To Nehru's distress, the Delhi administration seemed powerless, or unwilling, to stamp out the violence.

By 1951, Delhi's demography was transformed. The city's Muslim numbers had declined from almost a third (in 1941) to just under six per cent.[60] Thousands of Muslim refugees fled to the mausoleum of Humayun, the second Mughal emperor, which lies a few miles south of the Old City. Perhaps its high sandstone walls gave them a sense of protection. Perhaps a sense of Mughal authority still attached itself to these proud relics of a bygone era, and perhaps they took comfort in this.[61] Rehabilitation for displaced Muslims was appalling. Attia Hosain's novel *Sunlight on a Broken Column* evokes their horrors.[62]

That their plight moved Nehru is plain: he wandered round Delhi like a man in shock (rather like the Mahatma had done in Noakhali in East Bengal), seeking to quell the lynchings himself. He admonished Vallabhbhai Patel, with whom his relationship was now worsening by the day. He confronted his home minister about the slackness and communal bias of the Delhi administration:

I realise that the situation was too big for almost any person to handle satisfactorily and it came with some suddenness . . . [But] as far as I can make out, we have had to face a very definite and well-organised attempt of certain Hindu and Sikh fascist elements to overturn the Government, or at least to break up its present character. It has been something much more than a communal disturbance. Many of these people have been brutal and callous in the extreme. They have functioned as pure terrorists . . . Last night's incidents when four Muslims in Safdarjung Hospital were killed in their wards is a horrible reminder of the type of persons we have to deal with.[63]

Patel demurred, and this was one of many points on which the two men fell apart.[64]

After the Delhi riots, Nehru began to recognise that minorities indeed required protections over and above the rights that all citizens of the free nation should enjoy – Jinnah had been right after all. Gingerly, and not always with courage, he began to take up the mantle of what would come to be deemed the 'secular' and 'Nehruvian' approach to nationhood, and began to speak about an India in which everyone had a place, in which the culture and faith of minorities would be guaranteed protection, and where 'unity in diversity' would be celebrated.[65] This was a very particular sort of secularism, which mixed elements of the 'composite nationalism' of old with new discourses of citizenship, economic uplift and development.

In developing this vision, Nehru drew on the thinking of Muslim intellectuals and 'nationalists' who had stayed on in India – Muhammad Mujeeb and Zakir Hussain in particular,[66] but also Maulana Azad, who served as India's first minister of education. French-style *laïcité* this was not: it did not seek to deny religion or drive it totally out of the public domain. (That would have been fruitless anywhere in South Asia.) It was a vernacular secularism evolved in the particular context of India after partition, designed to enable religious minorities and their rich cultures to survive, perhaps even to thrive.

In 1947, however, it was not at all clear that this vision of India would triumph, because others drew a different lesson from the carnage. Those on the Hindu right veered further to the extreme, finding proof in partition's violence that all Muslims were murderous – a danger to all Hindus. In their uncompromising view, the thirty-five million Muslims who remained in India should be disarmed and cowed. India should be declared a Hindu nation forthwith. Muslims should be denied all citizenship rights, and forced to leave for the Pakistan 'they' had demanded. Those who stayed on in India should know that they did so on sufferance, provided that 'they behaved'. On 28 July 1947, eighteen days before independence and partition, an all-India conference of Hindu Congressmen resolved that they

> must exert their influence to see that this partition becomes real and those who clamoured for a 'homeland' of Pakistan for themselves leave this country and make themselves comfortable in their homeland, so that this partition plan may become a real and lasting solution of the

Hindu–Muslim problem once and for all. All Muslim members of the constituent assembly should be debarred from the membership of the assembly, as they have ceased to be the nationals of Hindustan.[67]

Muslims had to assimilate into the Hindu way: they must stop eating beef and stop publicly performing *go-korbaani* (cow sacrifice) during Eid. That many Muslims accepted these terms without protest did not appease the extremists.[68] The Hindu Mahasabha (the Hindu nationalist political party), whose leader Dr Syama Prasad Mookerji by this time had joined the cabinet, pushed for a war with Pakistan to grab more territory from it on which to house Hindu refugees. In October 1947, a brief and contained war had already begun in Kashmir, but the Hindu hawks wanted to go further still. They also bitterly opposed giving Pakistan its due in the division of assets and liabilities inherited from the British Raj.

Gandhi, in contrast, was vocal about the need to be fair to Pakistan in these negotiations. Long a bogeyman in the eyes of the extreme right, they now attacked the old man for 'selling out' to Pakistan.

In late January 1948, the Mahatma was staying at the mansion belonging to wealthy industrialists, the Birlas, in Lutyens' New Delhi. My husband Anil (then a child) happened to be staying with a family friend next door. On 29 January Gandhi, who delighted in children – often interrupting serious political business to join in their games – joined the 'tennis ball' cricket match that was underway. Anil was at the crease. Using a slow, wily, underarm technique, the Mahatma bowled him out with his first ball.

The next evening Nathuram Godse, a Hindu nationalist, shot Gandhi three times in the chest at point-blank range. The Mahatma, then seventy-eight years old, was at one of his daily prayer meetings. In the last months of his life he had been a Lear-like figure, refusing to participate in the independence celebrations, rushing hither and yon trying to quell the communal fires, whether in the Punjab, Calcutta or Noakhali in Bengal.

Godse, Gandhi's killer, was a Chitpavan Brahmin (from the same caste as Gokhale and Tilak). He was a school drop-out who had had a curious childhood. The fifth child of a clerk in the postal services, his three older brothers had all died in childhood; only his older sister had survived. After these successive tragedies, his grieving parents came to believe that all their sons were cursed. So when yet another son was born to them, they disguised the baby Ramachandra as a girl, even going to the extent of having his nose pierced and making him wear a nose-ring (*nath*). They brought him up as a girl, and it was only when his mother bore another boy that they revealed Ram's male identity. His name, 'Nathuram', was actually a nickname ('Ram with a *nath*'), mocking his piercing and the feminine upbringing that went with it.[69] Who knows, perhaps his attraction to the muscular and violent Hinduisms of the time derived from an anxious masculinity. His parents sent him to Poona to live with an aunt, but he did not thrive. He dropped out of school and took up with local members of the Mahasabha and the extremist Hindu nationalist volunteer organisation, the Rashtriya Swayamsevak Sangh (RSS). For years its leader, Vinayak Damodar Savarkar, had been heaping calumny on the Mahatma as the main enemy of Hindutva, or 'Hinduness', and expressed the determination to fight for its dominance in India. Godse himself set up a Marathi newspaper, *Agrani*, later *Hindu Rashtra* (*Hindu Nation*), which also attacked Gandhi for 'sabotaging' Hindu interests.

In hindsight, the fact that Gandhi was killed in those murderous times is not surprising. But the response to his assassination was. All over India people, apparently inured to brutality, reacted with shock and disgust. As soon as it was made known that the murderer was not a Muslim but had links with the Mahasabha, angry crowds began to attack the party's offices all around the country. A mob ransacked Syama Prasad Mookerji's home in Calcutta, and pelted Savarkar's home with stones.[70] In Bombay, riots broke out: shots were fired, fifteen people died and fifty more were injured before 'an uneasy peace was established'.[71]

But, the Congress leadership – and Nehru in particular – took control, orchestrating the funeral procession, the cremation, the outpouring of sorrow and the distribution of the Mahatma's ashes to remarkable effect. In a choreographed performance of national mourning, Gandhi's bier was not carried by his kinsmen, according to tradition, but placed on a carriage covered in flowers and sandalwood. In a show of India's newfound sovereignty, troops pulled the cortege through Lutyens' Delhi, previously inhabited by the most senior (chiefly white) officers of the British government. It moved down Queensway and Kingsway (now Janpath, 'People's Way'; and Rajpath, 'Ruler's Way'), through the Memorial Gate (now India Gate), down to the banks of the river Yamuna. Nehru and Vallabhbhai Patel sat alongside the body with Gandhi's eldest son, the chief mourner. This emphasised Nehru's figurative position as heir to the 'father of the nation' (and also the two adversaries' newfound resolve to work together).

But the most fascinating part of this 'invented tradition' was how, after inconsolable crowds, party members and dignitaries watched Gandhi's pyre burn to the ground, a special train carried the Mahatma's ashes through North India to the *prayaag* – where the Ganges, the Yamuna and the mythical river Saraswati have their confluence at Allahabad. Leaders from each province of India received a portion of ash and bone, which in turn was split into three parts, and taken to a different river or lake to be immersed. As rivers, lakes and creeks across India were thus consecrated with the remains of the Mahatma, Nehru sought symbolically to weld the partitioned nation into a new whole. By this elaborate ritual, India's dismembered geography was metaphorically cleansed and reunited, taking on, by association with the Mahatma's ultimate sacrifice, a novel and wholesome meaning.[72]

This was a powerful move in the context of the propaganda unleashed by the Hindu right that it would never accept the vivisection of India, demanding *akhand Bharat* (undivided India), despite the part it had played in bringing about that partition.[73] With this ritual interment of Gandhi's ashes across the new, smaller India, there was a sense that the nation could accept its loss – physical and spiritual – grieve, and move on.

A second consequence of the murder was that the extreme Hindu right, which until now had appeared to be an unstoppable force, was driven into the shadows. On 4 February, the government of India banned the RSS. Across India, police rounded up some 200,000 RSS *swayamsevaks* (members of the RSS).[74] Nor did the Mahasabha come out unscathed: as its own General Secretary admitted, the party's reputation was 'besmirched' by the assassination. On 14 February 1948, a fortnight after Gandhi's death, the Working Committee of the Mahasabha resolved (strategically) 'to suspend its political work and focus on *sangathan* [building up Hindu unity] and the solution of our diverse social, cultural and religious problems for the creation of a powerful and well-organised Hindu society in India'. In its years in the wilderness, the party fragmented, with Mookerji soon decamping to set up a new party, the Jana Sangha (People's Party). For decades the two organisations limped along, at war with each other as much as with the Congress, and performing dismally at elections.

Yet contrary to popular belief, during Nehru's ascendancy the Hindu right did not melt into thin air. The hard Hindutva brigade held fast to its hardline views. On 22 April 1949, for instance, Bishen Chandra Seth, the President of the Provincial Hindu Sabha UP (Uttar Pradesh, India's largest province), wrote saying,

> from history to the creation of Pakistan and till today, the clear policy of the Muslims has been to drink the blood of our country and like foreigners create different problems for us. Despite this, our govern-ment is tolerating the Muslims (Muslims consider Hindus as cowards) and the Kashmir problem is a good example of this policy. I would like to state that I consider the Muslims as fifth-columnists and in their hearts they have no love for the country.[75]

Many persons of a 'soft-Hindutva' persuasion had already joined the Congress years before 1947; after 1948, evacuees from the deci-mated Mahasabha joined their ranks, strengthening the Hindu right flank of the party.[76] If anything, the hard right within the Congress party was bolstered by Gandhi's death, even as its reputation was damaged among the population at large. This was made clear by the victory of Purushottam Das Tandon (1882–1962) in the 1950 elec-tion to the Congress Presidency, winning by an increased share of the vote. A darling of the Hindu right, Tandon was an orthodox Hindu from Uttar Pradesh, with powerful anti-Muslim views. A staunch opponent of Pakistan, he was a fanatical proponent of Hindi against Urdu and resisted any change to Hindu custom or tradition (which meant that his views on questions of the reform of family law, and caste, were unbending).

Sardar Vallabhbhai Patel backed Tandon in his campaign against Nehru. Patel was also a protégé of the powerful industrialist Ghan-shyam Das Birla, from whose house in Hardinge Avenue (now Tilak Marg) Gandhi had made his last journey. The 'iron man', as he was known, Vallabhbhai Patel, like so many fellow Congress leaders, was a London-trained barrister who rose to the top of Gandhi's inner cir-cle leading peasant protests in Gujarat during the Kaira and Bardoli *satyagrahas* (non-violent movements). Perhaps for this reason, he had a more earthy image than his rival, Jawaharlal. He dressed the part too, preferring rough *khadi dhotis* to Jawaharlal's elegant ensemble of *bandgala-churidaar* (a high-necked long jacket with jodhpurs). Both men wore, of course, the Congress cap.[77] Patel was a stocky, bald, bull of a personality, who browbeat and dragooned most princely states into acceding to India by 'the stroke of the midnight hour' on 15 August 1947, and in so doing laid the foundations for an independent India. Moral in a traditional sense, upright and proud, he had little time for those weaker than he was. (He placed Jawaharlal, with his wide and eclectic reading, his charm and his relationships with women, in this category.)

But Tandon and the Hindu right were never able to wrest control of the prime ministership from Nehru, who had been strengthened by the Mahatma's murder and by his inspired handling of it. Their dominant position within the Congress party was undermined, moreover, when on 15 December 1950, Sardar Patel, who had been ill for some time, died of a heart attack in Bombay. Patel, like Gandhi, died at Birla House, a coincidence that reveals the extent to which industrialists and businessmen like Birla had penetrated the party's innermost circles.

Patel's death weakened Purushottam Das Tandon's bid for the leadership of the Congress party at the centre, although intense battles would rage, over the next year, over its 'moorings' and its 'soul'.[78] Nehru would eventually see off the challenge, forcing Tandon to resign as the President of the All India Congress Committee. Nehru stood for election to that post himself, winning decisively by 295 votes to 4. He then invited Tandon to join his Working Committee. In conceding, with some grace Tandon admitted that Nehru 'represents the nation more than any other individual today'.[79] This was a moment of India's history at which Nehru's strength of conviction, his strategic nous and his newfound talent for compromise prevented the Congress party from falling apart. Such moments were rare, but when they came round, they helped cement both party and nation.

But it would be a mistake to see the era of Nehru's leadership of India as one in which his variant of social-democratic 'secularism' triumphed over all else. The UP Congress, of which Tandon was a representative, continued to do its own thing, ignoring Nehru's attempts to force it to follow the 'national' line. Full of Hindu rightwingers like Tandon and Charan Singh, India's new largest province promoted Hindi in the Devanagiri script in schools, denied support to Urdu and took active measures to make sure that Muslims in government service, particularly policemen, were driven out of their jobs.[80]

A shrunken West Bengal under Dr Bidhan Chandra Roy's leadership allowed Muslims to be ghettoised and marginalised.[81]

Nehru as prime minister had to learn to compromise with these provincial power-brokers. He gradually became more like his father Motilal – a liberal surrounded by pragmatists and party-machine politicians, having to work closely with Hindu nationalists, even if it meant holding his nose. Sometimes he chided them, often he pleaded with them, to little effect. His first fortnightly letter to his provincial chief ministers reveals the tenor of his relations with them. India's Muslims, he reminded them, 'have got to live in India. That is a basic fact about which there can be no argument.' But while he urged them to give Muslims 'security and the rights of citizens', he left the details up to them: 'How exactly you should do it is a matter I must leave to your judgement; it must depend on local factors.'[82] For the most part, he turned a blind eye to their excesses, which were legion.[83]

Fortunately for the stability of India – even though 'Nehruvianism' was not all that it was cracked up to be – Nehru not only saw off his challengers, but lived until 1964.[84] For nigh on twenty years after independence, Indians – who took to calling him 'Chacha (Uncle) Nehru' – experienced a measure of political continuity that was foundational. (Chacha means uncle, father's *younger* brother, suggestive of affection rather than fear, significant given the patriarchal structure of the Hindu family. More of this in Chapter 5.)

Indeed, born three months before Nehru's death, I grew up taking my liberal rights – to equality (before the law), to the freedom of speech and religion, cultural and educational rights – for granted. An entitled and spirited youngster, I wrote a book critical of the Congress in the era of Nehru, *because I had the right of freedom of speech and expression.* Before that, I had written a book that (in hindsight) was even more daring, about Hindu communalism inside the Congress party in Bengal. This earned me death threats but no judicial punishment. I was exercising my fundamental rights.

When India slid into authoritarianism, first in the 1970s, and again in the 1990s, losing these liberties was a shock. Losing the fundamental rights that citizens had become blasé about made many fight all the harder to regain them. But more of these battles later. For now, it is enough to know that Nehru lived and was prime minister of India until 1964. When he died, there was a search for alternatives. The Congress party machine filled the breach – after trying a few people out – by appointing his daughter Indira Gandhi to succeed him.

Let us now step across the Wagah border, to see what was happening in the newborn state of Pakistan.

In 1947, Wagah was a dusty spot in the middle of nowhere, about forty kilometres from Amritsar, the site of the Golden Temple and the scene of the Jallianwalla Bagh massacre. By the end of the twentieth century, Lahore had grown so much that Wagah had come to nestle in its outskirts. Today Wagah is perhaps the most Kafkaesque border post in the world, a point at which each country performs, in perfect symmetry, a choreographed display of its sovereign relationship with the other.

The ceremony is held in the orange-mauve dusk of the Punjab plains, between the villages of Attari (on the Indian side) and Wagah (on the Pakistani side). The name 'Wagah', however, has stuck, both to the ceremony and to the border. It is a name dense with history – the history of partition and the refugee caravans – and rich with allusion. 'The border in the middle of nowhere' could be the title of a short story by Sadat Hasan Manto, the writer of the most famous partition short story, 'Toba Tek Singh', about the exchange between India and Pakistan of inmates of 'lunatic' asylums. Manto questioned who the true lunatics were: those doing the partitioning or those incarcerated in asylums. (He questioned almost everything about partition. We will meet this extraordinary man again in Chapter 7.)

But Wagah is no longer 'nowhere'. By the end of the twentieth century it had become a destination in itself. Crowds on both sides gathered every day to watch the spectacle. On the Indian side before the ceremony, they whooped and cheered; spilling over into the military area to dance. Viewers are less boisterous, though no less fascinated, on the Pakistani side of the stadium. (Both countries have built towering pavilions, extraordinary structures, intended to conjure up 'the nation', to accommodate 'its' multitudes.)

The pageant involves Indian and Pakistani troops bringing down their country's flags before nightfall. Held in the cool of the evening, a phalanx of thirteen high-stepping soldiers, dressed like turkey cocks, wearing high red turbans topped with tall red fans (shaped like Japanese fans and adding a foot to their height), march towards each other in step. Both hold their position, for seconds. Both turn around, only to return and perform the most striking (if aggressive) dance steps, in unison. There are many such moves, each one more breathtaking than the previous one.

Viewers are stunned by the virtuosity of these dancing soldiers. But as one gazes at them for a while, one notes their different uniforms, their huge red fan-topped turbans matching better the Pakistanis' black 'pathani' tops and trousers, than the Indians' regular camouflage fatigues. But this difference only makes the symmetry of their dance poses more striking, and their increasing intensity more gripping. At a gesture, during a pause in the dance, the two sides draw open the metal gate between the two countries. As a drum rolls, the soldiers dance closer to each other, although no one puts one foot across the border line. Their moves grow more and more elaborate, to the extent that you lose sight of the fact that you are not watching modern dance, but armed soldiers at Wagah.

As the ceremony draws to an end, both sides lower their flags, in careful coordination – so that one flag is never higher than the other. They close the gate again, but not before exchanging a quick handshake. Both then do an abrupt about-turn, marching to the more sombre music of the 'beating of the retreat'. Bearing their respective flags like divine heralds, they march, their legs raised to an impossible angle, back to their positions.

This happens every single evening.[85]

Wagah is as famous in South Asia as the Berlin Wall was in Europe, and indeed the western world. But the differences are striking, because it is the joint performance of a relationship between the two countries. Not quite what you'd expect, given the catastrophising about India–Pakistan relations. (I will return to this in the Epilogue.)

In 1948, however, the Wagah–Attari border was little more than two flagpoles bedded in hastily constructed brick pediments, canvas army-issue tents on either side. It stood as a symbol of the pressures Pakistan faced after independence – some of which were akin to the pressures that face all nation states: the contradictory claim that the nation had always existed, and that it had to be forged anew.

The idea of 'Muslim nationhood' had a pedigree going back to the days of Syed Ahmed Khan; but that consisted of the notion that Muslims were a nation because they were numerous, important and *different to other Indians*. The poet Iqbal had offered a more positive definition in his famous Allahabad speech in 1930, stating that Islam had furnished those basic emotions and loyalties which had gradually unified scattered individuals and groups, and finally transformed them into a well-defined people, possessing a moral consciousness of their own. 'Indeed it is not an exaggeration to say that India is perhaps the only country in the world where Islam, as *a people-building force*, has worked at its best.'[86] In a rousing speech in the United States in December 1946, Jinnah had taken on aspects of the poet's thesis while reiterating some of the ideas of Syed Ahmed Khan, insisting Indian Muslims were 'a people', dissimilar from Hindus in their 'history, language, culture, architecture, music, laws, jurisprudence, calendar, and the entire social fabric and code of life'.

But now that Pakistan had been achieved with such amazing speed, the question arose: how similar were the Muslims of Pakistan to each other? How far had history transformed them into 'a well-defined people'? What hopes and values did they share? Did they have a common vision of nationhood? If not, how could such unities be achieved? What kind of state did they want Pakistan to be? These conundrums were not easily resolved. As Iqbal himself had warned, 'nations are born in the hearts of poets; they prosper and die in the hands of politicians.'[87]

Iqbal had died in 1938, and although he was hailed as Pakistan's spiritual founder, his thought (much of it expressed in Urdu, which only the migrant North Indian intellectual elite could read and understand) was so rich, changeable and open-ended that it could not serve as a guide to the nation. If anything it stimulated debate and interpretation, rather than consensus.[88] It could not provide a blueprint for building Pakistan.

Jinnah's authority among the people of Pakistan was profound. But he (with his Parsi wife and uncertain faith) was no 'pious caliph' of Islamic history, whose personhood could represent the common Islamic consciousness that the poet had claimed for the people. He could and did represent Pakistan, for the last year of his life. His personal influence, I think it is safe to say, was greater than that of any other living person in the new state.

This was not true of the party he led, the Muslim League. Its sway in the areas that became Pakistan was tenuous. Other parties had much deeper roots in these parts. They had grown in response to provincial social conditions and colonial constitutional structures and – whether the Unionist Party in the Punjab, the Krishak Praja Party in Bengal or the Khudai Khidmatgar in the North West

Frontier – they were often more interested in provincial issues and hence less 'national' in their outlook.[89]

Weaker still in these parts was the sense of nostalgia for a lost golden age that was so characteristic of the *ashraf* Muslims of North India, hundreds of thousands of whom now migrated to Pakistan. The provinces or princely states that made up Pakistan had robust linguistic and cultural traditions of their own, often very distinct from each other, more earthy and folksy than the Islamicate high culture of the old Mughal heartlands. Punjab had its own rich traditions, drawing heavily on the genre of the *qissa* (legend, fable or folk-tale).[90] The Lahore district's *Gazetteer* in 1883 observed that the ballads of Waris Shah (1722–98), and his famous love story, *Heer-Ranjha*, were universally popular among all creeds. Bulleh Shah (1680–1757), who composed *kafis* (poems) on the mystical Sufi *tariqa* (way), was, and remains, admired in Sind and Punjab.[91] *Qawwaali* singers (of devotional music), including the great Nusrat Fateh Ali Khan (1948–97), put many of his *kafis* to music; and this vibrant musical culture remains celebrated today, straddling the boundaries between creeds, between elite and popular culture, and even between India and Pakistan. (On a recent visit to Lahore, my colleague and friend Kamal Munir drove me at reckless speed over the 'Jinnah Flyover', to the accompaniment, on his car's CD player, of Nusrat Fateh Ali Khan singing Bulleh Shah: a memorable moment in which centuries, cultures and countries seemed to bend, collapse and fold into each other.)

Nor was it clear where exactly East Bengal fitted into the emerging Pakistani national imaginary. Separated from the western wing by more than 2,200 kilometres, East Bengal was a distant and unfamiliar land to most people settled in the west. Its 'national' poet, Kazi Nazrul Islam (1899–1976), was born into a family of traditional religious *kaazis* (judges), but he was a rebel from an early age, leaving school as soon as he could to join a troupe of rural actors and then setting up as a journalist. In 1917 he joined the army, and he encountered Persian poetry only much later in life. His verses and plays were about poverty, peasants, women and rebellion. He borrowed more readily from Rabindranath Tagore and the Bengali Hindu *bhajan-kirtan* (devotional singing) tradition than from Rumi, Ghaleb and Hafez.

Nazrul was so loved among Bengali-speakers that when he died in 1976 both Bangladesh and India claimed his body. Yet for the very reasons he was so loved in India and East Pakistan, the cultural elites of western Pakistan found him hard to grasp, and were never wholly persuaded that the East Bengalis who adored Nazrul were proper Muslims at all.

To complicate matters further, the majority of the people of Punjab, Bengal, Sind and Kashmir followed local *pir* cults of exceptional power. These were shrines associated with the relics of 'saints', managed by descendants, who had an extraordinary ability to retain – indeed, expand – the founder's discipleship (*muridi*): devotion from people in the region near them, and further afield. The austere message of Islamic modernisers like Mawdudi had made little headway with them. Shah Jalal of Sylhet in East Bengal and the *pirs* of Pagaro in Sind were figures to contend with in the new Pakistan; their followers' loyalty could not easily be displaced by the abstract idea of the nation (although it could, and did, sit alongside it). This is not to say that the people of these regions did not support Pakistan. Most did, with enthusiasm.

It is just that they did not quite know what it meant to them in all their particularity, now that it had so suddenly come about.

Welding these disparate localities and regions into a nation would always have presented a challenge, even without the strain of absorbing refugees. It did not help that many refugees were convinced that they were superior to the people among whom they had come to live. In two regions in particular – Bengal and Sind – the gulf of class and culture between refugees and their hosts overlapped to produce, with extraordinary speed, a toxic mix.

Refugees had been glad to assume the appellation bestowed on them by a government that was struggling to help them in more practical ways: *muhaajirun*, a title that linked their own emigration to the era when Islam was founded. This implied that their hosts should receive them just as the good people of Medina had received the Prophet and his followers, *ansars*. Having lost their all in India, most refugees were deeply invested in Pakistan's Islamic character. Often Urdu-speaking, they stretched the *muhajir–ansar* analogy to imply that they (the refugees) were bringing all that was good and great in Indo-Islamic civilisation from upper India to the 'less-developed' parts that had become Pakistan.

Sindhis and Bengalis found this attitude hard to digest, even when it came from the very top, from the Quaid-i-Azam himself.

If these social, racial and regional tensions were not enough, early Pakistan was torn apart by a battle for its soul that pitted religious traditionalists (the *ulema* of Pakistan, newly organised under the Jamiat Ulema-e-Islam) and fundamentalists (with Abu-l-Ala Mawdudi at their head) against the pragmatists and liberals, or 'secularists'. The latter group were not 'secular' in a western sense. Including most politicians (led by Jinnah himself), senior bureaucrats, officers, commercial men and urban middle classes, Pakistan's 'secularists' were largely men and women of faith who believed that simply by coming into existence, Pakistan had created the conditions necessary for the Muslims of Pakistan to flourish. Their goal was to design a modern (European-style) constitution by adapting the 1935 Government of India Act for Pakistan's post-colonial conditions. They were in a hurry to build an effective modern state apparatus with separate executive, legislature and judiciary, and to achieve a modern form of citizenship. They did not want a theocracy of any sort; they wanted to 'modernise'. Interviews conducted in the 1950s suggest that most urban, western-educated Pakistanis, both in the government and outside it, tended to look down upon the traditional *ulema* who pushed for a theocratic state as a bunch of 'misguided *mullahs*'.[92]

The birth of Pakistan placed these religious groups in a dilemma. A great many *ulema* and most fundamentalists had previously denied the validity of the concept of Pakistan, because classical Islamic political theory does not recognise the existence of an Islamic nation that is not identical with the *entire global community* of believing Muslims – the *ummaa*.[93] Just before partition, Mawdudi had denounced nationalism to be 'the antithesis of Islam, for it sets up the nation as a god'.[94]

Now, given the drastic changes in circumstances, both groups shifted their stance. They had to. Both now wanted Pakistan to become an Islamic state, and were determined that it should have an Islamic constitution. Although it was clear to no one precisely what that meant (since the concept of constitutionalism fits poorly with Islamic jurisprudence), the men of faith were determined to push for this.[95]

For their part, the secular political class believed that the support of the men of faith had won the Muslim League the 1946 elections. Whether this was right or wrong is a matter of debate. What matters is that they were convinced that the religious leaders had great influence. So they were chary of alienating them.

As for Mawdudi, thus far the bête noire of the *ulema*, he now saw cause to ally with his former foes. He had good reasons for so doing.

The nascent government of Pakistan regarded his version of Islamism as particularly dangerous, even if it was less influential among the public than the *ulema*. Before 1947, Mawdudi had denied that the League (whose leaders he denounced as secular and 'wordly') was capable of building an Islamic state. After partition, he changed his tune, deciding instead that his purpose was to advise 'worldly' League politicians to bring an Islamic state into being, in his words, to encourage 'a lemon tree to grow mangoes'. In a series of famous lectures, he began to outline how Pakistan's government could be made more Islamic. His key demand was that the Constituent Assembly should not make new laws unacceptable to the Sharia and should repeal all laws repugnant to it. His Jamaat-i-Islami group, established in 1941, now began to act like an Islamic vanguard party critical of the state. It challenged the League government's legitimacy, forbidding Pakistanis to take an oath of allegiance to the state until it became truly Islamic. He even declared that Pakistan's war in Kashmir was not a true jihad.

For his pains, he was jailed, and his party charged with sedition.[96]

After his release, he continued to maintain relentless pressure upon the government to adopt an Islamic Constitution for Pakistan.

These bald facts help to explain many of the conundrums of Pakistani nation-building after 1947. Most of the regions that became Pakistan had weak, or recent, histories of attachment to the cause of the Pakistani nation, whose meaning, everyone agrees, had been vague and contested until the elections of 1946, and remained freighted with tension afterwards. During those elections, the notion of 'Pakistan' had been injected with all manner of millenarian hopes for transformation, whether moral or material. One hugely popular election slogan was '*Pakistan ka matlab kyaa? La Ilaha ila'allah*' ('What does Pakistan mean? There is no God but Allah').[97] It rallied the pious but had all the specificity of 'Brexit means Brexit'. The campaign opened up contradictory aspirations – both for the universal rejuvenation of Islam *and* for individual freedom, economic development and citizenship guaranteed by the nation state. Sources tell us little, so we have to assume that Bengali peasants who voted for the Muslim League had voted for 'Pak-Bangla'[98] and 'Islamic socialism',[99] but whatever utopias they imagined were surely worlds apart from the aspirations of the educated middle classes of North India, or the *biraadiri* lineages (the clans and 'tribes') of the Punjab and their *sajjada nashins* (*pir* shrines), or the landed elites of Sind and their tenantries. Pakistan's claims to legitimacy rested, 'at least in part, in its moral juxtaposition against the very structures of local power and claims to . . . identity that brought it into existence'.[100] Yet, after independence (and indeed during the 1946 elections) the nation would rely upon these very 'traditional' structures and claims to buttress itself on the ground – and indeed, to locate itself in time and place.

Let us pause for a moment to consider the nationalism of Pakistan's generals: it is important and instructive. They have often been regarded as a Machiavellian force, manipulating the Pakistani *pablik*'s sense of vulnerability to gain ascendancy in the shifting and unstable balances of its politics.

Although there is much truth in this picture, it would be a mistake to ignore the particularities of the nationalism of an army that had to reconstruct itself from the fragments of regiments and units of a partitioned British Indian Army, and to which India denied its fair share of ordnance and munitions. Having served the British, their nationalism was not anti-imperial in tone. Mohammad Ayub Khan, who took over as Chief Martial Law Administrator after what he described as the 'Revolution' of 1958, was Sandhurst-trained, the son of a Risaldar Major in Hodson's Horse. His relations with his British superiors, and later with western counterparts including the US President Nixon, were comfortable. But he raged against India for its unfairness after partition, and he was frustrated by what he regarded as incompetence, corruption and the self-serving ambition of Pakistan's politicians. In his view, only a soldier who was ready to die for the nation knew what true patriotism was. In his memoirs, he wrote:

> Pakistan is my passion, my life. A look of happiness in the faces of people thrills and sustains me. Just as the shade of anxiety in their eyes causes me anguish. I have woken up from sleep to see whether the sound on the window-panes is of the long-awaited rain. I feel parched inside when I see a drought-stricken field. The soil of Pakistan fascinates me, for it is my soil. I belong to it.[101]

He simply could not accept – given what he saw of the manoeuvrings of the political classes – that they felt as he did for their country. From day one, when he took over as Commander-in-Chief of a fragmented army, he was sure that the main threat to Pakistan was India.

Our first concern was the defence of Pakistan against any possible aggression by India. We knew the war with India would be a national one in every sense of the word. India's aim is to expand, dominate and spread her influence ... our strategic aim cannot be the conquest of India because that would be a negation of the very concept of separation. Our aim must be to make India realize that it is not worth her while to maintain a hostile attitude towards us.[102]

Historians have suggested that Pakistan's national identity became a wholly negative one, bound up entirely with rivalry and enmity with India. Pakistan was a country that was 'not-India'. While there is a measure of truth in this – India provided a useful foil and external 'other' against which Pakistan's emergent identity could be fleshed out – there is more to modern Pakistani nationalism than negativity: the generals' vision of nationalism is not the only strand.

Pakistani nationalism, I suggest, also had a powerful internal dynamic, whose driver was the (positive) search for unity. Contrary to legend, it was only after 1947 that Jinnah's much-vaunted drive to be 'the sole spokesman' truly emerged. Increasingly, Jinnah himself (and those in his inner circle) assumed that unity could result only from a unitary state. The logic that had driven the Congress to this way of thinking before partition appealed to him more once he had a state, first to create and give an identity to, and then to govern. Indeed his unitarism became so extreme that he outdid in his advocacy even the Nehru of pre-independence years. He heard all the many aspirations – for greater federalism, for religious debate on the nature of the state – but his impulse was to deny them. These different desires were not accommodated in Jinnah's Pakistan to even the extent they were in India. Federal impulses, which were powerful indeed, Jinnah's government ignored or repressed. Provincialism was now seen as a threat of disunity. Very soon it became associated with treason.

For those at the helm in 1947, Pakistan's quandary was stark. The only thing unifying its disparate constituents was the fact that they were all Muslims – barring the large Hindu minority in East Pakistan – but being 'Muslim' meant many different things.

Moreover, Pakistan, as it was constituted until 1971, could not be an Islamic nation. They were clear it could not become another Israel, a Muslim Zion, a beacon and potential homeland for all the subcontinent's Muslims, let alone for Muslims around the world.[103] Their reasons could not have been more unsentimental. These lay in the mass migrations that began in 1947, which had slowed down but never wholly stopped: migrations that, in Jinnah's view, had threatened the existence of the new nation.

Pakistan, with an infant state, struggled without success to cope with the ten million or so refugees who flooded into it. As its leaders were all-too aware, after partition India still contained thirty-five million Muslims. Pakistan could not accommodate them should they too decide to flee their homes. On 9 June 1947, addressing the general assembly of the All-India Muslim League, Jinnah urged Muslims who were left in India after partition to 'stick to their respective homeland(s)', live as Indian citizens and avoid the 'temptation' to migrate.[104] He stuck to this position in the face of vigorous opposition from many members of the Pakistan Assembly who wanted the new nation's constitution to be based on Islamic foundations.[105] Already by late 1947, as panicking refugees in their millions ignored the Quaid, the Government of Pakistan's Ministry of Relief and Rehabilitation began to argue that West Punjab had received a 'surplus' of 12 *lakh* (hundred thousand) refugees (over and above the numbers of Hindus who had left for India). This surplus would have to be redistributed over finite territory. Very quickly, 'a political common-sense' emerged about how many refugees the Pakistani state could accommodate.

In this equation, the Pakistani state was a finite territorial entity that could accommodate only exactly 'as many . . . "non-Muslim refugees" who were leaving'.[106]

This left little room for any real compromise between Pakistan's 'secularists' and the 'Islamic state' protagonists about the kind of nation Pakistan could be (before 1971). Its rulers turned their face firmly against accepting more Muslims from India, fearing a flood of millions more refugees who would sink the uncertain ship of state that was Pakistan. But they also began to recognise the need to reassure the country's minorities (particularly the millions in East Bengal), lest another exodus of Hindus to India sparked a reciprocal wave in the other direction which Pakistan did not have the resources to absorb. Whatever the religious lobby demanded, those in charge could not leave Pakistan's Hindus unprotected and without religious and cultural rights. The nation's survival was at stake, and they recognised that.

Jinnah's response to this series of conflicting pressures was to cen-tralise. He ignored the religious lobby and treated those who demanded recognition of their differences with the same contempt Nehru had once shown him. Weeks after independence, he dismissed Dr Khan Saheb (brother of Khan Abdul Ghafar Khan) as chief minis-ter of the North West Frontier Province, because he feared he would push a Pashtun national agenda. Weeks later he dismissed Muham-mad Ayub Khuhro of Sind, who opposed Karachi (Sind's capital city) being made the capital of Pakistan, and resisted absorbing more refu-gees. In Quetta, in June 1948, Jinnah denounced 'provincialism' as a 'curse'. 'We are now all Pakistanis – not Baluchis, Pathans, Sindhis, Bengalis, Punjabis, and so on, and as Pakistanis we must feel, behave, and act, and we should be proud to be known as Pakistanis and noth-ing else.'[107] Two months later he declared a state of emergency in the Frontier Province and Sind to force these recalcitrant provinces to take 'quotas' of 500,000 refugees each.[108] He held fast to the notion of a unitary secular Pakistan, and tried, as one scholar has put it, to create a new man, 'a Homo Pakistanus' who would transcend pre-existing regional cultures.[109] His speech on Urdu in East Bengal (of which more below), which sparked protests among students in Dacca, showed his general direction of travel.

By the middle of 1948, however, it had become clear to those close to him that Jinnah had not long to live. The Quaid had smoked a tin of Craven cigarettes every day for fifty years. He had long suffered from tuberculosis, a secret this guarded man had held close to his chest. Now he began to show signs of lung cancer. A photograph of him splashed across the League's newspaper, *Dawn*, to celebrate his seventy-first birthday, displayed (with unintended irony) the ravages of his disease: his aquiline nose juts above lips too dry to smile; his cheekbones, always prominent, spread like wings over gaunt cavern-ous hollows. Ever slim, he was now skeletal. As his body began to fail him, his doctors moved this proud and lonely man from Quetta, where he had retreated, back to Karachi.

But, in a cruel metaphor for early Pakistan, the Red Cross ambu-lance scheduled to take him closer to medical help broke down, and the Quaid was forced to wait on his stretcher by the side of the road in the oppressive dust, heat and humidity. By this stage he weighed only thirty-six kilos. He died later that night, just as India launched its 'police operation' against Hyderabad.[110] The League government decided to bury him at the highest point in Karachi, some three miles from his home. Eyewitnesses recall that on 12 September 1948, every member of the grief-stricken crowd of a million or more wept as they followed the cortege of the Quaid-i-Azam to his burial place.[111]

Today Jinnah's resting place is a mausoleum, designed in the 1960s in an austere modernist style by the architect Yahya Merchant. Its cool marble elegance reflects the man it commemorates. There could be no dispersal of his physical remains across Pakistan, like Gandhi's across India: as a Muslim, the Quaid was buried, not cremated. Instead, a touched-up image of Jinnah as a younger, rosy-cheeked (and fuller-faced) man wearing a Turkish fez has become the symbol of Pakistan's sovereignty. This curious image – Jinnah was never chubby-cheeked or pink, as he is shown in it – hangs in every government office, be it so lowly. (In Lahore, when I presented my Indian passport to the police for a routine check, this version of the Quaid stared at me from behind a tower of dusty files. I stared back, discombobulated.)

Whether Pakistan might have got onto a more even keel had Jinnah lived longer is a moot question. The popular view is that it might have done: Jinnah, 'like Nehru', could have held Pakistan together by sheer force of personality, or so people say. A man who could terrify a viceroy could have dealt with a general. I think there is something in it.

Yet unlike Gandhi months earlier, Jinnah was not murdered, so his death did not lead to a backlash (as Gandhi's had done) against Jinnah's opponents and a profound restructuring of Pakistan's emergent politics (as Gandhi's had done).

Indeed, months afterwards, Bengal's most prominent leaders – the 'Red' Maulana Bhashani, Huseyn Suhrawardy and Fazlul Huq – were emboldened to set up a new party, the Awami Muslim League (later, the Awami League).

The religious lobby also sought to take advantage of the Quaid's passing, seizing the moment to put pressure on Liaquat Ali Khan, prime minister and one of Jinnah's closest allies, to Islamicise the constitution of Pakistan. In March 1949 Liaquat appeared to succumb, adopting the controversial Objectives Resolution on Pakistan's constitution, which declared that 'sovereignty over the entire universe belongs to God Almighty alone, and the authority which He has delegated to the State of Pakistan through its people for being exercised within the limits prescribed by Him is a sacred Trust'; that 'the principles of democracy, freedom and equality, tolerance and social justice, as enunciated by Islam, shall be fully observed'; and that Muslims would be enabled 'to order their lives in the individual and collective spheres in accordance with the teaching and requirements of Islam as set out in the Holy Quran and Sunna'.

However, Liaquat saw to it that it did not swing in the opposite direction. The Resolution thus also guaranteed fundamental rights and equality of status to all, to safeguard the legitimate interests of minorities, backward and depressed classes, and an independent judiciary.[112]

As this sophisticated policy of accommodation suggests, scholars have underestimated Liaquat Ali Khan (1895–1951). He was as different from Jinnah as a man could be. Whereas Jinnah, like Cassius, wore 'a lean and hungry look', everything about Liaquat was round, including his face, his head and his pebble glasses. But if he looked a bit like Falstaff, he was nobody's fool. From a state near Karnal in Indian East Punjab, he was of aristocratic stock: his family traced its origins back to Nausherwan the Just, the Sassanid king of Persia.[113] In 1857 the British had stripped the family of its princely status, but allowed it to retain some land and its title. Liaquat had the typical upbringing of the North Indian *ashraf* elite, graduating from Aligarh and then from Oxford's Exeter College, later being called to the bar. But in many other respects he was uncharacteristic of his class.

On his return to India in 1923, 'his lifestyle was *deceptively* lavish': he was the only *zamindaar* in the area who was not in debt.[114] He threw himself into politics; but far from just blustering in the Council, he proved to have an extraordinary command over matters fiscal and financial, often blinding his opponents with the mathematics of compound interest. His command over detail was legendary. Among the central issues that preoccupied him was the role of 'capitalist' moneylenders in the countryside, whose loans at exorbitant interest rates threw both peasants, and also the landlords who might have helped them in times of hardship, into crippling debt. In the UP Legislative Council he asked: 'Can my friend (Thakur Hanuman Singh) point to a single instance in which the capitalists have forgone their legal dues to the same extent as landlords ... during these years of depression?'[115] (This gives a foretaste of his approach to land reform as prime minister.)

At the centre, he backed Jinnah on all the great issues of the day, and he remained loyal to the Quaid unto his last. In 1946, Jinnah appointed him Finance Minister in the Interim Government, a role in which he revealed brilliant political skills. In 1947–8, he announced a budget which is remembered as one of his most remarkable achievements, and which, in all likelihood, was the final straw that pushed the Congress to opt for partition. That budget aimed to root out tax evasion, to abolish the Salt Tax (against which Gandhi had led a *satyagraha* in 1930) and impose a tax of twenty-five per cent on business profits exceeding Rs 1 *lakh*, with Liaquat seeking to drive a wedge between Congress right-wing big business allies and its socialist outriders.[116] (His wife, the distinguished economist Begum Raana, may well have helped him work out the craftier details of a budget that made Patel and other Congressmen apoplectic with rage.) What is interesting about Liaquat, who is often seen as a bland stand-in for the Quaid, was that his politics had a distinct flavour. It was the countryside that he knew best. Agrarian issues – looming large in these years – animated his politics. The Quaid, by contrast, was a far more urbane man. He knew only the city.

On taking up Jinnah's mantle in 1948, Liaquat proved that, besides being loyal and savvy, he was tough. He did not blink when both Britain and India devalued their currency in 1949, refusing simultaneously to devalue the Pakistani rupee. He told a secret session of the League that 'unless India accepts the value of our rupee, not even an ounce of jute could be given to her'.[117] He refused to budge from this position, and eventually it was India that folded.

He was decisive in his dealings with provincial factions, dismissing the provincial government in the Punjab in January 1949. He was also clear that Pakistan needed a functioning army. Given that Pakistan had received few complete regiments after the division of the British Indian Army at partition, he made the armed forces a national project for Pakistan and set up new centres for the instruction of army personnel and training, evoked with such wit in Mohammed Hanif's *A Case of Exploding Mangoes*. In a move that reveals his political nous, he instructed service chiefs to 'recruit as many Bengalis as possible' – a shrewd move, given growing Bengali discontent, which perhaps Jinnah himself would have been loath to make.[118] In 1951, in another act of great significance, he appointed Mohammad Ayub Khan, a handsome young Sandhurst-trained soldier's soldier, as Commander-in-Chief of the Armed Forces.

Like the Quaid, a proud nationalist vis-à-vis the British and the Commonwealth, while always ready to defend Pakistan's sovereignty,

Liaquat's preferred option, particularly in relations with India, was diplomacy. In 1948 he accepted a ceasefire in Kashmir and referred the dispute to the United Nations – a controversial but not unwise move, given the situation on the ground. In the same year Liaquat and Nehru signed the historic Calcutta Agreement on Minorities, by which both countries agreed to protect minority rights and avert conflict. This helped to secularise South Asia's diplomatic practices and institutions.[119] (More about this in the Epilogue.)

Critically, the Objectives Resolution with its Islamic overtones (much like the Indian constitution's 'Directive Principles of State Policy') was not justiciable. It was a fudge, much as the 'directive principles' in India's constitution were. They were not enforceable. Liaquat was a shrewd pragmatist, making allowances where pressures built so as to recalibrate expectations and achieve a new balance in Pakistan.

Immediately after making this concession to the religious lobbies, moreover, Liaquat launched a policy of rapprochement with India, working with Nehru on the minorities question. He announced that he was taking Pakistan in the direction of what he described as 'Islamic socialism'. What this meant, however, was not particularly Islamic, or even socialistic: his object was to provide the 'common man' with 'food, clothing, shelter, medical aid and education'. As the scholar Leonard Binder notes drily, Liaquat's Islamic socialism was 'no more than capitalism plus social security plus God'.[120] It was, in fact, no more than the good old-fashioned pragmatic liberalism of the centre-right, with a bit of social democracy thrown in, cloaked in language to satisfy domestic aspirations while negotiating the new global politics of the Cold War.

Liaquat continued to cleave to Jinnah's centrist position on states' rights and on language, while making important concessions to Bengalis. His response to other internal and external challengers was tough. Like Nehru in India, he came down hard on the Pakistani communists, not least the poet Faiz Ahmed Faiz. In the Rawalpindi Conspiracy Case (Pakistan's first attempted coup), those involved were given harsh sentences. Like Nehru, who banned the Communist Party of India and had Gandhi's murderer hanged despite an appeal from Gandhi's sons for clemency, Liaquat's soft contours hid a hard centre.

On 16 October 1951, an assassin shot Liaquat Ali Khan twice during a public meeting of the Muslim City League at Company Bagh (Company Gardens) in Rawalpindi. The police shot dead the presumed assassin, Saad Akbar Babrak, who was later identified as an Afghan known to the police. Liaquat Ali Khan was rushed to a hospital and given a blood transfusion, but it was too late to save his life.

Liaquat's assassination remains one of the great unsolved mysteries of the South Asian twentieth century. All manner of conspiracy theorists have transformed Saad Akbar Babrak into the Lee Harvey Oswald of the subcontinent. Perhaps more Panama and Paradise leaks will, one day, unlock the secret. The point here is that this murder (whatever and whoever inspired it) deprived Pakistan of shrewd and experienced leadership at a time when it was most needed. Aspects of Liaquat's pragmatic domestic and foreign policy continued to guide Pakistan long after his death, lasting even into the age of Ayub Khan. Yet perhaps, had Liaquat survived, there would have been no Ayub Khan, certainly not as Master of the State, and then no Yahya Khan. Perhaps, of the four untimely deaths after 1947, this murder was the one that most undermined the subcontinent's stability in the years after independence.

In South Asia, larger-than-life personalities had come to the fore during the battle for independence. (They would continue so to do in the era of nation-building.) Their deaths – particularly deaths by assassination – led to huge shifts; as fragile alliances broke down, building new ones took time, effort, negotiation and compromise. (Recall Chapter 1.) Periods of instability allowed extremists of one or other stripe to step forward and make their own insistent demands.[121]

In the five years between Liaquat's death and the army's takeover of the state, seven coalition governments rose and fell in Pakistan, under a changing guard of prime ministers. The bureaucracy, under the career ICS man Ghulam Muhammad, took upon itself a role that went beyond its remit as civil servants; they entrenched themselves whereas politicians, who were in power for such short periods, could not exert authority over them, as they played musical chairs with increasing desperation.

Into this whirligig stepped General Ayub Khan, with his 'Revolution' in 1958. Pakistan's era of martial rule had begun.[122] Ayub would remain in charge until 1969. During his rule, for that is what it was, he amalgamated all of western Pakistan into a single province, both to stamp out 'provincialism' and to water down East Pakistan's majority. (East Bengal's demographic majority was one of the big challenges that Pakistan faced. How could the Punjabi and Sindhi landed elites tolerate a government of those lesser beings, 'Bengali Muslims'? 'I mean, were they even Muslims?' was a common attitude.)

Ayub tried to avert this possibility by making minor concessions for indirect representation, of which it is best to know little: because it was designed to confuse, it was a most confusing system. But in the end, he could not ignore the groundswell of popular demands for full democratic elections that came not only from the unruly East, but also from 'West Pakistan', where Zulfikar Ali Bhutto (a member of the Sindhi landed elite) had taken up the fight.

It was at this point that General Ayub handed over power to Yahya Khan (he of the eating-with-elbows fame) to negotiate an election based on a full adult franchise.

What everyone in office feared came to pass. East Bengal's Awami League, led by Sheikh Mujibur Rahman, won that election. This was the moment of truth: would West Pakistan's politicians follow the rules and declare Mujib the elected leader of Pakistan? No. They could not bring themselves to do that. Days passed while Mujib, Bhutto and Yahya sat down to negotiate a compromise behind locked doors in one of Dacca's hotels. Meanwhile, people outside were getting restive.

There were localised scenes of violence against Bihari-speakers – a horrific straw in the wind of massacres to come.

When talks broke down, and Mujib addressed the crowds – still not calling for independence – he was arrested and charged with conspiracy. Meanwhile a crackdown began in Dacca. Soldiers yanked academics out of their homes and shot them dead in front of their families. Students in hostels were gunned down. The civil war that tore Pakistan apart had begun. So had Bangladesh's 'War of Liberation'.

The Pakistan of 1947 proved impossible to hold together. Two new states were born in 1971, and both had to embark on new nation-building projects, of which more below.

III

LANGUAGE TROUBLES: BABEL IN SOUTH ASIA

In December 1952, 'a great commotion' (*pedda galata*) broke out at Nellore railway station in India. A crowd of hundreds gathered. They looted wagons and ransacked the station. Police opened fire and four people died in the shooting. Three others succumbed to injuries sustained during the four days of violence that followed. The *galata* was a response to the news that Potti Sriramulu (1901–52) had starved himself to death to demand a separate province for Telegu-speakers within India.

Nellore was then a district in the sprawling Madras province, where Telegu, rather than Tamil, was the dominant language. Yet given Tamil's cultural dominance in Madras itself, and its strong sense of a proud literary tradition going back centuries, Tamil-speakers were wont to look down on Telegu-speakers as lesser mortals. Potti Sriramulu spoke Telegu.

A fine-featured man whose intense eyes stare out accusingly from his portrait, Sriramulu from Nellore trained as a sanitary engineer, but worked for the railways until 1930. In 1928, a tragedy changed his life: he lost his wife and infant child. Already an idealist, he now gave up his job and joined Gandhi's *aashram* at Sabarmati. Active in every one of Gandhi's campaigns before independence, he was jailed several times during the Quit India movement: indeed a more dedicated Gandhian it would have been hard to find in southern India. His particular passion was Gandhi's campaigns for the 'upliftment' of Dalits. The assassination of his mentor in 1948 seems to have struck a very deep blow. During the remaining years of his life, he took to walking barefoot through the streets of Nellore, wearing placards calling for Dalit uplift. Many locals believed he had lost his mind.

When, however, news spread that he had died demanding a separate province for Telegu-speakers, a small rebellion broke out.

After independence, Nehru was loath to create provinces on linguistic lines, despite the Congress party's long-standing commitment to the principle. But his stance towards linguistic provinces evolved in much the same way as his policy had changed in the face of angry partition refugees. Immediately after partition he had tried to do the liberal thing and set up a committee to examine the case for linguistic provinces. That committee, headed by S. K. Dar, concluded that this was not the time to examine the question, and suggested that it be postponed for a decade. At its Jaipur session in 1948, the Congress party set up its own high-powered committee to consider the issue. Headed by the party's most powerful leaders – Jawaharlal Nehru himself, Vallabhbhai Patel and Pattabhi Sitaramayya – it agreed that it was 'not an opportune time for the formation of linguistic provinces ... [it would] dislocate our administrative, economic and financial structures [and let loose], while we are still in a formative phase, the forces of disruption and disintegration'.[123] It thus also tried to loft the issue into the long grass.

But when the Nellore violence suddenly erupted in 1952, Nehru buckled in the face of popular pressure and violence, which, although a spark and not a conflagration, seemed frighteningly reminiscent of the partition riots. He announced the creation forthwith of a new Andhra state, carved out of the parts of the old Madras Presidency where Telegu was indisputably the dominant language. The Telegu agitators also demanded Madras city itself as Andhra's new capital, but much to their rage, it remained the capital city of the province of Madras. The four dead of Nellore are remembered to this day as the *mrita viralu* (dead heroes) or *Andhra rashtra mrita viralu* (the dead heroes of Andhra state).[124]

Sriramulu was not the first of the subcontinent's 'language martyrs': that distinction goes to the young men who had died in 1939 in mass protests in Madras. But in a fascinating symmetry, five Bangla-speaking activists died on 21 February 1952 in Dacca in East Pakistan, a few short months before Sriramulu. The Bengali *shaheed* (martyrs) were part of a vast rally defying a Pakistan government order banning all processions and demonstrations in the city on the day that language activists had declared State Language Day. The protestors, both Muslims and Hindus in the province of East Bengal, demanded that Bangla, a language spoken by an overwhelming majority in East Bengal, be included as a state language and as a medium of education in schools. The dead were mainly students and activists, although onlookers also got caught up in the violence: a nine-year-old boy died of bullet wounds. On 22 February, the agitation spread; shops closed and some 30,000 protestors joined the crowd of mourners following the *janaaza* (bier). More firing ensued, and thousands were wounded fighting pitched battles with the police.

After this, language campaigns gathered momentum elsewhere in the subcontinent. In 1956, the Samyukta Maharashtra Samiti, led by the bespectacled cartoonist Bal Thackeray (who later founded the Shiv Sena, 'Shivaji's army'), won its decade-old campaign to create the state of Maharashtra for Marathi-speakers. Salman Rushdie's *Midnight's Children* captures the temper of the times in a scene in which

Saleem Sinai, the child protagonist, accidentally finds himself at the
heart of a Samyukta Maharashtra Samiti throng. They goad him, asking if he wants to join the Samiti, in Marathi, a language he barely
understands. 'Dazed into telling the truth, [I] shake my head No.'
Forced to speak Gujarati, he recites a doggerel he has learned at
school and which he used when he was bullying Gujarati boys, a
rhyme designed to make fun of the speech rhythms of the language:

Soo che? Saru che!
Danda le ke maru che!

(How are you? I am well!
I'll take a stick and thrash you to hell!)

A nonsense, nine words of emptiness . . . but when I'd recited them, the
smiles began to laugh; and then voices near and further away began to
take up my chant, How Are You? I Am Well! . . . becoming, as it went,
a song of war . . . To the tune of my little rhyme the first of the language
riots got under way, fifteen killed, over three hundred wounded.[125]

Nehru's government once again reacted much as it had done in the
face of angry partition refugees. First it tried to do the liberal thing
and carve the cosmopolitan city of Bombay, the financial capital of
India, out of Maharashtra state and govern it directly from the centre.
But more fighting broke out, leaving more than eighty people dead.[126]
In 1956, as part of a new compact, six new 'linguistic states' were
established, Maharashtra at the head of the list. By taking the total
number of states to thirteen, India's States Reorganisation Commission thus tried to quell the furies of language movements which
everywhere challenged the central government's drive to achieve a
unitary nation state. The lid soon blew off. Today there are twenty-
nine provinces defined by language in India. The success of previous
movements merely spurred on new demands.

In 1956, Pakistan adopted its first constitution. Its prime goal too
was to deal with the challenges of Bengali and Sindhi 'regionalism'. To
achieve this it took the drastic step of abolishing all provinces in West
Pakistan. This left only two 'units' in the country, West and East Pakistan. The constitution bestowed parity upon both units, but in practice
this left East Bengal under-represented and dissatisfied. By abolishing
provinces, Pakistan's leaders hoped to abolish what they described as

'provincialism'; but just as their peers in India had failed, so too did they.

Neither of these devices – conceding linguistic provinces or denying them altogether – succeeded in defusing the passions driving language activism, and its close cousin, nativism (and their coeval histories are well worth noting). A pamphlet published by the Shiv Sena in 1967 claimed that 'there was definitely something rotten in the state of Maharashtra ... out of 1,500 executives on the rolls [of the leading industrial houses of the City of Bombay and government departments], only 75 were Maharashtrians while an overwhelming majority (above 70%) were South Indians'.[127] Bombay remains to this day the heart of nativist campaigns to rid the city of non-Marathi-speaking immigrants and Muslims. Dacca is rife with hatred of Urdu-speakers. In 1960–1, Sant Fateh Singh and Master Tara Singh led the Punjab Subah movement, fasting for forty-eight days to establish a Punjabi-speaking province; and in 1966 India created a shrunken state of Punjab, shorn of its Hindi-speaking territories, and a new 'Hindi-speaking' province of Haryana. This did not satisfy the Sikhs, among whom calls for a separate state of Khalistan grew louder. This movement would grow into a war of secession – very different in nature from the war fought in Bangladesh in the same decade, but with the same intention. India's state, under Indira Gandhi, expanded its deployment of the tools of repression open to it, and met Sikh separatists' fire with fire.

Meanwhile, thousands of miles to the south, in January 1964, a twenty-seven-year-old day labourer named Chinnasami, educated to the fifth standard but so infatuated with Tamil that he named his only daughter Dravidacelvi (Lady Dravida), walked to the railway station in Tiruchirapalli, south of Madras. There he doused himself with kerosene, shouted '*Inti olika! Tamil valka!*' ('Death to Hindi! May Tamil flourish!') and set himself ablaze. In 1965, eight more suicides followed, each proclaiming their devotion to the cause of the Tamil language.[128]

These events raise fascinating questions. First, how was it that language changed from being something that one used, one medium among others in a polyglot world rich with dialects, to being a primary marker of one's identity, the subject of intense, sometimes fanatical, devotion? How was it that, even as communal identities seemed to be defining themselves more sharply against each other, language devotion appeared to transcend (for a while) the schism between Hindus and Muslims?

The fact that something rather peculiar has happened to language in South Asia was brought home to me one day soon after I had come to teach at Cambridge. I was lunching with a new colleague, the historian of Britain Peter Mandler. This was our first of many collegial lunches and coffees. We sat in the Hall at Trinity College where Jawaharlal Nehru and Muhammad Iqbal had both lunched, like us, under the pouting, barrel-chested gaze of Henry VIII.

Peter asked me where I was from. I replied that I was Bengali. His puzzled questions shook my assumption that this was a 'natural' category, whose meaning was stable and easy to comprehend. I told Peter I was born in Delhi to a Bengali father and an English mother, and (before Cambridge) had been educated all my life in North India; but that I was a Bengali. Peter looked mystified, so I tried again. We had a family home in Delhi, but our 'ancestral home' was in North Bengal, so I was a Bengali. He persisted with his probing. Was I educated in Bengali? No, I replied. Although I learned Bengali as a child, and persevered with its study as a teenager and adult, in fact my Bengali is not as good as it should be, since I went to English-medium schools and Bengali was not spoken much at home in Delhi (even though it was the only language used in our 'ancestral home').

As I spoke, I realised that I was gabbling. Why, given this complexity, did I insist on defining myself as a Bengali? Peter asked. Because that was what I *felt*, I tried to explain. My sense of family history, and of my cultural legacy, was Bengali. My beloved *Pishima* (aunt), my father's sister, a widowed poetess who spent several months with us each year, saw to it that I learned the language as a child from the lyrical primers by Tagore (*Sahaj Paath*, 'Easy Lessons'). She put me to sleep with stories (in Bangla) from the epic *Mahabharata*, and if I woke up afraid at night, she comforted me with Sukumar Ray's nonsense rhymes, *Abol Tabol* ('The Weird and the Absurd'). She would laugh as she told them to me for the umpteenth time. She never stopped finding them funny, and nor did I. My father held strong, even essentialist, views about Indians who spoke languages other than Bangla (no one was remotely as cultured as we Bengalis were!). As a consequence, no matter how hard I argued with my father that he was wrong, my relationship to other Indians was framed by my

'Bengaliness'. I saw myself, and perhaps as importantly, other Indians *saw me*, as a Bengali.

How did these powerful linguistic and regional identities come to be so much a part of South Asia's landscape of affiliation and emotion? Another question that demands an answer is why the Bangla movement and the Telegu movement erupted at exactly the same time, the one in Pakistan, the other in India. This raises further questions about why South Asia's language movements refused to observe the new national borders; if anything, they seemed energised by the drawing of the Radcliffe Line.

Of course, turning language from a neutral medium of exchange with porous boundaries into a 'hard' marker of identity was a long process; it started at much the same time as the rise of nationalism, in the late nineteenth century. The concept of a mother tongue, in its South Asian sense, is a late-nineteenth-century construct. Linguistic and regional movements were propelled by many of the same motors as nationalism itself. Indeed they *were* forms of nationalism, except for the fact that they didn't, or didn't usually, seek sovereignty. At the forefront were elites versed in both English and the regional languages, and also scribal groups whose patrons had once been maharajas and *nizaams*, but who in the colonial era had no choice but to seek support from paying subscribers; and who used the lithograph to reach (and indeed create) wider reading publics.

A major turning point in Telegu's role 'from medium to marker' came in 1893, when Gurujada Sriramamurti solicited support for his *Lives of (Telegu) Poets* from 'those having affection of pride in the language of the Telegu country'.[129] Sriramamurti's source of inspiration, oddly enough, was Macaulay, whose biographical essay on Samuel Johnson was on the syllabus of Madras University: and it encouraged Sriramamurti, whose forebears might have written hagiographies of kings, to write instead biographies (*charitramu*) of Telegu poets. In 1893, P. Gopala Rao Naidu (influenced by current philological discussions about languages and their distinct 'histories') published his *Summary of the History of the Andhra Language*. This work attributed birth to languages, and 'the possibility that they might one day die'. This notion of the possible death of languages helps explain why these apparently arcane, scholarly works were shot through, and read, with intense emotion. Languages not only had to be described and recovered, they also had to be saved.

In some parts of the subcontinent, particularly where Hindus were in a majority, the next stage in this process would be the personification of the language as a mother goddess. Poets represented Telegu Talli ('Mother Telegu') as a beautiful woman, garlanded with jasmine flowers, wearing a diadem. Idols portrayed her as holding a sheaf of harvested crops in one hand, signifying the prosperity of Andhra, and in the other bearing a *kalasam* (a vessel signifying fertility).

In 1913, when Sriramamurti's work went into its third edition, the newly formed Andhra Mahasabha took up the cause of a separate province for Telegu speakers. By 1942, when cinema halls had begun to draw large crowds into the towns, Sankamrambadi Sundaraachari wrote the song 'Maa Telegu Tallika' ('To Our Mother Telegu') for the film *Deena Bandhu*. It opened thus:

> To our mother Telegu, a garland of jasmine flowers
> Camphor flames to the mother who gave birth to us
> Our mother, who showers us freely with gold in her heart,
> Compassion in her gaze, riches and good fortune in her smile.
>
> When the rippling Godavari River flows
> When the rapid Krishna river runs
> Golden crops ripen
> And milky white pearls appear
>
> The rare arts of Amravati city
> The notes which spring from the throat of Tyagayya
> The sweet beautiful sounds from the pen of Tikkayya
> She is present and endures in all of these.[130]

This song – in its way as lyrical as Bankim's 'Ode to the Motherland' and Tagore's 'Our Golden Bengal' – would become the official song of the province of Andhra Pradesh.

Meanwhile, in the Oriya-speaking region of Bengal, the lawyer-poet Madhusudan Das led a campaign to separate 'Utkal' from Bengal. He achieved this in 1935, making Orissa a 'linguistic province' a decade before independence.

But while the agency, devotion and creativity of men like Sriramamurti, Sundaraachari and Madhusudan Das must be recognised, changing technologies and governmental processes also played a part. I have already mentioned the humble lithograph, which drove so many cultural transformations in South Asia in the long twentieth century. The colonial census did much to encourage Indians to identify with discrete languages. In 1881, when the first complete census was carried out, 'mother tongue' appeared as a head of information gathered. To begin with, census-takers did not ask any direct questions about people's mother tongue; they simply read back the number from the total population of a region and assumed that its people had a single mother tongue – despite the fact that in large parts of Madras Presidency, as officials themselves admitted, people often spoke Tamil, Telegu, Hindustani, Malayalam, Marathi and, indeed, Urdu. (All these languages flourished in Hyderabad.) By assuming that people identified with, and prioritised, one language above others, the census helped to create a certain kind of value, and a sense of connection with one language, that had not previously existed. (Kings in South India had typically composed verses in eight languages as a mark of good kingship.)

Furthermore, by calling this one language a mother tongue, and implying that it was learned at the mother's breast, language-identity came to be loaded with an intimacy that it lacked when language was used and understood as simply one medium (among others) of communication.

This sense of intimate physicality would soon be represented in statuary and iconography, particularly of Tamiltay, the goddess of Tamil. Sculptor-artisans and poets often portrayed her as a Rubenesque figure, demurely seated, the perfect 'maternal' nurturer.[131]

Missionary-grammarians were also significant protagonists in this story. Hoping to convert heathens into Christians, they sought to master 'native' languages to a far greater depth and proficiency than did colonial officials; and their modern grammars had the effect of standardising and ordering languages, distinguishing each from the others as distinct objects. The missionary Robert Caldwell's *Comparative Grammar of the Dravidian or South-Indian Family of Languages* (1856) gave rise to the hugely influential notion of a 'Dravidian' language community that not only had a great literary corpus, even a canon, in its own right, but also was culturally distinct from the language communities of the North. In the hands of non-Brahmin or Dravidian campaigners, Caldwell's work lent itself to projects to rid South Indian languages of accretions and borrowings from Sanskrit (a 'northern', 'Aryan', language of conquest).

These projects took many forms. Maraimalai Adigal's (1876–1950) life's work was to 'purify' Tamil by removing every 'borrowed' Sanskrit word from Tamil texts. The product of an inter-caste marriage – his father came from the influential but non-Brahmin Vellalar caste; his mother was born into a Chettiar trading family – Adigal, like many boys of his social set in Nagapattanam, went to the Wesleyan Mission High School, but he later began to learn Tamil from teachers 'beneath' him in the stifling caste hierarchies of Madras.[132] (He also learned, and grew devoted to, Saivism, producing a rather peculiar resolution to the problems of caste through an invented history of 'Tamil Buddhism' and the promotion of vegetarianism.) He became a considerable scholar, particularly after Madras Christian College relieved him of his duties (the Indian Universities Act of 1904 having declared Tamil to be a mere vernacular, and not a 'classical' language). A proud and austere man, he had contradictory interests and cravings: he read and wrote every day in Tamil but translated Kalidasa's (Sanskrit) *Sakuntalam* into Tamil and kept his personal diaries in English. He enjoyed rowing and collected 'pictures of famous nudes' who were not all drawn from a Tamil pantheon.[133] But his consuming passion was for books. His personal library, valued at Rs 25,000 in 1943, 'exceeded four thousand volumes and contained rare works in Tamil, English and Sanskrit ... The critical marginal notes in most of the books show that they had all been studied ... with the greatest care ... They were all cased in new jackets and arranged in perfect order in wooden almirahs.'[134] An obsessive-compulsive personality, he spent hours each day dusting them.

Adigal's approach to the language issue was scholastic (indeed he reminds one rather of Mr Casaubon in *Middlemarch*); but others in the Dravidian movement were more aggressively political. The language issue, in their view, was bound up with power, with the tyranny of caste and the oppression of the Brahminical north (and an immigrant Brahmin culture) over the South. Questions of power, inequity and inequality loomed large as India's independence approached. Perhaps no single person posed these issues more powerfully than E. V. Ramasamy (1879–1973), who came to be known as *Periyar* ('the great leader'), or just 'EVR'. Born in Erode, the son of a coolie turned stone mason who had prospered through trade, Periyar joined the Congress in 1920 (serving as its president in 1920 and 1924) and led one of its most successful *satyagrahas* to demand the right of 'lower castes' to enter the streets near Mahadevalar temple in Vaikkom. (It earned him two stays in jail and the title *Vaikkom Veerar*, 'the Hero of Vaikkom'.)

But he rapidly became disillusioned by Brahmin dominance within the Madras Congress. He broke ranks with the party in 1925 on the issue of 'communal' representation for 'non-Brahmins', founding the Self-Respect movement the same year. He went on to publish the *Communist Manifesto* in Tamil, resist the introduction of Hindi into Madras schools and set up the Justice Party or the 'Dravidar Kazhagam'. As M. S. S. Pandian notes, this party became the vehicle of his implacable rationalism, and his (sometimes ribald) critique of Hinduism, Brahminism and Indian nationalism. An iconoclast, indeed a force of nature, by 1922 Periyar had threatened to set fire to the *Ramayana* and the *Manusmriti* (the Vedic texts that lay down the rules of the caste order), and later in life, he actually consigned these texts to flames.

As his rationalism grew more entrenched and more pugilistic, he used his weekly Tamil journal *Kudiarasu* to denounce superstition, in one memorable issue describing the worshippers of gods as barbarians. In his version of the *Ramayana* he recast Ravan, the abductor of Sita, as a Dravidian hero who repelled the invading 'Aryan' armies led by Ram. It was deliberately provocative. He depicted Ram, who many Hindus revere as the incarnation of Lord Vishnu (see Chapter 7), as a scheming aspirant for the throne of Ayodhya, a disloyal brother who mutilated, killed and disfigured women.[135] Ramasamy set out to write with 'polemical flamboyance', to create a public 'discourse for a group much larger than his relatively small band of followers'.[136] In 1953, he smashed idols of Ganesh to 'prove' that they were hollow shells. He also burned copies of the Indian constitution, which, in his view, upheld the caste order.[137]

Caste cruelty, the overweening Brahminical dominance of jobs and education, and the domination of the north over Indian politics all came together to fuel the politics of language, even as the Hindi–Urdu divide provided a model (if not always a savoury one) for these movements. Whatever their primary motive (and the motives of individual actors were inevitably mixed), the cause generated enormous dedication. A great many Tamil scholars lived and died in penury because they turned down jobs that would have taken them away from devoted service to Tamiltay, spending their lives teaching 'pure' Tamil, gathering old Tamil manuscripts or publishing their own works in the great language they sought to restore to her glory.

The history of Bengali language devotion before 1947 has parallels with the language movements of the South, but also differences, since there the deepest social cleavages were not along lines of caste but along those of religion. In Bengal as in the South, Christian missionaries played a significant part in producing a standard grammar and alphabet: in 1800 the British Baptists at the Serampore Mission Press published the Gospel according to St Matthew in Bengali; and the Press churned out over 200,000 Bengali books (mainly Christian tracts) by 1832. But Bangla began to develop as a modern literary language when Bengal's bilingual, English-educated Hindu intelligentsia took it up as their medium of choice – when the likes of Bankimchandra Chatterjee and Rabindranath Tagore began to write in the language, developing its vocabulary, rhythms and genres. In the 1920s, Sarat Chandra Chatterjee, a clerk in the public audit office in Rangoon, took Bengali literature to new heights of popularity. Less poetic than Rabindranath and less highbrow than Bankim, his phenomenal flow of thrilling and sentimental works in Bengali – over twenty novels or novellas, and as many short stories – created a vast reading public. He remains the most translated, most adapted and most plagiarised author in the Bengali language, and his lovelorn drunk, Devdas, is probably the best recognised character in Indian fiction and cinema. Between 1928, when the first silent version appeared, and 2002, fifteen cinematic versions in Bengali, Hindi, Urdu, Tamil (*Devdasu*), Malayalam and Assamese have brought him to life. Chashi Nazrul Islam's version showed on screens in Bangladesh in 2012.[138]

Peasants and poverty were among Sarat Chandra's main themes; and most of Bengal's peasants were Muslims. Yet – and here lay the rub – hardly any of his characters, and none of his heroes, were Muslims. If, by the early twentieth century, literary Bengali was perceived as a Hindu language, there were good reasons for this. While writers in the South were excising Sanskrit from their lexicon, 'purifying' Tamil and Telegu, Bengali writers were drawing heavily upon 'the language of the gods'[139] to create a vocabulary to suit their thematic preoccupations.[140]

But modern Bengali was also beginning to develop, hesitantly, as the language of a province with a Muslim majority, and remnants of courtly culture. In the mid-nineteenth century, the religious reformer Keshub Chandra Sen, a caste Hindu attracted to Christianity and monotheism, translated the Quran directly from Arabic into Bengali, perhaps in search of 'eastern' sources of monotheistic inspiration. In 1891, Mohammad Naimuddin (1832–1908) published his own translation and commentary, *Koran Sariph*, 'directed specifically at a Muslim audience whose primary language of communication was Bengali'.[141] The context for its production was, as with so much else at this time, reformist and revivalist tensions within Islam: but crucially, Mohammad Naimuddin wrote in a modern Bengali prose style and innovated specifically for a Muslim readership by starting the work from the right leaf, as in Urdu texts, rather than the left (although Bengali is written from left to right). By the 1930s, thousands of (often less scholarly) tracts had been published by Bengali-speaking pious Muslims, devoted to the 'improvement' of Muslims and the reform of their religious practices.[142]

In Bengal there were also signs of a growing resistance to Urdu. Some elite Muslims (the *ashraf*, Urdu-speakers trained in Persian and Arabic) were by the 1930s seeking to position Urdu as the language of Bengali Muslims. But this was no less divisive than the moves to promote Hindi beyond its heartland. By the early twentieth century, many educated Muslims had begun to look upon Bengali with affection, if not with the single-minded devotion of Adigal to Tamil. In 1900, for instance, Maulvi Delwar Hossain Ahmad, an inspector general of registration in Bengal, demanded a *fatwaa* (legal clarification) from the *ulema* 'authorizing every race to say their prayers in their own language'.[143] In the early 1910s and 20s, a new generation of Bengali-speaking Muslims, whose agriculturist parents prospered from the boom in jute prices, had gained a higher education; and they too had also begun to experiment with the Bengali language, establishing newspapers, writing short stories and poetry which they discussed avidly at reading rooms in Calcutta. Nazrul was among them. The pioneering generation of Bengali Communists was drawn largely from this stratum of Muslims, and their first journal – *Ganabani* ('The Voice of the People') – published essays and poetry (including songs by Nazrul Islam) in a vernacular Bengali peppered with a 'Muslim' *dobhashi* (more hybrid) idiom.

Ironically though, it was probably Muhammad Akram Khan (1868–1968), a leading figure in the Muslim League in Bengal, who did the most to popularise modern Bengali, spewing out writings and publishing religious and political tracts in the language. Unlike the Persian and Urdu-speaking Muslim *ashraf* elite of the province, Akram Khan had been born into a family of modest means and was educated at the local *madrassa*, and he first made his name as a *maulana* (religious leader). During the First World War, he became an ardent Khilafatist and founded several successful journals, including the *Mohammadi* and the *Azad*, both of which had a wide circulation among the Muslims of Calcutta.[144] I describe his role as 'ironic' because after partition, the Bengali language movement all but destroyed the Muslim League in Bengal, a party that Khan had expended huge energy to help create.

The rise and spread of literary Tamil, Telegu, Malayalam, Marathi and Bengali before independence, as well as Hindi and Urdu, was the work of at least three generations of committed writers and poets. As one observer of modern India reminds us:

> as late as the 1860s, the number of Bengalis earning more than seventy-five rupees (a little less than £6) a month was only a few thousand. One could just about maintain a small family on such meagre incomes ... Yet there was something profoundly compensating about the cultural efflorescence – the discovery of concerns and new interests that was life-enhancing. ... An outburst of creativity in the mother tongue was chief among these new experiences.[145]

Vernacular printing presses sprang up in their thousands to publish their works, often for no gain, and libraries and reading rooms began to proliferate, broadcasting more widely, to new reading publics, the 'passions of the tongue'.

These were, of course, long-term processes. In the short term, two critical moments helped transform these cultural movements into political battles. The first flashpoint occurred during the brief era from 1937 to 1939, when the Congress party was elected to power in six Hindu-majority provinces. In these provinces, Congress governments introduced the Wardha scheme of education, a Gandhian scheme based on instruction in the mother tongue (as well as practical training in manual and productive work).

Some years before this, the Congress had committed itself to the notion that British provinces should be broken up into 'linguistic provinces', and indeed from 1920 onwards, the party organised itself into an agglomeration of 'linguistic' provincial committees. But it had also grown wedded to the contrary idea that India should have only one 'national' language, and that that language should be Hindustani (a mélange of Urdu and Hindi) written in the Devanagiri or Sanskrit script. Ignoring the fact that India was a society of 3,000 dialects, and ignoring the emotions raised by language movements in the preceding decades, the leaders of the Congress – influenced no doubt by the example of European nations and nationalisms – felt that without a single language, the nation would lack cohesion. They took the view that Hindustani must have a distinct and superior status to regional languages and vernacular mother tongues. Many nationalists, Gandhi included, believed that the English language – a mark of imperial dominance and the colonisation of Indian minds – eventually had to go, and when English went, it had to be replaced by a single Indian language shared across the whole country. Since no such language existed on the ground, but the Hindi language family was the largest, Congress leaders agreed that non-Hindi speakers would have to accept Hindi/Hindustani as their national language in order to cement national unity, and to help official communication and public consensus. The Nagari Pracharini Sabha (Society for the Promotion of Hindi) began to promote Hindustani, with Gandhi's backing, in the 1930s.

When it was elected to power in 1937, the Congress Ministry in the Central Provinces introduced the *Vidya Mandir* (Temple of Learning) programme. The very name of the programme was redolent of Hinduism. What is more, it reeked of Sanskritised Hindi and Brahminism. It was profoundly unpopular with Muslims, and gave Jinnah a convenient peg on which to hang his anti-Congress politics. It also upped the ante in the battle between Hindi and Urdu that had been raging in North India since 1900, when the Chief Commissioner of the United Provinces ruled that Hindi (a version of Hindustani purged of Arabic and Persian words, written in one Sanskrit script) would be used as a language of government in the province. It also had casteist undertones, which its authors were too tone deaf to realise.

The *Vidya Mandir* controversy also hit a raw nerve in South India, where language devotees took it as a sign that Congress governments of the future would seek to impose 'Hindu Hindi' onto the 'Dravidian family'. When C. R. Rajagopalachari, the Congress Chief Minister of Madras, a Brahmin and an ardent advocate of Hindi as the 'national language', introduced the compulsory study of Hindi into the Madras school syllabus, suspicions hardened into certainty. The first anti-Hindi protests were launched in 1938, when the 'Tamilian Brigade' marched from Tiruchirapalli to Madras. In 1939, Dhalamtthu, Natarajan and Stalin Jagadeesan died in battle against the authorities, becoming India's first language martyrs.

Inspired by them, Karunanidhi (born in 1924 into a working-class family in Tanjavur) joined the militant fringe of the movement, organising fellow students to march every evening through the streets of the town carrying a giant poster of Rajagopalachari stabbing the language goddess Tamiltay in the heart, chanting a battle-cry that Karunanidhi had composed: 'Let us all gather together and go to war! Let us chase away and drive back that she-devil, Hindi!' As Karunanidhi later recalled, his 'blood and breath pulsed with Tamil'.[146] Karunanidhi's insistent movement made Rajagopalachari a hated figure in his home province. After independence, this brought Rajaji's career as an active politician in South India to an abrupt end and he was shipped off up north to become West Bengal's governor. Karunanidhi's star, by contrast, would rise and rise. He went on to become a cabinet minister in the first Dravida Munnetra Kazhagam (DMK) government in 1967, and later Chief Minister of the province, renamed Tamil Nadu, from 1969 to 1976 and again from 1989 to 1991.[147]

Long before independence, then, language had become tied up with all manner of social and political tensions – North versus South, Hindu versus Muslim, Brahmin versus non-Brahmin, English versus vernacular, elite versus popular. Prospects of power and employment in a decolonising dispensation fanned these glowing embers into flames. Even before 1947, these movements were in many respects 'government-regarding'. There was the vital matter of being able to communicate with government: as P. Raghunadha Rao summed up the issue in 1911, 'Andhras laboured under a double disadvantage.' On the one hand, 'the British officers who ruled them had very little knowledge of Telegu'; on the other hand, 'their subordinates were mostly non-Telegus who had very little acquaintance with the Telegu language or people. As such, the grievances of the Telegus were not brought to the notice of the Government.'[148] And then there was employment, crucial in a context where government was the largest employer and offered the only secure jobs available. Everyone recognised that if English remained the language of officialdom, presidency elites schooled in English would continue to enjoy a huge advantage over speakers of vernacular languages, however 'purified'. Many argued that this meant that colonial intermediaries and erstwhile collaborators (and their high-faluting liberal conceptions) would continue to hold sway after the Union Jack came down, and felt that independence would be a sham.

But there were also more personal concerns in their minds. People wanted jobs. They wanted their children to climb up the social ladder, particularly their sons. Nationalism had promised these prospects, or so they believed. But if the independent government did not employ people who spoke their mother tongue, they stood no chance. Nor did their children. As South Asia's population exploded after independence, competition for jobs grew ever more fierce: particularly the jobs that people most desired for the security they offered, *government jobs*. This competition fuelled the language wars.

When independence came suddenly in 1947, the leaders of both India and Pakistan had to make a call on the language issue. Neither Nehru nor Jinnah had any instinctive appreciation of the seething, creative, literary passions driving language devotion; nor did they have much sympathy for it. When they read, they read in English. Teenmurti House in Delhi, where Nehru lived as prime minister, retains Jawaharlal's chattels; they were, until its recent makeover, rather poignantly displayed just as he left them on his death in 1964. His large personal library included hardly any works in Hindi, Urdu, or any other Indian language. Although both men could speak Hindustani fluently, they seldom wrote in that language. (I have never seen a letter by either man in any language other than English. They may exist, but they are rare. Indeed Jinnah rarely wrote at all, being an early convert to the telephone.) Having had his early education at the Sind Madrassah, Jinnah no doubt could write in Urdu as well as Arabic, but he seems to have chosen not to; he was a man of few words. (All the same, he never forgave Gandhi for showing him up in public to be less than fluent in Gujarati.)

It should not surprise us that these two English-educated, anglicised liberals, so like each other in so many ways, plumped for the same decision. There would be *only one national language* in India and Pakistan: Hindi in India and Urdu in Pakistan. Perhaps the chaos after partition influenced this choice, but it is likely they would have made it regardless. English, Nehru decided, the language with which his social group was most comfortable, would remain an official language for fifteen years in the first instance, but all the people of the subcontinent would have to accept the 'national' language imposed upon them from on high.

At a speech in Dacca on 21 March 1948, Jinnah declared:

> There can ... be only one lingua franca, that is the language for inter-communication between the various provinces of the State, and that language is Urdu and cannot be any other. The State language, there-fore, must be Urdu, a language that has been nurtured by a hundred million Muslims of this subcontinent, a language understood through-out the length and breadth of Pakistan, and above all, a language which, more than any other provincial language, *embodies the best in Islamic culture and Muslim tradition* and is nearest to the language used in other Islamic countries.[149]

Bengali students in the huge audience cried out 'No, no', in the first shocking public challenge to the Quaid's authority.

The reaction to these decisions was akin to the response of a healthy human body exposed suddenly to a virulent infection: an inflamma-tory response. In both countries, language devotion that had hitherto been primarily cultural movements transmuted, overnight, into bel-ligerent political campaigns to challenge the unitary centralising policies on language.

By late 1947, Bengalis in Pakistan, both Muslim and Hindu, had already begun to demand that Bangla be declared a state language alongside Urdu. This was wholly reasonable: Bengali (and its various dialects) was spoken by the great majority of the population of East Pakistan, both Muslim and Hindu, eighty-two per cent of whom were still illiterate in 1961.[150] Their demands went unheeded.

Urdu's claims to be the national language of Pakistan lay in the long history of the Hindi–Urdu conflict, which by the twentieth century had turned Urdu, in the popular view, into the 'Muslim language' par excellence.[151] The problem was that for all that, it was not the mother tongue of more than a tiny proportion of Pakistan's population: it was spoken only by the *muhaajirun* from North India, and a small educated elite had read Urdu's fine literature and poetry. These groups, not surprisingly, shared the Quaid's view that they and their language represented 'the best in Islamic culture and Muslim tradition'. Easily, and as if by right, in both East and West Pakistan, they moved into the places in the bureaucracy of the nascent state that had been vacated by the British and by Hindus, in both wings of the new nation.

But their attitude was repugnant to the Bengali Muslim writers and activists, already in shock at having lost Calcutta – the heart and centre of Muslim Bengal's cultural world. East Bengal now found itself under the domination of a government in Karachi that had little sympathy with their crises or priorities, and no love for Bengali, which they regarded by a distant and uninformed leadership as a 'Hindu language'.

In due course, both dispensations, in Karachi and Delhi, made concessions when faced with these violent reactions against the national language policy. Nehru, who had no great love for 'Hindi-wallahs' (as he described them), made concessions to language agitations more readily than did Jinnah and his successors.

In Pakistan these concessions came a little too late. After Jinnah's death in 1948, when his heirs (some of them from Bengal) maintained the 'Urdu only' policy, students responded furiously with the slogan *Raashtrobhaasha Baanglaa Chaai* ('We demand Bangla as a national language'). Dacca University went on strike.

On 21 February 1952, students – boys and girls – all over East Pakistan broke the ban on assemblies. While the 'Red' Maulana Bhashani (of whom more in Chapter 3) played a prominent part in the movement in the coming months, students were its shock troops. Much of what followed in the first wave of the *Bhasha Andolan* (language struggle) movement was spontaneous. A generation reared on Tagore and Nazrul was shocked that the language they spoke, in which they were the first generation to be educated and which they had grown to love with a very modern kind of devotion, was to be denied its place in Pakistan.

The Ekushey (21 February) rally was joined by both Hindu and Muslim students. It is commemorated to this day as the foundational moment of Bangladesh's national movement. In the celebrated song of the 1950s, Abdul Gaffar Choudhury asked: '*Aamar bhaier rokte raangano ekushe February aami ki bhulite paari?*' ('Can I ever forget 21 February, coloured red with the blood of my brothers?') Few have forgotten it, and the date continues to be commemorated, albeit in different ways in different locations. In London's East End, on Ekushey the Shaheed Minar (or martyr's tower, now permanent after years of politics and lobbying) receives – in post-Diana displays of British–Bengali sentimentality – bouquets, and even teddy-bears.[152]

Ekushey, 21 February, is now recognised as International Mother Language Day. It is heralded as the date when Bangladeshi nationalism was born, although this is a post-facto rationalisation. Every nation needs a 'history of its national movement', and Bangladesh, born suddenly in the midst of war, did not have one: it had to be found, created, contrived. Ekushey provided the raw material for a long and (this is important) uncomplicated history of national sacrifice.

But it was also the beginning of a campaign against 'internal enemies', Urdu-speaking immigrants from North India, who were perceived as having taken all the plum jobs. This community, known pejoratively as 'Bihari', would come to be seen as collaborators in Pakistan's 'internal colonialism' over Bengalis, and as traitors, *rajaakaar*, in the 1971 war. Most were killed in reprisals after the Liberation War ended. Those who survived still live in camps, and in fear. The passionate loves of language have led to South Asia's only major war, and two genocides in East Pakistan/Bangladesh. They continue to simmer. There may have been devotion and heroism involved in the language movements of South Asia, but there was also plenty of hatred and contempt for the languages, cultures and mores of others.

If South Asians in the late twentieth century continue to identify themselves as Tamil, Telegu, Punjabi, Bengali or Urdu-speakers, in an un-reflexive way (as I did at that lunch with Peter Mandler), it is because decades of creativity and bloodshed, war and devotion have hardened and glazed these identities liked fired earth.

IV

HOW WE BECAME 'INDIANS' AND 'PAKISTANIS' DESPITE THIS: 'NATION-BUILDING' BY THE STATE

So how, in the midst of this chaos, did my generation grow up knowing that we were not just Bengalis or Tamils, but Indians and Pakistanis (or Bangladeshis), and have some sense of what that meant? We were told, is the simple answer. But how we were instructed is an interesting story (and how much of it we believed is yet another).

India's early leadership launched a series of concerted initiatives to educate the people about 'their history' and 'their united-but-diverse culture'. It droned on, ponderously, sonorously and repetitively, about what the nation stood for, its history and everything the nation state was doing for the people's benefit. This propaganda (put bluntly, this is what it was) emphasised that the nation was united by a single unbroken history, and that science and technology were now being harnessed on a grand scale to deliver it from poverty. The museum, the documentary film and the postage stamp were as much instruments of the national publicity drive as the school syllabus and the Republic Day pageant.

It is not so much that this publicity was executed with brilliance. It was not. It was more the case that it was repeated ad nauseam, and that its everydayness made the message 'natural'. Pakistan lagged behind, but never far. The banalities of official nationalism turned most, if not all of us, on both sides of the border, into unthinking Indian and Pakistani nationals.[153]

The pedagogical emphasis of these initiatives was crucial to their purpose. It was almost as if, in the aftermath of the partition, violence, mass migration and the language wars, a moral panic about politics set in. After 1947, the leaders of both countries began to regard citizens (hitherto the heroic supporters of mass movements) as unruly, ungrateful and irresponsible: like children, they had to be taught to behave like responsible adults.[154] Political debate was now deemed disruptive, a churlish repudiation of the nation, of all the sacrifices made for its freedom, and of the long hard battle against imperialism.

Like Saleem Sinai, midnight's children and the generations born after 1947 had to be rescued from 'infantile' behaviours, and fashioned into solid Indians and Pakistanis who fell into line. Most importantly, we had to forget the fact that 'Pakistan' had once been part of India too, and vice versa. To prevent awkward questions about how much that was 'Pakistani' (or 'Bangladeshi') remained in the mix of our 'Indian' collective memory and identity, our 'national' history had to be presented to us in a brisk and seamless narrative. The cracks and fissures in the storyline, allowing space for questions to which there were no easy answers, had to be covered over with rice paper and paste. We had to remember some events and forget others. These acts of remembering and forgetting, after all, shape the national identity of every country; in South Asia, we had an immense amount of forgetting to do.[155]

Curious though it may seem, the Indian National Museum in New Delhi was at the heart of a fascinating story of how India's 'national history' was curated, and where this process of air-brushing took place at its most rarefied and ideological levels.[156] Even more remarkable was the pivotal role played in it by the Glaswegian archaeologist Sir Mortimer Wheeler (1890–1976). Raised in Yorkshire, Wheeler studied Classics at University College London, and later lectured there. His star began to rise when after a 'good war' (service on the Western Front won him a Military Cross) he developed the Wheeler Method, a scientific approach to dating archaeological objects that became influential. By 1926, aged thirty-six, he was already Keeper of the London Museum.

In the 1950s, he brought archaeology to a mass audience in Britain through the BBC programme *Animal, Vegetable, Mineral?*, of which he was the most frequent and famous participant. (My English grandfather, a shy, sax-playing entomologist who was the Librarian of the Natural History Museum in London, taught us to play this game as children. I grew up believing that Granddad had invented it. I was crushed to learn that it too, like much else about our curated history, was Wheeler's creation.) In 1954 – by which time he had lost all hint of a Scots burr and spoke cut-glass BBC English – his Robert Redford looks, his burly moustache (which rivalled Diwan Singh's), and his jocular authority won him recognition as the TV Personality of the Year. Appointed General of the Archaeological Survey of India in 1941, this larger-than-life personality took Indian archaeology by storm, training and inspiring a generation of South Asian archaeologists who would go on to establish and run national museums in both India and Pakistan.

Wheeler believed that the 'relics of Indian art, architecture and material civilisation ... represent ... accumulatively ... a very notable part of the basis upon which a new India may be founded'.[157] He was also convinced that '"the relics" of art, archaeology and architecture embody the greatness of a civilisation, and that a museum is an essential toolkit that all nations, but especially new ones, need'.[158]

By happenstance, a large collection of the subcontinent's 'great' art, and some of its archaeological heritage, was in 1946 gathered together at the Royal Academy in London to display to the British public samples of '(undivided) India's art rich in masterpieces of marked individuality of character'.[159] Despite Sarojini Naidu's gushing telegram to the Academy that the collection demonstrated 'the full range and splendour of *India's* art as represented in noble stone and radiant colour through the centuries', the exhibition closed with significant financial loss.[160] The British public was not impressed: the strangeness of the objects displayed put people off.

However this collection – the largest assemblage of South Asian artefacts ever gathered at one site, borrowed from a host of personal, princely and regional museums – became the basis of the national museums of India and Pakistan, and also a matter of dispute over ownership between the two countries. Pakistan demanded the return of objects that had been shipped to London from the museums of Peshawar, Karachi and Lahore, and also art from Lahore's museum which had been on temporary loan to New Delhi before it departed for London. India challenged the return to Pakistan of this last group of objects. Months of bargaining saw the two sides get more entrenched in their positions.

In the end, since keepers on both sides were his students, they agreed to leave it to Mortimer Wheeler to divide the objects between India and Pakistan, including, in an apt metaphor for the wider process of partition, a girdle and necklace from Mohenjodaro.[161] What benefit each side perceived in having half a girdle and half a necklace one can only guess, but each insisted on its pound of prehistoric flesh. This quarrel points to the enormous significance both countries attached to the ancient sites of Mohenjodaro and Harappa, both now in Pakistan.

Until the excavations of Harappa and Mohenjodaro in the 1920s (during the Khilafat movement), the Bronze Age was believed not to have existed in India. The 'Indian *tradition*', although old, was therefore considered to be something of a johnny-come-lately compared with the truly ancient civilisations of Egypt and Mesopotamia.[162] The discovery of these prehistoric sites in the Indus Valley gave South Asia a Bronze Age civilisation of its very own.[163]

Mohenjodaro thus represented far more than simply an archaeological find. It embodied the fact that India had had a 'civilisation' during prehistoric times, as my father would sometimes put it, 'when white men still lived in caves'. (He would say this when enraged by some casual assumption of white superiority.) '*We*' now had an antiquity and a *civilisation* to rival the recent and shallow achievements of the imperial west, for all its hubris and its bullying of the rest of the world. In 1947, Indian archaeologists felt its 'loss' to Pakistan acutely, as did Wheeler himself. It would spark off a competitive hunt for alternative prehistoric sites in India.

In 1950, the Indian archaeologist Hasmukh Dhirajlal Sankalia (1908–89), Professor of Proto-Indian and Ancient Indian History at Deccan College Poona, proposed the exploration of the 'holy' Narmada Valley specifically to compensate for the 'loss'. Sankalia had taken his PhD at London; his first excavation was with Wheeler at Maiden Castle in Dorset, and the two men remained firm friends.[164] For its part, the Indian government lavishly supported his archaeological hunt for 'prehistoric' India (which actually lay within independent India's borders) throughout the 1950s.[165]

This explains why the museum was such a priority for both India and Pakistan. It signified, for both countries, a celebration of a recently revealed, unbroken history of civilisation. Given the chaos and devastation they faced (which they dealt with cack-handedly), it is remarkable how swiftly both countries got on with establishing their respective national museums, using the objects gathered together at the Royal Academy as the foundation of 'national' collections. The Indian cabinet gave the go-ahead for the establishment of the national museum in Delhi in December 1947, *while refugee transfers were still underway*.[166] In 1950, while riots were sweeping through East Bengal and Calcutta, the Pakistan government commissioned Wheeler to write *Five Thousand Years of Pakistan* to construct an ancient past and pedigree for a new nation. It was almost as though the more violence and migration disrupted these nascent states, the more determinedly they focused on creating a national past.

Wheeler helped to establish Pakistan's Archaeological Department, and served as archaeological advisor to the Government of Pakistan from 1950 to 1958.[167] In India, meanwhile, the National Museum opened to the public in the state rooms of Rashtrapati Bhavan (the former Viceroy's House) on 15 August 1949, just two years after independence. In 1960, it moved to its longer-term home in a purpose-built structure on the junction of Rajpath (Ruler's Way) and Janpath (People's Way) in the heart of New Delhi. Its location was no accident.

The Indian National Museum set out to create a novel notion of the national aesthetic, and a true 'Indian masterpiece'. The catalogue of the 1948 exhibition in Rashtrapati Bhavan claimed that Indian art held up a mirror to 'all India has stood for through the ages', to 'the religious thoughts and aesthetic emotions of the people'.[168] It gave sculpture priority above all else. This allowed the Museum's curators to sharpen the distinction between western 'realism' and 'Indian idealism' (a trope of nationalist thought) and to claim a 'national' aesthetic that had survived intact through the ages. Their vision drew on the scholarship of the Tamil Ceylonese-English auteur Ananda Kentish Coomaraswamy (1877–1947), the mission of whose unusual life was to wrest the assessment of South Asian objects from archaeologists and return it to artists and art historians; and to break the stranglehold of a Eurocentric view of Indian arts and antiquities as 'much-maligned monsters'.[169] Born in Colombo and trained mainly in London, Coomaraswamy was a botanist, geologist, metaphysicist and art historian, who married four times and became the first Keeper of Indian Art in the Boston Museum of Fine Arts in 1917. His complex personal life notwithstanding (despite his four wives he converted to Roman Catholicism in his later years), he wielded an enormous influence in fashioning a nationalist and non-Eurocentric conception of what was beautiful.[170] That vision remained palpable in the Indian National Museum until the end of the twentieth century. (At the time of writing it no longer exists, having been pulled down by a government with an altogether different vision of India.)

Building on Coomaraswamy's scholarship, the curators of the National Museum downgraded the Greco-Buddhist tradition (in which European connoisseurs had discerned harmony), replacing it with more 'indigenous' art from the age of the Mauryas (322–187 BCE) and Guptas (319–485 CE). The monumental Asokan bull, the standing Sarnath Buddha (c. fifth century CE), the flying sandstone 'Vidyadhars' of the Gupta period and the Didarganj *yakshi* (mythical female being) with her full-hipped sensuality, her breasts heavy with milk, these objects came to constitute the Indian canon. Replicated on thousands of postcards, they came to be widely recognised even if the context of their production was poorly understood. The Chola bronzes of the late tenth century – above all the dancing Nataraja, depicting the Hindu god Shiva in *taandava nritya* pose, dancing in cosmic ecstasy – also joined this select group of canonised objects of indigenous 'Indian' aesthetic creativity, stretching back, unbroken, into the hoary past. Whereas colonial experts had underlined the

Hellenic (European) influence on 'good' Buddhist sculpture, the nationalist account emphasised an outward spread of 'Indian' artistic influence to China, Japan and Southeast Asia.[171]

But there is another striking feature of this choice and arrangement of objects. A clear pecking order informed it, the exhibition in the National Museum as a whole propagating 'a distinct hierarchy of genres and periods'.[172] Sculpture was singled out. Curators presented stone sculpture, in particular, as the acme of ancient and early medieval Indian art. They gave statues, particularly those with Hindu or Buddhist motifs, pride of place; paintings, relegated to a secondary status, were consigned to a single gallery (the Long Drawing Room) at the back of the display, where they merged with a small display of decorative textiles, carpets, and arms.[173]

The subtext could be taken to mean that paintings (let's say Mughal miniatures) were not true 'Indian' art, and although they were certainly decorative, they were not masterpieces. It was a way of marginalising (deliberately or otherwise) the 'Muslim' contribution to India's material heritage – a pathetic attempt, given that much of the north of the subcontinent (and many parts of the south) was littered with Indo-Islamic, or Islamicate, architecture. There was just no place to hide it.

In much the same manner, in 1950 the Pakistan government established a National Museum in Karachi in what had been the Frère Hall. Pakistan, as we will see in Chapter 3, had far fewer resources than India, and its first museum reflected this. To begin with, and indeed until the 1970s when it moved to a larger purpose-built building, it had only four halls, and its curators filled them with the precious prehistoric and protohistoric objects they had fought over with India. Among its highlights (and there were many) were the famous dancing girl of Mohenjodaro and its priest-king, whose noble profile had decorated the front page of the *Illustrated London News* when it was first discovered.[174] It was expanded to include a gallery of stunning antique versions of the Quran, including a volume written in the era of the Abbasid Caliphate in the Nuksh script. Precious gemstones, gold, silver and copper enrich its ornamental borders, and the paper on which the *surah* (verses) are written is said still to carry the fragrance of roses.[175]

The display of the personal belongings of the Quaid (including his pen and cufflinks), of Allama Iqbal (his chair) and Liaquat Ali Khan's watch and *itar* (scent) bottle indicate the 'national' purposes the museum was intended to serve. After Bangladesh had broken away in 1971, the museum included manuscripts documenting Pakistan's political history, and an Ethnological Gallery with dioramas of the different 'ethnicities' living in the four remaining provinces of Pakistan. But despite these efforts to sideline 'Hindu' art, it could not erase from Karachi its older Hindu quarters with their distinctive Indo-Saracenic buildings, any more than Lahore could efface the massive mausoleum of Raja Ranjit Singh, founder of the Sikh Kingdom of the Punjab, which abuts the Badshahi Mosque and the Lahore Fort.

So although the museums were important agencies in the business of remembering and forgetting history, on their own they were not enough. The idealised 'publics' they hoped to conjure up remained 'illusory and elusive'.[176] Their message faced quotidian challenges from the everyday encounters people had with the 'relics' outside them.

For instance, Delhi, where I grew up, is a palimpsest of a city, layered with monumental architecture dating back to the twelfth century. The soaring Qutub Minar, a tapering tower almost seventy-five metres high, dates from 1192 CE. Once seen, it is impossible to forget, pointing as it does simultaneously to man's frailty and his ambition. It has imprinted itself upon me – as it has, I suspect, on all denizens of Delhi since it was built: no doubt each had or has their own Qutub Minar story. My father too loved each of Delhi's several layered, juxtaposed cities, so I visited the Qutub tens of times as a child before the government ordered that its upper balconies be sealed. (Suicidal people had taken to jumping from them: many were students who had performed badly in examinations.) It was on those delicate balconies I developed vertigo. But I then began to appreciate more fully the stunning splendour of its base. I noticed the huge arched gateway, the famous iron pillar – in its time portraying man's mastery over material – and the Alai Mosque. Over time, the Minar grew associated with more, rather than less, enchantment, beauty, pathos, history.

Think about this. Delhi's students, in the 1960s and 70s, brought their sorrow and shame to the Qutub. They sat on its high balconies, thinking of their lives, prospects and loved ones, before they jumped. How could we forget this?

I now live in the next two of Delhi's layered cities. Alauddin Khalji excavated the Hauz Khas (great tank) between 1296 and 1316 to supply the 'second city' of Delhi with water: my home is in the adjacent

Hauz Khas Village. The village, when we moved there in the 1980s, was a small rural outpost in a city overrun by refugee-migrants. By the 2000s it was flanked by nightclubs, exotic eateries, bric-a-brac dealers and Airbnbs. In the late fourteenth century, Firoz Shah Tuqhlaq, the modest legatee of an impoverished empire, built Firoz Shah Kotla, home to the city's cricket grounds. Everyone, but everyone, has heard of Firoz Shah Kotla, even if they don't know the first thing about Firoz Shah himself. But he also made a mark on the city's fabric. Firoz Shah Tuqhlaq re-excavated the tank, which had fallen into disrepair, and built an ethereal *madrassa* along one end of it. By the late twentieth century, young lovers had etched their names ('Deepak loves Sonu') onto its stonework.

My father and I used to take daily walks around the tank. (At one end of it lies the base of a tower begun by Iltutmish who married into the Qutub line. Another juxtaposition of cities, if you notice it.) As he aged, I noticed the slowing of my father's gait, although his back remained ramrod straight. After he died, I continued with the practice – days in archives and libraries followed by evenings around the tank – along with the throngs of walkers, lovers and friends. I would stop where we always stopped, the place where we got the best view of the tank, the *madrassa* and its ramparts. (It was on one of hundreds of such walks that I had my first known seizure.) Childhood, filial love, romantic love, illness, ageing, suicide and death: all are conjured up for me by this monument or that, which litter Delhi much as built heritage does Rome. I am not alone. Although I speak of my own encounters with these places, I was always but one among millions, since 'eating the air' is an urban pastime. We 'eat the air' in such open spaces, where monuments prevent traffic, and loved ones can gather. Do not underestimate their grip on our imagination, on our deepest emotions.

Moving due south, one encounters Sher Shah Suri's Purana Qila (Old Fort), which came up in the 1540s. Within it lies his personal mosque, a little gem. But in the twentieth century it housed (and still houses) Delhi Zoo, where tigers roar as they pad around their cages. We went there again and again as children; as parents we took our children there, even when we had begun to worry about the ethics of zoos. The flocks of migratory birds that came were not held there by force. As for those that did not migrate, like the sarus cranes, the tallest flying birds in the world, did they stay at the zoo because they knew we would come to admire them? They seemed so confident, so proud of their beauty. The Old Fort set off that beauty, just as it sets off the city's native brush tree, the humble *kikar*. It was there I learned the name of the remarkable colour of its sage grey-green leaves.

Buildings have always been recycled in South Asia, put to new uses when old ones became redundant: the Old Fort is not alone in this respect.[177] Probably every child in the city whose parents could afford the bus fare and the cheap tickets has been to the Delhi Zoo. So how could we forget the ramparts of the Old Fort?

Before we moved to Hauz Khas, we lived south of those that came before it, in the part of the city originally founded by the Lodhi dynasty (1451–1526). This city's highlight, in terms of built heritage, is the Lodhi Gardens. Every morning, my father and I, along with thousands of city-dwellers with diabetes and heart conditions (the classic diseases of urban South Asia) took their constitutionals along the pathways round the tombs and mausoleums. As for us children, as soon as we were let out of school (even during the high summer before the monsoon clouds broke, when the hot dry *Loo* (dust storms) burned our eyelids), we rushed there to play hide and seek, ride our bikes, and buy puffed rice and gram from the scary old man who sold snacks. We came home only as dusk began to fall, when thousands of parrots screeched in unison and settled in the trees in clouds of green. How could we forget the Lodhi Gardens?

As for the monuments built under the reign of the Mughals (1527–1857), what can one say? Everyone has heard of the Taj Mahal, but Mughal Delhi has its own splendours. Humayun's Tomb (Akbar's monument for his father) and Safdarjang's Tomb, the Red Fort which still guards what is left of Shah Jahan's in the Old City, their grandeur, their symmetry, their high red sandstone walls, their domes inlaid with white marble and lapis lazuli, these made a profound mark on us. This, we knew intuitively, was beauty. These may have been 'dead monuments', protected by the state for tourists and urban elites and alienated (even when there were mosques within them) from the faithful who would have used them for their intended purposes, but they were grand spaces around which we denizens of Delhi lived our little lives. In a thousand ways, we remained entranced by them.[178]

The Archaeological Survey tended to some of the built heritage of this monument-studded land, but it could not afford to look after all our treasures. So they have just stood, as they have done for centuries, gathering layers of dust, history and pollutants, acting as dense sites of place-making. Since the late 1980s and 90s, given their state of neglect, non-governmental organisations (NGOs) such as the Indian National Trust for Art and Cultural Heritage (INTACH) and the Aga Khan Foundation have taken up the restoration of some neglected buildings and streets, to dazzling effect. If you can, visit Lahore Old City and Delhi's Humayun's Tomb. Some citizens feel so deeply about this heritage that they have devoted their lives to saving it.

Often neglected by states too poor to tend to them, these were the landmarks by which we navigated our city. This was so as the city expanded, even if the overwhelming majority knew little of the history of these places. They make their way into Bombay cinema. In the film *Silsila* ('The Connection', 1981), the most controversial scenes of passion between Amitabh Bachchan and Rekha take place in the Lodhi Gardens in Delhi – not Bombay, which has no pre-Portuguese monumental architecture. (More of this in Chapter 7.)

The only way to challenge the hold that these places exerted on us would be to claim that they were constructed from the fabric of temples destroyed, as Hindutva campaigners began to do as early as the 1950s, when Nehru's government in its wisdom allowed the Babri Mosque in Ayodhya to be reinstated as a site of Hindu worship.

But it would be some years before their crusade made headway, and in the meantime the national narrative was delivered to us in other forms. Schoolbook history was a key device to teach us the authorised version of the 'national past', which we had to memorise by rote, or fail. In January 1948, the Assistant Secretary at India's Ministry of Education argued that 'nothing is more important today than the orientation of historical studies from the primary to the highest stages . . . India is One and Indivisible – geographically, historically, culturally. This is the first article of the creed of Indian Nationalism.'[179] Pakistan's 'creed' did not differ much in style, even if there were variations in substance. As Krishna Kumar notes, the foundation in 1961 of the National Council for Educational Research and Training indicated India's willingness 'to turn nation-building into an ideology and to see education as the prime instrument of propagating it', and Pakistan's Federal Curriculum Wing echoed the sentiment.[180]

The Indian curriculum (in which History was a compulsory subject until Class X) covered 'Indian' history from antiquity to independence, in a chronological linear framework designed to give equal weight to all periods. The problem was information overload:

students had to memorise a huge number of 'facts' pertinent to the 'national story', as teachers galloped through an inflexible syllabus.

What is remarkable is 'blurred divergence' in history teaching in India and Pakistan, particularly as it relates to 'the Freedom Struggle'.[181] History textbooks in both countries identify the starting point of the Freedom Struggle with the Rebellion of 1857, although in neither do they pay heed to the complexities of the Rebellion; nor do they account for the awkward fact that the subsequent leaders of 'the nationalist movement' – the western-educated middle classes – had in fact opposed the Rebellion.

This is only the first of many uncomfortable issues glossed over or ignored. The narrative of the nation abounds with non sequiturs as students are taken from event to event, without any attempt to contextualise them or link one to the other causally: 'periods when nothing dramatic occurs seem to shrink or vanish into a time warp'.[182] Pakistan's textbooks, in particular, 'take recourse to brevity' when faced with awkward facts that don't fit.[183] They fail to mention, for instance, the rather important matter that Jinnah was a Congressman in 1906, who opposed the partition of Bengal; indeed Jinnah first appears in these texts only in 1927 with the Fourteen Points and the Nehru Report. No detail that humanises him is allowed to enter the story. The same is true of the handling of India's 'great leaders': with the exception of Gandhi, they are all cardboard cut-outs. Students are encouraged to view history as the actions of a pantheon of heroes, whose high politics lack any social context, but whose values ('love of the nation') they are encouraged to embrace.

There are differences between the two countries' textbooks, of course: particularly in regard to periodisation. Pakistan Studies took history forward beyond 1947 but not so far as to include difficult bits. (More of this below.) Indian textbooks, by contrast, stopped dead in 1947, as if history itself came to a halt with the birth of the nation.[184] Even though Indian textbooks grew more sophisticated in their content after leading professional historians began to write them in the late 1960s, they showed little awareness of the pedagogical challenges of delivering the subject to students too young to understand irreversible processes and complex causality.

The problems with this approach are almost too numerous to list, but let me stress the most important ones. First, it turned history into a catalogue of facts, a body of knowledge that had to be memorised as part of a grand teleological narrative of the nation. There was no room or time for questioning, reflection or debate. It offered a series of 'memory posters', hanging free of a sense of diachronic time or analytical reasoning: the syllabus offered students no insight into historical method, how historians work with partial fragments and arrive at their (always contingent) conclusions.[185]

Further, it perpetuated the colonial heritage of the prescribed textbook which had constructed official knowledge. Textbooks and examinations emerged in post-colonial Pakistan and India as two vital instruments to control what was taught and what was learned to consolidate the nation.[186]

However, only a fraction of the children of the subcontinent have had the dubious pleasure of exposure to this 'national history'. In India, as late as 2001 (the first year for which stratified data are available), only seventy-one per cent of the national population for the Class VIII age group (equivalent to Key Stage 3) were in school.[187] In Pakistan, even in the 2010s, forty-two per cent of children above the age of ten could not read or write.[188] Primary education, bizarrely, was not a budgetary priority for either government. For India, tertiary education, particularly of a scientific nature, was. Institutes of technology had money thrown at them, while village schools languished.

Even I, whose love affair with history was intense, remember barely anything of the history syllabus. Mohenjodaro, yes; the figure of the dancing girl, yes. Perhaps all I ever had of her was a 'memory poster'. I was lucky to have a remarkable teacher who read, in her first lesson with us in Class XIII, a section from a primary source. No matter that it was Zia-uddin Barni's *Tarikh-i-Firoz Shahi* ('The Age of Firoz Shah') and that the lines she read concerned the sacking of Hindu temples by Mahmud of Ghazni, one of India's first Muslim invaders from the north-west. I understood nothing of the subtext. I understood only that this stunning source transported me to another place, to a past that was more vivid than the present. It wedded me for life to history, but the 'national' message was lost on me, receptive vessel though I was.

So other media were needed to reinforce our sense of nationality, and into the gap stepped the documentary film. Information Films of India was a British wartime propaganda vehicle. But while the refugees were pouring in, Nehru revived it, telling all chief ministers to 'utilise this powerful medium to reach the masses, more especially for them to understand the various development plans that you are undertaking. These films will also help develop a sense of social consciousness and a sense of corporate endeavour.'[189] His government also made it compulsory that approved documentary films made by the Films Division of India be shown before the main feature film in cinemas. Anyone seeking popular cinematic entertainment (and growing numbers were doing so, not only in the metropolises but also in second-tier cities and towns) had to swallow a dose of government indoctrination like the fast before a feast.

The furious rate at which these documentaries were churned out is a testament to the importance the government attached to them. In 1948–9, the Films Division made twenty-eight newsreels. Less than a decade later, in 1956–7, it was making 132 documentaries and newsreels in five languages each year. By the mid-1960s, it was reaching on average three films a week, in addition to the weekly newsreel. In 1973 alone, it made 227 films dubbed in more than fifteen languages.[190] It employed a staff of 860, including cameramen stationed across India, its documentaries and newsreels reaching as many as twenty-five million Indians a week.[191] Having originally focused on urban consumers, by the late 1960s the Films Division began to target rural audiences with different levels of education and exposure to cinema. As Ram Mohun, who joined the division's cartoons unit in 1957, told Peter Sutoris: 'This was the accepted attitude – that people have to be told . . . Generally it was taken for granted that people were ignorant about what was going on. There was a lot of talking down to people. Which was a major problem of the films.'[192]

These films focused not on the past but on the future. They showed us Wizard-of-Oz worlds in which the sky was always clear, children with well-oiled, combed and parted hair in neatly pressed uniforms worked diligently in classrooms, jolly turbaned farmers smiled as their tractors ploughed fertilised fields abundant with harvest, and huge dams ('the temples of our times') brought us water and electricity. The documentaries with their 'voice-of-god' narratives were mind-numbingly boring partly because we were coerced into seeing them, and because they had no plot and no real characters. When they concentrated on the present, it was only to hector people to have fewer children and to stop criticising the government. Even as their technical and cinematic qualities improved, the films remained tedious in the extreme. (The famous documentary *Temples of Tomorrow* showed the Nataraja temple in Chidambaram and a dam under construction in quick succession, both shot from a low angle emphasising the grandeur of these structures by portraying them as almost touching the sky. Great camera-work, no doubt, but dull viewing.)[193] India was all about its glorious future. The present, with its troubles, tensions and anxieties, was simply a vantage point. This was the message of the documentary, the medicine that Indians had to swallow before they could watch the films, of whose pleasures more in Chapter 7. So they took the medicine. How much of it they remembered after the movie is uncertain.

And then there was the bizarre Republic Day parade, which made very little sense even if you were a child. (Of all the people I know, only my husband Anil enjoyed it live on a freezing January morning, but that was because 26 January, India's Republic Day, fell on his birthday; as a child he thought the whole wretched Parade was being held in his honour. Some friends, with heavy irony, call him 'Meek'.)

Probably the most effective of all in creating a sense of belonging to a defined national unit were the most quotidian of objects – the yellow 'inland' postcard, the blue 'inland' letterform, the exotic blue, red and white 'aerogramme' and the stamps that adorned real envelopes. The distinction between the 'inland' and the 'aerogramme' reminded us, if only subliminally, of the nation's limits, the distinction between inside and outside, between insiders and outsiders. As for the real stamps that were attached to actual envelopes, the mystery and romance of a sealed letter drew our eyes towards them. They were a promise of something: something too important or too private to communicate on a mere postcard or an 'inland', something that required more words and more pages to articulate. Bulky envelopes with franked stamps had a mystique in my childhood; and as we gazed at them with a longing for worlds beyond and within, these tiny humdrum objects communicated (unbeknown to us) the government's message to us.

Whereas in the British era, stamps had invariably shown the monarch, with only the background colour changing, the stamps of India and Pakistan were more inventive. They were like each other in that they commemorated particular people, national heroes and national achievements. In the 1950s and 60s, 'achievements' were understood as related to large-scale development.[194] For instance, in 1960, in the wake of signing the Indus Water Treaty with India, Pakistan issued a fifteen-paisa stamp announcing the Mangla Dam and the Indus Basin Project. The stamp showed a wide canal with green irrigated fields on either side, and a vast reservoir in the background – reflecting the state's control over 'nature's sovereignty'.[195] Beyond the reservoir, near the horizon, were rolling hills. India produced a similar, rather beautiful, green one-anna stamp of the Damodar valley barrage, showing water rushing down the sluice at one end, a reservoir in the background and hills in the far distance. India, Pakistan and latterly Bangladesh too produced stamps that depicted the map of the country, its flag, its great men and women, its great objects and its national history.

It was not that we noticed the details of the stamps consciously, although their design was rich with meaning. The Mangla Dam stamp not only showed an image of electricity being generated by the dam in one corner – a promise of the energy to be released even at the cost of displacements in Kashmir – but also used three scripts, English, Urdu and Bengali, to spell out the word 'Pakistan'. Perhaps the odd stamp showing the map of East Bengal alone (again in Urdu, English and Bengali) was intended to indicate that this province was already irrigated by rivers, green with paddy and Islam, and needed no further dams to irrigate it. In 1965, India issued a five-rupee high-value stamp commemorating the 1965 war with Pakistan, captioned *Veerta aur Balidaan* (Valour and Sacrifice), which showed a photograph of soldiers carrying rifles running across rough terrain. The same year, Pakistan issued stamps inviting the public to recognise the sacrifice of 'our army' and 'our air force'. In 1976, to commemorate 200 years of the light cavalry, in India we got the image of a tank, its gun pointing directly at us. (Whether or not it is relevant that this coincided with the Indian Emergency is moot.)

Bangladesh's first one-rupee stamp showed merely its map and flag.

V

OFFICIAL NATIONALISM IN BANGLADESH

For Bangladesh, too, there were things to be forgotten and things to be remembered. The war of 1971 was the independent subcontinent's first 'total war'. It sucked almost all of the province's households into it, whether as irregular freedom fighters, the Mukti Bahini, and their families, and the villages and families who had hidden, fed and backed them; or as soldiers and their collaborators (*rajaakaars*) – willing or unwilling – on Pakistan's side. The brutality of it all is best left to the reader's imagination.

The Bangladeshi official claim is that three million people were killed during the war; Pakistan suggests only 26,000 died. The most reliable estimate of lives lost is 1.7 million – almost a million more than during the partition of 1947.[196]

The war generated, according to the United Nations refugee agency UNHCR, 9.9 million refugees (both Hindu and Muslim) who fled to India to escape the violence. On their return home they found that their homes had been devastated, often looted by soldiers on the rampage, sometimes even by their own neighbours.[197] Pakistani soldiers hunted down the Mukti Bahini everywhere, and raped women and girls. They looted homes in more villages than it is possible to count. It is not clear how far these soldiers ran amuck, given the vacuum in leadership in Pakistan.

This was a war that Pakistan should never have fought. Even if we set aside the ethics of crushing the majority of the nation's population (which I do not), no army can defeat insurgents on their own terrain. Military brutality simply deepened the burning hopes, in Bengali hearts, for independence, for democracy. It fanned the flames of their hatred of 'Pakistanis' – a term that almost overnight, came to mean 'West Pakistanis'.

There were two genocides in 1971. One against Bengalis, the 'official national dead', the officially recognised martyrs. If you can find a translated version of Sheikh Mujib's Parade Ground Speech in Calcutta in 1972, do watch it. In it, he recalls every type of atrocity Pakistani soldiers inflicted upon Bengalis. It is a list of mounting horrors, narrated, in ascending cadence, *with pride*. This suffering forms a crucial part of the narrative of the new nation.

The second was a genocide of reprisal against so-called collaborators, which began after the Liberation War ended on 16 December 1971. This was of the Urdu- and Bhojpuri-speaking people who had migrated to East Bengal after partition but who, in the context of 'passions of the tongue' raging in the region, had become a distinctive minority with an attachment to the 'wrong' language. People were 'violently settling scores' that had nothing to do with the war. They were also hunting down and killing 'collaborators' in their thousands. These 'Biharis' (not all of whom had been collaborators, some had been forced to join the *rajaakaars*) now became convenient internal enemies against whom 'the nation' could rally. Very few survived. Those who remain do so penned in camps, in Dacca, where they are stateless people.[198] About 300,000 are thought to be scattered outside Bangladesh's capital. This second massacre was also critical to Bangladesh's nation-formation, even if no one has dared build a memorial to recognise it.

The challenges of nation-building in this context were both easier and more difficult than in India and Pakistan twenty-five years earlier.

On the one hand, nation-building was easier because these stories are Manichaean and the emotions surrounding them are so potent, even if they underplay India's role in Bangladesh's breakaway from Pakistan, insisting on 'the purity of victory'.[199] The Indian Army entered the war formally only in December 1971, but supported the Mukti Bahini months before that.

Indeed, many Bangladeshis have forgotten that there is still a West Bengal in India. During my first visit to Bangladesh in the late 1980s, after a sweaty day in the archives I sat in a park to rest and 'eat the air'. A young boy, aged about fifteen, sold me a cold drink. We got chatting in Bangla, and this surprised him, for my daily archive wear of battered *churidaar kurtaa* (jodhpur trousers and long tunic) was unusual attire then, for a Bengali woman, in Bangladesh. He asked me where I was from. India, I said. Then how come you speak Bangla, he asked, mystified. I said that I was a Bengali, from West Bengal in India. He shook his head in wonder. He did not know that there had been a partition of Bengal in 1947. He did not know that there had been a partition at all in 1947. As a scholar researching that partition, I was dumbstruck by the amnesia about 1947 that I encountered everywhere.

Nation-building was more complex in Bangladesh, because to build the nation, one partition (1947) had to be forgotten to give the second (1971) centre stage. It was only by forgetting that they were partition refugees from India that 'Biharis' could be turned into internal enemies in Bangladesh. (This nation-building business leads to some strange loops and erasures in the national historical narrative.)

The nitty-gritty of the political challenge ahead was, moreover, to construct a peaceful Bangladesh out of a brutalised society at arms. A gigantic task.

Sheikh Mujibur Rahman (1920–75) had returned triumphantly from jail to become Bangladesh's first prime minister. He had languished in jail in West Pakistan during the Liberation War, so had played no part in the fighting, and this was to prove significant. The son of a court clerk in Gopalganj, he had qualified as a lawyer, but had spent much of his youth involved in student politics, rising in the 1940s to become one of the most significant leaders of the Muslim League in Bengal. In the 1960s, however, as a member of the breakaway Awami (National) League, he had been at the forefront of opposition to West Pakistan's 'internal colonialism' in East Bengal, and it was under his leadership that the Awami League had won every seat in the first ever free and fair elections in Pakistan.

Sheikh Mujib's eyesight was as weak as his aura was powerful, and in his adult years, he wore heavy horn-rimmed glasses with thick lenses. But they could not disguise him. A man of striking looks – his jet-black hair swept back from his high forehead, his thick moustache, his sensitive mouth in contrast to a strong cleft chin – he made a vivid impression. What a hero he was, not just in Bangladesh, but in India, which had watched the war with horror and received, with sympathy and panic, almost ten million refugees. He was lionised at home and abroad. I had a Bangladeshi playmate, a seven-year-old called Humaira, and there was a large framed photograph of Mujib in the front room of her house. I grew up with his face imprinted on my childish mind. It is an unforgettable face.

However, to function as prime minister, he had to persuade a series of poorly equipped, uncoordinated but determined vigilante forces, the dispersed Mukti Bahini (they were never a single organised force), to surrender their weapons. He tried to persuade them either to give up their arms and return to civil society or to join the Bangladesh Army, which was then being built from Bengalis who had deserted the Pakistan Army during the war. The fact that he had not fought in the war put him on the back foot in these negotiations.

Recall Ayub's thoughts about politicians: no doubt members of the Mukti Bahini and the army also believed they were more patriotic than Mujib, who had 'done' politics (as we put it in Bangla) since his teens, after his eyesight put a stop to his education.[200]

Adept at leading protest against governments, he found it harder to create or lead a government of his own.

Mujib failed to persuade sections of the public, and the army, that his efforts at development would lift Bangladesh out of poverty. (To be fair, he was given barely two years to succeed.)

After the Liberation War, people wanted wholesale transformation. They wanted change, and they wanted it now. They wanted renewal, and something on which to rest hopes for the future. Just as their sacrifices had been great, their hopes were boundless.

Mujib tried. He was tireless in pursuit of agrarian upliftment projects, more so even than India and Pakistan had been. But gigantic development projects – it was being realised in newly independent countries the world over – can put a blight on economies because of their inflationary effects on everyday commodities, including food, their ecological impact, and their disastrous effect on inhabitants of the regions chosen for development. Small was beautiful. So Mujib's well-intentioned but inexperienced government went against the grain of a growing global consensus. Indeed, they seemed to be driving the country ever deeper into an abyss: by 1973, agrarian production had fallen to eighty-four per cent of what it had been before the war, industrial production had shrunk to sixty-six per cent of pre-war levels, and the cost of living for agricultural labourers had risen by 150 per cent.[201]

By 1974, full-scale famine had broken out. One and a half million people are thought to have died of starvation and hunger-related illness between 1974 and 1975, a demographic catastrophe no less shocking than the war itself.

In 1975, in the midst of the famine (and a drive against hoarders which some allege protected Mujib's Awami League supporters), the army, by now composed of some 55,000 men, began to plot Mujib's overthrow. India is said to have warned him that something was afoot, 'but he laughed at the suggestion that any Bengali could raise his hand against him, "No, no. They're all my children."'[202]

Mujib was too complacent. On 15 August 1975, three strike forces of junior officers based at Dacca headed to his home, where they assassinated him and murdered no fewer than forty members of his household. His daughter, Hasina, survived. At the time of writing Sheikh Hasina is the prime minister of Bangladesh; but Mujib's death was followed by three military coups in quick succession.

General Zia-ur Rahman (1936–81) was a career soldier in the Pakistan Army. He abandoned that army during the war to join the Mukti Bahini. A war hero, he was first to declare Bangladesh's independence, in a famous speech on the radio broadcast live on Kalurghat station in Chittagong. He had a considerable following of his own among both the armed forces and the former Mukti Bahini, each of whom was a local hero in his own village and beyond. It is important that we understand this. He was the rare general who had the intelligence to establish a political party, the Bangladeshi National Party (BNP), and it was not just an office with a flag. It had a following among people who believed they had sacrificed more than anyone else for the liberation of Bangladesh.

So it should not surprise us to learn that he assumed office in 1977, after Mujib's murder, and that it was as leader of this party that his wife, Khaleda Zia, has since twice held office as prime minister.

Zia-ur Rahman, too, was murdered in an abortive military coup in 1981.

Both of the nation's foundational figures thus died at the hands of assassins. No wonder the control of their legatees – Sheikh Hasina and Khaleda Zia – over the nation's identity remained so tenacious and so contested. No wonder their followers have fought each other as if they are fighting a war all over again. Two different iterations of the Bangladesh War: Mujib's war, Zia's war.

Politics by assassination has punctuated, and in part shaped, the history of Bangladesh. During periods when the generals took charge, nation-building was largely about army-building and control. Given its history, the fact that it has been a mutinous army should not strike us as unexpected. The answer to these problems, as the generals saw it, was further expenditure on the army.

Policies that Mujib had begun to develop with the help of Bangladesh's great scholars of agrarian history, economics and constitutional law to help the 'people of Bangladesh' and secure their democratic rights were put aside under army rule. But a system of two-party democracy emerged nonetheless from these unpropitious beginnings (between interludes of military rule). The BNP and the Awami League have won elections, and formed pretty stable governments, despite their violent antipathy towards each other.

Bangladesh's relationship with big development, post-Mujib, has been rather different to that in India or Pakistan.

On an imaginary level, the nation could not look towards the future, as did the India of the cinema documentaries, since that future was so contested; it had to look to a past, to an era of Bengali consensus. The moment of the nation's birth was pushed back to Ekushey, to the first language movement back in 1952.

It had to have, after all, a story of common sacrifice in which all could share, Awami League or BNP. The first language martyrs overwhelm later figures of all stripes as the founders of Bangladesh. They *are* the monuments in Dacca, outside Dacca. They are celebrated wherever Bangladeshis gather, even in the diaspora. National history, here as in India and Pakistan, is teleological.

Another figure that has emerged as a symbol of the nation is the *birangana*: Bengali women raped or abused during the war. Here, as in India, national identity is carved onto the body of an unnamed woman, whose honour the Pakistanis have destroyed. Fighting to avenge her becomes the duty of every Bengali man. Here too, the nation is gendered: the tortured woman represented the enemy's vileness and the authenticity of Bangla nationhood.

The treason of 'Biharis' has also had to be emphasised, both to whip up hatred against an internal enemy, including those born long after the war had ended. 'Biharis' was the label given to migrants from up-country who survived the violence of 1971 and stayed on in Bangladesh. Rendered stateless after 1971, they were unwanted by all three nations – Pakistan, India and Bangladesh. Descendants of the *poorbea* labour migrants of the imperial age (discussed in Chapter 4), and of post-partition refugees, there were nearly 300,000 'Biharis' in Bangladesh in 2008, over half of whom lived in camps all over the country. Denied, or refusing to claim, citizenship rights until 2008, most were unable to get their children into government schools, to rent housing outside the camps or be employed in formal jobs, whether in government or the private sector.

In this context of precarious statehood, the story of the war had to be remembered, and repeated again and again: the sacrifice of the language martyrs of Ekushey being folded into the history of sacrifice for the nation. The glories of battle and sacrifice of the Liberation War (it is, at the time of writing, illegal in Bangladesh to describe the war in any other terms), and the brutalities committed by the Pakistan Army, have to be recalled and retold in gruesome detail. These atrocities (and the victory against the forces of oppression) represent the foundations of the nation's identity.

But in practice, the friction between the Awami League and the BNP has escalated, against this violent backdrop, into a battle neither side can afford to lose. The parties have tended to act more like war-ring countries than as parliamentary oppositions, with a 'winner takes all' mentality that sits uneasily with the concept of democracy. They often appear to be more loyal to the party than to the country, and to their *begum* (whether Hasina Begum of the Awami League or Khaleda Zia of the BNP) than to the state. Warring dynasties are not unique to Bangladesh, or even to South Asia (see Chapter 1); but in Bangladesh they have taken their country to the brink again and again.

So if the nation has been built, in Bangladesh, on the ground, a far greater role has been played by NGOs than by parties. I mention only one of them, the largest: BRAC (Bangladesh Rural Advancement Commit-tee, now just BRAC), whose founder Sir Fazle Abed (1936–2019) was among the first to emerge and to see the importance of microcredit in breaking the rural cycle of poverty and debt. By the twenty-first century it had become the largest NGO in the world, with a global footprint.

In a nation born in crisis – cyclone, civil war, famine – the NGOs with their quiet, dogged, on-the-ground engagement with the issues that in their view affected the Bangladeshi 'people' (endemic poverty and debt, above all) created a sense of a coherent narrative of what the 'nation' and 'nation-building' are about. The spectacular events (of open warfare between Awami League and BNP supporters, army mutinies, periods of emergency and military rule) could then be seen for what they were: moments of rupture within the more organised, continuous project of nation-building and self-help activity that con-tinued from 1971 to the end of the twentieth century. These projects have shades of the economic nationalism of Romesh Chunder Dutt and Dadabhai Naoroji. Their 'national' subjects are the rural poor. They regard themselves as enablers from below, rather than as devel-opers from on high.

If we look at Bangladesh from this perspective, far from being 'a rural slum', it is the neighbourhood's success story.

On 'internal enemies', while NGOs are active in the Bihari camps, society is still intolerant of their inhabitants. An incident in 2008 made me think that even India (then under the powerful influence of the Hindu right) was more tolerant of its Muslim communities than Bangladeshi society was of Biharis.

Modhu's canteen is a well-known landmark in the Dacca Univer-sity area. (Here sites of murder act as 'monuments'.) One humid summer's evening, Annu Jalais (my research assistant and a member of the Bengal Diaspora research team) had gone to tea with a group of people to watch Tanvir Mokammel's documentary *Swapnabhumi* ('The Promised Land', 2007).[203] This Bengali film portrays the dilemmas of Bangladesh's Biharis in a sympathetic light. The film's reputation had preceded it, and so Annu did not expect heated arguments about it: she assumed they all shared a similar perspective just because they were going to see this particular (brave) movie together. But the discussion at Modhu's café was fraught. The group included a Bengali Bangladeshi, 'Nazibul Islam', and a 'Bihari', 'Saif' (not their real names). Despite Saif's presence, Nazibul, a man in his mid-thirties who worked as a photographer, made no bones about his feelings. The director, he said, had been 'too kind to these bastard "Biharis"'. Tempers rose, and Nazibul walked out.

Saif was silent throughout this discussion. They were, after all, sitting in the notoriously 'Bengali' space of Modhu's canteen, where images of the proprietor Modhu, slain in 1971, hung on the walls. Finally he spoke, but softly, almost under his breath. Quoting the (communist) Urdu poet, Faiz, he murmured: 'How many monsoons will it take to wash away the blood?'[204]

Many, many more, I fear. The image of the Bihari traitor is so central to the structure of official (and indeed popular) Bangladeshi nationalism that it is hard to see how it can fade without the whole edifice crumbling, or at least changing beyond recognition. This process may be beginning, as I write, with the increasing Islamisation of political and personal life and the savage axe attacks on liberal bloggers, but as Chairman Mao said about the French Revolution, it is too early to tell.

Nation-making in Bangladesh offers some contrasts when compared with its siblings, India and Pakistan. Whereas India and Pakistan quickly drew a veil of silence over the violence of 1947, both in terms of state discourse and at the granular level of the family and community, Bangladeshis deliberately, repeatedly and publicly revisit the violence of 1971 in art, poetry, film and on national TV. This 'birth in blood' story is essential to the nation's founding narrative.

In India, it was only with the publication of Urvashi Butalia's ground-breaking study *The Other Side of Silence* in 1998 that the voices of women who had suffered horrors during partition were heard for the first time: finally they spoke, quietly, in private interviews, sharing harrowing details of what they had seen and undergone. Butalia's book builds on the history of her own family and relies on searing personal testimony, all the more excruciating to read because these memories are being rehearsed for the first time in fifty years. She is aware of the ethical conundrums of asking people to remember travails long past, of opening up tin trunks full of trauma.

By contrast, in Bangladesh, the claim that '200,000 women lost their honour for their country' is an inalienable part of nationalist rhetoric.[205] In the 1990s, Bangladesh's national TV aired a programme, *Aami Beeraangona Bolchhi* ('I, a war victim, speak'), in which woman after woman recounted, some in halting tones and others with pride, how Pakistani soldiers had raped her.[206] The raped woman symbolises the violence done to the national community – indeed it is she who turns the nation into a community.

But if there were contrasts, there were also continuities and blurred divergences. Once again in South Asia's twentieth century, women's bodies were made to represent the nation. At least in Bangladesh, *beeraangonas* spoke, instead of merely being spoken about.

VI

NATION-BUILDING IN PAKISTAN AFTER THE BANGLADESH LIBERATION WAR

In 1972, Pakistan emerged as a new entity. It had less than half the population it had had in 1971. The old eastern wing was gone for ever.

Pakistan's leaders had to embark on a new nation-building project; that was clear. They could not admit it; that too was clear. In that project, 'strategic forgetting' required an enormous veil to be drawn over the history of East Pakistan and the defeat of 1971.

Of course this was no easy task, not least for those Pakistanis who had been posted in East Pakistan as civilians or soldiers. There were never that many to begin with – most Pakistanis in the civil service saw East Bengal as a punishment post. Surviving soldiers have grown older and, for the most part, have held their peace. There is a great deal about the army's activities in the war that had to be locked up, hidden from scrutiny, for the new Pakistan to cohere and have a positive sense of national identity. Raking over Bengali coals was in no one's interests. Certainly not 'the national interest'. That seems to have been the general view among the leaders of the new state. So there was a cover-up operation, the result of which is that Pakistanis were handed a doctored version of 1971. So bland that they could forget it.

Pakistanis of my generation, who were children when the Indo–Pakistani war of 1971 broke out and are now in their sixties or younger, have childhood memories (just as I do) of the war. But each generation after us has 'forgotten' with greater ease.

I say this with no ill will towards the forgetful. Had I not grown into a historian, perhaps I too would have put aside Diwan Singh's Yahya Khan stories with a laugh, but never stopped to think beyond them.

Be that as it may, since the 1990s, I have taught undergraduate, MPhil and PhD students – brilliant young people – from Pakistan, whom I first met in their early twenties. (They were thus among the first graduates of the post-1971 generation.) They experienced shock or profound puzzlement after my lectures on the subject. They weren't sure they had heard me right.

'Was this what you said, Ma'am?'

'Did I hear you correctly, Professor?'

Yes.

Former students still contact me to check things, although excellent studies of Pakistan's pre- and post-1971 history, Bangladesh's history and East Pakistan's history, are now available.

Even distinguished colleagues have looked baffled when I have raised the East Pakistan question in relation to the minorities' question in early Pakistan; even *scholars* have 'forgotten' that in 1947, Pakistan had a larger Hindu minority (about twenty-five per cent) than India's Muslim minority, which then constituted about thirteen per cent. All forgotten. It was in East Pakistan, you see.

I speak here not of the average member of Pakistani society (whoever that might be) but of its intellectual elite – its brightest graduate students, its academics and intellectuals – the group tasked with questioning power and holding it to account.

If that group has forgotten (although there are notable exceptions), it is a testament to the success of one crucial aspect of the nation-building project: amnesia.

One tool of this is Pakistan Studies, in which 'national' history is presented (just as in India) via the school curriculum. It was, in the twentieth century, an odd course, which kept the narrative arc going through strange loops and whirls, from early Muslim dynasties and the Mughals to the history of the Pakistan movement and the early years of Pakistan, leaving centuries or decades out as it weaved its baffling way.

'Alia', born in 1983, went to school in her hometown in the 1990s, before doing a master's degree at the London School of Economics. Having taken her doctorate from Cambridge, she is now teaching in Pakistan. She writes to say how even as a teenager, Pakistan Studies left her curious but dissatisfied. 'The gaps were never explained.' She gathered (when she was young) that these parts were taught because they were 'the Muslim bits'. Their relationship to other 'bits', or even to each other, was no part of the syllabus as taught. ('Alia' is very bright, so this left her wanting to 'fill gaps' and make those connections herself.)

The syllabus took her class through 'the Pakistan movement' but did not extend, or so she remembers, much past Liaquat Ali Khan: 'I don't even remember reading about Ayub Khan, let alone Bhutto or Zia-ul-Huq. I think it more or less ended with the creation of Pakistan.'

Crucially, 'there was very little mention – if at all – of East Bengal'.[207]

It led students from a rather 'vague Islamic past, that leapt from Mohammad bin Qasim (712) to Mahmud of Ghazni (1020 or so I think)' and then on to the Mughals (1526–1721) to the Pakistan movement, to Iqbal, Jinnah and Liaquat. Jinnah came with no backstory: his long period as a Congressman had to be erased, of course. There was no mention of the Punjabi bureaucrat and governor-general Ghulam Muhammad, whose reign (for that seems the most apt word) consolidated the hold of bureaucrats in general and the Punjab bureaucrats in particular, over the levers of state power.[208] General Ayub found no place, despite the successful performance of the economy in that era. Nor did Zulfikar Ali Bhutto.

By this strategy of brisk editing, Pakistan Studies sidestepped the secession of over half the country in 1971, giving Pakistan a seamless history from 1947 to the present day. Pakistan Studies and Islamic Studies put the onus on schools to churn out educated citizens who 'knew' their history and national identity as Pakistanis and Muslims.

As for the unlettered poor, well, perhaps the hundreds of thousands of pictures of the Quaid-i-Azam have been deemed to be enough. A memory poster onto which all manner of hopes and dreams can be projected, or mourned.

But there also have been reorientations. One has been the ramping up, in a Cold War context, of anti-India rhetoric. The generals put Pakistan's defeat in Bangladesh in 1971 down to the Indian Army's military interventions. (This would mean – oh dear – mentioning the 1971 war.) One can see why they might have done so: they had face to save. The narrative is awkward, however. Indian troops were in there for the fighting for only thirteen days, from 3 December to 16 December 1971. (They had helped arm, and even train, some Bengali irregulars, but that is not quite the same as helping them win the war, as the case of Ukraine should make plain.) The war was unwinnable, given the total insurgency against Pakistan's crackdown and the globalisation of support to the Mukti Bahini from the Bengali diaspora. If the French and the Americans could not break the Vietcong, napalm and all, how could Pakistan's army break the Mukti Bahini?

The fact that Pakistan Studies sidestepped the war (or sought to) showed that at its foundation, in the new Pakistan, while there was still civil control over the army, the generals were never back in the barracks. The war had helped strengthen the Pakistan Army. For long at the centre of Pakistan's politics, they saw scant need to concede to the politicians, long before General Zia-ul-Huq's military coup.

In 1972, the leader whose party had won the most seats in the elections *in West Pakistan* before the war, became the new Pakistan's leader.

Zulfikar Ali Bhutto was, like so many South Asian politicians, a lawyer who went to the bar at Lincoln's Inn, with degrees also from Berkeley, California in the United States. He was a member of Pakistan's Sindhi landed aristocracy, but had the demotic touch. He was not handsome in a classic way – his lips were a tad too fleshy, his forehead a tad too high, his jowls a tad too heavy – but he radiated energy and enthusiasm. He was as true a populist as could be found (unless one looked across the border at Indira Gandhi). He founded the Pakistan People's Party (PPP). Who 'the people' were remained vague, but he personally was going to fix their problems. He became the object of a personality cult, as populists tend to do, soon after he assumed power in the shrunken state of Pakistan.

His notion of nation-building was first to help obscure that diminution by a blitzkrieg of measures 'to restore democracy', and secure the uplift of 'the people'. One could hear the echoes of the economic nationalists in his programme, as well as shades of Sheikh Mujib and Indira Gandhi. As we will see in Chapter 6, Bhutto and Gandhi even had the same slogan (*Roti, kapdaa aur makaan*, 'Bread, cloth and a home') as their rallying cry. The problem, of course, with such slogans, powerful though they may be, is that they are impossible to satisfy in a poor county. And there could only be a semblance of a beginning if there was far-going land redistribution in the countryside, which would have meant alienating Punjab and Sind's powerful landed aristocracies and the *pirs* they patronised.

I say 'restore democracy' in quote marks because democracy had never prevailed to start with. Bhutto only liked democracy when he won elections: recall his behaviour in the Bangladesh saga, in which his actions flew in the face of the logic of demos.

Bhutto's political manoeuvres bring to mind Monopoly games with my niece Aki when she was a smart ten-year-old, to whom I would lend Monopoly money when she was broke or wanted to build a hotel. When I – ever prudent, even at play – was broke, and asked for my money back, she'd say, 'Money? What money?' Bhutto's approach was similar: he forgot what democracy meant when it came to the crunch in March 1971, when Sheikh Mujibur Rahman had won an absolute majority in the elections in pre-war Pakistan. Bhutto's approach then was: 'Majority? What majority?' Let us be clear-eyed about our dear leaders.

His first act upon assuming the reins of government in Pakistan was to declare a state of emergency. Before this, he had held positions under General Ayub Khan, and had worked closely with Yahya Khan. He was a man of the world, was Bhutto. It is only if you recognise this that his whole career adds up.

As a man of the world, his most significant actions and legacies were in the area of relations with India. The war had left many loose ends; tying them up required mutual understanding between the neighbours. Pragmatic in his engagement with India, Bhutto organised for an exchange of prisoners of war, and a settlement of other pending disputes between the two nations, much as Liaquat Ali Khan had done in 1950. He also recognised, believe it or not, the new nation state of Bangladesh.

Bhutto may have been willing to work with Ayub and parley with General Yahya Khan, but with these very public gestures towards India and Bangladesh, the military top brass grew more irritated with him.

As the saying goes: 'You can please some of the people some of the time, but you can't please all of the people all of the time.' Bhutto could not please all the people all of the time, and his attempts to do so earned him powerful enemies.

He pleased those who yearned for democracy, socialism and reforms that addressed the concerns of Pakistan's poorest. In a curious way, the greater the violence there has been in South Asia's politics, the stronger the yearning has been for democracy, for real social change on the ground. This is as true of Pakistan as it is of India or Bangladesh, and Bhutto sensed this.

In a style that matched that of Indira Gandhi, on assuming power Bhutto nationalised swathes of industry, from iron and steel to chemicals, cotton factories, flour mills and the insurance sector. In February 1972, he made it more difficult for employers to sack workers, and gave employees a say in company policy.

In March 1972, Bhutto announced land reforms: no one could hold more than 150 acres of irrigated land and 300 acres of unwatered land. This may have been a small step (land reform in India was a provincial subject, and different states had established these ceilings far lower than this). But it went straight for the interests of a powerful constituency – Pakistan's landed gentry – the very milieu from which he was drawn.

No wonder he inspired students and intellectuals of the 1968 generation. The communist party may have been crushed in Pakistan in the early 1950s but that did not mean that the utopian dreams that had inspired the Maoists in India and Bangladesh had not leapt across borders. No wonder they grew hazy about the details surrounding Bhutto's complicity in the Bangladesh Liberation War, and have become rather vague about the whole thing. Nations need their founding heroes, and the hero of the new Pakistan was Zulfikar Ali Bhutto. For Pakistani liberals and socialists, these moments were the high point in their nation's history. And I share that view. But holding it is consistent with remembering the war – so perhaps many among them now recognise that the time for recalibration has come. Whether the new Cambridge O Level on Pakistan Studies delivers is too early to tell, but it does include a full section on the war.[209]

There was much in all of this for the generals not to like, but Bhutto's foreign policy on India was the hardest to swallow. It flew in the face of their own interests. As he tried to strengthen ties with China, (after the Sino–Soviet split), generals fretted about Pakistan's ties with the United States, which Ayub had striven hard to foster. Bhutto was not as concerned as he should have been with these: he was more keen to align with India.

While he was rushing his policies through, Zia-ul-Huq was brooding in the wings. He was his own man, whom Bhutto had promoted out of turn to the pole position in the army's pecking order. That angered the generals he passed over. Events would prove Zia to be a dangerous ally.

Meanwhile, at home, provincial tensions grew in Sind. The Muhajir Qaumi Movement (MQM, later the Muttahida Qaumi Movement), which claimed to speak for all refugees, grew more and more restive. The collapse of the government in Balochistan, and the resignation of the government in the North West Frontier Province, put increasing pressure on Bhutto's government. While he remained popular enough to push through a new constitution in 1973 (a considerable feat) and win (albeit in an alliance) a second term, he was spooked by his own magic. (In this way again he was like so many popular leaders of the subcontinent who had gone before him. He did not understand his admirers and devotees.) When, in 1977, a rally against vote-rigging turned into a violent melee, Bhutto called in the army to restore order.

While the Punjab courts struggled to keep the stuttering flame of democracy alive, declaring martial rule illegal in June 1977, they could not pre-empt what followed: General Zia-ul-Huq's arrest of Bhutto that July, and his condemnation to death (on the grounds of ordering the murder of a political opponent) in March 1978. The courts had thrown out the case, but this did not stop the tide; the judiciary in Pakistan had not been able to accrue as much influence as the judiciary had done in India – an irony in a state founded by a lawyer.[210] The higher judiciary was cowed, the Supreme Court buckled, and mercy petitions fell on deaf ears. Bhutto was hanged in 1979.

By this 'judicial murder', as it is still known, General Zia-ul-Huq handed his nation a martyr. Newspapers the next day led with banners shrieking 'Bhutto Hanged'. Thirty years later, on 4 April 2009, *Dawn*, the largest and oldest English-language paper in Pakistan, republished the long article it had printed after Bhutto's hanging, detailing his last days, hours and minutes. Repetition of the narrative does important work: the manner of his death is critical in sustaining the myth, and post-mortem glorification, of Bhutto. (My sense of these matters is that Zia was not the shrewdest of men, for all his degree from Delhi's elite St Stephen's College.)

I think it is helpful to bear in mind that this career officer, with dark clean-cut looks and the erect posture of a soldier, was a refugee. I suspect he hid behind his hooded deep-set eyes a fierce hatred of 'spineless' politicians and disorderly crowds who had let Pakistan down. (This leitmotif runs through General Ayub's autobiography; no doubt his disaffection with politicians was by this time widespread in the Pakistan Army.)[211] Perhaps Zia was indeed pious, as so many partition refugees had been, and shared their belief that Pakistan should have Islamic moorings. Perhaps his actions in 1977 harked back to the events of 1947.

Be that as it may, having murdered the nation's latest icon, General Zia (1924–88) needed to start afresh. He needed, urgently, to provide Pakistan with yet another national narrative. He turned to a strand of Islam reformed to its 'fundamentals', which was relevant only to the country's Sunnis and the reformed fundamentalist pious among them. (I use the word 'fundamentalist' here to refer to people of Mawdudi's persuasion.) How far he believed in it is moot. In February 1979, however, he declared the Hudood Ordinances, which ordered 'Islamic' punishments to be given to drunkards, thieves and adulterers. In 1980, he brought in the Zakat and Ushr Ordinances to bring in 'Islamic' taxation.

So Zia's thrust was to rebuild a nation of orderly, pious, reformed Sunnis, governed by certain radical interpretations of the Sharia and the Hadith that harked back to the life of the Prophet in Arabia.

The difficulty was that the Muslims of Pakistan had never been easy to corral into such a tidy box. In practice, 'lived Islam' was too varied, too strongly rooted in the diverse social spaces in Pakistan, its languages, and its regions.[212] True, Bengal was gone, but the problem of regional and linguistic identity was not so easily solved. Baloch, Pathan, Sindhi and Muhajir identity (under the more militant leadership of Altaf Hussain) grew more pressing in their claims.

Doctrinal differences, too, still mattered: it was no use pretending they did not. For a start, there were the Ahmediyas, who believed that a new prophet had been born in India, and whom most Muslims condemned as apostates. In 1953 and 1974, there had been huge pogroms against them in Pakistan: once at the country's birth, then again at its 'rebirth'. The fate of internal minorities has always been most precarious as each wave of nation-making has got underway.

Then there were the Shias (themselves not a tidy or united group:

there are several branches that make up this vast tree). In July 1980, the Shia Convention protested against the *zakaat*, a religious tithe which is not part of Shia tradition. They thus drew attention to themselves as a national minority of a distinct type, and for this they have paid a heavy price.

Even among the radical 'Islamists', as they are known in the West, many parties and factions disputed text, context and strategy.

It turned out that Zia's project of consolidating a majority was fraught with challenges, since even Sunni 'extremists' disagreed among themselves about a great many things.[213] Zia himself died a mysterious death, in all likelihood by assassination – fictionalised in Mohammed Hanif's brilliant *A Case of Exploding Mangoes*.

But although Zia was dead, military dictatorship was not. Shifting geopolitics had intervened to propel Pakistan increasingly to the forefront of a proxy war against the Soviets. American backing of Pakistan's generals – soon fighting against a Soviet-backed regime in Afghanistan – was assured. Their star had risen. If democracy could return, it could be only at the bidding of the Americans (widely resented in Pakistan for their now unabashed interference in the country's affairs). It was thus only in 1993, when the Americans saw no other option to Benazir Bhutto (Zulfikar Ali Bhutto's gifted but entitled daughter) as a solution to the mess of a new disastrous operation, that they allowed her to return to power via the ballot box. (The Taliban came to power in Afghanistan the following year, 1994.) In the context of George W. Bush and Condoleezza Rice's 'regime change' policy, Benazir Bhutto came back from exile once again to fight for a third term in office in 2007.

Benazir Bhutto fell to an assassin's bullets in 2007, in the very same place as Liaquat Ali Khan had done. A shooter gunned her down in her open electioneering vehicle. He then blew himself up.

So if Pakistan's leaders, and indeed its intellectuals, have struggled with nation-building, it is because the narrative of the nation – so ruptured and jagged and shot through by bullet holes – makes sense only if you push the moment of foundation back into the distant past, to 'the Pakistan movement' and to Jinnah, the Quaid, the Great Leader. The struggle to remember what is best forgotten was already so hard, even before Zia's Islamisation project, and the vast spread of army power and wealth that was the creation of 'Military Inc.'[214] A recent cartoon proposed a new 'two-nation theory': one the area called 'defence', prime property owned by the army and people with connections; and, outside a high security wall, the impoverished, ignored *awaam* (the people).

Only monuments stand, occupying space in neither zone. The entrance to Lahore's Old City is by the towering Delhi Gate. What can this mean? The one-eyed Sikh warrior king's huge mausoleum abuts the grand Badshahi Mosque: it draws no attention to itself but one's eye cannot help being drawn to it. Perhaps as in Delhi, their scale, and their juxtaposition, reminds us that one empire succeeded another right here where we stand. No national narratives can encompass such rich and tessellated histories of place.

So they stand there as question marks, leaving us to reflect on these things. Methinks the nation protests too much.

VII

'AFTER NEHRU, WHO?'
TWO FACES OF AUTHORITARIANISM IN INDIA

In India, well before his death, Nehru's illness in his last years had prompted much discussion of the question: 'After Nehru, who?'

A better question might have been: 'After Nehru, what?'

The answer to that would be that India has witnessed two phases, and two distinct types of authoritarianism, interspersed by more or less stable coalition government. Each variant of tyranny represented a different facet of nationalism and urged a new national future. The first was Indira Gandhi's slide into dictatorship in the mid-1970s. The second was the Bharatiya Janata Party's vision of a Hindu nation built on the repression of non-Hindu minorities and critics.

In 1964, when Nehru died after several years of failing health, no one in the Congress party seemed a suitable successor. The party had several powerful provincial bosses who ran large electoral machines in their states – this is what the Congress units had become by this time – but it lacked powerful leaders at the centre, although Morarji Desai of Gujarat believed he was a contender.[215]

Instead, Indira Priyadarshini Gandhi (1917–84) rose to occupy the office of prime minister in 1966, after two other prime ministers had died, in quick succession, of natural causes. (Morarji was overlooked.)

The Congress party machine politicians of the provinces had elevated Indira Gandhi to this role for their own ends. Because she was quiet in Parliament, they called her 'the dumb doll'; they thought she would be pliant, and they thought they could manipulate her. They were wrong.

She proved to be an adroit politician and a powerful, indeed dictatorial, prime minister. With fifteen years in office, she served a long stint by Indian standards, the longest after Nehru.

Because she presided over emergency rule in India and developed a new idea of what the nation was for, it is important that we take seriously her time in office from 1971, after early elections gave her a strong majority, until 1977, when she abrogated the Emergency. It is important not to look at the Emergency years in isolation, because what came before them helps us interpret what sort of political project this was. It was not a brief rupture in the history of Indian democracy. It was an attempt to reorient the state, its powers and its goals. This project was based on ideas established some seventy years previously, long held to be a 'truth' among nationalists of all hues, within the Congress party and outside it. In this sense, its intellectual roots were deep. If people failed to notice them in assessing the 1970s (which few historians have tried to do), it was because their tentacles and root balls had grown so deep.

What manner of authoritarianism was this, in a subcontinent where military rule provided an alternative, and robust, form? This question also deserves attention.

Far too many people believe that the Emergency was a product of Indira's ultra-defensive personality, and that of her 'sociopathic' younger son, Sanjay. But biographies paint a rather different picture of Nehru's daughter, who emerges from them as a person of many facets.[216] Both her parents adored 'Indu', as they affectionately called her. True, her childhood was unusual, and sometimes lonely. With her father so much at the heart of things in the Congress in her early years, and so often in jail, the fact that she became a part of its 'monkey brigade' as 'a child of the party' was perhaps inevitable; so also was the fact that she grew up in the Congress movement, with other children of the movement, but without much sight of her father. They developed, nonetheless, a close epistolary relationship. Jawaharlal wrote to her infinitely more often than the average Indian elite father, or indeed the average European father, of his time, as his *Letters from a Father to a Daughter* (1929) and his *Discovery of India* (1946) attest. Her mother Kamala suffered from tuberculosis, and Indira was her closest companion. She died in a sanatorium in Lausanne when Indira was only eighteen, but pictures of Indira in the years after this do not suggest an isolated, obsessive or inward-looking personality. She is often wreathed in smiles.

The Nehru household in Allahabad was not always a haven of comfort. Her paternal aunt, Vijayalakshmi Pandit, a strong and notable woman in her own right who became the United Nations General Assembly's first woman president, was a bit of a bully, it seems, and was unkind to both Kamala and Indira. Yet her father's nationalist choices saw to it that she was away from Allahabad for long spans during Indira's childhood and after Kamala's death. Indira was schooled away from Allahabad at Tagore's Santiniketan, and she seems to have imbibed its aesthetic sensibilities. (Her sense of style, which was distinctive, showed the *swadeshi* brand's stamp.) Soon after, Indira left India to read Modern History at Somerville College, Oxford, before her own health made further study impossible.

Nonetheless, by the time she had completed her unusual and truncated education and returned to India, she was, unlike her father and the party machine politicians, fluent in French, Hindustani and English. She could also understand Bengali.

There was nothing in her genetic inheritance, childhood or adolescence to push her towards almost insane degrees of defensiveness (and the aggression that often comes with it), which are often thought to have led her to declare the Emergency. Indeed, if we compare her childhood and youth with those of others in politics – Aurobindo Ghosh, for instance – her young life was sheltered. A 'psychological' understanding of her authoritarianism is just not good enough. No psychiatrist ever left any sort of diagnosis.

Tall and slender by the time she returned to India, her features were arresting: large eyes under delicate brows (one of which she often raised in a quizzical arch), a high forehead, a narrow oval face and a proud aquiline nose, which gave her face an imperious hauteur even if other features hinted at vulnerability. Later she developed the signature shock of white hair that lent her strong visage even more distinction. She brushed it back with pride, and in so doing, she acquired, like Mujib, one of the twentieth century's most unforgettable faces. She wore elegant bobs all her adult life, refusing to become a 'traditional girl' with 'tamed' long braid or bun. Indira must be counted among one of Asia's most iconic 'cosmopolitan modern girls' of her generation.[217]

Still they thought her a 'dumb doll'.

In 1942, Indira married outside her overweening and endogamous Kashmiri Pandit community, having fallen in love with a Parsi Congressman and journalist, Feroze Gandhi, her father's resistance notwithstanding. (To understand just what was at stake, see Chapter 5.)

Still they thought her 'weak'.

Although by the alchemy of this union, Indira Nehru turned into Indira Gandhi (a transformation that has confounded millions) and had two sons, Rajiv and Sanjay, the marriage did not last. The Gandhis parted quietly, with little fuss, years before Feroze's death in 1960. Indira, who had acted as her father's hostess often before this, now moved in to live with him and began to run his prime ministerial household full time. This also gave her an insight into the workings of power and high office she would never otherwise have had. It was from this perspective that she developed the view that the Congress party was spliced through with corruption. (The papers of the All India Congress Committee for this period make it plain that members of the public, and indeed of the Congress itself, shared this view.)

This should have given the 'Syndicate', as the leading provincial politicians were known, cause for concern, but they judged her to be pliable despite it. (If anything, their assessment reveals more about their own misogyny than it does about her. More on these subjects in Chapter 5.)

Everyone agrees that the Congress system had worked thus far through consensual accommodation between states and the centre, and managed disagreements over how best to share a limited cake of resources. In so doing, it had kept India stable through a period, whereas Pakistan had not enjoyed democratic stability for long. But everyone agrees that it had hitherto acted as a break to economic and social change.[218] One scholar describes it as creating and sustaining 'a democracy of the elite', and he is spot on.[219] Another speaks of the partnership between businessmen, landlords and a tiny rent-seeking civilian intelligentsia on which that democracy rested, and although the terms may seem old-fashioned, they do capture a sense of who precisely 'the elites' were.[220] Little had changed on the ground. The rich were still rich, with both social and economic capital; the poor were still poor, bereft of both. Dalits, despite all the promises of the constitution, were still Dalits, subject to all the cruel forms of oppression that society had designed for them. Tribal people still lived in poverty, despite all the breaks the constitution afforded them. (See Chapter 6: their poverty was so great that cooked food was a luxury.)

Perhaps Indira Gandhi's assault on the Congress system, and later on state institutions, came out of a genuine desire to change things for the better for those who had not seen any gains from independence. If we look at her actions from 1971 to 1977, when she was firmly ensconced in power, this interpretation holds. This is not to justify its excesses.

Indira seems to have decided that the Congress system, far from being a solution, was part of the problem. In her determined rise to power, she therefore split the party, creating her own breakaway faction (the Congress-I [I for Indira], as opposed to the Syndicate-led Congress-O [O for Organisation], headed by her arch-rival Morarji Desai). It was a bold strike against the system, which she had perceived (under her father's leadership) to be self-serving. The move succeeded, and she came to office in 1966. But her position – weak to begin with – was rendered more uncertain still after the Congress got its worst ever results in the 1967 elections. These results had their various roots in the states that booted the grand old party out, but they shook Indira Gandhi. She was, for a while, too insecure for comfort in her position. She had to act to gain authority in her party.[221]

It was in this period (1967–72) that she 'came out' as a left-leaning populist. Her main rivals outside the Congress represented a spectrum of views from the extreme right to the extreme left. But her enemies *within the Congress* were legion, and in the main they were social conservatives. So her lurch to the left was a way of rebranding *her* Congress under her leadership as something fresh. It declared a break from the system of the past. She, Indira Gandhi, would act as a direct link between 'the people' and a state that supported their interests: she wanted no party machine politicians or Congress system standing between them.

So she announced a ten-point programme that would ensure 'social control' over banks, limit urban incomes and property, curb monopolies, push through more aggressively with land reforms and abolish the privy purses of princes.[222] This last action broke an explicit pledge made in 1947 to the princes. The bending of the law to achieve social goals had begun. Power structures in the countryside were not trans-formed by depriving the princes and *ranisahebas* (princesses) of these monies, but the gesture was symbolic. 'Feudalism' was dead. She was coming after the old ways of agrarian oppression.

Next Indira went on to enact new licensing policies which hobbled the abilities of large industries, whether Indian-owned or foreign, to expand in the country. Message to capitalists: watch out! No matter that business had played a large role in the Congress movement, and that the Tatas and Birlas were achieving what Nehru had hoped they would – import substitution by manufacturing goods in India. She was after them. Also, to make sure they understood, she made it harder for them to sack workers, and ensured that workers had some voice in their company's management.

She would also soon curtail the rights of workers in the 'essential services' to take strike action. But the individual elements of her pro-gramme were not all part of one theoretical system. They came out like bullet points on a PowerPoint slide: ten-point plans, twenty-point plans and so on, with no clarity about how each point related to the other.

Indira was not much given to analysis but she was schooled in the basic teachings of the economic nationalists. She would have read Dadabhai's treatises and Dutt's *Open Letters* to Curzon on famines, and would have heard them discussed around her. These books would have been on her literary father's bookshelves. Her thinking, and her programmes, were grounded in some of their basic precepts. Once we understand her intellectual legacy, her policies are easier to interpret.

The idea that the nation did not produce enough to feed and clothe itself was a central precept of these men, which influenced her approach to productivity. ('Work More, Talk Less' was one admon-ishment during an emergency that eroded labour rights hard won over almost a century.) So when she both promoted the right of work-ers to join company boards while curtailing the right of essential workers to strike, the question of national productivity appears to have been on her mind.

Indira Gandhi also appears to have held the received view that the nation's compact with its people was to avert famine, and even severe food shortages. It was at times when such shortages were at their most acute – in 1966, after two successive monsoons had failed and a depression loomed, and in 1974, in the wake of the global oil crisis – that she took her most extreme actions. These were also the times when she was at her most destructive, believing herself to be acting in the interests of 'the people'.

After 1966, she did all she could to destroy the Congress system and accumulate power at the centre, in the Prime Minister's Office.

The attack on the judiciary, whose independence Indira Gandhi strove with her utmost to undermine, had also started before the Emergency began in 1975. By promoting judges out of turn (against every norm of Indian governance hitherto), she sought to do what the US judicial system allows for but the Indian one does not – packing the Supreme Court. Superseding three senior judges, she appointed Justice Ajit Nath Ray as chief justice of the Supreme Court. She did this, once again, not on a whim but for a reason: she wanted a 'progressive' judiciary which would prevent landlords from exerting their fundamental right to property, and in A. N. Ray she found a like-minded judge with whom she could work. Still, she was tampering with the state's institutions in ways that broke from the past. This is important, because this represents one significant similarity between this phase of authoritarianism and the one that followed it in the 1990s and 2010s (and also a common point with Pakistan).

After the spiralling food crisis of 1974–5, Indira's twenty-point programme focused on making food available in cities (hotbeds of 'rumour') and on dealing with those who smuggled, hoarded and adulterated food, cheating and short-changing the consumer. This indeed went on and was not a product of her 'fevered imagination'. Every afternoon, time in our kitchen was spent on fishing out tiny bits of stone from the daal, and even from rice. Filling these daily foods with stone made us, like all consumers, get less for our money, and crack our teeth if we failed to spot any of the stones. Diwan Singh was too grand to do this job himself, so I would help our *ayah*, Mary, to do it. It took two people a couple of hours for a household of eight. He, meanwhile, would relay his version of the latest news to anyone who would listen.

One scholar describes Indira's programme as being driven by 'the politics of consumption': political opinion in the climate of sky-high price rises. Given Indira's close notes on the prices of everyday food, about making sure that edible oil was not adulterated, and her war on the 'anti-social elements' who were making hay while 'the people' went hungry, his argument is persuasive.[223]

And then came the 1971 election, in which the Congress (I) won a healthy majority. (Soon she would drop the 'I' in a gesture that her Congress was the real Congress.) Then came the Bangladesh Liberation War, after which India hailed Indira Gandhi as a conquering Mother Goddess. An acolyte (and they proliferated around her now) coined the slogan 'India is Indira, Indira is India'.

So what did this prelude mean? The slogan provides a clue: the centralisation of power in Indira's hands. Everyone, be they so mighty, had to be her supplicant.

Not only was the *party* hollowed out in many provinces, in ways that started it on its path to decline, the state was centralised in ways not envisaged by those who had drafted India's constitution.

The constitution's authors had given the Indian executive authorities the right to suspend civil liberties in the event of internal or external disturbance, in provinces and at the centre. It had also the right, under specific circumstances, to detain persons without trial. These were colonial-era laws which, interestingly, the constitution-makers adopted, despite the grave reservations many legislators had expressed at the time. But it also, in a balancing gesture, gave authority to the judiciary to keep the executive in check,[224] and gave the public the right to approach the higher courts on matters of concern through writ petitions.[225]

It is not as though these 'emergency powers', or even military rule, had never been resorted to before the Emergency: they had, many a time. Hyderabad experienced army rule between 1948 and 1950. The states of Nagaland, Kerala and Kashmir had been governed by a mix of police terror and central intervention in state elections. The Armed Forces Special Powers Act of 1958 was used to control the 'disturbed areas' of Assam and Manipur. And then of course there were the emergency provisions embedded in the constitution, which Delhi's rulers before Indira had used eight times (between 1947 and 1966) to dismiss provincial governments. Indira Gandhi would use them twenty-six times between 1967 and 1974.[226]

So until the Emergency, Indira Gandhi's government represented, to many, a government acting lawfully (just), in a heroic attempt to push back against the political and social forces ranged against 'her and the people'. True enough, there were concerns about her 'excesses', within the Congress, the political commentariat (which was lively in India), and the judiciary, and an array of political opponents ranged against her.

Matters began to deteriorate in 1974. The oil shock of 1973 was a global crisis, but it tipped Indians into a new stage of political resistance against government. India produced hardly any oil of its own and the sudden oil shortages, then as now, led to huge inflationary pressures. Food prices shot up, causing consternation across the land, 'food movements' sprung up and some rice mills began to be looted. Given that food prices were controlled by government, this represented a political crisis.

A moral panic around food electrified a politicised citizenry. Indira Gandhi began to keep a watchful eye on the price of everyday food: potatoes, onions, chillies – the food of the poor. Government found new internal enemies: hoarders of grain, smugglers of food and mysterious people who adulterated everything, from spices to milk.[227] It is a strange memory; but as a small child I learned a big word: 'adulterer', which is 'Hinglish' for adulterator. Diwan Singh explained it all to us as we picked stones out of the daal. He persuaded me of the virtues of *ghee* (clarified butter) rather than *vanaspati* (vegetable oil), because solid ghee could not be subject to 'adultery'. That it had another meaning I learned only when I was old enough to read fiction and consult the huge Webster dictionaries my parents had on their bookshelves. This produced, at first, a curious conflation in my head – I thought an adulterer was someone who did shady food deals *and* had affairs with other men's wives. I suppose it goes to show how voluble political discussion was in India at the time, that even children aged ten learned these words.

These were not diversions from the real challenges – Indira grew obsessive about the price of the cheapest foods. But political opposition now began to mount, and not in the usual forms. The Naxal Maoist insurgency in West Bengal had been crushed locally with a brutal savagery which shocked even her friends, but it had spread to neighbouring states, where it still rages. No sooner had Indira begun to regroup from the events in Bengal, when in Gujarat, the provincial base of Morarji Desai (her arch-rival), students began to protest about the price and quality of food served at the hostel canteens. This swelled into riots waged against the minister responsible for food, whose effigies students began to burn in a four-day rampage through the city. Medical students from the university joined in, conducting mock autopsies on his 'dead body', claiming to have found grain, edible oil, and wads of cash hidden in his innards.[228] When police fired on protestors and the army was called in, Morarji Desai began an indefinite fast. Faced with these twin instruments of popular protest on the ground and Gandhian fasting at the top, Indira Gandhi found herself exactly where the British had been during the non-cooperation movements. She reacted much as they might have done. She dissolved the elected assembly.

But this was small beer in terms of what was to come. Another student movement began to coalesce around the food question in Bihar, which again led to clashes between students and the police. It was this student movement and the police killing of twenty-two students that propelled a movement about food prices into a campaign for a new kind of democracy: a real 'people's democracy'. Jayaprakash Narayan (1902–79) came out of retirement to become first the totem, and then the leader, of a battle against corruption and misgovernment, of which he refused any longer to be a mute spectator.

'JP', as he was known, was a product of the non-cooperation and civil disobedience movements, which did not bode well for Indira. Having retired from public life after independence, refusing (like Gandhi, but unlike so many fellow Congressmen) to accept the dividends of independence, he had acquired a reputation for high moral probity. His clean-cut face mirrored a clean-cut personality. Like Gandhi, he strove for truth, and like Gandhi, many people revered him almost as they would a saintly figure. Just as worryingly, his unusual journey through life had taken him not to Britain but to the United States, where he read Marx and supported his studies by doing menial labour. He was no barrister at Lincoln's Inn, then. His actions in 1975 could not be predicted: he was no dyed-in-the-wool liberal such as Nehru had been. JP's family had close ties with Jawaharlal, forged through politics, but what he saw after independence had led to a gradual straining of that relationship. Indira tested the bond between the two families to breaking point. After the dismissal of the Gujarat government, JP felt he could no longer defend the indefensible. No matter that the prime minister was acting within constitutional limits, her actions went against its spirit, and against natural justice.

He launched his movement of peaceful non-cooperation, recognising that it broke the law, 'for what were people to do when constitutional methods and democratic institutions failed to respond to their will or solve the problems under which they have been groaning?'[229] Curiously, Indira probably agreed with this assessment of the failure of constitutional methods and democratic institutions to respond to the will of 'the people' or to solve their problems. What she could not countenance was being toppled, which JP's movement seemed to threaten.

The spearheads of the student campaign went on to have a major role in national politics, not least Laloo Prasad Yadav, who came from a 'low caste' group of cattle herders and would later help alliances of 'backward castes' rise to power in Bihar. This brand of politics eventually ousted the Congress from its home bases in Uttar Pradesh and Bihar. At this time, however, Laloo was the able and energetic head of the Patna University Students' Union.

At a speech at which JP addressed many hundreds of thousands on 5 June 1975, he explained further what he meant: the people, rather than the central government, would seize the right to dismiss governments, if they failed to deliver. He described what he called for as a 'total revolution'. All over the country – not only in Bihar – his message struck a chord among millions of Indians, disgusted by local corruption and enraged by the failed promises of independence.[230] Indira might well have panicked. Could it be her government that 'the people' (led by JP) were planning to dismiss?

When he arrived in Delhi with his followers, camping in the Ramlila Maidan, she could see that it was.[231]

In the midst of all of this, the Allahabad High Court upheld a bold appeal against Mrs Gandhi for electoral malpractice. Her attempt to pack the courts had not gone far enough. The court held her election invalid, and barred her from standing for election for six years. In response to this judgement, JP and all other opposition parties except the CPI (the Communist Party of India, which supported Indira for her radical policies) urged her to resign.

It was at this point that her long flirtation with authoritarianism burst into a full-blown love affair. At midnight on 25 June 1975, without consulting her cabinet, she urged the president to declare a state of 'internal emergency'. (The president is only a nominal head of state, except at moments of constitutional crisis.) Whether he protested or not is moot. The next morning, by which time the country woke up to a new life altogether, the cabinet had given its sanction. Only one person raised a question. The fact that Indira did not address it, meant that no one else dared.[232] The pattern of intimidation that lay at the heart of the Emergency thus was turned, in those early hours of 26 June, against the country's most powerful men.

There was no one to check her hand thereafter, as motley advisors and fixers took the place of wiser heads, pretty much overnight. The prime minister's house at 10 Safdarjung Road became an extra-constitutional 'shadowy' space, which lacked authority in law, but from which orders issued were executed by grafters half-killing themselves to please.[233]

The orders came thick and fast. 'Arrest political opponents!' (Done, ma'am, before dawn.) 'Cut electricity supply to the press!' (Done, ma'am, the next day.) 'Arrest more political opponents!' By this stage, those arrested were being tortured, *laathis* (bamboo batons) covered in red chilli powder stuffed up their anuses. 'Round up political subversives!' Oh dear. What, and who, were subversives? An unwieldy category into which fell students, of course. Gujarat and Patna had suggested that student activists posed a huge threat so they had to be locked up. Inevitably many were caught up in cases of mistaken identity, but they festered in jail regardless under the Maintenance of Internal Security Act (MISA). (In this respect it was not unlike the infamous Rowlatt Bills of 1919 that led to the upsurge in Punjab and the carnage at Jallianwalla Bagh.)

Indira Gandhi's first instinct was clearly to protect herself against those calling for her to go.

But the list of the 'disappeared' during the Emergency also included a great many 'adulterers' or traders whom she held responsible for the situation by charging too much for diluted goods. A few of the points of her twenty-point programme had to do with these 'anti-social elements'. Several others pointed to ways of lowering prices, some of which were frankly odd. So traders in essential commodities were picked up and locked away. They too festered in jail for the duration of the Emergency under MISA. They counted as 'anti-social elements' because they were profiting from the misery of 'the people'.

Her populism, while strident and dictatorial, remained rooted in a particular understanding of what ailed India. It was hunger. The lack of productivity. Hence she urged people to 'work more and talk less' and avoid rumour, which she believed was a political flame that could light fires of panic across the population. She was particularly concerned about rumours in cities, at food markets, about the prices and quality of food. (Diwan Singh was lucky not to have been arrested.)

She monitored rumours: indeed a new panoply of investigative tools were put in place. (Rumour simply went underground but became more lurid. I remember following, with my close friend Emma, a woman who wore dark glasses day and night, which we thought was 'suspicious'. We began noting her comings and goings. We believed she was a CIA agent: there was much talk of CIA agents backing Indira at this time. Our jejune grasp of intelligence-gathering reveals both its existence, and the intense anxiety about it.)

Indira Gandhi's trusted officers monitored the press, of course, but also private conversations. (One vivid memory I have of the Emergency era was the house rule that *no* conversation, other than the banal, could be conducted within the house. 'Walls have ears,' my father told us. Since, as a politicised family, it was impossible for us not to discuss politics between ourselves or with friends, we did so sotto voce, in the middle of the garden, seated on cane chairs. Mosquito bites evoke the fury and fear of those days.)

This snooping went hand in hand with pushing through the goal of bringing more food to the market at reasonable cost. That Indira went about it the wrong way is indisputable. Rather than frightening the horses and driving grain stocks underground, she could have offered incentives through government procurement schemes to buy grain at a slightly higher price from the peasant, and sell it to the consumers in the city at the reduced price. Or she could have offered incentives to traders to sell more stocks at lower prices. But she had driven away her economic advisors who might have helped her devise such policies.

So she did neither. Instead she imprisoned food traders. This achieved nothing, except build up a pool of resentment among traders against the Congress, which parties of the right would soon exploit.

It is easy to see why she targeted students, but harder for the police to list all the 'subversives' in the country, and more difficult still to identify and catch them. (We, for instance, were right under her nose, sitting a mile from her house on cane chairs, while sheltering a well-known journalist who was critical of Madam. The Indian state has frailties and blind spots, of which more in Chapter 3.) But Indira also made it an objective to improve the quality of food for students in hostel canteens, and to make it more affordable. This was part of the twenty-point programme.

The police threw all these motley 'subversives' in jail without trial of course. The first rule of the Emergency was the suspension of citizens' fundamental rights, which the constitution-makers had placed as the coping stone of all else: it was 'the basic structure'. So when attacks came on personal liberties and freedoms in a form not seen since the days of non-cooperation and Quit India, these were soon followed through by an amendment that challenged that 'basic structure'. The numbers of those 'subversives' arrested (c.110,000), interestingly enough, is almost identical to the number rounded up by the British during Gandhian non-cooperation.

How far her drive to change the structure of the state (and its constitution) was fuelled by a genuine sense of frustration at its blundering impotence and corrupt elitism – or by a desire to protect herself – we can only guess. The constitution, for instance, protected the right to property (a fundamental right), which the judiciary had upheld in several test cases. This had acted as a bulwark against wide-ranging programmes of agrarian land reform. I suspect that by dismantling the constitution in the 'omnibus' 42nd Amendment, she was torn between a zeal to serve the interests of 'the people' and to protect her own interests, and the line between the two blurred in her head.

Increasingly the orders came from Madam's son Sanjay; if anything, these orders had to be implemented faster. They were so bizarre, violent and notorious that to a great extent, other aspects of Indira's political programme (which lent it coherence) have faded from view. The most inglorious was the mass sterilisation programme, which turned an existing policy (and indeed a global consensus) about the urgent need to tackle population growth into a savage campaign of target-driven, and sometimes forced, sterilisation.[234] The Shah Commission Report into these excesses concluded that 10,757,234 people underwent vasectomies and tubectomies, with a male to female ratio of 3:1 in the peak year of the campaign, 1976–7.[235]

The other notorious programme was the 'city beautification' plan, which led to violent slum-clearance drives. Once again, the idea that having clusters of poor people in cities was unsightly and dangerous has a long pedigree, dating back to the brutal assault on the fabric of Old Delhi – Shah Jahan's city – after the Mutiny and Rebellion in 1858, and the creation, in the late nineteenth century, of 'White Towns' apart from 'Black Towns' in British India. The Indian 'democracy of the elite' had a similar attitude towards housing the poor in cities.

Governments, whether in Delhi or in the states, were anxious at the thought of cities being 'overwhelmed' by the ('unsightly', 'rowdy', 'unhygienic') refugee poor, and devised policies to exile them to distant places.[236] (More of this in Chapter 4.) So the resettlement and demolition of slums had been underway in every Indian city since independence, where it faced often powerful movements of resistance. Delhi, as the capital of the new nation, was the subject of particular pressure to manage the problem. It is against this wider context that Sanjay Gandhi's slum-clearance drive in Delhi in best set.

A critical event in that programme (for which it has become a metonym) was a confrontation between protestors and policemen at the Turkman Gate area in Old Delhi. The regime's yes-man and over-zealous cop, Deputy Inspector General of Police Bhinder, led the police's chaotic response to a local community holding its ground in complex urban terrain. At one point, Bhinder tried to seize a constable's rifle and start firing at the crowds who would not yield to intimidation. The incident ended in horror, blood flowing inside a mosque, between six and twelve protestors shot dead, and a slum demolition programme in overdrive.[237] (This was one of the only mass protests against the Emergency. Those involved were almost all Muslims. So too were the dead. This is a point of some significance.)

But Turkman Gate was only one of the 150,105 demolitions carried out in Delhi alone during the Emergency. Sanjay's men and women took things further, faster and in more brutal directions than leaders before had dared to go. He acted with arrogant, entitled, lawless impunity. The doting mother's role in these events remains in the shadows: no one will ever know what she sanctioned herself and what went on despite her. This doubt (among, I need to remind you, a frightened but politicised public) led millions of large-hearted people to pity Indira for her wayward son.

I don't know anyone who wept when Sanjay Gandhi died in a plane crash in 1980, doing a swaggering loop manoeuvre. By contrast, I know all too many people who were shocked to find themselves grieve when Indira Gandhi died in 1984. (Her Sikh bodyguards gunned her down after Operation Blue Star, in which their sacred Golden Temple became a battleground between security forces and Sikh secessionists.) Many of these people were part of the anti-Emergency crowd. Perhaps they did then what so many Indians had done when they re-elected her to power in 1980: disaggregate Indira from Sanjay, and blame the son for the 'excesses' (as if the fundaments were acceptable, based on ideas grounded in consensus). They heaped calumny on the son and forgave the mother, for after all, what can an Indian mother do but indulge her sons? (More on this theme in Chapter 5.)

Despite Turkman Gate, Indira's Emergency never took the lurch to the Indian right into Hindu identity politics. Her claim was to be its antithesis.

By contrast, the Hindu nationalism which re-emerged from the shadows during, and in opposition to, Indira Gandhi's Emergency (1975–7), proposed a 'conservative revolution' as the bedrock of nationality.[238] Its intellectual roots were just as old as those of economic nationalism, but its accent was not on problems economic or social, but on questions of Hindu identity (and its 'other', the Muslim invader-pretender-interloper). Bankimchandra Chatterjee was its foundational thinker, and his play *Ananda Math* ('The Abbey of Bliss', 1882) created an imaginary history in which pure Hindu sons of India rose up in an armed uprising against a corrupt Muslim nawab.[239] (It is by no means his finest work, but its impact has been profound.) Bankimchandra also created the potent figure of 'Mother India' as a supreme and powerful deity. He wrote the poem 'Bande Mataram' before the play, but when he inserted it into *Ananda Math* it gathered charge and potency; in the play its calls to violence – embedded in a story about a righteous crusade – gain even more traction.[240] After its lyrical opening stanzas (rendered in English in Chapter 1), in which the poem dwells on the natural beauty and bounty of Bengal, the following stanzas move into an almost martial meter and mood. One line asks Hindus: 'Brothers, will that day come when we demolish their mosques to build temples for Radhamadhav?'[241]

Yes. It would.

In another, there is a call to 'raze their buildings to dust'.[242] That day, too, would come.

In the early twentieth century also, Bal Gangadhar Tilak, already well known to readers for his role in the controversy over the age of consent and his battle with Muslims for urban public space, made another significant intervention. He wrote an influential commentary on the *Bhagavad Gita* (a passage of divine mentorship in the epic *Mahabharata*), as a prisoner in Mandalay jail. Published in 1915, it espoused *karmayoga*, a philosophy of action. Well before this, Bankimchandra had given the *Gita* the status of '*the* religious text' for a modern, fit-for-purpose 'Hinduism', rid of its accretions (in its existing form a religion by no means monolithic, and one consisting of a range of philosophical, textual and oral traditions, but no single book). Some have argued Tilak's *Gita Rahasya* justified 'fraternal violence',[243] but very quickly, with the publication of Savarkar's *Hindutva*, the idea that Hindus and Muslims were not even of the same species had begun to circulate, so the concept of violence between Hindu and Muslim 'brothers' was soon overtaken.[244]

Vinayak Damodar Savarkar (1883–1966) was the man who made the next great leap forward for Hindu nationalism. Savarkar was a former revolutionary terrorist who had been exiled in the Andamans' Cellular Jail, and then in Ratnagiri, for the trouble he (and his coadjutors) had caused the Raj. In jail, this rather stern-faced but intelligent man had time to read and think. (The extent to which British jails were spaces where Indian public and political culture developed in the twentieth century is quite astonishing.) In the infamous Cellular Jail, Savarkar read books by the Italian nationalist Giuseppe Mazzini, who had imagined a culturally homogeneous nation of Italy, and this inspired him. The product of his ideas – in a milieu in which some Hindus perceived 'everyday anxiety', 'a sense of disorder' in the context of plural modernity, and developed 'ideological fantasies' of the savage Muslim threat[245] – was his influential book *Hindutva: Who Is a Hindu?*[246] In it he declared that Bharatvarsha was the sacred land of true Indians. Its takeaway line was: 'Hindus are only those persons for whom India was their Fatherland and Holy land.' This tense definition of 'Hinduness' had a logical premise for arguing that Muslims (and indeed Christians and Jews) could not be Indians. Their loyalty to the nation could never be proved.[247] But it allowed him to argue this despite caste, because 'we feel we are bound together, so it must be so', and to claim that all Hindus, by this definition, were also bound together by their love for their ancient land. India *was* Hindustan, historically the land of Hindus, and so it should aspire, after centuries of oppression, to become that once again.

Another critical pillar of the book's message was its stress that the state 'pandered to Muslim minorities'. (This became a reason for later generations to slam the Congress government for 'pseudo-secularist' pandering to minorities. This would lead, in more recent times, to an attack on all individuals deemed pseudo-secularist: a curious formulation used to describe an intelligentsia committed to open contestation and debate about the 'facts' and assumptions of history, and which shares the constitutional premise that India should remain a society in which religion does not dominate the official sphere of state power.)

More than any other, Savarkar's *Who Is a Hindu?* became *the* book for those looking for such guidance, since it was short, simply written, and had a headline claim that everyone could grasp and remember. In fact, few Hindus (by this definition or any other) could read the *Gita* in the original Sanskrit, which is, in contrast, profoundly metaphysical; Tilak's commentary is a challenging read as well. Although the hymn 'Bande Mataram' had become a nationalist anthem, only well-educated Bengalis could read and grasp the inwardness, and sleights of hand, in *Ananda Math* itself. Some Hindus, by the early twentieth century, could relate to Mother India, in the way that people had responded with such intensity to the goddesses of languages. (But Muslims could not, as it went against a central pillar of their faith.) Such simple messages, songs and iconographies have bedded these ideas down as more complex ones were lost in translation.

Perhaps following the logic of this conclusion, in 1925, a man of medicine, Dr Keshav Baliram Hedgewar, made a decision of huge historical impact. He established a 'grassroots' organisation called the Rashtriya Swayamsevak Sangh (RSS, the National Self-Service Organisation) in Nagpur. *Swayamsevak* is a labile word of which there are many possible readings. Self-defence, self-protection, Hindu defence, and a need for Hindus for self-protection from threatening others, can all be read into this one word. Do not be misled by literal, or indeed official, translations.

Readers will recall that it was about this time that Gandhi began to build the Congress at the grassroots too, with his six-anna membership scheme open (in theory at least) to all, and that many women, and members of middle castes, and groups who were already identified as 'minorities', joined the party. But the RSS was a very different kind of organisation. It recruited only Hindu boys and young men. (Readers will also recall that Nathuram Godse, who assassinated Gandhi, was one recruit.) It was disciplined in a way that the Congress was not. Every day of the week, early in the morning, members of RSS *shaakhas* (training centres) would meet to perform exercises (physical culture development being a watchword of Hindu nationalist outfits), martial drills and parades, to salute the saffron flag, and to sing 'Bande Mataram' in its entirety. Yes: a song written in Bengal in the late nineteenth century became the anthem of the RSS in the twentieth century. (The fact that the original song was a Bengali song *laden with Sanskrit* made its travel across north and central India smoother. That fact should also give a hint at who these recruits were: most were Brahmins, who had access to 'the language'.)

The RSS had grown into a large organisation before partition, particularly in its heartland (Bombay Presidency, Central Provinces and the United Provinces), but also in the wider Gangetic zone. Police reported the existence of similar (possibly linked) outfits as far afield as Calcutta.[248] It had flourished in the rising communal tides of those decades.

Partition provided this trained force with the chance to fight the war for which it had been preparing. However, in 1948, it took things too far with Gandhi's assassination. The public mood turned against it, and all organisations associated with it. The government briefly banned the RSS. The RSS, indeed the whole Sangh Parivar (of RSS-associated organisations) went on the defensive in the political sphere. Some even closed down.

But it then launched a counter-offensive in the 'cultural sphere'. (These spheres were then seen as divided. That was, after all, the premise of Indian secularism.) In 1954, the supremo of the RSS decided to establish a host of primary schools, first in Uttar Pradesh, and then in Delhi, Bihar, Madhya Pradesh and Andhra Pradesh. Named after the Hindu goddess of learning, Saraswati, these Saraswati Shishu Mandirs and Bal Mandirs (temples for children) spread like bindweed, so that by 1991, they were the largest chain of schools in the country after government schools. There were some 300,000 children in this alternative system of education by 1991.

On offer in this alternative educational model – which was more expensive than government schools but far cheaper than exclusive private schools – were literacy and numeracy, 'religion', 'patriotism' and 'Indian culture'.[249] The last three were contested fields, as we have seen, but this version was presented as the 'truth'. (This kind of pedagogy had no room for debate or independent ratiocination; less so, even, than the national histories that preceded it.) Children were expected to join *shaakhas*. Morning assemblies, rather than being devoted to the students' moral well-being and emotional development, gave contemporary politics much airtime. There was far more interaction between teachers and the families of students than in other school systems, so much so that whole localities were made into extensions of a public space with the school at its heart. The worship of the *tulsi* plant, the chanting of 'Om', the display of the symbol of 'Om', the ownership of a copy of the *Gita*: the system strongly encouraged these activities, so much so that they became gestures that made inhabitants of these localities into mid-twentieth-century 'modern' Hindus.

This version of a 'national education', unlike the *swadeshi* variety of the early twentieth century, was to create the ideal Hindu who would help refashion India and make it a Hindu nation.[250]

Monuments have been a crucial element of this discourse. India's 'Muslim' architectural heritage, in this view, is a defacement of Bharat Mata (Mother India) – to whom students daily affirm their loyalty in cries of '*Bharat Mata ki Jai!*' ('Victory to Mother India!') – and a constant reminder of her past humiliation under 'Muslim' rulers. The Babri Masjid Mosque at Ayodhya, built (possibly) in 1527 by the first Mughal emperor Babur, was the movement's particular focus because it was (allegedly) situated at the *precise spot* where Lord Ram had been born, and was constructed out of the remains of a temple dedicated to him. It is of course impossible to tell exactly where Ram of the Hindu epic – discussed at length in Chapter 7 – was born. But *bhakts* (devotees), a large number of whom were products of the Shishu Mandir system, are not interested in archaeological or historical niceties. So intellectual debate on the subject, with which many historians tried to engage, fell on deaf ears.[251]

Straight after partition, Hindu nationalists had attempted to lay claim to the Babri Masjid. (Of course they would try to do this. Given their perspective on things, this particular mosque was their prime target.) Under cover of darkness, a crowd of men placed an idol on its premises, declaring that the infant Lord Ram (*Ram lalla*) had returned to his birthplace to claim what was his. Nehru's government suspected, and found evidence of, illegal trespass by a mob of about sixty men. By the time it did anything, however, the story had spread.[252]

When I was growing up, people far and wide who had never been to Faizabad, Ayodhya or its environs, had heard 'all about' the Babri Masjid. (My source of news was, of course, Diwan Singh. He was from Rajasthan, a desert away from Ayodhya, but told me a version of the story twenty-five years afterwards. I now recognise that his version of the story was based on discrete events between 1947 and 1950 which, in his narrative, he collapsed into a single night. In his telling, the 'idol' was 'a doll'. I focused, as a child might, on the doll.)

As these debates began to ripple through India, circulating through society by *bhakts* and RSS-associated newspapers, Muslims too began, in the late 1970s and 1980s, to demand the restoration of 'dead monuments' to the community of the faithful, so that they could be restored to their original purposes.[253] For instance, in 1984 the All India Muslim Majlis-i-Mushawarat, an umbrella pressure group established in Lucknow in 1964, appealed to the central government to open all 'protected' mosques for prayer.[254] This helped turn the Babri Masjid into an even more impassioned issue (despite the fact that it was actually a functioning mosque and not a 'dead monument' at all). By the early 1990s, it had become a national cause célèbre for the RSS, and the ever-larger numbers of Hindus persuaded by it. Votaries of minority rights (whom *bhakts* deride as pseudo-secularists) also entered the fray.

Polarities had always been a feature of Indian politics, but by the 1990s, as the clash between the left and right grew more deafening, they reached new extremes. What was at stake was the very soul of the nation; its survival into the future. The left (which included liberals) wanted liberal secularism to survive, and fought to save it; the right wanted to destroy it and build something new in its stead: a religious state, of and for Hindus.

The Bharatiya Janata Party (BJP; literally, Indian People's Party) – the political wing of the RSS – placed monuments in general and the Babri Masjid in particular at the heart of its campaign to return to the centre of India's politics. The BJP was born in 1980 after the Emergency: it was a lineal descendant of the Hindu Mahasabha, founded in Bengal in the 1920s, and the Jan Sangh, born in 1951. The latter was one of many parties fighting the Emergency.[255] The Jan Sangh had joined the short-lived coalition Janata government that came to power after Indira Gandhi lost a general election in 1977, ending the Emergency for reasons that few claim to understand. That coalition lasted until 1980, when Indira Gandhi was returned to power. After her assassination in 1984, her older son Rajiv took up 'the mantle', which he held until he too died a gruesome death in 1991. (The assassin, a Tamil Sri Lankan, was protesting against India's policies regarding its island neighbour. Her suicide vest blew up in his face. We have come to expect this approach to assassination now, but then we did not.)

Just before this, in 1990, the BJP launched a Rath Yaatra (chariot procession or journey) that left havoc in its wake.[256] Relations between the BJP and the RSS were not, in the last century, always frictionless. Both had their respective roles, but the BJP's task was to gather votes on the basis of a programme grounded in Hindutva. Its political rise was slow, based on decades of quiet 'consciousness raising' in schools across North India, careful cultivation of the Indian diaspora, and a demand of increasing shrillness that a temple for Lord Ram be built on the site of the Babri Masjid, allegedly the site of Ram's birth. History, myth and monuments combined, by the 1980s and 90s, in a potent nationalist discourse that insisted that the Hindu male was still oppressed and emasculated, despite the end of colonialism, because of the Congress party's opportunistic and weak-kneed 'pandering' to Muslims. The Hindu woman was still in danger, susceptible to the wiles and aggression of the lascivious Muslim male, a target of 'love jihad'. It was time for the Hindu male to rise and claim his women and his nation, and make India shine.

The founders of the BJP were Lal Krishna Advani, a Sindhi refugee, and Atal Bihari Vajpayee, a noted Hindi poet. Advani held a seat in the Lok Sabha (Parliament's 'House of the People') in the 1980s and was already, at the time I met him as a research fellow at Trinity College, Cambridge, a totemic figure in India's political landscape. This brief encounter took place at an awkward college event to welcome parliamentarians from India. The soft-spoken, bald, bespectacled man was placed next to me at lunch and, as is the custom in this part of the British Isles, we had a conversation. It turned out that not only had he read my first book (this took me by surprise) but he described it as 'well researched' and went on to discuss its finer points with me. He was polite to his hosts, as is the custom in South Asia. He came across as a genteel and gentle man.

The Rath Yaatra was anything but gentle. A Toyota jeep was dressed up to look like the chariot that so many – brought up on the *Ramlila* and *Amar Chitra Katha* picture books – imagined to represent a chariot worthy of Lord Krishna advising Arjun in the epic to go to war.[257] Men dressed as characters from the Hindu epics accompanied him.

The journey – it is important to register – was from Somnath, an ancient temple near the western coast of present-day Gujarat (a monument allegedly vandalised by 'Muslim invaders' in the past). The jeep-chariot covered about 300 kilometres a day, through villages and towns across north and central India. It often stopped, giving Advani a platform to address as many as six public rallies a day.

Spot the difference: this was a more organised form of populism than Mrs Gandhi's hectic buzzing about the country. It was deliberate, planned, and intended to cause maximum impact. It had a clear message, and – recognising the party's linguistic limitations – it did not use only speeches to send it out, in an India where regions had become more committed to their mother tongues. Somnath, the chariot, the route, the end point: these all had a symbolism that was easy to comprehend by viewing. If riots followed (they did, some of the worst since partition), so be it. Lord Krishna's counsel in the *Gita* is that it is one's duty (*dharma*) to go to war for righteous reasons.

Hindu nationalism has remained obsessed with war. Vajpayee's first coalition government in 1996 may have lasted only thirteen days, but in his second term in office (1998–9), it set off five nuclear blasts. Vajpayee made no effort to pretend that these were anything but nuclear weapons. (Earlier governments had tended to present 'nuclear science' as being developed for peaceful purposes.) The Kargil war with Pakistan (of which more in the Epilogue) followed in 1999. The Hindu right's fascination with force has deep roots. By the end of the twentieth century, the sapling had grown into a tree with many long and small branches, all of strength and significance.

But the authoritarians of the right had learned from the Emergency *what not to do*. Their strategies would go on to be more subtle than Indira Gandhi's mode of full-frontal attack on her enemies. When established in power again from 1999 until 2004, Vajpayee did not begin by filling jails with politicians, traders and students. Nor would he lock up journalists and hinder free speech as obviously as Indira Gandhi had done: instead the government would put pressure on presses and news media channels. Traders were its friends. Vajpayee rather agreed with Sanjay Gandhi that the voluble Jawharlal Nehru University (JNU) was a grade-ten-level migraine, but rounded up and arrested a few individuals rather than thousands. Making examples of people was more his style. In case those who were supposed to be intimidated missed the point, there were other, more sophisticated, ways of trying to frighten them: delivering proximate threats (a sealed envelope via courier, say, containing just a newspaper cutting: 'X died when a bus ran over him'); or, as techies in the diaspora brought their talents into the game, ringing the targets' mobile phones or landlines several times a day. A few people were made examples of, and too many lost their lives or liberty. The majority were from the 'wrong', hated, community. But compared with the scale of (say) the sterilisation programme, in which more than a million were caught up, the numbers arrested or detained were small. Until the end of the century, under Vajpayee's watch, that is.

In this sense, BJP-led India at the end of the twentieth century could be described more as despotic than authoritarian. Generating a climate of fear is a different thing; minorities began, more than ever, to live in fear. Those who spoke up on their behalf wondered when their turn would come. In a rule by exception, crushing a little dissidence is deemed to be enough. (The rest will watch their words, and their step, is the logic. A great many did. Walls, phones, tablets and computers all have ears.)

However, the party took *some* leaves from Indira's book. Where Mrs Gandhi targeted political enemies and subversives, their target group is much larger: an entire religious community of Muslims that constituted, by the end of the century, some fifteen per cent of the population. Where Indira Gandhi had promoted one judge out of turn, there appears to have been a more systematic establishment of placemen and -women in the judiciary. The independence of the bureaucracy too, and even of the Election Commission, has been undermined. So too has the army. These erasures, not least on the firm line between the civil and military spheres that India had long succeeded in maintaining (and which Pakistan and Bangladesh had not), mark this out both as a radical departure from the past and a blurring of old subcontinental distinctions.

Going back to Advani and his Rath Yaatra. India is a vast country and, travelling at this leisurely pace, Advani and his chariot could not go everywhere. But he defied the limits of geography by exhorting followers to send *Ram sheelans* (bricks consecrated to Ram) to the site of the temple.

This was a masterstroke. Hundreds of thousands of bricks poured in, from around the country and even the diaspora. On 9 November 1989, the first brick with which Hindu activists hoped to construct the new Ram temple was put in place, with much fanfare, in Ayodhya. At the same moment, Hindus across the country were called upon to face Ayodhya, Mecca-like, and make an offering of flowers. As Hindus in the north, south, east and west of the country turned their faces to Ayodhya, many living overseas also participated in Hindu nationalist rituals.

This was of huge existential significance for those in the diaspora who participated, but also widened the scope, ambition and confidence of *karsevaks* (devotees who act) in India. The 'expansive geographies' of procession not only staked a claim to the territories in Bharatvarsha, but also incorporated and developed global dimensions of the Hindu nationalist movement.[258] Bricks carrying the inscription '*Jai Shri Ram*' ('Victory to Ram') travelled across the globe and, after sanctification, returned by airmail to their eventual resting place in Ayodhya.

The *yaatra* created a stupendous response. Some have described the militant upsurge in its wake as one of India's largest mass movements. It also triggered riots in cities across India on a scale not seen since partition.

On 6 December 1992, several hundred *karsevaks* broke the flimsy police cordon that protected the Babri Masjid. Many were dressed in black, and wore red bandanas to show that they were organised and united. They were armed with pick-axes, hammers and rods: builders' tools. They climbed the dome quickly, with remarkable agility, yelling and chanting as they attacked the old building. Viewers across India and the diaspora watched, mouths agape, eyes wide in horror or pride. The police stood by, doing nothing. While the provincial government attempted to prevent Rath from entering UP, the Congress national government, which had promised to protect the 'disputed structure', did nothing. Over a couple of hours, the mosque was reduced to rubble.

This act of vandalism has changed India. The model of the nation that evolved under Nehru had been able to accommodate diversity, and diverse claims to recognition, if only up to a point. 'Unity in diversity' as a national framework allowed for it in theory. In practice, concessions were made only in the face of intense popular pressure. The state acknowledged linguistic demands when a head of steam had built up around them, but Nehru's government had come down hard on anything that smacked of secession, whether on the eve of independence by the Naga leader Angami Zapu Phizo; or Hyderabad's moves to take his princely state to join Pakistan; or Sheikh Abdullah's calls for the autonomy of Indian Kashmir; or the Mizo uprising in 1966. Indira Gandhi was no less harsh to the Khalistan movement for a separate Sikh homeland in the 1970s and 80s; or the long-standing (but waxing and waning) movements in Kashmir by people who have felt let down and alienated by India.

This opportunistic flexibility of the Nehruvian national model itself made it better suited to adapt to a post-colonial context in which identity claims, far from ebbing, proliferated.

However, the Nehruvian state also thwacked down left-wing extremism hard. It never challenged the 'conservative revolution' of the right, even after the partition violence and the assassination of Gandhi. (The rumour of India's leftism under the Congress is just that – a rumour. Ask those Naxalites who survived.)

By the 1990s, India was no longer a 'soft state', as some feared. It could have dealt with this movement as it had done so ruthlessly with others, had it chosen to. Why did Nehru, Indira Gandhi and Rajiv Gandhi all fail to protect the secular 'idea of India'?

It seems to boil down to that hoary colonial principle: where religious matters are concerned, discretion is the better part of valour.

As the threats to India's minorities escalate, the historian's role is to remind readers that the saffron hues of Hindutva have always coloured one powerful thread of Indian nationalism. Liberal, Hindu extremist, secular and composite nationalisms have always been just some of various parallel discourses that have walked side by side like bickering siblings – arms sometimes entwined, at other times kicking and punching – for more than a century. For the larger part of the century, composite nationalisms have been on top, although Hindutva's popularity has never been negligible. At present Hindutva is triumphant, but it may well be pushed aside at some point in the future by its less flamboyant, more inclusive, siblings. This is how Indian nationalism has been structured since its inception, and so it remains.[259] The Hindu idea of India has been with us for a century at the time of writing, and is an intrinsic part, warts and all, of the nation's fabric.

VIII

CONCLUSION

At almost exactly the same moment that Mrs Gandhi began to ride high on a populist wave in the 1970s, promising to get rid of poverty, Zulfikar Ali Bhutto emerged as a populist hero in Pakistan. In 1977

Indira Gandhi was ousted by an election after the Emergency; that same year Bhutto was deposed in a coup named, with some irony, Operation Fair Play. Both leaders were later murdered: Mrs Gandhi by her Sikh bodyguards in 1984, Bhutto by 'judicial hanging' in 1979. Just as the Hindu right rose to power in India in the 1980s, in the same decade the Islamisation of Pakistan began in earnest under General Zia-ul-Huq, fulfilling, at long last, Mawdudi's demand. The lemon tree was forced to grow mangoes. Ahmediya minorities were barred from possessing and reading the Quran. Zia's regime amended Pakistan's Penal Code to provide for punishment for the desecration of the Quran and to penalise blasphemy with death or life imprisonment. The Objectives Resolution – which Liaquat had cobbled together as a compromise in a preamble to the constitution – now became a substantive part of its main text.[260] The Hudood Ordinances came into force. (*Hudood* means limits or restrictions, as in limits of acceptable behaviour in Islamic law.) The ordinances added adultery and fornication as new criminal offences under Pakistani law, and new punishments of whipping, amputation and stoning to death, for theft and robbery. The ordinance punished *zina* (extramarital sex) with flogging for unmarried offenders, and stoning to death for the married. At the time of writing, the Modi government in India has yet to enact ordinances of this extreme nature, but the harassment of women in bars, the persecution of 'love jihadis' (Muslim men who form relationships with Hindu women), the threats to those who wear short skirts, and the lynching of Dalits and Muslims presumed to be eating beef carries on every day. Houses are bulldozed as retribution. Muslim students disappear from campuses, and many of those who support them gag themselves. Hinduvta's moral code may not yet have become part of the constitution, but it is part of India's everyday life.

Am I alone in noticing these common trends, these infinite mirrors?

3

The State in South Asia:
A Biography

The first time I heard the phrase 'the state', I was sitting in the winter sunshine under a *langra* mango tree,[1] a curious child chatting with her father's old friend.

Amar Raha had spent years in an Indian prison for 'waging war against the state'. He had, for his pains, taken a bullet in the chest, and this ached in the winter. After his release, Amar would come and stay with us every year during Delhi's (then) crisp winter months, when the sky was blue and the monsoon had washed leaves clean; when the aroma of roasted peanuts wafted on the breeze.

The phrase 'the state' bemused me. What was it, where was it? How could one 'wage war' against something that one could not see? 'After independence?' I asked. 'You mean you shot at Chacha (Uncle) Nehru?'[2]

He chuckled as he told me the story – chuckled until he coughed. I was about seven years old then. I did not get the joke. (I was a rather literal-minded little girl.) He replied no, he hadn't shot at Nehru. Amar was then a wizened man, his raven-black hair swept off a high furrowed brow; bespectacled, with the largest, thickest, black plastic frames I had ever seen. (They would probably be fashionable now.)

He had once been young, he told me. He had held up Dumdum, Calcutta's only airport, with a handgun. And he had shot a policeman who had fired back at him. (Guffaws between each unbelievable sentence.)

Meanwhile, another of my dad's pals had attacked the Jessops armoury, hoping its workers would rise up. They did. They went further than the two revolutionaries thought they would, throwing its white manager into the furnace.

Each of these facts sounded implausible; still I persisted. An airport and policemen are 'the state'? What's a British man's factory got to do with it? I badgered Amar to explain it to me. He had gained a law degree while a convict, so he gave me a vague, legalistic-yet-Marxist idea of what it meant. I pestered him with questions. Dusk had fallen before he stopped trying.

Now I think that the clues to their idea of the state lay in what the two young men tried to capture: ordnance, an armoury, strategic infrastructure, state force. For them, the state was a violent assemblage whose interconnections they could not see, but could sense. It was, like its British predecessor, a mélange of coercive practices – some subtle, some blatant – designed to keep the powerful protected and the poor powerless.

Rather young, I had taken on board the notion that this shadowy phenomenon mattered a great deal.

Another incident some years later confounded the picture I had gleaned from Amar's story and his attempts to explain it.

In the mid-1980s, I travelled by train on a tour of southern India with a group of friends. We were innocents, city-bred, of the generation that didn't oil its hair. Late at night as we dozed on wooden berths, the train jolted to an abrupt stop. Peering out of barred windows, we could make out the ghostly shapes of the Chambal valley, its red ravines the mythical heart of dacoit country. The carriage doors swung open. Half a dozen extravagantly moustachioed men, wearing the long shirts and turbans typical of those parts, entered. They made eye contact with no one and said not a word. They carried the muskets and bayonets of an older era of warfare, belts studded with cartridges strapped round their torsos. A few strode up and down the carriage, others guarded the doors. Not one of us dared move. About twenty minutes later, they got off the train as silently and suddenly as they had entered it. This was on a mainline service from Delhi to Bangalore in the Republic of India, almost four decades after independence.

By this time I had learned Max Weber's pithy definition of the state – as an entity that claims the monopoly of the legitimate use of physical force within a given territory – but it did not seem to apply to South Asia.

I would go on to discover that the colonial state in India did not have that legitimacy. Nor did it have a monopoly over violence, ever, in its history.

The Raj's post-colonial successors also struggled, in the twentieth century, to impose their writ over many parts of the land within their borders. Their hold over their subjects was never as firm as they wished it to be, and although their legitimacy may have been more widely accepted, it was challenged right from the get-go. The successor states tried, but failed, to establish a monopoly over the use of force. They unleashed greater degrees of violence, with more urgency, over some parts (and people) of the subcontinent.

But trying to control people is one thing; succeeding is another.

Getting one's head around the causes of this predicament is crucial to understanding the state in South Asia, in both its colonial and postcolonial guises. And to grasp South Asia's politics, which are animated by a yearning to capture the state and force it to turn this way or that, making sense of the states of the region is vital.

Over the long twentieth century, the state has struggled – with varying degrees of energy – to tackle different tasks: to maintain its sovereign powers, support large armies, 'know' the people and govern them, and to raise revenue to pay for all this.

In their post-colonial guise, the states of South Asia also struggled to deliver development, to 'modernise' the economy, and feed, clothe and educate their people. Some of these goals still remain to be achieved, or have been quietly binned.

The question often asked, by the late twentieth century, was: were these weak states or strong ones? My answer would be that it depended on where you poked them. If insurgents challenged their physical unity and integrity, they could jump on them from a great height, all guns blazing. If there was a 'crisis of governability', you might get a spell of dictatorship Emergency-style in India, or a stretch of vigorous military rule in Pakistan or Bangladesh.[3] Yet low-grade chaos and lawlessness – whether within the family or neighbourhood, in large estates in the countryside, or on the long coasts where smugglers flourished, or in the stalking lands of the banditti – officials had little time (or stomach) to deal with. The independent states of South Asia tolerated a remarkable degree of disorder in matters that their leaders regarded as being peripheral to their core purposes. They also presided over growing scales of violence, provided that their targets were women, Dalits, minorities or party enemies (depending on the state).

The state, then, has focused on what it needed to do for its physical survival (and the survival of those who ran the *Sarkar*). Let us not forget: this was a bureaucracy and an army that succeeded in partitioning themselves, and also the colonial state's assets, while transporting and sorting the tsunami of refugees. This had been a matter of survival, and whatever the individual human cost, at their birth in 1947, both India and Pakistan performed rather well as 'states'. (Or so it seemed to the western world, which wanted nothing to do with this particular refugee crisis.)

Yet on all other matters deemed to be of low priority, they were ineffectual, indeed disinterested. A young wife in a working-class neighbourhood (whom I met in Delhi in 1990) was thrashed half to death, gagged and tied up with the goats. When begged to intercede, the policeman of the *basti* (slum) just giggled. Deep wells of cynicism about 'the *pablik*' flourish within 'the state', not least among its police. (The '*pablik*', in turn, have learned to expect little by way of protection from the police.)

If the Indian state's impotence in the face of such crimes says much about its limitations, it is also revealing about the extent to which late-colonial 'customs of governance' persisted despite independence.[4]

A striking feature of the colonial state in South Asia was its patchy coverage. Parts of the subcontinent were barely touched by British rule and, after decolonisation in 1947, new nation states tried (often in vain) to penetrate regions that had remained beyond the reach of the Raj.[5] Some of the challenges were geographical: in the wet, hilly jungle tracts of north-east India, and the dry, rocky uplands of the North West Frontier, on the border of Afghanistan. This unevenness was in part a legacy of the Mughal empire, itself a medley of different layers and idioms of authority. It was never ironed out by company or crown. In the seventeenth century the Dutch merchant Francisco Pelsaert described Mughal emperor Jahangir as 'the king of the plains and open roads only', a vivid phrase that alludes to the limits of Mughal sovereignty.[6] The Great Mughal did not seek to be, and knew he could not be, the sole source of authority in the land.

The difference was that the Raj believed in a notion of singular, uniform, total sovereignty. British rule would never achieve this.

To be sure, from its uncertain beginnings as a trading company, the British Indian state gradually grew more powerful and ambitious than its predecessor had ever been; and by 1947, many mountains, valleys, scrublands and forests were under its sway. Its *hukum* (command), whether by stealth or by fiat, had changed the fortunes, ways of life and even the identities of many of its subjects.[7] It was a far stronger state than its predecessor had been. Even so, in 1947 when the Union Jack came down, its grip over large parts of the subcontinent remained uncertain. There was not just the matter of the third of its territory that remained under 'indirect rule' in princely states, although this was significant: the largest of these states retained power and fealty over their subjects. But huge tracts within British India still remained only under a facsimile of control. The paradoxical combination of a violent state with a soft underbelly, a laissez-faire attitude to 'traditional' social crimes, legal and administrative incoherence, are crucial elements of the state's biography. Its inability to raise revenues beyond a certain limit is also of huge significance, as is the fact that Indians paid every rupee and anna of those revenues. What this meant in practice, and in politics, is also significant.

Again, to what extent have South Asia's post-colonial states been able to break the mould? Again, I suggest that it depends on where you poke them.

How do such states work? What does such a *Sarkar* mean for the governed, and how do they experience or imagine it? This chapter will try to shed some light on these fascinating, but challenging, questions.

I

SOVEREIGNTY: A MONOPOLY
OVER THE MEANS OF FORCE?

Bear with me while we take a brief glance back to the East India Company state, which governed India until the Rebellion of 1857. We must, because the state in South Asia is like a mille-feuille, its layers so many relics of different regimes. That, one might argue, is part of the problem.

A trading company working at first with Mughal sanction, the East India Company had expanded tentatively, and then more bullishly, into dominion. In the eighteenth century, as Mughal authority had waned outside its north Indian heartland, the Company – in a pattern not dissimilar from its Portuguese and French counterparts – had established toeholds on the water's margin in Calcutta, Madras and

Bombay. Eighteenth-century India, beyond the Mughal heartland, was a patchwork of 'successor' kingdoms large and small, with European outposts on the seaboard of a land-based empire.[8] In contrast to previous conquerors and marauders who had swept into the Gangetic plains through the mountain passes of the north-west, the companies of the West arrived in India by sea. This may be why the Mughal court did not, at first, regard them as a threat.

The Company first got drawn into Indian politics at London's behest: French moves in South India were a driving geopolitical factor. Its involvement in the principalities of Bengal around Fort Saint William was in part energised by wealthy Indian merchants keen to trade with it. The Company also began to recruit an army – the Bengal Army – attracting growing numbers of 'native' infantrymen, high-status *sipahis* (sepoys). It trained this army in modern European fighting techniques. It was soon able to challenge nawabs and rajas who stood in the way of free trade.[9]

At this stage, the East India Company had little appetite to govern. It farmed out the work of tax collection in its *parganas* (Mughal units of administration) to Indian entrepreneurs, some of whom became millionaires even as Bengal went into devastating famine. But the Napoleonic wars, and the increasing value of Bengal as a base from which to trade eastwards with China, led to the Company's expansion from a minor regional player to a formidable rival for dominion over India.

Richard Wellesley, governor-general of India from 1798 to 1805, exemplified the Company's new aggressive imperialism. Wellesley's circle argued for Britain's right to India by conquest. They pushed to topple rival polities, and strove to disarm India. Controlled violence enabled them to conquer much of India, but taking away weapons from all its inhabitants? The Company never achieved this goal.

One reason is that it lacked the power and depth as a state. The Indian states that the British Indian Army fought were often strong and legitimate. Some were also prosperous enough to support standing armies; they were not easy to topple. In the eighteenth century, India's economy was in many respects as buoyant as that of Britain, its technology on a par with Europe's, and several of its armies just as resilient, having been trained in European warfare methods by the French.[10] It took no fewer than four major wars (and crafty diplomatic alliances with his enemies) for the East India Company to best Tipu Sultan of Mysore.[11]

'Tippoo's Tiger', today in the Victoria & Albert Museum, evokes the ferocity of these battles. It also reveals, in Tipu's time, a different perspective on the relative balance of power between East and West than the one we now take for granted. This stunning creation is an almost life-sized wooden automaton of a tiger mauling a prostrate European. A key turns an organ hidden in the tiger's body, and as it does so, the European raises his arms and emits the screams of a man in his death throes. Tipu Sultan, by all accounts a courageous, brilliant and vengeful enemy, surely turned that key many times.

The 'pacification' of India – conquest by another name – continued under Wellesley's successors. The Company's bosses at Leadenhall Street in London wanted this expansion to stop. Nonetheless, the Company in India continued to pick off Mughal tributary states one by one. 'The Company state' was an aggregation of such smaller polities. But each of these tributary states was different. Although most adopted Mughlai courtly etiquette and diplomatic norms, they had in fact distinctive regional idioms and modes of rule.[12]

With each conquest, then, the East India Company was making a bigger problem for its successor – the British Raj – whose goal would be to become a tidy, bureaucratic state. With London and Calcutta pulling in different directions, 'men on the spot' serving the Company went ahead with more annexations. A case that best illuminates this is Lord Napier's conquest of all of Sind, when his instructions were limited to putting down a revolt among a few hostile tribes. Having asked for no permission, he made no apology after conquering the entire vast territory. He just sent his superior a (rather superior) one-word message: '*Peccavi*' (Latin: 'I have sinned').

These campaigns created unforeseen problems. The Company (and later the Raj) had to set up institutions to govern and tax these domains, and that was not the work of a day. It proved not to be the work of decades. Often it was easier simply to allow previous systems to continue with only cosmetic changes. Since the path of least resistance is often deemed to be the most prudent, this was often the path 'men on the spot' chose.[13]

So kings lost their heads or were exiled for life. (The 'last Mughal' lived out his declining years in exile in Burma.) But old institutions, old elites and dominant castes maintained their authority. Family patriarchs continued to run their households with an iron fist (see Chapter 5). In an age of reform, the British remained squeamish about interfering in matters of religion; and post-Mutiny, Queen Victoria's proclamation of 1858 pledged that the Raj would not interfere in this domain. Both the East India Company and the Raj were reluctant to intervene in the domestic sphere. By 1856, Thomas Babington Macaulay had codified Hindu and Muslim 'personal law'; but the codes sought to reflect the status quo, not to contest it, so there was never a plan to go about trying to reform households to give women more rights,[14] or to free men and women from servitude.[15]

The Company state (and indeed the Raj) was not a zealous reformer, imperial cant notwithstanding. It could never have been one because it lacked the force to drive through reforms or alienate the powers-that-were in South Asia.

(This is not the same as saying that empire did not change India. It did, without always intending to. More of this below.)

One challenge, however, the British could not ignore. What was to be done about all the soldiers of disbanded armies? Having lost their paymasters, these freebooters rejoined the vast pool of Indian military labour.[16] Peasant soldiers in the main, these bands of 'part peasant, part watchmen, part bandit or cattle thief' now had few Indian rulers left to serve.[17] *Kallars* (thieves) in Tamil country, likewise, were former cultivators who turned to plunder in the extreme instability of the times.

A commercial enterprise no longer deriving profit from its trading monopolies in an era of free trade, the East India Company, meanwhile, was retrenching its own armies to bring down costs.[18] The British state in India always lived precariously. It was never flush with cash, its mantra being that empire in the East should cost the British taxpayer nothing. So it could not afford to absorb all these (laid-off) part-time soldiers into its own army. Disgruntled former warriors began to raid areas now under British control; an early instance of British policy aggravating a problem it was designed to solve.

In the mid-nineteenth century, quelling the 'troublesome' *poligars* (chiefs of the regions around Madurai) became a preoccupation for the Company in South India.[19] It ran down many *poligars*, hanged some and exiled others. In 1849 the Sikh empire, consolidated and led by Ranjit Singh, fell. The one-eyed raja had been a skilful commander and statesman; during his lifetime, his empire was strong enough to keep both the Afghans and the British at bay. But Ranjit Singh died in 1839. A decade after his death, the Company's Bengal Army conquered Punjab. The Koh-i-Noor diamond – the 'mountain of light', one of the world's oldest, largest and most brilliant diamonds – disappeared from the possession of Ranjit's heir Dalip Singh, emerging in London as a 'gift' to Queen Victoria. The story behind this 'gift' is as fascinating as it is murky.[20] Yet it stands as a glittering symbol of a new vision of Britain's sovereignty over India that had, by this time, emerged: empire by subjugation, a rule of absolute power.

But even as India was subdued, the problem of bandits raised its head in another form, or at least under a new name: *thuggee*. In 1839 Captain William Henry Sleeman (1788–1856), an accomplished self-publicist, took credit for supressing the murderous Thuggee Secret Society. Thugs, so he claimed, were a 'caste' spread right across India with their own special language. In a self-congratulatory account, *The Thugs or Phansigars* [Stranglers] *of India, Comprising a History of that Extraordinary Fraternity of Assassins*, Sleeman maintained that these highwaymen robbed groups of travellers, suffocating and strangling their victims: 'villains as subtle, rapacious, and cruel as any who are to be met in the records of human depravity'.[21] Legend – much of it manufactured by Sleeman and popularised by his fans – has it that Sleeman disbanded the Thuggee Secret Society by penetrating it and deploying the thug 'approvers' who fell into his hands.

Sleeman's account is a classic example of the colonial state's will to dominate India failing in the face of social realities it could not fathom, except through the prism of its own distorting categories.

I do not claim that bandits were a figment of Sleeman's fevered imagination, or a spectre thrown up by Britain's drive for 'colonial knowledge'.[22] The point is rather that India's new rulers got it wrong about who these brigands were and why they became more (rather than less) active after the British had deposed the rulers in whose armies they had served. Increasingly they now morphed into dispersed and resilient gangs bound by quasi-religious codes, resolved to hang on to their arms and their way of life. (There was no all-India bandit 'caste', despite Sleeman's claims. 'Caste' did not work that way, as Chapter 6 shows.) Just as states 'encouraged sedentary agriculture for its "easy pickings"', so too did the raiders regard rural villages as attractive places, both to plunder and to lend their protection.[23] They refused to accept the *hukum* of a faraway British sovereign who, from their angle of vision, stole property in much the same way as they did.[24]

The East India Company did not, and could not, disarm, disband, or in any way hinder the great majority of dacoits. Its forces were spread too thin.

And then came the moment of truth: the Mutiny and Rebellion of 1857, in which disenchanted landlords, all manner of supporters of deposed rulers, Indians put off by missionaries, and soldiers of the Bengal Army rose up against the Company. The ferocious war (for we must call it that) ended the Company's reign over India.

In that confrontation, the Company turned on its enemies all guns blazing. It took no hostages. It was determined to hold on to India by fair means or foul. (The rebels, too, fought with everything they could muster.)

After 1857, one thing was clear. Force was the base on which British rule rested. But it had to use violence sparingly. It could never again afford to alienate 'rural notables' and 'landowning classes'. It had, if anything, to win them over.

After the Mutiny, moreover, a nervous British Raj felt it had to reform its army straight away. It is easy to see why. Hitherto the army had been made up largely of men drafted from the Bhojpuri-speaking areas in the neighbourhood of Lucknow, the seat of the Nawab of Oudh. These soldiers, famed for their fighting skills, now had to be turfed out of it, given their role in the uprising. Horrified by the way in which Indian soldiers had – 'all of a sudden' – turned round and killed white officers, the Peel Commission decided that white officers must never again be left isolated in a sea of brown sepoys. (It was not 'all of a sudden', in fact. The signs of disgruntlement had been there for a while, had they been able to recognise them for what they were.) The officers must have white 'other ranks' to support them. It recommended that a garrison of 80,000 British soldiers be stationed at all times in India; and that Britons never be outnumbered by two to one Indians in the north (and three to one in the south, where the rebellion had caught up fewer in its fury).

By 1905, there were 78,379 white soldiers garrisoned in India to 150,410 Indian ones.[25]

The army now became a huge burden on India's resources, since expensive white 'Tommies', imported to India like the pale ale they loved to drink, had to be paid almost ten times more than Indians in the imperial scheme of things.[26] From first to last the army was the single most burdensome outlay of the imperial state. The Raj spent thirty to forty per cent of its total yield from taxation on its standing army, 220,000 strong in peacetime. Its officers, until 1919, were all British.

Under the Raj, the army's use changed. Parliament now took decisions over the big strategic issues of the day. London's view was that the job of the Indian Army was not only to control India; it was also to be put at the service of an expanding British Empire. It thus became available for wherever the British needed it, whether to conquer new lands, or to hold on to older ones.

Nonetheless, the problem of controlling India still haunted those responsible for it in Calcutta. After 1857, therefore, recruitment policy underwent a radical change. The Raj took care to recruit Indian sepoys from regions and social groups (particularly the Punjab) which either had been loyal during the Mutiny, or had taken no part in it at all. It would replace mutinous Bhojpuri recruits with 'martial races', who had proved loyal (or neutral) towards the British during the Mutiny, and were also 'good fighting men'. (It never did succeed in ridding the army of all Bhojpuris, however. They remained about fifteen per cent of the reformed army.) 'Good fighting men' from Ranjit Singh's Punjab, of all faiths and creeds, were prime recruits. Mountain dwellers – Pathans from the North West Frontier, Dogras from Kashmir, Gurkhas from Nepal and Garhwalis from the Himalayan hills in the United Provinces – also fitted this bill. They were less educated and 'insulated' from politics, or so officials believed. They now formed the core fighting forces.

To a degree, this system worked. The fourteen mutinies between 1886 and 1930 were minor affairs involving only a handful of men. Half occurred abroad, or when the troops were about to depart for a new destination overseas and were restive about where they were being sent. The most significant was in Singapore, in February and March of 1915. Half the battalion of the 5th Light Indian Infantry, mostly East Punjabi Muslims, responded violently to the rumour that they were going to be sent next to the Middle East to fight the Ottomans, guardians of the Holy Places of Islam. (This was linked to Khilafatist ideas already in circulation. The army was not insulated from politics.) Another was in 1930, when two platoons of Garhwali soldiers in Peshawar refused orders to fire on Indian protestors at the height of the civil disobedience movement. (Ditto.)

By and large, though, the sepoys did their job. A court of enquiry in 1938 found that the most common reasons that sepoys gave for murdering officers – which happened on and off – were disputes over promotion or caste, inter-district feeling, bullying, abuse or sodomy.[27] Despite their privation, there were no mutinies of any note until 1942, when thousands of prisoners of war in Malaya, Singapore and Burma joined the Japanese as an Indian National Army (INA) under Netaji (honoured leader) Subhas Chandra Bose to fight the British. It achieved little, but the mutineers and their leader Netaji – who disappeared, and is thought to have died in a plane crash – live on in the hearts of many South Asian patriots. The British made an ill-advised decision to hold a public trial of the 'INA accused' at Delhi's Red Fort (a powerful symbol, harking back to a time of Indian glory and British wanton destruction). The men became instant heroes. One Hindu, one Muslim and one Sikh, led by a Bengali, they seemed to belong to the whole subcontinent. The participants in the INA uprising in the streets of Calcutta demanding the release of all the INA rebels who had been jailed, were just as mixed by faith; and for a few weeks, in late 1945, it seemed that communal animosity was held at bay.[28] It was not, sadly. But their sacrifice in the nation's cause still stirs public imagination across borders in South Asia. There are some who still believe that Netaji will one day return.

From the point of view of state power, however, the INA got nowhere, and the British, while losing control over Burma, managed to keep the Japanese forces out of India.

So, of all the structures of brute force supporting the late-colonial state, the post-Mutiny army was the most solid.

Nonetheless it would be a mistake to overlook the fissures and cracks within it. There were the 'little mutinies' I have mentioned – significant in hindsight given the role of mutinous soldiers in South Asia's politics after independence.

During the First World War, concerns about army loyalty became more serious, when ill-clothed, ill-shod and ill-equipped Indians were sent out to fight in Ypres, Flanders, Gallipoli and the Somme. Those who survived these killing fields could not be shielded from politics of a new and revolutionary kind brewing in German prisoner-of-war camps, where the potential for subversion was enormous.[29] There they learned, in the aphoristic words of Sib Singh, a Sikh peasant from Amritsar, about the frailties of empire:

> The Angrez [Englishman] is *badshah* [Emperor] in India and we did not know there were other *badshahs* [elsewhere]. When the War began we heard of several *badshahs*. One flaw in India is that people are without *ilm* [knowledge] ...[30]

Returning from the front, soldiers brought this *ilm* (knowledge) to the villages and towns of upper India, as well as other 'seditious' ideas. The 'martial races' were in danger of being transformed into *Homo politicus*. This was a danger for the British and they knew it, spending many resources in the following years tamping down sedition.

Another worrying problem was that with 'Indianisation' of the army during the Great War, discrepancies of approach divided Indian officers in senior ranks from their British counterparts. The former were expected to report to British superiors when trouble was brewing among the men (sepoys), but often they did not. Imperial military logic demanded that sepoy insubordination, once discovered, be dealt with by rounding up ringleaders and punishing them with spectacular harshness – shooting dead during wartime, or transportation (sometimes for life) during interludes of peace. Yet it was not always easy to pick out the 'inciters' or 'instigators' from the rest. One colonel wrote to his superiors that in his mutinous regiment 'there were virtually no ringleaders'. Facing severe censure for this admission, he was told that he should have made an example of some men 'even if no ringleaders actually existed'. Or else he should have arrested native officers for failing to report imminent disturbance, and for not showing 'that good example and submission to discipline which was to be expected from them'.[31]

The native officer became a vulnerable part of the system: not being quite of it, he risked being arrested for being a brown man if brown men in his regiment broke discipline. Where did his loyalties lie, then? With the regiment, the Raj or the nation? Biographies and studies suggest that first generations of Indian officers stuck together, forming strong bonds with each other. This suggests a certain aloofness from white officers. Forms of patriotism began to emerge among them that, it appears, were akin to nationalism. The army was not an island.

One might have expected that with the abrupt and enormous expansion of the army during the Second World War – from about

220,000 men during peacetime to almost 2.5 million men at its peak – the bias towards 'martial races' became impossible to sustain.[32] To make up these numbers, the British had to look beyond the 'martial' recruiting grounds, and bring greater diversity to the army.[33]

But the change was more at the hugely expanded base than at the top.

As one scholar has shown, it was not so easy to dislodge the British generals' long-cherished ideas about who were 'martial races' and who were not. Instead, during the Second World War, just as in the First World War, the British Indian Army operated a two-tier system.

During the First World War, by various means amounting to press-ganging, the army had managed (by its own admission) to have raised about 850,000 'good fighting men' from its usual recruiting grounds over four years under the 'voluntary' system.

As Major General George Molesworth later admitted: 'We did not spread our net very much wider than the '"martial classes", but we drained those to the last drop. . . . In other words we exhausted Fortnum and Mason, without tapping Marks and Spencer or Woolworths to any great degree. I believe that under any system, excluding Gurkhas, that remains (850,000) India's figure for really good troops.'[34]

The problem, during the Second World War, was that in the process of dragging every packet off the shelves of Fortnum & Mason, the army's dependence on the Punjab grew rather than declined. This would prove to be of crucial importance to both India and Pakistan after independence.

Meanwhile, non-martial groups from regions beyond the army's old hunting grounds provided only twenty-four per cent of all recruits during the war. Newcomers from new regions did little or no frontline fighting, which was reserved for tried and tested ('martial') troops. Instead they were assigned auxiliary and support roles as 'hewers of wood and drawers of water'.[35]

Bengal was the source of only seven per cent of the vast war army.[36] Bengal was the front: it was from Bengal that the army fought the war against Japan in Burma and the Bay of Bengal. This lack of involvement of Bengalis in the war was all the more striking given that Bengal was also the largest province in British India.

India emerged from the war with a slightly more diverse army, but it remained an army of the masses and the classes.

It also remained dominated by British officers until the last.[37]

With partition and independence came sudden and shocking changes to the character of the army, on both sides of the Radcliffe Line.

At a stroke, the British Indian Army had to divide itself between the two newborn countries.

This took place in a context of extreme violence in which units of the armed forces were implicated – standing by to watch, or even participating in, some of the most shocking incidents of brutality.

After this, in India as in Pakistan, leaders believed that the state had to wield force to protect the people from themselves, and from each other.[38]

At this juncture, Nehru and Liaquat Ali Khan, the prime ministers of India and Pakistan, thought it wise to allow Muslim regiments based in Pakistani areas to accompany refugees to Pakistan, and Hindu and Sikh units based in India to protect refugees moving towards India.

This decision had a huge impact on the minority question in both countries, as discussed in Chapter 2. It also shaped these two partitioned armies. Religious affiliation tended to determine which units went where in 1947. Sikh, Punjabi Hindu, Dogra and Garhwali 'martial' soldiers (and units) went to India, and (Hindu Nepalese) Gurkha regiments continued to serve it; whereas Punjabi Muslim and Pathan troops (and whole units) went to Pakistan. Individual soldiers had the right to opt for one country or the other. Except for the regiments based in Madras, which remained mixed, the Indian Army became essentially a 'Hindu and Sikh' army, of whose proportion Muslims remined at most 1.5 per cent,[39] whereas the Pakistan Army became a Punjabi-Muslim dominated army, afforced by Pathans.

This legacy of partition differed, in another crucial respect, in the two new states. Pakistan inherited most of divided Punjab and Bengal, respectively the most and least represented regions in the lopsided British Indian Army. It therefore ended up, at its birth, with a huge imbalance of state force (and military force at that) in its western wing. One province – Punjab, with twenty-five per cent of the population – 'now had 72 per cent of the army', whereas East Bengal, which represented fifty-five per cent of Pakistan's population, ended up with 'basically no representation in the army'.[40]

India, by contrast, inherited small parts of Punjab and Bengal, so inherited an army that was far less Punjabi-dominated. West Bengal's tiny contribution to it was less shocking when placed in the context of other tiny provinces. (West Bengal emerged from partition as India's smallest province.)[41]

India got lucky, in this respect at least. Very lucky, in fact, because it did not have the resources to recruit more soldiers from other regions, or make any major military reforms. The Indian Army already took up almost fifty per cent of its annual budget, after the division of the spoils of independence with Pakistan.[42] Remember that fifty per cent. There was only so much India could do with the other half, but it is significant that Nehru's government chose to keep this skewed balance.

But it tried to keep the army out of politics – no easy task since Nehru's government called the army in twice in the first years of independence, in Kashmir and Hyderabad, in short order.

India was lucky in other ways too. It inherited not only the legal identity, but also most of the 'hard power' of the British imperial state. Most army cantonments, barracks, ordnance factories and prisons remained in Indian territory. Of the forty-six pre-partition military training units, India inherited thirty-nine. Unlike Pakistan, it faced no shortages of officers. The army's officer corps had been slowly but surely Indianised since the early twentieth century.[43] Given the exigencies of the hour, it was impossible to reorganise the army to make it less reliant on Punjabi and other 'martial' soldiers, as Nehru wished to do, but he 'pushed back strongly in 1948 when regional leaders demanded that new regiments be created to represent their regions or communities'.[44] Advised by the brilliant bureaucrat H. M. Patel (who oversaw partition) and his successor M. K. Vellodi, he moved fast to 'coup-proof' the civilian government.

On taking office, Nehru occupied the mansion of the former commander-in-chief of the armed forces. This was not out of self-aggrandisement, as some have suggested: it was a symbol of the army's diminished place in India.

He downgraded the role of commander-in-chief to 'chief of army staff', and placed it on a par with the heads of India's much smaller navy and air force, encouraging (deliberately perhaps) inter-service rivalries. (Pakistan's Inter-Services Intelligence agency had the same structure, but did not achieve the same outcome.) Between 1947 and Nehru's death in 1964, only one chief of army staff was from the

Punjab. Nehru and the Defence Ministry kept a close eye on the senior generals, limiting their tenure and retiring them in their prime. Nehru's government allegedly snooped on them. When they retired, he often sent them on diplomatic assignments that took them far away from India's shores: he packed off General K. Cariappa (a bit of a star) as high commissioner to Australia, General J. N. Chaudhuri as high commissioner to Canada, and General K. Thimayya to a UN peacekeeping role in Cyprus. Nuclear capacity was kept strictly out of the hands of the army, leading to a divided structure of command.

Scholars agree that although these measures protected Indian democracy, they weakened it as a military power.[45]

In India, civilian leaders since Nehru thus ringfenced the armed forces, keeping them as far from politics as possible. Only one Indian officer had seen frontline service before partition, so after the British were sent home and British officers departed, there were weaknesses at the top. These gaps were filled by the recruitment of under-represented groups in the 1950s and 60s. Field Marshal Sam Manekshaw, a Parsi, was an iconic figure, whose name still resonates through the ages. General Chaudhuri, who led Operation Polo in Hyderabad and became its military governor from 1948 to 1949, was a Bengali Hindu from an 'upper caste' – a group that was under-represented in the army and likely to complain about it. One might argue that India replaced its lost British officers with eye-catching appointments that signalled that the Indian state did not favour any region (at a time of heightened regional feeling).

Perhaps this helps to explain why – despite its inability to drive through major reforms in its army – there has been no Indian equivalent of General Ayub, or General Zia-ul-Huq, or General Zia-ur Rahman, all of whom seized the state from the grasp of civilian politicians.

Nor would there be, as far as we know, as much siphoning off of public resources into a parallel economy. (As far as we know. These things are not easy to know.) In India there has been rumoured corruption in military procurement on a grand scale: the Bofors howitzer 'kickbacks' scandal being the best known, which resulted in the fall of the Rajiv Gandhi-led Congress government in 1989 – but it was likely neither the first nor the last instance of corruption. (A whistleblower in the Swedish police first leaked the news of the scale of the

Bofors kickbacks. India's dynamic investigative journalists knew nothing about it. These things, I repeat, are hard even to get a whiff of.) Another aspect of India's state capacity is the army's rule of *omerta*, or code of silence. It has blindsided historians just as much as it has stymied the media.

Nonetheless, I think it is safe to say that no phenomenon appeared in India equivalent to 'Milbus' (the military's business activities) in Pakistan, where the armed forces have emerged as big players in the private economy.[46]

One scholar suggests that the armed forces in Pakistan – usually acting through welfare organisations for veterans – have diverted significant, but undisclosed, assets towards the personal benefit of their members and retirees. Companies set up by, or acting on behalf of, 'the boots' (that is, the Pakistan Army) have bought land banks, indeed a mini empire's worth of prime property in neighbourhoods called 'Defence' (in Lahore) or 'Naval' (in Karachi), and built elite private housing societies. 'Civvies' (civilians) can buy or rent in these areas, but at rates far more expensive than elsewhere in the city. Those seeking security sometimes feel that they must pay these rents to protect their children against the lawlessness of Karachi.[47] The state fails to address routine disorder, and then private companies (run and owned by military men) step in, as businessmen, to exploit the insecurity of citizens.[48]

Soon after General Zia seized power in 1977, private organisations run by (often retired) army brass took over the huge business of bus cargo transport, the construction of roads and bridges (and charging tolls to use them) as well as rail cargo transport. By the mid-1980s, the army veterans' Fauji Fund (Soldiers' Fund) had private stakes in the strategic sector of oil and gas, with significant chunks of shares in the Pak Stanvac Petroleum Project and the Oil and Gas Corporation Ltd. Likewise, the Army Welfare Trust invested in sugar mills, rice ginning, oil mills, fish farms, bicycle manufacturing and hosiery. If that is not enough to boggle the mind, the Pakistan Rangers (the country's border security force) took control of fishing in the province of Sind.

The philosophy guiding this army-isation of Pakistan's business sector is that senior personnel in the armed forces have fabulous managerial experience. They can therefore run these vital businesses far more efficiently than mere civvies. That they do so is not a problem, in their view: it is a solution to the failings of civilian-run enterprises.

(For a sense of military contempt for civilians, read Mohammed Hanif's *A Case of Exploding Mangoes*.)

Since Zia's death, the army (and indeed Pakistan's much smaller navy and air force) has extended itself far further as a commercial actor. As a consequence, not only has the army accrued more power, but its senior members are better rewarded (by themselves).

Even during interludes without overt military rule, in the late 1980s and 90s, democracy has functioned only when the ISI – the shadowy Inter-Services Intelligence – allowed it to do so. The ISI, founded in 1948 by a British major general during the Kashmir War (of which more in the Epilogue), approached its role through the lens of 'threat perception' and covert intelligence. Since 1972 it has been headed by three-star generals of the army, navy and air force. Its budget is classified information. Its remit includes both internal and international security. Imagine it then, to be rather like the CIA and the FBI combined in terms of its power and sphere of action, with far weaker executive and judicial checks upon it.

In their turn, democratically elected governments by the end of the century have kowtowed to the ISI to keep it, however briefly, on side.

Bangladesh, for its part, was forged by a nation-at-arms, by the dispersed Mukti Bahini, as much as by the Awami League party. The role of force in that country's development has been discussed in Chapter 2. Let me just point out here that its army – composed in the main of Mukti Bahini fighters persuaded to join a structured force – has been the most challenging in terms of its civil–military balance. From the Mukti Bahini's standpoint, to speak of such a distinction made little sense. They were a vigilante force *of* society, and *for* society, protecting it from the depredations of the Pakistan Army. They were war heroes, patriots, martyrs. Whether in the state's official army or outside it, they had as much stake in the nation's direction as anyone else, if not more. If Bangladesh's army has been rambunctious and mutinous, it should not surprise us. It is just that the world has ignored Bangladesh, while keeping India and Pakistan in the blazing glare of light.

In this respect India and Pakistan (and then Bangladesh) turned out differently. We all know that. India's love affair with democracy has been noted and celebrated; Pakistan's failure to build a vibrant democracy has been held up as the defining difference between the neighbours. This divergence has dominated the discussion about the two countries to the extent that it has obscured all else.

This discussion is stuck, like a needle in a vinyl record of the last century. It does not take into account that these differences were born with the two partitions, and that the fault lines lay in the respective hands of cards they were dealt with the division of the British Indian Army in 1947.

Further, given how great the contrast is on this front, the remarkable parallels in their deployment of their armies have been missed, underplayed or denied outright.

Neither India nor Pakistan, after independence, used their considerable armies on behalf of Britain's global empire. Both countries stopped (at the same time) putting their armies at the service of the British Commonwealth, leaving the British chastened and disappointed. Where they have been drawn into proxy wars on their frontiers, realpolitik has spurred both countries on. (The war in Afghanistan was as much in Pakistan's perceived self-interests as those of the United States; India's brief war in what was to become Bangladesh was fuelled by Indira Gandhi's assessment of the refugee crisis. The less-known and less-understood Indian engagement in Sri Lanka – which led to the assassination of Rajiv Gandhi – was a response to the impact on India of the war against Tamils in Jaffna.)

Both India and Pakistan contribute, rather listlessly, to the UN's peacekeeping force.

There is a second common factor, and this is of great significance. India and Pakistan have both unleashed their armies upon 'their own people' every time there has been a whiff of 'secession'. India used its army to occupy Nagaland on the eve of independence (1947), in Kashmir (1947–8), to crush Hyderabad (1948–50), and to 'deal with' the Mizo uprising (1966). Sikh demands for an independent state of Khalistan turned violent in the 1970s, the numbers of hapless victims grew, and then a new kind of force came after them, the 'Supercop' K. P. S. Gill, who became a novel type of policeman who specialised in giving his enemy no quarter (and no law. This type of 'encounter cop' is now the ideal. More of this to come). Yet when the Khalistani leader Jarnail Singh Bhindranwale took shelter with his arms and supporters in the Golden Temple, the army followed him in there, and mowed down him and his supporters in Operation Blue Star (1984). In the 1990s, once again, there was the Kashmir intifada (as some have described it), and since then, the army and the Border Security Force (a twin of the Pakistan Rangers) have managed widespread discontent with varying degrees of threat, coercion, persuasion and violence.

On Pakistan's side of the border, concerns about secession from the nation prompt 'the boots' to show up pronto, and in full force. By 1948, East Bengal and Balochistan, two very large provinces, were already making demands that Pakistan's leaders were determined to resist. Both were remote frontier areas, from Karachi's perspective. That East Bengal constituted the majority of the new nation's population was hard to digest, as were its implications. It took, therefore, just a hint of secession for General Ayub to reach, metaphorically, for his gun.

The language movement of 1948 was asking for the inclusion of Bengali as one of the official languages. In 1966, all Sheikh Mujib was asking for was more autonomy and more resources for East Bengal. When Cyclone Bhola struck East Pakistan in November 1970, killing about half a million people in the region, all that activists wanted was more (and prompter) relief from the government. Each of these was read as a more threatening demand.

After the 1970 elections, which Mujib's Awami League won hands down, anxiety levels in Islamabad (the new capital) rose. Mujib gave a speech in Dacca that was rousing, but stopped short of demanding immediate independence from Pakistan. Pakistan reacted as if he had, throwing him into prison in West Pakistan. The crackdown began. The Pakistani army had been told what to do. Perhaps it went beyond its brief. The result was a gruesome bloodbath and the birth of Bangladesh.

The Baloch situation, although less well known than Bangladesh or Kashmir, has been an open wound since 1948. Formerly the princely state of Kalat (just as with Hyderabad in India), it was unwilling to secede to Pakistan. Insurgents began to resist incorporation into Pakistan in 1948 (another parallel with Hyderabad). The large dry state shares a long border with Shia Iran, and this made Pakistani forces – army and civilian – nervous.[49] This huge territory, and the long history to hold it, has simmered ever since, sometimes boiling over into open warfare. The discovery of raw minerals in this largely arid terrain upped the ante for the Pakistani state. Tying Balochistan to Pakistan, and crushing the insurgency (which remains ongoing) has been the work of many arms of state force: the Pakistan Army, the paramilitary forces, the ISI, and even the Balochistan Police.

Pakistan has thus been willing to expend all its considerable armed power against Baloch and Bengali 'secessionist' insurgents and all those who support them. India's approach has been no different. Perhaps partition's end game over the Radcliffe Line made both countries react in such a disproportionate way when talk of changing borders has come up.

By contrast, neither state had full control of its very long borders elsewhere, whether on land or at sea, and during the twentieth century neither seemed much concerned to impose it. (There was a limit, after all, to the number of men and munitions at their disposal, and where they could be deployed. The state's perspective was to throw power at its top priorities.) It has been strangely fragile on other frontiers, particularly in the north-west and north-east, and at sea. In the north-west, now known as the Af-Pak frontier, stretches of steep rocky terrain make for hard fighting conditions (as the British found in the four Afghan wars between 1839 and 1919; the Afghans regaining in the later wars what they had ceded to the British in the first).[50] Delineated borders such as the Durand Line of 1896 were observed more in the breach than in reality, and neither Pakistan nor Afghanistan accepts the frontier to this day.[51] It remains porous, particularly in Pakistan's northern zones: Khyber-Pakhtunkhwa, Swat and North Waziristan.

As for British India's north-eastern boundary, it was just as difficult to control. Hill tribes mounted an almost continuous barrage of raids against the plains which the British were unable to stop: a low-grade war that continued until and long after 1947.[52] Before 1947, rifles were being smuggled across that border into India. Even after the British settled 'villages' where none had existed before and appointed hand-picked 'chiefs' to govern them, the chiefs soon became enemies of the state. They became authors of the narrative of the powerful 'Jumma' movement (which later would demand recognition and a degree of autonomy) in Bangladesh.[53]

The 4,096-kilometre border between India and Bangladesh remains porous, despite India's stop–start effort to seal sections of it.[54] These things are hard to document (the files are closed to scholars) but journalistic observation suggests that both frontiers were still conduits for gun-running into India in the 1980s.

Along the mountainous frontier with Tibet, the state – colonial and post-colonial alike – hardly had a presence at all. Trade and travel continued unchecked across the notional borderlines, and Lhasa (in Tibet) continued to exercise more influence over the mobile inhabitants of these Himalayan regions than Itanagar, in India. Nepal had an open border with India until 2000, and its soldiers still fight in the Indian Army.

After independence, in the mountainous zones where it faced China, India's 'state presence had feet of clay'.[55]

Maritime borders, to the best of our knowledge, remained as porous for India (and Bangladesh) as they had done under British rule until 1947, if not more so. The Arabian Sea coast is notorious for smuggling (whether guns, explosives or drugs) by sea, as is the dangerous Arakan coast in the Bay of Bengal. Bombay's dock area, just as Calcutta's, remained under the writ of mafias.[56] With its small navy and its rather casual approach to its coastline, India did little to stop this. It certainly did not prioritise it. Which is why, perhaps, the young men who attacked Bombay in a spate of suicide killings across four days in 2008 – memorably at the Taj Hotel, whose attack was screened live on TV – were able to enter (indeed chose to enter) India by sea.

It took special forces flown in from god-knows-where to end the killing spree at the Taj. The regular cops were not up to it.

Policing

In contrast to all this kerfuffle about the armed forces – and here lies the rub – policing was thin on the ground. In the colonial era, as one might expect, at the top were British police officers, well educated and well rewarded, but they were about one per cent of the force at the provincial level. This 'thin blue line' was razor-thin everywhere, and it had very little white in it. At the bottom, in the countryside as in the city, the force was entirely Indian. It included very poor people seeking a route out of destitution. The gulf between 'state authority' and society was huge – differences in race, language, class, education, attitude and habit divided top-ranking (white) police officers from 'native' subordinates in the force.

In broad swathes of the countryside, about eighty-five per cent of the area under British rule, the imperial state depended upon *chaukidaars* or watchmen, who ran around for the state on their bare cracked feet. These humble men were supposed to be the state's eyes and ears in all the subcontinent's villages.

The imperial state did not pay them a salary, despite the many bets they covered in the countryside. A *chaukidaari* tax raised by local Indian elites was supposed to pay for them. Often these elites chose not to pay the tax for months, claiming hardship, and village servants survived on the verge of starvation. They were brown servants of the Raj, but their 'low-caste' and menial status (and unpaid arrears) often pitted them against their Indian neighbours.[57]

Even the police, supposedly the buttress of state sovereignty when the peace was threatened, were not as strong a force as one might think. While the army lived apart in cantonments some distance from towns and cities, and were visible only to populations deemed recalcitrant, the police force was the face of state power on the ground. In particular, it was the humble constable whom subjects encountered: most people in large villages, small towns or cities had seen at least one. The extent to which the constable figured in the public imaginary of state power (and Hindi cinema's imagined publics) is seen in the larger-than-life presence of constables in the movies, from the cult classic *Deewaar* ('The Wall', 1975) to *Mumbai Meri Jaan* ('Mumbai My Life', 2008). In the former, the constable gleams with idealism. In the latter, he is jaded, but wise. A significant number of 'hits' depicted a bright-eyed, bushy-tailed constable, a young man of valour, honesty and courage. He usually is clever too, having come 'first class first' in some exam or the other. He is shown to be studying hard.

At the start of the twentieth century, however, less than thirty per cent of Bengal's constables were literate, despite 'training'. In the Punjab, the figure was lower still, at twenty per cent.[58]

British officers spoke of recruits for the Bengal constabulary as 'freshly emerging from farms and jungles'. One of them described the 'gibberish sounds' he heard during drill:

> For example: 'Billing sthop giring grong' were words I had never yet encountered, and 'comenshe laf pot' were equally foreign to my ears ...
> My companion had, however, noticed my bewilderment and guessing the cause, explained that Drill Instructors, being often illiterate men, learnt their Drill by rote, and the strange words I had heard were intended to represent 'Balance step gaining ground,' 'commence left foot.'[59]

Frustrated officers reported that the men lacked the ability to identify suspicious characters or events. Recruited from the same social groups as millhands fleeing hunger in the countryside, paid only a few annas more (and sometimes less), the constables of colonial India worked in harsh conditions: often with only a *laathi* or bamboo stick to protect them against the forces of darkness. In 1919, a representative year, almost fifty-five per cent of the Bengal constabulary was admitted to hospital.[60]

In British times, the South Asian policeman earned too little to eat well, or dress for the weather. They were weak of body, and morale was low. This is significant, since each constable represented the strength, or weakness, of the state's grip over society.

The British Indian police force was based on the model of the Irish constabulary, with modifications appropriate to the conditions and budgetary constraints of India. Most constables in India did not carry weapons. But a small elite was always armed and kept in reserve as a paramilitary force whose role it was to escort bullion and prisoners and quell local disturbances. (When more serious trouble broke out, the army was called in.)[61] For 'political' tasks, the British again used men from particular groups deemed 'martial' and 'loyal', drawn from outside the troubled region, since officials felt it would be unwise to ask Indians to beat up co-religionists or neighbours. This much the Mutiny had taught them. It was not enough, though. There were simply not enough 'shoes on the ground'.

All too often, isolated and unarmed constables were overwhelmed, facing brickbats from crowds who were enraged with the *Sarkar* they represented. In one incident notorious in the annals of Indian history, protesting crowds in Chauri Chaura burned twenty-two constables alive for attempting to block a procession. But it represents only one of hundreds of thousands of situations in which police power proved fragile, and policemen vulnerable.

It is therefore no surprise that desertion rates in the constabulary were high, despite the prevailing wisdom that South Asians will sell their grandmothers for a government job.[62] In 1862–3, one in ten constables in Madras resigned or deserted.[63] In 1919, of 20,736 policemen in Bengal classified as men (as opposed to officers), 1,170 resigned and 343 deserted.[64]

Even if most constables stuck with their jobs for the prestige (often bound up with caste; working for the state had more status than labouring in mills), they were not always content. Ramanand Tiwari (1909–80) was one such youth. Born into a poor peasant family in

Bhojpur in north India, he had survived from the age of ten by doing odd jobs, joining the Bihar police as a constable in 1930. In an interview, Tiwari (who later became a socialist leader) spoke of the life-changing incident that drew him to politics. In December 1936, Tiwari and another constable, on an errand to the house of the British deputy superintendent of police (DSP), found the DSP sahib was out, and was not expected to return until later that night. So he and his friend huddled on the floor of the verandah, using a greatcoat as a blanket in the cold, eventually falling asleep. Tiwari awoke after midnight:

> I got up to pee. I felt let me see how our Sahib sleeps (he had arrived by then). I saw that Sahib and Memsahib were sleeping in a large bed. They were sleeping above a cotton-filled mattress and under a cotton-filled quilt. Then, as I turned around, I saw that there were two black dogs sleeping on a mattress, under a mosquito net. I was stumped. I was surprised to see that a dog's life could be this comfortable and happy ... Humans like me have lives that are worse than the dog's.[65]

This experience drove him to the politics of protest. From the 1920s onwards, constables began to resort to collective action to demand that the state redress their grievances. In Calcutta, they deployed, again and again, the tactic of the threatened strike to demand better conditions, more rations and higher wages. Anonymous letters and mysterious pamphlets would circulate announcing a grand city-wide police strike on a particular date if their demands were not met. Alarmed, the British would announce concessions. On the day itself, nothing unusual would happen; work would continue as normal.[66] The threat of trouble was a stark reminder that constables represented the shaky realities of colonial rule on the ground.[67]

But just as the state itself, its lowly agents were vulnerable. As hostility to the Raj grew, police authority attracted hatred among a population who saw them as the nailed fist of the state. Vilified by the nationalist press for their venality and collusion with colonial overlords, they were very exposed. In their khaki and blue uniforms, they were the physical symbol of the state's authority.[68] They instilled fear and loathing in the general public; but their weakness revealed, and continues to reveal, the true limits of the everyday state's power in its South Asian setting.[69]

There remains little understanding of the extent to which the colonial state relied on informers to do its policing.[70] These people were a bit like *chaukidaars* – not of the state, but acting as its eyes and ears for modest pecuniary gain. My years of research in the police archives in Calcutta left me dumbfounded about the extent to which informers spied on subjects (and later, on citizens). Letters to suspects were opened, text copied and translated, and envelopes resealed and posted on. The police maintained files on everyone who was deemed politically active, in any way whatsoever, and watched them until they died, it seems: files opened in the 1940s were still open in the 1980s. This required a vast network of informers spread through Calcutta (and every other city, and rural district). In Calcutta, informers' names were never shown on files. Each had a number. The size of the network is suggested by the fact that in the files I looked at, an individual informer's number was not in the hundreds or thousands, but in *lakhs* (100,000s).

This looked great on paper, however grubby the files. They provided an unambiguous sign of continuity between the colonial state and its successor – the same files on the same people were still 'live', fifty years after independence. They included prominent nationalists. The police, through informers, watched the Raj's enemies before independence and its leaders after it, as well as socialists, communists, refugees, student activists, intellectuals – all sorts.

The difficulty, for both, lay in the quality of that information. It was currency. Informers gave their information for money, so they had to say something interesting about a suspect. They were thus prone to exaggerating, claiming to have been eyewitnesses when they relied on hearsay, or even brazen invention.[71] The state's vision, thus, was blurred, and even occluded, by its reliance on this form of knowledge.

How much changed after independence? In terms of structure, rather little until 1977, in India where, after the Emergency, an enquiry into police brutality led to some change.[72]

Police stations had begun to be built in the districts at the start of the twentieth century, with more added in fits and starts, with interruption during the world wars and partition. These were squat, humble structures of brick and cement, unornamented, with only a lime wash. Furnished with an *almirah* (cupboard), a couple of tables and chairs, and two hurricane lanterns, they had little colonial pomp about them. A sign in English and the vernacular hung outside each station house.

Each, on average, kept an eye on 150 square miles.[73] For most people in the subcontinent, the station was the only face of state power that they (knowingly) encountered. The coppers had *laathis*, and wielded them. They represented sovereign violence.

It was a bit of a show, however. One scholar has argued that the police tried to optimise their capacity by deploying their knowledge of habitual offenders, 'criminal' and 'bad' castes.[74] (This knowledge was dodgy, of which more below, so it was an odd form of optimisation.) They protected the wealthy from these 'criminal elements'. That was their version of 'the peace'.

This situation did not change much with independence, as independent India concentrated more on bringing telephones to existing stations than on building new ones in the countryside. That said, there was more recruitment. By 1960, the number of policemen per square mile had almost doubled.

Yet elite Indian Police Service (IPS) cadres still hovered far above the constable rank, just as in the old days. Although the old racial divide was gone, a yawning chasm of caste, wealth, connections, language competence (in English) and elite education distanced the new DSP (deputy superintendent of police) sahibs and their ilk from constables and *their* ilk. The anthropologist Beatrice Jauregui, who studied policing at different levels in the sprawling Indian province of Uttar Pradesh in the 2000s, writes that senior officers admitted that they had no idea how 'the system' worked on the ground. They advised her that she would be better off hanging out with constables at a local station in the districts. Which she did.

What she discovered there was just how provisional and contingent their authority was.[75] In every situation, police authority had an indeterminate quality. In some situations, local powers (landlords, crime lords, or moneybags) could use their 'pull' or influence to neuter the constable, or give him a cut of their take. In other situations, the police constables might catch someone without power or pull committing an offence, and either demand a bribe to let him go or drag him to the *thaanaa* (police station) and, if the 'offender' couldn't pay up, thrash the living daylights out of him. Let's not look away from the violence of policing. As with everything in South Asia, the unlettered poor with no clout and nil influence experienced – and continue to experience – the worst brutality.

Take the story of Murugan, who has sold *dosas* (flatbread) in

Bombay for more than twenty years. Aged sixteen, he ran away from home with a few hundred rupees in his pocket. His plan was to sell snacks on trains, and then to set up a stall on a railway platform in Bombay. He had no idea that vending in public places was illegal. He learned the hard way that space on platforms, as in all public places in India, could be made available with the help of a nexus of municipal workers, politicians, hoods and cops. To set up and run his stall, Murugan had to pay protection money (*hafta*) every week.[76] I can't say how much of that money ended up in the pocket of the local constable, and how much went to other, more powerful players in the *hafta* racket. But I suspect the cop's slice of the pie was not huge.[77]

For these reasons, policing in South Asia even at the end of the twentieth century had a 'now-you-see-it, now-you-don't' quality about it.

Unless you understood the social context, its outcomes were incomprehensible. Even to the DSP sahib in his air-conditioned office in Lucknow.

The constables remained vulnerable to *pablik* retribution in the 1990s, even after more had been armed after the crises of the 1970s and 80s. After a little incident, for instance, involving a minor car accident at the High Court, lawyers in black robes attacked constables and chased them through the streets of Lucknow.[78]

The records suggest that corruption in the police was endemic in the colonial era; cynics insist that it grew worse after independence. There is smoke behind this fire. Yet I have never encountered it in person, and I don't think I have led a particularly sheltered life. I have seen constables beating beggars; slapping 'vagrants' and 'lunatics' ('moving these people on' is a legacy from colonial times). I have challenged them, only to be threatened with arrest. Constables have beaten me up for taking part in demonstrations. During the first Iraq War, a burly woman constable wearing purple lipstick threw me into a truck after giving me a few hard thwacks with her *laathi*. I've spent a night in a stinking cell. (No doubt there is a small file on me in Delhi, full of informers' half-truths, fantasies and approximations.) But no one has ever asked me for, nor have I offered, *chaai paani* (a bribe).

In the late 1990s, I encountered the police every day, for months on end. I was the only scholar working in the Special Branch intelligence headquarters in Lord Sinha Road in Calcutta, a colonial-era building with high ceilings, stuccoed walls and heavy shutters. The dear friend of a dear friend – a DSP sahib no less – facilitated my access to this

Aladdin's cave. (He also did so because he himself was of a scholarly bent and approved of the tenor of my published work. DSP sahibs are often rather erudite men and women.) Its walls were lined with ugly open-shelved steel *almirahs* full of grubby files. The cabin they found for me to sit in was tiny, no more than eight foot square. A fan hung from a long pole, stirring the humid air like soup. The cobwebs were so thick I could not see the ceiling. No one had disturbed the spiders since the British had left: what was the point? I sat there for months taking notes, returning day after day. (That's when I noticed all those informers.) But never once did the constables who brought me files ask me for an explanation, let alone for a bribe. They looked at me with narrowed eyes, wondering what this strange young woman was doing, but they delivered the files I asked for at once. In no other archive or government office in South Asia (or indeed the world) have I encountered such efficiency.

An introduction from a friend to the DSP worked far better, you see, than *chaai paani* to the constable on the frontline. The latter had few powers. The DSP sahib was a 'big man', and may have been angered by the assumption that he could be bought.

A lot hinges on where you poke the state.

The urban rumour is that constables take bribes from lovers in the park holding hands and waiting for the dark. A British-era law banning 'unnatural' sex remained on the statute book until the end of the century in all three countries, and this meant that queer people were particularly vulnerable to police predation. (I use the term 'queer' to cover all forms of sexuality and gender identity that the Act would have outlawed, had lawmakers been aware enough to know of them.)

The venal and violent policeman exists then, but his most defenceless victims are those who have broken some rule, regulation or by-law and who cannot intimidate him in return with their own connections. ('Don't you know who I am? My father is the DSP,' would be a great line, almost as good as 'My mother is the Prime Minister.') People deploy their social standing and connections to threaten humble *havildaars* (policemen). Social hierarchy bumps up with state structure to render the latter near toothless.

Don't get me wrong – I am not claiming that the constables don't take their cut. I am pointing out that there are structural constraints on their ability to 'eat bribes'. (*Ghoos khana*, the Hindustani term for taking bribes, describes it as an act of eating.) A growing number of scholars maintain that the rumour of corruption (and 'anti-corruption talk') is more pervasive than the phenomenon itself.[79] I believe they are right.

The police remained the face of the everyday state until the end of the twentieth century. The lure of the uniform was still substantial, but the reality behind it was still poor pay, hard nights alone on the beat in extreme weather, long spells in hospital, and a fear of 'the people' they were expected to control.[80] They remained vastly outnumbered when faced with agitated crowds. As the mood against British rule grew ugly, they became symbols of colonial violence.

During popular uprisings after independence, crowds singled them out for punishment. They still do: in India, charging the police barricade is still the most common form of political escalation. The cops' tendency, then as now, has been to look away, or to lock up the 'ringleaders' for a night. A nice punishment they thought up in the face of protests in the 1980s and 90s was to round up activists, load them into police buses and drive them to the middle of nowhere far from the city, leaving them to walk the long way home, and reflect on their folly. A form of saying 'stop wasting our time'. It did not work.

Let's return to the matter of the monopoly of the use of force.

By the 1970s and 80s, Naxals and Khalistanis had procured guns in large numbers, but by the 1990s, gun ownership was not limited to those fighting political causes, meeting force with force (as they saw it). By then, it had spread far wider. The gun had become – in India at least – the must-have accessory for the mafias. It had also become the latest toy for the rich kid who had it all. Liberalisation boosted the number of such brats beyond counting.

Nothing highlights this more than the shooting of Jessica Lall in 1999, at a bar at Hauz Khas Village (right next to my home, as it happens). The victim served drinks at the bar. The assailant – an entitled young man from a VIP family – wanted drinks after last orders. She declined to serve him, and held her ground. He shot her dead.

What happened next is interesting. The first trial acquitted the assailant, the police claiming not to have found sufficient evidence. (The family had 'pull', plenty of it.) The *pablik* was outraged. They sided with Jessica – a single young woman who modelled, working on her own late at night in a bar. (That in itself was extraordinary.) The assailant could hardly have been better connected. He went down for murder in a retrial, nonetheless. (How come? Was it because the owner of the bar was a person of clout too? We will never know. The file is still closed under the Official Secrets Act, and there will be no answers for a long time to come.)

Such shootings became frequent after that. Pointless killings. Tired hardworking men collecting tolls at highways were shot dead by impatient braggadocios who couldn't bear to queue, or perhaps just couldn't accept that they should pay like everyone else. Did anything much happen? Not clear. It appears only where the *pablik* – driven by 24-hour news coverage – got invested in a case that much seemed to happen.[81] Then suddenly the wheels of the judiciary, which otherwise took years to act, moved fast. (Or relatively fast. Let's not get carried away. The Indian judiciary has often checked the executive; in that role, it has done a fine job, whereas Pakistan's judiciary has been more hamstrung.[82] But the wheels of justice have moved so slowly, that 'justice denied' doesn't begin to capture the scale of the problem. People fear court, because they fear losing their lives to court cases.)

As for the everyday, no one asks. I have lived in Hauz Khas Village since the 1980s, with long stretches in Cambridge. Our house is yards away from where Jessica Lall was shot. My youngest brother, a tearaway since he was a toddler, by 1999 cut a dashing figure about town. He knew Jessica well. One might expect the police to have dropped round to ask him questions. No one ever did.

Now you see it, now you don't.

One didn't see it, at first, when 'encounter cops' emerged as a special (perhaps self-selected) group of sharp shooters in India. One heard of 'encounters' in which *dreadedterrorists* (pronounced as a single word in Hinglish) died in an encounter with the police in, say, an ambush. When enough of these encounters had taken place, people began to ask questions. Why were so many happening? It was impossible to know all the details but journalists began to investigate. Were these encounters actually murders of suspects in cold blood? It turns out that they were. We now know a lot more, since these lawless cops boast about their crimes and have Wikipedia pages. At the time of writing, Pradeep Sharma of Bombay currently holds the record, having killed, at the latest count, 312 people. This seems an unlikely role for this migrant from Uttar Pradesh, son of a professor of English, but he seems to relish it. In 2014, he was celebrated in Marathi cinema in the film *Rege*. The English-language media describe him as Bombay's

'Dirty Harry'. His work is an open secret and has political and popular support.

This is, of course, evidence of the lawlessness of the Indian state. The judiciary, for its part, has again and again turned a blind eye, letting Mr Sharma walk free, because his team (as with other encounter cops) is careful to destroy the evidence. (*Class of '83*, a 2020 feature film about their emergence and modes of operation – you might want to watch it.)

This kind of violence, in India, tends to be meted out to (usually Muslim) bosses of the underworld, Maoists and Muslim or Sikh *dreadedterrorists*.[83] But unarmed dissidents of other stripes, as well as poachers, are also targets.

What, you might ask, of the brigands?

The *daakus* (bandits) remained alive, well and active after independence. Along the 'inner frontier' in the Chambal valley, British India had never been under the command of its rulers.[84] Following an established habit of rule, neither post-colonial state did much at all when the problem of dacoity persisted after independence.

In 1952, independent India repealed the Criminal Tribes Act. In theory the new Habitual Offenders Act ended the categorisation of people as criminal tribes, but in practice, policing on the ground changed remarkably little.[85]

In 1969, while shooting the film *Pakeezah*, the crew, director and the legendary film star Meena Kumari ran out of petrol in Madhya Pradesh in central India, in the heart of dacoit country. Around midnight, sure enough, a dozen armed men surrounded their convoy of cars. They almost came to a sticky end until the dacoit chief – a Meena Kumari fan – learned that the actor was in one of the cars. He organised food, music and dancing for his honoured guests, and found a place for them to sleep. He even sent out his minions to fetch petrol for his new friends.[86]

Indeed, *daakus* are the theme of one of the most popular Bollywood films of all time, the dacoit-western *Sholay* ('Embers'). Made in 1975, its anti-hero, the *daaku* Gabbar Singh, is one of Bombay cinema's best-loved, most-remembered characters. In one grisly scene, Gabbar hacks off both arms of the policeman whose mission was to capture him: a metaphor, perhaps, for the limits of state capacity. In another such allusion, the policeman recruits two 'habitual criminals' to catch Gabbar and his gang, and they succeed where the state failed.

Of course, *Sholay* is not a mirror of its times, but millions of Indian viewers instantly grabbed its themes, despite the novelty of its genre. Small boys, including my youngest (later dashing) brother, memorised Gabbar's dialogue word for word. Aged five, he would growl, Gabbar-style: '*Kitne aadmi thhe?*' and '*Arre o Sambha!*' ('How many men were there?' and 'Hey you, Sambha!') – the whole scene, which includes some of the most celebrated lines in Hindi cinema's history.[87] To brush up my Hindi, which was not up to scratch when I went to boarding school aged nine, our supply teacher narrated every unfolding scene of *Sholay* (discussed in Chapter 7). I still remember whole glorious chunks of it.

In 1981, Phoolan Devi, a woman *daaku* leader (of whom more in Chapter 5) wreaked bloody revenge on the twenty-two men who had gang-raped her. In the 1980s, a government of Uttar Pradesh persuaded some to give up their arms, but in the 1990s, dacoit gangs still roamed the badlands of India and Pakistan.[88]

Meanwhile, 'habitual offenders' continue to practise the cattle theft which so irritated the British.

In the 2000s, the anthropologist Anastasia Piliavsky spent sixteen months in a village of Kanjars, a former 'notified criminal tribe'. Far from denying their fearsome reputation, Piliavsky's respondent boasted of it. Piliavsky writes:

> One conversation with my Kanjar host, whom I will call Gopal, went like this:
>
> AP: Is there anyone in this village who can tell me about Kanjar history?
>
> Gopal: Yes, I can tell you all about it myself! We, Kanjars, are a very old caste.
>
> AP: What kind of work did your people do in the past?
>
> Gopal: Thieving (*gaimi*) is our old vocation, [emphatically] we are old-time thieves. I am a thief and my father and my grandfather's grandfather were all thieves.
>
> AP: But don't people of other castes steal as well? Say, if I went now and stole some sugar from your wife's shop, wouldn't I also be a thief?
>
> Gopal: Naturally, people of all castes may steal, but they are all new players who know nothing about the thieving business. They steal in the daytime and they get caught. They are never good thieves because theft is not their *khandān* (caste business/heredity), it is not

in their blood. The youngest of our boys are better thieves than
these jokers.

AP: How is it that Kanjars are so much better at stealing than others?

Gopal: [laughing] Don't you understand? How can I explain this to
you? Look, you know the old cobbler who sits in the bazaar? He is
an old man. He is blind and deaf and you know that when we go to
him, I have to shout into his ear so he can hear me. But when he
makes shoes, they shine. You and I could not make shoes like that.
Shoemaking is in the old man's blood. The cobblers have their own
knowledge. This is why they make excellent shoes. It is this way
with us, Kanjars. Everyone knows that we are a caste of thieves and
we have our Mother's [Goddess'] special blessing.

Piliavsky continues:

If their neighbours dwelt on how low, lewd, and dangerous Kanjars
were, Kanjars themselves stressed their strength, valour and wit . . . In
the sixteen months I spent in their encampment, few nights passed
without at least one gang venturing on a thieving trip. Every night,
stolen goats and rams were brought to the camp and, because I lived
with a gang leader, every night I ate meat.[89]

What Piliavsky translates as thieving, I would describe as cattle
theft. It has elements of older banditry in it; it's just that itinerants
have been forced, by the Indian government, to settle in villages,
shrinking the perimeters of some of their hunting grounds, and changing what they do to earn their livelihoods.

The wife, after all, sells sugar – she does not steal it. History has
ushered in changes, be they hard to discern.

II

AN IMPERIAL BUREAUCRACY

After the last shots had been fired and Indian rebels punished (some
fired out of cannons to make sure the point was driven home), India
came under the Crown-in-Parliament. A key result of this was that the
country came directly under London's paw, and had to be seen to
serve its interests.

London had long wanted an end to annexations in India. After 1857, therefore, there were no further conquests. A third of the land-mass of South Asia, and a quarter of her people, remained outside British formal control, under 'native princes' and 'princesses'. (These names, too, did scant justice to the myriad kinds of sovereignty they exercised within their domains under the oversight of 'Residents'.)

The Raj tried to bring these 'princes' on side by restoring their priv-ileges and by inviting them to royal *durbaars* held with much ceremony in 1887, 1903 and 1911 – an 'invented tradition' if there ever was one. Each was more splendid than the one before it. They were kitsch affairs at which the Empire bestowed upon the princes, *begums* and *ranisahebas* (queens) – in a strict hierarchy – titles, gun salutes and other paraphernalia of the British system of honours adapted for an Indian colonial setting. The guns misfired. If anything, the system encouraged resentment against the Raj. Disagreements about jurisdic-tion led to continual conflict. The case of an English felon in Travancore became a landmark case, in which both Travancore and the Raj claimed the right to try to punish him. The British won that round, but by the 1920s many princes were dissatisfied with the British sys-tem, which was patronising and replete with the potential for offence. They felt little compunction about letting their irritation show.[90]

In 1947, over 550 states of this kind survived. Like the rest of Brit-ish India, they varied in the extreme. The largest, Hyderabad, was about half the size of France and boasted seventeen million subjects in the mid-twentieth century;[91] the smallest was less than one square mile with a population of about 200.[92] They interacted with the Raj in very different ways. Some, such as Hyderabad, had treaty relations with the East India Company and the Raj, and the Nizam of Hyderabad – the richest man in the world – was jealous of the priv-ileges this entailed. Others, like Tipu Sultan's Mysore, had been conquered, but ruled by a Hindu dynasty the British had 'restored' to the throne. Several were small fiefdoms, *zamindaaris* by another name. They were all informally ruled, but in certain states the British Resi-dent was intrusive and domineering, whereas in others he played the relationship with a lighter touch.

In the late nineteenth century, the differences between the princely states and British India were so marked that nationalists, including Gandhi, described the states as 'Indian India'. As historians are com-ing to recognise, in the twentieth century, many states subverted

British authority in subtle ways, using religious ceremonies to enhance their authority within their kingdoms.[93] Several princes financed anti-colonial nationalists and revolutionaries.[94] The states also represented actual limits to British jurisdiction. Indians fleeing British justice – whether criminals or revolutionaries – could simply slip into a princely state and shelter there.[95]

The princely states are often thought to have represented a major bulwark to the British Raj. In fact they represented a subtle challenge to its *hukum*.

But there were other swingeing changes. Long critical of the East India Company, Parliament now stripped away its role in governance. Eager to change the tone and style of British rule in India, Queen Victoria promised her Indian subjects a new deal.[96] The Queen's 'charter' of 1858 assured Indians that there would be no interference in their faith, and they would have as much right to progress in her service as all her other subjects. The era of imperial subjecthood had, apparently, dawned. A new top-down, autocratic but responsive bureaucracy was to govern India, headed by the Secretary of State in London to which it would report. The viceroy and his council in Calcutta represented the apex of the Raj in India.

The structure of the new state was meant to be a break with the past. It was to have the clear bold lines of a pyramid. The Secretary of State for India in London was its apex, the viceroy in India reported to him. Governors or lieutenant governors ran each province and reported to the viceroy. Divisional commissioners reported, in turn, to them. The new state's all-white officialdom dominated the top of the pyramid. Indians were an overwhelming majority at the many layers of the pyramid the closer it got to the base.

At the heart of the Raj was that figure of imperial nostalgia – the district officer. He represented the state's authority on the ground. His role was to remain in touch with the people, to understand them and their concerns. He was to tour 'his' district on horseback, talk to (invariably male) village elders and headmen, settle disputes and report back any signs of discontent to his superiors. He was to be their *maai-baap* (their mother and father – a role the Raj fondly imagined it could occupy).

The Rebellion, which had caught a complacent army and civil administration by surprise, had provoked an information panic, and the district officer was to be one means to rectify that failure.[97] He was to sniff out the first hint of discontent against rule by the *firang-hee* (foreigner).

Other modes of knowledge-gathering would soon proliferate: censuses, gazetteers, surveys and district histories. As 'colonial knowledge' weighed down shelf upon shelf in government offices, it produced the illusion that the state knew everything that was knowable about India. An army of officers and clerks had measured and surveyed every square mile of arable land, counted people in decennial censuses, having noted their myriad religions, races, castes and tribes, languages, customs, festivals, fairs and modes of livelihood.[98] These might be rather special, as for 'criminal tribes'. Some Indians had distinct qualities that made them, as a group, apparently 'unreliable'. Bengalis would find themselves in this category, and learn also that they were 'effeminate' and 'lazy'. Others needed watch and ward, because of their unique 'addiction to crime'. Still others had the qualities of 'good, fighting men' and became typecast as 'martial races'. These were ways of seeing India that reassured the Raj that its actions were based on a wealth of knowledge.

They in fact produced cookie-cutter stereotypes. Moreover, because the British would have failed in these recondite enterprises without the help of Brahmins, they were skewed in a certain direction.[99] 'Lower castes' were (congenital) bad sorts. 'Upper castes', above all Brahmins, were models of rectitude.

The Punjabis were not one 'race', as the British would discover to their amazement in 1947, when they tore Punjab apart. Bengali men were not all effeminate and lazy – they are a mixed bag of people with a mixed bag of proclivities. Some of the greatest men in South Asia's great wrestling tradition (of which more in Chapter 7) have been Bengalis. They have been farmers, bankers, traders, poets, merchants, clerks, servants, retainers, artisans and of course hardworking girls, wives and widows – women who held up half the sky.

Despite being armed with its 'knowledge', the Raj remained anxious and fearful. It was fractured and divided about policy. It sometimes acted with authoritative arrogance, but typically it was tentative, seeking to unpick as little as possible of the social fabric of Indian society.[100] There would be a few ambitious interventions, particularly building railways in a drive for security after the Great Rebellion; the tracks would also connect modern sectors of the economy to the hinterlands from which they recruited labour and sourced cash crops. Canals were another grand design to irrigate dry land and raise more revenue. But these projects were the exception, not the rule.

After 1857, the colonial state wanted to work with the grain of Indian tradition, which it struggled hard (and usually failed) to identify. It did not wish to work against it. Colonial rule, after 1857, was even more conservative than it had been in the times of the East India Company.

Yet it got much wrong. More changes to tradition flowed from these low-key non-interventions than from large-scale actions from above.

The deceptively simple process of asking Indians who they were for the purpose of counting them ('What is your religion? What is your caste? What is your language?') transformed the ways in which religious, caste and regional identities emerged and came to express themselves, and became major forces shaping the politics of the twentieth century.[101] At the start of the twentieth century, an individual so interrogated might feel a close affinity only with members of his or her local sect or *jati* (sub-caste), so might wish to answer, for instance: 'My ancestors are Mustalli Dawoodi Bohras.' Given the option of describing himself as either Hindu, Muslim, Sikh, Parsi or Christian, he would have had no choice but to opt for Muslim, despite the fact he was not even understood as a Twelver by most Shias. (It is not so simple, you see. The term 'Muslim' was a construct.) The census rubbed away this granularity and forced people into large communal categories that, a century ago, had little meaning. (Likewise, the fact that most Indians were bilingual would have been lost in censuses that allowed one person only one language.)

So in fact, although officials thought the knowledge-gathering operations to be unintrusive, they proved to have serious ramifications.

Meanwhile, grandiose projects to develop India were often disasters. The much-vaunted Canal Colonies in the Punjab, created by diverting and connecting the five tributaries of the river Indus (from which India derives it name), in an attempt to build a new Jerusalem in the scrub, came to nothing. In 1946 when Malcolm Darling, the maverick ICS officer and expert on the Punjab, visited the Canal Colonies, he discovered to his horror the scale of this fiasco. In village after village, he heard the same stories, of waterlogging, salination, leprosy, malaria, hunger.[102] One of the great 'achievements' of British rule was condemned by its own officers as a monumental failure.

If the Great Mughal's sovereignty had been limited to the high roads and plains, *Pax Britannica* was more like a threadbare eiderdown; it covered up vast zones into which the state, for all its drum-beating, dared not venture.[103] The efforts to rationalise its administration notwithstanding, heterogeneity, unevenness and incoherence remained essential features of British India. The state acted, all too often, like a delusional and drunken giant, staggering about, quick to take umbrage and lash out at the slightest offence, always wanting more tax even where there was no one to pay it, refusing to hear what its own officials were reporting if the facts were inconvenient, always preferring to believe that the nub of the problem was that 'corrupt Indian intermediaries' were misleading upright, incorruptible British officers.

So who were these upright British officers? And who were the 'corrupt native intermediaries' on whom they relied? In 1922 Lloyd George described the Indian Civil Service – the thousand or so British bureaucrats who ran the Indian empire – as the 'steel frame' of the whole structure. 'Their every word is a command, every sentence a decree, accepted by the people, accepted willingly with trust in their judgement and fairness which might be the pride of our race.'[104]

This purple prose bore little resemblance to the relationship between the ICS and the Indians they encountered. Yet this tiny cadre was the most powerful official force in the British Empire, if not the whole world – each officer (spread across about 250 districts) by the late nineteenth century governing on average 300,000 subjects.[105] It was also the best paid. Officers started at about £400 a year and ended their careers at over £2,000; annual pensions after retirement gave them £1,000 a year. The high flyers among them could expect to earn large additional allowances.[106] This was at a time when the per capita income of South Asians was between Rs 20 and Rs 30 (depending on whose figures you believe), a shocking £2 or £3 a year.

In theory, 'the ICS directed all the activities of the Anglo-Indian state.' Also in theory, 'they collected the revenue, allocated rights in land, relieved famine, improved agriculture, built public works, supressed revolts, drafted laws, investigated crimes, judged lawsuits, inspected municipalities, schools, hospitals and cooperatives.' The list is endless, and one historian suggests that 'the long lines of petitioners, choking their verandahs and waiting patiently outside their tents, paid tribute to their power'.[107] The foundations of the 'steel frame' rested on the district officer who had both judicial and executive functions. He collected taxes, punished offenders, maintained order and upheld the 'law'.

But this was the theory. Practice on the ground was very different: 'civilians' had to negotiate unfamiliar terrain and subtle forms of resistance. For one thing, Anglo-Indian law was a slippery beast. It was influenced by Henry Sumner Maine's historical, case-by-case approach; but this gave no clear guidance to a harried district officer faced with a huge number of cases to settle. Furthermore, Macaulay had divided it into two parts: criminal law (which applied equally to all) and civil law (which dealt with matters of inheritance, property, marriage and adoption). The latter worked differently for 'Mussalmans', 'Gentoos' (Hindus) and those of other faiths. Yet these neat distinctions meant little where local 'Hindu' practice had nothing to do with the high Brahminic injunctions the British had codified, or where common law and practice defied the idealised protocols set out in arcane textbooks.

Officers were seldom fluent in the languages of plaintiffs, petitioners or defendants. The 'knowledge' – about who in fact was entitled to till which particular parcel of land, and who should be taxed – if recorded, was held by *qaanungos* and *patwaaris* in the north and *karnams* in the south. These local accountants were the only ones who could interpret the local geld books. And yet the state was always hungry for more resources – its burgeoning size, its reconstructed army and its public works making it ever more expensive to run.

A 'steel frame' resting on such an unsteady yet impenetrable base was always going to be dependent on a host of Indian intermediaries and interpreters.

As R. S. Swann, a thoughtful Scots officer, recalls of Orissa in the 1930s:

> [My] first experiences of revenue collection and magisterial work – all extremely amateurish – left me with mixed feelings; fascination with the job or case immediately at hand, coupled with a growing realisation – not diminished by later experience in the districts, of how little could be achieved ... one slaved away regardless, perhaps with the subconscious wish to escape from a sense of futility.[108]

At the end of the day, reality for the ICS officer in India meant coming to terms with the fact the emperor had few clothes. It meant accepting your daily reliance on the very people you had conquered.

The 'Lords of Human Kind' had to accept that to rule, they had to work, day in and day out, with 'natives' they distrusted, even reviled.

These men had joined the ICS as boys still wet behind the ears. Just out of university, they went to crammers and took competitive examinations in London (hence aristocrats dismissed them as 'competition-wallahs'). While a few had been schooled at Eton, most came out of minor public or grammar schools – they were bright sons of clergymen, bank clerks and even shopkeepers, for whom colonial service provided a route up the social ladder of Mr Mother Country.

Many had made it to Oxbridge, where most achieved second-class degrees (firsts were rare in those days; but a handful of senior wranglers in mathematics, and graduates with distinguished degrees in Classics, supported the 'frame' at any given time). The 'Mandarins' were so named because they belonged to a meritocracy that had mastered enough Greek, Latin, British legal and constitutional history, the languages and histories of Europe, mathematics, moral sciences, and enough Arabic and Sanskrit to pass the rigorous entrance examination into the service.[109] Inevitably this meant that they were men of an intellectual bent of mind who (having somehow passed the test of horse-riding), once in India had to pretend 'to be men of action . . . to escape the stigma attached to cleverness by the Victorian middle-class'.[110] It is no great surprise that so many went on to become amateur historians. Or that so many wrote ethnographies, censuses and treatises on law, literature and the languages of India. One officer – the redoubtable Lewis Sydney Steward O'Malley – wrote almost a hundred such treatises.

The system of recruitment thus produced a ruling elite that was ill at ease with itself. Thinking men sailed out to India, and had to pretend upon landing that they loved nothing more than a bit of pig-sticking.[111]

It was also profoundly ill at ease with India. Most recruits found India's climate unbearable, its elites inscrutable and repellent, and its common people too lazy or too stupid to know what was best for them. Writing to his wife in November 1941, Clive Jenkinson, a talented pianist with a sensitive ear for music, wrote: 'It was extraordinarily sultry. I don't think I should stand the climate for very long. And I don't wonder now why they have to pay white people so highly to come out to it.'

On his arrival in Bombay, Jenkinson ventured into the Indian 'bazaar', where, to his eyes, everyone appeared to be 'either scrofulous or blind'. Having arranged with shipboard friends to meet at the Jay Hotel that evening, he turned up to find that its walls were covered in pornography. He was shocked to find that 'hotel' was a euphemism for a brothel. In a 'sex-starved' society, the red-light districts prospered.[112]

When he got to Bannu in 1942, Jenkinson's aversion to India grew deeper. It showed in every facet of his relationship with his Indian bearer, Ayaz, whose duty it was to serve him at mealtimes. (All British civil servants *had* to have a bearer. Although most had never enjoyed such domestic service at home, the first thing they had to do on their arrival in the district was employ one.)

Jenkinson found Ayaz irksome in the extreme. 'Like all bearers, he is trying to give me a bath,' he writes. 'I have stared him off and insisted on a *small* quantity of water.' He later wrote: 'It is a good thing to let one's bearer do your shopping, for while he will cheerfully rob you, but not for too much as he knows not to kill the golden goose, he will prevent others from robbing you.'

On one occasion, having not quite recovered from a dreadful cold, Jenkinson insisted on going to a party: European social occasions were rare and he yearned for the companionship and music of his fellow whites. Ayaz tried to persuade him to stay indoors as the skies were growing dark with clouds. Jenkinson tramped off anyway and got caught in a huge thunderstorm. When he discovered that his bearer had been following him at some distance with his mackintosh, he was furious rather than grateful. One gets a sense, in this vignette, of the impotent rage of the white man in India who, be he so powerful, could do nothing and go nowhere without the help, and intrusive presence, of the brown 'native'.[113]

Yet while almost all civil servants (whether they admitted it or not) were racists – these were, after all, times of high racism – they were not cardboard cut-outs. The very same Jenkinson who so loathed Ayaz displayed a remarkable openness of mind when his adored wife 'Chick', who had remained in England, took up with another man. In one of his thousands of letters to her he wrote: 'I am pleased to think you have found someone nice. I am glad he can give you a good time in these shortage times . . .' Chick rented out their house, moved to a flat in another town to get away from her mother-in-law's disapproving gaze, and seems to have entertained several male suitors during the war. Jenkinson accepted these arrangements without demur, signing off one of his letters with this poignant thought: 'Love cannot be held. It holds of itself, and that I think is what so few people understand. Go your own way sweetheart. If it is yours it is mine.'[114]

Men like Jenkinson were also aware of the hierarchy and snobbery within the ICS, and white society in India more broadly. Consider his description to Chick of his effort to learn Urdu: 'The trouble is that Urdu consists of two separate languages. One for speaking to servants and another for speaking to superiors or equals ... and they cannot realise that *in English the same things happen by difference in the arrangement of sentences and by tone of voice.*'[115]

Others – men perhaps more worldly than the talented Mr Jenkinson – learned the rules of white society fast. Writing to his 'dearest Mater', Roderick McLeod explained that 'the etiquette about calling is very strict. The first call must be made between 12 and 2; to call at any other time, unless you know the person well, is a heinous offence.' So he spent much time at the Byculla Club in Bombay 'inhabited by [white] bachelors' (not far from a fruit-juice bar on Marine Drive still known as Bachelors' Juice House). Even though when he arrived he was discomfited at being saluted by all Indian sepoys, regardless of rank ('it was a trifle embarrassing for a modest individual like myself'), he learned soon enough to accept their *salaams*. On his arrival at his first post in Benares, he followed the 'custom of a [white] newcomer to go round and visit *everyone* [white] without delay. Introductions are not required, you introduce yourself. I have been going round according to a list Mr Ch[urchgate] made for me.' Churchgate made sure that McLeod, with whom he later shared a house, introduced himself to people in the correct order.[116]

The civil service was, in some respects, like an Indian caste. It was a closed and hierarchical world, refreshed each year by new entrants, dining only with members of the 'club', steeped in its own mythology and heavy with (sometimes ludicrous) ritual.

Learning to govern a district was not easy. By this time, as one scholar has pointed out, the imperial state relied on paper; every decision required a file, with officers initialling every order to display responsible governance, and dating every decision to show swift action.[117] Writing in the *New York Tribune*, Karl Marx described the British state in India as 'one immense writing machine'.[118] But the files themselves were often unintelligible. McLeod complained bitterly about the '*shikasta* writing' he encountered at the *kutcheri* (local

court) every day, which was so unlike the formal Urdu he had learned
in England:

> It is a series of scrawls and flourishes. Letters in Hindustani are distin-
> guished by dots, the same may mean five different things depending on
> the position of the dot ... well in *shikasta* writing, there are no dots!

He had to entertain a stream of Indian visitors:

> Then baboos, baboos, baboos [Indians officials or clerks], who or what
> I know not ... [there is no end of signing]. Imagine you are trying to
> discover what a witness is driving at in a language you can't under-
> stand, and that at the same time half a dozen baboos are bent on getting
> your attention ... there is [just] no end of signing to do.[119]

As for the law itself, even if McLeod had been able to comprehend
the cases before him, it pulled in different directions. Some laws
upheld contract and the right of persons to engage in free and paid
labour – all necessary for the modern industrial sector that the state
was striving to encourage. Yet it was, at the same time, unwilling to
disturb the 'grain of tradition'. Civil law, which governed property
disputes, was complicated by the 'religion' of the plaintiffs, and here
too, British officials would discover that faith in India was rich and
strange, and customs did not follow Brahminic codes.[120]

The daily routine for McLeod and his ilk was a ride in the morning,
a frustrating day at the *kutcheri*, signing files and listening to a babel
of foreign tongues, retiring to the club to play tennis or billiards and
a gin and tonic (or three) with other Europeans in 'whites only' surroundings. Whites only, that is, except for the army of bearers,
pankhaa-wallahs (fan-pullers), cooks, the menials who washed dirty
plates, who swept, scavenged and cleaned privies that made possible
a sense of white style, privacy, even domesticity, and comfort.

It was a strange, and strangely barren, life. Even in the mid-1930s, there
were only half as many British women as there were British men at civilian posts, and if the white army is thrown in, British women were an even
smaller fraction in the Indian empire. There were very few older white
people in India, parents seldom making the trip out to visit their offspring
across the seas. A handful of older white women came out as chaperones,
or as governesses for Indian noble families, and their scarcity was such
that Dr Aziz, the central character in E. M. Forster's *A Passage to India*,
jumps out of his skin when he encounters the 'very old' Mrs Moore.

White children born in India were entrusted in their early years to Indian *ayahs* (nannies) and grew up speaking Tamil, Telegu, Marathi or Hindustani, and if they spoke English at all, they did so with a *chi-chi* (Indian-English) accent.[121] Many never quite got over their sense of displacement and exile when they left India.

Ken Miln's father John ran a jute mill just outside Calcutta. Ken's 'first memory is the smell of mustard oil on my *ayah* . . . Old Bhutair, as she was known, would rub it onto her skin to protect it from the sun.' As he recalled in a poignant interview: 'I grew up with that smell. I liked it. It was familiar to me. It eased me.' Old Bhutair was an ageing Bhutanese woman who always wore a white sari. (This would have been at the Memsahib's behest; a Bhutanese woman would normally dress in a *kira* – a colourful sarong appropriate for her mountainous 'land of thunder dragons'.) She was at Ken's disposal day and night. If he woke in the early hours it would be Old Bhutair who comforted him. The first words Ken spoke were in Hindi, which he learned from her. To communicate with his mother, the *ayah* would translate Ken's words into English. She would sing nursery rhymes in Hindi which he sings today with a strong Dundee brogue.

> *Nini baba nini*
> *Makhhan roti cheenee,*
> *Makkhan roti ho gaya,*
> *Soja Baba soja.*

> Sleep baby sleep
> Butter flatbread and sugar
> The flatbread and butter are all gone
> Sleep baby sleep.

Ken still has dreams he is in India, living as an Indian.[122]

Most British children were packed off to boarding schools at 'home' (in Britain) to cure them of embarrassing *chi-chi* habits, to learn *pucca* English with the right upper-class accents and to be schooled in British manners. They endured separation from their parents for inordinate lengths of time.[123] A study of some of them in their later years revealed how they had longed for India. They spoke of the sounds, tastes and smells that reminded them of India: the crowing of a cock, the clip-clopping of a pony and cart, the sweetness of mangoes, the scent of a wood fire, and the spicy aromas emanating from Indian restaurants.[124]

Or there would be the occasional cases of children of Indian officers recruited to the ICS in the 1920s and 30s, who went 'home' to
Britain to be educated. Anil Seal, the son of a Bengali officer in the
Engineering Service, was among them. Before his exile to Britain, Anil
went to Bishop Cotton School in Simla, the summer capital of the Raj,
and clip-clopped to school on a pony. His earliest memory is of a
monkey stealing his father's waistcoat. The first thing Anil did after
leaving 'Tercanbury'[125] in England was to return to India, where he
sought out and found his beloved *ayah* Panchami. By this time, his
chi-chi accent had been beaten out of him, and he had won a scholarship to Trinity College, Cambridge. But he returned to India year after
year. He still holds his Indian passport. Despite this, people mistake
him for a *firanghee*.

There is a tendency to berate white wives for being standard-bear-
ers of Anglo-Indian racism, for raising the snobbery of the ICS bubble
to a whole new level. My hunch is that this is a caricature, and a poor
one at that. Perhaps these women ached for home. Perhaps they were
lonely in their 'stations' while their husbands rode all morning,
worked all day and retired to the club at night. Perhaps the anguish of
losing their children so early drove them to seek intimacy elsewhere.

And temptation there was aplenty. Affairs within 'the bubble' were
commonplace. By all accounts Simla was alive with white mischief. A
few unusual women strayed outside the white world. In 1883, an
Indian employee allegedly raped a Mrs Hume. Hurroo Mehter, the
supposed perpetrator, was a Dalit, a sweeper. Her husband – James
Hume, public prosecutor – returned home early one day, he maintained, to find the two having sex on the bathroom floor. He 'thrashed'
the 'assailant' and filed a case against him. Hurroo remained
undefended but denied the charge of rape to the end. To no one's surprise, he was found guilty and sentenced to eight years in jail.

But two years later, a different picture emerged of what had happened, albeit in private letters. Allan Octavian Hume (a relative of the
Hume family and founder of the Indian National Congress) admitted
to the viceroy, Lord Dufferin, that in fact Hurroo and Mrs Hume had
been romantically involved for six months.[126] It was her husband's
punches that had bruised Mrs Hume, not Hurroo's assault. The relationship between Hurroo and Mrs Hume was consensual. This was
dynamite. It was impossible in Anglo-India, in the throes of the white
backlash against the Ilbert Bill (discussed in Chapter 1), for such truths

to be made public, as they would undermine the foundations of white colonial order.

Perhaps it was liaisons like these that embarrassed white men into admitting women to Indian clubs long before their counterparts were admitted to clubs in Britain. Club activities, however repetitive and male-oriented, allowed the men to keep an eye on their wives.[127] Perhaps it is not the case, then, as is often assumed, that British women were inevitably more racist than their husbands. Perhaps the ambiguity at the heart of *A Passage to India* – in which we never discover whether Dr Aziz attacked Miss Adela Quested or whether she was herself attracted to him – is more than an allegory.

The odour of hypocrisy lingered on in these clubs long after the British had left the subcontinent. It was palpable when I visited Delhi's Gymkhana Club, previously 'whites only', after independence 'Indianised'. I was in my teens then, so this was in the 1970s. After chicken sandwiches and coffee served by bearers in full livery, my friend and I retired to the ladies' loo. This was a stuccoed suite of rooms large enough to house five families. The vast outer chamber was lined with heavy chesterfield sofas upholstered in velveteen chintz; and against one wall stood a row of ugly glass-topped dressing tables made of carved mahogany. Victorian prudery still reigned in these women-only domains – the legs of these ugly objects were draped in even uglier fabric. I never returned. I am not sure what offended me more – the Indian metropolitan elite's desire for faux-Englishness decades after independence, or the vulgar opulence of empire.

Going back to our friend Roderick McLeod. In 1878, he rose to magistrate (second class) and assistant collector (first class). As he boasted to his beloved 'Mater', this gave him powers to sentence a man to six months' imprisonment, including solitary confinement, and to inflict a whipping. He sounded rather pleased about this. One could read his reaction as a sign of his inherent disregard for 'native' bodies, and there would be some truth in that. One might claim that the culture of physical punishment and bullying in British public schools had inured him to a culture of 'lashes'. He assured his sister Lily that she could 'set her mind at rest about the 50 *lashes*. It is all humbug. It is not a lash at all. It is done with a cane, and the average is about ten whacks. It must be mild indeed compared with what is given at home.'[128]

Or one might interpret it as a mark of the white officers' pent-up frustration at his inability to assert authority, the impossibility of ruling India without Indians. Whipping some poor felon demonstrated power, if not hegemony. As one scholar notes, the late-colonial state developed an armoury of coercive techniques that went well beyond the rule of law, and indeed had little to do with it. Public flogging, collective fines upon villages, forced 'flag marches', crawling orders, firing on unarmed crowds and even aerial bombardment were illegal techniques by which the British ruled India.[129]

One sees these tensions in the army as well. R. H. G. Johnstone, who joined the 21st Punjab Company in 1915, stayed on in India until 1946. He left a fascinating memoir. He writes that his training involved trying to learn how to read maps – the great survey maps by which the British believed they 'knew' and could 'see' every square mile of their Indian territory. Johnstone recalls:

> Much time was devoted to maps. We had to be able to read them properly, to understand the meaning of compass bearings ... and the intricacies of contours. Using the clinometer we attempted a contour map of a given area, but a number of us found that the contour lines had a nasty habit of running to the end of a spur and then vanishing like a Cheshire cat. With only a little more experience we would have got over this, but here too time pressed. Field sketching was included with some remarks on how to deal with puzzling perspective.[130]

This left them ill prepared for irregular warfare against 'natives' who knew their territory in an intimate, physical and even emotional sense; for them, every boulder represented a memory, every bush the taste of its berries in season, every contour cover against attack or an opportunity to surprise their enemy. During the Great War, Masuds in Waziristan invaded a British Army post, killing Captain Frederick Hughes, its British commander. Johnstone writes: 'This shook me into understanding that though there might be a Beau Geste romance to the frontier, there was real danger too.'[131] In a reaction typical of the late-colonial state, Johnstone's battalion responded by burning down an entire village.[132]

The state, it turned out, could not see.[133] Or it saw India only through grimy lenses. Their private papers reveal that at its highest echelons – despite their arrogant display – men like Johnstone were painfully aware of the state's inadequacies, and had no idea how to remedy them.

The 'steel frame' thus held up a curious kind of order. For all its hubris and high moral claims, the Raj was a jumble of incoherent policies and practices. Most officers were mindful of their failings as 'rulers' and of their ignorance of 'the natives'. They feared the brown man's intentions. They lashed out against individual misdemeanours with disproportionate violence against whole communities – the very opposite of the rule of law. Few befriended brown men or saw them as equals. Malcolm Lyall Darling, who spent most of his career in the Punjab and became something of an expert on its peasant society, developed a deep (and probably unfulfilled) homoerotic love for his ward Tukoji Rao Puar III, the Raja of the tiny Maratha state of Dewas. E. M. Forster – part of Darling's unconventional set – was no less enthralled by the stunningly handsome, mercurial prince, and writes about him in *The Hill of Devi*. But the relationship between Darling's set and the Raja collapsed in mutual misunderstanding.[134]

Perhaps the only Indians for whom white officers could feel affection were the 'peasants' of their imaginations, but this was a distant, paternalistic sort of regard; any idea that they actually understood their problems is belied by the famines of the late nineteenth and twentieth centuries. They valued the fighting skills and courage of the 'martial races' but did not see them as equals. Right until the end of empire, and indeed until very recently, the prized Gurkha soldiers earned a fraction of the wage that the Tommies received.

And let's be quite clear: the Mandarins held Tommies and white working-class 'squaddies' in low regard: the average British private was still on a wage of one shilling a day (about £1 10s a month) until after the First World War.[135] The fact that this state survived as long as it did has something to do with the brute force that backed it; but also, as Gandhi recognised, has much to do with the willingness of so many Indians – who understood their country rather better than their masters – to work with it, for a host of reasons that the British never wholly grasped.

Intermediaries

If British officers felt ill at ease with themselves in India, not all Indian intermediaries who worked for the Raj were discomfited by their role. This was marked in the countryside where the state relied heavily on

Indians to carry out its basic tasks. Neither tax collection nor adjudication at the district level was possible without the ever-present *qaanungo*, *patwaari* or *karnam*.

Take District Magistrate Symington's account of a day in the life of a district magistrate in the Bombay Presidency:

> When Dost Mohamed [the *qaanungo*, or registrar of property] said he would check the register, Mahars – village servants – were sent running in all directions to summon the interested parties to the pipal tree in front of the village office. A sizeable gathering had already collected there and went on growing through the afternoon.
>
> A series of dialogues ensued, calculated to try the patience of any officer who might fancy himself in a hurry, and to afford entertainment to the audience.
>
> 'Vinoba Ramya Koli.' Dost Mohamed read out the name of the first name belonging to the uncertified entry in the register.
>
> A dark-skinned figure in a high-girt dhoti – public opinion permitted only superior folk to wear their dhotis below their calves – was hustled forward.
>
> 'Are you Vinoba Ramya Koli?'
>
> The man addressed smirked sheepishly and looked around at his friends as if in doubt whether he should make such a daring admission. 'Yes, yes,' cried the audience, 'he is Vinoba.'
>
> 'Vinoba, are you the owner of field number 372?'
>
> 'Yes.'
>
> 'Have you mortgaged it to Tolaram Bhansali?'
>
> 'No sahib. How could I do so? I do not know what a mortgage is.'
>
> 'Then what happened about the field?'
>
> 'I have given it for three years.'
>
> 'And what has Tolaram given you?'
>
> 'Given? He has given me nothing. He gave me some cloth.'
>
> 'Did he give you money?'
>
> 'Yes.'
>
> 'How much?'
>
> 'One rupee and nine annas.'
>
> Approving murmurs came from the crowd as it settled down to enjoy itself. Obviously, Vinoba was not going to disappoint.
>
> 'Was that part of the loan?'
>
> 'It was to buy liquor.'

A cackle of laughter greeted this tit-bit and Vinoba felt encouraged to go on.

'It was to buy liquor at his shop. I had no money to drink at his shop, so he gave me money. When I had drunk I signed the paper.'

'And the cloth?' Dost knew he would have to ask that sooner or later, and decided to get it over.

'That was for my nephew's wedding.'

'So the one rupee nine annas and the cloth have nothing to do with your land?'

'Who knows? I gave him the paper.'

'What was the paper you signed?'

Here the village accountant [*patwaari*] intervened: 'It was a mortgage. Here is the true copy from the sub-registry.'

Dost Mohamed examined it. He pointed to a cross at the foot of the page.

'Did you make that?'

Vinoba hesitated. He recollected that two witnesses had seen him do it and decided not to disown it.

'Who else?'

'What is written here?'

'Tolaram is renting my field for three years.'

'What is the rent?'

'One hundred and twenty-one rupees.'

'Do you have to pay that back, with interest also?'

'I will pay when my cousin sends me money.'

'What if he doesn't send you money and you cannot pay?'

'Tolaram will take my field instead of the money.'

'Then it is not rent. It is a mortgage. This entry seems correct and I must approve it. Have you any objection?'

Vinoba sat back on his haunches. It was someone else's turn now.[136]

Note the cast of characters in this cameo. Symington, the district officer, seems to have said not a single word. Every other actor – from the hapless Vinoba to the rather scary but efficient Dost Mohamed – was Indian. The Mahar village servants who went to bring Vinoba to the 'court' under the peepal tree were Indians, as was the innominate *patwaari*, and the crowd. One gets no sense that either Dost Mohamed or the *patwaari* were uncomfortable with the proceedings, or their role in them. Even taking account of Symington's paternalism, Dost Mohamed comes across as a commanding figure. The *patwaari* had a more modest role. Both seemed conscious that their local clout was enhanced because they represented the *Sarkar*.

The British Raj relied on hundreds of thousands of such men who, without fuss and often with dignity, worked for the state. Indeed, many held this position because they had been scribes, *qaanungos* and *patwaaris* for previous *Sarkars*; the Persian word *qaanungo* (expounder of law) was in use in Mughal times. Nationalists (and some historians) denounced these men as 'collaborators' with imperial rule. Yet the powers who had ruled India before the British had also relied on *qaanungos* and *patwaaris* who held and interpreted land and revenue records, even if these had been less numerous, complex and bulky than the records the British Raj gathered.[137] Their service for the state reinforced their other privileges in local settings: their modest wealth, local standing and caste status. They come across as phlegmatic characters, going about their business with little fuss.

It is in such contexts that the British (and indeed post-colonial states) have feared their laws are being subverted by local intermediaries. They have worried about 'corruption' among Indians working for the state since the late nineteenth century. (This anxiety is not a post-independence phenomenon.) The problem for the British is that they would have needed an Indian intermediary to interpret what was indeed corruption and what merely looked like it but was not.

'Favours' and gifts are as much its currency as cash, so corruption was not easy to see. It was a complex matrix, bound up with law, power (and its lack), cultural performance and social connections. Getting a file moved or disappeared, changing the records in favour of the powerful, granting permission to build (or encouraging the right person to turn a blind eye to an 'unauthorised structure'), the licence to sell or to trade, to get a place for a child at school or university – all this is difficult in South Asia, given the sheer pressure of numbers and competition for scarce resources. Realising these goals may involve transactions that cannot always be measured in rupees or takas (the Bangladeshi currency). One may take a phone call calling in a favour; another might rest on relationships of gifting.

There is, and I imagine has been over the last century, a 'going rate' at any time in any place to persuade a *patwaari* (who remained the face of the state at the village level after independence) to register (or manipulate) a title to land in the revenue records.

But it is hard for a novice to figure out exactly what that rate is, since the euphemism is 'give what you want'. (That phrase is repeated, with laughter, when the amount offered is too small.)[138]

'Moving a file' might require one to bring over a box of sweets in a way that inverts hierarchies in the outside world. So if I, a professor of history at Cambridge, were to take a large box of the best *sandesh* and an imported mobile phone to a clerk at the Lord Sinha Road police station, hoping that my gift would encourage him to bring up my files more quickly, that would be a bribe. (*Sandesh* is a delicate Bengali sweetmeat, which is a treat even for someone without a sweet tooth.) Alternatively, it could be a way of thanking him for his efficiency on a previous visit, cementing our good relations. (A gift.) To the outsider it would be difficult to distinguish one transaction from the other, since both transactions would look and sound (almost) identical.[139] (There is no such clerk at the Lord Sinha Road police station.)

Context thus helps to differentiate corruption from the complex practices of gifting in the subcontinent, and without knowledge of that context, observers often see corruption under every bush.[140] Sending basketfuls of dried fruits to 'big people' at festivals may involve no corrupt transaction: the goal may just be to build a respectful and courteous relationship in case the big man's help is needed in the future – whether to get a 'permission' from the *Sarkar* or a hospital bed. It may simply be a gesture, adhesive binding to a relationship.

At other times, corruption is invisible because it involves calling in a favour without reminding the bribee about that favour. Etiquette in corruption is all, but that etiquette can be mysterious to outsiders. The conventions of gifting are no easier to grasp. That perhaps explains the tendency to see the whole of South Asia, and indeed the 'Third World', as irremediably corrupt. It's the new Orientalism and, like its predecessor, it does not help us understand much. It is an easy, but lazy, way of thinking about the issue.

This brings us back to the government of files – the *kaaghazi raj* – and the literate Indians involved in its production.[141] In 1863, Satyendranath Tagore became the first Indian to pass the ICS entrance examination. It was an extraordinary feat by a gifted young man whose high-browed face exudes a reflective sensitivity: extraordinary because the examination was weighted towards subjects not much studied in India such as Greek and Latin, and British and European history, in which his British competitors were infinitely better trained. His achievement would likely have been impossible without the backing of his exceptional family: the Jorasanko branch of the Tagore clan which also produced the poet and Nobel laureate Rabindranath (his brother), Debendranath (his father, the philosopher and social reformer) and Dwarkanath (his grandfather, one of India's first industrialists). They could afford to pay for him to take the examination in London. Only a handful of Indians followed in his steps. The 'steel frame' remained overwhelmingly white until the 1920s.

In the inter-war years, however, this pattern began to change. Demand for ICS jobs in Britain fell. Britons who took the ICS examinations increasingly did so for pecuniary reasons rather than any sense of calling. V. G. Matthews, born in 1907 and educated at Latymer School and the University of London, was attracted to the ICS 'especially, to be frank, [by] the high rate of emoluments offered by the ICS. With the economy of the world collapsing in ruins, security and high pay were considerations of the highest appeal.' He admitted as much in his *viva voce* interview at Burlington Gardens, on a summer morning with rays of sunlight shining 'full in [his] face . . . [My] reply was greeted with a long silence from my examiners and the rapid termination of the interview.' Matthews failed the viva, his candour duly punished. He got into the service only because he had done so well in the written component of the examination.[142]

But the lure of the ICS continued to fall when diarchy in 1920 and provincial self-government in 1935 gave elected Indian legislators a role and the ICS gained new Indian masters.

Meanwhile, more and more bright Indians took the ICS exams and passed. But if a 'guardian' in the mould of Matthews could be so calculating about serving in the ICS, it is easy to imagine Indians having a complex mix of feelings about it. As G. P. Woodford recalls of his Indian fellows in the Civil Service:

> *All* the Indian probationers were keen nationalists, some with family connections in the Congress Party. At first, the British element found this rather odd . . . in practice, I think they [the Indians] made a subconscious distinction between the Government as an instrument of foreign rule . . . and in its purely administrative capacity, as the established Government of the country, which, *in all non-political matters, they*

expected to operate impartially in the public interest and hence had no inhibitions about taking part in it.[143]

Hence Gandhi and other nationalists would often visit B. N. Rau (ICS from 1909) when he came to Delhi. One of four sons of a *hakeem* (physician) from a small village near Madras, Rau was an alumnus of Madras Christian College, and Trinity College, Cambridge, where he was a contemporary of Jawaharlal Nehru. In letters to his father, Nehru describes the 'strange' south Indian who worked so hard and yet was so good at sport (Rau won a tennis blue). Bets were laid as to whether he would defeat a British student at St John's College to become senior wrangler at mathematics. A handsome, gentle man of great charm and wit, he married an Englishwoman but, for reasons never discussed, lived alone. Until his death in 1953, he played a large role in many crucial moments in India's transition to independence, helping draft the Hindu Code Bill in the early 1940s and India's constitution in 1947, drawing up its first electoral roll, representing India at the United Nations and ending up at the International Court of Justice at the Hague.[144] Sir B. N. Rau was on intimate terms with the Nehru family. Neither saw any contradiction in bridging the ICS/ nationalist divide.

Below these lofty heights, the civilian 'paper state' had always been Indian (just as the *laathi* state was, and continued to be after independence). Indian clerks and copyists – *keraanis* who went about their business filling ledgers all day long – turned the information officers needed into signs in a strange language. They wrote with new implements – scratchy quill pens dipped into inkwells that smell, to this day, of a bygone era – and later with typewriters. They worked in new settings. No longer sitting cross-legged on the floor, as they had done in times past, now they sat indoors, at small desks in dingy cubbyholes set apart from the sahib's large office. They laboured to different rhythms. Just as for the *babus* (Indian clerks), for *keraanis* the nine-to-five day was an innovation as novel as the English language, and they struggled to cope with this unrelenting regimen. For his labours, the clerk was paid a pittance. He barely made ends meet while keeping his office clothes fresh, his boys' school fees paid, and his wife able to manage the household with the meagre income he brought home. By the early twentieth century the average clerk earned Rs 20 a month, a fraction of what his English ICS sahib earned in a day. Even though he was employed, his life lacked the dignity to which, as an educated man in Indian society, he felt entitled. The new form of drudgery that was his lot grated on him. So did the everyday racism of the everyday state. The British made no pretence of their allergy to *babus*: they despised their alleged effeminacy and mimicry and labelled them, as noted, WOGs.

The irony was that the British could not have run India for a day without them. These offices, then, like Writers' Building in Calcutta with its warrens of offices, courtyards and cubbyholes, were toxic hothouses, throwing people together in quotidian relationships marked by racism, snobbery, frustration and seething resentment. Thousands from the clerical classes of Calcutta sought the consolations of religion, turning to modern-day saints to seek meaning in their lives.[145] Others turned to politics. Nationalists, revolutionaries and communists found ready recruits among them.

Right at the heart of the British colonial state, then, was a connection which had never been comfortable and which curdled more and more as the decades progressed. It was here, in the offices of the Raj, that western-educated Indians and Britons came into most regular contact. It was in these close, hierarchical surroundings that the system began to unravel. Educated Indians who could do the dreary office jobs on which the Raj depended as years passed could not be depended upon. The 'paper state' – that vast edifice of files and ledgers and correspondence that went up and down departments, and back and forth between secretariats, which for better or worse determined who would pay tax (and how much), who could vote, or whose land title would be registered and recognised – was run by people who couldn't give a fig about the future of the government they served. In fact, many quietly supported the people who were trying to bring it down.

Post-Raj: independence with partition

The Second World War shattered Britain's metropolitan economy and changed the balance of profit and power that had long sustained the Raj. It destroyed London's capacity and its will to hold onto an empire ravaged by famine, by swelling tides of labour unrest and by communal violence.[146] Other casualties of the war were the die-hard Conservatives who wanted to hang on to India whatever the cost,

Churchill their most strident spokesman. After Labour won the election in 1945, Clement Attlee's government declared that it intended to transfer power to Indians as soon as possible. The 'end game' had begun.

The first move in that game required Britain to perform a volte-face. During the war, London had wanted to hang on to power in India and found Muslim demands a convenient bulwark against the Congress, so it had made promises to Muslims and Indian princes that their concerns would be addressed in the final settlement of India's future. Post-war, Britain's power, priorities and timetables changed. Britain wanted to get out of India as quickly as possible, and these guarantees were an embarrassment.

For its part, with the power at the centre (and control over the centralised state apparatus of the British Raj) almost within its grasp, the Congress leadership was in no mood to make any concessions to Muslims which might weaken that state and encourage particularist demands by other regional satraps. The Congress had always insisted that India was indivisible. Now it threw down a joker. It was ready to countenance a limited partition that would cut out troublesome Muslim-majority districts in the west and east, thereby allowing the Congress to inherit the rest of British India with its powers at the centre intact.

In arriving at this historic decision, there was a rare unanimity between the Congress leaders: liberals, socialists and those on the Hindu right all backed the high command's new line. It also had the support of Hindu nationalists in Bengal, the largest Muslim-majority province, who refused to be subjected to 'Muslim rule' and demanded a partition (ironically not dissimilar to Lord Curzon's partition of 1905; see Chapter 1) that would give them a homeland of their own inside a divided India.[147] The departing viceroy, Lord Louis Mountbatten, lacked the vision or the will to resist a solution that offered Britain a sharp exit from a desperate and dangerous situation. With his particular admixture of opportunism and vainglory, Tricky Dickie (as his critics dubbed him) persuaded London to accept the Congress' demand for a limited partition, and presented it to India and the world as his own idea.

Pakistan was thus the product at least as much of Muslim aspirations for nationhood as of the dramatic collapse of British power. The Congress party's single-minded drive for a strong centre for India forced a de-territorialised, variously imagined 'Muslim nation' into a 'moth-eaten and truncated' state. Cyril Radcliffe delineated the boundaries between the two states according to the terms of reference he was given. But since these terms were influenced by the Congress, in the end, he carved Pakistan, like an inexpert butcher, out of those parts of the empire that India's leaders no longer wanted.[148]

In the subcontinent, the mid-twentieth century was a time of darkness and light, of genocide and liberation, of shadows at noon. Both India and Pakistan faced agonising crises at the moment of their birth as new nations. Both had to deal with a bloodbath in the two parts of Punjab, now divided by the border between Pakistan and India. Delhi itself, many Rajputana states (now part of the tourist's 'golden triangle'), Bahwalpur, Hyderabad and other smaller principalities were soon swept up in tides of carnage. Between 750,000 and 1,000,000 people perished. More than 20 million people fled their homes. Both India and Pakistan had to accept millions of refugees, many of whom were militant in their demands for protection and shelter.

Both countries strove to deal with these pressures while ordinary people's expectations of what freedom would bring were sky-high, even utopian. In East Bengal, the charismatic *aalim* (religious scholar) Maulana Bhashani spoke of a 'land of eternal Eid'.[149] In Calcutta, crowds stormed the governor-general's house at Belvedere, wreaking havoc upon the upholstered furniture, damask curtains and paintings in heavy gilt frames. They tore these into shreds, taking fragments away with them as tokens that they were free.[150] The states of India and Pakistan both had to manage heady popular expectations. They had to curb soaring inflation and deal with shortages of everyday commodities. They had to deal with these crises *while the state itself was being divided*. Both new republics that emerged from partition bore its blood-stained imprimatur.

Literally everything that belonged to the state, that *was* the state – employees, files, land records, gold reserves, weaponry, army, down to its tables, chairs, cupboards and typewriters – had to be partitioned, according to an agreed ratio. Its civilian personnel – all the hundreds of thousands of brown people who had formed the base of the imperial pyramid – were given the right to opt to serve either nation. Most (but by no means all) Muslims opted for Pakistan, most (but by no means all) Hindus and Sikhs for India. Two senior servants of what had been a combined civil service, H. M. Patel and Chaudhri Muhammad Ali, oversaw this division in the seventy-two days they were given for this task with goodwill and courtesy.[151] Each then went his own way: Patel joining India's bureaucracy and Chaudhri Muhammad Ali, Pakistan's.

Despite the goodwill between the two civil servants, in India, from 1947 itself, the home minister Sardar Patel kept up sustained pressure to drive Muslim employees out of their jobs.[152] This, as we have seen, also happened in the army.

Yet in this division of the spoils, India did much better than Pakistan. In part this was because most of the immoveable physical infrastructure of the state – its capital city, its Reserve Bank, its ordnance factories, its railheads – lay in India. But in part it was the result of a more fundamental problem: Pakistan was a nation born without a state. It had to create one from scratch.[153] It may have acquired a capital city by decree – Karachi – when Jinnah declared that his old hometown on the shore of the Arabian Sea would play this role. But Karachi was already the capital of the province of Sind and its official buildings were occupied by Sind's government. Its reluctance to give up these premises was the first hint of tension between Sindhi regional patriotism and the federal government of Pakistan which would plague the nation's history.

So the central government, as well as its military command, operated from tents.

Pakistan's leader, Muhammad Ali Jinnah, was a refugee, as were most of his trusted Muslim League allies. *Muhajirs* (as refugees were known in Pakistan) dominated the civil service: ninety-five of the 101 Muslims in the ICS chose to leave India and found themselves senior government positions in Pakistan. Junior positions formerly filled by brown men – well, north Indian elites rushed to snap them up too. Both in its eastern and western wings, they loomed large in the new state's bureaucracy.

Pakistan was thus a state governed by a migrant bureaucracy.[154] The language of the migrants (Urdu) became Pakistan's national language, even if only refugees knew how to speak it. As late as the mid-1960s, refugees (a tiny fraction of the nation's population) still occupied more than a third (34.5 per cent) of all official posts.[155] Of Pakistan's forty-two largest companies, thirty-six belonged to *muhajirs*.

A new state was born and refugees ran its 'steel frame'.

I have tried to teach this history to students for over a quarter of a century. Every year, as a fresh cohort heard these befuddling facts in

Seminar Room 6 of Cambridge's freezing History Faculty, I have had to pause for a minute – sometimes five minutes – as they absorbed them. I could see thought bubbles rise over their heads. What would it be like if Lithuanian, Romany, Libyan or Afghan refugees not only came to Britain in such vast numbers but also imposed their language upon it? They cannot imagine anything so bizarre, and struggle to think through its implications.

India's experience was different, at least in this respect. It too received refugees in their millions. (Details follow in Chapter 4.) Like Pakistan, it took in refugee 'official displaced persons' (ODPs as they were known in the jargon of the time; South Asians adore acronyms). These were Hindu and Sikh state employees who had crossed the border, and wanted to fill jobs that Muslims moving in the other direction had left vacant.

But given India's size, refugee personnel could not swamp government. At its highest echelons, the government of new India was made up of 'locals': people who had long been settled in parts of the country that remained Indian after the vivisection.

Meanwhile, there were drives to expel Muslims from government at the state and central levels.

India decided early on to keep the 'steel frame' in place, but it did make minor changes to it. Perhaps the most important of these was to create the post of section officer, recruited from local qualified (but not ICS) men. These men provided a vast middle rank between the ICS (later renamed the Indian Administrative Service, IAS) at the top, and the clerks, *qaanungos*, *patwaaris*, *karnams* and their ilk at the base. The goal was to strengthen, and in fact create, a middle layer of the pyramid.[156]

This reformed service remained cast, however, in the British mould, 'backward-looking and precedent-based', shuffling files back and forth, passing the buck with a few annotations on every file.[157] It was not up to the job of 'delivering development', which the government had promised 'the people'. It was compromised by the distortions of 'colonial knowledge' which had become truisms by this time. On top of this, officials were no longer insulated from politics as had been the white guardians before them. They were embedded in a vibrant and violent political society. Some brought to their roles its charged political perspectives.[158]

For all this, the independent Indian state had much to be grateful for. It did not have to be conjured out of thin air, as in Pakistan. Nor did it have to function from tents. India inherited most of the physical fabric of the state at its highest levels. Lutyens' Viceroy's House on Raisina Hill, a monumental Edwardian-Baroque palace of buff and pink sandstone embellished by Indian motifs – *chhatris*, *chhajjas* and *jaalis* (umbrella-shaped roofs, ledges and latticework), and a towering *stupaa* that forms its dome – is the largest residence of any head of state in the world. When planned in 1911, it was an audacious statement of imperial power and permanence. When the empire fell, all this, and much else, went to India: the grand pillared offices of state that bookend it; the Central Secretariat (India's Whitehall) of Henry Baker's design; the stately tree-lined avenues and the bungalows for senior civil servants designed by Lutyens, each set in six acres of lawn – all became part of the *jaageer* (inherited property) of the Indian state. India Gate – New Delhi's answer to the Arc de Triomphe – dominated the network of boulevards at the heart of independent India's capital city. ('The smooth, polished roads of Delhi … the finest in all of India', as the murderous driver Munna observes in Aravind Adiga's *The White Tiger*.) The Supreme Court and the Central Legislative Assembly went to India. The grand *mahal* of the commander-in-chief – a white-chocolate confection in a sea of green lawn with peacocks strutting across the grass – was also in Delhi.

Five out of six high courts – Madras, Bombay, Calcutta, Allahabad and Patna – went to India. Only one, Lahore, went to Pakistan. Madras High Court in the later twentieth century still had a Dickensian feel to it. Its Gothic architecture embellished by 'saracenic' knobs, in which porters at the end of the century still carried around reams of parchment on their heads to and from the court, parchment later 'filed' in cages.[159] The state still churned out Himalayan massifs of paper: digitisation was impossible given the absence of internet coverage beyond (and indeed within) the cities.

Writers' Building in Calcutta, appropriately named and crowned by a statue of Minerva, once housed the secretariat of all India; after empire, its warrens of offices served the government of West Bengal. Files – the very stuff of government – that spilled out of the shelves of official headquarters went, in the main, to India. (It would be decades before all files pertinent to Pakistan were weeded out and sent across.) The General Post Office sits at right angles to Writers' Building in Dalhousie Square. Once it was British India's central post office.

Today it may have lost its dominance over communication and covert surveillance, yet it remains a proud emblem of the state. (The incessant anti-government protests in the city have always targeted Dalhousie Square, and continue so to do.[160] Bengal's people believe, with reason, that the *Sarkar* dwells in these structures.)

In Pakistan, by contrast, state capacity, and symbols of statehood, had to be built from the ground up. Syed Shahid Hamid (Sandhurst-trained former personal secretary to Field Marshal Sir Claude Auchinleck, who in 1947 became a refugee) wrote: 'There is no Government of Pakistan, but it is being created overnight. There are no government offices, no ministries, and no office furniture, or stationery. Typewriters are a luxury. It is utter chaos.'[161]

The Pakistan Army's general headquarters was makeshift and understaffed. To fill key posts, British officers took up short-term contracts. Even the role of commander-in-chief was filled by British officers: General Sir Frank Messervy held the job until February 1948; his successor General Sir Douglas Gracey until 1951.[162] Given the chaotic circumstances of its birth, and the ambivalent position of these officers who had all the archetypical biases of the British Indian Army, little was done to change the pronounced regional particularism in Pakistan's army, which remained overwhelmingly Punjabi and Pathan.[163] Ayub Khan, the bluff no-nonsense Pathan officer who was then general officer in command of East Bengal, wrote that it had only two infantry battalions and hardly any accommodation. 'At Headquarters there was no table, no chair, no stationery – we had virtually nothing at all; *not even any maps of East Pakistan*.'[164]

'Building a state structure from such an unstable [starting] point' was a mammoth task.[165] Given that at the start Pakistan had little bureaucracy to speak of – it was some years before it could regroup – the nascent army (also in the process of being divided) was called upon to discharge many civilian roles. Soldiers provided a semblance of administration in urban areas, protecting urban property, refugee camps and convoys, and dealing with civil unrest. Ayub insisted that from the start, 'the army was the instrument of Pakistan's sovereignty and the shield of the people'.[166]

But in other respects the two states, for all their bluster and claims to be so different from each other, were akin. After independence both were in much the same boat, and that boat often looked as if it was about to capsize.

A Raj family: District Magistrate
Cruishank, Mrs Cruishank and
their child.

William Robert Cornish:
surgeon and scientist of diet.

Pages from Irene Mott's diary: the Wellington Race Week.

Page from a Rai Bahadur's diary.

The glorification of violence: Santi Ghose and Suniti Chowdhury.

The iconisation of violence: the hanging of Khudiram Bose.

Dadabhai Naoroji (1825–1917): 'grand old man' of economic nationalism, mathematician and MP for Finsbury.

Bal Gangadhar Tilak (1856–1920): editor and militant.

Annie Besant (1847–1933): socialist, theosophist and President of the Congress in 1917.

Muhammad Ali Jinnah (1876–1948):
a very liberal lawyer and
leader of Pakistan.

Sarojini Naidu (1879–1949): poet
and advocate of communal unity.

Jawaharlal Nehru (1889–1964): nationalist hero and
first prime minister of India.

India–Pakistan border,
1947.

India–Pakistan daily border ritual,
Wagah–Attari, 2010s.

The paper state of
independent India.

Mortimer Wheeler:
archaeologist-in-chief
of India *and* Pakistan.

The dancing girl of
Mohenjodaro.

Phoolan Devi's defiance:
stolen police uniforms
and guns.

The destruction of Babri Mosque.

CULTURAL ICONS

Rabindranath Tagore
(1861–1941): poet, writer, artist.

Nazrul Islam (1899–1976):
poet, radical and musician.

Amrita Sher-Gil (1913–41):
trail-blazing artist.

Periyar (1879–1973): champion
of Dalits, critic of 'Brahmin' ideas.

Iqbal (1877–1938):
philosopher and poet.

Both were post-colonial 'nation states', which prized loyalty to the nation above all else.

Both, despite this, preserved the structure of the 'steel frame' that had undergirded British rule, even if in Pakistan the bureaucracy has had to come to terms with the overweening power of the army, and later the Inter-Services Intelligence (ISI). In both India and Pakistan, the civil services retained all the pomp, power and perks of the colonial bureaucracy; so much so that for decades, passing the civil service examination was the ultimate goal for educated young men and growing numbers of women.

Both Pakistan and India denounced, and then tried to stamp out, narrow provincialism. (The means by which they tried to achieve this, sometimes with devastating results, have been discussed in Chapter 2.)

As we have seen, both states soon came to fear insurgent refugees, who insisted that they had sacrificed their all for the nation and were owed full rehabilitation.[167] The only good refugees, they soon came to feel, were state servants, so these people got rehabilitation packages that the *pablik* most certainly did not.

So refugees in both countries occupied vacant property (which was empty only because previous residents had fled in terror). Both states lacked the will or capacity to protect the private property of original owners: they dithered while angry refugees divested minorities of their homes. Both states, blindsided by these actions, passed ordinances and laws to support this dispossession.[168] In both countries, the property of fleeing refugees became the cornerstone of governmental attempts to rehouse and rehabilitate the incoming tides.

Their models of citizenship soon began to look like mirror images of each other. Very rapidly, in both India and Pakistan, it was 'the enemy within' who began to emerge as the focus of state anxiety and surveillance.[169] As disscussed, the Muslims of India and the Hindus and Sikhs of Pakistan came to hold a new kind of minority citizenship, a second-class status that left them bereft of the secure rights of property capable of being defended in the courts. Even the right to free movement was denied to them, since anyone, anywhere, at any time could be labelled an 'intending evacuee', a quisling inspired by 'anti-national sentiment' secretly planning to flee with their assets to the enemy nation across the border.[170] No member of these minorities was safe.

But they were not alone in their vulnerability. The governments of

India and Pakistan had other internal foes in their sights. Both feared the power of princely states to diminish their new-found sovereignty. The leaders of India and Pakistan had powerful notions of national sovereignty, developed over decades of nationalist politics. Both could see that the princes were a potential focus of regional loyalty, and might challenge that sovereignty.[171] Both set about dismantling these states at once – something the British had not dared to do. By the end of 1948, both had integrated the states into the nation. Pakistan quickly folded Bahwalpur into Punjab; it tried, but failed, to force Kalat into Balochistan.[172]

India, meanwhile, bulldozed hundreds of principalities into signing instruments of accession, and in 1948 in Operation Polo (politely described as a 'police action') India forced the Nizam of Hyderabad to surrender his independence.[173] These 'instruments of accession' were quasi-treaties, promising their signatories the right to retain power over internal affairs. But in practice by 1950 New Delhi had wrested these powers from them.[174] In 1969 Indira Gandhi went further still and abolished their privy purses, leaving the princely states with palaces too expensive to maintain. Many have been turned into hotels. They tout a *Best Exotic Marigold* vision of India to tourists nostalgic for a past world of maharajas.

III

TAXATION: THE NUB OF GOVERNMENT

If the colonial state's sovereignty remained patchy over different spheres of government, and its capacity to intervene in Indian society was limited, and its capacity to rule was undermined by its stereotypes and attitudes, there remained the problem of the bottom line.

How were Indian revenues going to pay for all of this?

The expanded army, the policemen in their stations, the white officers with their fat-cat pay and pensions, all those grand buildings and all that 'knowledge gathering', the railways and canals, as well as the deployment on the frontiers, internal frontiers and overseas – how on earth was India to stump up the cash, in a period of recurrent famine?

The empire's limitations were visible, like light through cracks, in the ways it raised taxes.

The state could not survive without revenue – no state can. Since London's golden rule was that the Indian empire had to pay for itself (and then more), the state had to squeeze as much tax as it could without raising the hackles of Indian elites. (Gandhi had been right. No state could be run without the cooperation of the elites.)

After the Mutiny and Rebellion of 1857, Charles ('Clemency') Canning, the first viceroy, sued for peace with the rajas, ranis and *taluqdaars* who had risen up against the East India Company. This deepened the state's innate conservatism. From this point onwards, the Raj would strive with every sinew not to offend India's rural elites.

So now it was even more 'gently-gently' in the countryside, at least as far as the dominant castes and classes were concerned.

Most of the tax burden, in the first century of dominion, however, fell on the vast Indian countryside. So it was the peasant, the tenant farmer and the village artisan who had to bear the brunt.

Yet the East India Company had to recognise its limitations in gathering tax from these hamlets. It did not know who owned the land – indeed it never really understood the hierarchy of titles to land that co-existed in India – and how much each cultivator or tenant could afford to pay. It had established different revenue-gathering systems in different parts ('presidencies') of India. These were, to an extent, inventions of 'men on the spot'; and in part derivations of tax systems that had been in place under polities the British had conquered, and which they now thought it prudent to be guided by. These were glorious decades for conservatism in Britain, when Edmund Burke thundered in Parliament about ruling India in tune with its ancient traditions. Three different systems of agrarian taxation would survive across India until the Union Jack came down in 1947.

The British relied on Indian intermediaries to collect the tax, of course. In the huge region of Bengal, where landlords and petty kings had been crucial allies in helping the British gain control, a 'permanent settlement' gave these *zamindaars* (landowners) absolute rights of ownership of their land (a novel concept in the subcontinent, where the great majority held titles to a share of the crop, not the land itself). The British also gave them a duty to pay a quantum of annual tax fixed for all time.

The government hoped that the *zamindaars* might reinvest gains from the land into agrarian improvement, but that hope was belied: what developed instead was a rentier system from which the *zamindaars* gained much and the *Sarkar* nothing at all. The state turned a blind eye to what these *zamindaars* did within their estates, to how they treated tenants and peasants, and by what means they extracted that revenue. The state permitted *zamindaars*, right until 1947, to maintain small private armies of *paiks* (foot-soldiers) and *laathials* (stave-wielding heavies) to force tenants to pay up. Tentative efforts at reform in 1885 and 1928 did little to diminish the *zamindaars'* authority within their domains.

Meanwhile, the value of the tax each estate paid by 1900 had fallen; and it would continue to fall as the world wars created huge inflationary pressures. Partition would exacerbate a bad situation, from the taxman's point of view.

Having subjugated much of southern and western India by the sword, by contrast, the East India Company felt more confident about sweeping away 'intermediaries' and dealing directly with the cultivator (*raiyat*). The *raiyatwaari* system drew partly on Tipu Sultan's model, and in part on the fiscal ideology of the day back in England and partly on the notion that by getting the peasant cultivators to pay revenue themselves, the state would bypass Indians who were supposedly hoovering up the bulk of the peasants' surplus.[175] This system, put in place in most parts of the Bombay and Madras presidencies, was more energetic and interventionist than in Bengal, though not always in ways that helped the *raiyat*. The tax extracted from peasants remained too heavy to allow them to build up surpluses to invest and increase their yields. So these yields had begun to decline by the start of the twentieth century, not just in these areas but in Bengal too.[176]

In yet another system, in Punjab and the north-west of the subcontinent, tax was deemed payable by whole villages. How the village shared the tax burden, the British did not want to know.

However here the tax burden was light. The Raj did not want to alienate the region from which it recruited its 'good fighting men', so it was careful about squeezing Punjab as hard as it did other regions.

If anything, in vast expanses of the country under British rule – from the dry tracts of Madras to the wetlands of Bengal – the domination of local elites over cultivators grew more entrenched. The latter grew poorer, and more liable to seek credit from landlords. This debt would eventually push them into conditions of bondage (of which more in Chapter 4).

Even in the areas where it sought to tax and govern more closely, the East India Company soon found, as did the Raj after it, that it had to accommodate Indian social realities, notably Brahmin privilege and the role of dominant castes.[177] In other parts, as in the Punjab, it would impinge upon and change Indian circumstances often without realising what it was doing, or 'settling' the tax of villages where none existed, bestowing upon them the duty to pay revenue that never arrived.[178]

The goal was to get every bit of revenue possible from the cultivator himself. Everything above his basic subsistence needs was deemed 'excess' that belonged to the state. Almost everywhere the British strove to keep accurate and updated 'geld books' in the form of survey settlements, based on who owned land where.

This was not easy to discover, however. *Patwaaris* and *qaanungos* had the job of telling district magistrates and settlement officers who held the title to a large plot of 'good land' – or a smaller plot of sublet poor land, *inaam* land (rewarded for services), or charitable *waqf* property and so on – and report who owned what, who had mortgaged what, and who owed what sums. The potential for subversion of the system was enormous. A study of Guntur district in the Madras Presidency suggests just how hollow the structure had been in the era of the East India Company.[179] A close study of the Punjab in the Company period suggests that even in the late-colonial era, the Raj never got a handle on the problem, although this was a matter of the highest priority.[180]

The late-Victorian famines suggested that there was more than a grain of truth in the criticism of the economic nationalists about the burden of agrarian taxation. Three further points are important. First, the Rebellion was believed in London to have been caused, at least in large part, by rural discontent: and so there were disputes about whether it was a good idea to bear down so heavily on the land. The land itself had its limits. South Asia is a large subcontinent, but it had only so many acres that were cultivable and cultivated. Agrarian taxes would not grow. There was only so much land that could be brought under the plough to yield a bare subsistence.

Second, the 'cake' would only go so far. Agrarian yields per acre began to stagnate, and even decline, in the early twentieth century.

Third, such taxation had become a hot potato, already in the first decade of the twentieth century, when R. C. Dutt wrote his open letters to Curzon. Even British surgeon-generals – men such as William Cornish (whom we will meet in Chapter 6) – were creating almighty storms about how much food was enough to sustain life.

In this context, the British Raj began to think hard about raising other sources of revenue.

Pressing down harder on the forests in the subcontinent was one key plan. It was not as if such efforts had not started before the Mutiny or the Rebellion – they had, during the Napoleonic wars, when Malabar teak began to be used for ship building. It was rather that they now became more aggressive and far-reaching.[181] In 1865, 1878 and 1927, the Raj put successive Forest Acts onto the statute books that reserved the largest swathes of the subcontinent's forests (for use by the state itself to manage timber felling) for commercial use, and to permit only the most limited use of forest produce to those Indians whose lives depended on it. It worked. If commercial groups were given licences to fell timber, this raised revenue. Felled teak forests turned into ships in Bombay; softer woods could be made into millions of railway sleepers. And there was fun to be had in the bargain: more good *shikaar* (hunting) for British entertainment.

But it did what it was supposed to do, in spades: produce revenue. Table 3.1 has the figures.

Table 3.1
Revenue and surplus of the Forest Department[182]

Annual average	Period	Revenue (Rs million)	Surplus of Forest Department (Rs million)
1869–70	To 1873–4	5.6	1.7
1873–4	To 1878–9 (Year of the 1878 Forest Act)	6.7	2.1
1879–80	To 1881–4	8.8	3.2
1884–5	To 1888–9	11.7	4.2
1899–1900	To 1903–4	15.9	8.4
1904–5	To 1908–9	19.7	11.2
1914–15	To 1918–19	37.1	16.0
1919–20	To 1923–5	55.2	18.5
1924–5	To 1925	57.6	21.3

This policy used up only ten per cent of all trees 'captured' in South Asia's multi-species forests. It had no regard for the interests of forest dwellers or forest users. It was destructive of the subcontinent's habitat (by mass planting single-species forests to replace older heterogeneity). That this was a wasteful policy is another scandal of empire less well known than slavery, but no less devastating in its consequences for humans and habitats.[183]

As for forest dwellers, of whom many had lived by shifting *jhum* cultivation, or as hunter-gatherers, what of them? The government proved hell-bent on putting a stop to it, believing that these farmers, rather than the timber merchants, were responsible for the degradation of the forests. The state did not always succeed – no government can outwit all the people resisting it on their own terrain – but it did enough to begin to drive them out of the ecological niches they had long occupied. In time, this would yield a further benefit to the state that perhaps they had not anticipated. Many chose to migrate, and they proved to be among the few groups desperate enough to travel to the plantation colonies. (More of this in Chapters 4 and 6.)

Another strategy was for the government to look at what it could tax in the city. It was at this stage that 'vice taxes' came into operation – on western-style alcohol and cigarettes, mainly the addictions of the urban elites and middle classes. (These groups were among the Raj's loudest critics, but they had to tax someone, and at least these 'soft' city folk were not likely to rise up and attack the taxman with swords.)

Soon, the colonial government started to tax sales, beginning to hurt Indian merchants and traders. During the Great War, it alienated them further by charging 'supertaxes' on profits.

Customs duties became a major source of revenue now. Britain was no longer 'an empire of free trade', as it had been in its heyday of economic power. Lancashire's ability to dictate Indian tariffs now ended for good.[184] Before the Great War, duties on British imports already hovered at 3.5 per cent; by 1917, they had risen to 7.5 per cent; in the 1920s they hit eleven per cent, and by the 1930s, were a whopping twenty-five per cent. Goods from elsewhere in the world – the growing economic powers of the United States, Japan, Germany – attracted customs duties of fifty per cent.

It's a marvel that anyone bothered to trade with India at all. But they did, as India already had a huge market for cheap yarns, coarse but mill-made fabrics, and hosiery.

Stamp duty came in too in this new era, but since urban property (for instance the vast Palladian townhouses of the Calcutta Bengali elite) did not come on the market every day, it helped only at the edges. Custom and law militated against the sale of ancestral property. Hindu law forbade it. Sentiment revolted against it among many South Asians, whatever their sect or creed. When my brother wanted to sell our house in Delhi, my Christian Adivasi carer, Saroj, gave him a good talking to. She was in fine fettle! I have never seen her so angry.

The British should have known this. God knows they had been there long enough. They had spent an age codifying law. But institutional memory, or cross-department discussion, seems not to have been good, despite all that furious information gathering about 'the tribes and castes', not to mention the languages, avocations, laws and customs, creeds and practices, of India.

On and off, the Raj imposed income taxes. It was not sure it could do this, because by Hindu law, traditional Hindu families consisted of seven generations of men, all (including those unborn) sharing equally in the gains and losses of the whole household group. In a curious turn of fortune, successful Hindu men in the professions fought to pay tax on their 'gains of learning'. Why they offered themselves up in this way is discussed in Chapter 5. Here, it is enough to say that income from a few thousand professional men in the cities hardly began to pay for even the uniforms of a regiment.

All of this will explain why the Raj started to devolve tax gathering to districts in the late nineteenth century, and to the provinces in 1920. Indians, elected by other Indians, were charged with raising taxes and spending them locally on everything irrelevant to its sovereignty. They could run sanitation projects, build roads, 'develop' their districts. The Raj – having developed thousands of kilometres of railways – was now washing its hands of all that.[185]

India and Pakistan after independence could not take the same approach. They had to be seen to deliver the dividends of freedom to the people. No more famines, for one. And a future-oriented, optimistic approach about what a developing state could and should do for its people.

First, there would be a sharp separation of what the centre would tax, and what taxes the provinces would raise. Land revenue on agricultural land was allocated to provinces – but how could they squeeze juice out of this bitter lemon? Instead they were stuck with sales taxes (except where such sales had an impact on inter-provincial commerce), 'taxes on animals and boats', taxes on professions, and on newspaper advertisements.[186] A few 'vice taxes' were thrown in, hitting the urban consumer and trader where it hurt.

Raising tax at the local and municipal level (as in British times) was game over.

So the state had no choice but to wait for handouts from the centre – the size of which was calculated by the central Planning Commission. (More about this below.)

Meanwhile the centre grabbed all the juicy watermelons, as Table 3.2 indicates.

Table 3.2
Taxes under central or Union jurisdiction
(List I of the Seventh Schedule of the Constitution of India)[187]

No.	Entry no. on List	Description of tax/duty
1	82	Taxes on income other than agricultural income
2	83	Duties on customs including export duties
3	84	Duties on excise except on alcoholic liquors and narcotics, including medicinal and toilet[te] preparations
4	85	Corporation tax
5	86	Taxes on the capital value of assets, exclusive of agricultural land
6	87	Estate duty in respect of property other than agricultural land
7	88	Duties in respect of succession of property other than agricultural land
8	89	Terminal taxes on goods and passengers carried by railway, sea or air; taxes on railway fares and freights
9	90	Taxes other than stamp duties on transactions in stock exchanges and futures markets
10	91	Rates of stamp duty in respect of bills of exchange, cheques, promissory notes, bills of lading, letters of credit, policies of insurance, transfer of shares, debentures, proxies and receipts
11	92	Taxes on the sale and purchase of newspapers and advertisements published therein
12	92A*	Taxes on sale and purchase of goods other than newspapers where such sale takes place in the course of inter-state trade or commerce

13	92B*	Taxes on consignment of goods (whether the consignment is to the person making it or to any other person), where the consignment takes place in the course of inter-state trade or commerce
14	92C*	Taxes on services
15	97	Any tax not enumerated in List II or List III of the Seventh Schedule

92A*, 92B* and 92C* are amendments introduced in 1956, 1982 and 2003 respectively

Point 97 on the list – any tax not enumerated in the constitution – would be of growing importance as the century progressed. Telecommunications had not been so listed. When these appeared in a new, blue, snazzy (we thought then) form, with STD booths on every urban street corner, this became lovely revenue for the Government of India. The world wide web was still in its infancy at the end of the twentieth century, but guess who would get a slice of the growing tax income it generated? The centre, not the provinces.

Agrarian taxation, meanwhile, fell through the trapdoor of history. Given what we know of economic nationalism, this should surprise no one. (Agrarian taxation fell in Pakistan too, although for different reasons. There, landlords were seen as being benevolent old-school rajas who would care for their *raiyats* better than the British state had done. Recall Liaquat's views on the countryside.)

Gathering revenue from forests, meanwhile, continued with little change, although no one thought to mention it in India's constitution.[188]

This search for new sources of revenue was the need of the midnight hour, given the heavy burden of their armies, and the developmental goals of both states.

IV

THE 'DEVELOPMENTAL' STATE

It would be a mistake to see Nehru's 'socialism' as a watered-down variant of communism. It was a mode of governance with a focus on state-led, top-down development. The idea was that with effective, energetic and targeted development, India could leapfrog the stages of progress that western countries had been through to become 'modern'. The underlying assumption was that the countries of the West had all achieved progress in the same way, and that progress in and of itself was a good thing. Nehruvians believed it could be achieved only by harnessing the power of the state, since the poor illiterate masses and under-capitalised business groups, left to their own devices, could not go forward.

But it would be misguided to think that Nehru owned the copyright to the brand. Pakistan shared this grand vision, as did most newly independent states in the 1950s which came together at Bogor, in Colombo, and indeed in Bandung, in 1955.[189] Inspired by the Soviet achievements before and during the Second World War, the leaders of Pakistan, like India under Nehru, believed that, given insufficient capital accumulation and credit in their countries, only the state could deliver meaningful development. India's captains of industry had a considerable hand in guiding Nehru's vision. In their Bombay Plan of 1944–5, they stressed that for the private sector to grow, the state would have to step in.[190] With state intervention in the economy providing this support, they envisaged a doubling of the output of the agricultural sector and predicted a five-fold growth in the industrial sector. This dream may have failed, but the principles set out at Bombay shaped Nehruvian economic policies for decades to come.[191]

In some arenas, Pakistan lagged behind India in delivering development on these terms; in others it forged ahead. In certain fields, such as the advances in the biosciences that undergirded the Green Revolution, there was more collaboration between the two than is often recognised;[192] whereas in the development of nuclear power, competition with the other drove advances in both countries.

But the model was essentially the same. It was a planned and target-driven approach, in both cases inspired by the Soviet model. Both countries adopted five-year plans with specific goals in mind. Pakistan produced eight plans in all; India continued to churn them out until the end of the century and beyond. The five-year plans of both countries focused on catching up with the West, promoting self-reliance in industry and food, achieving economic growth, and stimulating the private sector.

Food security was a vital issue. Legitimacy in both states was, for reasons already discussed, tightly bound up with defeating famine. India, with supplies from the United States under the Public Law 480 programme, succeeded at keeping outright famine at bay.[193] Pakistan struggled more, East Pakistan experiencing regular food crises throughout the 1950s.[194] Developing better strains of food crops, insecticides and fertilisers, improving irrigation and stockpiling grain were pressing goals for both India and Pakistan. Nationalising banks, raising high import duties, putting in place 'support prices' for food, controlling trade in essential commodities; all these created what cynics and some scholars describe as a 'licence-permit Raj'. Import-substitution and controlling inflation generated autarchic pressures on both sides of the border, and (some would argue) two bloated, rent-seeking states.

In India, planning is associated with the eccentric polymath Prasanta Chandra Mahalanobis. Legend has it that his career was influenced by a missed train. In 1913, having registered to read physics at the University of London, this tall, gaunt, young Brahmo from Calcutta went to visit a friend at Cambridge and didn't make the last train back.[195] He was so impressed by King's College that he decided to stay on in Cambridge to study there, and this was somehow arranged. (Today, this would never happen, but we are speaking of another century.)

Mahalanobis seems (unlike Nehru) to have hung out with the Indian mathematicians at Trinity, in particular the genius Ramanujan, and their fascination with numbers seems to have rubbed off on him. Sometime in the next decade, he chanced upon a copy of the journal *Biometrika*, and a lifelong passion for statistics was born.

On his return to India in the 1930s, he founded the Indian Statistical Institute. Mahalanobis was elected Fellow of the Royal Society for a significant technical achievement (the Feldman–Mahalanobis distance); but it was as an institution-builder (and some would say empire-builder) that he made his mark on history. The Indian Statistical Institute is his memorial.

In Pakistan, strangely enough, the man who drove planning through was General Ayub Khan. Like Nehru, Pakistan's first prime minister Liaquat Ali Khan was impressed by Soviet planning; but he was assassinated in 1951. Numerous short-lived civilian governments rose and fell thereafter, and development was only taken up in earnest after Ayub's 'Revolution' (his declaration of martial rule in 1958). Ayub justifies his actions as being driven by the desire to 'get on with the reconstruction of the country and rehabilitation of society'. His view was that 'what the country needed was a positive effort to move forward, to build itself and the economy into a dynamic and progressive force'.[196] Anatol Lieven goes so far as to describe Ayub Khan as having come to power as the CEO 'of that great meritocratic corporation, the Pakistan army', which he regards as Pakistan's most 'modern' institution.[197] This is a provocative statement. I doubt Lieven himself takes it seriously. (It's the sort of quotation one might set as a question in an undergraduate examination paper, asking students to 'discuss'.) But it does encourage one to think, or rethink, the presumed relationship between democracy and development.

The goals of planning were wide-ranging, indeed, all-encompassing; but rather than give chapter and verse, I'll discuss three of them.

Refugees and cities were key targets of the drive for development, as were rivers.

This may sound an unlikely combination, but it's not, if you stop to think about it.

Refugees made a beeline for cities in search of shelter and a livelihood. Unlike the new nation's other citizens, they had been wrenched out of their contexts as whole families, and when the state was forced to get involved in their rehabilitation, it sought to develop this 'human material' according to its modernist vision. The goal was to turn refugees into ideal citizens: future-oriented (as opposed to backward-looking), progressive and self-sustaining. But this was to happen *outside* existing cities, which the refugees had (in the official gaze) rendered more chaotic.

Existing cities and industrial hubs, meanwhile, had to be electrified to enable them to drive the economy forward. Urban populations had to be fed, so agrarian communities had to become more productive and have more regular access to water. This meant that rivers had to be tamed, and nature's sovereignty had to be yoked to the goals of the state.

In India, the government's aim was to establish 'model' refugee colonies some distance away from existing cities. West Bengal's government kept up its constant drive to disperse refugees from Calcutta to 'empty spaces': to the dense forests of Dandakaranya in Central India, to the Andaman Islands in the Bay of Bengal, to the rocky arid plains of Koraput and Kalahandi in Orissa, and to abandoned marshy malarial tracts like Jirat. When these failed, government packed them off to 'model' townships.[198] The Indian government was particularly determined to keep Delhi, the capital city, clean and orderly; so Punjabi refugees were offered housing far beyond its limits, chiefly to its south and west.[199] Their new houses were planned on modern lines. Brick-built, with square large windows for air, they had distinct bedrooms, living rooms, kitchens and toilets – most unlike the homes most refugees had left behind, where (as Chapter 6 will show) the same living space tended to be used in a variety of ways for different purposes throughout the day, where windows and doors had tended to be small to keep out the scorching heat and lashing rain.

These homes, moreover, were arranged in an orderly fashion, in straight lines, along a road, facing (or close to) a park in which children could play. The park might have had only a patch of brown grass, a peeling bench, a climbing frame and a slide; but for most refugee children, it was an experience light years away from older kinds of play set in forests and fields, as in the magical (if often tragic) world of Apu and Durga in *Pather Panchali*.[200] Each camp would have a school, where children were to be educated to become modern adults and responsible citizens. Each would also have a hospital or dispensary, and a bus service to the city. Refugee families were to be modernised. They were encouraged to turn to western medicine when they were ill. The Bombay Refugees Act, which came into effect in June 1948, prescribed compulsory vaccination for refugees. If they failed to follow any of the Act's provisions they could be sent to jail or forced to pay a fine, or both.[201]

Refugees in Nehru's India and Ayub's Pakistan were also expected to have few children (two was the ideal number), birth control and family planning being the dicta of the age. These children were to go to government schools in clean white and blue uniforms, canvas shoes and khaki rucksacks, their hair oiled and parted (and, for girls, neatly plaited and tied with red ribbons). They were to be taught to serve the nation while making few demands upon the state.[202]

These plans reveal just how intrusive the post-colonial states strove to be, in contrast to their colonial predecessor (if only with refugees, but we are talking in India of about fourteen million people and growing, with refugees continuing to spill across the Bengal border).[203] The colonial state had only just begun to tinker with the market in the 1940s, during the war and the Bengal Famine; and was terrified of intervening in the domain of the Indian family. In free India and

Pakistan by contrast, not only were large sectors of the economy controlled and regulated by the state, but intimate areas of life – hitherto untouched by a nervous Raj – became the object of a liberal desire to cleanse and modernise every aspect of social life. Homes, toilets and even sexual relations between spouses were not spared. In their turn, these early programmes, during the Emergency, became blueprints for the harsh slum-clearance programmes of future decades, and even for the notorious mass sterilisation drive and forced vasectomies of India's Emergency.

These plans were a spectacular failure, whether in Calcutta, Delhi or Karachi; the subcontinent's three largest refugee cities. One of the ironies of the biography of 'the state' is that it matters not a jot that a plan has failed in the past; a decade or two later, the plan can be pulled out of a dusty drawer and reused as the plan for the next exciting social experiment. As they were, during the Emergency, and with the 'rehabilitation' of village dwellers ousted by big-dam development projects.

The model towns and model homes were either never completed, or else they were so badly built and illogically situated that the refugees abandoned them in droves.[204] Very often they sold their tiny government-allotted plots to property sharks – who in turn built on them dodgy, double-storied, unlicensed structures which they rented out to poor commuters – producing, over time, vast unplanned outskirts around Calcutta, Delhi and Karachi.[205] Meanwhile, the refugees drifted back to the slums of the very cities that they had been ordered to leave.

These failures were inevitable, given the scale of the refugee crisis, and given how the planners believed they knew what was best for the people they were trying to help, even when they patently did not. But it was also a sign of the extent to which government across South Asia had come to believe that modernisation was the solution to every problem, however large and complex.

Dare I say the unsayable: the bureaucrats of post-colonial South Asia were no more in touch with 'the people' than the British Mandarins had been. 'English, August' Sen, the IAS probationer in Upamanyu Chatterjee's cult classic novel of that name, could hardly have been more distanced from, or bored by, the little world of Madna, his first posting.[206] Funnily enough, only a few shades distinguish August's relationship with his cook Vijay from Clive Jenkinson's constant fury with his bearer, Ayaz. The modern English-speaking Indian middle-class officer barely saw his 'servant' as a human being. The class differences were too vast and the caste perspective too entrenched.

Meanwhile: back to cities.

As old cities tried without success to drive refugees out, new ones emerged to reflect the states' modernist aspirations. Though not often seen as such, Chandigarh (in India) and Islamabad (in Pakistan) are mirror images of each other. Both were designed by European architects. Chandigarh in the Punjab plains, in the shadow of the Himalayan foothills, was the work of Le Corbusier, one of the twentieth century's great modernist architects. Punjab, having lost its capital city Lahore to Pakistan, needed a new focus, so Nehru believed; although by the time Chandigarh had eventually come into existence, it became the shared capital of Punjab and the new state of Haryana. Chandigarh's masterplan was its sluice-gate against the 'ordered disorder' of the old South Asian city.[207] It divided Chandigarh into neat grids and sectors, with its heart in the business district. It even had a park of modern design: the Rock Gardens, complete with fake waterfalls and abstract sculpture.

Chandigarh divides opinion. Some describe it as the most beautiful city in the world; others as the ugliest. I have been spoilt by having spent my childhood in Delhi with its thousand years of history. To me Chandigarh feels brutal, temporary. Wags speak of 'Sector 25' (which houses the crematorium) as a euphemism for death.

The Greek firm of Constantinos Doxiadis designed Islamabad in 1958, when General Ayub's martial law 'Revolution' began. By this time, the Pakistan government had given up on Karachi – a refugee city par excellence – as its capital. It decamped first to Rawalpindi, where the army was headquartered, and then to Islamabad, twenty kilometres to its north. Like Chandigarh, Islamabad is cool in the winter and spring, being close to the Margalla foothills. A compact city, it is divided into eight zones.[208] The website of the Capital Development Authority describes it as 'a clean, spacious and quiet city with lots of greeneries'.[209] In other words, it is exactly the opposite of Karachi, Bombay or Calcutta, organic South Asian cities which are unplanned, dirty, crowded and raucous. They boast little foliage, their few trees wilting in the noxious air. I have never been to Islamabad, but that's because Pakistani friends have urged me not to bother.

('*Wahaan kyoon jaanaa hai? Wahaan to kuchh nahin milegaa.*' 'Why do you want to go there? You will find nothing there.') It is, they tell me, 'a city without a soul'.

The same spirit of hubris, on both sides of the border, drove the massive hydroelectric energy projects of the 1950s and 60s. In 1960, the two countries resolved their differences over the Indus waters. India gained rights to the waters of the Ravi, Sutlej and Chenab tributaries while Pakistan got the right to develop the Jhelum and Chenab, and the Indus river basin. It proceeded to build the Mangla Dam, one of the highest in the world, in Azad Kashmir (or Pakistan Occupied Kashmir, POK, as India prefers to call it). The dam submerged 280 villages and the towns of Mirpur and Dadyal, and displaced more than 110,000 people. Pakistan's government with Whitehall's connivance gave many of them permits to work in Britain, and their descendants are now clustered in Bradford and Leeds.[210]

Meanwhile, across the border, in 1963 India celebrated the realisation of the Bhakra–Nangal project, which dams the River Sutlej. In one of his most famous speeches, Nehru declared: 'This dam has been built with the unrelenting toil of man for the benefit of mankind and therefore is worthy of worship. May you call it a Temple or a Gurdwara or a Mosque, it inspires our admiration and reverence.'

This speech is often thought to encapsulate Nehruvianism; but, as a glance across the border shows, it reflected shared problems of irrigation in the two countries, common shortages of food and energy and perhaps the 'gigantist' zeitgeist of the time. There was nothing uniquely Nehruvian about it. The Bhakra Dam, at 741 ft (226 m), is one of the highest gravity dams in the world. The large reservoir created by the dam submerged over 370 villages from the district of Bilaspur and displaced their inhabitants. Sixty years after its completion, 'oustees' from the villages claim that they have yet to receive full compensation. They feel – and, knowing what I know about state rehabilitation practices, I am sure they are right – they were sold a lemon. They still are not resettled.[211]

Bangladesh's development story has been rather different. Or at least it has followed a different path since the assassination of its first prime minister Mujibur Rahman in 1975. This was in the context of a vast famine that challenged his government's legitimacy in the eyes of the soldiers who killed him, and which skewed its demography for decades afterwards.[212]

As prime minister, he was in a tearing hurry to 'catch up', not only with the West but with West Pakistan and India; and even friendly journalists believe that his haste to drive through governmental programmes in the countryside was a factor leading to the famine.[213]

Since then, Bangladesh's development has been far more of a story of 'bottom-up', non-governmental programmes.

Cyclone Bhola, the deadliest tropical cyclone ever recorded at the time, hit East Pakistan in 1970. It caused over 500,000 deaths, and small non-state groups (non-governmental organisations, NGOs) sprang up to help its victims. (The Pakistani state's failure to respond to this catastrophe was a proximate cause of Bengal's demand for *shaadhinota* or freedom.) Since its formation in December 1971, Bangladesh has teemed with NGOs. But the story of its largest NGO, BRAC (formerly Bangladesh Rural Advancement Committee), makes the point. A former executive with Shell, Fazle Abed (1936–2019), established it in 1972. BRAC's early focus was the rehabilitation of the 9.9 million refugees displaced during Pakistan's brutal crackdown and Bangladesh's war to liberate itself from Pakistani 'colonial' rule. By the mid-1970s, it had extended its remit to the vast problem of rural poverty that Sheikh Mujib had tried to solve with massive top-down state-driven projects. BRAC offered different solutions.

I first met Sir Fazle a few years ago in a small hotel at the centre of Cambridge, over a hearty breakfast of bacon and eggs. For me it was the crack of dawn (the drugs I take for epilepsy make me thick-tongued and foggy-headed in the mornings) but Sir Fazle had a spring in his step. I was in awe, but his soft-spoken charm drew me out. He was humble despite his staggering achievements, full of energy despite his years, and still interested in other people. His vision was the opposite of planning from above; it was empowerment from below. He introduced the idea of microcredit in 1974 as a tool to alleviate poverty.

BRAC, which also focuses on providing healthcare and literacy to the poor, is now the world's largest NGO, with about 47,000 regular staff and about 65,000 teachers working in some 70,000 villages spread across the sixty-four districts of Bangladesh. By 2003, according to its own data, the BRAC development programme had organised over 3.85 million landless poor, mostly women, into 113,756 'village organisations'. Each village organisation (VO) with about forty members serves as a forum where the rural poor collectively think through the impediments to local development.

Unlike the developmentalist models of India and Pakistan, BRAC encouraged the rural poor to work together to identify and tackle their own problems, with the help of small loans. By December 2002, Sir Fazle's massive team had disbursed Tk 86.61 billion ($1.8 billion) among VO members to develop their capacity to generate their own income. Meanwhile, in 1976, Professor Muhammad Yunus of the University of Chittagong devised and designed a credit delivery system to provide banking services (microfinance) to the rural poor. This led to the establishment of the Grameen Bank, which grew significantly after 2003, and in 2006, the Nobel Committee awarded Professor Yunus the Nobel Peace Prize. By 2011, the bank had 8.4 million borrowers, ninety-seven per cent of whom are women.

I do not suggest that these schemes have brought about a new dawn. Of course they have not, as numerous studies attest.[214] My point is rather that they couldn't be more different from the 'big-dam' approach to development.

Although underscoring these differences in Bangladesh's trajectory from those of India and Pakistan, I would not want to overplay them. By the late 1970s, both India and Pakistan also were rolling back on their grand promises of development and shrinking the state's role in the economy. 'Liberalisation', as it was called, was a condition that the two countries accepted in exchange for loans from the World Bank and International Monetary Fund (IMF). It proceeded further and faster in Pakistan, which in the 1980s moved towards the wholesale privatisation of national industries and liberalisation of the economy.[215] The difference can be overdrawn, however, given the Army's role in investment in large swathes of the sectors of the economy since that time.

India only really followed the script after an acute balance of payments crisis, exacerbated by oil shortages during the first Iraq War, forced it to its knees, bowl in hand, looking to the Bretton Woods institutions for a bailout. 'Every money lender has his rates, and the IMF and World Bank are far from charitable institutions.'[216] The quid pro quo was structural adjustment. Subsidies to farmers, for instance, had to go, and many public sector utilities were sold. 'Reform' was the mantra of government across the subcontinent, and massive state investment was now in the *development of infrastructure, rather than people*. This was the new liberalised route to making GDP grow. 'Reform' now meant making it easier for businesses to thrive. It also meant a retreat of the states' ambitions to transform society.

Meanwhile, civil society organisations and NGOs have sprung up throughout the subcontinent to take up some of the slack. They are not, of course, on the scale of Bangladesh's BRAC and Grameen Bank, but there is a sense in which the differences can be exaggerated. Despite conflict and hostility in the neighbourhood, the three states of South Asia have moved on parallel tracks more often than the world, or even South Asians themselves, realise.

Thinking about the state: what the *pablik* imagines the state is

Recall Sheikh Mujibur Rahman – the raven-haired, pipe-smoking, handsome leader of the Awami League, who died just three years after Bangladesh was born.[217] Some years before this, in a discussion with like-minded friends, Mujib had once claimed that the secession of the eastern wing would be no problem. All he needed was a can of kerosene and a matchbox. 'When all of us questioned how he would do it, Mujib said he would go to Kurmitola Airport, splash kerosene on the runway and ignite fire with a match stick.'[218] As with Amar Raha in 1948, so for Mujib in the early 1960s, the airport – strategic infrastructure – was a critical site of the state's violent sovereignty.

But these were men steeped in political theory and practice.

How do the ordinary folk of the subcontinent – the *pablik* as they often characterised themselves – regard the state? Do they see it as a single, interconnected and sublime structure, with a clear purpose – perhaps to keep power in the hands of those who already have it?

Or is it the chaotic useless mess they encounter at the police station?

Perhaps it is both? I believe that they know that the state is both the big structure run from Delhi, Islamabad or Dacca, and the local, every-day state that issues BPL (below poverty line) cards, has incompetent cops and some corrupt *patwaaris*. South Asians, in my experience, are smart enough to put that together.

Are they prepared to negotiate with, pressurise, or even resist, different levels of government authority – whether *patwaari*, block development officer (BDO), or the district magistrate (DM) – to pursue their own goals? You bet they are.

The story of a man-eating leopard, oddly enough, shows how.

Such a leopard emerged in the town of Chamoli, in one of India's most remote districts, in the Himalayan folds of Uttarakhand.

The anthropologist Nayanika Mathur happened to be based there for a year in 2006 (studying the state, funnily enough) when the big cat began to stalk Chamoli town and its surroundings. The cry went up: '*baagh lag gaya*' ('a big cat is on the prowl, the big cat has returned'), striking terror in every heart.

Women were (as they have always been) easy prey for leopards and tigers, since it is their duty, according to established norms, to gather firewood and fodder from the surrounding Himalayan forest. The *pablik* also feared for their small children who were vulnerable to attack.

The *baagh*'s first victim was a woman. Although mauled and battered, she survived.

'After this first attack, Chamoli became a veritable ghost town … Shops shut well before sunset. Doors were bolted firmly all day and people were wary of stepping out onto the porch.'[219]

There was little the DM could do. The state in Chamoli seemed paralysed. Leopards are a protected species in India, which has had one of the world's most ambitious conservation programmes – Project Tiger – since 1973.[220]

To respond to local fears, Chamoli's DM needed to put pressure on the state's capital in Dehradun, which in turn needed sanction from the central government in New Delhi. This took time. Weeks passed. Many files had to pass backwards and forwards. Thick files of evidence had to be created, noted, signed, the buck passed onwards and upwards, to prove that the leopard was a threat to human life, and many 'suasive letters' written to persuade the higher-ups that local anger was bubbling over.

Meanwhile, the leopard grew more bold. He even took up residence in Kund Colony (the government headquarters). One night he even slept beside the DM's rose bed.

The denizens of Chamoli first waited. This is something that the *pablik* in India are used to doing.[221] Indeed, one might say that waiting is an art form in the subcontinent.

Their reactions, though, were not passive for long. They mocked the DM. They were cynical about the state. They laughed, much like Rabelais, at the helplessness of this *kaaghazi baagh* (paper tiger).[222] They expressed admiration (mixed with fear) at the leopard's audacity. They seemed concerned for Nayanika's safety, but cared less about the DM and his staff, explaining that the *baagh* 'doesn't know' that the DM or BDO are sahibs. The *baagh*, it seemed, was a great leveller: he didn't recognise class, caste or state-backed power.

One day, the cheeky *baagh* turned up outside the main government office at 5 p.m. – at the very time the office closed. Satirists claimed he was lying in wait for the *babus*. (Satire is not only a finely honed literary form, as in the stories of Hari Shankar Parsai or R. K. Narayan, but a mode of devastating political critique in South Asia.)

After a month of waiting, several sightings and maulings, the leopard killed a twelve-year-old boy. At this point, the public mood turned ugly. Residents of Chamoli organised a procession through the town and demonstrated outside the DM's house, shouting '*Uttarakhand shaasan hai hai*' ('Shame on the government of Uttarakhand'), and '*DM sahib murdaabaad*' ('Death to the DM sahib').

'Local anger' has alarmed Indian officials since independence. Since 1948, Nehru himself denounced it again and again, to no avail. Violent crowds humiliating officers, forcing apologies out of them, had become a regular feature of politics.[223] It is little wonder that the DM was panicking.

Eventually, the frightened DM's supplications prompted Dehradun to grant a hunting permit in mid-December. In early January 2007, three *shikaaris* (state-employed shooters) turned up in the town in a white jeep, 'clutching big guns, dressed in camouflage with sunglasses and safari caps', in the manner of Bollywood stars.[224] The wily leopard eluded them, however, and three weeks later, they left Chamoli, as the wits put it, like *bheegi billi* (with their tail between their legs; literally, wet cats).[225] It was only at the end of January 2007 that a local hero succeeded in hunting down the leopard, and the town heaved a sigh of relief.

Like the people of Chamoli, one might say, the people of the subcontinent have mixed feelings about the state. They fear its harshness but mock its impotence. When angered beyond tolerance, they make noisy – sometimes violent – demands. When outraged, they demean the state's officers in ways that would have been unthinkable under the Raj.

Most of the time, however, they tolerate its lugubriousness. They wait.

What's changed since independence and what hasn't?

With the benefit of hindsight, it is easy to see why academics have argued about this so much. It's a complex picture. The answers are made no easier by the facts that no state in the divided subcontinent is exactly like another, that no state exerts its sovereignty evenly, and that each state has changed over time.

Yet despite some similarities, certain differences between the colonial and post-colonial states are stark. Citizens of independent India and Pakistan expected more of them than they could ever hope to achieve. They had dreams of freedom that were utopian in a million and one ways. India and Pakistan had to try to deliver, in short order. The developmental state was the top-heavy, bloated, often dystopian, product of their effort to fulfil popular expectations – while also protecting the interests of elites within the state, and of the state itself in the international order. The difference is that they tried to 'develop' the country and assist its people, whereas the colonial state did not.

In other respects, the differences are more nuanced. The post-colonial states of South Asia are simultaneously strong and weak, in much the same way as was the Raj. They are also violent, particularly in response to specific threats on the border and secessionist challenges. Pakistan's crackdown in what is now Bangladesh is thought to have resulted in between 600,000 and a million deaths (although the number is a matter of dispute). India broke the Khalistan movement, which demanded an independent state for Sikhs, with summary brutality; and its war against the Maoist guerillas in central India has been relentless and ferocious.[226] Bangladesh's treatment of the Jumma activists in the Chittagong Hill Tracts has not been gentle either.

India's 'encounter cops' shoot certain kinds of targets in cold blood, claiming that the victims attacked first.

The judiciary of India is stronger than that of Pakistan, having been endowed by the constitution with equal weight as the executive. Scholars claim that Indians embraced it, and perhaps they did a bit too much – the huge backlog of cases and its extreme ponderousness undermine its functioning. (A case lodged by my grandfather in the 1950s was settled only in the 2000s.) Towards the end of the century it grew embroiled in politics (as much in South Asia eventually does), after a wave of public interest litigation caused a stir. There has been political pressure on promotion to the supreme court – a recurrent note that grew louder. The poor have always been denied justice. So let's just say, there is much to reform.

Despite the rumour that Pakistan was a 'failed state' (a term that came into fashion in the 1990s), it worked effectively, thank you, in the interests of its elites. So too did the state in India. The military and the Inter-Services Intelligence agency may routinely disrupt democracy and cow the judiciary, but when required to act in the national interest (as they see it) they work with ruthless efficiency. As in India, the police protect property urban and rural, and browbeat 'criminal tribes' and 'backward castes'. They too gather files, shuffle more files, and drive beggars and 'lunatics' from the streets.

The integrity of the nation is another mantra held by all three. No challenge to it will be tolerated. Bangladesh seceded, but paid the heaviest price for its freedom, and had the advantage of being more than a thousand miles from distant Rawalpindi, separated from it by hostile Indian territory. The Sikhs, Balochis, Muhajirs and Jumma peoples did not win their battles in the twentieth century; nor did the Kashmiris. These conflicts have been raging for so long that their leaders, goals and methods have changed and been made new like the images in a shifting kaleidoscope. But I doubt that they will succeed. The states of the subcontinent are terrifyingly powerful when they choose to be.

Yet there are within these states what the late historian Rajnarayan Chandavarkar called 'zones of lawlessness'. The states tolerate them, indeed turn a blind eye to them. They have come to understand, after the failures of the 1950s, that some matters are best left alone. 'Tradition' remains a delicate area.

The family is another. In the 1950s, Nehru tiptoed around reforming Hindu family law. (More of which in Chapter 5.) In 1986, his grandson Rajiv Gandhi struck down a court judgement that gave a divorced Muslim woman, Shah Bano from Madhya Pradesh, the right to maintenance.

The state ignores, and even collaborates with, honour killings by extrajudicial groups. In April 2007, Manoj Singh (aged twenty-three) and Babli Singh (twenty) eloped from Karoran village in the Indian state of Haryana. They went to a temple at Chandigarh and married according to the laws of the state.

Eight days later Babli's relatives dragged them off a bus in broad daylight.

Ten days on their mutilated bodies were found in a canal. Their crime: they were of the same *gotra*, or sub-clan, and from the same village; but they had ignored traditions that prevented such 'incestuous' unions. The *khap panchaayat* took matters into its own hands when Manoj and Babli defied tradition. (The *khap panchaayat* is a council of male elders, an institution that has grown stronger in the last few decades and has become the self-appointed guardian of patriarchy and caste.) In turn it defied the state and its law.[227]

'Honour killing' is by no means restricted to Pakistan. Both states are cagey about implementing their own laws when it comes to dealing with such murders.

Above all, like the Raj before it, South Asia's independent states are chary of messing with religion and taking on fanatic zealots. Indira Gandhi was an exception: in June 1984 she launched Operation Blue Star, a military attack on the Golden Temple in Amritsar. Her goal, however, was *not* to intervene in Sikh religious affairs; it was to flush out from the temple complex Bhindranwale, the leader of the secessionist Khalistan movement, and his followers. In October 1984, her Sikh bodyguards shot her dead.

Since then, the state has become even more reluctant to intervene in the religious domain. On 6 December 1992, Hindu nationalists who had been demanding the construction of a temple in honour of Lord Ram at the site of the Babri Mosque, flooded into the city of Ayodhya. The Congress government led by Narasimha Rao stood by and did nothing while hundreds of young men armed with iron rods climbed on top of the mosque and began to smash it down, while armed police stood by and watched. In Pakistan, meanwhile, Osama bin Laden's hideout in Abbottabad was about thirty miles from Islamabad, the capital, and from Rawalpindi, the army headquarters. For years he remained 'undiscovered'.

And then there's the little matter of the monopoly of violence.

The other day I went to visit an old friend from my schooldays. Let's call him Ravi. He is an ophthalmologist who operates at an illustrious hospital in the heart of New Delhi. I know it well because my son was born there. As Ravi examined a tear to my cornea, he asked about the chapter I was writing and we got talking about *daakus*. Ravi told me about one of his patients who had been coming to see him for decades to deal with problems with his retina. He always came with a rifle and a sidekick. Eventually, after years of this, rushed between patients as all doctors are, Ravi got round to asking him: 'Bhai sahib, this is a hospital. *Bandook kyun hamesha yahaan le aate ho?*' ('Why do you always bring a gun here?') He said: 'Oh, this old *bandook*, doctor sahib? This is my profession! I am a killer. Do you have anyone you want bumped off? Any cousin or uncle, any property matter? For you I'll do it for free.'

'Doctor sahib', nervous, denied that he had any problems with anybody, and his patient left. But the *daaku* returned to his clinic a year or two later. This time his retina was detached and there was nothing that Ravi could do to fix it. But his patient asked Ravi to 'adjust' his *other* eye so that he could see clearly, one-eyed, through the rifle's sight, and shoot his victims dead with a single shot.

All this in the heart of the capital city, in plain sight of the thousands of policemen, paratroopers and 'blackcat' commandos who protect our leaders and, purportedly, our citizens. *Plus ça change, plus c'est la même chose?*

4

Migration at Home and Abroad:
South Asian Diasporas

'Indians are a stay-at-home people,' colonial ethnographers of the late nineteenth century were wont to complain.

You might ask: why then have a chapter on migration at all? My answer: because they were wrong, because they had looked at the issue with only one possible conclusion in view. That is never a good way to start.

The difficulty the British Indian government faced was that Indians were reluctant to travel to the destinations it wanted them to go to – the sugar islands and plantations across the oceans, and the British-owned tea plantations in Assam in north-east India. On the sugar plantations, after the abolition of slavery, planters hungry for cheap labour hoped that India would supply them with it; the colonial state in turn believed this might remedy the problem of 'overpopulation' (a condition from which it believed India suffered even in the mid-nineteenth century) and poverty. A happy solution all round, they thought.

But Indians proved reluctant to be drawn into the indentured system that was on offer, and were no more keen to work in the plantations in India itself, so bad was their reputation for conditions of employment. Hence the stereotype developed. Indians were deemed to be 'too rigidly stuck in villages and households', which needed the labour of both men and women to keep going. The grain of truth in this view, as this chapter will show, was not the whole picture. Under freer conditions, they have proved happy to travel both inland and further afield. Had this not been the case, the South Indian diaspora today would not rival that of China.

Indians were *not* reluctant migrants, in fact. In the more distant past, before the British established their dominion over India, mobility was far from exceptional; in 1800, perhaps half the population of

South Asia was peripatetic for much of their lives. Thousands of young men, particularly in the mid-Gangetic plains, volunteered to serve in a thriving market for military labour.[1] Graziers moved with their herds in search of new pastures, and shifting cultivators regularly sought out new land to plant their crops. Artisans often migrated with their families and the tools of their craft to work in the courts of petty kings.[2] Itinerant traders – Banjaras or Lambadis – took their *kaafilaas* (caravans) from the north-west of the country all the way to the south, selling mainly salt, but also grain, firewood and cattle in volumes that were huge by the standards of the time: a *kaafilaa* sometimes had as many as 100,000 bullocks, each loaded with goods weighing 250–300 pounds.[3] Astrologers, jugglers, acrobats (*baazigars*), conjurors, dancing bears, musicians, and monkeys and their handlers accompanied them, earning their crust in the *kaafilaa*'s train.

Pedlars from Afghanistan, coming down to the plains in the winter months to sell woollens and dried fruit, formed part of another web of itinerants that straddled colonial North India from the west to the Gangetic belt.[4] Rabindranath Tagore's *Kabuliwala* – a story of filial love between an Afghan merchant and a five-year-old Bengali girl – suggests how commonplace it was for Afghan pedlars to travel all the way east to Bengal, where a large community of Pathans eventually settled.[5] Earthworkers and stoneworkers (*wudders*) and cartmen were also always on the move. Pilgrims and traders criss-crossed the Indian Ocean in their dhows, regarding the sea not as a barrier to mobility but an enabler of it.[6]

By the late nineteenth century, when our story opens, this picture of mobile South Asia had been transformed.[7] In large measure this was a consequence of British policies that (deliberately or otherwise) destroyed, criminalised or, at the very least, changed these itinerant lifestyles. Technology had much to do with this. The railways made redundant the Banjaras' role as long-distance bulk commodity transporters;[8] and humble oarsmen, despite their astonishing ability to harness the monsoon winds, were pushed aside by iron-hulled steamships.[9]

Distrustful of Indians who carried arms and were on the move, and who could not easily be taxed, the Raj hunted down, disarmed and 'pacified' roving 'tribes', throwing them back on the land in search of livelihoods. In 1872, British officials clamped down on the activities of Banjaras and their like, classifying them as a 'criminal tribe'. They stigmatised *wudders* as 'skilful burglars and inveterate robbers'.[10] (The epithets used to describe the Romany in Europe and Travellers in Britain have an uncanny resonance.)

Meanwhile, the destruction of Indian kingdoms and courts, which had been the chief consumers of fine Indian wares, created what several historians have described as a crisis of 'de-industrialisation'.[11] Some artisans, to be sure, were able to resist this crisis by setting up little *karkhaanas* (small factories) or workshops in small towns, using family, kin and caste labour in ways that enabled them to adapt to the fluctuations in the market; but others were forced to abandon their hereditary crafts and ways of life.[12] Many in this category were also thrown back upon the land.

By the mid-nineteenth century, sedentary Indians had largely replaced their mobile ancestors. A great many more relied for their livelihood on agriculture, to their peril. The total area under cultivation had grown, but yields had not increased in proportion. Because the soil newly tilled was poor, more peasants struggled to cultivate land of inferior quality. The burden of tax varied across the subcontinent, but it fell hard upon those who could least afford to pay it. Countless peasants earned little above subsistence and paid eye-watering interest on loans.[13] During the long agrarian depression from the 1820s to the 1850s, and the devastating famines of the late nineteenth century, most cultivators lived life on the edge.[14] By the early twentieth century, the landless in western India were chronically hungry, while peasant cultivators all over the subcontinent suffered from the cumulative pressures of inflexible land revenue demands, chronic debt, and fluctuating prices for their produce.[15]

In those times when famine stalked the land, young men had every reason to move to towns, public works, coal mines and railway construction sites close enough to home that they could return in time for the annual cycle of harvesting crops after they had ripened.[16]

The distance they were willing to travel stretched further with the coming of the railways, which were built from the 1880s onwards – extending from 23,627 route miles laid by 1900 to 40,524 miles by 1947. The twentieth century saw a (linked) expansion of railway lines and loss of forests, and migration's changing forms and directions are connected to both. From the 1920s onwards, in response to a sudden rise in population and spurts of growth in Indian industry during the two world wars and the depression, the march of rural migrants to cities began. The cities in turn were shaped in profound ways by their arrival.

But the story of railway building is not simply one of turbocharged mobility. As we have seen in the previous chapter, it is a story of deforestation and dispossession. Tribal peoples who had lived off the fruits of the forest lost the right to their habitat when, in 1878, the British Raj declared 'reserved' forests in the subcontinent to be state property; and when timber merchants under licence began felling trees at a rate of knots to make hundreds of thousands of sleepers for the railways. These forest dwellers had been mobile folk in the past, circulating between pastures and practising *jhum* (or swidden) cultivation.[17] Now, as their world changed, they began to migrate in new directions to the neighbouring lowlands in search of work, any kind of work, in the fields, factories, cities, and even the dreaded plantations. The Santhali, Gondi and Jharkhandi diaspora from their woodlands across the Indian landmass began in the late nineteenth century. It continues to this day.

In another twist, big-dam building after independence washed away whole villages.[18] The villagers had nowhere to go in the end, but to towns and cities. The 'green revolutions' of the 1960s sparked off another spate of migrations. (This is discussed in some detail in Chapter 6.) As rich farmers swallowed up small plots, poorer ones broke for ever their ties to the land, and whole peasant families began to move to cities, changing their character once again.

Less conspicuous but far more numerous has been the migration of brides to the homes of their husbands and in-laws. It has rarely been captured in censuses, which counted as migrants only those who crossed district lines (and South Asia's districts were very large), whereas brides more often moved from one village to another one several miles away, within the same district. Everyone knows it exists, given that marriage was almost universal in South Asia in the twentieth century. One of the century's early literate women wrote of terrors of such marriages.[19] It is common knowledge that it was the bride who allowed the man to migrate in the first place, by taking on his responsibilities and work at home and in the fields. These women constituted almost half the population in the early years of the century. Without them, men could not have moved as easily or as often as they did. One kind of migration enabled another.

Halfway through the century came the shadows at noon. Between 1946 and 1964, huge waves of refugees, more than twenty-five million people, were caught up in currents of migration throughout the subcontinent, migrating as full families – creating new conurbations that changed the character of the towns and cities to which they fled. And as each independent nation made new citizens, it also created 'minorities' who were driven into new ghetto-like spaces. This process happened right across the subcontinent, not least in Bangladesh after its Liberation War.

South Asia, then, is not just an exporter of peoples to the West, a 'source region', as most people believe. It is made up of internal diasporas, small and large, layered like mica over time. Every city and town is full of outsiders – *pardesis*.

If you visit Bombay for the first time, or Delhi, or Lahore, or Calcutta, or Dacca, or Panjim, or Madras, or Karachi, or Cochin, bear this in mind. Almost everyone there is a foreigner. It is just that some have been around longer than you, long enough to learn the dominant language perhaps, or have been born there to parents who were 'foreign', born in another part of the subcontinent. Try and get your head around that. If you can do it – it will take a minute or ten – you might agree with me that migration is the most important driver of social, political and cultural change in twentieth-century South Asia.

I

THE OVERSEAS DIASPORA: CHANGE OR CONTINUITY?

In 1862, a 'coolie' named Virgagan, or Vergegen as the Boers pronounced it, gave evidence to a commission investigating a sugar planter in Natal. The east coast of South Africa, and Natal in particular, grew a lot of sugar – a precious global commodity at the time – and relied on Indian 'coolies' to plant, weed and harvest the crop.

The word 'coolie' had Telegu, Tamil and Turkic usages, and meant 'day labourer' when used in South Asia. In the overseas contexts where Indian indentured migrants worked on plantations, it had ugly, pejorative undertones. In South Africa, it was as racist and dehumanising as the word 'kaffir'.

Of his treatment at the hands of the planter, Henry Shire, and his jobber (*sirdaar*), Virgagan said:

I am in the service of Mr Shire. I have no complaint whatever to make against my master. I have to complain that Ramasammy[,] the present Sirdar, calls us out to work at six o'clock in the morning and makes us work until six o'clock at night. He then reports that we have not done a full day's work and then our master fines us. I was never fined until Ramasammy became Sirdar. We have done as much work since Ramasammy became Sirdar as before.

The Sirdar has several times struck me with a stick or anything he might have in his hand and kicked me but he never hurt me. I told my master this. I never reported this to my master through an interpreter but spoke to him in my own language. I left my master because I have received no wages since Ramasammy has been Sirdar. I understood the Magistrate [said] that he would see my wages paid in full. We left because Mr Shire Jnr. said that we should receive no more wages. I did not get sufficient food at Mr Shire's. I get 10 and a half lbs of rice for seven days' rations. The only reason I left was because Mr Shire Jnr. said that I should not get any more wages. I understood this from the other coolies.[20]

His testimony gives us a glimpse into the life of South Asian 'coolies' indentured in their millions on plantations in faraway islands and lands across the Atlantic, Pacific and Indian Oceans, from Jamaica to Mauritius to Fiji. Virgagan absconded, breaking the terms of his indenture, because of the harsh conditions that he (and twenty-two others who testified with him) experienced on Shire's plantation. Yet from the start it was clear that 'the master', Henry Shire, would get off scot-free. The line of questioning was designed to exonerate him. Artful interrogation had got Virgagan to admit that his complaint to Shire about the *sirdaar*'s maltreatment was '*in his own language*', which the planter could claim not to understand. Blame was pinned on the Indian intermediary, the *sirdaar* Rama*sammy* (note the racialisation of his name, 'Ramaswami').

Virgagan's brief statement laid bare the various ways by which South Asian labour, extracted from the subcontinent and scattered in bondage across the world, was kept docile – by beating, flogging, starvation and the withholding of wages. Assisted and loosely regulated by the empire and the British Indian colonial state, plantation owners, *sirdaars* and other professional intermediaries were part of a complex, interlocking global system of labour recruitment and management.[21]

And yet the Shire Commission of Enquiry whitewashed the planter's role in the system, attributed all gross abuses to the Indian jobber, and presented the empire as a neutral, paternalistic protector of the interests of all its subjects, white and brown. Imperial ideology spun its webs through many such obfuscations.[22]

It also gives an insight into what indenture was. In theory, it was just a binding contract for five years, renewable to ten, to work for one master. The workers' pay, rations and sometimes 'lines' (huts) were (in theory) assured for this period, after money had been docked from their wages for the cost of their passage. In practice, as Virgagan's account illustrates, it was a form of bonded labour involving extreme violence. Indenture ended in 1917, in part because of nationalist pressure, after Gandhi and Gokhale took the lead in exposing its iniquities. But its legacy lives on in a huge and far-flung South Asian diaspora which has never returned.[23]

So why did South Asians go to these places at all? One answer is that they were desperate. Between 1876 and 1902, between 12.2 and 29.3 million people died during famines across India, the imprecision of these staggering numbers being a comment on how cheap life had become.[24] Of El Niño weather systems and globalised commodity markets, peasants knew only this: hunger hovered over them like a baleful spectre. Tribal folk displaced from the forests had lost everything they knew how to live by. They now had nothing at all. Their response was to migrate.

Yet where were they to go? Those who had a stake in the countryside, however small, preferred not to travel far. Peasants had a powerful attachment to their holdings – the classic 1953 Hindi film *Do Bigha Zameen* ('Two *Bighas* of Land') gives a sense of this. Households tended to make these decisions jointly; and most patriarchs decided to send young able-bodied men and boys out to seek work paid in cash, while wives and daughters stayed behind to labour in the fields, grow a few vegetables, and forage for food, all the while caring for the aged and the young.

As for the migrants themselves, their constant refrain was to be able to return home, often to lend a hand at the heavy times of the agrarian cycle: to plough and harvest, and to repair their humble homes after the monsoons. They also had to perform *begaar*, or customary unpaid labour, for local elites. In Ratnagiri in western India, for instance, *khots* (people with land-revenue farming rights) claimed from their tenants one day's labour in eight, demanded that they plough their fields and carry these lordlings around in palanquins.[25] If they failed to return home on a regular basis to perform these tasks, the families of migrant workers in the countryside paid the price, as *zamindaars* claimed their 'dues' in harsher, more abusive ways.

So for many migrants, their preferred choice was to seek employment nearby. About two in five of Ratnagiri's population sought work in Bombay, only 200 miles away. The great bulk of Calcutta's migrants came from the neighbouring provinces of United Provinces and Bihar, a stream that turned into a flood as the railways connected these places to the city. Many other migrants gravitated to construction sites that were even closer to home, flocking to public works designed to improve India's 'moral and material progress'.[26] They broke rocks to build roads, and excavated earth to erect embankments for the railways. They needed no inducement to labour at these locations; nor did employers need penal contracts to bind them.

But railway companies soon took against such workers, whose labour dried up in the sowing and harvesting seasons. Other employers followed suit. They began to look for more 'reliable' workers who came to construction sites from places too far to return home whenever it suited them. Very quickly, employers in the emerging industries – jute, tea, coal and cotton, and also the merchant marine – came to the same conclusion: what they needed was a stable, reliable and disciplined labour force composed of long-distance migrants. *Pardesis* who 'had travelled too far from their villages and fields to be drawn back into the cycle of sowing and harvesting, and were not trapped into forms of servitude by local agrarian elites, were emerging as the modern employees of choice'.[27] Indentured workers, then, were at the extreme end of a spectrum of a system of labour control.[28]

The competition between and within sectors for such 'good' workers grew fierce as industrial capitalism (in its South Asian guise) took root. It was particularly ferocious in Calcutta, until 1911 the capital of the Raj and the second city of the empire, where coal, jute, railway and construction workers were all in demand. Most tea gardens – almost exclusively British-owned – were also in eastern India, not far from Calcutta. But these plantations were so unpopular with migrants (for a host of good reasons) that labour recruitment had to develop into a coercive industry. Calcutta was also the funnel through which all indenture ships sailed. So migrants seeking work abroad could board ships bound for 'Mirich' (as Mauritius was known. Mauritius was the largest destination of Indian migrants overseas, but by no means the only one).

There is much debate about how much agency the migrants were able to exercise when they signed (or put thumbprints) on indenture *girmits*, as these 'agreements' came to be called. The law of contract was itself only just developing in Anglo-Indian jurisprudence, so its widespread use among people without literacy raises issues. Given the scale of the professional 'recruitment industry' involved, my guess is that more were coerced than persuaded.[29] Either way, by 1901, 1.37 million Indians had gone overseas to Ceylon, Malaya and Burma, where they were most numerous, and also to sugar plantations.[30] By 1917, when indenture came to an end, there were over a million Indian migrants in the 'King Sugar' colonies in the Caribbean, Mauritius, South Africa and Fiji.[31]

However, indenture was only one of several forms of penal contract that emerged in this period to ensure that a labourer, once employed, stayed employed, even if the terms of work were harsh to the point of being unendurable. Comparable binding contracts emerged in other sectors of the economy where Indian migrants were reluctant to venture. The prime example is the tea gardens of Assam, whose reputation was so fearsome that planters depended on systematic trafficking in order to trap, ensnare and drag workers to the estates, and then keep them there.[32] Indian *lascars* (seafarers) were likewise bound by long labour contracts; they were denied land leave and had no right to terminate their labour contracts outside India.[33]

Indenture was also a response to global factors. The abolition of the global slave trade (Wilberforce and his works) was a key stimulus.[34] Sugar barons had hoped that freed slaves would return to work on plantations as free men and women. They were wrong. Right across the British Empire, they found that 'staying clear of the hated plantation was a high priority for many persons liberated from a lifetime of forced labour ... Where land was available, former slaves preferred to devote their energies to scratching out a humble existence on their own farms.'[35] This led to a crisis for the planters, and for the sugar economy.

Another engine driving the demand for indentured labour was the explosion in the demand for granulated white sugar. Already by 1750 'the poorest English farm labourer's wife took sugar in her tea', becoming 'the first mass-produced exotic necessity of a proletarian working class'.[36] In industrialising countries, workers spooned so much sugar into their tea and the better-off ate so much cake and confectionery that between 1790 and 1914, the global production of sugarcane rose from 300,000 tons to ten million tons. The British government believed that Indians were more docile than Chinese workers, and more suited than Europeans to the warm regions where sugarcane grew, and hence favoured the export of indentured Indians to the sugar islands to replace slave labour. Between 1846 and 1932, Indians made some twenty-eight million journeys abroad, ninety-eight per cent of them to labour on plantations in hot climates.[37] This 'global colour line' was not produced by accident.[38]

Indenture has acquired a dark reputation for good reasons. The ships that carried the workers across the *kaala paani* (black water) were larger than slave ships but no more salubrious. In the late nineteenth century, the smallest ships carrying indentured workers from British India weighed approximately 1,226 tons, and were desperately cramped.[39] Few ships were designed to transport workers, so indenture ship masters partitioned cargo holds by adding long shelves on each side, creating 'berths' six feet long and between twenty-one and twenty-four inches wide.[40] After the 1870s, rules about space per coolie (now seventy-two cubic feet per adult) came into force (but how often they were breached we cannot know; the state does not 'see' these minor details).[41]

Conditions on voyages remained unspeakable. Mortality rates were on a par with those in the Atlantic slave trade.[42] Totaram Sandhya, a migrant to Fiji, wrote in his memoir:

> Twice a day we were given a bottle of water to drink. Then no more, even if we died of thirst. It was the same about food. Fish and rice were both cooked there. Many people suffered from sea-sickness. Those who died were thrown overboard ... After three months and twelve days we reached Fiji.[43]

It is not as if some Indians did not collude in their misery. In fact, *arkatis* or *maistries* (professional labour contractors) had the most to gain from the system.[44] They recruited workers by fraud, deceiving them about their destinations, work conditions, pay and benefits in order to get them to affix their thumbprints on *girmits* that they could neither read nor understand. As Fazal from the Bengal-Bihar region puts it:

> i come to wuk for money
>> an go back
> i been wukking in de ship
>> i come Calcutta
> dem muslim fellar fool me
>> bring me dis country
> e say
>> e ha plenty money
> e axe me
>> how much you getting every month
> i say
>> three rupee
> e say
>> you chupid
> over dey *sara bara anna rogh*
>> every day.[45]

('You will earn ten times more there than you do here.')

But like Fazal, many were ensnared because they had *already* determined to leave home in search of work to pay their debts to the *sahookar* (moneylender) or taxes to the *sirkar*.

Consider the story of Saivaroodian, who, having left home of his own volition, was kidnapped by professional recruiters.

> I had one and a half *valy* [about ten acres] of land in [my] village. I was involved in debt to the extent of about 100 rupees and had no means of discharging it, also I was unable to maintain myself and family. I therefore determined to proceed to Mauritius, make some money there and return home ... I set out alone from my village, without taking leave of my wife and my only child, a boy of seven years of age, and proceeded to take the high road with a view of going to Madras. At the village of Audodotray in the Coottallum Taluka, I was joined by four persons who had come from the North ... They said that they were also going to Mauritius; took me with them, and together we reached Karrical in the French Settlement.

It was a little fishy to have ended up in the French Settlement, but Saivaroodian, glad for company, seems not to have questioned it.

Then came the awful turn in the story.

As soon as we arrived at Karrical I learned that one of my comrades was a resident of that place, and that he had brought thither the other three persons. For five days I subsisted on what I had brought with me and lived in the house of the above whom I found to be a maistry [a professional labour recruiter]. He then assured me that the coolies were not to be conveyed to Bourbon [present-day Réunion] but to Mauritius . . . he then led me to a godown which was enclosed on all sides by walls, and shut the door after me. There were already about 100 or 150 persons in this . . . somehow or other my wife accompanied by my little boy came to the godown in which I had been lodged and called to me from the outside. They refused to permit me to go out or even to open the door. The same day, some gentlemen visited the godown, informed me that 15 rupees would be first advanced to me for proceeding to Mauritius, and told me to accept the amount from the hand of the maistry. The maistry paid me 11 rupees . . . Out of it I retained 1 rupee, and through a chink in the door, gave the remaining to my wife; she refused to take them and threw them down on the ground. Some persons who were outside picked them up and gave them into the hands of my boy. My wife then returned home with the boy.[46]

Nothing is said about Saivaroodian himself in his case history; but his recounting of the story suggests a man of quiet dignity, narrating a harrowing experience without self-pity. His wife, too, emerges in her actions – we see her fury at being abandoned, her pride, her courage.

This case lays bare the subtle interplay between the agency of the migrant – his will to leave – and the violence and deception by which he was trapped. The cheating *maistry* in this case was just one cog in a wheel of intermediaries who tricked and even kidnapped workers, having sold them lies about wonderful work and high wages. The men who left their wives for the sugar islands often did so by stealth, and out of desperation, only to fall into the hands of unscrupulous murky men, about whom, thus far, we know little.[47]

Brave wives often hunted their husbands down, walking hundreds of miles, showing remarkable resolve and courage. Like Saivaroodian's wife, Ratna also chased her husband who left home because he had been 'rebuked' by his father.

I was told he had gone to Calcutta. I went to . . . to search for him. I was told he had already left two or three days earlier. I went to the wharf and there I saw a steamer, some people took my boy off me, and threatened me. I was put in the depot with my child for two or three days and stayed there for two or three days before embarking on the ship.[48]

Once they arrived on the plantations, labourers encountered work as harsh as it was unrelenting. Sugarcane takes about eighteen months to mature, so it was planted seriatim on ten acres or so of a plantation, so that different batches would mature in quick succession. When the cane ripened, it grew to almost one and a half times the height of the average Indian man.

As 'the tall fields shot up grey-blue arrow-like flowers' the stalk thickened to the size of a poor man's arm, its outer bark as hard as bamboo, its sugary pith unyielding.[49] Time was of the essence from the moment the sugarcane was cut and carried to boilers, the boiling arrested at the precise moment when it was ready to be poured into moulds to drain and dry into the crystalline product the world had come to love.

Work in the boiler rooms was hot and dangerous: fingers and arms were routinely lost as millers and firemen fed 'cane-trash' to keep the fires burning. As for work in the cane fields, it was often unbearable. Pandoo, a *sirdaar* who had worked for twenty-eight years in Mauritius, in a complaint against his estate manager wrote that:

> [Mr Raynal] was in the habit of beating and kicking them ... that he obliged them after weeding with the hoe to gather up the weeds stooping instead of squatting. That such work continued throughout the whole day is very severe and that your Petitioner's band were beaten and kicked whenever they attempted to do this work squatting ...[50]

Other forms of punishment were to force caste Hindus to clean excreta, or to eat food cooked by someone of a 'lower caste'. The records speak of outlandish, even satanic, forms of brutality. Colundaveloo was locked in the 'dead house', the estate mortuary, for almost three weeks after running away from his 'master'. Because he refused to renew his contract, his 'master' beat him 'with a rope ... for twenty days in a row', before locking him up with corpses.[51] It is little wonder that suicide rates were high.

Let's go back for a moment, in the light of this, and consider Ratna's unwillingness to stay at home with her ill-tempered father-in-law. It chimed with another aspect of imperial grand designs. The presence of women, it was felt, would lower the rate of suicide among indentured workers while also fostering more 'wholesome' plantation communities. Both the planters and the state wanted women 'of good character' to accompany men to the plantations, to create stable communities that would reproduce themselves and thus lower the cost of procuring labour. 'Decent' Indian women would carry with them, they presumed, 'the culture and morals of the homeland', and create god-fearing and sober communities on the plantations. In 1868 the government of India fixed by statute a minimum of forty women for every hundred men per shipment.[52]

But this stricture raised a host of problems. Were Indian women free to enter into such contracts without the consent of their husbands or fathers? Indian men thought not, and most British district commissioners tended to agree with them.[53] If they were free, as the indenture statutes presumed, this challenged the patriarchal family's control over women's work, their bodies and their sexuality; this, in turn, threatened the stability of colonial rule on the ground back in India. Once on a plantation, women could, and often did, use their freedom from the family to become more assertive, to choose and discard partners and create what the planters described as 'sexual anarchy'.[54] Fights over women and jealousies among men threatened to break bonds between *jahaaji-bhais*, men who had made the dreaded voyage together and regarded each other as brothers.

Women who arrived on their own thus were often kept penned in depots until single men had been found to 'marry' them. In Trinidad, a Brahmin widow called Maharani described her reluctance to enter into such a relationship (arranged by the plantation manager):

> Maharani you want de man
> > I say no
> E say why
> > I say
> I go go India
> > Just so I tell him
> E say you fall sick an ting
> > You have no body
> You have to take somebody . . .[55]

Or take this plaintive song about another woman who yearned to leave her petulant partner:

> Alas, I will have to run away with another man,
> For my beloved has turned his mind away from me.
> How eagerly, as I cooked rice and dal,
> do I pour the ghee,
> But as soon as we sit for dinner, you start quarrelling
> And my heart is weary of you.
> I put hot fire in the basket,
> Carefully I make the bed.
> But as soon as we lie down to rest,
> you start quarrelling
> My heart is weary of you.[56]

To leave this man, she would have to go 'with another man' for protection and support.

For their part, many Indian men were angered by what they saw as free-and-easy behaviour by 'their women'. A group of Telegu returnees roundly criticised the government (or lack of it) in Mauritius, for failing to recognise marriage and to punish 'abductors' who ravished 'their women':

> We are now going to our respective villages and on our arrival there, we will go to say to our friends who are also anxious to settle at Mauritius and fifteen or twenty thousand will come with their wives but whenever the wife of a person is ravished or carried away by another we are afraid no punishment will be inflicted on the perpetrator ... In our country if we go and complain to the Police that our wife has been ravished or taken away, the fugitive and ravisher are both condemned to prison ... We therefore request that a police of our own nation be established there to judge our own disputes.[57]

The government eventually obliged, introducing Hindu and Muslim marriage law in some sugar colonies. But this story also brings out the larger point that in diaspora, it is not the case (as is so often assumed) that women did the job of 'recreating culture and tradition'. Men do so too, perhaps more often, seeking to recreate patriarchal family structures in new places, keeping the wife, her labour and her sexuality strictly controlled by the family. They didn't always succeed, of course, and 'wayward' and 'degraded' women would soon become the focus of a nationalist critique of indenture.

The Telegu men's petition also points to another development in the indenture islands. On the whole migrant men preferred wives or companions from their own communities or castes, although women from their own region were also seen as highly desirable. Some seemed to want any woman, regardless, to cook for them and care for their children. So Kumally pleaded with the Protector of Emigrants, an office established by the British government in these colonies, 'to facilitate him in getting one [wife] as I find the impossibility of getting my breakfast cooked in the morning on account of the distance sometime I have to work, and to take care of my orphan children'.[58] Others were more finicky, particularly men from regions that had sent the greatest number of migrants. A study of the immigration registers in Mauritius suggests that marriage patterns changed insofar as migrants increasingly married outside their castes – but within their region. (I examine caste in Chapter 6.)

The same picture emerged in Trinidad.[59] Only the largest Hindu castes remained endogamous; only they were able to pick partners from the same caste: hence they have survived as distinctive groups (albeit not unchanged) to this day.[60] The highest castes also strove to marry within caste, regardless of circumstance or material standing. In V. S. Naipaul's *A House for Mr Biswas*, the widowed Mrs Tulsi, wealthy among time-expired labourers, married her fourteen daughters to any Brahmin man she could find, regardless of whether he was a field labourer, a crab catcher or a sign painter.

But men and women on the plantations formed other forms of solidarity and even community – most strikingly represented by the performance of the Islamic month of Muharram. Wherever Shias dwell, the age-old commemoration of the Battle of Karbala, in which the Imam Husyan and his brother Hassan were slain, is a month of grief and mourning. Wherever Indian indentured labourers went, however, Muharram for them changed into something quite different. From Natal to Fiji, from Mauritius to the Caribbean colonies, 'Hosay', their version of Muharram, emerged 'as the most important and spectacular festival of Indian immigrants': a show of solidarity between workers of different castes, religions and sects, a carnivalesque procession that enabled them to leave the stifling confines of the plantation by creating and asserting an identity grounded in immobilised migrant labour. In 1884, Sunni Muslims and Hindus even laid down their lives to assert their right to observe Hosay, facing down policemen who tried to block their path.[61]

Over time, a new social world emerged around the 'time-expired' labourers – those who had served the stipulated five years and were technically free to return to India. Only about twenty per cent ever did. While some travelled from island to island in search of higher pay and better working conditions (information networks being remarkably robust across indentured diaspora), many stayed on in the sugar island where they were first indentured. As Ram Bahadur put it:

> After five years indenture you could go back at your own expense – but on 8 annas a day how could you save the fare. After five more years the government would pay your fare back; but this was cunning, they knew that after 10 years most would have settled, have a wife and family, and wouldn't want to go back.[62]

There was also the matter of being re-admitted to caste after returning home. Having crossed the black water, 'high-caste' migrants were deemed to have lost their caste. To regain it, they had to perform expensive *praayaschitt* (purification) ceremonies of the kind that had so irritated Motilal Nehru (in Chapter 1). Gobardhan Pathak, a returnee from Demerara, had to pay between Rs 300 and Rs 400 on penances 'to get back into caste'. Nankhu, meanwhile, paid Rs 100 to achieve this.[63] For Nehru these were trivial amounts, and he had the clout to refuse to get involved in the ceremonies. For indentured men, by contrast, these were princely sums, often larger than the debt that had driven them to the sugar islands in the first place, and they could not afford the consequences of becoming outcastes on their return home.

Given these realities back in the subcontinent, many chose to stay on in the islands after their time had expired. Jobbers were most likely to have accumulated enough capital to buy some property on the islands. Often they were able to set up small shops. Others cultivated crown lands employing poorer time-expired workers to do the heavy lifting, replicating, on their small 'plantations', old hierarchies in new contexts. Little villages sprang up which were more likely to celebrate Eid and Holi than Hosay, whose practice today remains confined to the northern town of St James and the Cedros district in the southwest of Trinidad. Naipaul's acid account of the Tulsi family, which grew sugar on its own fields employing family labour, owned a modest shop selling hosiery, and gained status through extreme displays of Hindu piety and caste, gives a sense of how these communities were formed, and how caste and class hierarchies were reconstructed and negotiated within them.[64]

Indenture petered out before it was formally abolished in 1917. One might argue that it was always a failing enterprise, despite the millions of Indian workers exported overseas. The high cost of labour recruitment combined with global fluctuations in sugar prices made the indenture plantations risky ventures. The exorbitant cost of recruitment is only beginning to be understood after the scholar Samita Sen showed labour recruitment to be an industry unto itself with its own profit model. It was in the interests of the recruiting agencies, *arkatis* and *maistries*, to keep the cost of labour as high as they could, while planters called for cheap labour. If the recruiters won that arm wrestle, they killed their golden goose in so doing.[65]

This also helps to explain why indenture was such a violent system. Plantation owners were without exception racist: that was the zeitgeist. But they were not monsters. The structure of their business made them behave like sadists. Given how much these workers had cost them, planters were determined to get their money's worth – hence the beatings, the fines and the punitive incarcerations. No wonder, then, that indenture from day one had powerful critics who denounced it as 'a new form of slavery'.[66] In the 1830s the Anti-Slavery Society brought the attention of Parliament at Westminster to the plight of 'coolies', and raised such a hue and cry that indenture was temporarily suspended, only to be restored in 1842 under new regulations. But opposition grew increasingly powerful, and when in the 1910s, Gokhale and Gandhi took up the cause, the indenture system came to an end in Mauritius and Malaya. In 1911, after Gandhi's first *satyagraha*, it stopped in Natal too. The degradation of the indentured woman 'provided the most potent symbol' in the armoury of nationalist critics, and this should not surprise us, given how central womanly purity had become to many nationalist conceptions of the nation.[67]

Nationalists were outraged by the fact that many indenture colonies did not protect Hindu and Muslim marriage. Women workers were seen as helpless and 'wholly unprotected' from the lascivious assaults of white planters. In 1918, Gandhi's friend Charles Andrews made much of a medical report from Fiji, which showed that Indian women 'have to serve three indentured men as well as various outsiders'. Neither London nor India, weakened by war and assaulted by the suffragettes, could be seen to condone this.[68] In the end, indenture foundered on the politics of the 'sex question', then, quite as much as the unremittingly high cost of labour and the global slump in the price of sugar.[69]

Decolonisation brought transformations. The question is: how large? What trends of the old order persisted?

By 1947, South Asians were spread across fifty-eight countries in the world.[70] Almost all became either Indian or Pakistani nationals, although it was not always clear who was who. Some – and this is significant – retained British subjecthood or citizenship, as they were entitled to do under the British Nationality Act of 1948. By 1947, the diaspora was in the main settled in the Indian Ocean littoral: in Ceylon (732,258) and Burma, where after the war there were some 700,000 Indians. Other clusters of South Asians were in Malaya and Singapore (604,508), East Africa (184,000) and South Africa (232,407), while the sugar islands also had significant numbers of 'time-expired' South Asians.[71]

All, whether Indian, Pakistani or British, now found themselves unwelcome in these countries as they became independent. Malaya after the depression had already begun to repatriate Indians.[72] In 1948, when Burma and Ceylon became independent, they too set to drafting new citizenship laws that distinguished between 'ethnic' citizens and immigrants.[73] Already in 1939, Ceylon had banned the further entry of Tamil migrants to its coffee plantations. Among the 700,000–800,000 Tamils who had migrated to Ceylon before this date, most had left their wives and children behind in South India. This population, for the most part unlettered and unorganised (few independent unions were allowed to operate on the plantations), had now to negotiate the complex business of acquiring Ceylon citizenship for themselves and their families.[74] The Indian Mission in Colombo concluded that 'the best thing would be for all Indians who were qualified to be Sri Lankan citizens to apply for citizenship without hesitation', but the Mandarins did little to help them in this process.[75] Nor did New Delhi support the Ceylon Indian Congress in fighting a test case in the Privy Council to challenge this discriminatory law.[76]

For its part, in 1948 Burma defined its own nationality law on blatantly ethnic grounds, giving citizenship only to persons deemed to belong to an 'indigenous race' or having one grandparent from an 'indigenous race'. Indians who had lived in British Burma since before 1942 could register as citizens, but were soon to be victims of government drives to acquire their land by force and without fair compensation.[77] This generated a new wave of migration as Indians from Burma began to trickle back into India as refugees and, in the case of Arakanese Muslims (now better known as Rohingya), to East Pakistan. Neither India nor Pakistan – both still struggling to rehabilitate millions of partition refugees – was able to do much to help them, beyond allowing them (with greater or lesser degrees of reluctance) the right to enter and remain in their countries 'of origin'. The rising tides of ethnically defined nationalisms throughout the Indian Ocean region meant that 'Anglo-Indians', as mixed-race Eurasian families were now known, also began to seek new destinations in other parts of the world where their British subjecthood still allowed them rights of entry.[78]

Meanwhile, between 1948 and 1962, Whitehall resisted pressures to introduce formal controls for entry to Britain that were blatantly discriminatory. But that did not mean, as is often claimed, that the United Kingdom in this period remained open to all comers. 'Informal control' was now the name of the game.[79] In a throwback to imperial times when London had introduced emigration controls in response to pressures from white dominions, Britain now used its good offices with governments in the 'source' countries to encourage them to prevent unregulated emigration from their shores to the United Kingdom. In the mid-1950s, when South Asian migrants replaced those from the Caribbean as the prime focus of official concern, Whitehall persuaded the governments of India and Pakistan not to issue passports for travel to the United Kingdom to certain categories of their nationals. Both countries agreed to deny passports to their own citizens if they lacked adequate resources, proof of literacy and knowledge of English. Both put systems into place by which the police looked into the character and antecedents of would-be migrants. Significantly, India began to vet and then weed out applications for passports from 'low-class citizens' (by unpublicised arrangements with the UK Home Office) and to scrutinise claims that they had secured work and accommodation in Britain.[80] It was only in 1960, when India's Supreme Court declared this practice to be discriminatory, that the 'outsourcing' of UK migration controls against Indians to India came to an end.[81] In 1961, Pakistan too lifted restrictions on emigration, encouraging the people uprooted by the Mangla Dam to go to Britain.[82]

Getting local policemen to verify the 'character' of applicants for passports continued well into the 1980s, at least in India. I was alarmed one winter morning when, soon after my first marriage, I opened the door of our tiny *barsaati* (a room on a roof) in Delhi to find a cop staring at me, eyeball to eyeball. I had never committed a crime, except taking part in a few rallies against the Gulf wars of those times, marches that broke police cordons for which I had had my punishment. The policeman was about as young as I was, about the same height and build: five foot five and around fifty kilos. Yet his khaki uniform, buzz cut and burly moustache lent him menace, and his *laathi* frightened me.

He was checking my credentials, he said, in connection with my application for a new passport (with British rights of entry, of which more below). He sauntered into the one-room flat and inspected it with an elaborate display of suspicion. If he was disappointed to discover how the other half lived – a small fridge, a pressure cooker, an LPG cylinder, a battered typewriter and 500 books being our most valuable possessions – he did not show it. My passport came through several months later. (Those were the high days of bureaucratic inertia. I sometimes look back to them with nostalgia, missing their leisurely rhythms.)

As for Britain: after a decade of pressure to restrict immigration from the 'New', dark-skinned, Commonwealth, the Commonwealth Immigrants Act went onto the statute book in 1962.[83] Although it did not openly discriminate on the grounds of race, the Act was designed to restrict the admission of 'coloured immigrants', and this was its outcome in practice. Prospective migrants from South Asia now had to obtain employment vouchers from London's Ministry of Labour before being allowed in. Vouchers went mainly to people who had the offer of specific jobs in Britain, or who had particular skills and qualifications which Britain wanted. Only the wives and children of migrants already in Britain still had an absolute right to enter the country.

This was the first in a series of measures that changed the character of South Asian migration to Britain, and indeed to the western world. Hitherto that flow had been dominated by single, able-bodied but relatively unskilled working men, who were sojourners rather than settlers, circulating as often as possible between Britain and their homes back in the subcontinent. Forced to choose between bringing their families to Britain or returning once and for all to the subcontinent, many chose now to settle permanently in Britain.

This was also the context in which smuggling and people trafficking took root, to begin with as village-based self-help schemes. Nadir from the Gujrat district of Pakistan described how returnees used kinship networks to develop more sophisticated mechanisms to supply labour, much like the *maistries* of old:

> They would have a reference [voucher] and would take one or two. Then subsequently, group migration started. People would adopt kids, declare that so and so is their son just to help someone in the village. *It started as help. But then a business developed.* Someone clever would take 10–12, and work out a way to get them to the UK. This was in the early sixties. Even graduates and educated boys would look for a way to leave. A van which would take five or six to the UK would go through Turkey.[84]

But on their arrival in Britain, many found themselves trapped and alone. For some, their isolation was total, and their illegal status prevented them from getting jobs outside the restaurant trade where they faced regular abuse by drunk punters wanting a curry after a night on the town. In 2007, our Bengal Diaspora team interviewed 'Maruf', a forty-two-year-old illegal worker in London who had worked in Britain, moving from restaurant to restaurant, for several years.[85] His interview speaks of the trauma that illegal migrants experience, above all, their desperate homesickness. He said:

> I have already made my mind up that I will go back home in December ... mentally and physically, I am tired. That is the basic reason. Money is not the issue here ... Moreover my kids are growing up. There is no need to say that they miss me. Definitely they miss me. Then, my family miss[es] me. And me, I am mentally devastated. Living abroad without family for five years is very painful. Those who have experienced it will understand it. Otherwise, it is not possible for anyone to understand it. There are some issues which you can explain, make people understand. But this is not like that. It stays within you. It becomes [like a] stone. After five years of staying here my body and mind have reached such a position that I cannot say whether I am alive or not ... I have to say that I am mentally and physically sick ... I call home every day. Sometimes three to four times in a day ... I talk every day to my mother, brothers, sisters.[86]

Since 1962, the immigration laws of Britain have become ever more complex and restrictive. For a brief and inglorious episode in the 1980s, the Home Office decreed that migrant brides from South Asia be subjected to virginity tests.

Space does not permit a detailed discussion of these laws, but two points stand out. In 1963, Kenya gained independence, and four years later, in 1967, passed an Immigration Act that obliged all those without Kenyan citizenship to acquire work permits. It also introduced laws that deliberately targeted Kenyan South Asians in business and trade. This followed a drive to 'Africanise' the newly independent national government and economy of Kenya.[87] Uganda's President Idi Amin soon implemented his own, more terrifying, version of this policy, and South Asians began to flee East Africa. Many of them were British citizens and wanted to come to Britain. To prevent their entry into the country, in 1968 Britain passed a new Commonwealth Immigrants Act which restricted the number of Asian families from East Africa permitted to enter the United Kingdom to a mere 1,500. This broke an explicit pledge, given in 1963 to East African Asians who retained their status as citizens of the United Kingdom and Commonwealth, that they would have unrestricted rights of entry into the UK. It also meant that Britain now had denied the right of entry to a specific class of its *own citizens*.

In 1971, a Conservative government passed an Immigration Act which gave citizens of the 'New' (dark-skinned) Commonwealth the same status as 'aliens' in Britain. It also introduced 'patriality' as a condition for the right of abode in the UK. This was a thinly disguised racial qualification – 'patriality' being 'ethnic qualification' by another name.[88]

Aged seven, I did not understand much about it, but I do remember lying on dry grass under a mango tree trying to catch fat grey aphids while my parents (Indian father and English mother) discussed whether they should apply for 'patriality' for my brothers and me. After pondering the pros and cons, and the ethics of making such momentous choices for young children, they agreed to do this, concluding that we could always change our minds when we were adults. As a result, we were dragged off to have haircuts, and then to be photographed. I ended up with bizarre bangs under which my large eyes stared out in horror – a photograph of such spectacular awfulness that I have not lived it down fifty years later. Next we were dragged off to a government building reeking of phenyl (India's ubiquitous disinfectant) with cobwebbed, peeling walls, where these ghoulish black-and-white images of us were stapled to forms in triplicate, and stamped again and again in purple and red ink. In this way we got 'patriality', a liminal status granted to us because my mother, and her parents, were born in Britain (a code for white). I still have the stigmata of my racial ancestry stamped in my Indian passport. It still allows me to enter the United Kingdom as I wish.

Since these legal changes, migrants from South Asia in Britain tended to have rather different profiles from those who came before them. The men (and indeed, many women) among them were highly qualified. After 1965, Britain issued 'Category B' vouchers only to doctors, dentists, teachers, science and technology graduates, as well as skilled, qualified and experienced non-graduates.[89] Thirty per cent of doctors in Britain's National Health Service have South Asian primary qualifications and more than a third of Britain's IT industry employees are Indian 'techies'.[90]

In another huge shift, women began slowly to outnumber men: a scattering of trained nurses (usually single) could be found among larger numbers of brides or young married women, often accompanied by their children. Latterly, elderly people have started to migrate to Britain as well, to join their emigrant children to pass their twilight years on its grey shores.[91]

But what has been most marked is the tendency of government to embrace a hierarchy of preferences for certain types of migrants within a system of controls that caps overall numbers.

In the United States, meanwhile, since the passage of the Hart–Celler Act of 1965, preference has been given to two groups. (Refugees and asylum seekers are the third category of migrants who still have access under these systems, but there is not space to discuss these here.)

The first, based on the notion of 'family reunion', are the children and dependants of migrants who are already permanent residents.

The second predilection is for 'highly accomplished' migrants whose skills match the needs of the domestic economy. Since the Act of 1965, the annual quota for Indian entry to the United States has risen from 20,000 to 60,000. With their H1-B visas and precious 'green cards', by 2000 Indians with skills had become the 'model-minority' in the United States. In that year, sixty-seven per cent of 'Asian-Indians' possessed at least a bachelor's degree (compared with a US national average of twenty-eight per cent). Some forty per cent also had a master's or higher degree (compared with a national average of eight per cent). Almost sixty per cent of Asian-Indians worked in managerial and professional jobs. The median income in 2000 was $51,000 for men and $35,000 for women. This is the highest for any ethnic group in the United States, including 'white Caucasians'.[92] At least 35,000 doctors with Indian MBBS medical degrees worked in the health system; and in 2002, Asian-Indians owned 223,000 registered companies with combined revenues of more than $88 billion.[93]

By and large, with local and temporal variations, these preferences have also guided the immigration policies of the developed countries of the English-speaking West since the latter decades of the century; Australia, Canada and Britain have all adopted this model. Although the common perception is that Britain closed her doors to South Asians at the same time that the rest of the world began to welcome them, in fact, since the 1960s and 70s, different immigration regimes have converged on common ground.

Of course, among the South Asian diaspora there had always been a scattering of elite migrants – students like Jawaharlal Nehru studying at Harrow and Trinity or Jinnah at the Inns of Court;[94] and princes taking summer holidays abroad.[95] In the late nineteenth and early twentieth centuries, men of commerce who traded in Indian wares had also become visible and influential at imperial entrepots. Well before 1947, Sindworki and Shikharpuri merchants from Sind had spun far-flung webs of commerce that spanned the world from Bukhara to Panama; they concentrated their business within the British Empire.[96] Sindworkis from Hyderabad Sind first began to sell curios in Bombay which they sourced from different parts of the interior of Sind: lacquer work on wood, delicately painted *kashi* vases, jugs and jars, *ajrak* quilt covers from Dadu, embroidery from Nawabshah and bronze-alloy *kansa* work from Larkana.[97] (My former doctoral student Uttara Shahani, who works on the Sindhi diaspora, has a *kansa*-bronze lion door-knocker with a ring in its maw on her front door – so common on English houses. Very likely it travelled to Britain from Sind via Spain.)

The Sindworkis set up shop in Cairo when tourism to Egypt in its modern form took off, and when visitors became eager to buy oriental curios in the marketplace. They started small, never wholly displacing the Armenian, Levantine or Jewish traders who had come

before them, but nonetheless carved out a sizeable niche for their
wares. In 1888, one probate valued a single Sindworki shop in Alexandria at £637 – no mean amount by the standards of the day.[98]
From Egypt, these enterprising traders fanned out into Mediterra-
nean ports, with branches in Malta, Algiers, Gibraltar, Tunisia,
Tangiers and Italy by the 1890s; later venturing into West and East
Africa.

Another prominent community of traders with interests in cash
crops in Burma, Malaya, Indonesia and East Africa were the Nattukottai Chettiars of southern India.[99] These wealthy merchants bought
their own fares (as the students of law did) and were known as the
'passenger class'. They stood apart from, and looked askance upon,
the 'assisted' coolie classes in the hold or on deck whose fare had been
paid for by others.

In the late twentieth century, similar stratifications re-emerged, as
the better-off and highly skilled migrants turned up their noses at the
poor of Tower Hamlets, Bradford or Queens. A relative by marriage
(also half-Indian, with degrees from Cambridge and Oxford) described
Bangladeshi residents of Tower Hamlets to me as 'niggers'. A Pakistani PhD student at Cambridge gesticulated like a monkey while
describing Bangladeshis. Dacca's elite migrants in London do not rub
shoulders with the Sylheti restaurant workers of Banglatown.

Familiar forms of subordination and unfreedom have resurfaced
in the Gulf. Migrants there are often young and able-bodied men,
although large numbers of single women have joined the flow as
cooks, maids and childminders or *ayahs*. The oil-rich emirates have
become patterned by race and hierarchy.[100] Europeans (and a handful of highly skilled elite South Asian ex-pats) have prestigious jobs
and considerable freedoms, whereas poor South Asians work on
astonishingly illiberal terms. These new helots have few, if any,
rights.[101] The noxious practice of employers confiscating the passports of 'labour-class' employees has become commonplace; in the
past, the government of British India simply denied passports to
indentured migrants. 'Assisted' poor migrants travel to destinations
in Malaysia or Dubai, or indeed to Britain, with great expectations
of decent pay and working conditions, only to have their travel documents confiscated on arrival and their pay docked or withheld.
Some are effectively imprisoned until they have earned enough to

pay off the costs of their passage. Human trafficking in the twenty-first century has many of the features of indenture in the twentieth.[102]

On the face of it, then, migration in the late twentieth century bore an uncanny resemblance to that of the late-imperial world. Just as the old order was stratified by class and status, with a clear legal distinction between the self-funded free passenger class and the 'assisted' unfree coolie class, the late-twentieth-century order was characterised by the chasm that separates green-card holders (and their ilk) from trafficked or otherwise 'assisted' migrants.

But the distinctions are important, and ironic. In the late nineteenth and early twentieth centuries, the imperial state managed, admittedly with limited success, the migration abroad of unskilled South Asian workers in its capacity as 'protector of emigrants'. Today's national governments are less willing and less able to take on that regulatory role. The impoverished South Asian migrants of today not only face greater challenges in breaking through much tougher border controls of contemporary nation states, but they are also more dependent on the uncertain and profit-driven goodwill of labour contractors and traffickers who 'assist' their passage. This renders them more vulnerable to abuse, or at least to new forms of abuse, by agents and employers.

Only in 2003 did the Indian government first decide to celebrate its global diaspora with a Non-Resident Indians Day (*Pravasi Bharatiya Divas*) in Delhi. The migrants the government was most keen to embrace were, of course, the high-skilled green-card holders and the inward investment they generated. For their part, NRIs (as non-resident Indians are known) have played an increasing role in Indian domestic politics. They were involved in resisting – and in some famous cases, supporting – the Indian Emergency.[103] They were particularly prominent in the agitation for the Ram Temple at Ayodhya, sending consecrated *Ram sheelans* or bricks inscribed with '*Jai Shri Ram*' ('Victory to Ram') to build the temple, by airmail from the United States to India.[104] Likewise, Bengali migrants from East Pakistan were crucial propagandists for their country in its battle for liberation from Pakistan. More recently, Pakistanis in Canada have tried to tip the balance in the domestic politics of Pakistan.

Another distinction is that, from the nineteenth century to the mid-twentieth century, it was well understood that both free and 'assisted' migrants would typically leave families behind, remitting monies home and returning periodically to their villages. In the late twentieth century, the push by western governments has been to promote family reunion, in part, no doubt, for humane reasons, but quite as much to ensure that the few migrants they accepted did not have divided loyalties.

In practice, of course, migrants are not prepared to make such definitive choices, as the proliferation of *Londoni gaon* (villages with connections to London) in Bangladesh attests. Large mansions complete with satellite dishes, smoked-glass windows and arabesque pillars stud Sylhet's green landscape. Most are empty but for a caretaker – who, more often than not, is a migrant from another part of Bangladesh. Some have great concrete aeroplanes on their roofs to proclaim to the world the owner's success abroad. *Londoni* villages typically have grand mosques; some boast schools funded by remittances from abroad.[105] Migrants still refer to them as *desh* (home). Brides and even grooms are often 'sourced' from Sylhet.[106]

Since I was diagnosed with epilepsy and lost my driving licence, many of Cambridge's Sylheti taxi-drivers have befriended me. Often they show me photographs of their bride from the *desh* on their mobile phones. One driver is passionate about the Bangladesh Nationalist Party (BNP) and, learning of my interest in Bangladesh, keeps urging me to facilitate an honorary Cambridge degree for Begum Khaleda Zia (see Chapter 2). (Even if I had been minded to help the Begum in this way, it was far above my pay grade to try.) Another driver tells me with pride how many times he has taken Amartya Sen, Nobel laureate and former Master of Trinity, to the railway station. 'What a good man, what a great man. Do you know he was originally from Bangladesh?' Of course I do, I reply, and for a brief moment, we share pride in our *Shonar Bangla* (Golden Bengal), united in our diasporic hearts despite the border fence that divides Bengal today; the high-skilled but disabled one-time globe-trotter achieving a brief moment of connection with the low-skilled but able-bodied migrant. Ironies abound.

The final distinction between the old and the new is the preference today for 'permanent settlement', by those chosen few who have 'earned' their right to stay in the nation states of the West. To get a green card in the United States, the applicant has to demonstrate *continuous unbroken residence* and legal employment. In Britain, those with 'leave to remain' have not only to demonstrate an unbroken stretch of domicile before they are granted such leave, but they cannot leave the United Kingdom for any length of time without losing that entitlement. The paradox for today's skilled migrants is that they can regain their freedom to come and go only by taking the ultimate step, of applying for the citizenship of their host country and renouncing their affiliation with their homeland. India does not allow dual citizenship so NRIs must relinquish their Indian passports. Only by professing unalloyed loyalty to the adopted nation, through ever more elaborate rituals of citizenship, can today's migrant regain the right to leave it. And yet, in another irony, the technologies of today also make it easier for them to resort to the many forms of subversion that are collectively understood as 'transnationalism'.

Despite these strenuous efforts to bar the gates (or 'build a wall' in our century's rhetoric), through natural growth, family reunification and high-skilled migration, the South Asian global presence has grown considerably since 1947. By 2000, the diaspora of India, Bangladesh and Pakistan, taken together, hovered at about 40 million.

The UK census did not count Indians, Pakistanis and Bangladeshis as distinct 'ethnicities' until 1991. In 2011, it recorded 1,451,862 persons of Indian, 1,174,983 of Pakistani and 451,529 of Bangladeshi ethnicity, making a total South Asian population of just over three million (almost five per cent of the total population). In bare statistics, these numbers may seem alarming or reassuring, depending on your point of view.

But each number represents a person, with their unique history and personality. Let me tell you about one 'British Asian' I know. When I met him at the London School of Economics, Jasdeep was twenty. He was born in Hillingdon in 1985, to a working-class family of Punjabi Sikhs who had owned some land in Moga in Punjab, near the Pakistan border. This family had had a peripatetic history: Jasdeep's great-grandfather was in the police and had served in Singapore (then a British colony that imported Indian policemen), where he stayed until Japan's occupation. He returned to India when his troop was disbanded at the end of the Raj. By this time, of course, partition had ripped through Punjab, and they struggled to reclaim their land from, I expect, new refugee occupants. A partition family, then, of a kind.

They succeeded, but it was not enough to support them. So they moved back to Singapore, and later to Britain in the early 1960s.

They managed to give their five children a good education. After Jas did well at school, they wanted him to do something sensible, something that would make money, something like law or accountancy. Instead he read History, taking my classes on India's partition. Slight, sensitive and brilliant, he flourished, graduating with honours. Soon afterwards, to my surprise, he got a job in the City. I don't think his heart was in it.

Jas never got a chance to live the high life. The next I heard, he had been in a dreadful accident.

Since then, Jas has lived with the consequences of a shattered spine. After several operations, he remains in a wheelchair, dependent on carers who are not always kind. Yet he gained a postgraduate law degree, having taught himself to type with the one finger he could still use. In 2008, he took his local council to the ombudsman for failing to provide him with an independent apartment and adequate care. Since then he has raised donations for others by pushing himself in his chair along the length of the Camino de Santiago. As he put it in a casual WhatsApp to me: 'So here's the plan: Me pushing 100km (min) to raise £3,250 for two charities: Bakhita House and St Jude Children's Cancer Research Hospital. Doing this over 10 days although planning for 14 days to allow for rest/maintenance.' Remarkably, *he* writes to *me* regularly to inquire after *my* health.

Jas is a hero, an inspiration. But his story is instructive in other ways too.

His family would have qualified as low-skilled migrants when they first arrived in the United Kingdom. He himself is highly skilled and, but for his accident, he would have been yet another British Asian super-achiever. At a stroke, his identity changed. He was supported, for the most part, by the local council. He has had to reinvent himself again, to struggle with enormous courage to retain his dignity and independence. He hopes to be a qualified lawyer in 2023. My guess is that he will. (He has trained, in recent times, at a prestigious law firm.)

Just as in Jas' case, identity is fluid. 'Peoples' and 'ethnicities' do not have a singular character or quality; individuals are in a constant state of becoming. It is useful to remember this in our neo-nationalist and xenophobic times.

II

INTERNAL MIGRATION: THE LANDMASS AS A MOBILE LANDSCAPE

Kingsley Davis, the pioneering demographer of the subcontinent, estimates that between 1926 and 1930, when overseas emigration peaked, some 3.2 million Indians travelled abroad, mainly to the plantation colonies. During that period, 2.8 million returned.

By contrast, the Census of India showed that in 1921, in that single year alone, more than fifteen million South Asians were internal migrants, a figure that underestimated the true extent of internal movement by a huge amount, as it only counted people who had crossed administrative boundaries. It missed most brides.

South Asia's internal diaspora is a story, then, on a far grander scale than the forays of its people abroad. It is so large and so complex that it makes the mind boggle. But it has some clear lines and drivers.

In 1921, South Asia's population began its unstoppable rise. This new stage in the subcontinent's demographic history was one of continuing, exponential growth, decade after decade. Each decade broke the record of the previous one. From 1921 to 1931, the population grew by eleven per cent, the highest rate on record. The next decade saw an increase of fifteen per cent, another record. Between 1921 and 1941, eighty-three million people were added, as the cliché has it, 'to India's teeming masses'.[107] By 1947, internal migration had already produced vast male-dominated cities. Today these are dizzying megalopolises.

This new demographic surge reversed the age-old relationship between labour supply and demand. In the late nineteenth century, labour was a scarce commodity and the new industries competed for workers (resorting, as we have seen, to all manner of wiles and penal contracts to trap and bind workers), but after the 1920s, the supply of hungry humans at the mill gates (and wherever workers were needed) seemed inexhaustible. Industry could squeeze labour for all it was worth. It found ways of doing so, by keeping urban migrants in a constant state of precariousness. They had to move between formal and informal sectors of the economy simply to survive, returning to the village to die when their health was finally broken.

Poverty deepened in the first half of the twentieth century, albeit not in a uniform way. It cast deep shadows in areas the railways had bypassed. In the early decades of the century, as the ratio between humankind and the land that sustained it was inverted, scarcity was ever more evident in swathes of rough, dry land, wholly dependent on the monsoon rains and drying tanks.[108] Small plots of poor soil could no longer support the many mouths that depended on them for sustenance. And, as Chapter 5 will show, within a single household some were poorer than others: widows, women and girls.

Poverty, then, was not a blunt (economic) instrument: it interacted with different cultural norms of patriarchy, varieties of micro-environment, local demographies and epidemics, provision or absence of infrastructure, as well as global slumps and urban retrenchments. It was multidimensional.

Before 1920, demographic growth had been uneven. So too was its distribution: indeed, one scholar describes India as having 'a veritable patchwork of different demographic regimes'.[109] Populations were regularly decimated by famine, drought and epidemic. The famine of 1876–8, which hit South India particularly hard, caused between five and eight million deaths. In the 1890s, western India suffered two major famines, which together killed between 4.5 and nine million people. In 1896, rats on ships brought the plague to the Mazagaon docks in Bombay, leaving twelve million dead before it had worn itself out. And then came the influenza pandemic after the First World War, also entering the subcontinent by ship through Bombay. It took between fifteen and eighteen million lives, mainly in the Bombay Presidency and North India. India's population thus grew by only 0.3 per cent a year between 1871 and 1921.[110]

After 1920, by contrast, growth was steep and sustained. India's population of about 300 million in 1921 grew in two decades to about 400 million in 1941.[111] Its sharp rise continued in the decades that followed. One cause of this rise was a fall in the death rate, but this does not adequately explain it. Canals extending irrigation to dry tracts were a significant factor. Famine relief in the nineteenth century had been 'miserly'; but the Famine Commission reports of 1880, 1898 and 1901 challenged some of the old laissez-faire paradigms on which such policies had rested; and in the new century, more systematic early intervention began to reduce famine mortality.[112]

The control of epidemics – particularly of the swift killer

cholera – also helped. Pandemics had broken out with terrifying frequency: in 1863–5, 1875–7, 1891–2, 1894–7, 1900, 1905–8, 1918–19, and again in 1921. Cholera wiped out whole households and villages, and even 'White Town' areas, in a few hours or days. Frances Hodgson Burnett's *The Secret Garden* evokes the panic, the mysterious disappearances, the sounds of death witnessed by a peevish little English girl:

> Many things happened during the hours in which she slept so heavily, but she was not disturbed by the wails and the sound of things being carried in and out of the bungalow. When she awakened she lay and stared at the wall. The house was perfectly still. She had never known it so silent before. She heard neither voices nor footsteps, and wondered if everybody had got well of the cholera and all the trouble was over. She wondered also who would take care of her now that her old *ayah* was dead ... But if everyone had got well again, surely someone would remember and come to look for her. But no one came, and as she lay waiting, the house seemed to grow more and more silent.[113]

In 1928 an effective cholera vaccine was invented, but large-scale inoculation was a tremendous epidemiological challenge. In any event, vaccines alone could never be enough to improve public health: without addressing their poverty, and making improvements to the economic, social and sanitary conditions in which South Asians lived, inoculation alone would never subdue cholera. (It is still endemic, crossing social strata with ease. My younger brother had it in the 1990s. He almost died.)

After the 1920s, however, power over public health and works was devolved to Indian local governments; and some improvements began, but these sanitation measures were not sufficiently wide ranging (nor well funded) to rid the subcontinent of the many diseases with which it was afflicted. Indeed, public works sometimes made matters worse. Road, canal and railway embankments all created stagnant pools in which the larvae of mosquito-carrying malaria bred – so much so that by the time Davis wrote his treatise on population in 1951, he estimated that each year 100 million Indians and Pakistanis suffered from malaria, even if relatively few of them died of the disease.[114] If you know anyone in its grip, you will know how malaria patients suffer, again and again, all through their lives.

This rough and ready account only hints at why the people of the subcontinent began to live longer from the 1920s onwards; but the fact that they did so is of immense significance. Between 1911 and 1921, the average life expectancy in the subcontinent was twenty years. In the next decade it rose to twenty-seven years. Between 1931 and 1941, it rose again to thirty-two years.[115] Falling death rates, with no associated decline in birth rates, meant that South Asia's populations expanded at a record-breaking pace.

This happened in an era when the expansion of the railways brought cities closer, in real terms, to hinterland villages. Poor Indian villagers began to experience the 'space–time contraction' engendered by these new modes of transport as they set off to the city in search of work. Coolie wagons were so overcrowded and unsanitary that only the able-bodied could face the grim prospect of travel in such conditions: and many migrants, by definition, would have been weakened by hunger before they entered them.[116] Railway staff (Indians or Anglo-Indians) manhandled and abused the poor, 'especially ignorant villagers' and treated them 'worse than brute beasts'.[117] Lower-class carriages, into which passengers were stuffed like sardines in a tin, had no lighting or toilet facilities fifty years after rail travel began. Many carriages still had no seats.[118] For the elderly, the frail and the disabled, travelling by train was not an option. Unaccompanied women and girls entered at their peril. (If anyone hectors you about the marvellous railways the British 'gave' India, as happened to me on *Newsnight* some years ago, think about these carriages.)

Yet because journeys were relatively short (compared with the voyages by sea), the coolie compartments were always bursting with hopeful men and boys. The city, its opportunities and excitements, beckoned.

Consider the arrival of a teenage boy from the Konkan coast, getting off the train at Bombay's Victoria Terminus.[119] He is covered in sweat, grime, coal dust; his clothes smell of urine. Let's call him 'Cajetano', son of Philomena, father unknown. The Goan coastal fishing villages to the west of the hilly *ghats*, since the turn of the century, were a source of migrants to Bombay. Cajetano, born in the late 1950s (he thinks), was from one such tiny village, but where he was born I have not asked. (You will understand why, soon enough.)

Imagine his shock as a tide of bodies swept him from the carriage to the platform. Never before had he seen so many people gathered at one place. Even the pilgrimage to the Church of St Francis of Assisi in Panjim had not prepared him for the sight.

As for the architecture of the Victoria Terminus (VT), it was designed to shock and awe. Situated on the shores of the Arabian Sea, the Victorian Gothic complex, spread across three hectares, was an architectural statement of the might of the British Empire. Completed in 1888, at the time of writing three million commuters each day use VT, now renamed Chhatrapati Shivaji Terminus after the seventeenth-century warrior-king Shivaji from western India. When Cajetano came to the city, millions of travellers passed through the terminus every year. For a poor boy from the Konkan coast, it would have been an overwhelming, terrifying and exhilarating sight. (A beautiful film that makes you *feel* a migrant's first arrival to the city in that period is Satyajit Ray's *Aparajito*, 1956. Do watch it.)

Totally unlettered, Cajetano was a bright spark. He had struck up conversations on his journey in the coolie wagon with other Konkanis; and also with *Ghatis* from the stunning but barren escarpment that separates the Deccan Plateau from the Arabian Sea. He had learned something about Bombay from them. He befriended people who knew people in Bombay, and learned a little about the city. Clutching his little bundle close – station platforms were notorious sites of theft – he made his way hesitantly, asking directions as he went, to the mill district of Girangaon.

Double-decker trams had been introduced in Bombay in 1920, but they were not for the urban poor, let alone for rural migrants. He watched them rumble past, dumbstruck no doubt, and started to walk the five kilometres to Girangaon in the heart of the city.[120]

By 1921, the cotton textile industry employed more than a quarter of the city's population, and Girangaon exerted a magnetic pull on new migrants seeking work.[121] Owned almost exclusively by Indians, eighty-four cotton spinning and weaving mills employed some 1,800 workers each, and more than 550 manufacturing units employed almost ninety workers each.[122]

But in fact the great majority of the city's labouring population worked in much smaller 'factories' or *karkhaanas* producing goods for the local markets in the 'informal economy' – although Cajetano would not have known this. As he trudged to his destination, he would have passed hives of small units 'turning out carved blackwood couches, screens, writing desks and chairs; innumerable small bakeries, garment-factories, shoe shops, tobacco shops and *beedee* manufacturers; sugar refining factories and sweet-meat makers; match factories ... Dyers, printers, workers in cotton and silk, wire, tinsel and kincob workers in Bhuleshwar and Bhendi Bazar, brassworkers, black-smiths and potters, goldsmiths and jewellers'.[123] Artisan capitalists worked flexibly out of small workshops that employed skilled artisans. These workshops drove manufacturing in Bombay quite as much as in small towns and employed more people than did industry.[124]

But the chances of a complete outsider getting work in one of these family-run units, where skills were passed down through generations, were negligible.[125] Cajetano may not have had an education, but he had an intuitive grasp of structures of power and 'gate-keeping'. So he walked right on by.

Another sight that would have amazed Cajetano was the different garbs men wore, particularly their distinctive headwear. Writing in 1912 about the by-ways of Bombay, S. M. Edwardes had been struck by the 'dazzling assortment' of Muslims he saw in the city:

> of the lower class with their long white shirts, white trousers and skull caps of silk or brocade ... traders from the Gulf, in Arab or old Persian costumes and black turbans with a red border. Here again comes a Persian of the old school with arched embroidered turban of white silk, white 'aba' or undercoat reaching to the ankles, open grey shaya and soft yellow leather shoe; and he is followed by Persians of the modern school in small stiff black hats, dark coats drawn in at the waist, and English trousers and boots. After them come the Afghans, their hair well-oiled, in the baggiest of trousers ... Malays in English jackets and loose turbans, Bukharans in tall sheepskin caps and woollen gabar-dines, begging their way from Mecca ... singing hymns in honour of the Prophet, or showing plans of the Ka'ba or the shrine of the saints of saints.[126]

And these were just the city's Muslims, a sizeable part of an eclectic mix in a cosmopolitan city where almost eighty-five per cent of the population were migrants.[127] Hindu men from different regions and castes also wore different clothes, and above all distinctive turbans, whereas Englishmen out in the midday sun wore pith helmets or 'sola topis'. (This was the context in which Jinnah's belated adoption of the Turkish fez made such an impact on his followers.) There were also many sahibs, white and brown, wearing tailor-made suits. Cajetano's

Goa had a mixed population of Catholics, Indo-Portuguese Jesuits, Hindus and Muslims, but the sheer heterogeneity of Bombay's population, its languages, religions, sects, modes of dress, fashion and comportment would have been unlike anything he had ever encountered before. This was an India of which he had no conception.

After a long, tiring, if scenic, walk, Cajetano made it to Girangaon. The sight of the great towering stacks of mills belching out smoke would have stunned him no less than the collection, in a single place, of some 150,000 millworkers. By the early 1920s, most of them lived within a fifteen-minute walk from work, and their dwellings surrounded the mills themselves.[128]

On the face of it, the *chawls* (tenements) where workers lived, ate and slept were chaotic, cramped and dirty. Yet within the apparent disorder lay an order that may not have been visible to the western gaze, but has been teased out, in intricate detail, by historians (above all, Rajnarayan Chandavarkar).[129] Between thirty and forty per cent of the population of Girangaon lived in single-room tenements. Each room or *gala* of about eight cubic metres housed twenty or more people (this remains true today). The *chawls* that Cajetano would have encountered were two or three storeys high, their rooms arranged side by side along a long common corridor, at the end of which were shared washing areas (*mori*) and toilets.

The narrow streets between these crowded buildings 'were an extension of the home', part of the neighbourhood and its social life.[130]

Each *chawl* consisted of 300–400 *galas*. The twenty or so men who shared a *gala* were able to get by only because they did shift work and would sleep in turns in batches of six and seven. Shivaji Divte (a former tailor in his fifties) recalls: 'There [were] about twenty to thirty people in each room. How [did] we manage? Well, because there [were] three shifts. That is why there [was] a problem when the mills close[d] down or there [was] a general holiday. Then people [slept] outside on mats. Each [had] his own stuff which he [hung] on a nail behind his place.'[131]

Ties between *gaalekars* tended to be strong. When a worker got sick, or when he married, other *gaalekars* would pitch in to help him pay his bills.[132]

Three or four *chawls* were usually set around a central courtyard, where working men and boys played sports. Wrestling was particularly popular. Proficiency in the wrestlers' *akhara* (gymnasium) earned *gaalekars* local celebrity. (Cajetano was quick to take up wrestling, of which more in Chapter 7.) Community festivals took place in these courtyards, as did family celebrations. These spaces helped create and strengthen the bonds between the residents of small neighbourhoods; even as they quarrelled over water, fretted about debts owed for rent, or fought each other in alcohol-fuelled rages.

Since most workers at a particular mill came from the same region, the same community and often the same caste, and since those who lived in *galas* and *chawls* had relatives in the same *chawl*, Cajetano zeroed in on the tenement where Goans lived. By 1931, there were already some 34,000 Goans in Bombay who, like him, had made their way to Bombay from the Konkan coast, and many of whom worked in the mills. By the 1950s, their number had almost doubled. Cajetano joined them. Having insinuated himself in a Goan Catholic *gala*, he began the hunt for work.

This was easier said than done. Mill owners preferred to employ labour on a casual basis, responding to the variation in demand, seasonal or otherwise, for cloth. 'Not only were a significant proportion of cotton-mill workers hired at the factory gates [where they presented themselves each morning], but those who were permanently employed could easily lose their jobs and find themselves forced to take up casual employment.'[133] Even long-term, more highly skilled employees had a precarious hold over their jobs.

An outsider like Cajetano could only hope to get work at a mill by going every morning to the gate of a factory where many Goans were employed, eventually getting in with the help of an acquaintance from the village, *gala* or *chawl*, and then clinging on to his job by sheer hard work, and by making himself indispensable, which he had a knack of doing. Still, by the time he had paid his rent at the *chawl*, bought the odd bottle of country liquor and paid his dues at the *khanaval* (the cook house, of which more below) he often found he had little or nothing to send back to his mother in the village. Even though he loved the social life of the *chawl*, particularly the wrestling that became his hobby, and the *goondagardi* (hooliganism) that came with the drinking, he grew more and more worried about her.[134] Eventually he brought her to live with him in Bombay.

We know little in detail about Philomena's personal history up to this point, other than that she was a single mother. Perhaps she had once had a husband who had abandoned her; perhaps her in-laws threw her out after her husband, like many Goans, became a *lascar* on a British merchant ship and disappeared from her life. At the time of the 1931 census, there were only 554 women for every thousand men in Bombay.[135] In Calcutta in the same period, most women who migrated to the city did so because they had been widowed or abandoned.[136] Philomena joined their number and began to live with her son in the Goan Girangaon *chawl*.

Philomena was a small but striking woman. She was beautiful, intense, and had attitude. How she fended for herself in Girangaon is no mystery: Cajetano's body language and Philomena's flashing eyes made it plain that she did sex work at night. During the day she ran a *khanaval*, a cook house. Just as Indu Patil who ran a *khanaval* like her mother before her, Philomena concluded that her little family could not manage on one precarious income.

As Indu recalls, running a *khanaval* was not easy work:

My mother fell sick often. So I had to help out after I came home from school at 1 pm ... I would light the *sigdi* [clay oven or stove] in the afternoon and wake my mother. Then she would do the cooking. Dinnertime was at about 7 or 8 pm – everyone did not come at the same time. But the *dabbas* [lunchboxes] would have to go at the dot of 5 pm for the workers in the mill, on shifts. If anyone came after 10 pm we would not serve – their food would be kept in the *dabba* for them. My father kept accounts.[137]

And so they got by, until tragedy struck. The kerosene stove on which Philomena cooked exploded. She was horribly burned. Her neck and chest bore the brunt of the damage, and she was no longer able to work. With great reluctance, Cajetano (who by this time had a drug habit) took her back to the village. He could not leave her alone there now. But like her son, Philomena was a sharp (if foulmouthed) woman. She managed to find work as a cook in the house of a 'sahib' who was seldom around, but who had taken it into his head that he wanted to pitch his tent on Baga Beach. Today heaving with tourists and all the baggage that comes with them, Baga was, in the 1970s, just a strip of virgin sand overlooking the Arabian Sea. It had no road, no water, no electricity.

This time it was Philomena who found Cajetano a job: his only duty was to carry clean well water in buckets to the sahib's hut. The sahib in question was a Cambridge don. (Yes, the ways of the world are many and strange.) Cajetano is now diabetic and bad-tempered (not unlike his sahib). But they rub along.

I could go on about Cajetano. He has now become a traveller of a different kind. Despite being born a Catholic, he is a regular pilgrim at the shrine of Sai Baba, a guru who died in 1918, so a convert, of sorts, to a type of Hinduism. After his mother's death, he travelled so many times to Shirdi (250 times and counting) that the chief minister of Goa gave him an award in recognition of his devotion. Whether or not Cajetano has acquired mystical powers as a result, I cannot say. I do know that children, dogs, cats and even crows follow him around. Violent and unpredictable dogs that might otherwise have had to be put down grow calm around Cajetano. Children stop their crying. Mangy strays limp alongside him, sure that he will throw them some food. Cats wait for him to feed them the fish heads he saves for them. Birds seem to know that he will give them water, and perhaps stale crumbs. With his pockmarked face, wrestler's biceps, bulging chest and *goonda* past, he is an unlikely saint; but the people of Goa have come to believe that he has special powers. They flock to him to intercede with Sai Baba on their behalf, to pray for them and for their sick children.

I know that Cajetano prays for me. (He calls me *didi*, which is elder sister. I try not to be insulted, because he is much older than I am.) He sends me ashes from the shrine in little packages wrapped up in newspaper. He is sure that these prayers will cure me: 'Cent per cent pukka, *didi*, 100% guarantee, *didi*!' Who knows, perhaps they will.

But back to migrants in the city. As with Cajetano and Philomena, this pattern of keeping links with the village, of to-ing and fro-ing, of holding on to a plot in the village, however tiny, as a base to fall back upon when life in the city was no longer tenable, this was a common feature of male migrants in all the big cities. As Maruti Gyandeo Satkar recalls, he tried to bring his wife and children to the city, but it wasn't possible for them to settle down together:

> My wife and children lived in the village. I did bring them here for two years but it was too difficult to manage, so I sent them back. I have land and cultivation in the village. But it is not enough for my family to survive on. Otherwise, why would I come here, [to Bombay] to live alone and work?[138]

The links with the village remained strong, and *goankari mandals*, or village associations, were able to influence life in both the village and the city. They also helped sick workers to go home. Many of these men became ill by breathing in, for years, cotton fibres that had come to block their nostrils and airways with a thick gummy black residue. Others lost limbs. The city *chawl* was no place for the ill or disabled, and they returned home to be cared for by wives and daughters-in-law. Most died in the village.

The story of rural migration to Calcutta is somewhat different. Because Calcutta was, until 1911, the second city of the British Empire, and the base from which the British – post Mutiny and Rebellion – launched their reconquest of India, it was the first to be connected to its hinterlands by rail. (Troops could then be sent wherever they were needed, fast.)

If threat perceptions guided the building of the railways, they did not stop Indians from using it for their own ends. The Bengal and North Western Railway (1,468 miles long) linked Bengal to the populous, labour-exporting districts of Oudh, Rohilkhand, Benares, Jaunpur and Shahbad, and by 1904 carried thirteen million passengers each year.[139] The Bengal–Nagpur Railway linked Calcutta and Bombay, transporting another eight million passengers annually. More than twenty-five million passengers jostled for space on the East Indian Railway from Howrah to Kalka and Simla, the distant Himalayan summer capital of India. The Assam–Bengal railway, 740 miles long, ran from Chittagong on the south-eastern seaboard of Bengal, through the Surma river valley and Sylhet, and across Cachar into North Assam.[140] It transported over two million passengers a year by the turn of the century, not to mention the numerous smaller gauge 'feeder' railways that criss-crossed Bengal itself, carrying local traffic.[141]

Another difference was that the jute mills of Calcutta (unlike the cotton mills of Bombay) were almost all owned by Britons, often Scotsmen. Calcutta's satanic mills were situated in the southern suburbs of the city, rather than being at its core as they were in Bombay. Hence Palladian 'Bengal Baroque' Calcutta, with its grand mansions, esplanade and *maidan*, its cathedral and cemetery, and its hideous memorial to Queen Victoria, remained at some distance from the mills. The city's 'Black Town' was more clearly set apart from its 'White Town' than in Bombay, and most other cities and towns of British India.

Calcutta was also unique in that the city was surrounded by four major 'modern' industries: jute, tea and coal, and railway workshops. Construction was another growing employer, as in every city and town. As already noted Calcutta was also the funnel through which most indentured migrants went overseas, most depots being located there. Railways crossing peninsular India originated in Calcutta and passed through many of India's most famine-prone districts, not least the Gangetic belt of eastern Unirted Provinces and Bihar. Calcutta was thus close to a much larger hinterland of would-be migrants than Bombay. Inevitably it attracted migrants from a wider catchment area. Most came from the Gangetic belt, where pressure on land was particularly intense, and the monsoons capricious. Agriculture in north Bihar depended largely on the rains; its wells were insufficient to meet the needs of cultivators. As one folk song summed it up, referring to the sixth and thirteenth mansions of the moon, *Adra* and *Hast*:

Charhat barse Adra, utrat barse Hast,
Kitna Raja dandi le, sukhi rahe girhast.[142]

If it rained at the beginning of *Adra* and at the end of *Hast*,[143]
The cultivator would be happy, no matter how much the Raja demanded.

If the rains failed, however, drought often led to famine. Given that these rains often arrived at the wrong time, or were too heavy, or not heavy enough, Bhojpuri-speakers from the region migrated in droves in search of work. Stereotyped by the British as strong, brave but hot-headed, and after 1857, suspected of being involved in the Mutiny and Rebellion, they were no longer welcome in the army. So, many now flocked to the jute mills. By 1907, nearly half a million natives of the United Provinces had sought employment in the mills of Calcutta and Howrah and the coal mines of Burdwan.[144]

Men and some women from the dry areas of Orissa and northern Madras also swarmed to the city, some joining the mills while others found casual work. By 1914, one observer described mill towns as 'practically foreign towns planted in the middle of Bengal'. In Bhatpara, in the jute mill area, for every person who spoke Bengali four people spoke Hindustani. In Titagarh, also a centre of jute processing, seventy-five per cent spoke Hindustani, eight per cent Telegu, four per cent Oriya – and just over one in ten (eleven per cent) spoke Bengali.[145]

Owners often laid off millhands to drive down the price of labour, and then these workers would slip into the vast informal sector, finding work where they could: on construction sites, as palanquin bearers, as *darwaans* who guarded the mansions of the rich, or (increasingly as widowed and abandoned women began to throng to the city in this period) as domestic servants. The barriers between the formal and informal sectors of the modern urban economy were permeable; and as workers were increasingly 'casualised', they moved seamlessly into the world of informal work which dwarfed the mills, for all their size. They also moved between jobs within the formal sector – petty constables, who were paid little more than millhands and whose duties included being on the beat all night, often deserted to take up jobs in the jute mills when these became available.[146] Jute millhands, you will recall, were paid about as much as the 'guardians of the peace'.[147]

It is not as though there was no distress in eastern Bengal. The depression had hit its peasants hard. It was here that jute was mainly grown, and the fall in global jute prices left many destitute. But other than very particular niches in shipping and dock work (men from Noakhali and Sandwip in East Bengal were ubiquitous on Calcutta's docks, while Sylhetis monopolised the boiler rooms of steamships), most struggling Bengali peasants chose not to go west to Calcutta, but migrated instead eastwards, up the Brahmaputra river valley, to colonise hitherto uncultivated land in Assam and Burma. By 1907,

> Assam contain[ed] three-quarters of a million immigrants, or one eighth of its total population. These belong for the most part to the hardy aboriginal tribes of the Chota Nagpur plateau in Bengal and the adjacent parts of the Central Provinces and Madras; and upon the expiry of the labour contracts which they execute on coming to the Province, large numbers settle down as cultivators, or as carters, herdsmen, and petty traders . . . In Burma, as in Bengal, the profits of cultivation are so great, and the amount of wasteland so enormous, that very few labourers [were] available locally and the Province [was] dependent on outsiders for its harvesters and workmen in the rice-mills. These aggregated nearly half a million at the time of the last Census [1901], about three quarters of whom were natives of Madras and Chittagong . . . The aboriginal tribes of the Chota Nagpur Plateau [were] spreading to the north-east [of Bengal], and [were] bringing under cultivation the desolate uplands of the Barind, while large numbers of them [went] to the tea gardens of Jalpaiguri, whither they find their way without the elaborate recruiting agency on which the Assam tea gardens depend. Again, three or four hundred thousand persons born in Upper Burma were found in Lower Burma at the Census.[148]

As the century progressed, this migration became more and more controversial. Nativism emerged in Assam.[149]

Meanwhile, a quarter of a million people had migrated from Nepal into North Bengal, where the Darjeeling tea plantations relied on their work. More than half settled in contiguous British Indian districts, which went on to have profound political implications.[150] In the 1980s, North Bengal witnessed an insurgent movement seeking the establishment of an independent 'Gorkhaland', which has yet to be wholly resolved.

In eastern India, even more than in Bombay, South Asia's internal diasporas took dramatic shape, giving rise to political tensions that endured through the century and creating new jigsaw puzzles of peoples on the ground. In Assam, for instance, Bengali became an official language of the state.[151] Imagine that. Imagine Bengali becoming an official language of Great Britain, or Gorkhali in the United States. You cannot. But this is what has happened in South Asia. This, and much more.

But as with migrants to Bombay, many of Calcutta's migrants kept their connections to the village. If conditions of life and work in Bombay were bad, in Calcutta they were worse. In 1929, the average mill worker there earned only Rs 5 a week; at the time, the Royal Commission on Labour in India estimated that it cost a small family at least Rs 7 just to subsist.[152] In a note to the Royal Commission, a doctor described the *bastis* (slums) in which they dwelt as 'vile, filthy, disease-ridden hovels'. Their one-storey thatched huts had no windows, and their doors were so small that adults had to crawl to get in. There were no sanitary arrangements, no clean water, and mosquitoes and flies hovered. Such was the stench 'that one fears to strike a match lest the atmosphere, being combustible, should explode'.[153] In Kankinara, an aged worker told a visiting MP from Dundee, Calcutta's twin jute city in Scotland, that half the babies born in the *bastis* died. No wonder, then, that women tried to go back to the village to give birth, and returned to the *bastis* only when their children were old enough to be put out to work themselves.[154]

There have been particular pressure points in the subcontinent's history which forced migration levels to ratchet upwards. The post-depression decade was one such time, especially in parts of the subcontinent most closely integrated into the global economy. The Second World War was another such critical event. India (particularly Bengal) was once the frontline in the war against Japan. In a drive to deprive the oncoming enemy of food and means of movement in a riverine terrain, the government declared a Food Grains Control Order in 1942 and a Bengal Rationing Order in 1943. To implement these orders required assembling and importing a workforce of Adivasis – assisting new waves of labour migration – while stopping the normal movement of grain. At this time there were waves of emigration, too, from Calcutta, as Japanese bombs rained down on the city. Once again, a shift in the jigsaw, even if one that is seen only close up.[155]

Put together, these wartime orders are now understood to have had a disastrous effect, leading to the catastrophic Bengal Famine of 1942–3. If there was ever a man-made famine, this was it. There was no drought that explained it, but a drop in the import of Burma rice raised prices. This was followed by administrative bungling (at times well meaning, at others callous) and mismanagement on a grand scale.

The famine, in its turn, drove starving people off the land in their thousands in search of food, forging new migratory pathways through the disaster. For the first time in its history, Calcutta witnessed a mass influx from eastern Bengal, but it was composed of starving people looking for gruel kitchens rather than work. In 1931, the city had a population of about 1.2 million people. By 1941, 'flight from the impoverished countryside and migration related to wartime industrial production' saw the population of the city rise to 2.1 million (a figure that does not include military troops stationed in the city). Between 1931 and 1941, the size of the average household rose from sixteen to 27.5. Despite the shocking death toll among victims of starvation (between three and six million died from hunger and disease), the city continued to grow during the famine.[156]

It was during these crises that many peasants finally had to sell their tiny plots, or lost their right to cultivate the land, and began to dwell permanently in the city.[157] Up-countrymen from the Bhojpuri-speaking belt now began to see Calcutta as their primary home. Links with the village remained, but largely as ties of sentiment. In the 1990s, on one of my bi-annual visits to Calcutta, returning from the Writers' Building archive, I found myself stuck in one of the city's traffic jams. Dripping with sweat, I fanned myself with my research file and resigned myself to a long wait. As minutes turned into hours, I got chatting with the driver of the taxi, an ancient yellow Ambassador that had seen better days. The elderly driver had a world-weary manner. He spoke in Hindustani (rather than Bangla), so I asked him (in Hindustani) how long he had lived in Calcutta. He said: 'Always, *didi*. My family has been here for almost a hundred years. Of course we are from Bihar, our village is Bihar but Calcutta is our hometown.'

Rural poverty continued to drive migration until the end of the century. Consider the story of Sushila Devi, aged (she thinks) twenty-eight. A tiny spitfire of a woman, she looks like a child but works on a construction site like three men. Her skin is darkened by the sun – she works as a daily wager every single day and cannot afford to stop – but a bright smile lights up her face. When I asked her if I could take a life-history interview, she agreed readily, saying: 'My heart will feel lighter if I can tell someone everything.'

Sushila was born in a village near Rourkela, an industrial hub in the Indian province of Orissa. Her father was a construction labourer in Rourkela, as was his father before him. As soon as Sushila was old enough to go to school, her mother also returned to work as a *beldaar* (day labourer) on construction sites. With two incomes, they managed to send their youngest and brightest child to school, hoping that she would have a better life.

Sushila excelled at her studies, but her education was cut short when her father, to save his honour (*izzat*) after his elder daughter's elopement, got her married off to the older girl's prospective groom. Sushila was only twelve years old, and this was long after the legal age of consent for girls had been raised to eighteen years.

The marriage did not turn out well. Her husband drank himself to death, leaving her with a baby boy.

Meanwhile, Sushila's mother had been contacted by an 'aunty' (a professional recruiter, who visited Rourkela each year) who said there was better work and better pay in Delhi. Her parents took the decision to migrate to Delhi, where they went on to live and work for many years. (Whether the loss of *izzat* was a factor in that decision I cannot say, since Sushila believes that she saved her father's reputation.)

Upon being widowed, rather than staying with her in-laws, Sushila picked up her son and left for Delhi, where she, too, became a construction worker. (This was not, as we have seen, an unusual move for widows or abandoned women.)

Some years later, another aunty, a friend of her mother, suggested that Sushila ought to marry again: that she was too young to remain a widow all her life. And so she married Sher Singh (not his real name), also a construction worker, who is a migrant in Delhi from Rajasthan. He 'knows some plumbing work', she says, but mainly gets 'daily wage' jobs like her on construction sites. He too works seven days a week.

Sher Singh has adopted Sushila's first child as his own. (His mother most certainly has not.) Sushila now lives with him, his mother and his four unmarried brothers, and her three children; and after each day's hard labour on the site, she goes home to cook for ten people. She wakes up at 4 a.m. to cook for the same ten people, and bathe and dress her children. She makes light of it; she says she is used to it. She tells me that her house is very nice (*bahut achcha*). It is a small room in a little alley of shacks near Delhi's Fortis Hospital. It has a tin roof and was hot when we spoke (Delhi being in the middle of a heatwave) despite the new fan, but she has made it pretty inside, she tells me. She asks me if I will visit her when it is cooler. Of course I will.

Sushila speaks five languages: Sambhalpuri Oriya (that of her birthplace), Cuttacki Oriya (learned at work in Rourkela), Sadri (the language of Adivasi migrant co-workers in Rourkela), Hindi (flawless, acquired since her migration to Delhi) and Rajasthani (less good, she says), used by her husband's family at home and in their village, where as his bride, she goes often.[158] Her layered acquisition of languages gives one a sense of the richness and complexity of her migration history.

Every one of South Asia's internal migrants has to be seen not just as a statistic, staggering though these numbers are. Each has a story that, almost on page one of their telling it, rips away all the easy clichés. As with Philomena and Cajetano, so with Sushila – each one's history is full of twists and turns, and critical events.

Now try to see this subcontinent again. Not only is everyone, pretty much, a foreigner there, but each has a very curious (and often tragic) history that brought them to the places where you encounter them. There are no 'teeming masses'. There are people. People with migration stories.

III

PARTITIONS AND MIGRATION, 1947–2000

If cities before 1947 had been youthful, male-dominated places, that changed with partition.

Commemorating the seventieth anniversary of partition in 2017, the world's media represented the violence that accompanied it as anarchic, frenzied, wild.

In reality, it had clear patterns. Some places experienced more butchery than others. Punjab, above all, saw elemental violence akin to ethnic cleansing, as demobilised troops used their training and arms to try to change the demographic facts on the ground. 'Muslims' and 'Hindus', operating as mobs, wreaked violence of such magnitude that its effects linger to this day. Sikh *jathas*[159] on horseback surrounded Muslim villages in western Punjab, and either murdered their inhabitants or drove them out.[160] The plan, if such a fury can be called a plan, was to create more areas with non-Muslim majorities, so that India would be the legatee of more Sikh-owned land and holy sites. In fact, this strategy was doomed, since Sikh villages, fields and *gurdwaaras* (places of worship) were spread right across the Punjab; so theirs was a rage-fuelled, pain-driven but impotent drive to challenge the (il)logic of partition at the eleventh hour by drawing a border in blood.

It was, of course, too late for all this. India and Pakistan had both accepted the Radcliffe Line, broad-brush though it was. The poet W. H. Auden, whose brother married an Indian, was not wrong when he described the Radcliffe Line as having 'settled the fate of millions'. Auden's 1966 poem 'Partition' is worth revisiting:

> The maps at his disposal were out of date
> And the Census Returns almost certainly incorrect,
> But there was no time to check them, no time to inspect
> Contested areas. The weather was frightfully hot,
> And a bout of dysentery kept him constantly on the trot,
> But in seven weeks it was done, the frontiers decided,
> A continent for better or worse divided.
>
> The next day he sailed for England, where he quickly forgot
> The case, as a good lawyer must.

Whether in fact Radcliffe ever forgot (he did not) is irrelevant. Hindus, Muslims and Sikhs could not. Nor could they forget (or forgive) crimes committed by one 'community' against the other. Muslims in eastern Punjab retaliated with ferocious tit-for-tat attacks. The war for territory in the Punjab spilled over to Delhi, Ajmer, Alwar, Bharatpur, Bikaner and parts of Sind, and challenged the authority of the newly independent states and their borders. It shook the new status quo to its foundations. It is no exaggeration to say that it shaped those foundations.

Another pattern is that many princely kingdoms, even those situated in the plains of the Punjab, were, for the most part, peaceful.[161]

Within this mayhem, specific kinds of people were singled out for attack. Refugee columns moving in one direction, enraged by what had happened to them, attacked refugee *kaafilaas* moving the other way to the other country. Refugee trains were stopped and their inhabitants slaughtered, as Khushwant Singh's *Train to Pakistan* describes in unsparing detail. Satish Gujral, the Indian artist who trained at Lahore and later was apprenticed under Diego Rivera, made works that captured the horror of the Punjabi refugee experience. I had not seen Edvard Munch's *Scream* when I first saw an exhibition of Gujral's work, nor had I thought much about what had happened in 1947 but, like it, Gujral's canvases are etched into my mind, a visual metaphor for horror and disbelief.

But if refugees in general were a focus of violence, they were often implicated in it themselves. Victims became perpetrators just as perpetrators became victims.[162]

It was young girls and women who were singled out as targets. If, while under cover of the havoc, some young women eloped with lovers from the 'enemy' community, many thousands more (we think) were kidnapped, abducted or murdered.

Their attackers, when they were men from the 'other' community, killed them in the most gruesome ways, cutting off their breasts, slashing open their vaginas, violating their bodies in ways that they believed would most humiliate their male counterparts in the other community. Given all that we know about the evolving role of women as bearers of cultural and religious purity, as icons of community, these attacks had a barbarous logic – they destroyed the very thing the 'enemy' most prized. Sadat Hasan Manto's Urdu short story *Thanda Gosht* ('Cold Meat') is well worth reading; although it does not translate well into English, it conjures up the psychological trauma this brutality wreaked upon those who committed great crimes.[163] Perpetrators suffered too, Manto suggests.

This led to another phenomenon: men murdering 'their own women' to prevent them from falling into the hands of their foes. In countless instances, men murdered their own daughters, sisters and mothers. Thus Mangal Singh, a survivor in his eighties, was a legend in Amritsar Bazar when Urvashi Butalia interviewed him in the 1990s. He had killed seventeen women and children in his own family. He described them as 'martyrs'.[164] In the village of Thamali, Gurmeet Singh told Butalia that the men:

> took a decision that . . . all the young girls and women [must die] – two or three persons were assigned to the task of finishing them off. Those in the *gurdwara* were asked to set it on fire . . . first, we killed all the young girls with our own hands; kerosene was poured over them inside the *gurdwara*, women and children, where could they go?[165]

In other instances, women were encouraged to commit suicide en masse, often by jumping into wells, so that they would not fall into the hands of the enemy.

Fathers beheaded daughters. In one case that I have never been able to forget, a father in Thoa Khalsa told a young girl: 'Child, all the other sisters have gone, there is no one left, it is time for you to go.' Bir Bahadur admitted to Butalia that:

> Maan Kaur, my sister, came and sat in front of my father, and I stood there, clutching his *kurta* [shirt] as children do. I was clinging to him . . . but when my father swing the *kirpan* [sword], perhaps some doubt or fear came into his mind, or perhaps the *kirpan* got stuck in her *dupatta* [scarf] . . . no one can say. Then my sister, with her own hand she removed her plait and pulled it forward and then he swung the *kirpan* and her head and neck rolled off and fell . . . there . . . far away.[166]

These patterns explain why refugees moved as families: when surrounded, killing 'their women' before being killed themselves; when able to flee, taking women and girls with them as they travelled – a point of huge significance to which I will return. They also account for the decision by both states, India and Pakistan, to evacuate (under military guard) all Hindus and Sikhs from West Punjab and all Muslims from the eastern part of Punjab that remained in India. In an exchange of population that dwarfed the exchange of over a million Turkish Muslims and Greek Orthodox Christians after the Treaty of Lausanne of 1923, the Indian and Pakistani states collaborated in transporting about eleven million refugees moving in both directions within six months of 15 August 1947. By the time India and Pakistan undertook their first censuses as independent states, both counted about 7.5 million refugees *in each country* across the western border.

The mirroring effect seen across so many areas of South Asian life since independence was evident in this joint operation too.

Outside the divided province of Punjab, however, both states left minorities to get by as best they could, and leaders from both sides – even Gandhi and Jinnah – exhorted them to stand their ground.[167] Those who had the ability to move paid scant heed to this advice. They moved anyway, sometimes in trickles, sometimes in waves. And they too moved as families, ensuring that young women and vulnerable girls came with them.

This form of family migration continues to this day although, in the late twentieth century, some families moving were also environmental refugees, driven out of their settlements by the drying up or shifting of rivers.[168]

These migrations, too, have clear configurations. The great majority of refugee families moved to cities or large towns where they thought they could be absorbed into the urban economy.

Unlike the male working-class migrants who had gone before them, partition refugees had severed their connections with their villages or hometowns for all time.

Another feature marked out partition migrants from the rural poor who had previously migrated to the city. Most were moderately prosperous, well networked, skilled and healthy, with few obligations to people or places left behind.[169] The Hindus who left East Pakistan for India were chiefly of the 'higher castes', educated, with some capital, connections on the other side, and vigorous in body, whereas many Sindhi merchant and clerical families with similar qualities left Pakistan voluntarily and unassisted, for India.[170] This does not mean that they did not grieve, or mourn all that they had lost, even the precious earth that was left behind.[171] They still do.[172]

Today, as life has become more difficult for them in Pakistan, Dalits and other marginal groups (who were in the past less affected by this type of violence) make the hazardous journey across the border, but whole Dalit and Adivasi villages remained in Bangladesh after 1971.[173]

Muslims have continued to leave India in the second half of the century, just as Hindus have left in fits and starts, particularly after riots and calamitous events such as the violent incorporation of Hyderabad (1948) and the strange disappearance of Hazrat Bal (1964).[174]

For many, moreover, long after they moved across borders lock, stock and barrel, the 'remembered village' remained a source of nostalgia so powerful that it affected their children born long after partition.[175] Some children – the product of consummations of those violent times – are the true midnight's children, whom history has forgotten. The Indian and Pakistani states were determined to 'recover' abducted women, whether they wanted it or not. But who wanted these children? And where did they want to go? No one knew or cared.[176]

Kanakotpal Ghosh moved from Tangail in East Bengal to India in 1947. (He was the father of my friend Shohini Ghosh, whom you will meet in a different guise in Chapter 7.) Until his dying day, he longed for his place of birth. No, that is not strong enough. It's as if he were a mango tree whose root ball still lay buried deep in the *maati* (soil) of his village. (It is remarkable how many partition refugees long for that soil – some even carry a bit of it with them.)[177]

Kanakotpal refused to apply for a permit, passport or visa to go to East Pakistan, or later to Bangladesh, saying that if a visa were needed to travel to his own country, he would rather remain in exile. He would talk about the little village school and its headmaster, the date palms, the village tank, 'the air, the sky, the birds'; about long-lost Muslim friends and neighbours; indeed he spoke with such ardour about 'home' that Shohini and I felt a longing to 'return' to a place we had never been.[178] Our deep friendship was born out of this shared nostalgia for a place we had never seen.

Kanakotpal never did return. The village was lost for ever, the skein of connections it represented a spider's web brushed aside.

Because I have written so much about partition, people often ask me if I come from a family of refugees. I don't.

It is true that our ancestral home, in Hill Cart Road, nestles between three frontiers – India's borders with Bangladesh, Nepal and Bhutan – but in my childhood this was a serene setting, with only the rushing River Teesta disturbing its verdant calm. When I was a little girl, my father would lift me on his shoulders and point to the distance where the Teesta widened as it reached the plains. 'There is Bangladesh,' he would say. I could see nothing, just a beautiful emerald river in wild green Himalayan foothills.[179]

I did not associate that place with hatred, violence or enmity, rather with the deep peace that becalms one in an environment of quiet majesty.

What was probably more relevant to my direction as a historian was that I was in Delhi in 1984 when Indira Gandhi's Sikh body-guards assassinated her, and that I witnessed the carnage that followed.

I was twenty years old, a student at Lady Sri Ram College, attending a lecture of stupefying boredom about Mesolithic sites (I think. It could have been about kitchen midden cultures. My long-term memory is acute, but oh dear, those lectures). I was at the back of the class, hunched over a transistor radio a friend had been smart enough to smuggle in. We were listening to the cricket commentary. Suddenly the coverage was interrupted with a newsflash – Prime Minister Indira Gandhi had been attacked and was in a critical condition at the All India Institute of Medical Sciences. Since our college was not far from AIIMS, day scholars could not leave the campus until long after classes had been suspended. Fear clutched at our hearts.

By the time my elder brother was able to collect me from the campus that evening, the pogroms had begun. I could see burned-out cars and motorcycles; could smell burning rubber tyres and could see dense smoke rising from familiar buildings: from Sikh *gurdwaaras*, and Sikh-owned shops. I smelled what I recognised to be the odour of burned flesh. That night I heard people running in panic as they were chased down. Two mornings later, when curfew was briefly lifted, I shopped for stale vegetables for our household. As I crossed the main road, I saw lorry-loads of armed men carrying huge kerosene cans, roaring as they drove by. High on testosterone and hungry for revenge, they were hunting down Sikhs. They were going to pour kerosene on their homes, shops and bodies, and set them aflame. The police stood by and watched.

This horrific episode in 1984 is one of South Asia's watersheds in the twentieth century.

I suddenly sensed that this was what it had been like in 1947. For years afterwards I had a recurring nightmare in which I found the charred remains of my favourite aunt, Pishima, among the corpses, and would wake up gagging and sobbing. The smell of fear and the sounds of violence haunt us all, I think, even if we were born long after 1947. We all react to it in different ways. My response has been to write about partition. After 1984, I began to see my own city as one on which partition had branded its brutal legacy. Its imprimatur is unmistakable. It is everywhere.

Until the end of the century, Muslims continued to leave India in waves, after riots and calamities such as the violent incorporation of Hyderabad in 1948 (in which between 25,000 and 40,000 Muslims died); the Hazrat Bal incident in Kashmir in 1964 and the violence of that time; the demolition of the Babri Mosque in 1992; and the Gujarat riots of 2002.[180] Hindus also left Pakistan and Bangladesh. The fear of minorities spanned borders at such moments: some leave, others huddle together more closely and live in dread.[181] It is as if all of South Asia shudders in their wake. One little Bengali Hindu boy's growing awareness of this is rendered with a delicate, but unforgettable, touch in Amitav Ghosh's *The Shadow Lines* (1988) – a book that sparked in me an interest in partition's afterlives that still has me in its grip nearly forty years on.

The memory of the trauma of partition, of riots and retaliation, of pogroms and mass migration, is so deeply embedded in the South Asian psyche that any sudden political shock can open wounds so deep one barely knows they are there.

They are the violent drum beats of the South Asian twentieth century.

Inevitably influxes on such a grand scale (and emigrations and re-arrangements of peoples) over such a short time transformed South Asia's cities, especially those that bore the brunt of partition: Karachi, Delhi, Calcutta and Dacca.

IV

PARTITION CITIES

A couple of years ago, on a research trip to the subcontinent, my son and his girlfriend (now wife) came with me. Ciara had not been to India before. As we drove from the airport to my family home in Hauz Khas Village, past the sprawling medium-rise suburbs of Dwarka and Vasant Kunj, past the shanties that crowd their interstices, past the superior neighbourhoods off Olof Palme Marg, past temples under peepal trees, past roadside barber's shops and past stray dogs looking for scraps, she asked, where is the city centre?

I found that I didn't have a ready answer.

I did know that refugees had changed not only their built environments but transformed cities as dynamic lived spaces. They fought pitched battles with the state and resisted drives to remove them from the city. They proved to be militant, recalcitrant in defence of the rights they felt they had earned. They changed the power balances within neighbourhoods and between neighbourhoods and the city.

They also generated bitter local wars over space.

Partition created dispersed, disordered cities across South Asia, which no amount of master planning could contain. 'Partition cities' had multiple, changing structures. Some denizens emerged as winners in these battles over urban space. Others lost their footholds. Survival in them was a scramble, often defended with violence.

Beneath Karachi's apparent chaos, which appears unruly to the western gaze, lies a new kind of order that follows a logic that makes sense to Karachi's inhabitants. While colonial Karachi was, like every major imperial city, divided into 'White Town' and 'Black Town', today, one scholar of the city suggests, it is divided between the 'planned city' and the 'unplanned city'.[182] But I suggest that neither the transformation nor what has emerged has been anything like as tidy. The new urban patterns of the partition cities of the 1980s were not so easy to categorise: different kinds of space bled into each other. Urban politics, furthermore, bridged the divide between them.

In the Raj era, 'White Town' had tended to consist of four separate zones, connected to each other by large roads, each supplied by the municipality with water, electricity, roads and sanitation services. In Calcutta, it had housed the 'civil lines': the key offices of government, Writers' Building (which still stands, its red paint regularly renewed while stacks of files crumble within), the stately Grand Post Office, Belvedere (the governor-general's house), the courts, other municipal and official buildings, libraries, clubs, universities and churches.

Abutting this lay the commercial heart of the colonial city: Burra Bazar, its financial hub; and then the clubs, shopping centres, banks, restaurants, cinema halls, theatres and company headquarters. In Calcutta, this included Hogg Market (now New Market); Theatre Street (now named after Shakespeare – the one Briton who has, far from being trashed with all his countrymen, been elevated by being given a main street of his own); and Park Street with its expensive eateries, notably Flurys, established in 1927, which specialised in European confectionery and for years represented the epitome of colonial chic.

(The style was Palladian, so much so that I do a double take when I am in similar settings in London. Perhaps the best comparison is with the London of Charles Dickens' *Bleak House*.)

Close to these public buildings were residential areas for different classes of British government servants, with each class of employee allotted quarters appropriate to his station. Adjacent residential areas housed non-official Britons – the 'box-wallahs' and men of business whom the bureaucrats looked down upon (including the jute magnates who often lived in palatial residences within the mill compounds).[183] A few exceptionally wealthy 'natives', like Lord Sinha and the Singh Roys of Teota, moved into White Town in Calcutta, just as Motilal Nehru (as we saw in Chapter 1) had done in Allahabad. Indian habitations in White Town often emulated colonial styles, some (in Calcutta) a vernacular version of the neo-Palladian, in Bombay mock Tudor-Gothic, in Karachi and Delhi, Indo-Saracenic, Anglo-Mughal and modified *haveli* forms.[184] As the century progressed, these mansions found themselves surrounded by colonies of upwardly mobile 'native' middle classes who had migrated to the city in search of white-collar work, and their houses 'with no garden'.[185]

Lutyens' New Delhi with its sandstone official buildings, its straight boulevards and its roundabouts bright with bougainvillea, represented the acme of a colonial White Town. Planned from scratch, its political heart was the sandstone-clad, domed Viceroy's Palace atop Raisina Hill, while its commercial heart at Connaught Circus was a stuccoed Palladian arcade so white that it blinded one in the Delhi sun. Civil servants occupied much of the rest of the city, the top officials living in grand and spacious Lutyens bungalows (which in fact were dingy), set in acres of lawn; while rajas and princes built mansions in different styles in adjacent streets.[186] For its part, Karachi (still a small city) was dominated by the Port Trust financial district and Sadar (the administrative zone) and its glamorous sea-facing homes in Clifton.

At a safe distance from these areas lay the cantonment, the barracks of those at hand set apart to protect gentlemanly Britons from restive natives and from their own white lower orders, the unruly lower ranks of the soldiery, and to keep these supposedly 'rough' men as far as possible from the seething temptations of Black Town.[187]

In contrast to the zoned White Town, with its wide boulevards and green spaces, colonial Black Town, to the untutored eye, appeared anarchic. Kipling was obsessed by its 'stench'. In *The City of Dreadful Night* he described it as resembling 'the essence of corruption that has rotted for the second time – the clammy odour of blue slime'. In 1888, when he first visited the city, Calcutta was experimenting with local self-government, of which he wrote: 'In spite of that stink, they allow, even encourage, natives to look after the place! The damp, drainage-soaked soil is sick with the teeming life of a hundred years, choked ... with natives born in it and raised off this surfeited muckheap!'[188]

Yet this description of Black Town as an arena of teeming, chaotic, stinking Indian life was misleading. Bombay, Delhi, Karachi and Calcutta, and even smaller towns such as Surat, had distinctive neighbourhood (*mohalla*) modes of organisation.[189] Members of the same occupational groups (hence often the same sub-caste, sect and region) inhabited these *mohallas*, which were more or less self-regulating. With few resources (and little or no state provision of water or sanitation), they had no choice but to be organised: to share scarce water, to keep the areas as clean as possible with the help of *mehtars* (sweepers), to resolve disputes between members, to support each other in sickness and bereavement, and to protect their homes and families from outsiders.

Calcutta's poorer neighbourhoods, whether Hindu or Muslim, housed distinct enclaves of particular occupational groups: bookbinders, soap and candle makers, tailors, and *kumors* who crafted idols. Each of Old Delhi's narrow alleys, *galis* and *kuchas*, likewise, accommodated bangle makers, cock-fight organisers, sweetmeat sellers, *zaardozi* embroiderers, washermen and butchers; while *paraathewali gali* exuded the aroma of fresh fried flatbread. Traders, most of them Hindu, were prominent in Karachi's old city. They too lived in discrete enclaves, along winding streets with narrow entrances that could be protected against thieves and intruders.

Labouring neighbourhoods were more densely packed but were clearly structured around courtyards. Each *chawl*, as we have seen, had a distinct regional, linguistic and caste personality of its own, based on historic networks of recruitment built up by jobbers of various kinds, and the male chain migrants whose roots took them along these routes.

Leadership in the neighbourhoods was provided by a range of *mohalla sirdaars*, who were usually senior craftsman and the heads of small production units or *karkhaanas*; and sometimes factory *sirdaars*. Near the docks they were the *ghaat serangs* who recruited *lascars* for the merchant ships sailing out of the ports of Calcutta and Karachi, or *baariwallahs* (rentiers) who made a tidy living by renting out rooms to urban migrants (usually to men from their own villages or regions). These *sirdaars*, *serangs* and *baariwallahs* were also often money-lenders, and their power within neighbourhoods derived from complex overlapping structures of petty rentierism, recruitment to employment and, above all, loans. Shopkeepers too were important figures as suppliers of basic necessities on credit to the local poor. Young men like Cajetano trained in *chawl akharas* and provided muscle power: they protected communities from petty harassment by the police, and extracted rents and dues on behalf of neighbour landlords, creditors and shopkeepers.

Before the Second World War, these distinct parts of the city were often spatially separated from each other, often surrounded by large uninhabited lowlands, marshes or drainage canals. Often they had grown up close to long-settled villages, whose inhabitants continued to live by agriculture and cattle breeding, milk production and market gardening, selling their produce in the city's bazaars.

To be sure, these cities had grown substantially in the inter-war period, and more and more migrants crowded into urban spaces. The depression of the 1930s, and the rapid rise in population from the 1920s onwards, saw to that. By 1947, Karachi's population had risen to 400,000 after the building of the Sukkur barrage across the Indus threw thousands of Punjabi and Sindhi peasants off the land and into the cities. The expansion of cities continued through the Second World War. In Delhi and Calcutta, government requisitioned much empty land for barracks, airfields or industrial units to produce goods for the war effort, and to house military personnel. In Calcutta, the city swelled further as the Bengal Famine of 1942–3 pushed the starving into it.[190] Despite this, these imperial cities continued to have large tracts within and around them that remained thinly populated or uninhabited, even during the war. After its end, many wartime buildings and barracks were abandoned.

Yet despite this backcloth of urban expansion in the last days of the Raj, there is no way of overstating, or exaggerating, the impact of partition on these cities. The explosion in urban population after 1947 was not incremental, as growth had been hitherto. It was sudden, and its sheer scale was unlike anything witnessed before. By 1951, Karachi's population had increased by 168 per cent, taking it over the one million mark. It continued to spiral upwards so that by 1981, it had crossed five million, becoming the fastest-growing city in the world.[191] By 1970, parts of Calcutta had become the most densely populated parts of the planet.[192] As for Delhi, between 1941 and 1951, its population almost doubled, from just over 900,000 to over 1,700,000 (despite losing a sizeable proportion of its long-resident Muslims). By 1971 it had crossed four million.[193]

But raw numbers tell us only the headlines – they need careful interpretation. For one thing, this was not the familiar chain migration of pre-independence days. Most of these new immigrants had no *sirdaar* or *gaalekar*, no job to go to, no *baariwallah* who could give them a roof over their head, no caste fellow or kinsman to offer them temporary shelter.[194]

What is more, this wave of migrants flooded in not as single young men but as whole families – men, women, children, sometimes with elderly grandparents in tow. Their links with the rural countryside or the small town from where they came had been snapped suddenly and for ever.

Their needs were thus radically different from those of the migrants these cities had previously absorbed. Their impact on cities where they clustered was revolutionary.[195] No part of the city, whether the old White Town or Black Town, emerged unscathed.

Refugees and urban space

The most far-reaching changes were to the areas previously known as Black Town. As Black Town morphed into the 'unplanned' city, three new kinds of settlement emerged within it: the refugee squatter colony, the ghetto and the 'slum'.[196] Each was different, in some cases dramatically and in others more subtly, from the *mohalla*-based neighbourhood of the past. Each was grabbed, often with force, and defended with equal vigour, if threatened with dispossession. Each represents a facet of the angst of the city, its undertone of violence, and its fragile peace.

On the face of it, these places look similar, like chaos in the shadow of a skyscraper. In fact, they are quite different. The cities of South Asia are even more complex than they look.

Refugees who stormed the cities felt entitled to citizenship, even compensation, for their sacrifice of their all for the nation.[197] They had left everything they knew behind for the nation, and now, they thought, the nation would come to their rescue.

Did it? Not so. Neither India nor Pakistan had the will or capacity to attend to them. Bleeding hearts had turned to stone, it would seem.

Refugees, therefore, grabbed what they could, wherever they could.[198] They were most conspicuous in the public spaces of former White Town areas, now the base from which the *sarkars* of the new states sought to operate. Delhi's municipal committee got the police in to remove refugee hawkers from pavements in the business areas of Old Delhi, but the refugees were not for moving.[199] Homeless families camped at night in salubrious parks intended only for the enjoyment of the city's elites. This was enough to prompt panicky officials first to lock up parks at nightfall (they are locked up at dusk to this day), and then to build high iron fences around them.

Next the guardians of the nations tried to seal off whole cities to keep refugees out. As we saw in Chapter 2, in late 1947 governments sought to prohibit refugees from entering Delhi and Karachi. Calcutta tried again and again to establish cut-off dates for refugee ingress; it kept turning away new refugees and tried to shut down camps, with little success.[200]

The West Bengal government then began to plan the wholesale removal of refugees from the city, above all from its former White Town areas.[201] Everyone was determined to rid the city's old centres of refugees. All attempts failed.

As an adolescent visiting Calcutta in the late 1970s, I walked past refugee families who huddled on the footpath of 'genteel' Southern Avenue. Refugees were still there in the 1980s and 90s, when I returned on research trips. If Kipling's 'stench' emanated from their tarpaulin shacks, I do not remember it. All I recall are rake-thin women, wizened and weather-beaten by sun and pounding rain, holding tiny children on their hips as they bathed naked babies at communal taps and scrubbed utensils with ash. These children, if they survived, were among the first generation born in the city. I still associate Calcutta in my mind's eye with silver-grey ash.

To the unwitting eye, ash perhaps looks dirty. It is, in fact, what the poor used to scrub their utensils clean.

As refugees flowed into West Bengal in their millions, its government devised dispersal strategies, acquiring large plots of land at least twenty-five to forty kilometres distant from the city's 'heart'.[202] It used buckets of coercion, and homeopathic doses of incentive, to push refugees into these new 'colonies', where part of their job was to clear the land, fell trees and construct shelters. Some of these colonies were in the dense jungles of central India. Others were even further away, on the Andaman Islands off the southern tip of Burma, an erstwhile penal settlement of the Raj.[203]

Official reactions to the influx of refugees in Delhi and Karachi were very similar: to drive them as far away as possible. The ratio of carrot to stick varied across the cities, depending on state capacity. Delhi offered the most attractive incentives. Calcutta, Bombay and Karachi vied for top spot in the callous lack of humanity in crafting the stick.[204]

Even if these locations for refugee settlement in Delhi had been suitable, which they were not, the refugee colonies, planned and built between twenty-five and forty miles away from the heart of the old White Town, displaced or surrounded the Jat villagers who had previously occupied land adjacent to the city. The phenomenon of the 'urban village' marooned among islands of refugee colonies, which so characterises Delhi, was thus born.[205]

In Karachi, General Ayub ordered in bulldozers to flatten and clear dozens of refugee tenements and squatter colonies that had sprung up.[206] Just as in New Delhi, around Karachi the refugee 'satellite townships' displaced hundreds of villages; in turn their inhabitants (for instance, the Baloch residents of Lalukhet) began to drift towards the city.

With few exceptions, the new townships purpose-built for refugees failed to keep them there. Korangi near Karachi, Salt Lake and Jirat near Calcutta, Faridabad and Kalkaji south of Delhi, and Dandakaranya in the central Indian forests, are all examples of policy assumptions and failures that crossed subcontinental boundaries.[207]

Their failure could have been predicted. Unemployment was its cause. There was simply no work to be had in the middle of the countryside, or in the heart of a forest, and such facilities that the government had provided for travel to the city where work might be available were uncertain and expensive.

That state officials refused to see this right across the borders of divided South Asia reveals just how little stomach there was to address their huge – indeed catastrophic – problems. The nation was otherwise occupied.

If refugees began to take matters into their own hands, it should not have come as a surprise.

The refugee squatter colony

The refugee squatter colony represented, more than any part of the old Black Town, something novel in South Asia.

One such colony in Calcutta was Azadgarh ('fortress of freedom'). Four young refugees established it in Calcutta in 1950. These 'ringleaders', as the police described them, were all refugees of 'high caste', literate but impoverished, who met by chance. One of these men, Indu Ganguly, was already squatting (as were thousands of refugees) in a building on a large plot of land owned by an absentee landlord, almost certainly a Muslim.[208]

This angry squatter-activist circulated a notice among homeless refugees of the area, declaring that plots would be allotted on this 'empty' land on a first-come first-served basis. 'The rush was considerable and many of them had to go back disappointed.' The source does not tell us who the lucky ones were, but the fact that they were still living on the streets in 1950 suggests that they were lesser *bhadralok* (gentlefolk) proletarianised by partition, as well as artisans and a good number of people lower down the social scale.[209] (Ganguly is a Brahmin name.)

Unlike the neighbourhoods and *mohallas* of old, then, people from a variety of castes and regions lived cheek by jowl in Azadgarh.

The fact that women and girls outnumbered the menfolk was another novel – indeed striking – feature. The 'feminisation' of urban space had begun.[210] (A population boom would soon follow, making the refugees' situation even more precarious.)

The ringleaders, though, were all men, and they organised the young male and able-bodied among the refugees. They worked by stealth, at night. By early 1950, they had annexed almost an acre of land. They carved this tract into tiny lots of three *cottahs*, and distributed them among the refugee families.[211] Together they made pathways, levelled agricultural land and removed scrub and jungle. By the end, they had created a colony of almost 400 plots of equal size.

Their rigorous planning shows that the ringleaders were critical to the leadership of the Azadgarh community. But they also set up an elected central committee and three ward committees. They raised funds by subscriptions from the plot-holders: Rs 15 per plot at the start, after which everyone paid a monthly contribution of one rupee. This money paid for the construction and upkeep of common areas, a school and a marketplace.

Committee members, all men, met often to discuss the infrastructure needs of the community. They appointed a community doctor, a homeopath. They paid him no fees, but different households fed him each day. Similar arrangements were made for the schoolteacher. (If this were accurate, it would be revolutionary. It would mean a man of 'high' caste, a doctor, ate in the house of a man of much 'lower' caste. Unlikely. Many sources do, however, speak of the breakdown of caste barriers between young men and women in refugee colonies. So the space itself seemed to galvanise social change.)

But these were the only two men 'employed' by the Azadgarh community. The rest had to fend for themselves. Most seem to have integrated themselves as best they could into the wider workforce and marketplace of neighbouring Calcutta, selling home-made goods that ranged from straw baskets to earthenware lamps, in the city's vast informal sector. The women hawked a few vegetables grown on their tiny plots, but also sold their labour, working as maidservants in neighbouring wealthy and middle-class households. (More on this in Chapter 5.) Some men set themselves up as electricians, others as mechanics.

The Azadgarh families built their own houses. The fact that they made them from materials that ranged from brick and tiles to *hogla* thatching and cardboard soaked in tar, indicates the different degrees of poverty in which these families lived. This heterogeneity was a new feature of the social organisation of urban space. A *hogla*-thatched hut might sit adjacent to a grand brick and tin neighbour, a 'lower-caste' *nabasak* or *sudra* family next to that of a Brahmin. Very little remained of the spatially distinct occupational, regional, artisan-based or caste grouping that had characterised the urban *mohalla* of the past.

Another change was the structure of the central committee. Although it was in charge of the colony, the notion of participatory democracy was strong, and elections were held regularly in each ward. Yet the flip side was that their little democratic republic depended on the violent dispossession of the original owners of the plots, Muslim 'others' no longer able to fight for their rights.

Azadgarh's relationship with the city was something new. It did not live with the city in symbiosis, as *mohallas* had done in the past – it had been seized by force and against the law. Azadgarh's very name reflected its inhabitants' attitude to the city: *garh* means fort. Its inhabitants defended their space like beleaguered warriors defending a fortress in times gone by. *Arjun*, Sunil Gangopadhyay's novel, captures the refugees' constant round-the-clock armed vigilance.[212] Manas Ray's paper 'Growing Up Refugee', an autobiographical analysis of the refugee predicament, also underscores the constant sense of danger, and preparedness for violent attack.[213] The *para dadas* and *mastaans* – the musclemen so ubiquitous in Calcutta neighbourhoods in their armbands and headscarves at the end of the century – were a legacy of these vigilantes of the squatter colony.

The parallels between them and Karachi's Muhajir Qaumi (MQM) ward bosses are too striking to be missed. There is no question that in Karachi, the MQM with its huge refugee base of support began to run the city in a way that Calcutta's refugees never quite did. The violence (and for some decades success) of their battle for control over a city was more remarkable than anything else the subcontinent witnessed after partition. For decades, for all its armed force, Karachi was a no-go area for the Pakistani state. The war that ended the MQM's reign was brutal, grotesque (on both sides). It ended with Altaf Hussain, its firebrand leader, in exile in London. It is not impossible to understand the MQM phenomenon. Remember the fear, the sense of betrayal and the righteous rage, of refugees.

V

MIGRATION TO GHETTOS

Innumerable ghettos exist all over the subcontinent. Some are tiny, in the deep hidden shadows of refugee camps, where only a few dozen still dwell. Selimpore, south of Calcutta, is one such place. When I first visited it, I had not done much interdisciplinary work. Selimpore pushed me to seek a new path.

What happened was this. I had come across an account of a dispute ('fracas', to use police jargon) over the use of a graveyard in Calcutta. It mentioned refugees, graves, footballs and staves. Similar incidents occurred in the same place until the mid-1950s, and then the records fell silent. Frustrated and intrigued in equal measure, I decided to go looking for the place, in case anyone could tell me what had happened. This was in 1997. I behaved, in other words, as an anthropologist might have done.[214]

I had thought it would be easy to locate. Not so. The neighbours – all refugees – denied that the place existed. But find it I did, in the end, with the help of a Muslim rickshaw puller, who led the way.

When I got there, it was clear that the refugees of the surrounding area had 'swallowed up' a Muslim settlement, leaving only a part of its graveyard behind. Only the custodian of the graves, and his extended household, still live there, in the deepest poverty I have ever seen. Their grief was so palpable that it is imprinted on me still. No one smiled, not even the children. Something in the old custodian's eyes looked broken. Having gone nowhere, they had lost everything – their dignity, their peace, their place in the city, and the communities among which they had lived.

To make matters worse, the local refugee boys took pleasure in rubbing it in – they used part of the graveyard as a football pitch.

The graves of the ancestors were key sites in the faith of many Sunnis of Bengal and Bihar, accorded their own ritual observance: Shab-e-Baraat. So this was an insult they felt like a wound, opened afresh every evening as the boys came out for a kickabout.[215] It was one of the saddest places I have seen.

After this, I spent the rest of that hot summer going from graveyard to graveyard, speaking to their custodians, and walking in their – remarkably serene, rather beautiful – grounds. My family and friends thought I had gone mad. No doubt I had gone a little crazy with grief.

Because, you see, each one was like Selimpore, in macrocosm.

There are other types of ghettos, right at the heart of cities. Some are huge, like Geneva Camp in Dacca. Town Hall Camp, also in Dacca, is a newer urban ghetto. Both are products not of the first partition, but of the second in 1971 after the Bangladesh Liberation War. Town Hall Camp grew up after mass killings of 'Bihari' migrants to Bengal, who were all dubbed as traitors to the new nation of Bangladesh. It is one of the many camps in which survivors have lived since 1972. 'Bihari' or 'Urdu-speaking' minorities of Bangladesh were, in the twentieth century, stateless. In 2008 five young men, including 'Pappu' from the camp, filed a petition in the Supreme Court suing for citizenship for 'Urdu-speakers' like themselves who had been born after the Liberation War had ended. They won the case. But Bangladesh remains a dangerous place for them. (Hence 'Pappu' must still be referred to as 'Pappu'.)

Despite its recent history, no one is sure who set up Town Hall Camp.[216] The camp's 'leader', Musharraf, claimed that it was situated on government-owned land (which was empty scrub before 1971), although the sign at its entry gate proclaims that it was 'doneted [sic] by Muslim hands'. This is just one example of the complex array of versions of its history (and politics) that emerged in oral histories and interviews. It suggests, if nothing else, that its establishment was not remotely as organised as the formation of Azadgarh. Flight and panic, rather than assertive militancy, produced it.

Like Azadgarh, Town Hall Camp is an entirely new settlement in the city, built on previously uninhabited (in all likelihood, minority or 'Bihari'-owned) land. But its construction gives no hint of centralised planning by ringleaders. Its members are all non-Bengalis, in that their first language is not Bengali, but that is all they have in common.

Most, but not all, have what we might call urban proletarian antecedents – they were part of the Bhojpuri- and Awadhi-speaking diaspora from eastern United Provinces and western Bihar who built and manned the railways of undivided Bengal, and who worked in a variety of niches in Dacca's economy as *darwaans* (guards), masons, *lascars* and tailors. But most did not know each other before 1971. They did not share relationships of kinship or clan, or have village ties. Catastrophic violence, rather than chain migration and professional recruitment, threw them together.

Camp dwellers lived by a variety of avocations, chiefly in the informal sector. One worked as a guard at a local cinema hall; another had a 'saloon' or barber's shop; several deployed their railway workshop skills to work as mechanics. One man, Usman, ran a tiny corner shop, and also kept goats. Many women worked; like the women of Azadgarh many laboured as domestic servants in nearby homes. Most also sewed sequins on garments in their spare time.

Some of these women have never left the camp.

Salima is a widow. She was in her fifties in the 2000s when we met her. She had lived in the camp in one tiny room, about nine foot square, for more than thirty years. A thin, bespectacled woman, she shares the room with her adult son and his wife, her daughter and her grandchildren – of whom one, Taukir, about fourteen years old, is disabled. Salima's husband used to work in the railways, but during the troubles of 1971, he was tortured, and eventually died from his injuries. For several months, Salima nursed him and tended their children. After he died, she went to Dacca, as she had relatives in the city. She became a squatter in what would eventually become the camp:

> This was then a market place. It was empty. We put jute curtains up and started to live here. Things were very difficult. There were no fans – only light bulbs tied to bamboo poles, one providing light to a few families together.

This room is now one of hundreds of similar rooms in Town Hall Camp, itself one of several 'Bihari' camps in Dacca.

Salima's room has no windows or vents; when we interviewed her, the stale air smelled of kerosene. None of her children has had any education. She works as a cleaner for a local NGO and supplements her meagre income doing piecework for garment manufacturers.

Unlike in Azadgarh, the political leadership seemed very diffuse. There is a camp committee, but its leader is known as 'Baldy' behind his back. Baldy shares influence with members of the Stranded Pakistanis General Repatriation Committee (SPGRC) which, as its name suggests, demands that 'Biharis' be repatriated to Pakistan, a country that few of them have seen but to which they claim allegiance. Baldy also has to contend with aid workers and NGOs, with the

schoolteacher and the imam, and with the Khalifa groups that organise the annual Muharram procession. Each is an influencer in his own
way.

Baldy, let's just say, is no Indu Ganguly. No 'ringleader'.

'Bihari' ghetto areas are not controlled spaces, despite being gated
in. When outsiders enter – whether census-takers, microcredit bank
workers, hawkers, drug-dealers, NGO workers, guests, the police, or
even researchers like ourselves – the inhabitants go out of their way
to ask where they want to go and who they want to meet. There
seemed no sign of community policing.

The relationship between the camp and the city could hardly be more
different from that of Azadgarh. Its inhabitants still recall the horrors of
1971 and 1972; almost everyone lost family members in the killings. But
they do not fight it, they dare not. They mainly lie low, keep their heads
down and try to survive. They are anxious, at all times, about their
security, but they do not arm themselves. They make no political
demands. They do not look to government for help. Aid workers step in
to help provide civic amenities. The NGO Al-Falah had built twenty-
two latrines in the camp, and an Islamic charity helped repair the local
mosque.

Town Hall Camp has the feel of an island, its inhabitants marooned
in a hostile city. By the 2000s, it had a certain resilience.[217] The boundaries between the camp and the world had blurred over time, as outsiders
moved in and the upwardly mobile, like Baldy himself, moved out.

Taken together, these 'unplanned' settlements represent outcomes –
ever unstable – of struggles for space in the city. They were vulnerable
to attacks by lynch mobs after 1972, and the threat of the municipal
bulldozer always lurks. Existence there is always fraught, always anxious, always precarious. But as Sanjay Gandhi realised too late at
Turkman Gate in Old Delhi: when pushed beyond endurance, some
ghetto dwellers have, on occasion, been ready to fight for these footholds with everything they have.

The 'slum'

The *basti* (slum) is, at first sight, the least transformed settlement in
the city.

If you look closely, it is anything but.

The number of such settlements, their density and the make-up of their population have changed. In 1945, after the famine and the war ended, there were almost 5,000 slums in Calcutta alone.

By 1951, their population and density had risen. By that year, Calcutta's slums contained 22,000 huts which housed more than 600,000 people, and over the next decade their numbers continued to grow. Most of those who lived there were migrants from the countryside. Roughly twenty per cent of this growing population were refugees. There were even a few white-collar men and their families, employed but paid too little to live elsewhere. Or who were just unemployed.

Patwarbagan was one among such *bastis*.

A private landlord owned the land on which Patwarbagan stood. He had, in days gone by, rented it out to middlemen, *thika* tenants who became the key figure in the *basti*, where they played a role similar to that of the infamous *dalaals* of Karachi, the wheeler-dealers of its property market.[218]

In Patwarbagan, a *thika* tenant built tenement 'houses' at his own cost and then rented them out to sub-tenants, known as *bharatiyas* (rent-payers). In 1951, such sub-tenants paid between Rs 7 and Rs 8 a month in rent. Often the *thika* tenant also lived in the *basti* himself, where he was a powerful and authoritative figure.

This had been the pattern since the late nineteenth century. Colonial governments seemed to have been content to let these *bastis* endure with a bare modicum of regulation. Their low rents made them viable to their inhabitants. If they had no civic amenities: well, beggars could not be choosers.

As for their social organisation, depending on their location, *bastis* resembled either mill neighbourhoods such as Girangaon, or (more commonly) a version of the caste- and craft-based *mohalla* settlement. Calcutta's *bastis* tended to house large numbers of artisans. Most were identified with a particular craft – for instance, tailoring in Metiabruz, timber and plywood in Ultadanaga, tanning in Tiljala and Tangra, papermaking and bookbinding in Patwarbagan. Given the supply of cheap labour, many small more 'modern' enterprises also operated out of these *bastis*, such as leatherwork and footwear manufacture, printing, chemical and rubber production.

After independence, the West Bengal government began to view these settlements, and particularly their refugee inhabitants, with concern; and *bastis* became caught up in wider drives to clear the city of 'unruly elements'.

In 1954, the government amended the Calcutta Improvement Act. It presented a direct challenge to the existence of Patwarbagan, which was, by this time, more than a hundred years old. Its population was largely Muslim. While papermaking and bookbinding were the main occupations, some of its residents worked in factories and tiny units making *beedees* (humble tendu-leaf and tobacco mini-cigars). Two committees vied for leadership. The president of the *basti* committee was a local man, Babu Lal Mia, but the second committee, established by the Communist Party of India (CPI), also had influence: by this stage the Communists had unionised bookbinders. Both set aside their differences when faced with the prospect of eviction.

Their resistance had some fascinating features, which represented something new in the politics of the city. First, women were the most militant. They were more determined than men to fight eviction. They did so tooth and nail.

By this time, whole families had begun slowly to abandon the countryside and women had become the main breadwinners as domestic servants (more in Chapter 5). By 2000, eight million rural families had given up agriculture in India and had begun to migrate, as small families, to cities. The situation of those who stayed behind was so dire that all over the country thousands of farmers began to commit suicide. There was a brief moral panic about this in polite circles, but little changed in practice. (The 2010 film *Peepli Live* offers biting satire on this theme.)

The government had failed to take note of this point, even though many civil servants were getting their floors swabbed and their clothes washed by these very women (or others like them). Recall: the state sees only what it wants to, and that through distorting categories.

As for the women, they put their feet down, refusing to accept the 'carrot' of better accommodation elsewhere. Most worked as domestic servants in neighbouring households, and regarded this work as critical for the survival of their families. They could not see how they could possibly rebuild – in new locations – their long-standing relationships of 'pragmatic intimacy' with the local middle-class women who offered them jobs with a stable (if low) income, leftover food, old clothes and, critically, interest-free credit in times of crisis.[219] Given that their husbands worked in the informal sectors of the economy and were out of work for several weeks a year, these women's employment was critical for the survival of families living on the margin.

These women now demanded that they be allowed to stay in Patwarbagan.

If they were to be moved temporarily, they insisted that they be housed nearby – no more than one mile away from Patwarbagan. They pressed to be allowed to return to the *basti* after the government had improved their existing shacks and had provided better facilities to the tenement.

Faced with this combined resistance, the government caved in: the plan was first stalled and then quietly dropped. Patwarbagan lived on for another fifty years, until the century came to a close.

Patwarbagan *basti* dwellers stood firm on one point: that the existing tenements be improved where they were.

This became a common cry of the *basti* movement which raged in the 1950s. More tenements have developed all over every city in the subcontinent as agriculture failed to provide livelihoods for marginal farmers. These new tenements too have become adept at dragging urban amenities towards them, whether by stealing electricity or by extracting promises at election time (in India).

The success of the Patwarbagan campaign owed something, of course, to the leadership of the Communists, who were able to rally some sections of the middle-class public behind them. But it would be unwise to overlook the role of the *basti* residents themselves, and of *basti* women, in pushing back against the government. As with the refugee camps, they demanded urban citizenship.

Their demands, which swiftly became the demands of the *basti* movement at large, dragged in civic amenities and basic provision to areas of the city that had previously been ignored by the planners.

So, you see, there is more to the *basti* than meets the casual eye. It is a complex social world, a hive of economic activity tied to the city. It provides labour and services to the city. Yet conurbations give back nothing in return unless *basti* dwellers fight for it. Whether it is Dharavi in Bombay, made famous by Gregory Roberts' 2003 novel *Shantaram*, or the more humble shanty wedged behind Green Park in Delhi, or those by the lakes in Calcutta, look again. So many migrants. Hope drew them there, and perhaps destitution and despair. Yet they have been cauldrons of political resistance. Of battles – even bloodbaths – for space. Of women's agency. Of urban citizenship.

The history of South Asian cities is not to be found in their sky-scrapers, flyovers or sea links, dramatic through these may be. It is about the life-worlds of those who built them, and where, how, and in what states of mind, they live; and how they came to live there.

The city's heart throbbed in these interstices and peripheries. These are various and complex places, whose right to exist was never secure. Extremes of precariousness were evident, in different ways, in different urban envelopes.

Each contained ways of finding joy, to be sure. The laughter of children playing tag in the rain is real, not faked for the camera. What is hidden from it is the anguish, the fear, the fury and the resolve.

Perhaps you can sense it in the air.

The rich did. By the end of the century they had begun to secure themselves in gated communities that locked out the city – its fraught moods, its madding crowds, and everyday violence – as dusk fell.

VI

MIGRATING BRIDES

Most migration in South Asia has little to do with cities, or even towns. It happens in the countryside.

At the start of the century, people who lived off the land made up ninety per cent of South Asia's population. By 1947 that proportion had fallen to roughly seventy-five per cent, and by 2000, to sixty per cent.

Almost half of these rural people were women and girls, who married at an early age and migrated to their husband's home after marriage.

Stop, for a moment, to think about the numbers. This was in a society where at the start of the century, almost 300 million people lived in undivided India. By 2000, the inhabitants of divided India alone had crossed the billion mark. Almost half were women. Almost all were married or would marry very soon.

Marriage was, and remained until 2000, nigh on universal in South Asia. Statistical data makes it plain that a very large proportion of intra-regional migrants in South Asia itself were women, moving in the context of marriage (see Chapter 1).

Matrilocal societies, where a husband joins his wife's community, are rare in South Asia (a point to which I will return in Chapter 5). So the burden of marriage migration – upping sticks to live with another family, for ever – has fallen, in the main, upon young brides.

They were, more often than not, girls marrying men many years their senior, so their fear of being 'taken by strangers' was great.[220] Wedding songs were not fun in South Asia until the 1990s Bollywood movies made them appear that way. The *shehnaai* (woodwind instrument) created the mood of *bidaai* (parting), playing music that tugs at the heart and reminds you, throughout the 'festivities', of the girl's impending departure. No: the leave-taking of the child bride was a time of great pain and fear for the little girl herself, and also sadness (mixed with fear of the future) for her siblings and friends. Her parents would likely have felt a mix of emotions – relief that one of their daughters had been 'married off', and anxiety about how she would be received in her new home as a vulnerable little outsider.

The common presumption has long been that these migrant brides were cultural migrants, not least when they travelled overseas; that they carried 'tradition' with them in their little suitcases or bundles. Further, almost all scholars took the view that they reproduced tradition wherever they went, sprinkling it like the attar of roses, or imposing it like a stifling weight.

The stories women tell show us something rather different.

Like the economic migration of labour, marriage migration too involved a distinct form of recruitment and control, in which the wife's labour, reproductive capacities and person were transferred from one household to another.[221]

The documents on which social historians tend to fall back throw little light on the history of these girl brides before, during and after migration. Census officers mentioned the number of these marriage migrations, but are otherwise silent about it. When they gave any details about female migrants, these were about women whom they regarded as 'deviant': who had run away, been abandoned, expelled or widowed, and had turned to sex work or other forms of labour to sustain themselves. District gazetteers were no more informative. Standard chapters about 'the people' of a district said nothing about young girls or wives. There might be the odd observation about how village elders dealt with young women who broke the rules of caste and marriage, and who were thus also, in some senses, 'aberrant'. But they said nothing about the millions of women who, at least on the face of things, did as they were told.

Here I attempt to piece this hidden history together.[222]

The first thing that stands out in these accounts is that the norms for the socialisation of girls, and the expectations of their behaviour, were widely shared across the region, cutting across different social groups and religious communities. A classic study of kinship in India posited, in 1953, 'a north Indian region' across which rules of marriage were 'essentially similar'. I suggest that this region was not limited to the North India of 1953, but included Pakistan and Bangladesh as well.

The first rule was that whereas 'the man lives with his patri-kin among whom he is born and reared . . . the woman . . . spends her life, *except for her few childhood years*, with her . . . [marital] family with whom she is not acquainted up to the moment of her marriage'.[223]

Marriage for girls, then, involved living among strangers.

Girlhood involved preparing the child-bride-to-be for life as a permanent migrant.

Think of it this way. Every wife, every mother, in every village in the subcontinent, arrived there as a little stranger. She grew to maturity, and then brought up her own children there, but remained an insider/outsider. A migrant settler.

The women who spoke to the Bengal Diaspora team were all born in South Asia between 1930 and 1970, in a region that included the eastern districts of Uttar Pradesh (formerly the United Provinces), the Indian states of Bihar and West Bengal, and in Pakistani East Bengal (later East Pakistan) and Bangladesh. They grew up predominantly (but not exclusively) in Muslim households. They experienced 'girlhood' between 1940 and 1980. There is no Bengali translation for the word 'girlhood'. (In Bangla, the term *chhelabela* (boyhood) means 'childhood'.)[224]

Sushila, my youngest informant, was born in the early 1990s.

As late as the 1970s, about one in five of all marriages between 1971 and 1975 involved girls aged twelve or younger.[225] This rose gently over the next three decades, most rapidly between 1971 and 1975, when the average age for girls at marriage was 14.8 years (see Table 4.1). Our cohort, then, married as legal minors, often as pubescents.

Table 4.1

Mean age at first marriage by year of marriage, for females[226]

Year of marriage	Age at first marriage (females)
1947–50	11.7
1951–55	12.0
1956–60	12.1
1961–65	12.9
1966–70	13.8
1971–75	14.8

That Sushila Devi, whom we have come to know, was married off aged twelve in the 2000s is unfortunate. But in South Asia, such marriages were by no means rare.

I stress: she was a girl when she married. Her hips were so narrow that when she had her first baby, she had to have a Caesarean that left a scar right across her slender body. (She showed it to me, laughing, as a badge of sisterly honour, when we shared our childbirth stories. In my social milieu, my personal story of a labour thirty-six hours long with no pain relief at all produces gasps. 'What? Not even gas and air?' Set beside Sushila's experience, it is trivial.) Her next two children also had to be born this way, since hunger and maternity did not leave her the strength to grow herself. She still, aged around twenty-eight, looks like a child. Her third child almost killed her.

To untangle the complex relationships between marriage, migration and culture, our first task must be to try to tease out what that experience of girlhood and leaving home might have been like for girls and young adolescent females, the hundreds of millions of Sushilas of South Asia during this time.

Although anthropologists have questioned some of the details of the model, the broad picture of a 'north Indian' set of norms of marriage held up in our team's study.[227] The universal expectation was that girls would marry and leave the parental home for the house of their in-laws at (or before) puberty. This was true both for Muslim and Hindu girls.

Rules about 'prohibited relations' differed somewhat between the communities. Caste Hindu girls and men were expected to avoid marriage to anyone removed by fewer than seven degrees from their fathers and five degrees from their mothers.[228] Muslim families were expected to obey Quranic proscriptions on incest and exogamy.[229] Our life histories suggested that, by and large, these rules were recognised. (Incest is a sweeping category in South Asia; the punishment for it can be death at the hands of community male elders. See Chapter 5.)

Among Muslims of Bangladesh, an anthropologist in the early 1970s spoke of 'a certain extent of mimesis': upwardly mobile Muslims adopting many Brahminical taboos in relation to marriage practices.[230]

This was not a recent phenomenon, nor was it restricted to Bengal, or indeed to marriage. When, in the 1930s, Maulana Thanawi, the Islamic theologian, wrote his religious manual *Bihishti Zewar* ('Heavenly Ornaments'), his goal was to persuade north Indian Muslim mothers and wives to give up the practices of marriage borrowed from Hindus and other non-believers.[231] In the 'Sixth Book', for instance, he bemoaned the 'sinful' practices of Muslim parents at the time of their daughters' weddings such as the excessive rewarding of the barber who attends the engagement (*mangni*): 'The heart of this custom is a sin, namely, pretension ... the deed itself is worthless frivolity and hence wholly wrong.' Marriage customs that involve placing the bride on a low platform, filling her lap with puffed rice and sweet *batasha*, rubbing ointments on the bride's body to make her 'clean and fragrant', were 'irrationalities and absurdities' that, in his view, had to be rooted out by educating women themselves.[232] It should be noted that Thanawi was in no doubt that women needed re-education in the 'right ways', and that the time to do this was upon their marriage: *Bihishti Zewar* was (and still is) given as a gift to millions of South Asian Muslim brides.

As with Hindus, it was expected that Muslim girls would, upon marriage, travel to another village to live with their husbands and in-laws. This too was widely followed across the region. As Thanawi writes reprovingly:

> [When] the day of the girl's departure come[s], a curtained sedan is placed before the door ... The girl's relatives bid her farewell and seat her in the palanquin. Then they raise up cries and wails against all sense ...[233]

The good Maulana was tin-eared on this one. Why he could not understand why they cried is a mystery to me.

The status of *ghar jamaai* (the son-in-law who lives with his wife's parents) was anomalous to the point of being 'shameful'. As Taslima Nasrin recalls, when she was growing up in a Muslim household in Mymensingh in East Pakistan in the 1960s, her own father's status as *ghar jamaai* was an enduring source of strain and tension in her family.[234]

It was the girl who was supposed to live with her in-laws, not the man, and this meant that married girls travelled. Even among 'tribal' groups such as the Gonds, whose rules of marriage were less proscriptive, an analysis of 315 marriages conducted in the 1960s showed that almost sixty per cent of all marriages took girls outside the village, and almost twenty per cent took them between five and ten miles away.[235]

This raises the question of how far rural migrant brides travelled and why this mattered. Part of the answer had to do with wealth: the poor could only afford to walk and five miles was a long way to carry a palanquin on a *kucha* muddy footpath. If a family could afford to send their daughter off in a bullock cart, it was deemed a rather grand send-off.

But, as the century progressed and bus services reached more villages, these distances grew further. In 1981, at a caste Hindu Bengali village in western Bengal, 'the wives of Palashpur [came] from 87 different villages and towns, most within a *thirty-five mile radius*', and the daughters of the village had also all been married to men from eighty-seven different places outside its limits.[236]

Cross-cousin marriage, prevalent in southern India, and marriage within the *biraadiri* or *kunba* (clan) as practised in a few parts of Pakistan, was so rare that we didn't come across it, although we expected to.[237] None of our respondents in India or Bangladesh had married a close cousin or uncle.

This distance between the childhood home and the bride's new home, in rural South Asia, seems to have varied from five to thirty-five miles, at the moment of marriage. It was rarely shorter than this. The 'girl next door' was not an option. (She was likely to be related to you. Such a relationship would fall foul of draconian rules about incest and marrying outside the village and the clan. You could both end up dead.)

Why between five and thirty-five miles? one might ask. Because this was deemed just long enough to keep a safe distance between the bride and her kin and also to loosen her ties with them; thus reducing the risk of the bride's own family getting involved on her behalf if problems arose – such as bigamy, cruelty or violence – after her marriage.[238]

In Bangladesh, as trains and above all buses became more accessible to more people, the extent of inter-district female migration grew, showing a sharp upwards trend from the 1970s onwards. In 1974 the census showed that in several districts, women made up between a third and two thirds of all inter-district migrants.[239]

For the women we interviewed, over our period, it meant travel over longer distances.

Yet even if that movement involved relatively short distances, as it did for some, it was nonetheless a migration that was profoundly transformative, as there was little possibility of a return 'home'. A Hindu wife could return to her *baaper-baari* (father's house), but only at times pre-ordained by custom or permitted by her in-laws, such as the birth of her first child. If widowed, she was expected to stay in her late husband's home. However, as a widow (*bidhaba*) in that home, she would be treated as an 'inauspicious' person, with little authority and no autonomy.

If she had no adult sons of her own, her condition was even more precarious. Despite the passage of the Hindu code bills in the 1950s that entitled daughters to a share of their paternal property, rural women rarely exercised these rights, if indeed they knew about them. In the 1980s scholars found that among the Hindu village dwellers of Palashpur, the law's writ did not run: 'after her wedding a girl belongs to her husband's family, and she loses all rights in her father's house. She is ... expected to visit her parents' house only as an honoured guest. The length and frequency of her visits are controlled by the elders of her husband's family.'[240] These women stayed in their husband's villages, even if they took on second wives.

'Alia' lives in Pakistan. She was born in the 1980s and married in the 1990s. She is well read, a teacher, born to an educated 'liberal' family. Like most women, she travelled only a short distance to her new household, but that migration was enough. When abused and beaten at her in-laws' home, she went back to her parents' home. They put her up for a few days, and then told her to go 'home'.

'That is your home now, *beti* [daughter].'

She protested: 'When did this stop being my home?'

I don't believe she got a clear answer, but I think it stopped being her home the day she married.

Nor was widowhood a state to be envied for Muslim women, even though Muslim family law entitled them to a half-share of what their brothers inherited from their fathers, and an eighth of their husband's estate. Across North India (and Bangladesh) in the twentieth century, they were not given these rights, nor did they claim them. Thanawi denounced this most strongly in the *Bihishti Zewar*:

> The real point ... has to do with the fact that when a Hindu father dies
> in Hindustan, the daughters receive no share at all from his wealth.
> Ignorant Muslims have imitated the Hindus ... How is it legitimate to
> deny – indeed, to suppress – the right of any claimant established by
> God and his Apostles?[241]

Every study confirms that many decades later, right into the 1970s and 80s, in practice, Muslim women renounced their share to their paternal inheritance so as not to lose the goodwill and support of their brothers.[242] So most women, even after their husband's death, after having their heads shaved and their ornaments wrenched from them, remained tied to the village where they had married. Many were thrown out; others were exploited and abused.

As for Hindu widows, particularly those of 'high caste', their plight is better known. 'Indur Thakuran' in Satyajit Ray's 1955 film *Pather Panchali* ('Song of the Road') is a widow dependent on the charity of relatives. Ray's handling of her precarious standing is subtle. (If you have time to watch only one South Asian film, this is surely it.)

As a result, widowhood meant a life of vagrancy and begging for many women.[243]

Very few had the extraordinary good fortune, like my beloved aunt Pishima, who was widowed young, of being welcomed back to the family household at Hill Cart Road. But then, her father (my grandfather) was a *swadeshi*-era whiskey-brewer, and a high liberal when it came to women's rights. So this was not, in his time, a typical Hindu 'high-caste' household. He left Pishima property of her own after the Hindu Marriage Act of 1955 permitted him so to do.

Few fathers, or surviving brothers, were as generous, so the phenomenon of shunned, impoverished widows grew into a scandal of huge proportions. Tapan Sinha's film *Nirjan Saikate* ('The Desolate Beach'), released in 1963, gives one a sense of its horrors.

Marriage, then, was a moment not of *au revoir* but of *adieu*. Little girls spent years being prepared for it. Village studies suggest that until about the age of seven or eight, young girls enjoyed childhood, in that they were treated much as other children. But already, in Bengal, they may well have been rocked to sleep as infants to a popular lullaby evoking their impending dislocation:

> *Dol, dol, duluni, ranga mathaye chiruni,*
> *Bor ashbe ekhuni, niye jabe takhuni.*
>
> Rock, rock, little bride, with your forehead adorned,
> Your groom is about to arrive, and he will take you away.

They might not have understood its meaning. I used to hear my nieces Maya and Meghna sing it again and again in the late 1980s as three- or four-year-olds as they dressed up their dolls, or as Maya dressed up Meghna as a bride. No doubt millions of tiny Bengali girls also sang it as they played, too young to understand its significance for them.

In their early childhoods, girls as young as Maya and Meghna were allowed to run around the village with other children playing games. I imagine them as tiny little laughing stars, not yet aware of the future that lay ahead of them.

Then, rather abruptly at about the age of eight, they entered 'girlhood', a state evoked by Taslima Nasrin in her autobiography, *Meyebela* ('Girlhood').

> In this house [in the village where her family fled in 1971], the girls my age were wrapped in saris . . . At dawn they let out the ducks and hens. They lit the stove, ground spices, used the dheki to remove the husks from the rice, and poured the rice onto a wicker basket to shake it clean.
>
> 'Want to play hopscotch?' I asked. They smiled but did not move.[244]

Scholars also witnessed this transition in a village in Bangladesh, in 1974.

> We saw several girls going through these changes during the year we were in Jhagrapur. Girls who in the beginning had been running around freely, often naked breasted and wearing only a skirt, had become little ladies by the end of the year, restricting their exuberancy [while] waiting to be married off.[245]

In Palashpur, another little hamlet, by the age of eight, girls' mothers began to ask them to take on domestic chores. Their mobility was restricted. 'They [began] to recognise some of the disadvantages of their gender. Boys ... enjoy[ed] the freedom of being able to move about the village and pastures', while girls were 'expected to stay close to their mothers and other women of the neighbourhood, and in this way learn much about the proper behaviour of women'. Girls went to school for a few years, perhaps four or five years of formal schooling, often in a *madrassa*, where they also learned how to write and to read the Quran. Any further education was 'regarded as redundant, if not harmful for a happy married life'.[246]

After their first period, their movement outside the home was limited further still. The majority of adolescents stopped going to school altogether, if they had ever been there in the first place.[247] When you watch Ray's *Pather Panchali*, as I hope you will, focus on the little girl, Durga, as she goes through this transformation.

What mothers taught their daughters did not involve customs or rituals. The focus of her training was how to labour in the ways that would be required of her in her husband's home.

In the village of Char Gopalpur, for instance:

> Young girls spent most of their childhood learning work roles, skills, and tasks that constitute the women's share of the division of labour. The process is largely one of learning by doing ... the sexual division of labour manifests itself from the very beginning ... For male children there is little overall participation in housekeeping or food preparation; likewise, for females there is very little participation in marketing or, with the exception of harvesting chillies and potatoes, in agricultural field operations.[248]

This restriction on movement outside the home was because 'girls' sexual coming of age [was regarded as] potentially explosive, adolescent girls being highly vulnerable to their own and others' volatile sexual impulses'.[249]

Young men, on the other hand, were free to roam the village, shop and 'time pass' and visit relatives.[250] In the Bengal region, they typically married much later in life, as young men in their twenties (see Table 4.2). Whether they were landed or landless made little difference: *men* married girls.

Girlhood, then, was an anxious time, for girls and their families. This was, of course, particularly marked in the case of families of high status. One scholar, writing of Kashmiri Pandit girls after his fieldwork in 1957, observed that unmarried girls of the family were 'always referred to as *amaanat*, that is, someone held in trust on behalf of her lawful "owners". A young girl's upbringing is completely over-shadowed by the fact that she is to be married and sent away to live with her husband and parents-in-law.'[251] She was expected to arrive at her husband's house as a virgin: the critical moment of marriage being *kanyadaan*, or 'the gift of the virgin' by one family to another.[252] But even in households of lower status, even among 'tribal' groups such as the Gonds of Madhya Pradesh, it was believed that a man's 'soul neither goes to heaven nor rests in peace if he has not married a virgin'.[253]

Table 4.2

Mean age at marriage, by sex and economic class, Char Gopalpur, 1976[254]

Mean age at marriage	Landowner of large estate	Landowner of small estate	Landless
Male	21.9	23.2	23.0
Female	13.9	13.5	13.1

It is vital to recognise the ways in which girlhood was a time in which girls were trained to expect, and adapt to, the huge changes that were certain to befall them after marriage. A girl was transformed from a child of the village into a virgin in a cultural sense, a clean slate upon whom her husband (and his family) would inscribe their ways of life. As marriage approached, her parents taught her to be docile, obedient and adaptable. A girl did not belong to her natal family but was in a state of apprenticeship for her true achievement of person-hood as a bride in her husband's family. Everyone, grown women above all, knew that this process would involve trauma, hardship and self-sacrifice.

Both Hindu and Muslim brides, on arrival in their *shoshur-baari* (in-laws' home), were expected to learn their duties and responsibili-ties as wives, mothers, daughters-in-law and household workers in their new setting. They had to adopt the ways of their husbands' line-ages, and absorb, fast, their particular codes of conduct. (Each household is a little different, you see.)

The new bride also had to learn the *stri aachaars* (the rites performed by *stri*, married women) of that household, which were often different from such rites in her father's home; and from which, as a virgin (*kumaari*), she would in any event have been excluded.[255]

She would be instructed in her household duties by her *shaasuri* (mother-in-law). On the day of her arrival at this destination, her training began. After the rituals and rites of entry were completed, 'the bride [was] shown around the house by her mother-in-law'. She was shown the cooking area, where a large part of her time would be spent; and in the case of Hindu girls, the *thakur ghar*, where her new family ancestral deities 'resided': she was expected to share the rituals of their worship.

'In the course of the first day, the *shaasuri* will specify what she wants the bride to do in the *sangsaar* [household]'s daily work and how she expects her to behave towards the people of the house.' The mother-in-law would decide whether the new bride should cover her head in the presence of the elder males of the house, and how to greet her husband every time he entered or left the house.[256]

(Yes. The mother-in-law laid down what the little bride could say, in public, to her new husband. She determined every single detail of the migrant bride's comportment in her new setting. This happened in Hill Cart Road too, after my grandfather had died, in one of my uncle's wings of the household. I did not so much see it as glean it. There were sarcastic looks of admonishment from my aunts – *Je-ma*, my aunt with a sceptical eyebrow – and confusion and misery in my sister-in-law's lowered eyes. It was all in a sign language I soon learned to decipher.)

Full 'acculturation' for the girl bride thus began only in her husband's household. Her mother would have taught her to expect change, to learn to labour, and to adopt the ways of the husband's household. This was reinforced by the fact that marriages, for women, were expected to be to men of higher status. Particularly among 'higher castes' and Brahmins, a girl's father was required to do all he could to marry her into a family of the same caste but of superior social standing.[257] (Imagine what this meant for the standing of the little bride in her new home.) But the practice seems to have spread much more widely, leading to marked preferences in Bengal of marriages of girls from certain districts with men from particular neighbouring districts where more suitable 'high status' grooms were available.[258] On the festival of Jamai-sashti, observed widely in Bengal every summer, the son-in-law made an annual visit to his in-laws. They treated him as a visiting deity, feeding him special dishes and giving him lavish gifts, such as their budgets permitted.

Such, then, were the norms and expectations of wives and husbands, parents and in-laws, in the mid to late twentieth century across northern India, East Pakistan and Bangladesh.

But norms are only norms. Life is more complicated, shot through with disruptive events that can sometimes give space for a spirited woman to make sudden breaks and U-turns in a supposedly clear storyline.

Let me tell you about Bibi Ruha. She came from an itinerant group of peasants (loosely Muslims by faith) who specialised in capturing new alluvial sandbanks as they were thrown up by Bengal's vast, deltaic river systems. She was born around 1938, before partition, in Rajshahi, which would end up on the East Pakistan side of partition's borders. But many of her relatives, including her mother and husband, had been born in what became India in 1947. Local people suspected these communities of harbouring loyalties to no nation state, and I think they were right. Their loyalties were to the soil they had broken and tilled, and to each other. They were known as Chapaiyas. They grew a little more prosperous after partition, when they found new soil and new forest land to conquer. Neighbouring communities did not like them.

Bibi Ruha recalls her own wedding with pride. Scheming womenfolk did not organise her marriage (as is the common assumption). Men did, rather casually, from the two sides (and this again was a common theme among our respondents).

> Both my father's youngest brother and my father-in-law were looking for partners for their wards at the same time and were happy to find each other. For my wedding two cows and two goats were killed, and we also had *pithas*, *pulao* and *rasogollas* [special food and sweetmeats] and invited about fifty people. Then a cart pulled by buffalo was brought in ... and we drove all the way to Kandopur in the Birol district where my in-laws lived.

But Ruha's migration story did not end in this hamlet near Birol.

Seven years after her marriage, she and her husband traded in the expensive land they had in Birol for cheaper property in Dinajpur. 'He had 25 bighas there and each bigha sold for 1,200 takas, we got our bighas for 600 takas each, so we bought 50 bighas here.' (A bigha is about 1,500 square metres.) This was not an inconsiderable amount for a peasant family. So the environmental migrant, briefly settled, migrated upon her marriage (in a bullock cart, no less), and shifted once again in a bid for greater prosperity.

But perhaps their success was the cause of the catastrophe that befell her in 1971, during the Bangladesh Liberation War.

> It was a Wednesday morning. People came and *gheraoed* [surrounded] him [her husband. Like many older Bengali (and South Asian) women, she does not refer to her husband by his name]. They tied him and his brothers and father up and put a handkerchief on their mouths and shot them. They killed my father-in-law, my husband and three of his brothers. Then they stole our cow and cart.

Asked who the killers were, Bibi Ruha replied: 'They said they were *mukti joddhas* [freedom fighters]. Bengalis, the group of them, whoever they were, they were *saitan* [devils]. The locals of course helped them. We were from Rajshahi so they thought we were from India.'

Her history, after this, is one of inconsolable anguish. Of course she was left destitute. As a 'minority' suspected to have the wrong affiliations, she was in mortal danger. So she moved to a ghetto-like space, where she somehow eked out a livelihood as a domestic servant. No wonder she has warm memories of her wedding day.

The 'Train Lady' told us an even more complicated story, in which the theme of multiple upheavals and migrations comes through once again. (She was so fearful that her identity would be uncovered that we discussed and described her as 'Train Lady' to protect her identity, and I will use that tag for her here.) She was born in 1958 in Calcutta. Her mother was an Urdu-speaking Muslim from Calcutta's Zachariah Street area, and her father was from a Bengali-speaking family with shipping connections, which had business interests in Chittagong and Dacca, where he worked and lived. 'Train Lady' spent her childhood in Calcutta with her maternal family. Unusual.

However, during 'the troubles' (probably the riots in 1964), her frightened mother fled with her and her siblings to join their father in Dacca, where it was safer for them as Muslims. But her mother 'hated Dacca', where people 'were all the same kind, all Bengalis'. She missed Calcutta's variety and cosmopolitanism, and returned to the city as soon as she could, taking 'Train Lady' and her siblings in tow.

(Calcutta does have a way of binding its people to her, of seizing their imaginations. Ghosh's *The Shadow Lines* gives a flavour of this.)

'Train Lady' and her mother went once more to Dacca when trouble broke out again, but her mother 'did not want to live there'. During the 1971 war, her mother was able, through her Urdu-speaking connections, to get tickets 'for all of them to go to Karachi'. But her husband 'was furious'; and despite the fact that he had lost his home and possessions, he refused to accompany his wife to Karachi under the 'Bihari quota'.

Note that it was 'Train Lady's' mother who took all these decisions for the safety of her family, and organised their multiple migrations, and her eventual settlement, with her children, in Karachi. This must have required great ingenuity since the 'Bihari quota' was very small indeed, and tickets were desperately hard to come by.[259]

'Train Lady's' father never joined her mother in Pakistan.

'Train Lady' grew up, then, and was married in Karachi. She says relatively little about that event, although her story tells us much more about her mother's marriage migrations. But she still misses her *khaalaa* (maternal aunt) in Calcutta, whom she loves dearly and has often visited.

As for herself, she has become a constant traveller. She and her husband have visited India more than a hundred times, going again and again to the shrine at Ajmer *sharif* (known by many South Asians as the Mecca of the poor). Although she and her husband still live in Karachi in Pakistan, she longs to visit Bangladesh. She is so peripatetic, we met her on a train.

As she told Annu Jalais this story,[260] she began to weep. She begged Annu not to reveal her identity to anyone, as she feared she might 'get into trouble' – although it was not clear which authorities she feared. Perhaps she feared the guardians of all South Asian borders.

Where is 'Train Lady's' marital home, then? What is her 'culture'? As a child, she spent years in many different South Asian cities: Calcutta, Dacca and Chittagong, and later Karachi. Born into a mixed Urdu- and Bengali-speaking household, to parents whose marriage broke down during the upheavals of 1971, she herself married a man who had grown up in Karachi in Pakistan (no doubt following the orders of her powerful mother). Her husband was most likely a refugee from North India, as are most people who live in her neighbourhood (and indeed in Karachi). Yet she seems profoundly restless. Her emotional world includes a beloved aunt in Calcutta (India) and a daughter (in Kashmir). She and her husband clearly invest much of their time and money in travel, mainly to the holy shrine at Ajmer in India. Is it too far-fetched to suggest that she is creating her own sense of an interconnected South Asia?

In these life histories, there is a shimmer of the 'South Asia' of this book, and some of its deepest notes. We hear it as much in their stories as in their silences, their sighs, their jagged pauses. We see it in their averted eyes, their inward gaze, their moments of sudden confusion. We sense it in their despair, their yearning, and their hope for a better life for their children.

5

The Household, Marriage
and the Family

When my brothers and I were still young enough to be told what to do, my father would insist that we all travelled – en famille, by train from Delhi for forty-odd hours – to spend the summer holidays in the ancestral household. This was a sprawling set-up in north Bengal, in the foothills of the eastern Himalayas. I looked forward to these visits as much as my mother dreaded them. For me the Hill Cart Road household offered freedom from the constraints of an urban nuclear family, with all its boring restrictions. 'Oh no, you must never go out alone, you must never wander away in the park, the *budhdha baba* (scary old man) will take you away!' our *ayah* never tired of warning us. 'Do your homework! Change out of your uniform! Don't pat stray dogs! Don't eat street food!' The list of my mother's admonitions seemed endless.

The Hill Cart Road establishment – a large high-walled compound of adjacent houses of different sizes and styles, workers' cottages, wells, kitchens, fruit trees, coconut palms and cowsheds – was for me brimful of pleasures. The elders left a host of cousins, ranging from their early twenties to children just out of nappies, pretty much un-supervised. All my cousins played with me; none was too superior. The older ones, who were training to be doctors or lawyers, taught us card games like rummy and cut-throat (a lowbrow version of bridge, but for me far more glamorous than snap). The younger cousins were always up for a game of marbles, carom, badminton or hide-and-seek, or a vicious but short-lived quarrel. There were trees to climb (the jackfruit was my favourite) and quiet places to read. The household had its own milkman (*goala*) and cows, and no one stopped me when I petted the calves. I frolicked with Kanchha's children and rode on his shoulders – Kanchha being the Nepali driver and gentle gofer of the household. Aunts (*je-ma, pishima*)[1] and cousin-sisters-in-law (*bou-di*) showered us with treats.[2] The Brahmin cook gave us dough to play with as he set about making *luchis* (puffed fried flatbreads) for dinner. One special *je-ma*, her left eyebrow raised in a permanent look of scepticism, taught me how to make *zardaa paan* on the sly. This was betel leaf laced with tobacco: very naughty indeed.

I never asked my mother why she didn't look forward to these holidays, but sensed it had to do with the lack of privacy at Hill Cart Road. There was a level of constant scrutiny to which she, an Englishwoman, never got accustomed. The patriarch was my grandfather of *swadeshi* toddy-brewing fame, but by the time I was old enough to register intimate structures of authority, a stroke had paralysed him and my grandmother was de facto in charge. *Dudurani* (our grandmother) put us up in an airy room with a cool marble floor and shuttered windows overlooking the courtyard.[3] My parents slept in a vast carved four-poster bed covered with mosquito netting; we had cotton mattresses on the floor beside them. What they didn't get was downtime for their gin and soda, time alone as a couple. My mother spent her days with a throng of aunts, nieces, cousin-sisters, cousin-sisters-in-law, my grandmother, and the cook, sweating in the mud-and-thatch kitchen set at some distance from the more imposing main houses that faced the street, and took turns with the other women of the house to tend to my grandfather's needs. Meanwhile my father and his brothers sat drinking fine Darjeeling tea (served to them by the *bou-dis* and the lovely Malati, a 'domestic servant') and chatted about politics. All the senior Chatterji men, with the exception of my father and grandfather, were doctors. But most had their clinics on the property too; so to me it seemed that they would occasionally pop in to say hello to their patients, only to return to the more serious business of politics.

Although she wore them elegantly, my mother's saris were never quite as perfectly draped as my aunts' saris; her cutting of *rohu* (carp) lacked finesse; she could not (and would not) blow the conch shell to welcome Goddess Lakshmi at dusk. I never heard her complain, but her stress showed in the tense set of her mouth.

My father tried to make things better by taking her and us children out for long drives around Darjeeling district, whose views of emerald paddy fields, of bamboo thickets and coconut groves, of densely forested foothills, and of the dazzling Kanchenjunga (the third highest mountain in the world, so high and so close one felt one could reach out and touch it) were as glorious as any I have seen in the world. Often we saw spectacular wildlife. One evening, a Royal Bengal tiger stepped out of the tea bushes and ambled across the road, blinking lazily at the car's headlights. Sometimes we stopped to marvel at the river Teesta, roaring as she rushed down steep hillsides to burst upon the plains. But I sensed that despite the beauty, to which my mother was acutely sensitive, these breaks from the household were not enough.

From an early age, then, I registered that the South Asian household was riven with tension. Far from being the solid harmonious unit imagined by census-takers, it was divided and hierarchical, patriarchal and autocratic. It was not, and still is not, a unit of congruent interests.[4] Children were indulged but daughters-in-law were not. The latter seemed to work from dawn to dusk, cooking and serving meals in ritual order: first to the elders, then to the menfolk, then to the children. Only then would they bathe again and wash and oil their long hair, and sit down themselves to eat together. (This did not mean that they were friends. I got a hint that rivalries, even enmities, bubbled beneath the calm surface.) Our Brahmin cook must have prepared well over a hundred *luchis* every evening, yet his position seemed precarious as he made a great point of displaying his sacred thread. My father's brothers worked in prestigious professions; our household was probably the wealthiest in the town and my grandfather, like Motilal Nehru in Allahabad, was the first Indian in the locality to buy a motorcar. But they also found time to do an awful lot of *adda* (talking).[5] In hindsight I can see that they were part of a social class in decline, rich in land and assets that produced dwindling returns.

But my grandmother was in charge: of that there was no doubt. With an enormous bunch of keys tied to the end of her sari, she controlled access to dry foodstuffs – sugar, *gur* (molasses), rice, vegetable oil and ghee. She added the final touches to dishes that her daughters-in-law had prepared; she watched the cows being milked; she pointed out the ripest coconuts, which little boys trained in the art brought down in seconds.

Thinking back on it, she supervised all household labour with her small bespectacled eyes. She was a tiny, frail woman with a determined jaw and, unusually for her time, was educated in Bengali and Sanskrit. At the start of the century, only two per cent of India's Brahmin women could read and write. The daughter of a professor of

Sanskrit, she was one of them. She said very little and never raised her voice, but the household obeyed her every gesture. At dusk, each child of the family presented themselves to her for her blessings.

The household was not united by blood, a common hearth or even a common roof, even though the male Chatterjis and their children shared a common male ancestor. Their wives, and the small platoon of *bou-ma*, *je-ma* and visiting maternal cousins and aunts, did not. Kanchha, the driver, had his own little cottage; the Brahmin cook had his own shack; and the *goala* lived within the compound in a tumble-down manger with his family and the cattle. Malati and her son Jugnu as well as Ratan – shy boys who swept, swabbed and cleaned dishes – lived outside the compound's walls and came to work every day. Malati was almost certainly single – either widowed or abandoned by her husband. Kanchha was a migrant from neighbouring Nepal who had settled in Bengal with his wife and children – a more nucleated unit within a larger one.[6] I loved him dearly, but now it strikes me as odd (or typical of the times) that we called a grown man *Kanchha*: it means 'boy' in Nepali. The milkman's family lived on site so that my grandmother could ensure that the cows were well fed, and that the *goala* got no chance to add water to the frothing brass buckets of milk. The cook was from a 'lower' Brahmin sub-caste than ours, which is why he served us. We called him *daadamashay*, 'respected elder brother'. Ostensibly a term of esteem, this was in fact a signal that he was of lower status than us. He seemed indigent, and without close relatives of his own.

What united the household, then, was not blood, kinship or even co-residence: it was submission to the authority of its patriarch (or, in the case of the patriarch's incapacity, its matriarch).[7]

Of course Hill Cart Road was a big fish in a small pond. Our household was set among much humbler homes. For much of the twentieth century, it represented a certain kind of lifestyle, rich in property but less so in cash. It is much diminished now. But although it was 'elite' in one sense (my grandfather was a wealthy man from the *kulin* Brahmin sub-caste, the highest in the region's caste hierarchy), his household contained people of both genders who belonged to different classes, castes and sub-castes, whose standing was often changed by their manner of entering it. Often their position, particularly those of women, rose or fell within it.

You might wonder what is uniquely South Asian about this. I

suggest that many things are. Caste, for one: the milkman had to live in the household so that our milk was pure, and the cook was a Brahmin because we 'could not eat' unless served by Brahmins. Yes, even revolutionary Communists, and Congressmen like my grandfather, thought like this. Or were blind to the inequalities of caste. (More of this in Chapter 6.)

Also, their received ideas about patriarchy were of a different order. The Chatterji clan of Hill Cart Road included men of seven generations, some unborn, some ancestors. This unit was the core. All held the unit's property for all, in line with their needs. Everything earned and owned by one male householder was the property of the unit. Even the *karta*, or patriarch, was in theory an equal shareholder, albeit one who administered the unit and commanded its respect. So the South Asian household was a mighty structure. (This holds true for large 'upper-caste' Hindu joint families, but Muslim elite *khandaans* are not that different.)

Women – even Chatterji daughters like me – were 'outsiders' even at birth, held in trust for their husbands' households.

Further, there was no law of primogeniture.

By the late twentieth century, my own nuclear (city-dwelling) branch of the household was not atypical: my father ran an advertising agency and my mother worked part time at an embassy. But it remained connected to the ancestral home by marriages, deaths, by the annual summer holiday, and long visits from relatives from Hill Cart Road. Cousin-brothers came to live with us for years when they came to the city for their higher studies. My father's widowed sister Pishima was a poetess (and Maoist) who sheltered Maoist revolutionaries on the run. She stayed with us for three months each year. Frail but garrulous, she was full of contradictions: she observed the penances of widowhood, ate a widow's diet (free of any spices deemed to incite passion), and wore the widow's white sari. But she had a man friend who visited her often while she stayed with us – a platonic connection, I am sure. I was the lucky beneficiary of her eclectic interests: she taught me Bengali, the Hindu epic *Mahabharata*, and the history of the Naxalite movement. The Naxalites were and are Maoists; Naxalbari, where the movement began, is close to Hill Cart Road. Charu Mazumdar (leader of the movement in its early days) went to school with my father. My eldest uncle financed the movement for many years, so the relationships were close.

In Delhi my parents employed domestic workers who were all migrants from elsewhere. They, in turn, maintained their connections to rural families left behind, taking a month off each year to visit them. Since not all lived on site, they also had ties with urban neighbours, landlords, creditors, lovers and friends.

'Elsewhere' was, and still is, the countryside. The vast majority of South Asians lived as cultivators, yet rural households had different structures. For a start, they were much smaller: they had to be. Women often did the heavy lifting: in some villages, most young men had migrated to the cities in search of work. Despite their labour in the fields and the household, women's work was taken for granted. Like their sisters in elite households, they lived under the thumb of their in-laws. But they too were linked to their natal families, and connected to the cities by their ties to male emigrants, brothers and husbands upon whose 'money orders' they depended for cash.

These households might appear to be discrete – indeed colonial census-takers took them to be the fundamental building blocks of South Asian society. Social scientists likewise describe them as discrete units of production and consumption. But they are far from solid or unchanging. They are better imagined as shoals of fish, always on the move, some following in the wake of bigger fish, some being swallowed up by them. Their composition was constantly in flux. They did not share resources equally. They often lost members (whether by marriage, death, feuds or even internecine warfare), and gained new ones by marriage, adoption and natural increase.

Nor were they discrete entities. They were intimately connected to other households, some of which were thousands of miles away. It is this dense, cross-hatched web of ties – skeins of authority, love, rivalry, dependence and (let's call a spade a spade) exploitation – that gives South Asian society its texture. It *is* society. Households, this chapter will show, are nodes of connection (and disconnection) within this fabric.

Over the course of the twentieth century, there have been changes in the weave. Many complex households have given way to 'joint families' or 'nuclear families', recognised by law and taxed in different ways. But these transitions have been neither seamless nor complete. Old forms of authority and old divisions of labour persist. Some domestic servants are still much like the slaves of old. Others are more like retainers; and novel forms of domestic labour have also emerged to cope with demand for part-time female help in middle-class urban households.[8] By the end of the twentieth century, the size of the urban middle classes had ballooned,[9] and 'love marriage' had become an aspiration.[10] But it was seldom realised, and marriages that break rules of caste and degrees of kinship still attract violent forms of opprobrium.[11] Bollywood has sold the romantic dream to a yearning young audience: but even in the movies, in the end the lovers are reabsorbed, after marriage, into the patriarchal household.[12] Their acceptance by the household is the happy ending.

By uncovering the conflict and negotiation within South Asia's households, and the interdependencies and inter-linkages between them, this chapter challenges persistent myths. By looking inside the home – warts, love, violence and all – it invites readers to go beyond the obvious clichés. It shines a torch into the small flats along the motorways to reveal how their occupants, and those who serve them, live as families, and how they function. I suggest that these places are connected to other places far away, and to the countryside, whose economic decline is now leading farmers to commit suicide. I take you to the world of a village household. I suggest why some people (usually women) flee the world of households to seek a life at its margins.

These are dark matters. But one has to lift up the rough blanket to uncover the complex, often grim and sometimes mind-boggling histories that lie beneath. Without looking at them square in the eye, one is left with only the most superficial understanding of South Asia. That is not good enough. One might as well throw a flat pebble and watch it skim the surface of a lake.

I

UNFAMILIAR RELATIONS[13]

In 1899, a dispute over inheritance in the household of the *zamindaar* of Pittapore came before the Privy Council in London.[14]

Pittapore, in the Godavari region of Madras in southern India, was a permanently settled *zamindaari* estate, where the revenue it paid to the state was fixed for all time. Scions of one of several high-status clans in the region, the Pittapore rajas had strengthened their position by strategic marital alliances with other elite clans of the area. In 1861, the then *zamindaar*, Raja Rama Rao, had married Mangayamma, a woman from a clan of somewhat lower status, the Vellankis. There was nothing unusual about this – *anuloma* marriage (between a man of higher status than the woman) was the norm, indeed the ideal, across much of Hindu South Asia.

What *was* troubling was the fact that the marriage appeared strained. Mangayamma spent years away from the Pittapore household with her natal family. She also failed to produce an heir – one of the chief expectations of South Asian wives, then as now. Rama Rao married again. This was not unusual: Hindu men who could afford to often had several wives and concubines. Polygamy was not only a Muslim practice, as many believe. But still no child was born.

In 1873, Rama Rao adopted Nayana, son of the high-ranking Raja of Venkatagiri, to build links with the latter's household and to shore up his own position in the local pecking order.[15]

Still uneasy about his status among the jousting clans of Godavari, Rama Rao next married Subbamma, the only surviving daughter of the elite Appa Rao clan of Nuzvid. Subbamma was a woman of imperious bearing, and was proud of her own family. One might wonder why she married Rama Rao at all; by all accounts he was obese, had a violent temper and was in poor health. However, I suppose she had to marry someone (marriage being pretty much universal in South Asia), and his estate was large. In any event, in an ostentatious display of her high rank, she brought with her from Nuzvid a huge retinue of servants and slaves and established a large and distinct household within the raja's greater establishment in Pittapore. Her relatives from Nuzvid visited often, sometimes staying with her for several months, eating not at the raja's table but in Subbamma's quarters.

The Rama Rao household thus lived under different roofs and cooked at different hearths. The 'fort', as the British described it, was not a single structure, but had many buildings dispersed behind its ramparts. Some members of the household, notably adult *daasis* (female slaves), lived outside the compound having married local men, but they remained integral members of it. *Aranam daasis*, who had grown up with the queens when they were children and had accompanied them to Pittapore when they married and left home, were particularly close to 'their' rani; but when they grew up, they too married local men. The household, thus, had many connections, at every level, with worlds beyond it.

To return to the story: the Raja visited his new consort Subbamma often. Everyone seems to agree that she became his preferred wife. But still there was no heir.

Thereafter, in rapid succession, the Raja married three more women, all from eminent households; again each carefully chosen to strengthen his connections with the leading clans of Godavari. But still there was no heir.

And then, miraculously, Mangayamma (the senior but less favoured wife) delivered a boy. She persuaded the Raja that the baby was his. The delighted Rama Rao recognised the infant as his own, willing him his entire estate. Nayana, his adopted son, was left with only a pension. Rama Rao died soon afterwards, and Nayana cried foul. The two sides went to court in an epic contest that reached the Privy Council.

The case hinged on whether the baby was the true child of Mangayamma and Raja Rama Rao.[16] Nayana's lawyers pointed out that Mangayamma was more than forty-five years old at the time of the child's birth, and had lived apart from the Raja for many years. Other wives told graphic tales that challenged Mangayamma's claim. All ranis gave evidence from behind a curtain, because all were *gosha*, living in seclusion, as most elite women did at the time. (Purdah was a widespread practice among South Asian elites: it was not, as is assumed, restricted to Muslim women.) But despite their isolation from the world, the women of Rama Rao's household were willing to share with it the household's most intimate secrets. One rani testified that the Raja was not only impotent, 'he . . . suffered from considerable pain in his sexual organ, which she treated by applying leaves and coconut oil'.[17] Other co-wives supported this account, adding that his penis was shrivelled and that he had venereal disease. He could not have sired the child.

Mangayamma gave a very different account, stressing Rama Rao's vigour. In her version, he had 'strong sexual desire for her' before Subbamma came between them. Her suggestion was that in her sexually active days with the Raja, she had conceived the child, who was only born some ten years later. While he was alive, the Raja supported her story, saying that Mangayamma had had an unusually long pregnancy, which, although uncommon, was not unheard of. When someone dared to point out to him that the child was dark-skinned while he was fair, the Raja had an answer for this, saying that because the child had been in the womb for so long, his skin had grown dusky in hue. The Raja's desperation for a male heir perhaps made him more than usually credulous.

Note how the standing of Nayana, Subbamma and Mangayamma rose and fell within the Rama Rao household. Its internal hierarchies were never uncontested; they were fought out, and openly so, during the crisis of succession.

The case became even more interesting when Mangayamma's *daasis* gave evidence. As the historian Pamela Price points out, Mangayamma's *daasis* were with her day and night – they took turns to spend night shifts with her so that she was never alone, except when the Raja visited. They bathed and dressed her; they served her food. (In return for this work they received Rs 4 a month, and took turns to take home the valuable leftovers, *tavu*.) Most *daasis* were loyal to their mistress, particularly her *aranam daasis*, and their status was correspondingly high. All her slaves knew every detail of their mistress's naked form. One *daasi* painted an unflattering picture of Mangayamma's ageing body which suggested she was too old and ill to conceive a child:

> I noticed Mangayamma's body on such occasions. I noticed some pecu-
> liarities on her body. She had lines (*striae*) on her right thigh and
> left thigh and on the sides of her breasts and on the right side of her
> abdomen . . . Her breasts were hanging . . .[18]

Other *daasis* gave evidence that Mangayamma had given birth. The (junior) Chitrada rani was close to Mangayamma, and *her* daasi testified that she *had* witnessed Mangayamma's labour. She gave a detailed description of her delivery, recalling that it was Satti, Mangayamma's *aranam daasi*, who had cut the umbilical cord. There was, it has to be said, a certain verisimilitude in her evidence, however far-fetched the story of a ten-year pregnancy might seem. (There's a vague hint that another woman may have been smuggled in through a back entrance and delivered the boy in her stead. We'll never get to the bottom of it. In any case, the wench is dead, and it was in another century.)

Nayana lost the appeal, albeit on technical grounds.[19] But the Privy Council judgement gives us a fascinating glimpse into the workings of a large and wealthy *zamindaari* household at the start of the twentieth century. The evidence of the sex lives (or absence thereof) of Rama Rao and his wives is fascinating, of course. But the more prurient aspects are less important than its other revelations: the intricate and shifting picture of power, rivalry and intimacy behind the walls of the fort, and the connections that extended well beyond it.

For one, Rama Rao was the head of the household, a patriarch who wielded authority over all who lived and worked in the fort. But his household was not a world unto itself: it was bound to other establishments around it.[20]

The ranis who came to Rama Rao's palace did not sever their ties with their own families. They brought with them retinues of retainers and slaves, as small fish follow larger ones. 'Haughty' Subbamma, the favoured queen, showed off these links by having her relatives to stay for months and entertaining them herself. She displayed her dominance over the other wives, despite the fact that she was number two in the batting order. The other queens seem to have accepted this, even if they didn't like it. The first wife was *not* always the senior wife, as British administrators (and latter-day sociologists) have assumed. Mangayamma, the first wife, went home to her parents for many years, but then played a trump card by producing a male heir.

Within large households, wives, concubines and even slaves jockeyed for pole position; their status could rise or fall. We see this even more vividly if we move our eye far to the north of Pittapore, to Chakla-Roshanabad in present-day Bangladesh. There humble women entered and rose up the ranks in the royal household of the Raja of Tipperah.[21] This little kingdom was on the violent frontier between Tipperah and the uplands around it.[22] In the late nineteenth century, Tipperah's rajas had frequent skirmishes with Kuki hunter-gatherers of the hills, and captured female slaves by the dozen. These young girls and women often ended up as *kachua* (irregular) wives, and, by the 'alchemy' of marriage and war, strangers became kin.[23]

In theory, as former slaves, the standing of *kachuas* was lower than that of the *bibaahita* (or ritually married) first wife. But that could change if a *kachua* wife bore sons. A *kachua* wife could rise higher still, if, upon the reigning king's death, her son won the battle for succession. Thus, as one scholar shows: 'Eshan Chunder's mother was Kachooa before, but after the appointment of Eshan Chander as Joobraj [the young prince and heir], coins having been struck in her name, she was made a Rani.'[24] There is also a hint that a devoted mother and loyal wife (of whatever ritual status or background) could improve her position in the royal household by 'meritorious deeds', such as organising the building of a temple or the digging of a tank in which to store water.[25]

The status of wives could fall too. Age generally increased the standing in the household of women with sons, and gave them authority over their daughters-in-law – this stereotype often resembled the facts on the ground. But women without sons could face harsh destinies. In 1907, when Malcolm Lyall Darling reached Dewas as the young raja's tutor, he paid a courtesy call on the 'Maharani Sahiba, the raja's grandmother, who for some years during his minority had been Regent of the State'. When Darling arrived, to his great surprise he found that she had been expelled from the palace and lived in a dirty house in the town in a single room, divided in half by a bamboo screen (she remained in purdah). To reach the room, he had to climb up a 'mud-plastered staircase'.[26]

It is unclear who had driven her out of the palace, or why or how she came to live in such reduced circumstances; but it is plain from Darling's account that the position of women – even elderly and powerful women, Maharani Regents – did not stand still. Likewise in Bhopal, an Afghan state in central India dominated by women rulers, Kudsiya Begum, 'the oldest and most venerable member of the Bhopal family', was relegated to the fringes, for reasons unknown.[27] In 1874, when the new Begum of Bhopal, Nawab Sultan Jahan Begum, married with enormous pomp and eye-watering expense, Kudsiya Begum received no invitation.

If the position of wives was uncertain, that of slaves was even more so. Slavery was not a fixed status. Formal manumission did not turn a slave into a free woman or free man; but marriage, loyalty, devotion and good deeds could. ('Freedom', moreover, has to be understood as a relative term, given the overweening authority of patriarchs over *all* members of their households.) Slaves were not alike in standing, any more than were the patriarch's sons, their wives, concubines or members of their respective retinues. Certain *daasis* grew particularly close to their mistresses, and to each other. Their intimacy with their rani, and their knowledge of every detail of her life – her body, her illnesses, her diet, how often the raja visited – gave them a certain power in the household, even though many dwelt outside its walls. Much of this was opaque, of course, to outsiders.

One reason why these households were so rambling and messy, from a British point of view, was that South Asians had no law of primogeniture. Nor did rivals for the throne always accept a successor chosen by a reigning king during his lifetime. Sons of *nikaah* wives and concubines could press their case as much as sons of *shaadi* wives.[28] Legitimacy rested not so much in the purity of the bloodline, but in the recognition of a child by its father. Even when a prince came to the throne, there-fore, his position was never secure; rivals were all around him. Nor was he safe. Tukoji Rao of Dewas, Darling's friend and tutee, was convinced that the Rani, his mother by adoption, was trying to poison him.

> Once, he said, [he, Tukoji Rao] had been very ill after a meal due, he
> thought, to poison. Since then he has always had his food first tested on
> a *pye* [stray] dog, and once, he declared, the dog died in ten minutes.
> When dining . . . with the Rani, his mother by adoption, he [now] always
> offered [the dish] to her first, and if she refused it, he did not touch it.[29]

Succession could, and often did, lead to open warfare, as faction fought faction with all the ferocity they could muster. Rana Khagda Samsher of Nepal 'was not quite thirty years old when he . . . contrived to make himself the army's Commander-in-Chief'. He did so by mur-dering his uncle, the reigning monarch, shooting him in his bed at point-blank range, and killing two other male relatives.[30] He later had to flee to India, then under the vice-royalty of Lord Curzon, setting himself up in Central India, where the mountains and lakes reminded him of the home from which he was exiled.[31] Nor has intra-household violence on a spectacular scale remained a thing of the distant past. On 1 June 2001, Crown Prince Dipendra of Nepal shot and killed his father (the reigning monarch, King Birenda), his mother (Queen Aish-warya), and seven other members of the royal family, including his younger brother and sister, before shooting himself in the head. (Mon-archy has since been abolished in Nepal.)

These levels of fratricide were not restricted to families with royal pretensions. Even among more humble households, sisters-in-law were not natural allies, brothers were not always harmonious teams, and succession to property often caused rifts. In 1921, in the Betul district in Central Provinces, 'an avaricious illegitimate son, deter-mined to secure an inheritance, hired an assassin to kill his father and three legitimate half-brothers. The three sons were slain at night with an axe while they lay sleeping in a hut, and a stranger who was also sleeping there, shared their fate. Their father was murdered the fol-lowing morning.'[32] In R. K. Narayan's novel, *The Man-Eater of Malgudi*, set in the 1950s, the printer protagonist falls out with his brothers and their common property is subdivided, leaving him alone in a house much too large for him without any cash. In the 1980s, on the death of my eldest uncle, his sons (my rummy-playing cousins) fell out with each other, much to my father's distress. One cousin-brother left Hill Cart Road with his mother, wife and daughters to establish a new home and clinic. The other stayed at Hill Cart Road. The old household is now partitioned, sad and denuded – a moss-covered, leaking fraction of what it was in its glory days.

But even in more peaceful times, households were noisy, quarrelsome places. Bankimchandra Chatterjee gives a sense of this in his fictional account of the household of Nagendra Datta, an 'upper-caste' Hindu in Govindapur in Bengal:

> The establishment had three outer buildings and three inner ones. In one, groups of priest 'were bathing the images of the gods, ringing bells, arguing, making sandal paste . . .'; in another 'a group of *bairagis* [wandering ascetics], wearing garlands of *tulsi* [holy basil] around their withered necks . . . were playing drums'; 'in the middle in the dancing hall, the neighbourhood's idle boys were wrestling, quarrelling and hitting each other, and directing various kinds of refined abuse at each other's parents . . .'[33]

Unlike Nagendra's dwelling, which was 'well ordered', the *puja* house was

> old and poorly constructed; the rooms were low, small and dirty. This house was filled day and night with the continuous loud talking of countless daughters of kinsmen, maternal aunts and their cousins, paternal aunts and their cousins, widowed maternal aunts, married nieces, wives of paternal aunts' brothers, daughters of maternal aunts' brothers, and other such female relations like a banyan tree full of crows. And it was constantly filled with various kinds of outcry, laughing, joking, quarrelling, arguments, stories, gossip, the fighting of boys and the weeping of girls, calls of 'Bring me water', 'Pass the clothes', 'You haven't washed the rice', 'The boy hasn't eaten', 'Milks and curds', and other such sounds, like a troubled sea.[34]

Chatterjee, a district magistrate who wrote in his spare time, is credited with inventing the novel as a form in Bengali. He had a subtle ear for the tone of women's conversation among themselves. His novels have a marvellous auditory feel, a stereo soundtrack of their busy world of work, talk, more talk and more work.

In households on this scale, orphaned grandchildren, poor relatives and down-at-heel retainers were cared for as kin. But, whether Hindu or Muslim, the basic rule was the same: they had to follow the norms that the patriarch imposed upon them. In *Sunlight on a Broken Column*, Attia Hosain's semi-autobiographical novel set in the 1930s, the *taluqdaar* Baba Jan's Lucknow household (in its turn connected to an even larger one in the ancestral village) includes two young orphaned girls. Laila is convent-educated in line with her late father's wishes, a rebellious bookworm troubled by the political and cultural turmoil of the times; Zahra is the prettier of the two, more conventional, uninterested in books and politics. Other members include widowed aunts, companions of widowed aunts and a host of loved servitors. Laila, the protagonist, speaks of:

> Ustaniji, who had taught my aunts Urdu, Persian and Arabic, [whose family had served the court of Awadh for generations]; . . . Hajjan Bibi, whose husband had been a companion of Baba Jan's. He had spent his last impoverished years with us after losing all his money through speculation at the end of the war. Also Asad, eighteen, and Zahid, sixteen, who were orphaned sons of poor relatives . . .[35]

'Sad-eyed' Asad falls in love with Zahra, who returns his feelings. The minute this is discovered by the girls' spinster aunt, Abida, who runs the household and estate with brisk (and ruthless) efficiency after Baba Jan's death, she finds a suitable boy for Zahra. Asad is banished from the house. Just as there were numerous ways of entering a household, there were many doors out.

A household, then, was not the tidy, self-contained, inward-looking unit of the census-takers' imagination. Nor was it a mere sump of sunken wealth that could be taxed rather like a firm. It was a web of relationships of blood, power, dependency and servitude.

These relationships, moreover, were always in flux.

Ties could abruptly be severed. Households were as much a space of humiliation and exile as of affection and support. This was particularly the case with women, whose status was always more precarious than that of men. Widows could be cast off, wives abandoned. Abandonment left women of lower status than Magayamma in a desperate situation, since a bride was expected, particularly in 'upper-caste' Hindu northern India, to dissolve her whole being in her husband's household (*shongshaar*) once she had left her paternal home.[36] She was, by the act of marriage, born anew into a different clan.

'Acculturation', for the girl bride began anew in her husband's household and village, as seen in Chapter 4. This requirement expected the bride to change, to learn to labour, and adopt the ways of the husband's household: an expectation reinforced by the fact that marriages, for women, were hypergamous, to families in distant places, and which did not share a prohibited degree of kinship. This exile was intended to loosen the bride's ties with her own family. She was to expect no property from her father's estate, lest a new male (her husband) entered and destabilised patriarchal authority in her paternal household, with all its practical consequences. This was the ideological bedrock upon which 'upper-caste' Hindu society rested, well into the twentieth century.

Muslim family law permitted divorce and gave daughters a small stake in their paternal property; however, except in the wealthiest households, they were rarely able to exercise these rights. So Muslim women too had to adapt to their role as wives, and were no less vulnerable to the caprices of husbands and patriarchs.

Censuses of Calcutta in the early decades of the century registered growing numbers of female beggars and prostitutes, as well as others who described themselves, sometimes euphemistically, as 'maidservants'.[37] Most such women had transgressed norms or flouted patriarchal authority; or were widows without dependable sons.

That this was a wider trend is borne out by the findings of a meticulous survey in Matlab, a small part of Comilla district in Bangladesh. Between 1968 and 1978, one in three emigrations among women was due to 'marriage disruption'.[38] Some such women were lucky enough to be accepted back by their parents, but usually this was a temporary arrangement rather than a permanent return 'home'. Others were not even permitted to re-cross the threshold. Nor could these Muslim women claim their rightful inheritance.

The impoverished widow casts her 'inauspicious' shadow across modern Bengali literature. She is usually described as ugly and hunched with age, meddlesome and troublemaking. Consider this description of Thakrundidi, the friendly neighbourhood widow in Taraknath Ganguli's serialised novel *The Brothers*:

> Her house was ten or twelve ropes from Sashibhusan's. It had two small rooms, one for living in, one for cooking. In the front was a small

courtyard, and in the south of the courtyard a little garden, in which were some flowering plants, one or two pawpaws, and a coconut palm . . . In this house Thakrundidi lived alone 'by choice'.

The heavy satire loaded onto the phrase 'by choice' leads the reader to understand that she has been abandoned.

And then let's see how ugly this status renders her:

Her complexion did not resemble hibiscus, it did not resemble roses, it did not resemble *bel*-blossoms or jasmine . . . It was like the ink on a zemindar's records, the soot of a cookhouse, tar, and other such substances. Thakrundidi was dwarfish and stocky, her head was nearly bald, her teeth were like spring radishes, her eyes were bloodshot, her legs were like pillars, her toes sprawled, one here, one there, as though they had quarrelled and separated.[39]

When filming *Pather Panchali* in the 1950s, Satyajit Ray struggled to find an actor who could play the role of Indir Thakrun, the wizened, emaciated old woman, her shorn hair a mark of the widow's fate. He eventually found Chunibala Devi, a retired stage actor living in one of Calcutta's red-light districts. The overlap between widowhood and prostitution – conventional society and its margins – is discernible, then, in one of the finest films of the twentieth century.

The cruel culture of abandonment should not close our eyes to the numbers of women who *wanted* to leave their husbands. Only among the wealthy could they hope to return to their parental homes but they did not always find much succour there. For poorer women, often the only route out of unhappy marriages was emigration. Even after the indenture system came to an end in 1917, the demand for female labour remained high, particularly in Assam, where the number of tea plantations ballooned over the decades. The scale of their flight was such that the colonial government took fright. In 1901 the Government of India passed a new act that required the consent of (male) guardians before women could enter into labour contracts, endorsing familial claims to a women's labour within the home and a wife's lack of agency as an individual to work outside it. 'Men – husbands, fathers and other "guardians" – now could exert legal as well as extra-legal powers to deny women entry into plantations', which were the only industry with a high demand for female workers.[40]

But leave they did, regardless, taking huge risks secretly to flee oppressive households and unhappy marriages. This is not to romanticise their agency, deny the role of traffickers or downplay the horrific conditions of 'unfreedom' they faced in the plantations; but merely to point out that married women often migrated for quite different reasons than men, and that it is well that we bear this is mind. These women left to break away from the 'power of the paterfamilias' which bore down upon them in harsh and oppressive ways.[41]

Among the middle classes and the upper middle classes, though, exit from a marriage by entering the labour force was not a viable option: caste, class and status made it unthinkable. Divorce carried (and still carries) huge stigma. In colonial India, although it was not easy, divorce was not impossible. Muslim wives could ask for *khulaa*, release from the marital bond, in return for all or part of their *mehr* (money or goods given by the groom at the time of marriage). (This did not guarantee that they would get it, of course.) Christian women could sue for divorce if they could prove their husband's adultery, and one other betrayal of the marriage, say by cruelty.[42] For Hindu women, 'Hindu law' as interpreted by the colonial state did not sanction divorce until after independence, with the passage of the Hindu Marriage Act in 1955. But before this, apostasy was the only route out of the so-called sacramental bond. Few women dared to exercise it.

Two cases highlight just how narrow was this eye of the needle, how perilous the journey towards freedom from marriage. They are different, but the women's stories and social locations were different too. Their desire for freedom makes them alike, I believe.

Atreyee Devi was the only child of a well-educated Brahmin man who had risen high in the service of the colonial state, as manager in the Office of the Court of Wards. In 1941, when she was about fifteen, in accordance with her father's wishes, Atreyee married an indigent Brahmin of the locality. The young man, unemployed at the time, came to live in his father-in-law's household. This was atypical in a patrilocal society, but I imagine the father's expectation was that the young man would behave as a responsible and obedient *ghar jamaai* (house husband) and help manage his household affairs.

Things did not turn out as Atreyee's father had intended. The

son-in-law began to demand that Atreyee give him money. At first, her
mother tried to help her daughter, secretly passing small sums to the
insistent son-in-law. The demands escalated. On a visit to his relatives,
he stole Atreyee's jewellery. He then took to kicking and beating her.
On one occasion he struck her so hard that she collapsed and lost
consciousness. It was only then that her father discovered what had
been going on under his roof.

In 1944, when Atreyee turned eighteen, she decided to convert to
Islam, and by that conversion, to end her marriage. Her father tried to
dissuade her, but she replied in a trenchant voice – gold dust from the
legal archive: 'You have spoilt my life once. You have no right to spoil
my life any longer. You should allow me in all fairness to act according to my determination.'[43] She took the name Ayesha Bibi, having
converted to Islam at the Nakhoda Mosque in Calcutta. In the end,
her father supported her.

What makes Atreyee's case so striking is her determination to withstand parental pressure and social condemnation. Also remarkable
for the times is that Atreyee's father came round in 1944, supporting
her conversion at a time of intense Hindu–Muslim conflict, and the
dissolution of her marriage by this unconventional means. Most parents in a similar situation would put unrelenting pressure on their
daughters to return to their husbands, however hard their life with
them. Most still do.

But this pressure to return to the in-laws' home did not equate to a
shattering of a wife's connection to her parents once and for all. Life
on the ground was not, and is not, so snip-snap. Strands of love and
interdependence continued to connect women to their natal families
long after marriage. Among Hindus, sisters literally tied, and continue
to tie (ever more gaudy) braids on their brothers' wrists at the festival
of Rakhi each year – braids that represent the sister's affection for her
brother and her hope that he will protect her in hard times.

This is well known. But I was particularly struck by the capacious
network of familial support that Baby Haldar drew on when she tried
to leave her violent husband. Baby, who went on to become a domestic servant and write a stunning autobiography (the first ever by an
Indian domestic servant), was married off by her father to a much
older man. When I say violent – let me be blunt – the man raped her
again and again and then beat her with a log until she miscarried. Her
woman friend across the road took her to hospital. After being

discharged, she recuperated for a long time at the house of her *pishima* (aunt), and then returned to her father's for a while. She could not stay there long, because of tensions with her stepmother, and so she went back and forth, between her father, *pishima*, married elder sister, cousins, uncles, all of whom gave her shelter. So these connections remain strong, even for the poor. But she could enjoy their hospitality for only a while. She played endurance while she tried, this way and that, to break free. Eventually she became one of the many women who migrated to the city in search of work.[44]

Morium's story is very different. In it we see how women mobilise their energy, kin and connections to help their (various) families. These are strong women too, but they did not want to leave the marital home, and never did. Yet they remain involved (richly so) in the lives of their own natal families. They were often denizens of diasporas.

Morium (not her real name) was born in Sylhet (now in Bangladesh) in the 1920s. She was in her sixties when she arrived in London. She had married at the age of fourteen. For nigh on fifty years, she lived in her husband's household in Bangladesh, which was close to her parents' home, while her husband worked in London. She was happy where she was. Finally, in the 1980s, the elders (of both households) persuaded her husband to take her to London where he lived and worked. She did not want to move to Britain 'because I had everyone – parents, relatives – back in Bangladesh'.

After she arrived in England, Morium was lonely and homesick. Despite her husband's efforts to lift her spirits by taking her and the children sightseeing, she struggled; only the alleviation of short visits to her family in Bangladesh made life tolerable. As she aged, her parents aged too, and died. Her husband also died. When we interviewed her in 2008, her closest ties were with her children in Britain and her youngest sister 'back home' in Chittagong.[45] Her 'base' had changed, and now she had less urgent desires to 'go back home'. She remained involved in it however, if less achingly so.

Or let's consider Humeira's story. One of my dearest friends is a Pakistani Muslim woman, Humeira Iqtidar. Brilliant, witty and generous to a fault, she teaches Politics at King's College London. We have kept in regular touch by email and WhatsApp for several years now because, since the late 1990s, the moment that term ended, she left for Lahore. There she spent much time with her father – a widower who had dementia – and helped organise his home and the care of her disabled brother. She flew back when term began and started teaching again, doing the gruelling daily commute from Cambridge to London and back. Every single day, though, at a given time, she spoke to her father's carer, and then to her father, for ten or fifteen minutes, in reassuring, melodious, Urdu. If you didn't know the background, you would never know the extent to which Humeira remained embedded in *three* households: one in Lahore, with her father and brother and their carers; a second in her father-in-law's home (also in Lahore); the third in Cambridge, where she lived with her husband, two children, and a rosebush that flowered unpredictably in a garden she had little time to tend.

Sticky like a spider's web then, invisible unless a sunbeam throws sudden light upon them, the gossamers that connect members of one household to another, and to households beyond them, are far stronger than one might imagine. They also link families to worlds far beyond. These outward-facing dimensions of the household, and the manifold possibilities of their breakdown, are quite as important as the closeness of internal bonds, their patterns of sociability and structures of power.

II

LAW, ECONOMY AND THE FAMILY

What did the British make of all this? How far did they understand, or even try to understand, these delicate webs, these changing constellations?

Only as much as they felt that they had to. After the Mutiny, they believed (not without reason) that the rebels of 1857 had been led by a particular class of disgruntled householders: *taluqdaars* like Baba Jan in *Sunlight on a Broken Column* – landholders of North India with significant alliances and armed peasantries behind them.[46] After the Rebellion had been crushed, and after Queen Victoria's proclamation of 1858, the officers of the Raj wanted a truce. They were loath to get sucked into the domestic affairs of innumerable households and upset the fragile peace. They took the view that family matters were best left alone; it made more sense to uphold the status quo. Just as

Indian nationalists were representing the 'traditional' household as the vital essence of India's culture, so British officials backed away from that space: these were hornets' nests best left undisturbed.

Yet sometimes they had no choice but to get involved, particularly when quarrelling parties took cases of inheritance, succession, adoption and stipends to British courts. Some, as we saw in the Pittapore case, dragged on for years. Lawyers like Motilal Nehru began to make fortunes fighting inheritance cases at about this time.

Despite its firm intention to keep out of these murky waters, step by step, wittingly or otherwise, the Raj changed and narrowed the legal definition of the Indian household and family.

In 1861, Henry Sumner Maine published his celebrated work, *Ancient Law*. He did not write it in India; nor was it about India. Yet it had a powerful impact on how 'Anglo-Indian' civil law evolved. In *Ancient Law*, Maine argues that societies move 'from status to contract': from close-knit communities trussed together by codes of honour, to individuals capable of entering into binding contracts with one another.[47]

In 1862, Maine was appointed member for law in the Viceroy's Council in India, and even though he became preoccupied with the needs of 'unorthodox Hindus', officials who shaped law came to believe that there was such a thing as an 'orthodox Hindu family', which represented the ideal and also the norm. This was the Hindu Undivided Family (HUF), in which all the men of the family owned equal shares of a hereditary estate. It was run by its head, a *karta*, usually the eldest surviving male. He managed the estate, but held the same stake in it as his dead ancestors, brothers, uncles, nephews and sons, and grandsons, generations still to be born. According to this definition of the Hindu family, which was based on certain scriptures, women had no right to property. No male member of an HUF had the right to sell any part of this jointly owned estate without the agreement of all the others. The *karta*, although an equal shareholder, was in fact *primus inter pares* when it came to making day-to-day decisions on investment and expenditure. All earnings and profits were fed back into the household, and were spent according to the needs of individual members, as decided by the patriarch. That was the theory.

Even British judges recognised that that was all it was. In 1877, a judge in Madras declared that the Hindu law administered in British courts was a 'phantom of the brain, imagined by Sanskritists without law, and lawyers without Sanskrit'.[48]

Yet, despite everyone knowing this, the concept of a unified body of Hindu law underlying the Hindu Undivided Family persisted because it was convenient. It was the product of a long 'search for certainty'.[49] It imposed upon the perplexing variety of Hindu households across India the same school of law: the *Mitaakshara*, also known as the Benares School. This was despite the fact every learned British jurist, including Maine, knew that there was an alternative legal system in eastern India: the *Dayabhaaga*, the Bengal School, which gave rights of inheritance to some Hindu women.[50] The 'semi-autonomous' judges of colonial India were, of course, aware of a rich and strange variety of religious laws and regional customary practices, including matrilineal and 'lower-caste' forms of marriage, which bore no relation to *Mitaakshara* notions of the united family.[51] Yet *Mitaakshara* prevailed because in the perspective of officials, homogeneity was easier to administer than the bewildering diversities of the subcontinent.

As this gradual move to standardise Hindu family law progressed, it redefined who was, and who was not, a member of the family. This sanforised the household, which came out of the legal washing machine shrunken in size, shed of outriders and distant dependants. Anglo-Indian Hindu law recognised only a lineal line of descendants – from father to sons. According to this emerging definition, Hindu Undivided Families were not so different from the co-parcenaries (joint heirs) of English common law, and therefore easier for the British to understand; and their understanding had an impact on the legal context in which the household and family developed.[52]

Moreover, although in principle the *karta* had the same share of the household's property as his male lineal relatives, his age and seniority gave him more clout. He was de facto, if not de jure, the patriarch. Law thus created something that resembled primogeniture, which the British understood and liked, because they saw it as a force for good and for the progress of their own society. The *karta* was almost invariably the eldest surviving son, and the estates under his control remained undivided as long as the Hindu Undivided Family prevailed. Given the growing concern in this period (in both official and nationalist circles) about the fragmentation of agrarian holdings and its ill effects on agricultural yields, giving legal backing to the Hindu Undivided Family seemed an excellent idea.

The finances of the Raj also had a part to play in the story (as they do in every story about the Raj). It made fiscal sense for the British to try to narrow down the membership of large households, because where the East India Company had conquered territories, it had undertaken to pay stipends to former rajas, nawabs, their multiple heirs, queens, concubines and retinues: in fact their entire households. Indian elites too had much to lose (or gain) from the definition of the terms 'family' and 'household'. Almighty arguments raged about who was, or was not, a member, and therefore entitled to a pension or stipend.

The stakes were high on all sides. Perhaps they were highest in Muslim households, where women enjoyed rights of inheritance and entitlements to stipends denied to Hindu women. The consequences were sharpest among the well-to-do. Many (perhaps most) Muslim householders had established *waaf-ul-aulaad*: family trusts to protect their estates and descendants, exempt from taxation and other liabilities for all time.[53] But how were their beneficiaries to be recognised? Persian texts offered a host of usages of 'household' and 'family', and English dictionaries added to the confusion. John Richardson's classic dictionary of English, Persian and Arabic 'lists four Persian words for "family" in the sense of those who live under the same roof and fifteen more for "family" as those sharing a common ancestor'.[54] In the same dictionary, the (still commonly used) word *khandaan* is translated as 'family', 'house' and 'royal court'.[55] Indian petitioners could lay claim to stipends by playing on the capacious definitions of 'family' that the Persian tradition offered.

As time went on, the British began to feel these pensions were 'overly burdensome'. In the Carnatic region of South India, the number of members of one particular stipendiary's household started at ninety-two; other more distant dependants then successfully petitioned to be added to the list of beneficiaries.

Reader, I expect you are getting overwhelmed. Imagine the desperation of a British official faced with these complexities of law, religion and custom. The Raj, as we have seen, was struggling to balance its books, given other pressures on the exchequer at this time. So officials grew more zealous in seeking to limit the number of claimants it supported. Yet however hard they tried, with each decade, the number of pensioners grew bigger as a result of natural increase and the admission of new individuals. Family *waqfs*, they felt, were sumps of hoarded wealth that they could not tap; and they chafed against the constraints that were imposed on their ability to tax.

As the nineteenth century drew to a close, this official reluctance to honour old debts began to be mixed with a sense of disdain for this 'defeated class'. As they saw it, these pensions were 'a drain not only on the exchequer but on the moral fibre of the entire Muslim population'.[56] The matter came to be coloured by emotion: by imperial contempt for the conquered, their laws, customs and ways of life.

Even before the Rebellion, the East India Company had begun to interfere in matters of inheritance. In 1855, Edward Balfour (government agent at Chepauk and paymaster dealing with Carnatic stipends) recommended that the inheritable portion of a deceased woman's stipend be divided among four of 'her closest relatives', rather than divvying it up among all twenty of her dependants. He thought it made more sense to give four people a meaningful legacy rather than give twenty 'respectable' people a sum not capable of supporting a household.[57] 'Closeness', which might previously have included the intimate bond between a slave and her queen, or between a *zamindaar*, his concubine and their children, now began to be interpreted as the nearness of blood relationships.

In 1894, the Privy Council in London struck out in the same direction. It ruled that family *waqfs* were not true charities, because to leave money to one's heirs was not a charitable purpose. It decreed that *waqfs* of this sort had a duty to repay loans to creditors, and could be taxed like any other property.[58] This abolished, in law and in the eyes of the taxman, an age-old institution. The ruling was a blow to Muslims of all sects and creeds, giving them a common grievance.

So in 1913, when a bright young Bombay lawyer named Muhammad Ali Jinnah pushed back against the Privy Council ruling, much rode on the outcome. His Mussalman Wakf Validating Bill of 1913 argued that in the case of family trusts, after the extinction of all family members, such property was reserved 'for the poor or other religious, pious or charitable purposes'. These trusts were, then, charities, and could not be deemed invalid 'by reason of remoteness of benefit to [the] poor'.[59] This shrewd move was typical of Jinnah's gamesmanship, and it succeeded. As we have seen in Chapter 1, it helped cement Jinnah's reputation as a lawyer, as a politician able to unite different Muslim sects, and as a dangerous adversary of the Raj.

Despite this setback, during and after the war years, the colonial state grew ever more keen to tax more people and encourage the free flow of money in the market. Officials continued to regard family *waqfs* as cesspits of hoarded wealth and idle labour, which it was eager to 'liberate'.[60] They also grew more committed to taxing the personal incomes of all Indians as a means of stretching the state's resources. In the old century, viceroys had been tentative about income tax, but after 1918 they had to be more daring. The Raj (as it saw it) now had no option but to squeeze every last drop out of the Indian lemon.

This was the context behind a move to identify the 'nuclear family' as a target for the taxman, even if its male head also belonged to a Hindu Undivided Family, which had come to be taxed separately at a fixed (high) rate. In effect, the urban working man was to be taxed twice: on his personal income as a city-based professional, and also on the income that he received as part of the HUF to which he belonged.

But here was the rub. Far from protesting, as they were so ready to do, Hindu professionals who had made good in the city *supported* the move. In fact, they led it. They had their own reasons for wanting their professional incomes kept apart from, and out of the control of, the Hindu Undivided Family and its 'head'.

In 1929, Mukund Ramrao Jayakar, a reform-minded Marathi barrister who would become the first vice-chancellor of Poona University, pressed for the Hindu Gains of Learning Bill. This would 'secure a man's salary as his individual property ... and enable him to look after the daily needs of his wife'.[61] Jayakar was a commanding figure: the sheer strength of his personality shines through in photographs of him in every mood. Looking at his handsome, intelligent, stern-lipped face, his huge forehead half hidden by a Congress cap, one wouldn't guess that behind his aggressive visage lay a talent for consensus-building. But he had that gift in full measure. It is worth mentioning that he was Jinnah's co-director at the *Bombay Chronicle* and shared many of Jinnah's liberal instincts.

Given these skills, and the synergy between the interests of the colonial state and those of the growing number of Indian urban professionals, Jayakar's bill went onto the statute book in record time. The nuclear family thus became a legal entity.

But here we must pause to consider other nuances and implications of this development. We must note in particular Jayakar's emphasis on the modern urban man's (primary) responsibility towards his wife. But we should not for a moment imagine that this new dyad of husband and wife supplanted the patriarchal household of old. Rather, for wives, the authority of the husband replaced the patriarchal control of the *karta* or the authority of her mother-in-law. To be more accurate, the two forms of control over a wife's labour and social identity became intertwined, because her husband was still a fully paid up (and taxed) member of the HUF.

Nor did the emergence of the husband–wife partnership as the centre of the urban family mean that they were two individuals who met independently, fell in love and decided, of their own volition, to marry. As I will show below, the picture was more complicated than that.

Furthermore, although the legal and fiscal setting is crucial to understanding how the nuclear family appeared, with apparent suddenness, to replace the sprawling household structure of the past, the transformation of family life was neither abrupt nor seamless. Law cannot transform society, much less colonial law, which could be (and was) denounced as an alien attack on traditional and hallowed forms of domesticity. Tax breaks could provide incentives for social change, but these would affect only the 'learned' few – urban Hindu professional men. And reformist causes were unpopular, particularly where they involved the family.

One remarkable exception was the Child Marriage Restraint Act, also passed in 1929 (known informally as the Sarda Act, after its sponsor, Harbilas Sarda). This raised, in a trice, the age of consent for girls to sixteen years. In Chapter 2 we saw how, in the late nineteenth century, Bal Gangadhar Tilak won fame by *resisting* a bill to raise the age of marriage of Hindu consent to twelve years. This time round, in 1929, Indian politicians of all hues and creeds, and a significant phalanx of women, united behind Harbilas Sarda's bill.

What triggered this alliance between disparate groups, in the context of growing Hindu–Muslim tension outside the legislature, was the publication in 1927 of Katherine Mayo's book *Mother India*, which vilifies Indian society, and Indian men in particular, in the harshest terms.[62] Mayo's diagnosis is that India was an appalling society, and its worst badge of shame was child marriage. This institution, she argued, had become such a feature of society because India's men were disgusting hyper-sexual specimens of humanity. Their behaviour had led to all manner of social ills; but also homosexuality, masturbation, rape, prostitution and venereal disease.

> The whole pyramid of Indians' woes, material and spiritual – poverty, sickness, ignorance, political minority, melancholy, ineffectiveness, not forgetting that subconscious conviction of inferiority which he forever

bares and advertises by his gnawing and imaginative alertness for social affronts – rests upon a rock-bottom physical base. This base is, simply, his manner of getting into this world and his sex-life thenceforward.[63]

Mayo claimed (with justification) that child marriage led to maternal illness and early death. Given these horrors, she announced in strident terms, but with a total lack of logic, that colonial rule was not only required, but that the British would have to remain in charge in India for many decades to reform India's terrible society.

The book caused an uproar. For its time, it was as incendiary as Rushdie's *Satanic Verses*. Critics burned copies of the little red volume all over India, and cast effigies of the author ablaze. Gandhi described the book as a 'cleverly and powerfully written' drain inspector's report. More than fifty books and pamphlets, authored by furious Indians, repudiated Mayo's findings. In one of them, *Father India*, C. S. Ranga Iyer denounced Mayo's 'tirade on India, written in the style of a Cassandra-like propagandist' as 'slander'.[64] Indian critics asked why the British had done so little to stamp out these ills, if British rule was – as Mayo suggested – the panacea. Thirty years after Mayo's book came out, in 1957, Mehboob Khan made the Hindi film *Mother India*. Challenging Mayo's portrayal of the Indian child-mother as weak and oppressed, Radha (played by Nargis) is a young widow who manages to survive and bring up her young sons *in the world*, outside the inner walls of the home. This *Mother India* personified courage, strength and self-sacrifice. Regarded as one of Bollywood's greatest films of all time, *Mother India* was nominated for an Academy Award for Best Foreign Language Film in 1958. Nehru attended one of its first screenings.

Coming back to legal reform in the last decades of the Raj, the reformist coalition soon fell apart. The issue of women's rights was soon subordinated to the need to keep a wider alliance of Congress supporters together. Changes in legislation continued to be promoted, but they could not harness the outrage that Mayo's *Mother India* had generated. Instead, marriage law legislation began to assume communal and competitive dimensions. Muslim legislators sought to show that their religion was already modern, in that under Islamic law Muslim women already had rights to property and divorce. The Shariat (Application) Act of 1937 was therefore put forward as a 'clarifying measure', which presented Islamic law (properly followed) as more 'progressive' and 'women-friendly' than Hindu law.[65] (This construction helped keep the *ulema* on side.)[66] The Dissolution of Muslim Marriages Act of 1939 permitted Muslim women 'to divorce their husbands in terms that were far in advance of Indian women of other communities, particularly Hindus'.[67]

Attempts to 'reform' Hindu family law, by contrast, could not claim to have the sanction of textual tradition behind them. Likewise, the efforts of the Hindu Law Committee, chaired by B. N. Rau in 1941, soon ran into the sands. Nehru's Hindu Code Bill faced powerful headwinds of resistance after independence. It was only by breaking the Code Bill into five discrete bills (each separately covering divorce, adoption, succession, guardianship and inheritance) and by facing down a rebellion led by India's president after the Congress' landslide victory in India's first general election in 1952, that Nehru was able to drive these laws through the Lok Sabha (the lower house of parliament).

These were not radical measures. To take the example of the Hindu law of divorce, it was novel in that it recognised that only 'upper-caste' Hindus could break their 'sacramental' bond. (Other sorts of 'Hindus' had never had much of a problem about so doing.) But, as I learned the hard way, it applied to people born to Hindu parents (in my case, great-grandparents) who were not practising Hindus. The grounds for seeking divorce included mental illness, leprosy, venereal disease and desertion. Oh, and conversion to another faith. Later, cruelty was added to the list of grounds, but the act of cruelty had to have witnesses. It took one woman I knew thirteen years to get a divorce, despite her children acting as witnesses on her behalf. My divorce would have taken as long had history not played a sudden googly. So for a Hindu woman to get a divorce if her husband opposed it was like getting a peacock through the eye of a needle.

All of these reforms were 'softly softly' steps. Nehru may have won an election but he could not frighten the horses – conservatives dominated the Congress from the centre to its base.

Contrary to public perception then, India had to play catch-up with Pakistan in the matter of women's rights to property and divorce. This context explains, at least in part, why family law remained dangerous political terrain; until the end of the century, few governments dared to tread near it. In both Pakistan and Bangladesh, the Dissolution of Muslim Marriages Act of 1939 (barring a few amendments) remains the foundation of family law to date.[68] There have been no major amendments to Hindu or Muslim law in India, despite cries from both left and right of the political spectrum for a unified civil code for all citizens.

In 1985, an ageing Indian Muslim woman showed just how tricky this subject is for governments. Shah Bano Begum, from Indore, had married Mohammad Ahmed Khan. They had five children together. Time passed. Ahmed Khan then took another wife and, some years on, he divorced Shah Bano and stopped paying the small sum he had previously given her for her upkeep and for the children.

Shah Bano Begum did not take this lying down. Then in her sixties, this brave women took the matter to the courts and in 1985 won the case at India's Supreme Court.[69] Angry Muslim groups formed a coalition denouncing the judgement, which they saw as an unacceptable interference in Muslim Personal Law. A panic-stricken government facing an election back-pedalled. In 1986, Rajiv Gandhi's Congress government passed the Muslim Women (Protection of Rights on Divorce) Act, which allowed maintenance to a divorced woman only during the period of *iddat*, or until ninety days after the divorce, according to the provisions of Islamic law. In all but name, it succumbed to the Muslim conservative opposition.

The Shah Bano affair shocked me, then a twenty-one-year-old history student at Cambridge. Shah Bano's large kohl-rimmed eyes – her gaunt, lined, inscrutable face – stared out of the front page of every daily in India. Editorials raised more questions than they answered, as did learned debates about the law; nonetheless I rushed to join the brigade of people furious with the government for its betrayal of this woman. Demonstrations followed. I was probably there at some of them. (I can't remember. I demonstrated against so many things in India in my twenties; there was so much to protest about.)

Had I read more history at that age, perhaps I would have been less scandalised by the events as they unfolded in Shah Bano's case. I would have grasped that even as the century was drawing to a close, reforming the South Asian family – above all in ways that gave new rights to women – remained fraught with political danger. Just as the British had, post-colonial governments have preferred to look the other way, turning their face away from the family and household. Across South Asia, the state (as seen in Chapter 3) has left these spheres of society ungoverned, allowing instead communities, patriarchs and guardians of 'tradition' to police them.

III

LOVE AND MARRIAGE: HORSE
AND CARRIAGE?

Change, therefore, was slow to come. But come it did, in fits and starts; more in certain areas of life than others; driven by the *jugaad* (makeshift) engines of political, demographic, social and economic transformations, and novel cultural expectations. Some parts of the subcontinent witnessed more rapid change, cities in particular. By and large, urban elite and middle-class households began to look more like nuclear families (until one examines them closely), whereas those in the countryside tended to have rather different structures, with absent husbands and wives carrying more and more of the burden of production. But in this broad arc of change, there are so many exceptions that I hesitate to call it a rule.

Certain stories come to mind as I write this. A few years ago, as mentioned, I visited Lahore University of Management Sciences (LUMS), Pakistan's foremost private university. I was there to give some lectures and build links between LUMS and Cambridge. The LUMS campus with its flowering trees and carefully tended borders was full of young men and women strolling from lecture to lecture. I noticed, however, that once one was driven outside the campus, past the three barriers and heavily armed men who protect it, few women were visible. This leads other Pakistani intellectuals to dismiss LUMS as a bubble, cut off from the realities outside. In many senses they are right, but then so are most universities in most countries; and like them, LUMS is full of able and driven young men and women.

One day, my host and friend Kamal Munir (now pro-vice-chancellor at Cambridge) arranged for me to meet students at an open-air restaurant overlooking the Badshahi Mosque. The view was magical and the kebabs to die for, but what I remember most about the dinner is the conversation I had with the erudite young woman sitting next to me. We spent most of the evening talking about literature and critical theory. She went on to win Cambridge's most celebrated scholarship to take an MPhil degree. It was clear from day one that she was a star: eloquent, gently spoken but robust in her views. To no one's surprise, she came top of the course she enrolled in, and won yet another major scholarship to pursue a PhD. However she never took up her place.

She just disappeared. Her parents, my Pakistani friends told me, were from a 'backward' region, and it was unlikely that they would allow her to come back to the West alone. She never did.

Another incident from some years earlier was revealing in its own way. In the early 1990s, I took my baby son Kartik to the mountains, to one of India's most remote districts, not far from Chamoli as the crow flies. The purpose was to introduce the six-month-old to his paternal grandmother. It was a long journey from Delhi, more than twenty hours by bus, and we stopped midway at a guesthouse at dusk – which falls swiftly in India – in the middle of nowhere. Being an urban innocent, I strode in, and was surprised by the hushed tones and anxiety of the men around me, including my then husband, and his sweet brother. It turned out the guesthouse was on the property of a landlord notorious for exercising his droit du seigneur over the women in his domain – especially the wives and daughters of his workers and servitors. Would I be safe? At the end of the twentieth century, there were places in India where this kind of thing went on, unchecked by state authority.

The third incident took place more recently, in Delhi. It is known to most Indians, but not to all in the worlds beyond it. On a freezing December night in 2012, a twenty-three-year-old woman intern in physiotherapy was returning home with a male friend after an evening at the cinema. It was not late, about eight o'clock. They waited for a bus in 'genteel' South Delhi, in a 'decent' neighbourhood in the heart of the nation's capital. What looked like a private bus picked them up. The other passengers, and the 'driver', were drunk young men. They gang-raped the woman, and when they had had their pleasure, forced an iron rod into her vagina. They beat her friend with the same rod when he tried to fight back. The Indian media named the young woman *Nirbhaya* (Fearless), because of the courage with which she fought for her life and helped the police identify the perpetrators. The pseudonym was a legal necessity: Indian law gives rape victims anonymity to protect them from the stigma that they (rather than the rapists) suffer. Nirbhaya died of her injuries. When women's movements across India demanded better protection for women in cities at night, senior male politicians dismissed the Delhi activists as 'dented-painted' ladies for wearing jeans and lipstick, questioning their morals and also questioning their right to bring an action to court.

But something unusual happened next. Nirbhaya's father announced her true name to the world. She was Jyoti Singh Pandey. Her father, far from being shamed, claimed his raped and battered daughter. He told Jyoti's story: of her striving to study, of her move to the city to learn more, of her moral example to the children of her village.

So as I give you my account below of change and continuity over the century, I present these extraordinary stories as caveats to the general view I sketch out.

Historically speaking, several processes worked to take us from where we were then, in 1900, to where we are now. Some were driven by western-educated elites who, as we have already seen, have played a disproportionate role in the subcontinent's history. In the late nineteenth and early twentieth centuries, ideas of conjugal and companionate marriage captured the imagination of many men of this background. Seeing themselves as reformers, many having studied abroad, they wanted wives who were not devoted servants but true soulmates. Raja Tukoji Rao of Dewas was one unlikely Pygmalion figure of this period. He longed to 'modernise' his wife but failed; she remained a 'lovely wild creature with "gazelle" eyes'.[70] Rabindranath Tagore's novels contain vivid portraits of other would-be Professor Higginses and their Eliza-project wives. In *Ghare Baire* ('The Home and the World'), Nikhilesh is a young man from the 'highest' *kulin* Brahmin caste; he is wealthy, from a household that prides itself on its culture and its beautiful women. But he has an unusual and sensitive cast of mind. He marries Bimala, a 'traditional' and rather plain woman who, at the beginning of the novel, is so dutiful in the old-school style that she 'takes the dust from his feet' every time she sees him. Slowly, gently, he educates her, and encourages her to take part in the world outside the *antahapur* (women's quarters).

But his plan goes wrong. Bimala becomes the educated and independent-minded woman he had hoped for, but falls headlong in love with Sandip, her husband's friend. Nikhilesh does not share Sandip's political views (the latter being involved in the *swadeshi* movement). In a betrayal that goes beyond infidelity, Bimala decides to steal her husband's money and give it to Sandip. She is caught in the act, but there is a reconciliation between husband and wife.

The short novel pulls in two directions. It is dismissive of the claustrophobic world of the *antahapur* and presents Nikhilesh as its 'broad-minded' antithesis; but is wary of the danger that a woman of spirit and education could represent to the institution of marriage and to the stability of the larger household. (Interestingly, 'broad-minded' is the phrase still used in matrimonial columns to describe potential grooms who are not that fussed by a potential bride of a different caste, with a job, an independent mind, and just perhaps by inference, a past.)

In Tagore's novella *Nashtanirh* ('The Broken Nest'), Charulata is the beautiful, intelligent and talented wife of Bhupati, a fin-de-siècle intellectual who publishes a nationalist newspaper. They live in the city, a nuclear couple away from the larger household. But Charulata gets bored and lonely. Bhupati is fond of her but is always busy; she has nothing to do but sit around as an unfulfilled ornament draped in beautiful saris while a fleet of domestic servants manage her home. Sensing her ennui, when his cousin Amal comes to visit, Bhupati encourages him to spend time with Charulata to nurture her poetic talent. But the inevitable happens. The two grow more intimate. Amal falls in love with the enchanting Charu, and she with him. Yet Amal, torn by guilt and out of a sense of loyalty to Bhupati and the wider household, runs away. Bhupati finds Charulata sobbing over Amal's farewell letter to her. The novel closes on an ambivalent note.

The rumour is that the novella is more than semi-autobiographical. Tagore himself fell in love with his older brother's wife, Kadambari Devi, who committed suicide soon after the poet married. The poet knew, at a deep and intimate level, of the transgressive loves possible within the larger world of households. (Satyajit Ray's 1964 film *Charulata* is an adaptation of this work, and one of the finest films made in twentieth-century South Asia.)

These novels reflect aspects of the changing world that Tagore inhabited. In the early twentieth century, the relationship between husband and wife became more central to how elite households were imagined. Wedding invitations (now printed on stiff cards) increasingly focused on the couple coming together in marriage, even though bride and groom are still referred to as 'daughter of', and 'son of' their respective parents. After the wedding, the newly-weds would pose for (rather stilted) photographs, usually with the wife seated on a chair, and the husband standing behind her with an arm draped over the back of the chair in an attitude of possession.[71] By the 1950s and 60s, wedding photo albums had become a craze. (My first exposure to one was at Hill Cart Road, where my aunt with the sceptical eyebrow showed me a shiny plastic album bursting with pictures of her daughter's wedding.) Later in the century, video recordings of the marriage ceremony, with a focus on the couple in all their finery, became de rigueur in middle-class, and even some blue-collar, circles.

But this shift in emphasis did not mean that the nuclear unit was set free of the household. Nor did it imply that after the Hindu Code reforms of the 1950s, the Hindu Undivided Family fell apart. The nuclear married couple remained part of it, even if, like Charulata and Bhupati, they lived in the city. Households, to begin with, became spatially dispersed as cities grew and as migrants of all social classes moved to them. Some families lived in cities in what appear to be, from a western point of view, much like 'modern' western families: mother, father and 2.4 children. But this misses the extent to which they remain stacked like spoons within the moral worlds of the wider household. This created tensions, of course: of precisely the kinds that Tagore alludes to in his stories.

It also misses the extent to which those who now lived in the new urban flats tried to recreate around them the rambling family structure, by buying or renting other flats in the same building. One of my friends (let's call her the Hammersmith professor) is a great example. Her maternal family is from Santiniketan, Tagore's settlement in rural Bolpur. In the 1940s and 50s, her maternal uncles and aunts, and also her mother, migrated to cities, for work or marriage or because they were political activists. In their middle age, the surviving brothers and sisters regrouped, investing in flats in the same new building, some on the same floor. As if drawn by a powerful magnet, the Hammersmith professor also bought the small flat opposite her mother's. Her brother lived (and still lives) in her mother's flat. At least part of the old household structure has thus been recreated within a 'modern' multi-storey apartment block, although you would never grasp this if you did not know the dramatis personae, and just happened to be driving by.

Let's get one thing clear at this point. The new nuclear family was not based on love. These spatial reconfigurations of the household did not mean that pre-marital passion became socially acceptable. Outside a tiny bubble, love was, and still is, regarded as the greatest moral threat to *dharma* (duty), to honour (*izzat*), and to the order of things. Love before marriage brings shame upon both households and the lovers themselves. It is understood as lust: a vice. As one character puts it to his son in *Pakeezah* (the film that Meena Kumari was shooting when she encountered the dacoits in central India), his lover 'is not our daughter-in-law. She is your sin.'[72]

True love, in this moral world, grows and matures only *after* marriage, within the household. It is shaped, above all, by duty. It is only by parents choosing their son's bride that their authority over him remains intact: it is therefore essential that they arrange his marriage. If he 'loves' his wife-to-be *before* marriage, he will be torn between her and his parents. He will no longer be a reliable and obedient son. His mother's command over his wife (and her other daughters-in-law, *bahus*) will be diminished, and that will upset established hierarchies. The US anthropologist Gloria Raheja points to a common proverb in North India:

> Whoever kicks . . . his mother and father to strengthen his relationship
>   with his wife
> His sins will not go away even if he wanders through all the pilgrimage
>   places.[73]

Likewise, a daughter who chooses her own husband for 'love' faces excoriation, recapture from the clutches of her husband, and forcible remarriage.

In her debut novel of 1997, *The God of Small Things*, Arundhati Roy writes of 'Love Laws' that lay down rules about 'who should be loved, how and how much'. The list is long. One can break them in a host of ways – by transgressing prohibited degrees of kinship, by adultery, by crossing caste, class or religious boundaries, or by loving someone of the same sex or gender. All these forms of love meet severe social sanction, in some cases backed by the courts.

In 1923, the Indian Penal Code (Amendment) Act strengthened an act of 1860 so that any man found to have forced a woman under the age of eighteen with the intent of sexual intercourse could be put away for ten years in jail.[74] The woman herself faced no charges; the state assumed that the eloping girl had no agency of her own and was taken by force, or lured away. This denial of her sexuality and intelligence was convenient for any family that accepted back into its fold a victim and not a sinner,[75] because otherwise the family itself would face ostracism.[76]

Until it was repealed in 2018, Section 377 of the colonial-era penal code outlawed homosexual intercourse in India, and offenders were liable to ten years in jail. Homosexual men were often beaten when caught making love privately to another man. My late friend Siddhartha Gautam, who helped launch the movement against discrimination towards AIDS victims, was one of countless victims of police battering and public abuse. In his short life, lived with joyous intensity as he fought cancer, he educated many people, including me, about the challenges and politics of being gay in late-twentieth-century India.[77]

Siddhartha died in 1992. He was born in Calcutta (his parents still lived there when the cancer came back) but was not a Bengali-speaker. Being an anti-caste radical in his teens, he had dropped his 'caste' surname and adopted a new one: Gautam (one of the Buddha's names). Buddhism and anti-caste movements are closely related, as I had still to learn. Siddhartha was light years ahead of us, and there were some clever clogs in his tribe.

I last saw him alive when he came to take me home from hospital with newborn Kartik. (One reason Kartik got his name was because Kartikeya was Siddhartha's nom de plume.) A few weeks later, when the baby was six weeks old, I received that dreaded phone call before dawn. Siddhartha was dead. His was the first death to tear me apart. But his was the first life ever to inspire me.

I first met Siddhartha Gautam at Cambridge where I encountered so many brilliant South Asians. Our endless conversations bestowed on me quite a different pair of spectacles, through which I saw a different world. He transformed me, and many others, without being didactic. He had a whacky sense of humour (I still cry with laughter at his jokes) and a daredevil streak that could land all us groupies in trouble – we followed him though he made no attempt to lead us. ('We' are a crowd dispersed across continents.) As I write three decades later, his alma mater, Yale University, is honouring him posthumously for his courageous advocacy of gay rights and AIDS victims. But whether Yale knows just how much courage it took to be openly gay in India in the 1980s, to dress (when he felt like it) in drag, to have lovers outside his social class, to visit sex workers to educate them about HIV-AIDS, I don't know. I rather doubt it.

To this day, transgressors of Hindu caste rules prohibiting marriage with a certain degree of kinship continue to face the rough 'justice' of the 'community'. In 2007, as Chapter 3 shows, a *khap panchaayat* (a body of village elders) condemned Manoj and Babli to death because they had ignored the rules governing prohibited degrees of kinship.

Both were butchered. Research suggests that the trend has been on the rise since the 1980s.[78]

That's not to say that the Love Laws were never broken. Of course they were. Privacy surrounded such breaches, for the most part; only a few brave people faced down families and communities to follow their hearts. (Jawaharlal Nehru, notably, was not among them.)[79] Of the more famous examples from the early part of the century was Sarojini Chattopadhyay, the passionate Congresswoman and poet, friend and admirer of Jinnah who had helped engineer the Lucknow Pact in 1915 (discussed in Chapter 1). Sarojini was a Bengali woman, born in a *kulin* Brahmin household, and her father expected her to marry a 'suitable boy' with matching caste and regional antecedents. Sarojini would have none of it. She insisted on marrying Govindara-julu Naidu, a non-Brahmin of southern India, against the wishes of her conservative Bengali Brahmin father.

Ruttie Petit's decision to leave her Parsi millionaire father's home to marry Jinnah was another case that shocked Bombay, if not all of South Asia. Ruttie had coolth. Barely seventeen, she was already a 'society beauty' and heiress with glittering prospects. But she lost her heart to Jinnah. When she strolled out of her father's mansion to Jin-nah's flat on Malabar Hill, the barrister was forty-two years old. Their marriage caused an uproar. Her father was apoplectic. (He threatened legal action. Only the thought of facing a certain Muhammad Ali Jin-nah in court deterred him.)

These lovers broke rules of community, caste and inter-regional marriage. Ruttie also challenged expectations of the 'right' age difference between husband and wife.

Another woman who broke every rule of propriety was Amrita Sher-Gil (1913–41), the Indo-Hungarian artist often likened to Frida Kahlo. An opinionated, cosmopolitan, talented beauty, she told the truth as she saw it. (This was at a time when 'respectable' South Asian women were neither seen nor heard.) Like Kahlo, she travelled widely, living for stretches in Hungary, Turkey, Italy and France; but grew increasingly drawn to her Punjabi father's homeland, and to the world of simpler Indians whom she painted: villagers on their way to the market, simple preparations for a bride's toilette, a village scene. She denied a lesbian affair but had intense female friendships and declared herself open to the idea of a same-sex relationship.[80] Her most striking canvases depict women, including herself, often nude, in a range of moods and attitudes. She had an affair with her first cousin, whom she later married, breaking every taboo about degrees of kinship. He in turn performed a botched abortion upon her – we don't know why, but possibly the child was not his – which killed her. Like a shooting star on a dark night, she dazzled and died young. But, like Kahlo, she left a legacy that was more than her art; she provided a model of almost abrasive courage for South Asian women; a model of how one might break every social rule and, by sheer creative energy, get away with it.

Others spurned the limelight, seeking love secretly, without marriage. For the early part of the century, there are more hints and mysteries than there are open and shut cases. As noted earlier, whether or not Tukoji Rao of Dewas and Malcolm Lyall Darling ever consummated their love for each other we'll never know for sure, but a brief letter from Tukoji to Darling speaks of hours spent 'lying side by side' in carriages, on beds and railway berths, hinting that they might have done.[81] In her Urdu short story *Lihaaf* ('The Quilt'), Ismat Chughtai writes with great delicacy of lesbian relationships within the household that crossed boundaries between mistress and servant 'under the quilt'. (This led to her being tried for obscenity. She did not back down, and went on to win the case.) One only has to look at Ian Stephens' photographs taken in the late 1940s and 50s to sense his homoerotic attraction to beautiful brown young men. Perhaps this is one reason why Stephens, editor of the Calcutta daily *The Statesman*, stayed on in Pakistan after partition.

One might have thought that as the century progressed, it became easier for lovers in South Asia. Not so. Perveez Mody tells the story of Kamiyar, a young man from the city of Kanpur in North India. In the freezing winter of 1998, he climbed the microwave tower in the centre of New Delhi, close to the president's palace, Rashtrapati Bhavan. His demand was that the president help him to recover his wife Priya from her family. Kamiyar went on hunger strike, staying there in the freezing cold. In one of his letters to the president he wrote:

Dear Sir,

I would like to tell the reason for climbing this tower for the second time . . .

Me and Priya (my wife) were in love since 1993. Unlike in the cares of love we are the inspiration for survival for each other. She is respectable to me after my Mummy. She gave me reason to live. Anyway we married on the 4 Nov. 97 and I let her go to her paternal family and I tried my best to make reason our parents and family but failed. It was an effort which was a five years period ... When I saw nothing is going to happen I called finally PRIYA on 18 Nov 97 morning 8.00 and we went to Akbarpur to my uncle place.

The family of PRIYA came to know about our stay through someone and within 24 hours they make such terror on my family that they have handed over my marriage papers as well as my marriage photographs. They forcefully took my PRIYA my life away from me. They warned me not to take any legal action.[82]

The assembled crowd and journalists likened Kamiyar to one of the heroes of the dacoit western *Sholay*, in which 'Veeru' gets drunk, climbs to the top of a water tower and threatens to commit suicide unless he is allowed to marry the heroine. (More of this in Chapter 7.) As with 'Veeru' so with Kamiyar: love was understood to be a *nashaa* (intoxication) that had no place in marriage.[83] Despite their great love and Kamiyar's vertiginous hunger strike, Priya's parents married her off to someone else.

There are of course exceptions. Couples who have married for love can be found in the great metropolises, among the urban poor as well as the anglicised elites. The cities' most wretched parents have been known to welcome 'elopements' because of the relief they bring from wedding expenses and the dowry.[84] University professors, doctors, lawyers and journalists dwell in a social world of their own in which love is okay. But even here, in this space, crossing certain lines is shocking. My own first marriage to Prakash, a university lecturer of the same caste but from a poor family, shocked Delhi's liberal literati. My father (1921–2004) could hardly have been more broad-minded for an Indian man of his generation; but for two years he refused to speak to me to try and stop the inevitable, although the Coventry to which he banished me broke both our hearts. The sticking point in our case was class. Prakash is village-born and was the first person of his clan to go to university. I was from a landed family which for generations had produced doctors and lawyers, not to mention literate women since the early twentieth century. My determination to enter this 'love marriage' was too much for my father to swallow. (He reconciled himself to the situation in the end, but it took a while.)

Love across caste lines – particularly between 'touchable' and 'untouchable' castes – remains perilous in the extreme. 'Untouchables' who dare to love 'touchables' risk their lives, and they know it. The barbaric custodial killing of Ammu's *Paravan* Dalit lover, Velutha, in *The God of Small Things* rings true; the facts of South Asian life often being more brutal than fiction.

And as for crossing religious boundaries, it became more fraught as communal tension heightened. In the late 1920s, a Muslim man named Mahiuddin Ahmed fell in love with his neighbour, Sovana Ray, the daughter of a distinguished Hindu lawyer of Barisal in eastern Bengal. In 1929 the couple eloped, marrying under Muslim law after Sovana converted to Islam. The police pursued them for months as the lovers moved from town to town across India. They caught them in the end, arresting Mahiuddin and sending Sovana to a rescue home. The court found 'Mahi' (as Sovana fondly called him) guilty of rape, abduction and conspiracy.[85] Soon after partition, Narendranath Nabis, a Hindu from Assam, fell in love with Suraiyya Begum, a Muslim from Burdwan district. The Hindu newspapers hounded them.

In 2007, Rizwanur Rahman, a thirty-two-year-old Muslim man from a poor family fell in love with a young woman born into a wealthy Marwari Hindu household.[86] He had met Priyanka Todi at the graphics training school where he taught, and where students admired him for his teaching and kindliness. Both were adults. They married secretly under the Special Marriages Act. Priyanka moved to Rizwanur's paternal home in a working-class neighbourhood. Priyanka's family called in the police to force her to return to her parental home. She did this under duress. Soon afterwards, Rizwanur was found dead by the railway tracks.[87] The police claimed that he committed suicide. Others believe that he had died after being tortured in police custody.

Love, then, continues to be a dangerous business in South Asia.

There are exceptions, of course. Tribal groups such as the Sora did not obey the Love Laws for much of the century. Among them, live-in 'affairs' were permitted, and the language had no equivalent word for 'marriage'.[88] From the 1930s until the late 1960s, when the ethnographer-crusader Verrier Elwin studied Muria village 'dormitories' in the Bastar region of central India, he found that the majority promoted brief pre-marital flings. (Muria people believed that continuous relations with one partner were likely to lead to an undesirable pregnancy.) These sexual peccadillos were seen as a part of the 'fun and games' of growing up. That they broke all rules against endogamous marriage and intimacy – whether Hindu or Muslim – seems not to have concerned them.[89]

But things have not remained unchanged throughout the century. The story of Ankalu's 'errant' wife reveals that.[90] (Let's call her 'Anima' to remind ourselves that she was a person as well as a wife.)

Ankalu had come into money the hard way: through a terrible accident at work for which he got some compensation. It was only a small sum, but with it he bought a tiny field, built a small hutment, and had something left over for luxuries. He had already been married three times – each marriage ending a different way. His sons by an early wife were grown men by the 1990s, when he entered his fourth marriage. His new wife was the stunning Anima.

One night, a neighbour was caught scaling a wall near Anima's hut. Village gossips, and Ankalu's sons, were sure that she was having an affair with this man. They persuaded Ankalu to throw her out, which he did with some reluctance. The sons tried to get their father to marry again, pronto, to a better woman. They failed. Ankalu tried to woo Anima back. She moved back to the village.

What this life history makes plain is that the sons' values were different from their father's. They were becoming more aligned to the values of most South Asian men. Adivasi life-worlds have changed over time: they were never stuck in aspic. And with them, perspectives on marriage. And it's not only men who have changed. Remember Sushila from Chapter 4: the firecracker and wage-labourer. She now observes *Karva Chauth*: an 'upper-caste' penance whereby Hindu wives fast for the well-being of their husbands. (More on this in Chapter 6.) Hers is as extreme a case of realignment as one is likely to find over a single generation.

Returning to nuclear families, don't be deceived into thinking that those in South Asia are the same as those in the West. With the explosion of cities over the twentieth century, and the rise in the number of educated professionals working in them, new modes of living emerged. What Nikhil Rao evocatively describes as 'the house with no garden' (the small urban flat) is full of 'nuclear' families. Some estimate that South Asia's middle class has mushroomed to 350 million people over the century – the size of the subcontinent's entire population in 1901.

The flats they live in are just too small to accommodate more people than 'Mummy-Papa' and two or three children, and perhaps Papa's Mummy, *Dadiji*. ('Mummy-Papa' has become a ubiquitous urban term for parents, replacing older kinship terms such as *Ma, Baba, Abba, Ammi, Amma, Nana, Appa, Petrohal*.) But even in such small units, as Amitav Ghosh shows in *The Shadow Lines*, where the young protagonist lives with his parents and paternal grandmother, the notion of the household is expansive. It crosses borders, even continents.

Ghosh does not dwell on other figures who penetrate the middle-class domestic space he inhabits – domestic servants. Their changing worlds and households structures are crucial to understanding the twentieth century, however. As anthropologist Sara Dickey suggests, they signify what it is to be middle class: to shun manual labour, to pay others to do the housework that wives previously did, while always fearing the 'outsiders' who enter the most intimate spaces of the home.[91] Yet they too have had lives, hopes and fears. Attempting to grasp these is harder, but is essential to understanding the broad sweep of social history in the twentieth century.

IV

THE PEASANT-PROLETARIAT HOUSEHOLD AND ITS DECLINE

So much for the wealthy or middle classes, then. Throughout the twentieth century they formed only a tiny fraction of South Asia's population (albeit a growing one), but they changed the rhythms of the canticles of times past.

If we move our angle of vision to the countryside after independence we can still see the tall poppies. *Zamindaars* with thousands of acres became less prominent in the countryside in India, thanks to land reform, however patchy and imperfect. A delicate political matter left to provinces, each provincial landed elite resisted land reforms for the longest time in its own particular style. (Remember Chapter 3: revenue systems and estate structures varied across South Asia.) Various provincial governments tried to introduce curbs on how much land one householder could own, but these plans were leaked ahead of their enactment, because most of these elites were Congressmen themselves. So they had enough time to devise strategies of obfuscation – a central theme of Vikram Seth's *A Suitable Boy*.[92] Dominant castes and dominant households continue to wield disproportionate power unto this day. In Pakistan, there has been little successful land reform since 1947, and there are many famous landed families with well over a thousand acres.[93] Their power in politics has been significant, and their households have remained large.[94]

But it's important to remind the reader that by wealthy households I do not mean a cluster of connected people who jointly owned or controlled substantial resources. I mean a household dominated by a wealthy patriarch, whom all manner of people depended upon and obeyed: wives, concubines, children, younger siblings, aged, distant and poor relatives, retainers, live-in servants, slaves and other attendants. Using class as a lens to understand such groupings fails to capture their dynamics.

We might expect class to offer a more certain lever to prise open the worlds of the poorer people of South Asia who lived in the countryside, worked on the land and, as late as the 1970s, made up three quarters of the population. But here too, the story is more complicated. Not everyone was equally poor, or poor in the same ways. These conundrums are my focus here.

Women entering poor rural households as brides are no Subbammas. They bring very little with them when, as do most wives in South Asia, they move to their husband's house after marriage. The young bride's father might well have been a poor man, made poorer still by the cost of the wedding, the dowry expected of him when he gave his daughter in marriage, and by the debt incurred in so doing. The bride's father-in-law would likely have been a poor man too, a subsistence tenant cultivator perhaps, or a share-cropper, or even a landless labourer mired in debt.

(There are, as with everything in South Asia, notable exceptions to the rule of patrilocality – that is, migration to the husband's village after marriage. Some castes of the Tamil- and Kannada-speaking regions in the southern peninsula, and certain groups in north Pakistan, practised cross-cousin marriage; but given its relative rarity I will not discuss it here.)[95]

But within these struggling rural households, just as in their wealthy counterparts, there were hierarchies and rules of difference. Men were far more likely to possess titles to land than women, and to control its use.[96] Women's dependence upon men rendered their class status 'tangential, vicarious and temporary'.[97] Rural brides were made vulnerable by being wrenched out of their natal homes and sent to live some distance away among strangers. A woman's status in a poor man's house was even more precarious than his, and subject to sudden change. Widowhood and barrenness left her at risk of being driven out of the household altogether. Wives whose husbands belonged to relatively large landed households could shift some of the childcare and domestic chores onto female servants or slaves, but they still had to tolerate domestic violence and bear the full weight of reproduction.[98] (As we have seen in Mangayamma's story, barrenness – assumed or otherwise – could lead to sudden exile.)

In rural South Asia, moreover, women remained much poorer in absolute terms than men and boys. Women routinely ate less than their fair share of the small evening meal. This self-denial was extolled as virtuous womanly sacrifice; thus it became an ideal that mothers handed down to their daughters to emulate. In 1990, one scholar concluded that discrimination in food allocation was greater in the north of the subcontinent than the south, but that throughout it was 'least fair' for very young and very old females, as well as those in greater need of food on account of pregnancy and breastfeeding.[99] In extreme cases, families neglected, and even starved, girl children to death. In the North-Western Provinces, divided between India and Pakistan in 1947, female infanticide was common, and mothers or wet-nurses, *dais*, were known to poison baby girls or leave them to starve. In the 'bandit queen' Phoolan Devi's household, her mother bemoaned the fact that she had borne four daughters and only one son. The boy ate well; the girls ate scraps. The mother refused to breastfeed Phoolan's youngest sister, so the older girls fed her using a cloth dipped in rice water.[100]

The adverse ratio of women to men has persisted across the century throughout the subcontinent. New ultrasound technologies have given wealthy parents the power to determine sex before birth, and pay doctors to abort female foetuses. In 1991, when I was pregnant with Kartik, then a tiny boy-foetus, the clinician who tested me beamed '*Mubaarak ho!*' ('Congratulations!') even though I did not want to know, and had chosen that clinic because it announced that it did not reveal the sex of the child before birth.

In 1992, Bangladesh, India and Pakistan still had shocking

female-to-male sex ratios (94, 93 and 92 females per 100 males respectively).[101] By contrast, between 1990 and 1995, sex ratios in South America and Western Africa were 105 females per 100 males.[102]

Rural wives felt the sharp edge of agrarian decline throughout the twentieth century. It was women who laboured more and more in the fields, hefting the work of absent migrant men onto their thin brown shoulders. But they also had to keep doing all their traditional tasks – threshing grain, collecting firewood and fodder, carrying home pitchers of water from rivers, tanks or springs, making dung cakes, cleaning and decorating their huts, repairing mud floors, spinning yarn, and growing a few vegetables and spices. They also cooked, washed clothes and utensils, bore children, and tended to them and to the elderly.

From a very young age, girls contributed to the domestic economy by foraging for food. A recent study suggests that they were indulged by parents who knew what the future held for them and how hard they would work after marriage.[103] Others indicate, by contrast, that by the age of seven or eight, play for girls became a thing of the past. They helped their mother with domestic chores, learned to cook and looked after their younger siblings. Their mobility was increasingly restricted as they adapted to their role as a 'proper woman' and future wife.[104] As dicussed in Chapter 4, in the Bangladeshi village of Char Gopalpur, for instance, 'young girls spent most of their childhood learning work roles, skills, and tasks that constitute the women's share of the division of labour. The process [was] largely one of learning by doing . . .'[105] Girls were given some schooling, but this largely consisted of learning how to read the Quran and write.[106]

After the onset of puberty, girls were subject to 'strict sexual segregation, close supervision and physical seclusion from the world outside'.[107] Most adolescent girls stopped going to school altogether.[108] The mean age at marriage for rural girls in Bangladesh in 1976, almost fifty years after the Sarda Act, remained 13.5 years.[109] (The marriage of even younger children remained common throughout rural South Asia, although often the girl and boy lived with their parents until her clansmen deemed the girl old enough to be sent away.) Law remained a papery thing, however hard the fight had been to change it.

Young men, by contrast, were expected to stay in the villages in which they were born and to uphold the norms and status of their paternal families. In their childhood, they roamed the village and pastures, playing games. They had a few tasks too, but they were not onerous – like taking an animal, if the household could afford one, to graze. As adolescents and young adults, they visited the local market town to go to the cinema, shop or attend political meetings.[110]

In the Bengal region, as in much of the subcontinent, young men typically married much later in life than girls, usually in their mid-twenties.[111] In her fascinating autobiography, Baby Haldar describes her marriage at the age of thirteen to a taciturn man in his late twenties. Days after she came to live in his house – a one-room shack – he raped her. In a state of shock and trauma, she ran home to her father but he persuaded her to return to her husband. When she became pregnant with her second child, the husband beat her so violently with a hunk of wood that she miscarried.[112] He was not drunk at the time. Class cannot capture these brutalities, nor can poverty and country liquor account for them.

As I've mentioned, I had an exposure to village life in the early 1990s. When my son Kartik was about six months old, his father and I thought it would be nice to take him back to 'Leemli', the paternal village household. And so we set off, baby in tow. It was an endless journey along winding mountain roads – buttocks bumping on hard seats; carsick passengers vomiting out of windows as the driver hurtled round hairpin bends. The child wailed, needing food and a change. All of us needed sleep.

So the village, when we got to it in the end, seemed like heaven. Four thousand feet high in the northern Himalayas, it nestled against the forested mountainside. Dozens of tangerine trees added splashes of orange that mirrored the deep pinks and crimsons of the enveloping dusk. Across a deep gorge and river lay Nepal. At dawn, mist rose from the river and rolled over the mountains.

The village itself was tiny: a terraced row of stone cottages with sloping slate roofs. Each hut was the hearth and home of a male descendant of the same bloodline; and the *padhaan* (headman) was its ultimate authority. Each had a carved wooden threshold on the 'first floor', accessed by a few rough steps. Each mud-floored unit backed into the mountainside and consisted of two small rooms. One, relatively bright and airy, was for sleeping; it faced the front of the house. All members of the family rolled out mats at night and slept in a row in this room. The other room, windowless and chimneyless, backed onto the mountainside. It was for cooking on a clay *chulah* (wood-fuelled stove), and was dark, airless and smoky. This room also served as the store, housing the battered tin trunk in which the family kept its few valuables and winter quilts.

Under these rooms were mangers in which cows slept at night, safe from leopards and tigers. (Like Chamoli in Chapter 3, Leemli was in a part of the Himalayas where big cats lived and hunted.) Prakash's cousin, master at the primary school, lived apart in a *pucca* brick-built house with a separate bathroom (no flush, just a cesspit, much envied nonetheless). The others used the high meadows to attend to the needs of nature in the open, the women rising together at dawn long before the men, staying close together to avoid attack from a leopard, tiger or black bear as they bathed, modestly washing and drying their only 'everyday' saris, teeth chattering in the cool morning breeze, without taking them off.

The women grew turmeric, ginger, garlic and chillies, as well as lentils and seasonal vegetables in tiny patches close to their cottages. The fields, terraced against the monsoon rains, yielded a nutty pink short-grained rice. A tiny shop sold cheap blue washing soap, tooth powder, stale dry rusks, and white crystalline sugar in glass bottles around which lazy flies hovered. Dust had settled on ancient bottles of Coca-Cola. The men liked to boast that the village was self-sufficient in everything but salt, which it bought every few months from a 'Bhutia' trader from Nepal.

Except that it wasn't. As the days passed, I noticed things about the village that had so charmed me at first. It was denuded of men of working age. The *padhaan* was an exception to this rule, as was the schoolteacher, who had clambered into white-collar status when, after independence, primary education finally reached the region. So the village depended on money orders from the cities, which were never large or frequent enough. The emigration of the poorest rural men in search of work in the 'modern' sectors of the economy often exacerbated rather than relieved the agrarian crisis of subsistence. The dividends of migration from the woman's point of view, for the rural end of the household, proved smaller than expected – this was true of most villages, not this one alone. Working men in the cities often had a few crumpled, sweaty, rupee notes (first introduced in 1940) to send home after months of work. This was because employers paid them a wage sufficient only to support a single body: the jute and cotton mill owners were counting on the village to subsidise the urban worker, rather than the other way round. As shown in Chapter 4, demographic changes had meant that there was always an overabundance of labour in supply. So there was no fat in the urban labourer's wage packet. Even if he scrimped and saved – and often he did not: he drank, whored, gadded about with friends and developed a *beedee* habit[113] – the numbers didn't add up.[114] Whereas women tended to live on the lean and spend all their earnings on the whole family's subsistence, men spent a significant proportion on their personal needs. The evidence from all corners of the subcontinent shows the same pattern.[115]

These working men returned home rarely. In 'British times', of which he rather approved, my father-in-law had served in the British Army in Burma. He returned to the village only every two or three years, siring a baby each time. He was not unusual in this respect. As late at the 1970s, when Mead Cain did his ground-breaking research in Bangladesh, male migrants would leave home in their late teens and, barring attending marriages and the odd death, returned to the village only in their late twenties for their own weddings. Most would then head off to the city again. Semi-detached wedlock was part of the marital architecture in the countryside.

Leemli also depended on other settlements close by for the supply of services – particularly those that involved dirty, 'polluting' work. A village of poor Brahmins, it relied on the services of barbers, smiths, agricultural labourers, drummers and priests even poorer than themselves and lower down the purity index. These groups lived apart, but close by, and served the village in return for cash or grain. I never saw them but heard much about them, particularly the so-called 'Doms' who played 'polluting' leather drums at festivals.

There has been much debate about whether there ever was a 'traditional *jajmaani* system' that tied landed people of 'high caste' to 'lower-caste' menials, giving the latter a share of 'the grain heap' in return for particular services.[116] Anthropologists argue that it is a fiction,[117] but something like it seemed to be still in practice in remote regions in the 1990s (a theme for Chapter 6).[118]

Leemli also relied on distant villages to supply its young men with brides, and sent its own girls to good homes of another *gotra* (clan). Matches were made not so much by comparing genealogies, but by gathering information about girls of the right caste and lineage, and about the 'character' of the girls' mothers. If the mother was 'good' – that is, hard-working, modest, dutiful and pious – her daughter would probably make a good *bahu*. If she was fair-skinned, that was a bonus. (By this stage, in the cities, traditional genealogists had long been redundant, matrimonial columns having taken their place.)[119] In villages too, they seem to have been replaced by other forms of local knowledge.

After the wedding was done and dusted, these young wives took up the lion's share of the work in households in which their absent migrant husbands held a proprietary interest. So I observed the conundrum of families that could not be pigeon-holed by class – one part of it laboured in the city while the other worked on the land.[120]

The women's frail in-laws kept a critical (and, it seemed to me, harsh) eye on them. Occasionally they would sneak off with me – I was, like them, a daughter-in-law of the village – and giggle as they told me funny stories about the elders, even about the *padhaan*, the alarming head of the village. True enough, as Raheja and Gold found in their fieldwork in Uttar Pradesh and Rajasthan, the women's ribald humour sometimes challenged the structures of authority that governed them. They were frank about matters that I, with my urban, westernised, ways, was shy to speak about.[121] They grilled me about how I managed my periods, and whether or not I enjoyed sex, and shrieked with laughter at my discomfiture.

Yet I can't romanticise their lives. I soon discovered how impoverished their worlds were – and how hard they found it to imagine different ones. Their stories began to stifle me as it became clear that once out in the open, back in the claustrophobic space in front of the male elders, they kept their heads down and followed the rules. The cows received more affection than they did. Patted, cossetted and fed with love, her cow was my mother-in-law's pride and joy. She churned its milk into butter and ghee, which she served on rotis first to men and then to boys. Its urine was 'known' to disinfect wounds. Strong in personality, my mother-in-law was in her seventies when I met her, but age had not withered, nor custom staled, the mobile eloquence of her face. Despite her tattered sari and her thin grey plait (tied, incongruously, with a child's red ribbon), she was beautiful. But she had suffered a terrible neck injury when, as a much younger woman, she had fallen out of a tree while cutting dead branches for firewood, and she had a conspicuous tremor. She too had been a *bahu* of the village and had suffered for it. Yet she played by its rules and accepted, indeed perpetuated, its values.

The young women's husbands, when they returned to the village, beat them, sometimes to the point of unconsciousness. The children hated their distant, unfamiliar fathers, for the violence they were unable to prevent. They worshipped their mothers for forgiving these men, and for continuing to serve them all their lives. Seeing this close up, I began to get some idea of the source of the intense connection between South Asian sons and their mothers. Guilt and shame at having failed to protect their mothers from violence has produced an anxious masculinity, eased only by placing mothers on a pedestal as symbols of self-sacrifice. Many men then go on to expect the same qualities of their wives, and so the cycle continues. Or perhaps this is just cod psychology. Either way, the levels of domestic violence have to be seen to be believed.

Why did these women – so strong and brave in other ways – put up with the status quo? I heard stories in Leemli that gave me a hint as to why. Not only did law and society give them no land of their own to fall back upon, not only was it impossible for them (as it was for Baby Haldar) to return to a poor father's house, but they had seen worse things happen to their co-*bahus*.[122] After 1950, the *padhaan* and male elders cast out a *bahu* of the village when she became pregnant too long after (or so they calculated) her migrant husband had left for the plains. Unable to return to her paternal home, for months she lived in a cave in the mountainside, subsisting on wild fruit, berries and spring water. She was somehow accepted back – starving, her sari torn into rags, her matted hair full of briars. Some years later, another *bahu* defied the male elders. They locked her in a casket in which threshed grain was stored before milling. She would have died if the other women hadn't begged for her release.

But she was still in the village when I arrived as a new daughter-in-law. She had nowhere else to go.

V

THE RUPTURE OF FAMILY TIES

Among poorer rural families, then, returning home to paternal families was seldom an option if their husband's household rejected them. Marriage for them was a sharper tear in the web of ties with the natal village. When driven out or abandoned by the husband's village for one reason or other, many women had little option but to drift towards the cities in the hope of finding work.

In Bengal for instance, in the 1920s and 30s, census officials began to observe a new trend, of single women headed towards Calcutta. As Samita Sen puts it, these women became South Asia's first true proletariat, because they did not, and could not, circulate between village and city, as men did.[123]

The census officers assumed that while these female migrants hoped for jobs as factory workers or domestic servants, most would end up as sex workers. They were not always wrong. By the mid-1920s and early 30s, factory Acts had made it more complicated for employers to take on women, with health and safety standing in the way of women's work in the formal sector (the tea plantations being the one major exception to the rule).

Instead they were driven into the informal sector, where they began to establish novel modes of life. Evidence suggests that they drifted to working-class tenements, where (like Philomena in Chapter 4) they worked as cooks in the workers' kitchens, and also as sex workers, while sometimes establishing liaisons with men who afforded them some protection, in yet another form of household that began to spring up in mill neighbourhoods and slums. These were less hidebound relationships than marriage. They were less permanent and gave women greater autonomy. Given that there were few women in a largely male environment, they had some scope to make their own sexual choices and decide how they spent the money they earned. This is not to say they were liberated or empowered: male pimps often enticed them into brothels and beat them brutally to surrender their earnings. But here too, there were great variations: Shohini Ghosh's 2002 documentary *Raatparider Katha* ('Tales of the Night Fairies') shows that Calcutta's 'night fairies' had carved out some space in which they had intimate friendships among themselves, took lovers, brought up their children and backed each other up. More of this below.

As the century progressed to a close, however, a novel trend emerged. Rural nuclear families began to migrate *as a whole* to the cities: wives, husbands and children together. Partition, which pitchforked whole families across new borders, had done this in 1947 and its violent aftermath. Now something new was afoot, albeit with the same outcome: the poorest peasants began to lose whatever little stake they had in the land, and poverty drove them to the cities. By the 1990s, more than one third of all Indians lived below the poverty line (which in 1998 was pegged at Rs 88 per person per month).[124] The agrarian sector bore the brunt of the liberalising policies that came into play in India in the late 1980s and 90s (and in Pakistan at much the same time). This dismantled – quite fast, and under World Bank pressure – the complex structure of subsidies that the state gave the poor, urban and rural, while constraining the free play of the market. The loss of this protection was the end of an era in India, which was marked by the policies of a Cambridge-trained economist and finance minister, Manmohan Singh, in the early 1990s. With these policies in place, which no government since has tried to roll back, autarky ground to a halt and India was hurled into the global race with no trainers and no training.[125]

What this meant for the rural poor was that the game was over. They could no longer survive on the land, however much it meant to them. They left (as families) for the cities, never to return.

In Bangladesh, meanwhile, constant migration from the countryside to towns, at a rate of more than three per cent a year between 1975 and 2009, propelled the country to having one of the highest rates of urbanisation in the world.[126] In all three countries of the subcontinent, the most vulnerable agriculturists in the countryside felt the unforgiving consequences of globalisation. They got up and left the land for ever.

These destitute small families found a foothold for themselves either on the outskirts of cities, where they squatted without state sanction, or in long-established *bastis* in the cities. Both wives and husbands looked for work. One fascinating feature of this fin-de-siècle era is that the wives found it more easily. Some found work on construction sites, which were numerous as cities expanded sideways and upwards. Husband and wife sometimes worked for the same contractor, though in different roles; but these jobs were not easy to find, as established ties with contractors and tradesmen determined who was hired. Often to hold down a job with a contractor, the wife had to offer him her body. The lines between women's labour in 'respectable' professions and sex work were thus never neatly drawn.[127]

But the most defining feature of this era was the explosion in the size of the middle class. Most lived in nuclear households, in which having a domestic servant had itself become a marker of upper- or middle-class status, defining who was respectable and who was not.[128] Status-markers had transmogrified over the century. Once upon a time women in better-off households shunned work in the fields; now they would not do the rougher kinds of domestic work. As a result there were millions of jobs as domestic servants to be had, and these impoverished migrant women – who knew only too well how to cook, swab floors, clean dishes, scrub clothes and look after children and the elderly – had the required skill set.

Of course, because these were womanly domestic skills – skills 'of little value' – employers paid them a pittance. Shockingly, when scholars studied domestic workers in Calcutta in the early 2000s, they found that middle-class couples paid these women (who usually worked part time in two or more households, returning home between jobs to feed their own children) roughly Rs 200 a month. Because her employers depended on servants so much, the domestic worker could find regular and often secure employment; but it was so low paid that it was barely enough to feed two people.

Why were domestic servants so much in demand? Two reasons, really. Upper- and middle-class women had begun to go out to work and, given unchanged notions of domesticity, could not leave home if they did not hand over 'their' jobs to a servant. A single day's absence of a domestic servant could create havoc in such a household, upsetting carefully planned schedules.[129] This gave the employee a measure of bargaining power (though not much, given the glut in the market).

But there was another side to it as well: even if the middle-class woman did not work herself, merely to have servants gave status to a household. In Madurai in southern India, where one scholar did fieldwork among employers, she found them to be uneasy about letting 'outsiders' into their homes, bringing dirt in and taking gossip and secrets out.[130] For all that scholars argue that feudal 'cultures of servitude' have persisted among families that keep on generations of retainers, among middle-class households that never previously had domestic servants, attitudes towards them seem to be watchful and uneasy rather than 'feudal'.[131]

What was in it for the domestic workers themselves? Few large studies exist, but those that do suggest that the very regularity of this kind of employment made it something to which poor women gravitated, given that their husbands' earnings were so erratic.[132] The men from the villages found it tough to find work in the city. Most ended up in irregular jobs as house painters, day labourers (doing unskilled poorly paid work on construction sites) or rickshaw pullers, and they were as often out of work as they were employed. So the wife's regular earnings brought stability to these poorest of urban households. The irony is that these poor working women depended on this stability so much that they did not bargain for wage increments.

There are also other factors in play. Domestic work is, by definition, intimate work. Maidservants and mistresses built up relationships of 'pragmatic intimacy'. By washing their employers' clothes, making their beds and sweeping their floors, maidservants knew a great deal about their private lives. They bathed, changed and carried the babies of their 'madam' or '*didi*'. Maidservants spoke of 'love' and 'trust' as emotions that undergirded the more contractual aspects of their relationship, and were particularly affected by gestures of trust such as being handed a set of keys to the flat or access when no one else was in the house (which was rare). This gave them a sense of worth: 'Are we not human, after all?' being a common refrain in a hundred voices.

In more practical ways, these long-term relationships helped domestic workers by giving them access to credit to tide them over bad times. Few employers charged interest; they docked an agreed sum off each month's wages. Given the extortionate interest rates that prevailed in the informal market for credit, this was a perk of huge significance.

Some employers gave maidservants leftover food to take home and share with their children. (This led to a cut in her wage package but, with inflation, this payment in kind sometimes worked in the maid's favour.) Generous employers even paid medical bills. Women employers often gave their servants faded or torn old saris and *shalwaar kameezes* they had become too plump to wear. (The sedentary quality of an average rich woman's day, whether she worked or not, combined with her role as baby-producer – she needed that son, remember? – piled the kilos on.) Employers also gave maids cash bonuses, and sometimes new clothes, during high ritual days of the year. Puja, Eid, Diwali, Christmas (*Bada Din*): depending on the employer's faith, there was an expectation that once a year, one of these days would be 'bonus day'.

These working women hoped that their children would not grow up to be domestic servants, and they spent what they could on their education. They had aspirations for the future of the next generation. One of them, Sipra Sarkar, put it across in simple but powerful words: 'We are struggling so hard so that we can educate them. We are blind despite possessing eyes. We are struggling so hard so that they can see . . .'[133] But Sen and Sengupta suggest that their dreams were often dashed. Their children dropped out of school early, either because it was difficult to keep up with its intellectual demands, or because they didn't fit in.

So in metropolitan South Asia, it is important to look at the face of the domestic worker in the house. There is bound to be one. You will notice her lowered eyes ('I see no evil'), observe her faded sari or *shalwaar kameez*, her jutting collarbones. She is often skin, bone, muscle and tendon. Although she looks older than her years, she has achieved the fashionable body of the West through constant work and privation. (Male employers take advantage of that body where they can. 'They lie in wait like snakes watching a frog.')[134] Sometimes she may smile and chatter; at other times retreat into herself.

And should you ever drive past slums and railway lines, as I have done, and see bedraggled little children running around with not a single adult in sight, their bellies distended with hunger, their hair an unnatural shade of ochre, you might wonder where their parents are.

They are abandoned while their own mother looks after other women's homes and children.

Some of them are old enough to play, laugh and giggle among themselves. It is not as if they are unloved. But I doubt that many will grow up to be Slumdog Millionaires.

The savage juxtaposition of wealth and poverty in urban South Asia is usually described in terms of the contrast between gleaming sky-scrapers and stinking slums, flyovers and limbless beggars at the traffic lights. I suggest that we understand it in more human and intimate terms. That juxtaposition takes place every day, within 'decent' homes and households. The life of the female domestic worker, her attempt to juggle her burdens in her own tiny home (where she still does all the domestic work) and at her employer's home; her impossibly low wage and her family's needs and aspirations; and the texture of her relationship with her 'madam' or *didi*, not to mention her own husband and her *didi*'s husband, and her struggle to do her best for her children, encapsulates it. She represents the quiet underbelly of South Asia's late-twentieth-century 'neo-liberalism'.

VI

HOUSEHOLDS ON THE MARGINS

In 1981, in Behmai in Uttar Pradesh, the woman dacoit Phoolan Devi shot dead twenty-two men. She killed in cold blood, for revenge. The dead men had been members of a rival gang of a 'higher caste'. They had raped her again and again over several days and then had paraded her brutalised and naked body through the village. This gruesome act of gang rape created few ripples, but the Behmai murders did. In response to the uproar, the state's chief minister, Vishwanath Pratap Singh, resigned. The police offered grand sums to anyone who could deliver Phoolan to them, dead or alive.

Phoolan Devi was born to a poor family in a village on the banks of the river Yamuna. They were of the 'low' Mullah caste of boatmen; within her own village, her household was at the bottom of the heap, her father having lost his money in a court case over land, her mother struggling to feed four daughters and one son. Phoolan became a dacoit when she was eighteen. The circumstances that led to this are controversial – my account is based on her autobiography. At the age of eleven (so much for the Sarda Act), her parents married her off to a vile man in his forties who raped her, a mere child, using a knife to 'open her up'. (The details of her marital rape are chillingly reminiscent of Phulmonee's infamous rape unto death by her much older husband in 1889. Phoolan, Phulmonee.)[135]

Several times Phoolan returned home to her father, only to be persuaded to go back to her husband Putti Lal. But each time she left again, repelled by his violent sexual demands. Eventually Putti Lal threw her out. Phoolan's respect for authority in general, and men in particular, dissolved to vanishing point.

Small, skinny and raven-haired, she grew ever more rebellious and foul-mouthed: an embarrassment to the powerful families in her home village. In her autobiography, Phoolan suggests that her own cousin arranged for her to be kidnapped by a dacoit, Vickram Mullah, of the same caste.[136] In an ironic twist, he protected her from the sexual demands of other gang members, particularly of the 'upper-caste' men who wanted her. Later, he became her lover, his tenderness gradually breaching the wall of her hatred and fear of men. After Vickram's death, she established her own small gang, and later 'married' Umed Singh, her 'lieutenant'. He was by her side when she surrendered in 1983. He was 'tall and bearded with long and wavy hair that tumbled to his shoulders. Deep lines ran across his heavy brow; he had the penetrating gaze . . . of an eagle.'[137] Later she would describe him as 'my lieutenant, my friend, my brother'.[138] For me, this was one of the most interesting lines in the book, suggesting as it does all manner of inversions of traditional relationships between men and women. She was the boss. She chose to take her 'brother' as a lover. For her, love and sexual fulfilment meant 'friendship'.

In 1994, a new state government led by a new party released Phoolan from jail, and offered her a ticket to stand for election. She won the seat. She was a sitting member of Parliament when, in 2001, a gang of Rajput youths shot her dead to avenge the Behmai killings.

Phoolan lived an extraordinary life, by any standards. But I tell her story here because her gang of bandits was a marginal household of a very particular kind. Hers and those of other 'outliers' seem to me to throw aspects of the South Asian mainstream into sharper, and starker, relief.

Dacoit gangs were households in the sense that they had leaders who made every decision and brooked no dissent. They shared the proceeds of their plunder as the leader dictated – hence they were an economic unit not unlike a Hindu Undivided Family. And they watched each other's backs: they protected each other from the police and other rivals. They cooked and ate together. (Sometimes friendly villages fed and sheltered them, but never for long.) They had internal hierarchies which could lead to schism, faction and even murder – but then we have seen instances of this in conventional households too, most recently in the royal household of Nepal, mentioned at the start of this chapter. Succession often led to crisis, but that too is familiar in South Asian (and other) contexts. Lieutenants fought it out, and unless one was killed, they often split into two gangs. Again this is not unfamiliar. *Alag ho jaanaa* (separating) or *jaidaad ke maamle main kasheedgi* (tensions over property) are everyday expressions used across independent North India and Pakistan when brothers fall out and, with much rancour, divide the paternal legacy among themselves.

But of course, dacoit 'households' are different too, and examining these distinctions is a helpful way of understanding the conventional social worlds.

Usually dacoit gangs are all male, Phoolan's gang being an exception. That's not to say that they rejected gender norms – far from it: most dacoits seemed constantly to be trying to prove their machismo, their fearlessness. But there *was* a great deal more flux in their composition than a common-or-garden household with its patriarch. Gangs changed their composition far more often than mainstream households as men died or deserted, and had to get new recruits from a small pool. 'Recruitment' in typical households happened through marriage and was dictated by strict norms; in gangs, it was rather more haphazard. Conventional endogamous marriage, then, stands out as a pillar on which the mainstream household rests, women doing the job of reproduction across the generations.

In gangs there was no natural reproduction to keep them going. They survived by recruiting other male refugees from society. By definition, they were shorter-lived. Ancestry and genealogy, and all that goes with their fraught claims, have no place in the mythology of gangs.

Dacoits could also abandon their gang more easily, disappearing from one day to the next. Phoolan's autobiography is replete with stories of gang members running away (and perhaps joining other gangs), and of new members being absorbed in their stead. The size of her own gang fluctuated between about twenty at its largest and four at its smallest. Households show no comparable trend. They too fluctuate in size, but not on this scale or frequency. Even in their shrunken form, they are multigenerational units.

Another difference was that gangs were constantly on the move. They travelled by night through forests and slept, when they could, during the day. Sometimes, like big cats, they napped in the branches of trees. They had no fixed address, or even territory of operation – so when things became too hot for Phoolan's gang in UP, she crossed the border to Madhya Pradesh. The fact that they had no fixed property, no roof over their heads, marks them off so sharply from the mainstream that one must conclude that property and its control lie at the heart of conventional households. Women's lack of control over property takes on a different import: their powerlessness in that context is rendered sharper by the contrast.

This contrast also makes one ponder more deeply on the spatial structures of the mainstream world of households. Compound walls, halls, kitchens, prayer niches, bathrooms, verandahs, *zenanas*, back rooms, front rooms, bedrooms, wells and cowsheds, for instance, and how they are situated in relation to each other, are all rich with meaning.[139] This becomes clear as daylight when we compare them with groups who live in the open air, for whom there are only two kinds of space: safe space and dangerous space.

Also, there's the multi-caste, multi-community nature of gangs. Vickram Mullah's gang had 'high' and 'low' castes, Thakurs and Mullahs in the main. They appear to have stored cash with a pious Muslim, although this part of the story is more ambiguous. For obvious reasons, they could not use banks.

Gang leaders had close ties with famous spiritual figures, but these men (and sometimes women, *maataas*) were both Muslim and Hindu, of 'high' or 'low' caste. In this sense too they were rather more fluid than your average household. They often gave a large share (up to a third) of their takings to the holy men and women, and this lent them a certain charisma. (South Asians are often rather prone to extreme devotion: think back to Cajetano's transformation from small-time thug to quasi-saint.) The fact that Phoolan was elected to Parliament says something about their influence.

And they gave much to the poor. They gave much more of their loot than the alms that pious Muslims typically donated to the poor, or at the shrines of saints, or the sums that Hindus donated to temples. Especially Phoolan, who handed out rolls of rupees (she could neither read nor count) to the poor in towns and villages. She loathed the rich with every fibre of her being; and remembering the hardships her own marriage had imposed on her family, she and Vickram would often donate money quite randomly to poor people they came across. Sometimes they would pay a bride's dowry in an unknown village. On one occasion Phoolan performed the *kanyadaan* ritual instead of a bride's father, and gave presents to the groom.[140]

All were refugees from rural society yet they continued to have a close relationship with it, and with their paternal villages in particular. Thus Vickram and Phoolan, now dressed in stolen police uniforms and armed with rifles, returned every now and again to see their parents and give them some cash. But it was, of course, out of the question to return to the village for good.

One could therefore argue that they were Hobsbawm's 'social bandits' in their relationship to wider rural society. Even if, like Robin Hood, they robbed Peter to pay Paul, they did so without challenging, or trying to overturn, more fundamental inequalities of the social order from which they had escaped. (Here Phoolan, such a natural feminist in so many ways, by giving a dowry and performing the *kanyadaan*, supports Eric Hobsbawm's celebrated argument about the inherent conservatism of social banditry.)[141] Hunger for money drove others to the badlands. Some were blinded by bloodlust – they wanted vengeance in personal vendettas. But either way, they destabilised agrarian society by their predations; they threatened its fabric of rural order. They hovered in the background as an instrument of rough justice where the state and its courts failed, or never even tried to intervene.

The brothel, I suggest, was another quasi-household at the margins. Much has been written about the gradual decline under British rule in the status of courtesans (*tawaifs*) – celebrated singers, dancers and entertainers, who had offered sexual services only to a small elite – and *devadaasis* (girls dedicated to temples) to the position of 'common prostitutes'.[142] It is a remarkable story. The old courtesan households had attracted aristocratic connoisseurs of beauty, dance, poetry and song; and *tawaifs* had taught young men etiquette and courtly ways. By the twentieth century, few aristocratic patrons survived, and many *kothas* of old became brothels, having lost much of their considerable wealth after the Mutiny. The colonial state's position was that the 'common Indian prostitute' was a member of a 'hereditary caste'.[143] This was a load of nonsense dressed up as ethnography. Most brothel workers were refugees from hellish existences in ordinary 'conventional' households, and they came from all castes and creeds. (More of this in Chapter 7.)

From the standpoint of the Raj and the East India Company before it, the brothel was a necessary evil.[144] Necessary because the colonial white troops, men of the lower orders too 'base' to control their sexual urges, had to be given access to these fallen women, or else they might fall prey to even more dangerous vices: habits of sodomy and same-sex liaisons, which would make them (allegedly) unfit to serve.[145]

The state's goal was to cut down and control venereal disease which had become rife among white troops. Segregation and treatment of prostitutes under lock and key was for long the favoured solution, even though it was inefficacious and expensive; it went in and out of fashion. Prostitutes believed to be diseased were captured, examined, locked up and treated by force in 'lock hospitals', mercury being forced into their genitals under the cold eyes of a disapproving 'matron'. They were only let out when cured. The state's concern, at every point, was for the health of the soldier, rather than of the Indian prostitute. It is not a pretty part of colonial history.[146]

The gruesome details of Akootai's death in a brothel in 1917 brought home to me the awful similarity of her circumstances with those of her sisters confined in lock hospitals. It also occurred to me that brothels were both like conventional households and yet unlike them: that tension pointed to an intriguing history of 'the normal'.

Akootai lived, worked and died in a brothel in the Duncan Road area of Kamathipura.[147] This was Bombay's 'red-light district', so described because of the enticement that such areas represented for red-coated British Tommies.[148] (The term 'red-light district' has stuck, long after 'our boys' packed their bags and went home.)

To return to Akootai: this young woman had, in all likelihood, been trafficked to the brothel run by Syed Khan Mirza, his 'wife' Gomtibai, and Gangabai, their 'daughter'. She seemed to be under pressure to work off her 'cost' to her purchasers. A few days before her death, Akootai developed excruciating venereal disease and began to refuse customers. Gomtibai and Gangabai, her keepers, forced 'caustic' into her genitals to try to cure her. They may well have learned these treatments, and other methods of incarceration, as inmates of lock hospitals themselves. Who knows. The files are silent.

Her story is hard to bear, but I must tell it. Four young women worked in the brothel alongside Akootai: Phooli, Moti, Paru and Jajibhai. They took customers in three rented rooms on the ground floor of a tenement block. Bars replaced the wall facing the street, giving these rooms the appearance of cages, keeping the women in and unruly punters out. An older woman, Tarabhai, cooked for them in a room rented across the street. The brothel keepers, workers and servant all slept together in this room. In this 'familiarity' – eating and sleeping together, the single hearth, the single roof – it is easy to see in the brothel the hazy structure of a household. Likewise Mirza's absolute control over the five prostitutes and his 'wife', 'daughter' and servant resembled the traditional control of the patriarch in a conventional household. There is no physical description of Mirza in the court records that I was able to see, but he sounds both ordinary and terrifying.

Akootai was close to her fellow workers. They had lived together for a while and had become fond of each other. *Akku* and *tai* mean 'sister' in two Indian languages; and as a scholar notes, a flickering light of sisterhood glimmers through their testimony in court. So does Akootai's spirit. Mirza and Gomtibai forced Akootai to take customers just three days after the 'caustic' treatment, while she was still in agony.[149] She refused. Paru, who shared a room with her, agreed to do the work on her behalf – another flash of Paru's affection for her and the solidarity among the five women. And, indeed, of Akootai's personality. Mirza and Gomtibai then offered her to a customer for sodomy. Akootai's fear upon hearing this was so extreme that the customer refused the offer, leaving without his deposit. And then this brave wounded woman made a break for freedom. Mirza caught her. Together with Gomtibai, he beat her so hard – as a lesson to the others – that she died.

Syed Mirza and Gomtibai may not have meant to kill her – she was an asset after all – but in beating the young woman senseless with an iron rod and a heavy grinding stone, they probably wanted to break her will, which had shown itself to be too strong for the *kotha*. Instead they broke her ribs and battered every part of her body. They were caught only because, when her wrapped body was being taken for burial, a policeman came past, and Syed Mirza, who had been following the corpse, turned around and walked in the other direction. Fishy. The copper became suspicious and insisted that the body be uncovered. (The Indian state could see what was right under its nose. Sometimes.) And then the 'Duncan Road Murder Case' hit the headlines.

Was this brothel typical of the Bombay sex industry? Ashwini Tambe suggests that it was, and other court cases of the early twentieth century support her view.[150] Can one describe it as a quasi-household? Small details about the four survivors that emerged in the court case amplify a sense that it was.[151] All the money they earned (about three quarters of a rupee per client: less than a shilling in English money) went straight to the brothel owners. The women themselves got nothing but their board, lodging, clothing and some jewellery. (This seems to have been the general practice at this time. Other cases from the same period in Bombay confirm this. When Akootai tried to break free, she took her jewellery with her.) The women were forced to put their thumbprints on moneylenders' bonds, which made them feel trapped in debt, or their earnings were going to pay off that debt. They may have been trafficked, sold on by their own family members, deep in debt. It is unclear: shadowy creditors are much in evidence in these cases. But the resemblance between what a South Asian paterfamilias gives his daughter – beatings along with food, shelter and clothing, and jewellery when he gives her to another man – is too striking to be missed. When she marries, she too has to accept sex, however violent, and beating, without protest.

And then there's the enforced immobilisation. All five women were locked in at all times. What Akootai went through in her cage may have been more extreme than the captivity most pubescent South Asian daughters and wives experienced in the early decades of the century. But not much.

In 1910, there were only about 5,000 women in prostitution in Bombay.[152] Their numbers have proliferated since. Some claim that Bombay's Kamathipura is Asia's largest sex district, rivalling Dacca's Daulatia. But it retains a ghastly reputation, even among sex workers. In her remarkable autobiography, Nalini Jameela describes Kamathipura's brothels as 'simply, totally, unacceptable', as places of 'utter wretchedness'.[153]

But sex work elsewhere varies a great deal. We know much more about the brothels of the mid and late twentieth century, and it becomes clear that generalisations are unsafe. The differences are huge, whether by region or structure. Even within a single city, disparate kinds of establishments flourish. Lucknow provides some of the most remarkable material on *kotha* life in the 1970s. One account of a *kotha* in Lucknow suggests that it could hardly be more like a household, and a rather embracing one at that. All thirty women Veena Oldenburg interviewed told her that they were driven there by the horror of the *shareef* (respectable) life they endured, whether at the father's or husband's home. None had been kidnapped or trafficked. 'The problem', according to Saira Jan, a plump woman in her forties, was that there were no obliging kidnappers in her *mohalla* (neighbourhood). 'Had there been such *farishte* (angels) in Hasanganj I would not have had to plot and plan my own escape at great peril to my own life, and my friends, who helped me.'[154]

Most women echoed Saira Jan, describing their earlier homes as *jahannum* (hell). Rahat Jan, their *chaudhuraayan* (keeper/manager), saw her most difficult task as undoing the particular socialisation these desperate creatures had undergone in their previous homes – helping them to forget all the conventional expectations of girls and women. Teaching them the professional skills they needed came later. For the women themselves, in learning these skills and earning their own money (of which they kept a good portion, unlike in the brothels of Kamathipura), they began to recover some self-confidence. In fact, a great deal of confidence. The women whom Oldenburg interviewed were scathing about the 'joys of marriage' which they had escaped. They laughed and joked about the wiles they deployed to make their male clients mad for them, making the clients believe – not unlike in Mirza Muhammad Hadi Ruswa's classic novel *Umrao Jan Ada: The Courtesan of Lucknow* – that they (the women) were besotted with them (the clients). In this state of intoxication, this *nashaa*, men would shower gifts and money upon them (worlds away from the violent sex forced upon wives in the *shareef* or genteel world). The beautiful *tawaif* Umrao says:

> I am but a courtesan whose professional currency is love. Whenever we want to ensnare a man, we pretend to fall in love with him. No one knows how to love more than we do: we heave deep sighs ... threaten to take arsenic ... But I tell you truthfully, no man has ever really loved me, nor did I love any man.[155]

The actor Rekha plays this game with brilliance in Muzaffar Ali's 1981 film *Umrao Jaan*. If you don't have time to watch the whole film, do watch the song 'In Ankhon ki Masti' ('Thousands are Entranced by the Spell of My Eyes'). It will give you a flavour of the courtesan's art.

These women told Oldenburg that they sought emotional intimacy and support within the *kotha* itself. Eight admitted to being lesbians.

There appeared to be a hierarachy in the *kotha*, with the *chaudhu-raayan* and her 'partner' running the show. Below this, it was more nebulous; one gets a sense that more attractive and skilled women had higher standing because they were more highly prized among men (not unlike in the world outside), while those less favoured attended to other duties.[156] Alas, scholars have not fully explored these dimensions of *kotha* life.

Nalini Jameela's stunning *Autobiography of a Sex Worker* provides a less celebratory view of a life spent in the trade. It is never salacious, but its Malayalam and English versions were controversial. She has walked a finer line between the 'inside' and the 'margin'. She is, and has been, both a Hindu and a Muslim. She has married, and then left the world of domesticity. Life on the streets has not been easy. In Kerala, until the 1970s and 80s there were 'company houses', some run by 'high-caste' Nair *tharavads* (households), and Jameela worked at a few of these. While working for Nair-owned 'companies', she had to behave much as she would have done in a conventional household: rising and bathing at dawn, as if readying herself to go to the temple.[157]

But by 2000 there were few companies left in Kerala; clients rented rooms, which made the business more dangerous. Jameela managed, though, to manipulate clients into taking rooms where she knew the owners: without the men realising it, she was in charge (not them). For most of her life, Jameela has been 'self-employed'. Bold, funny, outspoken and irresistible, she describes her wares and her wiles, explaining how she learned the ropes. She tells us that she was beau-tiful, with long and plentiful hair; and that when dressed in a typical Kerala gold-bordered cream sari, with a sandalwood-paste mark on her head, she turned heads. (Again there's the premium on conven-tional idioms of beauty, which gives an otherwise amazing story a conservative edge.) She learned to keep out of harm's way very young, by seducing powerful men and cops, especially (*saars*, sirs); and by avoiding bad gentry – the types of elite young men who were most likely to be violent. She had regular relationships with clients, some of whom wanted her to act like a wife, or to explain to them what their unhappy wife's sexual needs might be.[158] Others demanded less. She writes wryly of one elderly 'regular' whose only desire was that she travelled with him by bus, stroking his ugly bald head.

But she is no Umrao Jan. Nalini Jameela has 'married' clients she has grown to love. She has given up sex work for a while and lived as a 'traditional' married woman. But these men have always let her down; and she brought up her daughter on her own. As long as she was able to, Nalini Jameela supported her mother, still living unhappily in her marital home, under the thumb of her husband and bullying sister-in-law. Her life, therefore, was never totally outside the realm of the conventional 'family'. She has moved betwixt and between, inside society and beyond its margins. She has had close and intimate friendships with sex workers (she writes with particular poignancy of her attachment to a gay man, also a sex worker), and is proud to be an activist in the sex workers' movement, which blossomed at the end of the century. For all her brio, her life has not been easy. For years she was too ill to work and she lived off alms outside a mosque. She writes, nonetheless, that sex workers are *free*. They are unlike housewives in four respects:

> We don't have to cook for a husband; we don't have to wash his dirty clothes; we don't have to ask for his permission to raise our kids as we deem fit; we don't have to run after a husband claiming rights to property.

Her laughing, unrepentant voice in her autobiography suggests that she has enjoyed these freedoms.

In 1994, 26,000 people were involved in the business in Calcutta, where the structure of sex work is different again. Sonagachi is Calcutta's best-known red-light district. It has three kinds of brothels – those that hold *chhukris* (bonded women working off a debt, like Akootai); those with *adhiyas* (notionally a fifty-fifty partnership where earnings and overheads are shared between workers and brothel keepers); and self-employed sex workers who rent rooms in Sonagachi, where working conditions are safer than for freelancers out on the streets.[159] (All they have to do is yell 'rape' and throngs of women come round to investigate.) They all live in close proximity to one another; rickety buildings looming across lanes so narrow that a large car could not drive along them. There appears to be some upwards mobility here: as *chhukris* strive to work off their debts and become *adhiyas*, who in turn work hard to save enough money to set themselves up on their own. To work rather like Nalini Jameela, but within the relative safety that Sonagachi offers to a sex worker.

Last evening, as it drizzled with rain in Cambridge, I watched a DVD of *Born into Brothels*. The documentary by Zana Briski and Ross Kauffman, which won every major prize in 2005, is about children who grew up in Sonagachi. The children were charming, but the film made me uncomfortable. The narrative was about an earnest white woman (Briski) saving 'innocent' brown children by giving them cameras and removing them from their 'bad' brown families. But, as often happens, the documentary showed a lot more than Briski had intended.

The brothel in which the children lived was shared by men and women of all ages. There were families among them, albeit difficult ones. Many children, boys and girls, were looked after by grandmothers while their mothers entertained clients. Working aunts in the trade paid little nieces to do their own 'housework' – in other words, to play the usual role of the good daughter, but in return for cash. (Women's household labour was paid for in this context, in contrast with the conventional world beyond, where it was taken entirely for granted, for 'free'.)

The children who lived in the tenement block had different mothers, and only a few knew their fathers. While their mothers took clients, they often escaped to the roof together, flew kites and played. Many of these homes had pets – sparrows or even parrots in cages – which seemed to bring cheer to these multigenerational families. Relatively few men were in sight, punters hiding their faces, the pimps no doubt concealing themselves from the camera. One haunting image is of a young boy's 'father'. Avijit's frail and ragged mother is still on the job, and clearly not earning much; his father ('previously a man the size of two men, feared by everybody', Avijit boasts) has been reduced to a shadow by his drug habit. His grandmother looks after the young boy, perhaps eleven years old. The child is talented, and Briski has high hopes for him. But during the shooting of the documentary, his mother dies. The official line is that a kerosene stove exploded in her face while she was cooking (the same story is proffered when brides are burned to death in 'dowry murders'). Within the household, one woman admits that her pimp burned Avijit's mother alive, and no, there would be no police investigation. Avijit changes after this. And though, in the documentary, he is the only child who survives being 'saved' (the rest escaping the boarding school which was to be their road out of the brothel), one can see how new pimps and hooligans are 'born into brothels'.

The point is that one must not be seduced into celebrating brothels as the radical 'free' other world that upturns society's social conventions; a female-only space of female power and sexuality. There is that element to them of course, and the late-twentieth-century movement for the rights of sex workers to be recognised and protected as 'workers' has been a radical step.[160] But brothels themselves are complex, multilayered spaces. Power structures within them vary. At the extreme bonded-labour end of the spectrum, there are more Akootais than Nalini Jameelas. In large varied red-light spaces like Sonagachi, power is more diffuse: madams, pimps, thugs, more experienced workers who keep half their earnings, self-employed women like Nalini, drug dealers, liquor vendors, all occupy an ecosystem alongside children, grandparents, sparrows and kites. They may be on the margins but they interact every day with men from the conventional world by sating the men's lust and strange desires.

They don't challenge convention head on. It is in their interests, in a curious way, for conventional sexual norms and repressions to survive.

Let me end with a story, based on *The Prisoner*, the quasi-autobiographical novel of a Pakistani policeman. Between the 1980s and 90s, the refugee-backed Muhajir Qaumi Movement (MQM) lost ground to an even more militant new generation: under Pakistan-born Altaf Hussain's leadership, the MQM morphed into the Muttahida Qaumi Movement (also known as MQM). Between 1992 and 1996, the Pakistani army and police dismantled the Muttahida Qaumi Movement's 'secondary [refugee] state' in Karachi in a war of shocking brutality. The gloves were off on both sides. The police and army invaded MQM areas and 'cleansed' them with state-sanctioned violence. The MQM's 'quasi-sovereign spaces', previously run by armed gangs, were all but destroyed.[161]

The author visited Cambridge with his family, to read from his book. A retired policeman, he had been a part of the Karachi operation. He looked more like an academic than a policeman: slightly stooping, shy, smiling, uncertain. He peered through spectacles and wore a sensible (if unfashionably donnish) jumper. He read well. His book, *The Prisoner*, is astonishing. Why it matters here is because the protagonist writes of a high-class *tawaif* – a woman of stunning beauty and courtly manners who has been the love of the protagonist's life. She knows everyone important in Pakistan. She is both an informant and a keeper of secrets. She loves him in return but they acknowledge that their relationship can go nowhere: she must remain in the *kotha*, and he in polite society, married and with conventions to be observed. The Love Laws must be obeyed.

Years later, these worlds suddenly collide. The policeman's family is threatened by MQM gang members who have discovered the family's hideout. Desperate, he seeks the courtesan's help, asking her to take in his wife and children and keep them safe during the years of war. She agrees. His wife agrees. No one finds his family there. It is the last place they would look.

It's an astonishing twist – the state itself seeks refuge at its margins. The conventional household is protected by a courtesan. The two nest together like spoons.

The tale points to the courtesan's enduring power. It may lie in the margins, in the crevices of society, but it is no less important for that.

6

Fasting, Feasting, Gluttony and Starvation: Consumption, Caste and the Politics of Food in South Asia

In the mid-1960s, Indira Gandhi began to demand '*roti, kapdaa, aur makaan*' (food, clothing and shelter) for the people of India. Dressed in block-printed cotton saris – a 'national dress' she favoured – she addressed thousands of audiences from jerry-built stages across the country, mics crackling as she rallied the crowds. This was part of the populist campaign that brought her to power in 1967. Across the border in Pakistan, Zulfikar Ali Bhutto also dressed in a style he invented as 'national dress' – the loose *shalwaar kameez*.[1] He too toured the country (or at least its western wing), addressing mammoth crowds from rickety platforms wherever he went. Bhutto also called for '*roti, kapdaa, aur makaan*'. A sense of crisis about food gripped South Asia, transcending its borders, tense though they were after the 1965 Indo–Pakistani war.

A few years later, Mrs Gandhi took to measuring public opinion in terms of the price of onions.[2]

Moral panics and the politics of hunger are core themes of South Asia's long twentieth century. Food commands my attention here, as it has preoccupied South Asians since the late nineteenth century. *Kapdaa* and *makaan* take a back seat: they must.

Food 'is a highly condensed social fact ... Unlike houses, pots, masks or clothing, food is a constant need but a perishable good.'[3] This makes it the nerve centre of an almost unbearable load of meanings. Consumption in South Asia does not end with food, but any serious analysis must start with it.

What follows is not a story about the rich and their changing appetites. Affluent elites have their place: they ate far too much to be ignored and their tastes drove demand and hence production by social groups far beyond them. Nationalists – Gandhi above all – used food and fasting to demonstrate their views about ethical consumption to the public. White doctors had notions about what foods were best for Europeans and Indians; these views influenced, in different and changing ways, what Indians ate. The Indian middle classes too, even when small in numbers, had cultural sensibilities about desirable and permissible commodities. By the end of the century the middle classes were 300 million strong – as large as the entire population of the subcontinent in 1900. So their appetite for 'modern' but also 'moral' commodities is part of my story.

But what the poor – the Dalits, Adivasis, 'outcastes' and 'pariahs' – ate, or could not eat, is central to it.

Class and caste are lenses through which I make sense of all this. Here, people of different class and caste status jostle with each other and with the well-to-do consumer on an imaginary berth in a railway compartment that, in real life, they would never share. Or if they did, only fleetingly. In the twentieth century, 'local' trains tended to stop often during the day, picking up passengers without reservations. These sojourners hovered around jam-packed compartments, hoping that people with expensive reserved tickets would give them a place on a berth. ('Local' was a relative concept; they might otherwise have had to stand for hours.) 'Please adjust' was their request. And adjust people did – warily, sometimes resentfully – making a tiny amount of room available by resettling their bottoms a little. The train stopped, strangers went their different ways, while new strangers boarded saying 'Please adjust'. The cycle began anew.

The food story is a bit like that. It has a cast full of strangers. It's important that they remain strangers: reluctant co-passengers rather than acquaintances.

The glory of the saffron-scented biryani, the aroma of the *hilsaa* fish curry, the religious power of the temple *prasaadam* (ritual food offerings) are not only part of the recipe. Their true magic is the trick that hides 'dirty' people beneath layers of rice, mustard oil and ghee. Their fine ingredients depended on the work – ill-rewarded, ill-regarded and, for the most part, ignored – of others.

This is the true 'Indian rope trick': disappear their 'dirty' work.

You might wonder again: what is 'South Asian' about this? Does anyone care about where food comes from?

The answer is that South Asians care more about 'whose food they eat' than any other people in the world. It is a fundament of caste, you see. Food and caste are so closely intertwined that it is hard to talk about one without the other.

For South Asian elites it is not just laziness not to think about where food comes from. They have to strive hard not to know.

Fine dining for them involves an unspoken compact not to think about food producers and gatherers, and cleaners and scavengers of food waste. To airbrush uncomfortable images out of memories. (Those thin-limbed lads who brought coconuts down from swaying treetops in our childhoods. Who were they? Why weren't they at school? Who was that little boy who did this for our household at Hill Cart Road? I can't remember his name: I probably never knew it. Why? He sat on the berth and yet I never even saw his face.) To erase from our minds any curiosity about the fisher-folk who went out to the dangerous tidal estuaries of the Bay of Bengal to catch the prized *hilsaa*. Women of 'low' status did most of the work of gutting and cleaning fish in most coastal regions, and still do. They were considered 'dirty' people, rank, stinking of the entrails they cut out. They did not cross the threshold of elite homes, so they did not impinge upon our consciousness.

We who ate well did not ask ourselves why fishermen were deemed 'lowly' while fish was so prized. Nor why ghee was elixir, while those who tended cattle were 'low-born'.

The zeitgeist among the urban literati was: let's have another *chaai*, another conversation about politics, or literature. Across borders, South Asia's intelligentsia read and discussed *Our Lady of Alice Bhatti*, Mohammed Hanif's stunning 2011 novel. But I doubt that many dwelt on Joseph Bhatti's line 'These [people] will make you clean their shit and then complain that you stink.'[4]

A *paandaan* is a special box with the ingredients and tools needed to make betel-leaf *paan* to suit different tastes. Secateurs to cut the betel nut just so. Little boxes and trays of different sizes to hold the assortment of ingredients: lime, *gulkand* (rose-petal jam), tobacco paste, cloves, soaked areca nuts, which different people like in different quantities. And instruments to apply each, as well as the one that all have in common – the betel leaf itself. This chapter prises open this *paandaan* to reveal the various compartments within. (In real life, society holds them apart.)

This chapter, like a *paandaan*, has many such little containers.

There is disturbing, indeed horrific, detail in some of them; but the story is as interesting as it is distressing.

Food held people apart as it tied them together, even if they knew little of each other and cared less. It changed society even as social structures resisted change. Food linked town and countryside; the huge urban *mandis* (markets) depended on complex rural supply chains. It linked the state to the producer: after independence, state-run ration shops bought up stocks directly from the farmers in rural India, and supplied essentials to the urban poor and middle classes. It connected retailers to producers. Wholesale markets – those famous around the subcontinent include Dhanmondi (now in Bangladesh), Azadpur Mandi in Delhi, and Subzi Mandi in Lahore – were sites where town and country met. They attracted thousands of retailers to the towering piles of fruit and vegetables that arrived in cities at dawn each day, and who in turn rushed like so many ants to neighbour-hoods to sell their produce at a higher price.

By 2000, however, *mandis* kept out many of the small producers and retailers. Small vegetable sellers from the hinterland were often unable to ply their wares at these big markets. Access to the markets had come to be controlled by political parties and their musclemen. Instead the smaller suppliers tried to sell at lower prices straight to *thhelawaalas* (cartmen) or hawkers, local dealers who supplied differ-ent localities at (often illegal) stalls – a jute bag on the roadside each morning or a cart in the evening, lit up by a hurricane lamp.[5] These were perishables that had to be consumed fresh, so there was a palp-able fervour about sales at every node of the network, prices falling as the evening approached. Only onions stayed fresh for longer. Humble vegetables, their price was more stable: a rise in the price of onions was a bellwether of inflationary conditions in food markets. Hence Indira Gandhi's anxious eye on their price.

And so the city ate, and slept. But urban man remained only dimly aware of the feverish activity that brought food to his plate.

Habits and tastes have changed, of course. New global commodi-ties had become so familiar that in 2000, only the aged remembered the days when 'there was no coffee'.[6] Until the 1950s and 60s even wealthy farmers of North India ate their meals outdoors, but by the end of the century, a 'dining room' area had become a must, even for families at the lower end of the middle classes.[7] In it, a refrigerator gleamed like an ornament on display. Street food, one of the (illicit) joys of urbanisation, had fallen by the wayside by the end of the century, as many middle-class women (and men) ate so much they began to diet to lose weight, and to watch what they consumed (fewer carbs, more salads, domestic workers doing the chopping, of course). Their children ate store-bought snacks in shiny silver packaging, high in salt, sugar and monosodium glutamate. Grandma's home-made treats were no longer good enough for them.

But hunger sat on the same berth as gluttony, and blindness has never gone out of fashion.

In a worm's-eye study of caste in southern India, a scholar observes that those at the bottom of the heap stressed not its ritual dimensions but its economic exploitation.[8] Caste and class are closely related, but they are not the same thing: the caste system gives the majority of the poor a particular ritual position – outside the system. It stigmatises the destitute Dalit (formerly described as 'untouchable') as polluted, defiled, unclean. Dalits have had to force their way onto the political agenda, with little or no backing from traditional class warriors. Many of their battles have been fought locally, around food.

This chapter looks at caste through the lens of food. Anthropologists tend to do it the other way round, but the reader might judge this chapter's approach to have its uses.

When I was well and strong and had just started teaching at Cambridge, I learned to make a fine biryani. I got the recipe from a Madhur Jaffrey book, and cooked it for twenty, thirty, sometimes seventy people. (Arjun Appadurai has shown that cookery books are not neutral objects, and have played a role in shaping the concept of the nation. I will return to this theme later.)

My biryani took days to prepare. I loved cooking on a grand scale in those days, having tired of the predictable and unforgiving routine of the evening family meal. I remember one party in particular. My goal was to prepare fourteen different dishes, each with different spices, from different regions of the subcontinent, to challenge the prevaling British stereotype of Indian food as a handful of red, hot and greasy dishes. It took me three days and the help of an old friend to produce this meal for seventy friends and their children. It was gone in a flash. I was worn out for a week.

Our cook in Delhi, Mohan Singh, a Dalit, did this sort of thing often, for my parents' 'superb' dinner parties. We didn't notice his fatigue, or even give it a thought, although the guests raved about the food. Voltaire puts it well: 'Appreciation is a wonderful thing. It makes what is excellent in others belong to us as well.'

I learned to cook only when I arrived in Cambridge as a student. I had never spent time in the kitchen in Delhi with Mohan Singh. From the Almora region in the northern Indian Himalayas, he had migrated to the plains as a young man and ended up working for us when I was a little girl, under Diwan Singh, graduating to *khaansama* when that gentleman left. He became a chef of genius who could cook every single dish in the Bengali Hindu repertoire (which is enormous), as well as many European ones and dishes from other parts of South Asia. (My father was a connoisseur of food, and although he didn't know where the fridge was, he was always on the lookout for new recipes. My job was to translate and transcribe these into Hindi; Mohan then improvised on them.) Our family's Sunday lunches consisted of several courses of Bengali food, each more glorious than the preceding one. My father had a South Asian approach to hospitality: all guests were welcomed and fed; and somehow many friends found themselves 'just passing' every Sunday when the Chatterjis sat down to lunch. I think back now on the work Mohan did to cater for this motley crew every Sunday – I never thought about it then. I was too young (and, I am ashamed to say, too thoughtless) to conceive of all the work Mohan did to feed us, to memorise and improve upon these recipes, to wash up (messily) afterwards, to shop and keep accounts. Preoccupied with literature, history, modern art and teenage crushes, I learned not a single thing from him. I didn't even think about what it meant for him to do 'woman's work' in the house of a brown 'burra sahib'.

It is this frustration with myself as well as with those who sit like me with expensive reservations on the berth, with so little curiosity about the 'strangers', that fuels this chapter. Why was food so political that it continued to drive politics long after the era of famines, after independence, in the 1960s and until the 90s, decades after the British had quit India? What, if anything, changed in the subcontinent's dietscapes, and why? What were the staple foods and how had they transformed with time? Did national governments succeed in making citizens eat 'national diets'?

There is much that a history of consumption can reveal about all this. But, as with everything about South Asia, there is nothing straightforward about it.

I

THE 'INDIAN' DIET: AN ANGLO-
BRAHMIN INVENTION?

In the late nineteenth and early twentieth centuries, the notion that there was an 'Indian diet' dominated the British view of South Asian eating habits. British medical men thought that the Indian diet was unusually light on meat, compared with western man's consumption, and heavy on foods such as rice, curds, lentils and greens. James Johnson, a surgeon in the Royal Navy in the early nineteenth century, painted a picture of considerable homogeneity in the diet of 'natives'.

> It may be observed, that the natives themselves make their principal meal at sunset, when the heat is less distressing, and insects neither so numerous nor teasing; but it must be recollected, that they, in general, eat nothing between breakfast and dinner; and that among *the Hindoos and lower classes of Mahomedans, &c,* the evening meal is by no means of a stimulating quality, while no provocative variety, or other adventitious circumstances, can have much effect in goading the appetite beyond its natural level.[9]

Johnson's sweeping generalisation about 'the natives' was misguided, even though it persuaded many readers.

To begin with, British medical men viewed India's 'vegetarianism' with approval, believing such light fare to be better adapted to the subcontinent's climate – so much so that they urged their own countrymen to borrow some of these 'habits'.[10] James Johnson went so far as to encourage greenhorns from Britain to adopt the 'Indian diet' for two years after their arrival in the subcontinent, shunning the usual white officers' meals heavy with meat, washed down with alcohol. This, he thought, would bring down the rates of illness and death among Britons in India, making redundant the adage of British India that 'two monsoons are the age of man'.

He found few converts among officers, however. Until they left the subcontinent, the British were still dressing for vast dinners of many courses. As John Beames, an Indian Civil Service (ICS) officer of the Bengal cadre, recalled in his *Memoirs*:

Our *chota haziri*, or little breakfast, was at five-thirty to six, and consisted of tea, eggs boiled or poached, toast and fruit. Breakfast at eleven
consisted of fried or broiled fish, a dish or two of meat – generally fowl
cutlets, hashes and stews, or cold meat and salad followed by curry
and . . . claret. Between four and five there was tea and cakes. Dinner at
half past seven or eight consisted of soup, an entrée, roast fowls or
ducks, occasionally mutton, and in cold weather once or twice beef, an
entremet of game or a savoury, and sweets.[11]

Intelligent medical men, like Johnson and those who followed in his
stead, thought that 'native' attitudes about food flowed from religion
and cosmology. Since they got most of their understanding about 'the
Gentoos' from Brahmin priests, British scholars learned a great deal
about values which were those only of a tiny segment of society. But
they assumed these to be of disproportionate significance to the whole
subcontinent; to be central to the mystical and impenetrable creed to
which India's people were 'fanatically' committed. As usual, the picture they received was skewed by their priestly interlocutors and their
own premise that they were rational men. A few sharp British observers saw beyond the official wisdom, and my account would be poorer
but for their meticulous research, and their sometimes enraged debates
and communications with their own colonial government.

But let's first hear the 'Brahmin' version of 'righteous food', on
which the British came largely to rely. But before that, a clarificatory
word about 'caste', given that I will use the term often in this
chapter.

The Brahmin *pandits* or scholars would have told the British that
the caste system was a four-fold structure, with Brahmins, of course,
on top. They would have called this structure the *varnashramadharma*, and explained it by reference to ancient texts that spoke of
society as an organism emanating from the Primeval Being.[12] The
Creator, according to this scheme of things, produced Brahmins from
the Being's mouth, *khattriyas* (warriors) from his arms, *vaishyas* (traders) from his thighs, and *shudras* (labourers) from his feet. (The first
three groups were 'the twice-born' and, given their higher callings, the
men could wear, after an initiation ceremony, the sacred thread.
Shudras could not.)

'Untouchables' lay outside this system. In status they were far
beneath the *shudras*. In parts of the South, *paraiah* was the term used

for these groups. Some of its meaning is redolent in the English borrowing, pariah. But stripped of locale and social context, it lacks the violent charge of the original.[13]

In practice, as the British came to learn, matters were far more complicated and nebulous. The four-fold model was more the ideal than the norm. Brahmins were not always 'on top', and although Brahmin sub-castes did exist throughout the country, not all intermarried. (It would have been considered most unsuitable for a *kulin* Brahmin 'boy' of Bengal to marry a Kashmiri Pandit 'girl'. When my cousin-brother did this in the late 1970s, my aunts and cousins reacted like flustered mynah birds.) Regional, indeed local, sub-castes (*jatis*) or even sub-sub-castes, were the relevant units to contend with. Caste Hindus married within their own regional group (*jati*) or sub-*jati*, and accepted food from each other, while observing rules about which other *jatis* they would accept water from, or eat or feast with.

As the social anthropologist M. N. Srinivas noted, it's not all about hierarchy, as the Brahmin view suggests. (A view that Louis Dumont's book *Homo Hierarchicus* crystallised in the West.)[14] Most *jatis*, or sub-*jatis*, were specific to a locality and could not be ranked outside it.[15] So a Taga, locally dominant in rural Maharashtra where the Dalit writer Om Prakash Valmiki grew up, might have been a tyrant in his village, but his local dominance and social identity would have meant little outside it.[16] If he migrated to a larger town or city, he was hard to place.

A *jati*'s status compared with another, moreover, was uncertain, and often was renegotiated with gains in socioeconomic and political status. Most often, as one sub-*jati* gained in standing, its members began to demand advantage in the ritual game of snakes and ladders by refusing to accept food and water from a close neighbour and former equal. Such a battle could be fought over years, even lifetimes.

Who ate what, where and with whom was the public mode of registering these shifts. Food was (and still is) a critical marker of caste behaviour. One cannot be talked of without the other. Some *jatis* were deemed so lowly that even the River Ganges was deemed to be polluted by their touch.[17]

What's more, within every locality, there was a dominant *jati*. This was by no means always Brahmin. Dominance was a matter of control over land and labour, and of political influence (with local leaders, policemen or officials).[18] These dominant castes could be *Shudra* (although in such cases, they might persuade the local Brahmin who served their caste to rewrite their genealogy to turn them into Rajputs or Thakurs, giving them a new genealogy).[19] Often they, as a group, began to ape 'Brahmin' modes of conduct, such as vegetarianism, in a mark of what Srinivas called Sanskritisation.[20]

Dalits remained everywhere at the bottom of the heap. They were outside caste, 'beyond the pale' in the terms of social interaction. Their touch was, and in many quarters still is, thought to pollute food and water. In Maratha country in western India, even in the late 1960s, the Mahars had to drag a thorny branch behind them to wipe away their footsteps and prostrate themselves (at some distance) if a Brahmin walked by. In the Punjab, scavengers like Joseph Bhatti had to carry a broom with them at all times to warn others of their 'polluting presence'.[21] No one, of any *jati*, would accept food from a Dalit. Although not a single caste, Dalits are a universal feature of South Asian society. Their treatment in the twentieth century, as in preceding centuries, is a horror unique to the subcontinent.

(The 'Criminal Tribes', branded as such by the British in 1871 and apparently 'freed' by independent India and Pakistan, had a similar, but not identical, status.)

But back to Brahmins and what they ate. They did not share a common diet. Some were strict vegetarians, Tamil Brahmins being prize-winners in this purity parade. Others delighted in fish and goat and, by the turn of the century, chicken. Wealthy and even middle-class Bengali Brahmins could not imagine life without freshwater fish. They ate fish heads. (Fish heads cooked in *moong daal* are – I speak as a Bengali here – a true delight.) The brains and eyes of the fish also have a place on the plate. These Brahmins also adored the large and luscious prawns available in the region, eating every part of the sweet crustacean, cracking it open with their fingers and teeth, arguing which was the best bit – the legs or the head. Kashmiri Brahmins were confirmed goat-eaters, as were Brahmins of the Himalayan belt.

However, this is not intended to suggest that religious views and orthodox behaviours did not matter, even if the number of practitioners of rigid food orthodoxy was always small, and has shrunk over the century. They were one of the single most important issues in South Asian society throughout the century.

For 'lower' sub-castes, one way of rising up the social ladder has been to adopt some of the food practices of Brahmins.[22] This has not always been easy. When promoted by Hindu political movements seeking to boost census numbers of 'the Hindu fold', caste Hindus welcomed such attempts at upward mobility; but when self-initiated, 'upstart' behaviour has not gone down well.[23] Punishment might be an economic boycott. So when milk vendors of the Goala *jati* claimed Vaisya status in the 1910s, 'high-caste' Hindus boycotted them, preferring to buy their milk (shock, horror) from Muslims.[24] Or it could be more violent: Yashica Dutt's father was pulled from his horse on his way to his wedding for daring to act like a caste Hindu.[25] From the 1980s onwards, press reports about the lynching of 'uppity' Dalits who 'didn't know their place' became so frequent that one wondered if caste attitudes had changed even a jot, or whether caste conflicts were turning into open warfare when the Dalit Panthers emerged as a party committed to fight oppression of 'pariahs' everywhere. In this context, Indians well beyond the tiny handful of the high Brahmin castes were, and remain, finely attuned to the political danger that hovers around food. They understand its tense relationship with social mobility.

I do not suggest, however, that all practitioners of Hindu food orthodoxy are aware of the conceptual ideals that undergird the system. Quite the opposite. I was not conscious of them myself, even though I watched members of our household play out these practices, day in and day out, at Hill Cart Road. As a child and teenager, I watched my aunts and cousin-sisters-in-law bustling about preparing and serving food, observing set rhythms and patterns. I did not understand what gave a certain food high status, or why others were deemed less worthy. (I thought ghee was prized for its aroma!) It's a bit like the rules of a big institution: no one ever sits you down and explains them to you. You watch and follow others, without quite knowing why you are doing what you are doing and how it fits into the larger scheme of things. Or whether there actually *is* a larger scheme of things.

This is particularly true of women. They have been, and remain, responsible for food preparation and serving, but were, until recent times, denied a religious education. When the century began, they were denied the right even to read. There were few women scholars of Sanskrit, Tarabai Shinde (1850–1910) and Pandita Ramabai (1858–1922) being notable exceptions.[26] At the start of the twentieth century, my grandmother was one of the tiny number of women who could read.[27] But she never explained to me why things in the kitchen had to be done in a certain way, even once. I did try to understand because it puzzled me. But she said nothing at all.

Most other women who learned the language did so in secret, because the conservative majority believed that the act of reading by a wife was a threat to her husband's life.[28] (When, in the 1930s and 40s, some Muslim girls began to be encouraged to learn to read and study at least some parts of the Quran, they were trained in Arabic, not in their mother tongue, so they learned by rote and understood little. Maulana Thanawi's *Bihishti Zewar*, a compilation of instructions in literacy and a basic reformed Islamic faith for women, did not suggest that they become learned *ulema* in their own right.)[29]

By definition, then, women had no access to the metaphysical concepts that shaped their everyday cooking and serving routines. By 2000, about a third of all South Asian women had basic literacy – just enough to sign their names and gain access to microcredit. I doubt, though, that many were quoting from the Sanskrit *shastras* (sacred texts). State education in India was largely secular, and Sanskrit was introduced only at the secondary level, by which stage most poor children (particularly girls) had dropped out. Across the border, the curriculum of the Pakistan Studies module did not equip its learners, male or female, with such knowledge or understanding.[30] For a woman to become a theologian was, and still is, a rare occurrence, both in India and Bangladesh. In 2019, my niece Maya married her long-term partner, Shamaun, in a *nikaah*. Two women *aalims* conducted the brief ceremony. One could sense the shock this caused among many of the assembled wedding guests.

Women served patriarchs first and then children, often fanning them as they ate. (Watch, for instance, how in Satyajit Ray's 1956 film *Aparajito*, his widowed mother, who cooks his every meal, fans the growing Apu as he eats.) They themselves ate last. They also bore the burden of most of the fasting that goes on in 'high-caste' Hindu India – this should come as no surprise.

Women tended to fast for others. In much of northern India, Hindu wives fast from dawn to dusk on *Karva Chauth* (the fourth day in the lunar month of Kartik), praying for the long life of their husbands. Women fasted for the well-being of their husbands and children on *Ekadasi*, twenty-four times a year for twenty-four hours, on the eleventh day of each lunar fortnight. Usually the fast involved giving up all cooked food for a day. The most devout were stringent in their observance as late as the 1950s, but by the 1960s and 70s, when the anthropologist of Hindu food Ravindra Khare was conducting his last studies, he sensed changes afoot. Some urban wives had become more lax; some while fasting could be seen buying and eating fruit in the market or even drinking coffee at a café.

The largest 'collective' female fast I observed as a young girl took place across North India at Janamasthami, the celebration and re-enactment of the birth of the Hindu god Krishna at midnight.[31] As I watched fasting women make fevered preparations for the big event, it was never clear to me that they were sure why they were fasting. They chatted and laughed a lot, and enjoyed the group activity but never discussed what it meant. Perhaps they did it because it displayed their credentials as 'good' women, and 'self-sacrificing' and 'righteous' Hindu wives. Perhaps, as Tanika Sarkar suggests, this sense of righteousness has led to their participation in Hindu right-wing politics outside the home; but my point here is that little theological knowledge undergirded either their fasts or daily cooking routines.[32]

Hindu men, by contrast, fasted seldom and fasted alone. They did so to accrue spiritual credit (*punya*) for themselves. Early in the twentieth century, political prisoners adapted the fast to protest against injustices – these were novel in that they were acts of communal abstinence by men demanding humane treatment for themselves in jail. Gandhi's fasts created such a frisson because he fasted alone (like a man), but for the benefit of others (like a woman). No one could grasp how exactly to handle this. Certainly not Nehru or other members of his close circle, nor the British who were terrified that he would die. The Gandhian 'fast unto death' has remained an instrument of great political power, demonstrated in 2011 by the Gandhian campaigner Anna Hazare's fast in New Delhi. The plump activist's cause was to fight corruption. As he withered in front of their eyes, people – often apolitical before this event – flocked to his side, wearing a Gandhi cap marked 'I am Anna'. His fast lasted 290 hours. Just like the British before it, the Indian government in power was paralysed. Each day Anna starved, he further eroded the moral foundations of its authority.[33]

Starving like Gandhi was an act of inordinate power, in a society that had peculiar notions about food.[34]

It is worth, then, setting out some core Brahminical precepts about cooking and eating: the pure and the impure, the raw and the cooked, stale food and leftovers, fasting and feasting, within the Hindu caste 'ideal'. But always recognising that these were only ever ideals, and that they too have undergone changes and challenges in the twentieth century.

Despite the fact that few understood the rules, breaking them was a political act. You could eat your way into caste war or mob lynching in South Asia. Food was also fertile terrain for resistance and rebellion.

Theory and practice of food and caste: a brief introduction

In Brahminical precepts, foods, like people, are changeable in their very essence. Just as a particular food's ritual rank or status is fluid, so too is the status of people, whose individuality is unstable and who can change moral and physiological character through interaction with others.[35] This is so because, according to these cosmologies, man is made up of small particles (*pinda*), such as those found in hair, saliva and sweat; his borders are porous so he can be 'invaded' by touch. Bad particles might enter him by the food he eats. Good and bad particles also float through the air and can be caught, unwittingly, in clothes. It is vital for the caste Hindu to wage a constant struggle against bad *pinda* and to accept only good particles 'through right eating, right marriage and other right exchange and actions'.

Crucially, a Hindu's identity can change with his or her encounter with food. What is at stake, scholars claim, is the preservation, and the transformation for the good, of the caste Hindu's moral substance and character.[36]

In the same way, food can attract or shed good or harmful particles.

Food is central to this concept of personhood because the status of food is transformed every day. Cooking is the process by which raw things are changed into pure edibles, provided the cook follows the right codes and practices. The same raw material, if treated differently, could achieve a different (polluted) status.

Food, for the orthodox 'high-caste' Hindu, is thus a bio-moral substance. Eating appropriate food transforms the human body so that its physical health and energy, as well as its spiritual power, are optimised in a state of balance.[37] Food is central to Ayurvedic medicine, which treats the body and mind as a single whole, and seeks to cure through diet, yoga and meditation, by achieving a balance of the humours. Foods are classified into three categories: *taamsik* (unduly exciting the system, stimulating lust, anger and other intemperate 'hot' states of mind); *raajsik* (hot but energising, appropriate to contexts such as exercise, hunting or war); and *saatvik* (cool, enabling tranquillity, celibacy and meditation). During an illness, an Ayurvedic practitioner might advise orthodox patients who normally only eat *saatvik* food to include *raajsik* foods in their diet so as to restore the balance of physical, mental and spiritual energy. An example of a *taamsik* food is highly spiced meat; an example of a *raajsik* food is spiced chickpea curry cooked with chillies, spices, onions and garlic; *saatvik* food could be any non-spicy light vegetable dish cooked without garlic or onions.

But the classification of foods gets more and more complicated. Superimposed upon this broad categorisation is one of ritual purity. This depends on a food's proximity to the gods and on how, where, and by whom it is prepared.[38]

So food that might otherwise be looked upon askance – say a guava from a humble orchard – if offered to the gods in sacrifice, achieves high rank as *prasaad/prasaadam* offerings to the deity and is shared by the whole congregation of caste Hindu worshippers. Brahmins of the highest ranks eat it raw, with heads bowed, palms open in supplication.

'Leftovers', here, were 'purified' by their role in the worship of the deity. (This is not the case in everyday life, particularly for 'lower castes', when the term *joothan* acquires more pejorative meanings, more akin to slops.)[39] Yet even in such cases of 'divine leftovers', not all worshippers are equal. At the Sri Parthasarathi Swami Temple in Madras city, in the 1940s and 50s, non-Brahmin worshippers launched a protest against the manner in which the priests gave them their *prasaadam* – sometimes flinging it at them. This was after the Vaikkom *satyagraha* had been won (see Chapter 2); and the movement continued after the Indian constitution enshrined the right to equality and dignity for all. In a context where the temple, prestations to it and its *prasaadam* were more central than anywhere else in India, food was (and continues) to be the medium by which the twice-born enacted their caste status by humiliating the 'low-born' in public.[40]

But there are also wide distinctions determined by the mode of preparation. Here the most significant applied to food is whether it is *kachcha* (raw or boiled) or *pakka* (fried). This rule is broken only in the case of the produce of cows – milk, curds and ghee – which could be consumed in their raw state given the quasi-divinity of their producer.

Every other food was deemed more humble, and is subject to the *kachcha/pakka* distinction. A 'high-caste' person would be unwilling to accept *kachcha* food from one of a different (and possibly 'lower') *jati*, although in the last century extremism in this regard varied across the subcontinent.

Speaking in the broadest terms, the South had a much more 'highly developed' body of ideas and practices regarding rank and pollution than the North, but there are all too many exceptions to the rule.[41] The Methars (scavengers) of Calcutta whom Tanika Sarkar has described with such vividness were the North's answer to the South, as were the Joseph Bhattis of Punjab and Sind in the West.[42]

The most valued cooking medium was ghee (boiled and clarified butter). If ghee is the first food that comes into contact with the heated saucepan, the next food (say, raw chopped cabbage) added to it transmutes into a *pakka* food by virtue of being fried in ghee. It can no longer 'catch' harmful particles floating in the atmosphere; it can no longer threaten the body and character of the consumer. It achieves a high rank. The fact that the cabbage was grown in a muddy field by members of a ('lower') *maali* (gardener) caste, and handled on its way to the market or local stall by god-knows-who, is wiped away by the simple act of frying. It is now transformed into something edible for the smuggest of self-respecting Brahmins. Just how blasé Brahmins were about what was *in* the fodder and manure in which crops grew – the dung of many animals, human faeces very likely – is shown by the fact that would-be gentleman farmers in Bengal took up bone meal with enthusiasm as a form of fertiliser.[43] After all, all polluting particles could be 'fried off' in ghee.

A *kachcha* food, by contrast, is more humble. Its medium of cooking is water. Lentils, pulses, coarse grains and rice are therefore lesser foods. (They are, inevitably, the food of the poor.) In wealthy, 'high-caste' households, they were always cooked after *pakka* foods and eaten just as they came off the boil. In many kitchens, where there is space so to do, cooks would keep *kachcha* and *pakka* foods apart even before they put them on the stove. Some 'high castes' went to great lengths in observing these distinctions: a proverb has it that three Kanaujia Brahmins needed no fewer than thirteen hearths, so punctilious were their needs in cooking their foods separately and in the proper order.[44]

The high rank of milk, ghee and curds did not depend on who owned the cattle, where they were herded and grazed, or how the milk entered the house. Those castes and classes of Hindus who could afford to own cattle did so at the start of the century, and many did so even in the 1970s and 80s, as did my family at Hill Cart Road. Less prosperous but locally dominant castes, such as the Tagas whom Om Prakash Valmiki writes about, also owned cattle.[45]

Those who could not afford this luxury bought milk, either directly or indirectly, from cowherds. Writing in 1909 of Ahirs and Goalas, pastoralists 'who tend flock', Lewis O'Malley, prolific author of gazetteers on greater Bengal, noted that they sold milk on to the Gauras, who churned cream into ghee, which *mahaajans* (moneylenders and small shopkeepers) purchased wholesale. They then sold on this prized commodity to local consumers at a higher retail price. What we might today call the 'supply chain', I call the berth, because no one thought, as they poured a spoonful of golden ghee over their steaming rice, of how close they sat to the roaming Ahir (classified as 'criminal') or the industrious but 'lowly' Gaura.[46] Few were even aware that Gauras existed.

Milk drinkers also depended on 'lower' castes or tribes for the supply of fodder. Over the nineteenth and twentieth centuries, cowherds of 'inferior' status – by their very nature nomadic groups who moved from one pasture to another – strove to maintain access to grazing land. Most struggled to survive against the drive of the colonial states to settle and tax mobile populations and to seize and possess forests, and later by the post-colonial states' management of forests and approach towards conservation. Studies of India in the late twentieth century show that the bargaining power of the pastoralist has been in free fall: Rajasthani pastoralists now get less cash for the manure they sell to farmers and pay more for the right to graze.[47] A few groups, such as the semi-pastoral Gaddi of India's Himachal Pradesh, have improved their standing by turning themselves into a political 'vote bank' in a democracy where such strategies sometimes work. But in general, pastoral groups in a subcontinent ever more densely settled have had to make desperate efforts to get forage for their cattle under a huge variety of property regimes.[48]

Yet these problems counted for nothing for 'high-caste' milk consumers of the twentieth century. The untended dry meadows or the health of the cattle were not among the Brahmin's priorities. Few registered the dire poverty of pastoralist groups. I can bet you this: most would have looked at you with a wild surmise if you put this question to them, most would do so even today. The survival of the milk trader is not their concern; their only worry is about adulteration of the precious white, frothy commodity, which is why, by the 1970s in small towns, Goalas came to their consumers' households each morning bearing tightly sealed churns full of milk. Adulterated or otherwise, once it crossed the threshold of the 'upper-caste' household it became the purest of pure foods.

Even Gandhi, who lacked neither imagination nor empathy, had this to say about the cow:

> Mother cow is in many ways better than the mother who gave us birth. Our mother gives us milk for a couple of years and then expects us to serve her when we grow up. Mother cow expects nothing from us except grass and grain. Our mother often falls ill and expects service from us. Mother cow rarely falls ill.
>
> Our mother, when she dies, means expenses of burial or cremation. Mother cow is as useful dead as when she is alive.[49]

Let's leave aside what this says about Gandhi's dim and utilitarian view of mothers and wives. He was clueless about what cows ate, where that food came from, and the human beings whose livelihoods depended on providing it. He hadn't any idea about how diseased many of India's cows were. Here again is an example of the blindness at the heart of consumption, and of the imaginary berth at work. Herdsman, farmer, milkman, ghee maker and seller, cow lover and consumer of dairy products all sit together on the berth. The consumer and cow lover is oblivious to the shadowy strangers who sit beside him.

Nor, curiously enough, has the health of cattle been a pressing concern of the cow lovers of the twentieth century. South Asian cattle were sickly in the late nineteenth century, and remained so in the twentieth. Even in the mid-nineteenth century, William Robert

Cornish, iconoclastic assistant surgeon in the medical department of the Madras government, observed this. Grazing land had been so eroded that India's cattle were skinny, diseased and dirty eaters, subsisting on anything they could find. The fodder available to them during the hot and dry seasons of the year was so insecure that 'horned cattle [got] miserably thin and perished by thousands . . . from contagious epidemics'.[50]

Cow protection movements sprang up soon after Cornish wrote this. The Kuka sect of Sikhs in the Punjab were first off the mark in 1870; soon after, in 1882, the Hindu social reformer Dayanand Saraswati founded the first *gaurakshini sabha* (cow protection society). His *sabhas* put up cattle shelters, and Dayanand also urged the reform of the caste system. His influence continued to grow in the twentieth century, mostly by stealth, through a web of Dayanand Anglo-Vedic schools, but not infrequently in association with communal campaigns against Muslim 'perpetrators' of the vile deed of *gau hatya* (cow killing), even though the largest consumers of beef during his lifetime were in fact the British in India.[51]

In 1950, the Indian constitution included cow protection as one of its long-term aims ('directive principles') but many provinces enshrined it in law. In 1966, two years after Nehru died, an alliance of Hindu right-wing parties led a rally of several hundred thousand people demanding a national ban on cow slaughter, and eight people died in the violence. (Mrs Gandhi did not relent – her election speech, available online, stressed the importance of dealing with poverty first.) In 1979, the venerable old Gandhian Vinoba Bhave (1895–1982) launched a hunger strike demanding that the government put an end to cow killing. The Gandhian figure had charisma in his old age, and his long white beard lent him the air of an ascetic.[52] Vinoba could not be ignored. Here again, the hunger strike was martialled as a potent weapon. Morarji Desai, then the prime minister of a shaky alliance, made promises he could not fulfil. In 2002, a band of Hindu nationalist groups, local and global, came together and threatened to enlist thirty million activists against cow killing.

The cow thus became an ever more emotive political symbol over the course of the twentieth century. But I doubt whether cow protectors in the early, mid or late twentieth century had more practical knowledge of how and what cows ate, who provided that fodder and how. They likely had even less knowledge than Gandhi. In the late 1970s, cow lovers (*gau bhakt*) began to provide shelters for diseased cows in their last and painful throes before death – rather like Mother Teresa's Missionaries of Charity did for the urban poor dying on the streets of Calcutta. In the cow 'hospices', *bhakts* rubbed down the suffering cows with Diclofenac to ease their pain as they died. (Some scientists and ornithologists argue that this killed off India's entire population of vultures, who were poisoned by feeding off the cows' flesh; this may or may not be the whole story behind their sudden and almost complete disappearance.)

But the mechanics of the life of a cow have mattered, and still matter, only to the 'lowly' cowherd. Visitors to India's towns and cities in the second half of the twentieth century will remember seeing cattle squatting in the middle of the roads, nibbling the patchy grass and shrubs that municipal corporations had planted in half-hearted attempts to beautify the streets, munching banana skins, husks of toasted corn and other urban waste. Cattle owners whose grazing lands were engulfed by towns, particularly after partition, took to letting their cattle roam the city all day, confident that they would not be harmed and hopeful that they might find something to eat.[53] Many outsiders thought their presence to be part of India's 'oriental' and 'traditional' charm. Few asked why they were there. This question of why serene cows blocked urban arteries seems not to have bothered anyone, even those who had a horror of cow killing. The answers would have made them uncomfortable. They were there grazing among scraps for fodder.

Yet once the cow's milk crossed the threshold of the Brahmin kitchen, it attained the status of the ultimate food. In southern India, Tamil Bramins were (and still are) wont to eat 'curd rice' for lunch; in affluent northern India, children drink milk for as many years as their households can provide it; in Punjab, salted buttermilk (*lassi*) cools and nourishes the thirsty on hot summer afternoons. In Bengal in eastern India, milk-based sweets, including *mishti-doi*, yoghurt sweetened with the jaggery of date palms, gave many a Bengali (and Bangladeshi) diabetes. These are foods that make people dreamy-eyed with desire. Of the starving cowherd and his diseased bony cattle they know nothing.

A turnaround of sorts began after independence, in India. In Kaira in Gujarat (the scene of one of the major protests against the British

Raj), three men – Tribhuvandas Patel (a Gandhian activist from the area who set up a milk producers' union in 1946), H. M. Patel (who helped achieve the technicalities of the partition of India) and Verghese Kurien of Kerala, a Michigan-trained scientist with some knowledge of animal husbandry – played a role. Together with the members of the milk producers' union, they set up a cooperative and then put into place rudimentary technology to process the milk, hitherto often provided by cows with tuberculosis or other illnesses. The cooperative at Anand began to provide parts of urban India with pasteurised milk, and butter made from it. This product was called Amul.

In an inspired decision, the Amul team hired the talented young Sylvester DaCunha to advertise Amul. (DaCunha, from Goa, had worked with my father, who ran an advertising agency, before he set up on his own.) DaCunha ran a most inventive advertising campaign: 'Utterly, butterly delicious – Amul', a slogan cleverly adapted to connect to current events, pushing back against state pressure to take a less cynical view of politicians and current affairs, and resisting the tendency to hire glamorous female models, a feature of Indian (and indeed global) advertising after the 1980s. The *Guinness World Records* shows the Amul campaign (still running) to have been the world's longest-lasting advertising campaign. It appealed to the urban Indian's sense of humour (believe it or not, despite the daily horrors they look away from, satire is much appreciated in the subcontinent). Amul captured markets to such a degree that, by 2000, it was hard to find any butter in urban India that was not manufactured by the Amul group or inspired by its model.

At the time of writing, Amul is owned by 3.6 million milk producers. They are all members of the cooperative. In 1976, they came together to support the making of a film, *Manthan* ('The Churning'), each contributing two rupees towards its production costs. Shyam Benegal's film, the first crowd-funded film ever, anywhere, is about the history of milk producers and their hardships, and of the Amul cooperative, but in no crude sense. Benegal was a significant artist who also worked in advertising.[54] (Advertising agencies in those days were refuges for people with creative talent who could not otherwise have made a living.) Even though it was critically acclaimed and aired on national television, I doubt that the film encouraged many middle-class or elite Indian milk consumers to think, and think again, about the webs of production and supply that link them to this everyday product without which they 'cannot live'.

Amul spearheaded the White Revolution in India, which eventually made India the world's largest producer of milk. In 1974, the National Dairy Development Board scaled up the Amul model with the goal of making India self-sufficient in milk. Tactically named 'Mother Dairy', mechanised booths stood in for 'Mother Cow' all over urban India by the end of the twentieth century, with early-morning queues for the pasteurised, unadulterated product a thousand miles away from its producers.

But in rural India (and much of Pakistan and Bangladesh), where there is no regular electricity and few can afford or sustain fridges, milk must still be procured in the (not so good) old ways.

II

ORTHODOX COOKING AND EATING: OF TABOOS AND CONTRADICTIONS

Moving on from milk in its various forms, so adored by the 'upper castes' of South Asia, there's the matter of the cooking space and its maintenance. Cleaning kitchens between meals and readying them for the next round of cooking was labour-intensive. The kitchen had to be rendered spotless. Every pot had to be scrubbed until it was gleaming. At the start of the century, the pots were scoured with ash. By 1948, Unilever's blue detergent powder Surf begun to replace ash and Vim (an older Unilever product) in towns in Pakistan. It entered the Indian market in 1959. But my memory is not of a simple urban–rural divide. Surf was there for the brown sahib's kitchen while his servants, like other urban workers, used ash. Many of the poorest city dwellers still do.

Next the floor had to be swept clean, and the room cleared of smoke, the *chulah* (wood-burning stove) brushed free of every speck of fallen food. In villages with mud houses, a thin mud floor often had to be laid anew in 'upper-caste' homes. When Ravindra Khare did fieldwork near Lucknow and Gopalpur in 1958, he found that Kahars – a 'low-ranking' caste – did this work. 'Dirty' people, in Brahmin India, cleaned the 'high-caste' home owner's sanctum sanctorum.[55] They saw no contradiction in this.

Within the household, lower-ranked people – women – did the cooking. But before they entered the kitchen they had to bathe and put on a clean sari. (Clothes could, in theory, capture bad *pinda*, after all.) Once they started cooking, they could not leave and re-enter the kitchen without bathing again. (In theory at least. It's hard to imagine how this could be practised.) 'Upper-caste' women rendered 'impure' by menstruation or childbirth could not cook, or even come close to the clean areas of the house. Only 'pure' women cooked, and by their work they transformed raw elements into 'morally edible victuals'.[56] In smaller, poorer, 'upper-caste' families, the delicious irony of telling husbands how to cook basic food was not lost on their wives. However, there were men who could not tolerate this world turned upside down, even for a few days for ritual reasons. As Baby Haldar writes in her autobiography, they beat their wives hardest at this time of the month for their 'impertinence'.[57]

The consumer – the Brahmin patriarch above all – also had to follow certain codes in the orthodox order of things. He had to wash, don clean clothes but bare his upper body and pray, before eating alone in total silence (*maun vrat*). If he wanted something more, he had to point. Instead of saying, 'Please could you pass me more salt?', he had to signal at the 'pure' woman waiting to serve him; and she rushed to bring him the salt.

This makes me think of my father, who grew up in a Brahmin household. He learned the habit of pointing at things that he wanted passed to him at the table. As I have mentioned, he loved food, so he was often pointing for seconds. (Our family mealtimes were most un-Brahminical in the sense that we all sat around a common dining table, men, women and children eating at the same time, tucking into food prepared by a Dalit cook.) A lot of argy-bargy went on: my father and I were classic 'argumentative Indians'. While my mother and siblings tried to make themselves heard, a lot of pointing went on. It is a habit I have picked up, much to my husband's irritation. It's totally upside down too: I (as a woman and wife) should be awaiting his orders rather than demanding his services (in what he regards as 'an imperative fashion' having never been exposed to this world of pointing himself). I am unaware that I do this. So history plays itself out. The transmission of 'tradition' is never as linear as we might imagine.

This is the underlying principle – the purity of the cook, the cooking space and the eater transforms mere produce into food: pure food for the righteous, food for the pure man. *Ahara suddhau satvas-uddhih*. ('The purity of beings lies in the purity of their food.')[58]

Of course, class plays a big part in how far this 'purity' can be maintained, as does the built environment. So one wealthy Tamil Brahmin family I know of in Calcutta built an entirely separate space outside their palatial house in which 'assistant cooks' (who chop the raw vegetables for each meal, but are 'lower' in caste and class status) ate their meals – consisting of what was left over after the sahibs and memsahibs had sated themselves. In middle-class families, where there is far less space, domestic workers who cook, eat leftovers on the floor, on a plate designated for their use. They eat as unobtrusively as possible, shovelling the food into their mouths as fast as they can so as not to offend their employers.

But just as food can be transformed into something pure by moral cooking practices, it can, according to this logic, lose its purity just as quickly. Two modes of impurity are embedded practice, well known (if not well understood) in Brahmin society – their power to disgust extends far beyond it. One is *baasi* (stale). Any cooked food had to be eaten at once, or it could gather impurities. Some foods were more likely to become *baasi* (literally, stinking) and their quality would degenerate faster than others: these were *kachcha*, boiled foods. *Pakka* deep-fried foods like Bombay mix could retain their freshness for months, as did pickles soaked in oil. But 'lesser' foods like boiled rice and daal – well, you had to eat them or waste them. This meant that women tried to cook just as much as was needed only for a single meal. It followed that they cooked day in and day out.

This taboo survived long after the refrigerator arrived in middle-class homes. When Kartik was little – three years old, so this would have been in 1994 – his orthodox paternal grandmother came to stay for a few months. Nanhi (not her real name), one of her daughters, came along too, bringing her own small children. Nanhi was a schoolteacher, having taken a bachelor's degree in Education – a route by which women from orthodox village homes come out and join 'modern' sectors, imbibing in this way many middle-class aspirations. She had had a love marriage, also to a schoolteacher, and lived in a small town.

On the evening after their arrival, I cooked, with Nanhi's help, saucepans full of daals, curries and the like, thinking this would tide us over for a few meals. But no. Even though after our first supper I put all the leftovers (pots and pots of food) into the fridge, it had somehow turned *baasi* overnight. Nanhi said the food smelled a bit off; I said she was imagining it. But neither she nor her mother would eat it; I had to start afresh the next day. Every single meal. Nanhi is a lovely woman – gently spoken, intelligent and uncomplaining – but her aversion to our own hand-cooked refrigerated leftovers was too strong for her to overcome. My aversion to cooking three times a day stems from the time they spent with us.

The other taboo is as weird: *jootha* – tasted but wasted food. It carries an even more powerful charge.

Imagine that I am eight. I am sitting on a low stone wall with my best friend Priya: two little girls with matching bobs, bony knees and scratchy headbands. We are both swinging our skinny brown legs. We are sitting on a wall in Lodhi gardens eating ice lollies, having escaped from our *ayahs* and splurged our saved pocket money. We could not be more content, despite the flies buzzing round our heads. I have finished mine, but Priya, a small and finicky eater, gets a stomach ache; she offers her leftover ice cream to me. I can't eat it because it is *jootha*, touched by the saliva of another. Even though it is special for the 1970s – a Kwality's, no less – I am repelled by the thought of eating it. Both of us watch it melt, as if under a spell, unable to prevent a tragedy.

We were trapped, like millions of 'upper-caste' Hindus in the subcontinent, and indeed in its diaspora, who waste fresh, delicious and desirable food because they will not eat *jootha*. They don't know why they won't. It is a habit, they say. Or they put it down to hygiene. Priya and I never knew the theoretical logic; we only knew, instinctively, that it was 'eeeew'.

I have only come to grasp the religious rationale for this prohibition through reading and research. It's because, in Brahminical theory, my saliva is as much my own, intensely personal, bodily fluid as my menstrual blood (or, for a man, his semen). Eating food touched by another's saliva is akin to ingesting their semen.[59] Think of the ramifications. This is why only wives eat the leftovers of their husbands. Or domestic servants, and others so poor and 'lowly', who eat leftovers and ignore the taboo. Consider what it meant, and means, for the Dalits to queue up at wedding feasts and wait all day for the leavings, and to 'relish' them.[60]

III

THE *PAANDAAN*:
DIFFERENT BOXES, DIFFERENT
FOOD NORMS

The number of Brahmins as a proportion of South Asia's population has been declining since the early twentieth century. In 1901, they accounted for 6.2 per cent of British India's total population.[61] By 1931, the proportion was down to about five per cent. In 2011, the Indian Human Development Survey dataset showed that in the Indian republic's more Hindu-dominated population, the Brahmin share of the cake (now 4.86 per cent) was still dropping. I don't deny that their influence was, and remains, far greater than their numbers suggest. Nonetheless, it is worth keeping these numbers in mind.

The geographical imprint of Brahmin power changed after 1947, when it grew more robust in North India and declined in the south, the west and the east of India. Brahmin strongholds in South India were damaged by the Dravidian movement. After partition, most Brahmins fled from the territories that became Pakistan, settling mainly in North India and West Bengal (see Chapter 4). India's Brahmins are now concentrated in Delhi, Uttar Pradesh and Himachal Pradesh, Jammu and the hilly areas of Uttarakhand.

Yet Brahmin power did not penetrate the tribal areas in central India, or the hills of the north-east. Nor did their food cosmologies have much influence over the Muslims of South Asia (although here, as in so much else, there was mimesis in practice). Extreme vegetarianism, even at the start of the century, was always on the margins, even among Brahmins of most regions; and with the passage of time, strict orthodoxy has weakened its hold on each new generation. Tamil Brahmins ('Tam Brams'), meanwhile, have tended to cling on to vegetarianism, even until the end of the century, in many cases even in the diaspora.[62] This does not always have much to do with a commitment to the orthodox value system. I know a Tam Bram astronomer at Yale and a historian in Boston who are both vegetarians. The former simply doesn't like meat, the latter is committed to green politics. But many more cleave to it because it's the done thing in their *jati*.

But let's be clear: they do not represent the subcontinent in any way.

The story of Emmanuel Tigga demonstrates this point.[63] Emmanuel is a dark-skinned man of medium height and strong build, sharp as a needle and quick to take offence. He works as a *peon* (low-ranking gofer) at an office in Delhi but knows he is capable of achieving more. There is an air of dissatisfaction about him. He is an Adivasi – self-styled 'indigenous inhabitant of the land', of a community the British listed as one of many Scheduled Tribes. By 2001, there were 84.3 million such 'tribals' across India, representing 8.2 per cent of a population that was just over one billion in size.[64] In 2001, there were roughly twice as many 'tribals' in India as Brahmins.

As one scholar has observed, the notion of indigeneity is a slippery one.[65] Historically, mobility rather than rootedness defined these tribes – they roamed wide areas and often practised shifting cultivation.[66] But after the Forest Act of 1878, the colonial state began to alienate some forests and to restrict Adivasi access to forest produce. It also strove to force them to settle in villages, and to take up 'scientific farming'. Villages did spring up, as did new form of forest use.[67] Yet older habits of procuring food never disappeared.

Emmanuel belongs to a tribe that dwelt deep in the forested uplands in Jharkhand in eastern India.[68] He was born in 1975 in a dirt-poor village of about one hundred souls. He was one of seven sons. In better-off families, this might have been a matter for celebration, but in a household as poor as Emmanuel's, it meant nine mouths to feed with all the domestic labour falling on the shoulders of one woman, his mother. He speaks of his lack of sisters looking into the middle distance, as though he wished things had been different.

The village, Tabela Lota Kona, was so deep in the forest and so high in the uplands that no other village could be seen from it. On a clear night, the sky was like a dome lit up by stars. At almost 7,000 feet above sea level, no electricity or piped water reached it, and a road has only just begun to be built in the context of the Indian state's war against the Naxalites.[69]

Emmanuel's family, like most families in the village, was destitute. They were smallholders on a tiny scale, owning under five acres of land dispersed across different mountain slopes. The only 'rich' man in the village was the bald and bad-tempered *chaukidaar* (the state's 'watchman'), who had about twenty-five acres. It was his duty to go to the police station every week and file a report on goings-on in his area. He was a 'very big' (powerful) man; he shouted at everyone, but he only ever wore a *langot*, two pieces of cloth covering his private parts, held together at his waist by a piece of twine.

Emmanuel starved for most of his childhood. Although his wider household (his father's four brothers and their dependants) jointly owned a cow, it was not their practice to milk it. Instead they allowed calves to drink their mother's milk so that they 'grew strong; and could help them plough' their own small plots; and do the heavy lifting when they were ordered to plough the *chaukidaar*'s twenty-five acres.

After being weaned from his mother's breast, Emmanuel drank no milk at all.

Nor did his brothers. They grew up on rice water – *maad*. Milk played no part in the life of his village. Its inhabitants subsisted on handfuls of rice with salt, leavened by fruit and meat; in lean times the whole family might have to share one kilo of rice for a month. Rough, brown and short-grained, the rice they grew in their fields fed Emmanuel's family for only three months of the year. For the rest of the year, they bought rice from the market several miles away. This 'market' seems to have been the kind of tiny bazaar that Verrier Elwin, the Christian missionary and self-styled authority on tribals, described: 'the entire contents of it could have been bought up for about £10, and a liquor shop, which, in its dirt and stink, unhappily bears no resemblance to the pub in England.'[70]

This is what the marketplace may have looked like to a passing (and somewhat breathless) English do-gooder, but for Emmanuel's family, it was their lifeline. During the monsoon, his mother sold raincoats made from the broad leaves of a wild gourd (*laopatta*), which she gathered in the forest. She treated them by tying them into a damp bundle for two nights, after which she sewed the yellowed leaves together to make *goongoo*, cape-like raincoats that were more or less waterproof. She then made the long trek to the bazaar with a dozen or so *goongoo*, and a couple of her elder sons in tow. She sold the *goongoo* and bought rice (between four and five kilos for a family of nine) and salt, and sometimes a splash of mustard oil – much desired but often more than the family could afford.

A few trees in the village bore digestible fruit. One was the banyan, which produced the sweet and tasty *bargat*, so delicious that young children would rise early and climb the great root-like branches to reserve a spot before dawn for their family so that they could take the fruits from that particular branch. (I, a city-bred child from a well-to-do family who could eat any fruit I wanted – in season, within reason – had never even heard of the banyan fruit before I interviewed Emmanuel. So many worlds under one sky.)

Deeper in the forest and hence riskier to gather was the fruit of *dumbaaris* (cluster fig trees). Emmanuel's brothers would climb these tall trees when the fruit had ripened and share the figs with the family. They were not sugary-sweet like the European fig, but good to eat.

The *chaukidaar* – the lowest official in the state structure – was a very important person in the village. On his twenty-five acres, he owned six jackfruit trees and two mango trees, which he guarded like a hawk. In return for their labour in his fields, he paid men in jackfruits. Women would ripen these with care and, at the right moment, carve them up, uncooked, and divide them equally among members of the family.

There was little water to drink. The villagers had sunk a well some distance away, years before Emmanuel's birth. But he remembers only being parched.

This was the basic diet. They ate no vegetables at all.

Every Sunday, however, men of the village went hunting in the forest. (Until there was a road, there were no forest officers to stop them, and the *chaukidaar* seems to have turned a blind eye to this practice, which was technically against the law.) They carried a variety of arms – bows and arrows, spears, tridents (*trishul*), old guns, sometimes one licensed gun (the *chaukidaar*'s own), axes and catapults, most manufactured by the village ironmonger. (The area is rich in minerals.) They were excellent hunters and they killed what they could. Emmanuel once killed a cobra poised to strike from twelve or fifteen feet away, with only a catapult. He got it straight between the eyes. The game they hunted included foxes, deer, mountain goats, wild boar, wild fowl, hares, rats, squirrels and, on a few occasions, black bears – the most dangerous of all the mammals in the subcontinent. The technique was not unlike the beating of the hunt in Europe: the entire village would gather at one end and make a racket while the hunters hid behind clusters of trees and outcrops of rocks. They would then kill any wild bird or animal startled by the sudden brouhaha.

The most prized kill was a *junglee sooar* – wild boar. Pig (*sooar*) meat, then, is not just eaten, it was lusted after more than any other meat.

'Why?' I ask Emmanuel.

He shrugs as though my question is stupid. 'Well, it is the most delicious meat. But also the animal is large, and has a lot of flesh on it. So we all had full bellies for a change.'

He looks at me straight in the eye to judge whether I, who have never gone hungry, appreciate what this means.

Sometimes, of course, the hunters returned empty-handed and dejected late in the evening. But if they succeeded, the men would take the kill back to the village square, and cut it up with axes, and apportion shares equally among themselves. Thereafter the women took over.

The cooking process was simple. First, Emmanuel's mother would burn the hair off the kill. This would give jungle cooking its association with the aroma of burning meat: there was no barbecue in this part of the Adivasi belt.[71] Women made simple stews, slow-cooked in baked earthen vessels. The only condiment was salt. If the family were in luck, they added a drop of precious mustard oil; if not, the meat cooked in its own juices. They had no spices to add.

I have heard urban visitors to tribal zones describe local meat curries as 'bland', even 'disgusting'. I now understand why; elite palates are unaccustomed to meat, or indeed vegetables, unfried and unspiced. The rich must have their *pakka* foods.

Emmanuel's fellow Adivasis were not vegetarian. They ate no vegetable or lentil curries. They drank no milk. The most nutritious part of their diet was meat cooked in salt. By the 1980s, they ate rice, but never enough to fill their bellies. Mainly, they went hungry.[72] And thirsty.

Studies that go back to the previous century paint a similar picture of 'tribal' food. Cornish writes this of southern India in the late 1850s:

> The tribes inhabiting the forests ... live chiefly upon jungle produce, e.g. large and small game, honey, fruits and the starchy bulbs of various plants. They procure a little rice, salt, tobacco and betel from the plains, in exchange for the horns, hides, honey, wax &c, which accrue to them in the chase.[73]

Of course things have changed since then, and not all 'tribal' areas were the same.[74] But when it comes to food, Bastar's inhabitants were just as dependent on the shifting cultivation of mixed grains, hunting and trapping into the late-colonial period; and *jhum* cultivation (slash and burn) continued much as before, despite British admonitions.[75]

How much the state, whether colonial or post-colonial, was able to transform the food habits of these regions in practice remains moot. Emmanuel's story suggests only two significant changes since the late nineteenth century. The first is much greater dependence on rice. A second is less barter and a heavier reliance on small markets.

Although this is not easy to prove, it is a reasonable conjecture that the Indian state's war against Naxalites in Jharkhand has severed the links between many isolated villages and the small markets they relied on for supplies. Likewise, in Bangladesh, the battle against the Jumma secessionist movement in the Chittagong Hill Tracts (mentioned in Chapter 3) is likely to have had a similar effect. If we cast our minds back to Emmanuel's family's dependence on the little bazaar in the plains in the 1980s, one dreads to think how people in these areas coped, and continue to cope to this day.

In these contexts, Brahminical concepts of *saatvik*, *raajsik* and *taamsik*, *kachcha* and *pakka* meant little or nothing. Adivasi eating habits turned Brahmin food orthodoxy on its head.

This is not to say that Emmanuel's people had no moral codes about food. Equality and equity seemed to have been important principles. Also recognition of work: he who works, eats. So only those men who went on the hunt got to take home (an equal) share of the meat, and at home, the family ate equal portions. (Had there been a girl child in the family, this may have been different, of course.) For the villagers of Tabela Lota Kona, the berth was not imagined, it was real; they shared it in full knowledge of each other's contribution to the common weal.

As Emmanuel remembers it, the only crime was the theft of food. Often it was scrumping – the theft of the *chaukidaar*'s mangoes, which drove him mad – but also the pilfering of small bags of ripened rice from people's fields. The most heinous crime was sneaking into other people's homes to steal food. 'Bags of rice' come up more than any other item.

I asked Emmanuel: 'How did you know who was guilty?'

He replied: 'It was a small village. Everyone knew what the other families had. If you had just been to the market and bought five kilos of rice, people knew. If a family had gone without rice for days, you knew. If your rice disappeared and they suddenly started cooking it, you knew where your rice had gone.'

Punishment, to begin with, worked a bit like a university's human resources system. The village elders would go to the house of the thief and advise his parents or guardians to bring him into line. First warning. If a series of misdemeanours showed that he was an incorrigible recidivist, the young man (he was usually a young man or adolescent) would be summoned to the banyan tree which was the central meeting point of the villagers. The *chaukidaar* was present at these meetings, as was most of the village. The offender's family was fined – they had to compensate each household for their losses. This was a heavy burden: it often took them years to pay it off. (Emmanuel's face when he describes this reflects his memory of the shock and grief experienced by the thief's family.) The young burglar himself was awarded no punishment, although some fathers thwacked their errant sons with a stick. And then it was over. Life went on.

I reiterate: all crime was about food. And hunger. This was in the late 1970s and 80s.

There was much fear of ghosts, male and female, who lived in the forests. Now and again older village women were identified as witches, and diseases were thought to be spells they had cast. This resonates with older accounts of Adivasi regions, which attest to similar stories of enchantment. Verrier Elwin writes of witches who could cast spells on food procured by wrongful means. He tells the story of a hungry *chapraasi* (messenger) who took a cock from a Gond (Adivasi) 'witch' without paying for it, cooked it in a curry and ate it all.

> He had not been asleep for three hours before he was seized with internal pains, and the old cock was actually heard crowing in his belly . . . the most skilful men were employed to charm away the effects of the old woman's spell, but in vain. He died, and the cock never ceased crowing at intervals up to the hour of his death.[76]

By the end of the twentieth century, Emmanuel tells me, these ideas, and the cruel exorcisms that sometimes followed when a 'spirit had entered', were on their way out. Most people tried to get to government hospitals for allopathic treatment instead.

Steal not. If you steal, pay back what has been stolen. Expect only the share you have earned by your labour. Respect the forest's spirits, give 'witches' a wide berth. Simple principles, but a world away from those complex cultures of 'repulsion' of Brahminical and 'upper-caste' India.[77]

IV

DALITS: OF STARVATION AND SURVIVAL

If we move from these 'wild' regions to South Asia's heartland, the point is even more stark. If by heartland we mean its vast cultivated plains, studded with villages – so beautiful from afar as the huge glowing red sun sets over dusty fields – it is better described as a heartless land.

At the start of the century, each village was structured by caste. For decades to come in Hindu-majority India, dominant castes continued to hold the levers of social, economic and political power on terms that beggar belief.[78] In Muslim West Pakistan, the *biraadiris* or clans became an ever more powerful force; they too organised agrarian labour on terms no less rapacious or violent, while also observing caste-like strictures against the likes of Joseph Bhatti. Caste cross-hatches all major faith groups – Muslims, Sikhs and Christians – in a range of ways and to varying degrees.[79]

In the early years of the century, 'untouchables' constituted about a sixth of India's population. In 1935, the British drew up a list of Scheduled Castes, as they were termed, and India's constitution in 1950 made them the object of affirmative action to counter hundreds of generations of oppression.[80] By the time that anthropologist Joan Mencher conducted her studies in the 1970s, one in every seven Indians, roughly eighty-five million in all, belonged to a Scheduled Caste. She calculated that, taken together, they made up two per cent of the world's population.[81]

In the 1970s members of this scattered community began to self-identify as Dalit ('oppressed'). They drew inspiration from Dr Babasaheb Ambedkar, himself a Dalit and scathing critic of Hinduism.[82] In 1972, the Dalit Panthers emerged as a militant organisation to fight their corner, inspired by the Black Panther Party in the United States. It remains the case, as I write, their struggles and the state's affirmative action notwithstanding, that no government servant is permitted to use the word 'Dalit' in official correspondence – the term is too loaded.[83]

In the late nineteenth century they lived as slaves with no rights who performed various forms of labour for agrarian elites, paid for, at best, in kind.[84] In the 1870s, a few decades after William Wilberforce's 'Saints' had abolished the slave trade, British colonial officials in India justified the prevailing system as a form of 'gentle slavery'.[85] Most Dalits in rural India continued to live in this form of 'gentle slavery' for much of the twentieth century, in quarters of their own on the furthest outskirts of villages. They survived on scraps, *jootha*, *baasi* food and grain, and the occasional fallen animal. They spent most of their lives starving.

Sharankumar Limbale's autobiography, *Akkarmashi*, is the story of a boy who grew up in a Dalit family in rural India. It is so harrowing that for days after reading it I sat stupefied in my chair, unable to find the intellectual resources, let alone the words, to do justice to it. I still cannot, the horror is so overwhelming. Let me tell you the bare bones of his story, and let Sharan speak for himself.

Sharankumar was born a 'half-caste' – the illegitimate son of a Dalit Mahar woman and a man of the locally dominant Patil caste. He grew up with his mother and several half-siblings sired by different Patil men in the Mahar *wada* (quarters) on the outskirts of the larger village. His maternal grandmother, Santamai, and her partner 'Dada', were the mainstays of his childhood, giving him the tenderness that his mother, for some reason, denied him.

His is no classic autobiography. Born in 1956, Limbale provides few dates or places. The village is somewhere in western India: the book was first published in Marathi in 1991.

Limbale's central theme is hunger, hunger so profound that each day begins and ends with it. He writes:

> *Bhaakri* [flatbread] is as large as a man. It is as vast as the sky, and bright like the sun. Hunger is bigger than man. Hunger is more vast than the seven circles of hell. Man is only as big as a *bhaakri*, and only as big as his hunger. Hunger is more powerful than man. A single stomach is like the whole earth.
>
> Hunger seems no bigger than your open palm, but it can swallow the whole world and let out a belch.[86]

The family lived on pieces of *bhaakri* – a rough, thinly rolled, unleavened bread made of sorghum. One *bhaakri* was broken up to feed several mouths. The day would start with a meal of black tea sweetened with jaggery, and crumbs of *bhaakri*. How it ended depended on many things, most often on whether or not his Dada and Santamai got a chance to do some 'dirty' work. If they did, it was a good day.

Santamai, Sharankumar's grandmother, worked as hard as anyone else to support the family. Sometimes, on a good day, she plastered a house in the village with fresh dung and got a little ghee in return. One of her more regular jobs was to make cow-dung cakes for fuel. She searched the dung carefully for food as she did so:

> During the harvest, when the cattle grazed the fields, they passed undigested grains of *jowar* [sorghum] in their dung. The grains were yellow and swollen. Santamai picked up such lumps of dung and on the way home washed the dung in the river, collecting only the clean grains . . . She then dried them in the sun. As they dried they shrank. We went home when the grain was dry. When Santamai came home she ground the grains into flour. Santamai always sang while she ground grain.[87]

Sharankumar was repelled by the *bhaakri* she made from dung *jowaar*, but Santamai ate it without any fuss.

The family only sated their hunger when village cattle died. 'Whenever an animal died in the village, its owner came to Maharwada to ask the one under contract to remove the carcass.' The 'contract' to do various tasks for the Maharwada came in turns. It was regarded as a great privilege.

> Hindus see the cow as their mother. A human mother is cremated but when a cow died they need a Mahar to dispose of it.
>
> As a tough boy, I used to hold the legs. Men peeled the flesh with knives. I used to watch closely the things I had heard about in my school – liver, intestines, lungs, heart, spleen, everything. Dogs would hover on the fringes of the gathering and a boy was appointed to throw stones at them to drive them away.
>
> Everyone in the Maharwada appeared, one after another, bringing their vessels or plates with them. They almost leapt on the slaughtered animal to get their share. The one with the contract who had fetched the dead animal had the right to the first share and he always chose the best part of the meat. Others took away the remaining parts.[88]

Wild dogs devoured what was left. Vultures, still plentiful when Sharankumar was a boy, would pick the rotting carcasses and bones clean.

Later in life, Sharankumar would grow to hate the thought of eating fallen animals, but in his childhood, it was a lifeline to survival. His grandmother, ever thrifty, would carve wafer-thin strips of raw meat off the joint and dry them in the sun, curing them a bit like biltong. She would feed him one small strip when he returned from school starving. So much for *baasi*.

The other food after which the whole community lusted was leftovers – *jootha* by another name. Wedding feasts (or rather the waste from them) were the highlight of their lives.

Arjun Appadurai draws attention to the wedding feast itself, a staple of South Asian culture on which the bride's family tended (much to British disapproval) to spend 'far too much'. They did so because so much was at stake. Public honour was only one part in this. The bride's parents had to honour the bridegroom's family by feeding them as lavishly as they could, in an attempt to buy some kindness towards their daughter when she went to her new home as the youngest and most vulnerable daughter-in-law.

Appadurai points out the micro-politics and potential mishaps that occurred routinely in this exercise of performing and bestowing rank, under the full gaze of the community, by serving food. Feeding a guest in the first sitting, giving him a large portion full of the choicest items on the menu, displaying extra attentiveness to his needs and repeatedly insisting that he have a second or third helping – all were symbols that he was held in the highest esteem: possibly he was the father or a close male relative of the groom. A person served in the fourth sitting, by contrast, was likely to be a poor and distant relative of the bride. Her portion was likely to be ungenerous – more carbs and only a few delicacies – served up with little politesse. The signs may be subtle, indeed invisible, to the foreign guest, but as loud as trumpets to insiders.[89]

But Appadurai does not discuss the spectres at the feast: Dalits. The organisers knew they would be there. Indeed, they had an invitation of sorts, as the whole village was, by custom, invited. But they had to wait with their own plates until the 'caste' guests left. They dared not detain a wedding guest. South Asia was not that sort of place in the twentieth century. It is not that sort of place now.

Sharankumar writes:

> When there was an occasional wedding in prestigious village families, we
> grew as excited as wolves . . . Guests were invited to the feast. Outside we
> swallowed our own saliva. Before beginning to eat they uttered the names
> of gods like Pundalik and Vithal, and also the names of saints like Jnana-
> dev and Tukaram . . . We greedily heard the sound of mashed food being
> slurped. 'Has everyone had enough?' asked some older men. 'Don't hesi-
> tate, eat slowly, have as much as you like,' they shouted. Men rushed
> between the rows, serving diners who were busy eating. There were shouts
> of 'Kheer!' Someone would announce loudly, 'Chapati! Ghee! Curry!' A
> flock of crows fluttered in our stomachs. Throughout the feast the name
> of food items being called aloud assaulted our ears. Our stomachs entered
> our ears, they became the feast, they became a huge cauldron.[90]

Eventually they would be called in to eat what was left over. They
did so with gusto.

After a while, Sharankumar stopped going to feasts. There was too
much ill treatment associated with them, and besides, he worried
about what his 'upper-caste' schoolmates might think.

His mother chided him for having 'too much self-respect'.[91] Dwell
on that, for a moment. *Too much self-respect.*

Returning to their diet, then: no vegetables, no milk (the cup of tea
was served black), no rice, no curds, no lentils.

Only stale sorghum bread, then, a little jaggery, and the dried meat
of dead cattle their daily fare; *jootha* foods their special treats. A seventh of India's population. If they had something to celebrate – a
wedding, say – they killed a wild boar and ate pig curry and drank
strong, home-brewed liquor.[92] So much for Brahminical norms. Those
very norms were designed to shut out Dalits from their world. Dalits
were not supposed to feel human, to have personhood or dignity.
Throughout the book, others of 'high caste' never address Sharankumar by his name; they just yelled '*Ohe Makar ka!*' ('Hey there, you
son of a Mahar!') in his direction.

The book burns with anger. Limbale forces the reader to smell and
taste his world, and to inhabit it. Dalits can live only by inverting
Brahminical food norms. By so doing, 'his people' are further degraded
in the eyes of 'upper castes', and the 'repulsion' factor that the French
philosopher Célestin Bouglé first alluded to in the 1950s reinforces
the caste way of life.[93]

Laxman Gaikwad's book *The Branded* gives the educated 'upper-caste' middle-class reader another kick in the stomach. This autobiography, like Limbale's, was first published in Marathi in 1987 and translated into English only in 1998. Laxman belonged to another segment of Indian society that in 1871 the British government classified as 'Criminal Tribes'. By the time Laxman grew up, his community, the Uchalya, was less like a mobile 'tribe' and more like a settled *jati* living on the outskirts of a village near Latur in Gujarat. And yes, thieving was one means by which they survived: going out in gangs to crowded places like fairs, bazaars or bus stands, identifying victims, and working together to pick pockets. 'Schooling' for this work involved weeks of beating and torture, with chilli powder often stuck up the anus. This – let's call it 'kindergarten' – was to train the apprentice thief for the police brutality that lay ahead, and how to observe *omerta*, the code of silence, if they were caught.

But Laxman writes that not every member of his family or sub-*jati* was involved in this business; nor did all its sustenance come from it. Several had to become proficient hunters of game, and they ate anything that moved. Tata, his maternal grandfather, taught him to fish and hunt 'rats, rabbits, mongoose, deer, iguanas, fox, partridges, ducks, cranes, doves, tortoise, wild cats, pigeons, pigs, crabs, sheep, goats, water-hens, peacocks'.[94] (Killing peacocks is not permitted in India, but then, neither is stealing. An empty belly makes insistent demands.)

Of the many stories Laxman writes of his life, two demand retelling here. Laxman and his grandfather Tata were nothing if not inventive. They chased rats through the rubbish-strewn lanes of the Maharwada and threw them into a sack. They then used these hungry rats as hunters in their turn, to help them steal wheat from the fields that lay beyond. Just before harvest, they would let their rats free in the fields. The rodents would do their job: digging holes in the soil and hoarding grain in them. After the field was harvested, Tata and Laxman would amble up like innocent passers-by who had stumbled upon rats' store holes, and take what was in them. Farmers did not complain, writing it off as natural loss. The pair cleared up as much grain as they could in this way, and then ate their accomplices, the rats. The Pied Piper could have learned a thing or two from them.

But note here the balance of fish and meat of all kind against grain in the diet of the Uchalya. Milk and ghee barely get a mention.

The other narrative is of Sanskritisation. Laxman's father was too badly injured after one too many a brutal beating to work either as a thief or a hunter, and in the end got a job as a servant in the house of a local 'big man'. Poacher turned gamekeeper. He began to lecture Laxman and his older sons to 'live like the other village people. The village people do not allow us to take water from wells. They give us water from a distance without touching us. They do not allow us to visit temples.'[95]

The problem, in other words, was not with the society that treated them like animals, but with the Uchalya themselves, because they behaved like animals. This was the take of a father who had been removed a mile from the Maharwada by chance – a combination of bad and good fortune. But into that distance crept self-hatred; and with it a desire to see his sons embrace 'proper village values' – that is, 'upper-caste' values. He enrolled young Laxman in school, so that he could become more 'normal'. Every time the father heard that his sons had been thieving or hunting, he came to their tiny hut and beat the bejesus out of them. Laxman, who had hitherto bathed three or four times a year, in mud, now had to bathe and wash his clothes every other day with 'the sticky mud of the Ingle Lake' in a struggle to assimilate into the 'normal world'.[96] But outside school, he still survived on the occasional *bhaakri*, crabs, rats, carrion and handfuls of stolen grain.

V

MUSLIM FOOD PRACTICES

And then there are the Muslims of the subcontinent; over a third of the population of the British Indian Empire until 1947 and still thirteen per cent of India's population of 138 million in 2001.[97] Today, India's Muslims constitute over a third of the world's 1.8 billion Muslim population.

Theologically, all Muslims are equal though not identical in the sight of Allah, who distinguishes between them only by their righteousness and good works. In practice, however, there has been much stratification between the Muslims of the subcontinent. There is a sharp distinction between Muslims who regard themselves as 'of foreign descent', or *ashraf*, who form a distinct elite group that claims ancestry from Persia, Arabia, Afghanistan or Turkey; and *ajlaf* or *atrap* Muslims, local converts, deemed to be of lesser status. The *ashraf* further divide themselves into four groups: Sheikh, Syed, Pathan and Mughal, the first two claiming lineal descent from the Prophet. They were not castes per se, but rather like *jatis* – intermarrying circles. That was the ideal in the nineteenth century and remained so in the first half of the twentieth.

The creation of Pakistan has weakened some of these divides, not least among the refugee populations who flooded into the new nation, and for whom the *muhajir* or refugee identity (as opposed to local-born clan ties) became more and more salient. There are Muslims who are regarded as 'dirty' too, and like Dalit Christians have been forced to live in discrete quarters. Today, they self-identify, in India, as Pasmanda Mahaz, and towards the end of the twentieth century, demanded recognition of their historic oppression and access to the state's reservation programmes for ('Hindu') Scheduled Castes.[98]

Sanskritisation was evident among Muslim groups too. Sheikh Siddiquis were technically *ajlaf*, having converted from the Hindu Kayastha caste of record keepers of Allahabad district in North India. There was, as Imtiaz Ahmad suggests, some resistance to their absorption into the fold. But the creation of Pakistan provided opportunities for all literate Muslims, and the Sheikh Siddiquis, with their high levels of literacy, may well have found many opportunities for assimilation and upward mobility. I imagine it would have been easy, in the context of mass migration, for them to shed *ajlaf* status and become *ashraf muhajirs*.[99] Identity is, in the end, a mutable thing.

Muslims are also divided into sects, the differences between them going back centuries. Sunnis were, and remain, the great majority in South Asia. But Shias, Ismailis and Bohras (like Jinnah) were also a significant presence: indeed, one might argue that as with Brahmins, their influence far outstripped their numbers.

Fissures between Sunnis and Shias have grown deeper over the twentieth century. Sunni reformers and 'fundamentalists' attacked Shia religious practices with increasing virulence, leading to more and more violence (albeit of a localised variety) before 1947.[100] In Pakistan, after Zia's regime let loose a culture of violent intolerance of religious and political difference, matters grew worse. These clashes were ever more violent and more frequent as the century drew to a close. One author writes that some 4,000 people died in Shia–Sunni sectarian battles in Pakistan between 1987 and 2007.[101] Human

Rights Watch suggests that since 2008 'thousands of Shia' have been killed by Sunni extremists.[102] These sources have their own biases, of course; but no one reading the world news during the last three decades could have remained unaware of the increasing carnage this difference has caused. Those who follow heterodox versions of Islam, such as Ahmediyas or Qadiyanis, have also been targets of extreme violence since the 1950s.

So Muslims too were 'stratified' in the twentieth century. Often, they were at war among themselves. To speak of them as if they sang from the same *marsiya* (elegy) is to get it wrong. Yet one can see them as a congeries of religious groups who rejected Brahminical food ideals. Indeed, if Muslims shared anything beyond faith in Allah and Mohammad as His Prophet, they shared an approach to food.

No amount of political and societal pressure persuaded Muslims of South Asia to adopt Brahmin codes. They did not take up vegetarianism as a means of upward mobility. In the late nineteenth century, they ate a great variety of meats, fish and fowl, including beef, but those of high birth and the orthodox, as enjoined by the Prophet, abjured pork. The medical officer of Kurnool noted that 'the Mahomedans adopt the most varied diet, a considerable quantity of animal food being combined with farinaceous and other vegetable nourishment they habitually indulge in'.[103] By the end of the twentieth century, this was still the ideal.

This is not to say that there was as a 'Muslim diet', as such, save that it was non-vegetarian and that its *haute cuisine* at the highest strata showed elements of Persian, Turkic and Afghan influence. There are overlaps and some mimesis against which Maulana Thanawi railed. Muslims, like everyone else, were influenced by the foods nature made available in the regions where they lived and by local culinary traditions. So in Bengal (where the majority of South Asia's Muslims were concentrated), those who could afford to do so ate rice supplemented by fish, just as the Hindus who lived alongside them did. Even poor peasants, particularly if they lived by rivers or *bils* (large natural lakes that were so common in the Bengal delta), caught fish to add protein to meals that otherwise consisted only of rough rice, salt and chillies.[104] In 1930, the Bengal Provincial Banking Enquiry Commissioners found that 'beef is eaten by Musalmans', but did not specify which 'Musalmans' ate it, or how often. They observed that while both Hindu and Muslim agriculturists ate fish, the 'lowest' Hindu castes ate pork.

Significantly, Muslims 'hardly ever purchased' milk.[105] (Yoghurt, though, is prized.) In this sense too, their food norms appeared to have been distinctive.

Those in Lahore, Lucknow and Delhi, the old Mughal heartlands, were more influenced by Afghan, Turkic and Persian traditions of cooking. Prized foods include kebabs of rich and subtle varieties, often specific to each city, each of whose denizens liked to boast that theirs were the best. (Here too there was a melding in Muslim and Hindu *tandoori* culture – it would be unwise to miss regional hybridity.) Yet another kind of Muslim cuisine was the Hyderabadi. Hyderabad was the most significant Muslim state in southern India (at least its Nawab was a Muslim); and to this day, people from this southern region of India insist that theirs are the most flavoursome and aromatic biryanis, more robust, spicy and tasty than the effete varieties of North India, Pakistan, Bengal or Bangladesh. Its larger portions of meat, heavier lacings of saffron and lashings of local spices make it a hotter, spicier, chunkier dish.

It is for this reason that we served Hyderabad biryani at Kartik's wedding dinner. It was a controversial choice. My family is Bengali – as you must by now remember – so for them Calcutta biryani is the best biryani. It was hard to explain my shadowy logic to them over all the conch-blowing, music and laughter.

But these are the diets of princes and landlords, who tended to shower generosity on guests by serving them dish after dish until they were practically faint with eating. Biryani, to be sure, was an object of desire across the subcontinent – a fetish that transcended borders. It is a dish that has bucked the effort to turn people into 'nationals'. Even a Tam Bram I know of orders it and eats it (from his favourite outlet in Calcutta) for lunch.

But for the poor and even the white-collar classes, it remained a luxury, eaten only on the rarest of occasions.

The everyday food of the Muslim poor at the turn of the century was much like the everyday food of the poor Hindu peasant: rice, roti or *bhaakri* – unleavened bread made from wheat, sorghum, maize or cornflour – eaten with daals if they were lucky, or just salt and chillies. Rice was plentiful only in alluvial regions such as Bengal and Madras (albeit even there it was considered to be a Brahmin food; the poor ate rougher grains). Bengal began to depend on imported rice from Burma by the 1930s. In southern India, rice was not easily grown in dry districts before canal irrigation made it possible, so it was not often seen on the poor man's plate, whatever his faith. This would change as the century progressed.

But the aspiration was to eat meat whenever possible. My impression is that even at the end of the century, Muslims in Old Delhi, an impoverished area by the 1990s when I used to visit it often, ate (or strove to eat) a protein-rich diet. Even the poorest rickshaw pullers rose at dawn seeking out a small portion of offal before they started their day – *nihaari* (curried trotters) or *gurda kapura* (spiced kidneys and testicles). If not, they survived on roti and *namak* (salt), *beedees*, *paan*, *gutkaa* (a wad of tobacco) or *charas* (marijuana) to ease the pain of starvation. But meat, however humble, remained the dream.

Given injunctions to Muslims to eat only *halal* (permissible) meat, it was inevitable that Muslims specialised as halal butchers to supply this market.[106] Kenneth McPherson writes of Calcutta of the 1920s as a palimpsest, where almost four in ten people were Muslims, and where different groups specialised in the delivery of different foods to the city.[107] He writes that *kasaais* (butchers) operated as an independent artisan 'caste', with their own neighbourhoods and leaders. Throughout the century, they traded in halal fresh meat, everywhere in South Asia.

Their status in society was different from that of *mahaars* or *chamaars*. Butchers provided consumers with a prized and expensive commodity and they had expertise in different cuts. They tended to be more prosperous and organised. Before partition, they had standing within Muslim neighbourhoods, and indeed in wider society.

After partition, much changed. *Kasaais* and *khaansamas* (cooks, usually Muslim, who lorded over the kitchens of grand houses) were among the many skilled groups who fled to Pakistan. Those who stayed in India found their standing diminished because many of their most elite patrons had fled. A study of Muslim *bastis* in the 1970s found that few had survived partition intact, 'one casualty being the hereditary trades and the status associated with them'.[108] In the 1970s, eighty per cent clung on to their professions but twenty per cent were forced into manual labour.[109]

In the late 1980s, I began to buy meat for the household. I would go to Kallu the butcher in Hauz Khas Market in South Delhi. Kallu was a burly and rather handsome man who traded exclusively in goat meat. He always had apprentices with him: no doubt his younger kinsmen. But regular customers got Kallu's special attention. He cut the meat exactly as they wanted it: with or without bones, fat, ribs, with marrow bones or without them, or ground fine for *shami kebaabs*. The demands of his customers were exacting, and he took care to serve each one. Buying meat burned a hole in one's pocket, then as now, and Kallu was aware that most of his customers were spending more than the rest of their week's food budget on this one transaction. He regarded it with the respect it deserved: he sat erect and proud. He treated them with courtesy.

How consumers treated him is another matter. The shop – though he kept it as clean as possible – smelled of raw meat and attracted flies. For comfort, no doubt, he wore a *lungi* (a piece of cotton wrapped and tucked round the waist), and a vest, rather than the rayon pant-shirt combo that had become the average urban Indian man's attire by this time. Both his *lungi* and his profession marked him out as a Muslim, whose status as a loyal Indian was a little suspect.

Still, Kallu radiated pride in his work. He sat cross-legged on a raised plinth beside a large wooden block. His knives were of the old kind: sharp curved blades embedded in the blocks, and he operated them to devastating effect. These were old skills, honed over time and passed down through generations: his young apprentices watched and learned. Yet the same people who ate the *methi gosht* (goat) curry with such excitement at a middle-class dinner party might hold their noses as they walked past Kallu's shop.

It is the berth again. Wherever there's middle-class or elite consumption, the berth's right there too.

The other major difference in Muslim food culture was that there was no rigid concept of *jootha* (polluted food).

Muslim families (and sometimes guests) ate at home from a single large platter, placed on a *dastarkhwhaan*, a large piece of cloth covering the floor, on which members of the household gathered. This way of eating was considered *sunna* – the tradition or way of the Prophet. The biryani (say) was piled onto a platter as humble or fine as the household's circumstances would permit. *Haleem*, too, a special dish cooked typically during festival times, is often eaten in this way. Everyone gathered round a single bowl of slow-cooked grains, daals, meat and spices, and dipped pieces of flatbread into it.

My former student, Humaira Chowdhury, who has described her family's history to me, tells me that each member of the family approached the platter from a slightly different angle, creating their own notional portion, burrowing into it with their right hand to take food to their mouths. Humaira – long-necked, delicate and bright-eyed – recalls eating thus as a child, her tiny hand creeping into her little wedge of the platter of festive biryani. They ate until they were satisfied, when there was enough. If not, they ate what was there, and then went to bed hungry. If there was plenty, Humaira's family invited the Hindu *darwaan* (guard) of the culturally mixed and down-at-heel square at Marquis Street in Calcutta, where her family lived in a single room, to share their food.

Even if the family ate meals from separate plates (as some of my friends do, for everyday supper), different generations, and men and women and children, all ate together. Women did all the cooking and serving, but they ate alongside the men of the family – as can be seen from the many scenes involving family meals in the 1970s black-and-white movie *Garam Hawa* ('Scorching Winds'). Indeed, the film has a marvellous scene of a Muslim family who stayed behind in India after partition in a rambling, crumbling but beautiful *haveli*, built around a courtyard with pillared arches and lattice through which dappled sunlight brightens, but does not burn.

The sequence is shot from above as they gather to eat. It is striking because, despite all the space they have in their beautiful old house, they sit in a tight circle on the floor, talking and eating.

Eating culture among Muslims was thus more democratic in the eating of food, if not in its preparation. It was a far cry from the Brahmin principle of serving different status groups in different sittings: patriarchs first, children next and women last of all. (Oh, and the servants after them, if space permitted, outside.)

Another difference (from Brahminical norms) is in Muslim behaviours of fasting and feasting.

I write this in the month of Ramazan in 2020, after the outbreak of Covid-19. The great majority of the subcontinent's 650 million Muslims will be fasting all day, families having woken in the early hours and gathered together to pray and eat *sehri* (the morning meal) before dawn. They will then fast until the evening moon is sighted, when the men are called for the night prayer (*isha*). Traditionally, for men, this prayer would have been at a mosque.

All day, men and women will not have eaten any food, nor drunk even a drop of water.

In previous years, before the Covid lockdowns prevented this, they feasted together after breaking their fast. In better times, they had hosted *iftaar* parties at home, inviting friends and neighbours, often non-Muslims. It's the joy of community that seems to make Muslims look forward to Ramazan as *barakat ka maheena* (the month of good fortune). Even at Humaira's little home, at every single *iftaar*, every member of the wider community (Hindu, Christian and Muslim), who helped sustain the family, was invited to join their meagre *iftaar* meal of fresh fruit, dates and savouries, and, more rarely, *haleem paraatha* (flatbread with a stew of mutton and lentils).

For young lads, the joy was a matter of pouring into the streets and roaming the bazaars in search of the most delicious food. During Ramazan evenings, markets in localities where Muslims were concentrated after 1947, came alive with the aroma of kebabs and *nihaari*. Famous restaurants had their busiest days of the year. Groups of women chattered together as they shopped for the next morning's *sehri*. At the start of the century, *sehri* foods such as *kheer* (spiced rice pudding, so much more delicious than its English cousin), *phirnee* (a sweet milk dessert), syrupy *gulaab jaamun*, and pickles were made laboriously, by hand, by women of the household. By the end of the century, Gits, a company selling instant dessert mixes, had begun to do fifty per cent of their sales over Ramazan. Rasna, an instant drink powder (India's answer to Tang) had all but replaced hand-made *sharbat* (sherbet). Ready-made garlic-ginger pastes, which had taken South Asian markets by storm, also sold out during Ramazan.[110]

Here's another difference: there's no notion of *saatvik* (pure), *raajsik* (energising) and *taamsik* (unduly exciting) foods. Everyone enjoys their onions and garlic, eschewed by the purest Brahmins. There's a colloquial saying that reflects this, albeit in a snide way: *Naya mullah pyaaz zyada khaata hai* ('The new convert to Islam eats more onions').

To return to Ramazan: tailors would do great business after Ramazan, when the days of fasting ended. It meant new outfits, however cheap, for all members of the household. Cold-drinks stalls were ready to slake thirst close to shops famed for hot *galauti* kebabs. Date-sellers did well. This luxury has become a staple of the pre-dawn breakfast for some decades now, a mark of the extent to which Muslim South Asia increasingly looks westwards to the land of the Prophet to define 'correct' Islamic practice.

This year, the loudspeakers blasting out the muezzins' call to prayer have fallen silent. One of the most striking images has been of the Jumma Masjid – one of Asia's largest and most beautiful mosques – empty. It only emphasised the extent to which Ramazan, the month of fasting and feasting, is about community. Prayer too of course: in addition to the usual ritual daily prayers, those Muslims who know it (very few even at the end of the century) recite the Quran all through the month. During the pandemic, instead of inviting neighbours and friends home, people who could were helping mosques and dargahs prepare packages of *iftaar* foods to send to the hungry in the tenements around them (*zakaat*, or charitable giving, being an Islamic ideal).[111]

Otherwise, during the twentieth century where (barring the Spanish flu) no pandemic struck South Asia, fasting and breaking fast were very much a communal activity. Both men and women performed it together. Of course the burden of food preparation fell on the shoulders of women, and the men had most of the fun of gadding about after sundown. But it *is* a community activity, and a very public one at that.

Let me touch upon the matter of leftovers. And of *nihaari* in particular. A dish adored across the subcontinent and the diaspora (I ate a fabulous nihaari, once, in Leeds), it is made from trotters and leftovers. Leftover *nihaari* is called *taar*. *Taar* forms the basis of the new *nihaari* cooked up each day. Some *nihaari* shops in Delhi boast an unbroken *taar* going back a century.

So much for the orthodox Brahminical concept of *baasi*.

VI

THE MIDDLE CLASSES: CHANGING FOOD REPERTOIRES

Finally, challenges to these norms have come from within. Urbanisation and the growth of a middle class to the size of the subcontinent's entire population in 1901 have affected the food habits not only of migrant labourers (see Chapter 4) but also of the Hindu 'upper castes' and elites more generally.

I think it would be useful to place in context this ballooning crowd, this mob of 300 million which I must claim as part of my heritage. It has a history, and that history has not been straightforward. Its growth has been in waves: some gentle, some tidal. It has two strands, although discussion of the literary and professional streams has hitherto dominated the story. That history is well known. This class emerged from landed lineages whose personal income from their estates was relatively small, but whose education (paid for by wealthy parents and affluent households) enabled them to go to elite colleges or universities – whether Hindu College (later Presidency College) in Calcutta, St Stephen's College in Delhi, Madras Christian College and Elphinstone in Bombay, or to Aligarh Muslim University. (Some products of these institutions went on to Oxford and Cambridge.) That education, in its turn, equipped them with the skills needed to flourish in the new professions.

From this nascent class emerged adventurousness, if not iconoclasm, in matters of food. The Young Bengal movement – a group of young men who had studied under Henry Derozio (1809–31), an Indo-Portuguese poet who died young but whose influence lived on until the end of the century – was a trail blazer. The members of the group were mainly caste Hindus, or later Brahmos ('reformed' Hindus), and they flouted convention by eating beef, drinking beer and sherry. A notorious moment was when one member of the group visited the Kali Temple in Calcutta, and greeted the terrifying goddess not by prostration but with a 'Good morning, madam'.[112]

But most had, soon enough, to get down to the serious business of earning a living, and put these pranks aside. They gravitated to the professions for which their 'English educations' had prepared them. They became doctors, lawyers, journalists and members of government service (and in time became part of nuclear households, with wives 'sourced' from similar backgrounds). All were educated in English, often to a very high level, and were also fluent in vernacular languages which they spoke at home, and in which they wrote poetry, newspaper articles, essays and novels in their spare time. *Charulata*, Satyajit Ray's film based on Rabindranath Tagore's novel, is a clear-eyed portrait not only of a lonely wife, but also of the birth of this social class. Charulata and her husband Bhupati live in a grand house in the Calcutta Palladian style. Every perfect frame shows the things these people inherited from their *zamindaar* forefathers: ornate hand-woven saris, ornaments inlaid with gemstones, fine muslin *dhotis* and tailored jackets, mirrors, cabinets, marble-topped mahogany tables and four-poster beds, and *paandaans* made of silver. They are 'cultured'.

They have read Shakespeare and Keats, Hali and Hafez, Tagore and Bankimchandra, and they write poems and novels of their own.

But the viewer realises, when Bhupati's nationalist journal goes bankrupt, that the family is property-rich but cash-poor. Bhupati (and his cousin Amal, with whom Charulata falls in love) must earn their living out in a new world of urban work. Modern work. They seem unsure how to face this challenge.

Debt, even bankruptcy, continued to constrain the spending power of this group for decades afterwards. One of the lesser-known facts about Chittaranjan Das, the dominant Bengali politician of the first half of the twentieth century, is that his father, a Brahmo social reformer and journalist, died in debt. Chittaranjan – a barrister trained at Emmanuel College, Cambridge, and at the Middle Temple – was unable to his repay his father's debts and declared himself bankrupt. When he had earned enough, he restored his family's reputation (and indeed his own) by paying off his father's creditors with interest.[113]

Nirad Chaudhuri's *Autobiography of an Unknown Indian* also shows how this class shaped itself, and how speaking English well, having the art of conversation and the ability to earn in the professions and public services, became its particular métier.

Chaudhuri's title is a paradox though. When you meet a South Asian in a prestigious setting abroad, they often have this sort of family history. You might say: 'By the way, do you happen to know X? I met him when I was at a conference in Seattle. He is from Delhi.' The reply is always: 'Of course I know X! My parents were at his parents' wedding! India is a village, you see . . .'

You might scratch your head and think 'a village of a billion people? Hmm.' But the English-speaking middle class of the first type was, and remains connected, by this gossamer web of marriage relationships ('his aunt's husband's father was my grandmother's father' – boy, do we know our genealogies), by school, college and university bonds, workplace ties, patron–client networks, unfulfilled or unacknowledged love affairs, deep friendships and passionate rivalries. No one is really 'unknown'. It's a matter of degrees of connection. This is profoundly irritating, I believe, to others who lack this form of social and cultural capital, who burn at the fact that this lot write with such eloquence and seem to glide through the world with such ease.

This section of the middle class has punched well above its weight in terms of its influence in both state and society right across the sub-continent and its diaspora throughout the twentieth century. But after its heyday in the early twentieth century, few really were 'rich' even when they held high-ranking government positions (by imperial standards). They were paid far less than their white contemporaries at a time when inflation was hitting everyone with a fixed salary, and felt the pinch quite as much as, if not more than, white *laat* sahibs some grades above them. Despite his title, the Rai Sahib Ashutosh Ghosh (1887–1966) kept a daily note of his expenditure on food and 'sun-dries', his budget was so tight. A civil servant who retired as deputy director of the Department of Posts and Telegraphs in 1941, Ashutosh Babu (as Bengali men of this type were known) was a grand figure in his day. But the diary reveals what it cost the emperor to wear clothes. Food – fish, vegetables, sweets, daal, milk and bread – were expensive by 1946, and he bought them fresh every day. A detailed *hisaab* (account) of how much he paid the barber sits alongside his electricity bill (Rs 11, 8 annas). He totted them up with increasing attention to detail as each decade passed. His diaries show that he grew more stressed about matching his income with the expenditure that a man of his standing felt he required to keep his household fed, shaved, clothed and shod.[114]

Ashutosh Babu's generation ate differently from his parents' gener-ation. Men like him were buying sliced white bread, *maidaa* (white wheat flour), and crystalline white sugar, and paying 'electric bills'.[115] Many successful men of his time had two kitchens at home, one serv-ing European food, the other an 'upper-caste' 'traditional' diet. Sarat Chandra Bose (1889–1950), elder brother of the famous Subhas, the Tiger of Bengal, was a considerable statesman in his own right. He had two kitchens at his house at Woodburn Park in Calcutta. A dis-tinguished and successful lawyer, he 'sourced' a chef from outside the home who served the *laat* sahib's food in European style. In the second kitchen, the women of the household cooked and served the meals traditionally eaten by Bengalis of this class. Sarat Babu often ate two breakfasts, one from each kitchen. He grew rather rotund in consequence.

Throughout the century, famous colleges and universities churned out matriculates with impeccable English among their other class credentials, and these young men came to patronise (often, to begin with, in secret) burgeoning restaurants or 'hotels' to satisfy their lust for the new and dangerous. In Parashuram's short story *Rata-rati* (published in the late 1920s), a staid father hunting for an errant son discovers him in an eating joint serving hybrid delights such as the *Murgir French malpoa* – spiced chicken stuffed in crêpes.[116] Restaurants with greater claims to sophistication, many with wine lists, began to pop up, serving Chinese and Japanese food. Chinese food, modified to suit the Indian palate, became a craze after some Chinese fled to India during the Sino–Japanese war, bringing with them recipes with exotic flavours and forbidden ingredients. It still is.

There are 'fancy' Chinese restaurants, of course. But interestingly, in Calcutta, the Chinese set up shop in the leather industry, specialising in shoes for wealthy men. In Tangra, where they lived, worked and had their factories, they set up tiny restaurants in their homes. The place smelled, as well it might, of rotting meat and leather in various stages of tanning. But it was a middle-class secret, among the young, that the best Chinese food was to be found in Tangra. And so we would set off, on the back of motorcycles or in autorickshaws. We would try to ignore the smells until we got to our favourite restaurant, where we gorged ourselves until we could eat no more.

I made my first visit to Tangra in the 1980s, when I was working on my doctoral project. I went with a colleague of my sister, a techie from South India (I didn't know enough to ask him where exactly) with vegetarian parents. He ignored the smell of drying hides. Was it the berth again? Or was it just exciting for him to break these codes? Again, I assumed he was 'cool' about such things and probed no further. I was twenty: that's all I can say in my defence.

So 'young food' became a 'thing'. Tangra first emerged as a young place, where young people of this milieu went without telling their folks. (Today it is a vast bourgeois sprawl of huge restaurants for the whole family.) Pastry shops – Flurys in Calcutta, for instance – are part of city lore, and young people of this ilk bought pastries and drank coffee there, romance blossoming under the watchful gaze of waiters. At the Machan in the Taj Hotel in Delhi, one could buy as much coffee as one could drink for the price of one filter coffee, in cool air-conditioned comfort. Middle-class young people gathered there to discuss matters of the heart, the marriages being arranged for them despite their love for another person, unrequited passions, disastrous exam results, talking much and spending little. Often they sat there for hours. (No wonder the restaurant had to change into a 'family restaurant'.) Nirula's headed in the other direction. The family firm, which in the 1950s set up 'The Chinese Room', went into the fast-food business in 1977, setting up the first pizza parlour in Delhi's Connaught Place. Later it opened another branch at Chanakya Cinema, one of the few halls that screened English films. I cannot count how many pizzas I have eaten there with my friends. My whole notion of what a pizza was, and ought to be, was forged by Nirula's: so much so that when I finally went to Florence in 1985, I was disappointed by what a 'real' pizza was.

Later still, Nirula's opened up an ice-cream counter serving twenty-one flavours. It too became a haunt for the affluent young of India's Gen X.

Relics of this class still exist. I am one. They still succeeded at the end of the twentieth century because of the intellectual and social capital they had accrued and inherited, long after land reform stripped them of land and luxury, even in provinces where reform took place as seriously as it did in West Bengal after the Left Front came to power. (Others were less robust; see Chapter 5. The Chatterji clan lost much of the land they had owned along Hill Cart Road, and everywhere else.) This pattern of land reform has been uneven across the subcontinent so that in West Pakistan, for instance, a few landed clans retained their agrarian wealth until the end of the century. In India the pattern varied according to the political support base of the dominant parties. Bihar, where Aravind Adiga's *White Tiger* is set, was a notorious laggard. Vikram Seth's *A Suitable Boy* takes place against this backdrop in UP after independence, with the ancien régime beginning to crumble away.

So what did it mean to belong to this segment of the middle class? What united this group, if anything?

This takes me back to a memory from my childhood. One day, after reading Charles Dickens' *Oliver Twist*, I asked my father what class we belonged to. This would have been in the mid-1970s, so I was about ten. Recall that my grandfather had been a very wealthy man, by any standards, in 1900.

My father, born in 1921, gave the question much thought. Pulling me onto his lap, after a long pause he said: 'I think we are middle class in terms of wealth, but upper middle class in terms of culture.' I didn't understand him then. I do now. The fact that I was reading Dickens at the age of ten; that we lived in rented accommodation; that my mother grew white-lipped at the end of each month trying to balance the *hisaab*, all make sense in retrospect. So does the vast expense – in relation to earnings – that my parents spent on our education. My father finally bought a tiny plot of land on the (then) far outskirts of Delhi, where my brother, an architect in training, designed a house. We built it on the hoof, with the cheapest materials available. The cost, after paying for our expensive educations, swallowed up my father's meagre savings. He worked until he was seventy-five and he died, like Chittaranjan Das' father, in debt. It all adds up.

So I suppose an extreme emphasis upon ensuring their children got a 'proper' education – that is to say, a Western education – marked this group out.

Sagarika Ghose suggests that the 'People like Us', who populate her novel *The Gin Drinkers*, share liberal values. Anita Desai's many novels show how liberalism plays itself out in quotidian South Asian contexts, while Amitav Ghosh's *The Shadow Lines* gives the reader an insight into the global mental geographies which people of this class could inhabit while chatting in a Calcutta teashop. Christopher Bayly has argued for a global liberal conversation in which Indians have influential roles. Perhaps what unites them more these days than their precise source of wealth, or the size of their pocket book, is their cast of mind. Some would describe it as cosmopolitan. Others are more damning, insisting that they are unreconstructed anglophiles, incapable of decolonising their minds. There's something to be said for both viewpoints.

Either way, 'People like Us' are important to our story because of their attitudes towards food. These are people who have broken food taboos not because they had to, but because they wanted to.

Whereas middle-class food cosmopolitanism started out as defiance in the days of Derozio and Young Bengal, in the twentieth century two factors have been at work. One is the churning force of urbanisation, which has created hybrid food cultures by the very force of juxtaposition; the other is new family structures in which young couples (mainly young wives) experiment with cooking for the family. The culture of cookbooks, as Appadurai points out, created the notion of an 'Indian cuisine' where no such thing existed.[117] This cuisine incorporated into it and 'Indianised' global commodities (coffee, tea, white sugar and leavened 'modern bread', for instance) on a huge scale, as well as delights like 'Indian scotch', Old Monk rum, King-fisher beer and Blue Riband gin. These in turn gave rise to new forms of sociability – not just the coffee and tea houses but rough booze joints, bars and 'dinner parties'.

Street food also provided the urban middle-class teenagers with a special kind of joie-de-vivre. Breaking out in groups to gather at the *fuchka* stall was a rite of passage for middle-class adolescents of my sort and generation. *Fuchka* is a puffed fried pastry: you break its shell and the whole thing becomes a receptacle for some spiced potato or chickpeas and flavoured spicy tamarind sauce, delicious but brutal on the stomach. *Fuchka* was so hot it blew your head off, chillies and tamarind spicing the hot (and 'dirty') sauce inside. *Paanipuri* and *bhelpuri* were, likewise, 'naughty' foods. Hawkers sold these forbidden delights from handcarts, which I now know were illegal. The sauces were *kachcha*, made in water: dangerous in so many ways. The young ate these to bond by breaking rules together, to show off, laugh and flirt. The mixed-gender groups gathered around handcarts faces aflame from the burning heat of the sauce, laughing at the one who got hiccups first. It was a mini-rebellion against accepted rules of taste, parental authority and perhaps, though no one mentioned it, against caste.[118]

Here I must underline one thing we gave no thought to: how vulnerable the hawkers were to police bribery and petty predations. We who bought 'naughty fun' from them knew nothing about that. (Here comes the berth again; here comes wilful blindness.)

There was also a considerable chunk of people among the intelligentsia who were left-leaning or 'free-thinking', and the new post-1947 universities became sites where people of this sort developed new modes of social comportment and more inclusive attitudes towards those with less historic privilege than themselves. (Even older, stuffier, institutions would feel these winds of change.) Breaking food taboos was a rite of passage on this journey. So generations of university students churned out since independence have been less and less likely to comply with food taboos in their own, nucleated homes as the century drew to a close.

This class grew in size after the independence of India and Pakistan, and again when Bangladesh gained its freedom, because all the jobs at the highest levels in all states went to brown candidates who passed rigorous examinations. But it grew relatively slowly, the natural increase after 1920 and the refugee influx after 1947 producing surges of growth. Their opportunities for lucrative employment were limited, but the highly English-educated middle classes hogged them all, and reproduced themselves as best they could. The state was their chief employer, and this limited their horizons. The elites in this sector were those who joined the Indian Administrative Service (IAS, modelled on the Indian Civil Service) by excelling in an annual national examination, and 'toppers' took the most prestigious jobs in the new Indian and Pakistani Foreign Services. Levels of competition for entrance into the top schools and colleges grew more and more extreme as the century progressed: two-year-olds, some barely potty-trained, had to take IQ tests by the 1990s just to gain admission to school. An education at a 'fine' school is a badge of class in South Asia just as much as it is in the United Kingdom, and the cliques and networks these institutions produce survive into late life.

Opportunities for growth have expanded abroad since the 1960s, after the Hart–Celler Act permitted Indians with high qualifications to enter and settle in the United States by the green card route. New Indian Institutes of Technology (IITs) produced engineers for the infrastructure projects at home. IIT graduates also found work in the burgeoning Silicon Valley abroad and the booming telecoms sector at home after the latter was liberalised.[119] Likewise, in Britain, Indian and Pakistani doctors, trained in South Asia at their parents' expense, gravitated to the UK's National Health Service, which they now help to hold up.

Brahmins adapted to work in these new sectors, despite taboos against touch and artisanal labour which would have prohibited them from working as doctors or engineers. They did so by insisting that Brahmin values, with their emphasis on learning, and middle-class values were one and the same.[120]

But it would be a mistake to think that this sort of group of highly educated, English-speaking people is representative of 'the middle class'.

There has been another route into this amorphous mass – through trade. Merchants had always been part of the middle class: Jinnah's father had been a small-time cloth merchant, after all, and Gandhi was of a *baniya* trading *jati*. We're not talking of the Tatas and Birlas here, but of medium-sized family firms who operated as brokers and intermediaries between peasants growing cash crops and British export firms. Many were migrants from princely states in western

India to colonial port cities.[121] The most vigorous flows were from Rajputana, Cutch and Kathiawar, and also Punjab, Sind and other arid areas. These merchants grew adept at exploiting the difference between the lax tax regimes of the princely states and the harsher ones of British India. They prospered, but other than building *havelis* (ornate courtyard houses) and endowing temples in their home villages, they lived and ate austerely.[122] Despite being diverse, the British named them all *baniyas*, a tag that has stuck.

This group continued to grow in size after the 1919 Government of India Act introduced fiscal autonomy, and during the interruption to world trade in 1929–30, the Great War and the Second World War. In the inter-war years merchants grew close to the Congress, but it is an oversimplification to say that at this point the professional and commercial bourgeoisie became one.[123] For starters, they were usually outsiders – for instance, Marwaris in Bengal, or Gujarati Bohras and Parsis in Bombay, with their own languages, caste and religious practices. Even when they were 'ethnic' insiders (as were the Chettiars of Madras), Brahmins kept aloof from them.

Furthermore, putting it at its crudest, Indian traders prospered at inflationary times when the Indian economy provided them with avenues for investment and growth. Both world wars, the depression, the Bengal Famine, the refugee crisis, the economic depression of the 1960s, the war of 1971: all these were moments of opportunity for Indian traders who could hoard goods (food especially) and sell high, fill gaps that had opened in the Indian market, or rent rooms and sell on credit to a refugee family.

Interest rates were high (sometimes as high as twenty-four per cent) and 'it did not appear that any money lender pure and simple had failed in business'.[124]

The English-educated salariat, its links to power notwithstanding, struggled during such times. So the interests of these two segments have been at odds.

It was only after the first five-year plan (1951–6) that state autarky hit the retail trade. At this point, traders began to see the value of sending their sons (and later their daughters) to English-medium schools and universities, rather than, as was their practice, getting their boys to join the family business as soon as they were old enough so to do. In 1929, when the Bengal Provincial Banking Enquiry Commission was doing its work, it had tried to get traders, retailers and moneylenders to fill in its questionnaire. Not a single one replied. Traders could not and would not do so. This is not to say they were not sophisticated keepers of records: they were. It is just that they had learned no formal English. Eventually the Commission had to interview a few of them in person to take their views on board.[125]

But after independence, this began to change. For one thing, getting a licence to trade in India meant clearing it with a member of the IAS – a little English was needed for this; sending presents of dried fruits (a classic gift from merchants to friends and patrons) did not always do the trick. Increasingly by the 1980s and 90s, as liberalisation of the economy began in India, this group has prospered in a way that the western-educated gentry has not.

With liberalisation in the late 1980s, the state reduced red tape (licences for trade in controlled commodities like food) and subsidies (such as fertiliser, which affected yields). The impact in towns, where food became dearer, varied from the impact in the countryside, where only larger landowners could afford to continue to cultivate without subsidies. (Farmers' movements have become an important factor in Indian politics.) Given the 'free market ideology' that had returned at the end of the century, the impact varied depending on global prices for cash crops. It increased vulnerability and risk in the agrarian process. And it removed food security from all those not classified as Below Poverty Line – a new, far smaller category of people given food support. But as far as our middle classes were concerned, the westernised salaried gentry struggled to cope with these pressures. Traders, however, benefited from them.

In this changing context, investing in MBAs for sons and even daughters seemed like a good idea, even if they then came back to run the family firm, as in the old days. It is this group that multiplied, with dazzling speed, into the 'new middle class' after economic liberalisation was imposed by the World Bank upon a desperate, dollar-starved, Indian government in the 1990s. These sons and daughters became the icons of Indian globalisation, whether by sitting on the boards of every big global corporation one can think of, or by running a business back in India that ballooned as it cut corners – in cahoots with the state of course. (They now spoke English, so could offer incentives and deals to 'buy' the franchise for all 3G services from the Government of India. This was just one example of a series of scandals that were as epic as the numbers of zeros involved in the deal.)

The world has watched this development with awe (among other reactions). Quite suddenly, India emerged from nowhere as a global economic power.

But this is not a new social group. If at the start of the century it shared values, these were about the reproduction of the family, its assets, honour and prestige: merchant groups valorised personal restraint, austerity and public *seva* – good deeds, temple endowments and charitable works.[126] By the end of the century, it had merely begun to change its spots. Their appetite for club memberships, sharp suits and Hermès ties suggests the direction of the change. But they still, for the most part, are conservative eaters.

Let me give you an example. My spouse, Anil, happens to know a family of this kind who figure near the top of the Forbes Rich List. They are a Hindu Undivided Family of (mainly) Non-Resident Indians. For some reason they value Anil's advice – I don't quite know why, but that's neither here nor there. The point is, he once invited them to Trinity College in Cambridge for an annual feast. He asked the catering staff to prepare a beautiful vegetarian meal for them, and the catering team worked hard to come up with a menu plan. This did not meet with the family's approval. They insisted on bringing their own food, and their own chef, to prepare and serve their meal. This was in the early 2000s.

By the start of the twenty-first century, this part of the great Indian middle class, now wildly rich, became a key driver of the world economy. Now their wives do not stay at home. Some of their grand-daughters wear diamonds when they visit beauty parlours for a wash and blow-dry. They carry Louis Vuitton bags. Perhaps there are diamonds on the soles of their shoes.

But they remain, for the most part, vegetarians.

There is, to be sure, intermarriage between the two strands – indeed three of my own (*kulin* Brahmin) nieces married their Marwari (businessmen-trader) boyfriends in the 1980s and 90s. Yet each marriage caused consternation on both sides. The two segments have not become one: there is no united 'great Indian middle class'. It's a myth. The two sides are still at odds with each other.

Indeed it is probably this anger – of the trader against the over-educated – that was one large driver in the swing to the Hindu right in Indian politics in the 1990s.

Even at the end of the century, the first strand, with its heritage in land ownership and its earlier and deeper engagement with the intellectual and artistic heritage of the West, may have less cash than the latter group but is snobbish about its erudition and command of a wide cultural repertoire. They love to hate the 'new' bourgeoisie for its arriviste taste in furniture and clothes, and to mock its ostentatious display of wealth. Mukesh Ambani of the Reliance group, a vast conglomerate that has prospered by refining petroleum and now owns Jio, India's largest mobile phone network, can look down on them from the gleaming windows of his billion-dollar skyscraper home in Bombay, yet they still can mock his building. They have taste, you see.[127]

Vivek Shanbhag's *Ghachar Ghochar* is not only one of the best novels you will ever read about India, but it also deals with this subject with insight and sensitivity. Published originally in Kannada, it tells the story of a trading family who grew rich by importing spices from Kerala wholesale, dividing them into bite-sized packs and selling them at high retail prices in the city. The younger brother of the businessman has a 'job' in the business, but no work. On moving from their humble home, he feels strange in the large house his brother has bought for the family. The ornate, heavy and cumbersome furniture oppresses him. His years of sharing a mat and secrets with his sister on the kitchen floor come to an abrupt end in the new house. Sleeping in his separate bedroom, he experiences a new kind of solitude. Out of loneliness, he begins to go every day to a coffee house called Coffee House. His closest relationship, until he is 'married off', is with the waiter there.

The protagonist marries Anita, the daughter of a college lecturer with little money but much learning. Anita is a feisty woman from the educated segment of the middle class. She has a BA degree and 'was never shy of speaking her mind, especially when she disagreed with something that was happening around her'.[128] She disagrees a lot with her conservative mother-in-law, and with what she regards as the family's hypocrisy. Anita, we understand, is of the other sort of middle class, rich in cultural capital but poor in cash.

The whole family knows about the rich wheeler-dealer brother's affair with a woman worker at his factory (caste unknown but not likely to be 'high'), but blame the woman for it. They protect him like wild cats protect their cubs, because he is their provider.

In a striking scene, his lover comes to the house with some cooked daal, curried in a way he enjoys, but nonetheless a *kachcha* food. The matriarch hurls her gift back at her, and the aroma of splattered daal fills the air. Anita leaves her husband in the inevitable unfolding of a Greek tragedy. Their marriage is *ghachar ghochar*: a tangled knot of new and older middle classes, intertwined by the end of the century, but still unable to find a common ground.

VII

THE TIFFIN BOX: FOOD, CASTE AND URBANISATION

There are a great many more clerical workers who fit somewhere in between, and lower down the scale. For office workers in towns and cities, the struggle for existence meant that they had no choice but to ignore some caste proprieties while commuting to cities and towns from distant suburbs. This does not mean that they rejected caste values or the food taboos associated with them. Every day they had to jostle for space in buses or commuter trains with people of all sorts. For all that they looked straight ahead, ignoring the crowds around them, their bodies could no longer be kept free of impurities in the old way.

And what of eating and drinking at work? Obviously all that business about oaths of silence and pointing, bathing and bare-chestedness while eating, against which Motilal Nehru fulminated at the start of the century, would not do in this new context. Who you stood next to, or bumped into on the pavement (if there was a pavement, a rare luxury in South Asia), and what you trod on, was anyone's guess.[129] You could be contaminated from without in a thousand ways. But you could still, with great effort, protect your purity within by eating food cooked at home by your forbearing wife. Or your doting mother.

This is where the tiffin box comes in. Every middle-class and lower-middle-class house began to invest in these boxes as soon as they came onto the market. For school-going children, they might be little plastic boxes into which a mother (long-suffering, patient, selfless . . . I am running out of adjectives) might stuff a *paraatha* with a little pickle; each child would also be given a plastic water bottle to ensure he or she drank only 'pure' water (in the caste sense). But for the man of the house, the tiffin box was a more expensive and complex object, a veritable tower block. Made of stainless steel, tiffin boxes come in different sizes, with three or four different compartments. The wife/mother loaded one with rice or roti; one with daal or curry; one with a vegetable or curd-based dish; and one with a little pickle; and perhaps one with a sweet treat. In the south, working folk of this sort still carry lightly spiced rice and curds in their tiffin boxes. (Few can afford biryani every day, even aficionados.) In most cities and towns, men carry these *dabbas* (boxes) to work, their wives or mothers (or both) having woken at dawn to cook them. (No leftovers will do, remember.)

But of course Bombay was better than every other South Asian city. As early as 1800, enterprising Mumbaikars came up with a system of *dabbawallahs* (tiffin-box deliverers) who deliver hot food from the home to the office-goer at lunchtime every day. By 1968 this had become a business. The Bombay Tiffin Box Suppliers Association prided themselves on never getting it wrong. And so the city's 'upper-caste' elites and middle classes trust the *dabbawallahs* (caste, religion, regional origin unknown) to protect them from caste contamination.

Yet of course, sometimes there were mistakes. (Everyone knows mistakes must happen, given the scale of the *dabbawallah* business. Everyone knows this but they pretend not to know. Another instance where blindness is the only resort for the caste-minded.) *The Lunchbox* (2013), an epistolary romance starring Irrfan Khan, one of India's finest (late) actors, and Nimrat Kaur, shows how a *dabbawallah*'s mistake leads to a deep friendship between two lonely people. Instead, they get to know each other through the medium of food, and then through the hesitant letters smuggled in the tiffin box – a wife stuck at home cooking for a distant husband, and a widower approaching retirement. They begin to communicate with that honesty that sometimes opens up between strangers, each solitary in a different way.

So yes, many urbanites have fought hard to maintain elements of caste propriety even in the improbable setting of the city, and walked an uneasy tightrope. This happens even inside urban homes, as high-status guests come by for a cup of coffee. In the 1920s and 30s, coffee was a new, global and rather expensive commodity.[130] It did not have a place in the Brahmin system of categories. But in early twentieth-century South India, where Brahminism was then a powerful force, elites loved its flavour, and they incorporated it into their lives as a drink (made at home, of course) with snob value. Coffee became all the rage, as did debates about how best to make and serve it. To this day, I hear southerners in general and southern Brahmins in particular arguing in favour of their decoction method and small cup (in which the lip didn't have to touch the cup) versus the French cafetière and mug. So Columbo and Colombia came to Chennai: hybridisation occurred by stealth, while the 'high-castes' guarded their 'purity'.

But it would be a mistake to ignore the millions who have gone the other way – who have embraced hybridisation and broken the rules with glee. Whether influenced by the liberal/secular education they received both before and after independence, by Ambedkar and his message against the caste system, or by greed, a great many urban people abandoned the old rules and embraced these pick-'n'-mix ways of eating. These ways were neither Muslim nor Hindu, neither northern nor southern, neither veg nor non-veg, nor western or indeed 'modern' – often influences travelled and merged.[131]

VIII

GLOBALISATION AND URBAN STREET FOOD

I observed the changes to the morphology of urban neighbourhoods as autarky gave way to the liberalisation of India's economy and the market forces of globalisation rippled through them.

Close to my home in Delhi is Green Park Market: a long row of shops set in a middle-class neighbourhood. As that middle class began to balloon in size and its pockets grew heavier, it changed beyond recognition.

In the 1980s, there was just a narrow pavement in front of the row of shops. By the turn of the century it had given way to a promenade, South Asia style.

On cool autumn evenings in the 1970s and early 80s, nuclear families would come out of their homes to 'eat the air', as we put it in Hindi, and also to eat. The big attraction would be fresh outdoor street food – *aaloo tikkis* (spiced potato cakes) or fresh deep-fried *samosas* or sticky-sweet *gulaab jaamuns*. The more adventurous would try *paapri chaat*, a more expensive and complicated treat that involved fried pastry, yoghurt and ('dirty') tamarind chutney, while those who had alimentary canals of iron might indulge in *gol gappas*, the Delhi variant of Calcutta *fuchka*. Punjabi refugees have shaped Delhi's street-food culture more than any bar the Coca-Cola franchise. Bottles of Coke and Fanta – or their made-in-India competitors Limca, Thums Up and Campa Cola – were expensive treats, but those with money left bought the cold glass bottles to cool the fire in their mouths.

Mouth-watering smells would waft over the forecourt as women chose glass bangles or peered at the rainbow colours of sari blouse fabrics, little girls begged for pompom hair-ties or erasers that smelled of chewing gum. (One treat was a chewing gum called Chiclets, which came in a yellow packet, looked like a small pillow and hardened in two chews.) Home-made *aam paapad* (dried mango) was still much loved. The women wore saris and *shalwaar kameezes*, almost without exception, as they searched in their gaudy plastic purses for change. The men wore 'Made in India' terylene pant-shirts and Indian watches. (Terylene was a drip-dry fabric of cotton mixed with large doses of polyester. It was robust if sweaty, needed no ironing, and was all the rage for Office-Going Man.) Most people used hair oil (women in copious quantities) and also talcum powder. Talcum powder was used more to protect against prickly heat than to provide fragrance. Hair oils were manufactured to appeal to local notions of delightful and soothing aromas. They also 'tamed' the hair of women, and by doing so, tamed them. All of these things (except Coca-Cola and Fanta) were made in India, for Indians – if sometimes following western models.

In the 1990s, Green Park Market changed. There was now, of all things, a McDonald's. I went in there once (when little Kartik's 'please please please' wore me down). It was revealing. Globalisation had a localising effect: the meaty fillings were spicy, moist and chicken-based: a 'French chicken malpua' perhaps? No beefburger was on offer.

Where there had been tailors, now there were 'boutiques'; where there had been barbers, now there were 'salons'; where there had been clothes, there were now 'brands'. The outdoor food stalls had pretty much disappeared, having been replaced by a massive indoor air-conditioned Haldiram's, the local branch of a huge global company listed on the US stock exchange. Since 1937, Haldiram's had sold a variety of 'Bombay mixes', or Bikaneri *bhujias*, spicy snacks from the arid region of Bikaner. After liberalisation it transformed itself into something new. It began to sell its products in shiny silver packets all over the subcontinent and its diaspora. Western-style 'chips' (with some South Asian flavours) were big. It has achieved global reach with an annual revenue in 2019, it claims, close to a billion US dollars. I admit I am addicted to its Magic Masala chips: they are available at the Pakistani grocer's Al-Amin in Cambridge – a Mecca for all South Asians seeking to buy spices in bulk. I've never been into the branch at Green Park Market, but from the outside have seen chairs and tables, and mirrors on all the walls, mall-style.

There are few hawkers to be seen any more. No street-food sellers. Who knows where they have gone? Perhaps they ply other products now, or work in other niches of India's bloating informal economy. Perhaps some work even at the lowest ends of the food chain at Haldiram's.

IX

MAKING THE 'NATIONAL' DIET

Appadurai remarks that in the 1970s and 80s women in India began to write cookery books that were gustatory in emphasis, stressing flavour and taste. They were silent about the relationship of food preparation to the bio-moral world that had previously so occupied caste Hindu India's concerns about cooking. These women were revolutionary in their quiet way. They communicated the cuisines of their own regions to other women of the subcontinent. Some were first published in English. Shock, horror: Aroona Reejhsinghani's *Tasty Dishes from Waste Items* of 1973 advised homemakers on how to use up leftovers.

Soon compilations of regional recipes emerged, in English, Madhur Jaffrey being a pioneer in this genre.

These cookbooks hint at the very different roles that middle-class women played in the provision and service of food by 2000. They had to be excellent cooks of 'their' religious, caste and regional cuisines for when the in-laws came to stay, and be experimental and inventive over a wide culinary repertoire for when the husband's boss and colleagues were visiting for a drinks and dinner party, being charming, 'cultured' and attentive hostesses. These were new burdens for every woman to juggle; new male fantasies to fulfil. Of course every middle-class woman had her Mohan Singh in the kitchen, but she had to curate her meals from this much larger, heavier recipe collection. When in doubt, she resorted to recipe books, just as I resorted to Madhur Jaffrey for my huge dinner parties in Cambridge.

Recipe compilers like Jaffrey had, by the 1990s, created something like 'an Indian diet', which put together a medley of regional favourites and called it 'Indian'. The diaspora, which tried to recreate the tastes of an imagined home, fell back on her volumes armed with Kenwood blenders. They too cooked the Indian diet of their memory and imagination. I learned to cook what I thought of as 'Indian' food, not from my Pishima or Mohan Singh, but from Jaffrey's cookbooks. Somehow, the tapestry of regional diets was 'nationalised', despite the fact that many – like the biryani I learned – were South Asian rather than Indian. Bordered ways of thinking made us 'nationals' even in humdrum ways.

The thing was that, when I got to know fellow South Asians at Cambridge, I learned that this 'food India' had little do with my partitioned country. Weeks after my arrival in Cambridge, a medic friend invited me to supper at his college – St John's, which then had a cluster of medics with South Asian connections. Shaffiq Essajee is a Bohra Muslim of Indian descent from the East African diaspora, and he was a brilliant student, packing his medical degree, and much cooking, into two years rather than three. He had grown up in Britain, so had a British accent. This surprised me. I was 'fresh off the boat'.

Supper started (to my amazement) with the familiar process of chopping onions, garlic and ginger. He had forgotten to check whether there was turmeric, and if there wasn't, oh dear. Fortunately, there was, but in relief he put in so much that for the first time in my life I tasted raw *haldi*. There was no *dhaniya* (coriander) powder (a shame) but we'd make do with *sabut dhaniya* and *jheera* (coriander and cumin seeds). What emerged was a good old *aaloo mattar* (potato and pea curry).

This experience knocked me off my comfortable nationalist perch. It began to dawn on me – a slow beautiful dawn, as in South Asia – that food could never be national.

Pulao (rice with chopped vegetables), which I learned as an 'Indian dish' from Jaffrey, remains a regular offering at the dinner table of my friends from Lahore. I can't count the number of times that Humeira has chosen to serve it, rather than plain rice, to guests. Rather as we do, if we can afford to, in India.

But let me make things clear. Jaffrey (and those like her) were not the only curators of 'national diets'. The state was far more influential; it created the bog-standard model through the railways. Trains were, for the twentieth century, the primary mode of long-distance travel for both the middle and the white-collar classes. (Budget airlines had not yet quite taken off.) Railway kitchens played a large part in improvising a version of an Indian diet for this type of sojourner. Food was boiled down to two options: veg and non-veg. Since journeys could last days, I opted for mix-'n'-match. I usually ate non-veg for dinner. It consisted of a tray of spicy chicken curry, wholewheat chapattis, daal, a vegetable curry and pickle – a pick-'n'-mix of what middle-class northerners might eat on a good day. My veg choice for breakfast was a more southern tray, with *upma*, *idlis*, *vadas* (semolina, lentil cakes, lentil snacks) and curds. These trays collapsed many regional cuisines into one with which the Indian traveller became familiar, and perhaps even came to identify as an all-Indian diet.

By the turn of the century, air travel became more affordable for middle-class folk: budget airlines proliferated in the age of globalisation. Airport lounges were full of people rushing to buy food. As a participant-observer, I would say that while Japanese, Chinese and Italian food were sought after, biryani (veg or non-veg) emerged as the default position. (The idea of a non-veg biryani is like roast duck without a duck, but it was still a favourite.) The Indian airline Indigo Air served freeze-dried *upma* and chicken 'junglee' sandwiches too. The coffee areas were packed and blueberry muffins went down like hot cakes. But chai and samosas have held their ground.

Who made all these dishes? Where did all this food come from? Who serves it? Is it *baasi*? Consumers cannot know, so they don't let themselves ask.

This is not to say that there are no longer guardians manning the gates of the caste-commensal order. Of course there are. Sometimes they are right there, among the liberal cosmopolitan elite; people you might know, from whom you'd least expect it.

On 10 April 2014, a notice in *The Hindu* newspaper announced that employees had complained about colleagues bringing non-vegetarian food into the canteen. (*The Hindu*, as readers may recall, was the doughty and prestigious paper established in Madras in 1878 by a group of Brahmin journalists.) 'All are aware non-veg food is not permitted in our canteen as it causes discomfort to the majority of the employees who are vegetarian.'

The next day, the *Dalit Camera* picked this up and reported the story. It generated anger and indignation. Dalits and other non-Brahmins could see through *The Hindu* management's strategy of not labelling them in caste terms (now illegal) but shaming them as carnivores. Rules about inter-dining have always been critical to caste distinction, and it is clear that Tamil Brahmins run *The Hindu* and still constitute the majority of its employees – whereas Brahmins make up only three per cent of the population of Tamil Nadu.[132]

This puts the veg breakfast of Indian Railways in a whole new light. It is a Brahmin breakfast. The social domination of the Brahmins has made vegetarianism the dominant norm in South India, to the extent that railway caterers imagine South Indian food to be a plate of southern vegetarian dishes.

But although they are a force to contend with, vegetarians do not represent India, let alone South Asia. They never did, whatever British medical men thought. At the time of writing, a poll suggests that only twenty-nine per cent of Indians are vegetarians.[133] If you took all of South Asia that figure would be lower still, but no one has crunched the numbers.

But vegetarians are a powerful minority, and they aren't going anywhere soon. So I expect that the veg option will remain on the Indian Railways menu for this century, and that 'upper-caste' vegetarians will continue to feel 'discomfort' in non-vegetarian settings. As vegetarian merchants grow more wealthy and powerful, so too will the clamour for 'veg only' spaces.

Food will continue to bear, for times to come, an 'unbearable load of meanings'.

X

STAPLES AND THE MARCH OF STANDARDISATION: THE STRANGE STORY OF RICE

There is a sense, then, in which the story of twentieth-century food in South Asia is one of an increasing variety of foodstuffs imported, grown, cooked and consumed. Yet there's another history to discuss which is both different and no less compelling. It is a story of reduction in the variety of staple foods consumed: above all, food grains. It's a strange but fascinating tale of how chronic famine gave way to persistent malnutrition, as the subcontinent came to depend ever more upon rice as its primary staple.

Already in the late nineteenth century, 'the whole of the inhabitants of India' were imagined to be 'peculiarly rice eaters'. This was not the case, as Cornish of the medical department of Madras emphasised with vehemence. 'Rice does *not* occupy the position of bread to the English labourer or the potatoe to the Irish. It is not the *essential* article of diet to the millions of people who form the bulk of the population.'[134] In the whole of southern India, 'raggy' (*ragi*) – or finger millet, a gluten-free wholegrain – was 'the staple food of the labouring man'.[135] Rice was intensively cultivated in wetlands because, to flourish, it needs a great deal of water. Elsewhere, other crops including wheat, maize, barley and millets were what the poor peasant ate, if he or she could afford to eat much at all. Cornish calculated that in all of South India, only *one fifth* of cultivated land was used to grow rice. The rest was planted up with dry, more hardy cereals: *ragi*, millets (particularly *cholum*), 'dholl [*daal*], gram, cotton, oilseeds, &c'. His conclusion was that eighty per cent of South India's people lived on 'dry cereals' as their staple food.

One reason for this was that rice cultivation – beyond a few deltaic and coastal regions – was laden with risk. It depended on heavy and reliable watering. Late, early or inadequate monsoons threatened harvests. The dry cereals coped better. They could withstand drought, up to a point. The peasants who farmed their tiny plots were not fools.

William Cornish (1828–96) would rise to become surgeon-general of the Madras Presidency. He had a beard like Karl Marx, features not unlike Tagore's and was born, of all places, in Glastonbury. His career in India began after the Rebellion when sympathy towards Indians was running low in British circles: his passionate campaigns for improved food standards for 'natives' are all the more remarkable in this context. He was the first scholar-administrator to draw attention to the relative nutritional deficiency of rice compared with other staples. It would be no great stretch to rank him as one of the medical pioneers of the notion of the glycaemic index of foods, and their relationship with health.

Cornish also drew attention to the shocking fact that in Her Majesty's prisons in India, 'native' inmates serving sentences of hard labour ate 24–28 ounces of grain (almost always rice, with little or no supplement except salt) a day. In contrast, a free labourer who could afford to ate 32–40 ounces of food grain (millet of two types, *cholum* and *cumboo*; raggy or rice), 2–3 ounces of daal, 'curry stuff', vegetables and fruit. Prisoners soon became ill; they developed strange diseases. They died younger and in larger numbers than the public at large.[136] Something was rotten in the state of prisons. Cornish put it down to inadequate nutrition.

The surgeon-general had a famous and public row with Sir Richard Temple, Famine Commissioner of India, during the Great Famine of 1876–8. The quarrel was about how much food was sufficient to support the life of survivors employed at famine works. Temple had previously recommended one and a half pounds of grain per person as an adequate daily ration by extrapolating from prison diets in Bengal and the food given to indentured migrants on board vessels. Accused of extravagance, he reduced the 'Temple Ration' to one pound (16 ounces) of grain per person. Cornish, furious, weighed in like an angry elephant in *musth*. He lashed out, hurling statistics at Temple like so many punches to show that a pound of grain was dangerously low, that rice on its own was not enough, that other foodstuffs had to supplement it. This included vegetables, condiments and even meat.

Indeed, one could argue that Cornish had already drawn out the rough contours of 'the balanced diet' by 1880.

Cornish also pointed out, in grim detail, what starvation did to the human body. A period of 'physical wasting' did irreversible physiological damage. The human body could 'recover with a timely supply of food', but

> when the supply of food becomes inadequate . . . the body itself begins to waste and be consumed . . . The skin gets thin and shrivelled, and the muscles become soft and flabby . . . the body, in lieu of other nutrients, begins to [consume] its own muscles . . . [and] the coats of the stomach and intestines waste away.

By this time, 'irreparable impairment had already occurred'.[137] It was the responsibility of the Raj not only to see that famine victims in camps survived, but also that they did not leave these camps in 'an irretrievably low physical state'.

One would have thought that a man of Cornish's scientific standing might have won the argument, but no. Temple clung on. In the end, the resolution was a typically British fudge – a small increase by the Madras Presidency to 20 ounces of grain a day plus one ounce of 'dholl'.[138]

This story fascinates me not only because it throws light upon figures like Cornish who went against the grain of an empire seeking to administer on the cheap, with little knowledge of Indian life and scant concern for it. It reveals the friction and division within what is all too often regarded as a monolithic machine.

But this debate also offers an insight into the forces that began to spread rice to the position of *primus inter pares* of staples long before the British had left India, despite the fact that its nutritional deficiencies were already well known.

Why the domestic market for rice grew in the late nineteenth and early twentieth centuries is something of a puzzle, which no historian has tried to answer. I suggest that its answer lies in a mix of state responses to local, subcontinental and global catastrophes.

Readers will recall the famines of the late nineteenth century, which took lives in the hundreds of thousands. They were, moreover, a recurrent phenomenon. Some, like the Orissa Famine of 1865, were localised, albeit over areas the size of a small European country; others engulfed almost the entire subcontinent.[139] The 1896–7 famines affected the North-Western Provinces and Oudh, Bombay, Madras, the Punjab, Berar, Bengal, Central Provinces and Burma. The number of people who lived in the 'distressed area' in British India, according to the report at the time, was nigh on forty-six million. In the ten affected princely states it was even higher: fifty-two million.[140] That is more than a quarter of the entire population of India in 1900. The actual numbers affected would have been even greater, because there were many parts of the country which the state did not reach. The survivors of starvation were never counted. As Chapter 1 has shown, imperial famines became charged political events, turning many a loyalist into a raging nationalist. The Raj had to act and had to be seen to act. Policies of famine relief had to be put into place. Grain had to be given to the starving.

But which grain? Rice almost immediately became the grain of choice (despite Cornish's thundering arguments against it). Why then? Because imperial policies to turn rice into a cash crop had come good.

The Raj had developed Upper Burma into a region producing rice for export. Parts of the subcontinent – newly conquered, as in the case of Upper Burma, or newly irrigated, as in Punjab – were specifically encouraged by government to grow rice and wheat respectively, as cash crops for export. By 1900, about one million and about half a million tons of these grains were sold abroad each year, respectively. In part this was a result of Britain's larger goal to export more from India to other parts of the world with which the metropole ran a trade deficit. Burma soon produced so much rice that the British were able to stockpile huge quantities for export. A part of that stockpile could be quickly diverted to avert famine or provide relief to famine-struck areas. The colonial state's public works – irrigation works and railways in particular – made such intervention in the agrarian economy possible.

So it was that Burma rice found its way to relief camps in southern India although, as Cornish noted when he visited them, the amount given to each person was tiny. In Monegar *choultry* in Madras, for instance, he was told that six bags of cooked rice were distributed among about 1,200 people.[141] (Six bags of cooked rice. For 1,200 people. Think about it.) The famished were in no position to complain.

By the time the twentieth century had rolled in, knowledge about the deficiencies of rice had spread beyond official circles into Indian civil society. By this time, vitamins had been discovered and their importance had begun to be appreciated. Nutritional science had come into its own, and its headlines had become well known, rippling far beyond the narrow circles of masters of western *materia medica*.[142] So much so that some rice-eating Bengalis who had already internalised the western denigration of themselves as an effete emasculated 'race' now blamed their diet for their 'lack of manliness'. In a little book called *Food*, published in 1930, the Bengali Chunilal Bose had this to say about the 'production of a proper dietary':

> The Bengal diet is far too rich in carbohydrates (starch [meaning rice] and sugar) and sometimes in fat (as in the case of well-to-do people), but markedly deficient in protein, the muscle-forming element, and in some of the vitamins. The result of taking such a poor and ill-balanced diet for a long time, especially in the growing period of one's life, is retardation in one's growth and development, disinclination for any kind of physical

exercise and any kind of active work, weakening the powers of endurance, lowering of vitality, loss of the natural resisting power against
infectious diseases, premature old age and, generally, an early grave.

All the poor Bengali had to do was to eat more like a Punjabi – lots
of 'wholemeal *atta*, dal, vegetables and milk, *with meat twice a week*.'[143]
(I don't know whether it was because my grandfather was influenced
by this discourse, but by the time I became a sentient Hill Cart Road
child, mutton and chicken supplemented a fish-heavy diet.)

Rice consumption and planting continued to spread despite these
cautionary words. The price of both rice and wheat had continued to
rise in the opening decade of the twentieth century and remained high
until the depression.[144] Landlords and farmers responded to this
incentive. Between 1881 (when the Famine Commission reported on
previous disasters) and 1897, in India as a whole, the area devoted to
the cultivation of these grains steadily increased from 166 to 188 million acres, or by thirteen per cent.[145]

Creditors too were willing to lend cash to entrepreneurs to set up
rice mills, which could husk the grain in bulk at low cost, and wealthy
Indian traders began to invest in Burma rice. By 1910, a new and
buoyant market in rice had emerged. In tandem with these trends,
new 'everyday technologies' found their way into the countryside.
Rice milling was one such adaptation that made its way via Burma
into the subcontinent where its penetration was 'gradual, if erratic'.[146]
The rice grain must be husked before it is ready to cook, and this used
to be done by hand, a long mortar grinding and pounding rice until it
was husked and polished. The job, heavy labour though it was, was
often done by women, and widows had earned their keep by doing it.
(Satyajit Ray's *Ashani Sanket*, translated as *Distant Thunder* – a 1973
film about the Bengal Famine – has a superb sequence of the old-
fashioned method of rice pounding.)

By the 1920s and 30s, several hundreds of mechanised mills had
been set up in their stead, which could do the job more quickly and in
larger volumes. Most mills were modest, consisting of 'little more than
a single oil-powered engine and a solitary milling apparatus, under a
thatch or corrugated iron roof with crude brick or even mud and wattle
walls'.[147] In 1900, there had been eighty-three such mills in Burma, and
only one in the large presidency of Madras. By 1910, there were four
oil-driven mills in the Kaveri tract of Madras, where rice production

was concentrated. By 1917–18, there were 215.[148] By 1939, Burma, now a colony outside British India but within the British Empire, had 692 mills, but the Indian provinces of Bengal, Bombay and Madras together had overtaken it with 745 in all. Without question, easy and cheaper milling was another incentive to grow rice in a more populous and more hungry market. By 1945, one district of Madras, Tanjore, boasted 1,071 mills, some of which were powered by electricity.[149]

Even in the Punjab, which Malcolm Darling visited after the Depression, he found that only two types of grain remained on the market: wheat and rice. The more complex grains – the barleys, millets and sorghums – he assumed, were consumed at home, since they fetched little in the bazaar. It seems that peasants diverted more and more of their land to growing these 'market grains', perhaps leaving only the worst, most difficult parts of their plots planted with the hardier (and more nutritious) ones. On his travels on horseback from village to village in 1930, Darling saw the same phenomenon. Wheat, wheat and more wheat was all that he saw at the shops. Some was of better quality, some broken and cheaper, but it was all that was available. Even gram, which had held its own in the early decades of the century, had been edged out as a staple food.

Wheat thus had a similar biography, if on a smaller scale. Flour mills too sprang up in wheat-growing regions. The competition from *aattaa* (wholemeal) and *maidaa* (white) flour was so intense that in 1930, when Darling visited some bazaars, he found no other grain being sold. Agricultural labourers were paid in kind: 25 *maunds* (almost 900 kilograms) of wheat a year and two meals a day.[150] A rare sight was of pedlars selling 'beautiful fresh cauliflowers by the roadside', although they too complained that prices had collapsed. Darling wondered whether this fall in the price of food meant that people ate better. 'The Inspector [he asked] thought not, as people generally ate what they were accustomed to. The Mohammedan generally eats large *chipattis* with a smear of ghee on them, but the more delicate Hindus go for *parauntas*, that is a girdle made of flour and ghee well mixed up.'[151]

Western and Central India witnessed a similar transformation. Already by the turn of the century British officers had begun to note that in Narsingpur in the Central Provinces, 'wheat is selling at twelve ... seers ... [and] juar never comes into the market'.[152] In Hoshangabad, the cropped area under *ragi* had fallen to thirty-seven per cent below normal, 'while inferior grains have been largely substituted for wheat'.[153]

By 1930, then, roti was king in the north-western and western parts of the subcontinent. Rice was emperor in the south and east.

Imagine the impact of these enormous and unsung changes from the point of view of hungry people, people who lived on the verge of starvation. Their famished stomachs would have found the polished rice doled out at gruel kitchens easier to digest. Perhaps they began to view this soft white food as more 'medicinal' than the hardier, more complex and nutritious grains they had previously eaten. Perhaps they even began to see rice as good, healthy food, when in fact it was quite the opposite.

The fact that rice was associated with Brahmins was also relevant. It already had a higher cultural value in the caste system of food, and so perhaps beginning to eat it gave famine survivors, and the other inhabitants of the worlds in which they were embedded, a sense of high status when they later brought home tiny amounts of rice to eat.

Tastes thus began to change, not among the rich, but among the most vulnerable members of society.

The fact that Indian sepoys were also fed on rations of rice (and, to a lesser extent, wheat) also mattered. The army enlisted many castes after the Rebellion of 1857: the Raj preferred 'martial races', although the Brahmins they had come to fear remained a part of the mix. During the Great War, when recruitment ballooned, beggars could not be choosers and the army accepted almost anyone who signed up. A larger mix of Indians then, began eating rice and wheat: day after day, year after year. Perhaps they grew used to it; even to prefer and expect it. For many Indians, joining the army was an aspiration: it was a ladder out of a precarious existence. Army rations, not surprisingly, became foods associated with upward mobility: 'better' foods.

There was no shortage of catastrophes for South Asians in the twentieth century to keep this fateful trajectory on track. In 1918, returning troops from the front brought with them the Spanish flu virus to India.[154] It was there, in India, that the pandemic wreaked its greatest havoc, killing between twelve and seventeen million people.[155] The focus was the Bombay Presidency, although the Central Provinces too were hard hit. Pandemics, as our Covid-era readers will know, hit consumption and trade hard.

If this were not bad enough, right across southern India, the south-west monsoon failed, sparking grain riots all over the Madras

Presidency.[156] For 'grain riots', read 'rice riots'. One consequence of the expansion of the railways and a cash economy was to encourage peasants to sell all their grain, keeping only a small part of it in reserve. By 1918:

> even the poorer classes of a traditionally cholam-eating district like Bellary were becoming rice-eaters, buying either rice from the Kistna delta or, if they could not afford that, broken Burma rice imported via Madras city and ground into flour to make rice cakes. Both varieties of rice were invading Bellary by rail.[157]

For a host of reasons, then, the subcontinent's 'able-bodied' men and their dependants found themselves eating the *sirkar*'s rice or roti, not once but again and again. Rice and wheat became market commodities while the coarser grains did not.

One can see how – without deliberate intention but through its interventions during catastrophes – the British Indian state had begun to change, for poorer South Asians, the concept of a nutritious meal. Markets were quick to respond. As peasants began to grow the grains in demand, other staples fell by the wayside. Peasants in South Asia are as responsive to market forces as those in the western world.

Cropping patterns no doubt changed gradually, field by field, *zamindaari* by *zamindaari*. But already by 1938, medical men and administrators were beginning to worry about what they had already begun to call 'the rice problem' in India.[158] Table 6.1 speaks volumes.

Table 6.1
Area under different grain crops, 1935–6 (British India)[159]

Crop	Millions of acres
Rice	80.6
Wheat	25.1
Jowaar or *cholum* (*Sorghum vulgare*)	21.5
Pulses	15.0
Bajra or *Cambu* (*Pennisetum typhoidium*)	13.1
Maize	8.2
Barley	6.2
Ragi (*Eleusine coracana*)	3.6

The problem, as William Cornish had warned in the late nineteenth century and as the League of Nations recognised in 1937, was that rice was the poorest of the grain crops in terms of nutrition. The more it was polished, the more it lost its nutritive value. Polished rice fetched high prices in the market, whereas unpolished rice (which held on to more essential nutrients, in particular B vitamins) did not.

This gave cultivators every incentive to grow, and subsist on, the less healthy food. This was not such a problem for the wealthy who could afford to supplement their diet with lentils, vegetables, milk, meat or fish. It was a huge problem for the poorest peasants, paid in kind in inflationary times, whose diets came to consist almost solely of rice. The 'invisible hand' of the market for grain – with help from the state – produced the barely visible body.

The Second World War brought its own challenges of recruitment, and of feeding the troops and the civil population of Bengal. This was a war fought close to home. After the fall of Burma, on India's borders, Japanese bombs rained down over Calcutta. People fled the city in panic, returning to a countryside that was being turned into a vast supply and support zone for Allied troops and Indian sepoys. 'Aboriginal people' were press-ganged into huge cadres to clear the scrub so that white troops could be billeted without catching fevers, and to build hundreds of airbases in a Bengal which previously had only one. All these war support workers had to be fed. Activity was feverish on all these fronts, and prices were already high when, starting in December 1941, Japanese forces attacked Burma. By 1942, the game was up: British imperial forces withdrew in one of the more inglorious imperial retreats in the Asian theatre.

The sudden withdrawal of Burmese rice from the Indian market set the scene for the Bengal Famine of 1942–3.

This is not the place to enter into a debate about the whys and wherefores of this horrendous episode in the ignoble history of empire. That would require another book.

The significance of this particular famine here is its impact on India's nationalist leaders' own debates about food as independence came closer. By the time the Bengal Famine began, a Muslim League government was at the helm in Bengal, and Leaguers drew their own conclusions from it. One was the dangerous role of markets in exacerbating shortages: so with one stroke, after independence, the government of Pakistan nationalised food markets across East Bengal.[160]

As for the Congress leadership, as Sunil Amrith points out, they were not of one mind about food policy. Chronic hunger, which became the norm since the 1920s, roused more muted responses than the visceral emotions that famines unleashed, but it did give them food for thought. With Gandhi, for whom diet was a vital part of his spiritual practice, the answer lay in going back to the old days of village self-reliance which he believed had subsisted before market forces destroyed these peaceful idylls. Au fait with advances in nutritional sciences and in touch with the old-school ways, he argued:

If rice can be pounded in the villages after the old fashion, the wages will fill the pockets of rice pounding sisters and the rice eating millions will get some sustenance from unpolished rice instead of pure starch which mill rice provides . . . Human greed, which takes no count of the health or wealth of the people who come under its heels, is responsible for the hideous rice mills one sees in all the rice producing tracts.[161]

But his friends on the National Planning Committee, led by Nehru and Subhas Bose, pulled in the other direction. They wanted malnutrition and undernutrition to be solved 'by systematic crop planning . . . stressing the production of heavy-yielding, energy-producing and also protective foodstuffs'.[162]

For this generation of Congressmen and women, the Bengal Famine was the first 'imperial famine' they would have seen. Most were in jail, but they still had news of the famine and saw photographer Sunil Janah's shocking portraits of the dead. This famine took place in the age of daguerreotype. Stark photographs asked questions about the moral failings of British rule, to which its spokesmen had no answer.

Already by 1929, Nehru had argued that British rule was the nub of the problem:

If the government as present functioning in India were really desirous of attacking and eradicating poverty, they would do something much more and vastly different from the petty relief they give in times of acute distress.

They would realise the responsibility for this poverty is theirs and therefore the speediest way of ending it is to remove themselves from the scene of action, liquidate their government and make room for others who could tackle the problem with greater disinterestedness and competence than they have shown.[163]

After the Bengal Famine, this view would prevail. About 5.1 million people died in Bengal: almost six times as many as those killed in the violence of partition. Those who witnessed its dreadful horrors were devastated by what they had seen: 'Gone are the cultivators, gone are the householders, rice is gone from the houses.'[164] They would be scarred by these images until they died.

Churchill's callous failure to feed India's subjects precipitated the end of empire. He pretended it wasn't happening. He took the cynical line that 'if Gandhi is still alive, then the famine crisis isn't that severe'.[165] For him, feeding Britain and fighting the war were the focus, and he would not be deflected from it. He thought that Indians were the 'beastliest people in the world next to the Germans', and declined to accept an offer of 100,000 tons of wheat for India.[166] Botched if well-meaning official policy in Bengal compounded the situation. Indians were not blameless either: some Indian traders sought to manipulate the grain prices to keep them high, and they did so by hoarding grain. That too is another story. But South Asians still blame imperial lack of accountability, and the callousness of racism, for the episode.

The Bengal Famine, however, clinched the argument in favour of Nehru and his supporters in the Congress. The scientific, planned route – for all 'modernist', 'right-thinking' technocrats – would become the obvious way to tackle the problem of hunger.

But it did not work. Plans have not worked. Or where they have worked, they have brought other problems in their train. History tends not to proceed along smooth tracks, and freedom's yields are never easy to quantify.

XI

INDEPENDENCE, PARTITION AND FOOD POLICY

With freedom came partition. Dividing the subcontinent played havoc with food supply in India and Pakistan. With the Canal Colonies going to West Pakistan, India lost large wheat-growing areas (discussed in Chapter 1). East Pakistan's severance meant the loss to India, likewise, of vast rice-growing tracts. India's food problem, coupled with the influx of some twenty million refugees, turned overnight into a food nightmare. A moral panic about food gripped political society and the Congress leadership. Freedom meant a new social contract between state and society in which the interests of the 'common people' and their welfare were paramount.[167] Now the time had come to deliver. But the new state, reeling from partition, lacked the capacity to honour it.

One obvious solution would have been for India and Pakistan to agree to a free trade treaty, or at least to bilateral trade on favourable terms, because Pakistan needed India's processing capacity quite as much as India needed Pakistan's food grains. This was a time when, elsewhere in the world, such arrangements were being forged. Yet in South Asia it could not easily be achieved, because by this time the two countries had taken different approaches towards the value of the rupee against sterling and the division of the Indus waters (of which more in the Epilogue).

So India's leaders, still in shock after the Bengal Famine, felt they were teetering on the precipice of a food emergency of gigantic proportions. India's first five-year plan of 1951 tackled many sectors, but the agricultural sector took priority (including the building of four major irrigation works at Bhakra, Hirakkud, Mettur and the Damodar Valley), and absorbed almost half the total allotted funds of Rs 2,069 *crores* (Rs 21 million). The goal was improved irrigation to promote greater agricultural yields. But of course dams took a long time to build and their gains (a controversial subject) could not be assessed. Nor were their benefits likely to be appreciated by peasants for many years to come. Many found, to their surprise and anger, that they were charged for the water supplied, and they made their opposition to this clear in the regions supplied by the Ajay and Damodar Valley.

Yet the years of the first five-year plan were kind to India (and Pakistan) with benign weather helping agriculture. Higher yields than normal – marginal though they were – kept up, just about, with the rise in their population. But those who read widely, Nehru among them (his dusty bookshelves at Teenmurti House show this), were aware of a second panic sweeping the world at this time. This was neo-Malthusianism, which in South Asia was sparked off by the publication in 1951 of Kingsley Davis' book *The Population of India and Pakistan*, and reached its apogee in 1968 when Gunnar Myrdal's *Asian Drama: An Inquiry into the Poverty of Nations* arrived on the bookshelves of South Asia's English-reading public. The latter was a three-volume tome on the shelves of every self-respecting 'cultured' middle-class household when I was growing up. It radiated a dark message even to those who did not read it.

Already in the early 1950s, post Davis, scholars had begun to brush up on their command of Thomas Malthus, going back to his 1798 *Essay on the Principle of Population*. Malthus' bold contention was that whereas agricultural yields grow in a linear way, populations grow exponentially. This premise led Davis to warn, Cassandra-like, of impending catastrophe for the subcontinent. The census of 1951 had recorded a remarkable surge in population on both sides of the border. Many South Asians agonised about the return of famines which Malthus had predicted.

The answer, many planners believed, lay in building up buffer stocks of grain. (There was agreement about this on both sides of the Radcliffe Line.) This would keep the prices of food grains low at a time of vast, inflationary state expenditure: the idea was that if grain prices began to rise, the state would dribble enough grain from its stocks into the market to lower them to affordable levels. But of course neither country grew enough to build up such a stockpile in short order.

This was the context in which India and Pakistan turned to the United States for food aid under the PL-480 scheme.[168] The first ship-loads of rice, wheat and maize began to arrive at Indian and Pakistani ports in 1956. (Aid to Pakistan, with its smaller population, would soon outstrip that which India received.)[169] Sacks of grain went first to 'fair-price shops' where the urban poor and white-collar classes could buy commodities at fixed prices. These were the 'ration shops' (pronounced in Hinglish as '*raashan shops*') on which Indian house-holds continued to depend, albeit with less security, until the 1990s. Pakistan abolished rationing in 1987, putting its 40,000 ration shops out of commission.[170]

The PL-480 programme had a philanthropic purpose, but its chief goal was to extend US influence over newly independent countries. So PL-480 food aid was controversial from the moment it arrived at the docks. For one thing, only a small part of it was actually 'aid'. Most was a loan, whose terms of repayment (especially in the second tranche) tied debtor nations to their creditor in knots. In the first major work on communism in India, two US authors concluded that rice-eating peoples were particularly susceptible to communism.[171] As far-fetched as this may seem to us now (Trinity College, Cambridge, a hotbed of communism in the 1930s, was not known for the quality of its biryani, or indeed its rice pudding), events in China, Malaya, Bengal and Kerala lent the thesis a veneer of credibility, and the Americans bought it. Cold War logic drove US largesse.

The Cold War entered South Asia first not by proxy wars, then, but by food. People experienced its consequences when they sat down to eat.

This led the politically minded to question how real was India's 'non-alignment'. Radicals muttered about neo-colonialism. Economists too entered the debate, suggesting that aid lowering the price of staples created disincentives for domestic production.[172] And that was one reason why both countries – India perhaps more urgently than Pakistan, although that is by no means clear – sought to be shot of their dependency on food aid.

This was the context in which plant scientists strove to produce high-yielding varieties of rice and wheat.[173] If the Malthusian dilemma could be resolved by developing varieties of rice that were higher yielding, then, they believed, agrarian productivity could keep up with population growth. Governments in South Asia could thus rid themselves of that spectre at the feast, and of humiliating dependency on the United States in a world ever more riven by Cold War rivalry.

Plant science thus became a vigorous field of research in Pakistan and India, and elsewhere in the developing world that was faced with the same dilemmas. By the mid-1960s, hybrid varieties of wheat had already shown great promise, but a sturdy high-yielding rice had proved less easy to create. 'Success' finally arrived in 1967, apparently overnight, in the nick of time. Two consecutive droughts in 1964 and 1965 had led to political crises, especially in West Bengal, where food marches and riots, and a more widespread insurgency, threatened Congress' grip on authority.

So the creation in 1967 of a dwarf rice variety by a team led by the American agronomist Norman Borlaug was hailed by governments falling at their feet with relief. (The team was a multinational one based in the Philippines, and included scientists from the subcontinent. When Borlaug received his Nobel Peace Prize in 1970, he was the first to recognise that 'his' achievement was the product of a huge, transnational cooperative endeavour.) In any event, the new miracle rice, a dwarf rice variety that grew fast, was resistant to pests and could, in good conditions, produce yields three or four times larger than those of ordinary rice. The variety was called IR8 – an ugly name that is made less harsh on the ear when we learn that some of the first farmers to take up the grain named their sons 'IR-ettu'.

In India, the Green Revolution is most closely associated with M. S. Swaminathan (MSS). Born in 1925 in Kumbakonam, a rice-eating part of Madras, Swaminathan studied at the University of Kerala and at the Plant Breeding Institute of the University of Cambridge. He started out as a student of medicine (like his father before him), but switched his field after witnessing the horrific images of the Bengal Famine. At Cambridge, he read zoology: a first step on a ladder of learning driven by a mission to end hunger.

MSS was still going strong in 2014, when I had the good fortune to meet and interview him. He was then in his eighties, but he was as sharp as he was generous with his time. He was gentle despite his strong features – high forehead, large eyes and square jaw. His mild demeanour did not hide his tenacity, his sense of urgency. His mission to end hunger was still far from reach, he said. He asked me to visit his Centre to see the steps he was taking to find remedies to the problems that the revolution, and climate change, had created. (Work in Cambridge beckoned. I could not go.)

In these interviews, he was modest in the extreme about his accomplishments as a scientist. MSS underlined not his own achievement but the international collaborative work that had made the Green Revolution possible, and gave much credit to Pakistani scientists who, since 1958, had been working in tandem on a shared problem.[174] This was something new to me: this scientific partnership across the border had popped up in none of the national histories of the Green Revolution I had read. It is particularly significant that, according to MSS, this work continued even when India and Pakistan went to war in 1965. It is also revealing that the best biography of Swaminathan is by the Pakistani scholar Anwar Dil.[175]

There is no doubt that the Green Revolution made India self-sufficient in food grains (it achieved this milestone by 1972). It enabled the government to build up the buffer stocks that had been its goal. It has used them thereafter to control food prices. By 2001, the sacks of grain in India's warehouses were so numerous that (according to one calculation) if piled up one on top of the other, they would have reached the moon.

But there have been complications too. The dwarf rice was no one-shot solution, and it brought problems in its train. 'IR-ettu', it turned out, needed watering at precise times. It also needed vast amounts of fertiliser to achieve the startling yields. The Green Revolution was not just the new seeds but this whole package of water and fertiliser, and few farmers had access to all three.[176] The dwarf paddy crop turned out to be prey to fungal attacks and blights (and needed pesticide). The rice itself was coarse, and fetched a price at the market lower than the finer local Indian varieties. Only for farmers with big fields did the sums add up. To grow it securely, groundwater had to be tapped by sinking bore or tube wells. These were larger investments than poor peasants could make, and they tended to sell their small-holdings to richer farmers, who needed more land to achieve the required economies of scale. Poorer peasants ended up working as landless labourers on these farms or drifting to the city in search of a livelihood. It is not an accident that it was in the 1970s and 80s that the poorest agricultural families began to migrate, *holus-bolus*, to cities, with the effects discussed in Chapters 4 and 5.

Of course, scientists did address some of these challenges. Soon they produced a variety of rice better suited to Indian tastes and conditions, and with a prettier name: *Japonica Indica*. Swamina-than has tried to address some of the social and environmental consequences of the Green Revolution. He worked with local groups of cultivators near his base in Madras city to help mitigate its ill effects, while thinking ahead about the need to develop seed vari-eties that will withstand salinity in the coastal zones as the oceans rise.

Yet its damaging outcomes have been profound, so much so that Vandana Shiva, a scholar and activist, writes about the violence of the Green Revolution.[177] Over the long term, the heavy use of fertilisers and pesticides turned soil toxic, unfit not only for cultivation but for human habitation. The loss of biodiversity destroyed unique ecosys-tems. Water was used more wantonly: by 2021, India had the highest demand for fresh water of anywhere in the world.[178] Damming rivers to divert water to these high-yielding areas came at a high human cost – destroying communities and the life-worlds of the people of the old river basins. These people have become a new type of refugee: the 'Big Dam refugee'.[179] Their rehabilitation has been as disastrous as the rehabilitation of other types of refugees.

But let me here focus on our central theme: diet.

Already by 1960, PL-480 aid had seen to it that Indians were eating more rice and wheat than ever before. Now the Green Revolution brought another factor into play: a huge incentive, for middling to rich landholders, to turn over more acreage to the new high-yielding varieties. Already when Francine Frankel published her classic work on India's Green Revolution in 1971, adopting this strategy had transformed the lifestyles of rich and middling farmers.

> The 50 per cent or 75 per cent or even 100 per cent [increase in yield] is sufficient to permit some significant improvement in the general standard of living: e.g. a cleaner home, cups and saucers (instead of metal glasses), in some cases the margin necessary to send a boy to school or to keep cows or goats for milk, and even to buy a luxury item like a transistor.[180]

In prime wheat-growing districts like Ludhiana, farmers bought refrigerators, telephones and even cars – after first investing in tractors.[181] The difference, previously wide, between the lifestyles of middle-class urban families and those similarly placed folk in the countryside began swiftly to narrow.

In the 1980s my parents sent me to a boarding school close to the Indian province of Punjab, and many of my friends were the children of agrarian beneficiaries of the Green Revolution (as I recognised then, but understand only now). Their families could afford the exorbitant school fees, not just for their sons but for their daughters too. One of my best friends at school – let's call her Kanika – came from such a family. Her father, a dashing Sikh of extraordinary energy and wit, threw himself into the new modes of farming. (I overheard 'the grown-ups', liberal city types who had never touched a plough, and by caste were 'prevented' from so doing, talking about his wheat yields with awe.) He was a new kind of revolutionary – a green revolutionary. The times they were-a-changing.

Kanika's house, where I spent much time, was not in Lutyens' New Delhi (indeed anglicised city types might describe its location as 'not ideal'). But it was far more luxurious than my own: there were air conditioners everywhere, fridges, fans, a large dining table and even larger sofa set in a very spacious living room, and separate bedrooms for each of the four girls. (This was perfect: she and I could spend days and nights undisturbed, talking about dorm bullies, boys, star signs and other matters of import.) They owned this house. We did not own ours. I registered this, without quite knowing what it meant.

I saw other similar homes in rural settings, when groups of students from our school went camping: we would turn up famished at someone's parents' doorstep for a meal and a wash. (I was part of the headmaster's group – sickening, I know – and no doubt he had arranged these stopovers in advance.) I would eat and chatter with the others. But I also soaked up my surroundings, probably because they challenged my idea of 'the rural'. (They had nothing in common with 'the rural' of Satyajit Ray, or Shyam Benegal, whose films formed me as much as the literature I read.) Of course, I now realise, these were 'Green Revolution homes'.

Why should middle farmers, and even some small farmers, not aspire to similar lifestyles? Why would they too not turn their holdings over almost entirely to wheat or rice production, since economies of scale were critical to success? Of course they would. For them, the lower price that dwarf rice fetched at the market was more than compensated for by the sheer volumes that they could produce. Frankel noted that by 1971, wheat farmers in Ludhiana were denying field workers payment in kind (in fodder, fuel and vegetables for instance), which they had provided in the recent past.[182]

Consider the impact on the diet of these working families. They had little bargaining power so would not get paid much cash, and could buy only cheap rice in the market. In the same period, she noted that in West Godavari in the south, only marginal upland farmers were still growing *jowaar*, *bajra* and other millets. Only those farmers with adequate and reliable supplies of water cultivated 'new' rice, because the seed was exacting in its demand for being watered at precise intervals.[183]

And so, to support the Green Revolution, successive governments have seen it as their business to provide water. Dams, Nehru's temples of the future, continued to be built long after Nehru was dead. They remained central to the national vision in South Asia long after Nehru was gone, and after new governments with different agendas had taken charge.

Almost the first big project the independent government of Bangladesh undertook was to build a dam across the Karnaphuli river in the Chittagong Hill Tracts. In 1987, the Indian government launched the construction of the Sardar Sarovar Dam across the river

Narmada. Both projects have continued in the face of powerful resistance movements – in particular the *Narmada Bachao Andolan* (Save the Narmada) movement.[184] Despite a temporary lull in 1995, governments of every stripe have powered through the political and legal hurdles. For the moment, let's just note that people of river-ine regions, activists who champion their rights and eco-warriors, have all fought long wars to stem the combined power of the state, science and financial incentive. It has been an uphill struggle, and there have been all-too-few victories.

Debal Deb's mission to create a seed bank in Orissa of 700 trad-itional varieties of rice before they too disappear must be understood in this light. He is not some crank. He argues that of the 110,000 var-ieties of rice that India had in 1970, only 6,000 remain.[185] But is he tilting at windmills? And what will happen to the lost varieties of millets and sorghums? Is it goodbye for ever to biodiversity?

And has the switch to the rice-heavy diet created the legend of 'South Asian' type II diabetes? Emmanuel, whose family of nine shared one bag of rice a month in the 1970s, now heaps his plate with rice. It is the core, rather than the periphery, of his diet. He has raging diabetes. A driver we knew and liked – Nana – died some years ago from the complications of diabetes, and Sebastian, another mate of his who used to drive a rented car, has had to stop working. I fear for him.

Recently, I encouraged Saroj, who helps look after me in Delhi, to seek advice from my old friend Vandana about a skin condition.

Vandana gave her advice. It proved invaluable. She also suggested – considering her weight – that Saroj ate less rice. To me she said: 'It's very hard to persuade tribals to eat less rice.' Saroj is an Adivasi.

Vandana Prasad is a formidable person. A slight, intense and bril-liant woman, she has been an activist in the field of paediatric medicine and public health for decades, and has been at the forefront of the *Jana Swasthya Abhiyaan* (People's Health Movement) in India. She is one of the brightest people I have ever known, and I say this as a fellow of a college that likes to boast that it has more Nobel laureates than France. (She arrived in my class in boarding school one day when we were both fourteen: her father had just died suddenly, and her touring officer mother could not give her two girls a settled education. So Vandana – all bones and a shiny 'boy-cut' – arrived in our class in the middle of term. Since then, rather like Lenu in Elena Ferrante's Nea-politan novels, I have regarded myself as a *chol*-able also-ran.)[186]

When she saw Saroj, Vandana was serving on the National Commission for the Protection of the Rights of Children, and had travelled all over India, observing children's diet and health in villages in 'tribal' areas. Everywhere she saw a rice-heavy diet. She is not a historian, and had not read Cornish – why should she? But she is smart, so Vandana presumed it had become the norm for Adivasis to eat plates of rice, and hence hard for them to change what had become an ingrained habit.

She was right – but, as we have seen, that was true not only of Adivasis. That South Asians are now such big rice eaters was the consequence of a perfect storm of forces at work in the twentieth century.

XII

THE RIGHT TO FOOD MOVEMENT IN INDIA, AND MIDDAY MEALS

That there have been no famines in India since independence is one achievement of its democracy, argue Amartya Sen and Jean Drèze. At the start of the twenty-first century, drought in Rajasthan prompted the provincial government facing re-election to respond with alacrity. It employed four million relief workers in one of the largest public employment programmes ever. Famine would have been fatal to its prospects at the polls, so it was averted in time.[187]

This is not the case with malnutrition, which one scholar has described as a 'silent emergency'.[188] As the crusading journalist P. Sainath pointed out, 'an exclusive focus on "starvation deaths" – disconnected from the larger canvas – seems to imply this: if they don't die, everything's all right'.

It is not all right. The figures make for grim reading. At the end of the twentieth century, only two countries – Bangladesh and Nepal – had a higher proportion than India of undernourished children, and India and Bangladesh languished at the bottom of the list when it comes to the proportion of babies born with a low birth weight. Child morbidity remained high. The second National Sample Survey (in 1998–9) showed rampant malnutrition among women and children: forty-seven per cent of all Indian children were undernourished. Only fifty-five per cent drank milk or ate yoghurt once a week, despite the

'White Revolution'. Thirty-three per cent ate fruit at least once a week, while a mere twenty-eight per cent got an egg.

Between 1992–3 and 1998–9, the time required for Indian girls to catch up, in nutritional terms, with their Chinese counterparts, was eighty years. *Eighty years.*

Chronic hunger has stunted the growth and affected the cognitive development of the subcontinent's poorest children.

No. It's not all right.

It was in this context that in 2001, the People's Union for Civil Liberties filed a civil writ petition in the Supreme Court, pressing it to recognise that the constitutional right to life guaranteed, *inter alia*, the right to food. The justices not only agreed that it did, but also on 28 November 2001 directed all state governments to introduce free school meals in state primary schools within six months.

Did this begin to tackle the 'silent emergency' of chronic malnutrition? Did the tide begin to turn?

Yes and no.

The free midday meal kept children in school for longer, its impact being particularly marked on girls. It provided them with at least one of the two meals they should ideally eat in a day. It also helped their impoverished families by taking some of the burden of feeding them. It provided work for the women who cook to supply these meals in bulk.

What did children actually get to eat? Official guidelines were 100 grams per day of food grains, 'supplemented with other items such as dal, vegetables, oil, spices etc'. There is no recommendation for how much of these additional and vital foods children ought to be fed. Even the excellent primer on midday meals issued in 2005 recommended '*lots of*' cereal grains such as rice, wheat, *jowaar* and *bajra*, and '*enough* pulses and legumes'.[189]

The challenges of cooking meals in bulk at the lowest cost suggest that what children were mainly fed was *khichri*, a gruel made of rice and lentils. The logistics of cooking hundreds of individual rotis (flatbreads) in a fixed and brief lunch break are mind-boggling. Most women work in tin shacks and the combined labour and heat, not to mention the fuel consumed, would make it impossible to provide rotis across most of the country, so it is unlikely that children were offered rotis, which are more nutritious. So milled rice became the base of the meal, almost everywhere in the country.

Given what we know about the nutritional hazards of an over-reliance on rice, the midday meal is not a one-shot solution to India's nutritional emergency. Yet despite this, in 2000, India's High Level Committee on Long Term Grain Policy recommended that 'a system of universal PDS [Public Distribution System] be rolled out for two grains only, rice and wheat respectively'.[190]

Health workers and activists on the right to food, Vandana Prasad among them, continue to push to improve the nutritional content of the midday meal, and advise local people of how to do so in turn. But the hurdles of illiteracy, caste, language and corruption make this a challenge of enormous proportions.

One ironic outcome of the midday meal programme, a crucial intervention in the health of children, is thus yet another fillip to the spread of rice-eating across India (see Table 6.1).

William Cornish was right: India was not a rice-eating country in the late nineteenth century. It had, however, become one by the end of the twentieth century, with milled wheat running a close second to rice. A complex mix of forces had made South Asians of us all by 2020, in terms of what we filled our bellies with (if we could fill them). Rice or wheat. Wheat or rice. That was all there was as staples as the twentieth century ended, whether in Pakistan, India or Bangladesh.

7

Leisure, Twentieth-century Style

Stopping to think about leisure – if one has time to think – it turns out to be a slippery concept.

Take the phrase in that sentence, 'time to think'. It is a type of time different in quality from routine time, when one is *not* engaged in work: whether domestic work, studies, labour in its various forms; whether paid or unpaid manual work, intellectual labour, artisanship, or business. Penumbral time in which the mind roams free of its usual constraints and routines.

But it also takes different forms. Leisure can be time spent enjoying organised fantasy. Choreographed make-believe tends to be a more prolonged escape from the drudgery of the everyday, for instance, during a festival or fair, or an outing to the cinema. You know the rules about what will happen. Good will triumph over evil on day ten of Ramlila, say, at the end of Durga Puja and the Bombay film. The outcome is the same every time. But the excitement lies in the detail, the energy, the sociability, and the contrast between this transformed time and the daily grind.

In South Asia, time spent in the enjoyment of organised leisure can be long. It can involve not just hours, but days and weeks. It is as if time itself slows down, for a while, and beats to a different rhythm.

In stage-managed escape, the most obvious example are the *filmi* fantasies of Bombay cinema. The classic dance sequence in the film *Pakeezah* ('The Pure', 1972), in which Meena Kumari dances on glass in front of her tormentors, is a huge favourite. The dialogue and scenes in *Sholay* ('Embers', 1975), in which the characters played by Amitabh Bachchan and Dharmendra take on dacoits and make chutney out of them, are scenes we love to remember, even westernised elites who love to hate Bollywood. In *Sholay*, good triumphs over evil, as it must. Its paean to the bonds of male friendship: the song

'Yeh Dosti Ham Naheen Todenge' ('We Will Never Break this Friendship'). We all knew it, however we interpreted its layered meanings. Songs of impossible love (since love is still such a difficult project) resonated long after they were written. People are still taken to another dimension when they listen to them decades later. They become different, less care-worn versions of themselves.

The other day I watched *Pakeezah* again. With my scholar hat on, I knew that Meena Kumari was dying as she filmed it. During that famous dance sequence, she worked so hard at her art that she made you forget that she – the real Meena Kumari – would be dead just days after the shooting wrapped up. As a member of her rapt audience, I forgot what I knew as I was transported into Pakeezah's predicament, her song, her tragedy. I forgot about Meena's work. Leisure creation has this effect: it makes one forget what one knows well, even when one is sober. It is, then, a particular kind of forgetting.

Or let's think about the disorder of things at festivals of bacchanalia. During the Hindu festival of Holi, say, when men and women pelt each other with colour, in a brief phantasmagoria in which routine social roles and behaviours dissolve. It's a crazy time when anything goes (within limits) for a few hours. Men drink milk mixed with pistachio and marijuana (*bhang*) all morning. Then they yell, '*Holi hai!*' ('It's Holi!') and pelt everyone around them with colour. Women and men (or men and men) play with each other in the open, for an hour or two. A great deal of groping is involved. Disguised by colour, the signs of their social location rendered less visible, people assault their 'superiors' in unthinkable ways. The scene in Vikram Seth's *A Suitable Boy* in which the irreverent multi-hued Maan throws the pompous professor in a tub of coloured water ('so that he looks like a beached pink whale') is typical of the transgressive spirit of the day.

Holi is also scary, particularly for women (and children) who don't want to play. For now, though, let's focus on the work behind the play. The manufacture, packaging, distribution and sale of *bhang* and *aabir* (the colours) and the special sweets for festival day, and – oh dear – the weeks of washing and cleaning up afterwards as order is restored. That's lots of work, mainly of a manual kind, when, after Holi, people return to the routine, almost as if that topsy-turvy day had never happened. They forgot while they played, and then they forgot that they had played, when the last bits of pink colour came out of their ears.

'Altered time' can often be quite brief, disorganised and fragmentary.

Consider an overworked doctor going home on a suburban commuter train in Bombay, suspended between the worlds of the hospital and of domesticity – and a second clinic perhaps. The train may smell of sweat, metal and hair oil, but this is the only time in the day he is not on call – South Asian doctors give their mobile numbers to all their patients – and he can't answer his ringing phone while hanging onto a strap with one hand and holding a briefcase with the other. So he thinks of nothing for a few seconds. And then of something strange – like what it might be like to travel to the North Pole. His mind roams free.

There are other, more everyday forms of escape, too. They are everywhere, even if some are under the *lihaaf* (quilt). *Daaru* (alcohol), *paan*, tobacco, hubble-bubble, *charas* (marijuana), sex with strangers. Listening to the cricket on a transistor radio while waiting for the boss. (Here the 'flunky' enjoys leisure while the boss 'works'. Nice.) Having a cup of milky sweetened tea at a chai shop with friends, shooting the breeze. Cheap intoxication (if the alcohol is toddy and the drug is *bhang*). Expensive leisure if the alcohol is Scotch whisky, or even 'Indian scotch', and the drug opium, fine marijuana or high-grade cocaine. Each of these activities is – in its own way, to a different degree – dubbed 'naughty' or downright filthy. Flouting taboos lends extra pleasure.

Leisure production is a particular type of work. Those who toil in this field seek to erase their own exertions from the viewer's mind – it's that erasure which makes the product. It is an unusual sector, teeming with both professionals and amateurs, artisans and specialists of a hundred kinds. Ventures in this sector can only succeed in producing leisure if the end product veils the work done backstage.

Yet leisure often challenges the order of things. Gossip, ribald songs, jokes, cartoons, all forms of adult play, at the expense of the social structure, are moments of time-out-of-time. They are forms of send-up, tiny acts of resistance, saying to the powers that be: 'Oh really? Do you think you can fool me?' Those who laugh with the joker join in looking at the world through the prism she creates, if only for a few seconds. A moment of dissent flashes round the group. Gossip can play out over months and years. It can be a form of bullying of the weak but, in the twentieth century, when internet trolls were yet to grow into the vicious powers they are today, more often it was gossip that undermined the powerful. The objects of the most vicious and consistent gossip tend to be the mighty. The millions of memes that have been recirculated so many times that they come with a warning remind us that jokes are serious. They undermine authority. There is a subtle power in just laughing at the powerful. Creating communities of laughter involves work: jesters, stand-up comedians and cartoonists do a real job.[1] The cartoonists – the great satirists of the twentieth century – were as necessary to the successful newspaper as the investigative journalist. In India, R. K. Laxman, employed full time by the *Times of India* from 1951 for almost fifty years, is still remembered and celebrated for his stamp-sized 'everyman' jokes long after the paper's illustrious editors and investigative journalists have slipped from memory.[2] In Pakistan, the ironic gaze of Khalid Hussain and the edgier images by Feica speak louder than a thousand editorials.

This chapter suggests that, for all its apparent diversity, every form of leisure depends on the work of others. The doctor's leisure is the train driver's work. Behind every chai lies a huge industry that employs almost as many people as the Indian Railways.

We have to bear this in mind, because it helps us remember that while those enjoying leisure at the movies might feel suspended outside the here and now, they remain very much part of it. Their pleasure draws upon the work of crews of people. The higher the order of fantasy, the greater the concealment of the work behind it, and the complexity of the artifice and illusion. Much of late-twentieth-century Bombay cinema was filmed at Filmcity in Goregaon, a walled city within a city in which a multitude of set builders, gaffers, spot boys, cameramen and women, actors, light artists, directors, on-set tailors and fitters, make-up artists, chai and *paan* sellers and cold-drink wallahs, painters, carpenters and security guards, all worked where each of any number of films is being shot.[3] Filmcity's high walls afford peace and security to the stars.[4] But they also perpetuate the illusion, leisure's closest companion, of the leisure–work dichotomy.

Friends have asked me, in true bafflement, about the phenomenon of Bollywood. Why are the films so long? Why are the plots punctuated by long fight sequences and romantic song-and-dance routines? How can a society that produced the most sophisticated Sangam poetry, Mir, Hali, Ghalib, Premchand, Bankimchandra, Tagore, Faiz, Nazrul and Satyajit Ray, churn out this rubbish?

In this chapter, I attempt to answer these questions. But I also challenge the premise: Bollywood is not rubbish. I also suggest why certain forms of leisure have evolved and gelled in the twentieth century, re-invented themselves during its huge social and political upheavals, while others have fallen by the wayside.

(I do not talk about cricket, which is a sport of Britain and its Commonwealth, and on which others have written substantial works.[5] Sorry. Instead I talk about wrestling, a South Asian sport that cricket, with its huge sponsorship, has come to overshadow. It was not always thus.)

While some answers lie in odd corners of history, most have to do with changing (moralising, nationalising) attitudes and the swings and roundabouts of patronage. It is a fascinating story, but it tells us as much about South Asia's twentieth century as the other, weightier subjects in this book.

I

MIRACLE PLAYS AND RELIGIOUS DRAMA: DANGER AND LEISURE

Imagine a fair, with bustling crowds, in the early 1910s or 20s. (This is the sort of occasion on which the British kept a watchful eye, concerned that conspiracies might bubble up in these settings of heightened spiritual tension, heroic performance and social disorder.) The site is western Bengal. The occasion is the annual Jhampan Mela (the snake festival). Coming at the end of the monsoon rains, it is connected to the worship of the snake goddess Manasa, a powerful deity who comes into her own in the monsoon season – a time when deadly snakes, flooded out of their holes, were everywhere.[6] The Jhampan offering to Manasa is a plea for her protection against death by snakebite.

In the north-east of the subcontinent, there were several versions of the festival. As far as we know, bards had written about it – interweaving it with different legends – from at least the seventeenth century.[7] The Flemish writer and artist Franz Balthazar Solvyns, who lived in Calcutta from 1791 to 1801, also drew and described it to the best of his limited understanding and ability, while Indian artists painted more humanising portraits of such men on mica.[8] Most of the subcontinent observed *Naaga Panchami* (the festival of the cobra), except for the icy mountains, as all parts of South Asia had their share of these timid but deadly creatures. But nowhere other than in eastern India – where rain-heavy monsoon winds met the vertiginous Himalayan slopes to create electric storms and thundering downpours – did snakes have their very own goddess.

The highlight at the Manasa festival was the congregation of non-Brahmin healers (*ojha*), exorcists and snake masters (*sapure*) at the Bishnupur palace. The Bishnupur rajas – owners of a large landed estate in south-central Bengal – had been patrons of the festival since the late nineteenth century, and the festival continued to be held (albeit in an attenuated form) at Bishnupur more than a hundred years later.

The snake masters are believed to have come from 'low caste' or tribal backgrounds, and their practice at Jhampan was to march to the palace from distant places. They walked with their snakes wrapped round their bodies, snake baskets in tow, with child mascots sometimes on their shoulders. They often hiked for weeks before arriving at Bishnupur. Drummers, always of 'low caste', and tambourine players, came with them. Disciples – whom each master was training in the art of 'snake-whispering', dancing with snakes, catching them, draining their venom and treating snakebites – escorted him. Their long trek continued until teams massed in a parade and marched to Bishnupur palace, where their performance reached its climax.

Manasa Puja was their day to shine. Early on in the day, in the first decades of the century, they displayed their skills to awed (but hushed) crowds.[9] There was a kind of magic in their mastery of virtuoso talents. The crowds shared a heightened sense of enchantment, and of suspense, as no one in the audience was quite sure whether the snakes they saw being 'charmed' were, at that moment, venomous or not. This prolonged thriller continued until the grand finale at the palace itself.

Note the sheer length of the performance (and worship): a whole day.

The following day was given over to an intense competition between the different masters. Each tried to outdo the other with acts of daring and skill. These competitions usually took place in the fishermen's quarters – 'low-caste' areas – but the crowds watching them were large, fearful and excited. Finally, after the best *sapura* had won, they all began the long trek home. Here's a lovely transition: from a performance of ritual propitiation overnight to a competitive sport. Two long days in a row, but quite different in nature and spirit.

I think we can learn a thing or two about festival leisure from the Jhampan Mela, as it existed earlier in the twentieth century. First: the festival is a morality play about good and evil. In all but a few cases, the virtuous triumph over the vicious: goddesses crush demons or snakes, heroic beings slay the wicked.

There are exceptions. For instance, Shia communities remember the histories of the vanquished during the Islamic month of Muharram. Muharram, the Shia annual commemoration of the Battle of Karbala – a battle that tore the Prophet's community asunder – is the largest and most significant of these. Shias have been an ever more embattled group – in India, Pakistan and Bangladesh, and in the diaspora. They have been, for many centuries, a significant part of South Asian spiritual life. Shias, although a minority among South Asia's sizeable Sunni-majority Muslim population, were influential patrons of aesthetic performance. Muharram was the time when they recited *marsiya* verses and remembered the suffering and sacrifice of the Imams.[10]

Going back to the Jhampan Mela, first note the length of festive time. Even the climax of the festival could last several hours; the festival itself, many days. For the snake masters for instance, who walk to Bishnupur, we're talking of weeks, because along the way, they gave smaller performances at the villages that hosted them. Large festivals, like Onam in southern India, last ten days. Ramlila could last as long as thirty-one nights, but almost always took up nine nights of Navaratri, ending with a bang on the tenth day when huge effigies of the 'evil' enemy went up in flames. As for Durga Puja in West Bengal, that has become a month of competitive madness in which everyone except the poorest forgets about trying to do paid work, so loud are each neighbourhood's blaring speakers. Altered time, in ritual performances, tends to be long and noisy.

It was not unbroken time, however. Viewer-participants at festivals that lasted for many hours or days dipped in and out for food, toilet and rest breaks or even work. Hence they moved in and out of profane and enchanted time, seamlessly and with ease.

Second: the Jhampan festival was patronised by a landlord so rich and powerful that in British times, he was given the status of a raja.

The Raja of Bishnupur gained merit and burnished his reputation by holding the festival at his palace. In the old days, he paid snake masters well for their part in it. There was, therefore, a transactional side to the event: economics lurked in the backdrop of magic. At the end of the century, after waves of land reforms, Bishnupur had no 'raja', and the old raja's heirs were not quite as rich as he once had been. In response to this crisis of patronage, festive forms had to change, and change again. The 1985 documentary *Serpent Mother*, by Allen Moore and Ákos Östör, provides a sense of the festival's later incarnation – more chaotic, less 'centred', and far less orderly, though still very central in the calendar of rural Bengal.[11]

Third: suspense, threat, dance and drama all had a part to play. Melodrama, even. The snake masters performed extraordinary feats of skill, taking on dangers unimaginable, unknowable and unquantifiable to their audience. On the day, they were epic heroes. Viewers were enthralled by the peril inherent in their performance as much as by their ritual obeisance to the goddess. Even though the audience was sure the goddess and her servants would triumph where they intervened, they couldn't be certain how powerful the performances would be, or what might go wrong (snakes sometimes bit their masters). So the same audiences and their children learned to watch the same plot again and again, appreciating the art in a more and more sophisticated way than Solvyns ever did or could. Good and evil (black and white) were drummed into the theme of these miraculous morality plays.

Last but not least: the snake masters were hard at work while the crowds enjoyed leisure. On Manasa Puja, they had a rare chance to display expertise of a very high order. Crowds watched them dance with snakes with a collective intake of breath, but for the snake master, this was his day job, his craft. According to old masters, crowds in the old days had watched in silence, tongue-tied by the astonishing sights they were witnessing. There was a sense of transcendence, of mystery, of profound authority, attached to these men. (They were always men.)

South Asian crowds are rarely silent, so this was something special. Carola Lorea's life history of a master shows that snake masters felt a respect flowing in their direction from the crowds, which was rare, given their social status.[12] 'They showed themselves to be repositories of authority, power and mystical knowledge in relation to [poisonous] snakes.'[13] Their capacity to amaze is understandable. Death by snakebite was so ubiquitous in the subcontinent that the British tried to keep district records of the numbers who died and work out how these deaths might be reduced. (They failed on both counts.)

Yet another dimension is this: play and religious ritual were not at odds with each other. The sacred and profane dimensions of the festival moved easily back and forth. The snake masters turned from Manasa worshippers to competitors overnight. Frank Korom observed this same flow at the annual three-day Dharmaraj Puja in Goalpara, also in West Bengal. The performers were, in the main, Hindu leatherworkers of 'low caste' who worshipped Dharmaraj. But pop-up chai and *paan* shops appeared near the *puja* area, to which worshippers drifted when they felt like it. Vendors were at work in the sphere of leisure and ritual. At intervals, an observer-participant would nip home for a meal and a nap, or slope off for a quick smoke of *beedee*. (This meal, conjured up by his wife or mother, was work for her. The *beedee* was work for tendu-leaf pickers, as well as all the actors in small-scale factories who produced them and brought them to the market. The *beedee* vendor, sitting cross-legged in his tiny stall, was hard at work selling his penny goods on holy days.)

A freelance journalist visiting India at the start of the century noticed this too. W. Knighton described, in rich detail, the fair in honour of Lord Vishnu held in Seepree, near Simla. Its patron was the Rana of Kothie, who charged a levy of Rs 1 on all his subjects at the fair. (There's an inventive way of gathering revenue if ever there was one.) According to Knighton, around the main event, the religious *puja*, 'conjurers, jugglers, snake charmers abounded, while the merry-go-rounds were filled with laughing tumblers snatching a fearful joy as they dashed through the air'.[14] (The merry-go-round was a South Asian diamond-shaped contraption, which rested on uprights on two sides. Men 'hauled this round and round in oscillating buckety-shaped things, hanging on the edge of the diamond and went up, up, up, and down, down, down'.)[15]

Drunkenness was hardly witnessed, unlike at similar fairs in Europe, and in South Asia there was little 'rude larking'. But 'other forms of indulgence, equally objectionable' were going on – some fair-goers were buying opium, *bhang*, *charas* and *gaanja*, the go-to intoxicants of male South Asian social life. And there were shops aplenty to supply all desires. 'Long lines of booths and stalls, with toys and sweetmeats stretched far away into the cedar groves, all teeming with looking glasses, beads, necklaces, rings, amulets, anklets, brooches, pins and ornaments for the head, while the cook shops sent forth pleasant odours and the sweetmeat men displayed their wares in tempting luxuriance.'[16]

Shopkeepers zoomed in on all festival sites, where they did their best business. So too did thieves and pickpockets. As Laxman Gaikwad reminds us, the Uchalya made a beeline for fairs, where they pocketed plenty of 'iron gold'.[17]

For women, festivals were a mixed blessing, since they were not freed from domestic tasks while men and boys joined the spectacle. If they were local affairs, like the Dharmaraj Puja, this was so obvious it hardly needs saying: all that fasting and feasting was a particular chore for them. But for larger festivals, which attracted families from far-flung places, things were different. South Asian women were expected to be models of prayer and piety. It followed that they had to be allowed to take part in the religious dimension of a festival, whether praying to Lord Vishnu in the Simla Hills, or by dipping in the Ganges at the Kumbh Mela in Allahabad, or visiting the shrine of 'Ghareeb' Moinuddin Chishti at Ajmer, 'the Mecca of the poor'. For them too, then, festivals became a kind of time-out-of-time. They still cooked sometimes, but meals rustled up while camping at a festival site were basic. Festive food at Benares, a major site of pilgrimage, consisted of little balls of baked flour (*litti*), *churmaa* (a sweetmeat of flour, ghee and sugar), spiced aubergines, rice and daal, served on banana leaves. Apparently this was delicious eaten outdoors cooked in clay vessels on cow-dung fires.[18] It was light work for the women who cooked and cleared up afterwards. They had time to participate in the larger events, if from a distance and in groups. Knighton described women at Seepree dressed in finery watching the fun, and laughing with and at each other 'as heartily as those in the swings'.[19]

The fact that so many goodies in the shops around festival sites and shrines were for women and children suggests that they delighted in the secular dimensions of the festival too. I can imagine groups of them haggling over 'iron gold' rings and headwear, buying jewellery, perhaps for a daughter soon to be given in marriage.[20] And since girls were married off so young (to men far older than them), one can imagine that new brides in the group were as drawn to sweet shops as the children of the household, although they may have been too shy to admit it. Many brides were younger than ten: let us not lose sight of that.[21]

Let's shift our attention to a much larger event – the Ramlila festival – and explore what it reveals.[22] Spread across North India and far beyond it, it is among the world's most popular dramatic traditions.[23] Based on an ancient Sanskrit text (Valmiki's *Ramayana*), the devout poet Tulsidas wrote a vernacular or Braj version, the *Ramcharitmanas* (the *Manas*), around 1650.[24] (I use *Ramayana* to denote the legend, Ramlila the festival/performance, and *Manas* the text.)

Ramlila, based on the Tulsidas version, had been performed over several days across most of the Hindi-speaking belt and beyond, in cities, *qasbaas*, palaces and bazaars, well before the century began. Already by the 1940s, Ramlila was performed in the Punjab, Bihar, Bombay Presidency, Central Provinces and Berar, Mysore, Rajasthan, Bengal, Srinagar and Nepal.[25] Philip Lutgendorf suggests that by the 1980s, Ramlila audiences were in the millions.[26]

The *Manas* (Tulsidas' text) is huge. Its print editions run to over a thousand pages, about the length of Tolstoy's *War and Peace*.[27] The Ramlila itself is a précis of this magnum opus: it has to be. The basic plot is about the birth, childhood, adventures, marriage and exile of (Lord) Ram, and his war against the ten-headed King Ravan of Lanka. While counter-hegemonic traditions challenge this storyline, and the reader must bear that in mind, the Tulsidas account has grown in popularity rather than diminished, with the rise and circulation of print.[28] Since its establishment in 1924, Gita Press has sold over 70 million copies of the *Manas* in Hindi, and several million in other languages. Print has a way of carving a story into stone – it is open to interpretation, of course, but it is far less labile than the oral traditions that preceded it. Ramlila performances, meanwhile, have proliferated.

Anyhow. In the dominant narrative, Dasharath, a noble king of Ayodhya, has, with his first wife Kaushalya, a boy called Ram. The child soon proves to have special qualities: *gambheerta* (sagacity), *dhairya* (serenity, wisdom) and depth.

With his second wife, Sumitra, Dasharath has two more sons, Lakshman and Shatrughn. (It was not uncommon for Hindus to marry more than once.) Dasharath next falls head over heels in love with the stunning but scheming Kaikeyi and marries a third time. She had a son too: they name him Bharat. But before this, the comely Kaikeyi extracts from the king an oath that once in her life he would give her anything her heart desires. (Hindu epics are full of miraculous boons and powerful oaths, hexes, spells and incantations.)[29]

The brothers grow up together in the royal household. Although of different temperaments – Ram is calm and wise, Lakshman brave but quick to anger – all four boys are devoted to each other. Their child-hood is idyllic. They grow up to be obedient sons.

But the Lila, like many miracle plays, flits back and forth between dramatic and spiritual modes. It is not pure entertainment (even though audiences enjoy the performance), because Ram, the first-born, reveals himself to be a personification of Lord Vishnu. The story begins to develop powerful religious and mythological themes. This happens at particular moments in the plot – subtle in the earlier stages but building to a crescendo towards the finale.

On reaching the age of marriage, Ram weds Sita, princess of the neighbouring kingdom of Janakpur. Sita is no ordinary woman, how-ever: she is the human guise of the goddess Parvati, consort of Lord Shiva. Sita cannot marry a mere mortal in this world. To make sure this does not happen, Sita and her father set her suitors a challenge: only the man who could lift a huge and heavy bow (the great bow of Shiva) can win her hand. Many try and all fail. Then Ram enters the contest. Draw-ing on his divine strength, he not only lifts the bow but also breaks it in half. Thus he wins Sita's hand in marriage. (Scholars suggest that Tulsidas sought to reconcile Shiva and Vishnu, two parts of the cosmic triad, and two great rival Hindu traditions, Shaivism and Vaishnavism, through this marriage. To a degree he succeeded: by the start of the twentieth century, Ramlila was performed in Shaivite parts of the country, and continued to bed down in these areas as the century drew to a close.)

To move back to the Ramlila story. Years later, Dasharath ages and tires of kingship, and wants to retreat to the forest to seek spiritual salvation (a key stage in the Hindu 'upper-caste' ethos of life stages). He decides to declare his first-born, Ram, as heir to his throne. (Even though Hindu customary law has no tradition of primogeniture, Tul-sidas, Ram devotees and Ramlila audiences believed that he *should* inherit the kingdom. In fact it is only now, on thinking and writing about it, that I have begun to think about this contradiction. Before this I took for granted Ram's claim to the throne, just like other mem-bers of the audience with a Ramlila 'habitus'.)

At this point, however, things begin to go badly for Ram. The wicked Kaikeyi shows her true colours. She now extracts her boon, forcing Dasharath to send his beloved Ram into exile in the forest for fourteen years. Her son Bharat, she insists, will inherit the throne.

Ram, ever dutiful, accepts these terms. To save his father's honour, he sets off for the forest, accompanied by Sita and his hot-headed younger brother, Lakshman. Bharat, for his part, refuses to rule, or does so only in Ram's name (even placing Ram's wooden slippers on the throne). For fourteen years, Bharat and the subjects of Ayodhya wait, as if in freeze-frame, for Ram to return.

The setting then shifts from Ayodhya to the 'forest', some distance apart. This is one interesting thing about Ramlila performances – they have had (until very recently) no single stage or proscenium: actors and audience move from setting to setting through bustling lanes to new scenarios. Its mobility is a vital feature of the performance, indeed the festival. (It has, dare I say it, a cinematic quality about it, except that the audience moves between sets, rather than having sets move around them.)

As they leave Ayodhya for the forest, much is made of exile and the pain of parting.

In the jungle, Ram and Lakshman develop an intense bond. This depth of their attachment is a leitmotif of the Lila.

Over the years, the brothers face down a hundred challenges, great and small. Every day is an adventure in the *Manas*; not so in Ramlila – the performance would be too long. The most dangerous of these is their encounter with Surupnakha, sister of the ten-headed Ravan of Lanka, and this encounter is the crucial turning point in the plot. Surupnakha takes on the guise of a beautiful woman to try to seduce the handsome Ram. (The taking on of guises, too, is a trope repeated in Hindu mythology. Both demons, *asurs*, and gods, *surs*, have this power.) Furious with this seductress, and true to his intemperate nature, Lakshman cuts off her nose.

This ugly scene, Nakkatayya or 'cutting off her nose', is one of the highlights of the Benares Ramlila. The story is thought of as hilarious, although even as a little girl, before my thoughts on matters feminist had even taken root, I thought it was horrible. Crowds of thousands (made up mainly of groups of men) gather in the evening to 'eat the air', wolf down sweet and savoury treats and marvel at the pageants of Nakkatayya. It is the only event of Ramlila that goes on all night.

In Benares, Tulsidas' city, the police presence has been much in evidence and alcohol is banned, but, as Nita Kumar's 1980s ethnography of the Chaitgang Nakkatayya suggests, that does little to dampen the euphoria of the crowds. Nai Sarak (new street), through which the actors and floats process, is brilliantly lit and decorated: shopkeepers compete to put up the best lights, hawkers sell everything from Bombay mix, street foods, *paan*, toys and trinkets, to papier-mâché figurines of the deities. It is like a massive all-night street party, minus the alcohol, a moment of carnival set within a much more 'sober, consensual' series of neighbourhood Ramlila performances.[30]

Going back again to the story: Surupnakha – bleeding, mutilated and humiliated – rushes to her brother Ravan and tells him how Ram and Lakshman have treated her.

Ravan promises his sister revenge. He proves to be a mighty and dangerous enemy, the ultimate baddie. With all the powers of an *asur*, he is far more macabre and wily than Bond villains. He first assumes the form of a dazzling golden deer, captivating Sita, who wants it as a pet. Ram, skilled though he is, cannot catch it alone – after all, it is no ordinary deer – and he cries out to Lakshman for help. But the younger brother is afraid to leave Sita alone in the forest. He draws a 'Lakshman *rekha*' (a line of protection) in the dust around their hut, telling Sita not to step beyond it. Inside its circumference, Sita is safe; her wifely purity is secure. She must, in all circumstances, stay within it.

Then he goes off to join his brother, leaving her alone.

At this point, Ravan sets another trap. Leaving the brothers hunting for the golden deer, he assumes the guise of an old man, a weak and thirsty sage. (The forest was the home of many sages who had given up the world in search of spiritual salvation. They lived on alms. It is a splendid disguise, since it was the caste-Hindu householders' duty to give them food and water.) This 'sage' begs Sita for water. When Sita tries to give it to him, he tricks her into putting a foot outside the *rekha*. He kidnaps her and forces her into his chariot which flies all the way to Lanka. More magic. There she remains prisoner in Ravan's palace for forty days. (The numbers are important. One woman. Two brothers. Forty days. Fourteen years.)

On their return, the brothers find Sita gone, and they are frantic. Seeing this, the birds and animals of the forest tell them what has happened. (Hindus regard all creatures as having souls. You wouldn't guess this from the way many treat them.) A vulture plays a key role, and so does a bear, and also squirrels (the striped markings particular to Indian squirrels are deemed to be a sign that Ram stroked them with his fingers). But it is Hanuman, the powerful monkey, who provides the two brothers with the critical logistical support they need to reach Lanka, to fight and defeat Ravan.

Ravan, for his part, had two brothers of his own: Vibhishan and Kumbhakaran; and a son, Meghnad, a brilliant warrior and learned scholar, who had famously vanquished Indra, commander of heavenly forces. In all versions of the play all members of Ravan's family wear scary black masks and dark clothes, as do Ravan's henchmen and his army of evil imps (underscoring the equation of 'fair and lovely'/'black and bad' in subcontinental eyes). Vibhishan crosses over to Ram's side (a 'good' traitor, unlike Judas). In the Ramlila, Meghnad fights hard but holds forth in Urdu (at least at the Ramlila that Norvin Hein watched in 1949, soon after partition). In other scenes, the evil imps of Lanka speak gibberish.

But Kumbhakaran is at the centre of one of the funniest scenes set in Lanka. Comedy leavens melodrama. This brother of Ravan is a renowned glutton and tippler, who eats meat (shock, horror) and drinks wine for six months, sleeping through the other six. (My witty handsome younger brother calls me Kumbhakaran, as my illness forces me to wake late. Ha ha.) The real Kumbhakaran, unlike me, is mighty when he's awake. But he happens to be in the sleep stage of his cycle when Ram attacks Lanka. Ravan implores him to wake up and help him ward off the enemy. But Kumbhakaran just rolls over, snores louder and belches. The imps jump all over him, trying but failing to wake him. The audience weeps with laughter, grateful for the comic relief even though they know that things are going to work out in the end. Everyone but babes in arms knows *that*.

Remember this: it's about two good men defeating a powerful demon and his huge army of henchmen to rescue a pure wife. Their only support is a horde of monkeys, whom Hanuman gathered in battle, a bear, a bunch of squirrels and brave birds. (Hanuman, too, is now a god – the monkey god. North India is littered with temples in his honour. Some wrestlers worship him as their particular deity. Hindu students are wont to recite the Hanuman *chalisa* before taking their exams.)

Finally, on Dassehra (the tenth day of the fortnight of the lunar month Ashvin when the night sky is bright), Ram kills Ravan in an epic battle. On Ramlila grounds across the subcontinent, crude effigies of the demon, stuffed with firecrackers, would – in the late twentieth century – go up in flames that could be seen from miles away. It is the cathartic moment of the Lila.

Another tremendous scene is when Ram and Lakshman meet their long-lost brothers, especially Bharat. Nati Imli, in Benares, is famed for its Bharat Milap. More of that in a second.

Then, on the darkest night of the month, Ram and his little group return in procession to the city from which they had been exiled. The townsfolk light up lamps to receive their true king, who goes on to rule as an exemplary monarch, establishing a period of bliss and plenty known as Ram Rajya.[31] Diwali, 'the night of the lamps', brings the festive month to a close.

Ramlila performances usually end here, even though the text on which they are based has several more chapters. One further scene is rarely performed but is nonetheless well known. This is Sita's trial by fire (*agnipariksha*) after her return to Ayodhya. The story is that gossips in the town begin to speculate about Sita's purity. After all, they conclude, her kidnapper held her for forty days; it was inconceivable that Ravan had not interfered with her. Sita insists that this did not happen, and Ram believes her. But to silence wagging tongues, as a good king must, he makes her walk through flames to prove her truth. Of course she proves blameless (although how being raped by Ravan could have been her fault ... well, then as now, the onus is on the 'defiled' woman to defend her 'character'). But even the earth is shocked by the event, opening up in grief, taking Sita to its breast.

One can see why Agnipariksha is not often performed. Its themes are uncomfortable, too close to the bone for contemporary male Ramayanis and their patrons. And it is hardly appropriate for little children. Most important, it robs Ram of some of his lustre – even Mother Earth recognises that. Another scene that does not make its way into mainstream Ramlilas, but is at the core of many Dalit performances, is Ram's beheading of the Dalit sage Shambuk for daring to be a seeker after truth in his kingdom.[32] The story goes that not all is well in Ram's Ayodhya. Monsoons fail and harvests wither, people go hungry and bemoan their fate. The city's Brahmins blame these ills on the fact that an 'untouchable' has had the temerity to become a sage in the forest near Ayodhya, within Ram's domains. This reversal of this order, so they claim, lies at the root of Ayodhya's misfortune.

Map of two nations:
newspaper coverage
of Independence Day,
15 August 1947.

Quelling
communal riots
in Calcutta
(*above*) and
Lahore (*right*).

Refugees rebuild their lives in Lahore (*above*) and Delhi (*below*).

Indentured labourers in Jamaica commemorate 'Hosay' (Muharram).

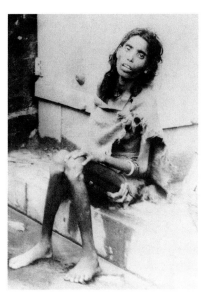

Famished girlchild during the
Bengal Famine, 1942–3.

Dalit worker at a brick
factory in Calcutta.

Mahatma Gandhi (1869–1948):
'father' of the Indian nation,
shot at point-blank range.

Liaquat Ali Khan (1895–1951):
first prime minister of Pakistan,
shot at close quarters.

Mujibur Rahman (1920–75):
gunned down with most of
his family in Dacca.

Zia-ur Rahman: coup leader and
founder of the Bangladesh National
Party (BNP), murdered in 1981.

Indira Gandhi: longest-serving
prime minister after Nehru, shot
at point-blank range in 1984.

Zia-ul-Huq goes down in
a mysterious plane crash in 1988:
a 'Case of Exploding Mangoes'.

Rajiv Gandhi: killed by
a suicide bomber in 1991.

Benazir Bhutto: slain by a shooter
and suicide bomber in 2007.

Indira Nehru Gandhi (1917–84): India's first and only woman prime minister.

Sheikh Hasina (born 1947): midnight's child.

Khaleda Zia (born 1945).

Benazir Bhutto (1953–2007): eleventh and thirteenth prime minister of Pakistan.

Snake master, as depicted by an unknown Indian artist.

Sushila Sundari (1879–1924): circus artist, with a Royal Bengal tiger.

Rukmini Devi Arundale (1904–86): maker of modern Bharatanatyam.

Fans celebrate Amitabh Bachchan's
seventieth birthday, holding a collage
of the poster of *Deewaar*,
and photos of his family.

Shah Rukh Khan: film star.

Madhuri Dixit: Kathak dancing queen,
sole woman 'leader' of movies.

Shabana Azmi: peerless actor,
renowned for activism.

They urge Ram to find and kill the man. He does so, beheading him with his sword.

Having grown up within the mainstream, sanitised, 'upper-caste', upper-class world, I was aghast when I first read about this episode. Unlike Sita's trial by fire, no one anywhere spoke of it, or performed it. You see, Tulsidas meant to show that Ram was a righteous king, doing everything possible to restore *dharma* and thus the prosperity of his kingdom and townsfolk. Dalit performers, by contrast, use it to show how Brahmins misled Ram into making his gravest mistakes.[33] Perhaps official attitudes towards affirmative action encourage Dalits to take up education, but schools and large city committees are still wary of performing the Agnipariksha. Still, the very existence of the Shambuk chapter underlines the *Ramayana*'s profound caste conservatism.

How it is that so many Indians know of Sita's trials I can't say for sure. Perhaps through word of mouth, dissemination by 'expounders', print and TV, and of course feminist groups. Or the publication of children's comic books based on the Hindu epics – the *Amar Chitra Katha* series, circulated widely among schoolchildren. But what of the millions who could not read? We know that in societies with strong oral traditions, information spreads far beyond the small communities of the educated.[34] So, like me, most probably can't remember how they learned of Sita's trial by fire, and her subsequent exile.

Returning now to the theme of time: Ramlilas usually varied in length, lasting for a week, nine days or, in the case of the Ramlila at Ramnagar, thirty-one days.[35] And these performances were not here and there, they were everywhere. At the turn of the century in the United Provinces alone, more than 300 towns put on one or more Ramlila performances.[36] One scholar suggests that in the first half of the twentieth century, 'there must have been few North Indian villagers who [did] not live within an evening's walking distance of a Ramlila during the Dassehra season'.[37]

The quality of performances varied of course – that is to be expected given that the actors were amateurs, children. But here is the scholar Philip Lutgendorf's eyewitness account of his experience of the Bharat Milap at Nati Imli in 1983. It attests to Ramlila's immense theatrical power even in an age of competing audio-visual media.

The scene unfolded thus. The Maharaja of Ramnagar arrived on a palanquin wearing silks and a jewelled turban, and the crowd greeted him with loud cries of '*Har-Har-Mahadev!*' ('Glory be to God, great one!'). The maharaja, patron of the largest, longest and most comprehensive Ramlila performance, was admired not just as a raja but also as patron of the greatest Ramlila.[38]

Lutgendorf describes how the drama built up.

While the maharaja, on his palanquin, perambulated round Ram's palanquin:

> Bharata and Shatrughna had arrived and had ascended the nearer platform. Everything was now in place, and as the magic moment approached, the dead hush of a great expectancy fell over the multitude. At the far end of the field, Rama and Lakshmana descended from their palanquin and stood at the edge of the runway; simultaneously Bharata and Shatrughna prostrated themselves full-out on their platform. A clash of the cymbals announced the presence of the *Ramaayanis*, who began singing Tulsi's description of the scene in the familiar chant special to Ramlila. So perfectly synchronized and dramatically effective was the timing that it seemed as if an invisible clock, of which all were aware, was counting off the few remaining seconds, bringing every onlooker to a calculated emotional peak. With measured steps Rama and Lakshmana began walking along the runway, but they soon broke into a trot, which gradually increased to a full run. The mass silence was replaced by a kind of involuntary and ecstatic roar . . .

As the brothers embraced, the crowd shouted '*Raja Ramachandra ki jai!*' ('Victory to King/Lord Ram!').[39]

And then it was over. The boys descended and walked to the waiting palanquin, which was hoisted on the shoulders of the Ahirs, a 'lower', herding caste – Dasharath and his wives were played by 'upper castes' and Ram by a young Brahmin – to process slowly to the Ramlila committee's headquarters, giving *darshan* (blessed view) to tens of thousands more en route.

Lutgendorf concludes: 'The Nati Imli Bharat Milap was one of the most dramatic events I had ever witnessed.'[40]

The *Ramayana* story is, at one level, just that: powerful drama, replete with good and bad characters (some with comic eccentricities), in which the goodies beat the baddies in the end. Like most epic tales, it has a strong moral architecture. The hero of the hegemonic version is Ram, whom Tulsi reveres as the human personification of Lord Vishnu. He is, then, a bit like Christ – at once human and divine.[41] Just as with Christ, Ram's story has bold clear lines which describe, in the most graphic way, moral and base conduct. It continues to exert a powerful appeal despite (or perhaps because of) its social conservatism. Everyone in the story plays their 'correct' (socially approved) role: Dasharath is a true patriarch, Kaushalya a devoted mother, Sita a loyal and self-sacrificing wife. Ram is a model of filial piety. Ram's brothers are loyal to a fault. Women who display any independent sexuality are 'wicked' (Kaikeyi) and deserve their humiliation (Surupnakha). As for the demons, they could hardly be worse. Ravan's sister is a loose temptress who deserves her fate, Kumbhakaran a lazy glutton and a drunkard to boot, the evil imps are ridiculous and inept. Meghnad is a complex figure, hard to reduce to caricature – but in Benares he speaks in Urdu, so he *must* be awful. As for Ravan, he is the personification of evil, and by god, every one of his ten heads is ugly. But like Satan, he is powerful; like Lucifer, he is full of tricks. Like Old Nick, he is a force to be reckoned with. It takes a divine hero like Ram to vanquish him.

Many urban residents boasted about their own 'very best' Ramlila performances, but the claims of Benares to be the best in the genre were strong. For one thing, Tulsidas, the author of the story, lived out his old age and died in the city, and so its connection with the author of the *Manas* is powerful. Next, the 'Maharaja' of Ramnagar (no longer one by law, but still with the comportment and style of a 'good Hindu king') hosted the longest and most elaborate Ramlila until the early 1990s. A number of groups of patrons, mainly merchants, supported different Ramlilas across the busy old city. Each of these was renowned for its particular enactment of one particular episode – say, Surupnakha's story, or the Bharat Milap. Discerning Banarasis move from Lila ground to Lila ground to catch the best enacted events at each location. Such is the depth and density of their understanding of this play, and their aesthetic judgement of the quality of each performance.

Pilgrims, meanwhile, have a different experience. They tend to come to Benares for *teerth* (pilgrimage) and usually are able to stay for only a few days. They might choose to attend the Ramlila closest to their lodgings; this might not be the best show in town, but is still, given its location, likely to be a cut above performances back home.

The players themselves were children, some as young as five. Little boys played the key roles, barring Surupnakha – a *'hijra'* (transgender person once spoken of as a 'eunuch') often played her part.[42] By the 1960s, middle-class girls began to perform, and still do. By the time hair began to sprout on a boy's upper lip, he was deemed too old to take part; he would then train a junior in his role.

In the first three quarters of the century, these miracle plays achieved the intended impact by a combination of tableaux, acting and speech, musical chanting, staging and costume. The reverence of the audience also was an essential part of riveting Ramlilas in small *qasbaas* and towns. The little actors, heavily made up and dressed in silken *dhotis* and *lehengas*, wearing paper crowns and carrying pretend bows and arrows, had to shout their lines to be heard. This made their speech a little singsong, rather in the way that BBC newsreaders have begun to cultivate, emphasising ev-e-ry syllable of each word. The effect was unnatural. (But tell me, was Laurence Olivier's talent spotted in his first role as a shepherd in his school nativity play? I doubt it.) Their gestures were meant to be neither realistic, nor subtle. The child actors tended to stick their little arms out in front of them and gesticulate as if speaking to a large crowd. Their body language – particularly for the main 'good' characters – suggested gravitas well beyond their years. (Seen through foreign eyes, this might seem absurd in children so young.) However, learned observers steeped in the study of drama did not see it this way, mid-century. Hein describes the actors speaking with 'a clarity, poise, feeling, and volume that would be highly credit-able anywhere', and notes that the best Ramlilas achieve aesthetic 'excellence'.[43]

I acted in my first Ramlila at the age of five or six. I was at nursery school, and I played the treacherous temptress, Kaikeyi. Who knows why I was given the role, which conservative iterations have lent such a dark charge. Perhaps I was a very bad girl? I don't remember being particularly naughty; if anything, I got heaps of gold stars, and I was a bit of a goody-two-shoes. (Yes, awful, I know.) So it's more likely they gave it to me because the headteacher knew my parents well, and judged that far from being offended, they would laugh. (They did. Other Hindu parents might have taken great offence.)

So I have been a Ramlila child. And before I had acted in it, and learned my own lines and everyone else's (as one does), I had watched it four years in a row. It was one of the highlights of the school year, when lessons took a back seat for nigh on a month. It was, if we are speaking of religion, Hinduism of the Vaishnava Bhakti variety. But it was not just religion, it was theatre, it was play, it was time-out-of-time. No other festival had week-long (or month-long) performances building up to it. (Christmas, which we also celebrated, seemed to be all about furtive present-wrapping, food and drink, the last of which interested me less then.) Gosh, how we rejoiced as the towering effigy of Ravan burst into flames that could be seen from a mile away! And how we delighted in Diwali! We were crazy for firecrackers: the acid smell of cordite still brings back to me gleeful memories of pyromania. (My older brother, now an architect of some renown, still bears a burn mark on his back from a dangerous game with a cracker that went whizzing in the wrong direction.) But we also knew that it was the end of the play: Ram, Lakshman and Sita had returned to Ayodhya. All over. The End. Back to normal time.

But my acting debut was in a nursery school play. Larger performances always have, as a key part of the act, adult Ramayanis to the side of the stage. They chant in singsong sections from the *Manas* in Braj – the 'common' language in which Tulsidas composed it – after which the young actors speak their parts in modern Hindi. This interweaving of musical chanting and acting in two languages adds to the Ramlila's dual flavour – it is an exciting performance even as it is worship. (Most Ramlila committees stage only the most melodramatic and cathartic scenes of the *Ramcharitmanas*.) Action, humour, wickedness, filial devotion, love, brotherhood, devoted womanliness and divinity are the themes you are likely to encounter at a regular neighbourhood Ramlila. All this is set within the clear frame of a morality play. Within it there is space for close readers of the text to enjoy the chanting, and hence the deeper meaning of the scene, while the majority who don't know the *Manas* can enjoy the musicality of the chant and the tableaux, plain speech, and action on stage. This interweaving of chant and action is a crucial feature of Ramlila's pleasures.

Indeed, if there are any directors at all of small Ramlilas, one should give Ramayanis credit for this role. Actors learned their lines alone, and dress rehearsals were unheard of mid-century. The producers and patrons were the Ramlila committees. (More about them in a minute.) There was no entry ticket – the performance was free and open to everyone.

This pattern would suggest that general Ramlila audiences, at least until the early 1980s, were very familiar with a few parts of the epic and knew little of the other parts. Each scene contains several layers of depth and meaning, but not all members of the audience grasped the same ones, or in the same way. Research in the Braj area in the 1940s showed that on average, each person interviewed had watched a Ramlila three times in their life. Their knowledge of the text, this would suggest, was patchy, but they knew the headlines very well indeed. Their grasp of its moral message was powerful.

Then there were people with an even higher level of expertise in Tulsi's *Ramcharitmanas* – known as *vyaas*. These 'expounders' held performances of pure speech alone, at which they sat before devout audiences and elaborated sometimes on the deeper meaning of a sin-gle passage of the text. In the late 1980s, when Lutgendorf was doing his fieldwork, a *vyaas* could command a substantial fee for an hour-long performance, ranging from Rs 200 to Rs 2,000. Some were famous across the length and breadth of the country, their diaries crammed with bookings.

What of the audiences? Lutgendorf observed in the 1980s, just as Hein did in the 1940s, that all members of the audience sat on the floor, on a rough cotton *dhurry* at best. These were not orderly occasions; often members fed their babies, ate peanuts or chatted with each other. Men and women sat apart. Since different parts of the play were staged in different localities, and since Ramlila is a mobile event – Ayodhya is set in one place, Lanka in another, Janakpur in a third and the forest in a fourth – viewers would jostle together along with the players as they rushed from one site to the other. Such chaos is part of both aspects of the festival: the scramble for seats at the show, and the performance of devotion to the gods. By being in the presence of (*darshan*), or brushing up against, 'Ram', members of the crowd felt twice blessed.

But Ramlilas, however demotic, were *not* democratic events. On one occasion when a respected connoisseur arrived late at a *vyaas'* performance, the expounder stopped his show to greet him and invite him to sit at the front of the audience, saying: 'Oh, Thakur Sahib! Please come forward! If a superior listener sits right in the front, the pleasure will increase, won't it?'[44] The income of a *vyaas* depended on patronage; though dealing in spiritual goods, the *vyaas* had to satisfy their most lavish patrons. This is nowhere more obvious than in Ram-nagar, where the maharaja is on stage with Ram in the finale of a month-long performance.[45]

So on to the economics of Ramlila. Who works, who earns a liveli-hood, who trades, who are the patrons? The actors were all unpaid amateurs, except for the *hijras* who played Surupnakha, who were, it seems, remunerated with a small amount of cash.[46] Ramayani chant-ers, even in the late twentieth century, received payment in kind – in food, shelter and (if performing at Ramnagar) gifts from the maha-raja. *Vyaas* expounders got cash at the end of their performance, and sometimes other gifts from wealthy fans. But there is a larger market around the event, these being occasions when small-time sellers of sweets and savoury snacks did a roaring trade (as, no doubt, did their suppliers). Artisans who made tops, toys, trinkets and other cheap merchandise would flock to these festivals because of the huge crowds (and markets) they attracted.

The town of Sivakasi in Madras would become India's main fire-cracker producer by the end of the twentieth century. With around 800,000 people employed in the industry and about 1,000 units, it is reputed to make huge turnovers and profits. It is also notorious for fires and deaths, mainly of frontline workers. The festivities have a price, in more than one sense. The ecological costs of the fireworks in cities grew enormous as the century ended.

Tailors all over India kept a careful track of fairs in their wider regions and headed to them, recognising huge opportunities to make sales at festivals.[47] Vendors of simple pleasures like chai and *paan* would be everywhere, and intoxicants would circulate through the crowds. The fair associated with every festival created a buoyant micro-economy in which a huge range of actors strove to make tidy sums (each by his own lights, of course).

There's the further question of how Ramlila performances were funded. Who raised the cash to pay the artisans who built the stages and effigies, the tailors who ran up the costumes, the cleaners of the site and general hands who set up *shaamiyanas* (the colourful mar-quees), the microphone providers and the Ramayanis? In certain places, a single patron might bear the whole cost, as in Ramnagar. More often, Ramlila committees were critical. 'Middle-level merchants and traders in grain, wood, metal or cloth as well as small shopkeep-ers, including those of milk and *paan*' were, in Benares, active as patrons.[48] Each gave what they could to their local committees, which consisted of about a dozen men, about six of whom were merchants, the others young Ram devotees or students of the neighbourhood.

These committees also raised some of the money from merchants and shopkeepers through 'general solicitation'.[49] But a surprisingly large portion came from small donors, local Hindus who were far from affluent. Lutgendorf's informants on one Ramlila committee told him (in 1983) that all that they had been able to raise was 35,000 rupees. ('Some people give just four or eight rupees, some give fifty-one, some give three hundred or more, according to their will.')[50] As a consequence, Ramlila even in Benares (with the notable exception of Ramnagar) was a low-budget affair, with most committees struggling to avoid going into the red by the time the festival ended.

This pattern changed in the late 1980s when the Indian state and its 'liberalised' broadcaster Doordarshan took up a role as 'patron' of Ramlila. In 1987–8, it aired a version for television in seventy-eight episodes. That made it more than twice as long as the Ramnagar Ramlila. Although the cost of the production is not widely known, it was the most popular TV serial of its time (the TV serial had just begun to come of age), watched by eighty-eight per cent of viewing households. One of the most seasoned actors of the Bombay cinema world – Ashok Kumar – narrated the tale, taking the place, one might say, of an expounder. The format of the small-screen Ramlila deviated from local performance culture in fundamental ways, but also fed off an existing bedrock, albeit of varying depth, of knowledge of the story, performance style and text. But by god was it a phenomenon. I remember my niece Maya, aged five or so, brought up in a secular home, insisting on putting up a poster from the epic in her little bedroom.

In a decision that was as political as it was popular, during the first wave of the Covid pandemic in India in 2020, the BJP-led government of India broadcast the series again. Seventy-seven million people watched a single episode. (I was in India at the time, but too ill with Covid to watch it.) The point is that the epic has reached a far wider audience, which now has a far greater command of the *Ramayana* based on the *Manas*, than did audiences of the early, mid and late twentieth century. Serial viewers saw far more segments of the tale than audiences in the 1950s or 80s who watched only a few scenes and heard rhythmic chanting but few words of speech that they could understand. By contrast, viewers in the late twentieth century watched, week after week, more than a year's worth of performances that used cinematic techniques honed in Bombay. All in modern, standardised Hindi/Urdu which, by this time, more South Asians could understand – thanks to popular cinema.

II

SECULAR DANGER: STRENGTH AND DARING AS ENTERTAINMENT

Baazigars: stuntmen before the movies

Like these miraculous traditions – whether Manasa Puja or Ramlila – secular performances also enthralled South Asian audiences. They knew that these players harnessed no miraculous powers, yet there was a huge appetite for their acts.

Let me first clarify what I mean by secular. These creators and enjoyers of leisure did not inhabit a distinct world of scientific reason; nor were they unbelievers. Throughout the twentieth century, South Asia remained a religious society, although the character of faith has changed over time. The subcontinent defied, and continues to defy, the prognosis that the whole world will march towards secularisation, playing catch-up with the West.[51]

Nonetheless, some forms of leisure operated in a different symbolic context, in which the sacred took a back seat. Feats of force and audacious courage fall into this category. Performers of these acts were admired, indeed patronised, by villages and kings.

Baazigars (magicians, tumblers and acrobats) were among several itinerant groups in the undivided Punjab and North India who performed their illusions by invitation, at festivals, fairs or weddings.[52] Consumers paid for their work in cash or kind. In undivided northern India, Naats ('tumblers' of a different clan and creed) entertained in much the same way. Performers of this type existed in many parts of India at the start of the century, but were concentrated in North India, particularly the Punjab.[53] Partition scattered them like chaff in a storm. Even though their attachment to 'Hinduism' or 'Islam' had always been tenuous, the conditions of the time, and their itinerant lifestyles, encouraged a process of 'unmixing' and border-crossing.[54] Baazigars, a clan of many intermarrying groups with its own dialect,

moved from West to East Punjab and North India, where they continued, somehow, to subsist.

The British had categorised Baazigars and other similar groups into
the catch-all category of 'vagrants', rather than as 'Criminal Tribes',
after 1872.[55] But after independence and partition, when many Baazigars migrated to India, they found themselves labelled as 'ex-Criminal
Tribes', and were rehabilitated in villages.[56] Oh, the wonders of the
Indian state, its myopia and inverted logic![57] However fatuous and
inappropriate, the 'criminal' tag stuck, despite the Baazigars' campaigns to fight it, and to be designated instead as a Scheduled Caste.

I focus on Baazigars because we now know more about them than
colonial sources reveal, and because of their grip on the popular
imagination. In 1993, the Hindi film *Baazigar* starred Shah Rukh
Khan as a murderous anti-hero. This was a bold move in Bombay's
cinematic history. The film, it was feared, would flop, and many reigning stars turned down the role. Like the Baazigars of yore, Khan's
character plays with death. Just as they were branded in 1947, he is a
criminal (indeed, a psychopath).[58] Nonetheless, he commands our
attention and wins our respect. Shah Rukh, a TV star but a relative
newcomer to the movies, took on the role and played it with brio.
Baazigar's huge success shows how the collective memory of Baazigars
lingers on. But by the late twentieth century, that figure of the Baazigar
had become a collage in which criminality, cruelty and violence had
been pasted onto courage and gumption: a mishmash of characteristics drawn from state-produced stereotypes. This is not to deny the
quality of this cult film (of which more below), but to place it in a long
historical context.

The Baazigars of British India performed 'physic and surgery, and
[were] not free from the suspicion of sorcery'.[59] But before partition,
their chief source of livelihood was *baazi*: feats of strength and daring. Acrobatics (*kalabaazi*) (including back flips, handsprings and
handstands) and *chaunki vali chhal* (a flip performed on a small platform) – acts we might compare with the top-end gymnastics at the
Olympics – were standard fare. Their contortions, though, were probably more astounding than those seen at your average Commonwealth
or Asian Games.

The shock factor ratcheted up as more crowds gathered. A typical
performance might involve a Baazigar shimmying up a tall pole resting
on the head of a fellow member of the troupe. Next, another might

vault off a raised springboard into the air, perhaps clearing a high wall.

Often they would demonstrate their skill and strength by lifting substantial objects, sometimes only with their teeth. A great favourite, in an age when brick kilns were becoming ubiquitous, was to smash bricks with a single blow.[60] A narrow iron rod might be bent across the body – sometimes across only the eyes of the Baazigar. In these demonstrations of strength, Baazigars resembled wrestlers. But the two cannot be confused. Baazigars worked more as a team. They had more of the circus approach to entertainment.

Their performances tended to walk closer to the jaws of death as the event progressed.

Two men would clash swords, blindfolded. Another would leap through a ring laced with daggers. A third would show off his blind-folded flip with a sword between his teeth.

In the most dramatic 'leap of doom' (*suli di chhal*), the performer did a back flip off a small platform raised high atop a bamboo pole, some thirty feet up, with a flaming sword in his teeth. Sarvan Singh, the Baazigar whom Gibb Schreffler interviewed in 1996, and who gave him these rich details about days gone by, told him that this was their crowning stunt. It was so dangerous, however, that some sponsors asked that it not be performed lest a tragedy occurred in the village.[61]

Children too were involved, in the main as contortionists. In Satyajit Ray's film *Aparajito* ('Undefeated', 1956), one such child performer makes a brief appearance, while the young Aparajito watches with the crowd. (Women, by contrast, did not perform.)

Baazigars lived by these performances. Much practice went into the production of this form of leisure for others. Baazigars, to be so adept and to save their own skins, had to spend most of their time training. In the first half of the century when they were not outlawed and their acts were much in demand, this made economic sense. Before partition, each group of Baazigars 'bagged' about thirty or forty villages as their turf, where they (and no other troupe) performed at marriages, festivals and fairs. These villages were their patrons, but of a particular kind: when a Baazigar daughter married into another clan, she could sometimes take performing rights in a village as a form of dowry. It took many villages, then, to sustain a single troupe. There was as little fat on their bodies as there were coins in their coin bags.

They were also a common sight at fairs, in turn often attached to religious events. These appearances no doubt earned them some extra cash, though it is not easy to learn how much.

With partition, Baazigars were torn from the networks of villages that had patronised them. Itinerants resettled as if they were criminal tribes; the state tried to reform them into becoming 'good and productive citizens'. Many began to live by manual labour, while occasionally performing *baazi* for a small sum. Today *baazi* makes up only the tiniest fraction of the occupations they practise. The vast majority have shifted to whatever unskilled labour was available, which was mainly agricultural work, and were thus de-skilled, shorn of their hereditary training and occupation. Some raised milch cattle, and sold fruit and vegetables on the roadside. Others had small businesses. By good fortune, partition also saw – with the influx of refugees from West Pakistan – a spurt in the popularity of *bhangra*, a vigorous dance of rural Punjab, of which they became skilled practitioners. They began to be invited to weddings and festivals again, but for *bhangra* rather than *baazi* performances.[62] *Sic transit gloria mundi.*

Some of their *baazi* skills survived too, albeit in a limited way, in the altered context of ticketed circus acts. These began to be a feature of middle-class entertainment as early as the turn of the century. Although the economics of patronage meant that they only reached large towns or cities, circus troupes were fascinating, mixing performers from India with actors from Russia, Hungary, Italy and even Syria.[63] They included women artists, not least Fearless Nadia, of whom more below, and Sushila Sundari, who posed lazily with a Royal Bengal tiger in a spangly glamorous outfit. It's hard to outdo a Royal Bengal tiger for sheer power and beauty, but Sushila sizzled in that context.

Animal taming had never been part of *baazi*, so one can see why acrobats and tumblers were never quite the stars of the big top. The greatest attractions were wild animals and their tamers, who showed courage of a different kind. I still remember the elephant and lion from the one circus I was taken to as a child. Everything else, bar the trapeze, is a bit of a blur. The 'walk of death' was an 'eyes-closed' moment: the acrobat unsupported, no net beneath him should he fall. No doubt the performer was a Baazigar.

I recall as a child seeing travelling groups of bedraggled acrobats who visited the back lanes of posh Delhi neighbourhoods, performing for the children and 'servants' of the burra sahibs. Such troupes, of at most seven or eight people, visited our close friends the Tullys twice when I was a little girl. Dressed in shabby clothes and rough turbans, they did not approach the main entrance: history had taught them to use 'the service entrance'. But their acts were riveting: poles balancing upon heads upon which more poles balanced more actors – more dangerous in a hard and confined, cemented space. It was clear, even to my young eyes, that they were poor, and Margaret Tully gave them dry rations and money. Yet they radiated a fierce kind of pride, a rage even, that lingers in my memory to this day. No wonder they were angry.

More than a quarter of a century later, in 1994, I took my son to the circus. Little Kartik sat round-eyed and open-mouthed, staring for two hours in unbroken concentration at the lion in his cage, paying scant heed to the acts of the other performers, leaping up only when the lion tamer came on stage. To my adult eyes, the circus appeared tatty: its fabric battered, its clown genuinely sad.

By the end of the century, the circus had become a rarity. The big tops faded out of existence and its star attractions – mangy lions and their tamers – were regulated out of existence. In 1998, the Indian government in Delhi banned bears, monkeys, tigers, panthers and lions from being exhibited or trained as performing animals.[64] After 2011, children could no longer act in circuses (never mind that children could still act in the cinema or modelling, or work as farmhands or manual labourers in fields and construction sites).[65]

These changes reflected late-twentieth-century shifts in the intellectual positioning of the thinking classes. With the decline of the Old Left, new causes emerged: wildlife protection became a default position for many left-leaning young people, and single-cause movements, like the green movement, the Right to Food Movement and the *Jana Swasthya Abhiyaan* (the movement for people's health) proliferated. In this context, the *Bachpan Bachao Andolan* (the Movement to Save Childhood) made a powerful case for children's rights. As well as losing some of its performers, the circus began to lose its customers of yore. In the main, they had been the children of the urban well-to-do, dragging their parents with them. Children had once constituted up to seventy-five per cent of the audience. By 2007, their proportion as viewers had dropped to thirty per cent.[66] Circuses still exist but have lost much of their glamour and financial wherewithal, with lower takings from poorer audiences. And those audiences have more exciting options.

I tell you so much about Baazigars because they represent something that South Asian audiences expected to see as 'entertainment' – daring in the face of danger – and were ready to pay for and wait for. These were stunts of the highest order before the word 'stunt' entered the lexicon of cinema-goers and cultural historians. One future for the Baazigar lay, it turns out, in Bombay.

The forgotten cult of wrestling

There's another group of daring men with whom South Asians have had a long love affair. They are wrestlers, *pehelwaans*. South Asia's obsession with wrestling (*kushti*) is one of the contemporary world's better-kept secrets. Few know of its history, not least because it is a sport of the poor (unlike cricket, which was first taken up by elites). Neither states nor corporations patronise it, though South Asian wrestlers continue to bring back medals. Their achievements received less and less airtime as the century progressed; indeed despite reading three newspapers a day I still had learned nothing about them.

My ignorance places me squarely in the social category to which I belong: the navel-gazing, western-educated (Bengali), 'upper-caste' elite, with its 'high' culture admitting only fine art, literature, sport (cricket), music and cinema. How much I have missed! I kick myself for not questioning this cultural snobbery before, despite my critical stance towards that elite. I offer this section to challenge myself, and to change the direction of our gaze.

Throughout the twentieth century, the young men of South Asia have wrestled. Indian wrestling has been a pastime and, in the past, a patronised form of entertainment. It was a way of life as much as a sport. Men of different social standing and religion wrestled together in the same *akharas* (clubs, albeit not of the western variety). At least until the 1940s, these were cross-communal spaces – no less diverse than Bombay cinema would later become. As disciples (*shaagirds*) of the same guru (*ustaad*), Muslims, Hindus, Sikhs and Christians practised, grappled and massaged each other seven days a week. For them it was an all-consuming world.

Rajas, maharajas, nawabs and ranas supported the best men and promoted wrestling competitions (*dangals*) which drew thousands of spectators. Among the pre-partition greats, the disabled had a considerable presence: the 'deaf-mute' Goonga was a name to be reckoned with, and 'Lame' Pataba was so good that the Maharaja of Rewa kept him on a retainer. Only caste has been a barrier, as one would expect, although Sahdeo, a 'Dom', was a famous exception to that rule.

Two anthropological studies of late-twentieth-century *akharas* (wrestling clubs) are well known to scholars, but because both are of Benares, this has somewhat skewed our understanding of their broader, deeper history. Joseph Alter (an amateur wrestler himself) suggests that although the number of *akharas* was huge at the start of the century, and has, if anything, proliferated, their membership had declined by the 1980s.[67] Both Alter and Nita Kumar suggest that by the 1980s, in India, these *akharas* tended to attract Hindu members who regarded the monkey god Hanuman, renowned for his strength in the *Ramayana*, as their patron deity. They had a strong Hindu ethos, even if a few disciples were Muslims by denomination.[68]

If so, much changed over the century.

Let me elaborate on the long history of wrestling through the story of one man, whose life reveals many contours of a South Asian obsession. His name was Ghulam Muhammad Baksh Butt, aka Gama. At some stage he began to be called Gama the Great, or the Great Gama, a tag that has stuck to this day. One only has to go online and search 'Gama' when up pop videos about Gama's history, his biography, training methods and victories. An international community of bodybuilders and grapplers still looks to him as a role model. Bruce Lee, the Hong Kong-American martial artist, borrowed some of Gama's training methods. Few outside this community, large and far-flung though it is, remember him.

Born circa 1880 in Amritsar into a Muslim family of wrestlers, Gama started training at the age of five. He lost his father and grandfather while still a small child. Given his talent, his extended household handed him into the care of a Madho Singh of Lahore, a friend of his father and a Punjabi Hindu wrestler of some repute.[69] In the *kushti* community, such religious borders meant little.

Gama was only ten years old when he took part in an endurance competition put on by the Maharaja of Jodhpur. Legend has it that more than 400 wrestlers from all of South Asia took part, performing the free squats (*baithaks*) which were part of their training. (And also a common form of punishment in schools when I was growing up. We had to do ours while holding our ears.) With only fifteen wrestlers holding out at the end, the Maharaja declared the youngest contestant, Gama, the winner. The ten-year-old Punjabi boy had already become a phenomenon in the Indian wrestling world.

The fact that Gama was Muslim hardly stood out. Most of the greats were Muslims in this period, from Punjab in the west to Bengal in the east, although Hindu 'touchable' castes were well represented. Even Catholics of the Konkan coast – like Cajetano of Calangute, a migrant from Portuguese Goa (see Chapter 4) – took to *kushti*.

Punjab's dominance in the sport is a persistent feature of wrestling history in India until partition. This is not to suggest that there were no great wrestlers from other parts of India. There were: Ramamurti of Madras, Syamakanta Banerji of Dacca and Gobar Guho of Calcutta were famous too.

Princes seem to have been the sport's main patrons, investing a great deal in *dangals* and in great wrestlers. Gama's patron was the Maharaja of Patiala, and most states of central and western India held tournaments. The Raja of Kohlapur maintained a league table of sorts and organised an annual tournament which 'gave Indian wrestling the appearance of order'. Kohlapur, Patiala, Jammu and Kashmir, Rewa and Nawanagar retained the best and most famous men; indeed Ranjitsinhji, the Jam Saheb of Nawanagar who would later go on to promote cricket, was an active referee of *dangals*. Tens of thousands of people collected to watch these bouts, so it made sense, from their regal perspective, to entertain the crowds. Just as with Benares and Ramlila, these men also valued and understood the sport.

Even the colonial state (whose officers did not understand it), looking for ways to keep its fighting arms fit and occupied, built time for wrestling matches into the few leisure activities of constables and sepoys.[70]

Where the state was not involved, whole *chawls* or shanty towns pitched in to set up training rooms and pit-like settings in which working men could wrestle. Bombay's slums heaved with *akharas*.[71] Cajetano learned to wrestle in a Goan *chawl* in Bombay. Until the century ended, part of his charisma derived not only from his reputation of 'sainthood' (which grew as he aged), but from his history as a wrestler. Calangute boys looked up to him as a wrestler and a fine figure of a man.

Other patrons tended to be Bengali *zamindaars* like Amboo Guha, an avid promoter of physical culture in all its forms.[72] (The British attack on the effeminacy of the 'Bengali Babu' propelled this movement.)[73] Even a sprinkling of eccentric intellectuals embraced it. Muzumdar, who fell in love with the sport at a young age, made a career for himself as a sports journalist, writing a book about the many 'strong men' of his time. He would also act as referee at major tournaments. 'Strangler' Lewis, the American fighter, described the Bengali fighter Gobar as 'the grappler who discussed Tagore'.[74] But it would be a mistake to think that Bengal's elite physical culture movement remained aloof from the *akhara* craze of North India – there was much borrowing, crossing of boundaries and mutual fascination.

But back to Gama. He was no intellectual. He could read only a little Urdu, yet he was, by all accounts, a thoughtful man who could explain in minute detail both the art and science of wrestling. Handsome, with cropped hair and a handlebar moustache, a small frown plays on his brow in most of his photographs, suggesting a contemplative personality. He looks the photographer straight in the eye in every portrait I have seen of him; no smile hovers at his lips as he holds his silver mace (a gift from the Prince of Wales) across his huge chest. There is no menace in his expression. Muzumdar, who spent many hours with him in 1934, attests to his high intelligence and his discomfort with strangers, even his shyness. We know of his extraordinary tenacity and ambition, and his ferocity in the ring. He was so quick off the mark, attacking his opponents with such aggression from the get-go, that he bested them within minutes, even seconds.

Gama's short bouts signalled 'a change in the time-rhythms' in wrestling.[75] Previously, bouts lasting two to four hours had been the norm (and they remained thus for rising stars), but the Gama style became the aspiration of all top wrestlers.

Gama attained supremacy first in the Punjab, and by 1910, in all of British India. He held his 'title' (a concept, I suspect, borrowed from the West, where Indian wrestlers were soon put on display) for decades, before surrendering it to his brother, Imam Baksh.

Long before Gama retired, British promoters tried to pit Indian greats against the big names from the West. At a much-publicised event in London's Holborn Empire, Gama faced the American Benjamin Roller, then the reigning world champion, and threw him in two straight falls. He next reduced the Pole Stanislaus Zbyszko to a defensive stance within minutes, the latter continuing in retreat through what was, by all accounts, a boring competition, but which left no one in any doubt about who came out on top.[76] Gama never lost a match after that. Despite issuing periodic challenges and offering cash sums to any world wrestler to take him on, few dared. Those who did regretted it.

After his victories in London, Indian newspapers declared him 'world champion', and Gama accepted that title, such as it was. In my view, there could have been no world champion in wrestling at this time. Although a South Asian won the Olympic title in 1908, after the Games were first revived, Gama beat Roller and Zbyszko in catch-as-catch-can wrestling, and US champions dominated the rather different style of Graeco-Roman wrestling. There were many great Japanese wrestlers too, with their own Sumo style, although Gama threw many of them also. There were just too many forms of the sport for a single world champion to have emerged.

In 1910, the Indian style was not 'the best'. It was neither less nor more. It was just different. In the Gama decades, the South Asian style was unbeatable.

So what was Indian wrestling?

First, it was fought in an open-air pit of modest dimensions, made of earth softened with ochre and sesame oil. The pit called for constant maintenance, and all members of the *akhara* joined in this work. In most *akharas*, wrestlers considered its soil to have sacred qualities.

Second, it had much in common with the Arabic and Turkish traditions. In early March 1928, an excited *Times* correspondent tried to describe it: 'bringing the adversary to the ground is not enough. An immense amount of time may be spent on the earth. The battle is not over until both shoulders (of the defeated man) are touched down', and kept down, for a long time. 'It is surprising how many wriggles and contortions will extricate' a felled wrestler to keep him in the game. 'The referees' work is important. Almost any hold is permissible [except strangleholds, and] the twisting of fingers and toes to breaking point.'[77]

Gama's preferred method was to bring his adversary to the floor within the first minute, by diving for one ankle with his arms while flipping his other leg from beneath him with one massive leg. He would then fall upon his opponent, pinning both shoulders down for as long as it took. It seldom took more than a few minutes.

What of training for the sport? Reading about it made me feel weak.

Like other South Asian wrestlers of his time, Gama used no barbells, no parallel bars, no equipment of any sort other than a *nal*, a heavy stone mace. This made wrestling a pastime, or mania, affordable for common folk.

Gama's routine focused on *baithaks* (free squats), *dands* (jackknifing push-ups) and, once he was powerful enough, wielding the backbreaking mace. But we are not talking about ten squats, or fifty squats, or even a hundred squats. Gama did 4,000 *baithak* squats and 3,000 *dand* push-ups every single day, getting these figures up towards 7,000 before every major tournament. He then grappled with other members of his *akhara* of about forty for three hours, every day. These figures are no doubt exaggerated: his fans were given to hyperbole. Even so, it's hard to demystify Gama's focus and discipline, and the punishing routine on which his greatness rested.

From the 1920s and 30s, Indian wrestling techniques were forced to change a little as wrestling became a transnational field and Indian wrestlers encountered a host of different styles. Nonetheless, given accounts by anthropologists in the 1980s, it would appear that training regimes in local *akharas* have changed relatively little. *Dands*, *baithaks* and *nals* were still the basic routine at the end of the century. Although some wrestlers had begun to show an interest in barbells, few *akharas* could afford the luxuries of modern gym equipment.

In consequence, Gama's body, like the bodies of all serious South Asian wrestlers, looked different from your average bodybuilder of the West at the time, and indeed in South Asia in the twenty-first century. He had a vast chest. His arms and thighs were like tree trunks, but these were not as sculpted as those of the fitness freaks of today.

Legends circulated about his weight (about 230 pounds) and chest dimensions. Gama's ability to expand his chest from its resting state of about fifty inches to fifty-eight inches with a sharp intake of breath, was one of the tactics for which he was renowned. A man of average height (five foot seven inches), Gama used this manoeuvre to floor much taller opponents in a trice, throwing them flat on their backs after squaring up to them.[78]

He is known as the wrestler who never lost. This too is part of Gama lore.

Another is the famous Gama stone. This was a huge piece of rock, weighing nearly 3,000 pounds. (The precision is part of the legend's faux authenticity; we know from the Baroda Museum that it is two foot six inches high, so let's just accept it is a crushing weight.) Inscribed with the legend that Gama lifted it in 1902, the stone turned up in Nazarbaug Palace in Mandvi. In 2010, when it was rehoused in the Baroda Museum, it took twenty men to lift it.[79] (These men were not wrestlers; most likely they were malnourished manual labourers. But it still says something about Gama: in 1902, he was an orphan in his teens, a shadow of his later self.)

So how did he do it? Much is made of his eating habits, which were unusual, even among the fraternity of top wrestlers. He seems to have drunk a gallon of milk, and a pound of crushed almonds mixed in fruit juice every day. When he grew up (depending on whom one believes) he drank the broth of a whole chicken, or of several whole chickens. Those who have read Chapter 6 will note the eccentricity of this diet. Whatever this did to his health – he died aged eighty-two of a heart condition – it 'gave him the strength of an ox and the quickness of a cat'.[80]

Gama fascinates me because of the way his life story intersects with the wider theme of this chapter, and indeed this book.

Indian wrestling in general, and Gama in particular, was drawn into the 'isms' of the times. Motilal Nehru started the practice of taking Indian wrestlers abroad and pitting them against European ones, to show off 'made in India' skills.[81] For people like Motilal, wrestlers became icons of nationalism, and again Gama was a giant among them. In 1910, when he had seen off every man pitted against him at the grand tournament in London, nationalist India was overjoyed.

British observers, meanwhile, were damning about the Gama vs Zbyszko match. Part of its bitty quality was a result of the fact that Gama (as he later told Muzumdar) didn't understand a word the referees were saying to him. Each time they spoke he thought that he was breaking the rules of the catch-as-catch-can format. He was not. But his tendency to hold back reined him in and ruined the fun.

So loud was British opprobrium that the British organiser of the event, R. B. Benjamin, questioned the newspapers' attitudes towards the Indian champions. He reminded them that these men were British subjects, in whose achievements Britons should take pride. Why, he asked, were they cheering on men from any and every part of the world that was *not* under the British flag against the Indians? The search among the Lords of Human Kind for a 'great white hope' had begun, then, half a century before the boxer Muhammad Ali became a household name.

These very public defeats of white men at tournaments in the heart of London by a bunch of Punjabi youths shook imperial confidence and wounded racial pride. Zbyszko, who had a point to prove, met Gama in Patiala on the condition that the Maharaja of Patiala paid his return fare and prize money, whether he won or lost (readers, he lost). But apart from him, few stepped forward to take Gama on.

Finally, partition. It turned his life upside down in his last decades. Perhaps that helps explain why he is now such a stranger in his own land.

Gama was born in Amritsar, now India, but trained in Lahore, which went to Pakistan. He was on the payroll of the Maharaja of Patiala (after 1947 in the independent nation state of India). Although he fought in many Indian princely states, his life was lived in undivided Punjab. In 1947 each of his crucial moorings became flashpoints, sites of some of the worst violence of India's partition.

We know little about Gama's partition story, except that he had one. Here is what I have gleaned from odd sources. Patiala, like all princely states, lost much of its power of patronage in 1947, and so Gama and his *akhara* were cut adrift. He tried to start up a bus travel business, without much success. Unaccustomed to failure, and out of tune with the world in which he found himself, he moved the forty miles across the Wagah border to Lahore, where he had grown up, now in Pakistan. Eventually, when the Pakistan government's rehabilitation drive got underway, he was given a piece of land. The Pakistani state also undertook to shoulder all his medical bills. (He was already a sick man by this time.) Of all people, the Indian industrialist G. D. Birla – said to have been a fan of the Great Gama – sent him a retainer of Rs 2,000 a month from across the border. (It boggles the mind to think that Birla supported both Gandhi, that apostle of non-violence, *and* Gama the Great, but no man or woman is easy to categorise, and Birla was a subtle man.)

Gama died in 1960. But his life was a South Asian life and remained one – despite partition – until his death.

With partition, Punjab's dominance as the heartland of wrestling declined, although the Punjabi Dara Singh (1928–2012) was so famous that his name reached even my childish ears. In 1953, long before I was born, his defeat of Japan's King Kong was celebrated with the heady nationalism of those times.[82] But by the time I was able to sign up as a Dara fangirl aged six or so, in 1970, his fame seemed to be restricted to the servants' quarters, where I loved hanging out.

But with the mass migration and dispersal of Hindu Punjabis in North India, the wrestling culture spread to parts it had not reached before. It is only after this point that it became more obviously Hindu, and more firmly associated with the worship of the monkey god of the *Ramayana*.

Low-key *akharas* after 1947 retained some of the features of old, but lost others: this was apparent by the time of studies made in the 1980s. All they needed was a piece of land near a shade-giving tree and some water, and a small shack to store whatever equipment they could afford. The pit remained the product of the greatest love and care. Wrestling, having lost its patrons, now had to be fitted around the demands of a working life. It remained more than a sport – the total submission to the gurus, who guided their flock, albeit with a light touch – and the commitment to a taxing regimen bordered on the insane. But given the loss of patronage of princes, it was not, nor could it be, a life-world.

This meant wrestlers had to work for a living. To practise, they woke before dawn (ideally at 3 a.m.), made their ablutions before entering the *akhara* at daybreak, trained for a few hours in the cool early mornings, and exercised again in the evenings after work, although much time at the fag end of the day was given over to relaxing with each other under the tree, and enjoying the evening breeze on sweaty bodies. Eating a diet heavy in ghee, with its Hindu connotations, was thought to be vital in producing the ideal body.

So too was massage. Each Sunday (after the holiday came out of nowhere – to use the idiomatic phrase – after independence) was given over to massaging each other with oil.[83] An easy intimacy with each other's bodies sat alongside complex views about sex. Some of the most famous wrestlers remained celibate all their lives, believing that careful harvesting of their semen prevented their strength flowing out of them.[84] (But by no means all wrestlers were celibate. Venkappa Burud had two wives and seven children and did 'not think that his much-married state interfered with his wrestling'.)[85]

Wrestling was more than a job, then. For some, its intense notions of discipleship, fraternity and discipline provided an all-consuming mania. For others, like Muzumdar – author, referee and wrestling freak – it was a wild and unstoppable passion. For yet others it is a hobby, albeit one they follow with the greatest seriousness. (Nabokov's butterflies come to mind – his obsession rendering his hobby more serious than most other things in a life of rare productivity.)

But what of the less-than-Gamas? There were vast numbers of wannabes with talent, and with the ambition to be supported by princely patrons. Even before partition, the also-ran wrestlers had put on other feats of daring to please wider audiences – and here their sport blurred lines with the skills of the Baazigars and stars of the big top. Stopping moving cars by running full tilt at them was very popular. Cars were a novelty, and stopping them was high drama. Having an elephant walk over a thin wooden bridge resting on the chest was a challenge that brave men, and even woman, took on. ('Indian' elephants weigh from 2,000 to 5,000 pounds.) Syamakanta Banerji even put his head between the jaws of a Royal Bengal tiger. That was a crowd-pleaser. Parts of what wrestlers did verged on, or were part of, circus acts. The mighty Tarabai (of whom Muzumdar writes: 'a lovelier woman I have never seen') ran her own circus. So after independence, the circus became one employer for down-at-heel wrestlers looking for a job.

But perhaps most importantly, the film industry emerged as another patron. It began to employ the best-connected 'dangerous men' – whether wrestlers or Baazigars – as stunt artists. The best (or most photogenetic) even made it as heroes. Dara Singh had a long run in Bombay cinema. I will not claim that his *Faulad* ('The Iron Man', 1963) is a good film, but the many fight sequences in it last a good ten minutes each, as long as Gama's longest and most ferocious bouts. More than an hour of time-out-of-time for the punters. Well worth a ticket in the stalls, many thousands thought. Why wouldn't they? Action films sustained Bombay cinema in the lean years in the 1960s. It even made its way onto the small screen: Dara Singh managed, late in his life, to bag the role of Hanuman in the TV version of the *Ramayana*. That was a good gig for him, and introduced wrestling (in an attenuated form) to a new generation. But he was only one among millions who made it. The rest remained far from the limelight, chasing their butterflies in the humble *akharas* that dotted the subcontinent.

But interestingly, the Indian state did not step in to back the sport where the princes had left off. By contrast, it did so for dance and music. Both India and Pakistan built museums, invested in art and 'artistes' (a new and ugly word of this era), albeit of the classical variety. This says much about what those in power thought it was important to rescue and propagate. In a strange irony, given its victories for the nation, *kushti* was not on that list. It was not deemed to be part of a national heritage that mattered, either to India or to Pakistan. Perhaps it was too inextricably linked to mixed geographies and communities, to social groups of no particular cultural merit, in elite eyes. (Not a silly mid-off among them, nor a true spin bowler.) Perhaps this made wrestling an embarrassment for both sides, indeed the makers of independent South Asia. Yet it lived on, albeit in changed forms.

III

SOUTH ASIAN MUSIC, DANCE AND SONG

Dance, music and song have always been central to leisure everywhere, and South Asia is no exception. The variation in genres across the subcontinent was vast in 1900 and was going through new modes of 'fusion' as the century drew to a close. In this respect too, South Asia is much like its neighbourhood and the rest of the world. But what makes it remarkable is not only its huge appetite for dance and song, but also the continued relevance at the end of the twentieth century of genres that were à la mode at its start.

In the early years there were, and continued to be, a large number of region-specific dance repertoires and musical forms, ever responsive to subtle changes in patronage. By the late twentieth century, however, this fluid mix of genres had been 'nationalised' and 'rationalised' by the independent nation states, national institutions, art and dance historians and social reformers into three distinct types of dance. These are now called 'folk', 'classical' and '*filmi*'.

Forms that were understood as 'tribal' in the early part of the century began to be categorised, after independence, as 'folk dance'. Folk dance had a special place in the new India and Pakistan, where the term 'the folk' was understood to mean 'the people' – rustic and crude perhaps, but *authentic*.

Meanwhile, out of older dance forms associated with temple worship (the Devadasi tradition) emerged the 'modern classical' form of Bharatanatyam.[86] Courtesan dance and *nautch* – a form of female performance with tones of sexual titillation, of which Indian nobles and elites and East India Company men were fond – were at the same time transformed into 'classical Kathak', by being reformed and formalised into a dance tradition 'as old as the newly discovered *Natyashastras*', and practised and 'held' by lineages or households (*gharaanas*) of male gurus (often Brahmin) and their disciples.

Meanwhile, in the *filmi* world of Bombay cinema, all tropes and genres of dance were up for grabs, producing a style that, on the face of it, lacks rigour, but draws heavily on existing classicised and folk genres in a plot-dependent way. But despite the light easy-breeziness suggestive in the word *filmi*, several Bollywood superstars are dancers trained in the new classical traditions: thus Waheeda Rehman (b. 1938) and Hema Malini (b. 1948) trained in Bharatanatyam; and Madhuri Dixit (b. 1967), trained in classical Kathak, is one of the greatest living exponents of *filmi* dancing. Bollywood has been eclectic in its choices of dance and music, but both classical Kathak and Bhratanatyam, and not-so-classical forms like *mujraa* (a raunchier, more sensual version of Kathak) and *bhangra* (a Punjabi 'folk', energetic dance) were on the menu. In the first seventy-five years of Bombay cinema, women actors and Kathak dominated *filmi* dance. By the end of the century, male actors had adopted elements of the *bhangra* style – indeed, some male stars became great dancers in their own right.

But the Kathak form simply would not lie down, even as the century drew to a close, perhaps because it lends itself so well to romance, erotic voyeurism and desire. Such is the importance of these song-and-dance routines to Bombay cinema that between thirty-five and fifty per cent of the average movie budget is spent on them. The *filmi*, then, is serious business. It is also work.

But to get back to the tripartite division of dance, which is the lens through which we are now encouraged to view the genre. There are heaps of scholarly tomes on it. But for the 'tribal' I'll go straight to Verrier Elwin, that intrepid missionary-turned-activist we have come to know in previous chapters, who wrote some of the most vivid accounts of dance in the 1930s and 40s: dance forms that would be later classified as 'folk'.

He writes: 'The Baiga dance whenever the season or their loves invite: give them a bright moon and a little liquor, and their feet begin to move unbidden, and their hands stray towards the drums.'[87]

They took their art 'seriously', Elwin observes.

> Men put on ornaments, tie big round turbans and stick tufts of pea-cocks' feathers in them. Girls put on every ornament they have, they often tie pretty red and orange shawls across their bodies, they bind their hair in loose pigtails with strings of mauve wool and little rings of *biran*-bark.[88]

Lovely. So lovely, in his eyes, that he married a thirteen-year-old Gond girl called Kosi in 1940. (Their first child was called Jawahar.)

Elwin writes that girl dancers also decorated their heads with pea-cock feathers. To accompany their dance, which was very rhythmic, they used wooden clappers called *tiski*, and three kinds of drums.

'The Baiga do not seem to attribute any magical efficacy to dan-cing.' For them it was 'simply a recreation, almost the only recreation, where friends and lovers meet, and the heart is warmed'.[89]

In Elwin's view, Karma was the main form of Baiga dance (and indeed all tribal dance), while others were variations on this theme. Karma had one key attribute: boys and girls danced and sang, but apart, on either side of an assembled group of drummers. At the start, the boys and men would huddle together and sing a verse of a song. The women and girls, holding hands, would repeat that verse until they got it right. Then one of two things could happen. In the first instance, girls would line up in a row, sway and sing softly, then bend down and begin to dance. The drummers would yell and advance towards the women, who would recede in steps, only to advance again. At other times, girls would move around the drummers in one direction, boys in the other, moving around the drummers in circles. 'They dance with great vigour and bang the *tiski* clappers as loudly as they can.'[90]

It was only in one variation of the dance, Dasseriliwar, that men and women actually held each other by the waist or shoulders, dan-cing slowly in a long circle.[91]

That the songs and dances of tribal peoples made a huge impres-sion on Elwin is evident from his autobiography, *The Tribal World of Verrier Elwin*.

On the poetry of the Gonds, another group of tribal peoples, he is at his most eloquent:

Gond poetry is simple and symbolic, free of all literary conventions and allusions. It is a poetry of earth and sky, of forest, hill and river, of the changing seasons and the varied passions of men, naked and unashamed, unadorned by any inhibition or restraint.

The most poetic were lyrics of the songs danced in the Gond variation of Karma dance, which was common to many tribes of Central India.[92] To give you a sense of Baiga poetry, let me cite my favourites:

When she puts oil on her hair and makes the parting, I feel very happy, friend.
How (lovely are) the breasts of my beloved. I feel very happy, friend.

Also:

Just in the mid-day you went out for water.
Like a thin bamboo sways your waist.[93]

The emphasis on romantic love and desire in 'tribal' song lyrics was frank. Karma song and dance performance had just a hint of the game *Antaakshari* (the game of the last letter) about it. It *was* a game, like charades, girls versus boys, in song and dance. Girls displayed a combination of boldness and shyness at different moments of the dance. Mood, which the classicists would define as *abhinaya*, was there in the drum beat and in the ebb and flow of song, and the tempo of the dance. There were no lead dancers, it appears, though some might have been better performers than others.

There was no single folk dance out there, you see. One or other would have to be made to represent all.

Of the more stylised genres now understood to form India's great classical dance traditions, I focus here on the form known as Kathak. I do so in part because its influence spreads across the north of the subcontinent, encompassing India, Pakistan and Bangladesh, and even to the south, Bangalore being an important centre. Its uncertain pedigree – by all accounts a product of the encounter between the Islamicate and Afghan traditions of the Mughal courts and the forms they encountered in the subcontinent – makes it relevant to the wider themes of this book. Kathak is neither this nor that, neither Muslim nor Hindu, neither elite nor degraded, neither 'upper caste' nor 'lower caste', neither male nor female. It is all of these things at once.

In the greater Bengal region, Kathak dancers had once been part of a popular cult of Vaishnavism, since the form lends itself to the depiction of *Raas Lila* (the erotic love play between Radha and Krishna) and popular regional practices of religious devotion. In this guise they had attracted female audiences from grand houses as well as poorer and 'lower-caste' homes. Visual and textual sources of East India Company rule speak of women, accompanied by male musicians, who danced with exquisite skill for wealthy patrons – English nabobs and writers, Indian kings, sultans, nawabs and gentlemen courtiers, from the seventeenth century onwards. Strange though it may seem, British men adored Kathak, for which they invented the term *nautch*.[94] The presumption grew that although it was stunning, it was a little too sexy to be proper. 'Nautch girls', many East India Company men thought, belonged to 'a caste of hereditary prostitutes' trained to sing and dance. This judgement (which was misguided) did not prevent them from being voracious voyeurs of the dance form, and female dance in particular.

My hunch is that it was in this context, with Indian princes outdoing each other to entertain British guests, that women dancers came to be seen as Kathak's main exponents. Patronised by Company-wallahs and their Indian friends, the dance became ever more the object of the European salacious gaze, and this, as much as its inherent sensuousness, led to the social reformers' attempts to ban it.

However, several different forces came together to push these dancers into the shadows. With the fall of many Indian states to East India Company rule in the mid-nineteenth century, Kathak lost many patrons. The greatest of these had been the Nawab of Oudh who, from his palace at Lucknow, had supported artists, singers, dancers and musicians. There's a marvellous scene in Satyajit Ray's film *Shatranj ke Khilari* ('The Chess Players', 1977) of Wajid Ali Shah, the last Nawab, watching a Kathak performance with some courtiers.

When Oudh fell in 1856, the Nawab migrated to Calcutta, but the Bindadin *gharaana* (household of Kathak performers) of Lucknow left for the princely state of Rampur. Birju Maharaj (1938–2022), a descendant of Bindadin, was, even in his lifetime, a legend. Recognised as one of Kathak's greatest exponents, he learned his art in Rampur.[95]

By the late nineteenth century, social reformers (influenced, many argue, by Victorian puritanical values) began to insist that *all* dancing was a pernicious moral influence.[96] Keshub Chandra Sen, a leading light of the reformist Brahmo Samaj, thundered in outrage:

Hideous woman ... hell is in her eyes. In her breast is a vast ocean of poison. Round her comely waist dwell the furies of hell. Her hands are brandishing unseen daggers ever ready to strike the unwary or wilful victims that fall in her way. Her blandishments are India's ruin. Alas; her smile is India's death.[97]

However, Edward Hall's discovery of the *Natyashastra*, a Sanskrit text which appeared to lay down the foundations of the dance in the hoary (Hindu) past, and its full publication in 1890, began slowly to shift attitudes among a handful of people. Let's call them the cultural literati of the time. Soon the *Natyashastra* began to enter the lexicon of the commentariat.

After this, *nautch* fell by the wayside. But women dancers had, all along, continued to dance and sing, accompanied by male musicians. The most talented became wealthy in their own right, having attracted the patronage of rich men. They passed this wealth down to their children. They also kept alive the art, and the musical forms associated with it, albeit at the margins.[98]

These developments and attitudes came together to bring about a revival of 'pure classical dance' in the 1920s and 30s, during which self-taught cultural historians, influenced by nationalism and the *Natyashastra*, began to invent classical dance traditions.

Rukmini Devi Arundale (1904–86) was one such impresario. A striking, bright and impetuous Brahmin ingénue, she was drawn as a teenager to the Theosophy society: her father, a Sanskrit scholar, was also a theosophist. To the horror of conservative elite Madras society, in 1920 when she was just sixteen, she married George Arundale, a theosophist many years her senior. Despite the fact that Annie Besant took young Rukmini under her wing, 'the storm broke fiercer than anyone had expected' and the couple fled to Bombay to register their marriage.[99] For more than a decade afterwards, she lived the cosmopolitan life of a theosophist 'mother' and world traveller. Indeed, she derived her first thoughts on ballet from Anna Pavlova.

Rukmini Devi returned to India in 1933. In the next decades she revived, or rather invented, Bharatanatyam. In so doing she broke its links with the sensuality and sexuality of Sadir, the genre associated with Devadasi 'temple dancers' and 'prostitutes'.[100]

Much thought, reading and research on ancient stone sculptures and iconography went into the creation of her new 'spiritual' dance:

she was a woman of high intelligence. She faced the challenge of bringing the dance to elite Indian Madras; remember, this was the very city that had once thrown her out. Her debut was performed on a stage built to look like a temple. She used an idol of Shiva dancing his 'cosmic dance' as a stage prop. Men (rather like Ramayanis) chanted Sanskrit verses before she appeared on stage. All of this gave the form of a (dubious) link with antiquity via the *Natyashastra* (which Rukmini herself had never read). She danced without any trace of eroticism, replacing the sensual curving movements of Sadir (and, indeed, of sculpture) with triangular and square shapes. The result was impressive. It was stark, beautiful, but in no way seductive.

By god, though, it had an impact on the respectable 'upper-caste' audience she was hoping to persuade. An eyewitness of her inaugural performance writes:

> Nearly a thousand people were seated under the great rain tree, through whose giant branches glimpses could be caught of the stars in an almost purple sky. The stage was at first in semi-darkness: *on one side the ensemble of musicians, including her guru, were seated on rugs; on the other a group of young men appeared chanting in unison a most impressive dedication of the dance recital . . . to Nataraja, that aspect of Divine life.* The music grew stronger, and the lights came on and against the green curtain of the background, Rukmini appeared in her archaic white and gold dress, looking like some *temple carving*, full of arrested movement.[101]

How could she not take their breath away? How could they not fall in love with a woman so brilliant, so brave, and so beautiful? However misguided she was, she was a force of nature whom historians of the twentieth century ignore at their peril. (Like many, I believe she was not only misguided, but too arrogant to admit it.)[102]

A formidable practitioner and teacher of her own 'invented' art, in 1936, Rukmini Devi set up Kalakshetra (the School of Arts) in Madras to teach her 'revived' Bharatanatyam to middle-class students, almost all of whom were women. She made dance respectable, you see, for this demographic. At the turn of the century, elite and middle-class 'high-caste' women would have braved a lion rather than surrender their prudery to the evils which dance was then seen to represent.

When it lost its base after yet another schism in the World

Theosophy Movement in 1950, Rukmini, who was as well networked as she was persuasive, acquired new premises of about a hundred acres to build a new Kalakshetra. It continues to this date to attract new generations of students and audiences hankering after a pre-colonial authenticity in which they might root their post-colonial identity. 'Cultured' visitors to Madras always take in a performance if they can. Some even build itineraries round them.

Meanwhile, high-minded dance historians were giving Kathak a new (ancient and Hindu) history. Kapila Vatsyayan (1928–2020) played a major part in this process. Born in Delhi, Vatsyayan grew into a thin, bird-like, scholarly woman. High-achieving herself – with a master's degree from Michigan University at Ann Arbor and a PhD from the Benares Hindu University – she could be condescending with others less gifted or learned. Maulana Azad had to advise her to be more courteous to civil servants.[103] Nor was she much constrained by convention – she married the Hindi poet Agneya and divorced him a few years later with little fuss. A force of nature, she wrote sixteen books on the history of dance and advised (or hectored) every Congress government on what it had to do to preserve India's classical traditions.

Arundale, Vatsyayan and Pupul Jayakar were the great women promoters of the new 'high culture' of independent India. This involved developing discernment: whether of exquisite saris from every region, of folk objects, of India's regional arts and crafts; as well as understanding, and perhaps mastering, classical dance, song and music – again, of every region and type. (Very few could gain a PhD in Discernment. I knew a few who did, who were kind without condescension.) Since the classical was itself being fashioned, one had to keep running to keep up. Their legacy endured until the end of the twentieth century. They established themselves as fierce 'guardians of the flame' which they assiduously fanned, and everyone, Nehru included, had to take note.

Nehru heeded the call of the culture vultures (as they came to be known) and the Indian state threw some energy behind their programme. After all, Nehru knew all the players well; they were part of a very small world on first-name terms with each other. (Kamaladevi Chattopadhyay (1903–88), a freedom fighter and social reformer, was Sarojini Naidu's sister; Nehru was close to Sarojini's daughter. And so on.)

Satyajit Ray's *Jalsaghar* ('The Music Room', 1958) depicts one *zamindaar*'s mania for the unsanitised forms of these arts. It's no surprise, then, to find that whereas once temple priests, princely courts and *zamindaari* elites had been the key patrons of these arts, when government stepped in to take over that role, it was in a clunky, heavy-footed way.

From the mid-1950s onwards, the central government established a host of institutions in the centre of New Delhi – the Sangeet Natak Akademi (National Academy of Music, Dance and Drama, 1953) and the Bharatiya Kala Kendra (Centre for Performing Arts), renamed the Kathak Kendra in 1952. Ministers invited the best exponents of the cleansed, high, pure, classical (and, by definition, Hindu, even Brahmin) form of this genre, to lead the Kathak Kendra. In the early twentieth century, Kathak had been reviled as the dance of the *nautch* girl and courtesan, who danced for a small, debauched, aristocratic circle of patrons. Government took it out of the naughty box. It reinvented Kathak as a classical art form with the most distinguished pedigree.

In the eighteenth and nineteenth centuries, princely courts also patronised singers and accompanying musicians. The Mughal court is said to have promoted *dhrupad* and *khayaal*, genres of music, and a cultural world in which the *ghazal* (a form of Urdu poetry) flourished. As the empire began to collapse, and when Delhi was sacked, singers, musicians and poets fled, heading for successor states. This was the context in which Lucknow emerged as a major new benefactor and patron of the arts, producing a fresh efflorescence of cultural riches. (It is said that Wajid Ali Shah, its last nawab, learned to dance Kathak himself. We'll never know whether it is true, but he did love and support it.) When he was deposed, he took all his artistic and other clients to his new settlement at Metiabruz in South Calcutta, which then became a legatee of Lucknow's artistic heritage. Other surviving centres of music and dance were in the princely states of Rajputana, Benares, Gwalior and Bhopal.

Perhaps aware of this history, the new nation state crowned the leaders of the Lucknow Bindadin *gharaana* – Shambhu Maharaj, Achhan Maharaj and his son, Birju Maharaj – as the torch bearers of a now-classical tradition, as gurus and indeed gatekeepers to the world of classical Kathak.

Don't get me wrong here. Birju Maharaj was a stunning exponent of the Lucknow *gharaana* form. A dancer since childhood, he was a hereditary performer who grew up with the dance, its unique musical accompaniment and powerful rhythms.[104] He conducted the musicians who accompanied him, choreographed his own performances, played *tablaa* and *dholak* (different types of drum), and often sang in accompaniment. He had a beautiful voice, but let his feet and body do most of the talking. He dressed simply, often in a plain turmeric-yellow or tussar silk *angrakhaa* (a flared long top), belted at the waist by a long sash. His *churidaar pyjama* were held tight at the ankles by *ghungroos* – the large anklets that Kathak dancers wear to accentuate the dramatic play of their feet. He was extraordinary. Magical.

Despite the efforts of the central government, nationalists, dance historians and other high-minded reformers to strip it of its 'debauched' associations with courtesan and 'low' culture, Kathak has confounded these pressures. Kathak's hybridity and malleability live on; its para-doxical flourishing make its history the more exciting for that reason. Kathak lives on as *mujraa*, a hyper-sexual version of the dance (do search online for references to live and cinematic representations). Birju Maharaj played a woman and a man in a single dance sequence. He visualised one of the most famous *filmi* dance sequences of the century: 'Dola re Dola' in *Devdas* (2002). He seemed just as at ease outside the world of 'high culture' as he was in it.

Millions enjoy Kathak 'high art' without knowing it. Hindi cinema has seen to that. Many readers will have seen Kathak even if they don't know they have, and have never been to a Kathak performance in a formal auditorium setting, or have never even heard the word 'Kathak'. It's there in Hindustani cinema in abundance. For a taster, watch *Pakeezah*, *Umrao Jaan* (1981) or *Devdas*, or indeed *Sahib, Bibi aur Ghulam* (1962), which has three Kathak dance sequences. It's there even in short-film ads. One only has to look at the Bollywood star Juhi Chawla dancing in the commercial for Lehar Pepsi of all things, to see how vibrant the form remained in the 1990s, and how dramatic and immediate its impact.[105] (The advertisement is far more erotic than I realised, I have to admit. I was too busy, focusing my limited energy on work, housework and parenting – and trying to pre-vent the sweet brown liquid from entering my little boy's innocent mouth – to pay attention to the ad itself, despite being the daughter of an 'ad man'. In hindsight, not one of my brightest moments. My son watched the short film on TV at least a hundred times. Happily he still has teeth.)

The striking thing about Kathak, as it is now understood and taught, is the distinctiveness between the moves performed by the upper and lower halves of the body. The dancers' arm and head movements are characterised by grace and feminine sensuousness, even when the dancer is a man; their arm and eye movements display a range of emotions and moods (*bhaav*, *abhinaya*). By contrast, their legs and feet have a different energy: often clean, crisp and bold, sometimes displaying languid steps forward (*chaal*), now dazzling with fireworks of footwork (*gat*) accentuated by the sound of the heavy anklets. Dizzying pirouettes (*chakkars*), which seem to unite the whole body, are a fourth element of an exquisite mix. The rhythm of the dance alters so that each segment foregrounds one or other of these elements of *bhaav*, *chaal*, *gat* and *chakkar*. Mastering the elements demands years, indeed a lifetime, of training. You will recognise this if you watch any classical Kathak sequence as performed on YouTube or in a film. I urge you to watch Birju Maharaj perform: many of his sequences are available on the internet.

Kathak is a treat. Dare I say it, it is more exciting than ballet. Men and women both wear the *churidaar pyjama* (jodhpurs), and the heavy anklets. Women used to wear what has come to be known as the Anarkali top – a tight bodice, a flared silken skirt (named after the heroine in the early Hindi film *Anarkali*). Another glorious iteration is Muzaffar Ali's *Umrao Jaan*. The courtesan Umrao's rich silk and brocade clothes, her bejewelled headdress and her gauze veil, in addition to the actor Rekha's beauty, might make the viewer's head reel, the accompanying music and songs awakening their every sense: it is thrilling, exciting and intoxicating all at once.

The outfit looked something like the dancers in Mughal miniatures, and in certain contexts – particularly in films – women performers sought to achieve twentieth-century approximations of the same aesthetic. The colour palates are sumptuous, their hands and arms are dressed in jewellery. Sometimes dancers play coquette with a gauze-thin veil; others mime these gestures.

Men have been, and remain, Kathak's great teachers, although that began to change mid-century. By 2000, women outnumbered men as students and performers of Kathak, but the status of the male heads of the *gharaanas* continued to reign supreme. Women dancers by then outnumbered their male counterparts but learned the same rules.[106]

The word *gharaana* (household, lineage of teachers and kin-students) has an uncertain history but has acquired glamour and mystique.[107] Perhaps the new rulers of independent India were daunted by the term. Nehru – educated at Harrow and Trinity College, Cambridge – wouldn't have known a *gharaana* from a *tablaa* (drum), or indeed from a *saarangi* (a stringed instrument), when Kapila Vatsyayan insisted that he patronise them. The Lucknow *gharaana* above all was to be the state's 'recognised' version of the high art of Kathak. It was 'classical Indian art' that it could use as soft power at festivals overseas. And so Birju Maharaj began to train students from all over India, in his role as head of the Lucknow *gharaana*.

Very soon, I think it is fair to say, a system of gatekeeping had come into place. The government of India set up a central institute of dance at which the greatest dancers of the three *gharaanas* of Lucknow, Jaipur and Benares gave disciples 'proper training'. More of this below.

But a short biographical documentary on Birju Maharaj casts *gharaanas* in a different, more human, light. The star of this black-and-white documentary was the legendary dancer. He speaks softly, seated on a *takht* (a seat that doubles as a bed) in a small, sparsely furnished room, surrounded by children of the household. His story is remarkable. Yet sunbeams from a window fall on a small child, a three-year-old boy, perhaps, who begins to touch, and then to play the *tablaa* near him, with tiny fingers. His drumming becomes more insistent. In another shot, the child is standing, dancing. As his cousins, brothers and sisters shout the beat for him, '*ta thai thai tak, aa thai thai tak; ta dhin, ta dhin, ta dhin dhin taa!*', their animation urges the little dancer on. Soon he is performing Kathak – all but the *bhaav*, or emotional element, of the dance. He is too young to understand these emotions, of course.[108]

So a *gharaana* is simply this: a large household whose hereditary occupation is dancing and music. Little children grow up learning '*ta dhin dhin ta*' before they learn A, B and C, *ka, kha ga*, or *alif be pe te*.

So there was no way, really, that the government could take up the patronage of the art where the princely states had left off. (Birju Maharaj, as mentioned, grew up in Rampur, under the patronage of Nawab Raza Ali Khan (1908–66), before being summoned to Delhi.) You see, the princes may well have been feudal – a view that has begun to be challenged – but they understood and appreciated the arts. The tenets of good kingship required them so to do, and to patronise great artists.[109] In the documentary, Birju Maharaj made it clear that the Nawab of Rampur's patronage had helped his *gharaana* to survive, and had provided him with all he needed to grow into the dancer that he became.

A shuttered concrete building, a hushed auditorium and an audience of not-so-discerning westernised elites could not, and cannot, take the place of the salon of the Nawab of Rampur; it couldn't provide an audience who knew or understood the form. In videos of his performances, therefore, Birju Maharaj took to teaching his elite (western-educated) audiences about his art – he spoke and explained as he performed. He was a great teacher, capable of displaying the genre's beauty, and explaining how it works: its combination of sinuous minimalism and controlled but astonishing energy.

But the dance form (even in its classicised form) has spilled out of the Delhi Akademi as hundreds of private schools started to teach Kathak across the land. Most pupils in the late century were young women. (Even I learned it for a few years, in the mid-1970s. I had little talent, but can attest that the genre is demanding in the extreme.) The most gifted dancers among them are now household names, like Maya Rao (1928–2014). Of a Saraswat Brahmin family, Rao trained first with a local (male) guru, before mastering elements of Jaipur *gharaana* style under Guru Sohal Dal, and of Lucknow style from Shambhu Maharaj, Birju Maharaj's uncle. She went on to form her own training school, the Natya Institute of Kathak and Choreography, in Bangalore.

Or take Kumudini Lakhia (b. 1930), another dancer of extraordinary talent. Like Maya Rao, she trained first at a local school, then under teachers from Jaipur *gharaanas*, and finally under Shambhu Maharaj, then the torch bearer of the Lucknow tradition. In 1967, she established the Kadamb Centre for Dance in Ahmedabad. It's almost as if this generation of female classical dancers had to go via this circuitous route before they could be pronounced 'great'. It is ironic, given that women had been great Kathak dancers for at least two centuries and had kept the form alive during its dark days when Indo-Victorians drove it out of polite society.

A further point is that the classical Kathak dancers simply would not be straitjacketed within the tight box of 'great tradition' into which government and dance historians sought to confine them. Kumudini Lakhia choreographed the film *Umroa Jaan*, set in a *kotha* (a courtesan's salon), from the short story about a renowned courtesan, Kathak dancer, poet and singer. Birju Maharaj sang himself in Satyajit Ray's film *Shatranj ke Khilari*, and helped visualise the famous dance sequences in *Devdas*. The 'classical' will cross borders – even, as we have seen, into the world of advertising.

IV

'BOLLYWOOD', AKA 'BOMBAY CINEMA'

Should I join the movies?

In 1939 an extraordinary event blew a hole through the hidden processes of film production in Bombay. A young actor, Shanta Apte, went on hunger strike against the studio that employed her. This strike involved Apte dressing herself in trousers and a shirt and lounging on a bench outside the studio's entrance. She lay there thumbing through magazines.

The 1930s was the start of the 'Talkies' era, with silent film in decline. In this milieu, Shanta Apte – who had a superb singing voice as well as a striking screen presence – was the kind of actor for whom studios competed. Apte's performance in the Marathi film *Kunku* (1937), released simultaneously in Hindi as *Duniya Na Mane* ('Whatever the World Says'), is a testament to her talent.

Once in its employ, however, the studio rarely used her. (Studios made relatively few films back then.) This was Apte's complaint – she was sick to death of waiting to be cast, waiting to perform, of training her voice and body for hours, turning up at the set every day all day, and hanging around waiting. She was enrolled as a 'star', although the word 'star' in Bombay then had different connotations from its counterpart in Hollywood: Indian stars were 'just' actors, employees with the potential to play lead roles.[110] As for Apte, she had grown sick of a kind of time that was the opposite of leisure – boredom that sapped confidence and broke the spirit.[111]

If Apte's hunger strike had been only about her own dispute with her studio, it might have remained a footnote in the history of leisure production. But she went further. Born in the Maratha region that had produced Dalit activists such as Jyotiba Phule and B. R. Ambedkar, this young Brahmin woman fired off an incendiary pamphlet, '*Janu Mi Cinemaanti?*' ('Should I Join the Movies?'), which insisted

that a seven-fold caste (or *varna*) system existed in the burgeoning
film industry:

1. Capitalists
2. Companies (managing directors)
3. Distributors
4. Exhibitors
5. Advertisers
6. Workers (directors, assistant directors, assistant technicians,
   cameramen, actors and actresses, music directors, other
   musicians, those involved in developing, printing, editing,
   recording, extras)
7. Public[112]

Two things fascinate me about Apte's ordering. The top five of her
filmi varnas include investors of different sorts in this novel form of
entertainment. Let me call them 'new patrons' of leisure. There's not a
mention here of a raja or maharaja, so prominent in other worlds of
leisure. Cinema's main investors in this early period, scholars insist,
were merchants, traders and rentiers with connections to the countryside.[113] They were people with capital, looking for projects in which
to invest, and the movies – a new and exciting product with tremendous potential – were worth a punt.[114] Cinema called for and created
a new kind of patron for a novel product, and then tried to create a
market for that product. These patrons could not double guess what
audiences might want, but could figure out what viewers already
understood as leisure, and give them stories and scenarios that worked
these various elements into their fabric. (As the film scholar Shohini
Ghosh puts it, Hindi cinema is 'a bit of everything'. Deciphering it,
therefore, is not straightforward.)[115]

Next is *varna* 6: workers. Note how Apte included everyone
involved in the making of the movie, from the director to the extras, as
workers, skilled or unskilled. Influenced as much by the *Communist
Manifesto* as various forms of anti-caste discourse (cinema would
soon be awash with writers influenced by the left-leaning Progressive
Writers' Association and People's Theatre Association), she sees them
all producing collectively, albeit in different ways, the goods in which
the capitalists invested, the advertisers promoted and the public
consumed.

This excited me because I think of complex forms of leisure as being produced by work that, by sleight of hand, is made invisible to the consumer. But it is fascinating to think that Apte, situated in a singular niche in India's hierarchical society, could see herself, a star, as being on a par with an extra. Also remarkable is her eagerness to rip back the curtain – like a plaster from an oozing wound – that hid this work from the audience, inviting them into the not-so-pretty world of Wonderland.

Cinema, then – good, mediocre or bad – was the product of enormous work, a collaboration between practitioners of different skills and forms of labour. To Apte's list of cinema workers we must add carpenters, set designers, set painters and hoarding painters (such as the feted artist M. F. Husain who earned his crust as a young man by painting posters, or B. B. Benegal, the Calcutta artist who nurtured the young Guru Dutt's talents).[116] We must also add tailor masters, costume designers, personal tailors to the stars, stunt artists, poets, storywriters, and continuity-script or scenario writers. (Sadat Hasan Manto, acknowledged as one of the subcontinent's finest authors, worked as a scenario writer for a while.) And also scriptwriters and lyricists (many of whom were North India's finest poets in their spare time), musicians and playback singers as well as sound engineers in dubbing studios. Continuity directors, tea boys, spot boys, the camera crew, light boys, assistant directors and hairstylists. What an ensemble. What a mélange of trained and honed human bodies, voices and hands and minds steeped in old and coeval genres of entertainment, with people with new cinematic imagination, with scientific and technical skills, that chiaroscuro of light and shade that changed the quality of darkness.

Imagine the stunning impact of that 'new darkness' on an audience used to rising at dawn and sleeping after dusk! Consider what it meant for people to hear for the first time music 'remembered', recorded and played back. This was cinema's unique lure. Despite its many difficulties, the enchantment has endured.

No wonder it was a heady world. No wonder so many wanted to join the movies. No wonder there were always extras available, the zero-contract workers of the early twentieth century. There were push factors that drove them to the studios (hunger and poverty, ambition) but there were also powerful pull factors – this potent brew of modern creativity, which attracted them like moths to a flame. Even I, a crusty professor, have known young people from 'cultured families' with the strongest yearning to join Bombay cinema. For years I watched as the talented daughter of a friend gave her everything for a 'break'. When would she get noticed? Would she ever get noticed? My own nephew spent years trying to establish himself. He is fit and handsome; he has the loveliest gentle brown eyes; he acts well; he performs in Calcutta cinema; he keeps prepared, and lives by modelling among other things. But, like Apte before him, he has waited a while, taking roles that have never quite matched his aspirations.

Why Bombay, one might ask? It was never inevitable that the 'Maximum City' would be its base, whatever film scholars say.[117] Mukherjee, in her otherwise excellent *Bombay Hustle*, argues that there was something exciting and dynamic about the city that made it the inevitable centre of the film industry.[118] The argument is, to a historian, teleological. By the time Bombay showed its first full-length silent film, *Raja Harishchandra* ('King Harishchandra', 1913), studios were up and running in most major cities of India. Throughout the twentieth century, Calcutta and Madras were large centres of the film industry, and Bengali, Tamil, Malayalam and Telegu cinema were still thriving in 2000.[119]

Nor was it inevitable that Hindustani, the language of Bombay cinema, would become the dominant language of the movies. Indeed, the subcontinent's most renowned director, Satyajit Ray, made all his films, with one notable exception (*Shatranj ke Khilari*), in Bangla. Nor has the flow of influence always been in one direction, from Bombay to these other centres. One of Bombay's greatest stars, Waheeda Rehman, first performed in the Telegu film *Rojulu Maraayi* ('The Days Have Changed', 1955). She points out that its hit song in which she danced (she trained in the new form of Bharatanatyam) was bowdlerised in the Hindi version of the Telegu original movie.[120]

But because it usually flowed that way, I focus on Bombay cinema here.

The migration of talent at every level to Bombay cinema from other regions was fuelled by cultural influences that are not easy to pigeonhole. Take the case of Guru Dutt (1925–64), producer, director and actor in the 1950s, a period many regard (with justification) as the high point of Bombay cinema. He produced, directed and acted in some of the era's greatest films. By birth a Saraswat Brahmin from western India, Guru Dutt grew up in Calcutta. He was often mistaken for a Bengali because of his (hard-to-define) Calcutta ways (marked even before he married the Bengali singer Geeta Roy in a Bengali caste Hindu ceremony). As a youngster he trained for a while at Uday Shankar's school for the creative arts at Almora, where he was a peer of Uday's brother, the sitar maestro Ravi Shankar. For their part, both Uday and Ravi Shankar grew up in present-day Rajasthan, where their father was in the employ of the Maharaja of Jhalawar, but their 'ancestral home', as we put it in these parts, is in present-day Bangladesh. (Uday Shankar was another sensation of the era, known for his avant garde choreography, his terrific talent as a dancer and his effort to revive old dramatic performance through modern dance fusion, rather than stilted classicism.)[121]

Given that some of Guru Dutt's best-known films are 'Muslim socials' (a genre depicting a Muslim urban aristocratic way of life), and given that Waheeda Rehman, Rahman and Johnny Walker (Badruddin Kazi, a former bus conductor), all Muslims, starred in some of his most famous films – *Pyaasa* ('Thirsty', 1957), *Chaudhvin ka Chand* ('The Full Moon', 1960) and *Kaagaz ke Phool* ('Paper Flowers', 1959) – and given his productive relationship with the scriptwriter Abrar Alvi, also a Muslim – it's clear that Bombay cinema was a cosmopolitan world, which drew gifted people of all sorts towards it.[122] Directors sought out talent wherever they could find it. It was a South Asian world of all the talents.

This brilliance was by no means born in Bombay, local to Bombay (or the British Bombay Presidency, post-independence Maharashtra after the former's division into two states), or even the Hindustani-speaking north of the subcontinent. It would be a gross misunderstanding to think of Bombay cinema as the film culture of 'Bombay-wallahs'. Bombay itself was being made by migration at the same time as its film industry. (See Chapter 4.)

A funny story illustrates this. A passionate movie buff from the Punjab, Raj Khosla, met Guru Dutt while the latter was directing a film. He wanted a job as a playback singer, but no such job was on offer. Guru Dutt, by all accounts a kindly man, asked Khosla whether he knew any Hindi. 'Yes,' he lied. He was hired, but he then had a problem: he knew some Urdu, like many Punjabis, but although Urdu has a similar vocabulary and grammar to Hindi, its script could hardly be more different. Keen Khosla went out and bought a Hindi reader the very next day. Of course he was caught out the minute he was asked to write something in Hindi. Far from sacking him, Guru Dutt found him something else to do and they became firm friends. The point here is that even Punjabi-speakers were flocking to what became known as 'Bombay cinema' (which was sometimes made outside Bombay).

Still, the city itself would become the hub of the great studios of the era where the first generations of Hindi movies were made. Studios like Bombay Talkies established themselves on the northern periphery of the city, in Andheri, where they had some access to its urban amenities but could just about avoid its accompanying cacophony. Bombay's wooded hinterland provided scenic backdrops to many a movie.

A caveat. There have been many points in the history of cinema in the subcontinent when Madras has produced a great many more movies than Bombay. In 1968, for instance, despite its smaller allocation of imported and expensive raw stock, it produced 227 films for Bombay's eighty-nine.[123] On his death, fans of the Tamil film star and politician 'MGR' Ramachandran (1917–87) grieved to the extent of burning themselves alive and slashing themselves with razor blades, while others looted and sacked Madras.[124] Scholars looking back fifty years down the line might ask whether he was the most popular film star of his time: history will have to judge this. To be fair to Amitabh Bachchan, the mass hysteria that followed his injury and near death from performing his own stunt while shooting *Coolie* (1983), when forty-five million fans are alleged to have prayed for his life, places him in the premier league. Let me just put it this way: the Big B (as Bachchan is known) is a strong contender for the top spot if we look at the subcontinent as a whole, and indeed the diaspora. A BBC News online poll rated him as the top star off stage or screen in the millennium, in the world.[125]

Here I will focus on Bombay cinema, though, because it has become the biggest-hitting industry in the world, and its Hindustani films are enjoyed by a huge fan base not only in the subcontinent but also worldwide. (My Pakistani friends Humeira and Kamal, whom readers have met in previous chapters, live diasporic lives between Cambridge and Lahore, and are far more knowledgeable about the Bombay movies than I am. One of the first questions Kamal asked me was 'Team Asha or Team Lata?' – a reference to the two sisters who were top playback singers, of whom more below. 'Team neither,' I replied. Kamal's knowledge of the Bombay song is encyclopaedic.)

In addition to Pakistan, Soviet Russia, Nigeria and practically the whole of the Middle East became a huge fan base, as well as the South Asian diaspora in Africa. (More recently, films have begun to be made with Euro-American and British cinema-goers in mind.) Since the 1970s, Bombay has become a locale rich with cinematic allusions – a 'cinematic city' onto and into which directors project scenarios.[126] This city, more than any other in India, has come to be known intimately as 'filmed space', even to those who have never been there.[127]

But I also chose it because it is so deplored. Because snobs despise it and cultural elites shun it. Because I myself was one such snob. Tejaswini Ganti recalls that while she was writing her PhD on the subject, she was invited to a party by neighbours in Bandra – a 'nice' Bombay neighbourhood – where one of her hosts' friends launched into a diatribe about the absurdity of Hindi cinema, exclaiming: 'What is there to study? All they do is run around trees. I mean how is it possible that so many bad films get made? I don't understand how people can stand to watch them, and what does it say about the mentality of the common Indian that he likes to watch them?'[128]

What follows is also my riposte to the party guest in Bandra. It will introduce the reader to a glorious cinematic rollercoaster; and, I hope, tempt a few to try it. To all those who damn Bombay cinema as overlong, boring, derivative, repetitive, filled with improbable fight sequences, coarse songs and dance routines, here is my answer.

What did Bombay not have (that Hollywood did)?

The answer can only begin to emerge if we drop the word 'Bollywood' to describe Bombay cinema, from the 1920s to the 90s. It pushes us to make misleading, wrong-headed comparisons with Hollywood. Bombay cinema could never play catch-up with Hollywood, nor would it try to, until the onset of neoliberalism in the 1990s. It would have flopped had it done so.

So it must be understood on its own terms. It is far too rooted in the entertainment and leisure worlds of South Asia to be seen as 'waiting to become like Hollywood'. It's a subject in which you can't assume progress. As I have already said, perhaps its best decade was the 1950s, or the 70s. Although it borrowed techniques of cinematography and the odd riff from Hollywood (the famous cowboy western opening music in *Sholay*, say, or tunes reminiscent of flamenco), and outfits from elsewhere (Italian peplums, for instance, were all the rage in the 1960s), and although the camera, sound and lighting technologies that go into making film have much in common the world over, they were not the same, nor could they be.

It seems bizarre to have to make the point that the film industry in South Asia faced quite different challenges, but I must.

For the pioneers of the industry, background noise, extreme rainfall and power cuts were a perennial problem. Power cuts were less frequent in favoured parts of the country by 2000, but many parts were not yet even 'on the grid'.[129] Despite considerable investment in sets to protect film work against inclement weather, much shooting is done on location, and clouds or thunderstorms prevent filming not only because they might damage equipment, but also because they challenge that precious thing, continuity. There's a well-known story about the making of *Sholay*. The film hinges on the scene when the good cop, played by Sanjeev Kumar, arrives home to find his whole family lying dead, slain by the dreaded dacoit Gabbar Singh. The sun is shining. When the crew return the next day to complete shooting, the sky has clouded over, and gusts of wind lift the white shrouds covering the bodies. Goodbye continuity! They must wait for a sunny day. They wait day after day, but the sunshine does not return. Eventually, in a film based on the principle of 'no compromise', they compromised. The same scene starts in bright sunshine and ends with the skies overcast. Look out for it.[130]

Finance was another major challenge. While Hollywood had few and large production companies managing every aspect of the business, the situation in Bombay could hardly have been more different. In South Asia, exhibitors – who owned the large movie halls and sold tickets to the audiences – called the shots. They made the largest profits however well or badly each film fared. Distributors, who bought the rights to have the film shown in particular provinces, were also big fish in the food chain. Bombay's producers and directors thus made movies in a context where they were weak players in a dispersed market.[131] The interests of each group were at odds with each other, as all could only make hay with mega hits, which covered everyone's investments and made a profit for them all. Only ten or so in every hundred films made were this kind of blockbuster.

In Hollywood, huge studios (like Metro-Goldwyn-Mayer, established in 1924) produced movies. They bought scripts or franchises and paid directors; they also held the distribution rights. They owned the whole process, therefore, and were thus far more secure. Profits from ticket sales fed back into the studio. By contrast, Bombay had no studio with that structure. South Asian producer-directors (many directors produced their own films – even the acclaimed Guru Dutt) went bankrupt if they took artistic risks. They invested in all the production costs, but only saw a small percentage of the profits from ticket sales, much of which went straight to distributors.

The balance of power between exhibitors, distributors and producers thus kept the directors and screenwriters (the actual 'authors' of the films) on a weak footing. But only the producers invested money in making the films within a fragmented sector until the last decade of the century.

Producers and directors also had a hard time raising capital to finance their movies. The ratio of hits to straight flops hovered between ten and fifteen per cent throughout the century. Banks would not lend, given these odds. So producers had to seek money from other sources. It appears that, from the early years, filmmakers strapped for cash had nowhere to turn but to the informal money market, where interest rates were as high as thirty-six to forty-eight per cent, with six months' payment having to be put down as a deposit.[132] Beneath the glamour, making films was a business fraught with risk.

One reason was that the cinema halls of old were enormous. Not quite as big as Wembley Stadium, but they could seat 800 to 1,000 people before the 'House Full' sign went up. Success was a cliff face to climb. To achieve blockbuster status, a film had to attract thousands upon thousands of bums on seats, again and again. (South Asians would happily watch the same film three or four times, which helped.)[133] Still, the maths, from the perspective of producers and directors, was awful.

It is hardly surprising that 'black' (untaxed) money began to prop up the industry, which grew to rely (allegedly) ever more on the very same underworld writ so large in its plots from the era of the Bachchan movies. If the movie industry had a sleazy reputation for 'immoral conduct' in the early decades, that image was tarnished further by its financial practices and circumstances by the century's end.[134]

The fact that the industry not only survived but grew to be the biggest in the world was thus an incredible feat.

The 'stepmotherly' (read uncaring) attitude of the state was also a real problem. Neither the Raj nor the Republic of India regarded it as their business to support Bombay cinema, affecting its access to bank finance and raw stock. It got no tax breaks either. For Nehru, radio was the prime modern technology for didactic preaching to the people, for cultivating the tastes of the nation. Bombay cinema occupied in the official mind a twilight zone that was neither 'industry' nor 'culture'. Yet it was both. As an industry it depended on imported raw stocks of film, but the government of India would not waive import duties to assist Bombay cinema. Nehru himself had little time for it. I fear he was a bit of a snob in this respect. His education at Harrow and Trinity made him uneasy with many aspects of India, and 'crude' films were not his thing.

What Nehru missed, for all his secularism, was that Bombay cinema until the 1990s continued to be an industry of all the talents, employing people of all religious backgrounds in every part of the process. No amount of subtle messaging could persuade the public not to love both Muslim and Hindu actors in Bombay: every decade of (surviving) Bombay film has been studded with Muslim stars. Waheeda Rehman, Meena Kumari (born Mehejebeen), Nargis Dutt, Saira Banu, Dilip Kumar, Zeenat Aman, Salman Khan, Aamir Khan, Shah Rukh Khan and Irrfan Khan were actors we loved to love in an India full of hatred. (Reader, most are 'Muslim names'.) Partitioned Indians still gobbled up their films and replayed their film songs. Even many of those born in the 1980s prefer the golden oldies. The transborder mourning of the death of Dilip Kumar (1922–2021, born Muhammad Yusuf Khan) is evidence that Bombay cinema could not easily be partitioned, nor could it be nationalised with ease.

No, Nehru did not watch enough films to understand all this. So, like the dinner guest in Bandra, he abhorred it. He went so far as to ban the construction of new cinema halls, the shortage of cement being the immediate cause, but showing just how low a priority Bombay cinema was given.[135] By the end of the century, India had only 1,300 cinemas, and its population-to-audience ratio was among the lowest in the world.[136] That gave exhibitors who had built huge halls before the ban even more bargaining power within the industry. Studios that actually produced films, like Bombay Talkies in the 1930s and 40s or Guru Dutt Studios in the 1950s, ran on perilous margins. However much they attempted to improve their production model by producing five or six films at the same time (as at Bombay Talkies), they were never far from ruin. The precariousness of the business was such that even an iconic producer like Guru Dutt, whose brilliance as a director, actor and producer is legendary, saw his studio go bankrupt after *Kaagaz ke Phool* tanked at the box office in 1959.

The film is perhaps Guru Dutt's finest, though it is hard to insist upon this because they were all so superb. It is now taught on cinema courses round the world. But for our purpose here, the film is a 'must-watch' because it gives us a sense of what an early studio looked like, and how it worked in Guru Dutt's day. The scenario involves the *mise-en-scène* of the filming of a movie: the many takes, the infrastructure, the somewhat chaotic style and the supporting team, whose place in the studio hierarchy is discernible but not clear; the dramatic play of light and shade that fall, in the main, on the 'director' (played by Guru Dutt) and the heroine (the peerless Waheeda Rehman). Looking at the decayed studio as shown at the beginning and end of the film, one can see how *jugaad* was its structure. The industry, at the producers' end, shared that precariousness.

There is another circumstance particular to the industry in Bombay. It has had to seek its own patrons. Unlike the forms of leisure discussed above, it was not patronised by the princes and *zamindaars* (who now at best lent them forts and palaces for 'historicals', once a popular genre). Neither the British colonial state nor the independent Indian state cared a toss for it, except in so far as they might 'corrupt the public morals'. India, and indeed Pakistan, took on the state-led revival of classical art, but the movies operated not only without state patronage, but also in hostile circumstances, until the turn of the century. This could not be more different from Hollywood, whose cultural impact and global 'soft power' US governments recognised and gave full backing.

When in 1998, in a surprise move – no doubt with an eye to its huge diasporic influence, and to a clean-up of the ('Muslim') mafia's role in movie finances – the BJP government finally recognised cinema as an industry, it thus made it eligible for government protection and promotion. But it still did not regard the Bombay film as 'culture'. The film industry was placed not under the auspices of the Ministry of Culture, but under (you won't believe this) the Ministry of Information and Broadcasting.[137] The regimes of the Hindu right, which claim to be more in touch with the Hindu 'masses', are in their own way (although for different reasons) as disdainful of Bollywood as their predecessors. They are guardians of the morals and chastity of Hindu women, so women actors and dancers (and the milieu in general) are not much loved.

That Bombay cinema continued to produce great films in these circumstances says much about the flow of brilliant people it attracted.

The 1950s were, many agree, among the best decades for Bombay cinema. Producers struggled but directors and actors made unforgettable movies. I have mentioned the oeuvre of Guru Dutt. There is also the marvellous *Mother India* (1957, directed by Mehboob Khan and starring Nargis), and the 'social', *Do Bigha Zameen* ('Two *Bighas* of Land', 1953), not to mention the Meena Kumari big-hitters. (More of this in the Note on Further Viewing.)

The 1960s were a difficult decade, and its films were more patchy.

Through the 1960s, the unfolding economics of the industry put a downward pressure on quality, favouring cheaply made sure-fire-hit movies that would cover the investments of producers, distributors and exhibitors while making them modest profits.

Recall: the lowest share of investment in the industry went into making movies. The largest share of profits went to the exhibitors.

Given the huge fan base of wrestling, and the wrestling films starring Dara Singh, one might even say the industry was kept afloat by millions of would-be Gamas. Dara Singh was also a very handsome man, and his co-star, Madhu Bala, was glamorous in ways that South Asians had not encountered. There was a lot in these films then, for women, not least new imaginaries of fashion.

In these circumstances, producers and directors worried themselves sick about potential audiences and what they might or might not like. The huge halls of that era had differential seating, ranging from the elite dress circle down to the cheap front benches, and so their goal had to be to make films that appealed to both the masses and the classes. Yet who were these faceless masses? Ganti recalls that even producers thought that the poor front benchers had 'low IQs'.

I imagine film directors worked in much the same way. They were conscious that their audience included the testosterone-fuelled 'low-class' urban male and the middle-class prudish 'aunty'. (Probably they had a face for each person: their tea boy or driver, say, or their second cousin's wife. Who knows.) To be hits, the films of Bombay had to strive to give the whole audience a bit of what it loved. Knowing what it loved must have been a real challenge if we bear in mind that the age of cinema coincided with the age of grand migrations referred to in Chapter 4. The city was full of rural migrants and partition refugees, all strangers in the city. Filmmakers did not, and could not, manufacture their market; they had to tantalise imaginary consumers whom they could see only in faint outline.

This explains why they dipped deep into the worlds of leisure they knew about, and had perhaps been part of themselves.

This is the context in which the 'masala movie' came of age. Until the 1960s, films were made in certain genres: historical, religious, romantic, melodramatic, action, social and Muslim social. The first film ever made was a historical about the (good) Raja Harishchandra. A religious one followed: *Lanka Dahan* ('Lanka Aflame', 1917). The finest historicals – including *Anarkali* (1953) and *Mughal-e-Azam* ('The Great Mughal', 1960) – were blockbusters in their own right. The early social focused on social issues – in the main, on rural poverty, this being soon after the Bengal Famine of 1942–3. *Do Bigha Zameen* is the classic in this genre. The Muslim social, by contrast, focused on the sociability of the urbane Muslims – *Chaudhvin ka Chand* being, in my view, the highlight.

Around the 1970s, however, cinema started to include all genres recognised as popular. Especially fighting, given that action films had helped sustain the industry through the 1960s; but also melodrama, festivals, bromance, romance, comedy, sibling rivalry, mother worship, son worship, worship, brothers-in-arms, heroes, anti-heroes and villains, comedy, songs and dances. This explains much about the length of these films, despite their tight plotting and – give credit where it is due – their lean, mean, dialogue.

Scholars argue (with rare unanimity) that the emergence of the 'Angry Young Man' movies starring Amitabh Bachchan have to do with the imposition of the Emergency in India in 1974–5, and the general public disenchantment with politicians and the nation state. There may be something in this. But as a historian, I can't help regard it as another teleology: an imposition of conclusions of the future (always in disequilibrium) upon the past.

History suggests a different reading. The film that broke new ground was *Zanjeer* ('Shackles', 1973). Imagine an axe breaking through red laterite stone: that was *Zanjeer*'s impact on the viewer. A stunning experience – both breathtaking and terrifying.

Zanjeer appeared before the Emergency. Javed Akhtar (co-author of the screenplay), who went to public cinemas to gauge audience reactions, recalls that in one theatre, a man sitting behind him in one momentous scene spoke out in a hall stunned into silence: '*Orre baap re baap!*' ('Oh my god!').[138] The reaction to the character was: 'What is this? What kind of hero is this? *Is* this a hero?' The character – Jai or Vijay depending on the movie – had the same name across many films (Javed Akhtar thought hard about his characters and gave them names that worked; the names stuck in the popular imagination). He shocked audiences; often he scared them. Yet his backstory made him legible even to middle-class viewers. Amitabh Bachchan's charisma (and his unacknowledged gifts as an actor) won over middle-class 'prudish aunty' viewers who might otherwise fear an encounter with such a person. They grew to love his 'Vijay' character. *Deewaar* ('The Wall', 1975), the next of the great Bachchan anti-hero films, also began to be made in 1973.

So there's a minor inconvenience in the dominant narrative: the timing is wrong. There's also the awkward fact that Bachchan himself was close to the Gandhi–Nehru family. The film press held Bachchan responsible for the press ban that began with the Emergency, and banned him. (He in turn banned them, a mistake he now admits.)

I suggest that there is indeed a mood music in Salim–Javed's 1970s screenplays (the pair grew almost as famous as Bachchan), but this was not about the Emergency at all.

The malaise these films cast in sharp relief was that of a generation of immigrants in the city, whose dreams of a better life had come to nought. They had no villages they could remember without pain, and no futures they could look to with hope.

These movies must be viewed as films about Bombay as a hub of immigration from south, north, west and east. 'Vijay', Bachchan's underdog Mumbaikar, speaks neither Gujarati nor Konkani nor Marathi (languages local to the region) but a Hindi patois that marks him out as a migrant. In *Deewaar*, he does 'honest labour' with other migrants as a dockhand, until – witnessing the mob's treatment of a newcomer who refuses the gaffer his tithe – he begins to resist them, and pays a huge price for his resistance. Rage and violence ratchet to higher and higher levels in the Salim–Javed films, reaching their apogee in *Sholay*. The audiences lapped it up. They proved not to be squeamish. And although the song quotient fell in this era (Bachchan being a fine enough actor to betray his interior self through the slightest movement of his face), the few songs they had were very good indeed. 'Mehbooba' ('Beloved') was a huge hit. I love it so much that I had it played at my fortieth and fiftieth birthday bashes, and indeed at my wedding party. Dames and knights, Trinity colleagues and friends looked on with amazement as my sisters, nieces and I rose in unison to try to match Helen's sexy faux 'belly-dance'. What a song. I hoped that my son and his wife would allow me to sneak it into *their* wedding song list. (Readers: they did.)

The problem arose as to how many times the audience could digest the 'masala'. It would accept almost anything from Amitabh, who rode out the 1970s ending his dramatic run of successes with *Don* (1978). It is a particular favourite of mine because it stars a Baazigar. (People still send each other WhatsApp GIFs of Amitabh dancing in *Don*. I received one from my friend Kamal – now a pro-vice-chancellor of the University of Cambridge, no less – in November 2021, forty-three years after the film was released. He's from Lahore and supports 'Team Lata', as you may recall.)

But problems arose when Amitabh himself, through his brother Ajitabh Bachchan, was believed to have been involved in and made money from the iffy Bofors arms procurement deal between the Indian and Swedish governments.[139]

After Amitabh's departure, the 1980s were patchy at best for commercial cinema, even as parallel (arthouse, non-commercial, realist) cinema began to emerge. (Again, more in the Note on Further Viewing.) Producers just couldn't get together the right mix of screenwriters, actors (male and female), cast and crew to make films that would gel. Why would they take risks on new themes, new actors? Two flops – one flop even (recall Guru Dutt) – could frighten the pants off a producer.

The financial challenge facing the industry lasted right through the 1980s, and its impact was discernible.

Another major challenge that Bombay cinema faced (which Hollywood did not) was finding female actors. Contrary to rumour, women have had a much larger presence in Bombay cinema than is often assumed: its female characters are often very powerful – watch *Mother India* for a sense of this. But sourcing women to take roles was not easy.

It was not so hard to persuade women from performing backgrounds to act in the films, such as the Australian circus artist Fearless Nadia (Mary Ann Evans, 1908–96), famed for playing the title role in *Hunterwali* ('Woman with a Whip', 1935); or Nargis or Meena Kumari, the stars of the 1950s and 60s, both born to poor performing families. They were entertainers; that was what they knew.

But it was a harder business altogether to get 'respectable' women to act, given the strict mores about the invisibility of 'cultured' women. Once dubbing came in – a technology that allowed recorded sound to be set free of background noise, with women playback singers who themselves remained invisible – more room opened up for talented actors who were not great singers. This also allowed women to enter the industry as singers only, golden voices behind the arras who retained a measure of propriety: hence the phenomenon of Lata Mangeshkar and Asha Bhosle, two sisters from Indore in central India, who sang in hundreds of movies without much dent to their bourgeois respectability.

'Mere actresses', who had to be visible, could not work without taking grave risks to their own reputations and to family honour. Durga Khote (1905–91) told of her social 'outcasteing' despite her high birth and learning. Khote, who began acting in 1930, recalls that the producers used her distinguished family background, trumpeting the status of both her natal family and her in-laws, in the publicity material for a film that was, in her frank and funny words, 'the very dregs'. After its release, she says, 'the Maharashtrian community' turned on her and the press reviled her. 'It became very difficult for her to venture outside her home and go anywhere in the neighbourhood'; 'both her natal and conjugal families were tremendously upset with her' for bringing shame on the good name of the families.[140] I doubt that Hollywood actors of her class and education faced this sort of venom.

So there were in fact subtle schisms within Apte's *filmi varna 6* – the workers. 'Actors' who were female, visible, famous, glamorous, on show because of the nature of their work, paid a price for being the face of cinema. Everyone else behind the scenes – the whole ensemble I have described – could work in Bombay cinema without their status changing so suddenly and irrevocably. Indeed the standing of some craftsmen, tailor masters in particular, could rise. This was not just because of the special demands of costume making but because of their close relationship with female stars, for whom, in the early days, they designed the one-dart blouse that produced a bosom that was more pointy than Ajanta-esque. The tailoring itself was part of the cinematic experience – it was as richly imaginative as it was fashion-bending and trend-setting.[141] By the end of the century, every star had her own personal tailor who accompanied her to the set.

So the industry has stuttered along in search of female talent.[142] There are the glorious exceptions that broke the rule: Meena Kumari (1933–72) and Nargis (1929–81) both died young, but their work outshines that of many actors who followed. Both started working by the age of five. By contrast, Waheeda Rehman, born in Chengalpet, Madras, in 1938, Sharmila Tagore, Hema Malini (from a Tamil Brahmin family) and Madhuri Dixit (born in Bombay in 1967) were middle-class girls from respectable households who had (as a part of their education) learned the 'new classical' dance. And how! I cannot imagine a viewer watching Waheeda Rehman act and not being blown away. Do watch Madhuri Dixit, a trained Kathak dancer, perform the Kathak sequence 'Dola re Dola' in *Devdas*.

That's another thing about Hindi cinema – the sheer number of remakes. *Devdas*, a romantic tragedy, has had twenty versions since its first appearance in 1955. I wonder if this is because South Asians are used to seeing the same miracle play every year, or whether new generations of directors think they can do it better. My hunch is that both factors are at work. Directors know that an audience will watch the same story filmed once, twice or even twenty times. Audiences watch them for many reasons (other than those mentioned by Mazumdar and Appadurai in their debate on the subject): because they love them, because they have a huge fixation on one of the stars, because they want to get a better grip of the plot, because they want to see that fight sequence or that Baazigar scene once again, because they want to hear the dialogue or songs again (and again and again) until they have learned them by heart. I speak here as a humble member of the audience: an 'aunty' but not a prude, and as a Ramlila child. There's no strangeness, for South Asian audiences, in repetition.

To come back to the twentieth version of *Devdas*, Birju Maharaj, the Kathak legend, sang and helped choreograph Madhuri's dance. ('Classical' and commercial art had a nice little conversation – it happens a lot more that the average snob realises.)

Hema Malini made Bharatanatyam move to *filmi*. Do watch her dance 'Haan Jab Tak Hai Jaan' ('Yes, as long as I have life, [I will dance]') in *Sholay*. Her dance speaks to *Pakeezah*, in which Meena Kumari danced *filmi* classical Kathak on glass. Here Hema Malini danced a *filmi* Bharatanatyam on glass. A nice border-crossing allusion lost on the casual viewer. Dixit came out of retirement and married respectability to perform the role of the courtesan Chandramukhi, hopelessly devoted to Devdas despite his cruel rejection of her. A married respectable woman played a courtesan, and danced Kathak in what must be one of the most popular of the twenty remakes of *Devdas*. Another little revolution is that she stole the screen from another respectable woman, playing a respectable woman – Aishwarya Rai Bachchan. (I could watch Madhuri dancing in it twenty times.)

But while South Asian women have been big characters in the cinema, Madhuri Dixit has been the only female actor who ever led movies in her own right: she has been cast first, male co-stars second. In the 1990s, films ran on her star power alone. She demonstrated considerable talent as an actor (seen most evidently in the very difficult film *Mrityudand* ('Death Sentence', 1997)). But it is as a dancer she will be remembered. Not only is she one of the best dancers that Bombay cinema has ever seen, but, as one scholar puts it, in her dancing she plays vamp and heroine all at once, opening up a space in which young women could be imagined to have desire.[143] By the late 1990s, India had moved on sufficiently for a woman actor like Madhuri to choose this trajectory.[144]

There are exceptions, then: women's ambition and flair have seen to that.

But often, the industry has relied on the offspring of movie moguls to play the female parts. Neetu Kumar, a star in the 1970s, came from a cinema family. The smouldering Rekha of *Umrao Jaan* and *Silsila* is the daughter of the huge Tamil movie star, Gemini Ganesan. Karishma Kapoor (b. 1974), a leading star of the 1990s, is a scion of the Kapoor movie dynasty. This happens with their sons too – the movies are like your regular South Asian family businesses in this respect.

And as the dynasts promote their own children, it is harder than ever for outsiders, however talented – middle class or otherwise – to break through.

Of course, many talented women aspirants who began to give it a go as the century entered its closing decades were outsiders. The industry always needed women and they remained a commodity in short supply. (It is for this reason, I now realise, that I was myself thus approached in my late teens, when I did a fair bit in amateur theatre.

The two famous directors who checked me out for roles had the wits to see that I was useless. I was relieved: the auditions had scared me.) Yet there were, as well as personal introductions like mine, other routes for young women to get noticed, chiefly by modelling and/or entering (and winning) beauty pageants.[145] (This gives you an idea of what the most desirable traits in a woman actor are, for the industry.) Some succeeded. Aishwarya Rai Bachchan, one of the stars of *Devdas*, made it by this route: first rocking it as a model, then winning the Miss World title, and next marrying Amitabh Bachchan's son (Abhishek Bachchan, also an actor, who began to make his way to the top in the new century). But for most aspirants, I suspect that great pressure was put on them to give up their childish fantasies of stardom and settle down.

My guess is that once the few succeeded, against the odds, in being cast in a film, they had crossed some invisible threshold, like Sita's 'Lakshman line'. They now belonged to a different world – an endogamous world not unlike a *jati* – because the road back was nigh impassable. The *filmi* world has its own norms and power structures, but these are (and are perceived to be) not those of polite society in Maharashtra, or Tamil Nadu, or West Bengal, or indeed any other region of South Asia. Javed Akhtar, the screenwriter and lyricist, describes it as 'a separate state in India', an apt and brilliant metaphor.[146] (I would describe it as 'a separate state in South Asia'.) Its 'abnormal' norms are the subject of a prurient fascination covered by journalism rich with innuendo.[147] Magazines like *filmindia*, *Stardust* and *Filmfare* were of course different to the dense offline and online chatter that created Hollywood stars as we know them.[148] But their own *raison d'être* was to speculate on the nature of 'the state of Filmistan', on affairs and elopements, broken marriages, two-timing, dating, flirting among Bombay actors and wannabes, and lately about the role of the casting couch in allotting female roles. It's a curious, parasitic relationship because, without the cinema and its stars, they would not exist. But it is symbiotic too: the magazines fund Bombay's version of the Oscars – so can make or break films, and stars.

Perhaps the tightest constraint on Bombay cinema (so unlike Hollywood) was the fact that both the story and scenario, whatever the genre, had to work within the subcontinent's social mores: above all its miracle plays and its forms of patriarchy. So the heroine has to be a good girl who does what her parents want her to do, even if it involves giving up the love of her life. Even if she is a courtesan (like Waheeda Rehman's Gulabo in *Pyaasa*, or Meena Kumari's character in *Pakeezah*, or Dixit's Chandramukhi in *Devdas*) – or a mistress (as she would then have been described), as with Parveen Babi's Anita in *Deewaar* – she must be as selfless and as devoted to her man as a girl from a cultured home would have been trained to be from childhood. Even in the ground-breaking film *Zanjeer*, which launched Amitabh Bachchan's rise to global superstardom, the character played by Jaya Bhaduri starts out by being a sharp-tongued, street-wise knife-sharpener, but ends up being a Sita-esque 'traditional good girl'. (There are always exceptions to any rule. My favourite is Zeenat Aman's kung fu fighter in *Don*. Do watch it.)

Even if she is an icon of all things that patriarchy expects of her, there's no guarantee of a happy ending. The hero must be a *mastaana* – crazy for his girl – but in the end, must either die or reject her if the family won't accept her.

There is a horrifying scene in the famous romance *Kabhi Kabhie* ('Sometimes', 1976), in which Amitabh Bhachchan's character, a well-known poet, says to his lover as he parts from her: 'We cannot erect a monument of our love upon the broken dreams of our parents.' His mellow voice turns harsh when he says this. He will brook no dissent. Her tears do not move him. So they each marry another chosen by their parents, leading lonely and unfulfilled lives. It is a shocking scene, but well worth viewing.

The number of Bombay films that broke this rule in the twentieth century were achingly few.

Only a handful of directors dared. Guru Dutt, a genius in his way, was among them. In *Kaagaz ke Phool*, he broaches marital break-down, 'unsanctified love' (between the hero, a divorcee director, played by Guru Dutt himself, and his accidental star, played by Waheeda Rehman), and the fall from grace, failure and ultimate death of the iconic director who created the new star. Hard themes, a diffi-cult film even today, which bombed at the box office. Another film, *Sahib, Bibi aur Ghulam* ('The Master, the Wife and the Servant', 1962), which Guru Dutt made with his friend Abrar Alvi, tells the story of a *zamindaari* family in which the daughters-in-law of the grand house are neglected by their gambling, courtesan-smitten dissi-pated drunk husbands. Desperate for her husband's love and desire, Chhoti Bahu (youngest daughter-in-law, played by Meena Kumari) learns to drink, play cards and act as a courtesan might, all in order to attract her husband. He is amused to begin with, and begins to stay at home at nights. Soon he tires of her and, complaining of claustrophobia, returns to the *kotha*. Desolate, she drinks more and more, becoming, by the end of the film, an alcoholic.

This was shocking stuff. More so was a scene that appeared in the original film. Chhoti Bahu's only confidant is the young migrant Bhootnath, who lives in their huge mansion (but does not work there, so has a liminal status in the household). In the electrifying shot, she rests her head briefly on him for comfort. In the early weeks of the film's release, audiences tut-tutted (nay, huffed and puffed) at this point. Guru Dutt watched this reaction. Already burned by the catastrophic reaction to *Kaagaz ke Phool*, he edited it out.[149] He was, after all, a commercial producer who had to sell films and fill the halls. His colleague Johnny Walker pointed out that he was the rare director whose films 'were liked by the gentry and the masses. That was his greatest quality.'[150] (Indeed, thinking about Guru Dutt's oeuvre, one begins to question the rigid line that most people imagine exists between commercial and arthouse cinema. His films crossed those borders.) But like many a great artist decades ahead of his time, he lost his zest for life and sank deep into despair. He killed himself at the age of thirty-nine.

Bombay cinema's novelty: the use of South Asian modes of leisure

So far, I have written about what the Bombay industry *didn't* have that makes it different from the industry in Los Angeles. Now let's move on to what it *did* have, what made it rich and distinctive. Situated in dense worlds of leisure upon whose traditions it could draw, the Hindi film directors had a good grasp of public leisure outside the cinema hall.

I have touched on some of these themes above, and I will unpack a few in the context of cinema.

Most ubiquitous is the miracle play. In it, as we have seen, good triumphs over evil against mighty odds. The *Ramayana*, to take one important example, has many features of a Hindi movie: a strong (and conservative) moral architecture, a love story between a man of noble character and a pure woman (Ram and Sita). The heroine was always – in the twentieth century, with a few notable exceptions – modelled on Sita: beautiful, chaste, devoted, committed to patriarchal norms of family and household.

Then there's the terrifying baddie, Ravan, with his evil underlings and henchmen. His style may have varied as the decades rolled on, but Ravan continued to shake (but not break) moral foundations. They are glimpsed again and again in one movie after another.

At its heart is the notion that a small group of skilled, powerful, virtuous but outnumbered men, men with whom the audience can identify, enter the baddie's kingdom and bring it down. (They are as outstripped in numbers as Ram and Lakshman were against Ravan's army. The 'numbers' on the baddie's side even look like evil imps, come to think of it. It probably has to do with the camera angles from which they are shot.) In *Sholay*, when our crooked heroes Jai and Veeru enter the dacoit Gabbar's lair, they are met by a small platoon of Gabbar's flunkies, including the still loved and remembered Sambha. They rescue Basanti, played by Hema Malini, whom the dacoit has held prisoner. A long and mighty stunt and fight scene follows, in which the forces of good and evil do battle, and good triumphs. (Snobbish viewers think of these fight sequences as ridiculous, laughable – but if we remember that the scenario invests our heroes with a sprinkling of divine qualities, they are anything but.)

In the end, the symbolic Lanka, Ravan's kingdom, burns. Billowing flames are cathartic sights in this cinematic context. Let's remember that the elements of this miracle play are so familiar that the subtlest of clues to the *Ramayana* tradition are enough for an alert paying audience to respond to them, even if they do not consciously analyse their reaction. Cinema is, after all, seen, felt, heard, viewed, enjoyed and analysed all at once. In the 'overlong' fight that is so much a part of Bombay action cinema, the viewer's heightened emotions are straining in support of the brave hearts and their survival against the powers of darkness.

Snobs, as I said, despise these scenes. The criticism began in the 1920s in British times, as the Indian film industry had just about found its feet, as the *Report of the Indian Cinematograph Committee* described the average Indian film as 'crude', poorly plotted, but saved its worst criticism for the fight sequences.[151] 'Episodes are long drawn out, so that the action is slow, and the multiplicity of captions accentuates the slowness of the movement [which, in turn, impedes plot development]. Generally the films are too long.'[152] The snobs of today echo this 'colonial' condemnation word for word, without being aware that this is what they are doing.

Meanwhile, non-elite audiences loved them.

> The bulk of the population, which is little acquainted with the English language, enjoys films with much action. If there is plenty of action, they can follow the sequence of events and they are very quick at grasping the significance of the scenes and picking up the story. *The hearty applause which is heard from the cheap seats when the hero administers summary justice to the villain or rescues the heroine in the nick of time shows a proper appreciation of the events and is very seldom at fault.*[153]

Why wouldn't they be so quick at 'grasping the significance'? They knew what it signified, even though they weren't aware of the cinematic techniques by which Tulsidas came to Bombay. One of the first ever films made in that city was *Lanka Dahan*. (One viewer/insider, the Parsi film entrepreneur J. B. H. Wadia, 'had a hearty laugh at the sight of a muscular Seeta played by a male artiste. ... But I was stunned by the spectacular burning of Lanka.')[154] In the later decades of the century, the *Ramayana*'s outlines remained visible in the subtext of much of Bombay cinema, albeit in different and often subtle forms. In some films it is explicit, as in *Tezaab* ('Acid', 1988), in which Madhuri Dixit plays Mohini, a girl forced by her father to dance to pay for his lifestyle. Anil Kapoor plays Munna, a good boy gone bad after life deals him a poor hand. The two fall in love. Mohini becomes Munna's soft underbelly as he strives to take on the gangmasters ruining the lives of so many, and undermining the state itself. Mohini is kidnapped and held prisoner by Lotiya, the evil genius and underworld don, in his 'badland', which significantly floats off the dry docks, Lanka-like, in a quasi-island. Munna marches in there, but his devoted friend Babban (perhaps Lakshman) is shot and killed before he reaches his destination. Eventually in a scene that could hardly be more like the rescuing of Sita from Ravan's clutches, Munna frees Mohini and takes her away to safety. Lotiya (read Ravan) dies while a good cop looks on. Lotiya's kingdom is put to the torch – the whole structure goes up in flames, just as with the burning down, in Tulsidas' *Ramcharitmanas*, of Ravan's palace.

The sheer number of films that draw upon elements of the

Ramayana – not least *Lanka Dahan* (setting the badland on fire) – is quite amazing. Once you notice it, you see it everywhere. In *Don*, a film that inspired remakes in several Indian languages, including Hindi, Amitabh Bachchan plays a Bombay mob boss. Despite its Bond-esque car-chase sequences (which led some myopic critics to dismiss it as derivative) and its heroine's unusual character (the karate-chopping Zeenat Aman), it too ends with the big baddie in flames. In *Dostana* ('Friendship', 1980), in which Amitabh Bachchan plays a gum-chewing, cool modern cop, the Ravan figure burns. The number of Bombay films in which the wicked villain dies by fire is so large that it cannot be accidental. Just off the top of my head, there's *Kabhi Kabhie*, *Shaan* ('Grandeur', 1980), and *Main Hoon Na* ('I Am Here', 2004), which even has the baddie announce: 'Rama and I are going into exile.'

Even in the slick and challenging action thriller *Parinda* ('Bird', 1989) – you must watch it, it is one of the best, if not *the* best, in the genre – the film ends with the anti-hero Kishan setting the underworld don alight in his own domain.

Indeed, the reference turns up in the most unexpected places. Even in *3 Idiots* (2009), which has an extraordinary anti-establishment plot, one 'idiot', an old college bro-friend, says to another: '*Ravan ki Lanka me ghoom gaya*' ('I got lost in Ravan's Lanka'). In Farah Khan's *Main Hoon Na*, the two brothers (unrevealed as such) are actually called Rama and Shyam. (Rama being the good brother, of course.) This reprises a famous Dilip Kumar film, *Ram aur Shyam* ('Ram and Shyam', 1967). In Khan's version, in a crucial action scene, the baddie announces: '*Major Rama banvaas jaa rahe hain*' ('Major Rama is going into exile in the forest'). The film ends in a series of fires and explosions.

Even in *Mission Kashmir* (2000) – a more complex, distressing and political movie, in which the actor Hrithik Roshan plays Altaf (a Kashmiri terrorist, no less) – bombs are thrown and explosions in terrorist hideouts precede Altaf's redemption. Fire seems to act as a metaphor for moral cleansing, the finale of the miracle play.

Now to a different point about those fight sequences that the cinema audiences (in the front benches, but not only in the cheapest seats) loved so much. Watch them with care. Every single good fight sequence ends with both sides unarmed, sidekicks seen off, and the goodies and chief baddies squaring each other off. All guns, all swords, all knives – and the other mechanised weaponry that has entered the action world – are out of reach. What you then get is a return to the wrestling format. This is when the sequence gets most exciting. If you are as much of a wrestling aficionado as I have become, you will recognise that many of the moves by which the hero turns a hopeless situation around, go back to the times of the Great Gama, and are still practised every day at hundreds of thousands of *akharas* across the subcontinent. There's the thundering *laafad* (slap), the leg pull and throw, the punching, the throwing of the full body on a grounded opponent, the multiple ways of getting up off the floor. *Akhara* wrestlers will love these moves, they will appreciate and admire them – forgetting that the actual action was done by a stunt double, or a wrestler, rather than the actor. Recall Amitabh was neither a wrestler nor a Baazigar, so he almost killed himself trying to perform a very simple stunt. These viewers will deplore the baddie's breaking of the rules of wrestling – using dangerous strangleholds, breaking fingers, not to mention cutting off arms (in *Sholay*) – which is depicted again and again in the movies. (After Bruce Lee became a star, kung fu made its way into the action moves; but the wrestling format held its ground.)

For informed viewers, as so many males were even in the late twentieth century, these scenes were not interruptions in the plot. They were entertainment of the highest order. Watching Dara Singh (if you were a mad *kushti*-head) at the movies was almost as good as going to Patiala to watch the Gama–Zbyszko rout, or Dara's flooring of King Kong. Or any of the wrestling tournaments held year after year in the princely states. Few amateurs could afford to watch the greats in action at such events. The zoom lens made it possible for the viewer to have a ringside seat, even to see the wrestlers' great bodies (about which there was so much excited speculation) close up.[155]

After the 1970s, such action movies became mainstream, and the fight was Amitabh Bachchan's bread and butter. If you watch a few action films, you will note that the goons do not have the sculpted figures of western stars. They look like wrestlers; they are big and bulky. (Do look out for Raj Babbar, who plays a goon in *Don*.) Many wrestlers, and indeed Baazigars, took to the movies as stuntmen and body doubles – so strongmen were doing the actual fighting, and Baazigars the leaping and falling in the stunts at which they excelled. There's a marvellous scene in *Don* in which a maimed character (a reformed thug who has had one leg cut off by the gang) throws a rope across two multi-storey buildings to form a tightrope, and carries his children to safety. A high-octane trapeze act with so much riding on it: what's not to love. And what can one say to the Baazigar stunt artist who actually performed the role except, '*Ustaad*! I wish there was *one frame* in which I could see your face.'

Wrestlers and wrestling pits also feature in scenes in several block-busters. In *Dabangg* ('Fearless', 2010), we have a character training with a stone mace, no less. My personal favourite is *Anand* ('Serene', 1971), in which the hero, a dying man played by Rajesh Khanna, per-suades the neighbourhood *akhara* guru to take on the gaggle of dirty-minded youths who harass his doctor's girlfriend every day. As recently as 2016, *Dangal*, a biopic, was named after a wrestling tour-nament. Its continuing presence tells us something important about Bombay cinema, its stuntmen and the appeal of wrestling.

(By contrast, few films draw on cricket. One is a must-watch: *Lagaan* ('Tax', 2001), which shows a group of men from a Cutch vil-lage take on the British at their own game, and win. Its premise and historical foundations are dubious, but watch it nonetheless. In another, *Masoom* ('Innocent', 1983), the lead male character is shown playing cricket with his friends on a lazy winter afternoon. It's shown to be a hobby of that layer of Delhi's elites who have huge lawns or 'farmhouses'.)

Another distinctive leisure world on which directors drew was that of song and dance. Guru Dutt is also a good person with whom to start a discussion of their place in Bombay cinema. He is recognised as being one of the best ever 'picturisers' of song in Bombay cinema's history. If you want a taster, try the song 'Chaudhvin ka Chand' in the film of the same name. It depicts a common experience: falling head-long in love. (Song sequences are often chosen for romantic moments in the film.) The brilliance here lies partly in the setting of the song sequences, at night, in a bright room. There are also the words, which convey the 'feeling of letting go' which most of us have experienced in an inarticulate way – the shock, the slowing down and unfurling of time – when falling in love. They reveal the character's emotions and inner dialogue with empathy. They permit a man to be tender in a hyper-masculine society. Mohammed Rafi's singing lends clarity to the words, which are themselves poetry of a high standard. They make me wish that every reader of this book could understand some Hindi and Urdu just so that they could appreciate how beautiful it is. If you don't, you have lost something, but do listen and watch. (The movie appeals to all senses.) The audiences, for the most part from the Hindustani-speaking north of the subcontinent, did, and fell in love with the hero and his song.

If you don't know Hindi, try a few of these films anyway: not knowing the language is not an insuperable obstacle to understanding them. Most of the blockbusters are available online and have subtitles. Whoever writes these subtitles rarely does justice to the poetic and lyrical aspects of the dialogue and song, but you can rely on them for a while. After a while you will, I think, begin to hear the language differently. If you don't believe this, let me tell you about Anil, my partner. His father was Bengali, his mother was Hungarian, and since his childhood he has lived in the UK: he speaks English with a posh accent having had a posh education. He loves going back to India though, so he had a smattering of Hindi words, no more. He was not fluent.

When I started watching Bombay films night after night, he got sucked in by the sights and sounds of 'home', and became as much of an addict as I was. Not knowing the language, he first used the subtitles. After we had watched about thirty-odd movies with subtitles, I moved on to those 'oldies' without them. He would ask me for some translations. But after a while, when we were on our fortieth movie or so, *he* started translating the movie to *me*, word for word (better than the subtitle writers). I would look at him, half amazed, half amused, and remind him that I already knew the language. One can learn much Hindustani – its metaphors, synecdoche, allusions and sibilance – just by watching the films. If you doubt me, ask South Asians who are not from North India/Pakistan, for whom Hindi/Urdu is not their first language. The Bombay film has made it their second or third language.

You see, when critics complain about 'running around trees', they reveal their own blindness. A great deal goes on in these songs which undermines social conventions. While the story may be conventional (and it almost always is), the songs are not. They point to the rich internal world of the individual self of the character – in a society that did not condone individualism, and even denied that it had begun to catch that disease. We see, in the 'Chaudhvin ka Chand' song sequence (sung almost as if in conversation with an interior self), Guru Dutt's character looking down at the sleeping beauty and object of his desire,

Waheeda Rehman. '*Chaudhvin ka chaand ho tum, ya aftaab ho? Jo bee ho tum, khudua ki kasam, lajawaab ho.*' ('Are you the full moon, or are you the sun? Whichever you are, I swear, you render me speechless.')

My translation does not scan and does scant justice to the song because, like all great directors, Guru Dutt worked with the greatest poets of his time. Majrooh Sultanpuri, O. P. Nayyar and Balraj Sahni were his close collaborators, and with them he did two things. First, he made sure that the song was not a pause in the narrative, but that it took it further. Second, he toned down the high-flown Urdu that most poets were prone to use, to the language the character might use. So whereas the aristocrat in *Chaudhvin ka Chand* speaks in Urdu and sings tunes based on the *ghazal* form, in *Aar Paar* ('This or That', 1954), Johnny Walker's head masseur sings '*Sun sun sun, arre beta sun, is champi me bade bade gun*' ('Listen, son, this massage will do you a world of good') in street Hindi. The song's rhythms were urban, pacy, with Spanish and American influences. But once again they spoke to the randomness of connections between one person and others, a tragi-comic reflection on the pathos and anomie of individualism.

And in this individualism, we can see that the song could play havoc with social mores. Love of this kind threatened them. Individuals who would not be fully absorbed into households and governed by patriarchs – individuals who rebelled, even in small ways – threatened conservative society.

Other renowned poets, including Sahir Ludhianvi and Shakeel Badayuni, also joined the *filmi* world of song-poetry. The classical Urdu *ghazal* tradition, verdant with imagery, enriched the many ways in which the deepest feelings of an individual could be expressed, well into the 1960s. To get a taste of this music in cinema, try '*Kabhi khud pe kabhi halaat be rona aayaa*' ('I wept sometimes for myself, and sometimes for how things were'); or '*Main shaayar badnaam*' ('I am a disgraced poet') in *Namak Haraam* ('Traitor', 1973).

Even the story was often a work of South Asian literature famous enough in its own right for its literary merit to have found its way into the hands of a filmmaker. For instance, Munshi Premchand, the much-admired Hindustani/Urdu writer, inspired the film *Godaan* ('The Gift of a Cow', 1963), based on his novel of the same name. Rabindranath Tagore wrote the story which became the stunning *Do Bigha Zameen.*

These stories were then converted into screenplays ('scenarios'), and then into cinema. Several brilliant left-leaning writers and poets joined the film industry in the 1930s and 40s: they include Kaifi Azmi, K. A. Abbas, Sadat Hasan Manto, Balraj Sahni and Chetan Anand.[156] They undertook the work of translating the story into spoken dialogue, action and lyrical song. By the 1970s, the scriptwriters had become stars, legends in their own right.

It was under their influence that one genre of film began to stand out. A different genre that shot across the cinema's darkness like a meteor in the 1950s was the 'social'. It explored, as the name suggests, society and its ills. Mehboob Khan's *Mother India* and Bimal Roy's *Do Bigha Zameen* are two other films you must try to watch before you write Bollywood off. Based on the themes of rural poverty and oppression, and migration to the city to escape it, these films create narratives and characters so powerful that we can still relate to them seventy years later. Indeed, so powerful is *Do Bigha Zameen* that I wonder whether arthouse cinema directors have not been influenced by it. Am I alone in imagining the resemblances in the frames of the arrival of the migrant in the city in this great film and Satyajit Ray's *Apur Sansar* ('Apu's World', 1959)? Allusions are subtle things, in the eye of the reader and viewer, but I for one believe that Ray had seen that film, and that it influenced him. I remain dubious about the rigidity of the line drawn between arthouse and popular cinema, as I have said before. Although freedom from the vicious circle of commerce has constrained the latter, writers, songwriters and directors have bust a gut to make their films as good as they possibly can be. (More of this in the Note on Further Viewing.)

Musicians have also played a vital role in this process. Rahul Dev 'Pancham' Burman (1939–94) was perhaps their greatest avatar (until a new star was born as the century ended – the glorious A. R. Rahman). Javed Akhtar has described the process by which lyricists would bow to the musicians, first telling them the song-scenario. Next, Burman and his peers wrote tunes that matched the mood of the scene. The lyrics were written straight afterwards, to match the tune.[157] The product was the child of this deep collaboration.

The tunes themselves drew on a variety of the subcontinent's musico-literary heritage – not only the *ghazal*, but the *shaayar*, *qawwaali*, *khayaal* and *dhrupad* among a legion of global and regional traditions of poetry, music and dance. Bombay's musicians have been eclectic in their choices. But the best have drawn on a huge repertoire of musical knowledge with ease, and so can pull a tune out of it to suit the particular song-scenario.

Other traditions on which songwriters and musicians drew (albeit less often) have been the classical *raags*, sets of a few notes which are associated with a mood, or time of day. Not originally a fan of Lata Mangeshkar, the empress of the Hindi film song, I was converted when I heard her sing 'Mohe bhool gaye sanwariya' ('My love has forgotten me') in Raag Bhairav in the classic *Baiju Bawra* ('Crazy Baiju', 1952).

The movies thus opened up South Asia's rich traditions of poetry and music to sections of society hitherto denied access to them. They have been part of a slow process of cultural democratisation. Far from dumbing down, Bombay cinema has made the poetic, literary and musical traditions of the subcontinent accessible to the ordinary viewer. These riches were now offered to the 'masses', even to front benchers, even to women. It has, in this sense, 'cultivated their taste', just as the modern nation state insisted – even though that dinner guest in Bandra thought Hindi cinema was 'trash'.

This tradition has continued, with the Urdu poets, the Progressive Writers' Association and other talents continuing to write lyrics. In the 1990s the poet Javed Akhtar, one half of the celebrated Salim–Javed duo, who scripted *Sholay*, *Zanjeer* and *Deewaar* and other big-hitters of the time, turned to writing lyrics. He brought to his songs a new sensibility. Just as Salim–Javed's screenplays had given a new tautness to screenplay and dialogue in the 1970s, he wrote lyrics of a new sort. The industry has demanding standards.

These standards have paid off. The songs have often been chart-busters in their own right. For South Asians, seeing R. D. Burman advertised as the music director of a film was as important, or almost as important, as its stars (who in any event only came into being, in the western sense, in the 1960s and 70s). It was a guarantee of good music, good songs – songs they would remember long after the movie itself was forgotten.

Since the earliest days of cinema, South Asian audiences had a huge appetite for these *filmi* song sequences. Their impact remains stupendous. In fact, if you ask a South Asian today about a Hindustani film they saw in the 1970s, they are likely to refer to a song. I hardly saw any Bombay films when I was growing up. (I hardly saw *any* films. I went to boarding school at the age of nine.) But if you ask me about a film that I happened to watch in school (literally – the reel was brought to the Welham Girls' High School's high-walled compound because we girls couldn't be seen in public), a song trips off my tongue: 'My name is Anthony Gonsalves, *main duniyan mein akela hoon*' ('I am alone in this world'). I could not remember the plot, however, until I rewatched the film – *Amar Akbar Anthony* (1977) – some months ago. Ask me about *Sholay*, which I've seen six times, and I have a vague memory of the plot (good cop and buddies versus charismatic bandit, and some of Gabbar Singh's dialogue) but I could sing every word of the bromance song 'Yeh Dosti' ('This Friendship').

You see, you need many senses on alert to be able to appreciate Bombay cinema. The aural was of particular importance to the ticket-buying public when the talkies began, reaching their golden era in the 1950s. Cinema-goers could luxuriate for a few hours in the poesy of *shaayars*, a form of which they were aware but in which they were not steeped. *Shaayar* is a form of performative poetry recited by poets for poets and a few select aficionados at long sessions (*mushairas*). The *shaayar* (which has a couplet form) lent itself perfectly to cinematic entertainment, allowing a wider audience to join a *mehfil* (a gathering for leisure). Films gave them access to these poetic, musical and lyrical traditions when they bought their tickets. The plots of this period moved slowly like a boat through rivulets thick with rushes, brilliant birds and butterflies hovering over as it rowed by. Dialogue and lyrics were magical things: rich, excessive, not of this world. They were not intended to be realistic: they aimed to enchant. Colonial critics found this slow pace unbearable. But for the consuming audience, many of whom had been barred from it before, the beauty and grandeur of the language was hypnotic.

As was the world of dance. I recently asked a research student (Humaira Chowdhury of Marquis Street) whether she had seen the film *Umrao Jaan*. The subject of Humaira's PhD is the history of tailoring, and there are some stunning tailored outfits in this film. In replying (in the context, recall, of a PhD supervision), she burst into song: '*In aankhon ki masti mein*' ('In the play of these eyes'). She also encouraged me to watch *Devdas* (2002), when I told her I was writing about Kathak. She was a little girl when she first saw it, ten years old perhaps, but as soon as she returned from the cinema to her little home, she began to teach herself the (Kathak-inspired) moves in the dance spectacular 'Dola re Dola', starring Madhuri Dixit and Aishwarya Rai

Bachchan. Her home had one room. Little Humaira had to leap over the sleeping bodies of aunties and cousins who had gathered for the special outing. She practised the complex moves again and again until, exhausted, she fell asleep. She is still a great dancer.

So devoted were South Asian audiences to these songs and dances that in India, Doordarshan, the state-controlled broadcaster, ran a weekly programme called *Chitrahaar* ('a garland of pictures'), which consisted only of song-and-dance sequences. I don't have primary evidence to back this up, but I am willing to wager a good sum that this was the most popular programme after the news. In the 1990s, when my nine-year-old niece Maya used to 'come over to play with Kartik' in Delhi, she would spend her time watching *Chitrahaar* with Meena Kumari, our cook Mohan's daughter (please note her name, after the star). They would huddle together watching *Chitrahaar* in Mohan's quarters. After the programme had ended, the two of them would burst into our front portico and sing and dance this or that sequence, repeating it again and again until their moves were flawless. (At this stage Maya knew no Hindi, although she spoke fluent Bangla. It didn't seem to matter. Like many Indians, she learned Hindi from *Chitrahaar*. Like Humaira, she dances like a dream. When she danced at our wedding party to the song 'Pardesi' ('Foreigner'), a family favourite, some of the guests almost fell off their chairs.)

When I was at boarding school, aged ten to twelve, a game we often played was *Antaakshari* (the game of the last letter). Two rival teams of girls would compete for the last word. The theme was songs from Bombay cinema. After tossing a coin (like Bachchan's character Jai in *Sholay*), one team would begin to sing a popular song. When the lead singer broke to catch her breath, or to match the rhythm of the song, the opposing team would leap in on the vowel or consonant on which she had ended . . . and ring out a song beginning with that vowel or consonant. This could go on, back and forth, for half an hour or so, before one side lost. In the last rounds of the match, players had to resort to quite obscure songs to hang on in the game. If one stops to think of it, the depth of knowledge that little girls had, before the days of TV or VCR, was astonishing. Transistor radios and small 'singles', the old HMV 78s, must be where we learned them so well.

By the end of the twentieth century, South Asians in their millions were choosing cinema songs as ringtones for their mobile phones.

But there is much more to these song sequences than just leisure, or pleasure.

At a deeper level, the song allowed the screenplay writer to give the character an interior, introspective self. The lyrics spoke from that space which was outside and beyond the character's social location. The songs gave the characters room to become modern individuals with personal desires and dreams. They hoped, they suffered, they despaired. As individuals. These were deep emotions and thoughts that were not tolerated, indeed could not be expressed, in the family context or in the household, in which individuals had no recognition.

The song, in other words, pointed to the emergence of a particular kind of modernity in South Asia. And to South Asian individuation, in theoretical parlance.

If we step back to think about this even more, we note that there are two or three settings in which Bombay cinema 'places' songs. All are spaces of transgression.

The first is the love affair. Recall that breaking the Love Laws is a dangerous business, but every Hindi movie, pretty much, allows its characters to fall headlong in love (at first sight, in the blink of an eye, often, as in *Devdas*, in childhood). That love cannot be turned into what they want: lifelong union. Social convention will not allow it. So they part and marry others, as in *Kabhi Kabhie*, or one dies alone (*Devdas*). This leaves us with two characters who, throughout a film lasting two or three hours, act out their personal emotions, often through songs full of anguish against the forces that have denied them their chosen beloved.

Another setting is the 'bromance song', the best known being 'Yeh Dosti' ('This Friendship') from *Sholay*. Since Guru Dutt's *Chaudhvin ka Chand*, in which two male friends fall in love with the same mysterious woman, and one kills himself to clear the way for his friend, bromance has been a pivotal element of many a Bombay blockbuster. In these films, male characters form bonds of such intensity that every other relationship pales into the background – families are either absent, minimal or deficient in some fundamental way. Girlfriends hover in the mid-distance.

The friendship itself is the theme, if not the plot. Friendship is shown to be a relationship between two well-defined individuals. The films often make them characters who are polar opposites, as with Jai and Veeru in *Sholay*: Jai is quiet, introspective and often wants space; whereas Veeru is all bounce, fun, drink and frolic. And in some films, the logic of their individuality is taken to the extreme – as in *Namak Haraam*, where the character played by Amitabh Bachchan goes to jail for fourteen years (like Ram in exile) to punish his father for killing his beloved friend. Friend trumps even family.

As to whether there is a layer of homoeroticism in these friendships, it is for the viewer to judge. My sense is that the movies vary; not every bromance movie develops that subtext, even though it might hint at it. Somu's song to Vicky in *Namak Haraam* – 'Diye Jalte Hain' ('Oil Lamps Burn') – is so full of grown-up love I felt I had to look away. That's not the case with the Jai–Veeru friendship in *Sholay*: the best buddies spend as much time romancing their chosen women as they do singing to each other. Or do they? Watch that last frame of them again. You might see it differently. There is room, in the movies' depiction of such relationships, to allow viewers to imagine them in a plethora of ways.

The third setting is the festival. In twentieth-century movies, it was almost always Holi. Holi is a few condoned hours of bacchanalia. Friends, relatives and neighbours (the men often high on *bhang*) cover each other's faces and arms (and other parts) with dry and wet colour. For a few hours, anything is allowed. The hero gets to touch his paramour in public. People touch each other in otherwise unacceptable ways, all in public.

Holi comes up in pretty much every twentieth-century movie I have seen (other than the Muslim social).[158] In *Sholay*, there are *two* Holi scenes. You have to ask yourself why. Holi sequences allow the audience to think (without being aware of it) of a world upside down. They allow directors to let their characters do things that buttoned-up family-minded South Asians would not do. For instance, dance with their girlfriends in full public view. Daub the scene with the colours of their love. These frames tear, and tear a thousand times, the fabric of conservatism in the 'picture' (as we call it in South Asia). The fact that there was no kissing, not least because the censors were concerned about public morality, is ironic. The directors were running rings round censors too unimaginative to see what was in front of them.[159]

Even so. These songs are not just an interruption to the plot. They present the expansion – beyond the literati – of a vernacular modernity and individualism in this part of the world. Whether they represented realities or created inchoate desires, either way they were doing important work, and it is best we understand that.

There is another sleight of hand that screenwriters often use to help create Bombay's cinema: inner dualism. In film after film, the main character or characters are orphans. I didn't notice this when I was watching these films as a schoolgirl – I tended to focus on the powerful, loving, doting, traditional mother figure who was so different from my own. But on second or third viewing I began to notice the orphans. Anthony Gonsalves of the famous song is all 'alone in this world'. Jai and Veeru of *Sholay* – who were they? They seemed to have no one but each other. They have no parents, as far as viewers can tell. Kishan and Karan in *Parinda* are orphaned as the movie starts, their sick starving father dying in an effort to migrate with his sons to the city. Vijay in *Zanjeer* is fatherless. Altaf in *Mission Kashmir* is an orphan. Ajay in *Baazigar* is an orphan. The death of their parents early in childhood contributes, of course, part of the narrative, because trauma animates their urgent desire for revenge, their uncompromising, violent, even psychopathic, behaviour.[160]

But the orphan status also seems to extend to the baddies and gangsters. They have only first names (Peter, Kaliya, Sambha, Taklu, Anna, for instance), but no surnames. I suggest that this has been a deliberate move to wipe each character clean of class, religious or caste marks, and give them a personhood outside the family/household. Their choices, for good or ill, are their own.

The fact that these characters have no social context makes it easier for a wide audience (from dress circle to front bench) to relate to them. Caste-conscious Hindus can't quite place them, and so will not necessarily see them as part of a different and inferior social group. They can relate to them as individuals themselves, in intimate contact – because this is what cinema gives you – with other individuals. And by sprinkling them with a little dust of the divine, even the caste- and class-conscious viewer can feel comfortable backing Jai and Veeru (and others like them) when they take on the forces of evil.

If the evil is unrealistic, it has to be. Realism is not the test of quality in these films. Hindi cinema is not realist, nor did it strive to be. In this respect too it was different from Hollywood.

It strove to connect to the imagination of viewers. Its baddies had to be so powerful, so over the top, and so outlandish because it had to conjure up a comparable dark force, a mythical lord of the under-world, Ravan. If Davar's or Peter's home and office are shown to be foreign and opulent in a grotesque way, that's all the better for the plot. No one can identify with them, not only because they are bad-dies, but because they are from another world no one can relate to, with their ostentation and hideous homes, cars and suits. None of them are recognisably Brahmins, Ezhavas, Vaidyas, Seals, Bohras, Shias, Sunnis, Tamil Brahmins, Catholics, Jats, Sikhs, Dalits or Adiva-sis. Only Gabbar Singh in *Sholay* has a surname – Singh – but he's not a Sikh (he has short hair) and no one could identify with such a sad-ist. Yet he is Hindi cinema's best-known character, and almost every South Asian I know can still act out the '*Kitne aadmi thhe?*' ('How many men were there?') scene, word for word, forty-five years later.

In that huge cinema hall, for three hours or so, audiences thus focused on individual people, with their own inner lives and few con-straining social ties.

All of this is, in a subtle way, quietly revolutionary. Cinema – quite as much as the novel or the newspaper – has been the site for the emergence of a form of vernacular modernity and somehow, histori-ans have missed this.[161] Films are also the setting that shows us, should we choose to see it, India's most modern city. Bombay was, in the twentieth century, the subcontinent's 'cinematic city': known and richly inhabited, if only through film.

The glib claim that Bombay cinema is derivative, then, is plain wrong. Of course there have been influences on almost every aspect of its movie-making from beyond. The world's transnationalism (and later globalisation) involved flows of ideas and technologies, within South Asia, from it to the rest of the world, and from the rest of the world to it. Javed Akhtar cites Kurosawa's *Seven Samurai* as an influ-ence, but also his training as a poet in the Indian Writers' Association. Ramesh Sippy, director of *Sholay*, is clear that he wanted to make a film with some of the feel of the Wild West in a sort-of Hollywood western, but if you watch *Sholay* you will be disabused of the idea that it is some sort of derivative 'spaghetti western'. Whatever the inspirations from beyond (and there have been many other than Hol-lywood), Bombay cinema has been constrained by the financial conditions, social norms, forms of leisure and expectations of enter-tainment particular to South Asia.

A word on the role of the anti-hero – such a feature of Bombay cinema in its most successful Bachchan-dominated phase. There isn't a comparable genre in Hollywood, barring, in a low-key mode, *Bonnie and Clyde* and a handful of Quentin Tarantino films.

The anti-hero is a baddie one identifies with. He may even be the right-hand man of the top mafioso. Yet a sense of desolation about him renders his actions (be they so vile) somehow legible to the audience. The film reveals him to be a lonely introvert, a reflective person. He has redeeming qualities: he loves his mother, his brother or his friend. In these loves he shows no limit. He can be tender to vulnerable waifs, and gentle to lovers. He has often experienced great suffering in his childhood.

From the 1970s to the 90s, some of the most powerful Hindi films have been based on the anti-hero premise. I would say that the greats started with *Zanjeer* and ended with *Parinda*. Salim Khan and Javed Akhtar were the scriptwriters who first took this risk and crafted a character of such power and charisma that you felt his pain, applauded his courage and empathised with his despair. They gave the character more layers in *Deewaar*. So many anti-hero films were made that this became known as the era of the Angry Young Man.

As I have mentioned, film scholars attribute the start of the trend to the Emergency. As an irritating historian I have pointed out that the dates don't work: both were made before the Emergency.

There was, however, a wider social context, which was the shattered hopes of two generations of poor migrants to the city. They had struggled and tried their hand at everything, but the city had slapped them in the face. The context for these films was social and economic – poverty, the plight of the footpath dwellers, the unemployable and daily-wage construction labour, and the casual cruelty of *maaliks* (their employers). The social (the genre of film that focuses on socio-economic or sociocultural issues) had taken over, albeit in a new urban form. It made Bachchan a superstar, despite his closeness to the Gandhi–Nehru family.

When I say that these were socials in a new sense, not only were they set in the city (the countryside fades from view), but psychology was now writ large in them. Vienna met Bombay. Each of these anti-heroes suffers from what we would today call post-traumatic stress disorder, the trigger being an event in early childhood. Thus the hero has a reason for becoming an anti-hero, and these reasons are always explained.

In the film I watched (again) recently, for instance, *Mission Kashmir*, the anti-hero Altaf is a Kashmiri terrorist, determined to do as much damage as he can to the Indian state. (It could hardly get worse.) But very early in the film, it's explained to viewers why Altaf has turned out this way: his parents and sister were shot dead in front of him while he was a small child; they were casual casualties in a police raid on extremists. His psychological maladjustment shows itself in his failure to speak. His wordless grief is revealed in every shot of him as a child. His desire to avenge their deaths is thus rendered personal (rather than political), his aggression is accounted for by post-traumatic stress. He confesses to his childhood love Sufi that he feels nothing, ever, so those who wish to can understand his buried, unspeakable, anguish.

And avenging harm to one's family sits comfortably with patriarchal values, so anti-heroes love their mothers if they know them. Watch Bachchan's character and his (rejected) mother-worship in *Deewaar*. The audience forgave Vijay many times, just as they did Altaf.

In a similar vein, in the 'must-watch' film *Parinda*, we learn that Kishan, who joins the underworld in Bombay as an enforcer, was the elder of two brothers abandoned (or orphaned) on their way to the city when fleeing starvation in the village. Kishan turns to petty crime to feed his little brother Karan, and then supports Karan's education in America so that he is kept out of the dirty world he works in.[162] The anti-hero proves to be sympathetic once the audience understands that he remains true to family values such as brotherly love, even as an outlaw.

If we look again at *Zanjeer*, we can reread Salim–Javed's new type of character. He first emerged as Vijay in *Zanjeer*. Played by Amitabh Bachchan, Vijay had witnessed his parents' murder in childhood by a stranger on a white horse. He had struggled as a growing child, always a misfit among his peers, and as a young adult with post-traumatic stress. (Javed Akhtar, co-screenwriter, admits to suffering something similar after the death of his beloved mother.) Vijay grows up to be a cop with the courage to take on the city's underworld, but (here comes the twist) he takes the law into his own hands when he needs to. A policeman-outlaw, a lonely man estranged from himself, Vijay finds relief only in violent outbursts of rage against players in the urban world's filthy underbelly.

This curate's egg character made a huge impact on the crowds. The Indian media dubbed him 'the angry young man', and the audiences of the 1970s wanted more. The label stuck, despite the Vijay archetype being developed further in *Deewaar*, in which he works for the Bombay underworld to support his hungry family after the death of his idealist father. His brother, played by Shashi Kapoor, becomes a cop, and the film becomes a complex moral tale of revenge, mother love and sibling rivalry. Here, this Vijay is seen in a consummated relationship with his lover (shock, horror) – but even when he is in bed with her, he seems alone. (The *deewaar* of the title, Akhtar explains, refers to the walls that these characters create between themselves and their emotions.)[163] There's a huge vulnerability about the character Vijay in his many avatars. Even as Jai in *Sholay*, where he is a recidivist petty crook – death-defying, bonded at the hip to his best friend, but always choosing to lose the bet (and his life) when it comes to the most difficult risks. If one thinks back on him tossing his coin in *Sholay*, is there a death wish? He won't say. Quiet, still, brooding, he plays his harmonica at dusk.

Still, the label stuck.

But if you look past the Angry Young Man, you will see something different: perhaps even the pain, anomie and despair that allowed every viewer to identify with Vijay/Amitabh, however 'bad' he was.

These are films worth watching, either way; they are full of plot, tense dialogue and complex characters, and replete with explosive tension. The Salim–Javed duo (of Salim Khan and Javed Akhtar) began to write rather different stories and scripts at this stage. It is not as though these men came from a different milieu: Javed Akhtar was the son of a poet whose pen name, or *takhallus*, was Akhtar (just as Amitabh Bachchan's father was a poet whose pen name was Bachchan) and who also wrote more lyrical screenplays. It is just that their approach to story and dialogue was more urban and gritty. 'The moral dilemmas posed were very much of their time,' Javed Akhtar has said.[164] They were, to an extent, the dilemmas of South Asia's struggling migrant urban youth. (Do recall Vijay's patois. He is not from Maharashtra.) This was the first generation of migrants born in towns and cities, and they knew nothing else. Their language was terse – Javed was a master of understatement. '*Mere paas Ma hai*' ('I have our mother') in *Deewaar* is one of the best lines in Bombay cinema's history, and it exemplifies the style. Short sentences build tension, as every author knows. These films, therefore, had a heightened pressure about them, as if something were about to explode. The story allowed for periodic violent catharsis.

The 1980s were a turning point for Bombay cinema, which all but collapsed under the combined challenges of satellite TV, VCRs and widespread piracy. Profits, always on a knife edge, disappeared, particularly after Bachchan retired from the industry. How to fill a big hall when the gentry (as producers called them) could watch films in the comfort of their homes? Answer: by making what producers thought the non-gentry (front benchers) wanted: bad films. Even Shah Rukh Khan, whose star began to be seen dimly on the horizon, decries these films as 'trashy'. In essence, these are elitist judgements about audience taste within the industry. It led to a vicious circle: because directors thought the front benchers wanted trash, they gave them forgettable movies.

There were bright spots too in this era, which had something to do with the state getting involved (at last) in supporting high-quality non-commercial cinema ('to cultivate the taste of viewers', there's that myopia again!). In consequence, some directors made movies that were very different from mainstream cinema. Many were exceptional films. Perhaps because I am a scholar of partition, Shyam Benegal's *Mammo* (1994) was for me one of the most powerful of these films, and its border-crossing character Mammo, most relevant to the themes of this book. *Mandi* ('Market', 1983) is also exceptional. By the 1990s, film festivals screened the pick of these films from India and elsewhere. (See the Note on Further Viewing.)

I fear that by the 1980s, when I was in my twenties, I was the type of person who watched films only at film festivals. Or at special screenings. These were films for the classes, rather than the masses. My father had a place as a 'liberal' on the board of censors. (There was always the odd liberal or two on the board.) So I also got to see the emerging stars of the twenty-first century – for instance the late Rituparno Ghosh's *Unishe April* ('April Nineteenth', 1994).

But snobbery did not cause the problem of splintering audiences, although it accentuated it. Distributors baked it into the system by beginning to build multiplex theatres to win back the gentry. These multiplexes ran many movies at the same time for much smaller audiences.[165] (That spread risk, while driving up demand. 'House Full' was achieved so much more easily.) These theatres were pricey, fancy (as little Kartik would have said) and had all the high-end technology of the West (like Dolby and surround-sound). Tickets cost well above what even the lower-middle classes could afford. On sale were snacks with silly prices.

So the entire multiplex became 'the new dress circle'. The films they showed appealed to niche, rich, westernised audiences. The rest could not afford to go even if they were interested. Everyone, even the government, began to worry that popular cinema would crash out of existence or drown in sleazy money, so finally in 1992, after almost a century of struggling without it, the industry was given 'industry status'. Producers could now go to banks to borrow at reasonable rates, breaking one of the shackles that had held the industry down. It could finally appeal to government for customs relief on the import of raw stock. Both risks and costs could, they hoped, come down. And indeed, the large theatres of old continued to run well into the 2000s.

But what was going to bring the gentry with their DVDs off their sofas and back to the halls? New kinds of crowd-pleasers. Films that drew on the new strand of Hindu nationalism emerging as a cultural force at the time. Films that valorised Hindu tradition. Films that erased all markers of poverty from the plot. Gone are the fights, the wrestlers, the Baazigars, the sexy dance sequences. Films that celebrated family values now were in, and indeed saved the industry. Films that appealed to a diaspora (a market on which the industry's profit model increasingly relied) that wanted to feel good about being a hyphenated Indian/South Asian. At last, Bollywood became a bit more like Hollywood.

Films like *Hum Aapke Hain Koun!* ('Who Am I to You?', 1994), a movie that one critic decried as a long 'wedding video', which had family values at its heart, and no fewer than fourteen songs. *Dilwale Dulhania Le Jayenge* ('The Bravehearted Will Take Away His Bride', 1995) is another film in the same genre, except here the couple are in the diaspora. The two meet on a Eurorail tour, and fall in love. The girl has been 'promised' to another family in the Punjab, but Braveheart, played by Shah Rukh Khan, rejects the idea of an elopement. He is determined to win his girlfriend's father's blessing. Ouch. The film has run at Bombay's Maratha Mandir Theatre for twenty years and counting.

These are slick films: their cinematic standards are high.[166] But in my humble view they fed into the zeitgeist of the 1990s in India, when Hindu traditions mushroomed, and non-Hindus were nowhere in sight. This could hardly be more different from, say, *Amar Akbar Anthony*, a celebration of the diversity that made Bombay cinema what it was.

It would be a mistake to see these films as harmless froth. They may be sophisticated, but they are ugly.

The other kind of film that made it big in this period, in every kind of theatre, was hard-core in its nationalism. This was the era of films like *Border* (1997), *Roja* (1992) and *LOC: Kargil* (2003). The goodies in these movies are the Indian security forces. The baddies are Muslim terrorists (with presumed ties to Pakistan).[167]

Roja was a phenomenal success, not least because it announced the arrival (in Bombay) of an astonishing music director, A. R. Rahman. Its theme song is remarkable, unforgettable. And yet the plot, set in Kashmir, is red-fanged in its depiction of the Kashmir question. In *Roja*, Kashmir is the new Lanka.

I was talking about it last year (in the intensive care unit, of all places) to the bunch of Malayali nurses who had gathered to chat in my bay. I gave one the nickname Roja because she looked a lot like the actor Madhoo who played the part. This led us all first to burst into song (quietly, so that the doctors wouldn't hear) and then to discuss the movie. I said I loved the songs but not the movie. Why, they asked, astonished. I gave them the reasons I have mentioned above. Slowly they began to nod their heads. Kerala has one of the most diverse populations (in terms of religion) of all the states in India, and my nurse buddies were a mixed bunch of Christians, Muslims and Hindus. They got my point.

Roja highlighted new trends at the close of the century. A Tamil pan-Indian film, it was an ode to the beauty of a language other than Hindustani. It was patriotic in a way that few films before it were (but many were to become, as a matter of routine).

It was not set in Bombay, the cinematic city of old. Kashmir has ever been a locale in which actors had long 'run around trees' – it is a beautiful place, an ideal location for shooting romantic songs. But its filmic portrayals in the 1990s and since are of the new 'Lanka', places in which the lost, overwhelmed, good cops and officers seek out the baddie terrorist and his goons in their lair. Their Gabbar Singh is now often across the border, in Pakistan.

But Bollywood is hard to repress. These would not be the only films to come. *Ek Tha Tiger* ('There Was a Guy Called Tiger', 2012) was shot in Dublin, Istanbul and Havana. The action is at a whole new level; the cinematography pioneering. But it is the plot that makes it important here. 'Tiger' is an agent of RAW, India's foreign intelligence agency, well capable of taking on many opponents single-handed. He falls in love with Zoya, whom he discovers works for Pakistan's intelligence agency ISI. She in turn falls in love with him. The two make a desperate break for freedom. In so doing they break the Love Laws, and worse still, their respective duties to their services and their nations, which they repudiate 'until there is no need for the ISI and RAW'. It was the highest-grossing film of the year, and one of the biggest hitters of all time.

As this book goes to press, the film *Pathaan* (2023) – starring Shah Rukh Khan – is being received worldwide with rapturous enthusiasm. It too asks challenging questions about the Indian nation's relations with its citizens, its 'broken people', and its neighbours. Bollywood South Asia continues to resist jingoism more often than it perpetuates it. That South Asians adore these movies so much raises crucial questions about how successful the state has been in turning us all into the nation's narrow, and narrow-minded, torch bearers.

Epilogue

The first decades of the twenty-first century brought to South Asia some of the heaviest monsoons ever recorded. In 2014 torrential cloudbursts caused floods to breach high mountain lakes, affecting both parts of Kashmir.[1] Water gushed across national borders, seeming to mock man's hubris.

In 1947 a British lawyer drew borders in line for an empire in a hurry to quit; the nation states of South Asia have invested considerable resources in sealing them tight. But the South Asian environment resisted such frontier lines, even before the era of climate crisis. From one end of the subcontinent to the other, the Himalayas tower over man and his works. They are the product of a great collision many million years ago when the 'Indian plate' landmass floated into Eurasia. This crash created an unstable, quake-prone fault along its entire length. Because of it, both upper India and southern Pakistan judder in unison, wherever the epicentre of any particular earthquake may be. Lahore, Quetta, Islamabad and Rawalpindi in Pakistan; Srinagar, Delhi, even Bombay, in India; and Sylhet, Mymensingh, Dacca, Chittagong, Comilla and Tangail in Bangladesh – all are prone to seismic reminders that South Asians are together on that tectonic plate.

The British threw huge resources at trying to seal the Afghan border from British India by drawing out the Durand Line.[2] Yet both Afghanistan and Pakistan have disputed this mountainous border after 1947, and people and goods still cross it with ease.[3] Running through communities of Pashto-speakers and Balochis, it makes little sense on the ground. If neither side cooperates with the other, the writ of the state cannot run. And so, at the end of the twentieth century, 'Af-Pak' was, as the term suggested, a vast frontier zone, rather than an impassable wall.[4]

As for the long boundary between India and West Pakistan – running through forests, pastures, fields and deserts – neither state had the capacity to defend it until late in the century. Smugglers operated in concert on both sides from 1947 onwards.[5] Even as barbed-wire fences came up in the final decades of the century, so have drug- and gun-running cartels that circumvent them.[6] Local people on both sides seem happy enough to subvert the state for a living. *Aakhir*, in the end, both might ask, in the same language and register, what has the nation ever done for us?

Fencing in the eastern border was a low priority for the British, and so it remained for India until the turn of the century. It was just as well, because this wild and verdant landscape was not made for a *subarnarekha* (golden line).[7] Many parts of it were impassable. Great rivers moved at will across the Ganges-Brahmaputra delta.[8] In spate, they burst their banks, often with catastrophic effects. Sometimes they swallowed up land, bridges and even mountainsides; at other times, they shifted course, creating fertile new land where waters had once flowed. Islands rose and disappeared in the Bay of Bengal. Radcliffe had divvied up the Sundarban Islands between India and Pakistan – but where the line lay, no one knew. All was water, mud, salt and mangrove 'forests of tigers', with humans struggling to survive.[9] It was only at the end of the twentieth century that a serious effort began to be made to build a border fence on Indian territory in some flat zones near border checkpoints. Political reasons drove this: the aim was to keep 'Bangladeshi Muslim migrants' out of India.[10]

Yet the monsoons, whose caprices affect all parts of the subcontinent, do not respect flat border areas. And Bengal's monsoons are something to contend with, with climate change making the seasons ever more extreme. By 2006 they had become so heavy that many roads were under water for several months, and to travel any distance, people either took boats, or draped themselves in waterproofs as they carried their bikes on their backs across bamboo bridges.[11] If the heavens opened in Bangladesh, neighbouring parts of West Bengal in India got drenched too. Whatever the nation state demanded, monsoon winds would hardly meet border security at a checkpoint, be rebuffed and turn back, head bowed in resignation. No, the monsoon was more likely to smite that checkpoint in a dramatic electrical storm.

So it's not surprising that nation states have been more successful at fencing in people's minds. The independent states of the subcontinent waged a relentless battle to persuade South Asians that they were Indian or Pakistani or Bangladeshi. That they were all citizens of fundamentally different types of states, based on different ideals, and therefore as different from each other as honey and arsenic. One's own side, of course, was 'honey'.

This was crucial to both India and Pakistan in 1947. Both nation-state projects were fragile: citizenship in neither country could be defined by language, religion or ethnicity. Ties that held people together – kinship networks, languages and dialects, household and clan relations, even burial grounds – cut across boundary lines, making it 'unclear exactly why people ought to have innate appreciation' for the nation state over and above these other ties.[12]

For the most part, top-down dissemination of nation-building ideology was by education in schools or public display and discourse; sometimes it was by rumour and word of mouth. I do not suggest that these ideas of nationhood always pulled in the same direction, or that there were no tensions in the concept of each nation. There were plenty, as this book has shown. Despite these, though, the goal of all was to make us identify with a new national identity: we were 'Indians' or 'Pakistanis' (or later, 'Bangladeshis'), and we were now as different from one another as species were. Indeed, we were told that our neighbours posed an existential threat to our survival. 'At the stroke of the midnight hour', by some strange alchemy, our fellow subjects had turned into aliens and now they were out to get us. That concentrated minds, to be sure.

But to what extent were 'the people of the plate' manipulated? Did they roll over and buy it?

The mission of nationalist pedagogy, this book has suggested, was not as resounding a success as one might assume. The goal was to make us identify with a new national identity: we were to be either Indians or Pakistanis, polar opposites of each other. If we had doubts about that difference, there was that reminder – the Punjab riots. Here 'they' had showed their true colours, remember? Soon, it was all we recalled about partition, the peaceful migrations fading, as memories of routine time tend to do.

Yet even in the last decades of the twentieth century, the people of the divided subcontinent could read little, so textbook histories of the nation passed them by. Nationalist rituals performed at school too had little impact. And visits to museums and parades could hardly be made to reach more than a billion people. This is not to say that attempts at nation-making have not been persistent. They have also grown more powerful as the independent states have developed greater institutional reach over citizens' lives. Radio, cinema newsreels and national anthems entered the life-worlds of people who did not have the privilege of literacy: repetition works well in a society with strong oral traditions. 'War talk' has helped to circulate these notions more widely; to deny its impact would be naïve.

But it would be no less cavalier to imagine that midnight's children had forgotten, or could forget, the anguish of partition, of people, friends and landscapes lost, of homes and families divided.

Many people with such inconvenient memories endured the rest of the twentieth century with that sense of bereavement, of painful incompleteness, of not wholly understanding. And they remembered that people on the other side were human beings. That their schoolteachers and neighbours had been kind people. They remembered their playmates, wondering what had become of them.

These were difficult – even insurgent – memories.

Unlike these citizens with their awkward recollections, children were thought to be a tabula rasa. Perhaps they could be turned into model citizens of the nation state's design. Perhaps they would buy the alien theory. Readers, they did. Mea culpa: I raise my hand. Our *khaansama* told me that the rain flowed back to the heavens in Pakistan, that its people ate with their elbows – and I believed him. I was all but seven years old then: it was the year of the Bangladeshi Liberation War – a big year for war talk.

But the process of education did not end at the school gates. I had the good fortune to go to university, where I discovered that not only were we all human beings – not an alien in sight – but we South Asians were *more like each other* than we resembled other people. We used the same spices in our cooking, liked the same flavours and preferred similar fabrics. And as I continued to learn through work and teaching, we laughed at the same jokes and shared the same assumptions about many things – not least when it came to hospitality and friendship. We dropped by uninvited, watched the same movies, adored the same stars, and argued about politics all the time. A great number appreciated the finer points of cricket. We still do all this today (despite the fact that cricket itself has changed).

This is not to claim that there have been no differences between

India and Pakistan, or between these two states and Bangladesh. I suggest, however, that to depict their relationship as an 'enduring conflict',[13] or a 'conflict unending'[14] mired in 'intractable' differences,[15] the inevitable consequence of the subcontinent's 'incomplete partition',[16] is not only hyperbolic: it concentrates on the glass half empty.[17]

There is, of course, that hoary old chestnut: the dispute over Kashmir. At the time of partition a Hindu maharaja ruled this Muslim-majority princely state (in this sense it was a mirror image of Hyderabad, but contiguous to Pakistan). For various reasons, including the deeds of non-state actors, the maharaja tried to crush an uprising in Poonch, a part of Kashmir hostile to his rule, after which 'raiders' from that region began to fight back. Other armed groups joined them as they began to invade and pillage other parts of the region; it became the site of tensions between the two countries.[18] India's approach was to repel the 'invaders', with limited success. It is not clear when Pakistan began to strengthen the raiders' hand by backing them with munitions, but it is almost certain that they did. By January 1948 the dispute had been referred to the United Nations. The actual war between the armed forces of the two countries only began on 11 December that year, and 'the guns fell silent' on 31 December, a mere twenty days later.[19] Both sides agreed to observe the Line of Actual Control (LOC) – the line at which the two armies stood down. This was still the de facto border in 2000.

The dispute is complicated by the fact that the two nations are not the only parties in it. There are the local raiders from Poonch and their motley supporters, the representatives of Azad Kashmir (the part of the state on Pakistan's side of the LOC). And there was Sheikh Abdullah (1905–82), the charismatic leader of the National Conference party, who claimed to represent Kashmiri interests in Indian Jammu and Kashmir, and indeed the state of Kashmir as a whole. This mélange of non-state actors proved not to be amenable to solutions proposed by either nation state.

Frustrated with the lack of progress in bilateral and multilateral talks, Pakistan launched a second Kashmir war in 1965, this one lasting forty-seven days.[20] Pakistan's president, General Ayub Khan, tried to use a perceived window of opportunity – China's defeat of India in 1962 – to change the realities on the ground in Pakistan's favour.[21] He failed.

And so the dispute has carried on, with both sides insisting that their version of events was the truth. But questions remain. Had the maharaja acceded to India when the raiders were reaching Srinagar? Were they backed by the Pakistani state and, if so, how, and at what stage? Was India a victim of an invasion, defending its sovereign territory, as it insists? Or did India intervene in Kashmir before its accession: in which case, did India act lawfully? India failed to grant a plebiscite in Kashmir (having at first promised one); Pakistan has since insisted that such a plebiscite is necessary. Many of the finer points are technical but, in essence, the dispute hinges on the question of sovereignty. Did India have sovereign authority over Kashmir in September 1947, when the invasion began?[22] Like everything else, it is unclear, and so the problem drags on.

There were no more wars over Kashmir for the rest of the century, yet it would be facile to suggest that the spectre of Kashmir does not loom large in both national imaginaries. It remains a screen onto which both nation states project their own notions of sovereignty, national identity, border truth, border governance and border anxiety. Divided Kashmir of course has its own populations and displaced people who, over the course of fifty-odd years, developed their own fractured, impassioned and shifting responses to their situation. All these have helped make a complex issue toxic.

The most significant war of them all, in December 1971, had nothing to do with Kashmir. After Pakistan's military crackdown in East Pakistan began in March 1971, Mukti Bahini forces were among the ten million refugees who spilled over the border into India. India played no official role in the conflict – let's be clear that it was Bangladeshi people fighting for the liberation of their own country. Until December that year, Mrs Gandhi's chief goal was to persuade the international community to urge Pakistan to cease and desist in its internal repression of Bengalis. She got nowhere. The US president Richard Nixon was too busy trying to open talks with China, through General Ayub, to pay heed even to his own envoy's 'blood telegrams'.[23] And the West followed Nixon. It was this failure, and India's growing panic over the refugee crisis, that led to the brief Indo–Pak war that followed.

That Indian forces assisted Mukti Bahini irregulars with shelter, training and provisions is common knowledge. So too did many ordinary people, shocked by the refugees' situation and their stories. Indians on East Pakistan's border acted as the Bengali fighters' supply line. In December 1971, India finally engaged Pakistan in battle. The third Indo–Pak war, which led to Pakistan's swift capitulation, lasted all of eleven days.

The wars between these 'implacable enemies' were brief. They lasted 168 days in the twentieth century, if we take into account the short war in Kargil (of which more below). I am not saying they were not important but unlike, say, the Vietnam War or the Afghan wars, they were over in the blink of an eye – despite all the talk of South Asia being the most dangerous place in the world.

In South Asia, then, there's a long era of 'not-war' to account for – or, dare I say it, of pragmatic peace. There's been a lot of hold-me-back-or-I'll-hit-you posturing, but even when that talk grew hysterical, the two countries strove hard not to hit each other.

Of those not-war situations, a prolonged, if little-known, dispute was over the rivers of the Indus basin. In the hurtle towards the partition deadline, administrators representing the two sides had agreed that the Indus river's tributaries on the Indian side would continue to supply British-built canals in Pakistan. But when the standstill agreements between the two countries ended in March 1948, this deal ended too, and some engineers in Indian Punjab thought it was a bright idea to turn the taps off. A million acres of Pakistani farmland faced drought.[24]

Though the water supply was soon restored, this incident was enough to cause Pakistan's leaders severe and lasting anxiety about their downstream status in the new order of things.[25] The subsequent Indo–Pak agreement over the Indus waters took so long to achieve in part because the river and canal system is so intricate (one river, with seventeen tributaries including the 'five rivers of the Punjab', in a river basin of 430,000 square miles, criss-crossed with an intricate system of canals and their headworks); in part because India held the advantageous upstream position while Pakistan depended far more upon these waters for irrigation; and in part because one arm of the river flowed through Kashmir.

Despite all these complexities, however, the two countries settled the dispute in the Indus Waters Treaty in 1960.[26] It is a strange agreement in that it shares the resource not on the basis of volumes of water but on the river's geographical location. That neither side got everything they wanted is a good sign: it tells you a great deal about the will to resolve issues by mutual compromise.[27]

It is to this more than half-full glass that I want to draw your attention in this final section of the book. Statesmen, bureaucrats and officers replenished it quietly, behind the scenes, so it never grabbed the headlines.

Politicians discovered that there were significant areas that required mutual cooperation, even during the first dark weeks after partition. The tidal waves of migration that threatened to overwhelm both nations straight after independence were primary among them. These tsunamis elicited surprisingly symmetrical responses in India and Pakistan, as discussed in Chapter 4. They also obliged the two countries to work together in efforts to stem the flows.

It is worth looking in some detail at the proceedings of the first inter-dominion conference held in Calcutta in April 1948, for it is here that Indo–Pak bilateral 'quiet diplomacy' first emerged. We are lucky to have a full stenographic record of every word that was exchanged at these meetings, over a period of two days, between the representatives of India and Pakistan.

Once the decision to divide India was announced on 3 June 1947, an enormous amount of work had to be done at breakneck speed to achieve the partition of British India and the transfer of power by 15 August. The Partition Council established a Partition Secretariat of expert committees, but the critical negotiations between the two sides took place in a Steering Committee headed by two senior civil servants, H. M. Patel and Chaudhri Muhammad Ali. As the latter recalled with some pride, the two bureaucrats 'were able to reach agreement in their recommendations over a considerable area . . . and the Steering Committee . . . was successful in reaching agreement on the bulk of unsettled points'.[28]

Yet despite the achievements of this remarkable duo, serious differences emerged between the two sides. Arriving at a mutually acceptable division of the assets (and liabilities) of British India proved challenging. In the matter of giving to Pakistan its share of the common pool of resources, India's Home Minister Vallabhbhai Patel deployed India's considerable advantage – physical control over the assets – to impose hard bargains on Pakistan. Even after India agreed, in December 1947, to accept Pakistan's claims to a portion of the public finance and the cash balances, Patel still refused to transfer any monies.[29] It was only in January 1948, after Gandhi undertook his last fast to compel the government of India to honour its commitments, that Patel reluctantly released monies to Pakistan. (As we know, Gandhi paid with his life for taking Pakistan's side on this issue.)

It seems rather curious that the Congress leadership, having insisted in the critical end game on a limited partition of the subcontinent, was so reluctant to countenance its fiscal, strategic and material implications. Insofar as the leadership had any clear plan for the way forward, the strategy (if such inchoate thinking can be elevated to that status) seems to have been based on two assumptions: first, 'that Pakistan was economically and financially . . . unviable', and in consequence, that it would soon collapse and 'return' to India.[30] (Nehru made remarks to the press about the partition being 'temporary' at this time.) Some of those pressing India's case in the division of spoils seemed ready to hasten Pakistan's collapse by denying it the wherewithal to establish itself; their plan thereafter was to force Pakistan back into the union, on India's terms. Certainly this is how it appeared to most contemporary observers, and not only those fighting Pakistan's corner.

Such evidence as there is seems to suggest that neither side had thought through what its national interest might be with respect to the other country in the fraught and chaotic aftermath of 3 June. To the extent that anyone had a plan, it seems to have been rather crude and basic: both concentrated simply on getting (or holding on to, as the case may be) as large a share as possible of the resources of British India, with little thought for anything else, in the spirit of letting the devil take the hindmost. And at this point, most Congress leaders had no intention of lifting a finger to help Pakistan get established.

In their different ways, both the Muslim League and the Congress had embryonic foreign policies before 1947, or at least had articulated points of view on the wider world. Their policies shared common ground, posited as both were on ideologies of anti-imperialism: the Congress and the League had espoused the cause of fellow subjects of colonial oppression, all the way from South Africa to Palestine and the Holy Places of Islam. Yet understandably, neither side had formulated a foreign policy towards the other before June 1947, since for a decade and more, they had got used to parleying with each other as political parties within the unified state structure of British India.

The partition negotiations were bitter and angry. The dealings of the party leaders with each other were characterised not by a spirit of give and take, but by the assumptions of a zero-sum game. (Kashmir is a legacy of that period.) At that moment, neither India nor Pakistan seemed to appreciate that they had to evolve ways of living together as neighbouring nation states in a changing and challenging world.

This approach began to change once violence swept over North India and the Punjab, and as Hindus, Sikhs and Muslims began to flee their homes on both sides of the new borders in the west in huge numbers. It was only on 17 August 1947 that the Boundary Commission's demarcation of the borders between India and Pakistan became public. Radcliffe's cartography had left minorities stranded on both sides of the Great Divide. Now, from mid-August to December 1947, the plains of North India witnessed ferocious outbreaks of civil disturbance – murder, pillage, rape and arson – in the main, though not only, in the divided province of Punjab. Hindus and Sikhs in the North West Frontier Province and West Punjab, Muslims in East Punjab, and Muslim Meos in the princely states in Bharatpur, Alwar and Faridkot all rushed across the border to seek the protection of the 'right' nation state, but found themselves even more vulnerable to attack in their convoys and refugee camps. Huge numbers left their homes and congregated in areas still on the same side of the border, but in places where their co-religionists were more numerous, seeking safety in numbers. Most still hoped to return home when 'normality' was restored.[31]

Both new governments had to respond at once to these challenges. Both recognised that restoring order was vital for the survival of their nations. Both saw at once that they would need each other's help if their response was to be effective. On 29 August, just six weeks after independence and partition, Liaquat Ali Khan and Nehru issued a joint statement that 'illegal seizure of property [would] not be recognized and both Governments [would] take steps to look after the property of refugees and restore it to its rightful owners'. The next day, they embarked together on a joint four-day 'peace tour' of the riot-torn areas.[32]

On 3 September, the two sides agreed to replace the failing Punjab Boundary Force with a new Military Evacuation Organisation (MEO), charged with protecting the refugees and escorting them safely across the borders.[33] On 9 September 1947, the Pakistan government in West Punjab appointed a custodian of evacuee property.

By ordinance, it charged the custodian with the duty 'within the area placed in his charge to take possession of the property and effects of evacuees and to take such measures as he considers necessary or expedient for preserving such property or effects'. East Punjab in India quickly followed suit.[34]

No sooner had Nehru returned to Delhi, however, than fierce communal riots broke out there too and mass exoduses began. The Punjab measures had to be extended to the capital city, and then to Bharatpur, Alwar and Bikaner as well.[35] In effect, both governments had been forced to recognise that these massive exchanges of population could not be reversed.

This realisation had an immediate impact on the tenor and substance of India–Pakistan relations. Over the next few months, representatives of the two countries had to meet several times to resolve problems arising from what were now state-sanctioned and state-assisted migrations – a repeat of the Lausanne Treaty but on a much vaster scale.[36] At a series of key (but little-known) conferences, they agreed to adopt common mechanisms for 'the evaluation of property on each side, the exchange of property records, settling the areas to which evacuee property legislation was to apply, and making arrangements regarding moveable property'.[37]

Chaudhri Muhammad Ali, who was closely involved on the Pakistan side in these decisions, recalled that 'arrangements *in concert with India* had to be made for all manner of things. From recovery of abducted women to the protection of sacred places . . .'[38] A spirit of compromise emerged as India and Pakistan, seeing they were in the same boat, realised that they had to work together to prevent that vessel from sinking.

By late October 1948, hostilities in Kashmir had escalated into open war between India and Pakistan. Yet war didn't stop these negotiations: as Ali noted, the controversial settlement over the cash balances was reached while 'the hostilities in Kashmir were in progress'.[39] What's more, neither side could afford to let the Kashmir crisis interfere with the urgent task of containing the migrations and managing refugee populations, whose number exceeded fourteen million by the winter of 1947.

By December, the MEO had evacuated most of the refugees in the two Punjabs and Delhi, and it appeared that the crisis was over. The Joint Defence Council had wound itself up in November. Yet no sooner had things begun to settle down in the northern and western tracts of the subcontinent than riots broke out in the east.

This was the context in which the first of hundreds of inter-dominion conferences took place, in Calcutta in April 1948. India and Pakistan had held several meetings to discuss arrangements in respect of the Punjab refugees and other matters, chaired either by the British military commander Claude Auchinleck or by Mountbatten himself.[40] The Calcutta Conference was different. It was the first 'international' encounter between the leaders of India and Pakistan, at which envoys from the two countries faced each other across the table without a white man in the chair.[41]

The agenda before them was:

- To discuss the causes of the present exodus of non-Muslims from Eastern Pakistan and Muslims from West Bengal and action necessary to create conditions in Eastern Pakistan and West Bengal which will make it possible for non-Muslims and Muslims respectively to continue to live there
- To discuss steps necessary to induce evacuees from Eastern Pakistan and West Bengal to return home and other ancillary action.[42]

This remit shows that neither side could countenance a reprise of Punjab. The delegates' goal was thus to agree the ways to create peaceful conditions on both sides of the border that would encourage Bengali minorities to remain at home, and allow those refugees who had already left to return home. The transcript of their discussions allows us, like flies on the wall, to see how they went about the business of producing peace.

At first, it seems remarkable that the conference succeeded. The meeting began with a furious outburst from Pakistan's Ghulam Muhammad about the Assam government's policy of 'pushing out' Muslim migrants into East Bengal. Indian Assam's Chief Minister, Gopinath Bardoloi, reacted with rage, insisting on his government's right to evict 'illegal' settlers. Only minutes after the conference began, Bardoloi threatened to walk out. He was persuaded to stay, after others around the table – both Indian and Pakistani – brokered a compromise by which all agreed to defer discussion of the Assam question to a later date. They thus prevented the collapse of the conference before any of the main issues had even begun to be addressed.[43]

Deferral was a strategy that the delegates used more than once over the course of the conference; indeed, it would become standard strategy in the strange and secret history of Indo–Pakistani cooperation. It was an important device that laid the basis for continued dialogue. Crucially, it presumed that the two sides would continue to talk to each other, and settle differences between themselves through discussion. The doors between India and Pakistan were thus never slammed shut.

Agreement was more quickly achieved once delegates began to speak to each other as members of the same social class, with common material interests and a common stake in a mutually beneficial settlement. One such instance was on the question of the scope of the proposed Evacuee Property Management Boards.

The two sides had agreed to set up these boards for the express purpose, as their name suggests, of protecting and managing the property of refugees who had fled their homes, since both India and Pakistan were keen that they should return home. However, H. M. Patel, the leading bureaucrat advising the politicians in the Indian delegation, proposed the word 'evacuee' in the agreement be replaced with the word 'minority'.

This amusing yet revealing exchange followed:

The Hon'ble Mr Neogy [India]: It is not evacuees who own property there.

The Hon'ble Mr Ghulam Muhammad [Pakistan]: I think there are men like Mr Kiran Sankar Roy and Mr Nalini Ranjan Sarkar [both prominent Hindu politicians who had vast estates in East Bengal, Pakistan] who own property there. They can keep their agents.

[. . .]

The Hon'ble Mr Ghulam Muhammad [Pak]: I do not want it to be made a sort of Court of Wards.

[. . .]

The Hon'ble Mr Nazimuddin [Pak]: You yourself suggested when this was discussed that it must be a question of people who have gone temporarily. We ought not to think of permanent absentees.

The Hon'ble Mr Hamidul Huq Choudhury [Pak]: *I have got some property in Kalimpong [India]. Will this Committee manage that property?*

The Hon'ble Mr Neogy [Ind]: Yes, certainly . . . I know of any numbers of landlords and businessmen who have never crossed the Padma, although they own property in East Bengal.[44] But having regard to the circumstances it may easily be imaginable that they may find it difficult to get assistance from their normal agents. In such cases they may avail of this statutory board.

The Hon'ble Mr Ghulam Muhammad [Pak]: We are considering here to safeguard the property of those people who have left against their wishes. You want to bring in all sorts of people ... so far I have received no complaint [from such people]. If you have any data, send [it] to me ...

The Hon'ble Mr Neogy [Ind]: *I have some personal property.*

The Hon'ble Mr Ghulam Muhammad [Pak]: Men like you [by remaining resident in East Pakistan] would have served us in a higher position and we are being deprived of that benefit. So we think these cases should be punished! (Laughter).[45]

Soon after, both sides accepted the revised clause. (I hope you got the joke, even if you aren't part of that elite South Asian world.)

They also swiftly agreed to the provision in the agreement to 'curb tendencies' against 'economic boycott and strangulation'. Here the discussion hinged on cases, on both sides, of unfair or excessive income tax demands levied upon individual members of the minority communities. Once again, there was much laughter and mutual leg-pulling, references to common acquaintances who had fallen foul of the tax-man, and jokes about rapacious finance ministers. ('The Hon'ble Mr Nazimuddin [Pak]: You don't know what the Finance Ministers have [up] their sleeves!') Not surprisingly, it did not take long for the two delegations to achieve 'absolute agreement in the matter'.[46]

Both sides also helped ease tensions by distancing themselves and their own class from any responsibility for the communal violence and discrimination against the minorities. It suited the delegates to insist that it was people lower down the social scale, and refugees themselves, who were to blame for the bigotry, the violence, which they as 'civilised' men had a common duty to stamp out. As Hamidul Huq Choudhury put it, 'nobody occupying high position can ever think of molesting or injuring the interests of the minorities ... It is generally the petty officers who [are] being misled by false patriotic feelings [and] are responsible for all this mischief ...' And 'it is only some [Muslim refugee] people who have gone from the Indian Union and who are themselves in difficulty about their own prospects, who are irritated for the sufferings they have undergone – it is they who are contributing ... to the problem'.[47]

By the evening of the second day of the conference, the delegates had relaxed into a mood of mutual trust, good humour and ease. Indeed, at several points that afternoon, they appear to have forgotten that they were at an international conference and not at a social occasion in the company of *bondhu-baandhob*, friends and equals. That night, when the meeting broke off for refreshments and dinner, there was time for *adda*, fabulous food (all loved their fish), jokes and laughter. As South Asians of a 'genteel' type, they shared the same good sense of humour.

Yet all the bonhomie should not blind us to the utmost seriousness of the decisions that were made at this conference, which were:

- To protect [the] life and property of minorities
- To safeguard their civic and cultural rights
- To discourage propaganda for the amalgamation of India and Pakistan
- To warn government servants against dereliction of duty towards minorities, towards creation of fear and apprehension in their minds
- To curb tendencies towards economic boycott and strangulation of their normal life
- Setting up of Evacuee Property Management Boards in districts or areas from which a substantial exodus had taken place
- To postpone discussion of the question of Muslim migration between Assam and East Bengal to a separate Inter-Dominion conference
- Pending this, not to take any action to force or precipitate migration to one province from the other on a mass scale.[48]

Nor should we forget that while these elite representatives of the states understood the critical underpinnings of their mutuality, it remained important to both their nation-building projects that the *pablik* should not know. These talks remained secretive, below the radar.

After Calcutta, the 'reciprocity of national interest' began to sink in among the leaders of the two new nation states. If neither nation could secure peace and stability at home without the cooperation of the other, it followed that when push came to shove, both India and Pakistan needed each other. And they needed each other not only to survive, but to be stable, to have viable economies, and to be strong

enough to protect their more vulnerable minority citizens, who might
be minded to flee across borders at the first hint of trouble. Only collaboration could prevent mass migration. In fact, ensuring Pakistan's
stability and survival now became the highest priority, bar none, of
India's foreign policy. And in an awesome (but veiled) symmetry,
India's stability and survival were also a necessity for Pakistan. All
Vallabhbhai Patel's threats to beggar Pakistan would henceforth be
just that: empty threats. India could not survive Pakistan's collapse,
and its leaders knew that.

Once this point is recognised, it should no longer come as a surprise
that both countries signed up to the Calcutta Agreement, or that the
troubles over jute that had threatened trade in March 1948 were settled at a new trade agreement months later.[49] Their trade relations
with each other were, of course, crucial for their economic survival,
because India bought sixty per cent of Pakistan's exports and supplied
forty-three per cent of her imports.[50] Nor should it astonish us to discover that in the matter of minority rights and refugee rehabilitation,
the two countries produced a whole series of entirely identical laws
and regulations, and that they did so in tandem (see Table 1). For
each, its domestic policies on these questions were irretrievably tied
up with the priorities in its foreign policies towards the other.

Table 1

Legislation and agreements regarding refugees and evacuees in
India and Pakistan, 1947–54

Liaquat–Nehru declaration establishing custodians of evacuee property	India, September 1947	Pakistan, September 1947
Joint Defence Council decision to establish the Military Evacuation Organisation	India, September 1947	Pakistan, September 1947
Calcutta Agreement (discussed)	India, April 1948	Pakistan, April 1948
Permit ordinances (requiring permits for travel across borders)	India, July 1948	Pakistan, October 1948
Evacuee Property Ordinance: all evacuee property to be captured by the custodian of evacuee property, for the settlement of refugees	India, June 1948	-------

Karachi Agreement	India, January 1949	Pakistan, January, 1949
Evacuee Property Act: (Ordinance ratified by parliament)	India, April 1950	Pakistan, April 1950
Liaquat–Nehru Pact: No War Pact after further outbreak of riots in both Bengals	India, 1950	Pakistan, 1950
Passports introduced for travel across India–Pakistan border	India, October 1952	Pakistan, October 1952
Displaced Persons (Compensation and Rehabilitation) Act: evacuee property 'pooled' to provide resources for refugee rehabilitation	India, 1954	Pakistan, 1954

And so the pattern has continued well beyond 1960, when India and Pakistan signed the Indus Waters Treaty. Even after two further wars between India and Pakistan and the creation of Bangladesh, cooperation was much in evidence when, in 1966, India and Pakistan signed the Tashkent Declaration (which sought to create a framework for lasting peace). Even after the 1971 War and the birth of Bangladesh, this spirit of mutuality was alive and well. A year later India and Pakistan signed the Simla Accord of 1972, which promoted friendly relations between them. In 1974, India and Bangladesh agreed on a comprehensive resolution to their disputes (more on this below).

Today these agreements are public, well-known if controversial milestones of public diplomacy. Although governments do not permit scholars to extend their research into quiet diplomacy far beyond the early years, ethnographic research reveals that it continued. Mutual arrangements for the travel of pilgrims, and the protection of sacred spaces, survived late into the century.[51]

None of this is intended to suggest that conflict has played no part in the relationship between India and Pakistan. But the point is that both sides knew that each of these conflicts had to be resolved, or at least contained. Moreover, the areas of conflict – the 'ignoble fratricidal strife' on which most observers have been wont to concentrate – must be understood within the context of the large and significant areas of agreement between the two countries.

Scholars have pointed to the paradox that the three Indo–Pakistani conflicts of 1947–8, 1965 and 1971 'were all characterised by a low threshold of violence, limited scope and short duration'.[52] We might add here the Kargil war of 1999, a quarrel over a single uninhabited spur of the Karakoram range: Pakistani troops allegedly tried to encroach on Indian-held parts of that jagged mountain outcrop, and Indian forces (again allegedly) repelled them. Each side has its own narrative.

To recall a metaphor used by another historian of South Asia, each was like 'a Dussehera duel', in which the two sides were locked 'in motionless and simulated combat'. The hidden history of collaboration suggests why this should be so. A full war between India and Pakistan is one that neither side can afford to win.

But what of Bangladesh? As ever, it plays its own hand. Here perceptions of Pakistan were, for a long time, shaped by its bloody Liberation War, and have been (for the most part) hostile. India has been viewed (for the most part) as a friend, despite Mrs Gandhi's callous repatriation of millions of refugees.[53] But with Sheikh Mujib's assassination and the rise of General Zia-ur Rahman, things became more complex, at least on the level of high policy that makes the headlines. The Bangladesh Nationalist Party (BNP) has a different line on India (and indeed on Pakistan) than the Awami League. So high policy waxes and wanes with the ups and downs of competing party politics.

On the boundary between Bangladesh and India, there is another dispute over river waters, this time over the Ganges. It is a long-standing, post-partition disagreement, batted into the long grass by Pakistan, but taken up in 1973 by Sheikh Mujibur Rahman and Indira Gandhi. Their comprehensive solution of 1974 gave India what it needed: dry-season water to flush clean the river Hooghly, a key tributary which flows through Calcutta, of some of its huge deposits of silt which have been choking the city's port for a century.

But the Farakka Barrage in India became a bone of contention after Sheikh Mujib's assassination, as Bangladesh's new leaders contended that it diverted flows that would have otherwise watered its peasants' fields. The Awami League and the BNP have rather different views on the issue. For the BNP the Indira–Mujib comprehensive solution worked better for India than it did for Bangladesh, and must be revisited. The two countries, meanwhile, continue to need the Ganges waters for different reasons: India to revitalise one of its key ports; Bangladesh for irrigating its farms and fields. By the turn of the century, climate change was bringing in high tides that bathed fields in salt, making the problem more acute for peasants in Bangladesh. That could have turned the disagreement into a flashpoint between a small country and its larger neighbour.

But Farakka is a modest skirmish. The dispute's details are barely known; it hardly figures in the Indian national imaginary. People in Delhi still ask me 'What? Where?' when I mention Farakka. (I have known about it since I was sentient, since it is less than fifty miles from Hill Cart Road. I witnessed its construction from the vantage point of my father's shoulders.)

The Farakka issue is well enough known in divided Bengal but it doesn't have much impact on relations between the two countries.[54] Indo–Bangla trade was healthy in 2000; and at the time of writing there is talk of a most-favoured-nation trade agreement between India and Bangladesh. (Needless to say, illicit trade, aka smuggling, also flourished here after partition, and remained healthy throughout the century.)[55]

Here too there is the detritus of partition, however. There are people – Muslims of course – whom India contends are not its citizens and regularly pushes over the Bangladesh border, forcing them 'home'. These frightened folk insist that they were born in India and produce documents to back up their claim, to no avail. Bangladesh protests, but in moderation. A small country with high revenues from migrants abroad, emigration is part of its idea of where it sits in the world. It thus refuses to have (now electrified) border fences on its territory, but raised no hue and cry when India built its own fence. It refused, in a quiet way, to cooperate with India on border control.

I do not suggest that the three countries see eye to eye, or even that their ruling parties share the same views about the neighbourhood. They do not. But warts and all, neighbourly relations – however tense or practical – were more important to them than their relationship with the rest of the world.

The neighbourhood was not an island unto itself, however.

India and Pakistan were both born during the Cold War, as was Bangladesh. While most think of that war as being confined to the United States, western and eastern Europe, and the USSR, it was in fact a global conflict, in which both blocs competed in the Third World (as it was then known) to gain strategic benefit over their rival.[56]

It follows that right through the Cold War, both the United States and the USSR (and later China) made overtures to the nation states of South Asia. The received wisdom is that India leaned towards the Soviets (or was in their pocket), while Pakistan was in cahoots with the Americans.

I fear I am going to say what I tend to say about such 'wisdoms': they miss the point, and make marshmallow out of layer cake.

Both India and Pakistan pursued a policy of anti-imperialism in global forums, both tended to vote the same way in the UN General Assembly. Both were at the Bandung Conference in Indonesia in 1955, regarded as the foundation of the non-aligned movement. Furthermore, for the critical decades before perestroika, they were non-aligned with either bloc. (Indeed, this was the case despite Pakistan's membership of the western Southeast Asia Treaty Organization defence bloc from 1954 to 1977. Pakistan's relations with the United States were more complex and shifting than is often understood.)

I suggest that the South Asian states' non-alignment was driven by the pragmatic need not to be too attached to one superpower so that that relationship prevented them from staying aligned (quietly) with the other.[57] That had to be their first priority.

If, in consequence, they were wooed (and misunderstood) by both sides – and they were – they both took what they could, when they could, from food to arms.[58] Both India's and Pakistan's relations with the western and eastern blocs were opportunistic, if 'supple'.[59]

So Nehru accepted food aid from the Americans and MiG fighter planes from the Soviets. Pakistan played both the Soviets and Americans against each other and the Chinese – until increasing pressure in the late 1950s began to draw it closer to the Americans, who had always been more interested in Pakistan's potential for airbases than India's dominant position in the Indian Ocean. Latterly, Pakistan has paid a high price in terms of sovereignty, vis-à-vis the United States, which has sought to influence its domestic affairs. Meanwhile, to counterbalance this, Pakistan pursued good relations with Beijing. Some now worry about an over-reliance on Beijing, but this is not a new anxiety. British Foreign Office documents reveal that Pakistan developed a subtle and astute foreign policy from its earliest days, and was aware of both the dangers and possibilities of its geographically divided setting. Friendship with China was a way of shoring up the defence of its eastern wing.

Yet Pakistan's relationship with 'Red' China did not sit well with the Americans, and so Pakistan's early rapport with the superpower was not all smooth sailing. Its 'always already' attachment to the United States is a post-facto narrative, and a persistent one at that. History, as ever, is more complex.

India also pursued peace with China. Sadly for India, China did not share its goodwill, settling its own border disputes with India instead by war in 1962.[60] As the century drew to a close, India permitted US jets refuelling rights during the Iraq War. There had been glasnost and perestroika, and the United States had emerged (if only for a brief period) as global hegemon. India's dependency on petrodollars brought it to its knees in the 1990s, and with petrodollars came debt to the International Monetary Fund – a hard bank that imposed western economic logic upon the Indian economy.

So of course both countries have had to continue to respond to these shifting global balances of power, as nimbly as they could. Their responses to the superpowers could have spooked each other, had it not been for all that 'track two' below-the-radar talking. India and Pakistan quietly continued to sign agreements, settle border disputes and discuss other mutual business with each other, week after week, month after month.[61] They still have a lot of talking to do.

Meanwhile, what's known as 'people-to-people' contact started to build up in the late twentieth century. Once it had been easy only for pilgrims to travel to holy places across the borders. More and more, others began to travel too, a process that snowballed with the establishment of the Samjhauta Express bus service between Attari and Lahore in 1977. By 2005, the number of such services connecting the two countries had multiplied, and there was just no stopping the travellers.

Some refugees went to the places where they were born, and were overwhelmed by the warmth of the welcome. Soon there were thousands, then tens of thousands, *lakhs*, of returnees. By the late 1990s and early 2000s, the memories of partition refugees, and their stories of return, reverberated among those who wanted to hear them. Even L. K. Advani, refugee leader of the Rath Yaatra – passionate hater of the Babri Mosque and all it had stood for – was changed by a five-day visit to Pakistan.[62]

As for a mere scholar like me – although interested in partition, I was not a refugee, evacuee or returnee – I developed a profound desire to hear these stories, and to see the 'others' with my own eyes. I first travelled to Bangladesh, where I was overwhelmed by the hospitality of strangers, who took me into their own home, looked after me as a daughter, and plied me with fish curry. And then to western Pakistan, across the Wagah border. I mingled in Lahore with scholars and students; to this day, I receive presents from Syed Babar Ali, the founder of Lahore University of Management Science. He, too, had once been a stranger. This wise and remarkable man adopted me, in a trice, as a friend.

I was hardly alone in wondering at this warmth. Truth be told, there was a part of me that had bought the idea – received from an aunt or a schoolmaster – that 'we' Indians were hospitable because we received visitors like gods. It turns out that despite the fact that many South Asians across the border know no God but Allah, they did know about hospitality.

Given all these first-hand encounters, the growing circles of warmth they have generated prove harder to repress. And unlike the top-secret track two diplomacy, they can't be hidden away from the *pablik*.

In 1999, as we have seen, there was a short war in Kargil over that outcrop. In the same decade, both India and Pakistan engaged in nuclear testing, with Pakistan's Chagai-I a response to India's Pokhran-II. Yet in 2004, as each country raced towards the target of missile delivery capability, they set up a direct 'nuke hotline' to communicate with each other. In the same vein, they had also agreed to alert the other side to conventional troop movements so as not to mistake routine training for war preparation.

I was teaching at the International History Department at the London School of Economics at the time, where my colleagues kept abreast of international affairs. (It was very different, in this sense, from Cambridge's Faculty of History.) When news of the hotline broke, a senior professor rushed up to me, his fine face etched with alarm, and pressed me for my view. Was India or Pakistan likely to push the red button?

'Relax,' I replied. 'No. The leaders of both countries are sensible human beings. They depend on the stability of the other. Both know that if they "nuke" Delhi or Lahore they would cause millions of deaths and catastrophic refugee flows. The powers that be in India and Pakistan are not stupid. They are no more insane than the leaders of any other country that has nuclear weapons.'

(This is not to suggest that nuclear armament, testing, proliferation and deployment are not in themselves insane, but that's another story.)

So despite all the shouty talk about eternal enmity, all the posturing, the war talk and the flag-waving, South Asia is not the most dangerous place on the planet.

Some people describe this region in more positive terms, as the most interesting place in the world. Whether they are right, I cannot say: it is an impossible claim to test. But South Asia is so surprising, so fascinating, so intricate and so disturbing that I, for one, remain spellbound, still powered by the drive to understand it all. Despite knowing that such comprehension is impossible, I continue to search for it like a meal moth battering itself on a hurricane lamp. I seek light, I see shadows. More and more questions reveal themselves in the small arc lit up by the lantern's light. Are there answers somewhere in the gloaming?

This book, I hope, conveys some sense of my compulsion to understand. If I have passed a little of it on to you, the endeavour will have been worth it.

A Note on Further Viewing

ARTHOUSE

This book has referred to many films. Not all are of the Bombay cinema variety, which Chapter 7 discusses. Many belong to the arthouse or parallel cinema genre (bearing in mind that the boundary between the two is porous).

So arthouse seems a good place to start.

(Note: this is my personal take. I speak or understand these languages: Hindi, Urdu, Bangla, English, Hinglish, Punjabi, and a smattering of Assamese. All, bar English, are languages of the northwest, north and north-east of the subcontinent. They are my prism; they are also my limitation.)

No such discussion can begin without mention of the films of Satyajit Ray (1921–92). Ray's first film, *Pather Panchali* ('Song of the Road', 1955), was a neo-realist film, set in the countryside, about the childhood of a poor boy called Apu. We see the world through his eyes, and those of his sister Durga. The film, based on a great Bengali novel of the same name, depicts a journey without a clear beginning or end. One could argue that there is an element of 'poverty display' about it, or that it was apolitical (as critics have done), but that would be to miss the point. As this book has suggested, intense wells of 'poverty feeling' animated not only the politics but also the art of this period. Ray's stunning depiction of its impact on one impoverished Brahmin household won him eleven international prizes. This, and the two other films in the 'Apu trilogy' – *Aparajito* ('Undefeated', 1956) and *Apur Sansar* ('Apu's World', 1959) – are among the best films you will ever see.

Another Ray film which is just as magnificent is his *Charulata* ('The Lonely Wife', 1964). Here Ray does something else he is brilliant at – watches his own social milieu being itself. He observes the subtle nuances of the ennui and intellectual isolation of the central character, Charulata, a lonely wife in an elite Bengali Hindu household. The film is based on a novella by Rabindranath Tagore; Ray tended to look to Bangla literature for inspiration, as did many directors. But the film surpasses the novel, in my opinion. Its every frame is a work of art. Ray himself considered it his most accomplished work, the film in which he 'made the least mistakes'. Do watch it also as a film that revolves around a woman: Madhabi Mukherjee is riveting in the central role.

If you develop a taste for Ray, as you well might, he made thirty-six films in all, several of which have their own cult following for good reason. They include *Jalsaghar* ('The Music Room', 1958); *Mahanagar* ('The Big City', 1963), which is, in its way, as woman-centred as *Charulata*; *Nayak* ('The Hero', 1966); and *Aranyer Din Ratri* ('Days and Nights in the Forest', 1970). There's also *Shatranj ke Khilari* ('The Chess Players', 1977), based on a short story by the Hindi/Urdu writer Premchand. Ray's only Hindi/Urdu movie, it is not as flawless as, say, *Charulata*, but it offers many riches to the attentive viewer.

Another unmissable film, in Bangla, is Mrinal Sen's *Ek Din Pratidin* ('One Day Like Every Day'; English film title: *And Quiet Rolls the Dawn*, 1979). It portrays, with minute attention to detail, the 'everyday' and its rupture, for a lower-middle-class family in Calcutta after partition. The disappearance of its main breadwinner, a young woman (played by Mamata Shankar), is the tear in the fabric through which Sen shows us every nuance of the relationships within that family. Luminous (if understated) performances light up the darkness of the everyday. It is a gem of a movie.

Another Mrinal Sen film well worth watching is *Akaler Sandhane* ('In Search of Famine', 1981).

Or instead, you might wish to jump back in time to another film that perhaps inspired Sen's *Ek Din Pratidin*: Ritwik Ghatak's *Meghe Dhaka Tara* ('Cloud-capped Star', 1960). Ritwik Ghatak (1925–76) was another precocious genius who died young. His locale was Calcutta after partition. The focus of his 'refugee trilogy' – *Meghe Dhaka Tara*, *Komal Gandhaar* ('E-Flat', 1961) and *Subarnarekha* ('The Golden Thread', 1962) – was the impact of partition on society. *Meghe Dhaka Tara* introduces us to a young woman breadwinner and the tribulations she faces as she tries to support her refugee

household. The plight of the refugee is his theme. His cinematography
is dark, hiding as much as it reveals.

Moving on to the mid-1970s and 80s, the era in which New Wave
Cinema (sometimes referred to as Indian parallel cinema) came into
its own. (Worry not about the terminology. We are talking about
movies with few, if any, song-and-dance sequences, no fights, and no
commercial investment from the industry as it then was.) Often patronised by the Indian National Film Development Corporation, one
could watch such films on TV – a great luxury at the time – or at 'high
culture' viewing halls, and, as the century drew to a close, at film
festivals.

The standout directors of the new wave, for me, were M. S. Sathyu
and Shyam Benegal.

M. S. Sathyu's *Garam Hawa* ('Scorching Winds', 1973) is one of
the most powerful films about partition you will see. Based on a story
by the gifted writer Ismat Chughtai, the screenplay (by the poet Kaifi
Azmi and Shama Zaidi) itself is a work of art. The opening sequences,
replete with *shaayar* poems and poetic banter between a Muslim
workshop owner and a tonga driver, are the best I have ever seen. It
also has excellent cinematography, showing 'lived space' from surprising new angles. The results are sometimes extraordinary.
Examining the predicament of Muslim families 'opting' to stay in
India or flee to Pakistan, the film has elements of the Muslim social
about it but shows just how vulnerable that sociability became when
faced with tides of bigotry and religiously defined nationhood.

Benegal's *Ankur* ('Seedling') came out in 1974. Just as in Ray's first
film, *Ankur* focuses on rural poverty, but this time in southern India.
It is also realist (no singing, no dancing, no fighting), but here we see
the contrast between lush environment and desperate humans. A style
of conversation emerges – best described as minimalist – because the
lead actor is the peerless Shabana Azmi. (We cannot talk about arthouse without a conversation about Shabana Azmi, of whom more
below.) A lot is conveyed in a few words. In my view, Shyam Benegal's
message is both more simple and more complex than Ray's. Where
Ray is a quiet observer of the pathos of the rural, Benegal's films are
more blunt, full frontal in the way that they shock the viewer into
recognising oppression, abuse and sexual exploitation. The rural, for
Benegal, is no idyll.

Two other Shyam Benegal films are memorable for different

reasons. *Manthan* ('The Churning', 1976), paid for by two-rupee contributions from dairy farmers, brought a major talent, Smita Patil, to the limelight, while narrating the history of a cooperative in a way the viewer can not only understand but also care about.

Mandi ('Market', 1983) tells the story of a brothel and its destruction by greedy politicians. Starring Shabana Azmi, Patil and the (still performing) theatre and film actor Naseeruddin Shah, it is studded with fine performances and political satire. Great performances are a feature of Benegal's films – his characters tend to have layers and backstories, and he works with very gifted actors. By this time, the National School of Drama in Delhi had produced a generation who would go on to become household names. Naseeruddin Shah went to the Film and Television Institute of India in Poona, another such centre. (Watch him, for instance, in *Monsoon Wedding* (2001), a good film but one I mention here chiefly for his performance.)

Of course, there were many commercial Bombay films before *Mandi* in which *kothas* (the homes and entertainment rooms of courtesans) had featured, or had even played a large part. But we had never before seen them quite in this way. Never had they seemed so vulnerable, yet never before had they been seen as agents – in ways that would presage the sex-workers' movements of the late twentieth century. Naseeruddin, as the *kotha*'s weak gofer, is as memorable as Shabana's madam. (It takes enormous talent to stand out at all in a Shabana Azmi film. The fact that Naseeruddin Shah did this in a striking performance says something about his defining role in the new wave.)

Another marvellous Benegal film is *Mammo* (1994). Its central character Mammo (played by Farida Jalal) is a Muslim woman in India whose life is turned upside down by partition. She loses her family in the bureaucratic quagmire of post-partition South Asia. Her predicament (and that of millions like her) is rendered legible on the screen to a new generation of viewers, through a charming character whose life teems with histories and stories in which borders, permits and passports make little sense. *Mammo* does not explain its politics, but if you have read Chapter 4, you will understand them.

Rituparno Ghosh (1963–2013) was a director whose rise to greatness was already inevitable in the 1990s. He was a border-crosser, in life as well as art, and his films were both popular and critical successes. His films tended to explore difficult family relationships, and the challenges the family posed to individual flourishing. *Unishe April* ('April Nineteenth', 1994) was the first of a series of stunners which took Bangla-speakers, and then many others, by storm. *Dahan* ('Crossfire', 1997), *Asukh* ('Illness', 1999) *Utsab* ('Festival', 2000), *Bariwali* ('The Landlady', 2000) and *Titli* ('Butterfly', 2002) all explore different dimensions of these conflicting pulls and pressures on individuals. Ghosh exposed the family to an intense scrutiny that it had thus far escaped.

Rituparno had already acquired a huge reputation by the time he made *Chokher Bali* ('Sand in the Eye', 2003), based on one of Tagore's novels.

His casting of Aishwarya Rai Bachchan in the main role saw to it that the film was available on Indian airlines under 'current hits'. It was shape-changing: Tagore met Bollywood after fifty years. Soon afterwards (for Rituparno was a prolific genius) he collaborated with Shohini Ghosh on the script of the superb *Shob Charitro Kalponik* ('All Characters Are Fictional', 2009). Here a self-indulgent engineer is creative all day while his wife puts food on the table. Familial relationships again, but seen through a conjugal prism.

Dev Benegal (b. 1960) is a director who has made relatively few films but has had an outsized impact. His breakout film was a stunner: *English, August* (1994). Based on the novel of the same name by Upamanyu Chatterjee, the film, in my opinion, is better than the book (which is excellent in its own right). There are all too few films about which one can say that.

Now a few words about women actors in this field. You may have already noticed their importance. Directors may have 'discovered' them (like European explorers 'found' continents), but perhaps they knew not what they had unearthed. Sharmila Tagore, Satyajit Ray's female lead in many great movies – *Apur Sansar*, *Devi* ('The Goddess', 1960), *Nayak*, *Aranyer Din Ratri* and *Seemabaddha* (English title: *Company Limited*, 1971) – lit up the scene like no other actor did. I remember no one but Madhabi Mukherjee in *Charulata*: no other character's face comes into high relief, and I have watched the film five times. Did Ray intend this to happen, or were Sharmila and Madhabi far more gifted than he realised? Let us applaud Ray's genius, but let's at least pose the question.

It is the same with Shabana Azmi. She is a border-crosser who has worked in both Bombay cinema and parallel cinema, and delivered bravura performances in both arenas. Shabana has acted in over a hundred films, but there is much more to her oeuvre than quantity.

Shabana needs few words – nay, sounds – to indicate volumes on screen. A subtle change of register is enough to suggest a significant shift of her character's thoughts and (shifting) emotional states. As for her films, there are *Ankur* and *Mandi* mentioned above, and also *Fire* (1996), superb movies rendered spectacular by Shabana's role in them.

But there are films less fabulous that I would recommend just on the basis of Shabana's performances in them. They include *Masoom* ('Innocent', 1983), in which she plays a woman who discovers that her husband (played by Naseeruddin Shah) has had a child from another relationship, and wants to bring that child home. There are also *Sparsh* ('Clear', 1980), *Arth* ('Meaning', 1982) and the genre-porous *Mrityudand* ('Death Sentence', 1997). All showcase talent and take up controversial, sometimes challenging, themes, but Shabana's performance in each lifts the movie from being 'brave' to being 'unforgettable'.

A final word. Observe just how conspicuous the female lead is. She is everywhere, once you notice her.

BOMBAY CINEMA/BOLLYWOOD

Moving on to Bombay cinema, a subject on which I have dwelt at some length in Chapter 7.

What is best added here is something about the qualities and characteristics of each decade (remembering that, like centuries, decades won't follow thematic rules).

We know that films began to be made in Bombay in the 1910s, but few early films still exist. References to them abound – for example, *Raja Harishchandra* ('King Harishchandra', 1913) and *Lanka Dahan* ('Lanka Aflame', 1917) – but little footage survives.

Documentaries do, however. One is recommended viewing: *Fearless: The Hunterwali Story* (1994). It shows fascinating glimpses into how Mary Ann Evans became Fearless Nadia, a star of Hindi cinema, above all of the stunt.

The first singing-dancing talkie that can be viewed in full online is *Alam Ara* ('Ornament of the World', 1931). As the first ever Indian movie with sound, it is invaluable for historical reasons, but also revealing because of the transition, for different actors, from the silent era to the talkies. The silent movie star Master Vithal leapt across the chasm to a talking (singing) role, whereas Ruby Myers, aka Sulochana (another silent star), did not, because of her lack of command of Hindustani. Being in the industry now required different skills.

In *Alam Ara*, Bombay cinema drew vigorously on other leisure worlds – which, this book argues, has been vital to the success of the form. Its opening sequence enthrals the viewer with music. The entire sequence is given over to the full performance of a *qawwaali*, very likely by trained *qawwaals* rather than actors. (*Qawwaali* is a form of devotional singing popular all over the subcontinent, usually sung at the shrines of Muslim *pirs* or saints.) Another feature of the film was the sense of travel and perspective it offered to viewers with its aerial shots of a famous shrine; even the opening camerawork reveals why it is considered one of the most important films of the early talkies era. It was a super hit of its time.

Probably the best decade in which to start serious viewing is the 1940s. The top hit (as well as the highest-grossing film) of the 1940s was *Aurat* ('Woman', 1940). That's a remarkable name for a movie – the word *aurat* suggests not just 'woman' but 'independent, strong, woman'. (There are many words for 'woman' in Hindustani's polysemic vocabulary.) In it, the central character, widowed young, struggles to pay off a greedy moneylender while she brings up her sons.

A fascinating border-crosser of the 1940s is *Neecha Nagar* ('Lowly City', 1946), inspired by Maxim Gorky's play *The Lower Depths*. A social (a film with a focus on social inequality), its daring theme was caste oppression, although it was anything but explicit about it. Its music director was the sitar maestro Ravi Shankar, although he did not steal the limelight in this movie which involved a 'team of all the talents', as so many Bombay films did. *Neecha Nagar* went on to share the first ever prize for Best Film at Cannes. (YouTube offers a version without subtitles. Watch it if you can understand the language, or when you come to understand the language, as you will, if you are planning to watch a few films.)

Then there's the very different *Andaz* ('Guess', 1949), in which Nargis plays Neena, a society beauty. Two men fall in love with her. If the love triangle is the plot, the theme is the westernised ways of the super-elite, and the subtext the many would-be loves and behaviours that society will not condone. The version on YouTube has no subtitles, but Nargis and her co-star Dilip Kumar deliver such extraordinary performances it is worth watching when you have learned the language. (Many readers, of course, will know it already.)

Cinema scholars I know take the view that the 1950s to the early 1960s was the best decade for Bombay cinema. I rather agree, although I have a lot of time for the 1970s too.

There is a problem of plenitude in the 1950s.

You could start with *Mother India* (1957), in which Mehboob Khan revisits some of the same themes that he explores in *Aurat*, with more explosive effect. Don't be fooled by the title – this is not a nationalist movie. Starring Nargis again, it is about one woman's strength, her courage, her values. About how she supports her sons, repels a moneylender's advances, fights for her dignity, rebuilds an impoverished, starving, all-but-emigrating community around her ideals. It repays careful viewing. And yes, we have to have a conversation about actors like Nargis, too. And a few male actors – above all, Dilip Kumar, thought to have been the first method actor in Bombay cinema. His role in *Andaz* was tremendous, but after the release of *Devdas* (1955), about a lovelorn man who has lost his childhood sweetheart to another, he became a sensation. Based on a story by Sarat Chandra Chatterjee, a Bengali writer, the film was a runaway success: viewers condoned his character's suicidal alcoholism. How could they not, when Dilip Kumar made Devdas' suffering so understandable, yet so heartbreaking to watch? His performance was so memorable that the very name 'Devdas' leapt across linguistic barriers to describe any man pining in vain for a lover beyond reach. 'Stop being such a "Devdas"' was a phrase one grew up with, even among South Asians who had not read Chatterjee's novel (or even knew that such a novel existed) or watched the film.

Many regard *Mother India* as one of the best movies ever made in Bombay. I think it is remarkable. Others might give the top spot to *Do Bigha Zameen* ('Two *Bighas* of Land', 1953). Based on a Tagore story, it is a film that is a social of its time, tracking destitution in the village and the emigration of the poor to the city, and their harsh lives there. It is not just a great film, which influenced many filmmakers to come, it also resonates with the themes of the twentieth century's social history. Its impact on Bombay cinema was palpable at least until the 1980s. Javed Akhtar, of whom more below, cited it as an inspiration.

But there were others just as good, if not better, than these. I am a particular admirer of Guru Dutt's oeuvre.

Guru Dutt was a producer-director-actor-picturiser of song – a brilliant man whose films crossed the boundary between commercial and artistic worlds, who challenged conventions by showing rule-breakers to have inner demons, psychological pain, often a fear of failure. In *Pyaasa* ('Thirsty', 1957), Guru Dutt played a failed poet, supported only by a kindly sex worker, Gulabo (played by Waheeda Rehman). Its extraordinary plot, script, cinematography and performances will disabuse you of the notion that Bombay cinema was all about 'running around trees'.

There's also his *Kaagaz ke Phool* ('Paper Flowers', 1959), in which Shanti (Waheeda Rehman) becomes an accidental star, and the great director who made her (played by Guru Dutt) spirals into decline as his marriage collapses, and he loses access to his child. (Did this film represent an attempt by a director to think through his making of a female lead? Perhaps.) Either way, it tanked at the box office but went on to achieve cult status worldwide. It is an exquisite film.

To recover, Guru Dutt next made *Chaudhvin ka Chand* ('The Full Moon', 1960), a beautiful tragedy in which two best friends fall in love with the same woman (unbeknown to each other). There is comic relief – the actor Johnny Walker provides it – and scenes of festivals, marriages and Kathak dancing give the audiences many moments of pleasurable viewing and listening. But there is tragedy too, and astonishing power in the play of light and shade. The songs by Jameela (Waheeda Rehman) and Aslam (Guru Dutt) are also outstanding, not least those in which the central characters reflect on society (even as they are part of it), and reveal interior (individual and torn) selves.

Chaudhvin is also one of Bombay's first bromance movies, in which the friendship between two men is the underlying theme. (Bromance movies remain on the menu as I write.)

This film was also a fine example of the Muslim social, a genre in Bombay cinema whose characters were urbane Muslims. It is remarkable that such a genre not only existed, but was so splendid, so soon after partition.

It's as if the cosmopolitan world of Bombay cinema resisted the crude forces of nation-making, which in turn resisted the world of cinema.

Finally, in 1962, Guru Dutt made *Sahib, Bibi aur Ghulam* ('The

Master, the Wife and the Servant'). Based on a Bengali novel, this showed the relationship between a devoted Hindu wife and her dissipated *zamindaar* husband. Here the star is Meena Kumari, who plays the devoted wife in perhaps her finest performance. It too is a remarkable film, a shocking film, perhaps one of the films that will haunt you for the longest time. Perhaps it was his masterpiece.

I find it hard to believe that, having watched these movies, you will not want more Guru Dutt films. There are more. My personal favourites are *Jaal* ('Trap', 1952), *Aar Paar* ('This or That', 1954), *Mr & Mrs '55* (1955) and *Baharen Phir Bhi Aayengi* ('Spring Will Come Again', 1966).

I think it is time to have another discussion about woman actors, this time in commercial cinema. In that great decade, along with Nargis and Waheeda Rehman, another star rose in the east: Meena Kumari (born Mehjabeen, 1933–72). Like Nargis, she was from a performing background, but by the early 1950s she had already grabbed attention for her roles in *Baiju Bawra* ('Crazy Baiju', 1952) and *Parineeta* ('Married Woman', 1953). A fine, if languid, dancer in the Kathak tradition, she soon came to be known as an actor who could capture the nuances of a role. (Kathak can have languid upper body movements, and she executed those well.) She was beautiful, of course. But she was also a fine actor. Her face was eloquent, her eyes hiding (yet sometimes revealing) her character's mischief or sorrow. The film for which she is best known is *Pakeezah* ('The Pure', 1972). Her finest performance was perhaps in *Sahib, Bibi aur Ghulam*, but *Pakeezah* overshadows it in popular recall, because her own death followed so soon after its release. (It is a must-watch in its own right.) Her personal tragedy mirrored the tragedy of Pakeezah, the character she played.

First, note just how important women were in Bombay cinema before the Big B (as Bachchan came to be known) seemed to cast everyone else into the shade. The plots had women at their heart. They were often heroine-driven.

But also observe that each of these women, from Fearless Nadia onwards, had a male patron who claimed to have discovered her. Guru Dutt's name is mixed up with Waheeda Rehman's all through the 1950s. Did Guru Dutt make her? Her ability to act for cinema was so extraordinary that it is hard to forget the moments when light falls on her face. I doubt she was Guru Dutt's discovery. Did *she* make *him*? I salute his genius, but let's at least pose the question. It seems that even he did.

What of Meena Kumari? She fell in love with Kamal Amrohi, an aspiring film director, while still a teenager. They married in 1952. Did he introduce her to the *filmi* creative world? No: she had been acting since the age of five. Did he make her? I don't think so: *Baiju Bawra* (a film that uses the classical *raag* form and eschews the use of Urdu) does not show Amrohi's pawprints. M. Sadiq directed *Bahu Begum* ('Daughter-in-law/Wife', 1967), a little gem of a movie, for which the poet Sahir Ludhianvi wrote the lyrics, but it seems not to show his imprint. Amrohi appears to have acted more as Kumari's gatekeeper, and much later (long after their divorce) as her collaborator in *Pakeezah*. He made less than a handful of films. I think we remember him because we remember Meena Kumari, not the other way round.

And then there is Nargis (1929–81). Do watch her in *Aurat* and *Andaz*. Neena in *Andaz* is a woman with a devil-may-care attitude to social conventions. We see her defy them in many scenes. Part of the tragedy is a doomed love triangle (with Dilip Kumar and Raj Kapoor as her admirers), but the theme is that society (and law) punish her harshly for defying its norms.

Indeed, Nargis made so many movies with Raj Kapoor that rumours spread of an affair and a secret child. But if you watch these few movies – and also *Shree 420* ('Mr 420', 1955) – you can see who has the talent and star quality. Raj Kapoor dresses, dances and walks as the (sometimes ludicrous, Chaplin-esque) object of her desire, while Nargis – whether in western outfits or in simple saris – steals every shot. The fact that people describe the 1950s as the best decade for the movies has something to do with Nargis.

The fact that out of a very small pool of female actors such talent emerged says much about what plots Bombay filmmakers were writing, and what characters they were inventing. It was not what you would imagine in a patriarchal society. But art did not imitate life. These filmmakers were artists – some of them great ones – for all that these films have been deemed lowbrow. In these movies they imagined worlds, and the characters who peopled them. The teams who made these films were often of many talents – composed of great poets, musicians and choreographers, stars in their own fields. They drew on great literature. Many of their films challenged hidebound tradition; indeed, some were subversive *if watched closely*. The plot was often conventional, as producers worried about pleasing censors, 'aunties' and front benchers. But the action was often off-piste, perhaps in a song or in a fight. It's a good idea to view these parts with attention, and to trust your eyes. Watch the tragic twist in *Sholay* ('Embers', 1975). Please. Press replay if you can. This is no spaghetti western.

The 1960s were a bit of a mix. The decade opened with a bang, with *Mughal-e-Azam* ('The Great Mughal', 1960), a historical film that was also about lovers who challenged convention. The errant lover in this case was Prince Salim, infatuated with Anarkali (a court dancer). His flouting of the Love Laws led to war between father and son – an unthinkable outcome. The film was the most expensive made in Bombay's history back then. It had powerful and resonant themes, and its soundtrack is rated one of the best ever in the industry. Madhubala's performance as Anarkali won her a nomination for an award for best actress. It was box office gold. No wonder a colourised version of the original was released in 2004.

The 1960s are otherwise known for the less-than-great wrestling movies, starring the wrestler Dara Singh. Few are memorable. Perhaps the best in this genre is *Faulad* ('The Iron Man', 1963). Mumtaz sizzles in new fashions while Dara does *kushti*. I am a big fan of *kushti*; even so, the movie left me cold. You might want to watch it to get a taste of Indian wrestling, but expect fantasy costume (Dara dressed in peplums, no less).

There is one other gem I'd watch before writing off the 1960s. It is *Aradhana* ('Worship', 1969), starring Sharmila Tagore and Rajesh Khanna. *Aradhana* is a remarkable film: it challenged social mores about sex before (formal) marriage.

Then on to the era of male superstardom.

Here we have to start with Rajesh Khanna (1942–2012), the sole hero of fifteen films made between 1969 and 1971. More classically good-looking than Bachchan, he acted alongside him in some marvellous films, the best of which (in my view) are *Anand* ('Serene', 1971) and *Namak Haraam* ('Traitor', 1973). In both, Rajesh Khanna got first billing. Amitabh Bachchan was the junior actor.

But then for a decade from 1973, the star of the Big B rose and rose.

Why? you might ask. The zeitgeist, as I have suggested in Chapter 7, had a lot to do with it. Of a generation of migrants born in the city, with no land to fall back on, nowhere to return to, and dwindling hopes for the future. Salim–Javed's anti-hero character Jai/Vijay had a vulnerability – even a death wish – to which even we, the middle-class dress-circle audience, could relate. Vijay was terrifying, but his back-story rendered him human. The tight plotting and lean dialogue, cutting down the song quotient and ratcheting up the action, all marked a shift to something new. Amitabh was not their creation – he had genius, in Akhtar's view. But he rose to fame in the context of the changes that the Salim–Javed duo ushered into Bombay cinema.

Amitabh Bachchan wasn't a looker in the mode of Bombay actors hitherto: he wasn't 'fair and lovely' (like the cream), nor was he well built in the way of male leads of the time. No: he was long of body and long of face, and a head taller than most male stars. He was skinny, and a tad gangly about the shoulders. He resembled neither the Great Gama nor Dara Singh nor Guru Dutt nor Dilip Kumar nor Rajesh Khanna. He was so unique in his appearance that few thought he could ever be a 'star'. It seems that the industry had fixed notions about male beauty too.

His costume artists describe him as a challenge to clothe. But watch him kill the dockworker look in *Deewaar* ('The Wall', 1975). And soon we wanted more of him; then, only him.

Nor did 'Vijay' speak like an actor of times past. Gone were the *shaayari*, the dancing with fireflies, the lyrical dialogue of old. This character spoke, thanks to Javed Akhtar, terse sentences – sometimes laconic, at others, angry – often in a Mumbaikar migrant patois. Akhtar brought in a sea change in scriptwriting: in Amitabh he had an actor who could deliver his novel less-is-more dialogue style with remarkable ability. (Soon we were all calling ourselves *apun*, instead of *mein*. *Apun* means I, in a faux-patois. We city-bred types identified with Bachchan's migrant character.)

He dominated the industry in a way no actor had ever done. And that was for two reasons. One was his remarkable gift; the other was the character he played. Salim–Javed (soon stars in their own right) had created a character – Jai/Vijay – an anti-hero of stunning novelty, and Bachchan injected into him layers, mysteries, hidden histories. Javed Akhtar gave him few words to play with, sure that Amitabh would make every single one count.

Still, it took a while for him to get top billing. It was with Salim–Javed's backing that he got his roles in *Zanjeer* ('Shackles', 1973) and

Deewaar. In both he played an anti-hero, yet stole the movie. These films stunned. They took people's breath away. The rumour of Amitabh spread with the wind. These are even more important movies, in the industry's history, than *Sholay*. They are necessary viewing.

Even in *Sholay*, Amitabh Bachchan got fourth billing, after his co-actors Dharmendra, Sanjeev Kumar and Jaya Bhaduri (a fine actor, soon to be his wife). It is hard for us to get our heads round this today because Bachchan has become a legend, a South Asian treasure. But it reminds us why history should never be read backwards.

Sholay enjoyed the top spot as the ultimate Bollywood film for the longest time. It is still also necessary viewing. Immensely pleasurable, it has more complicated subtexts than the mere plot suggests. (The plot itself is, of a very high order – a Salim–Javed triumph.) *Sholay* offers a panoply of larger-than-life characters: Amjad Khan's unforgettable dacoit chief Gabbar Singh, Hema Malini's voluble tonga-driving Basanti, and Jaya Bhaduri's strong but silent widow Bahu among a rich and strange variety. Yet Bachchan's Jai, his mixture of caustic and taciturn wit, his silent loves, his devotion to his male bro-friend, and his coin still shine today. This film about two career criminals hired by a retired policeman to catch a dangerous dacoit, Gabbar Singh, is the stuff of legend. And protest. Amjad Khan, then a novice in the industry, played Gabbar Singh: the character is still a household name. Characters who played bit parts in it are mobbed at airports. People remember whole chunks of it, almost fifty years on.

Amitabh starred in many movies between *Sholay* and the mid-1980s, when he crashed out of the industry for a while. You could well become an addict and want to watch every single one. My personal favourites are *Kabhi Kabhie* ('Sometimes', 1976), *Namak Haraam* (1973), *Don* (1978), *Silsila* ('The Connection', 1981) and *Coolie* (1983).

I like these films for different reasons: the plot, sub-plot, plot-subversions, the songs, the acting, or the representation of Muslims (in *Coolie* – not just urbane ones, as with the Muslim socials, but of all social strata, of all temperaments and quiddities).

Silsila is a brave film, about desire and extramarital passion. Amitabh delivers a fine performance in it. However, the film would not have worked but for the parts played by two female actors: Jaya

Bhaduri Bachchan as his wife, and Rekha as his lover. Passion, jealousy and guilt are their material. Some of their scenes together are the film's most memorable moments.

This is not the place to dwell on speculation that this romantic triangle had a real basis. I want instead to dwell on performances of actors other than Bachchan. Although it is true that he hogged the limelight in every film, in just a few, women shone too. Hema Malini and Jaya Bhaduri in *Sholay*. Parveen Babi in *Deewaar*, Raakhee in *Kabhi Kabhie*, Rekha and Jaya Bhaduri Bachchan in *Silsila*. Zeenat Aman in *Don* – another wonderful film. Dare I say it, necessary viewing. (By this time, our anti-hero has developed into a full-time, all-powerful mafioso. Ah, but he has a doppelgänger. Amitabh has two roles in a single film. And Zeenat Aman is doing kung fu. Her character represents an amazing challenge to expectations of how women could live, dress and behave, while still being 'good' people.)

Rekha had already shown her talent in Muzaffar Ali's border-crossing *Umrao Jaan* (1981). Based on Mirza Hadi Ruswa's novel *Umrao Jan Ada* (1899), Rekha carried the movie on her slender long neck. This is a must-watch, not only for the leisure worlds it introduces us to, but also for Rekha's performance.

After the mid-1980s, when Amitabh made an abrupt departure from the scene, the industry struggled to replace him. (The Salim–Javed duo split at around the same time.) One actor the industry thought it could use as another Vijay-style character was Jackie Shroff. This is nowhere more obvious than in the stunning movie *Parinda* ('Bird', 1989). Starring Madhuri Dixit, the next big thing, it offered novel techniques of filming and exposed audiences to astonishing degrees of violence. Bizarrely, however, even though it was allusive to, even derivative of, *Deewaar*, *Parinda* breaks the mould in how it ends. It did something shocking – the plot allowed the Sita figure (played by Madhuri) to die, gunned down in cold blood before our eyes. This was new, this was blue. It started like *Deewaar*, but its ending held out little hope, no moral redemption.

You must watch this film.

After this, yet another cult classic, *Baazigar* (1993), ratcheted up the violence to another level. A new actor, Shah Rukh Khan, had spent some time looking charming on TV (he has cute dimples). He now took a risk on a part – Ajay and his alter ego, Vicky – that many bigger stars had turned down. Do watch it. It represents the apogee of a certain kind of cinema, with a certain kind of plot, with the culmination in the murder of an innocent woman. Or two. Ajay/Vicky terrified even as they charmed.

Perhaps because of this – although there were several other reasons, discussed in Chapter 7 – the plots began to change. There was, in the mid to late 1990s, a shift towards family-friendly movies. Less violence, don't frighten the children. Dancing please, Hindu weddings please, but all polite, thank you. No poverty, no starving farmers, no social issues.

Many films of the 1990s were, as a consequence, rather bland. Romcoms were the name of the game. *Hum Aapke Hain Koun!* ('Who Am I to You?', 1994) is the one to watch in this genre, if you must. (There's a good historical reason to watch it: it won a prize for wholesome entertainment, while featuring Madhuri Dixit and Salman Khan, of whom more below. It had fourteen song-and-dance sequences. The plot involves sacrificing love for the sake of the family. It had an impact on the structure of the industry, on South Asian wedding culture, and even wedding fashion. It was one of the highest-grossing movies of the century.)

The only one I rate is *Devdas* (2002) – the twentieth remake of the 1955 movie – and that's in large measure because of the character that Madhuri Dixit played. Chandramukhi is a *tawaif* who falls in love with Devdas, who despises her with all his being. Drunken and heartbroken, he dies on the doorstep of his first love Paro (Aishwarya Rai Bachchan), who loves him in return but is married to someone else. Their love for each other was impermissible – her parents would not allow it because his mother has 'history'. Equally, in Chandramukhi's world, falling in love with a male visitor was hazardous. The movie, which created the Chandramukhi character (who has no parallel in Chatterjee's novel), is not as bland as others of the era. In fact, it is rather interesting. One you might just want to watch.

The saving grace of that era, then, was Madhuri Dixit. There were others, discussed below. But first, we need to talk about Madhuri.

Madhuri became the only woman star ever to have had top billing. She could act; she was radiant; her smile could set sail a thousand ships. But her unique selling point was dancing. Trained in Kathak – a challenging form – she could perform a range of dance moves from the raunchy, to the coy-but-sexy, to the classical, in a plot-dependent way. She was controversial in the 1990s, not least because some feminists took offence at her dancing to a number called 'Choli ke Peechhe Kya Hai' ('What is Under my Blouse?') in *Khal Nayak* ('Villain', 1993). Others celebrate her for depicting women not merely as objects of desire, but as people with their own desires. *Tezaab* ('Acid', 1988) and *Devdas* are my favourite Madhuri movies. *Devdas* is packed with talent, but Madhuri outshone everyone else, including poor dying Devdas (played in the 2002 version by Shah Rukh Khan).

But would the industry lie down and present only family-friendly movies? Would it behave? Yes and no.

In 2009, a huge hit was *3 Idiots* (2009). On the surface – even the idiotic typeface – it's a comedy, about three bro-friends at an elite engineering college. On the surface, family-friendly. But is it conventional? No. Not if we peel back the layers. For starters, one friend is a Muslim, the other is a devout Hindu.

Before we know it, violence enters the story, though not in the usual way. A character commits suicide. One of the bro-friends jumps off the roof. These scenes are deeply shocking. Poverty and social difference enter the plot: the musketeer who attempted suicide jumped because he thought news of his expulsion would crush his poor working mother and kill his sick father. And oops ... it celebrates one woman's intelligence and strength, in the form of a feisty, sexy, dancing doctor (Kareena Kapoor).

It's as though you can't keep the industry down.

Another remarkable feature of the 1990s – odd, given the political context – was the rise to fame of Khan, Khan, Khan (and Khan). That's Salman Khan, Aamir Khan, Shah Rukh Khan (and Irrfan Khan, 1967–2020). All are, as the name Khan suggests, Muslims.

First let us acknowledge the bizarreness of this phenomenon when anti-Muslim attitudes were mushrooming (rather than waning) in India, and indeed in the Hindu diaspora. Did the 'separate state of Filmistan' (to use the screenwriter Javed Akhtar's metaphor) resist these impulses? Viewers in their millions who wanted 'SRK' haircuts and 'Bhaijaan' or 'Tiger' hairstyles (public nicknames for Shah Rukh and Salman) seem to push back against easy assumptions about the nature and spread of Hindu communalism in the 1990s.

My favourite Khan is Irrfan Khan – a border-crosser in many directions. (There have been so many border-crossers that the border is proving to be more a large zone than a line.) Do watch *Salaam Bombay!* (1988). Like Shah Rukh Khan, Irrfan shone both as villain and hero. But unlike Shah Rukh, Irrfan acted in both Bollywood and Hollywood, and there was a reason for this: he was an actor of astonishing range. Watch him in *Maqbool* (2003), *The Namesake* (2006), *Life in a ... Metro* (2007), *Slumdog Millionaire* (2008), *Life of Pi* (2012), *The Lunchbox* (2013) and *Hindi Medium* (2017). There's also the biopic *Paan Singh Tomar* (2012), and the smaller film *Billu Barber* (2009), made important by Khan's performance as an unsuccessful barber in a very small town. Irrfan Khan's career was cut short; he died young. Tall and slender with enormous hooded eyes, he was not easy to cast. But his performances are extraordinary. He died soon after shooting *Puzzle* (2018), a huge critical success. He also acted in a fascinating film set in India and Bangladesh, *Doob* ('No Bed of Roses', 2017), in which characters move across the eastern border for all manner of quotidian reasons. If you are interested in the cross-border qualities of 'Bollywood', this is a must-watch.

The other Khans are good too. My favourite 'Bhaijaan' movies ('dearest brother', as Salman Khan is known to his fans) are *Bajrangi Bhaijaan* ('Brother Bajrangi', 2015) and *Ek Tha Tiger* ('There Was a Guy Called Tiger', 2012). The latter has a remarkable premise: two secret agents, one working for India, the other for Pakistan, fall in love. Their love trumps their allegiance to their respective agencies and nation states. Rather than sacrificing their love at the altar of the nation, they go into hiding from both RAW and the ISI. Beat that.

It also has some astonishing novel action sequences, using new cinematographic techniques. (There's a Tiger franchise, should you get hooked. When Tiger returned in the sequel *Tiger Zinda Hai* ('Tiger is Alive', 2017), it was a global blockbuster. Here, it brought back the ruthless Muslim terrorist as the arch enemy, but makes his perspectives easier to grasp.)

Salman Khan's *Hum Aapke Hain Koun!* was such a big hit that it has an acronym of its own, *HAHK*, yet is ranked only sixteenth on his list of global hits. It put him on the path to stardom, but (for reasons discussed above) it isn't the best movie you will ever watch. (My humble opinion.)

Aamir Khan has played many roles well, but is likely to be best remembered for his performance in *Lagaan* ('Tax', 2001). In this gripping film – the plotting is great – he plays a village youth in a drought-prone region forced to pay tax to a raja under pressure from the British. There's a cricket match, on whose outcome Khan's character wagers the entire village's taxes for three years. They have first to learn the rules of cricket, then to play, and then win this strange game to avoid mass starvation. The stakes are high.

There is not much history in the film, other than the fact that the British made few tax concessions to drought-hit peasants. The history of cricket is all wrong. The song-and-dance sequences have little merit. But it's the game itself that thrills and makes this movie good. It is not quite *Deewaar* or *Kaagaz ke Phool*, but it is well worth your time.

His other career best is as Rancho – the mysterious, brilliant bro-friend, in *3 Idiots*.

Returning to Shah Rukh Khan. I admire him because he has had the courage to play roles that established actors rejected. There's his performance in *Maya Memsaab* (1993), based on Flaubert's novel *Madame Bovary*. Shah Rukh Khan played Maya's young lover. (He is very good: this is perhaps one of his best ever roles, the other being a poor child turned liquor-dealer in *Raees* (2017).) His next shocker was his appearance as Ajay/Vicky, the revenge-seeking psychopath in *Baazigar*. In *Dil Se . . .* ('From the Heart', 1998), he played an executive from All India Radio, whose views about the legitimacy of the Indian state are challenged by a close encounter with the Assam insurgency.

In *Chak De! India* ('Go for it, India!', 2007), he plays a Muslim hockey player accused of having colluded with Pakistan in ensuring India's defeat – his character Kabir Khan addressing assumptions about Muslim minorities in India. This was a huge, if surprising, hit; in fact, Indians (including team captains) sing the theme song 'Chak De! India' at cricket matches. This despite the ever-darker days for Indian Muslims.

In *Veer-Zaara* (2004), a paean to undivided Punjab, Khan's charac-ter, the Hindu Veer, falls in love with a feisty Pakistani Muslim woman, Zaara. Surprising things happen.

Both films have been box office big-hitters. Remarkable, that; and also a testament to SRK's tremendous appeal.

There was also *My Name Is Khan* (2010), in which Shah Rukh Khan plays a character with autism/Asperger's traits, who introduces himself thus: 'My name is Khan and I am not a terrorist.' Imagine the impact of that title, those words, in a world (for this was a movie with a global audience) in which Islamophobia had rendered all the globe's

Muslims 'suspected terrorists'. It ran at my local cinema multiplex in Cambridge for almost four months.

SRK has also acted in several romances, many set in the diaspora, and as the tragic hero in *Devdas*. He has even acted as himself in several films, the best of which is the Irrfan Khan film *Billu Barber*. This left no one in doubt about who was the finer actor. SRK may be 'more-is-more' as an actor, or perhaps that is how he interprets his characters. He is often accused of playing himself (or the same kind of character) again and again (unfair, in my view). Nonetheless, he has earned his place as a star. He has staying power, he has charisma, and a chutzpah that his millions of fans adore. Above all, he has courage.

But there was more to the 1990s and 2000s than the rise of the Khans. There were the new pan-India movies, the best of which pushed back against communal hatred of minorities and showcased remarkable talent. The finest, in my view, was *Bombay* (1995). It propelled a new director, Mani Ratnam, who made films in Tamil and Malayalam, into the limelight, and also the musician A. R. Rahman. Here, a Hindu 'boy' and a Muslim 'girl' (as they are still called in South Asia) break the Love Laws – they fall in love and elope to Bombay, the 'Maximum City'. Watch what happens: you must.

You might follow this with Mani Ratnam's *Roja* (1992) and *Dil Se . . .* Together with *Bombay*, they are part of a cluster of films described as Mani Ratnam's 'terrorism trilogy'. Each one is worth viewing, though *Bombay*, in my view, surpasses the other two.

But – quite as much as these new directors, actors, action scenes, all-India format, use of language (in *Dil Se . . .*, characters speak in Telegu and Assamese) and plot lines – the 1990s offered something fresh: a novel and exciting director of music. A. R. Rahman is a genius in his own right, just as R. D. Burman was. It is now possible to search for films sorting by A. R. Rahman. I sometimes do that, and not only when I am tired. Movies are there to give pleasure too, even as they encourage us to think, let us not lose sight of that. His music challenges the conventions of Bombay cinema's musical history while lifting the heart and encouraging one to live. You may already have heard it in *Slumdog Millionaire* or *Roja*: do get to know it better.

Acknowledgements

This book would not exist but for Shane Delamont, neurologist at King's College Hospital, London. He planted the seed by advising me to write the one 'big' book I had in me and to drop all other work. His patient was stubborn, she was angry, she had other plans. He fought to keep her cognitively intact, able to chase this strange book down, to see its architecture emerge, to find a language in which to write it. For this I – now a little wiser – cannot thank him enough.

A small platoon of doctors kept me going as I wrote. I owe them more than I can say: no words I know in any language express the depth of my gratitude to Guy Leschziner, Melvin Lobo, Nicholas Gall, Fergus Rugg-Gunn, Giorgio Lambru, Shane Delamont, Jai Chitnavis and Farokh Udwadia. Guy and Mel took calls and responded to emails at all hours and advised me how to cope with the rollercoaster ride of a capricious malady. Giorgio always managed to squeeze me into an impossible schedule. He stuck injections into my head (for good reason), but so gently that we often chattered about his research, or my son's wedding, or his baby's life and times, while the procedure was ongoing. (We are friends now. It has been a long haul.) Paul Flynn, an old friend, has been there throughout, advising us in his wry way and holding Anil's hand at frightening times. Navin Sakhuja has been like a hawk in keeping a watch over my sight, while making me laugh at his stories. Vandana Prasad, a close friend since my teens, saw me through Covid in Delhi before there were vaccines or 'therapeutics', to use the mangled language of one notorious sufferer. Shane Delamont continues to help me with the challenges of Long Covid. Farokh Udwadia saved my life just as the last chapter was in progress. Jai Chitnavis pulled me through a crisis that developed when I was checking the proofs. John Brown's counsel informed our more difficult decisions. My deepest thanks to these brilliant people of medicine.

Mel Lobo advised me to take medical retirement in 2019. Even though it distressed me at the time, I am indebted to him. I thank the Faculty of History, the University of Cambridge and Trinity College for making that transition so smooth. Thanks, too, to the ever-generous Tim Harper for his words of farewell as Faculty Chair – I am still stunned by them, and feared letting him down while writing. I owe Leigh Denault much for years of fruitful collaborative teaching and examining. Sarah Pearsall and Peter Mandler: thank you for being colleagues from heaven.

At Trinity, I am grateful to my fellow historians – Boyd Hilton, John Lonsdale, Peter Sarris, Richard Serjeantson, Teresa Webber, Arthur Asseraf, Alexandra Walsham, Simon Keynes, Samita Sen and Sachiko Kusukawa. Years of working with them helped me raise my game. John, once my director of studies, has been a combination of moral sweetness and courage, supportive at all times. I have drawn strength from his example.

Another squad of allies believed in the 'bonkers book' (as my students dubbed it) and my ability to pull it off. Simon Longstaff – impresario of 'dangerous ideas' – helped me to think through a thematic structure. When Partha Pratim Shil first heard about this lunatic venture, his response – first stunned and then excited – persuaded me that the idea was worth pursuing. James Pullen at Andrew Wylie encouraged me to write *this* book, as against a standard political history. James went well beyond his remit as 'my agent'. He acted as my 'lay intelligent reader'.

It was only when I submitted it to my editor that I realised that James was anything but 'the general reader'. He reads and commissions books for a living, does dear lovely James; he is an expert! What a fool I was! (And remain.) But if this book has a co-author (it has three), one is James. He liked the thematic structure. He liked the style. But for him, there would have been no book: I wouldn't have had the courage to write it. He had this ridiculous, baseless, unwavering confidence that I could pull it off.

Tanika Sarkar's engagement with this project has also been pivotal. Like James, she was behind it all the way; like him, she is an expert. Her enthusiastic (but critical) reception of each draft of every chapter, her constant encouragement, and the pleasure she has taken in its style of delivery encouraged me to keep developing the book's genre and perspectives.

The third 'co-author' is Jörg Hensgen, the book's editor at The

Bodley Head, Penguin Random House. Jörg was handed a manuscript as unwieldy as a T-Rex. (Believe it or not, he wanted more.) He edited it with no holds barred. It was like being a PhD student again: an odd experience to be taken apart at this great age, but a marvellous one. I remember now why students admire their supervisors. Jörg has been an extraordinary editor: a true *ustaad*.

(All three may want to distance themselves from the very imperfect result. The responsibility for this book is mine alone.)

I also owe huge thanks to Stuart Williams, Leah Boulton and the wonderful team at The Bodley Head/Vintage/Penguin Random House for their amazing work getting this monster ready for the world.

Prasannan Parthasarathi spurred me on. He read the proposal and suggested the crucial change that helped it fly; and since then has not allowed me to give up, whatever the circumstances. Sarah Pearsall asked brilliant questions about a chapter, and continues to bestow on me her incomparable Sarah-brand affection, and to support me in writing. Samita Sen read a chapter and nodded. (That was enough.) Prasannan and Parth read chapters too, and were a little more forthcoming. Shohini Ghosh read a chapter and tore it to shreds – that was invigorating! She also read the Note on Further Viewing, and subjected it to gentle critique. (Given the parlous state of her eyes, I am beyond grateful.) Anil read every chapter and professed to love them all, and looked after, fed and watered their crazy author as she wrote.

The late David Washbrook, staunchest of friends, was this book's most constant reader until death snatched him away. The book is much the worse for his loss, that goes without saying. But to say I miss him every single day is an understatement. Polly O'Hanlon continued to read chapters after David left us so suddenly. Her support has been like adhesive that helped hold me together. Thank you, Polly.

Raj Chandavarkar's influence shows all over this book. It makes me sad that we will never have a rambling mysterious conversation about it. In the middle of New Court, in the rain, as was his habit.

The 'Pamir Knot' group of friends lives, thinks and breathes the 'South Asia' of this book. So it is not just for them, it is about them, too.

I have been blessed in my friends. It is wonderful to be able to acknowledge their place in my life. Tanika Sarkar, Shohini Ghosh, Humeira Iqtidar, Kamal Munir, Shaffiq Essajee, Shalini Sharma, Tim Hochstrasser, Ali Alavi, the lesser-spotted Saji Eapen, Eivind Kahrs, Sudeshna Guha, Simon and Suzie Longstaff, Sarah Pearsall and 'Boy

Wonder', Samita Sen, Polly O'Hanlon, Anuradha Roy, Vandana Prasad, Ornit Shani, Jennifer Davis, Claire Alexander, Benjamin Hopkins, Chandra Mallampalli, Navin and Puja Sakhuja, and Prasannan Parthasarathi: thank you for the laughter and camaraderie, and for being there in good times and bad. Rukun Advani, thanks – in addition – for the bad jokes and exquisite music. Neeladri Bhattacharya – in addition – for your gentleness. Siddhartha Gautam cannot be thanked in person – but his 'tribe', should they dip into this book, will recognise his continuing impact upon me.

My former doctoral students, to whom this book is dedicated, shower me with love and affection. To Anjali Bhardwaj Datta, my deepest gratitude for your friendship, red-wine-fuelled high-jinks ('ride to Edinburgh, anybody?'), help with filing, and for all those (hundred?) library books. Thank you, Parth, for your questions, your intellectual companionship, your *raags* and excitement about this book. Uttara Shahani, thank you for your mad acts of generosity, not just of bringing a special cake down from London by Uber, but of carrying *a whole suitcase* full of papers by train from London to Cambridge for me (your poor hip still hurts). Aishwarya Pandit, our laughter still makes me laugh. Anjali, Uttara, Parth, Aishwarya, Laurence Gautier, Ishan Mukherjee, Tamina Chowdhury, Sophie-Jung Kim, Teresa Segura Garcia, Pallavi Raghavan, Devika Singh, Mohita Bhatia, Mohammad Amir Khan, Derek Elliot, Hira Amin, Benjamin Meyer and Mrinalini Venkateswaran either allowed me to use material from their unpublished theses or taught me to see subjects from different angles of vision. Toni Jokinen also shared with me his unpublished Tripos work. Thank you all. Humaira Chowdhury hasn't quite finished her PhD yet, but has helped me in a thousand practical ways while advising me about many others far less mundane. Newal Osman has helped me think many things through – and helped with the research for this book. Of Erica Wald and Bérénice Guyot-Réchard – what can I say? They've dropped everything to help me, whatever, whenever. Uditi Sen, you are a wonderful whirlpool of conspiracies. Sundeep Lidher was my ally in several public causes, but she spared me the heavy lifting: huge thanks, Sundeep. Apurba Poddar sent me material, love and strength from Bangladesh.

I don't have words to thank Edward Anderson and Patrick Clibbens, former students and dear friends, who stepped in when the pandemic struck, making the last chapters of the book impossible to achieve in the ways to which I was accustomed. Without their superb research assistance in digital archives and materials, this project would have foundered. I feel this is as much their book as it is mine. (They are, of course, at liberty to distance themselves from it.) But for Meeraal Shafaat-Bokharee's back-breaking labour on the notes, this would be a far shabbier work. She is responsible, too, for the photography of some of the images. I don't know how to thank her either.

Former students at the LSE, too – Ben Hopkins, Taylor Sherman and Uther Charlton-Stevens – also taught me and learned with me. Boy, has it been fun.

These wonderful people have provided me with a posse of 'grand-children'. (One of them thought I was a *building* when she was little. I kid you not. I mean I was large, but not that large.) My 'brood', as Anil describes them, have become my all-but-family. But for their emotional and intellectual sustenance, this book would have remained a dream.

Current students keep me on my toes and encourage me to rethink my assumptions: Humaira Chowdhury, Rohit Dutta Roy and Anashya 'Ruru' Ghoshal – keep rocking it.

Colleagues and friends helped me with translation. I thank Aishwarj Kumar for his help with translation from Bhojpuri; Kamal Munir, from Urdu; and Eivind Kahrs, from Sanskrit.

Javed Majeed gave me an introduction to Lahore's Old City that I will never forget. But for Syed Babar Ali's generous friendship and hospitality, my experience of that city would have been less 'South Asian'. Thanks also to Tahir Kamran, Kamal Munir and the scholars and students at LUMS, for the warmth of their welcome to Lahore.

I owe Dayanita Singh a huge hug for giving me the right to use a brilliant photograph. I also owe a big one to Kavita Puri who allowed me to use material from a draft of her book.

This is a pandemic-era book. Without Sarfaraz Hamid's resourceful research assistance, I could not have seen some of the papers cited from the Nehru Memorial Museum and Library archives, and the National Archives of India. When international travel was impossible, I worked – pandemic rules permitting – at the Centre of South Asian Studies, Cambridge, where Kevin Greenbank was most helpful in bringing up the papers I needed. Thanks also to Kevin, and Rachel Rowe (now retired) for allowing me to borrow books on generous terms. Trinity's librarian Nicholas Bell went far beyond the call of duty to help me with books, papers and images, for which I am grateful beyond measure.

It was both a challenge and a delight to write a book of this length and range as a debilitated, 'co-morbid', person during a pandemic. Mirka Gruszczynska, Saroj, Shakeel Ahmad, Lucas Reali, Asha and Cyril, Emmanuel, Caitan, Dave (Pinky) Roberts, Alison Talbot, Jimmy Jolland and Richard Chalklin, all in their different ways, helped me function. Humaira, Alison – and my 'Khatija diaries' – reminded me which day of the week/month/year it was. At Trinity, the members of the College staff – on whom we all depend – made each day joyous. Thank you all, wonderful people. You made it possible for me to enjoy writing every page of this.

I owe debts of various kinds to my one-of-a-kind family. Many members appear in this book, others do not, but all hover over it. You are all amazing: crazy and wonderful as individuals, and glorious as a riotous whole.

Some cannot be thanked now. My father would have enjoyed seeing my child's-eye view of his 'ancestral home'. My mother might have been surprised by how much I remembered about her reaction to it. My Pishima would have laughed, no doubt, as she did at everything. It saddens me that none of the three people who fashioned me as a youngster will read this book.

Few of those mentioned at Hill Cart Road are still alive. My own generation have died or dispersed, our children have grown up and left. It is now a shadow of itself, and those who now live there as children will have a different experience of place, space and time. I am grateful to have my own memories of 'the olden days', however challenging it has been to make memory 'speak'.

This book would not be what it is without the memories of others. Above all, I owe enormous thanks to those who shared with me some of their most intimate and secret histories.

I have no words to thank my 'nuclear-but dispersed' family. Through all of this Kartik has given me reasons to fight on, to write, to live life to the fullest. He has listened and understood me when my guard was down. He's been that rare gift, a son who is also a best friend. Anil has risked his back to prevent my head hitting the floor, not once but again and again. (The poor chap even suffered endless episodes of *Masterchef* when the struggle to meet the deadline got really tough.) The duo have been my main carers, and I could not have dreamed of more gentleness and patience on their part: the journey has been hard for them too. I thank Ciara for her love for Kartik, for being her

caring, beautiful self, her plans to travel with us, and for her willingness to share Kartik with his old mum.

Khatija and David, Hufi and Sam, thank you for things too subtle
to put into words.

Jasdeep Brar has been my inspiration, Samuel Walker my role
model. When I struggled through 'bad patches', thinking of them
helped me get back to the book, and then to finish it. My sister, Louise
Priya Kernahan, is a hero. While writing, I imagined her reading it.
While struggling to the finishing line, I thought of her on the Camino
Walk. You are a wonder to behold, Louise. I am prone to magical
thinking. So I am sure you will hold this book, and read parts of it
(and argue with me about them!) since your example got me to the
bitter-sweet end.

Cambridge, January 2023

Glossary

aabir	colour (particularly the red colour used at the festival of Holi)
aachaar	ritual, rite
aakhir	in the end, eventually
aalim	scholar (of Muslim learning)
aaloo mattar	a curry made from potatoes and peas: simple food eaten even by white-collar folks
aaloo tikki	spiced potato cake shallow fried and served with a sharp tamarind chutney
aam paapad	layered dried mango
aamil	accountant
aattaa	wholemeal flour
abaa	loose garment, generally for men
abhinaya	mood; literally, leading an audience towards a sentiment
adda	talking, free-flowing conversation
adhiya	system where a sex worker is rented a room by a brothel keeper, who charges her rent based on her total earnings rather than at a fixed rate, so that the brothel keeper gets a share of the worker's earnings (notionally 50:50)
Adivasi	tribal people of the Indian subcontinent
ahimsaa	non-violence
ajlaf	'lower-caste' Hindu converts to Islam
ajrak	blockprinted
akhand Bharat	term for the concept of a unified Greater India; literally, undivided India

akhara	place of practice with facilities for boarding and training; gymnasium, where the main sport is wrestling
akku	sister
almirah	cupboard
amaanat	something (or someone) entrusted to somebody for guardianship
angrakhaa	a flared long top, which allows greater movement than the traditional long *kurtaa*
anna	currency unit formerly used in British India, equal to 1/16 of a rupee
ansars	local inhabitants of Medina who, in Islamic tradition, took the Prophet and his followers (the *muhaajirun*) into their homes; literally, the helpers
Antaakshari	spoken parlour game: each contestant sings the first verse of a song (often with Bombay film songs) that begins with the consonant of the Hindi alphabet on which the previous contestant's song ended; literally, the game of the last letter
antahapur	women's quarters
anuloma	a union between a high-born man and a woman of lower standing (by birth)
aranam daasi	personal attendant (enslaved) to a rani
areca nut	also known as the betel nut, known for its bitter and tangy taste, and routinely used for chewing
arkati	professional labour recruiter; person licensed to direct ships into or out of a harbour or through difficult waters
ashraf	cultured, noble
asur	demon
avataar	incarnation in human form
awaam	the people, general public
ayah	nursemaid, nanny
baagh	big cat (leopard, tiger)
baaper-baari	father's house
baariwallah	rentier
baasi	stale; literally, stinking
baazi	feat of daring

baazigar	a nomadic tribe, who go from village to village practising acrobatic feats
babu	Indian clerk
Bada Din	Christmas; literally, Big Day
badshah	emperor
bahu	daughter-in-law
bairaagi	wandering ascetic
baithak	squat; literally, seat
bandgala-churidaar	a formal high-necked jacket with classic jodhpurs
bandook	gun
baniya	trading caste
bargat	banyan tree
barsaati	a one-room apartment on the roof of a typical two-storey house in the 1980s; building regulations then did not permit a third floor
basti	slum neighbourhood, tenement
batasha	a semi-spherical crisp and spongy sugar-cake
beedee	short, thin cigar-like roll-up, filled with tobacco and wrapped in tendu leaves
beeraangonas	women raped during the Bangladesh Liberation War by the Pakistan army and their local collaborators; literally, war heroine
beggar	forced labour, usually without payment
begum	Muslim woman of high rank; wife
beldaar	day labourer
betel	plant cultivated for its leaves which are commonly used to make *paan*
beti	daughter
bhaakri	flatbread made from unleavened *jowaar* or sorghum
bhaav	sentiment, feelings
bhadralok	gentlefolk
bhajan-kirtan	devotional singing in the Hindu, often Vaishnava Bhakti, tradition
bhakt	devotee; a term used for believers of Hindu right-wing ideology
bhang	marijuana

bhangra	energetic dance of the Punjab
Bharat Mata	Mother India
bharatiya	rent payer
bhelpuri	a common street food made from crisp puffed rice, chutneys and spicy toppings
bhujia	a type of Bombay mix, made from spicy bean and chickpea flour
bibaahita	ritually married first wife
bidaai	parting
bidhaba	widow
bigha	measure of land, equivalent to about 1,500 square metres
bil	lake
biraadiris	clans, tribes, lineages
biran	a small tree with thick corky bark
biryani	mixed rice dish, made with spices and usually some type of meat
bondhu-baandhob	close friends, friendship groups
bou-di	sisters-in-law; cousin-sisters-in-law
bou-ma	sister-in-law (-*ma*, when added to a woman relation's name, means 'much-loved')
budhdha baba	scary old man
burra	big
burra sahib	big master
chaai paani	a bribe; literally, tea or water
chaal	motion
chacha	uncle (one's father's younger brother)
chakkar	whirling motion (in Kathak), pirouette (in Kathak)
chalisa	devotional hymn of forty verses
chapraasi	official messenger
charas	marijuana
charitramu	biographies, stories
chaudhuraayan	keeper, manager
chaukidaar	guard, watchman
chaukidaari tax	tax collected from farmers to provide funds to keep *chaukidaari* in the villages

chawl	tenement block
chhajjas	deep ledges built above windows to keep out the sun and monsoon rains
chhukri	bonded sex worker, typically working off a debt
chi-chi	pejorative label applied to many aspects of the Eurasian lifestyle, particularly speech and accent
cholbe	will do
cholum	variety of millet; *Andropogon sorghum*
choultry	inn, resting place, run by a charity
chulah	wood-burning stove
churidaar kurtaa	tightly fitting trousers with a loose overshirt/tunic
churidaar pyjama	long, tight-fitting trousers, jodhpurs
churmaa	a sweetmeat of flour, ghee and sugar
cottah	unit of area, which varies from place to place
cumboo	'cat-tail' millet, also called *baajra*; *Pennisetum typhoidium*
daadamashay	respected elder brother
daai	midwife, wet-nurse
daaku	dacoit, bandit
daal	boiled and tempered lentils
daaru	alcoholic drink
daasi	female slave or servant
dabba	lunchbox; typically a metal box used to transport hot food to a person's place of work
dabbawallah	lunchbox deliverer
dalaal	broker, middleman
Dalit	a member of the lowest rank in the Hindu social hierarchy
dand	a jack-knifing push-up
dangal	wrestling competition
darshan	a glimpse or view of, being in the presence of
darwaan	guard
dastarkhwhaan	tablecloth which is spread on the ground, floor or table and is used as a surface for food; also used more broadly to refer to the entire meal setting
Dayabhaaga	Hindu law treatise that focuses on inheritance procedure and does not give the sons a right to

	their father's ancestral property until after his death; also known as the Bengal School; different from the *Mitaakshara*
deewaar	wall, means of protection
desh	home, village, region, country, nation
devadaasi	female artist dedicated to the worship and service of a deity or a temple for the rest of her life
dewaan	chief minister
dhairya	serenity, wisdom
dhaniya	coriander
dharma	duty
dheki	large, heavy thresher used in the Bengal area for taking the husk off rice; no longer in use
dholak	a medium-sized drum
dhoti	type of sarong, tied in such a way that it looks like loose trousers
dhrupad	the oldest surviving classical style of North Indian vocal music
dhurry	rug
dida	paternal grandmother, father's mother
didi	elder sister
dosa	a flatbread from southern India made with fermented rice and lentil flour
dumbaari	cluster fig
dupatta	long scarf; girls and women, particularly in the north, drape *dupattas* across their breasts (and sometimes heads) as a sign of modesty
durbaar	court, assembly
ek dam	straight away
Ekadasi	the eleventh day of a fortnight in a lunar month
farishte	angels, messengers of God
fatwaa	ruling on a point of Islamic law given by a recognised authority
fauji	soldier
filmi	related to the Bombay film industry
fiqh	jurisprudence
firanghee	foreigner

fuchka	a puffed fried pastry, containing spiced potato or chickpeas and flavoured with spicy tamarind sauce; also known as *gol gappa* in North India and *paanipuri* in Bombay
gaalekar	inhabitant of the same *gala* (shared room) in a tenement
gaanja	cannabis
gaaonkari mandals	village associations
gaddi	low cushioned seat, the emblem of a particular type of sovereignty
gala	room
galata	commotion
galauti kebab	'festive' kebab made from lamb, rose water and cashews
gambheerta	sagacity
garh	fort
gat	a movement in Kathak
gau bhakt	cow lover
gau hatya	cow killing
gaurakshini sabha	cow protection society
ghaat serang	wharf headman
ghaats	range of stepped hills with valleys; stone steps near sacred rivers
ghar	house
ghar jamaai	resident son-in-law who lives in the house of his wife's family; house husband
gharaana	courtesan household; hereditary household of musicians or dancers
gharry	horse-drawn carriage
ghazal	a form of Urdu poetry
ghee	boiled and clarified butter
ghoos khana	to take a bribe; literally, to eat grass
ghungroo	a musical anklet tied to the feet of classical Indian dancers
girmit	agreement; indenture agreement with Indian labourers
goala	herdsman

go-korbaani	animal sacrifice (e.g. of a goat, sheep or cow)
gol gappa	a common street food, also known as *paanipuri* or *fuchka*
goonda	thug, member of a gang of toughs
goongoo	cape-like raincoats
gosha	a woman in seclusion or purdah
gotra	clan, lineage
grameen	rural; literally, of the village
gulaab jaamun	a syrupy sweet made of fried balls of cottage cheese, beloved throughout the subcontinent
gulkand	sweet preserve made from rose petals
gur	molasses; in Bengal, usually made of dates rather than sugar
gurda kapura	spiced kidneys and testicles
gurdwaara	Sikh place of worship; literally, doorway of the guru
gutkaa	chewing tobacco
Hadith	accounts of the deeds and sayings of the Prophet
hafta	protection money; literally, week
hakeem	practitioner of traditional medicine
halal	permissible
haldi	turmeric
haleem paraatha	fried flatbread, eaten with a stew made of mutton and different lentils
hartal	mass protest, strike
haveli	townhouse, usually with an inner courtyard
havildaar	policeman, soldier
hijrat	to migrate from one place to another place (of faith); religious procession
hilsaa	species of fish related to the herring; much sought-after and the national dish of Bangladesh
hisaab	account
hogla	perennial plant, also known as elephant grass, often used for thatching
hudood	limits, restrictions
hukum	command

iddat	the period a woman must observe after the death of her husband or after a divorce, during which she may not marry another man
idli	steamed cake made of fermented rice flour and black, de-husked lentils
iftaar	the evening meal with which Muslims end their daily Ramazan fast at sunset
ijaaza	licence to instruct; literally, permission to teach a subject
ilm	knowledge
inaam	gift
isha	night prayer; one of the five mandatory Islamic prayers
istri-waali	ironing lady
itar	scent, perfumed oil
izzat	honour, reputation
jaageer	land grant; colloquially, inherited property
jaali	latticework, in stone
jaggery	a cane sugar, similar to muscovado
jahaaji-bhai	literally, boat brother
jahannum	hell
jajmaani	economic system in which 'lower castes' performed various functions for 'upper castes' and received grain or other goods in return
janaaza	funeral bier
jatha	a formation of armed Sikhs
jati	sub-caste
je-ma	a term of affection for a beloved *jethi*
jethi	aunt (father's older brother's wife)
Jhampan Mela	snake goddess festival
jhum	slashing and burning, swidden
jootha	tasted but wasted food, scraps
jowaar	a type of millet, sorghum
jugaad	makeshift
kaafilaa	caravan
kaaghazi	paper

kaaghazi raj	a kingdom of recorded information; literally, the rule of paper
kaala paani	literally, black water: many Indians believed they would lose caste if they crossed the ocean
kaazi	civil judge
kachcha	raw or boiled
kachua	irregular wife
kafi	a monorhyme poem that is always meant to be sung
kalabaazi	acrobatics
kalasam	vessel signifying fertility; often seen on temples in the form of an inverted pot with a point facing the sky
kali yuga	the age of conflict/darkness
kallar	thief
kameez	long shirt or tunic
kanchha	boy (Nepali)
kansa	bell metal, bronze; a hard alloy of copper and tin
kanyadaan	marriage ritual of giving away the bride
kapdaa	clothing
karkhaana	small factory, often employing family labour
karmayoga	a philosophy of action
karnam	accountant who maintained the records used in collecting taxes
karsevaks	devotees who act, a modern neologism
karta	patriarch
Karva Chauth	the fourth day in the lunar month of Kartik
kasaai	butcher
kashi	enamelled
kathavachak	storyteller
keraani	clerk, scribe
khaalaa	maternal aunt
khaansama	cook, steward
khadi dhotis	long cloths of hand-spun cotton, draped in folds around men's torsos, covering their thighs and calves
khanaval	cook house

khandaan	family, clan
khap	community organisation representing a clan or a group of North Indian castes
khap panchaayat	assembly of *khap* elders
khattriya	warrior
khayaal	musical form based on a Hindi song in two recurring parts
kheer	spiced rice pudding
khichri	gruel made of rice and lentils
khot	person with superior land-revenue farming rights
khulaa	release from the marital bond
kikar	tree also known as gum arabic tree, babul, thorn mimosa, thorny acacia
kincob	a fine silk fabric embroidered with threads of gold or silver
kirpan	sword carried by observant Sikh men
kotha	brothel, courtesan's salon
kucha	very narrow alley, typical of the Walled City of Old Delhi
kulatyaagini	woman who brings dishonour to the family
kulin Brahmin	the 'highest' strata of intermarrying Brahmins in the Bengal region
kumaari	unmarried girl, virgin
kunba	clan
kurtaa	loose long tunic
kushti	wrestling; also known as *pehlwaani*
kutcheri	local court, accounts office
laafad	slap
laat sahib	a VVIP (very, very important person)
laathi	heavy stick of bamboo used as a weapon, especially by police
laathial	person wielding a *laathi* or stave
lakh, laakh	a hundred thousand
langot	loincloth
langra	a type of mango, particularly prized by Bengalis
laopatta	the leaves of the wild gourd

lascar	seafarer, sailor
lassi	salted buttermilk
lehenga	a long piece of pleated cotton or silk, tied or tucked into the waist; an ankle-length, very full skirt (and blouse and veil) for girls
lihaaf	quilt
litti	flour
Lok Sabha	lower house of India's Parliament
Londoni gaon	villages in Bangladesh with connections to London, or to the UK more broadly
Loo	a strong, dusty, gusty, hot and dry summer wind from the west which blows over North India and Pakistan
luchi	a small, deep-fried puffed flatbread made of white flour – an unhealthy staple of an upper-class Bengali meal, particularly in western Bengal
lungi	a piece of cotton wrapped and tucked round the waist; type of sarong
maad	rice water
maai-baap	public welfare government; literally, mother-father
maali	gardener
maalik	master, employer
maataa	mother; respectful form of address for a woman
maati	soil
madrassa	theological seminary
mahaajan	moneylender or shopkeeper
mahaar	Dalit caste found largely in the state of Maharashtra
mahal	palace, mansion
maidaa	white bread flour
maidaan	field, gathering place
maistry	master workman, foreman
makaan	shelter
Manas	traditional epic poem: *Ramcharitmanas*
mandi	wholesale market for grains, fresh fruit and vegetables
mandir	Hindu temple

mangni	engagement, betrothal
marsiya	an elegiac poem about the imams Hassan and Hussain; part of Shia religious observance
mastaan	tout, gangster
mastaana	lover
maulana	respected Muslim religious leader
maun vrat	vow of silence
maund	an Indian unit of weight, equivalent to about 35 kg
mazaar	tomb or shrine, typically of a saint or notable religious leader
mehfil	a gathering for refined leisure
mehndi	henna
mehr	also *Huqq mehr*; money or goods the groom gives to the bride at the time of her marriage, which then legally becomes her personal property
mehtar	sweepers
mela	fair, Hindu festival
methi gosht	goat curry cooked with leaves (rather than seeds) of asafoetida
mishti-doi	a sweet made from yoghurt with the jaggery of date palms
Mitaakshara	legal treatise which gives sons the right to their father's ancestral property at their birth; also known as the Benares School of Mitaakshara Hindu Law; different from the *Dayabhaaga*, which gave rights of inheritance to some Hindu women
mobed	Parsi priest
mohalla	neighbourhood, community
moong daal	yellow lentils, split mung beans
mori	washing area
mrita viralu	dead heroes
Mubaarak ho	congratulations
muhajir, muhaajirun	refugees; those who had accompanied the Prophet on his *hijrat* from Mecca to Medina
mujraa	a dance performance by women

Mukti Bahini	freedom fighters or liberation army; also known as the Bangladesh Forces
mukti joddha	freedom fighter
mullah, maulvi, maulana	Islamic religious teacher or leader
munsif	judge
mureed, mureeda	disciple or pupil of a religious instructor
murshid	master
mushaira	social gathering at which Urdu poetry is read
musth	a normal periodic condition in male (bull) elephants characterised by terrifying levels of aggression
muttahida qaumiyat	composite nationalism; concept that the Indian nation consists of people of diverse cultures, castes, communities and faiths
Naaga Panchami	a day of traditional worship of snakes
nabasak	a 'low' but respectable (usually agricultural) caste
naib	a deputy
nal	hollow stone cylinder with a handle inside; a weight-training device for wrestlers
namak	salt
nashaa	intoxication
nath	nose jewellery, e.g. nose ring
nautch	British term for Kathak performed by women
nawab	ruler of a princely state
nawabzaada	son of a wealthy person; literally, son of a Nawab
nihaari	curried trotters
nikaah	Islamic marriage ceremony
nizaam	ruler of the princely state of Hyderabad
ojha	folk healer
paan	leaves of the betel plant wrapped around tobacco, fruit, etc., and chewed
paandaan	container used to store betel leaf, betel seeds and other spices for making *paan*, and the tools needed

paanipuri	common street food consisting of a filled and fried flatbread
paapri chaat	a spicy snack with chickpea fritters, served with yoghurt, tamarind and assorted savoury titbits
paara daada	neighbourhood vigilante, lookout
pablik	a mass of politically alert yet 'ordinary' people (Hinglish)
padhaan	headman
paik	foot soldier
pakka	fried
panchaayat	a body of village elders who decide upon its social and customary matters
pandaal	marquee, tent
pandit	Brahmin scholar versed in Hindu religious tradition
pankhaa-wallah	fan-puller
paraatha	flatbread
paraathewali gali	a narrow street in Delhi; literally, the bylane of flatbread
paraiah	outcaste, 'untouchable'
pardesi	migrant, foreigner
pargana	Mughal province/group of villages, subdivision of a district
patwaari	recorder of local land titles, local accountant
pehelwaan	wrestler
peon	low-ranking worker, e.g. office gofer
phaansigar	strangler
phirnee	a sweet milk dessert made with ground rice
pinda	small particles
pir	religious leader, spiritual guide, charismatic leader (saint) or custodian of a saint's shrine
pishima	aunt, father's sister
poligar	(historical) territorial administrative and military governor in South India
poorbea	migrant workers from Bihar and eastern United Provinces

praayaschitt	purification ceremony
prasaad, prasaadam	ritual food offerings served to Hindu gods, after prayers, shared with the congregation of worshippers
prayaag	historical name of the area near the confluence of the Ganges and Yamuna rivers, and the mythical river Saraswati
pucca, pukka	genuine, authentic
puja	the essential ritual of many Hindus; the offering of light, flowers and water or food to the divine
pulao	rice with chopped vegetables
punya	spiritual credit, virtue
pye, pye-dog	stray dog
qaanungo	land revenue clerk/property registrar, often supervising ten *patwaaris* (recorders)
qasbaa	fortress, citadel, or fortified quarter of a city
qawwaali	style of devotional music particularly associated with Sufis
raag	melodic framework of notes
raajsik	one of three basic attributes of food: hot and energising, appropriate to contexts such as exercise, hunting or war
ragi	finger millet, a gluten-free wholegrain
raiyat	cultivator
raiyatwaari	land revenue system, which allowed the government to deal directly with the *raiyat* (cultivator) for revenue collection
rajaakaar	traitor, collaborator
Rajput	'warrior' community from north-west India
Ramayani	expert on the *Manas*
Ramlila	any dramatic re-enactment of the life of Ram according to the ancient Hindu epic *Ramayana*; literally, Ram's *lila* or play
ranisaheba	queen
rasogallah	dessert made from dumplings in a sugar syrup
Rath Yaatra	public procession in a chariot

rohu	carp, highly prized among Bengalis
roti	flatbread made from wholemeal wheat flour
ryot	British spelling of *raiyat* (see above): an agrarian smallholder, tenant or peasant cultivator
saarangi	a stringed instrument played with a bow which accompanies Kathak
saatvik	one of three basic attributes of food: cool, pure, enabling tranquillity, celibacy and meditation
sabha	group, society
sabut jheera	coriander seeds
saheb, sahib	a European man in colonial India
sahookar	moneylender
sajjada nashins	spiritual superior of a shrine
samjhauta	mutual agreement, understanding or pact
samosa	pastry, folded and stuffed with spicy potatoes and peas
sandesh	Bengali sweetmeat made of milk, clotted milk and sugar or date palm juice
sangathan	association
Sangh Parivar	umbrella term for the collection of Hindu nationalist organisations spawned by the Rashtriya Swayamsevak Sangh (RSS)
sangsaar	household
sapure	snake masters, snake charmers
sarkar	rule, government
satyagraha	non-violent protest; passive civil resistance
satyagrahi	someone who practises non-violent or civil resistance
sehri	the morning meal eaten by Muslims before the sun has come up during Ramazan
serang	head of a crew of sailors (*lascars*)
seva	selfless service; good deeds
shaadhinota	freedom, independence
shaadi	traditional Hindu wedding
shaagird	disciple

shaakha	daily training centre
shaamiyaana	ceremonial tent, marquee
shaasuri	mother-in-law
shaayar	a form of performative poetry
shaheed	martyrs
shaitaan, shoitaan	devil, evil spirit
shakti	primordial cosmic energy, force
shalwaar kameez	traditional combination dress worn by women, and in some regions by men, in South Asia. *Shalwaars* are trousers which are unusually wide at the waist and narrow to a cuffed bottom; the *kameez* is a long shirt or tunic
shami kebaab	kebab made with ground beef, yellow split peas and spices
sharbat	sherbet
shareef	respectable; literally, a descendant of the Prophet Muhammad through his daughter
shastra	sacred text
shehnaai	wind instrument, like a clarinet
sherwaani	a long coat, worn by Indian men, that is buttoned to the neck with the length usually extending just below the knee
shikaar	hunting
shikaari	hunter
shikasta	broken handwriting in which correspondence and reports are sometimes written
shishu	small child
shongshaar	household
shoshur	father-in-law
shoshur-baari	home of the in-laws
sigdi	clay oven or stove
silsila	connection
siphaahi	sepoys, Indian soldiers serving under British
sirdaar	foreman, labour recruiter; also *Sardar*: a respectful form of address for Sikh men
sooar	pig, boar

stri	married woman
stupaa	Buddhist commemorative monument shaped like a hemisphere; it usually houses sacred relics associated with the Buddha or other saintly persons; its finest iteration is believed to be the *stupaa* at Sanchi in Central India, in Madhya Pradesh
subarnarekha	golden line, golden thread
sudra	the fourth and lowest *varna* of the traditional, four-fold caste system
sur	a god
surah	chapter, verse
swadeshi	national, domestic, i.e. not imported
swayamsevak	a member of Rashtriya Swayamsevak Sangh (RSS)
taamsik	one of three basic attributes of food: hot, unduly exciting the system, stimulating lust, anger and other intemperate 'hot' states of mind
taandava nrtiya	cosmic dance of destruction and re-creation
taar	leftover *nihaari*
tablaa	a pair of small hand drums
tai	sister
taka	currency of Bangladesh, word used for 'rupee' in Indian Bengal
takhallus	pen name
takht	a seat or bench that doubles as a bed
taluqdaar	aristocratic landowner
tavu	leftovers
tawaif	courtesan
teerth	pilgrimage
thaanaa	police station
tharavad	household
thhelawaala	cartman
thika	urban leaseholder of property developed into *basti*-tenement quarters, and then sublet on; Calcutta, Bengal, Bangladesh
thuggee	robber, murderer

Tommy/Tommy Atkins	slang for a common British Army soldier, especially during the First World War
trishul	trident
tulsi	basil, regarded as sacred
ulema	plural of *aalim*: scholar and teacher of the (older) Islamic system of pedagogy
ummaa	community
upma	boiled and spiced semolina
urs	commemoration; literally, wedding
ustaad	maestro, guru, revered teacher
vada	fried, spicy doughnut-shaped snack made of lentils
vaishya	trader
valy/veli	one *veli* is about 6.67 acres
vanaspati	vegetable oil
varna	social rank within the caste system
vyaas	expounders
waaf-ul-aulaad	family trust (Islamic jurisprudence)
wada	dwelling quarters of different *jatis*, western India
waqf	a permanent dedication by a Muslim of any property for any purpose recognised by the Muslim law as religious, pious or charitable
watan	territorial nation
wataniyat	territorial nationalism
wudder, wadaar	stonemason
yakshi	mythical female being, in Hindu and Buddhist traditions, symbolising fertility
zaardozi	embroidery worked with gold and silver thread
zakaat	charitable giving; religious tithe
zamindaar	landowner, landlord of large rural estates
zardaa	flavoured tobacco used in *paan*
zardaa paan	betel leaf laced with tobacco
zenana	the inner apartments of a house in which the women of the family live
zina	extramarital sex

Picture Credits

A Raj family: District Magistrate Cruishank, Mrs Cruishank and their child (Centre for South Asian Studies, Cambridge)

William Robert Cornish: surgeon and scientist of diet (Wellcome Collection (CC BY 4.0))

Pages from Irene Mott's diary: the Wellington Race Week (Centre for South Asian Studies, Cambridge)

Page from a Rai Bahadur's diary (Centre for South Asian Studies, Cambridge)

The glorification of violence: Santi Ghose and Suniti Chowdhury (Centre for South Asian Studies, Cambridge)

The iconisation of violence: the hanging of Khudiram Bose (Anil Seal)

Dadabhai Naoroji (1825–1917): 'grand old man' of economic nationalism, mathematician and MP for Finsbury (Anil Seal)

Bal Gangadhar Tilak (1856–1920): editor and militant (Anil Seal)

Annie Besant (1847–1933): socialist, theosophist and President of the Congress in 1917 (GL Archive/Alamy)

Muhammad Ali Jinnah (1876–1948): a very liberal lawyer and leader of Pakistan (Joya Chatterji)

Sarojini Naidu (1879–1949): poet and advocate of communal unity (Centre for South Asian Studies, Cambridge)

Jawaharlal Nehru (1889–1964): nationalist hero and first prime minister of India (Anil Seal)

India–Pakistan border, 1947 (Centre for South Asian Studies, Cambridge)

India–Pakistan daily border ritual, Wagah–Attari, 2010s (Pacific Press Media Production Corp/Alamy)

The paper state of independent India (Dayanita Singh Studio)

Mortimer Wheeler: archaeologist-in-chief of India *and* Pakistan (PA Images/Alamy)

The dancing girl of Mohenjodaro (CC0 1.0 Universal)

Phoolan Devi's defiance: stolen police uniforms and guns (Photo 12/Alamy)

The destruction of Babri Mosque (AFP/Stringer/Getty Images)

Rabindranath Tagore (1861–1941): poet, writer, artist (Anil Seal)

Benazir Bhutto (1953–2007): eleventh and thirteenth prime minister of Pakistan (Robert Nickelsberg/Getty Images)

Snake master, as depicted by an unknown Indian artist (Wellcome Collection)

Sushila Sundari (1879–1924): circus artist, with a Royal Bengal tiger (Historic Collection/Alamy)

Rukmini Devi Arundale (1904–86): maker of modern Bharatanatyam (AGF Srl/Alamy)

Fans celebrate Amitabh Bachchan's seventieth birthday, holding a collage of the poster of *Deewaar*, and photos of his family (Indranil Mukherjee/Alamy)

Shah Rukh Khan: film star (NurPhoto/Getty Images)

Madhuri Dixit: Kathak dancing queen, sole woman 'leader' of movies (STRDEL/Stringer/Getty Images)

Shabana Azmi: peerless actor, renowned for activism (Georges de Keerle/Getty Images)

Notes

I THE AGE OF NATIONALISMS: COMPETING VISIONS

1. Henry W. Nevinson, *The New Spirit in India* (London, 1908), pp. 233–7, cited in S. R. Mehrotra, *A History of the Indian National Congress: Volume One 1885–1918* (Delhi, 1995), p. 231

2. Taylor C. Sherman, *State Violence and Punishment in India* (London, 2009)

3. Anil Seal, *The Emergence of Indian Nationalism: Competition and Collaboration in the Later Nineteenth Century* (Cambridge, 1968), p. 245

4. George A. Grierson, *Linguistic Survey of India* (Calcutta, 1898–1928). It is worth listening to some of the recordings of dialects that Grierson and his team made, at the British Library, if you ever get a chance. One can hear languages and dialects destroyed by their absorption and rationalisation into dominant languages. I do not support the view that the (formalised) 'vernacular languages' were superior to dialects. Language was going through an intense process of creation and formalisation at this time. Prachi Deshpande, *Scripts of Power: Writing, Language Practices and Cultural History in Western India* (Ranikhet, 2023)

5. *The Imperial Gazetteer of India: The Indian Empire. Vol. III: Economic* (Oxford, 1907), p. 273

6. *Report Connected with the Project for the Construction of Docks at Calcutta, Part I*, PWD Serial No. 1 (Calcutta, 1885)

7. Aparajita Mukhopadhyay, 'Wheels of Change?: Impact of Railways on Colonial North Indian Society, 1855–1920', doctoral dissertation (School of Oriental and African Studies, London, 2013), p. 53

8. Ibid., p. 63

9. Ibid., p. 558

10. M. K. Gandhi, *An Autobiography, or The Story of My Experiments with Truth* (translated from the original in Gujarati by Mahadev Desai) (Ahmedabad, 1958), p. 163

11. Mithi Mukherjee, *India in the Shadows of Empire: A Legal and Political History 1774–1950* (Oxford, 2009)

12. Sukanya Banerjee, *Becoming Imperial Citizens: Indians in the Late-Victorian Empire* (Durham, NC, 2010)

13. C. A. Bayly, *Recovering Liberties: Indian Thought in the Age of Liberalism and Empire* (Cambridge, 2011)

14. 1890 Presidential Address, in A. M. Zaidi (ed.), *Congress Presidential Addresses: Volume One: 1885–1900* (New Delhi, 1985), p. 88. See also Sanjay Seth, 'Rewriting Histories of Nationalism: The Politics of "Moderate Nationalism" in India, 1870–1905', *American Historical Review* 1 (1999), p. 110

15. George A. Grierson, *The Modern Vernacular Literature of Hindustan* (Calcutta, 1889), cited in C. A. Bayly, *Empire and Information: Intelligence Gathering and Social Communication in India, 1780–1870* (Cambridge, 1999), p. 343

16. Ibid.

17. For a discussion of the role of 'colonial difference' in helping to produce nationalist consciousness, see Partha Chatterjee, *The Nation and Its Fragments: Colonial and Postcolonial Histories* (Princeton, 1993), Chapter 2

18. Sumit Sarkar, *Modern India: 1885–1947* (London, 1983), p. 22

19. Cited in Seal, *Emergence*, p. 147

20. Seal, *Emergence*, pp. 147, 278

21. Others have seen this as a genuine and far-reaching engagement with European thought, albeit in a colonial, and hence intrinsically unequal, context. See, for instance, Tapan Raychaudhuri, *Europe Reconsidered: Perceptions of the West in Nineteenth-Century Bengal* (Delhi, 1988)

22. For the everyday humiliation of the western-educated Indians employed in offices in early twentieth-century Bengal, see Sumit Sarkar, '"Kaliyuga", "Chakri" and "Bhakti": Ramakrishna and His Times', *Economic and Political Weekly* 27(29) (1992)

23. *Amrita Bazar Patrika*, 26 April 1883, cited in Seal, *Emergence*, p. 259

24. Gayatri Chakravorty Spivak, 'Can the Subaltern Speak?', in Cary Nelson and Lawrence Grossberg (eds), *Marxism and the Interpretation of Culture* (Urbana, IL, 1983). Also see Ashis Nandy, *The Intimate Enemy: Loss and Recovery of Self under Colonialism* (Delhi, 1983); and Dipesh Chakrabarty, *Provincializing Europe: Postcolonial Thought and Historical Difference* (Princeton, 2000)

25. Sarvepalli Gopal (ed.), *Selected Works of Jawaharlal Nehru*, Volume 1 (Oxford, 1984), pp. 252–3

26. R. P. Masani, *Dadabhai Naoroji: The Grand Old Man of India* (London, 1939), p. 29

27. The Elphinstone Institute, or Institution, in 1856 divided to create Elphinstone School and Elphinstone College. Dadabhai held his Chair at the latter

28. Resolution III of the Seventh Indian National Congress, Nagpur, 1891

29. Major contributions were made by G. V. Joshi, Surendranath Banerjee, G. Subramaniya Iyer and William Digby

30. Dadabhai Naoroji, 'Poverty of India', paper read before the Bombay branch of the East India Association, 28 February 1876

31. Bipan Chandra, *The Rise and Growth of Economic Nationalism in India: Economic Policies of Indian National Leadership, 1880–1905* (New Delhi, 1966), p. 8

32. J. N. Gupta, *The Life and Work of Romesh Chunder Dutt, C.I.E.* (London, 1911)

33. Ibid., p. 17

34. Romesh Chunder Dutt, *Open Letters to Lord Curzon on Famines and Land Assessments in India* (London, 1900)

35. Romesh Chunder Dutt, 'Famines and Land Assessments in India: Open Letters to Lord Curzon', in Romesh Chunder Dutt, *Speeches and Papers on Indian Questions, 1901 and 1902* (Calcutta, 1902), p. 17

36. Romesh Chunder Dutt, *The Economic History of India*, p. vi

37. *Provincial Reports on the Material Condition of the People, 1880–91* (Simla, 1894), Bengal Report, p. 9, cited in Chandra, *Economic Nationalism*, p. 22

38. John Strachey, *India* (1894), p. 301, cited in Chandra, *Economic Nationalism*, p. 23

39. Dadabhai Naoroji, *Poverty and Un-British Rule in India* (London, 1901)

40. Naoroji, cited in Chandra, *Economic Nationalism*, p. 19

41. Meeraal Shafaat-Bokharee, 'The Untold Story of the India Office Library and Records, 1946–1982', doctoral dissertation (University of Cambridge, 2022)

42. Manu Goswami, *Producing India: From Colonial Economy to National Space* (Chicago, 2004), p. 70

43. Mushirul Hasan (ed.), *Proceedings of the Indian National Congress, Volume 2 1890–1894*, cited in Chandra, *Economic Nationalism*, p. 585

44. Arthur H. Nethercot, *The Last Four Lives of Annie Besant* (London, 1963), p. 55

45. L. S. S. O'Malley, *Bihar and Orissa District Gazetteers, Saran* (Patna, 1930; reprinted New Delhi, 2007), p. 36

46. Annie Besant, *India: A Nation: A Plea for Self-Government* (London, 1915), p. 1

47. Curzon, *Speeches, Vol. III: 1902–1905* (Calcutta, n.d.), p. 160

48. *Speeches by Lord Curzon of Kedleston, Viceroy and Governor General of India, Vol. IV: 1904–1905* (Calcutta, 1906), p. 212; Bipan Chandra, 'Colonial India: British versus Indian Views of Development', *Review (Fernand Braudel Center)* 14(1) (1991)

49. Chandra, *Economic Nationalism*, p. 19

50. Ibid., pp. 11–12

51. Gordon Johnson, *Provincial Politics and Indian Nationalism: Bombay and the Indian National Congress 1880–1915* (Cambridge, 1973), p. 79; Stanley Wolpert, *Tilak and Gokhale: Revolution and Reform in the Making of Modern India* (Oxford, 1990), pp. 52–6

52. Tanika Sarkar, 'A Nation of Husbands? Intimate Violence and Nationalism in Colonial Bengal', paper presented at the Centre of South Asian Studies, Cambridge, June 2016 (unpublished)

53. Wolpert, *Tilak and Gokhale*, p. 68

54. *Kesari*, 8 September 1896

55. *Kesari*, 15 June 1897; Cited in Queen Empress v. Bal Gangadhar Tilak and Keshav Mahadev Pal (1897), *Indian Law Review*, 22 Bom. 112. Lakshmi is the goddess of wealth. Here again, the recourse to double-entendre suggests that the Hindu goddess has been interfered with, and abducted, by the white man: a blow to Hindu masculine pride

56. For analyses of Chatterjee's varied works, see Tapan Raychaudhuri, *Europe Reconsidered: Perceptions of the West in Nineteenth-Century Bengal* (Delhi, 1988); Sudipta Kaviraj, *The Unhappy Consciousness: Bankimchandra Chattopadhyay and the Formation of Nationalist Discourse in India* (New York, 1995); and Partha Chatterjee, *Nationalist Thought and the Colonial World: A Derivative Discourse?* (London, 1986)

57. *Sujalam, suphalam, malayaja sheetalam, shasya shyamalam, mataram, bande mataram!* The English translation, penned by Aurobindo Ghosh, fails to do it justice, as the first lines suggest:
    Mother, I bow to thee!
    Rich with thy hurrying streams,
    Bright with orchard gleams

58. Joseph S. Alter, *The Wrestler's Body: Identity and Ideology in North India* (Berkeley, 1992)

59. Francis Robinson, 'Crisis of Authority: Crisis of Islam?', *Journal of the Royal Asiatic Society* 19(3) (2009), pp. 339–54

60. Masani, *Dadabhai Naoroji*, p. 57

61. Curzon's note, 'Minute on Territorial Redistribution', 28 June 1903, cited in Sumit Sarkar, *The Swadeshi Movement in Bengal, 1903–1908* (New Delhi, 1973) p. 15

62. David Gilmour, *Curzon* (London, 1994), p. 15

63. Ibid.

64. Denzil Ibbetson, cited in Sarkar, *Swadeshi*, p. 43

65. Sarkar, *Swadeshi*, p. 56

66. Ibid., pp. 135–6

67. 'The Present Situation', *Speeches of Aurobindo Ghosh* (Chandernagore, 1922), p. 36

68. Manmohan Ghosh to Laurence Binyon, 18 February 1888, cited in A. B. Purani, *The Life of Sri Aurobindo* (Pondicherry, 2006), p. 24

69. Teresa Segura Garcia, 'Baroda, the British Empire and the World, *c.*1875–1939', doctoral thesis (University of Cambridge, 2016)

70. Sri Aurobindo, *On Himself* (Pondicherry, 1972), p. 98

71. Haridas Mukherjee and Uma Mukherjee, *Sri Aurobindo and the New Thought in Indian Politics* (Calcutta, 1964), p. xxiv

72. Sri Aurobindo, 'Bhawani Mandir', cited in Mukherjee and Mukherjee, *Sri Aurobindo*, p. xxv

73. Sarkar, *Swadeshi*

74. Rabindranath Tagore, *Swadeshi Samaj* (Calcutta, 1962); Goswami, *Producing India*, pp. 252–3

75. Sarkar, *Swadeshi*, p. 55

76. Bipin Chandra Pal, *Swadeshi and Swaraj: The Rise of New Patriotism* (Calcutta, 1954); also cited in Goswami, *Producing India*, p. 242

77. Sarkar, *Swadeshi*, p. 258

78. Ibid., p. 259

79. Ibid., p. 261

80. Ibid., pp. 478–9; Peter Heehs, *The Bomb in Bengal: The Rise of Revolutionary Terrorism in India, 1900–1910* (New Delhi, 1993)

81. *The Statesman*, 2 May 1908. His age was a matter of dispute. 'Anglo-India' held that he was an adult, no doubt to ensure he got the maximum penalty

82. Kama MacLean, *A Revolutionary History of Interwar India: Violence, Image, Voice and Text* (London, 2015)

83. Gandhi, *Autobiography*, p. 58

84. Ibid., p. 49

85. Ibid., pp. 70–1

86. Leela Gandhi, *Affective Communities: Anticolonial Thought, Fin-de-Siècle Radicalism and the Politics of Friendship* (Durham, NC, 2006)

87. Dilip M. Menon, 'An Eminent Victorian: Gandhi, *Hind Swaraj* and the Crisis of Liberal Democracy in the Nineteenth Century', *History of the Present* 7(1) (2017)

88. Ajay Skaria, *Unconditional Equality: Gandhi's Religion of Resistance* (Minneapolis and London, 2016), pp. 40–1

89. Banerjee, *Imperial Citizens*

90. Anthony J. Parel (ed.), *Gandhi: 'Hind Swaraj' and Other Writings* (Cambridge, 2009), p. 38

91. Ibid., p. 40

92. Howard Spodek, 'On the Origins of Gandhi's Political Methodology: The Heritage of Kathiawad and Gujarat', *Journal of Asian Studies* 30(2) (1971); David Hardiman, *Gandhi in His Time and Ours: The Global Legacy of His Ideas* (New York, 2003)

93. Menon, 'An Eminent Victorian'

94. Ibid., p. 49

95. Chatterjee, *Nationalist Thought*; Uday Singh Mehta, 'Patience, Inwardness and Self-Knowledge in Gandhi's *Hind Swaraj*', *Public Culture* 23(2) (2011)

96. John Breuilly, *Nationalism and the State* (Chicago, 1994)

97. E. S. Montagu, note on 'Finance', Montagu Papers, Trinity College, Cambridge, 1/2/10; also see Keith Jeffery, '"An English Barrack in the Oriental Seas"? India in the Aftermath of the First World War', *Modern Asian Studies* 15(3) (1981), p. 374

98. Judith Brown, *Gandhi: Prisoner of Hope* (New Haven, 1991), p. 116

99. Montagu Papers, Trinity College Cambridge, 2/8/1, p. 134; Montagu, *An Indian Diary* (London, 1930), p. 58

100. Maia Ramnath, *Haj to Utopia: How the Ghadar Movement Charted Global Radicalism and Attempted to Overthrow the British Empire* (Berkeley, 2011)

101. Gandhi, *Autobiography*, p. 336

102. Ibid., p. 337

103. Ibid., p. 339

104. B. R. Nanda, *The Nehrus* (London, 1962), p. 165

105. Ibid., p. 166

106. Sherman, *State Violence*, p. 16

107. Banerjee, *Imperial Citizens*

108. Edward Thompson, *Rabindranath Tagore: Poet and Dramatist* (London, 1926, 1948), p. 259

109. David M. Laushey, *Bengal Terrorism and the Marxist Left* (Calcutta, 1975)

110. Sherman, *State Violence*, p. 5

111. Durba Ghosh, *Gentlemanly Terrorists: Political Violence and the Colonial State in India, 1919–1947* (Cambridge, 2017)

112. Judith M. Brown, *Gandhi's Rise to Power: Indian Politics 1915–1922* (Cambridge, 1972), p. 245

113. Shahid Amin, *Event, Metaphor, Memory: Chauri Chaura 1922–1992* (Delhi, 1995)

114. Gandhi, *Autobiography*, p. 347

115. Ranajit Guha, *Dominance without Hegemony: History and Power in Colonial India* (Delhi, 1998). Also see Sumit Sarkar, 'Popular Movements and National Leadership, 1945–47', *Economic and Political Weekly* 17(14/16) (1982)

116. Besant, *India: A Nation*, p. 2

117. Bernard Cohn, *Colonialism and Its Forms of Knowledge: The British in India* (Princeton, 1996)

118. David Gilmartin, 'A Magnificent Gift: Muslim Nationalism and the Election Process in Colonial Punjab', *Comparative Studies in Society and History* 40(3) (1998), p. 417

119. Percival Spear, *Twilight of the Mughals: Studies in Late Mughal Delhi* (Cambridge, 1951)

120. Seyyed Vali Reza Nasr, *Mawdudi and the Making of Islamic Revivalism* (Oxford, 1996), p. 10

121. Seema Alavi, *Muslim Cosmopolitanism in the Age of Empire* (Cambridge, MA, 2015), p. 19

122. Ian Douglas Henderson, Gail Minault and Christian W. Troll (eds), *Abul Kalam Azad: An Intellectual and Religious Biography* (Delhi, 1993), p. 1

123. Muhammad Iqbal, *Rumuz-i-Bekhudi* (*The Mysteries of Selflessness*), in W. Theodore de Bary (ed.), *Sources of Indian Tradition* (New York, 1958), p. 756. Also cited in Francis Robinson, 'Technology and Religious Change: Islam and the Impact of Print', *Modern Asian Studies* 27(1) (1993), p. 244. See also Muhammad Iqbal, 'The Mosque at Cordoba'

124. Robinson, 'Technology and Religious Change', p. 243

125. Seema Alavi, '"Fugitive Mullahs and Outlawed Fanatics": Indian Muslims in Nineteenth Century Trans-Asiatic Imperial Rivalries', *Modern Asian Studies* 45(6) (2011)

126. Javed Majeed, *Muhammad Iqbal: Islam, Aesthetics and Postcolonialism* (Abingdon, 2009), p. 1

127. Constance E. Padwick, *Muslim Devotions: A Study of Prayer-Manuals in Common Use* (London, 1961), p.119, cited in Robinson, 'Technology and Religious Change'

128. Abul Kalam Azad, *Zikra* (*Thoughts of the Past*) (1925), cited in Henderson, *Abul Kalam Azad*, p. 49

129. Robinson, 'Technology and Religious Change', p. 245

130. Nasr, *Mawdudi*, pp. 12–13

131. Abul Kalam Azad, *Azadi Ki Kahani*, p. 176, cited in Henderson, *Abul Kalam Azad*, p. 39

132. Mohamed Ali, *My Life: A Fragment: An Autobiographical Sketch of Maulana Mohamed Ali* (Lahore, 1942), pp. 5–6

133. Ibid., p. 477

134. Haraprasad Chattopadhyaya, *Internal Migration in India: A Case Study of Bengal* (Calcutta, 1987); also see Chapter 4

135. Ibid., p. 471

136. Henderson, *Abul Kalam Azad*, p. 51

137. Hafeez Malik, *Sir Sayyid Ahmad Khan and Muslim Modernization in India and Pakistan* (New York, 1980), p. 136

138. 'Sir Syed and the Word *Qaum* (Nation)', in *Writings and Speeches of Sir Syed Ahmed Khan* (Shan Mohammad, ed.) (Bombay, 1972), p. 267

139. 'The Indian National Congress', to Badruddin Tyabji, in *Writings and Speeches of Sir Syed Ahmed Khan*, p. 243

140. J. M. S. Baljon, *The Reforms and Religious Ideas of Sir Sayyid Ahmed Khan* (Lahore, 1949), p. 66, cited in Gail Minault, *The Khilafat Movement: Religious Symbolism and Political Mobilization in India* (New York, 1982; reprinted New Delhi, 1999), p. 14

141. Dufferin to Kimberley, 26 April 1886, cited in Seal, *Emergence*, p. 185

142. Rochana Bajpai, *Debating Difference: Group Rights and Liberal Democracy in India* (New Delhi, 2011)

143. Ali, *My Life: A Fragment*, p. 43

144. Minault, *Khilafat Movement*, pp. 93–4

145. Ibid., p. 95

146. Ibid., p. 123

147. Ibid., p. 73

148. Ibid., p. 137

149. Ibid., pp. 173–4

150. David Gilmartin, *Empire and Islam: Punjab and the Making of Pakistan* (London, 1988); Sarah Ansari, *Sufi Saints and State Power: The Pirs of Sind, 1843–1947* (Cambridge, 1992)

151. Alavi, '"Fugitive Mullahs"'

152. Ranajit Guha, *Elementary Aspects of Peasant Insurgency in Colonial India* (Durham, NC, 1999)

153. Ajay Skaria, 'Gandhi's Politics: Liberalism and the Question of the Ashram', *South Atlantic Quarterly* 101(4) (2002); and by the same author, '"No politics without religion": of Secularism and Gandhi', in Vinay Lal (ed.), *Political Hinduism: The Religious Imagination in Public Spheres* (New Delhi, 2009)

154. Nanda, *Nehrus*, p. 240

155. Joya Chatterji, 'Decolonisation in South Asia: The Long View', in Martin Thomas and Andrew Thompson (eds), *The Oxford Handbook of the Ends of Empire* (Oxford, 2018). Also in Joya Chatterji, *Partition's Legacies* (Ranikhet, 2019)

156. Ian Bryant Wells, *Jinnah: Ambassador of Hindu–Muslim Unity* (London, 2006)

157. Rohit De, *A People's Constitution: The Everyday Life of Law in the Indian Republic* (Princeton, 2018)

158. Motilal Nehru to Pandit Pritinath, 22 December 1899, in B. R. Nanda, *The Nehrus: Motilal and Jawaharlal* (New Delhi, 2007), p. 39

159. Mian Ata Rabbani, *I Was the Quaid's Aide-de-Camp* (Karachi, 1996), p. 173

160. Jinnah to K. M. Ashraf, 1921, cited in Hector Bolitho, *Jinnah: Creator of Pakistan* (Karachi, 2006), p. 9

161. Wells, *Jinnah*, p. 16

162. Ibid., p. 7

163. Ibid., p. 20

164. Ibid., p. 23. For more details, see Chapter 5

165. Ibid., pp. 35–6

166. Syed Sharifuddin Pirzada (ed.), *Foundations of Pakistan: All-India Muslim League Documents, 1906–1947*, Vol. 1 (Karachi, 1969), p. 258

167. A. M. Zaidi and Shaheda Zaidi (eds), *The Encyclopaedia of the Indian National Congress*, Vol. 6 (New Delhi, 1976), p. 442

168. 'Memorandum of the Nineteen', in Syed Sharifuddin Pirzada (ed.), *The Collected Works of Quaid-e-Azam Mohammad Ali Jinnah, Vol. 1, 1906–1921* (Karachi, 1984), p. 144

169. Montagu's Diary, 27 November 1917, Montagu Papers A/52/8/1. Also cited in Wells, *Jinnah*, p. 107. Montagu Papers, Trinity College Cambridge, 2/8/1, p. 138; Montagu, *Indian Diary*, p. 61

170. Jinnah to Gandhi, 30 October 1920, *Bombay Chronicle*; 1 November 1920. Also cited in Wells, *Jinnah*, p. 102

171. B. R. Nanda, *Jawaharlal Nehru: Rebel and Statesman* (New Delhi, 1995), pp. 10–13

172. Reading to Olivier, 13 March 1924, Reading Papers, Vol. 7

173. M. A. Jinnah, *History of the Fourteen Points*, p. 4

174. *Bombay Chronicle*, 12 December 1927, cited in Wells, *Jinnah*, p. 171

175. M. S. S. Pandian, *Brahmin and Non-Brahmin: Genealogies of the Tamil Political Present* (Delhi, 2007)

176. Rafi Ahmed Kidwai to Motilal Nehru, 5 December 1924, All India Congress Committee (AICC) Papers 37/1925. Cited in Wells, *Jinnah*, p. 144

177. Thakurdas to Sarabhai, 18 November 1930, Thakurdas Papers, File 126. Cited in Claude Markovits, *Indian Business and Nationalist Politics 1931–1939: The Indigenous Capitalist Class and the Rise of the Congress Party* (Cambridge, 1985), p. 74

178. Markovits, *Indian Business and Nationalist Politics*, p. 77

179. Vinayak Damodar Savarkar, *Hindutva: Who Is a Hindu?* (1923)

180. William Gould, *Hindu Nationalism and the Language of Politics in Late Colonial India* (Cambridge, 2004); Aishwarya Pandit, 'From

United Provinces to Uttar Pradesh: Heartland Politics 1947–1970', doctoral dissertation (University of Cambridge, 2015)

181. Maulana Abul Kalam Azad, *India Wins Freedom: The Complete Version* (Delhi, 1988), p. 17

182. Motilal Nehru to Thakurdas, 28 April 1928, Thakurdas Papers, F. 40, cited in Wells, *Jinnah*, p. 174

183. Wells, *Jinnah*, p. 187

184. Muhammad Iqbal's Presidential address at the All-India Muslim League Conference, 1930, Allahabad. Latif Ahmed Sherwani (ed.), *Speeches, Writings and Statements of Iqbal* (Lahore, 1977, 2nd edn), pp. 3–26

185. James Chiriyankandath, '"Democracy" Under the Raj: Elections and Separate Representation in British India', in Niraja Gopal Jayal (ed.), *Democracy in India* (New Delhi, 2001), pp. 53–81

186. John Gallagher and Anil Seal, 'Britain and India between the Wars', *Modern Asian Studies* 15(3) (1981), p. 407

187. Joya Chatterji, *Bengal Divided: Hindu Communalism and Partition, 1932–1947* (Cambridge, 1994)

188. Ayesha Jalal, *The Sole Spokesman: Jinnah, the Muslim League and the Demand for Pakistan* (Cambridge, 1985); Ishtiaq Ahmed, *Jinnah: His Successes, Failures and Role in History* (Delhi, 2019)

189. Venkat Dhulipala, *Creating a New Medina: State Power, Islam and the Quest for Pakistan in Late Colonial North India* (Delhi, 2015), p. 6

190. Ibid., p. 358

191. Ibid., p. 322

192. Ibid., p. 325

193. Faisal Devji, *Muslim Zion: Pakistan as a Political Idea* (London, 2013)

194. Mahmudabad to Jinnah, 8 April 1940, Rizwan Ahmed (ed.), *Quaid-i-Azam Papers, 1940* (Karachi and Lahore, 1976), pp. 98–102, also discussed in Dhulipala, *Creating a New Medina*, p. 207

195. Ibid., pp. 105–6, cited in Dhulipala, *Creating a New Medina*, p. 208

196. See, for instance, Ishan Mukherjee, 'Agitations, Riots and the Transitional State in Calcutta, 1945–50', doctoral dissertation (University of Cambridge, 2017); and Taylor C. Sherman, *Muslim Belonging in Secular India: Negotiating Citizenship in Postcolonial Hyderabad* (Cambridge, 2015)

2 CITIZENSHIP AND NATION-BUILDING AFTER INDEPENDENCE: SOUTH ASIAN EXPERIENCES

1. The capacity of European states, now all allies, assisted by the American Marshall Plan to rebuild Europe, was far greater than that of their

counterparts in South Asia. Tony Judt, *Postwar: A History of Europe since 1945* (London, 2005)

2. Joya Chatterji, 'Princes, Subjects and Gandhi: Alternatives to Citizenship at the End of Empire', in Naren Nanda (ed.), *Gandhi's Moral Politics* (London, 2018). Joya Chatterji, 'Princes at Midnight', Radhakrishnan Lecture series, Oxford, 2022

3. Decennial growth in the population of Karachi, Censuses of Pakistan:

Year	Population	% increase
1911	186,771	37
1921	244,162	30
1931	300,779	23
1941	435,887	45
1951	1,137,667	161
1961	2,044,044	80
1972	3,606,746	76
1981	5,437,984	51

Also see Vazira Fazila-Yacoobali Zamindar, *The Long Partition and the Making of Modern South Asia: Refugees, Boundaries, Histories* (New York, 2007), and Anjali Bhardwaj Datta, 'Rebuilding Lives, Redefining Spaces: Women in Post-Colonial Delhi', doctoral dissertation (University of Cambridge, 2015)

4. Sarah Ansari, 'Pakistan's 1951 Census: State-Building in Post-Partition Sindh', *Journal of South Asian Studies* 39(4) (2016), Table 1, p. 838

5. B. Shiva Rao (ed.), *The Framing of India's Constitution: Select Documents*, 5 vols (New Delhi, 1966), i, p. 6. The Nehru Report of 1928 (mentioned in Chapter 1) had taken a similar line. Ibid., p. 59

6. See the responses to the questionnaire 'safeguards' sent on 28 February 1947 to the subcommittees on fundamental rights and minority rights. Shiva Rao, *India's Constitution*, ii, pp. 391–2. Also see Pant's speech on the subject in the Constituent Assembly on 24 January 1947. *Constituent Assembly of India: Debates* (12 vols, Faridabad, 1946–50), Vol. II, p. 328; henceforth *CAID*

7. *CAID*, Vol. III, p. 417

8. Ibid., p. 419

9. See R. V. Dhulekar's question on this subject, ibid., p. 421

10. See Patel's remark urging K. Santhanam to withdraw his proposed amendment to this new clause, ibid.

11. Ibid., p. 527

12. See the remarks by B. R. Ambedkar and C. Rajagopalachari on 2 May 1947, ibid.; and Gyanendra Pandey, 'Can a Muslim Be an Indian?', *Comparative Studies in Society and History* 41(4) (1999)

13. *Constituent Assembly of Pakistan: Debates* (16 vols, Karachi, 1947–54), Vol. I, no. 2, pp. 16–20; henceforth *CADP*

14. Jinnah's speech 'Those who gave great sacrifices', 9 June 1947, is cited in Tahir Hasnain Naqvi, 'The Politics of Commensuration: The Violence of Partition and the Making of the Pakistani State', *Journal of Historical Sociology* 20(1–2) (2007), p. 56

15. *CADP*, Vol. I, no. 2, p. 16

16. Taylor C. Sherman, 'Migration, Citizenship and Belonging in Hyderabad (Deccan), 1946–1956', *Modern Asian Studies* 45(1) (2011)

17. Telegram from Patel to the governor of East Punjab, 24 August 1947, Durga Das (ed.), *India: Sardar Patel's Correspondence 1945–50* (10 vols, Ahmedabad, 1971–2), Vol. IV, p. 249; henceforth *SPC*

18. Ian Talbot, 'The August 1947 Violence in Sheikhupura City', in Ian Talbot (ed.), *The Independence of India and Pakistan: New Approaches and Reflections* (Karachi, 2013)

19. Telegram from Sampuran Singh to Patel, 27 August 1947, *SPC*, Vol. IV, p. 256

20. Government of India, Ministry of External Affairs papers, National Archives of India, F./2-1/48-Pak I (Vol. I); henceforth MEAI

21. Note from Lt Colonel Kirpal to the Joint Defence Council, 28 August 1947. Mountbatten Papers (Mountbatten Papers Database, University of Southampton), Section I (MB1), D/46/3

22. On the role played by social workers in shaping policy, see Joya Chatterji, 'South Asian Histories of Citizenship, 1946–1970', *Historical Journal* 55(4) (2012). Also see Uditi Sen, *Citizen Refugee: Forging the Indian Nation after Partition* (Cambridge, 2018); and Bhardwaj Datta, 'Rebuilding Lives, Redefining Spaces'

23. Salma Tasadduque Hussain to M. A. Jinnah, 22 August 1947, Z. H. Zaidi (ed.), *Quaid-i-Azam Mohammed Ali Jinnah Papers: First Series* (18 vols, Islamabad, 1998–2011), Vol. V, p. 90

24. Tahir Kamran, 'The Unfolding Crisis in Punjab, March–August 1947: Key Turning Points and British Responses', *Journal of Punjab Studies* 14 (2007), pp. 187–210

25. Ian Copland, 'The Further Shores of Partition: Ethnic Cleansing in Rajasthan 1947', *Past & Present* 160(1) (1998)

26. See Rajendra Prasad to Patel, 10 September 1947; and Patel's reply to Prasad, 12 September 1947, *SPC*, Vol. IV, pp. 340–1

27. See Patel's directions of 3 October 1947 that 'we should insist that our motor transport convoys bring in our refugees', ibid., p. 308

28. Baldev Singh to Patel, 6 October 1947, ibid., pp. 348–9

29. For example, Ritu Menon and Kamla Bhasin, *Borders and Boundaries: Women in India's Partition* (New Delhi, 1998)

30. M. S. Randhawa, *Out of the Ashes: An Account of the Rehabilitation of Refugees from West Pakistan in Rural Areas of East Punjab* (Chandigarh, 1954)

31. Joya Chatterji, 'Secularization and Constitutive Moments: Insights from Partition Diplomacy in South Asia', in Humeira Iqtidar and Tanika Sarkar (eds), *Tolerance, Secularization and Democratic Politics in South Asia* (Cambridge, 2018)

32. MEAI/F.8-15/48/Pak-I; for Pakistan, see memo by A. Rashid Ibrahim dated 25 May 1948 (Ref. no. 315-Cord/48, MEAI/F.8-14/48-Pak-I; and MEAI/F. 10(9)/Pak (A)/1949

33. Such cases run into the thousands. See, for instance, MEAI/F.9-10/48-Pak I

34. For examples from West Bengal, see Government of Bengal Intelligence Bureau (Calcutta) (henceforth GB IB), 1838-48 (KW) and GB IB 1809-48 (Nadia). For instances in Delhi, see Delhi State Archives (henceforth DSA), 16/48/DC and DSA, DCO/259/47

35. M. L. Mehra to the district commissioner of Delhi, 9 October 1948, DSA, DC, 16/48

36. Noor Ahmed to J. M. L. Prabhu (Custodian of evacuee property), New Delhi, 13 November 1947, DSA, DC, 191/1947

37. B. S. Guha, *Studies in Social Tensions Among the Refugees from Eastern Pakistan* (Calcutta, 1959); and Joya Chatterji, '"Dispersal" and the Failure of Rehabilitation: Refugee Camp-dwellers and Squatters in West Bengal', *Modern Asian Studies* 41(5) (2007)

38. Sarah Ansari, *Life after Partition: Migration, Community and Strife in Sindh, 1947–1962* (Oxford, 2005)

39. Engin F. Isin, 'Theorising Acts of Citizenship', in Engin F. Isin and Greg M. Nielsen (eds), *Acts of Citizenship* (London, 2008), pp. 17, 26

40. GB IB File no. 1838-48 (KW)

41. Nehru to Patel, 6 October 1947, *SPC*, Vol. IV, p. 400

42. Ordinance XXXIV of 1948, MEAI/ F.26-189/48-Pak I

43. 'Rules Regarding Permit System Introduced between India and Pakistan', Notification no. II (55)/48- General, *Gazette of India*, 14 September 1948

44. Zamindar, *Long Partition*, p. 82

45. V. D. Moray, Bombay C.I.D., to A. Jayaram, 14 September 1948, MEAI/Pak-I Section, F. 26-189/48-Pak I

46. See, for instance, the lengthy discussions about whether the permits of Noor Mohamed and Ishaque Khan, two Muslims 'found' in Nagpur, were fake or authentic, ibid.

47. C. N. Chandra, secretary, ministry of rehabilitation, to all chief secretaries, 9 May 1949, GB IB 1210-48 (4)

48. *AIR* 1964 MP 272 Bench: H. Krishnan, P. Sharma

49. For the difficulties appellants faced in proving their claims, see any of the 6,000 cases fought in the Indian courts, e.g. the State of Mysore v. Abdul Salam on 5/7/51; or Nazir Hussain v. the State on 13/12/51, in which the judge described the plaintiff's case as 'balderdash'

50. 'An Ordinance to Provide for the Administration of Evacuee Property and for Certain Matters Connected Therewith', Ordinance no. XXVII of 1949, *Gazette of India*, 18 October 1949, MEAI, F. 17-39/49-AFRI

51. The reasons why India excluded West Bengal, Assam and Tipperah from the evacuee property regime are addressed in Joya Chatterji, *The Disinherited: Migrants, Minorities and Citizenship in South Asia* (Cambridge, forthcoming)

52. Ordinance no. XXVII of 1949

53. T. H. Marshall, 'Citizenship and Social Class' (1950), reprinted in Jeff Manza and Michael Sauder (eds), *Inequality and Society: Social Science Perspectives on Social Stratification* (New York, 2009)

54. 'The problem of evacuee property and efforts made to solve it', MEAI/11(21)/49-Pak III

55. The Displaced Persons (Compensation And Rehabilitation) Act, Act 44 of 1954, 9 October 1954

56. Nazar Abbas Syed (ed.), *The Citizenship Laws with NADRA Laws* (Lahore, 2008)

57. Claude Markovits, Jacques Pouchepadass and Sanjay Subrahmanyam (eds), *Society and Circulation: Mobile People and Itinerant Cultures in South Asia, 1750–1950* (Delhi, 2003). Also see Chapter 4

58. Abul Barkat et al., *Political Economy of the Vested Property Act in Rural Bangladesh* (Dhaka, 1997); M. I. Farooqui, *Law of Abandoned Property with Principles of Administrative Law* (Dhaka, 2000); Papiya Ghosh, *Partition and the South Asian Diaspora: Extending the Subcontinent* (Delhi, 2007)

59. Giorgio Agamben, *State of Exception* (Chicago, 2005); Hannah Arendt, *The Origins of Totalitarianism* (1951); Seyla Benhabib, *The Rights of Others: Aliens, Residents and Citizens* (Cambridge, 2004)

60. Bhardwaj Datta, 'Rebuilding Lives, Redefining Spaces', p. 86

61. Hilal Ahmed, *Muslim Political Discourse in Postcolonial India: Monuments, Memory, Contestation* (Abingdon, 2014)

62. Attia Hosain, *Sunlight on a Broken Column* (London, 1961)

63. Nehru to Patel, 30 September 1947, *SPC*, Vol. IV, p. 298

64. Patel to Nehru, 12 October 1947, ibid., pp. 299–304

65. Benjamin Zachariah, *Developing India: An Intellectual and Social History, c.1930–1950* (New Delhi, 2005) and Sunil Khilnani, *The Idea of India* (London, 1997)

66. Laurence Gautier, 'A Laboratory for a Composite India? Jamia Millia Isla-mia around the Time of Partition', *Modern Asian Studies* 54(1) (2020); and Laurence Gautier, *Between Nation and Community: Muslim Univer-sities and Indian Politics after Partition* (Cambridge, forthcoming)

67. AICC papers, first instalment. F. No. G-18 KW-1 (P-II) 1947–48. Cited in Aishwarya Pandit, 'From United Provinces to Uttar Pradesh: Heartland Politics 1947–1970', doctoral dissertation (University of Cambridge, 2015)

68. Joya Chatterji, *The Spoils of Partition: Bengal and India, 1947–1967* (Cambridge, 2007), pp. 177–80

69. Robin Jeffrey, *India, Rebellion to Republic: Selected Writings 1857–1990* (New Delhi, 1990), p. 105

70. Sekhar Bandyopadhyay, *Decolonization in South Asia: Meanings of Free-dom in Post-Independence West Bengal, 1947–52* (Abingdon, 2009), p. 146

71. *New York Times*, 30 January 1948

72. Yasmin Khan, 'Performing Peace: Gandhi's Assassination as a Critical Moment in the Consolidation of the Nehruvian State', *Modern Asian Studies* 45(1) (2011)

73. Joya Chatterji, *Bengal Divided: Hindu Communalism and Partition, 1932–1947* (Cambridge, 1994)

74. Walter Andersen and Shridhar Damle, *The Brotherhood in Saffron: The Rashtriya Swayamsevak Sangh and Hindu Revivalism* (Boulder, 1997), pp. 51–2; also All India Hindu Mahasabha (AIHM) Papers, C-155/1947

75. Letter to Ashutosh Lahiry, Hindu Mahasabha Papers NMML, File no. P-120 Part-I, cited in Pandit, 'From United Provinces to Uttar Pradesh'

76. Chatterji, *Bengal Divided*; William Gould, *Hindu Nationalism and the Language of Politics in Late Colonial India* (Cambridge, 2004)

77. Stanley A. Kochanek, *The Congress Party of India: The Dynamics of One-Party Democracy* (Princeton, 1968), p. 32

78. Ibid.

79. Ibid.

80. Pandit, 'From United Provinces to Uttar Pradesh'

81. Chatterji, *Spoils of Partition*; Joya Chatterji, 'Of Graveyards and Ghet-tos: Muslims in West Bengal, 1947–67', in Mushirul Hasan and Asim Roy (eds), *Living Together Separately: Cultural India in History and Politics* (New Delhi, 2005), pp. 222–49

82. Letter from Jawaharlal Nehru to Chief Ministers, 15 October 1947, in Jawaharlal Nehru, *Letters to Chief Ministers, 1947–1949*, Vol I, (ed. G. Parthasarathi) (Government of India, 1985 edn), pp. 1–5

83. Jawaharlal Nehru, *Letters to Chief Ministers, 1947–1964*, Vol. I, (ed. G. Parthasarathi) (Government of India, 1989 edn)

84. Taylor C. Sherman, *Nehru's India: A History in Seven Myths* (Princeton, 2022)

85. If you can't make the journey yourself, video clips are available online

86. Iqbal's Presidential address at the All-India Muslim League Conference, 1930, Allahabad in Latif Ahmed Sherwani (ed.), *Speeches, Writings and Statements of Iqbal* (Lahore, 1977, 2nd edn), pp. 3–26. Emphasis added

87. Javid Iqbal (ed.), *Stray Reflections: The Private Notebook of Muhammad Iqbal* (Lahore, 2008), p. 142

88. Naveeda Khan, *Muslim Becoming: Aspiration and Skepticism in Pakistan* (Hyderabad, 2012)

89. See Ayesha Jalal and Anil Seal, 'Alternative to Partition: Muslim Politics between the Wars', *Modern Asian Studies* 15(3) (1981); David Page, *Prelude to Partition: The Indian Muslims and the Imperial System of Control 1920–1932* (Delhi, 1982, 1987); Imran Ali, *The Punjab Under Imperialism, 1885–1947* (Princeton, 1988); Ian Talbot, *Punjab and the Raj 1849–1947* (New Delhi, 1988); Andrew Sartori, *Bengal in Global Concept History: Culturalism in the Age of Capital* (Chicago, 2008); Layli Uddin, 'In the Land of Eternal Eid: Maulana Bhashani and the Political Mobilisation of Peasants and Lower-Class Urban Workers in East Pakistan, c.1930s–1971', doctoral dissertation (Royal Holloway, University of London, 2016); Mukulika Banerjee, *The Pathan Unarmed: Opposition and Memory in the North West Frontier* (Oxford, 2000)

90. Farina Mir, 'Genre and Devotion in Popular Punjabi Narratives: Rethinking Cultural and Religious Syncretism', *Comparative Studies in Society and History* 48(3) (2006); and Farina Mir, *The Social Space of Language: Vernacular Culture in British Colonial Punjab* (Berkeley, 2010)

91. Derived from the Arabic *kafa*, meaning group, this poetry lent itself to the Kafi genre of singing, popular throughout South Asia. A rich and varied poetic form, it has remained centred on the dialogue between the Soul and the Creator, symbolised by the Sufi *murid* (disciple) and his *Murshid* (Master), and often by the lover and his beloved

92. Leonard Binder, *Religion and Politics in Pakistan* (Berkeley, 1961)

93. Ibid., p. 35. Also see Iqbal, *Stray Reflections*

94. Abul A'la Maududi, *The Process of Islamic Revolution* (Pathankot, 1947), pp. 2–5, cited in Binder, *Religion and Politics*, p. 93

95. Binder, *Religion and Politics*

96. Seyyed Vali Reza Nasr, *Mawdudi and the Making of Islamic Revivalism* (Oxford, 1997), pp. 42–3

97. Cited in David Gilmartin, *Civilization and Modernity: Narrating the Creation of Pakistan* (New Delhi, 2017), p. ix

98. Neilesh Bose, *Recasting the Region: Language, Culture and Islam in Colonial Bengal* (New Delhi, 2014); Tariq Omar Ali, *A Local History*

of Global Capital: Jute and Peasant Life in the Bengal Delta (Princeton, 2018)

99. Abul Hashim, *In Retrospection* (Dacca, 1974); Abul Mansur Ahmad, *Amar Dekha Rajnitir 50 Bochor* ('Fifty Years of Politics as I Saw It') (Dacca, 1970)

100. Gilmartin, *Civilization and Modernity*, p. xxxvii

101. Mohammad Ayub Khan, *Friends Not Masters: A Political Autobiography* (London, 1967), p. viii

102. Ibid., p. 47

103. Faisal Devji, *Muslim Zion: Pakistan as a Political Idea* (London, 2013)

104. Jinnah's speech, 'Those who gave great sacrifices', 9 June 1947, is cited in Tahir Hasnain Naqvi, 'The Politics of Commensuration: The Violence of Partition and the Making of the Pakistani State', *Journal of Historical Sociology* 20(1–2) (2007), p. 56

105. *Constituent Assembly of Pakistan Debates* (16 vols, Karachi, 1947–54) Vol. I, no. 2, p. 16

106. Zamindar, *Long Partition*, pp. 68–9

107. Jinnah, 'Provincialism: A Curse', Quetta, 15 June 1948, cited in Philip Oldenburg, '"A Place Insufficiently Imagined": Language, Belief and the Pakistan Crisis of 1971', *Journal of Asian Studies* 44(4) (1985), pp. 711–33

108. Christophe Jaffrelot, *The Pakistan Paradox: Instability and Resilience* (translated by Cynthia Schoch) (London, 2015), p. 103

109. Ibid., p. 102

110. M. Rafique Afzal (ed.), *Speeches and Statements of Quaid-i-Millat Liaquat Ali Khan (1941–1951)* (Lahore, 1987)

111. Citizens Archives of Pakistan, 10 November 2011, oral testimony of Qutubuddin Aziz and Mahmud Zaidi

112. Binder, *Religion and Politics*, pp. 142–3

113. Muhammad Reza Kazimi, *Liaquat Ali Khan: His Life and Work* (Oxford, 2004), p. 4

114. Ibid., p. 13. Emphasis added

115. Ibid.

116. Afzal, *Speeches and Statements of Quaid-i-Millat Liaquat*, p. xiv

117. Ibid., p. xxi

118. Ibid. Also see text of speech

119. Joya Chatterji, 'Secularisation and Partition Emergencies: Deep Diplomacy in South Asia', *Economic and Political Weekly* 48(50) (2013); Pallavi Raghavan, *Animosity at Bay: An Alternative History of the India–Pakistan Relationship, 1947–1952* (London, 2020)

120. Binder, *Religion and Politics*, p. 186

121. Rakesh Ankit, 'Probing Early Pakistan: East Bengal Politicians and Their Exchanges with Prime Minister Liaquat Ali Khan, 1947–51', *Indian Economic and Social History Review* 60(1) (2023)

122. Ayesha Jalal, *The State of Martial Rule: The Origins of Pakistan's Political Economy of Defence* (Cambridge, 1990)

123. *Report of the Linguistic Provinces Commission of India* (New Delhi, 1948), pp. 29–30; also see Robert D. King, *Nehru and the Language Politics of India* (Delhi, 1997)

124. Lisa Mitchell, *Language, Emotion and Politics in South India: The Making of a Mother Tongue* (Ranikhet, 2010), pp. 192–3

125. Salman Rushdie, *Midnight's Children* (London, 2008), p. 265

126. Thomas Blom Hansen, *Wages of Violence: Naming and Identity in Postcolonial Bombay* (Princeton, 2001), pp. 41–3

127. Kapil Acharya, *Shiv Sena Speaks* (Bombay, 1967), cited in Blom Hansen, *Wages of Violence*, p. 47

128. Sumathi Ramaswamy, *Passions of the Tongue: Language Devotion in Tamil India, 1891–1970* (Berkeley, 1997), p. 1

129. Gurujada Sriramamurti, *Kavi Jivitamulu* (Chennapatnam, 1893), p. 1, cited in Mitchell, *Language, Emotion and Politics*, p. 11

130. Translation from Mitchell, *Language, Emotion and Politics*, p. 68

131. Ramaswamy, *Passions of the Tongue*, p. 95

132. M. S. S. Pandian, *Brahmin and Non-Brahmin: Genealogies of the Tamil Political Present* (Hyderabad, 2007), pp. 122–3

133. Ibid., pp. 120–35

134. T. S. Raghavan, *Makers of Modern Tamil* (Tinnevelly, 1965), pp. 39–40, cited in Pandian, *Brahmin and Non-Brahmin*, pp. 124–5

135. 'The Ramayana, A True Reading', *Collected Works of Periyar E.V.R.* (compiled by K. Veeramani) (Chennai, 1981), pp. 616–19

136. Paula Richman, 'E. V. Ramasami's Reading of the *Ramayana*', in Paula Richman (ed.), *Many Ramayanas: The Diversity of a Narrative Tradition in South Asia* (Delhi, 1992), pp. 194–5

137. K. Veeramani, *Collected Works of Periyar E.V.R.* (Chennai, 2005)

138. Vanya Lochan, personal communication, 2 January 2017

139. Sheldon Pollock, *The Language of the Gods in the World of Men: Sanskrit, Culture and Power in Premodern India* (Berkeley, 2006)

140. Jnanabrata Bhattacharyya, 'Language, Class and Community in Bengal', *Comparative Studies of South Asia, Africa and the Middle East* 7(1–2) (1987)

141. Sufia M. Uddin, *Constructing Bangladesh: Religion, Ethnicity and Language in an Islamic Nation* (Chapel Hill, 2006), p. 96

142. Pradip Kumar Dutta, *Carving Blocs: Communal Ideology in Early Twentieth-century Bengal* (New Delhi, 1999); Sartori, *Bengal in Global Concept History*; Omar Ali, *Local History of Global Capital*

143. *The Moslem Chronicle*, 22 December 1900, p. 1481, cited in Rafiuddin Ahmed, *The Bengal Muslims, 1871–1906: A Quest for Identity* (Delhi, 1988), p. 129

144. Chatterji, *Bengal Divided*, pp. 68–9

145. Tapan Raychaudhuri, *The World in Our Time: A Memoir* (Noida, 2011), p. 103

146. Ramaswamy, *Passions of the Tongue*, p. 225

147. Ibid., p. 227

148. Mitchell, *Language, Emotion and Politics*, p. 189

149. Muhammad Ali Jinnah, *Speeches as Governor-General of Pakistan, 1947–48* (Karachi, n.d.), p. 90. Italics added. Also cited in Oldenburg, 'A Place Insufficiently Imagined', p. 716

150. Willem van Schendel, *A History of Bangladesh* (Cambridge, 2009), p. 156

151. Christopher Rolland King, *One Language, Two Scripts: The Hindi Movement in Nineteenth-century North India* (New Delhi, 1994)

152. Claire Alexander, Joya Chatterji and Annu Jalais, *The Bengal Diaspora: Rethinking Muslim Migration* (Abingdon, 2016)

153. Michael Billig, *Banal Nationalism* (London, 1995)

154. Srirupa Roy, *Beyond Belief: India and the Politics of Postcolonial Nationalism* (Durham, NC, 2007), p. 20

155. Gerrit W. Gong, 'The Beginning of History: Remembering and Forgetting as Strategic Issues', *Washington Quarterly* (Spring 2001)

156. Tapati Guha-Thakurta, *Monuments, Objects, Histories: Institutions of Art in Colonial and Postcolonial India* (Delhi, 2004)

157. R. E. M. Wheeler, The Archaeological Survey of India, 'Director-General's Report on the Development of the Department, 1944–48', December 1947 (Wheeler Archive E/1/10), cited in Mrinalini Venkateswaran, 'Constructing a Nation through Museum Collections', unpublished paper, p. 1

158. Venkateswaran, 'Constructing a Nation', p. 5. I am grateful to Mrinalini Venkateswaran for sharing with me her knowledge of archaeology and the museum scene in the 1940s. Also see Himanshu Prabha Ray, *Colonial Archaeology in South Asia: The Legacy of Sir Mortimer Wheeler* (Oxford, 2008)

159. Guha-Thakurta, *Monuments, Objects, Histories*, p. 177

160. Venkateswaran, 'Constructing a Nation', p. 18

161. Ibid., p. 17

162. Sudeshna Guha, *Artefacts of History: Archaeology, Historiography and Indian Pasts* (New Delhi, 2015), p. 141

163. Ibid., p. 142; John Marshall (ed.), *Mohenjo-Daro and the Indus Civilisation* (London, 1931)

164. F. R. Allchin, 'Obituary, Professor H. D. Sankalia', *South Asian Studies* 5(1) (1989)

165. Guha, *Artefacts*, pp. 236–7

166. Wheeler Report, December 1947, p. 15, cited in Venkateswaran, 'Constructing a Nation'

167. Venkateswaran, 'Constructing a Nation', p. 6

168. Guha, *Artefacts*, p. 184

169. Partha Mitter, *Much Maligned Monsters: A History of European Reactions to Indian Art* (Oxford, 1977)

170. See, for instance, Ananda Kentish Coomaraswamy's *Art and Swadeshi* (Madras, 1912), *Bibliographies of Indian Art* (Boston, 1923–30), and *Essays in Indian Idealism* (Madras, 1911, reprinted 1981)

171. Guha-Thakurta, *Monuments, Objects, Histories*, p. 187

172. Ibid., p. 180

173. Ibid., p. 182

174. 'A remarkable relic of an unknown civilisation', *Illustrated London News* (27 February 1926). With thanks to Uttara Shahani

175. Muhammad Yousuf Ali and Malahat Kaleem Sherwani, 'National Museum of Pakistan, Karachi: Case Study', Conference Proceedings on Intellectual and Cultural Heritage of Pakistan, June 2010

176. Guha-Thakurta, *Monuments, Objects, Histories*, p. 204

177. Richard M. Eaton and Phillip B. Wagoner, *Power, Memory, Architecture: Contested Sites on India's Deccan Plateau, 1300–1600* (New Delhi, 2014)

178. Ahmed, *Monuments, Memory, Contestation*

179. *Proceedings of the Educational Conference held at New Delhi* (Simla), pp. 9–17, cited in Toni Jokinen, 'The Treatment of the Partition of South Asia in History Teaching in India, *c.*1960–2005', History Tripos dissertation (University of Cambridge, 2013), p. 5

180. Krishna Kumar, *Prejudice and Pride: School Histories of the Freedom Struggle in India and Pakistan* (New Delhi, 2001)

181. Ibid., p. 5

182. Ibid., p. 99

183. Ibid., p. 95

184. Ibid., pp. 76–7

185. Ibid., p. 82

186. Ibid., p. 63

187. Jokinen, 'The Treatment of the Partition', p. 17

188. *The Fourth Five Year Plan 1970–75* (Islamabad, 1970), p. 113. Courtesy M. Arif Naveed, to whom I am very grateful. Also see Muhammad Sabil Farooq, 'Millennium Development Goals and Quality Education Situation in Pakistan at Primary Level', *International Online Journal of Primary Education* 7(1) (2018)

189. Nehru, *Letters to Chief Ministers*, Vol. I (2 November 1947), p. 11

190. Peter Sutoris, *Visions of Development: Films Division of India and the Imagination of Progress, 1948–75* (London, 2016), p. 4

191. Ibid., p. 61

192. Ibid., p. 74

193. Ibid., pp. 153–4

194. On the 'age of development', see Benjamin Zachariah, *Developing India: An Intellectual and Social History, c.1930–50* (Oxford, 2012); and Markus Daechsel, *Islamabad and the Politics of International Development in Pakistan* (Cambridge, 2015)

195. David Gilmartin, 'Nature's Sovereignty: The Indus Basin and India's Partition', seminar paper presented at the Centre of South Asian Studies, Critical Pakistan Research Cluster, December 2017

196. Rudolph J. Rummel, *Statistics of Democide: Genocide and Mass Murder since 1900* (Munster, 1998), pp. 153–63

197. Van Schendel, *History of Bangladesh*, p. 172

198. Alexander, Chatterji and Jalais, *Bengal Diaspora*; Ghosh, *Partition*; Taj Ul-Islam Hashmi, 'The "Bihari" Minorities in Bangladesh: Victims of Nationalisms', in Mushirul Hasan (ed.), *Islam, Communities and the Nation: Muslim Identities in South Asia and Beyond* (New Delhi, 1998); Victoria Redclift, *Statelessness and Citizenship: Camps and the Creation of Political Space* (Abingdon, 2013)

199. Ranabir Samaddar, *Many Histories and Few Silences: The Nationalist History of Nationalism in Bangladesh* (Calcutta, 1995)

200. Sheikh Mujibur Rahman, *The Unfinished Memoirs* (translated from Bengali by Fakrul Alam) (Dhaka, 2012)

201. Van Schendel, *History of Bangladesh*, p. 177

202. Ibid., p. 182, citing Jyoti Sengupta, *Bangladesh in Blood and Tears* (Calcutta, 1981), p. 91

203. The Arts and Humanities Research Council funded the Bengal Diaspora Project (2006–10), of which I was principal investigator, and compared 'internal' subcontinental migration with long-distance overseas diasporic movements

204. For further details, see Alexander, Chatterji and Jalais, *Bengal Diaspora*

205. Chaity Das, *In the Land of Buried Tongues: Testimonies and Literary Narratives of the War of Liberation of Bangladesh* (Delhi, 2017), p. 97

206. Neelima Ibrahim, *Aami Beeraangona Bolchhi* (Dhaka, 2010; 1995). Kajalie Shehreen Islam, 'Breaking Down the Birangona: Examining the (Divided) Media Discourse on the War Heroines of Bangladesh's Independence Movement', *International Journal of Communication* 6 (2012)

207. 'Alia', personal communication, June 2022

208. Christophe Jaffrelot (ed.), *A History of Pakistan and Its Origins* (London, 2004), pp. 65–7; Jalal, *State of Martial Rule*

209. See the Pakistan Studies Syllabus for 2022: www.cambridgeinternational.org/Images/557081-2022-syllabus.pdf

210. Paula R. Newburg, *Judging the State: Courts and Constitutional Politics in Pakistan* (Cambridge, 1995)

211. Ayub Khan, *Friends Not Masters*

212. Magnus Marsden, *Living Islam: Muslim Religious Experience in Pakistan's North-West Frontier* (Cambridge, 2005); Uddin, 'In the Land of Eternal Eid'

213. Humeira Iqtidar, *Secularizing Islamists?: Jama'at-e-Islami and Jama'at-ud-Da'wa in Urban Pakistan* (Chicago, 2011)

214. Ayesha Siddiqa, *Military Inc.: Inside Pakistan's Military Economy* (London, 2007)

215. Chatterji, *Spoils of Partition*

216. Katherine Frank, *Indira: The Life of Indira Nehru Gandhi* (London, 2001); Sagarika Ghose, *Indira: India's Most Powerful Prime Minister* (Delhi, 2017)

217. Su Lin Lewis, 'Cosmopolitanism and the Modern Girl: A Cross-Cultural Discourse in 1930s Penang', *Modern Asian Studies* 43(6) (2009)

218. Rajni Kothari, *Politics in India* (Boston, 1970)

219. Partha Chatterjee, *The Politics of the Governed: Reflections on Popular Politics in Most of the World* (New York, 2004); and Sudipta Kaviraj, *The Trajectories of the Indian State: Politics and Ideas* (Delhi, 2012)

220. Pranab Bardhan, *The Political Economy of Development in India (Expanded Edition)* (Delhi, 1984, 1998 edn)

221. James Manor, 'Indira and After: The Decay of Party Organisation in India', *The Round Table* 68(272) (1978)

222. Gyan Prakash, *Emergency Chronicles: Indira Gandhi and Democracy's Turning Point* (Princeton, 2019), pp. 137–8

223. Patrick Clibbens, 'The Indian Emergency, 1975–77', doctoral dissertation (University of Cambridge, 2014)

224. Prakash, *Emergency Chronicles*; Chatterji, *Spoils of Partition*

225. Rohit De, *A People's Constitution: The Everyday Life of Law in the Indian Republic* (Princeton, 2018)

226. Prakash, *Emergency Chronicles*, p. 146

227. Clibbens, 'The Indian Emergency'

228. Prakash, *Emergency Chronicles*, p. 99

229. Ibid., p. 105

230. Shalini Sharma, '"Yeh Azaadi Jhooti Hai!": The Shaping of the Opposition in the First Year of the Congress Raj', *Modern Asian Studies* 48(5) (2014)

231. See the Jayaprakash Narayan (JP) Papers, National Memorial Museum and Library (henceforth NMML), New Delhi, File no. 280 (Correspondence between JP and Acharya Ramamurti concerning organisation and tempo of the Bihar movement, 1974); File no. 289 (JP's statement on his probable arrest and other speeches relating to the Bihar movement, 1974); File no. 297 (Statements/press releases by JP on Patna

Firing incident and various aspects of the Bihar movement, 1974–75; File no. 300 (JP's speeches on the Bihar movement at Sarvodeya's Workers' Conference, transcript of this speech at Patna, JP's manifesto for a new Bihar, his arrest and imposition of Emergency, 1974–75); File no. 273 (Speeches, writings, articles by JP, 'Press statement on Mrs Gandhi', 25 April 1976); File no. 278 (Correspondence received by JP on the Bihar agitation, dissolution of state assemblies and other miscellaneous matters, 1973–74); File no. 279 (JP's appeal to student organisation, inaugural address at the All India Youth Conference Allahabad, questionnaire on the Bihar movement and letters received on the aims and progress of the Bihar movement, 1973–76). See also 'Papers relating to the People's Peace March to the Parliament, 6 March 1975, led by JP against corruption and nepotism; his programme in Western Uttar Pradesh; summary of discussion on authoritarian regime; charter of demands on the struggle of Bihar people presented to the Parliament by JP and other leaders', 1975, in File no. 445, Janata Party Papers, NMML, New Delhi

232. Christophe Jaffrelot and Pratinav Anil, *India's First Dictatorship: The Emergency, 1975–77* (London, 2020)

233. Prakash, *Emergency Chronicles*, p. 167

234. Clibbens, 'The Indian Emergency'; Emma Tarlo, *Unsettling Memories: Narratives of the Emergency in Delhi* (Berkeley, 2003); Marika Vicziany, 'Coercion in a Soft State: The Family-Planning Program in India. Part 2: The Sources of Coercion', *Pacific Affairs* 55(4) (1982–3); Matthew Connelly, *Fatal Misconception: The Struggle to Control World Population* (Cambridge, MA, 2008)

235. Patrick Clibbens, personal communication, 25 July 2022

236. Chatterji, '"Dispersal" and the Failure of Rehabilitation'; Sen, *Citizen Refugee*; Bhardwaj Datta, 'Rebuilding Lives, Redefining Spaces'

237. Prakash, *Emergency Chronicles*, pp. 228–58

238. Thomas Blom Hansen, *The Saffron Wave: Democracy and Hindu Nationalism in Modern India* (Princeton, 1999), p. 4

239. Tanika Sarkar, *Hindu Nationalism in India* (London, 2021)

240. Sabyasachi Bhattacharya, *Vande Mataram: The Biography of a Song* (Delhi, 2003)

241. Sarkar, *Hindu Nationalism*, p. 45

242. Ibid., p. 46

243. Shruti Kapila, *Violent Fraternity: Indian Political Thought in the Global Age* (Princeton, 2021)

244. Sarkar, *Hindu Nationalism*, p. 131

245. Blom Hansen, *The Saffron Wave*

246. V. D. Savarkar, *Hindutva: Who Is a Hindu?* (Delhi, 1923, 1989 edn)

247. Pandey, 'Can a Muslim Be an Indian?'

248. Chatterji, *Bengal Divided*, p. 235, Table 8

249. Sarkar, *Hindu Nationalism*

250. Ibid., pp. 146 ff.; Tapan Basu et al., *Khaki Shorts and Saffron Flags: A Critique of the Hindu Right* (Delhi, 1993). *Shaakhas* were and are daily training centres at which participants wear (martial) khaki shorts

251. Sarvepalli Gopal (ed.), *Anatomy of a Confrontation: Ayodhya and the Rise of Communal Politics in India* (Delhi, 1991)

252. A. G. Noorani, *The Babri Masjid Question, 1528–2003: 'A Matter of National Honour'* (New Delhi, 2003)

253. Ahmed, *Monuments, Memory, Contestation*, p. 133

254. Ibid.

255. Edward Anderson and Patrick Clibbens, '"Smugglers of Truth": The Indian Diaspora, Hindu Nationalism and the Emergency (1975–77)', *Modern Asian Studies* 52(5) (2018)

256. See K. N. Panikkar, 'Religious Symbols and Political Mobilization: The Agitation for a Mandir at Ayodhya', *Social Scientist* 21(242–3) (1993)

257. The Hindu epic drama, the *Ramayana*, is discussed in Chapter 7. *Amar Chitra Katha* ('Eternal tales in speech and drawing') were much in circulation among children in the 1960s, 70s and 80s. See Nandini Chandra, *The Classic Popular: Amar Chitra Katha (1967–2007)* (New Delhi, 2008)

258. Edward Anderson, *Hindu Nationalism in the Indian Diaspora: Transnational Politics and British Multiculturalism* (London, 2023)

259. Sudipta Kaviraj, 'On the Structure of Nationalist Discourse', in Sudipta Kaviraj, *The Imaginary Institution of India: Politics and Ideas* (Ranikhet, 2010)

260. I. A. Rehman, '40 Years of Zia and the Far-reaching Repercussions of the 1977 Military Coup', *Dawn*, 5 July 2017

3 THE STATE IN SOUTH ASIA: A BIOGRAPHY

1. There are about 1,500 varieties of mango in India. *Langra* is prized, particularly by Bengalis

2. Nehru was known by this affectionate kinship term, particularly used by children

3. Atul Kohli, *Democracy and Discontent: India's Growing Crisis of Governability* (Cambridge, 1990)

4. Rajnarayan Chandavarkar, 'Customs of Governance: Colonialism and Democracy in Twentieth Century India', *Modern Asian Studies* 41(3) (2007)

5. Bérénice Guyot-Réchard, *Shadow States: India, China and the Himalayas, 1910–1962* (Cambridge, 2016)

6. *Jahangir's India: The Remonstratie of Francisco Pelsaert* (translated from the Dutch by W. H. Moreland and P. Geyl) (Cambridge, 1925)

7. Neeladri Bhattacharya, *The Great Agrarian Conquest: The Colonial Reshaping of a Rural World* (Ranikhet, 2018)

8. Philip J. Stern, *The Company-State: Corporate Sovereignty and the Early Modern Foundations of the British Empire in India* (Oxford, 2011)

9. Seema Alavi, *The Sepoys and the Company: Tradition and Transition in Northern India, 1770–1830* (Oxford, 1995), p. 2

10. Prasannan Parthasarathi, *Why Europe Grew Rich and Asia Did Not: Global Economic Divergence, 1600–1850* (Cambridge, 2011)

11. Kate Brittlebank, *Tiger: The Life of Tipu Sultan* (New Delhi, 2016)

12. Muzaffar Alam and Sanjay Subrahmanyam (eds), *The Mughal State 1526–1750* (Delhi, 2000)

13. C. A. Bayly, *Indian Society and the Making of the British Empire* (Cambridge, 1988)

14. Samita Sen, '"Without His Consent?" Marriage and Women's Migration in Colonial India', *International Labor and Working-Class History* 65 (2004)

15. Rupa Viswanath, *The Pariah Problem: Caste, Religion and the Social in Modern India* (New York, 2014)

16. Dirk H. A. Kolff, *Naukar, Rajput and Sepoy: The Ethnohistory of the Military Labour Market of Hindustan, 1450–1850* (Cambridge, 2002)

17. David Shulman, 'On South Indian Bandits and Kings', *Indian Economic and Social History Review* 17(3) (1980), p. 287

18. Alavi, *Sepoys and the Company*, p. 8

19. *Poligar* is an anglicisation of *Palegara, Palaiyakkarar, Palegaadu* or *Palegar*, as these territorial governors were known in the regions they controlled

20. Neeladri Bhattacharya, 'Koh-i-Noor: Violence, Law and the Moral Politics of Colonialism', Kingsley Martin Lecture, Cambridge, 2018

21. W. H. Sleeman, *The Thugs or Phansigars of India, Comprising a History of that Extraordinary Fraternity of Assassins, and a Description of the Measures that have been Adopted by the Supreme Government of India for its Suppression* (Philadelphia, 1839), p. 2

22. Anastasia Piliavsky, 'The "Criminal Tribe" in India before the British', *Comparative Studies in Society and History* 57(2) (2015), pp. 323–54

23. James C. Scott, *The Art of Not Being Governed: An Anarchist History of Upland Southeast Asia* (New Haven, 2009), p. 6

24. On the sense of moral equivalence between King and Kallar, see Shulman, 'South Indian Bandits'

25. David Omissi, *The Sepoy and the Raj: The Indian Army, 1860–1940* (London, 1998), p. 133; Lionel Caplan, *Warrior Gentlemen: 'Gurkhas' in the Western Imagination* (Oxford, 1995)

26. The monthly wage of sepoys crept up only very slowly – from Rs 9 in 1895 to Rs 11 in 1911. Courtesy Erica Wald. Also see Erica Wald, *Vice in the Barracks: Medicine, the Military and the Making of Colonial India, 1780–1868* (London, 2014)

27. Omissi, *Sepoy and the Raj*, p. 148

28. Joya Chatterji, *The Spoils of Partition: Bengal and India, 1947–1967* (Cambridge, 2007), p. 284

29. Ravi Ahuja, 'Lost Engagements? Traces of South Asian Soldiers in German Captivity, 1915–18', in Franziska Roy, Heike Liebau and Ravi Ahuja (eds), *'When the War Began We Heard of Several Kings': South Asian Prisoners in World War I Germany* (New Delhi, 2011), p. 19

30. Cited in Ahuja, 'Lost Engagements', p. 44

31. Omissi, *Sepoy and the Raj*, p. 143

32. *Official History of the Indian Armed Forces in World War II* (Venkateshwaran, 1967), p. 187

33. Anirudh Deshpande, *British Military Policy in India, 1900–1945: Colonial Constraints and Declining Power* (New Delhi, 2005)

34. Cited in Steven I. Wilkinson, *Army and Nation: The Military and Indian Democracy since Independence* (Cambridge, MA, 2015), pp. 75–6

35. Wilkinson, *Army and Nation*, p. 82. Also see Radhika Singha, *The Coolie's Great War: Indian Labour in a Global Conflict, 1914–1921* (London, 2020)

36. Wilkinson, *Army and Nation*, p. 82

37. Vipul Dutta, 'Gentlemen and Officers: The Challenges of "Indianisation" and Military Institution-Building in India, c.1900–1960', doctoral dissertation (King's College London, 2016)

38. Also see Thomas Blom Hansen, *The Law of Force: The Violent Heart of Indian Politics* (Delhi, 2021)

39. Wilkinson, *Army and Nation*, p. 96

40. Ibid., p. 99

41. Chatterji, *Spoils of Partition*; Wilkinson, *Army and Nation*; Stephen P. Cohen, *The Pakistan Army* (Berkeley, 1984)

42. Wilkinson, *Army and Nation*

43. Dutta, 'Gentlemen and Officers'

44. Wilkinson, *Army and Nation*, p. 21

45. Ibid., pp. 19–28

46. Ayesha Siddiqa, *Military Inc.: Inside Pakistan's Military Economy* (London, 2007), pp. 143–57

47. Interview with 'Alia', 19 August 2022

48. Laurent Gayer, *Karachi: Ordered Disorder and the Struggle for the City* (London, 2014)

49. Firoozeh Kashani-Sabet, *Frontier Fictions: Shaping the Iranian Nation, 1804–1946* (Princeton, 1999)

50. B. D. Hopkins, *The Making of Modern Afghanistan* (Basingstoke, 2008)

51. Nooreen Reza, 'Law, Space and Political Imaginations in the Northwest Frontier', MPhil dissertation (Centre of South Asian Studies, University of Cambridge, 2016)

52. Tamina Chowdhury, *Indigenous Identity in South Asia: Making Claims in the Colonial Chittagong Hill Tracts* (Abingdon, 2016); Sanjib Baruah, *Durable Disorder: Understanding the Politics of Northeast India* (New Delhi, 2005); Sanjoy Hazarika, *Rites of Passage: Border Crossings, Imagined Homelands, India's East and Bangladesh* (Delhi, 2000)

53. Willem van Schendel, 'The Invention of the "Jummas": State Formation and Ethnicity in Southeastern Bangladesh', *Modern Asian Studies* 26(1) (1992); Chowdhury, *Indigenous Identity*

54. Willem van Schendel, 'Easy Come, Easy Go: Smugglers on the Ganges', *Journal of Contemporary Asia* 23(2) (1993). By the same author: 'Working through Partition: Making a Living in the Bengal Borderlands', *International Review of Social History* 46(3) (2001); 'Stateless in South Asia: The Making of the India-Bangladesh Enclaves', *Journal of Asian Studies* 61(1) (2002); and *The Bengal Borderland: Beyond State and Nation in South Asia* (London, 2005)

55. Guyot-Réchard, *Shadow States*, p. 106

56. Unstructured interviews/conversations with a now-retired senior police officer in Calcutta, with much active dockland experience, 1996–7

57. Partha Pratim Shil, 'Police Labour and State-formation in Bengal, c.1860 to c.1950', doctoral dissertation (University of Cambridge, 2016); Erin M. Giuliani, 'Strangers in the Village? Colonial Policing in Rural Bengal, 1861 to 1892', *Modern Asian Studies* 49(5) (2015)

58. David Arnold, *Police Power and Colonial Rule: Madras 1859–1947* (Delhi, 1986), p. 45

59. Charles Elphinstone Gouldsbury, *Life in the Indian Police* (London, 1912), cited in Shil, 'Police Labour', pp. 81–2

60. Personal communication with Partha Pratim Shil

61. Arnold, *Police Power*, pp. 27–9

62. Shil, 'Police Labour'; Arnold, *Police Power*, passim

63. Arnold, *Police Power*, p. 53

64. R. B. Hyde, *Report on the Police Administration in the Bengal Presidency for the Year 1919* (Calcutta, 1920). Statement E, Column 5,

p. xiv. Ibid., Statement E, Columns 31 and 34, p. xv. With grateful thanks to Partha Shil for analysing the relevant data

65. Transcript of an interview with Ramanand Tiwari by Haridev Sharma in July 1978 for the Oral History Project, Nehru Memorial Museum and Library, New Delhi. Cited and translated from Hindustani by Shil, 'Police Labour', pp. 113–14

66. Partha Pratim Shil, 'The "Threatened" Constabulary Strikes of Early Twentieth-Century Bengal', *South Asian Studies* 33(2) (2017)

67. Martin Shipway, *Decolonization and Its Impact: A Comparative Approach to the End of the Colonial Empires* (Oxford, 2008), p. 19

68. Shil, 'Police Labour'

69. C. J. Fuller and Véronique Bénéï (eds), *The Everyday State and Society in Modern India* (London, 2001). General Zia-ur Rahman first rose to celebrity when he announced Bangladesh's independence (and hence its secession from Pakistan) by radio after the crackdown had begun

70. Although, see Radha Kumar, *Police Matters: The Everyday State and Caste Politics in South India, 1900–1975* (Ithaca, NY, 2021)

71. Rajnarayan Chandavarkar, 'The Perils of Proximity: Rivalries and Conflicts in the Making of a Neighbourhood in Bombay City in the Twentieth Century', *Modern Asian Studies* 52(2) (2018)

72. Kumar, *Police Matters*

73. Ibid., p. 31

74. Ibid.

75. Beatrice Jauregui, *Provisional Authority: Police, Order, and Security in India* (Chicago, 2016)

76. *Times of India*, 21 January 2019. *Hafta* (literally, weekly): in colloquial terms, a sum charged every week by a hood, usually serving a bigger hood, for letting a person run a business

77. *Times of India*, 23 January 2019

78. Jauregui, *Provisional Authority*, pp. 7–8

79. Nayanika Mathur, *Paper Tiger: Law, Bureaucracy and the Developmental State in Himalayan India* (Cambridge, 2015)

80. Shil, 'Police Labour'

81. This has led to the phenomenon of the 'media trial' in India, which subverts and ignores judicial due process. It has its dangers as well as upsides

82. Paula R. Newburg, *Judging the State: Courts and Constitutional Politics in Pakistan* (Cambridge, 1995)

83. Omar Shahid Hamid, *The Prisoner: A Novel* (Basingstoke, 2013)

84. J. C. Heesterman, 'The "Hindu Frontier"', *Itinerario* 13(1) (1989), pp. 1–17; J. C. Heesterman, 'Warrior, Peasant and Brahmin', *Modern Asian Studies* 29(3) (1995), pp. 637–54

85. Sarah Eleanor Gandee, 'The "Criminal Tribe" and Independence: Partition, Decolonisation, and the State in India's Punjab, 1910s–1980s', doctoral dissertation (University of Leeds, 2018); Chandavarkar, 'Customs of Governance'

86. Vinod Mehta, *Meena Kumari: The Classic Biography* (Delhi, 2013), p. 115

87. The spare tautness of the script distinguished *Sholay*'s dialogue from the lush, slow-moving poesy of most great films that came before it

88. On Pakistan, see Anatol Lieven, *Pakistan: A Hard Country* (London, 2011)

89. Piliavsky, 'The "Criminal Tribe"', pp. 339–40

90. Barbara N. Ramusack, *The Indian Princes and Their States* (Cambridge, 2004)

91. Government of India, *White Paper on Hyderabad* (Delhi, 1948), p. 2

92. Ramusack, *Indian Princes*, p. 3

93. Janaki Nair, *Mysore Modern: Rethinking the Region under Princely Rule* (Minneapolis, 2011)

94. Sophie-Jung Hyun Kim, 'Rethinking Vivekananda through Space and Territorialised Spirituality, c.1880–1920', doctoral dissertation (University of Cambridge, 2018); Teresa Segura Garcia, 'Baroda, the British Empire and the World, c.1875–1939', doctoral dissertation (University of Cambridge, 2016)

95. Eric Lewis Beverley, *Hyderabad, British India and the World: Muslim Networks and Minor Sovereignty, c.1850–1950* (Cambridge, 2015)

96. Miles Taylor, *Empress: Queen Victoria and India* (New Haven, 2018)

97. C. A. Bayly, *Empire and Information: Intelligence Gathering and Social Communication in India, 1780–1870* (Cambridge, 1996)

98. Bernard S. Cohn, *Colonialism and Its Forms of Knowledge: The British in India* (Princeton, 1996)

99. Rosalind O'Hanlon and David Washbrook, 'After Orientalism: Culture, Criticism and Politics in the Third World', *Comparative Studies in Society and History* 34(1) (1992)

100. Bhattacharya, *Great Agrarian Conquest*

101. Arjun Appadurai, 'Number in the Colonial Imagination', in *Modernity at Large: Cultural Dimensions of Globalization* (Minneapolis, 1996); Bernard Cohn, *An Anthropologist among the Historians and Other Essays* (Delhi, 1987)

102. Bhattacharya, *Great Agrarian Conquest*; Malcolm Lyall Darling, *At Freedom's Door* (London, 1949)

103. Chandavarkar, 'Customs of Governance'. The most ubiquitous was the household, whose power structures and practices it did not seek to reform. See Chapter 6 for details

104. Roland Hunt and John Harrison, *The District Officer in India, 1930–1947* (London, 1980), p. 3.This could not have been more ironic, given the non-cooperation movement which had just ended

105. B. H. Baden Powell, *The Land-Systems of British India* (Oxford, 1892)

106. Hunt and Harrison, *District Officer*, p. 24

107. Clive Dewey, *Anglo-Indian Attitudes: The Mind of the Indian Civil Service* (London, 1993), p. 3

108. Hunt and Harrison, *District Officer*, p. 37

109. *Examinations for the Civil Service of India*, R. H. McLeod Papers, Centre of South Asian Studies, Cambridge, Box 1

110. Dewey, *Anglo-Indian Attitudes*, p. 5

111. Erica Wald, *Everyday Empire: Social Life, Spare Time and Rule in Colonial India* (forthcoming)

112. C. Jenkinson Papers, Centre of South Asian Studies, Cambridge, Box 1. Also see Wald, *Vice in the Barracks*; Ronald Hyam, *Empire and Sexuality: The British Experience* (Manchester, 1990); and Kenneth Ballhatchet, *Race, Sex and Class under the Raj: Imperial Attitudes and Policies and Their Critics, 1793–1905* (New York, 1980)

113. Jenkinson Papers, Centre of South Asian Studies, Cambridge, Box 1

114. Ibid.

115. Ibid. Emphasis added

116. McLeod Papers, Box 1. Emphasis in the original

117. Bhavani Raman, *Document Raj: Writing and Scribes in Early Colonial South India* (Chicago, 2012)

118. Karl Marx, 'The East India Question', in Karl Marx and Frederick Engels, *On Colonialism: Articles from the* New York Tribune *and Other Writings* (New York, 1972), p. 2, cited in Raman, *Document Raj*, p. 1

119. McLeod Papers, Box 1

120. D. A. Washbrook, 'Law, State and Agrarian Society in Colonial India', *Modern Asian Studies* 15(3) (1981), pp. 649–721. Also see Sen, '"Without His Consent?"'; and Samita Sen, 'Wrecking Homes, Making Families: Women's Recruitment and Indentured Labour Migration from India', in Joya Chatterji and David Washbrook (eds), *Routledge Handbook of the South Asian Diaspora* (Abingdon, 2013)

121. The term *chi-chi* was a pejorative label applied to many aspects of the Eurasian lifestyle, particularly speech and accent

122. Pre-publication draft of what would become Kavita Puri, *Partition Voices: Stories of Survival, Loss and Belonging* (London, 2019)

123. Vyvyen Brendon, *Children of the Raj* (London, 2005)

124. Ibid., p. 157

125. King's School Canterbury, as referred to by W. Somerset Maugham in *Of Human Bondage* (1915)

126. Hume to Dufferin, *Dufferin Papers: Correspondence in India*, Vol. 78, 1885: thanks to Anil Seal for drawing it to my attention. The case is also discussed in Mrinalini Sinha, '"Chathams, Pitts and Gladstones in Petticoats": The Politics of Gender and Race in the Ilbert Bill Controversy, 1883–1884' in Nupur Chaudhuri and Margaret Strobel (eds), *Western Women and Imperialism: Complicity and Resistance* (Bloomington, 1992)

127. As Sinha has noted, these were particularly imperial institutions, distinct from male clubs at 'home'; they symbolised the particular intersections of power, race and gender in an imperial setting. Mrinalini Sinha, 'Britishness, Clubbability and the Colonial Public Sphere: The Genealogy of an Imperial Institution in Colonial India', *Journal of British Studies* 40(4) (2001), pp. 489–521

128. McLeod Papers, Box 1. Entry for 30 July 1878. Emphasis in the original

129. Taylor C. Sherman, *State Violence and Punishment in India* (London, 2009). Also see Jonathan Saha, *Law, Disorder and the Colonial State: Corruption in Burma c.1900* (London, 2013)

130. Johnstone Papers, Centre of South Asian Studies, Cambridge, Box 2, 'Memoir', p. 5

131. Ibid., p. 30

132. Ibid.

133. James C. Scott, *Seeing Like a State: How Certain Schemes to Improve the Human Condition Have Failed* (New Haven, 1999)

134. Dewey, *Anglo-Indian Attitudes*, passim

135. Personal communication with Erica Wald. The 'men' were seen as a rowdy, uncontrolled, drinking and whoring crew, to be kept under the strictest control. Wald, *Vice in the Barracks*, passim

136. Hunt and Harrison, *District Officer*, pp. 56–7. From the account of D. Symington

137. Rosalind O'Hanlon, 'In the Presence of Witnesses: Petitioning and Judicial "Publics" in Western India, c.1600–1820', *Modern Asian Studies* 53(1) (2019)

138. Akhil Gupta, 'Blurred Boundaries: The Discourse of Corruption, the Culture of Politics and the Imagined State', *American Ethnologist* 22(2) (1995)

139. Just to clarify, I have never taken a box of sweets to any public officer, least of all to a policeman at an archive

140. Gloria Goodwin Raheja, *The Poison in the Gift: Ritual, Prestation, and the Dominant Caste in a North Indian Village* (Chicago, 1988)

141. Martin Moir, 'Kaghazi Raj: Notes on the Documentary Basis of Company Rule, 1773–1858', *Indo-British Review* 21(2) (1996), pp. 185–93

142. Hunt and Harrison, *District Officer*, p. 9

143. Ibid., pp. 21–2. Emphasis added

144. Ornit Shani, *How India Became Democratic: Citizenship and the Making of the Universal Franchise* (Cambridge, 2018); B. N. Rau, *India's Constitution in the Making* (Calcutta, 1960); B. Shiva Rao (ed.), *The Framing of India's Constitution: Select Documents*, 5 vols (New Delhi, 1966)

145. Sumit Sarkar, '"Kaliyuga", "Chakri" and "Bhakti": Ramakrishna and His Times', *Economic and Political Weekly* 27(29) (1992), pp. 1543–66

146. Tanika Sarkar and Sekhar Bandyopadhyay (eds), *Calcutta: The Stormy Decades* (Abingdon, 2018); Ravi Ahuja, '"Produce or Perish": The Crisis of the Late 1940s and the Place of Labour in Post-Colonial India', *Modern Asian Studies* 54(4) (2020)

147. Joya Chatterji, *Bengal Divided: Hindu Communalism and Partition, 1932–1947* (Cambridge, 1994)

148. Joya Chatterji, 'The Fashioning of a Frontier: The Radcliffe Line and Bengal's Border Landscape, 1947–52', *Modern Asian Studies* 33(1) (1999); and Chatterji, *Spoils of Partition*

149. Layli Uddin, 'In the Land of Eternal Eid: Maulana Bhashani and the Political Mobilisation of Peasants and Lower-Class Urban Workers in East Pakistan, *c.*1930s–1971', doctoral dissertation (Royal Holloway, University of London, 2016)

150. Sekhar Bandyopadhyay, *Decolonization in South Asia: Meanings of Freedom in Post-Independence West Bengal, 1947–52* (London, 2009)

151. Joya Chatterji, 'Mutuality and Cooperation in South Asia: An Alternative History of India–Pakistan relations', unpublished lecture, Royal Asiatic Society, 2012

152. Aishwarya Pandit, 'From United Provinces to Uttar Pradesh: Heartland Politics 1947–1970', doctoral dissertation (University of Cambridge, 2015)

153. Ayesha Jalal, *The State of Martial Rule: The Origins of Pakistan's Political Economy of Defence* (Cambridge, 1990)

154. Christophe Jaffrelot, *The Pakistan Paradox: Instability and Resilience* (translated by Cynthia Schoch) (London, 2015), p. 104

155. Ibid., pp. 105–6

156. B. B. Mishra, *The Administrative History of India 1834–1947: General Administration* (London, 1970), p. 163

157. Ibid., p. 165

158. Indivar Kamtekar, 'A Different War Dance: State and Class in India 1939–1945', *Past & Present* 176 (2002) and, by the same author, 'Freedom and the Coercive Power of the Indian State', *Proceedings of the Indian History Congress* 78 (2017)

159. Communication from Boyd Hilton, who was granted special access to the High Court sittings

160. After independence, Dalhousie Square got a new name: 'Benoy Badal Dinesh Bag' (BBD Bag), after three revolutionary terrorists

161. Shahid Hamid, *Disastrous Twilight: A Personal Record of the Partition of India* (London, 1986), p. 228. Also cited in Owen L. Sirrs, *Pakistan's Inter-Services Intelligence Directorate: Covert Action and Internal Operations* (London, 2017), p. 14

162. Sirrs, *Pakistan's Inter-Services Intelligence Directorate*, p. 14

163. Wilkinson, *Army and Nation*

164. Mohammad Ayub Khan, *Friends Not Masters: A Political Autobiography* (London, 1967), p. 22. Emphasis added

165. Jalal, *State of Martial Rule*, p. 16

166. Ayub Khan, *Friends Not Masters*, p. 19

167. Joya Chatterji, 'Rights or Charity? Government and Refugees: The Debate over Relief and Rehabilitation in West Bengal, 1947–1950', in Suvir Kaul (ed.), *The Partitions of Memory: The Afterlife of the Division of India* (Delhi, 2001)

168. Joya Chatterji, 'South Asian Histories of Citizenship, 1946–1970', *Historical Journal* 55(4) (2012)

169. Chatterji, *Spoils of Partition*

170. Chatterji, 'South Asian Histories of Citizenship'

171. Joya Chatterji, 'Princes, Subjects and Gandhi: Alternatives to Citizenship at the End of Empire', in Naren Nanda (ed.), *Gandhi's Moral Politics* (Abingdon, 2018)

172. Yaqoob Bangash, *A Princely Affair: The Accession and Integration of the Princely States of Pakistan 1947–1955* (Karachi, 2015)

173. Taylor C. Sherman, *Muslim Belonging in Secular India: Negotiating Citizenship in Postcolonial Hyderabad* (Cambridge, 2015); V. P. Menon, *The Story of the Integration of the Indian States* (Bombay, 1956)

174. *White Paper on Indian States* (Government of India Ministry of States) (New Delhi: Manager of Publications, 1950)

175. David Ricardo's theory of rent, which held that all agrarian surplus beyond subsistence belonged to the state

176. Rajat Ray and Ratna Ray, 'The Dynamics of Continuity in Rural Bengal under the British Imperium: A Study of Quasi-Stable Equilibrium in Underdeveloped Societies in a Changing World', *Indian Economic and Social History Review* 10(2) (1973); Rajat Ray and Ratna Ray, 'Zamindars and Jotedars: A Study of Rural Politics in Bengal', *Modern Asian Studies* 9(1) (1975)

177. Burton Stein, *Thomas Munro: The Origins of the Colonial State and His Vision of Empire* (Oxford, 1990). For an analysis of caste, see Chapter 4

178. Bhattacharya, *Great Agrarian Conquest*

179. Robert Eric Frykenberg, *Guntur District 1788–1848: A History of Local Influence and Central Authority in South India* (Oxford, 1965)

180. Bhattacharya, *Great Agrarian Conquest*

181. Mahesh Rangarajan, *Fencing the Forest: Conservation and Ecological Change in India's Central Provinces 1860–1914* (Delhi, 1996)

182. Table source: Ramachandra Guha, 'Forestry in British and Post-British India: A Historical Analysis', *Economic and Political Weekly* 18(44) (1983)

183. For a classic exposition of the arguments, see Ramachandra Guha and Madhav Gadgil, 'State Forestry and Social Conflict in British India', *Past & Present* 123 (1989)

184. Clive Dewey, 'The End of the Imperialism of Free Trade: The Eclipse of the Lancashire Lobby and the Concession of Fiscal Autonomy in India', in Clive Dewey and A. G. Hopkins (eds), *The Imperial Impact: Studies in the Economic History of Africa and India* (London, 1978), p. 36

185. Ramachandra Guha, *The Unquiet Woods: Ecological Change and Peasant Resistance in the Himalaya* (Delhi, 1989)

186. M. M. Sury (ed.), *Finance Commissions of India, I to XII: 1952–57 to 2005–10* (Delhi, 2005), p. 23

187. Taxes within Union Jurisdiction enumerated in List I of the Seventh Schedule of the Constitution of India, cited in Sury (ed.), *Finance Commissions*, p. 26

188. Guha, 'Forestry in British and Post-British India'

189. Christopher J. Lee (ed.), *Making a World after Empire: The Bandung Moment and Its Political Afterlives* (Athens, OH, 2010)

190. Medha M. Kudaisya, *Tryst with Prosperity: Indian Business and the Bombay Plan of 1944* (New Delhi, 2018)

191. Ibid.

192. Author's interview with Professor M. S. Swaminathan, India's 'father of the green revolution', New Delhi, December 2015. Professor Swaminathan acknowledged the input of Pakistani scientists, and that of those of other hungry nations

193. Amartya Sen, *Development as Freedom* (New York, 1999)

194. New research suggests this was the unintended consequence of a drastic policy of nationalising markets in the State Acquisition and Tenancy Act, 1950 (also known as the East Pakistan Estate Acquisition Act, 1950) and the revised Hats and Bazars (Establishment and Acquisition) Ordinance, 1959 (East Pakistan Ordinance No. XIX of 1959). Apurba K. Podder, 'The Making of the "Illegal" Marketplace: State, Class and Space in Khulna *c.*1951–2008', doctoral dissertation (University of Cambridge, 2017)

195. Member of the Brahmo Samaj, a reformist sect founded by Raja Ram Mohan Roy

196. Ayub Khan, *Friends Not Masters*, p. 72

197. Lieven, *Pakistan: A Hard Country*, p. 65

198. Debjani Sengupta, 'The Dark Forest of Exile: A Dandakaranya Memoir and the Partition's Dalit Refugees', *Journal of Commonwealth Literature* 57(3) (2022); Joya Chatterji, '"Dispersal" and the Failure of Rehabilitation: Refugee Camp-dwellers and Squatters in West Bengal', *Modern Asian Studies* 41(5) (2007), pp. 995–1032

199. Anjali Bhardwaj Datta, 'Rebuilding Lives, Redefining Spaces: Women in Post-Colonial Delhi', doctoral dissertation (University of Cambridge, 2015)

200. Satyajit Ray's *Pather Panchali* ('Song of the Road', 1955) was his first, searing film. It was based on Bibhutibhushan Banerjee's novel *Pather Panchali*, a sensation in its own right

201. Uttara Shahani, 'Sind and the Partition of India, *c.*1927–1952', doctoral dissertation (University of Cambridge, 2019), p. 224

202. For Pakistan, see Lieven, *Pakistan: A Hard Country*, pp. 65–7

203. Chatterji, *Spoils of Partition*

204. Chatterji, '"Dispersal" and the Failure of Rehabilitation'

205. Gayer, *Karachi*; Arif Hasan, *Understanding Karachi: Planning and Reform for the Future* (Karachi, 1999)

206. Upamanyu Chatterjee, *English, August: An Indian Story* (London, 1988). The 1994 film *English, August*, directed by Dev Benegal, is another treat

207. Gayer, *Karachi*

208. C. A. Doxiadis, 'Islamabad: The Creation of a New Capital', *Town Planning Review* 36(1) (1965), pp. 1–28; Dusan Botka, 'Islamabad after 33 years', *Ekistics* 62 (1995), pp. 209–35; Sajida Iqbal Maria and Muhammad Imran, 'Planning of Islamabad and Rawalpindi: What Went Wrong?', 42nd ISoCaRP Congress, 2006, Istanbul, Turkey

209. Cda.gov.pk, last accessed on 13 January 2019

210. Daniel Haines, *Building the Empire, Building the Nation: Development, Legitimacy, and Hydro-Politics in Sind, 1919–1969* (Oxford, 2013)

211. '50 Years On, Bhakra Dam Oustees Wait for Rehabilitation', *Times of India*, 22 October 2013

212. Nahid Kamal, 'The Population Trajectories of Bangladesh and West Bengal During the Twentieth Century: A Comparative Study', doctoral dissertation (London School of Economics and Political Science, 2009)

213. Anthony Mascarenhas, *Bangladesh: A Legacy of Blood* (London, 1986)

214. For example, Milford Bateman and Ha-Joon Chang, 'Microfinance and the Illusion of Development: From Hubris to Nemesis in Thirty Years', *World Economic Review* 1(1) (2012)

215. Kamal Munir, 'Pakistan and India: Common Economic Challenges', unpublished paper delivered at the Cambridge Festival of Ideas, 2014

216. Amit Bhaduri and Deepak Nayyar, *The Intelligent Person's Guide to Liberalization* (New Delhi, 1996), p. 30

217. Sheikh Mujibur Rahman, *The Unfinished Memoirs* (translated from Bengali by Fakrul Alam) (Dhaka, 2012)

218. Salil Tripathi, *The Colonel Who Would Not Repent: The Bangladesh War and Its Unquiet Legacy* (New Haven, 2016), p. 61

219. Mathur, *Paper Tiger*, p. 147

220. Mahesh Rangarajan, 'The Politics of Ecology: The Debate on Wildlife and People in India, 1970–95', *Economic and Political Weekly* 31(35/37) (1996), pp. 2391–409. Also see Annu Jalais, *Forest of Tigers: People, Politics and Environment in the Sundarbans* (Abingdon, 2010)

221. Stuart Corbridge, 'Waiting in Line, or the Moral and Material Geographies of Queue-Jumping', in Roger Lee and David M. Smith (eds), *Geographies and Moralities: International Perspectives on Development, Justice and Place* (Oxford, 2004), p. 184

222. Mikhail Bakhtin, *Rabelais and His World* (Bloomington, 2009)

223. Dipesh Chakrabarty, '"In the Name of Politics": Democracy and the Power of the Multitude in India', *Public Culture* 19(1) (2007)

224. Mathur, *Paper Tiger*, p. 156

225. Ibid.

226. For example, Nandini Sundar, *The Burning Forest: India's War in Bastar* (Delhi, 2016); Atreyee Sen, 'Torture and Laughter: Naxal Insurgency, Custodial Violence and Intimate Resistance in a Women's Correctional Facility in 1970s Calcutta', *Modern Asian Studies* 52(3) (2018), pp. 917–41; Thomas Blom Hansen, 'Whose Public, Whose Authority? Reflections on the Moral Force of Violence', *Modern Asian Studies* 52(3) (2018), pp. 1076–87

227. Abhimanyu Chandra, 'Khap Panchayats and the Logic of Honour Killing in Contemporary Haryana', MPhil dissertation (Centre of South Asian Studies, University of Cambridge, 2016); Gemma Scott, 'Emerging from the Emergency: Women in Indira Gandhi's India, 1975–1977', doctoral dissertation (Keele University, 2018)

4 MIGRATION AT HOME AND ABROAD: SOUTH ASIAN DIASPORAS

1. Dirk Kolff, *Naukar, Rajput and Sepoy: The Ethnohistory of the Military Labour Market in Hindustan, 1450–1850* (Cambridge, 1990); Dirk H. A. Kolff, 'The Market for Mobile Labour in Early Modern North India', in Joya Chatterji and David Washbrook (eds), *Routledge Handbook of the South Asian Diaspora* (Abingdon, 2013); David Ludden, 'Presidential Address: Maps in the Mind and the Mobility of Asia', *Journal of Asian Studies* 62(4) (2003)

2. Prasannan Parthasarathi, *The Transition to a Colonial Economy: Weavers, Merchants and Kings in South India, 1720–1800* (Cambridge, 2001)

3. Ian J. Kerr, 'On the Move: Circulating Labour in Pre-Colonial, Colonial and Post-Colonial India', *International Review of Social History* 51(S14) (2006), p. 91

4. Neeladri Bhattacharya, 'Predicaments of Mobility: Peddlers and Itinerants in Nineteenth-Century Northwestern India', in Claude Markovits, Jacques Pouchepadass and Sanjay Subrahmanyam (eds), *Society and Circulation: Mobile People and Itinerant Cultures in South Asia, 1750–1950* (Delhi, 2003)

5. Also see Claire Alexander, Joya Chatterji and Annu Jalais, *The Bengal Diaspora: Rethinking Muslim Migration* (Abingdon, 2016), Chapter 1 in particular

6. David Washbrook, 'The World of the Indian Ocean', in Chatterji and Washbrook (eds), *South Asian Diaspora*, p. 13

7. C. A. Bayly, *Indian Society and the Making of the British Empire* (Cambridge, 1988); David Washbrook, 'Economic Depression and the Making of "Traditional" Society in Colonial India, 1820–1855', *Transactions of the Royal Historical Society* 3 (1993), pp. 237–64

8. Kerr, 'On the Move', p. 93

9. Sunil S. Amrith, *Crossing the Bay of Bengal: The Furies of Nature and the Fortunes of Migrants* (Cambridge, MA, 2013)

10. Kerr, 'On the Move', p. 98

11. Tirthankar Roy has recently qualified this view. See his 'De-industrialisation: Alternative View', *Economic and Political Weekly* 35(17) (2000), pp. 1442–7. For just the tip of the iceberg of the 'de-industrialisation debate', see Daniel Thorner, '"De-industrialisation" in India, 1881–1931', in Daniel and Alice Thorner (eds), *Land and Labour in India* (Bombay, 1962), pp. 70–81; Morris D. Morris, 'Towards a Reinterpretation of Nineteenth-Century Indian Economic History', *Journal of Economic History* 23(4) (1963), pp. 606–18; Toru Matsui, 'On the Nineteenth-Century Indian Economic History – A Review of a "Reinterpretation"', *Indian Economic and Social History Review* 5(1) (1968), pp. 17–33; Bipan Chandra, 'Reinterpretation of Nineteenth Century Indian Economic History', *Indian Economic and Social History Review* 5(1) (1968), pp. 35–75; T. Raychaudhuri, 'A Reinterpretation of Nineteenth Century Indian Economic History?', *Indian Economic and Social History Review* 5(1) (1968), pp. 77–100; Amiya Kumar Bagchi, 'De-industrialization in India in the Nineteenth Century: Some Theoretical Implications', *Journal of Development Studies* 12(2) (1976), pp. 135–64; Amiya Kumar Bagchi, 'Deindustrialisation in Gangetic Bihar, 1809–1901', in Barun De (ed.), *Essays in*

Honour of Susobhan Chandra Sarkar (New Delhi, 1976), pp. 499–522; Marika Vicziany, 'The Deindustrialization of India in the Nineteenth Century: A Methodological Critique of Amiya Kumar Bagchi', *Indian Economic and Social History Review* 16(2) (1979), pp. 105–43; J. Krishnamurty, 'Deindustrialisation in Gangetic Bihar during the Nineteenth Century: Another Look at the Evidence', *Indian Economic and Social History Review* 22(4) (1985), pp. 399–416; Colin Simmons, '"De-industrialization", Industrialization and the Indian Economy, *c.*1850–1947', *Modern Asian Studies* 19(3) (1985), pp. 593–622; Tirthankar Roy, *Artisans and Industrialization: Indian Weaving in the Twentieth Century* (Delhi, 1993); Tirthankar Roy, *Traditional Industry in the Economy of Colonial India* (Cambridge, 2009); and Parthasarathi, *Transition to a Colonial Economy*

12. Douglas E. Haynes, *Small Town Capitalism in Western India: Artisans, Merchants and the Making of the Informal Economy, 1870–1960* (Cambridge, 2012)

13. Sugata Bose, *Agrarian Bengal: Economy, Social Structure and Politics, 1919–1947* (Cambridge, 1987)

14. Washbrook, 'Economic Depression'; also David Washbrook, 'Economic Development and Social Stratification in Rural Madras: The "Dry Region" 1878–1929', in Clive Dewey and A. G. Hopkins (eds), *The Imperial Impact: Studies in the Economic History of Africa and India* (London, 1978), pp. 68–82

15. David Hall-Matthews, *Peasants, Famine and the State in Colonial Western India* (Basingstoke, 2005), p. 9

16. Prasannan Parthasarathi, 'Water and Agriculture in Nineteenth-Century Tamilnad', *Modern Asian Studies* 51(2) (2017)

17. For instance: Ramachandra Guha, *The Unquiet Woods: Ecological Change and Peasant Resistance in the Himalaya* (Delhi, 1989); Ramachandra Guha, 'An Early Environmental Debate: The Making of the 1878 Forest Act', *Indian Economic and Social History Review* 27(1) (1990); Neeladri Bhattacharya, 'Pastoralists in a Colonial World', in David Arnold and Ramachandra Guha (eds), *Nature, Culture, Imperialism: Essays on the Environmental History of South Asia* (Delhi, 1995); and K. Sivaramakrishnan, *Modern Forests: Statemaking and Environmental Change in Colonial Eastern India* (Delhi, 1999)

18. Amita Baviskar, *In the Belly of the River: Tribal Conflicts over Development in the Narmada Valley* (Delhi, 2004)

19. Tanika Sarkar, *Words to Win: The Making of Amar Jiban: A Modern Autobiography* (New Delhi, 1999)

20. Y. S. Meer et al. (eds), *Documents of Indentured Labour: Natal 1851–1917* (Durban, 1980), p. 96

21. Samita Sen, *Recruitment for the Assam Plantations, 1830–1930* (forthcoming)

22. Thomas R. Metcalf, *Ideologies of the Raj* (Berkeley, 1995)

23. Rattan Lal Hangloo (ed.), *Indian Diaspora in the Caribbean: History, Culture and Identity* (Delhi, 2012); Gijsbert Oonk (ed.), *Global Indian Diasporas: Exploring Trajectories of Migration and Theory* (Amsterdam, 2007); Jan Lucassen, Leo Lucassen and Patrick Manning (eds), *Migration History in World History: Multidisciplinary Approaches* (Leiden, 2010); Claude Markovits, *The Global World of Indian Merchants, 1750–1947: Traders of Sind from Bukhara to Panama* (Cambridge, 2000)

24. Mike Davis, *Late Victorian Holocausts: El Niño Famines and the Making of the Third World* (New York, 2000), p. 7

25. Rajnarayan Chandavarkar, *The Origins of Industrial Capitalism in India: Business Strategies and the Working Classes in Bombay, 1900–1940* (Cambridge, 1994), p. 135

26. Ravi Ahuja, *Pathways of Empire: Circulation, 'Public Works' and Social Space in Colonial Orissa (c.1780–1924)* (Hyderabad, 2009)

27. Alexander, Chatterji and Jalais, *Bengal Diaspora*, p. 28

28. Although, see Anna Sailer, *Workplace Relations in Colonial Bengal: The Jute Industry and Indian Labour 1870s–1930s* (London, 2022)

29. Sen, *Recruitment*

30. Kingsley Davis, *The Population of India and Pakistan* (Princeton, 1951)

31. Brij V. Lal, 'Indian Indenture: Experiment and Experience', in Chatterji and Washbrook (eds), *South Asian Diaspora*

32. Sen, *Recruitment*

33. Ravi Ahuja, 'Mobility and Containment: The Voyages of South Asian Seamen, c.1900–1960', *International Review of Social History* 51(S14) (2006), pp. 111–41; Laura Tabili, '*We Ask for British Justice': Workers and Racial Difference in Late Imperial Britain* (New York, 1994); Yousuf Choudhury, *The Roots and Tales of the Bangladeshi Settlers* (Birmingham, 1993)

34. Hugh Tinker, *A New System of Slavery: The Export of Indian Labour Overseas, 1830–1920* (London, 1974)

35. David Northrup, *Indentured Labour in the Age of Imperialism, 1834–1922* (Cambridge, 1995), pp. 19–20

36. K. G. Davies, *The North Atlantic World in the Seventeenth Century: Europe and the World in the Age of Expansion*, Vol. 4 (Minneapolis, 1974), p. 251, cited in Sidney W. Mintz, *Sweetness and Power: The*

Place of Sugar in Modern History (London, 1986), p. 45. See also Mintz, *Sweetness and Power*, p. 46

37. Davis, *Population*, p. 98. Net emigration was roughly 6.2 million

38. Marilyn Lake and Henry Reynolds, *Drawing the Global Colour Line: White Men's Countries and the International Challenge of Racial Equality* (Cambridge, 2008)

39. Northrup, *Indentured Labour*, p. 81

40. Ibid., p. 84

41. Tinker, *New System of Slavery*, p. 145

42. Northrup, *Indentured Labour*, pp. 87–99

43. Cited in Marina Carter and Khal Torabully, *Coolitude: An Anthology of the Indian Labour Diaspora* (London, 2002), p. 41

44. Sen, *Recruitment*

45. The phrase *sara bara anna rogh* means 25 cents a day, more than ten times what Fazal was earning in India. Cited in Frank J. Korom, *Hosay Trinidad: Muharram Performances in an Indo-Caribbean Diaspora* (Philadelphia, 2003), pp. 101–2

46. Indian Public proceedings, 188/46 deposition of Saivaroodian to Phillips, Magistrate of Tanjore, 13 June 1857, cited in Marina Carter, *Voices from Indenture: Experiences of Indian Migrants in the British Empire* (London, 1996), p. 77

47. Sen, *Recruitment* makes the case for the larger arguments here

48. Carter, *Voices from Indenture*, p. 83

49. V. S. Naipaul, *A House for Mr Biswas* (London, 2016), p. 216

50. Carter, *Voices from Indenture*, p. 119

51. Ibid., p. 111

52. Samita Sen, 'Wrecking Homes, Making Families: Women's Recruitment and Indentured Labour Migration from India', in Chatterji and Washbrook (eds), *South Asian Diaspora*, p. 98

53. Samita Sen, '"Without His Consent"? Marriage and Women's Migration in Colonial India', *International Labor and Working-Class History* 65 (2004)

54. Sen, 'Wrecking Homes', p. 97

55. Carter and Torabully, *Coolitude*, p. 43

56. Carter, *Voices from Indenture*, p. 148

57. Ibid., pp. 86–7

58. Ibid., pp. 140–1

59. Radica Mahase, '"Indian" Culture in Trinidad: Transportation, Reconstruction and Integration, 1845–1970', in Hangloo (ed.), *Indian Diaspora in the Carribbean*, p. 17

60. Carter, *Voices from Indenture*, p. 142

61. Prabhu P. Mohapatra, '"Following Custom"? Representations of Community among Indian Immigrant Labour in the West Indies, 1880–1920', in Rana P. Behal and Marcel van der Linden (eds), *Coolies, Capital and Colonialism: Studies in Indian Labour History* (Cambridge, 2007). Mohapatra argues that global sugar prices began to fall from the 1880s onwards, and planters tried to reduce the costs of production by squeezing labour harder; and that the 1884 Hosay riots were set against this backcloth. Also see Korom, *Hosay Trinidad*

62. Carter, *Voices from Indenture*, p. 201

63. Ibid., p. 200

64. Naipaul, *House for Mr Biswas*

65. Sen, *Recruitment*

66. Tinker, *New System of Slavery*

67. Sen, 'Wrecking Homes'

68. Lucy Delap, *Feminisms: A Global History* (Chicago, 2020)

69. Sen, 'Wrecking Homes', pp. 105–6

70. Memo by B. F. H. B. Tyabji dated 23 August 1952, Government of India, Ministry of External Affairs, AFR II Branch, AII/53/6491/31/ Secret. Also see Markovits, *Global World of Indian Merchants*

71. Figures taken from memo by B. F. H. B. Tyabji dated 23 August 1952, Government of India, Ministry of External Affairs, AFR II Branch, AII/53/6491/31/

72. Sunil S. Amrith, 'Indians Overseas? Governing Tamil Migration to Malaya 1870–1941', *Past & Present* 208(1) (2010), pp. 231–61. Also see Kernial Singh Sandhu, *Indians in Malaya: Some Aspects of Their Immigration and Settlement, 1786–1957* (Cambridge, 1969)

73. Valli Kanapathipillai, *Citizenship and Statelessness in Sri Lanka: The Case of the Tamil Estate Workers* (London, 2009)

74. Patrick Peebles, *The Plantation Tamils of Ceylon* (London, 2001)

75. Note by M. L. Mehta dated 5 April 1950, MEAI/7/49/BCI

76. MEAI (CAP Branch)/5/1951, MEA/F.7/49-BCI

77. 'Note on Land Nationalisation in Burma', GOI/MEA/F.9-8/ 48-o.s.II/1948

78. Robyn A. Andrews, 'Quitting India: The Anglo-Indian Culture of Migration', *Sites* 4(2) (2007). Also see Uther E. Charlton-Stevens, *Anglo-Indians and Minority Politics in South Asia: Race, Boundary Making and Communal Nationalism* (Oxford, 2017)

79. Sundeep Lidher, 'The Evolution of British Citizenship and Immigration Policy, 1945–1962', doctoral dissertation (University of Cambridge, 2021)

80. Pakistan agreed, in addition, to give publicity to the difficulties encountered by Pakistanis in finding work in Britain. Cabinet Memorandum. Commonwealth Immigrants. Memorandum by the Lord President of

the Council, 20 June 1958, UK PRO/CAB/129/93. Also see Joya Chatterji, 'From Imperial Subjects to National Citizens: South Asians and the International Migration Regime since 1947', in Chatterji and Washbrook (eds), *South Asian Diaspora*, pp. 183–97

81. Davis, *Population*

82. Judith M. Brown, *Global South Asians: Introducing the Modern Diaspora* (Cambridge, 2006), p. 42

83. Roger Kershaw and Mark Pearsall, *Immigrants and Aliens: A Guide to Sources on UK Immigration and Citizenship* (Kew, 2004), p. 14. Also see Rieko Karatani, *Defining British Citizenship: Empire, Commonwealth and Modern Britain* (London, 2003); and Lidher, 'Evolution of British Citizenship'

84. Ali Nobil Ahmad, 'The Production of Illegality in Migration and Diaspora: State Policies and Human Smuggling from Pakistan', in Chatterji and Washbrook (eds), *South Asian Diaspora*, p. 212. Italics in the original

85. The team included Claire Alexander, Annu Jalais and Shahzad Firoz. The Arts and Humanities Council (UK) supported the Bengal Diaspora Project (2006–10)

86. Joya Chatterji and Claire Alexander, with Annu Jalais and Shahzad Firoz, 'The Bengal Diaspora project', Arts and Humanities Research Council, Diaspora, Migration and Identities Programme, 2006–2010. Interview and translation by Shahzad Firoz

87. Sana Aiyar, *Indians in Kenya: The Politics of Diaspora* (Cambridge, MA, 2015); Avtar Brah, *Cartographies of Diaspora: Contesting Identities* (London, 1996)

88. Chatterji, 'From Imperial Subjects'

89. UK NA/HO 344/196; David Washbrook, 'Brain Drain, Exchange and Gain: "Hi-skill" Migrants and the Developed Economies', in Chatterji and Washbrook (eds), *South Asian Diaspora*, pp. 251–2

90. UK NA/HO 344/196; Washbrook, 'Brain Drain'

91. Katy Gardner, *Age, Narrative and Migration: The Life Course and Life Histories of Bengali Elders in London* (London, 2002)

92. *American Community Survey*, Washington DC, US Census Bureau, 2009, cited in Washbrook, 'Brain Drain', p. 251

93. Washbrook, 'Brain Drain', pp. 251–2

94. Shompa Lahiri, *Indians in Britain: Anglo-Indian Encounters, Race and Identity, 1880–1930* (London, 2000)

95. Rozina Visram, *Ayahs, Lascars and Princes: The Story of Indians in Britain 1700–1947* (London, 1986)

96. Markovits, *Global World of Indian Merchants*

97. Ibid., p. 116

98. Ibid., pp. 122–3

99. David Rudner, 'Banker's Trust and the Culture of Banking Among the Nattukottai Chettiars of Colonial South India', *Modern Asian Studies* 23(3) (1989), pp. 417–58; David West Rudner, *Caste and Capitalism in Colonial India: The Nattukottai Chettiars* (Berkeley, 1994)

100. Roger Ballard, 'The Political Economy of Migration: Pakistan, Britain and the Middle East', in Jeremy Eades (ed.), *Migrants, Workers and the Social Order* (London, 1987)

101. Robert Nichols, *A History of Pashtun Migration, 1775–2006* (Oxford, 2008), especially Chapter 6

102. Ali Nobil Ahmad, 'Production of Illegality', pp. 198–210

103. Patrick Clibbens, 'British Responses to the Indian "Emergency", 1975–1977', BA dissertation (University of Cambridge, 2009); Edward Anderson and Patrick Clibbens, '"Smugglers of Truth": The Indian Diaspora, Hindu Nationalism and the Emergency (1975–77)', *Modern Asian Studies* 52(5) (2018), pp. 1–45

104. Edward Anderson, *Hindu Nationalism in the Indian Diaspora: Transnational Politics and British Multiculturalism* (London, 2023)

105. Katy Gardner, 'Transnationalism and the Transformation of "Home" by "Abroad" in Sylhet, Bangladesh', in Chatterji and Washbrook (eds), *South Asian Diaspora*, p. 261

106. Joya Chatterji, Claire Alexander et al., 'The Bengal Diaspora Project', AHRC 2006–2010

107. Davis, *Population*, p. 28

108. Parthasarathi, 'Water and Agriculture'

109. Tim Dyson, 'India's Population: The Past', in Tim Dyson, Robert Cassen and Leela Visaria (eds), *Twenty-first Century India: Population, Economy, Human Development, and the Environment* (Oxford, 2004), p. 24. Also see A. Geddes, 'The Social and Psychological Significance of Variability in Population Change: With Examples from India, 1871–1941', *Human Relations* 1(2) (1947), pp. 181–201

110. Dyson, 'India's Population', p. 22

111. Davis, *Population*, pp. 26–9

112. Jean Drèze, 'Famine Prevention in India', in Jean Drèze and Amartya Sen (eds), *The Political Economy of Hunger: Volume 2: Famine Prevention* (Oxford, 1990), pp. 13–122

113. Frances Hodgson Burnett, *The Secret Garden* (Ware, 2018), p. 14

114. Davis, *Population*, p. 53

115. Ibid., p. 35

116. Aparajita Mukhopadhyay, 'Wheels of Change?: Impact of Railways on Colonial North Indian Society, 1855–1920', doctoral dissertation (School of Oriental and African Studies, London, 2013)

117. *Native Newspaper Reports*, cited by Mukhopadhyay in 'Wheels of Change', pp. 97, 74

118. Ibid., p. 76

119. The Konkan coast is a narrow strip of land south of Bombay that separates the Arabian Sea from the Deccan Plateau. Its sandy coastline is interspersed with fishing villages and terraced paddy fields where Goa's nutty red rice grows

120. Life history interviews with Cajetano, 2018–22

121. L. J. Sedgwick, *Census of India, 1921: Vol. IX: Cities of the Bombay Presidency, Part I Report* (Bombay, 1922), p. 37

122. Chandavarkar, *Origins of Industrial Capitalism*, p. 77

123. Ibid., p. 79

124. Ibid.

125. Ibid.

126. S. M. Edwardes, *By-Ways of Bombay* (Bombay, 1912), cited in Nile Green, *Bombay Islam: The Religious Economy of the West Indian Ocean, 1840–1915* (Cambridge, 2011), p. 5

127. Rajnarayan Chandavarkar, 'From Neighbourhood to Nation', in Neera Adarkar and Meena Menon, *One Hundred Years, One Hundred Voices: The Millworkers of Girangaon: An Oral History* (Calcutta, 2004), p. 14

128. Chandavarkar, 'From Neighbourhood to Nation', p. 13

129. See the concept of 'ordered disorder' in Laurent Gayer's book about Karachi: *Karachi: Ordered Disorder and the Struggle for the City* (London, 2014)

130. Chandavarkar, *Origins of Industrial Capitalism*

131. Cited in Adarkar and Menon, *One Hundred Years*, p. 96

132. Krutika Behrawala, 'Know About the Mill Lands of Central Mumbai Through an Interactive Exhibition', mid-day.com, 21 November 2017

133. Chandavarkar, *Origins of Industrial Capitalism*, p. 121

134. We know that Cajetano's past was not wholly savoury. The details he now forgets; he seems to have hung out with hooch-sellers and dealers in drugs. He has been a teetotaller, he says, for decades

135. Sedgwick, *Census of India, 1921: Vol. IX*, p. 31

136. By 1941, Calcutta had only 456 women for every 1,000 men. M. W. M. Yeatts, *Census of India 1941. Vol. I, Part 1: Tables* (Delhi, 1943), p. 76; Sen, '"Without His Consent?"'

137. Cited in Menon and Adarkar, *One Hundred Years*, p. 97

138. Ibid., p. 101

139. *The Imperial Gazetteer of India: The Indian Empire. Vol. III: Economic* (Oxford, 1907), p. 389

140. Misbahuddin Khan, *History of the Port of Chittagong* (Dhaka, 1990)

141. *Imperial Gazetteer: Vol. III*, p. 389. Also see *History of Indian Railways, Constructed and in Progress, corrected up to 31 March 1923* (Simla, 1924)

142. D. L. Drake-Brockman, *Azamgarh: A Gazetteer. Being Volume XXXIII of the District Gazetteers of the United Provinces of Agra and Oudh* (Allahabad, 1911), translated by Aishwarj Kumar, p. 22. Also cited in Subho Basu, *Does Class Matter? Colonial Capital and Workers' Resistance in Bengal, 1890–1937* (New Delhi, 2004)

143. *Adra* literally means the sixth lunar mansion, marking the start of the rainy season in eastern India. *Hast* is the thirteenth mansion of the moon. As the ditty shows, peasants held that if it rained in these periods, crops, particularly sugarcane and rice, would thrive. (Personal communication with Aishwarj Kumar)

144. *The Imperial Gazetteer of India: The Indian Empire. Vol. 1: Descriptive* (Oxford, 1907), pp. 467–8

145. L. S. S. O'Malley, *24 Parganas District Gazetteer* (Calcutta, 1914); also cited in Basu, *Does Class Matter?*, p. 43

146. Partha Pratim Shil, 'Police Labour and State-formation in Bengal, c.1860 to c.1950', doctoral dissertation (University of Cambridge, 2016)

147. Ibid.

148. *Imperial Gazetteer: Vol. 1*, pp. 467–8

149. Jayeeta Sharma, '"Lazy" Natives, Coolie Labour and the Assam Tea Industry', *Modern Asian Studies* 43(6) (2009); Jayeeta Sharma, *Empire's Garden: Assam and the Making of India* (Durham, NC, 2011)

150. *Imperial Gazetteer: Vol. 1*, p. 469

151. For a nuanced discussion of Assam's migration history and linguistic struggles for identity, see Sharma, *Empire's Garden*

152. *Royal Commission on Labour in India, Vol. V, Part II* (London, 1931), p. 132

153. Ibid. Note by Dr Batra, p. 31, cited in Basu, *Does Class Matter?*, p. 46

154. Basu, *Does Class Matter?*, p. 47

155. Tanika Sarkar and Sekhar Bandyopadhyay (eds), *Calcutta: The Stormy Decades* (Abingdon, 2018)

156. Janam Mukherjee, *Hungry Bengal: War, Famine and the End of Empire* (London, 2015), p. 213

157. For land sales and transfers in Bengal in this period, see Saugata Mukherji, 'Agrarian Class Formation in Modern Bengal, 1931–51', *Economic and Political Weekly* 21(4) (1986)

158. Interview with Sushila Devi, 5 April 2022, New Delhi

159. A *jatha* is a formation of armed Sikhs; Swarna Aiyar, '"August Anarchy": The Partition Massacres in Punjab, 1947', *Journal of South Asian Studies* 18(1) (1995)

160. Gurharpal Singh, 'Sikhs and Partition Violence: A Re-evaluation', in Ian Talbot (ed.), *The Independence of India and Pakistan: New Approaches and Reflections* (Karachi, 2013)

161. Anna Bigelow, *Sharing the Sacred: Practicing Pluralism in Muslim North India* (New York, 2009); Karenjot Bhangoo Randhawa, *Civil Society in Malerkotla, Punjab: Fostering Resilience through Religion* (Lanham, 2012); Joya Chatterji, Radhakrishnan Lectures, All Souls College, Oxford, 2022

162. Gyanendra Pandey, *Remembering Partition: Violence, Nationalism and History in India* (Cambridge, 2001)

163. Sa'adat Hasan Manto, 'Cold Meat', in Muhammad Umar Memon (ed.), *Black Margins: Stories* (New Delhi, 2003). The film *Manto* (2018), based on his life, handles the story, its reception and its author with sensitivity

164. Urvashi Butalia, *The Other Side of Silence: Voices from the Partition of India* (New Delhi, 1998), p. 177

165. Ibid., p. 155

166. Ibid., p. 156

167. Joya Chatterji, 'Princes, Subjects and Gandhi: Alternatives to Citizenship at the End of Empire', in Naren Nanda (ed.), *Gandhi's Moral Politics* (Abingdon, 2018); Joya Chatterji, 'South Asian Histories of Citizenship, 1946–1970', *Historical Journal* 55(4) (2012)

168. Alexander, Chatterji and Jalais, *Bengal Diaspora*

169. Joya Chatterji, 'Dispositions and Destinations: Refugee Agency and "Mobility Capital" in the Bengal Diaspora, 1947–2007', *Comparative Studies in Society and History* 55(2) (2013)

170. Joya Chatterji, *The Spoils of Partition: Bengal and India, 1947–1967* (Cambridge, 2007); Mohita Bhatia, 'Citizenship as Politics and Performance of Religious Identity: Hindu Refugees from Sindh', *Sociological Bulletin* 70(4) (2021)

171. Uttara Shahani, 'Sind and the Partition of India, c.1927–1952', doctoral dissertation (University of Cambridge, 2019)

172. Unpublished draft of Kavita Puri, *Partition Voices: Untold British Stories* (London, 2019)

173. Alexander, Chatterji and Jalais, *Bengal Diaspora*. After the 1965 war between India and Pakistan, over 8,000 people crossed over from Thar Pakar, a district with a large population of Dalits, Adivasis and other marginal Hindu groups. During the 1971 war, India occupied parts of Thar Pakar and a wave of 90,000 Hindus crossed over. Migration accelerated again after the fall of the Babri Mosque in 1992. Niraja Gopal Jayal, *Citizenship and Its Discontents: An Indian History* (Cambridge, MA, 2013), pp. 89–90

174. Veena Das, *Critical Events: An Anthropological Perspective on Contemporary India* (Oxford, 1995). Also see Arthur Kleinman, Veena Das and Margaret M. Lock (eds), *Social Suffering* (Berkeley, 1997)

175. Also see Dipesh Chakrabarty, 'Remembered Villages: Representation of Hindu-Bengali Memories in the Aftermath of the Partition', *Journal of South Asian Studies* 18 (1995)

176. Ritu Menon and Kamla Bhasin, *Borders and Boundaries: Women in India's Partition* (Delhi, 1998); also Nonica Datta, *Violence, Martyrdom and Partition: A Daughter's Testimony* (Delhi, 2009); Kavita Daiya, *Violent Belongings: Partition, Gender and National Culture in Postcolonial India* (Philadelphia, 2008)

177. Unpublished draft of Puri, *Partition Voices*. Also see Aanchal Malhotra, *Remnants of a Separation: A History of the Partition through Material Memory* (Delhi, 2019)

178. Kanakotpal Ghosh to Shameem Akhtar in a letter written just before his death, n.d. (Personal communication with Shohini Ghosh)

179. On the borderlands, see Willem van Schendel, 'Easy Come, Easy Go: Smugglers on the Ganges', *Journal of Contemporary Asia* 23(2) (1993), pp. 189–213; Malini Sur, 'Bamboo Baskets and Barricades: Gendered Landscapes at the India–Bangladesh Border', in Barak Kalir and Malini Sur (eds), *Transnational Flows and Permissive Polities: Ethnographies of Human Mobilities in Asia* (Amsterdam, 2012), pp. 127–50

180. Ornit Shani, *Communalism, Caste and Hindu Nationalism: The Violence in Gujarat* (Cambridge, 2007)

181. Das, *Critical Events*. Also see Kleinman, Das and Lock (eds), *Social Suffering*

182. Gayer, *Karachi*

183. Basu, *Does Class Matter?*

184. Gayer, *Karachi*, p. 34; Arif Hasan, *The Unplanned Revolution: Observations on the Processes of Socio-economic Change in Pakistan* (Karachi, 2021)

185. Nikhil Rao, *House, but No Garden: Apartment Living in Bombay's Suburbs, 1898–1964* (Minneapolis, 2013)

186. Stephen Legg, *Spaces of Colonialism: Delhi's Urban Governmentalities* (Oxford, 2007)

187. Erica Wald, *Vice in the Barracks: Medicine, the Military and the Making of Colonial India, 1780–1868* (London, 2014)

188. Cited in Louis L. Cornell, *Kipling in India* (London, 1966), p. 151

189. Haynes, *Small Town Capitalism*

190. Mukherjee, *Hungry Bengal*, p. 213

191. Sarah Ansari, *Life after Partition: Migration, Community and Strife in Sindh, 1947–1962* (Oxford, 2005)

192. *Delhi District Census Handbook*, 1971

193. For Dacca, see Elisa T. Bertuzzo, *Fragmented Dhaka: Analysing Every-day Life with Henri Lefebvre's Theory of Production of Space* (Stuttgart, 2009)

194. Uditi Sen, 'The Myths Refugees Live by: Memory and History in the Making of Refugee Identity', *Modern Asian Studies* 48(1) (2014), pp. 37–76

195. Ilyas Chattha, *Partition and Locality: Violence, Migration and Development in Gujranwala and Sialkot 1947–1961* (Karachi, 2011); Chatterji, 'South Asian Histories of Citizenship', pp. 1049–71; Haimanti Roy, *Partitioned Lives: Migrants, Refugees, Citizens in India and Pakistan, 1947–65* (New Delhi, 2012); Uditi Sen, *Citizen Refugee: Forging the Indian Nation after Partition* (Cambridge, 2018); Gayer, *Karachi*; Anjali Bhardwaj Datta, 'Rebuilding Lives, Redefining Spaces: Women in Post-Colonial Delhi', doctoral dissertation (University of Cambridge, 2015); Shahani, 'Sind and the Partition of India'; Rotem Geva, 'The City as a Space of Suspicion: Partition, Belonging and Citizenship in Delhi, 1940–1955', doctoral dissertation (Princeton University, 2014)

196. Known by different names in different cities: *bastis* in Calcutta, *katchi abadi* in Karachi and the *jhuggi jhhopri* in Delhi

197. Joya Chatterji, 'Rights or Charity? Government and Refugees: The Debate over Relief and Rehabilitation in West Bengal, 1947–1950', in Suvir Kaul (ed.), *The Partitions of Memory: The Afterlife of the Division of India* (Delhi, 2001)

198. Sarah Ansari and William Gould, *Boundaries of Belonging: Localities, Citizenship and Rights in India and Pakistan* (Cambridge, 2019); Rotem Geva, *Delhi Reborn: Partition and Nation Building in India's Capital* (Stanford, 2022); Shahani, 'Sind and the Partition of India'; Bhardwaj Datta, 'Rebuilding Lives, Redefining Spaces'

199. Chatterji, 'South Asian Histories of Citizenship'; Anwesha Sengupta, 'Bengal Partition Refugees at Sealdah Railway Station, 1950–60', *South Asia Research* 42(1) (2022)

200. Deputy Inspector General of Police to the Chief Commissioner, Delhi, 20 December 1947, Delhi State Archives, Deputy Commissioner's papers (DC), File 259/47

201. Vazira Fazila-Yacoobali Zamindar, *The Long Partition and the Making of Modern South Asia: Refugees, Boundaries, Histories* (New York, 2007); Chatterji, *Spoils of Partition*

202. Joya Chatterji, '"Dispersal" and the Failure of Rehabilitation: Refugee Camp-dwellers and Squatters in West Bengal', *Modern Asian Studies* 41(5) (2007), pp. 995–1032

203. Uditi Sen, 'Developing *Terra Nullius*: Colonialism, Nationalism and Indigeneity in the Andaman Islands', *Comparative Studies in Society and History* 59(4) (2017), pp. 944–73

204. Shahani, 'Sind and the Partition of India'; Markus Daechsel, 'Sovereignty, Governmentality and Development in Ayub's Pakistan: The Case of Korangi Township', *Modern Asian Studies* 45(1) (2011); Chatterji, 'Rights or Charity?'

205. Anjali Bhardwaj Datta, *A City in Motion: War, Migration, and Decolonisation in India, c.1939–1965* (forthcoming); Bhardwaj Datta, 'Rebuilding Lives, Redefining Spaces'; Anjali Bhardwaj Datta, 'Genealogy of a Partition City: War, Migration and Urban Space in Delhi', *Journal of South Asian Studies* 42(1) (2019)

206. Hasan, *Unplanned Revolution*, p. 202

207. The only case where the dispersal policy enjoyed some success was in the Andaman Islands. Uditi Sen, in *Citizen Refugee*, explains why

208. The plan of the colony shows several small mosques or *mazaars* (tombs of buried *pir* saints) on the site

209. The following account is based on B. S. Guha, Memoir No. 1, 1954, in *Studies in Social Tensions Among the Refugees from Eastern Pakistan* (Calcutta, 1959)

210. Bhardwaj Datta, 'Rebuilding Lives, Redefining Spaces'

211. One *cottah* is approximately 13 ft x 10 ft

212. If this subject interests you, this novel is a must-read: Sunil Gangopadhyay, *Arjun* (London, 1987)

213. Manas Ray, 'Growing Up Refugee', *History Workshop Journal* 53(1) (2002)

214. The courses and seminars in Anthropology and Sociology I had audited (as one can) at Cambridge, gave me some confidence in my evolving research methods

215. Joya Chatterji, 'Of Graveyards and Ghettos, Muslims in West Bengal, 1947–67', in Mushirul Hasan and Asim Roy (eds), *Living Together Separately: Cultural India in History and Politics* (New Delhi, 2005), pp. 222–49

216. The 'South Asian end' of the Bengal Diaspora team, which included Dr Annu Jalais and myself, studied the camp

217. For a fuller description, see Alexander, Chatterji and Jalais, *Bengal Diaspora*. On the resilience of minority settlements, see Humaira Chowdhury's study of Metiabruz, 'A Social and Economic History of Darzis (Muslim Tailors) in Calcutta, c.1890–1967', doctoral dissertation (University of Cambridge, 2023)

218. Hasan, *Unplanned Revolution*, pp. 202–4

219. Samita Sen and Nilanjana Sengupta, *Domestic Days: Women, Work and Politics in Contemporary Kolkata* (New Delhi, 2016); Samita Sen, 'Impossible Immobility: Marriage, Migration and Trafficking in Bengal', *Economic and Political Weekly* 51(44/45) (2016)

220. Samita Sen, 'Girls Marrying Men: Labour, Culture and Child Marriage in Colonial India', inaugural lecture at the University of Cambridge, 2021

221. Samita Sen, *Women and Labour in Late Colonial India: The Bengal Jute Industry* (Cambridge, 1999); Indrani Chatterjee (ed.), *Unfamiliar Relations: Family and History in South Asia* (Delhi, 2004); and Indrani Chatterjee, *Gender, Slavery and Law in Colonial India* (Delhi, 1999)

222. The picture that follows is a synthesis of existing scholarship, and draws on unusual source materials: anthropological treatises, religious manuals, demographic surveys, little-known village studies, reports on infectious diseases, analyses of case law, autobiographies, the interviews conducted in the 2000s by the Bengal Diaspora team, and my own life history interview of Sushila Devi. It is admittedly partial; but nonetheless it provides some idea of what the transition from girlhood to marriage was like for north Indian, East Pakistani and Bangladeshi women in the twentieth century, and how they experienced 'marriage migration'

223. Irawati Karve, 'The Kinship Map of India', in Patricia Uberoi (ed.), *Family, Kinship and Marriage in India* (Delhi, 1993), p. 60, emphasis added; Irawati Karve, *Kinship Organisation in India* (Bombay, 1953)

224. Thanks to Samita Sen for pointing this out

225. Armindo Miranda, *The Demography of Bangladesh: Data and Issues* (Bergen, 1982), p. 75, footnote

226. Ibid., p. 85

227. See, for instance, Louis Dumont, 'North India in Relation to South India', in Uberoi (ed.), *Family, Kinship and Marriage*

228. Karve, 'Kinship Map of India', p. 54

229. Hastings Donnan, 'Marriage Preferences among the Dhund of Northern Pakistan', in Uberoi (ed.), *Family, Kinship and Marriage*

230. Miranda, *Demography of Bangladesh*, p. 108

231. Barbara Daly Metcalf, *Perfecting Women: Maulana Ashraf 'Ali Thanawi's Bihishti Zewar: A Partial Translation with Commentary* (Delhi, 1992)

232. Ibid., pp. 113–17

233. Ibid., p. 127

234. Taslima Nasrin, *Meyebela: My Bengali Girlhood: A Memoir of Growing up Female in a Muslim World* (South Royalton, 1998), p. 20

235. K. S. Yadav, 'Some Gond Marriages', *Man in India* 50(3) (1970), p. 291

236. Ronald P. Rohner and Manjusri Chaki-Sircar, *Women and Children in a Bengali Village* (Hanover, CT, 1988), p. 45; emphasis added

237. Dumont, 'North India in Relation to South India', p. 91; Donnan, 'Marriage Preferences', p. 311; Hastings Donnan, *Marriage among Muslims: Preference and Choice in Northern Pakistan* (Leiden, 1988), p. 311

238. Mead Cain, Syeda Rokeya Khanam and Shamsun Nahar, 'Class, Patriarchy and Women's Work in Bangladesh', *Population and Development Review* 5(3) (1979), p. 406

239. *Population Census of Bangladesh, 1974. National Volume* (Dacca, 1974)

240. Rohner and Chaki-Sircar, *Women and Children in a Bengali Village*, p. 47

241. Metcalf, *Perfecting Women*, p. 106

242. Jenneke Arens and Jos van Beurden, *Jhagrapur: Poor Peasants and Women in a Village in Bangladesh* (Calcutta, 1977), p. 53

243. Cain, Khanam and Nahar, 'Class, Patriarchy and Women's Work', p. 409. Also see Mead T. Cain, 'The Household Life Cycle and Economic Mobility in Rural Bangladesh', *Population and Development Review* 4(3) (1978), pp. 421–38

244. Nasrin, *Meyebela*, p. 10

245. Arens and van Beurden, *Jhagrapur*, p. 62

246. Miranda, *Demography of Bangladesh*, pp. 76–7

247. Rohner and Chaki-Sircar, *Women and Children in a Bengali Village*, pp. 76–7

248. Cain, Khanam and Nahar, 'Class, Patriarchy and Women's Work', p. 423

249. Miranda, *Demography of Bangladesh*, p. 79

250. Rohner and Chaki-Sircar, *Women and Children in a Bengali Village*, pp. 97–8

251. T. N. Madan, 'Structural Implications of Marriage in North India: Wife-givers and Wife-takers among the Pandits of Kashmir', in Uberoi (ed.), *Family, Kinship and Marriage*

252. Lina Fruzzetti, *The Gift of a Virgin: Women, Marriage and Ritual in a Bengali Society* (New Brunswick, NJ, 1982)

253. Yadav, 'Some Gond Marriages', p. 289

254. Cain, 'Household Life Cycle', p. 435

255. Fruzzetti, *Gift of a Virgin*, p. 65

256. Ibid., p. 94

257. Karve, 'Kinship Map of India', pp. 52 ff.

258. Miranda, *Demography of Bangladesh*, p. 202. The patterns of 'female neighbourhood migration' were very variable, strongly favouring some districts while rejecting others. This is difficult to explain unless one takes into account strong biases or preferences in the choice of grooms

259. Ahmed Ilias, *Biharis: The Indian Émigrés in Bangladesh: An Objective Analysis* (Syedpur, 2003); Anthony Mascarenhas, *Bangladesh: A Legacy of Blood* (London, 1986)

260. A member of the Bengal Diaspora team; now an anthropologist based at the National University of Singapore

5 THE HOUSEHOLD, MARRIAGE AND THE FAMILY

1. *Jethi* means father's older brother's wife; in our household, we called all our jethis '*je-ma*', showing affection. *Pishi* means father's sister; in her case, '*ma*' signalled love

2. Across South Asia, 'cousin-sister' is the English term for female first or 'second cousins'. The latter term applies to children of one's parents' cousins. 'Cousin-brother' is used in the same way. In the vernacular, kinship terms are so widely used, by everyone for everyone, that they do not connote household relationships

3. In Hindu Bengali families, paternal grandmothers are called *dida*. The fact that we turned ours into a *rani* gives some sense of her place in the household after my grandfather's stroke

4. Bina Agarwal, *A Field of One's Own: Gender and Land Rights in South Asia* (Cambridge, 1994), p. 3

5. *Adda* is almost untranslatable. It is free-flowing conversation, often about serious topics like politics, books, poetry and cinema, leavened by laughter, gossip, food and song

6. David Gellner, 'Warriors, Workers, Traders and Peasants: The Nepali/ Gorkhali Diaspora since the Nineteenth Century', in Joya Chatterji and David Washbrook (eds), *Routledge Handbook of the South Asian Diaspora* (Abingdon, 2013)

7. This definition differs from that of Naomi Tadmor in *Family and Friends in Eighteenth-Century England: Household, Kinship and Patronage* (Cambridge, 2001), p. 27. But my thinking around the subject has been influenced by her work, in more than one way. I am also grateful to Sarah Pearsall for her comments

8. Samita Sen and Nilanjana Sengupta, *Domestic Days: Women, Work and Politics in Contemporary Kolkata* (New Delhi, 2016)

9. Sara Dickey, 'The Pleasures and Anxieties of Being in the Middle: Emerging Middle-Class Identities in Urban South India', *Modern Asian Studies* 46(3) (2012)

10. Perveez Mody, *The Intimate State: Love-Marriage and the Law in Delhi* (Abingdon, 2008)

11. Rochona Majumdar, *Marriage and Modernity: Family Values in Colonial Bengal* (Durham, NC, 2009), passim

12. M. Madhava Prasad, *Ideology of the Hindi Film: A Historical Construction* (Delhi, 1998)

13. The title of this section is taken from Indrani Chatterjee's edited volume of the same name: *Unfamiliar Relations: Family and History in South Asia* (New Brunswick, NJ, 2004), to acknowledge its influence on my thinking about these themes

14. The version of the case cited here is based on Pamela Price, 'Kin, Clan and Power in Colonial South India', in Chatterjee (ed.), *Unfamiliar Relations*; and the *Judgment of the Lords of the Committee of the Privy Council on the Appeal of Sri Raja Rao Venkata Surya Mahapati Ramakrishna Rao Bahadur v. The Court of Wards and Venkata Kumari Mahapati Surya Rao, 24 February 1899* (Judicial Committee of the Privy Council Decisions, 1899)

15. After 1857, the British had abandoned the unpopular 'doctrine of lapse', by which all estates or principalities where there was no lineal heir 'lapsed' to British rule. Instead these were now managed by the Court of Wards while the Dowager Rani ran the household, and brought up the heir

16. The Privy Council would eventually rule that this was irrelevant. *Judgment of the Lords . . . 24 February 1899*

17. Price, 'Kin, Clan and Power', p. 207

18. Ibid., p. 211

19. *Judgment of the Lords*

20. Also see Sumit Guha's critique of the idea that households are 'monadic units', in Sumit Guha, 'The Family Feud as a Political Resource in Eighteenth-Century India', in Chatterjee (ed.), *Unfamiliar Relations*, p. 74

21. Indrani Chatterjee, 'Gossip, Taboo and Writing Family History', in Chatterjee (ed.), *Unfamiliar Relations*

22. *The Imperial Gazetteer of India. Vol. X: Central Provinces to Coompta* (Oxford, 1908), p. 124

23. Chatterjee, 'Gossip, Taboo and Writing', p. 238

24. Ibid.

25. Ibid., p. 249

26. Malcolm Lyall Darling, 'His Highness? Or Tutor and Guardian or Guardian and Prince', an unpublished typescript of Darling's memoir of his early days in Dewas in 1907. Malcolm Lyall Darling Papers, Box 4, 3.2, Part 3 (Centre of South Asian Studies, Cambridge), p. 200

27. Sultan Jahan Begam Nawab of Bhopal, *An Account of My Life (Gohur-i-Ikbal)* (translated into English by C. H. Payne, late educational advisor to the Begam) (London, 1912), p. 54

28. *Nikaah* marriages then were basic, conducted with little ceremony, whereas *shaadis* were celebrated with much ado, and were opulent, ritual-laden affairs

29. Darling, 'His Highness?', p. 198

30. Vijayaraje Scindia with Manohar Malgonkar, *Princess: The Autobiography of the Dowager Maharani of Gwalior* (London, 1985), p. 5, passim

31. S. M. Edwardes, *Crime in India: A Brief Review of the More Important Offences Included in the Annual Criminal Returns, with Chapters on Prostitution & Miscellaneous Matters* (Oxford, 1924), p. 21

32. Ibid.

33. Bankimchandra Chatterjee, *The Poison Tree: Three Novellas* (translated by Marian Maddern) (Delhi, 1994)

34. Ibid., pp. 24–5

35. Attia Hosain, *Sunlight on a Broken Column* (London, 1961; reprinted 1999), p. 36

36. Lina Fruzzetti, *The Gift of a Virgin: Women, Marriage and Ritual in a Bengali Society* (New Brunswick, NJ, 1982)

37. Haraprasad Chattopadhyaya, *Internal Migration in India: A Case Study of Bengal* (Calcutta, 1987), pp. 429–35

38. Claire Alexander, Joya Chatterji and Annu Jalais, *The Bengal Diaspora: Rethinking Muslim Migration* (Abingdon, 2016), p. 143. Also see Armindo Miranda, *The Demography of Bangladesh: Data and Issues* (Bergen, 1982), p. 211

39. Taraknath Ganguli, *The Brothers* (translated by Edward Thompson) (London, 1931), pp. 28–9

40. Samita Sen, '"Without His Consent?" Marriage and Women's Migration in Colonial India', *International Labor and Working-Class History* 65 (2004), p. 79

41. Ibid., p. 80

42. Section 10, Indian Divorce Act, 1869. Also see Rohit De, 'The Two Husbands of Vera Tiscenko: Apostasy, Conversion and Divorce in Late Colonial India', *Law and History Review* 28(4) (2010), p. 1017

43. Point 15 of the Judgement, Musstt Ayesha Bibi v. Subodh Ch. Chakravarty, *All India Reporter* 1949 Calcutta 436

44. Baby Haldar, *A Life Less Ordinary* (translated by Urvashi Butalia) (Delhi, 2006)

45. Joya Chatterji and Claire Alexander, with Annu Jalais and Shahzad Firoz, 'The Bengal Diaspora project', Arts and Humanities Research Council, Diaspora, Migration and Identities programme, 2006–2010

46. Thomas R. Metcalf, *The Aftermath of Revolt: India, 1857–1970* (Princeton, 1964); Eric Stokes, in C. A. Bayly (ed.), *The Peasant Armed: The Indian Rebellion of 1857* (Oxford, 1986)

47. Henry Sumner Maine, *Ancient Law: Its Connection with the Early History of Society, and Its Relation to Modern Ideas* (London, 1861)

48. Cited in Alan Gledhill, 'The Influence of Common Law and Equity on Hindu Law since 1800', *International & Comparative Law Quarterly* 3(4) (1954), p. 576

49. J. Duncan M. Derrett, *Religion, Law and the State in India* (London, 1968), p. 237

50. 'A daughter, who is a mother of male issue, or who is likely to become so, is competent to inherit; not one who is a widow, or is barren, or fails in bringing male issue as bearing none but daughters, or from some other cause . . .' H. T. Colebrooke (translator), *Two Treatises on the Hindu Law of Inheritance* (Calcutta, 1810), pp. 184–94; cited in Eleanor Newbigin, *The Hindu Family and the Emergence of Modern India: Law, Citizenship and Community* (Cambridge, 2013), p. 36

51. Mitra Sharafi, 'The Semi-Autonomous Judge in Colonial India: Chivalric Imperialism Meets Anglo-Islamic Dower and Divorce Law', *Indian Economic and Social History Review* 46(1) (2009), pp. 57–81

52. Gledhill, 'Influence of Common Law'

53. Gregory C. Kozlowski, *Muslim Endowments and Society in British India* (Cambridge, 1985)

54. Sylvia Vatuk, '"Family" as a Contested Concept in Early-Nineteenth-Century Madras', in Chatterjee (ed.), *Unfamiliar Relations*, p. 168

55. John Richardson, *A Dictionary: Persian, Arabic and English*, 2 vols, (Oxford, 1780–1800)

56. Vatuk, '"Family" as a Contested Concept', p. 165

57. Ibid.

58. *Abdul Fata Muhammad Ishak (and others) v. Rasamaya Dhur Chowdhury and others* (1894), *AIR* 1894 22 I A 76; Newbigin, *Hindu Family*, pp. 50–1

59. Newbigin, *Hindu Family*, p. 53

60. Aishwarya Pandit, 'From United Provinces to Uttar Pradesh: Heartland Politics 1947–1970', doctoral dissertation (University of Cambridge, 2015); Ritu Birla, *Stages of Capital: Law, Culture and Market Governance in Late Colonial India* (Durham, NC, 2009)

61. Newbigin, *Hindu Family*, p. 103

62. Mrinalini Sinha, *Specters of Mother India: The Global Restructuring of an Empire* (Durham, NC, 2006)

63. Katherine Mayo, *Mother India* (London, 1927; 9th imp., 1928), p. 29

64. C. S. Ranga Iyer, *Father India: A Reply to Mother India* (London, 1927; 11th imp., 1928), p. 10

65. Newbigin, *Hindu Family*, p. 129

66. Rohit De, 'Mumtaz Bibi's Broken Heart: The Many Lives of the Dissolution of Muslim Marriages Act', *Indian Economic and Social History Review* 46(1) (2009), pp. 105–30

67. Newbigin, *Hindu Family*, pp. 131 ff.

68. The Muslim Personal Law (Shariat) Application Act replaced the Shariat Application Act in 1962 in (West) Pakistan, although the latter

remained in force in East Pakistan. See Sulemen Khan, 'Muslim Personal Law vs State Law – Marriage & Divorce', courtingthelaw.com, 28 March 2016

69. *Mohd. Ahmed Khan v. Shah Bano Begum, AIR* 1985 SC 945

70. E. M. Forster, *The Hill of Devi* (London, 1935, 1985), letter to his mother, 1 January 1913, p. 37

71. Majumdar, *Marriage and Modernity*

72. Cited in Mody, *Intimate State*, p. 1

73. Gloria Goodwin Raheja and Ann Grodzins Gold, *Listen to the Heron's Words: Reimagining Gender and Kinship in North India* (New Delhi, 1994), p. 121; also cited in Mody, *Intimate State*, p. 14

74. *India Penal Code Amendment Act 1923, Section 3*

75. A *kulatyaagini* – one who had broken her links to her parental household, to both maternal and paternal lineages. Flavia Agnes, *Law and Gender Inequality: The Politics of Women's Rights in India* (New Delhi, 1999); Flavia Agnes, *Family Law. Vol. 1: Family Laws and Constitutional Claims* (New Delhi, 2011); Flavia Agnes, *Family Law. Vol. 2: Marriage, Divorce and Matrimonial Litigation* (New Delhi, 2012)

76. Aparna Bandyopadhyay, 'Of Sin, Crime and Punishment: Elopements in Bengal, 1929', in Samita Sen, Ranjita Biswas and Nandita Dhawan (eds), *Intimate Others: Marriage and Sexualities in India* (Kolkata, 2011)

77. Siddhartha Gautam and others, *Less Than Gay: A Citizen's Report on the Status of Homosexuality in India* (1991)

78. Abhimanyu Chandra, 'Khap Panchayats and the Logic of Honour Killings in Contemporary Haryana', MPhil dissertation (Centre of South Asian Studies, University of Cambridge, 2016)

79. Aruna Asaf Ali, *Private Face of a Public Person: A Study of Jawaharlal Nehru* (New Delhi, 1989), pp. 12–13

80. Vivan Sundaram (ed.), *Amrita Sher-Gil: A Self-Portrait in Letters and Writings*, 2 vols (New Delhi, 2010)

81. Letter from Tukoji to 'his brother Malcolm', Darling Papers, Box 8.1

82. Date withheld. Mody, *Intimate State*, pp. xvii–xviii

83. Ibid., pp. xvi–xvii

84. Sen and Sengupta, *Domestic Days*, p. 185

85. Bandyopadhyay, 'Of Sin', pp. 107–10

86. The Marwaris, a diaspora of endogamous Hindu traders and moneylenders from Marwar in present-day Rajasthan, are thought of as typically wealthy

87. Pradip K. Datta, 'Collectives Today: The Novelties of the Rizwanur Movement', in Anjan Ghosh, Tapati Guha-Thakurta and Janaki Nair (eds), *Theorizing the Present: Essays for Partha Chatterjee* (New Delhi, 2011)

88. Piers Vitebsky, *Dialogues with the Dead: The Discussion of Mortality among the Sora of Eastern India* (Cambridge, 1993)

89. Verrier Elwin, *The Kingdom of the Young* (Oxford, 1968)

90. Jonathan Parry, 'Ankalu's Errant Wife: Sex, Marriage and Industry in Contemporary Chhattisgarh', *Modern Asian Studies* 35(4) (2001)

91. Sara Dickey, 'Permeable Homes: Domestic Service, Household Space and the Vulnerability of Class Boundaries in Urban India', *American Ethnologist* 27(2) (2000), pp. 462–89

92. For a broad account, see Francine R. Frankel, *India's Political Economy, 1947–2004: The Gradual Revolution* (New Delhi, 2nd edn, 2005). The nitty-gritty from one province, Bengal, emerges in Joya Chatterji, *The Spoils of Partition: Bengal and India, 1947–1967* (Cambridge, 2007)

93. For details, see Haris Gazdar, 'The Fourth Round and Why They Fight On: An Essay on the History of Land and Reform in Pakistan', paper for PANOS South Asia (2009)

94. Newal Osman, 'Partition and Punjab Politics, 1937–55', doctoral dissertation (University of Cambridge, 2013)

95. For details, see Irawati Karve, *Kinship Organisation in India* (Bombay, 1953), and Thomas Trautmann, 'The Study of Dravidian Kinship', in Patricia Uberoi (ed.), *Family, Kinship and Marriage in India* (Delhi, 1993). Also Hastings Donnan, *Marriage among Muslims: Preference and Choice in Northern Pakistan* (Leiden, 1988)

96. Agarwal, *Field of One's Own*, p. 12

97. Kate Millett, *Sexual Politics* (New York, 1970), p. 38

98. Agarwal, *Field of One's Own*, p. 15

99. Barbara Harriss, 'The Intrafamily Distribution of Hunger in South Asia', in Jean Drèze and Amartya Sen (eds), *The Political Economy of Hunger* (Oxford, 1995), pp. 351–424

100. David Arnold, 'The Politics of Poison: Healing, Empowerment and Subversion in Nineteenth-Century India', in David Hardiman and Projit Bihari Mukharji (eds), *Medical Marginality in South Asia: Situating Subaltern Therapeutics* (Abingdon, 2013); Phoolan Devi with Marie-Thérèse Cuny and Paul Rambali, *I, Phoolan Devi: The Autobiography of India's Bandit Queen* (London, 1996)

101. Agarwal, *Field of One's Own*, p. 50. United Nations Statistics Division, *World Population Prospects: The 2022 Revision*, data.un.org

102. UN Statistics Division, *World Population Prospects*

103. Samita Sen, *Recruitment for the Assam Plantations, 1830–1930* (forthcoming)

104. See Ronald P. Rohner and Manjusri Chaki-Sircar, *Women and Children in a Bengali Village* (Hanover, CT, 1988). Also see Taslima Nasrin, *Meyebela: My Bengali Girlhood: A Memoir of Growing up Female in a Muslim World* (South Royalton, 1998)

105. Mead Cain, Syeda Rokeya Khanam and Shamsun Nahar, 'Class, Patriarchy and Women's Work in Bangladesh', *Population and Development Review* 5(3) (1979), p. 423

106. Miranda, *Demography of Bangladesh*, pp. 76–7

107. Ibid., p. 79

108. Rohner and Chaki-Sircar, *Women and Children*, p. 76

109. Mead Cain, 'The Household Life Cycle and Economic Mobility in Rural Bangladesh', *Population and Development Review* 4(3) (1978), p. 435

110. Rohner and Chaki-Sircar, *Women and Children*, pp. 97–8

111. Cain, 'Household Life Cycle', p. 435

112. Haldar, *Life Less Ordinary*

113. Smoking tobacco, wrapped in a tendu leaf. Cheaper than cigarettes, for sure, but an expense they could ill afford

114. Rajnarayan Chandavarkar, *The Origins of Industrial Capitalism in India: Business Strategies and the Working Classes in Bombay, 1900–1940* (Cambridge, 1994)

115. For example, Joan P. Mencher, 'Women's Work and Poverty: Women's Contribution to Household Maintenance in South India', in Daisy Dwyer and Judith Bruce (eds), *A Home Divided: Women and Income in the Third World* (Stanford, 1988); S. Dasgupta and A. K. Maiti, 'The Rural Energy Crisis, Poverty and Women's Roles in Five Indian Villages', *World Employment Programme Technical Cooperation Report* (Geneva, 1986)

116. William H. Wiser, *The Hindu Jajmani System* (Lucknow, 1936)

117. C. J. Fuller, 'Misconceiving the Grain Heap: A Critique of the Concept of the Indian *Jajmani* System', in J. Parry and M. Bloch (eds), *Money and the Morality of Exchange* (Cambridge, 1989)

118. Susan S. Wadley, *Struggling with Destiny in Karimpur, 1925–1984* (Berkeley, 1994)

119. Rochona Majumdar, 'Looking for Brides and Grooms: *Ghataks*, Matrimonials, and the Marriage Market in Colonial Calcutta, c.1875–1940', *Journal of Asian Studies* 63(4) (2007)

120. I owe this observation to Samita Sen

121. Raheja and Gold, *Listen to the Heron's Words*, passim

122. Even where they had rights, as in parts of Sri Lanka and Bangladesh, they lacked effective control. See Agarwal, *Field of One's Own*; Cain, Khanam and Nahar, 'Class, Patriarchy and Women's Work'

123. Samita Sen, *Women and Labour in Late Colonial India: The Bengal Jute Industry* (Cambridge, 1999), passim

124. Alan Heston, 'Poverty in India: Some Recent Policies', in Marshall M. Bouton and Philip Oldenburg (eds), *India Briefing, 1990* (Boulder, 1990)

125. Deepak Nayyar, 'Globalisation, History and Development: A Tale of Two Centuries', *Cambridge Journal of Economics* 30(1) (2006)

126. Richard Marshall and Shibaab Rahman, 'Internal Migration in Bangladesh: Character, Drivers and Policy Issues' (UNDP, Bangladesh, 2016)

127. Jonathan Parry, 'Sex, Bricks and Mortar: Constructing Class in a Central Indian Steel Town', *Modern Asian Studies* 48(5) (2014)

128. Dickey, 'Permeable Homes', p. 466

129. Sen and Sengupta, *Domestic Days*, passim

130. Ibid., passim

131. Raka Ray and Seemin Qayum, *Cultures of Servitude: Modernity, Domesticity and Class in India* (Stanford, 2009)

132. Sen and Sengupta, *Domestic Days*, passim

133. Ibid., p. 195

134. Nalini Jameela, *The Autobiography of a Sex Worker* (translated with a foreword by J. Devika) (Delhi, 2007), p. x

135. Tanika Sarkar, 'A Nation of Husbands? Intimate Violence and Nationalism in Colonial Bengal', unpublished paper (Cambridge, 2017); and personal communication. Also see Chapter 1

136. Devi with Cuny and Rambali, *I, Phoolan Devi*

137. Ibid., p. 390

138. Ibid.

139. L. T. Denault, 'Publicising Family in Colonial North India *c.*1780–1930', doctoral dissertation (University of Cambridge, 2009) makes this point. Also see Nikhil Rao, *House, but No Garden: Apartment Living in Bombay's Suburbs, 1898–1964* (Minneapolis, 2013)

140. Devi with Cuny and Rambali, *I, Phoolan Devi*, p. 319

141. Eric Hobsbawm, *Bandits* (London, 1969)

142. For example, Veena Oldenburg, 'Lifestyle as Resistance: The Case of the Courtesans of Lucknow, India', *Feminist Studies* 16(2) (1990); Amrit Srinivasan, 'Reform or Conformity? Temple "Prostitution" and the Community in the Madras Presidency', in Bina Agarwal (ed.), *Structures of Patriarchy: State, Community and Household in Modernising Asia* (London, 1988)

143. I hesitate to use the word 'prostitute', which carries all manner of demeaning connotations. But I do so because its contemporary replacement, 'sex worker', would be anachronistic

144. Edwardes, *Crime in India*

145. Erica Wald, *Vice in the Barracks: Medicine, the Military and the Making of Colonial India, 1780–1868* (London, 2014)

146. Kenneth Ballhatchet, *Race, Sex and Class under the Raj: Imperial Attitudes and Policies and Their Critics, 1793–1905* (New York, 1980); Philippa Levine, *Prostitution, Race and Politics: Policing Venereal*

Disease in the British Empire (New York, 2003); Wald, *Vice in the Barracks*

147. Ashwini Tambe, 'Akootai's Death: Subaltern Indian Brothel Workers', in Tambe, *Codes of Misconduct: Regulating Prostitution in Late Colonial Bombay* (Minneapolis, 2009)

148. Wald, *Vice in the Barracks*

149. Ashwini Tambe also draws attention to these and other features in 'Brothels as Families: Reflections on the History of Bombay's *kothas*', *International Feminist Journal of Politics* 8(2) (2006)

150. For example, Emperor v. Bandu Ebrahim and Anr (1918), *Indian Law Review*, Bom. 181

151. Government of India Home, *Proceedings Report on the Conditions of Brothels in Bombay and the Murder of a Prostitute in the City*, Police-A, no. 128–30, December 1917; Tambe, *Codes of Misconduct*, pp. 81 ff.

152. Ashwini Tambe, 'Social Geographies of Bombay's Sex Trade, 1880–1920', in Prashant Kidambi, Manjiri Kamat and Rachel Dwyer (eds), *Bombay Before Mumbai: Essays in Honour of Jim Masselos* (London, 2019), p. 163

153. Jameela, *Autobiography of a Sex Worker*, p. 138

154. Oldenburg, 'Lifestyle as Resistance', p. 267

155. Mirza Muhammad Hadi Ruswa, *Umrao Jan Ada: The Courtesan of Lucknow* (translated by Khushwant Singh and M. A. Husaini) (Madras, 1982). This section is cited in Oldenburg, 'Lifestyle as Resistance', p. 276

156. Ibid.

157. Jameela, *Autobiography of a Sex Worker*, p. 171

158. Ibid., p. 163

159. Prabha Kotiswaran, *Dangerous Sex, Invisible Labor: Sex Work and the Law in India* (Princeton, 2011), pp. 138–9. Also see Swati Ghosh, *The Gendered Proletariat: Sex Work, Workers' Movement, and Agency* (New Delhi, 2017)

160. Rohini Sahni, V. Kalyan Shankar and Hemant Apte, *Prostitution and Beyond: An Analysis of Sex Work in India* (New Delhi, 2008)

161. Laurent Gayer, *Karachi: Ordered Disorder and the Struggle for the City* (London, 2014), p. 259

6 FASTING, FEASTING, GLUTTONY AND
STARVATION: CONSUMPTION, CASTE AND THE
POLITICS OF FOOD IN SOUTH ASIA

1. I. A. Rehman, 'The PPP at 50: Mid-life Crisis?' *Newsline*, November 2017, https://newslinemagazine.com/magazine/ppp-50-mid-life-crisis/

2. Patrick Clibbens, 'The Indian Emergency, 1975–77', doctoral dissertation (University of Cambridge, 2014)

3. Arjun Appadurai, 'Gastro-Politics in Hindu South Asia', *American Ethnologist* 8(3) (1981), p. 494

4. Joseph Bhatti, father of Alice, makes this blunt observation in the novel, in which the Bhattis are of the Choohra caste in an urban cluster in Karachi, Pakistan. Joseph makes his living as a sewer cleaner. Mohammed Hanif, *Our Lady of Alice Bhatti* (London, 2011)

5. Apurba Kumar Podder, 'The Making of the "Illegal" Marketplace: State, Class and Space in Khulna *c.*1951–2008', doctoral dissertation (University of Cambridge, 2017)

6. A. R. Venkatachalapathy, '"In Those Days There Was No Coffee": Coffee-Drinking and Middle-Class Culture in Colonial Tamilnadu', *Indian Economic and Social History Review* 39(2–3) (2002). Also see Lizzie Collingham, *The Hungry Empire: How Britain's Quest for Food Shaped the Modern World* (London, 2017)

7. Joyce Pettigrew, *Robber Noblemen: A Study in the Political System of the Sikh Jats* (London, 1975); Nikhil Rao, *House, but No Garden: Apartment Living in Bombay's Suburbs, 1898–1964* (Minneapolis, 2013)

8. Joan P. Mencher, 'The Caste System Upside Down, or the Not-So-Mysterious East', *Current Anthropology* 15(4) (1974)

9. James Johnson, *The Influence of Tropical Climates, More Especially the Climate of India, on European Constitutions; the Principal Effects and Diseases Thereby Induced, Their Prevention or Removal, and the Means of Preserving Health in Hot Climates, Rendered Obvious to Europeans of Every Capacity: An Essay* (London, 1813), p. 441. Emphasis added

10. Ibid., cited in David Arnold, 'The "Discovery" of Malnutrition and Diet in Colonial India', *Indian Economic and Social History Review* 31(1) (1994), p. 1

11. John Beames, *Memoirs of a Bengal Civilian* (London, 1961), p. 156

12. Crudely put, *varnashramadharma* referred to only four classes, types or colours of persons, and the (legal) duty of all to perform the duties and penances of their rank. (The term is ancient, in Sanskrit, and not easy to translate into modern English)

13. Rupa Viswanath, *The Pariah Problem: Caste, Religion and the Social in Modern India* (New York, 2014)

14. Louis Dumont, *Homo Hierarchicus: The Caste System and Its Implications* (London, 1966)

15. M. N. Srinivas, 'Varna and Caste', in his *Caste in Modern India and Other Essays* (Bombay, 1962)

16. Om Prakash Valmiki, *Joothan: A Dalit's Life* (translated from the Hindi by Arun Prabha Mukherjee) (Kolkata, 2003)

17. G. S. Ghurye, 'Features of the Caste System', in his *Caste and Race in India* (Bombay, 1969)

18. Gloria Goodwin Raheja, *The Poison in the Gift: Ritual, Prestation, and the Dominant Caste in a North Indian Village* (Chicago, 1988)

19. In these instances, where matters of genealogy needed to reflect actual changes on the ground, 'grand civilizational categories' of *varnashram-adharma* were often pressed into service, particularly that of the Kshattriya. McKim Marriott, 'Multiple Reference in Indian Caste Systems', in James Silverberg (ed.), *Social Mobility in the Caste System in India: An Interdisciplinary Symposium* (The Hague, 1968)

20. M. N. Srinivas, *Religion and Society Among the Coorgs of South India* (Oxford, 1952)

21. Ghurye, 'Features of the Caste System', p. 42

22. Like Yashica Dutt, I use the terms 'upper caste' and 'lower caste' only because they are common currency. I do not accept the implicit (or indeed explicit) inequality these terms connote. See Yashica Dutt, *Coming Out as Dalit: A Memoir* (New Delhi, 2019), p. x

23. For example, Joya Chatterji, *Bengal Divided: Hindu Communalism and Partition 1932–1947* (Cambridge, 1994), pp. 192–203

24. Sekhar Bandyopadhyay, *Caste, Politics and the Raj: Bengal, 1872–1937* (Calcutta, 1990), p. 101

25. Dutt, *Coming Out as Dalit*

26. Tarabai Shinde, who is often described as the subcontinent's first feminist, wrote *Stree Purush Tulana* ('A Comparison Between Women and Men') in 1882. For a sensitive introduction and translation, see Rosalind O'Hanlon, *A Comparison Between Women and Men: Tarabai Shinde and the Critique of Gender Relations in Colonial India* (Delhi, 1994)

27. H. H. Risley and E. A. Gait, *Census of India, 1901, Volume I* (Calcutta, 1903), Chapter V – Education, Subsidiary Table VI, Education by Selected Castes, pp. 180–3. Also see Maroona Murmu, *Words of Her Own: Women Authors in Nineteenth-Century Bengal* (Delhi, 2019)

28. Tanika Sarkar, *Words to Win: The Making of Amar Jiban: A Modern Autobiography* (New Delhi, 1999)

29. Since then, the Tablighi Jamaat has done much to enhance basic literacy among Muslim women, and encourage them to adhere to reformed religion. For example, Eva F. Nisa, 'Insights into the Lives of Indonesian Female Tablighi Jama'at', *Modern Asian Studies* 48(2) (2014)

30. *Curriculum of Pakistan Studies* (revised 2006)

31. Ravindra S. Khare, *The Hindu Hearth and Home* (New Delhi, 1976), pp. 145–6

32. Tanika Sarkar, 'The Woman as Communal Subject: Rashtrasevika Samiti and Ram Janmabhoomi Movement', *Economic and Political Weekly* 26(35) (1991), pp. 2057–62

33. Kisan 'Anna' Hazare, born in 1939, a long-time Gandhian social activist, was at this time frustrated by corruption. His 'fast unto death' in Delhi in 2011 was a sensation, shaking the foundations of one government and giving rise to a new and growing political party, the Aam Aadmi Party (the Common People's Party, AAP)

34. For an interesting discussion of the wider theme of the power of renunciation, see Louis Dumont, 'World Renunciation in Indian Religions', *Contributions to Indian Sociology* 4 (1960), pp. 33–62

35. McKim Marriott, 'Caste Ranking and Food Transactions: A Matrix Analysis', in Milton Singer and Bernard S. Cohn (eds), *Structure and Change in Indian Society* (Chicago, 1968)

36. McKim Marriott and Ronald B. Inden, 'Toward an Ethnosociology of South Asian Caste Systems', in Kenneth David (ed.), *The New Wind: Changing Identities in South Asia* (Chicago, 1977)

37. Appadurai, 'Gastro-Politics', p. 507

38. This discussion relies on the work of the anthropologist R. S. Khare, *The Hindu Hearth and Home*; the work of the chemist and food scholar K. T. Achaya: *Oilseeds and Oil-Milling in India: A Cultural and Historical Survey* (New Delhi, 1990); *The Food Industries of British India* (Delhi, 1994); *Indian Food: A Historical Companion* (Delhi, 1994); *A Historical Dictionary of Indian Food* (Delhi, 1998); and *The Illustrated Foods of India A–Z* (Delhi, 2009). Many long years of observation, as a participant, have also shaped my argument and point of view

39. Valmiki, *Joothan: A Dalit's Life*, p. xxx

40. Appadurai, 'Gastro-Politics', p. 506; see also Arjun Appadurai, *Worship and Conflict under Colonial Rule: A South Indian Case* (Cambridge, 1981)

41. Ghurye, 'Features of the Caste System', p. 39

42. Tanika Sarkar, '"Dirty Work, Filthy Caste": Calcutta Scavengers in the 1920s', in Ravi Ahuja (ed.), *Working Lives and Worker Militancy: The Politics of Labour in Colonial India* (Delhi, 2013)

43. Utsa Ray, *Culinary Culture in Colonial India: A Cosmopolitan Platter and the Middle-Class* (Delhi, 2015)

44. Ghurye, 'Features of the Caste System', p. 39

45. Valmiki, *Joothan: A Dalit's Life*, passim

46. L. S. S. O'Malley, *Bengal District Gazetteers 1909: Monghyr* (Calcutta, 1909), p. 92

47. Arun Agrawal and Vasant K. Saberwal, 'Whither South Asian Pastoralism? An Introduction', *Nomadic Peoples* 8(2) (2004), pp. 36–53

48. V. K. Saberwal, *Pastoral Politics: Shepherds, Bureaucrats and Conservation in the Western Himalaya* (Delhi, 1999); V. K. Saberwal and Mahesh Rangarajan (eds), *Battles over Nature: Science and the Politics of Conservation* (New Delhi, 2003), pp. 1–28. Also see Neeladri Bhattacharya,

The *Great Agrarian Conquest: The Colonial Reshaping of a Rural World* (Ranikhet, 2018)

49. *Harijan*, September 1940, Mahatma Gandhi speaking to Harijan workers, Sevagram Ashram. Cited in D. N. Jha, *The Myth of the Holy Cow* (New Delhi, 2009), p. 17

50. William Robert Cornish, *Observations on the Nature of the Food of the Inhabitants of Southern India, and on Prison Dietaries in the Madras Presidency* (Madras, 1864), p. 11

51. Peter van der Veer, '"God Must Be Liberated!" A Hindu Liberation Movement in Ayodhya', *Modern Asian Studies* 21(2) (1987); Anand A. Yang, 'Sacred Symbol and Sacred Space in Rural India: Community Mobilization in the "Anti-Cow Killing" Riot of 1893', *Comparative Studies in Society and History* 22(4) (1980); Jha, *Myth of the Holy Cow*; Prabhu Bapu, *Hindu Mahasabha in Colonial North India, 1915–30* (Abingdon, 2013); C. S. Adcock, 'Sacred Cows and Secular History: Cow Protection Debates in Colonial North India', *Comparative Studies of South Asia, Africa and the Middle East* 30(2) (2010), pp. 297–311; Peter Robb, 'The Challenge of Gau Mata: British Policy and Religious Change in India, 1880–1916', *Modern Asian Studies* 20(2) (1986); S. Chigateri, 'Negotiating the "Sacred" Cow: Cow Slaughter and the Regulation of Difference in India', in Monica Mookherjee (ed.), *Democracy, Religious Pluralism and the Liberal Dilemma of Accommodation* (Dordrecht, 2011)

52. Dumont, 'World Renunciation in Indian Religions'

53. Anjali Bhardwaj Datta, 'Rebuilding Lives, Redefining Spaces: Women in Post-Colonial Delhi, 1947–1980', doctoral dissertation (University of Cambridge, 2015)

54. See the Note on Further Viewing

55. Khare, *Hindu Hearth and Home*, p. 53

56. Ibid., p. 1

57. Baby Haldar, *A Life Less Ordinary* (translated by Urvashi Butalia) (Delhi, 2006)

58. Swami Lokeswarananda, *Chandogya Upanishada VII*, 26, 2, cited in Khare, *Hindu Hearth and Home*. My thanks to Eivind Kahrs, who seems not entirely happy with this translation (his own)

59. Khare, *Hindu Hearth and Home*

60. Valmiki, *Joothan: A Dalit's Life*, p. 9

61. Risley and Gait, *Census of India, 1901*, p. 351

62. Appadurai, 'Gastro-Politics'. On the Tamil diaspora see David Washbrook, 'Brain Drain, Exchange and Gain: "Hi-Skill" Migrants and the Developed Economies', in Joya Chatterji and David Washbrook (eds), *Routledge Handbook of the South Asian Diaspora* (Abingdon, 2013)

63. This account is based on the author's extended interview with Emmanuel Tigga, in New Delhi, over several sessions starting on 1 April 2020. He has consented to, indeed insisted upon, his name being revealed

64. Registrar General & Census Commissioner, *Census of India 2001: Primary Census Abstract – Scheduled Tribes, Table A-9* (2001). Also see Nitin Kumar Bharti, 'Wealth Inequality, Class and Caste in India, 1961–2012', *World Inequality Database* (November 2018), Table 13, p. 36

65. Nandini Sundar, *Subalterns and Sovereigns: An Anthropological History of Bastar, 1854–1996* (Oxford, 1997)

66. For example, Ajay Skaria, *Hybrid Histories: Forests, Frontiers and Wildness in Western India* (Delhi, 1999)

67. Tamina Chowdhury, *Indigenous Identity in South Asia: Making Claims in the Colonial Chittagong Hill Tracts* (Abingdon, 2016); Sajal Nag, *Pied Pipers in North-East India: Bamboo Flowers, Rat Famine and the Politics of Philanthropy, 1881–2007* (New Delhi, 2008)

68. Louise Tillin, 'Questioning Borders: Social Movements, Political Parties and the Creation of New States in India', *Pacific Affairs* 84(1) (2011)

69. The Naxalite movement in Bengal is discussed briefly in Chapter 5. In Jharkhand, most Naxals were, and are, Adivasis who have studied and gained qualifications but found no work, says Emmanuel Tigga. This may be a snip-snap answer, but it is his personal understanding of the problem

70. Verrier Elwin, *Leaves from the Jungle: Life in a Gond Village* (London, 2nd edn, 1958), p. 32

71. Francis Zimmermann, *The Jungle and the Aroma of Meats: An Ecological Theme in Hindu Medicine* (Berkeley, 1987)

72. For scholarly studies of chronic malnutrition in Jharkhand, see, for instance, Kiran Sharma, 'Hunger in Jharkhand: Dimensions of Poverty and Food Security in Palamu District', *South Asia Research* 39(1) (2019)

73. Cornish, *Observations on the Nature of the Food*, p. 11

74. Sundar, *Subalterns and Sovereigns*, passim. Also see Skaria, *Hybrid Histories*; and Archana Prasad, *Against Ecological Romanticism: Verrier Elwin and the Making of an Anti-Modern Tribal Identity* (New Delhi, 2003)

75. Chowdhury, *Indigenous Identity*; Sundar, *Subalterns and Sovereigns*, p. 114

76. Elwin, *Leaves from the Jungle*, p. 12

77. Célestin Bouglé, 'The Essence and Reality of the Caste System', *Contributions to Indian Sociology* 2 (1968)

78. Raheja, *Poison in the Gift*

79. Imtiaz Ahmad, 'Endogamy and Status Mobility among the Siddiqui Sheikhs of Allahabad, Uttar Pradesh', in Imtiaz Ahmad (ed.), *Caste and Social Stratification among the Muslims* (Delhi, 1973); and C. J. Fuller, 'Kerala Christians and the Caste System', *Man* 11(1) (1976)

80. Marc Galanter, *Competing Equalities: Law and the Backward Classes in India* (Berkeley, 1984); Granville Austin, *The Indian Constitution: Cornerstone of a Nation* (New Delhi, 1966)

81. Mencher, 'The Caste System Upside Down'

82. *Constituent Assembly Debates, (India), Official Report: Vols 1–5* (New Delhi, 2009)

83. 'Refrain from Using Term "Dalit": I&B Ministry's Advisory to Media', *Outlook*, 4 September 2018; S. N. Sahu, 'Telling People Not to Use "Dalit" Contravenes Both the Law and the Dalit Cause', *The Wire*, 11 September 2018

84. Viswanath, *Pariah Problem*, p. 6

85. Ibid., p. 5

86. Sharankumar Limbale, *The Outcaste: Akkarmashi* (translated from the Marathi by Santosh Bhoomkar) (New Delhi, 2008), p. 50

87. Ibid., p. 10

88. Ibid., pp. 14–15

89. Appadurai, 'Gastro-Politics'

90. Limbale, *Outcaste*, p. 8

91. Ibid., p. 9

92. Valmiki, *Joothan: A Dalit's Life*, p. 43

93. Célestin Bouglé, *Essays on the Caste System* (translated by D. F. Pocock) (Cambridge, 1971)

94. Laxman Gaikwad, *The Branded: Uchalya* (translated from the Marathi by P. A. Kolharkar) (New Delhi, 2005), p. 10

95. Ibid., p. 21

96. Ibid.

97. Registrar General & Census Commissioner, *Census of India 2001: The First Report on Religion Data* (New Delhi, 2004), p. xvii

98. For details and the political conditions under which this demand was made, see Theodore P. Wright, Jr, 'A New Demand for Muslim Reservations in India', *Asian Survey* 37(9) (1997), pp. 853–8

99. Ahmad, 'Endogamy and Status Mobility'

100. Justin Jones, *Shi'a Islam in Colonial India: Religion, Community and Sectarianism* (Cambridge, 2011)

101. David Montero, 'Shiite–Sunni Conflict Rises in Pakistan', *Christian Science Monitor*, 2 February 2007

102. 'Pakistan: Rampant Killings of Shia by Extremists: Disarm, Prosecute Militants, Protest Hazara Community', Human Rights Watch, 29 June 2014

103. Cornish, *Observations on the Nature of the Food*, pp. 32–3

104. K. C. De, *Report of the Bengal Provincial Banking Enquiry Committee, 1929–30, Vol. I* (Calcutta, 1930), p. 78; henceforth *BBEC*

105. Ibid.

106. *Halal* in Arabic means permissible. Meat or poultry is halal if animals or poultry are killed through a cut to the jugular vein

107. Kenneth McPherson, *The Muslim Microcosm: Calcutta, 1918 to 1935* (Wiesbaden, 1974)

108. Mahadeb P. Basu, *Anthropological Profile of the Muslims of Calcutta* (Calcutta, 1985); Joya Chatterji, *The Spoils of Partition: Bengal and India, 1947–1967* (Cambridge, 2007), p. 193

109. Basu, *Anthropological Profile*, p. 16

110. Namrata Singh, 'Food Companies Miss Ramazan Demand in Lockdown', *Times of India*, 8 May 2020

111. Amin Ali, 'Corona Clouds Ramzan: No Coming Together in Month of Plenty', *Times of India*, 26 April 2020

112. Rajnarain Bose, *Atmacharit* ('Autobiography' in Bengali) (Calcutta, 1909); and Anil Seal, *The Emergence of Indian Nationalism: Competition and Collaboration in the Later Nineteenth Century* (Cambridge, 2008), p. 196, fn. 2

113. De, *BBEC*, p. 32

114. The Rai Sahib's daily *hisaab* diary, Ghosh Collection Box 3, Centre of South Asian Studies, Cambridge

115. Ibid., September 1946

116. Ray, *Culinary Culture*, p. 1

117. Arjun Appadurai, 'How to Make a National Cuisine: Cookbooks in Contemporary India', *Comparative Studies in Society and History* 30(1) (1988)

118. See, for instance, Bhaskar Mukhopadhyay, 'Between Elite Hysteria and Subaltern Carnivalesque: The Politics of Street-Food in the City of Calcutta', *South Asia Research* 24(1) (2004)

119. Washbrook, 'Brain Drain'. Also see Joya Chatterji, 'From Imperial Subjects to National Citizens: South Asians and the International Migration Regime since 1947', in Chatterji and Washbrook (eds), *South Asian Diaspora*

120. C. J. Fuller and Haripriya Narasimhan, *Tamil Brahmans: The Making of a Middle-Class Caste* (Chicago, 2014)

121. Claude Markovits, 'What about the Merchants? A Mercantile Perspective on the Middle Class of Colonial India', in Sanjay Joshi (ed.), *The Middle Class in Colonial India* (New Delhi, 2010), p. 123

122. Ibid.

123. Appadurai, 'How to Make a National Cuisine', p. 6

124. 'Note on Indigenous Bankers and money-lenders in the Tangail subdivision by Rai Bahadur Sasadhur Ghosh', Appendix VI, *BBEC*, p. 316

125. De, *BBEC*, p. 18

126. C. A. Bayly, *Rulers, Townsmen and Bazaars: North Indian Society in the Age of British Expansion, 1770–1870* (Cambridge, 1983)

127. On the inwardness of 'taste', see Pierre Bourdieu, *Distinction: A Social Critique of the Judgement of Taste* (Abingdon, 2010)

128. Vivek Shanbhag, *Ghachar Ghochar* (translated into English by Srinath Perur) (London, 2018), p. 93

129. Ritu Birla, *Stages of Capital: Law, Culture and Market Governance in Late Colonial India* (Durham, NC, 2009)

130. Venkatachalapathy, 'There Was No Coffee'

131. Pat Caplan, 'Crossing the Veg/Non-Veg Divide: Commensality and Sociality among the Middle Classes in Madras/Chennai', *Journal of South Asian Studies* 31(1) (2008), pp. 118–42

132. Hugo Gorringe and D. Karthikeyan, 'The Hidden Politics of Vegetarianism: Caste and *The Hindu* Canteen', *Economic and Political Weekly* 49(20) (2014)

133. Ashris, *India in Pixels* (2020), Union Government Sample Registration System Baseline Survey 2014

134. Cornish, *Observations on the Nature of the Food*

135. *Eleusine coracana*; Cornish, *Observations on the Nature of the Food*, p. 3

136. Ibid., p. 30

137. J. M. Cunningham, *Fourteenth Annual Report of the Sanitary Commissioner with the Government of India 1877* (Calcutta, 1878), p. 180

138. Arnold, '"Discovery" of Malnutrition', pp. 6–7

139. Ravi Ahuja, *Pathways of Empire: Circulation, 'Public Works' and Social Space in Colonial Orissa (c.1780–1914)* (Hyderabad, 2009)

140. T. W. Holderness, *Narrative of the Famine in India in 1896–97* (Simla, 1897), p. 6, Table 1

141. *Fourteenth Annual Report of the Sanitary Commissioner*, p. 181

142. Arnold, '"Discovery" of Malnutrition'

143. Chunilal Bose, *Food* (Calcutta, 1930), pp. 92–3. Also see Arnold, '"Discovery" of Malnutrition'

144. Holderness, *Narrative*, p. 13

145. Ibid.

146. David Arnold, *Everyday Technology: Machines and the Making of India's Modernity* (Chicago, 2015), p. 63

147. Ibid.

148. Haruka Yanagisawa, 'Growth of Small-Scale Industries and Changes in Consumption Patterns in South India, 1910s–50s', in Douglas

E. Haynes, Abigail McGowan, Tirthankar Roy and Haruka Yanagisawa (eds), *Towards a History of Consumption in South Asia* (New Delhi, 2010), p. 53

149. Ibid. Also see Christopher John Baker, *An Indian Rural Economy, 1880–1955: The Tamilnad Countryside* (Oxford, 1984), pp. 379–80

150. Baker, *Indian Rural Economy*

151. Darling Papers, Box 2.1, 'Wisdom and Waste', p. 10

152. *East India Famine: Papers Regarding the Famine and Relief Operations in India, 1899–1900*, Vol. 1 (London, 1900)

153. Ibid., p. 19

154. Laura Spinney, *Pale Rider: The Spanish Flu of 1918 and How It Changed the World* (London, 2017)

155. David Arnold, 'Death and the Modern Empire: The 1918–19 Influenza Epidemic in India', *Transactions of the Royal Historical Society* 29 (2019)

156. David Arnold, 'Looting, Grain Riots and Government Policy in South India 1918', *Past & Present* 84 (1979)

157. Ibid., p. 117

158. W. R. Aykroyd, B. G. Krishnan, R. Passmore and A. R. Sundararajan, *The Rice Problem in India* (Calcutta, 1940)

159. *Indian Year Book*, 1937–38, cited in Aykroyd et al., *Rice Problem*

160. Podder, 'Making of "Illegal" Marketplace'

161. M. K. Gandhi, 'Polished v. Unpolished', *Harijan*, 26 October 1934, cited in Sunil S. Amrith, 'Food and Welfare in India, c.1900–1950', *Comparative Studies in Society and History* 50(4) (2008), pp. 1020–1

162. Radhakamal Mukherjee and K. T. Shah (eds), *National Planning Committee: Population: Report of the Sub-Committee* (Bombay, 1947), cited in Amrith, 'Food and Welfare', p. 1021

163. S. Gopal (ed.), *The Essential Writings of Jawaharlal Nehru, Vols I & II* (New Delhi, 2003), p. 10

164. Jnananjan Niyogi, noted Bengali social reformer, cited in Janam Mukherjee, *Hungry Bengal: War, Famine and the End of Empire* (London, 2015), p. 140

165. India: Government Policy, 1944, CHUR 2/43 A-B, p.23/ Churchill Papers, Churchill Archives Centre, Churchill College Cambridge

166. 'The Things We Forgot to Remember', BBC Radio 4, 7 January 2008, cited in Lizzie Collingham, *The Taste of War: World War II and the Battle for Food* (New York, 2012), p. 151. Also see Madhusree Mukerjee, *Churchill's Secret War: The British Empire and the Ravaging of India during World War II* (Gurgaon, 2018)

167. Selina Ho, *Thirsty Cities: Social Contracts and Public Goods Provision in China and India* (Cambridge, 2019)

168. CIA Memorandum, 'The India-Pakistan Situation', 3 December 1965, www. foia.cia.gov

169. Ibid.

170. Yassir Islam and James L. Garrett, 'IFPRI and the Abolition of the Wheat Flour Ration Shops in Pakistan: A Case-Study on Policymaking and the Use and Impact of Research', International Food Policy Research Institute (December 1997), pp. 11–13

171. Gene D. Overstreet and Marshall Windmiller, *Communism in India* (Berkeley, 1959)

172. Nilakanth Rath and V. S. Patwardhan, 'Impact of Assistance under PL 480 on Indian Economy', *India Quarterly: A Journal of International Affairs* 24(4) (1968); H. Laxminarayan, 'Indo–US Food Agreement and State Trading in Foodgrains', *Economic Weekly*, 24 September 1960; Paul J. Isenman and H. W. Singer, 'Food Aid: Disincentive Effects and Their Policy Implications', *Economic Development and Cultural Change* 25(2) (1977)

173. Jack David Loveridge, 'The Hungry Harvest: Philanthropic Science and the Making of South Asia's Green Revolution, 1919–1964', doctoral dissertation (The University of Texas at Austin, 2017)

174. Interview with M. S. Swaminathan, New Delhi, December 2014

175. Anwar Dil, *Life and Work of M. S. Swaminathan: Toward a Hunger-free World* (Chennai, 2005)

176. B. H. Farmer, 'Technology and Change in Rice-Growing Areas', in B. H. Farmer (ed.), *Green Revolution?: Technology and Change in Rice-Growing Areas of Tamil Nadu and Sri Lanka* (London, 1977), p. 3

177. Vandana Shiva, *The Violence of the Green Revolution: Third World Agriculture, Ecology and Politics* (Lexington, KY, 2016)

178. Daisy A. John and Giridhara R. Babu, 'Lessons from the Aftermaths of Green Revolution on Food System and Health', *Frontiers in Sustainable Food Systems* 5 (2021). Also see Mariane Silva de Miranda et al., 'Environmental Impacts of Rice Cultivation', *American Journal of Plant Sciences* 6(12) (2015); Sanjay Choudhary et al., 'A Review: Pesticide Residue: Cause of Many Animal Health Problems', *Journal of Entomology and Zoology Studies* 6(3) (2018)

179. Amita Baviskar, *In the Belly of the River: Tribal Conflicts over Development in the Narmada Valley* (Oxford, 1996)

180. Francine R. Frankel, *India's Green Revolution: Economic Gains and Political Costs* (Princeton, 1971), p. 34

181. Ibid., p. 26

182. Ibid., p. 37

183. Ibid., p. 57

184. Baviskar, *In the Belly of the River*

185. 'From 1,10,000 Varieties of Rice to Only 6,000 Now', *The Hindu*, 6 April 2012. Also Rohini Chaki, 'The Conservationist Saving India's Heirloom Rice Varieties', www.atlasobscura.com, 25 November 2019

186. '*Cholbe*' suggests that you (or something) will do, just. A 'Bonglish' word, '*chol*-able' has the same meaning as 'serviceable', but is injected with delicious irony. I suggest you add it to your vocabulary. You will need it more often than you think, and it will make you laugh at yourself for being 'just about okay'

187. Jean Drèze, Amartya Sen and Athar Hussain (eds), *The Political Economy of Hunger: Selected Essays* (Delhi, 1990)

188. Jean Drèze, 'Democracy and Right to Food', *Economic & Political Weekly* 39(17) (2004), p. 1729

189. Vandana Bhatia, Jean Drèze and Vandana Prasad (eds), *Mid-Day Meals: A Primer* (Right to Food Campaign, 2005), p. 20; emphasis added

190. *Report of the High Level Committee on Long Term Grain Policy*, 16 November 2000, Section 5.58 (vii)

7 LEISURE, TWENTIETH-CENTURY STYLE

1. Don Handelman, 'Play and Ritual: Complementary Frames of Meta-Communication', in Anthony J. Chapman and Hugh C. Foot (eds), *It's a Funny Thing, Humour* (Oxford, 1977). In the same collection, see the following: Harvey Mindess, 'If Hamlet Had Had a Sense of Humour'; Paul Kline, 'The Psychoanalytic Theory of Humour and Laughter'; Thomas R. Kane, Jerry Suls and James Tedeschi, 'Humour as a Tool of Social Interaction'; Lawrence E. Mintz, 'American Humour and the Spirit of the Times'; William F. Fry, 'The Appeasement Function of Mirthful Laughter'; Paul E. McGhee, 'A Model of the Origins and Early Development of Incongruity-Based Humour'; Mary K. Rothbart and Diana Pien, 'Elephants and Marshmallows: A Theoretical Synthesis of Incongruity Resolution and Arousal Theories of Humour'; Jerry Suls, 'Cognitive and Disparagement Theories of Humour: A Theoretical and Empirical Synthesis'; Göran Nerhardt, 'Operationalization of Incongruity in Humour Research: A Critique and Suggestions'; Chris Powell, 'Humour as a Form of Social Control: A Deviance Approach'; and Robert Barshay, 'Black Humour in the Modern Cartoon'

2. R. K. Laxman, *The Tunnel of Time: An Autobiography* (New Delhi, 1998); R. K. Laxman, *The Best of Laxman* (New Delhi, 1998); Ritu Gairola Khanduri, *Caricaturing Culture in India: Cartoons and History in the Modern World* (Cambridge, 2014); Sukeshi Kamra, 'The War of Images: Mohammed Ali Jinnah and Editorial Cartoons in the Indian Nationalist Press, 1947', *ARIEL* 34(2–3) (2003); Shazia Akbar

Ghilzai and Zubair A. Bajwa, 'Seeing Pakistan through the Gaze of Cartoonists: Editorial Cartoons Epitome of National Interest', *European Academic Research* 8(2) (2020)

3. Debashree Mukherjee, in her excellent *Bombay Hustle: Making Movies in a Colonial City* (New York, 2020), uses the word 'cine-ecology' in roughly the same way as I have used 'sector'. I do so because the latter is a concept with a rich literature in the study of labour, capital and the working classes. It has the further advantage of being widely understood

4. For a virtual tour of Filmcity, watch the short YouTube video of 2018, in the series '200 Journeys'

5. Prashant Kidambi, *Cricket Country: An Indian Odyssey in the Age of Empire* (Oxford, 2019); Ramachandra Guha, *The Commonwealth of Cricket: A Lifelong Love Affair with the Most Subtle and Sophisticated Game Known to Mankind* (London, 2020); Ashis Nandy, *The Tao of Cricket: On Games of Destiny and the Destiny of Games* (London, 1989)

6. By the term 'folk deity' I refer to a cult of a god or goddess that has a limited regional scope and following; unlike, say, the worship of Shiva or Vishnu, whose devotees can be found among Hindus across the sub-continent. For a discussion of the 'great' and 'little' traditions of Hinduism, see C. J. Fuller, *The Camphor Flame: Popular Hinduism and Society in India* (Princeton, 1992)

7. Sukumar Sen, *Vipradasa's Manasa-Vijaya* (Calcutta, 1953)

8. Pradyot Kumar Maity, 'The Early History of the Cult of the Goddess Manasa', doctoral dissertation (University of London, 1962), pp. 485–6

9. Carola Erika Lorea, 'Snake Charmers on Parade: A Performance-centered Study of the Crisis of the Ojhā Healers', *Asian Medicine* 13(1–2) (2018), pp. 255 ff.

10. See, for instance, Vernon James Schubel, 'Karbala as Sacred Space among North American Shia: "Every Day is Ashura, Everywhere is Karbala"', in Barbara Daly Metcalf (ed.), *Making Muslim Space in North America and Europe* (Berkeley, 1996), pp. 186–203; David Pinault, *Horse of Karbala: Muslim Devotional Life in India* (New York, 2001); J. R. I. Cole, *Roots of North Indian Shiism in Iran and Iraq: Religion and State in Awadh, 1722–1859* (Berkeley, 1988); Justin Jones, *Shi'a Islam in Colonial India: Religion, Community and Sectarianism* (Cambridge, 2011); Kamran Scot Aghaie (ed.), *The Women of Karbala: Ritual Performances and Symbolic Discourses in Modern Shi'i Islam* (Austin, TX, 2005); Syed Akbar Hyder, *Reliving Karbala: Martyrdom in South Asian Memory* (Oxford, 2006); Kamran Scot Aghaie, *The Martyrs of Karbala: Shii Symbols and Rituals in Modern Iran* (Seattle, 2004); Claire Alexander, Joya Chatterji and Annu Jalais, *The Bengal*

Diaspora: Rethinking Muslim Migration (Abingdon, 2016). So too, in a minor key, is the tradition of Ghazi Miyan, slayed (perhaps?) in a battle centuries ago but venerated as a hero, as a protector of 'the community'. See Shahid Amin, *Conquest and Community: The Afterlife of Warrior Saint Ghazi Miyan* (Chicago, 2016)

11. Allen Moore and Ákos Östör, *Serpent Mother* (1985), Documentary Educational Resources, www.der.org. Also see Lorea, 'Snake Charmers'

12. W. Crooke, *An Introduction to the Popular Religion and Folklore of Northern India* (Allahabad, 1894), pp. 20, 135; and Lorea, 'Snake Charmers'

13. Lorea, 'Snake Charmers', p. 251

14. W. Knighton, 'Religious Fairs in India', *The Nineteenth Century: A Monthly Review* 9 (1881), pp. 838–48

15. Mrs E. Tierney Papers (copies of letters from James McNeill ICS, CSAS); letter from James McNeill to his brother John from Malgadi, Madras, 2 December 1892, describing a 'Musalman' fair

16. Knighton, 'Religious Fairs'

17. Laxman Gaikwad, *The Branded: Uchalya* (translated from the Marathi by P. A. Kolharkar) (New Delhi, 2005 edn). Also see Chapter 6: 'gold was iron treated to look like gold'. See Pankhuree Dube, 'Rethinking *Melas* as Subaltern Spaces: Pardhan Blacksmiths and Some Aspects of "Caste-Passing" in Fairs, 1872–1931', *Social History* 43(2) (2018)

18. Nita Kumar, *The Artisans of Banaras: Popular Culture and Identity, 1880–1986* (Princeton, 2017), pp. 98–9

19. Knighton, 'Religious Fairs'

20. See Dube, 'Rethinking *Melas*'

21. Samita Sen, 'Girls Marrying Men: Labour, Culture and Child Marriage in Colonial India', inaugural lecture at the University of Cambridge, 2021

22. Ramlila means the sport of Ram. *Lila* has a different meaning to any secular sport in Hindu thought: it is the play of the gods with and in their different moods and avatars

23. Philip Lutgendorf, *The Life of a Text: Performing the Ramcaritmanas of Tulsidas* (Berkeley, 1991), p. 248

24. Valmiki's *Ramayana*, composed in Sanskrit, is thought to date from the first few centuries before the Christian Era. Or at least this is an authoritative, but not uncontroversial, view. Lutgendorf, *Life of a Text*, p. 3; and Robert P. Goldman (ed. and trans.), *The Ramayana of Valmiki: An Epic of Ancient India, Volume 1: Balakanda* (Princeton, 1985)

25. Norvin Hein, *The Miracle Plays of Mathura* (New Haven, 1972), p. 101; and W. Crooke, 'The Dasahra: An Autumn Festival of the Hindus', *Folk-Lore* 26(1) (1915)

26. Lutgendorf, *Life of a Text*, p. 248

27. Ibid., p. 13

28. See Paula Richman (ed.), *Many Ramayanas: The Diversity of a Narrative Tradition in South Asia* (Berkeley, 1991); and Paula Richman and Rustom Bharucha (eds), *Performing the Ramayana Tradition: Enactments, Interpretations, and Arguments* (New York, 2021)

29. For a useful account of Hindu beliefs and practices, see Fuller, *Camphor Flame*

30. Kumar, *Artisans of Banaras*, pp. 180–4

31. For fuller treatments, see F. S. Growse (trans.), *The Ramayana of Tulsi Das* (Allahabad, 1937); and W. D. P. Hill (trans.), *The Holy Lake of the Acts of Rama: A New Translation of Tulasi Das's Ramacaritamanasa* (Bombay, 1952). More readable versions include C. Rajagopalachari, *Ramayana* (Bombay, 1968). Works still banned in India include Aubrey Menen's *Rama Retold* (London, 1954)

32. For example, see Aaron Sherraden, 'Recasting Shambuk in Three Hindi Anti-Caste Dramas' and Om Prakash Valmiki and Aaron Sherraden, 'Shambuk's Severed Head', both in Richman and Bharucha (eds), *Performing the Ramayana Tradition*

33. Valmiki and Sherraden, 'Shambuk's Severed Head'

34. C. A. Bayly, *Empire and Information: Intelligence Gathering and Social Communication in India, 1780–1870* (Cambridge, 1996)

35. Richard Schechner and Linda Hess, 'The Ramlila of Ramnagar', *Drama Review* 21(3) (1977)

36. H. R. Nevill (ed.), *District Gazetteers of the United Provinces of Agra and Oudh*, Vols I and I (Allahabad, 1909), pp. 6–48

37. Hein, *Miracle Plays*, p. 102

38. Schechner and Hess, 'Ramlila of Ramnagar'

39. Lutgendorf, *Life of a Text*, p. 276

40. Ibid., p. 277

41. Christopher Fuller, in *The Camphor Flame*, argues that Hinduism sees no sharp divide between humanity and divinity. But it is, I would argue, not unique in that respect. Jesus Christ, as the son of God and performer of miracles, was certainly quasi-divine in some of the same ways that the Rama was. There are differences, but to think of them as polar opposites is unhelpful, not least for the general reader

42. The term '*hijra*' has pejorative connotations that I do not endorse. The alternative term '*khwaja sara*' is often used in Pakistan. See Shahnaz Khan, 'Khwaja Sara, Hijra and the Struggle for Rights in Pakistan', *Modern Asian Studies* 51(5) (2017)

43. Hein, *Miracle Plays*, p. 99

44. Lutgendorf, *Life of a Text*

45. Schechner and Hess, 'Ramlila of Ramnagar'

46. Lutgendorf, *Life of a Text*, p. 290

47. Humaira Chowdhury, 'A Social and Economic History of Darzis (Muslim Tailors) in Calcutta, *c.*1890–1967', doctoral dissertation (University of Cambridge, 2023)

48. Kumar, *Artisans of Banaras*, p. 185

49. Lutgendorf, *Life of a Text*, p. 283

50. Ibid.

51. Charles Taylor, *A Secular Age* (Cambridge, MA, 2007); Humeira Iqtidar and Tanika Sarkar (eds), *Tolerance, Secularization and Democratic Politics in South Asia* (Cambridge, 2018); Talal Asad, *Formations of the Secular: Christianity, Islam, Modernity* (Stanford, 2003)

52. Gibb Schreffler, 'The Bazigar (Goaar) People and Their Performing Arts', *Journal of Punjab Studies* 18 (2011), pp. 217–50

53. Aastha Gandhi, 'From Postcolonial to Neoliberal? Identifying the "Other" Body in Indian Circus', *Performance Matters* 4(1–2) (2018)

54. Aristide R. Zolberg, 'Managing a World on the Move', *Population and Development Review* 32 (2006); Joya Chatterji, *The Spoils of Partition, 1947–1967* (Cambridge, 2007)

55. Denzil Charles Ibbetson, *Panjab Castes: Being a Reprint of the Chapter on 'The Races, Castes and Tribes of the People' in the Report on the Census of the Panjab, published in 1883 by the late Sir Denzil Ibbetson* (Lahore, 1916), p. 285

56. They challenged this status for many decades. Schreffler, 'Bazigar (Goaar) People'

57. Sarah Gandee, 'Criminalizing the Criminal Tribe: Partition, Borders, and the State in India's Punjab, 1947–55', *Comparative Studies of South Asia, Africa and the Middle East* 38(3) (2018)

58. See the discussion of *Baazigar* in Ranjani Mazumdar, *Bombay Cinema: An Archive of the City* (Minneapolis, 2007)

59. Ibbetson, *Panjab Castes*, p. 285

60. Jan Lucassen, 'The Brickmakers' Strikes on the Ganges Canal in 1848–1849', *International Review of Social History* 51(14) (2006)

61. Gibb Schreffler's extended interview with Sarvan Singh in 1996, cited in Schreffler, 'Bazigar (Goaar) People'

62. Ibid.

63. Gandhi, 'Postcolonial to Neoliberal?', p. 84

64. Shashank Shekhar, 'In Welcome Move, No Circus in India Can Now Make Wild Animals Perform Tricks', *India Today*, 27 October 2017

65. Gandhi, 'Postcolonial to Neoliberal?', p. 86

66. Ibid.

67. Joseph S. Alter, *The Wrestler's Body: Identity and Ideology in North India* (Berkeley, 1992); Kumar, *Artisans of Banaras*

68. Alter, *Wrestler's Body*; Kumar, *Artisans of Banaras*

69. S. Muzumdar, *Strong Men over the Years: A Chronicle of Athletes* (Lucknow, 1942), pp. 64–5

70. Partha Pratim Shil, 'Police Labour and State-formation in Bengal, *c.*1860 to *c.*1950', doctoral dissertation (University of Cambridge, 2016)

71. Neera Adarkar and Meena Menon, *One Hundred Years, One Hundred Voices: The Millworkers of Girangaon: An Oral History* (Calcutta, 2004)

72. Muzumdar, *Strong Men*, p. 109

73. John Rosselli, 'The Self-Image of Effeteness: Physical Education and Nationalism in Nineteenth-Century Bengal', *Past & Present* 86 (1980)

74. Muzumdar, *Strong Men*

75. Ibid.

76. Muzumdar, *Strong Men*, pp. 66–70. Also see Graham Noble, 'The Lion of the Punjab: Gama in England, 1910', in Thomas A. Green and Joseph R. Svinth (eds), *Martial Arts in the Modern World* (London, 2003), pp. 93–110

77. 'Wrestling in India', *The Times*, 2 March 1928. On reading this account, the anthropologist Hornblower reported seeing similar bouts in Alexandria during the entertainments surrounding Ramazan at the turn of the century. G. D. Hornblower, 'Wrestling in India and Egypt', *Man* 28(43) (1928)

78. Muzumdar, *Strong Men*, p. 193

79. *Times of India*, 5 August 2010

80. Noble, 'Lion of the Punjab'

81. Muzumdar, *Strong Men*

82. Seema Sonik Alimchand, *Deedara aka Dara Singh!* (New Delhi, 2016), p. 121

83. Kumar, *Artisans of Banaras*; Alter, *Wrestler's Body*

84. Muzumdar, *Strong Men*

85. Ibid., p. 183

86. Pallabi Chakravorty, 'Hegemony, Dance and Nation: The Construction of the Classical Dance in India', *Journal of South Asian Studies* 21(2) (1998), pp.107–20. Also see Lakshmi Vishwanathan, *Women of Pride: The Devadasi Heritage* (New Delhi, 2014 edn)

87. Verrier Elwin, *The Baiga* (London, 1939), p. 431

88. Ibid.

89. Ibid., p. 432

90. Ibid., p. 433

91. Ibid., pp. 433–4

92. Verrier Elwin, *The Tribal World of Verrier Elwin: An Autobiography* (Oxford, 1964), pp. 103, 117

93. Elwin, *Baiga*, pp. 438–9

94. Margaret E. Walker, *India's Kathak Dance in Historical Perspective* (Abingdon, 2014)

95. 'Pandit Birju Maharaj. Rare Documentary', July 2020, YouTube

96. Sumanta Banerjee, 'Bogey of the Bawdy: Changing Concept of "Obscenity" in 19th-century Bengali Culture', *Economic and Political Weekly* 22(29) (1987)

97. Pallabi Chakravorty, *Bells of Change: Kathak Dance, Women and Modernity in India* (Kolkata, 2008), p. 45

98. Ibid.

99. Avanthi Meduri (ed.), *Rukmini Devi Arundale, 1904–1986: A Visionary Architect of Indian Culture and the Performing Arts* (Delhi, 2005), p. 9

100. Uttara Asha Coorlawala, 'The Birth of Bharatanatyam and the Sanskritized Body', in Meduri (ed.), *Rukmini*, p. 181

101. Gowri Ramnarayan, 'Rukmini Devi: Dancer and Reformer', *Sruti* 10, cited in Meduri (ed.), *Rukmini*, pp. 204–5

102. Just for starters, Amrit Srinivasan, 'Reform and Revival: The Devadasi and Her Dance', *Economic and Political Weekly* 20(44) (1985); Janet O'Shea, '"Traditional" Indian Dance and the Making of Interpretive Communities', *Asian Theatre Journal* 15(1) (1998); and Coorlawala, 'Birth of Bharatanatyam'

103. Jyoti Sabharwal, *Afloat a Lotus Leaf: Kapila Vatsyayan (A Cognitive Biography)* (New Delhi, 2015)

104. 'Pandit Birju Maharaj Puts Up a Magical Kathak Male Dance Performance', WildFilmsIndia, www.wildfilmsindia.com

105. 'Doordarshan: Childhood Memories of the 90s and 80s: Juhi Chawla's Lehar Pepsi ad', YouTube

106. Chakravorty, *Bells of Change*

107. Margaret Walker, who searched for the origins of Kathak, finds them hard to pin down, but rebuts the common version that they descend from the hereditary performing *kathavachaks* (storytellers). Walker, *India's Kathak Dance*

108. 'Pandit Birju Maharaj. Rare Documentary'

109. Bayly, *Empire and Information*, 'Patriotism and Nationalism'

110. Neepa Majumdar, *Wanted: Cultured Ladies Only!: Female Stardom and Cinema in India, 1930s–1950s* (Champaign, 2009), Part 1

111. Mukherjee, *Bombay Hustle*, pp. 239–57

112. Ibid., p. 257

113. M. Madhava Prasad, *Ideology of the Hindi Film: A Historical Construction* (Delhi, 1998)

114. Under the Raj, investment opportunities for Indians were limited in the extreme. See D. A. Washbrook, 'Progress and Problems: South Asian

Economic and Social History *c*.1720–1860', *Modern Asian Studies* 22(1) (1988)

115. Shohini Ghosh, personal communication

116. Nasreen Munni Kabir, *Guru Dutt: A Life in Cinema* (Delhi, 1997), p. 10

117. Suketu Mehta, *Maximum City: Bombay Lost and Found* (New Delhi, 2004)

118. Mukherjee, *Bombay Hustle*

119. See, for instance, Meena T. Pillai, *Women in Malayalam Cinema: Naturalising Gender Hierarchie*s (Hyderabad, 2010)

120. Nasreen Munni Kabir, *Conversations with Waheeda Rehman* (New Delhi, 2014)

121. For a taster, watch 'Uday and Amala Shankar (A glimpse). Some dance sequences', Facebook

122. The details of Guru Dutt's life are drawn from Kabir, *Guru Dutt*

123. Valentina Vitali, *Hindi Action Cinema: Industries, Narratives, Bodies* (Bloomington, 2008)

124. Film historian M. Madhava Prasad suggests that stardom in the south of India is different from that in the north, in that 'stars' become 'stars' only after they have entered politics. He cites the cases of M. G. Ramachandran and the Telegu politician star N. T. Rama Rao. I doubt that it's a universal truth though. Other actors from the south, often women, have become stars without ever being in politics – for example Waheeda Rehman, Hema Malini and Rekha

125. Robina Mohammad, '*Phir bhi dil hai Hindustani* (Yet the Heart Remains Indian): Bollywood, the "Homeland" Nation-State and the Diaspora', *Environment and Planning D: Society and Space* 25(6) (2007)

126. Mazumdar, *Bombay Cinema*

127. Priya Jaikumar, *Where Histories Reside: India as Filmed Space* (Durham, NC, 2019)

128. Tejaswini Ganti, *Producing Bollywood: Inside the Contemporary Hindi Film Industry* (Durham, NC, 2012), p. 3

129. Joya Chatterji, 'On Being Stuck in Bengal: Immobility in the "Age of Migration"', *Modern Asian Studies* 51(2) (2017)

130. Anupama Chopra, *Sholay: The Making of a Classic* (New Delhi, 2000), p. 73

131. Ganti, *Producing Bollywood*

132. Ibid.

133. Arjun Appadurai, 'The Ready-Made Pleasures of Déjà Vu: Repeat Viewing of Bollywood Films', *Cambridge Journal of Postcolonial Literary Inquiry* 6(1) (2019); and Ranjani Mazumdar, 'Repetition with a Difference: A Response to Arjun Appadurai', *Cambridge Journal of Postcolonial Literary Inquiry* 6(3) (2019)

134. Ganti, *Producing Bollywood*. Also see Prasad, *Ideology of the Hindi Film*

135. Ganti, *Producing Bollywood*. Also see Prasad, *Ideology of the Hindi Film*

136. Ganti, *Producing Bollywood*, p. 54

137. This section relies on Ganti, *Producing Bollywood*

138. Javed Akhtar in conversation with Nasreen Munni Kabir, *Talking Films and Songs* (New Delhi, 2017), p. 35

139. 'Amitabh Bachchan Speaks out on Media Ban & Bofors Scam', You-Tube, 11 October 2019. The video is in Hindi/Hindustani

140. Ganti, *Producing Bollywood*, p. 125

141. Chowdhury, 'A History of Darzis'; Clare Wilkinson-Weber, 'Behind the Seams: Designers and Tailors in Popular Hindi Cinema', *Visual Anthropology Review* 20(2) (2004), pp. 3–21; Rachel Dwyer and Divia Patel, *Cinema India: The Visual Culture of Hindi Film* (New Brunswick, NJ, 2002)

142. Majumdar, *Wanted: Cultured Ladies Only!*

143. Shohini Ghosh, 'The Importance of Being Madhuri', *Zee Premiere*, December 2000

144. Nandana Bose, *Madhuri Dixit* (London, 2019)

145. Ganti, *Producing Bollywood*

146. Akhtar with Kabir, *Talking Films and Songs*

147. Majumdar, in *Wanted: Cultured Ladies Only!*, refers to this as 'anti-gossip'. I am not sure that I agree with that. Sadat Hasan Manto, after his emigration to Pakistan, started a new journal – *Afaq* – which one outraged middle-class woman took him to task for: 'I am no child, but there are certain pictures I dare not look at, because to do so would lower me in my own eyes, as if I had violated privacy.'

148. Majumdar, *Wanted: Cultured Ladies Only!*

149. Kabir, *Guru Dutt*, pp. 113–14

150. Ibid., p. 131

151. *Report of the Indian Cinematograph Committee, 1927–28* (Calcutta, 1928), pp. 15–16

152. Ibid., p. 35

153. Ibid., p. 22. My emphasis

154. J. B. H. Wadia's unfinished autobiography, 'Those Were the Days', cited in Vitali, *Hindi Action Cinema*, p. 7

155. Vitali, *Hindi Action Cinema*

156. Mukherjee, *Bombay Hustle*, p. 253

157. Akhtar with Kabir, *Talking Films and Songs*

158. A Muslim social was a genre common in the 1950s in which all the main characters are Muslims, set in a twilight of their social status in India. The film *Chaudhvin ka Chand* is a superb example

159. On censorship in India, see Kobita Sarkar, *You Can't Please Everyone!: Film Censorship: The Inside Story* (Bombay, 1982). Another key work

for the interested is William Mazzarella, *Censorium: Cinema and the Open Edge of Mass Publicity* (Durham, NC, 2013)

160. Ranjani Mazumdar, in *Bombay Cinema*, is particularly fascinating in her discussion of *Parinda* and *Baazigar*

161. Francesca Orsini, *The Hindi Public Sphere 1920–1940: Language and Literature in the Age of Nationalism* (Delhi, 2009)

162. There is much more to be said about *Parinda*, one of Bombay cinema's finest films. See the Note on Further Viewing

163. Akhtar with Kabir, *Talking Films and Songs*, p. 34

164. Ibid.

165. Ganti, *Producing Bollywood*

166. Ashish Rajadhyaksha, 'The "Bollywoodisation" of the Indian Cinema: Cultural Nationalism in a Global Arena', *Inter-Asia Cultural Studies* 4(1) (2003)

167. On the films of the 1990s, see Shohini Ghosh, 'Violence and the Spectral Muslim: Action, Affect and Bombay Cinema at the Turn of the 20th Century', doctoral dissertation (Jawaharlal Nehru University, 2016)

EPILOGUE

1. Shekhar Pathak, *Dastan-i-Himalaya* (New Delhi, 2021); Ed Douglas, *Himalaya: A Human History* (London, 2020)

2. B. D. Hopkins, *The Making of Modern Afghanistan* (London, 2008); Benjamin D. Hopkins and Magnus Marsden, *Fragments of the Afghan Frontier* (London, 2012)

3. Magnus Marsden, 'From Kabul to Kiev: Afghan Trading Networks across the Former Soviet Union', *Modern Asian Studies* 49(4) (2015)

4. Nooreen Reza, 'Law, Space and Political Imaginations in the Northwest Frontier', MPhil dissertation (Centre of South Asian Studies, University of Cambridge, 2016)

5. Joya Chatterji, 'Secularisation and Partition Emergencies: Deep Diplomacy in South Asia', *Economic and Political Weekly* 48(50) (2013)

6. Hosna J. Shewly, 'Survival Mobilities: Tactics, Legality and Mobility of Undocumented Borderland Citizens in India and Bangladesh', *Mobilities* 11(3) (2016); Reece Jones, 'Spaces of Refusal: Rethinking Sovereign Power and Resistance at the Border', *Annals of the Association of American Geographers* 102(3) (2012)

7. A film called *Subarnarekha*, directed by Ritwik Ghatak, is discussed in the Note on Further Viewing; also see Amit Ranjan, 'Rivers and Canals as "Other Factors" in the Partition of India', *Water History* 13 (2021)

8. Iftekhar Iqbal, *The Bengal Delta: Ecology, State and Social Change, 1840–1943* (London, 2010)

9. Annu Jalais, *Forest of Tigers: People, Politics and Environment in the Sundarbans* (Abingdon, 2010)

10. Claire Alexander, Joya Chatterji and Annu Jalais, *The Bengal Diaspora: Rethinking Muslim Migration* (Abingdon, 2016)

11. Joya Chatterji, Claire Alexander and Annu Jalais, 'The Bengal Diaspora Project', AHRC 2006–2010

12. Pallavi Raghavan, *Animosity at Bay: An Alternative History of the India–Pakistan Relationship, 1947–1952* (London, 2020), p. 3

13. T. V. Paul (ed.), *The India–Pakistan Conflict: An Enduring Rivalry* (Cambridge, 2005)

14. Sumit Ganguly, *Conflict Unending: India–Pakistan Tensions since 1947* (New York, 2002)

15. Lars Blinkenberg, *India–Pakistan: The History of Unsolved Conflict: Volume 1: The Historical Part* (Odense, 1998)

16. Alastair Lamb, *Incomplete Partition: The Genesis of the Kashmir Dispute, 1947–1948* (Roxburg, 1997; Karachi, 2002)

17. Vali Nasr, 'National Identities and the India–Pakistan Conflict', in Paul (ed.), *India–Pakistan Conflict*; Ganguly, *Conflict Unending*

18. On the raiders, see Andrew Whitehead, *A Mission in Kashmir* (New Delhi, 2007). Other significant works on Kashmir and/or the dispute include Sumantra Bose, *Kashmir: Roots of Conflict, Paths to Peace* (Cambridge, MA, 2003); Alastair Lamb, *Kashmir: A Disputed Legacy, 1846–1990* (New York, 1991); Victoria Schofield, *Kashmir in Conflict: India, Pakistan and the Unending War* (London, 2003); Chitralekha Zutshi, *Languages of Belonging: Islam, Regional Identity and the Making of Kashmir* (London, 2004); and Mridu Rai, *Hindu Rulers, Muslim Subjects: Islam, Rights, and the History of Kashmir* (Princeton, 2004)

19. Srinath Raghavan, *War and Peace in Modern India* (London, 2010), p. 146. This work offers a careful history of wars and almost-wars between India and Pakistan. Despite its focus, and its Indian perspective, it is, at the time of writing, the best work on these subjects

20. Ganguly, *Conflict Unending*, pp. 31–45; Elisabeth Leake and Daniel Haines, 'Lines of (In)Convenience: Sovereignty and Border-Making in Postcolonial South Asia, 1947–1965', *Journal of Asian Studies* 76(4) (2017)

21. Bérénice Guyot-Réchard, *Shadow States: India, China and the Himalayas, 1910–1962* (Cambridge, 2016); Ganguly, *Conflict Unending*

22. Lamb, *Kashmir: Disputed Legacy*; Schofield, *Kashmir in Conflict*; Bose, *Kashmir: Roots of Conflict*

23. Gary J. Bass, *The Blood Telegram: Nixon, Kissinger, and a Forgotten Genocide* (London, 2014)

24. Aloys Arthur Michel, *The Indus Rivers: A Study of the Effects of Partition* (New Haven, 1967)

25. Daniel Haines, *Rivers Divided: Indus Basin Waters in the Making of India and Pakistan* (London, 2017)

26. They may not have been settled for all time, as Haines suggests in *Rivers Divided*. But because China sits upstream of India and is the river's source, its deepening relationship with Pakistan is likely to tie India's hands

27. In this case, the World Bank also played a part. See also FO 371/101218, FO 371/112324, FO 371/112325, FO 371/123678, FO 371/144470, FO 371/144471, The National Archives at Kew (henceforth TNA)

28. Chaudhri Muhammad Ali, *The Emergence of Pakistan* (New York, 1967), pp. 168–9

29. Ali, *Emergence of Pakistan*; Ayesha Jalal, *The State of Martial Rule: The Origins of Pakistan's Political Economy of Defence* (Cambridge, 1990)

30. Ali, *Emergence of Pakistan*, p. 181

31. Speaking of Delhi's displaced Muslims later that year, Nehru acknowledged that at least half of them had no wish to migrate to Pakistan. Nehru to Patel, 6 October 1947, in Durga Das (ed.), *Sardar Patel's Correspondence 1945–50* (Ahmedabad, 1972), Vol. 4, pp. 400–1

32. Ali, *Emergence of Pakistan*, p. 258

33. Ibid., p. 268

34. See the introduction to the *Government of East Punjab Evacuees (Administration of Property) Act, 1947 (Act XIV of 1947)*

35. Ian Copland, 'The Further Shores of Partition: Ethnic Cleansing in Rajasthan 1947', *Past & Present* 160(1) (1998), pp. 203–39; Shail Mayaram, 'Speech, Silence and the Making of Partition Violence in Mewat', in Shahid Amin and Dipesh Chakrabarty (eds), *Subaltern Studies IX: Writings on South Asian History and Society* (New Delhi, 1996)

36. Emma Haddad, *The Refugee in International Society: Between Sovereigns* (Cambridge, 2008); Peter Gatrell, *The Making of the Modern Refugee* (Oxford, 2013)

37. Ali, *Emergence of Pakistan*, p. 270

38. Ibid., p. 263. Emphasis added

39. Ibid., p. 183

40. Claude Auchinleck, a career soldier, had been Commander-in-Chief of the Indian Army in the last days of the Raj. After independence he was Supreme Commander of all British forces in India and Pakistan until late 1948

41. Chatterji, 'Secularisation and Partition Emergencies'; Joya Chatterji, 'An Alternative History of India–Pakistan Relations', Royal Asiatic Society (unpublished lecture, 2012)

42. Ministry of External Affairs of India, *Agreements between India and Pakistan Reached at Inter-Dominion Conferences held at New Delhi in December 1948, Calcutta in April 1948 and Karachi in May 1948* (National Archives of India, 1948), Pak-I Branch, File No. 8-15/48

43. Ibid.

44. The Padma river, metaphorically at least, divided East Bengal (Pakistan) from West Bengal (India)

45. *Agreements between India and Pakistan.* Emphasis added

46. Ibid., spoken by Mr Ghulam Muhammad, Pakistan

47. Ibid.

48. Ibid.

49. V. V. S. Tyagi, 'The Economic Impact of Partition on Indian Agriculture and Related Industries', doctoral dissertation (American University, Washington, DC, 1958)

50. Blinkenberg, *History of Unsolved Conflict*, p. 135

51. The story of the constant pilgrim, 'Train Lady', in Chapter 4 of this book, suggests how pilgrimage became an expression of inchoate, inexpressible, yearning. Also see Alexander, Chatterji and Jalais, *Bengal Diaspora.* Joya Chatterji, in 'Partition Studies: Prospects and Pitfalls', *Journal of Asian Studies* 73(2) (2014), draws attention to the work of Amritpal Khosa on the development of Sikh cultures of pilgrimage after partition. Amritpal Khosa, 'Sikh Sacred Spaces in Pakistan', MPhil dissertation (Centre of South Asian Studies, University of Cambridge, 2011); Safdar Ali Shah and Syed Javaid A. Kazi, *The Sikh Heritage of Pakistan* (Lahore, 2012)

52. Sumit Ganguly, 'Wars without End: The Indo–Pakistani Conflict', *Annals of the American Academy of Political and Social Science* 541 (1995)

53. Antara Datta, 'The Repatriation of 1973 and the Re-making of Modern South Asia', *Contemporary South Asia* 19(1) (2011). See DO 133/230, DO 133/219, DO 133/220, DO 133/221, DO 133/222, DO 133/223, DO 133/225, DO 133/226, DO 133/227, DO 133/228, DO 133/229, TNA

54. This is, in no small measure, because West Bengal is a small state under opposition rule since 1969. Its difficulties do not press down heavily upon Delhi

55. Joya Chatterji, 'The Fashioning of a Frontier: The Radcliffe Line and Bengal's Border Landscape, 1947–52', *Modern Asian Studies* 33(1) (1999); Willem van Schendel, 'Easy Come, Easy Go: Smugglers on the Ganges', *Journal of Contemporary Asia* 23(2) (1993)

56. Odd Arne Westad, *The Global Cold War: Third World Interventions and the Making of Our Times* (Cambridge, 2007 edn)

57. It of course also had to do with their post-colonial desire to be shot of power blocs and empires. See Mark Mazower, *No Enchanted Palace: The End of Empire and the Ideological Origins of the United Nations* (Princeton, 2013); Christopher J. Lee (ed.), *Making a World after Empire: The Bandung Moment and Its Political Afterlives* (Athens, OH, 2010). Many scholars have seen Nehru alone as the author of non-alignment; he was in fact one member of a group of like-minded post-colonials

58. Pakistan, having entered the Southeast Asia Treaty Organization and the Central Treaty Organization in the mid to late 1950s, still strove to join what had become an official non-aligned movement. It became a full member at the Havana Conference in 1979. Naveed Ahmad, 'The Non-Aligned Movement and Pakistan', *Pakistan Horizon* 32(4) (1979)

59. Raghavan, *War and Peace in Modern India*. See FO 371/101199, FO 371/123585, FO 371/144462, FO 371/170641, DO 133/99, DO 133/200, DO 133/218, TNA

60. Guyot-Réchard, *Shadow States*; T. V. Paul (ed.), *The China–India Rivalry in the Globalization Era* (Washington, DC, 2018)

61. DO 133/155, DO 133/154, DO 133/156, DO 133/157, DO 133/158, DO 134/11, FO 371/76090, FO 371/76091, FO 371/84253, FO 371/84254, FO 371/84252, FO 371/84255, FO 371/84256, FO 371/84257, FO 371/92870, FO 371/144467, FO 371/117367, FO 371/136177, FO 371/180960, FO 371/170637, FO 371/152540, DO 133/231, DO 133/232, TNA

62. Sukumar Muralidharan, 'L. K. Advani's Pakistan Yatra: Historical Revisionism', *Economic and Political Weekly* 40(24) (2005)

Index

aabir, 540
aalim, 54, 79, 262
aaloo mattar, 514
aaloo tikkis, 511
aam paapad, 512
Aami Beeraangona Bolchhi, 168
aap, 63
Aar Paar (1954 film), 618, 668
aashrams, 59, 126
Abadi Bano Begum, 54
Abbas, Khwaja Ahmad, 619
Abbasid Caliphate (750–1258), 150
Abbottabad, Khyber Pakhtunkhwa, 291
Abd-al-Aziz, Ottoman Sultan, 44
abductions, 93–4, 341–2
Abdul Bari, 54
Abdullah, Mohammad, 201, 639
Abed, Fazle, 166, 284
abhinaya, 581, 588
Abode of Peace (Chatterjee), 22, 192
Abol Tabol (Ray), 130
Acid (1988 film), 613, 675
acrobats, 563–8
adhiyas, 446
Adiga, Aravind, 265, 501
Adigal, Maraimalai, 134
Adivasi, *see* tribal peoples
adoption, 244, 339, 385, 387–8, 392, 401
Adra and *Hast*, 334
Advani, Lal Krishna, 198, 199, 200, 655
Af-Pak frontier, 225
Afghanistan; Afghans, 124, 207, 328, 635
    Anglo-Afghan wars, 225
    ashraf, 488
    Bhopal and, 391
    cuisine, 490, 491
    Durand Line, 225, 635
    Kathak and, 581

    Khilafat movement and, 58, 59, 81
    NATO War (2001–21), 176, 223
    pedlars, 294
    Sikh Empire and, 212
    Soviet War (1979–89), 176
Aga Khan, 52, 65, 68
Aga Khan Foundation, 154
age of consent debates, 20, 338, 406, 425
    Age of Consent Act (1891), 20–21, 406
    Child Marriage Restraint Act (1929),
      406, 425, 436
    Mayo and, 406–7
    Phulmonee case (1889), 20, 436
    Tilak and, 20
Agnipariksha, 554–5
Agra, Uttar Pradesh, 70
Agrani, 104
agriculture, 122, 163, 243, 279
    cash crops, 242, 318, 504
    cities and, 350, 355, 362, 363, 427, 432
    depressions, 16, 295
    droughts, 324, 334, 530
    green revolutions (*c.*1967–*c.*1978), 277,
      296, 531–6
    irrigation, 159, 173, 242, 278, 283, 324,
      492, 520, 528
    labour, 163, 299, 385
    land reform, 190
    liberalisation and, 432
    migration and, 299, 300
    staple crops, 516–27
    suicides and, 362, 386
    taxation, 17, 269, 271, 274, 276
    women and, 385, 425, 427–8
    yields, 528
ahimsaa, 32, 35, 39, 41
Ahirs, 466, 556
Ahmad, Imtiaz, 489

Ahmed Khan, Mohammad, 409
Ahmedabad, Gujarat, 590
Ahmediyas, 175, 490
Ahomiya, 336
AIDS, 416
air travel, 515
Aishwarya, Queen consort of Nepal, 392
ajlaf, 488–9
Ajmer, Rajasthan, 340, 378, 379, 548
ajrak quilt covers, 317
Akaler Sandhane (1981 film), 660
akhand Bharat, 105
akharas, 23, 329, 568–78, 615–16
Akhtar, Javed, 604, 609, 620, 629, 671–2, 675
   Deewaar (1975), 227, 604, 610, 620, 627, 628, 629, 671, 673
   influences, 626, 666
   on musicians, 619
   Salim Khan, partnership with, 604, 620, 628, 671–2
   separate state, film as, 609, 675
   Sholay, see *Sholay*
   Zanjeer (1973), 603–4, 610, 620, 625, 627, 628
Akkarmashi (Limbale), 483–6
Akootai murder (1917), 441–3
Akram Khan, Muhammad, 137–8
Alam Ara (1931 film), 664–5
alcohol, 273, 330, 497, 503, 541, 547
Algiers, 318
Ali Khan, Liaquat, 92, 120–24, 170, 172
   assassination (1951), 123–4
   Ayub Khan appointment (1951), 122
   budget (1947–8), 122
   countryside, views on, 121, 122, 276
   Indo–Pakistani War (1947–8), 123
   moneylenders, views on, 121
   Objectives Resolution (1949), 120, 123, 203
   Partition (1947), 92, 218, 644
   personal belongings, 150–51
   Soviet planning, influence of, 278
Ali, Muhammad, 575
Ali, Muzaffar, 444, 588, 673
Aligarh, Uttar Pradesh, 49, 53, 54, 63, 497
All Characters Are Fictional (2009 film), 663
All India Institute of Medical
   Sciences, 345

All India Muslim League, 52, 73–83, 137–8, 162
   Bengal Famine (1943), 525
   elections (1946), 114
   foreign policy, 643
   Fourteen Points (1929), 76, 155
   Lahore Resolution (1940), 79, 80
   Lucknow Pact (1916), 68–9, 417
   Nehru and, 73, 74, 78
   Partition (1947), 89, 118
All India Muslim Majlis-i-Mushawarat, 197
All India Radio, 84
Allahabad, Uttar Pradesh, 64, 70, 105, 179, 187, 265, 348, 382, 489, 548
Almora, Uttarakhand, 455, 595
Alter, Joseph, 569
Alvi, Abrar, 595, 610
Alwar, 340, 644
Aman, Zeenat, 600, 673
Amar Akbar Anthony (1977 film), 621, 632
Amar Chitra Katha, 198, 555
'Amar Shonar Bangla' (Tagore), 29, 132, 320
Ambani, Mukesh, 508
Ambedkar, Bhimrao Ramji, 482, 511, 591
Amin, Idi, 315
Amrita Bazar Patrika, 11
Amrith, Sunil, 526
Amritsar
   communal riots (1923), 70
   Gama in, 569, 575
   Jallianwalla Bagh massacre (1919), 38–40, 188
Amrohi, Kamal, 669
Amul, 470
Anand (1971 film), 616, 670
Anand Bhavan, Allahabad, 64
Anand, Chetan, 619
Ananda Math (Chatterjee), 22, 192
Anarkali (1953 film), 588, 603
ancestral property, 274, 384, 386–90
Ancient Law (Maine), 401
And Quiet Rolls the Dawn (1979 film), 660
Andaman Islands, 193, 279, 353
Andaz (1949 film), 665, 666, 669
Andheri, Bombay, 596
Andhra Pradesh, 127, 131–2
Andrews, Charles, 310–11
Anglo-Indian people, 249–50
Anglo-Mughal architecture, 348

angrakhaa, 587

Angry Young Man films, 603, 627, 629
  see also anti-heroes

animal taming, 566, 567

Animal, Vegetable, Mineral?, 146

Anjuman-e-Khuddam-e-Kaaba, 57

Ankur (1974 film), 661, 664

ansars, 113

Antaakshari, 581, 622

antahapur, 412

anti-caste movements, 416, 482, 511, 592

anti-heroes, 236, 564, 603–4, 626–30,
  671–2
  Jai/Vijay character, 603–4, 612, 622,
  623–4, 625, 628–9, 671, 673

anti-imperialism, 42, 116, 643, 654

Anti-Slavery Society, 310

anuloma marriage, 387

Anushilan Samity, 30–31

Aparajito (1956 film), 327, 461, 565, 659

Appadurai, Arjun, 454, 485, 513, 607

April Nineteenth (1994 film), 630, 663

Apte, Shanta, 591, 606

Apur Sansar (1959 film), 619, 659, 663

Arab nationalism, 53

Arabia, 43, 488

Arabian Sea coast, 226

Arabic, 4, 9, 45, 64, 137, 245, 461

Aradhana (1969 film), 670

Arakan coast, 226

Arakanese Muslims, 312

aranam daasis, 387, 389

Aranyer Din Ratri (1970 film), 660

Archaeological Survey, 153

archaeology, 146–50

architecture, 146
  colonial, 265, 273, 348, 497
  Islamic, 150–54, 196
  modernist, 120, 282

Arjun (Gangopadhyay), 356

arkatis, 302, 310

Armed Forces Special Powers Act (India,
  1958), 184

Army Welfare Trust, 221

Arth (1982 film), 664

artisans, 133, 241, 269, 294–5, 328, 354,
  356, 361

Arundale, Rukmini Devi, 583–5

Arya Samaj, 22

ash, cleaning with, 352–3, 471

Ashani Sanket (1973 film), 521

ashraf, 43, 44, 45, 48–9, 112, 121, 137, 488

Asian Drama (Myrdal), 528

Assam, 24, 86, 184, 293, 301, 335, 396,
  420, 646, 649

Assam–Bengal railway, 333

assassinations
  Benazir Bhutto (2007), 176
  Indira Gandhi (1984), 191, 197, 345
  Liaquat Ali Khan (1951), 123–4
  Mahatma Gandhi (1948), 91, 103–5,
  123, 194, 643
  Mujib (1975), 163, 283, 286, 652
  Rajeev Gandhi (1991), 197–8
  Zia-ul-Huq (1988), 176
  Zia-ur Rahman (1981), 164
  Zulfikar Ali Bhutto (1979), 174

astrakhan caps, 57

Asukh (1999 film), 663

atrap, 489

Attari–Wagah border, 109–10, 655

Attlee, Clement, 90, 261

Auchinleck, Claude, 266, 646

Auden, Wystan Hugh, 340

Aurat (1940 film), 665, 666, 669

Australia, 220, 317

authoritarianism, 83, 108, 177–203

Autobiography of a Sex Worker (Jameela),
  445

Autobiography of an Unknown Indian
  (Chaudhuri), 498

Awadhi language, 358

Awami League, 125, 162–6, 222, 224, 284,
  286, 652

ayahs, 9, 183, 249, 250, 318, 380

Ayodhya, 154, 196, 200–201, 291, 319

Ayub Khan, Mohammad, 116, 122, 124–5,
  170, 220, 278–9
  Bhutto, relationship with, 172, 173
  Commander-in-Chief appointment
  (1951), 122
  coup d'état (1958), 116, 125, 278, 282
  development policies, 278–9
  East Bengal/Pakistan and, 124, 162, 224,
  266
  family planning policies, 280
  Indo–Pakistani War (1965), 639
  Islamabad, development of, 282
  politicians, views on, 116, 162, 175
  refugee colonies, destruction of, 353
  US, relations with, 116, 173

Ayub Khuhro, Muhammad, 119

Ayurvedic medicine, 464
Azad, 138
Azad, Abul Kalam, 44, 46, 47, 48, 54, 55, 75, 102, 585
Azadgarh, Calcutta, 95, 354
Azadpur Mandi, Delhi, 453
Azmi, Kaifi, 619, 661
Azmi, Shabana, 661, 662, 663–4

baariwallahs, 350
baasi, 473–4, 483, 485, 496
Baazigar (1993 film), 625, 673–4, 677
Baazigars, 563–8, 605, 615
Babar Ali, Syed, 655
Babi, Parveen, 610, 673
Babri Masjid, Ayodhya, 154, 196–8, 200–201, 291, 319, 655
Babur, Mughal Emperor, 196
babus, 259, 499
Bachchan, Abhishek, 609
Bachchan, Aishwarya Rai, 608, 609, 621–3, 663, 674
Bachchan, Ajitabh, 605
Bachchan, Amitabh, 596, 599, 603–4, 628, 629, 671, 672–3
   Anand (1971), 616, 670
   Bofors scandal (1987–9), 605
   Coolie (1983), 596, 672
   Deewaar (1975), 227, 604, 610, 620, 627, 628, 629, 673
   Don (1978), 605, 610, 614, 615, 672, 673
   Dostana (1980), 614
   fight sequences, 615
   Jai/Vijay character, 603–4, 612, 622, 623–4, 625, 628–9, 671, 673
   Namak Haraam (1973), 624, 670, 672
   physical appearance, 671
   popularity, 596
   Sholay, see *Sholay*
   Silsila (1981), 154, 608, 672
   Zanjeer (1973), 603–4, 610, 620, 625, 627, 628
Bachchan, Jaya Bhaduri, 673
Bachpan Bachao Andolan, 567
Badayuni, Shakeel, 618
Badshahi Mosque, Lahore, 177, 410
Baga Beach, Goa, 331
Bahadur, Ram, 308
Baharen Phir Bhi Aayengi (1966 film), 668
Bahu Begum (1967 film), 669

bahus, 415, 429, 430
Bahwalpur, 262, 268
Baiga, 480
Baiju Bawra (1952 film), 620, 668
bajra, 524, 534, 537
Bajrangi Bhaijaan (2015 film), 676
Baker, Henry, 265
Baksh, Imam, 571
Bal Mandirs, 195
Balfour, Edward, 404
Balochistan, 72, 75, 93, 174, 224–5, 268, 635
'Bande Mataram' (Chatterjee), 22, 30, 194–5
bandgala-churidaar, 107
banditry, 205–6, 211, 212, 236–8, 291–2, 431–40
   in cinema, 236–7, 419, 539, 598
Bandra, Bombay, 597
Bandung Conference (1955), 277, 654
Banerjee, Surendranath, 1, 4
Banerji, Syamakanta, 570, 577
Bangalore, Karnataka, 205, 581, 590
Bangla language, *see* Bengali language
Bangladesh, 19, 159–68
   armed forces, 164, 222
   'Biharis', 144, 161, 165, 166–7, 358–60, 378
   coup attempt (1981), 164
   development, 283–6
   Famine (1974–5), 163, 283
   Ganges river dispute, 652–3
   ghettos, 358–60
   Jumma movement, 225, 289, 290, 480
   Kaptai Dam, 534
   Liberation War (1971), *see* Bangladesh Liberation War
   malnutrition in, 536
   marriage in, 366, 368, 369–70, 372–3
   migration, 318, 319, 320, 321, 399, 432
   Mujib assassination (1975), 163, 283, 286, 652
   NGOs, 166
   postage stamps, 159
   poverty in, 163, 166, 284–5
   Urdu in, 129, 144, 160, 358
   Vested Property Ordinance (1972), 100
Bangladesh Liberation War (1971), 3, 61, 83, 125, 159–60, 165, 167–8, 173, 377–8, 638, 640–41
   Adivasi and, 343
   'Biharis' and, 144, 161, 165, 358, 359

casualties, 289, 290
Dalits and, 343
diaspora and, 319
Indian intervention, 84–5, 161, 169,
171, 184, 223, 640–41, 651
merchants and, 505
Mukti Bahini, 160–61, 164, 171, 222,
640
refugees, 160, 161, 162, 165
women and, 165, 167–8
Bangladesh Nationalist Party (BNP), 164,
165, 166, 320, 652
Bangladesh Rural Advancement
Committee (BRAC), 166, 284,
286
bangle makers, 349
baniya, 504–5
Banjaras, 294
Bannu, 246
Banu, Saira, 600
banyan trees, 477–8
Bardoli Satyagraha (1928), 106
Bardoloi, Gopinath, 646
bargat, 477–8
Bariwali (2000 film), 663
barley, 517, 522, 524
Barni, Ziauddin, 156
Baroda, 16, 27, 574
barrenness, 386–90, 424
Bastar region, 420, 479
bastis, see slums
Battle of Karbala (680), 308, 545
Bayly, Christopher, 502
Bazmi, Syed Abu Syed, 80, 81
Beames, John, 456–7
Beck, Theodore, 49
beedees, 362, 428, 547
beef, 103, 203, 490, 497
Begum Raana, 122
Behmai murders (1981), 436, 437
Benares, 247, 333, 548, 551–2, 554,
555–8, 586
Benares School, 402
Benegal, B. B., 593
Benegal, Dev, 663
Benegal, Shyam, 534, 630, 661–2
Bengal, 29
Communal Award (1932), 78
Delhi Proposals (1927), 72
diet in, 469, 490, 520
Famine (1873–4), 14

Famine (1943), 280, 337, 350, 505, 521,
525–7, 528, 531, 603
Jhampan Mela, 543
Krishak Praja Party, 111
migration to, 336
partition (1905), 24, 29–30, 155, 261
partition, annulled (1911), 53
partition (1947), 87, 95, 143, 343, 344
pirs in, 113
policing in, 227, 228
rice production, 522
swadeshi movement (1905–8), 22,
24–31, 35, 52, 61, 371, 381, 412
taxation in, 270
wrestling in, 241
Young Bengal movement (1820s–30s),
497, 502
Bengal and North Western Railway, 333
Bengal Army, 209, 212, 213
Bengal Provincial Banking Enquiry
Commission, 490, 505–6
Bengal Rationing Order (British India,
1943), 336
Bengal School, 402
Bengali Brahmins, 47
Bengali language, 4, 29, 130–31, 136–8,
334, 366
cinema, 136, 594
Jinnah's speech (1948), 142, 224
literature, 29, 136–8, 195
State Language Day protests
(1952), 127
Benjamin, R. B., 574
Berar, 16
Besant, Annie, 17, 37, 583
Best Exotic Marigold Hotel (2011 film),
268
betel, 381, 452, 492, 541, 542, 547, 561
Betul, Central Provinces, 392
bhaakri, 483–4, 488, 491
bhaav, 588, 589
bhadralok, 24, 354
Bhaduri, Jaya, 673
Bhagavad Gita, 23, 35, 192–3, 194, 199
bhajan-kirtan, 112
Bhakra–Nangal project, 283, 528
bhakts, 196, 197
bhang, 540, 541
bhangra, 566, 579
Bharat, 550, 551, 554–7
Bharat Milap, 554, 555, 557

Bharatanatyam, 579, 583, 584, 594, 607–8
  Arundale, 583–5
  Kalakshetra, 584, 594, 607
  Malini, 579, 607–8, 612, 673
  Rehman, 579
  Vatsyayan, 585, 589
Bharati, Subramaniam, 18
Bharatiya Janata Party (BJP), 177,
  197–201, 562
Bharatiya Kala Kendra, Delhi, 586
bharatiyas, 361
Bharatpur, 340, 644
Bharatvarsha, 193, 201
Bhasha Andolan, 143
Bhashani, Abdul Hamid Khan, 120, 143
Bhashani, Maulana, 262
Bhatpara, Calcutta, 334
Bhave, Vinoba, 468
bhelpuri, 503
Bhendi Bazar, Bombay, 327
Bhindranwale, Jarnail Singh, 223, 291
Bhojpur; Bhojpuri, 17, 160, 213, 214, 229,
  334, 337, 358
Bhopal, 44, 391, 586
Bhosle, Asha, 596, 606
Bhuleshwar, Bombay, 328
Bhutan, 249, 344
Bhutto, Benazir, 176
Bhutto, Zulfikar Ali, 125, 170, 171–4,
  202–3, 450
bidaai, 365
Big City, The (1963 film), 660
Bihar, 47, 187, 337, 358, 366
Bihari language, 125
'Biharis' (in Bangladesh), 161, 165, 166–7,
  358–60
Bihishti Zewar (Thanawi), 368, 370, 461
Bikaner, Rajasthan, 340
Bikaneri *bhujias*, 512
Bilaspur, Chhattisgarh, 283
Billu Barber (2009 film), 676, 678
bils, 490
Bin Laden, Osama, 291
Bindadin *gharaana*, 582, 586
Binder, Leonard, 123
Biometrika, 278
biraadiris, 86, 115, 369, 482
Bird (1989 film), 614, 625, 627, 628, 673
Birenda, King of Nepal, 392
Birla House, Delhi, 103, 107
Birla, Ghanshyam Das, 36, 575

birth control, 280
biryani, 451, 454, 491, 493, 510, 514, 515
Bishnupur, West Bengal, 544
Bishop Cotton School, Simla, 250
Black Panther Party, 482
'Black Town' zones, 10, 190, 333, 347,
  348–9, 351, 354
'black water', 64, 302, 309
blasphemy, 203
Blavatsky, Madame Helena, 33, 35, 37
Bleak House (Dickens), 348
block development officers (BDOs), 286
Blue Riband gin, 503
Boer War (1899–1902), 34
Bofors scandal (1987–9), 220–21, 605
Bogor Conference (1954), 277
Bohras, *see* Dawoodi Bohras
Bollywood/Bombay cinema, 539, 542,
  591–633
  action films, 577, 603, 612, 614–16
  anti-heroes, 236, 564, 603–4, 626–30,
    671–2
  audiences, 630–33
  Apte's activism, 591–2
  Baazigars in, 464, 605, 615
  caste and, 625
  child marriage and, 407
  cricket in, 616
  dacoits in, 236–7, 419, 539, 598
  dance sequences, 539, 542, 579, 587,
    590, 605, 607–9, 616, 618, 620–22
  dialogue in, 603, 607, 617, 619, 620,
    621, 629
  diaspora and, 596, 631, 675, 678
  directors, 598–9
  distributors, 598–9, 630
  exhibitors, 598–9
  extras, 593
  female actors, 605–9
  festivals in, 624
  fight sequences, 603, 612, 614–16
  financing, 599–601
  friendships in, 621, 623–4, 667
  genres, 603
  global influences on, 626
  Hindu right and, 601–2, 631–2
  historical monuments and, 154
  inner dualism, 625
  labour, 592
  love and, 386, 414–15, 419, 623
  masala movies, 603

multiplex theatres, 630–31
Muslims and, 595, 600, 603, 661, 667,
    675–8
organised crime and, 599, 601, 631
orphans in, 625
Partition (1947) and, 600
piracy and, 630
power cuts and, 598
producers, 598–9
Ramayana and, 611–14, 626, 632
screenwriters, 592, 593, 599, 619
set design, 593
social mores and, 609–11
songs, 365, 596, 605, 616–25
state and, 600, 601, 630, 631
villains in, 625–6
weather and, 598
wedding songs, 365
wrestling and, 577, 602, 615–16, 670
Bolpur, Bengal, 28–9, 179, 414
Bombay/Mumbai, 5, 16, 595
    Bengali Brahmins in, 47
    Bollywood, *see* Bollywood
    chawls, 329–33, 570
    earthquakes in, 635
    East India Company in, 209
    Elphinstone Institute, 12
    High Court, 265
    INC foundation (1885), 3, 7, 10
    influenza pandemic (1918–20), 324
    informal economy, 327–8
    languages in, 604
    Malabar Hill, 99
    migration to, 297, 327–33, 603, 604
    mohallas, 349
    organised crime in, 226
    plague outbreak (1896), 324
    policing in, 231–2, 235–6
    raiyatwaari system, 270
    red light districts, 246, 441
    rice production, 522
    ship building, 272
    slums, 363
    street vending in, 231–2
    taxation in, 270
    terror attacks (2008), 226
    textile industry, 327–33
    Victoria Terminus, 326–7
Bombay (1995 film), 678
Bombay Chronicle, 405
Bombay cinema, *see* Bollywood

Bombay Hustle (Mukherjee), 594
Bombay mixes, 473, 512
Bombay Plan (1944–5), 277
Bombay Provincial League, 68
Bombay Refugees Act (India, 1948), 371
Bombay Talkies, 596, 600–601
Bombay Tiffin Box Suppliers Association,
    510
Bonnie and Clyde (1967 film), 627
Border (1997 film), 632
Border Security Force, India, 223
Borlaug, Norman, 530
Born into Brothels (2005 documentary), 447
Bose, Chunilal, 520
Bose, Khudiram, 31
Bose, Nandalal, 29
Bose, Sarat Chandra, 499
Bose, Subhas Chandra, 215, 526
Boston Museum of Fine Arts, 149
Bouglé, Célestin, 486
'box-wallahs', 10, 348
BPL cards, 286
Bradford, West Yorkshire, 283, 318
Brahmaputra river, 335, 636
Brahmins, 4, 47, 50, 63, 73, 384, 457–60,
    475–6
    bureaucracy and, 47, 241
    Chitpavans, 19, 103
    coffee consumption, 510–11
    cooking and eating precepts, 463–6,
        471–4, 515–16
    education, 4, 47
    diet, 459, 467, 469
    kaala paani and, 64–5
    kulin sub-caste, 383, 412, 417,
        458, 507
    language and, 4, 134–5, 139, 140
    indentured labour and, 306, 308
    marriage and, 306, 308, 368, 375
    milk consumption, 467, 469
    Ramlila and, 554–5
    rice consumption, 523
    RSS and, 195
    Sanskrit and, 4
    squatter colonies and, 354, 355
    taxation and, 271
    vegetarianism, 459, 475
Brahmo Samaj, 582–3
Branded, The (Gaikwad), 487
Bravehearted Will Take Away His Bride,
    The (1995 film), 631

bread
  bhaakri, 483–4, 488, 491
  dosas, 231–2
  flatbread, 249, 349, 493
  leavened, 499, 502
  luchis, 381, 382
  paraatha, 495, 509
  rotis, 429, 491, 523
'Bread, cloth and a home', 172, 450
breastfeeding, 424
Bretton Woods institutions, 285
bribery, 232, 233–4, 256–7
Briski, Zana, 447
British Broadcasting Corporation (BBC), 596
British Indian Association, 5
British Nationality Act (UK, 1948), 311
British Raj (1858–1947)
  Afghan wars, 225
  armed forces, 213–18, 252–3
  Baazigars in, 564
  Bengal partition (1905), 24, 29–30, 155, 261
  censuses, 24, 51–2, 133, 241–2, 323
  Chauri Chaura incident (1922), 41, 59, 228
  Child Marriage Restraint Act (1929), 406
  civil service, 7, 14–15, 54, 124, 240, 242, 243–60, 262
  clubs, 251
  coercive techniques, 251
  councils, 40–41, 50, 51, 60, 78
  Councils Act (1892), 50–52
  Councils Act (1909), 52–3
  'criminal tribes' in, 236, 237, 241, 294–5, 459, 487, 564
  Durand Line, 225, 635
  famines, *see* famines
  festivals in, 543, 545–6, 549
  film industry in, 612
  food in, 456–7, 517–27
  Forest Acts, 272, 476
  Government of India Act (1919), 40, 60
  Government of India Act (1935), 61, 71, 77–8
  Hindu Gains of Learning Act (1930), 405–6
  Ilbert Bill (1883), 10–11, 250
  indentured labour, 34–5, 66, 293, 297–311
  influenza pandemic (1918–20), 324
  intermediaries, 47, 141, 243, 244, 253–60, 269
  Jallianwalla Bagh massacre (1919), 38–40, 188
  Khilafat movement (1919–24), 35, 41, 54–60, 70, 79, 138, 214
  legal system, 9–11, 211, 244, 386–90, 400–408
  maritime borders, 226
  martial race theory, 214, 216, 217, 253, 520, 523
  migration, 293–311, 323–39
  north-eastern frontier, 225
  north-western frontier, 58, 72, 75, 111–12, 119, 174, 207, 214, 225
  Office of the Court of Wards, 397
  Penal Code, 9, 415
  policing, 226–30
  princely states, relations with, 208, 238–40
  prisoners in, 518
  prostitution in, 440–43
  railways, *see* railways
  rice consumption and, 517–27
  Rowlatt Act (1919), 37–8, 39, 188
  Scheduled Castes, 482
  Scheduled Tribes, 476
  state, 207–8, 210, 243
  taxation, 16, 36, 77, 209, 214, 227, 243, 244, 260, 268–74, 295, 403
  Victoria's proclamation (1858), 7–9, 57, 62, 211, 240, 400
  white community, 9, 87, 190, 213, 248–53, 325, 333, 347, 348
  World War I (1914–18), 34, 36, 54, 81, 138, 215–17, 252, 253
  World War II (1939–45), 5, 81, 215, 217, 260, 321, 336–7
Broken Nest, The (Tagore), 412
bromance movies, 621, 623–4, 667
Bronze Age, 147
brothels, 246, 440–48, 662
Brothers, The (Ganguli), 395
Buddhism, 134, 149, 150, 416
Bukhara, Uzbekistan, 317
Bulleh Shah, 112
bullock carts, 5, 377
Burdwan, 334
Burke, Edmund, 36, 269

Burma
  Bahadur Shah's exile to (1858), 43, 210
  cash crops, 318
  Japanese War (1941–5), 215, 217, 428, 525
  migration to, 301, 311–12, 335
  rice exports, 337, 491, 520, 521–2, 525
Burman, Rahul Dev, 619, 620, 678
Burnett, Frances Hodgson, 325
Burra Bazar, Calcutta, 347
Burud, Venkappa, 576
Bush, George Walker, 176
Butalia, Urvashi, 167–8, 342
butchers, 349, 492–3
Butterfly (2002 film), 663
Byculla Club, Bombay, 247

Cabinet Mission Plan (1946), 79
Cachar, 333
Cain, Mead, 428
Cairo, Egypt, 44, 317–18
Calcutta/Kolkata, Bengal, 5, 347–51, 377–8
  architecture, 348
  Azadgarh, 95, 354–6
  Bengal Famine (1943), 350
  Chinese community, 500
  civil service in, 260
  Dalhousie Square, 265–6
  East India Company in, 208
  expansion, 350
  film industry, 594
  General Post Office, 265–6, 347
  High Court, 265
  INA uprising (1945), 215
  INC Session (1901), 5
  Inter-Dominion Conference (1948), 642, 646–50
  lascars, 350
  Methars, 465
  migration to, 297, 333–7, 350
  mohallas, 349
  organised crime in, 226
  Palladian architecture, 273–4
  Partition (1947), 87, 95, 143
  population, 351
  red light districts, 396, 446
  refugees in, 281, 352
  riots (1964), 377
  RSS in, 195
  Selimpore, 357–8

  slums, 361–3
  World War II (1939–45), 336–7
  Writers' Building, 260, 265, 337, 347
Calcutta Improvement Act (India, 1954), 362
Caldwell, Robert, 133
Cama & Co, 12
Cambridge; Cambridge University, 63, 130, 170, 245, 250, 260, 317, 331
  Advani, 198
  Aligarh and, 49
  Das at, 498
  communism and, 530
  food at, 507, 514
  Gautam at, 416
  Ghosh at, 27
  Iqtidar in, 400
  LUMS, links with, 410
  Mahalanobis at, 278
  middle classes and, 497
  Munir at, 410
  Nehru at, 11, 64, 70, 600
  Rau at, 259
  Singh at, 432
  Swaminathan at, 531
  Sylheti taxi-drivers, 320
Canada, 220, 317, 319
Canal Colonies, 242, 527
canals, 44, 242, 324, 641
Canning, Charles, 269
Cape Comorin, 5
Cariappa, K. M., 220
Caribbean, 298, 301, 308, 312
Carnatic region, 403, 404
cartoons, 541, 542
Case of Exploding Mangoes, A (Hanif), 122, 176
cash crops, 242, 318, 504
caste, 2, 210, 384, 457
  Ahirs, 466, 556
  anti-caste movements, 416, 482, 511, 592
  bandits and, 212, 439
  baniya, 504
  Bollywood and, 625
  Brahmins, *see* Brahmins
  Buddhism and, 416
  censuses and, 242
  Dalits, *see* Dalits
  food and, 64, 305, 451–2, 454–60, 463–88, 490, 492, 509, 515–16

caste – *cont.*
    Gandhi and, 34, 36
    Gauras, 466
    Goalas, 460, 466–7
    indentured labour and, 308, 309
    jajmaani system, 428–9
    jatis, 242, 458, 459–60, 475, 487, 504
    kasaais, 492
    khattriyas, 457
    Khojas, 65
    marriage and, 306, 308, 365–6, 368,
        371, 375, 386, 397, 420, 458, 595
    mohallas and, 349, 351, 356, 361
    Nayyars, 58
    patriarchy and, 395
    ploughing, 533
    prostitution and, 440, 582
    Ramlila and, 554–5
    Self-Respect movement (1925), 135
    shudras, 457, 458
    snake masters, 544
    squatter colonies and, 354, 355
    Tagas, 458, 466
    travel and, 5–6
    Uchalya, 487
    vaishyas, 457, 460
    wrestling and, 570
    Yadav's campaigning, 187
Catholicism, 149, 329, 330, 332, 570
cattle, 22, 103, 203, 465, 466–71
Cellular Jail, Port Blair, 193
censuses, 24, 51–2, 87, 133, 241–2, 323,
    335, 342, 365
Central Intelligence Agency (CIA), 189
Central Provinces, 16, 139
Ceylon, 301, 311
chaai paani, 232, 233
chaal, 588
Chagai-I tests (1998), 656
chai, 515, 541, 542, 561
Chaitgang Nakkatayya, 552
Chak De! India (2007 film), 677
Chaki, Prafulla, 31
chakkar, 588
Chakla-Roshanabad, Bangladesh, 390
Chambal valley, 205, 236
Chamoli, Uttarakhand, 287–8
Champaran Satyagraha (1917), 37
Chanakya Cinema, Delhi, 501
Chandavarkar, Rajnarayan, 290, 329
Chander, Eshan, 390

Chandigarh, Haryana/Punjab, 282, 290
Chandni Chowk, Delhi, 94
Char Gopalpur, Bangladesh, 373, 425
charas, 541, 547
Charles III, King of the United Kingdom,
    571
Charulata (1964 film), 497, 659–60
Chatterjee, Bankimchandra, 22, 25, 30,
    132, 136, 192, 393, 498, 542
Chatterjee, Sarat Chandra, 136, 674
Chatterjee, Upamanyu, 281–2, 663
Chatterji clan, 384, 501
Chattopadhyay, Kamaladevi, 585
Chattopadhyay, Sarojini, *see* Naidu, Sarojini
Chaudhuri, Jayanto Nath, 220
Chaudhuri, Nirad, 498
Chaudhvin ka Chand (1960 film), 595,
    603, 616–18, 623, 667
chaukidaars, 226, 227, 230, 476–81
chaunki vali chhal, 464
Chauri Chaura incident (1922), 41, 59, 228
    see also non-cooperation movement
Chawla, Juhi, 587
chawls, 329–33, 349, 350, 570
Chenab river, 283
Chennai, Tamil Nadu, *see* Madras city/
    Chennai
Chepauk, Madras, 404
Chess Players, The (1977 film), 582, 590
chhajjas, 265
Chhatrapati Shivaji Terminus, Mumbai, 327
chhatris, 265
chhukris, 446
chi-chi, 249, 250
Chidambaram, 158
Child Marriage Restraint Act (British
    India, 1929), 406, 425, 436
    see also age of consent debates
childbirth, 367, 472
childhood, 366, 372, 426
children
    Baazigars, 565, 567
    marriage of, 20, 338, 366–7, 372–3, 406,
        425
    miracle plays, 557–8
    Partition (1947) and, 342
China
    Bengal, trade with, 209
    communism in, 530
    cuisine, 500, 515
    diaspora, 293

indentured labour, 302
India, relations with, 226, 639, 653, 655
Indian artistic influence, 150
nutrition in, 537
Opium War, Second (1856–60), 7
Pakistan, relations with, 173, 653, 654
US, relations with, 640
Chinese cuisine, 500, 515
Chitpavan Brahmin caste, 19, 103
Chitrahaar, 622
Chittagong, 164, 333, 377, 399, 635
Hill Tracts, 289, 480, 534
Chokher Bali (2003 film), 663
Chola bronzes, 149
cholera, 325
'Choli ke Peechhe Kya Hai', 675
cholum, 517–18, 524
Chota Nagpur plateau, 335
Chotani, Seth Mian Muhammad Haji Jan
    Muhammad, 57
Choudhury, Abdul Gaffar, 143
Chowdhury, Suniti, 31
Christianity, 33, 35, 274
    caste and, 482
    Catholicism, 149, 329, 330, 332, 570
    Dalits, 489
    divorce, 397
    missionaries, 133, 136, 477
Christmas, 435, 559
Chughtai, Ismat, 418, 661
chulah, 471
Churchill, Winston, 261, 527
churidaar, 587, 588
Churning, The (1976 film), 662
cinema halls, 599, 630–31
circuses, *see* Baazigars
cities; urbanisation, 432, 454, 496, 502
    chawls, 329–33, 349, 350, 570
    colonial era, 10, 87, 190, 325, 333, 347,
        348–9, 351–2, 354
    ghettos, 351, 357–60
    mohallas, 349–51, 354, 356, 361
    refugees and, 279–82, 346–56
    rural migration to, 326–39, 432–3
    slums, 190–91, 281, 336, 351, 360–64,
        432
    squatter colonies, 94–6, 354–6
citizenship, 88–90, 91, 94, 96–100, 267,
    321, 351, 637
    jus soli, 88–9, 94
    Non-Resident Indians (NRIs), 319–21

Partition (1947) and, 88–90, 91, 94
    passports, 98, 312, 313, 316, 318
    permit system, 96–8
city beautification, 190–91, 281
City of Dreadful Night, The (Kipling), 349,
    352
civil disobedience campaign (1930–31), 74,
    186
civil disobedience campaign (1932–4), 78,
    186
civil law, *see* family law
civil service, *see* Indian Civil Service
Class of '83 (2020 film), 236
classical dance, 578, 579
    Bharatanatyam, 579, 583, 584, 594, 607–8
    Kathak, 579, 581–2, 585–91, 607, 674
Clear (1980 film), 664
Clifton, Karachi, 348
climate change, 531, 635, 636, 652
Cloud-capped Star (1960 film), 660
cluster fig trees, 478
coal, 300
Coca-Cola, 512
cocaine, 541
Cochin, 297
cock fighting, 349
coffee, 502, 508, 510–11
Cold Meat (Manto), 341
Cold War (1947–91), 123, 171, 530, 653–5
Colombo Conference (1954), 277
Comilla, Bangladesh, 31, 635
common law, 244, 402
Commonwealth, 122, 223, 313, 315
Commonwealth Immigrants Act (UK,
    1962), 313
Commonwealth Immigrants Act (UK,
    1968), 315
Communal Award (1932), 77–8
communal violence, 70
    anti-Ahmediya (1953; 1974), 175
    anti-Bihari (1971–2), 144, 161, 165,
        166–7, 358–60
    Babri Masjid demolition (1992), 291, 346
    Calcutta riots (1964), 377
    Gandhi assassination (1984), 345
    Gujarat riots (2002), 346
    Hazrat Bal riots (1964), 343, 346
    Partition (1947), 91–2, 94, 262, 340–42,
        644
    Rath Yaatra (1990), 198–9
    Shia–Sunni conflict, 489–90

communism, 123, 135, 276, 530, 592
Communist Manifesto (Engels and Marx), 135, 592
Communist Party of India, 31, 40, 123, 187, 362, 384
Communist Party of Pakistan, 173
'communities', 51–2, 53, 78
Company Limited (1971 film), 663
composite nationalism, 3, 55, 76, 79, 102
Comrade, The, 54
concubines, 387, 390, 391
　see also courtesans
Connaught Place, Delhi, 348, 501
Connection, The (1981 film), 154, 608, 672
Conservative Party, 260–61, 315
Constantinople, 44, 55
Constantinos Doxiadis, 282
Constituent Assembly, India (1946–50), 88–9
Constituent Assembly, Pakistan (1947–50), 90, 115, 118, 120
Constitution of India Bill (1895), 88
contortionists, 564–5
cooking, 454–5
　caste and, 305, 384, 463, 471
　cookery books, 454, 513–16
　khanaval, 330–31
　tribal peoples and, 181, 478, 479
　women and, 425, 431, 447, 461, 472
　see also food
Coolie (1983 film), 596, 672
'coolies', 297–8, 310, 318, 319, 326
Coomaraswamy, Ananda Kentish, 149
Cornish, William, 271, 517–20, 536
　on cattle, 467–8
　glycaemic index, 517
　on prisoners, 518
　on rice, 517, 519, 520, 525, 538
　on starvation, 518
　on tribal diets, 479
　Temple Ration and, 518
corruption
　armed forces and, 220–21, 605
　intermediaries, 256
　police and, 232, 233–4
coup proofing, 219
courtesans, 440, 444, 449, 588, 590, 608, 610–11, 662
　dance and, 579, 582, 586, 587, 590, 608
　see also prostitution

Covenant of Medina (*c.*622), 79
Covid-19 pandemic (2019–23), 494–6, 523, 562
cow protection movements, 103, 203, 468–9
Crazy Baiju (1952 film), 620, 668
cricket, 85, 87, 103, 152, 345, 541, 543, 616, 638, 676–7
crime, 206, 208, 226–38
　banditry, 205–6, 211, 212, 236–8, 291–2, 431–40
　Bollywood and, 599, 601
　domestic violence, 207, 430
　honour killings, 290–91
　organised crime, 226, 599, 601
　people trafficking, 314
　policing, 226–38, 289
　rape, 20, 237, 250, 406, 411–12, 415, 436
　shootings, 234–5
　smuggling, 206, 226, 636
Crimean War (1853–6), 43, 45
Criminal Tribes Act (British India, 1924), 236, 459
criminal tribes, 236, 237, 241, 290, 294–5, 459, 487, 564
cross-cousin marriage, 369, 423
Crossfire (1997 film), 663
Curzon, George, 1st Marquess, 14, 15, 17, 24–5, 29, 182, 261, 271, 392
customs duties, 273
Cutch, 16, 505, 616
Cuttacki Oriya, 339
Cyclone Bhola (1970), 224, 284
Cyprus, 220

daadamashay, 383
daaku, 236–7, 291–2
daal, 183, 185, 473, 491, 493, 509, 517, 518, 519
daasis, 387, 389, 390, 391
Dabangg (2010 film), 616
dabbas, 331, 509–11
Dacca, 224, 297, 377–8
　'Biharis' in, 129, 161
　Daulatia, 443
　Dhanmondi, 453
　Jinnah's speech (1948), 119, 142
　Liberation War (1971), 125
　Modhu's canteen, 166–7
　partition protests (1905), 29–30

State Language Day protests (1952), 127
Town Hall Camp, 358–60
dacoits, *see* bandits
DaCunha, Sylvester, 470
Dadu, Sind, 317
Dadyal, Kashmir, 283
Dahan (1997 film), 663
Dal, Sohal, 590
Dalhousie Square, Calcutta, 265–6
Dalip Singh, Sikh Maharaja, 212
Dalit Camera, 516
Dalit Panthers, 460, 482
Dalits, 181, 206, 250, 454, 457–8, 482–8, 591
  Christianity, 489
  cross-caste love, 420
  food and, 203, 459, 460, 472, 474
  Gandhi and, 34, 126
  meat consumption, 203, 515–16
  Partition (1947), 343
  Ramlila and, 554–5
Damodar Valley, 528
dams, 285, 296, 312, 528, 532–3, 534–5
  Bhakra–Nangal project, 283, 528
  Farakka Barrage, 652–3
  Kaptai Dam, 534
  Mangla Dam, 159, 283
  migration and, 283, 296, 312, 532
  Sardar Sarovar Dam, 534–5
  Sukkur Barrage, 350
dance, 578–91
  classical, 578, 579, 581–91, 607
  filmi, 539, 578, 579, 587, 607–9, 618, 620–22
  folk, 566, 578, 579–81
  see also Bharatanatyam; Kathak
Dandakaranya, 279, 353
Dangal (2016 film), 616
Dardanelle Straits, 55
Darjeeling, Bengal, 26, 336, 381
Darling, Malcolm Lyall, 242, 253, 391, 392, 418, 522
Das, Chittaranjan, 60, 498, 502
Das, Ghanshyam, 106
Das, Madhusudan, 132
Dasharath, 549, 550–51, 556, 557
Daughter-in-law/Wife (1967 film), 669
Daulatia, Dacca, 443
Davis, Kingsley, 323, 325, 528
Dawn, 119
Dawoodi Bohras, 242, 489, 505

Dayabhaaga, 402
Days and Nights in the Forest (1970 film), 660, 663
Days Have Changed, The (1955 film), 594
Death Sentence (1997 film), 608, 664
Deb, Debal, 535
Deccan College, Poona, 20, 148
Deena Bandhu (1942 film), 132
Deewaar (1975 film), 227, 604, 610, 620, 627, 628, 629, 671, 673
Dehradun, Uttarakhand, 287–8
Delhi, 5, 151–3
  architecture, 103, 265, 348
  Azadpur Mandi, 453
  Baazigars in, 566
  Brahmins in, 475
  cuisine, 491, 492
  dance schools in, 586, 590
  earthquakes in, 635
  expansion, 350
  Firoz Shah Kotla, 152
  Fortis Hospital, 339
  Gandhi assassination (1948), 103–5
  Gymkhana Club, 251
  Hauz Khas, 151–2, 153, 234, 346, 492
  Humayun's tomb, 101, 153, 154
  India Gate, 265
  Indian National Museum, 146, 148–50
  Jumma Masjid, 496
  migration to, 297, 338–9
  mohallas, 349
  Nirbhaya rape case (2012), 411–12
  Partition (1947), 87, 93, 94, 96, 101, 340, 645
  population, 351
  Qutub Minar, 151
  Rebellion (1857–8), 7, 43, 44, 63, 190, 586
  refugees in, 280, 281, 346, 352, 353
  tenements, 190–91, 281, 363
  street food in, 511
  Turkman Gate demolition (1976), 191, 192, 360
  Viceroy's House/ Rashtrapati Bahavan 265, 348
Delhi Proposals (1927), 72
Delwar Hossain Ahmad, 137
Demerara, 309
democracy, 35, 36, 172, 173, 186, 222
demography, 51–2, 69, 100, 101, 124, 163, 283, 323–6

Deoband Madrasa, 79, 80
Department of Posts and Telegraphs, 499
Derozio, Henry, 497, 502
Desai, Morarji, 177, 181, 185–6, 468
Desher Katha (Deuskar), 25
Deuskar, Sakharam Ganesh, 25
devadaasis, 440
Devadasi tradition, 579
Devanagiri script, 53, 107, 139
Devdas (Chatterjee), 136, 607, 674
Devdas (1928 film), 136
Devdas (1955 film), 607, 666, 674
Devdas (2002 film), 136, 607, 609, 610, 623, 674, 675, 678
　dance sequences, 587, 591, 607–8, 621
Devi (1960 film), 663
Devi, Atreyee, 397–8
Devi, Phoolan, 237, 424, 436–40
Devi, Sushila, 338–9, 336–7, 421
Dewas, 253, 391, 392, 412, 418
Dhanmondi, Dacca, 453
Dharavi, Bombay, 363
dharma, 199, 414, 555
Dharmaraj, 547, 548
Dharmendra, 539
dholak, 587
dhrupad, 586, 619
diabetes, 469, 535
dialects, 4, 139
diarchy, 60
Dickens, Charles, 348, 501–2
Dickey, Sara, 422
Diclofenac, 469
Dil Se . . . (1998 film), 677, 678
Dil, Anwar, 531
Dilwale Dulhania Le Jayenge (1995 film), 631
dining habits, 453
　see also cooking; food
Dipendra, Crown Prince of Nepal, 392
Discovery of India (Nehru), 179
disease, 324–5
　cholera, 325
　Covid-19, 494–6, 523
　influenza, 324, 496, 523
　malaria, 242, 279, 325
　plague, 324
　venereal disease, 406, 441
Displaced Persons Act (India, 1954), 99

Dissolution of Muslim Marriages Act (British India, 1939), 408
Distant Thunder (1973 film), 521
district magistrates (DMs), 286
divorce, 290, 395, 397, 407–9
　apostasy and, 397
　Dissolution of Muslim Marriages Act (1939), 408
　Hindu Code reforms (1947–51), 408
　Hindu Marriage Act (1955), 397
　khulaa, 397
　Shah Bano case, 290, 409
　Shariat Act (1937), 407
Divte, Shivaji, 329
Diwali, 435, 554, 559
Dixit, Madhuri, 579, 607, 608, 610, 613, 621, 673–5
Do Bigha Zameen (1953 film), 299, 602, 603, 618, 619, 666
documentary films, 145, 156–7
Dodecanese islands, 55
Dogras, 214, 218
domestic servants, 362, 377, 398, 431, 433–6, 474
domestic violence, 207, 430
Don (1978 film), 605, 610, 614, 615, 672, 673
Doob (2017 film), 675
Doordarshan, 562, 622
dosas, 231–2
Dostana (1980 film), 614
dowries, 419, 423, 439, 447
drama, religious, 543–63
Dravida Munnetra Kazhagam (DMK), 140
Dravidar Kazhagam, 135
Dravidian movement, 2, 73, 133, 134, 139, 475
dreadedterrorists, 235, 236
Drèze, Jean, 536
droughts, 324, 334, 530, 536
DSP (deputy superintendent of police), 231, 232–3
Dubai, United Arab Emirates, 318
Dufferin, Frederick Hamilton-Temple-Blackwood, 1st Marquess, 250
dumbaari, 478
Dumdum airport, Calcutta, 204
Dumont, Louis, 458
Duniya Na Mane (1937 film), 591
Durand Line, 225, 635

Durga Puja, 539, 545
Dutt, Guru, 594–6, 600–601, 602, 605, 610–11, 667–9
  Benegal, influence of, 593
  Chaudhvin ka Chand (1960), 595, 603, 616–18, 623, 667
  death (1964), 611
  Kaagaz ke Phool (1959), 595, 601, 610, 611, 667
  Khosla, hiring of, 595–6
  Muslim socials, 595
  Pyaasa (1957), 595, 610, 667
  song and dance sequences, 616–18
  themes, 610–11
Dutt, Nargis, 407, 600, 602, 605, 607, 665–6, 668, 669
Dutt, Romesh Chunder, 14–15, 16, 17, 18, 27, 166, 182, 271
Dutt, Yashica, 460
dwarf rice, 530–32
Dwarka, Delhi, 346
Dyer, Reginald Edward Harry, 38, 40

East Africa, 315, 318
East Bengal (1947–55), 94, 101, 112–13, 117, 649
  Bengali language movement, *see under* language movements
  marriage migration in, 366
  rice production, 527
East India Company, 7, 48, 207, 208–13, 240, 242
  bandits and, 212–13
  brothels and, 440–41
  domestic sphere and, 211
  expansion campaigns, 209–12, 239, 403
  inheritance law and, 404
  Hyderabad, relations with, 239
  Mughal Empire, relations with, 208
  nautch and, 579, 582
  stipends, 403
  taxation, 209, 269–71
East Pakistan (1955–71), 124, 169
  Cyclone Bhola (1970), 224, 284
  diaspora, 319
  food crises (1950s), 278
  Liberation War (1971), *see* Bangladesh Liberation War
  marriage migration in, 366
  rice production, 527
  Rohingya refugees in, 312

economic nationalism, 13–14, 18–19, 25–6, 166, 171, 182, 192, 271, 276
education
  history, 145, 154–6, 169–70, 637–8
  middle classes, 497, 502, 504, 506, 508
  RSS, 195–6
  swadeshi movement, 25, 28, 196
  Vidya Mandir controversy (1937), 139
  Wardha scheme, 138
  western, 7–8, 11–12, 29, 45, 47, 49, 497, 502, 504, 506, 508
  women and, 382–3, 419, 425, 460–61, 473
Edwardes, Stephen Meredyth, 328
Egypt, 43, 45, 147, 317–18
Eid, 103, 262, 309, 435
Ek Din Pratidin (1979 film), 660
Ek Tha Tiger (2012 film), 632–3, 676
Ekushey Rally (1952), 127, 143–4, 165
El Niño, 299
Election Commission, 200
elections
  1936–7 British Indian provincial elections, 75
  1952 Indian general election, 408
  1970 Pakistani general election, 172, 224
  1971 Indian general election, 184
  1977 Indian general election, 197, 203
electricity, 598
elephants, 577
elopements, 338, 419
Elphinstone College, Bombay, 12, 497
Elwin, Verrier, 420, 477, 481, 579–81
Embers (1975 film), see *Sholay*
Emergency (1975–7), 83, 108, 159, 177–8, 179, 184–92
  Bollywood and, 603, 627
  city beautification campaigns, 190, 281
  diaspora and, 319
  Jan Sangh and, 197
  sterilisation campaign, 190, 281
Emmanuel College, Cambridge, 498
enemy property ordinances (1968), 99
English education, 7–8, 11–12
English language, 4, 139, 140–41, 249, 498, 499, 506
English, August (Chatterjee), 281–2, 663
English, August (1994 film), 663
Enlightenment (*c.*1637–*c.*1789), 11, 12
epidemics, 324–5

Essay on the Principle of Population (Malthus), 529
etiquette, 44, 210, 247, 257
Eton College, Berkshire, 245
Evacuee Property Management Boards, 647, 649
Evacuee Property Ordinance (India, 1949), 98
Evans, Mary Ann, 566, 605, 664
Exeter College, Oxford, 121
exorcisms, 481, 544
'extremists', 1–2, 18, 19, 73
  Hindu revivalism and, 20–23
  violence and, 2, 23–4

Factory Acts (British India), 431
Fadl, Sayyid, 58
Faiz, Faiz Ahmed, 123, 167, 542
Faizabad, 196
al-Falah, 360
family law, 106, 211, 244, 400–409
  inheritance, 64, 371, 386–90, 401–5
  marriage, 395, 405–9
Famine Commission, 324, 518, 521
famines, 14, 253, 260, 268, 277–8, 295, 299, 324, 334, 455, 536
  Bangladesh (1974–5), 163
  Bengal (1873–4), 14
  Bengal (1943), 280, 337, 350, 505, 521, 525–7, 528, 531, 603
  Bhojpur famines (1900s), 17
  economic nationalism and, 14
  Great Famine (1876–8), 324, 518
  green revolutions (c.1967–c.1978) and, 531–6
  Indian Famine (1896–7), 324, 519
  Indian Famine (1899–1900), 16–17, 324
  Indian food crisis (1974–5), 183, 185–6
  Orissa Famine (1865), 519
  rice and, 517, 519
Farakka Barrage, 652–3
Faridabad, Haryana, 353
Faridkot, 644
farmer suicides, 362
Faruqi, Arshad, 85
fasting; hunger strikes, 461–3
  Apte (1939), 591
  Bhave (1979), 468
  Desai (1975), 186
  Gandhi, 33, 38, 186, 450, 462–3
  Kamiyar (1998), 418

men and, 462–3
Punjabi Subah movement (1960–61), 129
Ramazan, 494
  women and, 461–2
Father India (Ranga Iyer), 407
Fauji Fund, 221
Faulad (1963 film), 577, 670
Fazal Dad, 97–8
Fazlul Huq, 120
Fearless (1994 documentary), 664
Fearless (2010 film), 616
Fearless Nadia, 566, 605, 664
Federal Curriculum Wing, 154
Feica, 542
female infanticide, 424
Ferrante, Elena, 535
Festival (2000 film), 663
festivals, 543–63
  Bollywood and, 624
  chawls and, 330
  Christmas, 435, 559
  Dharmaraj Puja, 547, 548
  Diwali, 435, 554, 559
  Durga Puja, 539, 545
  Eid, 103, 262, 309, 435
  Ekadasi, 461
  Ganapati, 21
  Holi, 309, 540, 624
  Jamai-sashti, 375–6
  Janamasthami, 462
  Jhampan Mela, 543–7
  Karva Chauth, 421, 461
  Muharram, 308, 360, 545
  Navaratri, 545
  Onam, 545
  Puja, 435
  Ram Navami, 38
  Ramazan, 494–6
  Ramlila, 198, 539, 545, 549–63, 607
fez, 328
Fiji, 298, 301, 302, 308
files, 120, 230, 233, 257, 259, 260
Film and Television Institute of India, 662
Filmcity, Goregaon, 542
Filmfare, 609
filmi dance, 539, 578, 579, 587, 607
filmindia, 609
Films Division of India, 157
fiqh, 46
Firangi Mahal, 54

Fire (1996 film), 664
Firoz Shah Kotla, Delhi, 152
Firoz Shah Tuqhlaq, 152, 156
fish, 459, 490
fishing, 221
Five Thousand Years of Pakistan (Wheeler),
    148
five-year plans, 277, 505, 528
flag parades, 40, 252
Flaubert, Gustave, 677
Flurys, Calcutta, 347, 500
folk dance, 578, 579–81
food, 181, 271, 382, 429, 450–538
    baasi, 473–4, 483, 485, 496
    beef, 103, 203, 468, 490
    bhaakri, 483–4, 488, 491
    biryani, 451, 454, 491, 493, 510
    caste and, 64, 305, 384, 451–2, 454–60,
        463–88, 490, 492, 509, 515–16
    Chinese cuisine, 500, 515
    cookery books, 454, 513–16
    cooking, *see* cooking
    dairy products, 466–7, 469–71, 487, 491
    dieting, 454
    dining habits, 453
    European cuisine, 499, 501
    famines, *see* famines
    fasting, 461–3, 494
    festivals, 548
    ghee, 185, 382, 429, 465, 487, 576
    globalisation and, 511–13
    green revolutions (*c.*1967–*c.*1978), 277,
        296, 531–6
    hybrid cultures, 499–503, 511
    'Indian diet', 456–63, 513–16
    Jhampan Mela, 543
    jootha, 464, 474, 483, 485, 493
    kachcha, 465–6, 473, 480, 503
    mandis, 453
    malnutrition, 536–8
    meat, *see* meat
    middle class and, 451, 496–509
    'Muslim diet', 490–96
    nation and, 454, 513–16
    pakka, 465–6, 473, 479, 480
    paandaan, 453, 475
    prasaadam, 451, 464–5
    raajsik, 464, 480, 495
    rice, *see* rice
    saatvik, 464, 480; 495
    shortages, 183, 185–6, 188, 278

    staples, 516–27
    street food, 231–2, 380, 454, 503, 511–13
    taamsik, 464, 480, 495
    tandoori culture, 491
    tiffin boxes, 509–11
    tribal peoples and, 181, 451, 476–81
    vegetarianism, 33, 134, 459, 475, 507,
        515–16
    women and, 425, 431, 447, 455,
        460–62, 472
Food (Bose), 520
'food, clothing and shelter', 172, 450
food crisis (1974–5), 183
Food Grains Control Order (British India,
    1942), 336
Forbes Rich List, 507
forests, 272–3, 276, 296, 299, 476
Forster, Edward Morgan, 248, 251, 253
Fort Saint William, Bengal, 209
Fourteen Points (1929), 76, 155
France, 55, 208, 209
Frankel, Francine, 533, 534
Fraser, Andrew, 40
Friendship (1980 film), 614
From the Heart (1998 film), 677, 678
fuchka, 503, 512
Full Moon, The (1960 film), 595, 603,
    616–18, 623, 667

gaanja, 547
Gaddi people, 466
Gaikwad, Laxman, 487–8, 548
galas, 329–33
galis, 349
Gama, 569, 571–5, 615
Ganabani, 137
Ganapati, 21
Gandhi, Feroze, 180
Gandhi, Indira, 29, 83, 84, 171, 173,
    177–192, 200, 202–3, 253
    assassination (1984), 191, 197, 345
    Bangladesh Liberation War (1971), 184,
        223, 640
    CIA conspiracy theories, 189
    'city beautification' campaign, 190, 281
    cow protection movements and, 468
    Emergency (1975–7), 83, 108, 159,
        177–8, 179, 184–92, 197, 281, 603
    'food, clothing and shelter', 172, 450
    food crisis (1974–5), 183, 185–6, 188,
        453

Gandhi, Indira – *cont.*
Ganges river dispute, 652
general election (1977), 197, 203
Hindu right and, 192
Khalistan movement, relations with, 201
Operation Blue Star (1984), 191, 223, 291
privy purse abolition (1969), 181, 268
sterilisation campaign, 190, 281
Gandhi, Mohandas, 5–6, 13, 32–42, 61
aashrams, 59, 126
Amritsar massacre (1919), 39–40
assassination (1948), 91, 103–5, 123, 194, 643
baniya jati, 504
Bardoli Satyagraha (1928), 106
Bengal Famine (1943), 526, 527
Birla and, 36, 575
caste, views on, 34, 36
cattle, views on, 467
Champaran Satyagraha (1917), 37
civil disobedience campaign (1930–31), 74, 186
civil disobedience campaign (1932–4), 78, 186
Dalits, views on, 34, 126
democracy, views on, 36
on elites, 269
fasting, 462–3
food, views on, 526
Gokhale, influence of, 20, 35
Hind Swaraj, 34, 35, 36
indentured labour, campaign against (1910s), 34–5, 299, 310
Irwin Pact (1931), 74
Kaira Satyagraha (1918), 37, 106
Khilafat movement, relations with, 55, 56, 57, 59
language, views on, 139, 141
Mayo, views on, 407
My Experiments with Truth, 33
non-cooperation movement (1920–22), 35, 40–41, 55–6, 59, 60, 61, 70, 186, 190
non-violence (*ahimsaa*), 32, 35, 39, 41
Partition (1947), 343, 642–3
Rau, relationship with, 259
Rowlatt Act (1919), 37–8
Salt Tax Satyagraha (1930), 122
Savarkar and, 74, 104
satyagraha, 35–6
Tagore, influence of, 28, 29

Gandhi, Rajiv, 180, 197–8, 202, 220, 223, 290, 409
Gandhi, Sanjay, 178, 180, 190, 191–2, 199, 360
Ganesan, Gemini, 608
Ganesh, 21, 135
Ganges river, 105, 458, 548, 636, 652
Gangopadhyay, Sunil, 356
Ganguli, Taraknath, 395
Ganguly, Indu, 354, 360
Ganti, Tejaswini, 597, 602
Garam Hawa (1973 film), 494, 661
Garhwalis, 214–15, 218
gat, 588
gaurakshini sabha, 468
Gauras, 466
Gautam, Siddhartha, 416
Gazetteer, 112
General Post Office, Calcutta, 265–6, 347
Geneva Camp, Dacca, 358
ghaat serangs, 350
Ghachar Ghochar (Shanbhag), 508
Ghadr, 37
Ghalib, Mirza, 45, 542
ghar-jamaai, 397
gharaanas, 440, 579
Ghare Baire (Tagore), 412
Ghareeb, 548
gharry, 5
Ghatak, Ritwik, 660
ghazal, 586, 618, 619
Ghaznavid Empire (977–1186), 156, 170
ghee, 185, 382, 429, 465, 487
ghettos, 351, 357–60
ghoos khana, 233
Ghosh, Amitav, 346, 378, 421, 502
Ghosh, Aurobindo, 26–8, 179
Ghosh, Kanakotpal, 344
Ghosh, Rai Sahib Ashutosh, 499
Ghosh, Rituparno, 630, 662–3
Ghosh, Santi, 31
Ghosh, Shohini, 344, 431, 592, 663
ghosts, 481
Ghulam Muhammad, 124, 646
ghungroos, 587
Gibraltar, 318
Gift of a Cow, The (1963 film), 618
Gill, Kanwar Pal Singh, 223
Gin Drinkers, The (Ghose), 502
Girangaon, Bombay, 328–33, 361
Gita Press, 549

Gita Rahasya (Tilak), 23, 192–3, 194, 196
globalisation, 432, 506, 511–13
Go for it, India! (2007 film), 677
go-korbaani, 103
Goa, 326, 329, 330, 331, 570
Goalas, 460, 466–7
Goalpara, West Bengal, 546
goat meat, 459, 493
God of Small Things, The (Roy), 415, 420
Godaan (1963 film), 618
Godavari, Madras, 386–90
Goddess, The (1960 film), 663
Godse, Nathuram, 103–4, 123, 194
Gokhale, Gopal Krishna, 6, 13, 61
    Curzon, relationship with, 17
    death (1915), 69–70
    Gandhi, relationship with, 6, 34, 35
    indentured labour, campaign against, 34, 299, 310
    Jinnah, relationship with, 63, 68
    Nehru, relationship with, 63
    Tilak, relationship with, 19–20
gol gappas, 512
Gold, Ann Grodzins, 429
Golden Temple, Amritsar, 38, 39, 109, 191, 223, 291
Golden Thread, The (1962 film), 660
Gonds, 369, 374, 481, 580–81
goondagardi, 330
goongoo, 477
Gopalpur, Orissa, 471
Goregaon, Bombay, 542
Gorkhaland, 336
Gorky, Maxim, 665
gossip, 541–2
Gothic architecture, 265, 348
gotra, 291
Government of India Act (British India, 1919), 40, 60, 505
Government of India Act (British India, 1935), 61, 71, 77–8, 114
Govindapur, Bengal, 393
Gracey, Douglas, 266
Graeco-Roman wrestling, 573
gram, 517, 522
Grameen Bank, 285, 286
Grand Trunk Road, 5
Grandeur (1980 film), 614
Great Depression (1929–39), 74, 75, 505, 522

Great Game (1830–1907), 25
Great Mughal, The (1960 film), 670
Greece, 55, 81, 342
Greek language, 245, 258
Green Park Market, Delhi, 511–12
green revolutions (*c.*1967–*c.*1978), 277, 296, 531–6
Grierson, George, 4
Guess (1949 film), 665, 666, 669
Guha, Amboo, 570
Guho, Gobar, 570
Guides on the Mazdayasnan Path, 12
Guinness World Records, 470
Gujarat, 186, 487
    riots (2002), 346
Gujarati language, 4, 13, 35, 141
Gujral, Satish, 341
Gujrat, Punjab, 313
gulaab jaamun, 495, 511
Gulf War (1990–91), 232, 285
gun ownership, 234
Guntur district, Madras, 271
Gupta Empire (319–485), 149
gurdwaaras, 86, 283, 340, 342, 345
Gurkhas, 214, 217, 218, 253
Guru Nanak, 39
Gwalior, 586
Gymkhana Club, Delhi, 251
gymnasiums, 23

Habitual Offenders Act (India, 1952), 236
Hadith, 46
Hadramaut, Yemen, 58
Hafez, 498
hafta racket, 232
hair oil, 512
halal meat, 492
Haldar, Baby, 398–9, 426, 430, 472
haldi, 514
Haldiram's, 512
haleem, 493
Hali, Altaf Hussain, 45, 498, 542
Hall, Edward, 583
Hamdard, The, 54
Hamidul Huq Choudhury, 648
Hanafi jurisprudence, 81
Hanif, Mohammed, 122, 176, 452
Hanuman, 553, 569, 576, 577
Harappa, 147
Harrow School, Middlesex, 11, 64, 317, 600

Hart–Celler Act (US, 1965), 316, 504
hartal, 38
Haryana, 129, 282
Hasina, Sheikh, 163, 166
Hauz Khas, Delhi, 151–2, 153, 234, 346, 492
haveli architecture, 348
hawkers, *see* street vendors
Hazare, Anna, 462
Hazrat Bal theft and riots (1963–4), 343, 346
healthcare, 284
Heavenly Ornaments (Thanawi), 368, 370
Hedgewar, Keshav Baliram, 194
Heer-Ranjha (Waris Shah), 112
Henry VIII, King of England, 130
Hero, The (1966 film), 660
high courts, 265
Hijaz, 43
hijrat, 58, 81, 113, 263
Hill Cart Road, 26, 85, 344, 371
    food culture at, 452, 460, 466, 521, 653
    household dynamics in, 375, 380–85, 393, 413
Hill of Devi, The (Forster), 253
Hillingdon, London, 321
hilsaa, 451
Himachal Pradesh, 466, 475
Himalayas, 214, 380, 381, 426, 544
Hind Swaraj (Gandhi), 34, 35, 36
Hindi Medium (2017 film), 676
Hindi, 9, 53, 106, 107, 138, 339
    Devanagiri script, 53, 107, 139
    in Calcutta, 334, 337
    cinema, 594, 595–6, 617, 620, 622
    literature, 138
    in Madras, 133, 135, 139–40
    Nehru and, 141, 143
    Urdu and, 53, 106, 107, 135, 139, 142
Hindu, The, 515
Hindu Code reforms (1947–51), 260, 408, 414
Hindu College, Calcutta, 497
Hindu Gains of Learning Act (British India, 1930), 405–6
Hindu Mahasabha, 72, 76, 103, 104, 105, 197
Hindu Marriage Act (India, 1955), 371, 397
Hindu Patriot, 9
Hindu Rashtra, 104

Hindu right, 74, 102–8, 192
    Bharatiya Janata Party, 177, 197–201
    Bollywood and, 601–2, 631–2
    cow protection movements, 103, 203, 468–9
    Emergency (1975–7), 192
    Gandhi assassination (1948), 103–5, 194
    Hindutva, 104, 106, 154, 193, 198, 202, 203
    merchants and, 507
    monuments and, 196–201
    Partition (1947), 102–3
    Rashtriya Swayamsevak Sangh, 72, 104, 105, 194–201
    Shiv Sena, 127, 129
    war and, 199
    women and, 462, 602
Hindu Undivided Family (HUF), 401–6, 414, 437, 507
Hinduism, 20–23, 42, 74
    ancestral property and, 274
    bandits and, 439
    castes, *see* caste
    cattle, reverence for, 22, 103, 203, 468–9
    Dharmaraj Puja, 547, 548
    Diwali, 435, 554
    Durga Puja, 539, 545
    Ekadasi, 461
    family law, 290, 400–409
    fasting, 461–3
    Ganapati, 21
    Ganesh, 21, 135
    Hanuman, 553, 569, 576, 577
    Holi, 309, 540
    Janamasthami, 462
    Jhampan Mela, 543–7
    Kali Temple, 497
    Karva Chauth, 421, 461
    Krishna, 23, 198, 199, 462, 582
    legal system and, 244
    Mahabharata, 23, 35, 130, 192–3, 196, 199, 384
    marriage customs, *see* marriage
    Onam, 545
    Partition (1947) and, 92–6, 262, 340, 342, 343, 346, 644
    prasaadam, 451, 464–5
    Raas Lila, 582
    Rakhi, 398
    Ram, 38, 135, 196, 198, 200–201, 291, 319, 549–63, 611

Ram Navami, 38
Ramayana, 135, 549–63, 569, 576, 577, 611–14, 626, 632
Ramlila, 198, 539, 545, 549–63
revivalism, 20–23
right wing politics and, *see* Hindu right
Saraswati, 195
secret societies, 31
Shaivism, 550
Shiva, 550
Vaishnavism, 550, 559, 582
Vishnu, 135, 547, 548, 550, 556
wrestling and, 569, 576, 577; *see also* wrestling
Hindutva, 104, 106, 154, 193, 198, 202, 203
Hindutva (Savarkar), 193, 194
Hirakkud Dam, Orissa, 528
History of British India (Mill), 11
HIV/AIDS, 416
Hobsbawm, Eric, 440
Hogg Market, Calcutta, 347
Holborn Empire, London, 571
Holi, 309, 540, 624
Hollywood, 597, 598–9, 601, 627, 631
Home and the World, The (Tagore), 412
Home Office, UK, 312, 315
Home Rule movement (1916–18), 37
Homo Hierarchicus (Dumont), 458
homosexuality, 558, 561
honour killings, 290–91, 416–17
Hooghly river, 652
Hooghly, West Bengal, 5
hooliganism, 330
horse-drawn carriages, 5
Hosain, Attia, 101, 394, 400
Hosay, 308
Hoshangabad, Madhya Pradesh, 522
House for Mr Biswas, A (Naipaul), 308
households, 380–49
    brothels, 440–48
    dacoits, 436–40
    inheritance, 274, 384, 386–90, 392, 401
    legal system and, 400–409
    marriage, *see* marriage
    migration, 296, 431–6
    nuclear families, 380, 384, 385, 405–6, 410, 413–15, 421–2, 432
    peasant-proletariat, 422–36

slaves, 387, 389, 390
    status in, 390, 394
Howrah, 333, 334
Hudood Ordinance (1979), 175, 203
Hughes, Frederick, 252
Hum Aapke Hain Koun! (1994 film), 631, 674, 676
Human Rights Watch, 489–90
human trafficking, 314, 319
Humayun, Mughal emperor, 101, 153, 154
Hume, Allan Octavian, 250
Hume, James, 250
hunger strikes, *see* fasting
Hunter Commission (1919), 40
hunter-gatherers, 273, 390, 476–81
Hunter, William Wilson, 52
Hunterwali (1935 film), 605
hunting, 272
Husain, Maqbool Fida, 593
Hussain, Altaf, 175, 356
Hussain, Khalid, 542
Hussain, Salma Tasadduque, 92
Hussain, Zakir, 102
Husyan, Imam, 308
Hyderabad, 4, 44, 86–7, 133, 239
    army rule (1948–50), 184, 219
    cuisine, 491
    Famine (1899–1900), 16
    Indian annexation (1948), 119, 220, 223, 224, 268, 343, 346
    Partition (1947), 201, 262
Hyderabad, Sind, 317
hydroelectric energy, 283

I Am Here (2004 film), 614
iddat, 409
idols, 349
iftaar, 495
ijaazas, 46
Ilbert Bill (1883), 10–11, 250
Ilbert, Courtney, 10
Illness (1999 film), 663
Illustrated London News, 150
Immigration Act (UK, 1971), 315
In Search of Famine (1981 film), 660
inaam land, 271
incest, 368
income taxes, 274
indentured labour, 9, 34–5, 37, 66, 293, 297–311, 318, 396

India, Dominion of (1947–50)
  armed forces, 218
  civil service, 264–6, 267
  Constituent Assembly, 88–9
  Evacuee Property Ordinance (1949), 98
  Gandhi assassination (1948), 103–5
  Hindu Code reforms (1947–51), 260,
    408, 414
  Hyderabad 'police action' (1948), 119,
    184, 219, 220, 223, 343, 346
  Inter-Dominion Conference (1948), 642,
    646–50
  Pakistan (Control) Ordinance (1948), 96
  Pakistan War (1947–8), 103, 123, 219,
    222, 223, 651
  Partition (1947), 82–3, 85, 86,
    89–96
  permit system, 96–8
India, Republic of (1950–)
  anti-imperialism, 654
  army, see Indian Armed Forces
  China, relations with, 639, 655
  citizenship laws (1955), 99
  civil service, 264–6, 267, 504, 506
  Cold War and, 653–4
  development, 277, 279–83, 285, 289,
    505
  Displaced Persons Act (1954), 99
  Emergency (1975–7), see Emergency
  enemy property ordinance (1968), 99
  five-year plan (1951–6), 505, 528
  food policy, 528–38
  Ganges river dispute, 652–3
  green revolution (1967–78), 296, 531–6
  history in, 145–7, 148–50, 155, 637–8
  Indus Waters Treaty (1960), 158, 283,
    641, 651
  judiciary, 235, 289
  liberalisation (1970s–90s), 285, 432,
    506, 511, 512–13
  malnutrition in, 536–8
  migration, see migration
  national dress, 450
  Naxalite insurgency (1967–), 85, 185,
    202, 234, 384, 476, 480
  nuclear power, 277
  nuclear weapons, 199, 656
  Operation Blue Star (1984), 191, 223,
    291
  Pakistan War (1965), 99, 159, 450, 639,
    651

Pakistan War (1971), 84–5, 161, 169,
    171, 173, 223, 640–41, 651
  Pakistan War (1999), 199, 641, 652, 656
  passports, 98, 312–13, 316, 318
  policing, 230–38, 289, 290
  postage stamps, 159
  Research and Analysis Wing (RAW),
    633, 676
  Simla Accord (1972), 651
  Tashkent Declaration (1966), 651
  taxation, 274–6
  United States, relations with, 277–8,
    529, 533, 654, 655
  Wagah–Attari border, 109–10
India Gate, Delhi, 265
India Office, 16
Indian Administrative Service (IAS), 264,
  504, 506
Indian Armed Forces, 218–21, 223
  Bofors scandal (1987–9), 220–21, 605
Indian Civil Service (ICS), 7, 14–15, 54,
  124, 242, 243–60, 262, 499, 504
Indian Councils Act (British India, 1892),
  50–52
Indian Councils Act (British India, 1909),
  52–3
Indian Human Development Survey, 475
Indian Institutes of Technology (IITs), 504
Indian National Army (INA), 215
Indian National Congress
  Calcutta Session (1901), 5
  civil disobedience campaign (1930–31),
    74, 186
  civil disobedience campaign (1932–4),
    78, 186
  Delhi Proposals (1927), 72
  extremists vs moderates, 1–2, 19–24, 73
  food policy, 526
  foreign policy, 643
  foundation (1885), 3, 7, 10
  Hinduism and, 42, 106–8
  Karachi Session (1913), 68
  Khilafat movement, relations with, 55
  Lahore Session (1900), 17
  left–right divide, 73
  Lucknow Pact (1916), 68–9, 417
  Muslims and, 42, 49, 55
  non-cooperation movement (1920–22),
    35, 40–41, 55–6, 59, 60, 70, 186, 190
  Nagpur Session (1920), 40–41
  Partition (1947), 89, 261

Pro-changers, 60–61
Surat Session (1907), 1, 2, 13, 19, 20, 23
Working Committee, 72, 75
Indian National Film Development
  Corporation, 661
Indian National Museum, Delhi, 146,
  148–50
Indian National Trust for Art and Cultural
  Heritage (INTACH), 154
Indian Penal Code (British India, 1860), 9
Indian Penal Code Act (British India,
  1923), 415
Indian Police Service (IPS), 231–38
Indian Statistical Institute, 278
Indian Universities Act (British India,
  1904), 134
Indian Writers' Association, 626
Indigo Air, 515
Indo–Pakistani War (1947–8), 103, 123,
  219, 222, 223, 651
Indo–Pakistani War (1965), 99, 159, 450,
  639, 651
Indo–Pakistani War (1971), 84–5, 161,
  169, 171, 173, 223, 640–41, 651
Indo–Pakistani War (1999), 199, 641, 652,
  656
Indo-Saracenic architecture, 348
Indonesia, 318
Indus Basin Project, 159
Indus river, 158, 242, 283, 350, 528, 641,
  651
Indus Valley civilisation, 147
Indus Waters Treaty (1960), 158, 283, 641,
  651
infanticide, 424
inflation, 262, 270, 278
influenza pandemic (1918–20), 324, 496,
  523
informal economy, 327–8, 334–5, 355, 431
Information Films of India, 156
inheritance, 274, 384, 386–90, 401, 402
Innocent (1983 film), 616, 664
Inter-Dominion Conference (1948), 642,
  646–50
Inter-Services Intelligence (ISI), 219, 222,
  224, 267, 633, 676
interest rates, 121, 434, 505
intermediaries, 47, 141, 243, 244, 253–60,
  269
International Monetary Fund (IMF), 285
International Mother Language Day, 144

Internet, 541–2
IQ tests, 504
Iqbal, Muhammad, 44, 45, 76–7, 79, 110,
  111, 130, 150
Iran, 224, 488
  cuisine, influence on, 491
  Safavid Empire (1501–1736), 43
  Sasanian Empire (224–651), 121
Iraq, 232, 285, 655
Iron Man, The (1963 film), 577, 670
irrigation, 159, 173, 242, 278, 283, 324,
  492, 520, 528
Irwin, Edward Wood, Lord, 74, 75
isha, 494
Islam; Muslims, 21, 42–60, 114–16
  aalim, 54, 79, 262
  Ahmediyas, 490
  ajlaf, 488–9
  architectural heritage, 150, 196–8
  ashraf, 43, 44, 45, 48–9, 112, 121, 137,
    488
  bandits and, 439
  beef and, 103, 203, 468
  Bollywood and, 595, 600, 661, 667,
    675–8
  caste and, 489
  censuses and, 242
  Communal Award (1932), 77–8
  Communist Party and, 31
  conversion to, 398, 420
  Covenant of Medina (c.622), 79
  Dawoodi Bohras, 242, 489
  Eid, 103, 262, 309
  fiqh, 46
  food practices, 488–96
  Government of India Act (1935), 78
  Hadith, 46, 49
  Hindu revivalism and, 21, 22, 31
  Holy Places, 643
  Kathak and, 581
  Khilafat movement (1919–24), 35, 41,
    54–60, 70, 79, 138, 214
  hijrat, 58, 81, 113, 263, 489
  Ismailis, 65, 68, 489
  legal system and, 244
  madrassas, 44, 53, 138, 373
  Mapilla Muslims, 58–60, 70; see also
    non-cooperation movement
  marriage customs, 368–70, 372–3, 374,
    395, 407–9, 420
  mosques, 196–8

Islam; Muslims – *cont.*
  Muharram, 308, 360, 545
  Muslim League, *see* All-India Muslim
    League
  Partition (1947) and, 92–6, 102, 261,
    340, 342, 343, 346–7, 644
  pirs, 44, 46, 58, 113, 115–16, 172, 665
  qawwaali, 112, 619, 665
  Qadiyanis, 490
  Quran, 4, 46, 48, 49, 137, 150, 203,
    368, 373
  Ramazan, 494–6
  Shab-e-Baraat, 357
  Sharia, 115, 175, 203
  Shiism, 65, 68, 81, 175–6, 224, 242,
    308, 489–90, 545
  Simla Deputation (1906), 52, 68
  Sufism, 46, 58
  sunna, 493
  Sunnism, 65, 68, 175, 308, 357, 489–90
  Tablighi Jamaat, 79
  ulema, 46, 49, 55, 56, 79, 114, 115, 137,
    408, 461
  ummaa, 43, 114
  waqfs, 67, 81, 271, 403, 404
  wataniyat, 48
  women's education, 461
  zakaat, 175, 176, 496
Islamabad, Pakistan, 282–3, 635
Islamic socialism, 115, 123
Israel, 117
Italian cuisine, 515
Italy, 55, 193, 318
Iyer, Ganapathy Subramaniya, 16, 18
izzat, 338, 414

Jaal (1952 film), 668
jaalis, 265
Jabalpur, 70
jackfruit, 478
Jaffrey, Madhur, 454, 513, 514, 515
jahaaji-bhais, 306
Jahangir, Mughal emperor, 207
Jainism, 32–3
Jaipur, 589, 590
jajmaani system, 428–9
Jalal, Farida, 662
Jallianwalla Bagh massacre (1919), 38–40,
    188
Jalpaiguri, Bengal, 26
Jalsaghar (1958 film), 585, 660

Jamaat-i-Islami, 115
Jamai-sashti, 375–6
Jamaica, 298
Jameela, Nalini, 442, 445–6
Jamiatul-Ulema-i-Hind, 79, 80, 114
Jammu and Kashmir, 475, 570
  see also Kashmir
Jan Sangh, 197
Jan, Rahat, 443
Jan, Saira, 443
Jana Sangha, 105
Jana Swasthya Abhiyaan, 535, 567
'*Janu Mi Cinemaanti?*' (Apte), 591–2,
    606
Japan, 215, 217, 336, 525, 573, 576
Japanese food, 500, 515
Japonica Indica, 532
jathas, 340
Jatin, Bagha 'Tiger', 31, 40, 41
jatis, 242, 458, 459–60, 475, 487, 489
Jats, 353
Jaunpur, 333
Jauregui, Beatrice, 231
Jawharlal Nehru University (JNU), 199
Jay Hotel, Bombay, 246
Jayakar, Mukund Ramrao, 405
Jenkinson, Clive, 245–7, 281–2
Jessop & Company Limited, 204
Jhalawar, 595
Jhampan Mela, 543–7
Jharkhand, 476, 480
Jhelum river, 283
jhum cultivation, 273, 296, 479–80
Jinnah, Muhammad Ali, 13, 62, 65–72,
    75–83, 111, 117, 170, 317
  Ali Khan, relationship with, 121–2
  Bombay Chronicle directorship, 405
  Cabinet Mission Plan (1946), 79
  communal riots (1923), 70
  Constituent Assembly speech
    (1947), 90
  Dacca speech (1948), 119, 142
  death (1948), 67, 91, 119–20
  Delhi Proposals (1927), 72
  education, 65
  fez, 328
  Fourteen Points (1929), 76, 155
  Lahore Resolution (1940), 79, 80
  language, views on, 141, 142
  legal career, 65–6
  Lucknow Pact (1916), 68–9, 417

Malabar Hill home, 99
marriage, 65, 72, 417
Mussalman Wakf Validating Bill (1913), 67, 404
Nationalist Party, 71
Nehru Report (1928), 75–6, 155
Partition (1947), 118–19, 263, 343
personal belongings, 150
'provincialism', views on, 119
Simon Commission (1928), 72–3
tuberculosis, 67, 119
Urdu, views on, 119, 142
US visit (1946), 111
Vidya Mandir controversy (1937), 139
Jio, 508
Jirat, West Bengal, 279, 353
Johannesburg, South Africa, 34
Johnson, James, 456
Johnstone, R. H. G., 252
Joint Defence Council, 645
jokes, 541–2
jootha, 464, 474, 483, 485, 493
Joshi, Ganesh Vyankatesh, 16, 18
jowaar, 484, 524, 534, 537
Judaism, 35
judiciary, 235, 289
Jugantar, 28
Jumma Masjid, Delhi, 496
Jumma movement, 225, 289, 290, 480
junglee sooar, 478
jus soli, 88–9, 94
Justice Party, 135
jute, 11, 122, 137, 249, 300, 333, 650

kaafilaas, 294, 341
Kaagaz ke Phool (1959 film), 595, 601, 610, 611, 667
kaaghazi raj, 257
kaala paani, 64, 302, 309
Kabhi Kabhie (1976 film), 610, 614, 623, 672, 673
Kabuliwala (Tagore), 294
kachcha, 465–6, 473, 480, 503
kachua wives, 390
Kadamb Centre for Dance, Ahmedabad, 590
kafis, 112
Kahlo, Frida, 417
Kaikeyi, 549–51, 557, 558
Kaira Satyagraha (1918), 37, 106

Kaira, Gujarat, 469–70
Kairanwi, Rehmatullah, 45
kalabaazi, 464
Kalahandi, Orissa, 279
Kalakshetra, Madras, 584
kalasam, 132
Kalat, 224, 268
Kali Temple, Calcutta, 497
kali yuga, 41
Kalidasa, 134
Kalka, 333
Kalkaji, Delhi, 353
kallars, 211
Kalurghat, Chittagong, 164
Kamathipura, Bombay, 441–3
Kanaujia Brahmins, 466
Kanchenjunga, 381
Kanjars, 237–8
Kankinara, Calcutta, 336
Kannada language, 423
Kanpur, Uttar Pradesh, 418
Kanungo, Hemchandra, 30
kanyadaan, 374, 440
Kapoor, Anil, 613
Kapoor, Kareena, 675
Kapoor, Karishma, 608
Kapoor, Raj, 669
Kapoor, Shashi, 629
Karachi, Sind, 65, 378
  capital status (1947–59), 119, 263, 282
  dalaals, 361
  INC session (1913), 68
  lascars, 350
  migration to, 297
  mohallas, 349
  MQM in, 356
  Naval neighbourhood, 221
  population, 351
  refugees in, 87, 95, 118, 281, 282, 347, 352, 353
Karachi Seven, 57
Kargil War (1999), 199, 641, 652, 656
karkhaanas, 295, 327, 350
Karma, 581
karnams, 244, 264
Karnaphuli river, 534
karsevaks, 201
karta, 384, 401–2, 405
Karunanidhi, 140

Karva Chauth, 421, 461

Kashmir, 63, 184, 201, 202, 290, 639
  Bollywood and, 614, 625, 628, 632
  Dogras, 214
  floods (2014), 635
  Hazrat Bal disappearance and riots
    (1963–4), 343, 346
  Hindu right and, 106
  Indo–Pakistani War (1947–8), 103, 123,
    219, 222, 223, 651
  Indo–Pakistani War (1965), 99, 159,
    450, 639, 651
  Indo–Pakistani War (1999), 199, 641,
    652, 656
  Indus river and, 641
  Mangla Dam, 159, 283
  Mawdudi on, 115
  Pandit community, 180, 374, 458
  Partition (1947), 86, 103, 639, 640, 644,
    645
  pirs in, 113
Kathak, 579, 581–2, 585–91, 607,
    674
  Chawla, 587
  Dixit, 579, 607, 608, 610, 613, 621,
    673–5
  Kumari, *see* Kumari
  Lakhia, 590
  Maharaj, 582, 586, 589, 590, 607
  Rao, 590
Kathak Kendra, Delhi, 586
Kathiawar, 16, 35, 65, 505
Kauffman, Ross, 447
Kaur, Nimrat, 510
Kaushalya, 549, 557
Kaveri tract, Madras, 521–2
Kayasthas, 47, 489
Kazi, Badruddin, 595
Keats, John, 498
kebabs, 410, 491, 493, 495
Kennedy, Pringle, 31
Kenya, 315
keraanis, 259
Kerala, 184, 445, 508, 530, 632
Kesari, 10, 21
Key to Theosophy, The (Blavatsky), 33,
    35, 37
khaansamas, 84, 492, 638
Khairuddin, Maulana, 46, 47
Khal Nayak (1993 film), 675
Khaleda Zia, 164, 166

Khalistan movement, 39, 129, 191, 201,
    223, 289, 290, 291
Khalji, Alauddin, 151
Khan Saheb, 119
Khan, Aamir, 600, 675
Khan, Farah, 614
Khan, Imran, 85
Khan, Irrfan, 510, 600, 675–6, 678
Khan, Mehboob, 407, 602, 619, 666
Khan, Nusrat Fateh Ali, 112
Khan, Salim, 604, 620, 628, 671–2
Khan, Salman, 600, 674, 675, 676–7
Khan, Shah Rukh, 464, 600, 630, 631,
    633, 673, 675, 677–8
Khan, Syed Ahmed, 47–50, 53, 110–11
khanaval, 330–31
khandaans, 384, 403
Khanna, Rajesh, 616, 670
khap panchaayat, 36, 291, 416
Khare, Ravindra, 462
khattriyas, 457
khayaal, 586, 619
kheer, 495
khichri, 537
Khilafat movement (1919–24), 35, 41,
    54–60, 70, 79, 81, 138, 214
Khoja Ismailis, 65
Khosla, Raj, 595–6
Khote, Durga, 606
Khudai Khidmatgar, North West Frontier,
    111
Khyber-Pakhtunkhwa, Pakistan, 225
Khyber Pass, 58
King's College London, 399
King's College, Cambridge, 27, 278
Kingdom of God Is Within You, The
    (Tolstoy), 35
Kingfisher beer, 503
Kipling, Joseph Rudyard, 349, 352
Knighton, W., 547
Koh-i-Noor diamond, 212
Kohlapur, 570
Komal Gandhaar (1961 film), 660
Konkan region, 326, 327, 330, 570
Koran Sariph (Naimuddin), 137
Korangi, Sind, 353
Koraput, Orissa, 279
Korom, Frank, 547
kotha, *see* brothels
Krishak Praja Party, 78, 111
Krishna, 23, 198, 199, 462, 582

kuchas, 349
Kudsiya, Begum of Bhopal, 391
Kuka, 468
Kuki people, 390
kulin, 383, 412, 417, 458, 507
Kumar, Ashok, 562
Kumar, Dilip, 600, 614, 666, 669
Kumar, Krishna, 154
Kumar, Neetu, 608
Kumar, Nita, 552, 569
Kumar, Sanjeev, 598
Kumari, Meena, 236, 600, 602, 605, 607,
    622, 668
  dacoit incident (1969), 236
  death (1972), 607
  Pakeezah (1972), 236, 414–15, 539, 540,
    587, 607, 610, 668, 669
  Sahib, Bibi aur Ghulam (1962), 587,
    610, 667–8
Kumbh Mela, 548
Kumbhakaran, 553, 557
kumors, 349
kunba, 369
kung fu, 569, 610, 615, 673
Kunku (1937 film), 591
Kurien, Verghese, 470
Kurmitola Airport, Dacca, 286
Kurnool, Andhra Pradesh, 490
Kurosawa, Akira, 626
kushti, 241, 329, 543, 568–78, 670

laathials, 270
laathis, 188, 228, 231, 232, 260, 313
lacquer work, 317
Lady Sri Ram College, Delhi, 345
Lagaan (2001 film), 616, 676–7
Lahore, Punjab, 112, 120, 341
  architectural heritage, 151, 154, 177
  cuisine, 491, 514
  Defence neighbourhood, 221
  diaspora, 399–400, 596, 605
  earthquakes in, 635
  High Court, 265
  INC session (1900), 17
  migration to, 297
  Museum, 147
  Partition (1947), 282
  Samjhauta Express, 655
  Subzi Mandi, 453
  Wagah–Attari border, 109–10, 655
  wrestling in, 569, 575

Lahore Resolution (1940), 79, 80, 81
Lahore University of Management Sciences
    (LUMS), 410
Lakhia, Kumudini, 590
Lakshman, 549, 550, 551, 552, 554, 556,
    559, 612
Lall, Jessica, 234–5
Lalukhet, Karachi, 353
Lambadis, 294
Lancashire, England, 26, 273
land
  inaam land, 271
  inheritance, 64, 386–90, 392, 401, 402
  middle class and, 508
  population growth and, 324
  reform, 121, 173, 181, 190, 422–3
  waqfs, 67, 81, 271
  zamindaars, see *zamindaars*
Landlady, The (2000 film), 663
langra mangoes, 204
language movements
  Bengali, 127, 136–8, 142–4,
    165, 224
  Hindi, 53, 106–7, 137, 139–40, 141
  Tamil, 129, 133–5, 136, 139–40
  Telegu, 126–7, 131–2, 136
  Urdu, 53, 106, 119, 137, 141–2, 143,
    263
languages, 4, 125–44, 201
  Ahomiya, 336
  Arabic, 4, 9, 45, 64, 137, 245, 461
  Awadhi, 358
  Bengali, *see* Bengali
  Bhojpuri, 17, 160, 213, 214, 334, 337,
    358
  chi-chi, 249, 250
  Devanagiri script, 107, 139
  dialects, 4, 139
  Gujarati, 4, 13, 35, 141
  English, 4, 139, 140–41, 249, 498, 499,
    506
  Hindi, 9, 53, 106, 107, 133, 138,
    139–41, 143, 334, 337, 339, 594
  Kannada, 423
  Malayalam, 4, 133, 138, 594
  Marathi, 4, 10, 21, 50, 127–8, 129, 133,
    138
  Oriya, 132, 334, 339
  Persian, 4, 9, 64, 403
  Rajasthani, 339
  Sadri, 339

languages – *cont.*
  Sanskrit, 4, 11, 22, 133–4, 139, 194,
    195, 245, 383, 401, 460, 461
  Tamil, 4, 126, 129, 133–5, 138, 139–40,
    297, 423, 594
  Telegu, 4, 126–7, 131–2, 133, 138, 140,
    297, 334, 594
  Urdu, *see* Urdu
  Wardha scheme, 138
  Vernacular Press Act (1878), 9, 10
  Vidya Mandir controversy (1937), 139
  white community and, 249
Lanka Dahan (1917 film), 603, 613, 614,
  664
laopatta, 477
Larkana, Sind, 317
lascars, 301, 330–31, 350, 358
lassi, 469
Latin, 245, 258
Latur, Gujarat, 487
Lausanne Conference (1922–3), 81, 342,
  645
Laxman, R. K. 542
Le Corbusier, 282
League of Nations, 525
Lee, Bruce, 569, 615
Leeds, West Yorkshire, 283
legal profession/system, 9, 63, 64, 65, 66,
    171, 244, 317, 400–409
  common law, 244, 402
  criminal law, 9, 244, 415
  Dayabhaaga, 402
  family law, *see* family law
  Ilbert Bill (1883), 10–11, 250
  inheritance law, 64, 386–90, 401–5
  Mitaakshara, 402
  Penal Code (1860), 9, 415
Lehar Pepsi, 587
leisure, 539–633
  alcohol, 273, 330, 497, 503, 541, 547
  Baazigars, 563–8, 605
  cinema, 539–40, 591–633
  dance, 578–91
  drugs, 540, 541, 547
  festivals, 540, 543–63
  secular performances, 563–8
  wrestling, 241, 329, 543, 568–78; *see
    also* wrestling
leopards, 286–8, 427
Letters from a Father to a Daughter
  (Nehru), 178–9

LGBTQ+ people, 406
  gay men, 233, 253, 415–16
  lesbians, 417–18, 441, 444–5
  transgender people, 558, 561
liberalisation, 285, 432, 506, 511, 512–13
liberalism; liberals, 10, 35, 60–69
  Constituent Assembly (1946–50), 88
  constitutionalists, 60–69
  Gandhi and, 36
  imperialism and, 8, 9, 10, 11, 39, 50, 62
  moderates and, 22, 32
  Partition (1947), 261
Lieven, Anatol, 279
life expectancy, 326
Life in a . . . Metro (2007 film), 676
Life of Pi (2012 film), 676
Lihaaf (Chughtai), 418
Limbale, Sharankumar, 483–6
Lincoln's Inn, London, 66, 171, 317
Line of Actual Control (LOC), 639
Linguistic Survey of India (Grierson), 4
literacy, 74, 227, 284, 296, 382–3, 419,
  460, 637–8
Lives of Poets (Sriramamurti), 131
LOC Kargil (2003 film), 632
lock hospitals, 441
Lok Sabha, 198
London, England
  migration to, 314, 318, 320, 321, 356,
    399
  wrestling in, 571
London India Association, 4, 6, 32
London School of Economics, 170, 321,
  656
London Vegetarian Society, 33
Lonely Wife, The (1964 film), 497, 659–60
Lord Sinha Road, Calcutta, 232, 257
Lorea, Carola, 546
Loreto Convent, Darjeeling, 26
Lower Depths, The (Gorky), 665
Lowly City (1946 film), 665
luchis, 381, 382
Lucknow, 232, 394
  Ali brothers in, 56
  All India Muslim Majlis-i-Mushawarat,
    197
  cuisine, 491
  Kahars in, 471
  Kathak in, 582, 586, 589
  Naval Kishore Press, 9
  policing in, 232

prostitution in, 443–4
Rebellion (1857), 7, 213
Lucknow Pact (1916), 68–9, 417
Ludhiana, Punjab, 533, 534
Ludhianvi, Sahir, 618
Lunchbox, The (2013 film), 510, 676
Lutgendorf, Philip, 549, 555, 560, 562
Lutyens, Edwin, 103, 265, 348
Lytton, Edward, 10

'Maa Telegu Tallika' (Sundaraachari),
132
Macaulay, Thomas Babington, 9, 11, 51,
211
Madame Bovary (Flaubert), 677
Madani, Husain Ahmad, 79, 80, 81
Madhya Pradesh, 236, 439
Madras city/Chennai, 32
Andhra state and, 127
coffee in, 511
High Court, 265
language in, 126, 127
migration to, 297
prasaadam protests (1940s–50s), 464
Vaikkom Satyagraha (1924–5), 135, 464
Madras province, 208
armed forces in, 218
film industry, 594, 596
language in, 126, 127, 129, 133, 134–5,
139–40
migration from, 334
Nellore riots (1952), 126–7
policing in, 228
rice production in, 521–2
taxation in, 270, 271
Madras Christian College, 497
madrassas, 44, 53, 138
Madurai, Tamil Nadu, 211, 433
mafias, 226, 599, 601
magicians, 563
mahaars, 492
Mahabharata, 23, 130, 384
Bhagavad Gita, 23, 35, 192–3, 196, 199
Mahadevalar temple, Vaikkom, 135
Mahalanobis, Prasanta Chandra, 278
Mahanagar (1963 film), 660
Maharaj, Achhan, 586
Maharaj, Birju, 582, 586, 589, 590, 607
Maharaj, Shambhu, 586, 590
Maharani Regents, 391
Maharashtra, 127, 595

Mahiuddin Ahmed, 420
Mahmud, Ghaznavid Sultan, 156, 170
Mahmudabad, Raja of, 68, 81–2
Mahratta, 10, 16
Main Hoon Na (2004 film), 614
Maine, Henry Sumner, 244, 401, 402
Maintenance of Internal Security Act
(India, 1971), 188
maistries, 302, 303–4, 310, 313
maize, 491, 517, 524, 529
Malabar Hill, Bombay, 99, 417
Malabar rebellion (1921), 58–60, 70
Malabar teak, 272
malaria, 242, 279, 325
Malaviya, Madan Mohan, 72
Malaya, 215, 301, 310, 311, 318, 530
Malayalam, 4, 133, 138, 594
Malaysia, 318
Malik Ghulam, Muhammad, 170
Malini, Hema, 579, 607–8, 612, 673
malnutrition, 536–8
see also famines
Malta, 318
Malthusianism, 528–9
Mamata Shankar, 660
Mammo (1994 film), 630, 662
Man-eater of Malgudi, The (Narayan), 392
Manasa, 543–7
Mandalay, Burma, 23
Mandi (1983 film), 630, 662, 664
mandis, 453
Mandler, Peter, 130, 144
Mandvi, Gujarat, 574
Manekshaw, Sam, 220
Mangeshkar, Lata, 596, 605, 606, 620
Mangla Dam, 159, 283
mangoes, 204, 478, 480
Manthan (1976 film), 470, 662
Manto, Sadat Hasan, 109, 341, 593, 619
Manusmriti, 135
Maoists, 85, 173, 185, 289, 384
Mapilla Muslims, 58–60, 70
see also Khilafat movement; non-
cooperation movement
Maqbool (2003 film), 676
Maratha Empire (1674–1818), 19, 21–2
Marathi language, 4, 10, 21, 50, 127–8,
129, 133, 138
marijuana, 540, 541, 547
maritime borders, 226
Market (1983 film), 630, 662, 664

Marquis Street, Calcutta, 494
marriage, 338, 364–79, 384
  age of, 20, 338, 366–7, 372–3,
    406, 425
  anuloma marriage, 387
  caste and, 306, 308, 365–6, 368, 371,
    375, 386, 397, 420, 458, 595
  cousins, 369, 423
  divorce, 290, 395, 397, 407–9
  dowries, 419, 423, 439, 447
  Hindu Undivided Family and, 405–6
  honour killings and, 290–91, 416–17
  indentured labour and, 307–8, 310–11,
    396–7
  in-laws, 367, 368–9, 370, 374–6, 405
  kanyadaan, 374, 440
  Karva Chauth, 421
  kinship and, 386, 395, 415, 416
  love and, 386, 412–22
  migration and, 296, 364–79, 395, 396–7,
    423, 424, 458
  natal families, 374, 385, 387, 398–400
  nikaah, 391, 461
  peasant-proletariat households,
    429
  polygamy, 387, 388, 390
  status of wives, 390, 394
  taxation and, 405–6
  virginity and, 315, 374, 375
  weddings, 413, 423, 474, 485–6
  widowhood, 370–71, 395–6, 424
Married Woman (1953 film), 668
Marshall, Thomas, 98–9
martial race theory, 214, 216, 217, 253,
    520, 523
Marwaris, 420, 505, 507
Marx, Karl, 247
Marxism, 19, 73, 186, 205
masons, 358
Masoom (1983 film), 616, 664
Master, the Wife and the Servant, The
    (1962 film), 587, 610, 667–8
Mathur, Nayanika, 287
matrilocal societies, 365
Matthews, V. G., 258
maun vrat, 472
Mauritius, 298, 301, 303–4, 305, 307, 308,
    310
Mauryan Empire (322–187 BCE), 149
Mawdudi, Saiyid Abu-l-Ala, 48, 79, 113,
    114–15, 175, 203

Maya Memsaab (1993 film), 677
Mayo, Katherine, 406–7
Mazagaon docks, Bombay, 324
Mazumdar, Charu, 85, 384, 607
Mazzini, Giuseppe, 193
McDonald's, 512
McLeod, Roderick, 247–8, 251–2
McPherson, Kenneth, 492
Meaning (1982 film), 664
Mecca, 44
Medina, 44, 79, 80
Meerut, 70
Meghe Dhaka Tara (1960 film), 660
Meghnad, 553, 557
mehfil, 621
mehndi, 63
Mehta, Pherozeshah, 1, 4, 8, 32
mehtars, 349
Mehter, Hurroo, 250
memes, 542
Meo people, 644
Merchant, Yahya, 120
merchants, 504–9
Mesopotamia, 55, 147
Messervy, Frank, 266
Metcalfe, Charles, 1st Baron, 51
Methars, 465
Metiabruz, Calcutta, 361, 586
Metro-Goldwyn-Mayer, 598
Mettur, Tamil Nadu, 528
Meyebela (Nasrin), 372
Mia, Babu Lal, 362
microfinance, 285
middle classes, 115, 155, 273, 348, 355,
    362
  domestic servants and, 433–4
  food and, 451, 496–511
  households, 385–6, 397, 410, 414,
    421–2
  merchants, 504–9
Middlemarch (Eliot), 134
Midnapore, West Bengal, 31
Midnight's Children (Rushdie), 127–8
migration, 293–379
  dam building and, 283, 296, 312
  famine and, 295
  ghettos, 357–64
  human trafficking, 314, 319
  indentured labour, 293, 297–311, 318,
    396
  internal, 323–39, 430, 431–6, 496

marriage and, 296, 364–79, 331, 423, 424
nomads, 293–5
overseas diaspora, 297–322
partitions and, 339–56
remittances, 319–20
wrestling and, 576
Military Evacuation Organisation, 92, 93, 644, 645
milk, 466–7, 469–71, 477, 487, 491
Mill, James, 11
millet, 517, 522, 534, 535
Miln, Ken, 249
Minerva, 265
Ministry of Information and Broadcasting, India, 601
Ministry of Relief and Rehabilitation, Pakistan, 118
Minto, Gilbert Elliot-Murray-Kynynmound, 4th Earl, 52, 66, 68
Mir Taqi Mir, 542
miracle plays, 543–63, 609, 611
Mirpur, Kashmir, 283
Mirror of Indigo (Mitra), 9
mishti-doi, 469
Mission Kashmir (2000 film), 614, 625, 628
missionaries, 133, 136, 477
Missionaries of Charity, 469
Mitaakshara, 402
Mitra, Dinabandhu, 9
Mizo uprising (1966), 201, 223
'moderates', 1–2, 19, 73
   Hindu revivalism and, 20–23
   violence and, 2, 23–4
modernisation
   economic, 206, 279–86
   religious, 12, 42, 48, 113, 114
modernist architecture, 120, 282
Modi, Narendra, 203
Mody, Perveez, 418
mohallas, 349–51, 354, 356, 361
Mohamed Ali Jauhar, 54–7, 60, 61
Mohammad bin Qasim, 170
Mohammadi, 138
Mohenjodaro, 147, 150, 156
Mohun, Ram, 157
Moinuddin Chishti, 548
Mokammel, Tanvir, 167
Molesworth, George, 217
Monegar *choultry*, Madras, 520

moneylenders, 121, 285, 303, 350, 434, 443, 466, 505
monopoly on violence, 206, 291
Monsoon Wedding (2001 film), 662
monsoons, 153, 204, 294, 299, 427, 477, 636
   failure of, 58, 182, 324, 334, 517, 523–4, 554
   floods, 635
   Jhampan Mela, 543–7
Montagu, Edwin Samuel, 37, 70
Mookerji, Syama Prasad, 103, 104
moong daal, 459
Moore, Allen, 546
Moradabad, 70
Morley, John, 1st Viscount, 65–6
Morley–Minto Reforms (1909), 52–3
Morocco, 318
mother goddess, nation as, 22, 28, 30, 32, 74
Mother India (Mayo), 406–7
Mother India (1957 film), 407, 602, 605, 619, 666
Mountbatten, Albert Louis Francis, 1st Earl, 82, 89, 92, 261, 646
Movement to Save Childhood, 567
Mr & Mrs '55 (1955 film), 668
Mr 420 (1955 film), 669
Mrinal Sen, 660
Mrityudand (1997 film), 608, 664
Mughal Empire (1526–1857), 58, 63, 101, 207–10
   architectural heritage, 101, 153, 190, 196, 348
   ashraf, 43–4, 112, 489
   cuisine, 491
   dissolution (1857), 43–4, 48
   East India Company, relations with, 208–10
   Kathak and, 581
   miniatures, 150, 588
   music, 586
   Pakistan and, 170
   qaanungos, 256
   Shivaji, conflict with (1657–68), 21
Mughal-e-Azam (1960 film), 603, 670
muhaajirun, 58, 113, 489
Muhajir Qaumi Movement (MQM), 174, 290, 356, 448–9
Muhammad, Prophet of Islam, 46, 48, 54, 79, 80, 113, 175, 328, 489, 490

Muhammad Ali, Chaudhri, 262–3, 642, 645
Muhammadan Anglo-Oriental College, Aligarh, 49, 53, 54
Muhammadan Educational Conference, 50
Muharram, 308, 360, 545
Mujeeb, Muhammad, 102
mujraa, 579, 587
Mukherjee, Debashree, 594
Mukherjee, Madhabi, 660, 663
Mukti Bahini, 160–61, 164, 171, 222, 640
multiplex theatres, 630–31
Mumbai, *see* Bombay/Mumbai
Mumbai Meri Jaan (2008), 227
Munch, Edvard, 341
Murgir French malpoa, 500
Muria people, 420–21
murids, 46
Mussalman Wakf Validating Bill (British India, 1913), 67, 404
music, 112, 365, 578–91, 586–7, 616–21
Music Room, The (1958 film), 585, 660
Muslim League, see All-India Muslim League
Muslim Women Act (India, 1986), 409
Muslims, *see* Islam
Mutiny (1857–8), *see* Rebellion
muttahida qaumiyat (composite nationalism), 55, 76, 79, 102
Muttahida Qaumi Movement (MQM), 174
Muzaffarpur, Bihar, 31
My Experiments with Truth (Gandhi), 33
My Name Is Khan (2010 film), 677
Myers, Ruby, 665
Mymensingh, Bangladesh, 369, 635
Myrdal, Gunnar, 528
Mysore, 43, 210, 239

Naaga Panchami, 544
Naats, 563
nabasak, 355
Nabis, Narendranath, 420
Nadia, Bengal, 14
Nagaland, 184, 223
Nagari Pracharini Sabha, 139
Nagas, 201
Nagpur Session (1920), 40–41
Naicker, Erode Venkatappa Ramasamy, *see* Periyar

Naidu, P. Gopala Rao, 131
Naidu, Sarojini, 62, 417, 585
Naimuddin, Mohammad, 137
Naipaul, Vidiadhar Surajprasad, 308
Nair *tharavads*, 445
Nakhoda Mosque, Calcutta, 398
Namak Haraam (1973 film), 624, 670, 672
Namesake, The (2006 film), 676
Naoroji, Dadabhai, 4, 12–13, 18, 23–4, 27, 63, 65, 166, 182
    drain thesis, 16
    economic nationalism, 18, 166
    at Elphinstone College, 12
    famines, views on, 15–16, 17, 18
    per capita income statistics, 15
    'Poverty of India' (1876), 14
    religion, views on, 23
    violence, views on, 24
Napier, Charles James, 210
Napoleonic Wars (1803–15), 209, 272
Narayan, Jayaprakash, 186–7
Narayan, Rasipuram Krishnaswami, 288, 392
Nargis, 407, 600, 602, 605, 607, 665–6, 668, 669
Narmada river, 534–5
Narsingpur, Madhya Pradesh, 522
Naseeruddin Shah, 664
Nashtanirh (Tagore), 412, 497, 660
Natal, South Africa, 34, 66, 297, 308, 310
Nataraja temple, Chidambaram, 158
Nati Imli, Benares, 554, 555–8
National Conference Party, 639
National Council for Educational Research and Training, 154
National Dairy Development Board, 471
National Health Service, UK, 316, 504
National Museum of India, 146, 148–50
National Museum of Pakistan, 150–51
Nattukottai Chettiars, 318
Natural History Museum, London, 146
Natya Institute of Kathak and Choreography, Bangalore, 590
Natyashastra, 579, 583, 584
Nausherwan the Just, Sassanid King, 121
nautch, 579, 582–3, 586
Naval Kishore Press, 9
Navaratri, 545
Nawabshah, Sind, 317
Nawanagar, 570

Naxalite movement, 85, 185, 202, 234, 384, 476, 480
Nayak (1966 film), 660, 663
Nayyar Hindus, 58
Nayyar, Omkar Prasad, 618
Nayyar, Sushila, 91
Nazarbaug Palace, Mandvi, 574
Nazrul Islam, Chashi, 136
Nazrul Islam, Kazi, 112–13, 137, 143, 542
Neecha Nagar (1946 film), 665
Nehru, Gangadhar, 63–4
Nehru, Jawaharlal, 11–12, 64, 72, 82, 106–8, 186, 201–2
  armed forces, relations with, 219–20
  Babri Mosque and, 154
  'Chacha' kinship term and, 108
  cinema and, 600
  Cold War and, 654
  dam building, 534
  dance and, 585, 589
  death (1964), 108, 177
  Discovery of India (1946), 179
  documentary films and, 156–7
  dress, 106–7
  economic policies, 277
  education, 11–12, 64, 317, 600
  family law and, 290, 408
  fasting, 462
  food policy, 526
  Gandhi assassination (1948), 104–5, 123
  general election (1952), 408
  Hindu right and, 106–8
  Hyderabad annexation (1948), 119, 184, 219, 220, 223
  language, views on, 141, 143, 201
  Letters from a Father to a Daughter (1929), 178–9
  Malthusianism and, 528
  marriage, 417
  Mother India screening (1958), 407
  Muslim League, relations with, 73, 74, 78
  Nehru Report (1928), 75–6, 155
  Pakistan War (1947–8), 103, 123, 219
  Partition (1947), 92, 96, 101, 218, 643, 644, 645
  provincial elections (1936–7), 75
  Rau, relationship with, 259
  socialism, 276–7
Nehru, Kamala, 179

Nehru, Motilal, 62, 63–5, 72, 108
  Brahminical ritual, views on, 64–5, 309, 509
  education, 64
  English language, 64
  Jinnah, relationship with, 70, 71, 72
  legal career, 64, 401
  Lucknow Pact (1916), 69
  Nehru Report (1928), 75–6, 155
  non-cooperation movement (1920–22), 70
  property, 64, 348, 382
  wrestling, 574
Nehru Report (1928), 75, 155
neo-Malthusianism, 528–9
Nepal, 214, 218, 226, 336, 344, 383, 392, 426, 427, 437, 536
New Market, Calcutta, 347
New Wave Cinema, 661
New York, United States, 318
New York Tribune, 247
Newsnight, 326
Nigeria, 597
nihaari, 495
nikaah, 391, 461
Nil Darpan (Mitra), 9
Nirbhaya case (2012), 411–12
Nirula's, 501
Nixon, Richard, 116, 640
No Bed of Roses (2017 film), 676
Noakhali, Bangladesh, 101, 335
non-alignment, 530, 653–4
non-cooperation movement (1920–22), 35, 40–41, 55–6, 60, 61, 70, 186, 190
  Chauri Chaura incident (1922), 41, 59, 228
  Malabar rebellion (1921), 58–60, 70
  see also Khilafat movement; Mapilla Muslims
non-governmental organisations (NGOs), 154, 166, 284, 286, 359
Non-Resident Indians (NRIs), 319–21
non-violence, 32, 35, 39, 41
Nordau, Max, 35
North West Frontier Province, 58, 72, 75, 111–12, 119, 174, 207, 214, 225, 644
nuclear families, 380, 384, 385, 405–6, 410, 413–15, 421–2
nuclear weapons, 199, 656
Nuksh script, 150
Nuzvid, Andhra Pradesh, 387

O'Malley, Lewis Sydney Steward, 245, 466
Objectives Resolution (1949), 120, 123, 203
'Ode to the Motherland' (Chatterjee), 25, 132
Oil and Gas Corporation Ltd., 221
oil crisis (1973), 182, 185
oil shortages (1990–91), 285
ojha, 544
Olof Palme Marg, Delhi, 346
Old Monk rum, 503
Oldenburg, Veena, 442–3
Oliver Twist (Dickens), 501–2
Olivier, Laurence, 558
Olympic Games, 573
'Om', 196
On Compromise (Morley), 66
Onam, 545
Open Letters to Lord Curzon (Dutt), 15, 182, 271
Operation Blue Star (1984), 191, 223, 291
Operation Fair Play (1977), 171, 174, 203
Operation Polo (1948), 119, 184, 219, 220, 268
opium, 541, 547
organised crime, 226, 599, 601
Orientalism, 257
Orissa, 47, 132, 198, 244, 279, 334, 338–9
Orissa Famine (1865), 519
Oriya language, 132, 334, 339
Ornament of the World (1931 film), 664–5
orphans, 625
Osman Ali Khan, Nizam of Hyderabad, 239
Östör, Ákos, 546
Other Side of Silence, The (Butalia), 167–8
Ottoman Empire (1299–1922), 43, 44, 45, 53–5, 57
Oudh, 6, 213, 333, 582, 586
'Our Golden Bengal' (Tagore), 29, 132, 320
Our Lady of Alice Bhatti (Hanif), 452
'overpopulation', 293, 528–9
Oxford University, 49, 63, 121, 179, 245, 497

Paan Singh Tomar (2012 film), 676
paan, 381, 452, 492, 541, 542, 547, 561
paandaan, 452, 497
paanipuri, 503
paapri chaat, 511–12
pablik, 95, 116, 207, 232, 234, 267, 656
padhaan, 426–7, 429, 430

Pagaro, 113
paiks, 270
painters, 593
Pak Stanvac Petroleum Project, 221
Pakeezah (1972 film), 236, 414–15, 539, 540, 587, 607, 610, 668, 669
Pakistan, Dominion of (1947–50)
    armed forces, 218
    Balochistan conflict, 224
    civil service, 263, 265–6
    Constituent Assembly (1947–50), 90, 115, 118, 120
    establishment, *see* Partition
    evacuee property appropriation (1948), 99
    India ordinance (1948), 96
    Inter-Dominion Conference (1948), 642, 646–50
    Islamic state proponents, 114, 118
    Objectives Resolution (1949), 120, 123, 203
    permit system, 96–8
    secularists, 114, 118
Pakistan, Islamic Republic of (1950–), 19, 44, 67, 77, 111–25
    Afghanistan War (2001–21), 223
    anti-imperialism, 654
    armed forces, *see* Pakistan Armed Forces
    Attari–Wagah border, 109–10
    Balochistan conflict, 224–5
    Bangladesh, secession of (1971), *see* Bangladesh Liberation War
    biraadiris, 482
    Bollywood in, 597
    China, relations with, 173
    citizenship laws (1951), 99
    civil service, 263, 265–6
    Cold War and, 653–4
    coup d'état (1958), 116, 125, 278, 282
    coup d'état (1977), 171, 174, 203, 221
    development, 277, 278–9, 280, 285, 289
    enemy property ordinance (1968), 99
    food policy, 528–9
    green revolution (1967–76), 277, 296
    history in, 145, 146, 147–8, 150–51, 155–6, 169–70, 637–8
    Hudood Ordinance (1979), 175, 203
    Indo–Pakistani War (1947–8), 103, 123, 219, 222, 223, 651
    Indo–Pakistani War (1965), 99, 159, 450, 639, 651

Indo–Pakistani War (1971), 84–5, 161, 169, 171, 173, 223, 640–41, 651
Indo–Pakistani War (1999), 199, 641, 652, 656
Indus Water Treaty (1960), 158, 283, 641
Inter-Services Intelligence (ISI), 219, 222, 224, 267, 633, 676
Islamisation, 175–7
judiciary, 235, 289
land reforms (1972), 173
landed clans in, 501
Liaquat Ali Khan assassination (1951), 123–4
liberalisation (1970–80s), 285
migration, 312, 317–18, 321
national dress, 450
nuclear power, 277
nuclear weapons, 656
passports, 98, 312
postage stamps, 159
Rawalpindi Conspiracy (1951), 123
Shia–Sunni sectarianism, 489–90
Simla Accord (1972), 651
Tashkent Declaration (1966), 651
taxation, 274–6
United States, relations with, 173, 529, 654
water supplies, 158, 283, 641
Zakat and Ushr Ordinance (1980), 175
Pakistan Armed Forces, 218, 219, 221–2, 223, 224
    corruption, 221
    development and, 279
    establishment (1947), 266
    generals, 116, 171, 220
Pakistan (Control) Ordinance (India, 1948), 96
'Pakistan ka matlab kyaa?', 115
Pakistan People's Party (PPP), 171
Pakistan Rangers, 221, 223
Pakistan Studies, 155, 169–70, 173, 461
pakka, 465–6, 473, 479, 480
Pal, Bipin Chandra, 29
palanquins, 334, 369, 555
Palashpur, Bangladesh, 369–70, 373
Palestine, 55, 643
Palladian architecture, 273–4, 348, 497
Panama, 317
pandemics, 325
    Covid-19 (2019–23), 494–6, 523
    Spanish flu (1918–20), 324, 496, 523

Pandian, Mathias Samuel Soundra, 135
Pandit, Vijayalakshmi, 179
Pandits, 180, 374, 458
Panjim, 297
Paper Flowers (1959 film), 595, 601, 610, 611, 667
paper state, 259, 260
paraatha, 509
paraathewali gali, 349
paraiah, 457–8
Parashuram, 500
pardesis, 297, 300
parganas, 209
Parinda (1989 film), 614, 625, 627, 628, 673
Parineeta (1953 film), 668
Park Street, Calcutta, 347
Parsai, Hari Shankar, 288
Parsi people, 4, 9, 12, 13, 43, 65, 75, 505
Partition (1947), 82–3, 85, 86, 89–96, 101, 109, 118, 241, 261–3, 339–56, 642–51
    armed forces and, 218–19
    Brahmins and, 475
    children and, 342
    cinema and, 600
    cities and, 279–82, 346–56
    civil service and, 261–6
    communal violence, 91–2, 94, 262, 340–42, 644
    cooperation and, 642–51
    food and, 527–8
    Gama and, 575
    Hindus and, 92–6, 262, 340, 342, 343, 346, 644
    inflation and, 262
    Kashmir and, 86, 103, 639, 640, 644, 645
    Line of Actual Control (LOC), 639
    merchants and, 505
    Muslims and, 92–6, 102, 261, 340, 342, 343, 346–7, 644
    National Conference Party, 639
    princely states and, 268, 644
    property, appropriation of, 98–9, 267, 644–5, 647
    Radcliffe Line, 85, 131, 218, 225, 340, 636, 644
    secular performers and, 563
    Sikhs and, 92–6, 262, 340, 342, 644
    women and, 93–4, 341–2, 344

'Partition' (Auden), 340
Pashto language, 4, 635
Pashtuns, 119, 175, 214, 218, 294, 635
Pasmanda Mahaz, 489
Passage to India, A (Forster), 248, 251
passports, 98, 312, 313, 316, 318
pastoralists, 466–7
Patel, Hirubhai Mulljibhai, 219, 262–3, 470, 642, 647
Patel, Tribhuvandas, 470
Patel, Vallabhbhai, 75, 88–90, 92, 96, 101–2, 104–7, 642–3, 650
Pathaan (2023 film), 633
Pathak, Gobardhan, 309
Pathans, *see* Pashtuns
Pather Panchali (1955 film), 280, 371, 373, 396, 659
Patiala, 570, 575, 615
Patil caste, 483
Patil, Indu, 331
Patil, Smita, 662
Patna, 265
Patna University Students' Union, 185
patriality, 315–16
patriarchy, 33, 108, 211, 324, 382, 383–4, 386, 389–90, 394, 395
   abductions and, 93
   Gandhi and, 36
   indentured labour and, 306, 307
   karta, 384, 401–2, 405
   migrant labour and, 299
   panchaayats, 36, 291, 416
   poverty and, 324
patrilocal societies, 365, 397, 423
patwaaris, 244, 255–6, 264, 271, 286
Patwarbagan, Calcutta, 361–3
peacocks, 487
peasants, 422–36
   indentured labour, 9, 34–5, 37, 66, 293, 297–311, 318, 396
   Malabar rebellion (1921), 58–60, 70; *see also* Khilafat movement
   migration, 296, 329–33, 337, 350, 431–6
   Rebellion (1857–8), 6
   satyagrahas, 37, 106
   taxation and, 15, 16, 17, 25, 36, 77, 269–70, 295
   women, 423–36
pedlars, 294

Peel Commission (1858), 213
Peepli Live (2010 film), 362
Pelsaert, Francisco, 207
Penal Code (1860), 9, 415
peons, 476
people trafficking, 314, 319
People's Health Movement, 535
People's Theatre Association, 592
People's Union for Civil Liberties, 537
peplums, 598
Pepsi, 587
Periyar, 73, 134–5
permit system, 96–8
Persia, *see* Iran
Persian language, 4, 9, 64, 403
Peshawar, 214–15
Petit, Ruttie, 65, 72, 417
phenyl, 315
phirnee, 495
Phizo, Angami Zapu, 201
Phoolan Devi, 237, 424, 436–40
Phule, Jyotiba, 591
Phulmonee case (1889), 20, 436
physical culture, 23
Piliavsky, Anastasia, 237–8
pinda, 463
pirs, 44, 46, 113, 115–16, 172, 665
Pittapore dispute (1899), 386–90, 401
pizza, 501
plague, 324
planning, 277–86
plays, 543–63, 609
poetry, 29, 112, 137, 142, 497, 542
   Bollywood and, 616–21
   ghazal, 586, 618, 619
   tribal peoples, 580–81
Pokhran-II tests (1998), 656
policing, 226–38, 289
poligars, 211
polygamy, 387, 388, 390
Poona University, 405
Poona/Pune, 20, 104, 148
population growth, 293, 323–6, 528–9
Population of India and Pakistan, The (Davis), 528
populism, 171, 181, 188, 199, 202
Port Trust, Karachi, 348
Portugal, 154, 208, 329, 497, 570
post office, 265–6, 347
postage stamps, 145, 159

poverty, 14–19, 324
  BPL cards, 286
  Dalits, 483–8
  grain and, 524
  migration and, 324, 323–39, 430, 431–6
  railways and, 324
  slums, 190–91, 281, 336, 351, 360–64,
    432
  tribal people, 181, 476–81
'Poverty of India' (Naoroji), 14
power cuts, 598
praayaschitt, 64, 309
prasaadam, 451, 464–5
Prasad, Rajendra, 75, 88
Prasad, Vandana, 535–6
Pratijna, 30
prayaag, 105
pregnancy, 424, 430
Premchand, 542, 618, 660
Presidency College, Calcutta, 497
press, 9, 30
  cartoons in, 542
  Emergency (1975–7), 189
  Urdu press, 45
  Vernacular Press Act (1878), 9, 10
Price, Pamela, 389
primogeniture, 384, 391, 402
Princely States, 239–40, 268
  Alwar, 340, 644
  Bahwalpur, 262, 268
  Baroda, 16, 27
  Benares, 247, 333, 586
  Bharatpur, 340, 644
  Bhopal, 44, 391
  Cutch, 16, 505, 616
  Dewas, 253, 391
  Faridkot, 644
  Gwalior, 586
  Hyderabad, *see* Hyderabad
  Jaipur, 589, 590
  Jhalawar, 595
  Kalat, 224, 268
  Kathiawar, 16, 35, 65, 505
  Kohlapur, 570
  Nawanagar, 570
  Oudh, 6, 213, 582
  Partition (1947), 268, 644
  Patiala, 570, 575, 615
  privy purses, 181, 268
  Rajputana, 16, 47, 262, 505, 586
  Rampur, 44, 54, 582

  Rewa, 570
  taxation in, 505
  Travancore, 239
prisoners, 518
Privy Council, 63, 311, 386–90, 404
privy purses, 181
Pro-changers, 60–61
Progressive Writers' Association, 592, 620
Project Tiger, 287
property rights, 274, 290, 384, 386–90,
  402
prostitution, 440–48, 662, 674
  Bollywood depictions, 610–11, 662, 674
  brothels, 246, 440–48, 662
  family law and, 395, 396
  Mayo on, 406
  migration and, 431, 433
  nautch and, 582–3
  red light districts, 246, 396, 441, 446,
    448
  tawaifs, 440, 443, 674
'provincialism', 117, 119, 124, 128–9, 267
Public Law 480 (US, 1954), 277–8, 529,
  533
Puja, 435
Pune, *see* Poona
Punjab, 37
  Amritsar massacre (1919), 38–40, 188
  army and, 218, 219
  Bengali Brahmins in, 47
  bhangra, 566, 579
  Canal Colonies, 242
  caste in, 459, 465, 482
  Communal Award (1932), 78
  Delhi Proposals (1927), 72
  East India Company conquest (1849),
    212
  martial race theory and, 217
  Partition (1947), 82–3, 91–2, 241,
    340–43, 637, 644, 645
  pirs in, 113, 115–16
  policing in, 227
  qissa, 112
  Rowlatt Satyagraha (1919), 37–8, 39
  stereotypes, 241
  Subah movement (1947–66), 129
  taxation in, 270
  Unionist Party, 111
  wrestling in, 570, 575–6
Punjab Boundary Force, 92, 644
Punjab Subah movement (1960–61), 129

Punjabi language, 4, 129
Purana Qila, Delhi, 152
Pure, The (1972 film), 236, 414–15, 539, 540, 587, 607, 610, 668, 669
Puzzle (2018 film), 676
Pyaasa (1957 film), 595, 610, 667

qaanungos, 244, 254, 256, 264, 271
Qadiyanis, 490
qawwaali, 112, 619, 665
qissa, 112
Queens, New York, 318
queer people, *see* LGBTQ+
Quetta, Balochistan, 119, 635
Quilt, The (Chughtai), 418
Quit India movement (1942–5), 190
Quran, 4, 46, 48, 137, 150, 203, 368, 373, 461
Qutub Minar, Delhi, 151

Raag Bhairav, 620
raag, 619, 620, 669
raajsik, 464, 480, 495
Raakhee, 673
Raas Lila, 582
Raatparider Katha (2002 documentary), 431
racism, 7, 10–11, 19, 62, 89, 246
Radcliffe, Cyril, 262, 636, 644
Radcliffe Line, 85, 131, 218, 225, 340, 636, 644
Radha, 582
Rae Bareilly, Uttar Pradesh, 70
Rafi, Mohammed, 616
ragi, 517, 522, 524
Raha, Amar, 204, 286
Raheja, Gloria, 415, 429
Rahman, Allah Rakha, 619, 678
Rahman, Mujibur, 83, 125, 160, 162, 171, 224, 283, 652
Rahnumai Mazdayasnan Sabha, 12
Rai, Aishwarya, 608, 609, 621–2, 663, 674
Rai, Lala Lapat, 38
railways, 2, 5, 44, 58, 295–6, 326–7, 333
	deforestation and, 272, 295, 296
	food and, 515, 516
	labourers and, 300
	poverty and, 324
	Rebellion (1857–8), 58, 241, 333
	taxation and, 16, 268, 274
	tribal people and, 294, 295–6

Raisina Hill, Delhi, 265, 348
raiyatwaari system, 270, 276
Raja Harishchandra (1913 film), 594, 603, 664
Rajagopalachari, Chakravarti, 139
Rajasthan, 93, 196, 338, 429, 595
Rajasthani language, 339
Rajputana, 16, 47, 262, 505, 586
Rajputs, 459
Rajshahi, Bangladesh, 376
Rakhi, 398
Ram, 38, 135, 196, 198, 200–201, 291, 319, 549–63, 611–14
Ram aur Shyam (1967 film), 614
Ram Navami, 38
Ram Rajya, 554
Ram sheelans, 200–201, 319
Rama Rao, Raja, 386–90, 401
Ramabai, Pandita, 460
Ramachandran, Maruthur Gopala Menon, 596
Ramamurti, 570
Ramanujan, S., 278
Ramayana, 135, 549–63, 569, 576, 577, 611–14, 626, 632
Ramazan, 494–6
Ramcharitmanas (Tulsidas), 549, 552, 556, 557, 613
Ramlila, 198, 539, 545, 549–63, 607
Ramnagar, Benares, 555, 557, 560, 561, 562
Rampur, 44, 54, 582, 589
Rana Khagda Samsher, 392
Ranade, Mahadev Govind, 13
Ranga Iyer, C. S., 407
Rangoon, Burma, 43, 136
Rangpur, Bengal, 30
Ranjit Singh, Sikh Maharaja, 151, 211–12
Rao, Maya, 590
Rao, Nikhil, 421
Rao, P. Raghunadha, 140
Rao, P. V. Narasimha, 291
Rashtrapati Bhavan, Delhi, 148–9
Rashtriya Swayamsevak Sangh (RSS), 72, 104, 105, 194–201
Rasna, 495
Ratarati (Parashuram), 500
Rath Yaatra (1990), 198–9, 200, 655

ration shops, 529
Ratnagiri, Maharashtra, 193, 299
Ratnam, Mani, 678
Rau, Benegal Narsing, 259, 408
Ravan, 135, 551–4, 557, 559, 612, 613, 614, 626
Ravi river, 283
Rawalpindi Conspiracy (1951), 123
Rawalpindi, Punjab, 91, 282, 290, 291, 635
Ray, Ajit Nath, 183
Ray, Kedarnath, 5
Ray, Satyajit, 534, 542, 659–60
    Aparajito (1956), 327, 461, 565, 659
    Apur Sansar (1959), 619, 659, 663
    Aranyer Din Ratri (1970), 660, 663
    Ashani Sanket (1973), 521
    Charulata (1964), 497, 659–60
    Devi (1960), 663
    Jalsaghar (1958), 585, 660
    Mahanagar (1963), 660
    Nayak (1966), 660, 663
    Pather Panchali (1955), 280, 371, 373, 396, 659
    Seemabaddha (1971), 663
    Shatranj ke Khilari (1977), 582, 590, 660
Ray, Sovana, 420
Ray, Sukumar, 130
Raza Ali Khan, Nawab of Rampur, 589
Reading, Rufus Daniel Isaacs, 1st Marquess, 71
Rebellion (1857–8), 6–7, 10, 20, 43–4, 45, 48, 50, 63, 155, 238
    arts and, 586
    Delhi and, 7, 43, 44, 63, 190, 586
    elites and, 269
    householders and, 400
    information panic and, 240
    middle classes and, 155
    military reform and, 213, 214
    punishment of rebels, 238
    railway building and, 241
    taxation and, 271
Red Fort, Delhi, 43, 153, 215
red light districts, see prostitution
Redford, Robert, 146
Reejhsinghani, Aroona, 513

Rees, Thomas Wynford 'Pete', 92
refugee cities, 279–82, 346–56
    Bombay, 349, 353, 603
    Calcutta, 281, 346, 347–51, 352, 353, 354–6
    Dacca, 346, 358–60
    Delhi, 280, 281, 346, 352, 353
    Karachi, 87, 95, 118, 281, 282, 347, 352, 353, 356
refugees, Burma citizenship law (1948), 311–12
refugees, Bangladesh War (1971), 160, 165, 297, 357–60
refugees, post-Partition (1947), 91–100, 113, 118, 262–3, 267, 296–7, 339–56, 642
    cities and, 279–82, 346–56
    development and, 279–82
    dispersal efforts, 279–80, 353
    evacuees, 94–100, 644–5, 647, 649
    as muhaajirun, 113, 263, 489
    property, appropriation of, 98–9, 267, 644–5, 647
    squatter colonies, 94–6, 354–6
    Urdu and, 263–4
    women, abduction of, 93–4
Rege (2014 film), 235
Rehman, Waheeda, 579, 594, 595, 600, 601, 607, 610, 618, 667, 668
Rekha, 154, 444, 588, 608, 673
Reliance, 508
religious drama, 543–63, 609, 611
rentiers, 350
Report of the Indian Cinematograph Committee, 612
Republic Day, 1, 145, 158
Research and Analysis Wing (RAW), 633, 676
returnees, 655
Réunion, 304
Rewa, 570
rice, 427, 456, 465, 473, 491, 516–27
    army rations, 523
    Brahmins and, 523
    Burmese imports, 337, 491, 520, 521–2, 525
    communism and, 530
    IR8 variety, 530–32
    Japonica Indica, 532
    mills, 521–2
    tribal people and, 477, 479, 480–81

rice water, 424, 477
Rice, Condoleezza, 176
Richardson, John, 403
Right to Food Movement, 537, 567
ringtones, 622
Ripon, George Robinson,
    1st Marquess, 10
Rivera, Diego, 341
rivers, 279
    Ganges dispute, 652–3
    Indus dispute, 158, 283, 528,
        641, 651
    see also dams
Rizwanur Rahman, 420
roads, 5, 44, 221, 274
Roberts, Gregory, 363
Rohilkhand, Uttar Pradesh, 333
Rohilla, 44
Rohingyas, 312
Roja (1992 film), 632, 678
Rojulu Maraayi (1955 film), 594
Roller, Benjamin, 571
Roshan, Hrithik, 614
Roti, kapdaa aur makaan, 172, 450
rotis, 429, 491, 523
Round Table Conferences (1930–32), 74
Rourkela, Orissa, 338, 339
Rowlatt Act (British India, 1919), 37–8,
    39, 188
Roy, Bidhan Chandra, 108
Roy, Bimal, 619
Roy, Geeta, 595
Royal Academy, London, 146–7, 148
Royal Commission on Labour (1929), 336
Ruha, Bibi, 376
Ruskin, John, 35
Russian Empire (1721–1917), 25, 43, 45
Ruswa, Muhammad Hadi, 444, 673

Saad Akbar Babrak, 123–4
saatvik, 464, 480, 495
Sabarmati Ashram, Ahmedabad, 126
Sadar, Karachi, 348
Sadiq, D. M., 669
Sadri, 339
Safavid Empire (1501–1736), 43
Safdarjang, 153
Sahaj Paath (Tagore), 29, 130
Saharanpur, 70
Sahib, Bibi aur Ghulam (1962 film), 587,
    610, 667–8

Sahni, Balraj, 618, 619
sahookar, 303
Sai Baba, 332
Saivism, 134
sajjada nashins, 115–16
Sakuntalam (Kalidasa), 134
Salaam Bombay! (1988 film), 675–6
sales taxes, 273, 274
saliva, 474
Salt Lake, West Bengal, 353
Salt Tax, 122
Sambhalpuri Oriya, 339
Samjhauta Express, 655
samosas, 511
Samyukta Maharashtra Samiti (1956–60),
    127–8
Sand in the Eye (2003 film), 663
Sandesh, 257
Sandhurst military academy, Berkshire,
    116, 122, 266
Sandhya, 30
Sandhya, Totaram, 302
Sandwip, Bangladesh, 335
Sangam poetry, 542
Sangeet Natak Akademi, Delhi, 586, 590
Sankalia, Hasmukh Dhirajlal, 148
Sanskrit, 4, 11, 22, 194, 245, 382–3, 401
    Bengali and, 195
    Brahmins and, 4, 139
    Hindi and, 53, 139
    script, 53, 139
    shastras, 4, 461
    Tamil and, 133–4, 136
    women scholars, 460, 461
Sanskritisation, 459, 488, 489
Santiniketan, Bolpur, 28–9, 179, 414
Sapru, Tej Bahadur, 62–3, 71, 72
sapure, 544–5
Saraswati river, 105
Saraswati Shishu Mandirs, 195
Saraswati, Dayanand, 22, 468
Sarda Act (1929), 406, 425, 436
    see also age of consent debates
Sardar Sarovar dam, 534–5
saris, 63, 372, 381, 384, 413, 427, 434,
    435, 445, 450, 497, 512
Sarkar, Sipra, 435
Sarkar, Tanika, 462
Sasanian Empire (224–651), 121
Satan, 557
Satanic Verses, The (Rushdie), 407

Sathyu, Mysore Shrinivas, 661
Satkar, Maruti Gyandeo, 332
satyagraha, 35–6, 37
Savarkar, Vinayak, 74, 104, 193, 194
Savile Row, 57, 65
Sayaji Rao Gaekwad III, Maharaja of
  Baroda, 27
Scheduled Castes, 482, 489, 564
Scheduled Tribes, 476
Schreffler, Gibb, 565
Scorching Winds (1973 film), 494
Scream (Munch), 341
Seal, Anil, 250
Secret Garden, The (Burnett), 325
secular performances, 563–8
secularism, 114–15, 193–4, 197
seed banks, 535
Seedling (1974 film), 661, 664
Seemabaddha (1971 film), 663
Seepree, Himachal Pradesh, 547, 548
sehri, 494, 495
Self-Respect movement (1925), 135
Selimpore, Calcutta, 357–8
semen, 576
Sen, Amartya, 320, 536
Sen, Keshub Chandra, 137, 582–3
Sen, Samita, 310, 431, 435
Sengupta, Nilanjana, 435
sepoys, 209, 213, 214–16, 247, 523
Serampore Mission Press, 136
Serene (1971 film), 616, 670
Serpent Mother (1985 documentary), 546
Seth, Bishen Chandra, 106
Seth, Vikram, 423, 501, 540
seva, 507
Seven Samurai (1954 film), 626
sex; sexuality, 541
  cross-racial relationships, 250–51, 253
  dance and, 579, 582–3, 587
  incest, 368
  LGBTQ+, 233, 253, 406, 415–16,
    417–18, 444–5, 558
  modernisation and, 281
  prostitution, *see* prostitution
  venereal disease, 406
  virginity, 315, 374, 375
  wrestling and, 576
  zina (extramarital sex), 203
sex ratios, 424–5
shaadi, 391
shaakhas, 195

shaamiyanas, 561
Shaan (1980 film), 614
shaayar, 619, 621, 661, 671
Shab-e-Baraat, 357
Shackles (1973 film), 603–4, 610, 620,
  625, 627, 628
Shadow Lines, The (Ghosh), 346, 378,
  422, 502
Shah Bano Begum, 290, 409
Shah Commission (1977), 190
Shah Jahan, Mughal emperor, 153
Shah Jalal, 113
Shah, Naseeruddin, 662
Shahajanabad, Delhi, 43, 101, 190
Shahbad, 333
Shahid Hamid, Syed, 266
Shaivism, 550
Shakespeare, William, 347, 498
shalwaar kameezes, 434, 435, 512
Shanbhag, Vivek, 508
Shankar, Ravi, 595, 665
Shankar, Uday, 595
Shantaram (Roberts), 363
Shariat Act (British India, 1937),
  407
Sharma, Pradeep, 235–6
shastras, 4, 461
Shatranj ke Khilari (1977 film), 582, 590,
  660
Shatrughn, 549, 556
Shaukat Ali, 54–7, 60, 61, 70
shehnaai, 365
Sheikh *ashraf*, 489
Sheikh Siddiquis, 489
Sheikhupura, Punjab, 92
Shell, 284
Sher Shah Suri, 152
Sher-Gil, Amrita, 417–18
Shia Islam, 65, 68, 81, 175–6, 224, 242,
  308, 489–90, 545
shikasta, 247–8
Shinde, Tarabai, 460
Shirdi, Maharashtra, 332
Shire, Henry, 297–8
Shishu Mandir, 196
Shiv Sena, 127, 129
Shiva, 550
Shiva, Vandana, 532
Shivaji, Chhatrapati of the Maratha
  Empire, 19, 21–2
Shob Charitro Kalponik (2009 film), 663

Sholay (1975 film), 236–7, 604, 620, 622, 670, 672, 673
  dance sequences, 607
  fight sequences, 615
  friendship in, 539–40, 621, 623–4, 625
  Holi scenes, 624
  inner dualism, 625, 626
  Jai character, 604, 612, 622, 624, 625, 629
  music, 597
  Ramayana and, 612
  suicide and, 419
  weather and, 598
  'Yeh Dosti', 621, 623
Shonar Bangla, 29, 132, 320
shootings, 234–5
shoshur-baari, 374
'Should I Join the Movies?' (Apte), 591–2, 606
Shree 420 (1955 film), 669
Shroff, Jackie, 673
shudras, 457, 458
Sidhwa, Rustom, 89
Sikh Empire (1799–1849), 151, 211–12
Sikhism; Sikhs, 39
  armed forces and, 214, 218
  caste and, 482
  cow protection movements, 468
  diaspora, 37, 321
  Gandhi assassination (1984), 191, 197, 345
  Golden Temple, 38, 39, 109, 191, 223, 291
  gurdwaaras, 86, 283, 340, 342, 345
  Khalistan movement, 39, 129, 191, 201, 223, 289, 290, 291
  Partition (1947), 93, 94, 95, 262, 340–41, 644
  Punjabi Subah movement (1947–66), 129
Silsila (1981 film), 154, 608, 672
silsilas, 45
Simla, Himachal Pradesh, 70–71, 250
  Muslim Deputation (1906), 52, 68
  railway links, 333
Simla Accord (1972), 651
Simon Commission (1928), 72–3
Sind
  British conquest (1843), 210
  Delhi Proposals (1927), 72
  diaspora, 317

fishing in, 221
hijrat (1920), 58
kafis in, 112
Karachi, capital status of, 263
  merchants, 317, 434
  Nehru Report (1928), 75
  Partition (1947), 86, 87, 89, 93, 340, 343
  pir cults in, 113
Sindworkis, 317–18
Singapore, 214, 215, 321, 322
Singh Pandey, Jyoti, 411–12
Singh Roy family, 348
Singh, Babli, 290–91
Singh, Baldev, 93
Singh, Bhagat, 40, 41–2
Singh, Charan, 75, 107
Singh, Dara, 575–6, 577, 602, 615
Singh, Diwan, 84–5, 146, 169, 183, 185, 188, 196, 455
Singh, Gurmeet, 342
Singh, Khushwant, 341
Singh, Madho, 569
Singh, Mangal, 341–2
Singh, Manmohan, 432
Singh, Manoj, 290–91
Singh, Mohan, 454–5, 514, 622
Singh, Sampuran, 92
Singh, Sant Fateh, 129
Singh, Sarvan, 565
Singh, Sib, 216
Singh, Tara, 129
Singh, Thakur Hanuman, 121
Singh, Umed, 437
Singh, Vishwanath Pratap, 436
Sinha, Satyendra Prasanna 1st Baron, 348
Sino–Indian War (1962), 639
sipahis, see sepoys
Sippy, Ramesh, 626
sirdaars, 350
Sita, 135, 550, 551, 552, 554–5, 557, 611, 612, 613
Sivakasi, Tamil Nadu, 561
slavery, 14, 273, 293, 301, 302
  concubines, 387, 390, 391
  daasis, 387, 389, 390, 391
  Dalits and, 483
  domestic servants and, 385
  kachua wives, 390
  see also human trafficking; indentured labour

Sleeman, William Henry, 212
Slumdog Millionaire (2008 film), 676, 678
slums, 190–91, 281, 336, 351, 360–64, 432, 492
smuggling, 206, 226, 636
Smyrna, 55
snake masters, 544–5
social democrats, 73
socialism, 35, 73, 115, 123, 276
Solvyns, Franz Balthazar, 543, 546
Somerville College, Oxford, 179
Sometimes (1976 film), 610, 614, 623, 672, 673
Somnath, Orissa, 198
Sonagachi, Calcutta, 446
Song of the Road (1955 film), 280, 371, 373, 396, 659
Sora people, 420
sorghum, 522, 535
    cholum, 517–18, 524
    jowaar, 484, 524, 534, 537
South Africa, 6, 34, 66, 297–8, 301, 308, 310, 643
Southeast Asia Treaty Organization, 654
Southern Avenue, Calcutta, 352
Soviet Union (1922–91), 176, 277, 278, 597, 653–4
space–time contraction, 326
spaghetti westerns, 626
Spanish flu pandemic (1918–20), 324, 496, 523
Sparsh (1980 film), 664
Special Marriages Act (India, 1954), 420
Spring Will Come Again (1966 film), 668
squatters, 94–6
Sri Lanka, 223, 301, 311
Sri Parthasarathi Swami Temple, Madras, 464
Srinagar, Jammu and Kashmir, 635
Srinivas, Mysore Narasimhachar, 458, 459
Sriramamurti, Gurujada, 131
Sriramulu, Potti, 126
St Paul's School, London, 27
St Stephen's College, Delhi, 174, 497
stamp duty, 273–4
staple grains, 524
    bajra, 524, 534, 537
    barley, 517, 522, 524
    maize, 491, 517, 524, 529
    millets, 19, 517, 518, 522, 534, 535
    ragi, 517, 522, 524

rice, *see* rice
    sorghum, *see* sorghum
    wheat, *see* wheat
Stardust, 609
starvation, *see* famine
state, 204, 205, 207
State Language Day, 127
Statesman, The, 31, 418
'steel frame', 243–4, 253, 258, 263, 264, 267
sterilisation, 190, 281
stipends, 401, 403, 404
Strachey, John, 15
street vendors, 87, 231–2, 352, 453, 503, 511–13
stupaas, 265
sub-castes, *see* jati
Subarnarekha (1962 film), 660
Subzi Mandi, Lahore, 453
succession, 386–90, 401, 438
sudra, 355
suffragettes, 310
Sufism, 46, 58, 112, 113
sugar plantations, 293, 301–11, 396
Suhrawardy, Huseyn Shaheed, 60, 120
suicide
    farmers, 362, 386
    indentured labourers, 305–6
    Qutub Minar and, 151
    Partition (1947), 342
    Tamil language movement, 129
Suitable Boy, A (Seth), 423, 501, 540
Sukkur Barrage, 350
Sulochana, 665
Sultan Jahan, Begum of Bhopal, 391
Sultanpuri, Majrooh, 618
Sumitra, 549
Summary of the History of the Andhra Language (Naidu), 131
Sumo wrestling, 572
Sundaraachari, Sankamrambadi, 132
Sundarban Islands, 636
Sundari, Sushila, 566
Sunlight on a Broken Column (Hosain), 101, 394, 400
sunna, 493
Sunni Islam, 65, 68, 175, 308, 357, 489–90
supertaxes, 273
Supreme Court, India, 312, 409
Sur Empire (1538–56), 152
Suraiyya Begum, 420

Surat Session (1907), 1, 2, 13, 19, 20,
    23, 32
Surf, 471
Surma river, 333
Surupnakha, 551, 552, 557, 558, 561
Sutlej river, 283
Sutoris, Peter, 157
swadeshi movement (1905–8), 22, 24–31,
    35, 52, 61, 371, 381, 412
Swadeshi Samaj (Tagore), 28
Swaminathan, Mankombu Sambasivan,
    531
Swann, R. S., 244
Swapnabhumi (2007 documentary), 167
swaraj, 59, 72
Swarajya party, 60, 71
Swat, 225
Sweden, 220–21, 605
sweetmeats, 257, 349, 548
Syed *ashraf*, 489
Sylhet, Bangladesh, 113, 318, 320, 333,
    335, 399, 635
Symington, D., 254–5
Syndicate, 180, 181
Syria, 55

taamsik, 464, 480, 495
taar, 496
Tabela Lota Kona, Jharkhand, 476–81
tablaa, 587, 589
Tablighi Jamaat, 79
Tagas, 458, 466
Tagore, Debendranath, 258
Tagore, Dwarkanath, 258
Tagore, Rabindranath, 28, 136, 143, 258,
    517, 542, 571
    Amritsar massacre (1919), 39
    Bengali language and, 29, 130, 136, 143
    Chokher Bali (1903), 663
    'Dui Bigha Jomi', 618
    on households, 414
    Ghare Baire (1916), 412
    Kabuliwala (1892), 294
    Nashtanirh (1901), 413, 497, 660
    and nationalism, 28
    Nazrul Islam, influence on, 112
    Sahaj Paath, 29, 130
    Santiniketan school, 28–9, 179
    Swadeshi Samaj, 28
Tagore, Satyendranath, 257
Tagore, Sharmila, 663, 670

tailors, 349, 358, 361
Taj Hotel, Bombay
    Machan, 500
    terror attack (2008), 226
takht, 589
talcum powder, 512
Taliban, 176
Tamil language, 4, 126, 129, 133–5, 138,
    139–40, 297, 423, 594
Tamil Nadu, 140
Tamil people, 50
    Brahmins, 5–6, 459, 469, 473, 475, 491,
        515–16
    kallars, 211
    in Sri Lanka, 223, 311
    Telegu-speakers and, 126
Tamiltay, 133, 135, 140
Tandon, Purushottam Das, 106
tandoori culture, 491
Tangail, Bangladesh, 344, 635
Tangier, Morocco, 318
Tangra, Calcutta, 361, 500
Tanjore, Madras, 522
Tarantino, Quentin, 627
Tarikh-i-Firoz Shahi (Barni), 156
Tashkent Declaration (1966), 651
Tasty Dishes from Waste Items
    (Reejhsinghani), 513
tawaifs, 440, 443, 674
Tax (2001 film), 616, 676–7
taxation, British rule, 16, 77, 260, 268–74,
    294, 394, 466
    agriculture, 16, 17, 269, 271, 274, 276,
        295
    armed forces, funding of, 36, 214
    chaukidaari tax, 227
    civil service and, 243, 244
    Hindu Undivided Family and, 405–6
    income taxes, 274
    parganas, 209
    supertaxes, 273
    vice taxes, 273, 275
    waqfs and, 67, 403, 404
taxation, India, Republic of, 274–6
taxation, Pakistan, Republic of, 274, 276
tea, 26, 293, 301, 336, 381, 502
teak, 272
Teenmurti House, Delhi, 141, 528
Teesta river, 344, 382
Tejpal Gokuldas Boarding House,
    Bombay, 10

Telegu, 4, 126–7, 131–2, 133, 138, 140, 297, 334, 594
    Nellore riots (1952), 126–7
Temple, Richard, 518
Temples of Tomorrow, 158
Teota, Bangladesh, 348
Teresa, Mother, 469
terrorism, 28, 30–32, 57
    Anushilan Samity (1900s), 30–31
    Bollywood and, 614, 628, 632, 676, 677, 678
    Bombay attacks (2008), 226
terylene, 512
textile industry, 25, 327–33
Tezaab (1988 film), 613, 675
Thackeray, Bal, 127
thakur ghar, 375
Thakurs, 459
Thamali, Punjab, 342
Thanawi, Ashraf Ali, 79, 368, 370, 461
Thanda Gosht (Manto), 341
tharavads, 445
Theatre Street, Calcutta, 347
Theosophy, 33, 35, 37, 583, 585
There Was a Guy Called Tiger (2012 film), 632–3, 676
thhelawaalas, 453
thika tenants, 361
Thimayya, Kodandera Subayya, 220
Thirsty (1957 film), 595, 610, 667
'This Friendship', 621, 623
This or That (1954 film), 618, 668
Thoa Khalsa, Punjab, 342
Thrace, 55
3 Idiots (2009 film), 614, 675, 677
thuggee, 212
Tibet, 225–6
tiffin boxes, 509–11
Tiger Zinda Hai (2017 film), 676
tigers, 382, 427, 566, 636
Tilak, Bal Gangadhar, 1, 10, 13, 19, 20–22, 23, 70
    Age of Consent Act (1891), 20–21, 406
    Gita Rahasya (1915), 192–3, 194
    Hindu nationalism, 21–2, 23
Tiljala, Calcutta, 361
Times of India, 542
Tipu, Sultan of Mysore, 43, 210, 239
Tipperah, 390

tiski, 580
Titagarh, Calcutta, 334
Titli (2002 film), 663
Tiwari, Ramanand, 228–9
'Toba Tek Singh' (Manto), 109
tobacco, 273, 362, 381, 428, 541
Todi, Priyanka, 420
Tolstoy, Leo, 35
Tower Hamlets, London, 318
Town Hall Camp, Dacca, 358–60
'Train Lady', 377–9
Train to Pakistan (Singh), 341
Traitor (1973 film), 624, 670, 672
transgender people, 558, 561
transnationalism, 321
Trap (1952 film), 668
Travancore, 239
Treaty of Sèvres (1920), 55, 57
tribal peoples
    Baiga, 480
    in Bangladesh, 343
    Bengal Famine (1943), 337
    dance, 578, 579–81
    food and, 181, 451, 476–81
    forests and, 296, 299, 476
    Gonds, 369, 374
    hunter-gatherers, 273, 390, 476–81
    jhum cultivation, 273, 296, 479–80
    migration, 337, 296, 299
    Muria, 420–21
    poverty, 181, 477
    Sora, 420
Trinidad, 306, 308
Trinity College, Cambridge, 50, 64, 130, 198, 250, 260, 278, 317, 320, 507, 530
tuberculosis, 67, 119
Tudor revival architecture, 348
Tukoji Rao Puar III, Maharaja of Dewas, 253, 391, 392, 412, 418
Tully, Margaret, 567
tulsi plant, 196
Tulsidas, 549, 552, 556, 557, 613
tumblers, 563, 566
Tunisia, 318
Turkey, 55, 57, 81, 342, 488
Turkic cuisine, 490, 491
Turkic languages, 297
Turkman Gate, Delhi, 191, 192, 360
Two Bighas of Land (1953 film), 299, 602, 603, 618, 619, 666

Uchalya, 487
Uganda, 315
ulema, 46, 49, 55, 56, 114, 115, 137
Ultadanaga, Calcutta, 361
ummaa, 43
Umrao Jaan (1981 film), 444, 587, 588, 590, 608, 673
Umrao Jan Ada (Ruswa), 444, 673
Undefeated (1956 film), 327, 461, 565, 659
unemployment, 353–4
Unilever, 471
Unionist Party, 111
Unishe April (1994 film), 630, 663
United Arab Emirates, 318
United Kingdom
    migration to, 311, 312–16, 318, 320, 321–2, 399, 504
    see also British Raj; East India Company
United Nations, 160, 179, 223, 639, 654
United Provinces, 47, 214, 334, 358, 366
United States
    Afghanistan War (2001–21), 223
    Bangladesh Liberation War (1971), 640
    Central Intelligence Agency (CIA), 189
    Cold War (1947–91), 530, 653–5
    Hollywood, 597, 598–9, 601
    migration to, 316–17, 320–21, 504
    Pakistan, relations with, 173–4, 176, 223
    Public Law 480 (1954), 277–8, 529, 533
University College London, 12, 15, 146
University of Chittagong, 285
University of Kerala, 531
Unto This Last (Ruskin), 35
upma, 515
urbanisation, *see* cities
Urdu, 4, 9, 45, 46, 100, 111, 113, 133, 137, 138, 141–4
    Bangladesh and, 129, 144, 160, 358
    Bengali and, 119, 129, 137, 143–4
    cinema, 596, 618, 620
    East Bengal and, 159, 160
    ghazal, 586
    Hindi and, 53, 106, 107, 135, 139, 142
    Pakistani national language, 141–2, 263
    postage stamps and, 159
    Ramlila and, 557
    refugees and, 263–4
    registers, 247
    shikasta, 247–8

Usmani, Shabbir Ahmed, 80
Utsab (2000 film), 663
Uttar Pradesh, 106, 107, 185, 231, 237, 366, 429, 475
Uttarakhand, 287–8, 475
Uzbekistan, 317

vaccinations, 280
Vaikkom Satyagraha (1924–5), 135, 464
Vaishnavism, 550, 559, 582
vaishyas, 457, 460
Vajpayee, Atal Bihari, 198, 199
Valmiki, 549
Valmiki, Om Prakash, 458, 466
Vancouver, British Columbia, 37
varnashramadharma, 457
Vasant Kunj, Delhi, 346
vasectomies, 281
Vatsyayan, Kapila, 585, 589
Veer-Zaara (2004 film), 677
vegetarianism, 33, 134, 459, 475, 507
Vellalar caste, 134
Vellankis, 387
Vellodi, Mullath Kadingi, 219
Vernacular Press Act (British India, 1878), 9, 10
Vested Property Ordinance (Bangladesh, 1972), 100
Vibhishan, 553
vice taxes, 273, 275
Viceroy's House, Delhi, 265, 348
Vickram Mullah, 437, 439
Victoria & Albert Museum, 210
Victoria Terminus, Bombay, 326–7
Victoria, Queen of the United Kingdom, 7–9, 57, 62, 211, 212, 240, 333, 400
Vidya Mandir programme (1937), 139
Villain (1993 film), 675
Vim, 471
Virgagan, 297–8
virginity, 315, 374, 375
Vishnu, 135, 547, 548, 550, 556
Vithal, Master, 665
Voltaire, 455
vyaas, 560, 561

Wacha, Dinshaw, 9, 16
Wagah–Attari border, 109–10, 655
Wah, Punjab, 91
Wajid Ali Shah, Nawab of Oudh, 582, 586

Walker, Johnny, 595, 611, 618
Wall Street Crash (1929), 74, 505
Wall, The (1975 film), 227, 604, 610, 620, 627, 628, 629, 671, 673
waqfs, 67, 81, 271, 403, 404
Wardha scheme, 138
Waris Shah, 112
washermen, 349
wataniyat, 48
water supplies, 158, 283, 349, 641
Wazir Hasan, Syed, 68
Waziristan, 225, 252
Weber, Max, 205
weddings, 413, 423, 474, 485–6
Wellesley, Richard, 209
West Bengal, 108, 219, 352, 353, 361, 366
'westernised oriental gentlemen', 11, 260
'What is Under my Blouse?', 675
wheat, 487, 491, 499, 515, 517, 521, 522, 523, 527
    army rations, 523
    Burmese imports, 520
    child nutrition and, 537, 538
    green revolutions and, 530, 533, 534
    PL-480 scheme, 529
Wheeler, Mortimer, 146–8
white community, 9, 87, 190, 213, 248–53, 333
    'box-wallahs', 10, 348
White Revolution, 471, 537
white sugar, 499, 502
White Tiger, The (Adiga), 265, 501
'White Town' zones, 87, 190, 325, 333, 347, 348–9, 352
Who Am I to You? (1994 film), 631, 674, 676
widowhood, 370–71, 395–6, 424
Wilberforce, William, 301, 483
wild boar, 478, 486
wild gourd, 477
witchcraft, 481
'wog', *see* 'westernised oriental gentlemen'
Woman (1940 film), 665, 666, 669
Woman with a Whip (1935 film), 605
women
    agricultural labour, 385, 425, 427–8
    Bangladesh Liberation War (1971), 160, 165, 167–8
    beggars, 395
    British Raj, 248, 250–51
    childbirth, 367, 472
    cooking and, 425, 431, 447, 461, 472
    domestic labour, 362, 377, 398, 431, 433–6, 474, 476
    domestic violence against, 207, 430
    education of, 382–3, 419, 425, 460–61, 473
    festivals and, 548–9
    film industry and, 605–9
    food and, 425, 431, 447, 455, 460–62, 472
    indentured labour and, 306, 396–7
    infanticide of, 424
    literacy, 382–3, 419, 460
    migration, 296, 306, 364–79, 331, 431–6
    Partition (1947), 93–4, 341–2, 344
    personal law and, 207, 211
    pregnancy, 424, 430
    railways and, 326
    Ramlila and, 557
    rape, 20, 237, 250, 406, 411–12, 415, 436
    sex work, 246, 396, 431, 433, 440–48, 582–3, 610–11, 662, 674
    sexual harassment of, 203
    slums and, 362
    squatter colonies, 354, 359
Woodburn Park, Calcutta, 499
Woodford, G. P., 258–9
World Bank, 285, 506
World War I (1914–18), 34, 81, 215–17, 252, 253
    Caliphate and, 54, 138
    rations, 523
    taxation and, 36
    trade and, 505
World War II (*c.*1937–45), 5, 81, 215, 217, 260, 336–7
    Bengal Famine (1943), 280, 337, 350, 505, 525–7, 528, 531, 603
    Burma campaign (1941–5), 215, 217, 428, 525
    Indian National Army, 215
    road building and, 5
    Singapore, Japanese invasion of (1942), 321
    Sino–Japanese War (1937–45), 500
    trade and, 505
Worship (1969 film), 670

wrestling, 241, 329, 543, 568–78
  Bollywood and, 577, 602, 615–16, 670
  British Raj and, 574–5
  Burud, 576
  caste and, 569
  celibacy, 576
  Dara Singh, 575–6, 577
  diet, 576
  Gama the Great, 569, 571–5, 615
  Goonga, 569
  Hanuman and, 569, 576
  kung fu and, 569, 615
  'Lame' Pataba, 569
  Muzumdar's journalism, 571, 574, 577
  Nehru and, 574
  patronage, 568, 570, 575, 576, 577,
    578
  training, 576
  Sahdeo, 569
  Zbyszko, 571, 572, 574, 575, 615
Writers' Building, Calcutta, 260, 265, 337,
  347
wudders, 294, 295

Yadav, Laloo Prasad, 187
Yahya Khan, Agha Muhammad, 84, 124,
    125, 169, 172
Yale University, 416
Yamuna river, 105, 436

'Yeh Dosti', 621, 623
Yemen, 43, 58
Young Bengal movement (1820s–30s), 497,
    502
Yugantar, 30
Yunus, Muhammad, 285

zaardozi, 349
Zaidi, Shama, 661
zakaat, 175, 176, 496
Zakat and Ushr Ordinance (1980), 175
zamindaars, 59, 121, 239, 300, 404, 422,
    524, 610
  middle classes and, 497
  Pittapore dispute (1899), 386–90
  taxation and, 269–70, 300
  wrestling and, 570
Zanjeer (1973 film), 603–4, 610, 620, 625,
    627, 628
zardaa paan, 381
Zbyszko, Stanislaus, 571, 572, 574, 575,
    615
Zia-ul-Huq, Muhammad, 83, 170, 174–7,
    203, 220, 221–2, 489
Zia-ur Rahman, 163–4, 220, 652
zina (extramarital sex), 203
Zolberg, Aristide, 86
zones of lawlessness, 290
Zoroastrianism, 12